ECONOMICS

An Introduction to Traditional
and Progressive Views

7TH EDITION

Howard J. Sherman, E.K. Hunt,
Reynold F. Nesiba, Phillip A. O'Hara,
and Barbara Wiens-Tuers

Foreword by Robert Pollin

Routledge
Taylor & Francis Group

LONDON AND NEW YORK

First published 2008 by M.E. Sharpe

Published 2015 by Routledge

2 Park Square, Milton Park, Abingdon, Oxon OX14 4RN
711 Third Avenue, New York, NY 10017, USA

Routledge is an imprint of the Taylor & Francis Group, an informa business

Library of Congress Cataloging-in-Publication Data

Economics : an introduction to traditional and progressive views / Howard J. Sherman . . . [et al.]. — 7th ed.
  p. cm.
Rev. ed. of: Economics : an introduction to traditional and radical views / E.K. Hunt, Howard J. Sherman. 6th ed.
Includes index.
ISBN 978-0-7656-1668-5 (pbk. : alk. paper)
  1. Economics. I. Sherman, Howard J. II. Hunt, E. K. Economics.

HB171.5.H83 2008
330—dc22

2007050485

ISBN 13: 9780765616685 (pbk)

ECONOMICS

Dedicated to
Barbara, Brandon, Dan, Jody, Nathaniel, and Rhoda
WITH LOVE

Contents

Foreword

ROBERT POLLIN

Economics should be an exciting subject for anyone who cares at all about the world we live in. What are the opportunities for getting a job and getting paid decently? Are the opportunities available today likely to erode over time, if businesses look to scour the globe for the cheapest possible pools of available workers? If we put our money in a bank, pension fund or the stock market, will it be safe, or vulnerable to the speculative excesses of Wall Street? Why do more than a billion people wake up each morning to lives of severe poverty while a tiny elite live in splendor? Why is our very existence as a species on earth threatened by our abuse of the environment? These are some of the basic questions on which economics is capable of shedding a clear, powerful light.

But if this is so, why is it also true that most economics textbooks are tedious, intimidating or some combination of both? One major reason is that economics does include technical issues that students should understand, such as why a bunch of bananas will cost perhaps $1.25 while a gallon of gasoline costs $3.00. Why don't they both cost $3.00, or for that matter, $2.00? Such price differences are part of our everyday lives, and we take them for granted. But explaining what's going on to set bananas at $1.25 and gasoline at $3.00 does entail learning a bit of technique.

Still, almost anything worth doing involves mastering some techniques, including hitting a baseball, playing a trumpet, or cooking. The problem with most economics textbooks is not that they present techniques, but that they get so bogged down in a welter of graphs, equations and terminology that the real substance of economics—the fundamental questions about our living standards, our sense of community and security, and viability of our environment—get shunted aside. It's as though we are taught the steps for baking a delicious cake but are never given a chance to eat it.

This brings us to *Economics: An Introduction to Traditional and Progressive Views*. This is no ordinary textbook. Its authors, Howard Sherman, E.K. Hunt, Reynold Nesiba, Phillip O'Hara, and Barbara Wiens-Tuers, do guide you ably through the steps of baking the cake. But—most important—they also give you a chance to sit down and savor the fruits of your effort. In other words, this textbook stays focused on the lively and challenging substance of economics.

I learned this first-hand as a student reading the initial edition of this book 30 years ago. I had the good fortune as a beginning economics graduate student of having a professor—indeed it was a quite eminent professor, the late Paul Sweezy—tell me that I needed to read this book. Until that moment, it had never occurred to me that a textbook, any textbook, in any subject, could actually be exciting. But *Economics*, in its initial edition, rose to that very difficult standard. Thirty years, six editions, and many revisions and improvements later, it still hits that mark.

Among the many strengths of this edition is its inclusion of a full section on economic history and history of economic thought that is far superior to any other general introductory work. This edition also pushes into new territory, including, among other things, a wide-ranging discussion of globalization. By now, the term "globalization" is a ubiquitous buzzword. But what does it really mean and what relevance does it have for the lives of ordinary people everywhere? This book guides its readers artfully through a bramble of complicated details to deliver a clear, compact but still authoritative discussion.

More generally, this book proceeds in a highly original fashion, as its subtitle, *An Introduction to Traditional and Progressive Views,* suggests. It presents the main issues in the field as a contest of ideas among thinkers who seek to both interpret the world in various ways and to change the world, in equally various ways. For example, the authors make clear that macroeconomics is anything but a frozen body of knowledge requiring that students merely memorize a standard collection of graphs. There are burning questions to face, such as whether capitalist economies can deliver an abundance of decent employment opportunities—something approximating full employment—without government intervention into the operations of free markets. And if the answer to that question is "no," then what types of government interventions, if any, might be capable of delivering full employment?

Equally with microeconomics: can we rely on the competitive pressures of a free market economy to, for example, force businesses to operate at an acceptable level of environmental responsibility? And if the free market isn't effective for addressing global warming and other pressing environmental concerns, then what do we do about it?

These are the types of questions that Sherman, Hunt, Nesiba, O'Hara, and Wiens-Tuers invite us to ponder on almost every page. This book won't give you all the answers, but it will force you to think in new and unexpected ways. *Economics* thus serves as an invaluable resource for all students interested in both interpreting the world and perhaps even changing it for the better.

Robert Pollin is Professor of Economics and Co-Director, Political Economy Research Institute, University of Massachusetts-Amherst

Preface

Most courses on economics present only the traditional point of view. We wrote this book so that people can teach the whole spectrum of views from very conservative, traditional views to nontraditional, progressive views.

EXACTLY HOW IS IT DIFFERENT?

This difference from most other texts is seen in each part of this book. In Part I we present the history of all of the points of view in economics, though this is ignored by most books. Part I explains the traditional views of the Classical and Neoclassical economists. But it also explains the nontraditional views of Marx, Veblen, and Keynes, as well as many other progressive viewpoints, such as feminist economics.

Part II presents microeconomics. Almost all other texts discuss these problems only from the traditional, neoclassical view. This book first presents the outlooks of feminists, institutionalists, Marxists, Post Keynesians and other progressive economists before discussing the traditional Neoclassical approach. This section also addresses problems such as poverty, discrimination and the environment. The traditional neoclassical approach is then presented in full, along with the criticisms of it.

Part III discusses macroeconomics, and explores business cycles, unemployment, and inflation. It presents the traditional views from J.B. Say to modern Neoclassicals. But it also presents the Keynesian, Veblenian, Marxist, and other progressive approaches.

Part IV presents the debates now raging over international relations and globalization. Both traditional and progressive sides of the argument are discussed.

WHAT'S NEW?

The seventh edition includes the history of thought in Part I as it always did. Part I in this edition also explains in historical detail the evolution of economic institutions from the earliest societies to the present.

Part II has been expanded, not only with newer progressive views, but with ten chapters of neoclassical economics. Both Parts III and IV have shed all their old data and illustrations and bring the story right up to date. Much of Part IV, dealing with the functioning and debates on international relations and the global economy, did not exist before this edition.

Finally, we have made the book more user-friendly. Learning Objectives at the beginning of each chapter tell the student where the chapter is heading and what questions will be answered in the chapter. Key Terms will appear in boldface type in the text and will be listed at the end of each chapter. A Summary of major points will appear at the end of each chapter. Review questions also appear at the end of each chapter. Suggested readings are also provided in many chapters for students who wish to delve more deeply into a particular topic.

HOW TO USE THIS BOOK

The instructor may choose among options as to how much Neoclassical economics to teach. The ten Neoclassical chapters each contain a basic presentation of the Neoclassical theory, followed by progressive criticism, followed by all of the technical details of Neoclassical economics. These chapters are separate from the progressive chapters, which precede them. It is thus possible for an instructor to present the technical material of Neoclassical economics in one of three ways: (1) in great detail; (2) in a brief, basic way; or (3) not at all.

The instructor is also given flexibility by the use of a large number of appendices in all parts of the book. Some of the appendices are far more technical than the chapter text. Some of the appendices are not technical at all, but contain interesting discussions of issues somewhat different than the chapter text. The existence of these appendices allows the instructor to pick and choose which ones to use for teaching.

WORDS AND CONFUSION

The nontraditional economists cover a wide spectrum of politics from mildly liberal to extremely radical, as well as a variety of schools from Keynesian to feminist. It is hard to find a single term to describe all of them. We shall use the term "progressive" to cover what is common among them, but will sometimes mention their disagreements.

Another area of confusion lies in the description of men and women. Many previous texts have described the economy on the assumption that only men work in the economy. Since half the human race is women, we shall not use "he" or "men" to describe all people. Sometimes we will use the term, "he or she." Because of the past discrimination against women, we will use male forms only when we mean men, not women.

Another difficulty with words is what to call the people of the United States of America. We shall speak of United States, U.S., or America as it is convenient to do so. The people living in the United States will usually be described as Americans, since that is the most common and convenient term. But Latin Americans also consider themselves to be Americans. Only when referring to Latin Americans will we make the distinction clear. By so doing, we mean no insult to Latin Americans.

COORDINATION

All of these terms and practices, plus many decisions about the content of the book, must be uniform and consistent throughout the book to avoid confusion. But we have five authors. In many books, the fact that there are five authors guarantees confusions and inconsistency in both style and content. We have tried to avoid that in the following way. One author was made the "coordinator," whose job was to rewrite every single chapter of the book until they were uniform in content and style. But in a long book, even a single author can be inconsistent. So we had another author follow after the coordinator and remove small inconsistencies from every chapter. We therefore hope that the whole text is a unified one.

Howard J. Sherman, Professor Emeritus of Economics,
University of California, Riverside and Visiting Scholar in
Political Science at University of California, Los Angeles

E.K. Hunt, Professor of Economics, University of Utah

Reynold F. Nesiba, Associate Professor of Economics,
Augustana College, Sioux Falls, South Dakota

Phillip A. O'Hara, Professor of Economics and Chair,
Global Political Economy Research Unit, Curtin University

Barbara Wiens-Tuers, Associate Professor of Economics,
Pennsylvania State University, Altoona

Acknowledgments

We would like to thank Lynn Taylor, Executive Editor at M. E. Sharpe for her generous contribution of time and effort to provide all-out cooperation and all-out encouragement.

We express our grateful acknowledgment to William S. Brown, who shared ideas, words, and diagrams from his out-of-print text on economic principles.

We thank Heather Brinkmeyer, Amanda Woockman, Carl Szabo, Andrea Krogstad, Megan Malde, and Paul Sherman for technical expertise and creativity in graphics and other tasks.

We are grateful for many constructive criticisms and extremely helpful advice from William Dugger, Robin Hahnel, Michael Meeropol, Robert Pollin, Paul Owen, Ira Sohn, Lisa Sherman, Dena Stoner, and Mayo Toruno.

We are grateful to Dell Champlin for preparing the Instructors Manual for this edition of the text. Finally, we acknowledge the students we have encountered over the years who have forced us to think more clearly about how the world works.

PART I

ECONOMICS OF HISTORY AND HISTORY OF ECONOMICS

PART I, SECTION 1

THE LONG ROAD TO CAPITALISM

CHAPTER 1

Prehistoric Communal Institutions in the Middle East

This chapter begins the story of the evolution of the earliest humans and their societies. It describes the key characteristics and advances of prehistoric communities. This chapter also introduces and explains how the four categories of technology, economic institutions, social institutions, and ideology provide a useful framework for examining human societies. The interaction of the four categories in prehistoric communal societies explains why those societies survived and also explains why these societies did not change for an incredibly long time.

LEARNING OBJECTIVES

After reading this chapter you should be able to:

- Comprehend* the genesis of human beings and early societies.
- List and explain the four basic institutions of human society.
- Describe the six ways in which the four basic institutions of society interacted in prehistoric society.

THE VERY BEGINNING

Our sun and planets evolved over an enormous amount of time. The earth was originally uninhabitable by life as we know it. Over billions of years the earth eventually developed an environment in which we can survive. The geological changes in the earth are revealed in its layers of rocks. For example, some rocks show plant fossils from a million years ago or reveal violent volcanic eruptions.

When the environment permitted, life evolved in spots where all the necessary elements happened to be together. Life evolved from the simplest virus-like creatures that lived at least three billion years

---

*To comprehend something means to have an understanding of it and the ability to describe it in your own words, to paraphrase, give examples, and translate it from one form to another (for example, words to numbers or numbers to words).

ago. Charles Darwin showed how *nature selects from the existing individuals the ones best suited for survival under particular conditions. Eventually this type of individual has the highest reproduction rate, and over a long period of time that fact leads to changes in the species.* This process of change is called **natural selection**. Thus new species evolved, including human beings.

At the time our first hominid ancestors (of the genus *homo*) evolved on grassy plains, they made simple tools and weapons from pieces of wood or stone or bone. Remnants of early humans are dated to six or seven million years ago, but the exact time is still controversial. Those with better brains could use tools and weapons more effectively, thus improving their chance of survival. This process led to slow enlargement of the brain. Hominids with a larger brain could improve the use of tools. An erect stance allowed early human beings to hold tools while running farther, increasing their survival chances. A new species of Homo sapiens (our present species) became dominant over 100,000 years ago. Eventually, the older species disappeared. There is much debate among scientists whether Homo sapiens wiped out the older types of hominids, interbred with them, or if they just died out.

The earliest societies developed by Homo sapiens endured through most of the last hundred thousand years. How do we know anything about societies that existed tens of thousands of years ago? Many societies of the past three to four thousand years had the ability to write down their languages, so scholars can translate their documents and learn a great deal about them. But earlier societies were **prehistoric** (*meaning before written history*) and had no written language. Two kinds of evidence are available on the earliest human societies. First of all, archaeologists dug up the earliest dwellings and graves containing weapons, tools, and ornaments, as well as skeletons. From this evidence, archaeologists deduce an amazing amount of information about how early humans lived.

Second, in the past two centuries anthropologists studied existing societies that resemble the prehistoric societies, though the numbers of such societies have steadily declined. One problem in using this kind of evidence is that we cannot say for sure whether existing societies that resemble the prehistoric ones behave exactly the way prehistoric ones did. Moreover, the evidence is contaminated because these societies were in contact with more advanced societies. If no one else, the anthropologist herself has contacted the communal society and therefore changed it. Nevertheless, in the past two centuries anthropologists accumulated an immense amount of reliable information on the earliest type of society.

THE FEATURES OF PREHISTORIC COMMUNAL SOCIETY

To understand prehistoric societies and how they changed, it is useful to examine the four key institutions of a society. **Institutions** are *sets of customs, laws and norms that influence, enable or constrain human behavior.* The four main categories of institutional structures of any society are technology, economic institutions, social institutions, and ideology.

What is meant by **technology**? We think of technology today as modern gadgets and machines, but it means far more than that. *Technology is the way that human beings produce goods and services.* Technology is based on the knowledge of how to do things, the available skills of the labor force or workers, the amount of production by each type of present equipment, and the quality of land and natural resources available. The technology of the early communal societies was based on knowledge about simple stone, bone, or wood tool making and was used for hunting, fishing, and the gathering fruits and vegetables. Since prehistoric societies lived off of hunting and gathering food, small groups had to roam over a large amount of land to find their food supply. The total labor force of each group was small, estimated at five to thirty-five people.

Table 1.1

Four Features of Early Communal Society

Technology	Earliest stone tools; hunting and gathering
Economic Institutions	Common ownership by extended family
Social Institutions	Group consensus
Ideology	Community togetherness and equality

An **economy** is *the process through which a society provisions itself with the goods and services that it needs to survive and grow.* **Economic institutions** are *sets of relations between people doing economic activities and the ways that people interact in the economy.* An economic institution is not a "thing" or a "place." The main prehistoric economic institution was an extended family of brothers and sisters, cousins, aunts, uncles, parents and grandparents. There was a division of labor between men and women and a division of labor between young and old. Men, usually as a group, did most of the fishing and hunting. Women, usually as a group, gathered fruits, nuts, and vegetables. The division of labor between genders, however, was far from absolute because the men probably often gathered fruits and vegetables, while women probably hunted small animals. These two collective groups delivered their food to the whole band and the whole band consumed the food. This little collective group was isolated and seldom interacted with other groups.

Such *family-based collective* or **communal societies** have been present for 90 to 95 percent of human existence. No one word describes all aspects of family-based societies, but the term "communal" emphasizes the collective nature of their economic institutions. Since everyone worked together and everyone consumed the product, the prehistoric communes had no use for the market. Thus, the communes were non-market societies. (Remember, of course, that such early, family-based communes had little or nothing in common with the utopian groups called communes in the nineteenth and twentieth centuries.)

Social institutions are defined as *all the non-economic ways that people interact, such as the political process, the family, or religious organizations.* The earliest institutions were very simple. There was no separate government and most decisions were made collectively. There were no separate, organized religious institutions. Instead, the whole community took part in various ceremonies. There was no separate education system. Education consisted of learning from your parents and the rest of the band by following their example. There were no separate media. News was spread by everyone around the campfire.

Ideology is defined to mean *a more or less coherent system of ideas about how society works and how we should behave within a given society.* We may believe that an ideology is good, like democracy, or bad, like the idea of burning witches. Everybody has an ideology or ideas about how things work. Ideology is simply a particular viewpoint that integrates many of one's ideas. The early communal social ideas (or ideology) reflected their life and environment. If the earliest groups behaved like similar small bands of people discovered in the nineteenth and twentieth centuries, then they valued cooperation among all individuals in the band. They also had a set of superstitious beliefs which were centered on animals and natural forces such as lightning.

The four features of communal society are summarized in Table 1.1.

Studying the four key institutions of early communal society raises many intriguing questions. When one asks how the four institutions fit together in the social whole that was prehistoric communal society, the tale becomes even more exciting!

Figure 1.1   **Four Basic Features of Society**

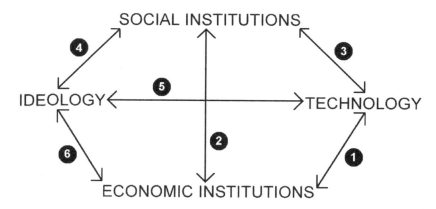

HOW THE FOUR BASIC FEATURES OF SOCIETY INTERACTED

At first glance, there seem to be hundreds of unrelated aspects to a society. In order to understand how society functions, the seemingly unrelated aspects must be looked at within a framework. The four categories—technology, economic institutions, social institutions, and ideology—will be our framework for understanding society as a whole. The four categories are not independent of each other. Rather, it will be seen that each of the four is determined by the other three. For example, technology provided quite reliable birth control devices. This new technology changed our ideas about sex. Thus technology can affect ideology.

A simple schematic picture of these interactions is presented in Figure 1.1.

Figure 1.1 illustrates six interactions:

1. Economic institutions with technology.
2. Social institutions with economic institutions.
3. Social institutions with technology.
4. Social institutions with ideology.
5. Technology with ideology.
6. Economic institutions with ideology.

We will explore how the interactions play a vital role in understanding the early communal society. The description of economic activity and **productivity**, *the amount of output produced by each input,* in this chapter relies on the archaeological evidence from the Middle East approximately one hundred thousand to ten thousand years ago. In addition, we know from studying small simple societies that every group devoted some time to leisure activities and recreation. More leisure time is found in early societies that lived in easier environments, such as a fertile Pacific island with a pleasant climate year round.

ECONOMIC INSTITUTIONS AND TECHNOLOGY

The technology of the prehistoric communal society was based on land for hunting and gathering, a small labor force and production based mostly on simple stone, bone, and wooden tools. Communal economic institutions were described as nothing but an extended family acting collectively. How did the communal institutions interact with the simple tools they used?

Each band of people was forced to form a communal group to protect themselves from large carnivores as well as to hunt large animals such as the mammoth. An individual who left the communal group usually died quickly. With the simple technology using bone, stone, and wooden tools, the prehistoric communal society was able to hunt animals, gather plant resources, and make leather and fiber implements, clothing, and shelters. Because technology was at such a simple level, if everyone worked together all day there was only enough food, clothing, and shelter produced for everyday survival. In other words, productivity was relatively low. For this reason, no one could specialize in any one trade since that would have reduced the production of needed supplies below immediate, daily needs.

Through peer pressure, the economic institution of the family encouraged work at a reasonable pace, but it did not encourage people to do anything differently than the family had always done. Because there were no specialists, no one focused his or her thoughts on how to improve tool-making technology. In fact, the prehistoric communal people did not dream that their tools could be radically improved. When the family is just above the starvation level, it cannot take chances with new ways of doing things that might result in death by starvation for most of the family. For all of these reasons, technological progress was very, very slow. In tens of thousands of years, there was very little improvement.

One consequence of the low technological level was that if there was a clash with another band, it made no sense to keep a prisoner as a slave because a slave could only produce enough to survive. Therefore, a prisoner from another band was either integrated into this band, or killed and left behind, or killed and eaten. Although it was rare, cannibalism made economic sense to some bands, but slavery did not. Only in a few exceptional cases, such as intensive fishing under good conditions, could slaves produce more than what the slave needed to survive.

Each small community was separate from the others, so there was little or no trade with other communities. There was no market exchange because there was rarely anything to exchange. Since there was no exchange there was also no money. The reason for the isolation was that each person required about a half a square mile or more for adequate food supply, though bands often moved in a nomadic life style from place to place following the food supply. Since it was a family and since everyone worked collectively to bring in the food, the food was distributed to everyone. People had almost no private possessions except for an animal skin as clothing and perhaps some simple implements.

Remember, economic institutions included the extended family, the collective production of the food supply, no division of labor except between men and women and by age, no specialists, no market, no money, no significant amount of wealth, and the collective consumption of the food supply. The economic institutions did not encourage technological experimentation, but tended to promote the use of the same technology century after century. Since there was little or no change in the available technology, there was no need to change the economic institutions. The entire set of economic institutions and the available technology fit together perfectly at this very low level and change was incredibly slow.

SOCIAL INSTITUTIONS AND ECONOMIC INSTITUTIONS

Given the technological forces and the economic institutions just described, the social institutions necessary to maintain the community were also very simple. No group of managers or complex corporate structure was needed to run the repeated economic tasks of hunting and food gathering by a small group of people. No separate government structure was needed in the political sphere to run such a small, highly integrated group. The simple tasks of governance and major decisions could be and were made by the group as a whole. There was a **direct democracy**, *government by the entire population usually through elected representatives,* but since all adults participated in the decisions of the group, there was no need to vote for representatives.

Since society was not complex and everyone knew what was happening, there was little opportunity for getting away with crimes of violence or theft. With very little crime, there was no need for police. The group as a whole punished or expelled anyone guilty of crime. Expulsion was an extremely serious punishment because it was very difficult to survive alone.

The total amount of personal wealth consisted of only a few tools, weapons, and ornaments that could easily be reproduced and carried. There was little reason for theft by individuals. Nor was there reason for war by communities, except skirmishes over hunting grounds. A bigger war was not profitable. Moreover, war not possible in much of an organized way over the vast spaces roamed by the different families, so there were no armies, navies, or air forces.

According to studies of similar bands still in existence today, life was mysterious to people with limited scientific knowledge. There was widespread belief in magic but there was no organized religion and no full-time priests. One reason was that there was no surplus above basic necessities to feed groups not engaged in production. Everyone had to work for the community to survive.

There was no **sexist discrimination** or *differential treatment of people based on prejudices or myths about their gender.* As noted earlier, men tended to do most of the hunting, while women usually focused on gathering food because pregnancy and childcare often did not allow them to go on long hunting trips. But it is quite possible that women often produced more resources for the groups than men did. The food gathering was often more important for the food supply than was the hunting, which was often unsuccessful. Women carried very heavy loads at least as often as men did.

There was no **racist discrimination**, *differential treatment of people based on prejudices or myths about differences in physical characteristics or ethnicity,* within the group because everyone was a family member. There was certainly ignorance of other families and wariness about all strangers. This was a result of the isolation imposed by the need for each group to roam a very large area for its food supply. Different bands occasionally met, mainly to find suitable mates outside the immediate family.

Of course the social institutions also help mold the economic institutions. The education and media systems, in which all of one's learning and news came from other family members, meant that all of the views reinforced the existing system of an extended family working cooperatively. The magic ceremonies involved the entire family, so they also reinforced the family unit as the center of activity. The whole group made the most important economic decisions, such as where to go next to look for food.

SOCIAL INSTITUTIONS AND TECHNOLOGY

We already discussed how the technology of prehistoric communal societies consisted of a small labor force, large areas of land for hunting and food gathering, a few simple tools, and an unchanging fund of technological knowledge. There was no radio, TV, or cable, but they were not needed for spreading news and education within the family. Because there was no long distance communication, hunters were constrained to work as a group within sight or calling distance of each other. These facts had important implications for social institutions. Hunters and gatherers had fairly stable populations. Their low level of technology and perilous existence meant that even a high birth rate was balanced by a high death rate. No chiefs had the right to have their children inherit their power. The low level of technology enforced a rough equality of power and wealth. In turn, the social institutions of the extended family, education by the family, news exposure within the family, and magical ceremonies within the family all tended to reinforce and support the economic institutions of cooperation among family members.

SOCIAL INSTITUTIONS AND IDEOLOGY

The extended family was not only an economic institution, it was also the most important social institution. As described in detail above, living within the extended family meant that it constituted one's early training and conditioning, education, exposure to news, and religious experiences. No wonder that the family dominated one's ideology and behavior. In similar isolated communal groups living today, the prime importance of the extended family is perhaps the most important ideology—the family is everything.

This potent ideology of the all-important family lasted for thousands of years. It was taken for granted and almost never questioned. Everyone agreed that the extended family was the proper and only possible economic institution. Therefore, this ideology was very powerful and went unchallenged. The ideology of the importance of the family helped shape the way this society behaved in every aspect of life.

The group was collectivist in its thinking, meaning that it was taken for granted that everyone must work together just to survive. Expulsion from the group usually meant death. The collectivism was not an outlook thought up by philosophers or politicians. Rather, the collectivism of the family was a result of dire economic necessity as the only way the group could survive.

For people in that era, economic necessity meant having enough food and shelter. Economic necessity shaped the main communal institutions such as working together. Economic necessity also shaped their ideology, the idea that it is good to have cooperation in the extended family. The ideology of cooperation became a powerful force holding the group together for tens of thousands of years.

We have noted that the work that women did was roughly equal to that of men in importance to the survival of the family. It is no surprise that this experience was reflected in the myths that portrayed men and women as roughly equal. There were no myths about the inferiority of women. Economic necessity and institutions shaped the egalitarian ideology of men and women and those ideas of equality then shaped the democratic institutions over great stretches of time.

TECHNOLOGY AND IDEOLOGY

The small labor force meant that everyone knew everyone else extremely well and made the ideology of cooperation seem natural. The simple stone tools produced little envy for the wealth of others. Other people had very little except their tools and ornaments. The use of the same simple tools for thousands of years meant that people came to think that this way was the only way that things could be done. People trusted these tools and ways of doing things and they come to distrust any change.

These ideas formed a strong ideology and reinforced habits and rigid traditions. But one should not assume that the belief that there should be no change in technology was merely a superstitious impediment to progress. For tens of thousands of years the technology represented reality and the best available wisdom. Prehistoric communal people did not look for brand new technology, but they did spend much time learning how best to use the technology they had. It was this belief in the unchanging technology that pushed them to do their best with what they had. You and I could not shape stone tools as well as they did without years of practice.

In the prehistoric communal period of technology, most myths had to do with nature. Nature was at the center of people's lives. They found nature to be dangerous and full of surprises. Their myths had to do with gods who were embodied in animals, fire, water, thunder, and lightening. Some of these myths encouraged magic rituals to accomplish goals. If a wise person correctly portrayed a mastodon in a magic ceremony consisting of song or dance or pictures, then the band might control it and kill it without losing members of the family. Myths about nature helped to give confidence to the whole band. These myths also reinforced the power of those who seemed to know the most about "spirits," animals, the weather, and other mysteries.

Art often meant pictures of the animals or dances depicting the animals, because that was part of the magic to control them. Science consisted of accumulated detailed knowledge of nature plus magic. In short, all of their ideology helped unify the family and helped it operate successfully for thousands of years. At the same time, the economic and political environment of the extended family, along with the level of the technology, helped shape their ideological views.

ECONOMIC INSTITUTIONS AND IDEOLOGY

The communal economic institution consisting of the extended family and cooperation and collective action lasted for at least 90 percent of the time that Homo sapiens existed and over 99 percent of the time since the first hominids came out of the trees. As noted earlier, the ideology was not planned by philosophers, but was pure economic necessity since people could not survive alone. The ideology of the extended family and cooperation and collective action was taken for granted. Any dissenter was handled harshly. Although the ideology at first represented necessity, it came to be a habit of thinking and then a rigid tradition.

The ideas of cooperation and collective action within the extended family did tend to hold back progress, but they were not silly ideas. Remember that this belief in cooperation and collective action allowed the society to survive for countless ages and was the glue that held it together. Since these ideas were vital to survival under these circumstances, any other social ideas (a different ideology) would have led to societies that may not have survived. Their ideological beliefs helped to enforce the unchanging technology as well as the economic, social, and political institutions that lasted for most of human existence.

SUMMARY

This chapter introduced and explained how the four categories of technology, economic institutions, social institutions, and ideology are a useful framework for examining human societies. The interaction of the four categories in prehistoric communal societies explained why those societies survived. Yet their interaction also explained why these societies did not change for an incredibly long time.

SUGGESTED READINGS

All of the facts in this chapter are discussed in detail in the suggested readings. This section does not necessarily provide the latest books and articles for specialists nor are they obscure or difficult books that would interest only specialists. Rather, the suggested materials provide the reader with some books that will be easy and, in some cases, fun to read. A few more difficult books are identified as advanced or scholarly, so the reader is warned. The same approach—expanding the facts in interesting and pleasant books or articles—will be used in all the Suggested Readings sections in this book. Note that all citations in the text are partial. Full citations are in the References at the end of the book.

Early communal societies are beautifully, but precisely, described in Jared Diamond, *Guns, Germs, and Steel* (1997). A good introduction to the geological evolution of the earth is Edmund Blair Bolles, *The Ice Finders: How a Poet, a Professor, and a Politician Discovered the Ice Age* (1999), which is very pleasant reading. A book that explains the disappearance of the dinosaurs and reads like a detective novel is Walter Alvarez, *T Rex and the Crater of Doom* (1998).

There are hundreds of books on Darwin and evolution, but by far the best is Stephen Jay Gould, *Ever Since Darwin* (1977). Gould was one of the best writers in science. A scholarly collection of articles on the role of women in prehistoric societies is by Frances Dahlberg, editor, *Woman the Gatherer* (1981).

KEY TERMS

communal society	prehistoric
direct democracy	productivity
economic institutions	racist discrimination
economy	sexist discrimination
ideology	social institutions
institutions	technology
natural selection	

REVIEW QUESTIONS

The Review Questions are organized by the Learning Objectives stated at the start of each chapter. The review questions represent the information and skills you need to master in order to meet each learning objective. The questions and problems represent an opportunity for guided, in-depth study and analysis of each learning objective as well as an opportunity for self-assessment or finding out whether or not *you* really know and understand the material. After reading the chapter, you should find these questions fairly easy to answer. If you cannot answer a question, go back to the chapter and reread the relevant section. When all of the questions under a particular learning objective are accurately answered, you can be assured that you have mastered that particular objective.

Comprehend the genesis of human beings and early societies.
1. How was natural selection important in the development of early humanoids?
2. What is the definition of a prehistoric society and why is it so difficult to learn about these early communities?
3. What are some characteristics of early human society?
4. What evidence is used to substantiate claims about early humans and early society?

List and explain the four basic institutions of human society.
5. List and describe the four basic features of society used as a framework for analysis in this text. Using this framework, what are the basic features of prehistoric society?

6. What is an institution?
7. What is an economy?
8. What is technology? What are examples of technology in early communal societies?
9. What are economic institutions? What is the key economic institution in prehistoric society?
10. Explain the importance of the communal group and the role of its members for ensuring the survival of all its members.
11. Can there be more than one way a society could organize to produce and allocate what it needs to survive and grow?
12. What are social institutions?
13. What is ideology as used in this text?
14. Give examples of ideas or systematic beliefs in early communal society.
15. We usually do not think of ideology as necessary for our day-to-day survival. In what ways is it necessary for the survival of the members of the communal society?
16. How could prehistoric societies survive so long with little change and without major technological advancements?

Describe the six ways in which the four basic institutions of society interacted in prehistoric society.

17. List the six possible interactions of the four basic institutions of society. Give brief examples of each interaction in prehistoric society.
18. What is productivity? Why was productivity so low in prehistoric communal societies?
19. What is a direct democracy? How does that differ from democracy as practiced in the United States today?
20. What is sexist discrimination? Why was it not practical in a prehistoric society?
21. What is racist discrimination? Why was it not a factor in prehistoric society?
22. What is the importance of the extended family?
23. Why is cooperation and collective action within the extended family so crucial for survival?

CHAPTER 2

Communal Equality to Slavery in the Middle East

This chapter tells the story of the evolution from the earliest communal societies to the first complex, class-divided civilizations where slavery played a key role. The process began with the Neolithic revolution, went through a long transitional period, and finally resulted in changes to all four main features of society. The slave society that emerged had technology, economic institutions, social institutions, and ideology that were all completely different from those of prehistoric society.

LEARNING OBJECTIVES

After reading this chapter you should be able to:

- Comprehend the components and processes of the Neolithic revolution.
- Explain the role that increasing productivity played in changing social and economic institutions.
- Understand the composition of a slave society.
- Comprehend the changing ideologies.
- Explain how the four institutions of society changed in the evolution from communal to slave-based society.

CHANGE IN PREHISTORIC COMMUNAL SOCIETIES

The technology available to early communal societies was shaped by the prevailing ideology, economic, and social institutions. Even after Homo sapiens became the clear winner among various types of hominids about a hundred thousand years ago, little or no technological change occurred during the next eighty or ninety thousand years.

As we saw, the basic economic institution was the extended family. The dominant ideology said that the technology could never change and, in fact, the way of life did not change much for thousands of years. Together, these facts perpetuated a tradition that no change was possible and that no change was good. As a result, for tens of thousands of years, people with about the same brain capacity as you or I kept on using crude stone tools, gathering fruits and vegetables, and hunting just as their ancestors had done.

However, over thousands of years, people learned a great deal about tools, plants, and animals. In spite of very strong traditions, imperceptible changes crept into their tool making, hunting, and gathering. Eventually, evolving institutions and ideology enabled humans to make three great discoveries, all somewhat linked together. The three great discoveries were *better tools, invention of agriculture (farming and herding), and invention of effective pottery. All three together were called the* **Neolithic revolution**.

When and where did the Neolithic revolution begin? As a very broad generalization, one can say that it began around 10,000 **B.C.E.** (*Before the Common Era*, that is, before year 1 of our present calendar) in the Middle East, but there is controversy over the date. There is some evidence that a few crops were planted in Syria and Palestine as early as 13,000 B.C.E., and a little later in Mesopotamia, especially around the Euphrates River in Iraq, but it was several thousand years later before there was full-scale farming.

In China, probably independently, there is some evidence of planted crops as early as 11,000 B.C.E. Full-scale farming in China did not start until thousands of years later. The only other independent beginning of agriculture was far later in Central and South America, with the potato coming from the Andes and corn (or maize) from Mexico. The Neolithic revolution—including new and better stone tools and pottery, as well as agriculture—spread from these three areas. From the Middle East it spread east into India and west into Africa and Europe. The Neolithic culture moved all around the Mediterranean and then slowly up the Danube, but took thousands more years to spread west to the Atlantic.

How exactly did this long process unfold in the areas where it began? First, the crude stone tools were improved very, very slowly over thousands of years. Eventually, Homo sapiens developed easier and more consistent techniques for making tools. They also figured out how to improve tools in many ways, such as sharper cutting edges. Although this does not sound like much, most anthropologists consider it a revolution. It was a revolution from the Old Stone Age to the New Stone Age. The move from the Old Stone Age to the New Stone Age did bring major results in increasing productivity in hunting and food gathering and helped strengthen the possibility of new and different economic activities. One way to measure productivity is to measure how much output was generated by each hunter or gatherer. Productivity thus means the amount that each person is able to make and bring to the table.

In a few exceptionally favorable environments, especially some river valleys in the Middle East, China, and the Americas, a simple sort of agriculture emerged. Agriculture consists of both farming and herding, so we must follow the story of how food gathering changed to farming, then how hunting changed to herding.

The revolutionary change from food gathering to farming was slow because it included many stages, such as weeding around favored plants, protecting the plants from other animals, and learning how and when to plant crops. All of this human activity eventually, over thousands of years, changed the environment of these plants and resulted in their genetic modification by natural and human selection. Therefore, different dates are given for the coming of farming, not only because of different evidence, but also because it matters exactly which point in the process one is trying to date.

The Middle East, China, and the Americas had fertile river valleys and just the right plants for a transition to farming. Climate, distribution of easily domesticated plants and animals, and geography played a big role in determining which locations would make the change from food gathering to farming. It also appears that geography helped determine the areas to which farming spread as people and news disseminated from the original areas. Europe and Asia is really one big continent with nothing blocking the way of communication, except distance, mountains, and deserts that people went around. Thus, farming spread along the entire latitude from the Middle East to India (and perhaps China) in one direction and to northern Africa and southern Europe in the other.

Farming in North and South America began with severe disadvantages compared with the Middle East. For instance, the alpaca and llama of the Inca civilization in Peru were far inferior beasts of burden and sources of nourishment than were the cattle, sheep, goats, pigs, and horses found in Eurasia. Similarly, the corn (or maize) of Central America was more difficult to cultivate and nutritionally inferior to the wheat, sorghum, and rice of Eurasia.

To further complicate matters, *the spread of knowledge of farming by the movement of ideas from one village to another* (called **diffusion**) was much more difficult in the Americas. The narrowness of Central America acted as a blockade between North and South. Apparently, plant domestication and civilizations appeared independently in both North and South America. Another blockade to diffusion of farming was that spreading farming practices to the North or South was much more difficult than spreading farming practices to the East or to the West. The reason is that the weather changes from North to South, so the agriculture that works in one latitude may not work in another.

Thus geography played an important role in determining the location of the earliest farming and the directions of its spread. Of course, geography remains an important part of the story of institutional change. Geography, however, is mostly a constant factor because the geography of mountains and continents has hardly changed in the last ten thousand years, except for human-made ecological disasters. Therefore, after the beginning of farming, further changes in institutions must be explained mostly by factors other than geography.

We have seen that the transition to farming did not happen overnight, but took thousands of years. The details of the scenario seem to have been something like this. When women did their age-old activity of gathering fruits and vegetables, they sometimes pulled the weeds to allow certain plants to grow that they especially favored. Eventually they learned how new plants came from the old, so they could replant new ones if they wished. When women learned how to plant their favorite fruits and vegetables and to protect them from weeds or from other gatherers, they were then practicing the beginnings of farming. Moreover, human processes, such as harvesting techniques, influenced the genetics of plants. For example, if you collect the seeds of native grasses, chances are you are selecting seeds that tend to stay on the stalk longer. Thus, if you replant them, you are selecting for those varieties of grasses.

With the simple stone tools, or even the improved ones, farming was very difficult, with low productivity. Nevertheless, the earliest farming meant an enormous increase in the food supply as well as the certainty of that supply. Using jars from newly developed pottery, people could put more food away for winter to prevent starvation in cold climates. Also, it meant that people became more dependent on these labor-intensive crops instead of what grew wild. People ate all the grains, such as wheat, oats, barley, and rice, and also sugar. Later, in the great cities of the slave empires, while the elite ate meat, the grains and sugar were fed to the masses of servile people.

Since women had most of the burden of gathering fruits and vegetables, they developed most of the earliest farming techniques and comprised most of the earliest farmers. Men did most of the hunting and therefore were instrumental in developing the techniques of herding animals. The process of changing from hunting to herding also took a very long time. A number of steps were involved and these happened gradually over thousands of years. First, men learned to follow a herd as it moved. Next, they had to fight off other predators. After that, men had to find ways to tame a herd. Finally, men had to find ways to keep the herd in some area where they wanted it to be. When men became herders, they increased the food supply greatly. The herders now produced far more food than the same number of hunters.

It is reasonable to describe this process of moving to farming and herding as the first agricultural revolution. As we shall see, this revolution had several effects along with increasing productivity of labor, the division of labor, the size of the population and the economic institutions. When farming and herding became the dominant way of life for society, productivity increased dramatically.

COLLECTIVE LABOR TO DIVISION OF LABOR

In the early communal period, everyone worked together. The women, collectively, did most of the plant gathering while men, collectively, did most of the hunting. Except between men and women as a whole, there was no division of labor and no specialists doing separate tasks. This resulted in very low productivity or product per worker. The agricultural revolution in farming and herding changed all of this and greatly increased productivity. When the herding and farming increased productivity, people could produce a **surplus**, or *food above the level needed for survival.* It became possible to have some people specialize in certain tasks. The specialists could be fed with the surplus food in exchange for their talents. The people who specialized in tool making further improved the efficiency of tools and weapons. As tools improved, the productivity of farming and herding improved. This was a cumulative process with the surplus from agriculture allowing specialization in tool making, while better tools in turn helped agriculture.

Division of labor affected many other processes. For example, some people could now specialize in making pottery while others could specialize in weaving. In the construction of buildings, specialists from many crafts could work together to do things much faster than before. The reason for the improvement was that each knew their craft better than any one person could have known all the crafts. Higher productivity also meant that some people could specialize in mathematics, astronomy, accounting, healing, or even fortune telling. This was the beginning of intellectual specialization. It was also the beginning of specialists in ideological **propaganda**, *selected information and publicity used to support and spread certain ideas,* in the service of those who had vested interests in the new society.

Farming meant that people could end their nomadic existence, at least for a year or two at a time, to harvest the crops they had sown in a particular place. Some people still roamed the countryside between the time of planting and the time of harvesting, but more and more chose settled living. The tendency to a settled existence gave more stability to their economy.

It should be noted that people did not just choose to go into agriculture. One reason for leaving hunting in favor of agriculture in many areas was over-hunting and the extinction of game. This cannot be proven, but it is a fact that most of the larger animals disappeared at about the same time that humans began to live in North America. Most of the large animals also disappeared at the same time as humans appeared in Australia.

The higher productivity of agriculture meant that there could be a far larger population per square mile than in the old hunting and food-gathering societies. Greater population density meant that people began to live in villages. Over the centuries, villages became small towns and towns became large cities. The economic unit grew from the small band of families, to the large tribe, to entire empires.

COMMUNAL EQUALITY TO SLAVE-BASED ECONOMIES AND CLASS DIVISIONS IN SOCIETY

The rising productivity of agriculture, including farming and herding, slowly undermined the old economic institutions of collective production within an extended family. Not only did higher productivity lead to more population and growth of towns, it also led to the first small accumulations of goods and wealth. Eventually, it led to a division between rich and poor—between those with a large accumulation of goods and wealth and those with very little or no accumulation of goods and wealth. The economic inequality between rich and poor was followed by political inequality between the powerful and the powerless.

There was not an overnight jump from the collective governance of the small communal economy to the wealthy slave owners, kings, and emperors of later times. Rather, those who had more wealth slowly gathered more economic and political power. Eventually, the differences between people made obsolete the old communal family band working in solidarity in collective activities. A transition began toward an economy with more private ownership (which included **private property rights**, or *control over an asset and the right to exclude any one else from using it*), more specialists, division into rich and poor, and division into ruled and rulers.

FROM COLLECTIVE TO PRIVATE OWNERSHIP

In the transitional period, some activity was still collective, but now some activity became private. As a few people amassed more private wealth while others remained poor, the differences in affluence also led to differences in influence. At the same time, the population of the economic unit grew from dozens to hundreds and then to thousands. The larger population meant that some governing body had to make decisions.

Those with a good reputation for leadership, as well as enough money to employ warriors, took political power. In the old system, people might become temporary leaders of hunting groups if they showed merit, or a temporary leader of the food gathering group if they showed excellence in that occupation. But now there were permanent chieftains for tribes of thousands. The chieftains usually managed to have their sons inherit their power. This is shown in detail for the Middle East in Diamond (1997). So far the story is one of widening differences in economic wealth and widening differences in political power. After a while, the chieftains could tell the people: "I direct and you do as I say." Usually, the same people held both wealth and power, yet this was still a fluid situation. There was not one class that owned all the wealth and another that worked for it under some kind of coercion. The differences began very gradually, with no class system set in stone. There may have been inheritance of the rule in one family, but others could aspire to a leadership position.

As is shown by traditions, myths, religious stories in later tribes with writing, and even in the traditions of the early Roman republic, there was still a view among many that equality is a good thing and the tribe should return to it. There were many conflicts between those holding to the old principles of equality and those who now wanted individual power. Those who advocated equality were for a return to the old ways. The advocates of equality often struggled long and hard, but they lost to those with power in the class-divided civilizations that survived.

SKIRMISHES TO WAR AND COMMUNAL EQUALITY TO SLAVERY

In earlier periods, there was communal ownership of land and communal production of food, but there was barely enough food to eat and few personal goods to own. In the transitional period, there was wealth in the form of buildings, belongings, fertile land for farming and herds of animals. This wealth meant that it was profitable to raid a village or town for loot. Since that had not been true earlier in the communal period, war had not shown its ugly face. There had only been brief skirmishes over hunting land and brides for marriage alliances. When there was wealth to be gained by conquest, there were significant wars.

Wars meant not only looting any wealth that could be moved or taking over fertile land, it also meant taking prisoners. A prisoner in the early communal period could not produce a surplus of food beyond his or her own needs, so the prisoner was useless as a slave. Therefore, the prisoner was either killed or integrated into the group. There were a few, extremely rare cannibal groups, who ate their prisoners. Within the band, there was solidarity and equality, but hostility toward other bands occurred primarily in squabbles over hunting grounds or brides.

With the higher productivity of farming and herding in the transitional period, a prisoner could produce a surplus. Therefore, progress was made by ending the killing of prisoners and occasional cannibalism. Higher productivity also meant that the winning side found it profitable to make slaves of prisoners of war. The slaves worked for their masters. They produced a surplus that could be consumed by their masters. Was the old situation of rough equality with very low productivity and killing of prisoners better or worse than the new situation of much higher productivity, vast inequality, and the cruelty of slavery? All we can say is that this was the path of change in some areas.

For better or worse, the new technology and higher productivity of agriculture meant the final end of the early communal economic and social institutions. Only a few isolated small-scale societies never changed from their hunting and gathering technologies. Now, some people owned slaves and some did not. Some were able to accumulate wealth and power and some were not. There was now a class of people who were slaves. Thus, the community became differentiated into permanent classes of top dogs and underdogs. As differences arose over economic rank, the old bonds of the extended family frayed and became far less important than class divisions. There were now dominant classes, subordinate classes, and innumerable subclasses.

MASTERS AND SLAVES

In some areas such as ancient Greece, the largest subordinate class was the slave class. This group was given little to eat, bits of clothing, and dirty, cramped shelters. They worked for the benefit of the dominant or master class from dawn till dusk. The master class had agricultural slaves to produce a large surplus over the immediate needs of the estate, so they had surplus on which to live in luxury. In addition, the estate owners had domestic slaves to cater to their every whim. The slaves did the cooking, made the clothing, minded the children—and were forced to fulfill the sexual needs of the male masters.

It is important to understand, however, that these were not simple two-class societies, but rather very complex ones. Even at the beginning of class-divided societies there were other types of forced laborers sometimes more numerous than slaves. There were many subclasses and degrees of forced or subordinate labor, some with very onerous tasks and some with a lighter burden. For example, some laborers were not owned in body as the slaves were, but had to give service to a master a certain number of days per year. In Western Europe, slavery was the dominant form of labor in ancient societies, but other types of forced labor became the dominant form in medieval, feudal societies.

In addition, the master class also employed free workers including warriors to fight, craftspeople to make things, and officials to collect taxes. Kings also made sure that the priests in their employ emphasized the major religious belief of the time that kings were gods or sons of gods, thus upholding their right to power. Beneath the master class and their employees were the slaves, who, due to higher productivity of farming and herding, could now produce enough to provide gourmet food, sumptuous clothing, and luxurious shelter for the master class as well as food, clothing, and shelter for the underlings of the master class.

There also emerged a class of independent farmers. Usually such independent farmers became a small minority in class-divided societies. At the end of the transitional period, the class of independent farmers was quite large in most places, but their numbers declined over time. In Greece and Rome, the independent farms tended to die out for several reasons. First, there was competition from large plantations with slaves. Second, the men from the independent farms were often drafted into the army for long periods of time. The ruling group was forced to draft independent farmers into the army because the slaves would not fight for their masters, so this was the only way to raise an army. Third, the independent farmers sometimes had to pay considerable taxes, but they did not have enough money to pay the taxes while they were in the army. Many soldiers lost their farms. This policy eventually lowered the number of free farms.

Greece and Rome were mainly slave societies, but in their cities they also had workers who were not formally subservient. These workers were free to produce and sell their goods and services at any price they could get. Because of the dominance of slave workers, independent workers could ask only low prices and therefore usually remained very poor. In Rome, they were given some free bread at times and they were also given free entertainment, called circuses, to keep them happy. These circuses were grisly affairs in which men killed each other, killed animals, or were killed by animals.

The rough equality and solidarity of the hunting and gathering band consisting of an extended family and its last vestiges in the transitional tribal society vanished. The population of the economic and political unit grew from hundreds to thousands to hundreds of thousands. It was, however, a very different kind of community, with new social and political institutions. Some now could exert more influence than others and some could become specialized as leaders and rulers. All of this was due to the greater productivity of herding and farming, the use of vast numbers of slaves, and the division of labor into many specialties. But it did not go without a struggle. People who had not acquired wealth and slaves preferred the old communal institutions. However, Pandora's box was open and there was no way to close it. As farming and herding became a fact, it allowed far greater profitability to those with slaves so the owners of slaves slowly acquired more wealth and power. Soon, society had its rulers and the ruled.

WOMEN: FROM EQUALS TO PIECES OF PROPERTY

In the early communal society, men and women were generally in rough equality, but that changed markedly with the introduction of slavery. Women were clearly subordinate in Greek and Roman society. The basic reason was that men were the warriors so the prisoners of war belonged to them. As slaves became important, the status of the men who owned them also rose. They became masters of people in the economy and their economic power and wealth allowed them to become rulers of the society. Only men above a certain level of wealth could become members of the Roman Senate.

Men used the slaves primarily in agriculture. This was no longer the light agriculture begun by women and conducted by women for a very long time. This was new agriculture, with the much better and heavier implements that could now be made. These included heavy plows that required either slaves or animals such as oxen to pull them. Since men were also the herders, they naturally took control of the animals as well, when these animals were used in agriculture. As men came to dominate production under slavery, they also came to dominate women. Myths developed that said women were inferior, in order to rationalize their subordinate position.

In order to pass on private property in ancient Rome, it was important to determine a legitimate heir. This was done by prohibiting women of the ruling class from having sex freely with men other than their husbands. If a ruling class woman had sex with a slave, she was punished in various ways and the slave was punished by death. Ruling class men could have sex anywhere they found it without fear of punishment, but husbands used every possible way to prevent their wives from having sex with other ruling class men. As a consequence, myths and legends came to be popular about the wonders of virginity and abstinence from extramarital sex by women, though not by men. It was in this way that a double standard for sexual behavior arose in which women were severely restricted to monogamous marriage, but men could do as they pleased. Thus, as the subordination of women emerged, the social mores and beliefs completely changed from the rough equality that men and women had shared during the communal period.

Under the laws of the Roman slave society, a woman who was the daughter of one of the master class was completely under the control of her father, and she had no rights of her own no matter how old she was. When she married, control of the woman was transferred to her husband and she still had no rights of her own. Women of the slave class belonged to their master. So the slave woman suffered under a double burden. She was exploited as a worker who was paid no money and had no rights, and she was also exploited sexually by her master.

RACIST MYTHS AND SLAVERY

In early Rome, the Romans had the same attitude as most other ancient cities, that is, most thought their city was the best one and acted patriotically toward it. They very slowly and reluctantly extended citizenship to the rest of the area under their control after several wars in the first century B.C.E. In the first century C.E., Rome became an empire and ruled most of the known world. As rulers of the world, at that time they considered themselves superior to most people.

They made slaves of many people, since that was a major purpose of military expansion. At that time, many Romans considered most Germans to be strong, but uncultured. So the Romans used German slaves for many difficult manual tasks. They also used some Germans, including whole tribes, as mercenaries.

Many Romans thought highly of the intellectual skills of the Greeks, though some Roman writers considered the Greeks to be decadent. Greek slaves were used for many skilled tasks, such as secretary, sculptor, or treasurer.

The Romans also made allies of some nations. And they slowly extended citizenship to the elite of all conquered countries. During the empire, however, being a Roman citizen gave one freedom, but not necessarily power. Increasingly, power was in the hands of the Emperor, while the Senate and the Roman citizens became less influential.

The ideology of racial superiority was very useful to the master class, first in Greece and then in Rome. Racism is defined as the ideology that one group is superior by birth to another group. Racism meant that the masters felt it was perfectly proper and legitimate to enslave other peoples. Racist ideology was so powerful that some of the slaves were also convinced of their inferiority. Racism meant that free Roman farmers felt that slavery was proper and supported it. Because of prejudice, free Roman farmers continued to support slavery even though slave plantations began to out-compete the independent farms and those farms often went bankrupt. The free Roman farmers were the backbone of the Roman army for a long time, so their loyalty to the Roman state was very important. Racism helped to cement that loyalty.

The masters had a vested interest in the racist myth that the slaves were inferior beings, so they reinforced it by every means possible. The priests of the early religions in Rome preached that the Romans were superior to all others. The philosophers of the ancient world all said that slavery was inevitable and natural, and even the great Aristotle argued that proposition. Politicians stated in their speeches to the population of Rome, rich and poor, that Romans were superior to all other peoples. Therefore, they said, even the poor should support the Roman state in its battles with others.

SLAVERY AND MYTHS OF DIVINITY

There was slavery in ancient Egypt, so a strong government was needed to prevent slave rebellions. A strong government was also needed to fight with other governments over slaves and ownership of land. The pharaoh was given absolute power and was proclaimed to be the divine son of a god. This was done to make the government more powerful; and thus this myth provided strong support for the political and economic status quo.

In order to expand this belief within the context of the religious mythology of Egypt, it was decided to protect the immortal body and soul of the pharaoh after his death by placing him for eternity in a huge pyramid. The pyramids also added to the perception of the awesome and impressive might of the Egyptian government. In order to build the pyramids, thousands of slaves were used as cheap labor. Thus the government's needs in a class society, the necessary religious myths, and the labor supply afforded by the class relations were all necessary to the building of the pyramids and the new technology that was developed during their creation.

TECHNOLOGY AND THE DIVISION OF LABOR.

The new agriculture was highly productive compared with the earlier light agriculture. With the new agricultural productivity, more specialists were possible because of the surplus of food. There emerged specialists in tool and weapon making, who were able to greatly improve the tools and weapons of Rome. It is interesting that these specialists were often slaves. There were police and soldiers to guard all the new wealth. The police and soldiers also had to keep the slaves under control. They intimidated the slaves with terror, and ruthlessly put down all slave uprisings.

There was also a class of priests, whose job was to advocate religion and lead religious practices. Priests, like soldiers, were paid out of the agricultural surplus by the ruling elite because the elite found these priests to be very useful. In some religions, such as that of the ancient Egyptians, the priests declared that the ruler was himself a god and could do no wrong. Mark Twain once observed that in every war, the priests on both sides declared that their side is morally superior and racially superior to the other side. Thus each side can call on God to help them kill their enemies.

Later, in the feudal period of Europe, priests declared that kings were divinely appointed by God, so everyone should obey them. During the American slave period, Southern clergy said that slavery was divinely ordained, while Northern clergy declared that God and morality demanded the abolition of slavery. Religion has often played a positive role in society. For example, sometimes religion was the only source of education. Religion also often played an ideological role in favor of retaining the existing institutions or in favor of revolution against the existing institutions.

GOVERNMENT AND SLAVERY

The change from communal to slave economies meant a big change in government. There was no separate government in the earliest communal period, only decisions by the leading members of the family. Sometimes someone was chosen temporarily to lead the groups in hunting or food gathering. After the Neolithic revolution, there was a long transitional period in government with increasing power going to chiefs. The eventual result was the emergence of a large, strong government with a slave economy. One task of government was to protect private property, especially property in the form of slaves, by using force to control slaves and put down their revolts.

In addition to starting wars to acquire more slaves, and repressing the subservient classes, and stopping bloody slave revolts, large governments were needed for the expansion and growth of the entire community. For example, in fertile river valleys, such as the Nile, the government had to control irrigation schemes, build dams or other means to control flooding, and establish laws for orderly landholding after a flood. But even these community service functions often had a class angle as well. For example, the Nile was controlled in ways that satisfied the landowner class but ignored the interests of the slaves.

The group that was governed was now far larger than a family. Although family interests were important for each individual, the ties that held the elite together in the governing system were mainly economic interests, not family ties. Of course, in Egypt and later in Rome, the close family of the ruler was on a much higher level than the families of the other nobility.

In the early communal society, the community as a whole decided on the use of force against an individual in the community or against outsiders. They made harsh but relatively democratic decisions. In a slave society, such as ancient Rome, the use of force was monopolized by the ruling elite of the master class. The use of force had to be authorized by the government, but that government was made up exclusively of the master class and contained no slaves. For most of its existence, the powerful Roman Senate had legal restrictions for membership that required a level of wealth attainable only by a small group. Since much wealth was in slaves, they had a common interest in repressing the slaves.

ECONOMIC INSTITUTIONS UNDER SLAVERY

The surplus produced by the slaves in agriculture and herding was used not only for the luxury living of the master class, but also for the employment of all kinds of specialists, including police, judges, and soldiers to uphold the government. The government employed scribes to record taxes as well as to write stories about kings' victories. This propaganda in favor of the kings was among the first uses of writing.

Once metal tools were invented, the master class employed craftspeople to make weapons, jewelry and other ornaments, pots for food, and pipes to carry water. This division of labor into many narrow specialties further increased productivity. There was now enough productivity to build large palaces and other monuments and to construct large cities. Although technology did not progress rapidly, the existing technology was used ingeniously to bring many comforts to the homes of the elite. The homes of the poor, by contrast, were tiny in size and lacked running water, plumbing, and other conveniences.

Civilizations based on slave labor and the labor of other subservient classes, with specialists and division of labor, with heavy agriculture and large cities, and with craft production, all followed the emergence of agriculture. To support such societies on an ideological basis, philosophers such as Aristotle proclaimed that it is natural for some people to be slaves and some to be masters, while it is also natural for women to be subservient to their fathers and husbands. It should be noted that philosophers received their living from the male nobility, who took it from the surplus produced by the slaves.

There was also a change in the values of people after communal life changed to slavery. Under early communal conditions, solidarity was vital, so the highest value was working for the good of the whole group of men, women, and children. In class-divided societies, it is every man for himself and a woman's duty is to support her man without asking questions. Traditions remained a long time after their basis had disappeared. In early Greek and Roman society, there were remnants of tales about the good old communal life and tales of heroism in its favor. However, most of the Romans in the later days of the empire came to have a completely individualist view, which claimed that only one's own welfare counted.

Table 2.1

Four Features of Ancient Slave Society

Technology	New stone tools to iron tools; farming and herding
Economic Institutions	Slaves work; masters take product
Social Institutions	Rule by masters in all social institutions
Ideology	Racism. Sexism, Classism

THE FOUR FEATURES OF SLAVE-BASED SOCIETY

We introduced in Chapter 1 four key institutional structures: technology, economic institutions, social institutions and ideology, which are the framework for understanding and comparing different societies at different points in time. Within our framework there are many features common to the ancient slave-based societies of the Near East, Egypt, Greece, and Rome that are summarized in the next few paragraphs and then developed in more detail in the rest of the chapter.

Technology was based on tools made of bronze and other metals. Most economic activity was agricultural, including farming and herding. Land was divided into large estates of the people who amassed land, goods and other forms of wealth, with a large slave labor force on each estate.

Economic institutions consisted mainly of the use of slaves by masters, with the slaves producing a surplus exploited from them by their masters. The slaves worked mainly in agriculture, domestic work, and service work in the cities. There also existed other types of unequal labor relations between the dominant group and the subordinate groups,

The **social institutions** supported slavery, from a priesthood that extolled slavery to an army and government that enforced it. Elite men were masters, and women were subordinate to them. Slave women were exploited both sexually and for their labor.

The dominant **ideology** strongly supported slavery, from the religious ideas to the philosophical arguments to the ideas stated by the politicians and the great orators. The ideology included racist prejudice against all foreigners, sexist prejudice against women, and elitist prejudice against all the subordinate groups that did the labor of society.

These four features are summarized very briefly in Table 2.1.

SUMMARY OF STEPS FROM COMMUNAL SOCIETY TO SLAVERY

First, the ideology, social institutions, and economic institutions of the early communal economy all held back rapid technological advance. Yet they were sufficient to promote extremely slow technological progress over tens of thousands of years. Eventually, the communal society produced new and better stone tools, changed from gathering fruits and vegetables to farming and changed from hunting to herding.

The new technology created the conditions for the emergence of slavery. The new technology of agriculture meant that a person could produce a surplus above their own **subsistence**, *a minimal level of goods and services needed to support life*, needs. The higher productivity of the new agriculture meant that there was some wealth to be gained by war, including prisoners who could be used as slaves. The heavy implements used in agriculture of that day were used by the slaves to produce a surplus large enough for their own needs, to support the luxury living of the masters, and to produce huge monuments (such as pyramids) and enormous cities.

The new technology and new economic institutions forced what was left of the old communal economy to change because it held back further progress. After a long transitional period of mixed communal and private ownership, the old system eventually disappeared and was replaced by slavery and other forced labor. The old ideology, based on ideas of community solidarity of all its members, was destroyed. Remnants of the old ideology lived only in folk tales. Communal political equality gave way to a transitional period of chiefs in large tribes. The tribes then gave way to empires, including very large cities with massive bureaucracies, police, and armies.

Men controlled the slaves in heavy agriculture, which was the main source of food. From their power gained by control of the slaves, men were able to exercise domination over women in society. The transition from early communal institutions, with roughly equal political and economic power among all adults to slavery with masters and emperors led to many bitter struggles. The struggles were between people defending the doomed old communal institutions and those in favor of the new, seemingly invincible, slave institutions. Few of these conflicts were described in writing at the time. Writing and literature emerged only during the time of slavery, so the accounts of events were written by members of the master class from their own viewpoint and in their own interest.

In a nutshell, society created new technology. The new technology undermined existing economic institutions and created tensions in the society that could not be resolved peacefully. Some people resisted change but, in a long transition, the struggle for change was won by the increasingly powerful master class. Slavery and other types of oppression became dominant. This revolution took place over thousands of years, but in the end this revolution changed all of human life.

SUGGESTED READING

We know much about slave civilizations from their own writing and also from archeological evidence. The most pleasant and fascinating introduction to archaeology is *Gods, Graves and Scholars* by Ceram (1986). It deals with the exciting discovery of some slave civilizations including Troy, ancient Egypt, and ancient Crete.

Many books in anthropology and archaeology deal with the transition from the rough equality of communal bands to the slavery of the ancient civilizations. The most wonderful to read is Diamond, *Guns, Germs, and Steel* (1997). It is clear and up-to-date in its facts but written in a popular style that fascinates readers. To read about how sugar played an important role in the industrial revolution of the nineteenth century see Mintz, *Sweetness and Power* (1986).

KEY TERMS

B.C.E.	propaganda
diffusion	subsistence
neolithic revolution	surplus
private property rights	

REVIEW QUESTIONS

Comprehend the components and processes of the Neolithic revolution.
1. What are the three key discoveries comprising the Neolithic revolution?
2. What and where is the earliest evidence of agriculture, better stone tools and pottery?
3. What is diffusion?

4. Explain the role of geography in early farming.
5. How did agriculture spread from where it originated?

Explain the role that increasing productivity played in changing social and economic institutions.

6. How is technology changing? How did the changing technology improve productivity?
7. Explain how productivity aids specialization and how specialization improves productivity.
8. What is the relationship of increasing productivity and the creation of surplus? Be sure to define the term surplus in your answer.
9. Why is surplus so crucial in the further changes in society?
10. How did increasing productivity enable towns to grow in size and population?
11. What is wealth and why are some people able to accumulate wealth?
12. Explain the significance of private property rights for accumulating wealth.
13. Why was war not practical or profitable in communal society? Why does increasing productivity and surplus now make war profitable?
14. How do widening differences in economic wealth translate into widening differences in political power?

Understand the composition of a slave society.

15. What main groups of people comprised the slave population?
16. Who were the independent farmers and why did independent farms die out?
17. Why did workers in the cities who were not slaves remain poor?

Comprehend the changing ideologies.

18. What is the sequence of events that led women's status to change from rough equality with men to being subordinate to men?
19. What is the explanation for the rise of the "double standard" for men and women?
20. What are examples of some racist myths or prejudice?
21. Why is the ideology of racial superiority so useful to the ruling class? Give examples to support your reasoning.
22. Explain the emergence of priests and religious leaders in the slave society. What role do they play in this society?
23. How does governing change in the slave society?

Explain how the four institutions of society changed in the evolution from communal to slave-based society.

24. Explain the common features of ancient slave-based societies for each of the four institutional structures in our framework: technology, economic institutions, social institutions, and ideology.
25. How are the features of each institutional structure different from communal society?

CHAPTER 3

Slavery to Feudalism in Western Europe

This chapter explores how slavery ended and feudalism emerged as the dominant system in Western Europe. It explains how most slavery in Western Europe changed, sometimes slowly and sometimes violently and rapidly, into serfdom. The institutions of serfdom were the main defining feature of the feudal economy though a small amount of slavery continued throughout feudalism.

LEARNING OBJECTIVES

After reading this chapter, you should be able to:

- Comprehend how slavery limited the economic institutions and technology of the Roman Empire.
- Explain the effects of slavery on the Roman army.
- Describe the motivations and the steps in the movement from slavery to serfdom.

RULING THE ROMAN EMPIRE

The political structure of ancient Rome was closely entwined with the slave-based economy. For some time during the second and third centuries B.C.E., Rome was a **republic**, *a nation in which power is held by the people or their elected representatives.* In the Roman republic, all of the male citizens not including male slaves were, at least in theory, equal. Democracy, government by the whole population usually through elected representatives, existed for those male citizens who could vote.

After titanic struggles and civil wars, Rome became an **empire**, *an extensive area of land or countries under a single authority, with no democracy.* There was an emperor who had most of the power plus a weak senate composed mostly of the wealthiest slave owners. The Roman senate pretended to function independently for a long time after the republic died, but it surrendered most of its power to the emperor. In both the republic and the empire, the slaves had no power.

Rome followed the same path as many other ancient peoples, from small bands of hunters and gatherers to large tribes with powerful chiefs. Eventually, the most powerful tribes became city dwellers with a government that also ruled the surrounding areas. Finally, Roman conquests created an empire. The empire was a collection of tribes, cities, and subordinate countries. In the transition from communal societies, the ruler gained ever more power, evolving from temporary leader to hereditary chief, then to king of a city, and finally to emperor, with absolute power over an enormous area.

When Rome was a republic, how could it justify the fact that the slaves had no rights? The answer was embedded in the racist view that slaves were only property, not people and certainly not citizens. This racist view was embodied in all of the Roman laws. Even when there was a form of democracy in ancient Greece and Rome, the slaves, who were the majority of the people in much of this period, had no rights. Of course, women were also excluded from democratic procedures. This was a democracy that was not made up of all the people, but was an exclusive minority of elite, slave-owning males, who did all the ruling.

SLAVERY, WORK, TECHNOLOGY, AND CHANGE

In the early period of the ancient world of slavery, there was tremendous technological improvement beyond whatever had existed under early communal economic institutions. As spelled out in the previous chapter, when slaves could produce a surplus, that surplus supported all kinds of specialists including a slave-owning master class. Specialization led to further technological development, the building of large cities and monuments, advances in astronomy, wonderful works of art, and a standardized and systematic legal system.

In the ancient slave civilizations, the specialists—who were often slaves—figured out excellent ways of improving life. The improvements were then used by the masters, so their homes were comfortable places with many conveniences. They had water piped to their houses and forms of central heating, in many cases. The architecture was beautiful. Of course, the slaves were excluded from using most of the comforts of Roman life, even though they had produced it all.

There was very little industry in the Roman Empire. Agriculture was dominant and it remained the largest economic sector until the nineteenth century. Agriculture remained dominant even longer in many areas of the world. At the peak period of ancient Rome, 90 to 95 percent of the people worked in agriculture. Most of the agricultural workers were slaves on large plantations. In addition to the masters and the slaves, there were always free farmers in agriculture, though their numbers declined over time.

The cities were tiny islands in a sea of agriculture, yet the cities grew to be enormous and controlled mighty armies. This was possible because the cities were supported by the surplus flowing in from the countryside, as well as the labor of the slaves and the craftspeople in the cities. Rome seemed so powerful that people thought that the empire and slavery would last forever. What led to the decline and fall of the mighty Roman Empire?

In Western Europe, the Roman Empire and its institution of slavery disappeared in the fourth and fifth centuries C.E. (*Common Era,* that is, *since year 1 of our calendar*). The decline of the Roman Empire culminated in the fall of Rome itself to Germanic tribal invaders in 456 C.E. The decline, however, started much earlier.

The great wealth of Rome was built by the device of slavery. The problem was that slavery put up barriers to further economic growth. Specifically, consider the following problems.

One reason for stagnation and decline was the attitude and behavior of the master class. In the ancient Roman Empire the ruling elite did no manual work and often no clerical or professional work, except to govern or lead armies. Slaves produced all of the food in agriculture. Slaves made custom clothing for their masters. Slaves prepared the food for their masters. Slaves were domestic servants, providing everything that was desired by the masters, including sex by the slave women. All heavy work was done by slaves. But, slaves also did much intellectual work, such as accounting and supervising other slaves. Moreover, some slaves were artists, dancers, and musicians.

Since only slaves did the actual production, the entire area of economic production came to be seen as a place for slaves. People at the very top of the elite ladder perceived anything associated with the dirty business of production to be beneath them. The elite had supervisors who handled the slaves on their plantation and sent the profits to the slave owners in Rome. They had supervisors for every kind of labor as well as treasurers to take care of their money.

The top elite looked down their noses at anyone who was interested in ways of improving production. With few exceptions, the elite took no part in science or technological improvement. This attitude was one of the reasons that after a certain point in their history, the Romans did not produce much new technology even though they made advances in governing and war making.

In addition, slavery produced a sufficient surplus for all of the masters' needs without further changes in technology.

Many plantation owners lived in absentia in Rome. A great many of the plantation owners knew nothing about agricultural technology. Moreover, the owners usually had enough money that they did not have a driving compulsion to get more profit from their estates. If they needed more money, they were likely to use the government. For example, a rich Roman could become a colonial governor and loot his province of its surplus in various ways, both legal and illegal. For all of these reasons, the slave-owning class allowed technology to stagnate in the later Roman Empire.

A second reason for technological stagnation was that some of the early impetus to improvements came from the free farmers and the free artisans. But farms were slowly taken over by slave plantations as the men were drafted into the army for long periods of time or the taxes were increased beyond their ability to pay. The free artisans had to compete with slaves who were paid a minimum subsistence, and many of the free artisans went out of business. As slavery became dominant, some of the groups who had the incentive to make technological improvements were greatly reduced in numbers.

A third problem tending to cause stagnation was that the slaves also had little interest in technological innovation. A more productive technique would not have reduced the number of hours or the intensity with which they had to labor. Their hours and intensity of work were not affected because they were always pushed to the maximum, no matter what technology they used. The slaves saw nothing for them in new technology and, as we shall see, often actively resisted changes in how they did their work.

A fourth problem for changing technology also was a result of the master-slave relationship. It was not profitable to give the slaves the expensive equipment necessary to increase production. If the slaves were given a large new device meant to improve their productivity, they acted against the introduction of the new technology. They acted this way for very rational reasons. For one thing, if the slaves could sabotage the equipment, this action would give them some rest time. As a stronger reaction, they could turn the new equipment into weapons in order to rise up and kill the masters. Therefore, putting money into developing new equipment made no sense.

Fifth, slavery meant that it was difficult or impossible to use a complex organization of work, such as many different crops in different fields. Slaves could only be effectively supervised if they all did the same work and if nobody was out of sight. But good agriculture required planting different crops and changing them from time to time. By planting just one crop to make supervision easy, the land eventually became exhausted. The less productive land was another reason for stagnation.

Sixth, even for simple types of production, a large number of supervisors were needed to prevent slave revolts. The masters were always terrified of the prospect of slave revolts. In fact, the Roman Empire witnessed many small slave revolts at fairly frequent intervals, but there were also some massive slave revolts. During the slave revolt led by the gladiator, Spartacus, the slaves defeated three Roman armies sent against them. When they were finally defeated, most of the slaves were crucified.

But if slaves did not get enough to eat and died at a young age, or if they were killed for revolting or for attempts to escape, it meant that the supply of slaves was often insufficient. This problem became worse and worse over time. There was a vicious circle because the supply of slaves could only be drastically increased by new conquests. On the other hand, slavery weakened the empire, so it became more difficult to make conquests.

For all of these reasons, although slavery at first brought great advances over earlier methods of production, after a certain point technological change and productivity stagnated and output stopped rising. The fact that slavery was so much more productive than the earlier communal system allowed the system of slavery to last for hundreds of years, but the system of slavery had limits to its progress, which led it to stagnation and an eventual fall to invaders.

SLAVERY AND MILITARY POWER

In addition to the economic problems, another problem linked to slavery was the weakening of the Roman army. Slaves could not be put in the army and given weapons because they could use them against their officers and lead even stronger revolts. The early Roman army was largely composed of free farmers. But, as noted earlier, the class of free farmers slowly declined. Farmers were forced to spend long years in the army and many were killed fighting. When a soldier came home after twenty years or more, his farm was often gone, taken by the government for unpaid taxes or sold to slave plantations. Even those who stayed home had to compete with the products of cheap slave labor, so a steady stream of free farms went bankrupt. When their owners could not pay debts, they often ended up as slaves themselves (see Anderson, 1974).

At any rate, fewer farmers to draft into the army—and other problems such as increasing corruption and lessened ability to pay the soldiers—weakened the army. Yet the threat of the surrounding Germanic tribes remained or grew as the tribes improved their weapons and strategy after contact with the Romans. The tribes were separate from each other, but were known collectively by the Romans as Germans or Goths. The tribes were all in various stages of the transitional period from communal societies to class-divided societies based on slavery or other kinds of labor. During this period, the tribes were led by chiefs, nobles, and priests, but the common people retained some rights.

After a while, in order to fill the ranks of soldiers needed, the Romans hired some of the Germanic tribes as mercenaries. One of their main jobs was to fight other Germanic tribes. They often had little desire to fight others like themselves so the Roman army became less effective. At the same time the army became filled with more mercenaries, the central power of Rome declined and it had fewer resources to pay the army. Various units decided to make money for themselves by taking extra taxes from conquered areas. Later, they even forced Roman plantations to pay for "protection." Paying for protection really just means paying someone not to attack you. The army just agreed not to attack a particular plantation as long as it paid money to the army.

As the army declined in power, the Germanic tribes advanced farther into the relatively affluent empire. Even while the Germanic tribes advanced, the Roman army generals perceived the weakness of the emperor. Therefore, some generals proclaimed themselves emperor. After ruinous civil wars, some of the generals did indeed become emperors until they in turn were overthrown.

Eventually, law and order declined and only military might mattered. The empire was slowly dismembered and each little area became to some degree independent of the Roman emperor. In some areas, there were bands of armed slaves trying to survive. In some areas there were Roman legions looking for loot in any form available. In some areas, the Germanic tribes conquered the region. Eventually, in 456 C.E. even the city of Rome was taken and sacked by a Germanic tribal army, marking an advanced stage of decline of the Roman Empire.

FROM SLAVERY TO SERFDOM

Even though slavery existed for many centuries, the decline of safety and productivity in the third and fourth centuries C.E. made slavery less appealing to the elite than other forms of subordination and exploitation. The Roman plantation owners wanted a workforce that would be less likely than slaves to revolt whenever there was an armed attack on the estate and more likely to help defend the estate. They also wanted a work force that would be more productive than slaves but would not need a great many supervisors with whips.

On many plantations slaves were given a little more freedom and graduated to the category of "serfs." A **serf** is defined as *someone who owes service to the land owner or lord for a certain number of days a year, but is given his or her own small amount of land for subsistence farming.* The serf is bound to the land, must remain there, and belongs to whatever lord captures the land. The serf, however, cannot be bought and sold as a slave, so the serf's children cannot be sold to another master. The serf is subordinate, is exploited, and produces a surplus for the lord, but has somewhat more freedom than a slave.

During the decline of the Roman Empire from the third to the fifth century, some bankrupt free farmers became subordinate to landlords. They were not called slaves or serfs and even continued to be called "free men" throughout their service, but they were subordinate to the lords and had to provide certain labor services. Serfdom meant varying degrees of subordination to the lord of the estate. There were varying obligations to perform work on the lord's land for a certain number of days a year and to give some kind of payment in goods or other services to the lord of the estate. Finally, a small percentage of slaves continued to exist through most of the feudal period.

During the decline of the Empire, exactly why did the Roman elite change from being slave masters to being lords of feudal estates with serfs? In economic terms, the serf had some motivation to work and provide goods or services to the lord in return for possessing a piece of land. To possess land meant to have a degree of independence and economic stability. That possession, however, would only last as long as the serf worked for the lord without additional compensation. The right of the lord to those services or goods in return for letting the serf use some land was strictly enforced, not only by tradition and law, but also by the use of force beyond the law. Each lord kept a group of armed men to hold down the serfs and force them to perform labor services.

A second reason why the masters were forced to change from the use of slavery to serfdom was a military one. If the estate or manor was attacked, slaves could seize the opportunity and revolt. Serfs, however, had some interest in the manor because they had their own small plots of land. Therefore, the serfs usually saw the attackers as a greater evil than their own feudal lord. Hence the serfs could be more of a supporting group in a military defense or at least they were not likely to be another hostile group. The serfs proved to be both more willing to work and far more helpful, or at least less dangerous, in military situations than slaves.

Serfs could not be bought or sold as a slave and had a plot of land that might be enough to feed his or her family. The serf had some incentive to work on the lord's land and not revolt. This concept—that the ideal way of life was for lords to protect and serfs to produce—was part of the powerful role of tradition in the feudal period. Yet serfs were still exploited and spent most of their time producing for the lord. Serfs were held down by two mechanisms. First the lord employed his own soldiers, who held the serfs down by force. In addition to the use of force, the lords used an ideology to convince everyone of the righteousness of what they were extracting from the serfs. They emphasized the idea that the lord was protecting the serf from roving armed bands. The next chapter will discuss in depth the system of feudalism. **Feudalism** may be defined briefly as *a system based on serfdom, where political power was mainly decentralized from kings to lords of estates, called feudal manors.*

In addition to the Roman elite, parts of the empire were controlled by chiefs of Germanic tribes. As they gained wealth, they came to have more power over their followers. They were attracted to the feudal scheme in which their leading followers became nobles and military supporters, while their less powerful followers became subordinate workers similar to serfs. Since this subordination was happening within their own ranks, it was also natural and convenient to make the conquered Romans or other peoples into serfs. Serfdom had the same economic and military appeals to the former tribal chiefs, who had now become feudal lords, as it had to the Roman elite.

Eventually, by different paths, all of Western Europe became a set of feudal manors, consisting of lords and serfs. There were also "free men" who were similar to the serfs, but with a few more rights. Trade and commerce had broken down because of both economic stagnation and the lack of any law and order. Each feudal manor became isolated from the others in an economic sense. They each tried to be completely self-sufficient. Each became a small society, isolated from all others.

The most powerful and ambitious lords became kings of large territories. They retained complete power over law and control within their own manors, and the lesser lords owed them allegiance. They only agreed to give military support as necessary. The king was usually just a greater feudal lord, so the king had to raise all the revenues of the kingdom on his own estates.

Feudalism provided the possibility of more productivity from serfs than there ever was from slaves. The possibility of greater productivity, however, did not materialize for several centuries. In the chaos of the decline of the Roman Empire, which had held Western Europe together as a unified area including much of the Mediterranean, the great Roman cities declined and some of them disappeared. Since the area was no longer a political unity, trade between distant places was no longer protected by the Roman army and trade declined for the next several centuries.

Moreover, the Roman level of technology was dependent on vast numbers of specialists available in each city. When the population centers mostly died and travel became very risky, there were no longer all the needed specialists available in most places. In the isolated feudal manors, only a few types of specialists were usually present. Therefore, the level of technology also declined for centuries. These were rightly called the Dark Ages, penetrated by little "light." Ignorance and illiteracy dominated the scene, as each lord tried to protect his own area and ruled over a system of subsistence production for his manor. The old centers of learning died as the Roman surplus disappeared, and much knowledge of science was lost in Western Europe.

CONCLUSIONS ON THE TRANSITION TO FEUDALISM

The myth of "inevitable progress" in technology and in civilization was proven false in the fall of Rome. In the modern world, we often take technological progress for granted and think of it as inevitable. Actually, this has not been the case in many areas at various points in time. One example was the stagnation of technology in ancient Rome for several centuries. Not only was there stagnation, there was a decline of technology in the Dark Ages following the decline and fall of the Roman Empire.

Rather than being inevitable, technological progress happens only when the social and economic institutions and the dominant ideology enable it to improve. That was not the case in the late

Roman Empire or the early feudal period. Slavery and all of its related institutions and ideology held back technology in the later Roman Empire. The chaos that followed the fall of the empire resulted in the isolation of each manor from all others. This caused a further decline of technology during the centuries of transition to the new institutions that followed

One can see this in a striking way if one compares the Roman cities of Pompeii and Herculaneum, both buried by volcanic eruptions, with the castles and villages of the feudal period. The Roman cities were filled with conveniences for the elite and with evidence of high culture and art works. The castles of early to middle feudalism were unpleasant, cold places to live and the villages of the serfs lacked any amenities. The lifespan of the serfs was short and filled with hardship and misery.

To summarize, the mechanism by which slavery was transformed to serfdom can be laid out in several steps. First, Roman economic institutions, the dominant Roman ideology, and Roman social institutions were permeated with slavery and its related effects. The institutions and ideology based on slavery resulted in technological stagnation.

Second, that stagnation created powerful tensions in Roman agriculture, Roman trade, and the Roman army. These tensions within the slave-based institutions of Rome were not solvable until slavery was ended and a new system of institutions created.

Third, the fact that the tensions could not be resolved within existing institutions led to the decline of Roman agriculture and weakening of the Roman army. This led to various types of social conflicts: class conflicts between masters and slaves seen in major revolts, as well as class conflicts in Rome between the aristocrats and the poor citizens. There were also ethnic conflicts between the Romans and surrounding Germanic tribes, who saw an opportunity to conquer their old enemy. The conflicts between wandering groups of slaves, Roman legions, and Germanic tribal armies produced great insecurity in the economically weakened agricultural estates. These conflicts led to the fall of Rome, which meant that the benefits of the Empire—common laws, maintained roads, shared currency, and a military to maintain order—vanished. This led to still lower technology and several centuries of decline. Finally, as a result of these conflicts, the system of feudalism was born, with isolated manors containing serfs, nobility, and armed retainers.

SUMMARY

This chapter explains how most slavery in Western Europe changed, sometimes slowly but sometimes violently and rapidly, into serfdom. The institution of serfdom was the main defining feature of the feudal economy (though a small amount of slavery continued throughout feudalism). There were three main sources of serfs in this region: former slaves, former free farmers, and the former rank and file of the Germanic tribes.

SUGGESTED READINGS

There are hundreds of books on the decline of the Roman Empire, but the best one that deals with both the decline of slavery and the rise of feudal serfdom is a book by Perry Anderson, *Passages from Antiquity to Feudalism* (1974). Anderson's book contains all of the factual knowledge and theoretical discussions relevant to this chapter. Although many earlier books on the issue have interesting things to say, Anderson includes the best of all of them and lays it out in a concise and readable manner.

KEY TERMS

C.E.	republic
empire	serf
feudalism	

REVIEW QUESTIONS

Comprehend how slavery limited the economic institutions and technology of the Roman Empire.

1. Who produced most of the goods and services for Rome?
2. How was production perceived by the slave owners and the ruling class? Why does this attitude limit technological change and motivation for technological change?
3. Why do slaves have little interest in changing technology?
4. Why might the slave owner not want to introduce new technology?

Explain the effects of slavery on the Roman army.

5. How did the composition of the Roman army change after the introduction of slavery?
6. Why is the changing composition of the Roman army a problem for the Roman Empire?

Describe the motivations and the steps in the movement from slavery to serfdom.

7. Discuss the two main reasons for the change from slavery to serfdom.
8. Explain the steps in the shift from slave society to a feudal society.
9. How is a serf like a slave and how is a serf different from a slave?
10. What incentives did a serf have not to revolt and how is this different from the slaves?
11. How did some of the chiefs of the Germanic tribes controlling parts of the Roman Empire move to feudalism?
12 Why was the possibility of increased productivity of serfs not realized for several centuries?

CHAPTER 4

Feudalism and Paternalism in England

Using our framework of the four categories: technology, economic institutions, social institutions, and ideology, this chapter starts out by describing the four features of feudalism. The four features show that feudalism was very different from the slave societies that came before it or the capitalist societies that came after it in England. The chapter stresses that feudalism is distinguished from other systems not only by its economic and political institutions, but also by its Christian paternalist ideology.

LEARNING OBJECTIVES

After reading this chapter, you should be able to:

- List and explain the four features of society under feudalism.
- Explain the concept and evolution of Christian paternalism and its role in supporting feudalism.

THE FEATURES OF FEUDALISM

The four features of feudalism that distinguish it from the slave systems that preceded it are as follows:

1. Economic institutions: Most production on the manor is performed by serfs while the feudal lord makes all economic decisions and owns the product of all labor on the land of the manor.
2. Social institutions: Power is decentralized from the king to the lords, so all legal, economic, and military power is held by the lord of the manor. A large part of the land and the power is held by the church.
3. Technology: The level of technology fell in the early feudal period and rose slowly thereafter.
4. Ideology: The ideas dominant at this period of time include the divine right of kings and the subordination of women to men. The lord of the manor was supported by the inertia of tradition and sanction of religious teaching. These brief descriptions of the four features are amplified in the rest of this chapter.

Economic Institutions

The economic institution of serfdom is defined by the fact that the serf had to work on the lord's land doing agricultural and other duties for a certain number of days a year, but could work on his or her own land the rest of the time. The last chapter showed that the feudal economic institution of serfdom originated in three different ways: Roman slaves were turned into serfs, Roman farmers were turned into near-serfs, and barbarian tribespeople became serfs.

Roman slaves became serfs partly because the land owners felt that the serf would have a greater stake in the land than would the slave. This meant that the serf would be more likely to support his or her own lord in an attack rather than revolt as the slaves did. The land owners also believed that the serf would work with higher productivity than the slaves on the lord's land because of the threat that they would lose their own land.

A second source of feudal labor came from free Roman farmers. Unlike the serfs, the free Roman farmers remained technically free, but they were coerced to work for the feudal lord in return for the "protection" of the lord. This was a protection in which the lord took services and goods from the peasant to "protect" them from other would-be "protectors," such as barbarian tribal kings. It was not clear that they would be any worse off under these kings. In fact, it was clear in much of the feudal period that the most dangerous predator to the peasant was the feudal lord. It was only a fiction that the lord agreed to protect the peasant from other predators out of a sense of duty. At any rate, the status of the "free" peasants on the lord's land eventually became very similar to that of the serfs.

A third source of feudal serfs was the free members of barbarian bands. After the barbarian tribes conquered parts of the Roman Empire, the ordinary members of the tribe slowly became mere subjects of their now powerful chiefs, who soon called themselves kings. Eventually, the ordinary tribal members came to have a status like that of the serfs, though they might still technically be free. Both serfs and free persons owed services and/or goods to the lord, while the lord had all the military power to enforce these traditional duties. In brief, the first feature of feudalism, the economic institution of serfdom, had three sources of labor: slaves, free farmers, and barbarian tribal members.

Social Institutions

The second feature of feudalism was its social and political institutions. The institutions of the feudal manor included the legal power of the lord to do as he liked. The lord was typically a "he" although there were a few examples of manors under the management of a lady, rather than a lord. Thus, the personal pronoun "he" is clearly the more typical title. The lord had both legal and economic power on his estate and commanded a large military force. There was little practical difference between military command, political power, and economic power.

The lords used military force as well as tradition and religious teachings to control the serfs. This meant that the lords could take their traditional dues and services, but could also demand arbitrary new dues, usually in the form of goods, and feudal law said that this was proper. The serfs, however, did resist, sometimes by force, so the lord in reality did have constraints on his greed. Even though the lords competed bitterly among themselves, they usually met a peasant revolt with a united force, so this enhanced the power of each individual lord. Since religious intolerance was considered normal in the period, religion and tradition were a powerful determinant of who did what in the feudal period. On the other hand, religion itself was shaped by feudal society. Remember that many of the feudal lords were part of the church hierarchy.

Technology

The third feature of society is technology. Technological progress declined for the first few centuries of feudalism after the breakdown of the Roman Empire. After that, it rose very, very slowly for the rest of the feudal period. There were many barriers to progress, but not quite as many as under slavery.

Ideology

Dominant feudal ideas included the God-given right of kings and nobles to rule. Another dominant idea was the subordination of women to men. Both of these ideas were advocated by the Roman Catholic Church, the only form of Christianity in Western Europe during the early and middle feudal period. Except for small groups of persecuted Jews and Muslims, the Catholic Church had a monopoly on religion. Its leader, the pope, held absolute power in the church and considerable power in society. The church was the largest single landowner and treated its serfs about the same as any other feudal lord. Theology ruled supreme under feudalism and science was considered subversive. Some scientists were burned alive for stating scientific ideas that conflicted with church doctrine. The church forced even the great scientist Galileo Galilei (1564–1642) to cease his attempt to prove that the earth travels around the sun.

DYNAMIC RELATIONS OF FEUDALISM

Some of the relationships of feudal society were obvious and some not so obvious. Each feudal manor had only one center of power and the lord was both the political power and the economic power. There was no separate political sphere in feudalism. Economics and politics were so closely interwoven that it made no sense to try to separate them. The economic system worked in part because the lord enforced the services owed to him by the use of force. Over the centuries, tradition came to play a big role. Serfs gave the traditional amount of service and lords demanded the traditional amount of service. Only in situations of crisis were the traditions sometimes challenged or overthrown.

Religion also played a central role in feudal society. The church hierarchy was shaped to look like the **secular** (*not related to religion or religious beliefs*) hierarchy, which consisted of lesser nobles, greater nobles, and the king. In fact, the church not only looked like the feudal system, it was very much part of it in concrete terms. The church owned large estates in every country. Altogether, the church owned more land than anyone else. Each of the church estates was run the same way as any other estate. The church representative who ran the estate used the services of serfs like any other feudal lord did. They used soldiers to enforce their decisions as did any other feudal lord. Just as the feudal lords owed their allegiance to higher feudal lords, the representative of the church who ran the estate owed allegiance to a bishop or someone else above him—or her, as the church system included both monasteries *and* nunneries.

Not only was the church a great landowner, it also was the main source of information and education. It was the media, it founded the schools, and it established the religious training centers. One of its primary messages was that the feudal system was ordained by God, so all good Christians must obey the feudal laws and traditions. Thus the serf was told to serve the lord in all he asked the serf to do, while the lord was told to follow the wishes of the higher lords and the king.

There were few written laws, but there were many traditional rights where the lord made all decisions and enforced them by might. Each feudal lord, secular or religious, had his own court to which the peasants must come for justice. Of course, a peasant had a good chance to get justice against another peasant, but no chance against the feudal lord himself. It would be very unhealthy to bring a case against the lord, because the lord was often close friends with the judges. There was also a higher justice from the king or from a bishop. In later feudalism, as kings became stronger, the kings appointed traveling justices who represented the king and presided over a system of courts.

Some feudal laws may seem very strange to people living under contemporary capitalism. There was, in theory, no land ownership. The serf merely was able to use his or her land as long as he or she gave service to the feudal lord, but the serf never owned the land outright. Even the feudal lord had the right to use his land only so long as he served the greater lord above him. In theory, even the king did not own his land, but could use it only as long as he served God, who was the greatest landlord, owning all the land. Property "belonged" to the lord because he possessed it and defended it with his knights. There were no land title documents, and most lords never even considered the possibility of selling off a piece of their kingdom.

MEN, WOMEN AND FEUDALISM

Peasant men, whether serf or technically free, were subordinate to the feudal lord. Women were subordinate to the feudal lord, but they were also subordinate to male serfs to some degree. Men usually served the lord in the fields, doing heavy labor such as plowing, and also herding animals. Women serfs performed long hours of service to the lord in domestic tasks, including making clothing from raw material—from shearing the sheep and preparing the wool, to sewing the finished garments. They might also cook in the lord's kitchen, mind his children, and clean his house. When they finished the day's work for the lord, they were allowed to go home and work about the house—preparing food, minding children, cleaning the house until the sun set. In England, as late as the twelfth century C.E., most serfs were too poor to afford candles.

Women were not only exploited for their labor, but were also sexually exploited. Many lords and their sons fathered children by serf women, who had conceived by having sex under coercion or threat. In some regions, the lord had the right of the first night, the right of deflowering a virgin before she could have sexual relations with her new husband. All marriages among the ruling class were arranged for purposes of enlarging a lord's power or allies. Many marriages were arranged when girls were very small or even just born. Frequently, a teenaged girl was married to an old man. Supposedly if a girl was engaged at a very young age, she could change her mind at age twelve. In practice, however, the pressure from her parents usually prevailed, so the marriage would go ahead.

Romantic love as we know it hardly existed in this age of arranged marriages and forced sex. However, when the lords went off to fight in the crusades they had to leave their wives at home. The lords had sex with women along the way to Jerusalem, but what about their wives at home? At this time there was a class of wandering minstrels who went to sing in every castle on their route. They often gave a special service to the women of the lords. Of course, the minstrel could never marry the lord's wife, even if the lord was killed in battle, so there were many ballads of love that was brief and beautiful, but had to end without a happy life ever after for the lovers. Thus, the notion of romantic love first appeared in literature (aside from a few earlier exceptions) during the late Middle Ages. This helped set the stage for further changes in the notion of love in later capitalist societies.

THE CHRISTIAN PATERNALIST ETHIC

The feudal lords, secular as well as religious, needed an ideology that would reflect and justify the feudal status quo. This ideology, which provided the moral cement holding feudal Europe together and protecting its rulers, was the medieval version of the Judeo-Christian tradition. This tradition evolved a moral code sometimes called the Christian corporate ethic, reflecting the fact that all of society was considered a single entity or corporation. To emphasize another feature of it, the *Judeo-Christian moral code as interpreted in the medieval period,* will be called the **Christian paternalist ethic** in this book.

The Christian paternalist ethic can be most easily understood by comparing society with a family. Those with positions of power and wealth can be likened to the father or keeper of the family. They have strong fatherly or paternalistic obligations toward the common people or, in our analogy, the children. The common person was expected to accept his or her place in society and to be willingly subordinate to the leadership of the wealthy and the powerful in much the same way that a child accepts the authority of his or her father.

The Old Testament Jews quite literally regarded themselves as the children of one God, and that God had given them, through Moses, certain laws to live by. Their relationship as children of God meant that all Jews were brothers. Note that the tradition thought only in terms of men and brothers, not women and sisters, because women were subordinate. The Jewish law was intended to maintain this feeling of membership in one big family. The brotherhood was one of grown children who acknowledged their mutual obligations even though they no longer shared possessions.

From the mass of duties and regulations governing the early Jews, the most salient feature is the large number of provisions made for the prevention and relief of poverty. Their humane treatment of debtors was also notable. Each Jew was to be his brother's keeper. Indeed, his obligations extended to caring for his neighbor's animals should they wander his way (Holy Bible, Deuteronomy 22:1–4). The first duty, and particularly the duty of the wealthy, was to care for the poor: ". . . Thou shalt open thine hand wide unto my brother, to the poor, and to the needy, in the land" (Deuteronomy 15:11). Another important element in this paternalistic code was the sanction against taking a worker's tools as a means of satisfying a debt: "No man shalt take the nether or the upper millstone to pledge; for he taketh a man's life to pledge" (Deuteronomy 24:6). The same point was made in the apocryphal biblical literature, written centuries after Deuteronomy: "He that taketh away his neighbor's living slayeth him" (Ecclesiasticus, 34:22).

All Jews did not, of course, live up to these lofty teachings. Great extremes of wealth and poverty existed that would have been impossible had the Mosaic Law (the Jewish law that started with Moses) been strictly observed. Many of the prophets were champions of the poor and eloquently denounced the rich for their abuse of their wealth, for their wicked, slothful luxury, and for their general unrighteousness. The important point is not that they failed to live up to the code, but that the moral code of this small tribe left such important an imprint on much of subsequent history.

The teachings of Christ in the New Testament carry on a part of the Mosaic tradition that is relevant to economic ideology. He taught the necessity of being concerned with the welfare of one's brother, the importance of charity and almsgiving, and the evil of selfish acquisitiveness and covetousness. His emphasis on the special responsibilities and obligations of the rich is even more pronounced than that of the earlier Jewish writers. In fact, on the basis of a reading of the Gospel according to Luke, one might conclude that Christ condemned the rich simply because they were rich and praised the poor simply because they were poor. "Woe unto you that are rich! for ye have received your consolation. Woe unto you that are full! for ye shall hunger. Woe unto you that laugh now! for ye shall mourn and weep" (Luke 6:24–25) (Gray, 1963, p. 41). However, on examining the other gospels, it must be concluded that this is probably Luke speaking, not Christ. Luke must be seen as the "leveler among the apostles" (Gray, 1963, p. 42).

In the other gospels there are warnings that wealth may be a stumbling block in getting to heaven, but there is no condemnation of wealth as such. The most important passages in this regard deal with the wealthy young man who wants to know what he must do to attain eternal life (Matthew, 19:16–26). Christ's first answer amounts to nothing more than a brief statement of the Ten Commandments. It is only after being pressed further that Christ goes beyond the binding, universal moral requirements to a counsel of perfection. "If thou wilt be perfect" (Matthew, 19:21) begins the statement in which he tells the young man to sell whatever he has and to give it to the poor.

The Christian paternalist ethic, with its parental-like obligations of the wealthy toward the poor, was developed more specifically and elaborately by most of the Christian Church Fathers, who wrote in the first few centuries after Christ. The writings of Clement of Alexandria (c. 150–211/216) are a reasonably good reflection of the traditional attitudes of the early church. He emphasized the dangers of greed, love of material things, and acquisition of wealth. Those who had wealth were under a special obligation to treat it as a gift from God and to use it wisely in the promotion of the general well-being of others.

Clement's *The Rich Man's Salvation* was written in order to free the rich of the "unfounded despair" they might have acquired from reading passages in the gospels like those found in Luke. Clement began by asserting that, contrary to anything one might find in Luke, "it is no great or enviable thing to be simply without riches." Those who were poor would not for that reason alone find God's blessedness. In order to seek salvation, the rich man need not renounce his wealth but need merely "banish from the soul its opinions about riches, its attachment to them, its excessive desire, its morbid excitement over them, its anxious cares, the thorns of our earthly existence which choke the seed of the true life" (Gray, 1963, p. 48).

It was not the possession of wealth but the way in which it was used that was important to Clement. The wealthy were given the responsibility of administering their wealth, on God's behalf, to alleviate the suffering and to promote the general welfare of their brothers. In decreeing that the hungry should be fed and the naked clothed, God certainly had not willed a situation in which no one could carry out these commandments for lack of sufficient material prerequisites. It followed, thus, that God had willed that some men should have wealth but had given them the important function of paternalistically caring for the well-being of the rest of society. In a similar vein, Ambrose, Bishop of Milan (c. 337–397), wrote that "riches themselves are not blamable" as long as they are used righteously. In order to use wealth righteously, "we ought to be of mutual help one to the other, and to vie with each other in doing duties, to lay all advantages . . . before all, and . . . to bring help one to the other" (Gray, 1963, p. 49).

The list of Christian fathers who wrote lengthy passages to the same effect could be expanded greatly. Suffice it to say that by the early feudal period, the Christian paternalist ethic was thoroughly entrenched in western European culture. Greed, avarice, materialistic self-seeking, and the desire to accumulate wealth were sharply condemned. The acquisitive, individualistic person was considered the very antithesis of the good man, who concerned himself with the well-being of all his brothers. The wealthy man had the potential to do either great good or great evil with his wealth and power, and the worst evil resulted when wealth was used either exclusively for self-gratification or as a means of continually acquiring more wealth and power for its own sake. The righteously wealthy were those who realized that their wealth and power were God's gift, that they were morally obligated to act as paternalistic stewards, and that they were to administrate their worldly affairs in order to promote the welfare of all.

THE NATURE OF FEUDAL IDEOLOGY

The philosophical and religious assumptions on which medieval people acted were extensions of the Christian paternalist ethic. The many particular additions to the ethic were profoundly **conservative**, *reflecting aversion to rapid change and bound to tradition,* in purpose and content. Both the continuity and conservative modifications of this ethic can be seen in the writings of Thomas Aquinas (1225–1274), the preeminent spokesman of the Middle Ages.

Tradition was upheld in his insistence that private property could be justified morally only because it was a necessary condition for almsgiving. The rich, he asserted, must always be "ready to distribute . . . and willing to communicate" (Gray, 1963, p. 57). Aquinas believed, with the earlier church fathers, that "the rich man, if he does not give alms, is a thief" (Gray, 1963). The rich man held wealth and power for God and for all society. He administered his wealth for God and for the common good of humankind. Wealth that was not properly used and administered could no longer be religiously and morally justified, in which case the wealthy man was to be considered a "common thief." The conservative addition to the Christian paternalist ethic of Aquinas and most of the fathers of the medieval church was their insistence that the economic and social relationships of the medieval manorial system reflected a natural and eternal ordering. The relationships were ordained by God. They stressed the importance of a division of labor and effort with different tasks assigned to the different classes, and insisted that the social and economic distinctions between the classes were necessary to accommodate this specialization.

If one occupied the position of a lord, secular or religious, it was necessary to have an abundance of material wealth in order to do well the tasks providence had assigned. Of course, it took little wealth to perform the tasks expected of a serf. It was every person's duty to labor unquestioningly at the task providence had assigned, to accept the station into which one was born, and to accept the rights of others to have and do the things appropriate to their stations in life. Thus, the evolving Christian paternalist ethic could be used to defend, as natural and just, the great inequities and intense exploitation that flowed from the concentration of wealth and power in the hands of the church and nobility.

Any account of medieval social and economic thought must also stress the great disdain with which people viewed trade and commerce and the commercial spirit. The medieval way of life was based on custom and tradition. Its viability depended on the acceptance by the members of society of that tradition and their place within it. Where the commercial ethic prevails, greed, selfishness, covetousness, and the desire to better oneself materially or socially are accepted by most people as innate qualities. Yet the commercial ethic was uniformly denounced and reviled in the Middle Ages.

However, the serfs (and sometimes the lower nobility) tended to be dissatisfied with the traditions and customs of medieval society and thus threatened the stability of the feudal system. It is not surprising, therefore, to find pervasive moral sanctions designed to repress or to mitigate the effects of these motives. One of the most important of such sanctions, repeated over and over throughout this period, was the insistence that it was the moral duty of merchants and traders to transact all trade or exchanges at the "just price." This notion illustrates the role played by paternalistic social control in the feudal era. A **just price** was *one that would compensate the seller for his efforts in transporting the good and in finding the buyer at a rate that was just sufficient to maintain the seller at his customary or traditional station in life.* Prices above the just price would, of course, lead to profits, which would be accumulated as material wealth.

It was the lust for wealth that the Christian paternalist ethic consistently condemned. The doctrine of the just price was intended as a curb on such acquisitive, and socially disruptive, behavior.

Then, as now, accumulation of material wealth was a passport to greater power and upward social mobility. Social mobility was eventually to prove totally destructive to the medieval system because it put an end to the status relationships that were the backbone of medieval society.

Another example of condemnation of acquisitive behavior was the prohibition of **usury**, or *the lending of money at interest or lending money at exorbitant or illegal rates of interest*. A "bill against usury" passed in England reflected the attitudes of most of the people of those times. It read in part:

> for as much as usury is by the word of God utterly prohibited, as a vice most odious and detestable . . . which thing, by no godly teachings and persuasions can sink in to the hearts of divers greedy, uncharitable and covetous persons of this Realm . . . be it enacted . . . that . . . no person or persons of what Estate, degree, quality or condition so ever he or they be, by any corrupt, colorable or deceitful conveyance, sleight or engine, or by any way or mean, shall lend, give, set out, deliver or forbear any sum or sums of money . . . to or for any manner of usury, increase, lucre, gain or interest to be had, received or hoped for, over and above the sum or sums so lent . . . as also of the usury . . . upon pain of imprisonment (Huberman, 1961, p. 39).

The church believed usury was the worst sort of acquisitive behavior because most loans on which interest was charged were granted to poor farmers or peasants after a bad crop or some other tragedy had befallen them. Thus, interest was a gain made at the expense of one's brother at a time when he was most in need of help and charity. Of course, the Christian ethic strongly condemned such rapacious exploitation of a needy brother.

Many historians have pointed out that bishops and abbots as well as dukes, counts, and kings often flagrantly violated these sanctions. They themselves granted loans at interest, even while they were punishing others for doing so. We are more interested, however, in the values and motives of the period than in the bending or breaking of the rules. It is the values of the feudal system which stand in stark contrast to those that were to later prevail under a capitalist system. The desires to maximize monetary gain, accumulate material wealth, and advance socially and economically through acquisitive behavior was to become the dominant motive force in the capitalist system. The behaviors that were most strongly denounced within the context of the Christian paternalist ethic were to become the behavioral assumptions on which the capitalist market economy was to be based. It is obvious that such a radical change would render the Christian ethic, at least in its medieval version, inadequate as the basis of a moral justification of the new capitalist system. The ethic would have to be modified drastically or rejected completely in order to elaborate a defense for the new system. Attempts to do both are explored in later chapters.

SUMMARY

Feudalism had four main features. The economic institutions were built on ruling lords and subordinate serfs, who produced food, clothing, and shelter for everyone. The technology consisted mainly of people or an animal pulling ploughs to provide subsistence farming. The political and social systems proclaimed the superiority of the secular and religious lords, who fought for power among themselves.

There was an ideology that supported feudalism. The ideology called the Christian paternalist ethic was used to justify the feudal economy and its attendant social and economic relationships. This ideology contained elements that were antithetical to the functioning of a capitalist market

Table 4.1

Four Features of Feudal Society

Technology	Iron tools; Very slow improvement
Economic Institutions	Serfs work; Lords take product
Social Institutions	Rule by Lords in all instiutions
Ideology	Christian Paternalism and sexism

system. Charging interest was a sin. Being rich was a sin unless most of your money was used to help the poor. Peasants had a moral obligation to work for the lords, and the lords had a moral obligation to protect and help the serfs to survive in emergencies. In later chapters we examine the ways in which people attempted to substitute new ideologies for the older Christian paternalist ethic or to modify this ethic in such a way that it could be used to provide a moral justification of a capitalist market economic system.

Feudalism in England is summarized in Table 4.1:

The four features show that feudalism was very different from the slave societies that came before it or the capitalist societies that came after it in England. The chapter stresses that feudalism is distinguished from other systems not only by its economic and political institutions, but also by its Christian paternalist ideology.

SUGGESTED READINGS

A very pleasant book that presents the lives of six actual medieval people, derived from documents of that time, is Eileen Powers's, *Medieval People* (2000). A more advanced work is Clapham and Powers, *The Agrarian Life of the Middle Ages* (1966). The relations of lord and serf were very complex; they are discussed more below, and also in great detail by Robert Brenner in many articles, such as his article in Aston and Philpin (1985).

KEY TERMS

Christian paternalist ethic	secular
conservative	usury
just price	

REVIEW QUESTIONS

List and explain the features of the four institutions of society under feudalism.
1. State the features of the four institutions under feudalism and explain how they are different from those in slave society.
2. What are the sources of serfs?
3. Why did feudal lords change from slave labor to serf labor?
4. How did the lords control the serfs?
5. How did religion play a role in inhibiting the technological and scientific advancement?
6. What is the impact of the church and religion in feudal society?

7. Discuss the status of women in feudal society.
8. Discuss the role of the church as a landowner in feudalism.

Explain the concept and evolution of Christian paternalism and its role in supporting feudalism.

9. How does a system of Christian paternalism compare to the pattern of a typical family? Who fills each role?
10. What are the duties and obligations of the wealthy?
11. In the movie *Wall Street,* Michael Douglas proclaims "greed is good." What would be the response to this statement by people who adhere to the idea of Christian paternalism?
12. What role does tradition play in feudal society? How did this affect development of trade and commercial interests?
13. What is a "just price?" What role does the idea of a just price play in the context of feudalism and Christian paternalism?
14. What is usury? How is usury related to the idea of a just price?
15. Does being poor necessarily mean you are righteous person?

CHAPTER 5

Feudalism to Capitalism in England

This chapter explains how feudalism ended and how capitalism was born. As in previous transitions, it involved various complex processes and all of these processes overlapped and interacted with each other. In England, the evolution from feudalism to capitalism was driven primarily by internal forces. Most other countries evolved to capitalism directly by diffusion from England or indirectly from the other European countries that became capitalist aided by the influence of England. Capitalism has had several stages in its development. During the transition from feudalism in England, merchants were the main representatives of the growing capitalist institutions. By the late eighteenth century industrial capitalism was the dominant system in England.

LEARNING OBJECTIVES

After reading this chapter, you should be able to:

- Explain the effect of the merchant class on feudal society.
- Understand the reasons for the shift from subsistence farming to commercial farming.
- Comprehend the connection of the emergence of capitalism and the English Revolution.
- List and explain the four features of capitalism.
- Understand the rise and impacts of the Industrial Revolution.

ECONOMIC INSTITUTIONS, SELF-SUFFICIENCY AND TRADE

There was very little trade and few merchants in the early middle ages. The merchants did not produce goods for a market, they merely bought goods cheaply and sold them to someone else for a higher price. Merchants largely traded in luxury goods for the rich and not in the basic goods necessary to life. However, merchants helped expand the range of trading under feudalism.

Each feudal manor was mostly self-sufficient, trading only for a few goods it could not produce. The lord who suddenly needed more food to feed his retainers simply told the peasants to give him more. Of course, if he asked the peasants for more than was traditional, and if they were all angry enough, there might be a rebellion. At a fair held now and then, a peasant might bring a pig to market and trade it for a coat, but there was no market exchange as a normal, daily routine. There was no use of money except by a few very rich merchants engaging in long-distance trade.

44

Most commodities were not produced for the market, but simply for the use of those who produced them or for the lord of the feudal manor.

By the mid-feudal era there were a growing number of towns. Large industrial towns emerged in Italy and Flanders in the eleventh and twelfth centuries. Trade and towns became a big part of feudalism because they were important for fulfilling the needs of the lord. Lords had a growing demand for military and luxury goods. The lords needed these goods because they had to build up larger military units and more ostentatious displays of power in response to competition with other lords. The towns and the merchants, who were often their chief citizens, were an important part of feudalism at its peak and were initially perceived as helpful to the feudal lords and not as a threat.

Great feudal lords often ran small towns while a few larger towns had some measure of independence, but they all owed allegiance to some great lord or directly to the king. As the merchants in the towns grew stronger in late feudalism, the people in the towns sometimes demanded more freedom from the lords and, after a fight, they sometimes got it. The struggles of merchants for rights in the towns were similar to the struggles of peasants for village rights. Both types of struggles existed, but were a normal part of feudalism and did not pose a major threat. In fact, the merchants were often in a coalition with certain lords.

As merchants grew stronger, they found obstacles to doing business under feudalism. One problem was that there were no laws, for example contract laws, governing the conduct of two people who were exchanging goods with each other. Serfs did not exchange much and did not need contract laws, while lords and merchants made only very few transactions needing a contract. Furthermore, the lords did not want written laws because the lords wanted to maintain their own arbitrary power of judgment. As the kings grew stronger relative to the lords, they granted the merchants a set of laws protecting their contracts. This change was part of the transitional struggle toward **market capitalism**. Market capitalism, or simply **capitalism**, is *an economic system based on production for markets in which the ownership of the means of production—land, buildings and equipment—is in the hands of a small group of individuals called capitalists.*

SELF-SUFFICIENT FARMING AND TECHNOLOGY

The fact that farming by peasants was for their own subsistence and not for the market had many important ramifications. Why did the peasants choose to do self-sufficient farming rather than market-oriented farming? The word "choose" is misleading here. The peasants had little choice. In the early and middle feudal period, the times were hard, so that one could barely scratch out a living and there were almost no surpluses to consider selling. There was little law and order outside the manor and no established markets, only occasional fairs. Where could a peasant safely sell goods? If there were a drought or other disaster, where could one safely expect to buy necessary goods? By taking the risk of not producing enough for the family in order to produce for an uncertain market, the peasant was courting starvation for the whole family. Therefore, for most of the Middle Ages production for a market did not exist. Subsistence farming was the rule for both peasants and lords.

The lords, in theory, might have been able to produce enough for subsistence and also produce a large quantity for the market. There were, however, good reasons for not doing so. In an emergency, such as a drought, the lords wanted plenty of reserves. They did not want to be dependent on a fickle and uncertain market for the price of the goods they were selling or for the price of the goods they would be forced to buy if they oriented their farms toward production for a market.

The lords relied on self-sufficient farms for centuries and there was nothing forcing them to change their traditions. When the lords wanted more production, there was no reason to do more intensive farming because they were able to expand into new lands for many centuries. If the lords wanted more surpluses, they could usually coerce more labor or more tithes in form of commodities from the serfs.

Rather than competing with other lords in an economic way which was contrary to tradition, they put their resources into military and political competition with other lords. As a result of the dominant institutions of the time, there was little economic development and little innovation. There were some innovations over the centuries, such as better ploughs and better harnesses for animals to pull heavy loads, but there was still very little specialization in the use of land or labor. Change was so slow that the dominant view of the medieval period was that change never occurs and the present form of work and life was eternal.

The peasant villages also had their own rigid rules about who could farm where, and often the village land was divided and redivided into many small plots. The tradition was that every peasant would have exactly the same quantity and quality of land, even if people had to get tiny plots in several different areas. On these tiny plots, new technology or ways of doing things made little sense. Since the lords spent their surplus on military expenditures or ostentatious displays of luxuries, the peasants themselves also had little or no **capital**—*materials, buildings and equipment used in the production of goods and services.*

What was the importance of the fact that peasant farming and most farming by the lords remained self-sufficient and not tied to the demands of the market? It meant there was little technological change and innovation. If the peasant was to produce enough food to feed his or her family, then it was impossible to plant any specialized crops designed for the market. Producing the same type of thing year after year, the peasant did not have the incentive or the capital or the knowledge to use new technology. Because the peasant had a very limited surplus, if any, there was no capital to accumulate more equipment or to experiment with new types of equipment. Since the peasant was not under the pressure of competition in the market, there was nothing to compel the peasant to make costly innovations. The peasant could make a technological innovation if he or she wished to, but was under no compulsion from the competitive forces of the market to do so.

For the lords, tradition said the lord could not force the peasants off the land no matter how low the productivity or output of the peasant. Indeed, the scarcity of labor—especially in the period following the Black Death epidemic of the 1300s, when the population of Europe was reduced by one-quarter to one-half—meant that lords wished to preserve their current peasant labor force, not antagonize them. It was not easy to get new tenants or to get free farmers if the lord got rid of an old peasant family. Coupled with the fact that lords put their own resources into military-political competition and not into improving production for a mostly nonexistent market, there was little innovation by the lords, and technology continued to stagnate during feudalism.

Remember that technology began the feudal period by going backward during the breakup of the Roman Empire. After a few centuries, there was just enough stability to allow technology to equal that of Roman agriculture although it did not equal that of Rome in domestic conveniences for many more centuries in most areas. The peasants did have more incentive than the slaves to use new technology, at least on their own land. The lords would not object to new technology on their land if it did not cost too much, so there was some very slow technological progress during the mid and late feudal period.

But technological progress remained excruciatingly slow for many reasons. First, as mentioned above, the peasants did only subsistence farming, so competition did not force technological change. Second, the lords also practiced subsistence farming on a larger scale and the lords normally thought first of squeezing the peasant for more revenue rather than the chancy and expensive business of technological innovation. Third, neither lords nor peasants had more than a tiny bit of extra revenue, if any, so purchasing equipment was close to impossible. Fourth, the traditions of feudalism, pushed hard by the church, said that nothing should change. Most people went their whole lives without seeing any significant change in technology, so the idea that it would never change was very believable to them.

WHY DID THIS PICTURE CHANGE?

For many centuries, the lords and peasants practiced self-sufficient farming while the merchants practiced the art of buying cheap and selling dear. Neither group engaged in production of goods for the market. Some crafts people practiced their trade in the lord's manor, being rewarded by subsistence goods like any other retainer. Some crafts people in the cities worked in associations of craft workers called guilds. Each guild master employed many apprentices. Most of the apprentices became masters in due course so that the relationship was only a temporary subordination and not a permanent one. The medieval guild was an integral part of feudalism and not an early sign of a new economic system. There were no industries, no industrial owners, and no industrial workers in the feudal period.

Where did industrial employers and employees come from? The transition occurred in different ways in different places in Europe. The first transition came in England, so the focus here is on England. What is most fascinating is that the transformation did not occur in the cities, was not due to the existing merchants, and was not due to the existing craft guilds. The transformation occurred first in the English countryside. Since capitalism is associated with industry, this seems strange.

One catalyst for change was the Black Death and other plagues that greatly reduced the English population in the last half of the fourteenth century. The landlords faced a big problem, since there was not enough labor to provide the amount of services they relied upon for a comfortable survival of their manors. What should they do? Most landlords in England first tried the traditional method of squeezing more service from the peasants. But times were very hard, so the peasants were not willing to give more time or more goods to the landlords without a fight. To give more to the landlord meant starvation for many peasant families. Rather than see their children starve, many rebelled in one form or another, including armed struggle. The landlords were forced to give up this attempt to increase exploitation of their workers in traditional ways.

As a result of the struggles between lords and serfs, the serfs began to fight to achieve freedom from traditional services. Not only did the lords face peasant resistance to more exploitation, but in the face of a shrinking labor supply, the lords were forced to compete with each other to get peasants away from other lords to increase their own labor supply. To get more peasants meant the lords had to give more concessions than their competitors. Thus, many peasants achieved liberation from onerous duties either by resistance or by the competition of the lords. Because of the competition for peasants in wake of failure to impose tighter serfdom in the later fourteenth century, lords were obliged to grant peasants full freedom from feudal dues and service. The courts upheld these rights, thereby implicitly recognizing the free status of the peasants.

The lords seemed worse off than before, but the peasants had only freedom, not land. The lords responded to the peasant struggles by changing the rules and no longer recognizing traditional peasant rights to the use of land. Besides their own plots of land granted to them by the lords, the peasants had traditional rights to an area known as the **commons**. This was *land where they could collect wood, graze animals, and get other benefits*. What they did on the commons provided enough extra goods and income to allow them to survive. Enclosure of commons land by the lords pushed many peasants out of farming and into unemployment.

Many of the uprooted farmers and craftsmen who were now denied access to their former means of production became vagabonds and beggars. Some attempted to secure a subsistence living by squatting on marginal, unused lands where they could grow crops for their own use. Harshly repressive laws were passed against such farming and against being an unemployed vagabond (Dobb, 1946, Chap. 6). When force, fraud, and starvation were insufficient to create the new working class, criminal statutes and government repression were used. Over a long period, the thousands of peasants who were forced off the land drifted into the cities to become an unemployed labor force, only very slowly getting subsistence jobs.

In the transitional fifteenth, sixteenth, and seventeenth centuries, many of the lords used the former commons area to pasture their sheep. In that period, wool became a very important industry in England. Wool became the largest single export and British wool was considered superior to most continental wool. An important industry was born by enclosing the former commons. At first wool production was still mainly feudal in nature. The lords who had sheep processed the wool for market themselves, often using serf labor. Peasants who had sheep produced the wool for market using their family labor. In some cases, the lords or peasants who owned the sheep sold it to other peasants who processed it into a form ready for sale. They then sold it to the merchants.

The merchants then sold the wool, mostly abroad. The wool merchants of England were a company with a **monopoly**, *a market characterized by a single seller*. At first they sold almost all the wool to Holland where it was made into cloth. For a long time the merchants produced no wool themselves. It was much later before the wool merchants began to have their own cloth woven from the wool in England. Eventually the merchants started to place orders with peasants in advance and then sell the resulting production. Placing orders in advance of demand was called the "putting-out" system. It was a long, long time before a merchant gathered the peasant weavers of wool into a factory of some sort. Such factories are discussed later when we look at the Industrial Revolution.

CHANGE FROM LABOR TO LEASE-HOLDERS

At the height of feudalism, the lords used military force to extract labor from the serfs in the form of service on the lord's land and/or payment of dues. But in the struggles of the fourteenth and fifteenth centuries peasants won a large degree of freedom from the traditional services and payments. Now the peasants were demanding even more. They wanted land with fixed rents rather than arbitrary changing feudal dues for the land. They wanted their children to inherit their traditional land. If they got that, they would be freeholders and, in effect, landowners. To prevent this, lords asserted their own right to ownership. They forced the peasants into renting the land with a temporary lease. Thus, the peasants were now free but had no guarantee of land. They had to pay for the land and a price change was possible every time the peasant renewed the lease.

The lords claimed the traditional land of the peasant as their own and the courts upheld this right. In their fight with the peasants, this tactic of the lords proved to be far more earthshaking than they could have imagined. The peasants won their freedom, but the lords insisted—and they had the law and military force on their side—that peasants could no longer use their own traditional land for farming. The lords would let them use the land only if the peasants paid rent under a lease to the landlords. The lords did not mean to change the system in any basic way, they merely meant to grab any revenue they could in their fight with the peasants.

But things did change. A market emerged in land to be leased from the landlords. For the first time, the peasant had to compete to rent the land. What's more, to rent the land the peasant needed cash to make payments on the lease. Therefore, the peasant was no longer self-sufficient and could not choose to remain in subsistence farming. The peasant had to sell enough goods in the market to make the money to pay the lease. Peasants were forced out of subsistence farming into **commercial farming**, that is, *farming for the market*. Peasants were now under the control of market forces and had to follow the competitive dictates. This meant that they may not be able to plant enough food for their families because they had to plant commercial crops that could be sold in the market. They would then have enough money to pay the lease and retain their land. The change had begun from feudal relations, maintained by tradition and force, to the monetary and market relations that characterize market capitalism.

Farming changed from self-sufficient subsistence to intensive production of commercial crops. When the peasants had produced only for their own families, they were under no pressure to use the latest technology. Now they were competing in the market to sell their crops. Therefore, in order to compete, they were forced, often with enormous sacrifice, to purchase the best equipment and fertilizer. The peasants became involved in the process of technological innovation. Many of the most important inventions of this period were discovered or first applied in the countryside, not the towns. Technology in England began to make progress, but it was still mainly agricultural technology.

Since the peasants could no longer produce all of the things they needed because of their focus on a few commercial crops, for the first time in history peasant families faced the need to buy many of their necessary goods on the market. Peasants who produced mainly commercial crops no longer had time for many of the necessary crafts. Therefore, much craft production moved out of its traditional place in the peasant home. Where would the peasants now get all of the craft goods they needed? They had to buy them in the market. Since it was forced out of the countryside to some extent, the production of craft goods moved to the city for the first time.

Very, very slowly, a market was born for the products of industrial production. During the same period, thousands of peasants had been forced off the lord's newly enclosed lands, both the former commons and the peasant holdings they could now not afford. These peasants roamed as vagabonds all over the British countryside looking for work without success for a very long time. Eventually, the newer industry of the towns needed workers, so it utilized many of the thousands of unemployed peasants in industrial jobs. Being used to the life of a self-employed peasant, most of them found it very hard to adjust to the discipline of the factory.

Eventually, the competitive leasing by peasants led to cash crops and many agricultural innovations in the countryside, and the purchasing of other goods from the city. One result was increasing agricultural productivity, which lowered the price of food. This meant that workers in the cities could eat and survive even at fairly low wages. Low food prices also meant that many people had income left over to buy things other than food.

In the cities, the combination of unemployed workers and relatively cheap food led to far more extensive craft production and the beginning of industry. Much early industry was simply craft production with no employees or with a few employees in the houses of merchants. In the countryside, much of the farming was done by families with no other employees. Although peasants were more and more tied to the market, the structure of industry or agriculture was still based on family production. It took a long time for production based on an owner and many employees to become widespread.

Slowly, the better-off peasants began to accumulate land. They started to improve their methods of production to compete on the market. They also increased their animals from the one per family common in the feudal times to many animals held by some families. They began to specialize in certain crops and in certain animals. All of this specialization and trade meant further increases in production. They began to employ landless peasants on their farms. Production was growing faster than the number of peasants. They were able to feed the growing population, ending the feudal crisis of a lack of supply of food. Since the richest peasants now had their own land by lease, owned their own equipment, and employed others to work for them, they fitted the definition of a capitalist entrepreneur in agriculture.

THE ENGLISH REVOLUTION OF THE SEVENTEENTH CENTURY

In the countryside, although there were still people called lords, much of feudalism disappeared by the time of the revolution that ended the remnants of feudalism in the seventeenth century in England. Tenants now leased their land and owed no feudal services. Lords were now landlords who received rents from a commercial relationship with the tenants. If someone says that the English Revolution got rid of the remnants of feudalism, what remnants are being discussed?

First, the British crown and court had vast powers which were used to enrich themselves in order to lead a luxurious life. This meant the power of the king and court remained a serious economic issue. In addition to the vast waste of the court, the king also imposed all kinds of minute regulations on business and industry, which the crafts and the newer industries found very irksome. Second, the high officials of the church also had vast landholdings and power that were used to enrich themselves and the church. Thus, the power of the church remained a very real issue. Third, the king gave monopolies to certain merchants—for a price. The stranglehold of the monopolies prevented market capitalism from flourishing in several important areas, for example, trading with the East Indies.

Altogether, the political-economic remnants of feudalism were seen as obstacles and burdens by those trying to make a living through the market. Eventually, there was a revolution in England in the mid-seventeenth century that ended the remnants of feudalism and established a state friendly to market-based industrial development. But it would be very wrong to think of the leaders of this revolution as typical industrial manufacturers since very few of those existed yet.

One of the most important groups in the revolutionary process was the former peasants, now becoming commercial farmers with the help of family labor. Another group was the merchants, who lived and died by market exchange. A third group in the English Revolution were the small crafts people, some still organized in medieval guilds. In feudal times almost all the apprentices eventually became masters, when they had demonstrated enough skill. The guilds, however, were changing as some masters became richer and many apprentices failed to become masters. Thus, as demand grew for their products, they slowly became more like modern market-oriented manufacturing enterprises. The commercial farmers, the merchants, and the craft masters could be thought of as a new middle class of merchant and industrial capitalists, but they were still a far cry from what we think of today as industrial capitalists. The revolution led to a new governmental and legal framework for the economy. The new economic relations plus the new legal and political framework is called capitalism.

The English Revolution that legalized capitalism was not fought under the banner of making the world safe for capitalism. The English Revolution of the mid-seventeenth century was not only fought by a pre-capitalist middle class and farmers, it was also fought under the banner of religion. In addition to the religious issues between Catholics and various groups of Protestants, there was also a stated political issue between parliament and the king, Charles I. Different political parties in the revolution were marching under various religious banners which masked the economic issues. The climax of the revolution appeared to be when the king's head was chopped off in 1649. But underneath the religious and political issues, a basic economic change occurred. The remnants of feudalism were destroyed and the stage was set for the emergence of industrial capitalism.

To better understand the true nature of the English Revolution, let us go back and recall briefly the sequence of events that led to this revolution. Remember that the story began with the struggle between the peasants and the lords under a feudal system that reshaped both of these classes and made them bitter antagonists. It was shown above that, in the crisis situation where both sides felt they were fighting for survival, the peasants won freedom from feudal services, but the lords won the right to enclose the commons and charge rents for the traditional peasant lands. This turned out to be a major change in economic institutions. The new rural relations led to commercial crops in the countryside and the slow growth of industry in its earliest forms in the cities. The new economic institutions in the countryside led to production for a market with profit maximization as the goal and technological innovation in agriculture.

The change in the relative power of different classes led to further conflict over peasant rights and over the power of the lords versus the town merchants, crafts people, and store owners. These conflicts culminated in revolution. The revolution in England set up a government friendly to capitalism. Three types of capitalism evolved over time. First, small scale trade led to large-scale international trade and very rich merchants. Second, small lenders grew into great financial institutions. Third, the new situation in agriculture and in the cities grew into industrial capitalism several centuries later.

After capitalism was established in England, overseas activities helped greatly to expand it further. The overseas activities were called "patriotic" by the British, but they included piracy against Spanish treasure ships, massive raids on Africa for slaves to be sold in the Americas, and establishment by military force of colonies all over the world. England had an enormous empire and all kinds of loot came from overseas to England. The English intentionally kept most of the colonies largely as producers of agriculture and raw materials, while selling manufactured goods to them at high prices. Thus, surplus from many countries was taken by piracy, slavery, and colonialism and brought to England. This surplus helped build English industry. That vast treasure, however, could not have built this industry unless England was already largely capitalist. Remember that Spain also received vast treasure from its colonies, but it could not build much industry because it still had largely feudal institutions.

THE FOUR FEATURES OF CAPITALISM

To understand the rest of this book, it is vital to understand exactly what is meant by capitalism. It may be defined in terms of its four basic features.

Economic Institutions

What are the relations and institutions of capitalism? Capitalism is an economic system in which a small group of people, called capitalists, own the natural resources, plants and equipment of industry and agriculture. Most of the population consists of employees who receive wages and salaries by working for the capitalist employers. The capitalist employers produce and expand production only so long as there is a market for their goods in which to make a **profit**. *Profit is the difference between the amount of revenue taken in and the amount spent for wages and materials (total costs).* Production is for profit and it declines if the expected profit declines.

Technology

The economic forces of capitalism are characterized by rapid improvement of technology, rapid growth of plants and equipment, and rapid growth of population as seen throughout the transitional fifteenth, sixteenth, and seventeenth centuries. Then technology, plants and equipment, and the growing labor force led to explosive economic **growth**, usually *measured in terms of the output goods and services in a country*, in the late eighteenth and the nineteenth centuries. This vast change was called the Industrial Revolution (discussed below).

Social Institutions

What are the social and political institutions of capitalism? The institutions included a government that eliminated all feudal restrictions and managed the economy in the interests of the capitalist employers. Private property rights are a crucial component. There was a whole new system of schools to train both skilled workers and professional workers as well as managers and executives. The religious system stopped supporting kings and feudal nobility and now began to tout the virtues of capitalism and the capitalist leaders of industry. The family no longer produced what was necessary for survival, but bought its goods in the market and sold its labor in the market. This changed the family from working together, usually under the dominance of the father, to dependence on the market and awareness of the monetary importance of marriage and divorce.

Ideology

The emergence of the institutions of capitalism was accompanied by an enormous change in ideology. No longer did people assume that nothing would ever change, but came to expect rapid change in technology, either welcoming it or dreading it depending on the circumstances. The status of women changed from being property to being free to work or starve or be dependent on a man, so there was a long ideological fight to view women as equals of men. There were no more slaves or serfs from some other race or ethnic group, so that basis for assumed superiority of one group disappeared. Yet under capitalism, there were still some groups mostly employed at the lowest wages and assumed to be inferior by many of the dominant group.

THE INDUSTRIAL REVOLUTION

The economic, political, and legal framework of capitalism, which reached its full flower in the late eighteenth century, formed the basis for the Industrial Revolution that took place in England in the last part of the eighteenth century and in the nineteenth century. The Industrial Revolution was composed of both technological changes and further institutional changes.

In 1750, a person could not get from Rome to London or send messages between cities any faster than in the days of the Roman Empire, using relays of fast horses in both cases. By the late 1800s there were railroad lines that could take passengers and freight rapidly from Rome to London. Moreover, the telegraph meant that a message could travel instantaneously from Rome to London. Clearly, transportation and communication were both changed in truly revolutionary ways by the end of the nineteenth century.

In 1750, most power was supplied by people or animals just as it had been in the Roman Empire. At night, people still had to use candles to read or do work, or go to sleep. By the last half of the nineteenth century, steam engines were used in industry, railroad engines were driven by steam or oil and eventually by electricity. Lighting by kerosene lamps and then electric lighting meant that people could pursue whatever activities they wished at night, as long as they could afford the fuel. Increased demand for power encouraged coal production to increase by leaps and bounds. The production of iron and steel also increased at an amazing speed. Cheap power and greater production capacity meant that vast quantities of consumer goods could be produced very cheaply for the first time. Altogether, the output of British manufacturing doubled from 1750 to 1800.

Industry needed people for its expansion. People moved from the rural areas to the cities, pushed out by landlords who enclosed the land to produce wool for commerce, attracted to the cities by the new factory jobs. Wool and other textile products became the most important industry for a while. The quality of English wool was highly regarded. There was a large foreign market and the large demand for textiles encouraged many new inventions in the textile industry. Production in textiles, iron and coal eventually changed England from a rural, agricultural country to a mainly urban, industrial country. As an example, the manufacturing town of Manchester, England had only 17,000 people in 1760, but had 400,000 people by 1850.

All of these changes that constituted the Industrial Revolution could not have occurred without the institutions of capitalism. Remember that it was the capitalist motives of landlords that convinced them to enclose their estates producing a homeless and unemployed class of workers available for industry. It was competitive market pressures on farming that raised productivity and supplied more food at lower prices to the cities. Only after these foundations were laid did the factory system emerge and produce more and more innovations.

The Industrial Revolution, which shifted the majority of production from agriculture to industry, resulted in a class of industrial capitalists whereas earlier capitalists had been in trade and finance. It was only after the Industrial Revolution that there were a significant number of rich manufacturers and vast numbers of employees who worked for wages in manufacturing.

In England, the revolution against feudalism was in the mid-seventeenth century, but the Industrial Revolution did not really begin until the end of the eighteenth century. It was the capitalist structure of industry (including private ownership and competition), plus a government friendly to capitalism, plus a set of laws defining capitalist relations, that made the Industrial Revolution possible. The new technology did not drop out of the sky, but emerged from an environment that encouraged it.

THE SOCIAL COSTS OF THE INDUSTRIAL REVOLUTION

Historically, in all cases in which society forced a bare subsistence existence on some of its members, it was those with the least economic and political power who made the sacrifices. So it was in the Industrial Revolution in England. The working class lived near the subsistence level in 1750 and their standard of living (measured in terms of the purchasing power of their wages) deteriorated during the second half of the eighteenth century (Hobsbawm, 1968, p. 72).

To facilitate rapid industrialization, resources had to be diverted from producing consumer goods to the production of factories and machines. In other words, less food, clothing and shelter was produced so that more factories and machines could be produced. In the long run, this meant economic growth, but in the short run it meant sacrifice of someone's standard of living. The sacrifice did not come from the elite of industrial capitalists, but from the working classes who had less to eat, less clothing, and poorer housing.

Moreover, workers found a brand new job situation. They had been doing many differing kinds of jobs in a day, each of which required some different skills. Now they were linked to one machine all day doing the same routine job hour after hour. The monotony and lack of freedom was a major cost of the Industrial Revolution. The extensive division of labor in the factory made much of the work so routine and simple that untrained women and children could do it as well as men. In many cases wages were so low that entire families had to work in order to earn enough to eat.

Many factory owners preferred women and children because they could be reduced to a state of passive obedience more easily than men. The widespread ideology of this period, that the only good woman is a submissive woman, was a great help to their employers. Children were bound to factories by "indentures" of apprenticeship for seven years, or until they were twenty-one years old. In these cases almost nothing was given to the children in return for long hours of work under the most horrendous conditions. Women were mistreated almost as badly. Work in a factory was long, arduous, and monotonous. Discipline was harsh. Many times the price of factory employment was submission to the sexual advances of employers and foremen (Mantoux, 1927, p. 416). Women in the mines toiled from fourteen to sixteen hours a day, stripped naked to the waist, working with men and doing the same work as men.

Conditions in the cities of this period were terrible. Smoke and other air pollution were pervasive, while there was overcrowding plus insufficient water supply or street cleaning. These conditions produced epidemics of typhoid and cholera (Hobsbawm, 1968, pp. 67–68).

The total destruction of the laborers' traditional way of life and the harsh discipline of the new factory system, combined with deplorable living conditions in the cities, generated social, economic, and political unrest. Chain reactions of social upheaval, riots, and rebellion often occurred in the years from 1811 to 1848. In many areas these were purely spontaneous and primarily economic in character. For example, in 1816 one rioter from the Fens exclaimed: "Here I am between Earth and Sky, so help me God. I would sooner lose my life than go home as I am. Bread I want and bread I will have" (Hobsbawm, 1968, p. 74).

Industrial capitalism was erected on the basis of the wretched suffering of a laboring class denied access to the fruits of the rapidly expanding economy and subjected to the most degrading of excesses in order to increase the capitalists' profits. The basic cause of the great evils of this period was "the absolute and uncontrolled power of the capitalist. In this, the heroic age of great undertakings, it was acknowledged, admitted and even proclaimed with brutal candor. It was the employer's own business, he did as he chose and did not consider that any other justification of his conduct was necessary. He owed his employees wages and once those were paid the men had no further claim on him" (Mantoux, 1927, p. 417).

Because of the terrible conditions, labor organizations spread rapidly as early as the 1790s. Along with the concurrent growth of social and economic discontent, the upper class became very uneasy. The memory of the French Revolution was fresh in their minds and they feared the power of the united workers. The result was the Combination Act of 1799, which outlawed any combination of workers whose purpose was to obtain higher wages and shorter hours. All workers' unions were banned because they might constrain the free action of their employers. Proponents of the anticombination laws couched their arguments in terms of the necessity of free competition and the evils of monopoly. The proponents did not, however, mention combinations of employers or practices of capitalists designed to undermine their competitors.

SUMMARY

How did England get from feudalism to capitalism? First, old economic institutions prevented new technology. Subsistence farming and limited incentives of serfs held back technological progress under feudalism. Second, vested interests fought the common people. The vested interests were the great feudal lords who wanted to hold on to the political and economic power vested in them by feudalism. The serfs fought the lords for a long time until they won freedom. But the serfs had no land and the lords required leases and rents. To pay the leases, former serfs turned to commercial farming and bought craft goods from the cities. The crafts and other early industries rose.

Table 5.1

Four Features of Capitalist Society

Technology	Industrial revolution
Economic Institutions	Employees work; employers get profit
Social Institutions	Democratic forms, but wealth dominates all institutions
Ideology	Market is always right, so employers and employees get what they deserve

Eventually, the merchants, crafts people and freed serfs fought the remaining power of the lords and won in the revolution of 1648.

Class conflicts led to a revolutionary change in ideology, which led to revolutionary political change, which led to new economic institutions. The conflict between the feudal lords and the serfs, crafts people, and merchants was reflected in a religious revolution from Catholicism to Protestantism.

The whole transition took three centuries. As in previous transitions, it involved various complex processes, and all of these processes overlapped and were entangled with each other. Only England had this evolution primarily from internal forces, though even there the rest of the world formed its environment. Most other countries evolved to capitalism directly by diffusion from England or indirectly from the other European countries that became capitalist aided by the influence of England.

Capitalism has had several stages of development. During the transition from feudalism in England, merchants were the main representative of the growing capitalist institutions. There were very few capitalist industrialists until the Industrial Revolution, so industrial capitalism is the first stage of capitalism as a dominant system beginning in England in the late eighteenth century. Table 5.1 summarizes industrial capitalism.

COMPARISON OF FOUR SOCIETIES

The story told in this book up to this point has focused on four societies that followed each other in Western Europe: prehistoric communal, slave, feudal, and capitalist. It must be emphasized that some of the four societies did not appear in every country, nor did they appear in the same sequence in every country. Moreover, evolution in some areas skipped different ones and in some places went back to an earlier one for a while. Other types of society have also appeared. Still, each of these types of society was the dominant for some time and they did follow in a sequence in some places.

At any rate, each of the four types was important enough that it is worth comparing the main features of all of them in one summary table (see Table 5.2, next page).

SUGGESTED READINGS

There has been a lengthy debate, with heated exchanges on exactly how feudalism ended in Western Europe and how capitalism began. The debate focused on England because it led the way to capitalism and so this chapter also focused on England. The whole complex history of the debate is clearly explained in Ellen Meiksins Wood, *The Origins of Capitalism* (2002) and she adds her

Table 5.2

Types of Society

	Communal	Slavery	Feudalism	Capitalism
Technology	Earliest stone tools; hunting and gathering	New stone tools to iron tools; farming and herding	Iron tools; Very slow change	Industrial revolution
Economic Institutions	Common ownership by extended family	Slaves work; masters take product	Serfs work; Lords take product	Employees work; employers get profit
Social Institutions	Consensus of group	Rule by masters in all social institutions	Rule by Lords in all social institutions	Democratic forms, but wealth dominates all institutions
Ideology	Community togetherness and equality	Racism, Sexism, Classism	Christian Paternalism	Market distributes income justly. All Employees get the wages they deserve.

own interesting contribution. The pioneering writer who set off the debate was Maurice Dobb, *Studies in the Development of Capitalism* (1946). An excellent collection of historians' essays was edited by Rodney Hilton, *The Transition From Feudalism to Capitalism* (1976).

For about the last three decades, however, the debate has centered on the outstanding work of Robert Brenner, whose work is also the best single source for these issues. Brenner's insightful work—along with his critics'—can be seen most conveniently in the book edited by T. H. Aston and C. H. E. Philpin, *The Brenner Debate* (1985), which includes two lengthy contributions by Brenner. The writings on the Brenner thesis and the earlier works on the transition from feudalism to capitalism, however, are difficult reading—so the reader is advised to start with the brief and far more readable survey by Ellen Wood, mentioned above.

The fascinating story of how law changed as institutions changed is told in clear but not fun prose in Tigar and Levy, *Law and the Rise of Capitalism* (1977). An authoritative and beautifully written history of the industrial revolution and its political and economic surroundings is Hobsbawm, *Industry and Empire* (1968).

KEY TERMS

capital
commercial farming
commons
growth

market capitalism
monopoly
profit

REVIEW QUESTIONS

Explain the effect of the merchant class on feudal society.
   1. What is the role of merchants in the early Middle Ages?
   2. Why did towns become increasingly important in this period? How did this impact trade?
   3. What were some problems for early merchants trying to conduct trade?

Understand the reasons for the shift from subsistence farming to commercial farming.

4. Discuss the reasons for technological stagnation in feudal society.
5. What role did the plagues that swept Europe play in changing the relationship of serfs and lords?
6. Why did feudal lords slowly lose power over the peasant class?
7. What is the commons and why was it important to the peasants? Why did the lords enclose the commons? What was the effect of enclosure of the commons on the peasants?
8. Describe the emergence of a market in land to lease. What impact does this have on farming?
9. How does the change to farming for the market (commercial farming) change the productivity or farming?
10. Discuss how changes in the productivity of farming impact the growth of cities.
11. Who made up the peasant class in the cities?

Comprehend the connection of the emergence of capitalism and the English Revolution.

12. What are the remnants of feudalism present in the seventeenth century? Why is this a problem?
13. Who are the three groups of people important to the English Revolution? Why?
14. How did the change in relative power of different classes lead to struggle between the classes?

List and explain the four features of capitalism.

15. Discuss each of the distinguishing features of capitalism in the four institutions.
16. Compare and contrast the features of prehistoric communal society, slavery, feudalism and capitalism. How are they similar and how are they different?

Understand the rise and impacts of the Industrial Revolution.

17. What was the first major industry in England? What factors enabled the development of this industry?
18. How did the institutions of capitalism facilitate the Industrial Revolution?
19. What are some of the social costs of the Industrial Revolution?
20. Why did workers attempt to organize unions?
21. Compare and contrast life in England before the Industrial Revolution (c. 1750) to life in the latter part of the nineteenth century.

CHAPTER 6

Mercantilism in England

Chapter 4 discussed feudalism and the Christian paternalist ethic in England, while Chapter 5 discussed the transition from feudalism to capitalism in England. In the transitional period of the sixteenth, seventeenth, and eighteenth centuries, the most important school of economic thought was called **mercantilism**. It reflected the economic conditions of the transition. The Christian paternalist ethic of feudalism thoroughly condemned the acquisitive behavior that was to become the dominant motive of the new capitalist system. It was therefore necessary to create a new *philosophical and ideological point of view that morally justified individualization, greed, and profit seeking.* Protestantism and the new philosophies of individualism furnished the bases for the new ideology. The new point of view emphasized the need for greater freedom for capitalists to seek profits and the need for less government intervention in the market.

LEARNING OBJECTIVES

After reading this chapter, you should be able to:

- Explain the importance of trade in the early phase of mercantilism.
- Comprehend the battle of ideas: Christian paternalistic ethic and mercantilism.
- Compare and contrast Christian paternalist view with those of emerging individualists and Protestants.

EARLY MERCANTILISM

In the transitional period of the sixteenth, seventeenth, and eighteenth centuries, the most important school of economic thought was called mercantilism. *The earliest phase of mercantilism,* usually called **bullionism**, originated in the period during which Europe was experiencing an acute shortage of gold and silver bullion. Bullion is gold or silver valued by weight. Remember, since there was no paper money European countries did not have enough money to service the rapidly expanding volume of trade. Bullion policies were designed to attract a flow of gold and silver into a country and to keep them there by prohibiting their export. These restrictions lasted from the late Middle Ages into the sixteenth and seventeenth centuries.

Spain, the country into which most of the gold from the Americas flowed, applied bullionist restrictions over the longest period and imposed the most severe penalty for the export of gold and silver: death. Yet the needs of trade were so pressing, and such large profits could be made by importing foreign commodities, that even in Spain merchant capitalists succeeded in bribing corrupt officials or smuggling large quantities of bullion out of the country. Spanish bullion rapidly found its way all over Europe and was, to a large extent, responsible for the long period of **inflation**, *a general increase in prices.* Spain did not legalize the export of gold and silver until long after the bullionist restrictions had been removed in England and Holland in the middle of the sixteenth century.

After the bullionist period, the mercantilists' desire to maximize the gold and silver within a country took the form of attempts by the government to create a favorable **balance of trade**. The balance of trade is *the relationship between a country's **exports** (what a country sells to foreigners) and **imports** (what a country buys from foreigners).* To them a favorable balance of trade meant that money payments into the country from exports would be greater than the money flow out of the country for imports. Thus, exports of goods, as well as activities such as shipping and insuring when performed by compatriots and paid for by foreigners, were encouraged, and imports of goods and shipping and insurance charges paid to foreigners were discouraged. A favorable balance of trade would ensure the growth of the country's treasure. Even though some gold and silver would be paid out in the process, more would come in than would leave.

One of the most important types of policies designed to increase the value of exports and decrease that of imports was the creation of trade monopolies. A country like England could buy most cheaply (from a backward area, for example) if only one English merchant bargained with the foreigners involved rather than having several competing English merchants bidding the price up in an effort to capture the business. Similarly, English merchants could sell their goods to foreigners for much higher prices if there was only one seller rather than several sellers bidding the price down to attract one another's customers.

The English government could prohibit English merchants from competing in an area where such a monopoly had been established. It was much more difficult, however, to keep out French, Dutch, or Spanish merchants. Various governments attempted to exclude such rival foreign merchants by establishing colonial empires that could be controlled by the mother country to ensure a monopoly of trade. Colonial possessions could thereby furnish cheap raw materials to the mother country and purchase expensive manufactured goods in return.

In addition to the creation of monopolies, all the Western European countries (with the exception of Holland) applied extensive regulations to the businesses of exporting and importing. These regulations were probably most comprehensive in England, where exporters who found it difficult to compete with foreigners were given tax refunds or, if that were not enough, subsidized. **Subsidies** are *grants of money from the government.* Export duties were placed on a long list of raw materials to keep them within England. Thus, the price English merchant-manufacturers would have to pay for these raw materials would be minimized. Sometimes, when these items were in short supply for British manufacturers, the state would completely prohibit their export. The English prohibited the export of most raw materials and semifinished products, such as sheep, wool, yarn, and worsted, which were used by the textile industry.

Measures aimed at discouraging imports were also widespread. The importation of some commodities was prohibited, and such high duties were placed on other commodities that they were nearly eliminated from trade. Special emphasis was placed on protecting England's principal export industries from foreign competitors attempting to cut into the export industries' domestic markets.

Of course, these restrictions profited some capitalists and harmed others. As would be expected, coalitions of special-interest groups were always working to maintain the restrictions or to extend them into different areas in different ways. Attempts such as the English Navigation Acts of 1651 and 1660 were made to promote the use of both British-made and British-manned ships in both import and export trade. All these regulations of foreign trade and shipping were designed to augment the flow of money into the country while decreasing the outflow. Needless to say, many of the measures also stemmed from appeals and pressures by special-interest groups.

In addition to these restrictions on foreign trade, there was a maze of restrictions and regulations aimed at controlling domestic production. Besides the tax exemptions, subsidies, and other privileges used to encourage larger output by industries that were important exporters, the state also engaged in extensive regulation of production methods and of the quality of produced goods. In France, the regime of Louis XIV (r. 1638–1715) codified, centralized, and extended the older decentralized guild controls. Specific techniques of production were made mandatory, and extensive quality control measures were enacted, with inspectors appointed in Paris charged with enforcing these laws at the local level. Jean–Baptiste Colbert (1619–1683), Louis XIV's famous minister and economic advisor, was responsible for the establishment of extensive and minute regulations. In the textile industry, for example, the width of a piece of cloth and the precise number of threads contained within it were rigidly specified by the government.

In England, the Statute of Artificers (1563) effectively transferred to the state the function of the old craft guilds. It led to central control over the training of industrial workers, over conditions of employment, and over allocation of the labor force among different types of occupations. Regulation of wages, of the quality of many goods, and other details of domestic production was also tried in England during this period.

What was the source of this extensive control of trade, commerce, and domestic production? It might seem at first glance that the state was merely using its powers to promote the special interests of capitalists. This view is reinforced by the fact that most of the important writers of this period who dealt with economic issues were either merchants or employees of merchants. Undoubtedly many of the particular statutes and regulatory measures were backed by special interest groups that benefited handsomely from them.

However, the rising new middle class of merchant and industrial capitalists was often constrained in its pursuit of profits by the maze of state regulations. Therefore, throughout the period one finds extensive arguments advanced by these capitalists and their spokesmen for greater freedom from state controls. Economic regulation increasingly became problematic to the capitalists and their spokesmen. In fact, the mercantilist period represents an era in which an outdated economic ideology, the medieval version of the Christian paternalist ethic, came into increasingly sharp conflict with a new social and economic order with which it was incompatible.

THE CONFLICT IN MERCANTILIST THOUGHT

The Christian paternalist ethic, with its condemnation of acquisitive behavior, conflicted with the interests of merchants throughout the feudal period. As the importance of trade and commerce grew, the intensity of the conflict grew. There were two principal themes underlying the development of English mercantilism. "One was the biblical injunction to promote the general welfare and common good of God's corporate world and its creatures. The second was the growing propensity to define God's estate as the civil society in which the Christian resided." (Williams, p. 33). During this period the state began to take over the role of the church in interpreting and enforcing the Christian paternalist ethic. The basic issue for the earliest formulators of mercantilist policies was whether the growing merchant class was to be allowed to pursue its profits recklessly, regardless of the social and economic consequences of that pursuit. The Christian ethic demanded that the activities of the merchants be checked and controlled in the interest of the welfare of the entire community.

The Medieval Origins of Mercantilist Policies and the Poor Laws

The first indications of a mercantilist type of economic policy can be traced to Edward I (r. 1272–1307), who evicted several foreign economic enterprises from England, established the English wool trade in Antwerp, and made various attempts to control commerce within England. A short time later, Edward III (r. 1327–1377) significantly extended these policies of economic control. The long war with France (1333–1360) led him to attempt to mitigate the harsh effects of wartime inflation on the laborers. He did this by fixing wages and prices in a way that was more favorable to the laborers. In return for this aid, Edward required all men to work at whatever jobs were available. "As this quid pro quo indicates, mercantilism was grounded in the idea of a mutual, corporate responsibility. God's way was based on such reciprocal respect and obligation, and Jerusalem provided the example to be followed" (Williams, p. 34).

Richard II (r. 1377–1399) extended and systematized his predecessors' policies. The principal problems facing England during his reign were the social and economic conflict that led to the Peasants' Revolt of 1381. The other important issue was the necessity of countering foreign competition more effectively. The latter led to the Navigation Act of 1381, which was designed to favor English shippers and traders and to bring gold and silver into England. This money was needed for his program of building England into a "well and rightly governed kingdom" in which greater economic security for all would mitigate the social tensions that existed.

Henry VII (r. 1485–1509) renewed these policies. He commissioned numerous voyages of explorers and adventurers and attempted in various ways to secure legislation and negotiate treaties advantageous to English merchants. At the same time he subjected merchants to many controls and regulations imposed by the crown, for he believed that the unlimited pursuit of self-interest in the quest for profits was often harmful to general social interests and harmony.

Henry was still balancing feudal and capitalist interests; neither was dominant enough to persuade him to favor one over the other. The rapid growth of mining and wool raising during his reign led to an unfortunate neglect of food production. Moreover, the general excesses of the merchants had alienated both the peasants and the agrarian aristocracy. The merchants seemed to understand these problems and accepted a relationship in which, in return for crown policies that would benefit them in foreign dealings, they submitted to domestic regulation of manufacturing and commerce.

The Secularization of Church Functions

During the reign of Henry VIII (r. 1509–1547), England broke with Roman Catholicism. This event was significant because it marked the final secularization (in England at least) of the functions of the medieval church. Under Henry, "The state in the form of God's monarchy assumed the role and the functions of the old universal church. What Henry had done in his own blunt way was to sanctify the processes of this world" (Williams, p. 36). During his reign, as well as during the reigns of Elizabeth I (r. 1558–1603), James I (r. 1603–1625), and Charles I (r. 1625–1649), there was widespread social unrest. The cause of this unrest was poverty, and the cause of much of the poverty was unemployment.

The movement of landlords to remove peasants from their lands to make way for sheep herding was responsible for much of the unemployment. Another factor, however, was the decline in the export of woolens in the second half of the sixteenth century, which created a great deal of unemployment in England's most important manufacturing industry. There were also frequent commercial crises similar to, but without the regularity of, the **depression** phase, a *severe downturn in production and output,* or of later **business cycles,** *upward or downward trends of output that deviates from the overall trend in output over time.* In addition to these factors, seasonal unemployment put many workers out of work for as many as four months of the year.

The people could no longer look to the Catholic Church for relief from widespread unemployment and poverty. Destruction of the power of the church had eliminated the organized system of charity. The state attempted to assume responsibility for the general welfare of society. In order to do this, "England's leaders undertook a general, coordinated program to reorganize and rationalize . . . industry by establishing specifications of standards of production and marketing" (Williams, p. 40). All these measures were designed to stimulate English trade and to alleviate the unemployment problem.

In fact, it appears that the desire to achieve full employment is the unifying theme of most policy measures advocated by mercantilist writers. The mercantilists preferred measures designed to stimulate foreign rather than domestic trade "because they believed it contributed more to employment, to the nation's wealth and to national power. Writers after 1600 stressed the inflationary effect of an excess of exports over imports and the consequent increase in employment which inflation produced" (Grampp, p. 59).

Among the other measures taken to encourage industry during this period was the issuance of patents of monopoly. These royal decrees of monopoly gave the exclusive right to some individual or company to do all the trade in a given sector such as glassware, or a particular region, such as India. The first important patent was granted in 1561, during the reign of Elizabeth I. Monopoly rights were given in order to encourage inventions and to establish new industries.

These rights were severely abused, as might be expected. Moreover, they led to a complex system of special privileges and patronage and a host of other evils, which outraged most mercantilist writers. The evils of monopoly led to the Statute of Monopolies of 1623. This statute outlawed all monopolies. Exceptions were made for those monopolies that involved genuine inventions or those that would be instrumental in promoting British exports. Of course these loopholes were large, so abuses continued almost unchecked.

The Statute of Artificers (1563) specified conditions of employment and length of apprenticeships, provided for periodic wage assessments, and established maximum rates that could be paid to laborers. The statute is important because it illustrates the fact that the crown's paternalistic ethic never led to any attempt to elevate the status of the laboring classes. Monarchs of this period felt obliged to protect the working classes but, like their predecessors in the Middle Ages, believed those classes should be kept in their proper place. Maximum wage rates were designed to protect the capitalists, and furthermore, the justices who set these maximums and enforced the statute generally belonged to the employing class themselves. It is probable that these maximums reduced the real wages of laborers because prices generally rose faster than wages during the succeeding years.

Poor Laws passed in 1531 and 1536 attempted to deal with the problems of unemployment, poverty, and misery then widespread in England. The first sought to distinguish between "deserving" and "undeserving" poor. Only the deserving poor were allowed to beg. The second decreed that each individual parish throughout England was responsible for its poor and that the parish should, through voluntary contributions, maintain a Poor Fund. This proved completely inadequate, and the "pauper problem" grew increasingly severe.

Finally, in 1572 the state accepted the principle that the poor would have to be supported by tax funds and enacted a compulsory "poor rate." And in 1576 "houses of correction" for "incorrigible vagrants" were authorized and provisions were made for the parish to purchase raw materials to be worked up by the more tractable paupers and vagrants. Between that time and the close of the sixteenth century, several other Poor Law statutes were passed.

The Poor Law of 1601 was the Tudor attempt to integrate these laws into one consistent framework. Its main provisions included formal recognition of the right of the poor to receive relief, imposition of compulsory poor rates at the parish level, and provision for differential treatment for various classes of the poor. The aged and the sick could receive help in their homes; pauper children who were too young to be apprenticed in a trade were to be boarded out; the deserving poor and unemployed were to be given work as provided for in the Act of 1576; and incorrigible vagrants were to be sent to houses of correction and prisons. (For an extension of this discussion of the poor laws, see Birnie 1936, chaps. 12 and 18.)

From the preceding discussion it is possible to conclude that the period of English mercantilism was characterized by acceptance, in the spirit of the Christian paternalist ethic, of the idea that "the state had an obligation to serve society by accepting and discharging the responsibility for the general welfare" (Williams, p. 41). The various statutes passed during this period "were predicated upon the idea that poverty, instead of being a personal sin, was a function of the economic system" (Williams, p. 44). They acknowledged that those who were the victims of the deficiencies of the economic system should be cared for by those who benefited from the system.

THE RISE OF INDIVIDUALISM

After the Civil War of 1648–60 and the Glorious Revolution of 1688, the English government was dominated by the gentry and the middle-class capitalists. The medieval worldview that underlay the Christian paternalist ethic was eclipsed. A fundamental shift in the philosophy of the role of the state in society took place over the next one hundred years. In 1776, with the publication of Adam Smith's (1723–1790) *The Wealth of Nations,* **classical liberalism**, a *new individualistic philosophy,* emerges. A **liberal** is *someone who favors political and social reform or change.* We use the adjective "classical" to differentiate from what is called "liberal" in the twenty-first century. Classical liberalism had definitely gained the ascendancy in England. This individualistic philosophy existed throughout the mercantilist period, struggling to break the hold of the older paternalist world view. In the end, the new classical liberalism prevailed because it, and not the older, essentially medieval world view, reflected the needs of the new capitalist order.

In condemning greed, acquisitive behavior, and the desire to accumulate wealth, the medieval Christian paternalist ethic condemned what had become the capitalist order's dominant motive force. The capitalist market economy, which had been extended by the late eighteenth century to almost every phase of production, demanded self-seeking, acquisitive behavior to function successfully. In this context new theories about human behavior began to emerge. Writers began to assert that selfish, egoistic motives were the primary, if not the only ones, that moved people to action. Yet they argued that this selfish action would actually help society.

This interpretation of humankind's behavior is expressed in the writings of many important thinkers of the period. Many philosophers and social theorists began to assert that every human act was related to self-preservation and hence was egoistic in the most fundamental sense. The English nobleman Sir Robert Filmer (1588–1653) was greatly alarmed by the large number of people who spoke of "the natural freedom of mankind, a new, plausible and dangerous opinion" with anarchistic implications (McDonald, p. 29). Thomas Hobbes's (1588–1679) *Leviathan,* published in 1651, articulated a widely held opinion that all human motives stem from a desire for whatever promotes the "vital motion" of the human organism. Hobbes believed that everyone's motives, even compassion, was merely disguised self-interest: "Grief for the calamity of another is pity, and ariseth from the imagination that the like calamity may befall himself; and therefore is called . . . compassion, and . . . fellow-feeling" (quoted in Girvetz, pp. 28–29).

Except for the few special interest groups that benefited from the extensive restrictions and regulations of commerce and manufacturing during this period, most capitalists felt constrained and inhibited by state regulations in their quest for profits. The individualistic and egoistic doctrines were eagerly embraced by such people. This view began to dominate economic thinking, even among the mercantilists. One careful historian asserts that "most of the mercantilist . . . policy assumed that self-interest governs individual conduct" (Grampp, p. 69).

The majority of mercantilist writers were either capitalists or employees of the great capitalist trading companies. It was quite natural for them to perceive the motives of the capitalists as universal. From the capitalists' views of the nature of humans, and their need to be free from the extensive economic restrictions that inhibited them in the conduct of their everyday business, grew the philosophy of "individualism" that provided the basis of classical liberalism. Against the well-ordered, paternalist view Europe had inherited from the feudal society, they asserted "the view that the human person ought to be independent, self directing, autonomous, free—ought to be, that is, an individual, a unit distinguished from the social mass rather than submerged in it" (McDonald, p. 16).

PROTESTANTISM AND THE INDIVIDUALIST ETHIC

One of the most important examples of this individualistic and middle-class philosophy was the Protestant theology that emerged from the Reformation. The new middle-class capitalists wanted to be free not only from economic restrictions that encumbered manufacturing and commerce, but also from the moral constraints that the Roman Catholic Church placed upon their motives and activities. Protestantism not only freed them from religious condemnation but eventually made virtues of the selfish, egoistic, and acquisitive motives that the medieval church had so despised. (The classic studies of the relationship between Protestantism and capitalism are Weber's and Tawney's.)

The principal originators of the Protestant movement were quite close to the Catholic position on such questions as usury. The crime of usury was charging interest for loans. On most social issues they were deeply conservative. During the German peasant revolt of 1524–25, Martin Luther (1483–1546) wrote a virulent pamphlet, *Against the Murdering Hordes of Peasants,* in which he said princes should "knock down, strangle and stab. . . . Such wonderful times are these that a prince can merit heaven better with bloodshed than another with prayer." His advice contributed to the general atmosphere in which the slaughter of over 100,000 peasants was carried out with an air of religious righteousness.

Yet despite the conservatism of the founders of Protestantism, this religious outlook contributed to the growing influence of the new individualistic philosophy. The basic tenet of Protestantism, which laid the groundwork for religious attitudes that were to sanction middle-class business practices, was the doctrine that human beings were justified by faith rather than by works. The Roman Catholic Church had taught that humans were justified by works, which generally meant ceremonies and rituals. In the Roman Catholic view no one could be justified on merit alone. "Justification by works . . . did not mean that an individual could save himself: it meant that he could be saved through the Church. Hence the power of the clergy. Compulsory confession, the imposition of penance on the whole population . . . together with the possibility of withholding absolution, gave the priests a terrifying power" (Hill, p. 43). These powers also created a situation in which the medieval doctrines of the Roman Catholic Church were not easily abandoned and in which the individual was still subordinated to society (as represented by the church).

The Protestant doctrine of justification by faith asserted that motives were more important than specific acts or rituals. Faith was "nothing else but the truth of the heart" (as represented by the church). Each person had to search his or her own heart to discover if acts stemmed from a pure heart and faith in God. Each man and woman had to judge for himself and herself. This individualistic reliance on each person's private conscience appealed strongly to the new middle-class artisans and small merchants. "When the businessman of sixteenth- and seventeenth-century Geneva, Amsterdam or London looked into his inmost heart, he found that God had planted there a deep respect for the principle of private property. . . . Such men felt quite genuinely and strongly that their economic practices, though they might conflict with the traditional law of the old church, were not offensive to God. On the contrary: they glorified God" (Hill, pp. 46–47).

It was through this insistence on the individual's own interpretation of God's will that the "Puritans tried to spiritualize [the new] economic processes" and eventually came to believe that "God instituted the market and exchange" (Hill, p. 49). It was only a matter of time before the Protestants expounded dogma that they expected everyone to accept. But the new dogma was radically different from medieval doctrines. The new doctrines stressed the necessity of doing well at one's earthly calling as the best way to please God, and they emphasized diligence and hard work.

The older Christian distrust of riches was translated into a condemnation of extravagance and needless dissipation of wealth. Thus, the Protestant ethic stressed the importance of frugality. A theologian who has studied the connection between religion and capitalism sums up the relationship in this way: "The religious value set upon constant, systematic, efficient work in one's calling as the readiest means of securing the certainty of salvation and of glorifying God became a most powerful agency in economic expansion. The rigid limitations of consumption on the one hand and the methodical intensification of production on the other could have but one result—the accumulation of capital" (Fullerton, p. 19). Although neither John Calvin (1509–1564) nor Martin Luther was a spokesman for the new middle-class capitalist, within the context of the new religious individualism the capitalists found a religion in which, over time, "profits . . . [came to be] looked upon as willed by God, as a mark of his favor and a proof of success in one's calling" (Fullerton, p. 18).

THE ECONOMIC POLICIES OF INDIVIDUALISM

Throughout the mercantilist period this new individualism led to innumerable protests against the subordination of economic affairs to the will of the state. From the middle of the seventeenth century, almost all mercantilist writers condemned state-granted monopolies and other forms of protection and favoritism in the domestic economy (as opposed to international commerce). Many believed that in a competitive market that pitted buyer against buyer, seller against seller, and buyer against seller, society would benefit most greatly if the price were left free to fluctuate and find its proper (market-equilibrating) level. One of the earliest mercantilist writers of importance, John Hales (1584–1656), argued that agricultural productivity could best be improved if husbandmen were allowed to:

> have more profit by it than they have, and liberty to sell it at all times, and to all places, as freely as men may do their other things. But then no doubt, the price of corn would rise, specially at the first more than at length; yet that price would evoke every man to set plough

in the ground, to husband waste grounds, yes to turn the lands which be enclosed from pasture to arable land; for every man will gladder follow that wherein they see the more profit and gains, and thereby must need ensure both plenty of corn, and also much treasure should be brought into this realm by occasion thereof; and besides that plenty of other victuals increased among us (quoted in Grampp, p. 78).

This belief, that restrictions on production and trade within a nation were harmful to the interests of everyone concerned, became increasingly widespread in the late seventeenth and early eighteenth centuries. Numerous statements of this view can be found in the works of such writers as Gerard de Malynes (1586–1641), William Petty (1623–1687), Dudley North (1641–1691), John Law (1671–1729), and Josiah Child (1630–1699). Of these men, perhaps Sir Dudley North was the earliest clear spokesman for the individualistic ethic that was to become the basis for classical liberalism. North believed that all men were motivated primarily by self-interest and should be left alone to compete in a free market if the public welfare were to be maximized. He argued that whenever merchants or capitalists advocated special laws to regulate production or commerce, "they usually esteem the immediate interest of their own to be the common Measure of Good and Evil. And there are many, who to gain a little in their own Trades, care not how much others suffer; and each man strives that all others may be forced in their dealings to act subserviently for his Profit, but under the cover of the Publick" (quoted in Lekachman, 1962, p. 185). The public welfare would best be served, North believed, if most of the restrictive laws that bestowed special privileges were entirely removed.

In 1714, Bernard Mandeville (1670–1733) published *The Fable of the Bees: or Private Vices, Publick Benefits,* in which he put forth the seemingly strange paradox that the vices most despised in the older moral code, if practiced by all, would result in the greatest public good. Selfishness, greed, and acquisitive behavior, he maintained, all tended to contribute to industriousness and a thriving economy. The answer to the paradox was, of course, that what had been vices in the eyes of the medieval moralists were the very motive forces that propelled the new capitalist system. And in the view of the new religious, moral, and economic philosophies of the capitalist period, these motives were no longer vices.

The capitalists had struggled throughout the mercantilist period to free themselves from all restrictions in their quest for profits. These restrictions had resulted from the paternalist laws that were the remnants of the feudal version of the Christian paternalist ethic. Such an ethic simply was not compatible with the new economic system that functioned on the basis of strict contractual obligations between people rather than on traditional personal ties. Merchants and capitalists who invested large sums in market ventures could not depend on the forces of custom to protect their investments.

Profit seeking could be effective only in a society based on the protection of property rights and the enforcement of impersonal contractual commitments between individuals. The new ideology that was firmly taking root in the late seventeenth and eighteenth centuries justified these motives and relationships between individuals. It is to a consideration of this new individualistic philosophy of classical liberalism that we turn in Chapter 8.

SUMMARY

There is a basic continuity between medieval and mercantilist social thought. State intervention in economic processes was originally justified in terms of the medieval Christian notion that those to whom God had given power were obligated to use this power to promote the general welfare and common good of all society. In early capitalism the state began to assume many of the roles formerly held by the church.

The Christian paternalist ethic, however, had thoroughly condemned the acquisitive behavior that was to become the dominant motive force of the new capitalist system. It was therefore necessary to create a new philosophical and ideological point of view that morally justified individualization, greed, and profit seeking. Protestantism and the new philosophies of individualism furnished the bases for the new ideology. The economic writings of the later mercantilists reflected the new individualism. The new point of view emphasized the need for greater freedom for capitalists to seek profits and hence the need for less government intervention in the market. Thus the presence of two fundamentally different general points of view in mercantilist writings created an intellectual conflict that was not resolved until the classical liberal philosophy, including classical economics, effectively ferreted out all remnants of the medieval Christian paternalist ethic.

SUGGESTED READINGS

For a more complete discussion of mercantilism, see E. K. Hunt, *History of Economic Thought: A Critical Perspective* (2002).

KEY TERMS

balance of trade
bullionism
business cycles
classical liberalism
depression
exports

imports
inflation
liberal
mercantilism
subsidies

REVIEW QUESTIONS

Explain the importance of trade in the early phase of mercantilism.
  1. What is bullionism? Why is it not possible for every country to achieve its main goal?
  2. Why is exporting so important for countries in the bullionist period? What did countries do to protect their exports?
  3. What is the motivation for creating trade monopolies?
  4. How did the restrictions on trade and production impact the new middle class of merchants and industrial capitalists? What was their response?

Comprehend the battle of ideas: Christian paternalistic ethic and mercantilism.
  5. What are the two themes underlying the development of English mercantilism? What does this mean for the role of the church and the role of the state in protecting the social welfare of its citizens?
  6. As the state begins to take over the role of the church in interpreting and enforcing the Christian paternalistic ethic, what are some early mercantilist policies?
  7. Mercantilists advocate for full employment policies. What problems is unemployment causing in the late 1500s and early 1600s? What is the cause of widespread unemployment in this period?
  8. In 1563 a *maximum wage* is set. Why? Who is this designed to protect? Why?

9. As the state assumes more and more responsibility for the general welfare of society, it creates the Poor Laws. What are the Poor Laws? What are they designed to do?

Compare and contrast Christian paternalist view with those of emerging individualists and Protestants.

10. What is classical liberalism? Why did it end up prevailing over the older paternalistic view of the world?

11. What is considered to be the dominant motive needed to function successfully in a capitalist market economy? How is this justified by classical liberalism?

12. Compare and contrast "human justification by works" and "human justification by faith." Why does individual interpretation of God's will appeal to the new middle class of capitalists?

13. Using individual self-interest as a foundation, what arguments are put forward supporting removal of restrictions on trade and production? Be sure to give specific examples as part of your answer.

CHAPTER 7

Pre-Capitalism to Industrial Capitalism
in the United States
1776–1865

Chapter 5 revealed that capitalist institutions first emerged in England in the countryside, then spread to the rest of England. After that, they spread to Western Europe and then to the rest of the world. The initial rise of market capitalism in England was due to the internal evolution of feudalism supported by the changing ideology explained in Chapter 6. The European powers spread capitalism by fire and sword to the rest of the world, whose independent evolution was cut off in mid-stream. The Europeans set up a system to extract wealth from the colonies, but allowed little development of the colonies.

LEARNING OBJECTIVES

After reading this chapter, you should be able to:

- Explain the economic relationship of England and the United States.
- Explain the gradual shift from agriculture to urbanization and economic development and the impact on society.
- Discuss the evolution of the women's rights movement.

COLONIALISM AND ECONOMIC DEVELOPMENT

The settlements and territories that ultimately became the United States were colonies of England until the Revolutionary War. During the colonial period, over 80 percent of the people in the American colonies worked in agriculture. It is not surprising that most of American exports at that time were agricultural products, including lumber. Some products from mining were sent abroad, but there was very little industry, just small craft shops. England tried to keep a monopoly in trade with the colonies and exclude other European powers.

In return for American agricultural and mining products, England sent finished manufactured products to the colonies. When the cheap raw materials came to England, they were changed by crafts and manufacture into finished goods, worth far more than the raw materials. Some of them were then shipped back to the American colonies at a high profit. The American colonies provided England with cheap food, cheap raw materials, and a market for more expensive finished goods.

The industrial, trade, and military domination brought a flow of profit from the American colonies to England. This was a pattern repeated with all the other European colonies.

This meant that America stayed dependent on England for many finished goods and did not develop its own industry. Moreover, England did everything it could to keep its American colonies agricultural and extractive, rather than develop manufacturing. In fact, England prohibited the import of new machines into the American colonies. The colonists felt, and correctly so, that England was extracting profit and taxes from them, while holding back their economic development. This was one major cause of the Revolutionary War. England tried to reconquer the United States in 1812, but did not succeed. Nevertheless, the economic power of England and economic weakness of the United States remained in place for many years.

Since the pattern of production and trade remained similar to the colonial pattern, the United States was a neo-colony of England. Being **neocolonial** meant that *it had formal independence and no occupying troops, but its economic relationship to England remained the same as the colonial one*. It was only very slowly as U.S. manufacturing increased, starting in the 1840s, that some degree of economic independence was slowly achieved.

PRE-CAPITALIST INSTITUTIONS IN THE UNITED STATES: 1776–1840

At the time of the American Revolution in 1776, the future United States was a colony of England. It was economically underdeveloped because of British restrictions, such as on importing new technology in most fields. The United States was largely rural, agricultural, poor, and dependent on English trade for vital goods. At that time, capitalist institutions did not exist in the United States to any large degree. For example, the South still had slavery. The discussion of slavery is very important to the story of U.S. development as a whole. Since the system of slavery was so different than the rest of the country, however, it will be discussed in detail in Appendix 7.1.

In the North and West, there were millions of farmers, each of whom owned their own farm and employed no one but their own family. In 1810, 81 percent of the U.S. labor force was in farming. The farmers were not part of capitalism because they were neither capitalists nor workers, but part of an independent type of economic system. Their farms were mostly self-sufficient, producing their own food, clothing, and shelter.

Gradually throughout the nineteenth century, the farmers became less self-sufficient and more tied to the market, both in order to buy vital goods and to sell their product for cash. As they became tied to the market, they had to compete by using better farming techniques and better machinery. The farmers and ranchers found that they were paying monopoly prices to a few large farm equipment producers, paying the giant railroad corporations monopoly prices to ship their products, and selling at relatively low prices to large wholesalers. As their costs rose and their prices were limited, they went into debt to the banks. Throughout the nineteenth and twentieth centuries, many farmers went bankrupt, left agriculture, moved to the cities and became workers in manufacturing and service industries. From 81 percent of the labor force in 1810, farmers fell to 63 percent of the labor force in 1840. The disappearance of small farms and the rise of a few giant farms continued steadily from then until today. By the year 2000, the number of farmers fell to less than 2 percent of the population. A large portion of that 2 percent was no longer independent farmers, but agricultural workers.

In the cities of the East Coast after the American Revolution there were both merchants and craftspeople but few manufacturing owners or manufacturing workers. The craft shops were small, usually with one or two apprentices who would eventually become masters. Craftspeople such as blacksmiths, silversmiths, cabinet-makers, and candle-makers did not produce a steady stream of goods, and then worry about selling them. Instead, they typically worked only on orders as they came in.

Crafts slowly became more market oriented, with shops turning out a steady stream of products and expanding their production, but it was a very slow evolution. Up until now, merchants mainly bought and sold commodities but they did not produce them. Over time the merchants started to order larger amounts from craftspeople or from farmers and even more slowly some merchants started their own production. By the early 1840s, there were the beginnings of manufacturing with a few hundred employees only in the biggest factories.

Most foreign trade was with England. The U.S. economy was clearly subordinate to England and shipped lumber and agricultural goods, while buying manufactured goods from England. This is a pattern of trade similar to that of many underdeveloped countries today. During the War of 1812 against England, some manufacturing businesses started to produce things previously imported from England, but England remained dominant over U.S. trade throughout the first half of the nineteenth century.

There were just a few banks, law firms, and insurance companies. The most important banks in the world were in London. U.S. banks remained subservient to English finance until long after the Civil War. For most of the nineteenth century, even the U.S. government borrowed money from London banks and tended to be bow to their wishes in financial matters. Transportation and communication slowly improved, but news, people and merchandise still moved at a snail's pace.

During this period, the corporate form of doing business emerged. A **corporation** is defined as *a business in which all of the assets are owned by people who buy shares of stock, or shares of ownership, in the business.* By law, investors may lose their investment if the share price falls to nothing, but creditors have no right to pursue the investors beyond the **assets**, *things of value that can be owned*, of the corporation. Thus the corporation is said to have **limited liability**, whereas noncorporate businesses, owned by individuals or partners, are liable to creditors, not only for the assets of the business, but for all of the personal assets of the owners as well. *The corporate form allows a large group of investors to work together with liability limited to their investments.*

At that time only a few businesses made use of the corporate form. After the Civil War, however, more and more businesses organized as corporations in order to limit their liability. Today, although corporations are a minority of total businesses, corporations produce something like 90 percent of all the output of the United States.

Output, measured by **gross domestic product (GDP)**, expanded and grew by 30 percent from 1810 to 1840. GDP is *the current dollar value of all final goods and services produced within the country in one year*. With the growth of crafts and merchandising, towns grew. Farms produced more per acre so fewer farms were needed to satisfy the market. Therefore, the number of farmers declined while towns grew. The urban population increased from 6 percent of the population in 1810 to 11 percent in 1840. Urbanization continued to increase throughout the century.

BEGINNINGS OF CAPITALISM, 1840–1860

Railroads grew rapidly in the eastern United States from 1840 to 1860. Building, supplying, and operating the railroads was the largest single industry at this time and helped start many fortunes as well as many financial empires. The railroads were helped by large government giveaways of land. It is estimated that the land giveaways amounted to 158,293,000 acres, a greater land area than that of many countries. Canals and telegraph systems were also subsidized by the government. With the help of the earliest telegraph and the railroads, some of the most important industries of the nineteenth century, such as the oil industry, began to be developed.

Building a transcontinental system of railroads and telegraph was an essential prerequisite to large-scale industry. The first small beginnings of the railroads and telegraph emerged in this period, mostly serving the East Coast. Total railroad mileage was only 2,000 miles in 1840, but had risen to 47,000 miles by 1860. At the beginning of 1840, only 10 percent of the labor force was in manufacturing. There were few enterprises with more than 200 workers and none over 500. The railways were the first large industrial firms, although they were still relatively small throughout this period. In fact, large, nationwide enterprises were impossible in this period because of the slowness of transportation and communication, which was little better than the Roman roads. Ships still had to go all the way around the tip of South America to bring heavy loads to the West Coast of the United States.

In addition to a material basis, industrialization requires the proper ideological climate. There had been no long history of feudalism in the United States, so the ideology of the 1840s supported unbridled capitalism. The dominant view was one of "rugged individualism," and that if one were willing to work hard enough, anyone could make a fortune. The economic possibilities were perceived as endless. The gold rush to California came in this period and men fought over every pretty pebble in the stream. Some became rich overnight but many faced years of misery for nothing. There were no income taxes, no regulations of business, and no safety net of unemployment compensation or welfare. This was perceived as the perfect basis for building capitalist industry once slavery was ended.

In the 1850s and 1860s when railroads needed vast sums, investment banks grew in importance. Railroads were 60 percent of all stock issues. Banks became very close partners to railroad corporations and to various other corporations to whom they loaned money. In this period corporations started having bankers on their boards of directors, so this increased the control of bankers over corporations.

Output began to rise consistently in this period as result of the new capitalist system. The earliest beginning of a system with a small elite group of owners and bosses, but many low-paid workers, meant the beginnings of increased inequality by the end of this period. By 1860, the top 10 percent of wealth holders owned 75 percent of all the wealth. The picture was becoming one of a pyramid with a few wealthy people at the top, but an enormous number of people at the bottom with little to no wealth and just enough income to survive.

THE STATUS OF WOMEN

This chapter has been almost purely on economics to this point, but economic development cannot be understood without considering the political institutions, social institutions, and ideas of society that influence the economy every single day. Politics and ideology are key components of every economic transformation. The story of ideas begins here with women's rights because the status and treatment of women in a society is important in itself, but it is also important for its reflection of a society and for its impact on society. In addition to the Native American women who were here already, women came to the United States as free immigrants, as slaves, or as indentured servants. Usually, indentured servants were people who agreed to pay for their passage to America by seven years of service to a master.

Leaving aside slave women (discussed in Appendix 7.1), what was the status of women after the American Revolution? In the early days of the United States, the treatment of women must be seen in the context of enslavement of African Americans, the extermination of many Native Americans, and laws preventing the poor and propertyless from voting.

Status of Women: 1776–1840

Early U.S. law concerning women was the same as British common law, which gave the husband all the rights, while a woman had none. Specifically, a wife had no right to hold property, even her dowry, and the husband owned and managed everything. Wives had no right to keep their own wages. Wives had no control of children, but had to give them up to their husbands in a divorce. Wives had no right to sue in court. Wives had no right to testify in court, nor could women serve on juries. Women could not vote.

During the American Revolution, the only man to speak for women's rights was Thomas Paine (1737–1809), but he was known to be a "troublemaker." Most towns would not employ women to teach in the schools and those that did required them to resign when they had children. There was little or no education for most women. A few rich women attended women's seminaries which usually taught sewing, singing, and French, along with a lady's manners. Some women produced textiles, but typically not in factories. They worked at home and sold their product to merchants.

Women on farms, which constituted over 80 percent of women, planted and tended and harvested crops. When they were not doing agricultural work, women made clothes, prepared food, cared for health needs, cared for children, and repaired the house. Men hunted, fought Native Americans (whose land they were taking), cleared fields, and built any extensions on the house. Women had higher status on the frontier than on the East Coast. Why? On the frontier, women were scarce, and their work was absolutely necessary to the survival of the farm.

Status of Women, 1840–1860

By 1850, there were some women in textile factories. They worked thirteen to sixteen hours a day and their wages were only one-fourth to one-seventh of men's wages. A few women tried to build unions, but found it to be very difficult. In the 1840s no women had any property rights, but this situation started to change by the 1850s in the North. In a campaign that had some early success in the northeast states, but took decades to be successful all over the country, the rights of women to hold property apart from their husbands were finally won. Women were aided by some rich fathers, who were annoyed at the control over their daughters' dowries by their husbands.

Some revolutionary ideas also emerged from the American and French revolutions about liberty and equality before the law for everyone. If "everyone" is equal before the law, why should women not be treated equally? Later, some women fought in the movement for the abolition of slavery. This question of abolishing slavery for black men also raised the question of abolishing the subordination of women. Not only were many women abolitionists, they also did some of the most difficult jobs. For example, the African-American woman abolitionist, Harriet Tubman (c. 1822–1913), was a conductor on the Underground Railroad, which meant that she helped move many slaves to freedom under very dangerous conditions. Women learned much about activism by working in the abolitionist movement.

The church and most public opinion said that it was not "lady-like" to work in a political movement, help the Underground Railway, or speak in public. Some male abolitionists wanted them to help very quietly and "stay in their place." For example, at the 1840 World Abolitionist Meeting in London, women were kept in the gallery and not allowed on the floor of the convention. Since the abolitionist movement taught many women how to run a movement while many abolitionists rejected the equality of women, a separate women's movement was organized.

In 1848 in Seneca Falls, New York, women met for the first time as a separate movement. They wrote a declaration in favor of the equal rights of women, including the rights to keep their own wages, to keep their own property, and to keep their children. There was fear, however, of something as revolutionary as the vote for women. It was only after a very long debate that the participants approved a demand that women should have the right to vote. All of the demands of women were met at first with ridicule. The big city newspapers attacked the women's movement, especially the demand to vote, as unfeminine and silly. One response of women was to organize at the local level. For example, women took control of many local newspapers.

LABOR RELATIONS AND UNIONS

Before the Civil War, the relationships of the U.S. economy were still dominated by rural, agricultural production and small craft businesses. There were few large concentrations of workers. Consequently, unions were weak and usually short-lived. Nonunion employees, who were most of the labor force, were oppressed in ways that seem hardly believable today. Remember that capitalism in the nineteenth century remained almost completely unregulated and employers were free to do as they pleased with workers.

Dry statistics do not make clear the extent of human suffering, so let us begin with a concrete example. This dramatic example of the oppression of free employees in the last half of the nineteenth century came during the building of the first intercontinental railroad from Omaha to San Francisco and shows that labor conditions had not improved from the period of the American Revolution, a century before.

At the time of the Civil War Abraham Lincoln strongly endorsed the idea of an intercontinental railroad that would make it easy to move goods, people, and soldiers, and helped push it through Congress. At the same time, the telegraph was extended along the same line for rapid communication. It was a daunting feat since it meant covering thousands of miles by rails where there was often no water, no wood or rock for building, hostile people, lengthy desert terrain, and very high mountains. Its accomplishment in only about seven years was amazing and had major positive consequences on the U.S. economy and on the unification of culture and the military.

Congress and the president agreed it could not be done without government aid, but there should be no government ownership or control because of possible corruption. The result was that a small group of railroad financiers received immense amounts of low-cost government loans and immense amounts of land—greater in area than France. One corporation set up by the financiers was the Crédit Mobilier, which robbed millions from the railway corporations actually building the railroads and from the government. These fortunes were not enough for the financiers, who also paid very low wages or did not pay the workers at all. When the whole scheme was exposed, it resulted in the biggest scandal of the nineteenth century. Until the exposure, these financiers all became fabulously rich—and most of them managed to remain fabulously rich even after the exposure.

Much of their money came from paying the workers miserable wages for backbreaking work.

The eastern part of the transcontinental railroad, called the Union Pacific, used thousands of Irish-American workers, who were new immigrants. There was a great deal of prejudice against Irish-Americans at this time and they had to take whatever work that was available. The western part or the railroad was called the Central Pacific and employed many thousands of Chinese-American workers, who faced even more prejudice than the Irish and received even lower wages. On the Central Pacific, white men earned three dollars a day, while Chinese Americans were paid one dollar a day.

The low wages seemed to barely compensate for extremely hard and dangerous work from morning to night, with many railroad workers hurt and many killed. For example, in the Sierra Nevada, the Chinese workers were lowered down the side of a sheer cliff, then had to drill a hole, set dynamite, and yell to be pulled up quickly. Many were killed.

The Chinese workers were stereotyped as docile and passive, but when conditions became bad enough, they went out on strike. The Chinese worked six days a week from sunrise to sunset, so they demanded a few less hours work a week. They wanted an increase from thirty-five dollars a month to forty dollars a month, at least for the most dangerous jobs. They also wanted the supervisors to stop beating them, a demand which gives a chilling picture of the work conditions. In response, the railroad cut off their food supply and starved them into submission at the same old salary, and with the same dangerous work, long hours, and beatings.

The economic oppression of the average employee was made much worse when prejudice was added to the picture. The existence of racial or ethnic prejudice caused public opinion to be against the employees, so they had even less bargaining power than the average employee. In short, although the average employee was oppressed economically, minority employees were twice as oppressed, and minority women employees were three times as oppressed. Although many things have changed, it will be shown that this basic pressure on employees to produce profit for employers remains in all countries with capitalist institutions.

ENVIRONMENTAL ISSUES

Since there was little industry until the 1840s, there was little industrial pollution in this period. There was, however, continual chopping down of forests in all regions. There was exhaustion of the land in the South, as shown in the next chapter. There was the near elimination of entire species, such as the disappearance of the vast herds of buffalo on the Great Plains. Killing the buffalo was part of a deliberate attempt to eliminate Native Americans from the Great Plains.

U.S. LAW AND ECONOMIC DEVELOPMENT

Laws reflect and are influenced by the institutions and the relationships among different groups of a given society. Laws change with each change of society and changing group relationships. At the same time, laws also influence economic institutions and relationships of different groups, locking them into place until changed. For example, in order to keep slaves subordinate, the Southern states passed laws making it a crime to teach a slave to read and write, with the death penalty threatened as a punishment.

The dominant group or groups in a society tend to control the laws according to their interests. The laws of the South before the Civil War, such as the law against slaves learning to read and write, not only reflected Southern slavery, but in turn helped to preserve and protect slavery. The object of the Southern laws was to freeze into place the existing slave institutions. The laws change in a fundamental way only after institutions change. After the Civil War ended slavery, the law changed when new amendments to the U.S. constitution were passed. How has this process, the interaction of law and institutions, developed in the United States?

Law: 1776–1840

The first period of U.S. law corresponds to the period of a mostly pre-capitalist economy before the market institutions of capitalism were well developed. That period lasted from the founding of the British colonies in the present borders of the United States until roughly the 1840s. In that period, besides slavery in the South, there were millions of small independent farmers who were neither capitalist employers nor employees. In the western United States, the early laws reflected the needs of agriculture with isolated farms and small communities. In these small farm communities, tradition played a big role in a society that appeared to be unchanging.

When the economy changed to one of expanding industry with rapidly changing technology, the law had to change. The groups that dominated the government no longer saw land and farming as most important, but rather favored the needs of industry. What was rational for a backwoods society was not rational for a modern industrial society. For example, under modern industrial capitalism, people think of contracts as inviolate and assume that things will be sold at the price agreed in the contract, no matter how much one party may be hurt by it. On the contrary, in the early period of pre-capitalist relationships, what counted for the courts was a "just price," which meant a fair price by community standards. This doctrine was especially upheld in the so-called "equity" courts, to which people could appeal a decision. This notion of a just price made sense for a small community where everyone knew each other and where profiteering from your neighbors was abhorrent and was denounced by most churches.

What counted in later contract law in a complex industrial society was simply the market price as set by supply and demand, whether it was fair or just or not. Often, the formal legal terminology remained the same, but talk about what was a "just price" slowly changed to talk about the market price by 1840.

Law: 1840–1865

Although capitalism was still young in the 1840s and 1850s, the whole period from the 1840s to the 1920s was the era of mostly unregulated industrial capitalism. In this period, contracts were enforced by the law. Moreover, property law was revised to meet the needs of the industrialists as opposed to the farmers. As an example, with respect to water rights, polluting a river was a terrible thing from the viewpoint of its use for farming. But water pollution was seen as secondary to production when the representatives of the industrialists wrote the laws. When industrialists came to power, labor law consisted of nothing but the right of the employer to do as he or she pleased. Again, it was a period of unregulated capitalism with private enterprise completely dominant.

SUMMARY

In 1776, when the Revolutionary War began, the United States was not yet capitalist. In the Northeast, there were independent farmers, craftspeople, and merchants. In the South, there were masters and slaves and some independent farmers. In the West there were independent farmers. By the 1840s, some industry was beginning in the North. Industry then grew by leaps and bounds in the first stages of an industrial revolution for the United States and made great strides forward by the time of the Civil War in 1860.

During this period, Native Americans were hunted and killed, African-Americans were in slavery, and women were completely subordinate to men. This situation was changed to some degree by the abolitionist movement and the Civil War. Slavery was abolished and on paper African-Americans were given equality, but it took another hundred years to gain a large measure of equality in civil rights and voting. After the Civil War the dominant system in the United States may be called industrial capitalism. It was the first stage in the evolution of U.S. capitalism that is still continuing.

SUGGESTED READINGS

An outstanding book on the economic aspects of U.S. history and the source of much data in this chapter is Richard DuBoff, *Accumulation and Power: An Economic History of the United States* (1989). The social aspects of U.S. history are covered excellently in Howard Zinn, *A People's History of the United States* (1999). The history of women and sexist discrimination is covered in a powerful book by Barbara Sinclair Deckard, *The Women's Movement* (1983). The story of the fight for women's right to vote, told in a wonderfully exciting style, is Eleanor Flexner, *Century of Struggle: The Women's Rights Movement in the United States* (1975), the classic on which much women's history has been founded. The book by Michael Reich, *Racial Inequality, Economic Theory, and Class Conflict* (1980), is a very thorough history and an insightful theory of racial discrimination, but it is more difficult than the other books listed here—which were chosen to be easily readable as well as excellent—so a noneconomist should read only Reich's first chapter plus the introductions and conclusions of each chapter.

The fascinating story of the financing and building of the first transcontinental railroad is told in beautiful prose in Stephen Ambrose, *Nothing Like It in the World* (2001). The history of the rise of the oil monopoly and its unscrupulous tactics is told as a biography of Rockefeller in Ron Chernow, *Titan: Biography of John D. Rockefeller* (1999). The history of the rise of finance is told in interesting and well-written prose in Ron Chernow, *House of Morgan: An American Banking Dynasty and the Rise of Modern Finance* (1998). The history of law and U.S. institutions is given in Anthony Chase, *The American Legal System: The Evolution of the American Legal System* (1997), a very clear book if you skip the footnotes, fun to read if you are a lawyer or historian, but more difficult if you lack the background. A book on the amazing history of the labor movement that is riveting and fun to read for anyone is Richard O. Boyer and Herbert Morais, *Labor's Untold Story* (1970). A very detailed, but accessible history is Philip Foner's *History of the Labor Movement in the United States*. It covers the period from the earliest colonial times to the 1920s (ten volumes, 1947–1994). Finally, the whole evolution of environmental problems is presented in a short, beautifully written, and fascinating book by John Bellamy Foster, *The Vulnerable Planet: A Short Economic History of the Environment* (1984).

KEY TERMS

assets	limited liability
corporation	neocolonial
gross domestic product (GDP)	

REVIEW QUESTIONS

Explain the economic relationship of England and the United States.

1. What was the nature of trade between the United States and England when the United States was still a colony? Why?
2. Why did the U.S. economy stay undeveloped for so long?
3. Describe how the United States remains a neocolonial country after the Revolutionary War.
4. Was the United States really independent from England after 1776? Explain.

Explain the gradual shift from agriculture to urbanization and economic development and the impact on society.

5. How did monopolies in farm equipment and railroads impact early farmers?
6. How is a corporation different from a business that is not organized as a corporation?
7. Why did the building of the railroad have such a huge impact on the economic development of the United States? How was the building of the railroads financed?
8. How were the workers who actually built the railroads treated in general? Give examples. How were ethnic minorities treated? Why?
9. How did the idea of "rugged individualism" support capitalism? Why did the ideology of the United States so easily support capitalism?
10. Unregulated capitalism was the predominate ideology of the era. In what ways is this ideology a good thing? In which ways is it bad?
11. How did unbridled capitalism affect the distribution of wealth in the United States?
12. In which ways did the law try and preserve social institutions? When was law used as a tool to change them?
13. Discuss revisions to property rights laws and contract law. What happened to the notion of "just prices?"

Discuss the evolution of the women's rights movement.

14. What was the legal status of women in the early history of the United States?
15. Why did women on the frontier have a higher status than women on the East Coast?
16. What was the first right won by women in the 1850s
17. How did the work of women in the abolitionist movement lead to a separate women's movement?

APPENDIX 7.1
SLAVERY IN THE UNITED STATES, 1776–1865

There are many similarities and differences between ancient Roman slavery and the system of slavery that existed in the Old South of the United States before the Civil War. The main features of society are similar. First, both had predominantly slave economic institutions, which produced most of the product of the society. Second, in both cases the political, religious, and military power was held by the slave owners. Third, in both cases, the ideology that supported slavery was based in part on racism. Fourth, both had a mostly stagnant technology, relying on heavy, but crude, agricultural implements. On the other hand, the two slave societies came into being by different paths. Moreover, they evolved in somewhat different social forms, though retaining the same basic institutions.

LEARNING OBJECTIVES

After reading this appendix, you should be able to:

- Describe how slaves were treated/exploited in America.
- Compare and contrast the Southern economy to the Northern economy.
- Understand the causes, forces, and motivations behind the Civil War.

FEATURES OF U.S. SLAVERY

Most of Southern agriculture was divided into large plantations. Slaves worked under supervisors who were often cruel and brutal. Slaves were sometimes whipped for tiny mistakes or for not working fast enough. In the fields, most slaves picked cotton which is a backbreaking job. On each plantation, there was a magnificent mansion for the master and little, rundown shacks for the slaves. In the mansion, slaves cooked the meals, cleaned the house, made the clothing, and performed other endless tasks. The master and his friends often sat on the veranda drinking mint juleps, while the slaves did hard, agricultural labor or tedious domestic labor from sunrise till after sunset. The master had all kinds of good food to eat, while the slaves were often not given enough for an adequate diet. Everything produced by the slaves belonged to the master class.

The state governments, under the control of slave masters, passed severe laws to protect slavery. It was perfectly legal to beat a slave or to sell children separately from families. It was a crime punishable by death for a slave to learn to read and write! Any slave revolts were punishable by death. Any attempts to escape also had severe punishments.

After the Revolutionary War, since the South was part of the United States, it had political democracy, in theory. It was, however, a democracy in which the slaves and women were not allowed to participate. Most of the power in every state in the South was held by male slaveholders with very limited representation by the free farmers, craftspeople, or even the merchants. There was an educational system, but it was limited to white, male students. Most of the churches were run by and for whites only. The white churches provided much of the social life and a great deal of information or misinformation to their members. The churches were the center of white life before the Civil War and the white churches played a major role in defending and perpetuating slavery.

But there was also an underground African-American church. The African-American churches were the center of the social, musical, educational, and political activity of the African-American population. The African-American churches were a center of social and political revolt as well as spiritual and social balm for their members.

Everywhere where slavery has arisen, there is racism. Those who made vast profits by capturing or buying slaves in Africa claimed that the slaves were little better than animals. Those who sold the slaves at a high profit in the South said that they were very useful "animals." The owners of slaves held them to be inferior beings, so they were justified in keeping them as slaves, making them work very hard all day, and giving them very little to eat, little clothing and little shelter. The vast majority of preachers of the white churches agreed that the slaves were inferior, but said it was the duty of white Christians to keep the slaves, provide them minimum provisions, and help them learn to be Christians so their souls would be saved. The slaves could be beaten in this world to teach them to live proper Christian lives, so they would go to heaven in the next world. Thus, racism and religion cooperated to support slavery with a rhetoric of saving the souls of inferior creatures.

In addition to racism, certain family values were an important part of the ideology. The family was considered to be vital to Southern culture. The family of the white master class was viewed and treated very differently than the family of the African-American slave. Within white families, all power was held by the father or husband. Women were placed on a pedestal as the finest product of Southern culture. But it was an isolated pedestal. The women of the master class was not allowed to mingle with other men, not allowed to wander freely about town, not allowed to get an education beyond sewing and perhaps French. Reading, except for the Bible, was discouraged for women. Women played no role in public life or politics. Women could not be doctors or lawyers or even teachers until after the Civil War. Women were expected to run the master's mansion by telling the slaves what to do, but the lord and master could always change their orders concerning the house or the children. If there were a divorce, which was rare, but sometimes granted at the request of the husband, women had no rights to money (even her dowry), no rights to property, and no rights to their children. It was rare that women of the master class did any work outside the house. In the South as in the North, if a woman did receive an income, it belonged to her father or her husband if she were married.

The rights of slave families were not recognized by the masters. Some plantations essentially raised slaves, encouraged children, and then sold the children. Slave women could be used for sexual purposes by the male master or his sons. If the slave woman had a child of her master, the child was often sold, thus getting rid of a problem while making more profit. If a woman of the master class had sex with a slave, the slave was killed. Moreover, the white woman could be divorced, beaten, or even killed by her husband with no legal repercussions. There was a strong double standard between men and women with respect to sex.

SLAVERY AND ECONOMIC PROGRESS IN THE OLD SOUTH

Although Southern plantations tried to be efficient profit makers, they were very different from capitalist enterprises. Most production was done by slaves, so there was little or no free labor market. Unlike free workers, slaves were bought and sold. Unlike capitalist enterprises, much of the assets of the plantations consisted of the slaves.

It has been argued by those economists who see the Southern plantations as part of the market that they were quite efficient and made good profits. Slaveholders were in fact intent on maximum profit and so they were part of the capitalist marketplace with capitalist motives. Slavery was usually profitable. The slaves produced varying degrees of surplus, which was sold by the masters at a profit. In the late eighteenth century after the Revolutionary War, the profit was fairly low and some talked of voluntarily ending slavery. Slave owners like Thomas Jefferson, who wrote the Declaration of Independence, were troubled by the contradiction between slavery and the high ideals of the Declaration. The Declaration of Independence said that "all men are created equal" and that all men have the right to "life, liberty, and the pursuit of happiness." Jefferson owned slaves, but fought to end slavery.

In the nineteenth century, the invention of the cotton gin made slavery more profitable, so slave owners ended any talk of voluntarily ending slavery and fought against abolition of slavery tooth and nail. As the Civil War began in 1861, the South was not in economic decline or stagnation.

In fact, the South experienced rapid growth for fifteen years before the war. This helps to explain why the Southern rulers were willing to risk war to keep slavery.

At first glance, it appears that Southern agriculture was doing even better that Northern agriculture. The average value of all Southern farms was $34,000 while Northern farms were an average of only $4,000 dollars. But averages can be very deceiving. The wealth of the South was all concentrated in the slave plantations. A majority of Southern farmers were not slave owners and they were backward and poor as compared with Northern farmers. The average farm belonging to free Southern farmers was worth less than $2,000 even though the average for all Southern farms was $34,000 dollars. Agricultural wealth in the South was highly concentrated, with the slave-owners plantations being wealthy and the free farmers being poor. In terms of acreage, slave plantations were five and a half times as large as free Southern farms.

Slavery caused three economic problems for the South. First of all, most of Southern agriculture consisted of small, nonslave farms. But the wealth of the slave owners let them dominate the South, even though the slave owners were a minority. They kept the best land for themselves. This meant the productivity on the lands of the free Southern farmers was far below that of the slave plantations and far below that of Northern farmers.

A second problem caused by slavery was that industry did not develop in the South. It is inconceivable to run a complex factory with slaves. Slaves would break complex machinery because any rational person would want to work as little as possible for a slave master. Third, and fortunately for the United States, slavery weakened the Southern army. It had no industrial base, so it was soon short of supplies. Moreover, the slaves would not fight for the South. They were much more likely to use any weapons against the Southern armies. In fact, many escaped to the North and became Union soldiers. Southern troops were required to be on guard at all times against slave revolts.

CONFLICTS OVER SLAVERY

The Civil War did not result directly from the existence of slavery in the South, but from the attempt to expand slavery into the West. Why did the slave owners wish to expand into the West? As part of the capitalist market system, the slave owners put a heavy emphasis on producing a cash crop for profit. Therefore, they did not plant a diversified crop, but rather planted cotton year after year. This practice tended to deplete the land. Depletion of the land was one reason for the policy of expansionism.

There was still a certain amount of land available in the South, but it cost money. The land in the West was free, so it drew Southerners as it drew Northerners. Even within the South, the plantations moved west to the more fertile land. This helped make Southern productivity look better than it had been in the older regions.

Another reason why Southern slave owners found the Western lands so attractive was that they could easily move most of their capital. Their most important capital was the slaves and they were completely mobile. Even in regions with scarce labor supply, the slave owners had their own labor supply. Finally, Southern state governments encouraged migration to the West because of the desire for more slave states. Thousands of free Northerners migrated to the West, so the Southern politicians worried over the need to maintain the balance between the number of slave states and free states.

There was one conflict after another between the free farmers and the slave owners in the West. A series of compromises were made by which slavery was restricted below a certain latitude, but escaped slaves were to be returned to the South. Compromises included explicit laws with regard to the Northwest Territory in 1787 and the state of Missouri in 1820. Eventually the intense struggle over the West could no longer be compromised. The war broke out, resulting in long years of bloody fighting. The Northern victory in 1865 finally put an end to slavery.

In the Civil War, the South faced the farmers of the West and the former slaves given weapons by the North, the Northeast farmers, workers, and industrialists. In the North, there was a growing industrial production, which was largely lacking in the South. Northern industrial workers resented any competing goods made by the South, since they were produced by cheap slave labor. This fact meant Northern workers tended to side with the abolition of slavery.

It was not only Northern workers, but also Northern industrialists who opposed slavery. On the subject of slavery, the Northern industrialists sounded like revolutionaries. Even the most powerful capitalist, John D. Rockefeller (1839–1937), made incendiary statements against slavery. Since the slave owners wanted to expand into the West and the Northern industrialists also wanted to expand into the West, there was an inevitable clash between these two giants. The clash over who was to expand was not limited to the West. The slave owners also had a negative impact directly on the North through their control most of the Congress, the presidency and the Supreme Court. The issues on which they clashed with the North included everything from laws on returning an escaped slave living in the North back to the South to the tariff laws (in which the industrialists wanted high tariffs on manufactured goods in order to protect their industries). After many years of fighting for the abolition of slavery in various political forums, the Republican Party was formed in 1854 with the abolition of slavery as one of its goals. The Republicans received much financial support from the Northern industrialists. It was the party of abolition but it was also the party representing the interests of the owners of industry. Eventually, in coalition with the Western farmers and the free workers of the North, the Republican Party won the election of President Lincoln.

The Civil War lasted from 1861 to 1865. After the war, the South was occupied by federal troops and forced to give democratic rights to all. African-Americans were even elected to the U.S. Senate. Three Amendments to the U.S. constitution were passed to end slavery, to give equal civil rights to former slaves, and give the former slaves the right to vote. It took another hundred years or more of struggle to make all of these rights effective.

SUGGESTED READINGS ON SLAVERY

A pioneering book on Southern slavery that is well-written and good reading is Eugene Genovese, *Roll, Jordan, Roll: The World the Slaves Made* (1976). A more scholarly book by Genovese is *The Political Economy of Slavery: Studies in the Economy and Society of the Slave South* (1989). A readable book on the economics of slavery is Roger Ransom, *Conflict and Compromise: The Political Economy of Slavery, Emancipation, and the Civil War* (1989).

REVIEW QUESTIONS

Describe how slaves were treated/exploited in America.
1. Describe the living and working conditions for most slaves.
2. What social norms and laws were in place that perpetuated slavery?
3. What was the role of religion and underground churches for the slaves?

Compare and contrast the Southern economy to the Northern economy.

4. What is the difference in assets for capitalist enterprises in the North and the plantations of the South? How might this affect innovations and productivity?

5. What invention improved the productivity of Southern plantation? How did this affect the attitude of the slave owners?

6. Compare and contrast the distribution of agricultural output and wealth in the North and the South.

7. What problems for economic development did slavery cause in the South? Explain and give examples.

Understand the causes, forces, and motivations behind the Civil War.

8. Discuss how slavery was a factor in the Civil War. Was the war only about the institution of slavery itself or are there other factors?

PART I, SECTION 2

CAPITALISM, ITS DEFENDERS, AND ITS CRITICS

CHAPTER 8

Classical Liberalism
Defense of Industrial Capitalism

In previous chapters it was shown that the Industrial Revolution in England changed that country from a primarily agricultural country to a primarily industrial country. England made that transition long before any other country. England in the nineteenth century had a great advantage in productivity of labor. It could outcompete any other country in most industries. Therefore, free trade among countries tended to mean the dominance of England.

This chapter outlines the triumph of the classical liberal capitalist ideology that occurred during the late eighteenth and early nineteenth centuries. Liberalism was the philosophy of the new industrial capitalism, and the new liberal ideas created a political and intellectual atmosphere in eighteenth-century England that fostered the growth of the factory system. In its medieval version, the Christian paternalist ethic had led to a pervasive system of restrictions on the behavior of capitalists during the mercantilist period. Liberalism created the philosophical basis for why these restrictions should be removed.

LEARNING OBJECTIVES

After reading this chapter, you should be able to:

- Understand the ideological basis for classical liberals to advocate for free trade and a minimum of government intervention.
- Explain Thomas Malthus's theory of population and how it impacts society today.

THE RISE OF CLASSICAL LIBERALISM

It was during this period of industrialization that the individualistic world view of classical liberalism became the dominant ideology of capitalism. Many of the ideas of classical liberalism had taken root and even gained wide acceptance in the mercantilist period, but it was in the late eighteenth and nineteenth centuries that classical liberalism most completely dominated social, political, and economic thought in England. The Christian paternalist ethic was still advanced in the writings of many of the nobility and their allies as well as many socialists, but in this era these expressions were, by and large, dissident minority views.

THE PSYCHOLOGICAL CREED OF CLASSICAL LIBERALISM

Classical liberalism's psychological creed was based on four assumptions about human nature. People were believed to be egoistic, coldly calculating, essentially **inert** (*unable to move or act, sluggish, lethargic*) and atomistic. The egoism argued by Hobbes furnished the basis for this view, and in the works of later liberals, especially Jeremy Bentham (1748–1832), it was blended with **psychological hedonism**: *the view that all actions are motivated by the desire to achieve pleasure and avoid pain.* "Nature," Bentham wrote, "has placed mankind under the governance of two sovereign masters, pain and pleasure. . . . They govern us in all we do, in all we say, in all we think" (Bentham, p. 341). Pleasures differed in intensity, Bentham believed, but there were no qualitative differences. He argued that "quantity of pleasure being equal, pushpin is as good as poetry." This theory of human motivation as purely selfish is found in the writings of many of the most eminent thinkers of the period, including John Locke (1632–1704), Bernard Mandeville (1670–1733), David Hartley (1705–1757), Abraham Tucker (1705–1774), and Adam Smith (1723–1790).

The rational intellect played a significant role in the classical liberal's scheme of things. Although all motives stemmed from pursuit of pleasure and avoidance of pain, the decisions people made about what pleasures or pains to seek or avoid were based on a cool, dispassionate, and rational assessment of the situation. Reason would dictate that all alternatives in a situation be weighed in order to choose that which would maximize pleasure or minimize pain. It is this emphasis on the importance of rational measurement of pleasures and pains (with a corresponding de-emphasis of caprice, instinct, habit, custom, or convention) that forms the calculating, intellectual side of the classical liberal's theory of psychology.

The view that individuals were essentially inert stemmed from the notion that pleasure or the avoidance of pain were people's only motives. If people could see no activities leading to pleasurable conclusions or feared no pain, then they would be inert, motionless, or, in simpler terms, just plain lazy. Any kind of exertion or work was viewed as painful and therefore would not be undertaken without the promise of greater pleasure or the avoidance of greater pain. "Aversion," wrote Bentham, "is the emotion—the only emotion—which labor, taken by itself, is qualified to produce: of any such emotion as love or desire, ease, which is the negative or absence of labor—ease not labor—is the object" (quoted in Girvetz, 1963, p. 38).

The practical outcome of this doctrine (or perhaps the reason for it) was the widespread belief of the time that laborers were incurably lazy. Thus, only a large reward or the fear of starvation and deprivation could force them to work. The Reverend Joseph Townsend put this view very succinctly: "Hunger is not only peaceable, silent and unremitted pressure, but, as the most natural motive to industry and labor, it calls forth the most powerful exertions." Townsend believed that "only the experience of hunger would goad them [laborers] to labor" (Bendix, 1963, p. 74).

This view differed radically from the older, paternalistic ethic that had led to the passage of the Elizabethan Poor Relief Act of 1601. The paternalistic concern for the poor had lasted for two centuries and had culminated in 1795 in the Speenhamland System, which guaranteed everyone, able-bodied or not, working or not, a minimal subsistence to be paid by public taxes. It was against this system that the classical liberals railed. They eventually succeeded in passing the Poor Law of 1834, the object of which, according to Dicey, "was in reality to save the property of hard-working men from destruction by putting an end to the monstrous system under which laggards who would not toil for their support lived at the expense of their industrious neighbors" (Dicey, 1926, p. 203).

Classical liberals were persuaded, however, that the "higher ranks" of individuals were motivated by ambition. This differentiation of people into different ranks betrayed an implicit elitism in their individualistic doctrines. In order to ensure ample effort on the part of the "elite," the classical liberals believed the state should put the highest priority on the protection of private property. Although the argument began "as an argument for guaranteeing to the worker the fruits of his toil, it has become one of the chief apologies for the institution of private property in general" (Girvetz, 1963, p. 50).

The last of the four tenets was atomism, which held that the individual was a more fundamental reality than the group or society. "Priority [was] . . . assigned to the ultimate components out of which an aggregate or whole . . . [was] composed; they constituted the fundamental reality" (Girvetz, 1963, p. 41). With this notion, the classical liberals rejected the concept, implicit in the Christian paternalist ethic, that society was like a family and that the whole, and the relationships that made up the whole, were more important than any individual. The liberals' individualistic beliefs were inconsistent with the personal and human ties envisioned in the Christian paternalist ethic. The group was no more than the additive total of the individuals that constituted it. They believed that restrictions placed on the individual by society were generally evil and should be tolerated only when an even worse evil would result without them.

This atomistic psychology can be contrasted with a more socially oriented psychology that would lead to the conclusion that most of the characteristics, habits, ways of perceiving and thinking about life processes, and general personality patterns of the individual are significantly influenced, if not determined, by the social institutions and relationships of which he or she is a part. Atomistic psychology, however, sees the makeup of the individual as somehow independently given. It therefore regards social institutions as both tools for and the handiwork of these individuals. In this view society exists only because it is useful, and if it were not for this usefulness each individual could go his or her own way, discarding society much as he or she would discard a tool that no longer served its purpose.

THE ECONOMIC CREED OF CLASSICAL LIBERALISM

Several explanations are necessary for an understanding of why the classical liberals thought society so useful. For example, they talked about the "natural gregariousness of men," the need for collective security, and the economic benefits of the **division of labor**, which society makes possible. When one man produced everything he needed for himself and his family, production was very inefficient, but if *men subdivided tasks, each producing only the commodity for which his own abilities best suited him*, productivity increased. The last item was the foundation of the economic creed of classical liberalism, and the creed was crucial to classical liberalism because this philosophy contained what appears to be two contradictory or conflicting assumptions.

On the one hand, the assumption of the individual's innate egoism led Hobbes to assert that, in the absence of restraints, people's selfish motives would lead to a "natural state" of war, with each individual pitted against all others. In this state of nature, Hobbes believed, the life of a person was "solitary, poor, nasty, brutish, and short." The only escape from brutal combat was the establishment of some source of absolute power, a central government, to which each individual submitted in return for protection from all other individuals (Hobbes, 1955, pp. 192–205).

On the other hand, one of the cardinal tenets of classical liberalism was that individuals (or, more particularly, businessmen) should be free to give vent to their egoistic drives with a minimum of control or restraint imposed by society. This apparent contradiction was bridged by the liberal economic creed, which asserted that if the competitiveness and rivalry of unrestrained egoism existed in a capitalist market setting, then this competition would benefit the individuals involved

and all society as well. This view was put forth in the most profound single intellectual achievement of classical liberalism: Adam Smith's *The Wealth of Nations*, published in 1776.

Smith believed that "every individual . . . [is] continually exerting himself to find out the most
advantageous employment for whatever capital he can command" (Smith, [1776] 1937, p. 421).
Those without capital were always searching for the employment at which the monetary return
for their labor would be maximized. If both capitalists and laborers were left alone, self-interest
would guide them to use their capital and labor where they were most productive. The search for
profits would ensure that what was produced would be what people wanted most and were willing
to pay for. Thus, Smith and classical liberals in general, were opposed to having some authority or
law determine what should be produced: "It is not from the benevolence of the butcher, the brewer,
or the baker, that we expect our dinner, but from their regard to their own interest" (Smith, [1776]
1937, p. 14). Producers of various goods must compete in the market for the dollars of consumers.
The producer who offered a better quality product would attract more consumers. Self-interest
would, therefore, lead to constant improvement of the quality of the product. The producer could
also increase profits by cutting the cost of production to a minimum.

Thus a free market, in which producers competed for consumers' money in an egoistic quest
for more profits, would guarantee the direction of capital and labor to their most productive uses
and ensure production of the goods consumers wanted and needed most (as measured by their
ability and willingness to pay for them). Moreover, the market would lead to a constant striving
to improve the quality of products and to organize production in the most efficient and least costly
manner possible. All these beneficial actions would stem directly from the competition of egoisti-
cal individuals, each pursuing his or her self-interest.

What a far cry from the "solitary, poor, nasty, brutish" world Hobbes thought would result from
human competitiveness. The wonderful social institution that could make all this possible was
the free and unrestrained market, the forces of supply and demand. The market, Smith believed,
would act as an "invisible hand," channeling selfish, egoistic motives into mutually consistent
and complementary activities that would best promote the welfare of all society. And the greatest
beauty of the market was the complete lack of any need for paternalistic guidance, direction, or
restrictions. Freedom from coercion in a capitalist market economy was compatible with a natural
orderliness in which the welfare of each, as well as the welfare of all society (which was, after all,
only the aggregate of the individuals that constituted it), would be maximized. In Smith's words,
each producer:

> intends only his own security; and by directing that industry in such a manner as its produce
> may be of the greatest value, he intends only his own gain, and he is in this, as in many other
> cases, led by an invisible hand to promote an end which was no part of his intention. Nor is
> it always the worse for the society that it was not a part of it. By pursuing his own interest he
> frequently promotes that of society more effectually than when he really intends to promote
> it. I have never known much good done by those who affected to trade for the public good.
> It is an affectation, indeed, not very common among merchants, and very few words need
> be employed in dissuading them from it (Smith, [1776] 1937, p. 423).

With this statement it is evident that Smith had a philosophy totally antithetical to the paternalism of the Christian paternalist ethic. The Christian notion of the rich promoting the security
and well-being of the poor through paternalistic control and almsgiving contrasts sharply with
Smith's picture of a capitalist who is concerned only with "his own advantage, indeed, and not
that of the society. . . . But the study of his own advantage naturally, or rather necessarily leads

them to prefer that employment which is most advantageous to the society" (Smith, [1776] 1937, p. 421).

Not only would the free and unfettered market channel productive energies and resources into their most valuable uses, but it would also lead to continual economic progress. Economic well-being depended on the capacity of an economy to produce. Productive capacity depended, in turn, on accumulation of capital and division of labor. For such a subdivision of tasks a market was necessary in order to exchange goods. In the market each person could get all the items he needed but did not produce.

This increase in productivity could be extended further if the production of each commodity were broken down into many steps or stages. Each person would then work on only one stage of the production of one commodity. To achieve a division of labor of this degree, it was necessary to have many specialized tools and other equipment. It was also necessary that all the stages of production for a particular commodity be brought together and coordinated, as, for example, in a factory. Thus, an increasingly fine division of labor required accumulation of capital in the form of tools, equipment, factories, and money. This capital would also provide wages to maintain workers during the period of production before their coordinated efforts were brought to fruition and sold on the market.

The source of this capital accumulation was, of course, the profits of production. As long as demand was brisk and more could be sold than was being produced, capitalists would invest their profits in order to expand their capital, which would lead to an increasingly intricate division of labor. The increased division of labor would lead to greater productivity, higher wages, higher profits, more capital accumulation, and so forth, in a never-ending, upward-moving escalator of social progress. The process would be brought to a halt only when there was no longer sufficient demand for the products to warrant further accumulation and more extensive division of labor. Government regulation of economic affairs, or any restriction on the freedom of market behavior, could only decrease the extent of demand and bring the beneficial process of capital accumulation to a halt before it would have ended otherwise. So here again there was no room for paternalistic government meddling in economic affairs.

THE THEORY OF POPULATION

Thomas Robert Malthus's population theory was an important and integral part of classical liberal economic and social doctrines. Malthus (1766–1834) believed most human beings were driven by an insatiable desire for sexual pleasure and that consequently natural rates of human reproduction, when unchecked, would lead to geometric increases in population, that is, the population would increase each generation at the ratio of 1, 2, 4, 8, 16, and so forth. But food production, at the very best, increases at an arithmetic rate, that is, with each generation it can increase only at a rate such as 1, 2, 3, 4, 5, and so on.

Obviously, something would have to hold the population in check. The food supply could not support a population that was growing at a geometric rate. Malthus believed there were two general kinds of checks that limited population growth: preventive checks and positive checks. Preventive checks reduced the birthrate, whereas positive checks increased the death rate.

Moral restraint, vice, and birth control were the primary preventive checks. Moral restraint was the means by which the higher ranks of humans limited their family size in order not to dissipate their wealth among larger and larger numbers of heirs. For the lower ranks of humans, vice and birth control were the preventive checks; but they were grossly insufficient to curb the vast numbers of the poor.

Famine, misery, plague, and war were the positive checks. The fact that preventive checks did not succeed in limiting the numbers of lower-class people made these positive checks inevitable. Finally, if the positive checks were somehow overcome, the growing population would press upon the food supply until starvation, the ultimate and unavoidable check, succeeded in holding the population down.

Before starvation set in, Malthus advised that steps be taken to help the positive checks do their work:

> It is an evident truth that, whatever may be the rate of increase in the means of subsistence, the increase in population must be limited by it, at least after the food has once been divided into the smallest shares that will support life. All the children born, beyond what would be required to keep up the population to this level, must necessarily perish, unless room be made for them by the deaths of grown persons. To act consistently therefore, we should facilitate, instead of foolishly and vainly endeavouring to impede, the operation of nature in producing this mortality; and if we dread the too frequent visitation of the horrid form of famine, we should sedulously encourage the other forms of destruction, which we compel nature to use. Instead of recommending cleanliness to the poor, we should encourage contrary habits. In our towns we should make the streets narrower, crowd more people into the houses, and court the return of the plague. In the country, we should build our villages near stagnant pools, and particularly encourage settlements in all marshy and unwholesome situations. But above all, we should reprobate specific remedies for ravaging diseases; and those benevolent, but much mistaken men, who have thought they were doing a service to mankind by projecting schemes for the total extirpation of particular disorders. If by these and similar means the annual mortality were increased . . . we might probably every one of us marry at the age of puberty, and yet few be absolutely starved (Malthus, 1961, pp. 179–180).

The masses, in Malthus's opinion, were incapable of exercising moral restraint, which was the only real remedy for the population problem. They were, therefore, doomed to live perpetually at a bare subsistence level. If all income and wealth were distributed among them, it would be totally dissipated within one generation because of profligate behavior and population growth, and they would be as poor and destitute as ever.

Paternalistic attempts to aid the poor were thus doomed to failure. Furthermore, they were a positive evil because they drained wealth and income from the higher (more moral) ranks of human beings. These higher-class individuals were responsible, either in person or by supporting others, for all the great achievements of society. Art, music, philosophy, literature, and the other splendid cultural attainments of Western civilization owed their existence to the good taste and generosity of the higher classes of men. Taking money from them would dry up the source of such achievement; using the money to alleviate the conditions of the poor was a futile, foredoomed exercise. It is obvious that the Malthusian population theory and the liberal economic theories led to the same conclusion: Paternalistic government should avoid any attempt to intervene in the economy on behalf of the poor. Malthusian views—that poverty is the fault of the poor, who have too many babies, and that nothing can be done to end poverty—are still held by many people today.

THE POLITICAL CREED OF CLASSICAL LIBERALISM

The economic and population doctrines of classical liberalism gave rise quite naturally to a political creed that rejected the state, or government, as an evil to be tolerated only when it was the sole means of avoiding a worse evil. Much of this antipathy stemmed directly from the many corrupt, despotic, capricious, and tyrannical actions of several European kings, as well as from the actions of the English Parliament, which was notoriously unrepresentative and often despotic. The liberal creed was not put forward as an objection against particular governments, however, but against governments in general. Thomas Paine reflected the sentiment of classical liberals when he wrote: "Society in every state is a blessing, but government, even in its best state, is but a necessary evil; in its worst state, an intolerable one" (quoted in Girvetz, 1963, p. 66).

What were the functions that classical liberals thought should be given to governments? In *The Wealth of Nations*, Adam Smith listed three: protection of the country against foreign invaders, protection of citizens against "injustices" suffered at the hands of other citizens, and the "duty . . . of erecting and maintaining those public institutions and those public works, which, though they may be in the highest degree advantageous to a great society, are, however, of such a nature, that the profit could never repay the expense to any individual or small number of individuals, and which it therefore cannot be expected that any individual or small number of individuals should erect and maintain" (Smith, [1776] 1937, p. 681).

This list is very general, and almost any kind of government action could be justified under one of these three functions. In order to understand the specific functions which the liberals believed government should have, it is necessary to deal first with an objection that is frequently raised when the writings of Adam Smith are said to comprise part of an ideology justifying capitalism. It is often pointed out not only that Smith was not a spokesman for the capitalists of his day but also that many of his passages show that he was in general suspicious and distrustful of capitalists. This contention is certainly true. Nevertheless, capitalists used the arguments put forward by Smith to justify their attempts to eliminate the last vestiges of paternalistic government when these stood in the way of their quest for profits. It was Smith's rationale that enabled them to quiet their consciences when their actions created widespread hardship and suffering. After all, they were only following his advice and pursuing their own profits; this was the way they should act if they wished to be of the greatest service to society.

Finally, most classical liberals interpreted Smith's theory of the three general governmental functions in a way that showed they were not hesitant about endorsing a paternalistic government when they, the capitalists, were the beneficiaries of paternalism. Thus "the original doctrine of laissez-faire . . . passed, for the most part, from the care of intellectuals like Adam Smith . . . into the custodianship of businessmen and industrialists and their hired spokesmen" (Girvetz, 1963, p. 81). **Laissez-faire** is *a policy of leaving the coordination of individuals pursuing their own self-interest to the market-the government should not be involved.*

First, the requirement that the government protect the country from external threats was to be extended in the late nineteenth century to a protection or even enlargement of foreign markets through armed coercion. Second, protection of citizens against "injustices" committed by other citizens was usually defined to mean protection of private property, enforcement of contracts, and preservation of internal order. Protection of private property, especially ownership of factories and capital equipment, is of course tantamount to protection of the sine qua non of capitalism. It was their ownership of the means of production that gave the capitalists their economic and political power. Giving the government the function of protecting property relations meant giving the government the job of protecting the source of power of the economically and politically dominant class: the capitalists.

Contract enforcement was also essential for the successful functioning of capitalism. The complex division of labor and the necessity for complex organization and coordination in production, as well as the colossal capital investments necessary in many commercial ventures, meant that capitalists had to be able to depend on people to meet contractual commitments. The medieval notion that custom and the special circumstances of a case defined an individual's obligations was just not compatible with capitalism. Therefore, the duty to enforce contracts amounted to governmental coercion of a type necessary for capitalism to function.

The preservation of internal order was (and is) always necessary. In the late eighteenth and early nineteenth centuries, however, it often meant brutally crushing labor union movements or the English Chartist movement, which capitalists considered threats to their profit-making activities.

Finally, the function of "erecting and maintaining those public institutions and those public works" that were in the public interest generally was interpreted to mean the creation and maintenance of institutions that fostered profitable production and exchange. These included the provision of a stable and uniform currency, standard weights and measures, and the physical means necessary for conducting business. Roads, canals, harbors, railroads, the postal services, and other forms of communication were among the prerequisites of business. Although these were often privately owned, most capitalist governments were extensively involved in their erection and maintenance either through financial subsidies to private business or through the government's direct undertaking of these projects.

Thus it may be concluded that the classical liberals' philosophy of laissez-faire was opposed to government interference in economic affairs only if such interference were harmful to the interests of capitalists. They welcomed and even fought for any paternalistic intervention in economic affairs that stabilized business or made larger profits possible.

SUMMARY

The Industrial Revolution and the triumph of the classical liberal capitalist ideology occurred together during the late eighteenth and early nineteenth centuries. Liberalism was the philosophy of the new industrial capitalism, and the new liberal ideas created a political and intellectual atmosphere in eighteenth-century England that fostered the growth of the factory system.

In its medieval version the Christian paternalist ethic had led to a pervasive system of restrictions on the behavior of capitalists during the mercantilist period. Capitalists and their spokesmen opposed most of these restrictions with a new individualistic philosophy that advocated greater freedom for the capitalist to seek profits in a market free of encumbrances and restrictions. It is not surprising that the triumph of this philosophy should coincide with the greatest achievement of the capitalist class: the Industrial Revolution. The Industrial Revolution vaulted the capitalist class into a position of economic and political dominance. This fact goes far toward explaining the triumph of classical liberalism as the ideology of the new age of industrial capitalism.

SUGGESTED READINGS

There is a more complete, in-depth discussion of the classical economists in E. K. Hunt, *History of Economic Thought: A Critical Perspective* (2002).

KEY TERMS

division of labor
inert

laissez-faire
psychological hedonism

REVIEW QUESTIONS

Understand the ideological basis for classical liberals to advocate for free trade and a minimum of government intervention.

1. List and explain the four assumptions made by classical liberals about human nature.
2. What did this doctrine imply about the motivations of workers and how they should be treated? What did it imply about the motivations of higher ranks of individuals?
3. Compare and contrast the ideology of the classical liberals with that of those supporting Christian paternalism.
4. How did classical liberals bridge the gap between egotistic humans who would only harm society if not for government and the need for an unfettered capitalist system?
5. How do Smith and Hobbes differ in their views of the outcome of human competitiveness?
6. What is the "invisible hand" of Adam Smith and how does it work?
7. What does Adam Smith mean by division of labor? Why is this concept important?
8. What three functions did classical liberals, and Adam Smith in particular, think that government should be responsible for? How did these three functions provide an additional advantage to the capitalists?

Explain Thomas Malthus's theory of population and how it impacts society today.

9. Malthus is often credited with giving economics the reputation of being the "dismal science." Why?
10. Compare the rates of growth for the population and the rate of grown for food. What is the outcome of this difference?
11. According to Malthus there are preventative checks and positive checks to population growth. Compare and contrast the two "checks." What is the implication for aiding the poor?
12. According to Malthus, whose fault is poverty and why? Do you see any parallels in today's society? Give examples.

CHAPTER 9

Socialist Protest Against Industrial Capitalism

The Industrial Revolution brought about increases in human productivity without precedent in history. The Industrial Revolution, however, was conducted at the expense of enormous human suffering. The workers bore the cost of industrialization as the new factory system reduced many of them to poor, unhealthy, dehumanized wretches. Classical liberalism was generally not only impervious to their plight but even taught that the desire to improve the conditions of the poor was doomed to failure. One response to the inequities of the Industrial Revolution was a socialist protest movement.

LEARNING OBJECTIVES

After reading this chapter, you should be able to:

- Comprehend the evolution of socialist thought.
- Compare and contrast the basic elements of socialism and capitalism.

SOCIALISM WITHIN THE CLASSICAL LIBERAL TRADITION

Socialism, *a theory of social organization which advocates ownership and control of production to the community as a whole,* had its origins in England in the late eighteenth and early nineteenth centuries. It was a protest against the inequality of capitalism and the social evils resulting from this inequality. This inequality, in the opinion of all socialists, resulted inevitably from the institution of private property, in particular the private ownership of the means of production. Socialism's most fundamental belief is that social justice requires the abolition of private ownership of capital.

Socialists have never accepted unanimously any particular social philosophy or body of doctrines, and on nearly any given issue one can find differences of opinion among them. The essential and defining feature of socialism, and the one idea that all socialists accept, is that private ownership of capital necessarily involves inequality and a host of other evils and that such ownership must be abolished if we are ever to achieve a just society.

Although there are today many schools of socialism, if we go back to the early 1800s we find that socialists can be divided into two groups, each having a distinctly different general social philosophy. The two traditions can be labeled the classical liberal form of individualistic socialism and its adversary, cooperative socialism. **Individualistic socialism** *states that capitalism exploits*

94

workers, but it asserts that an effective socialist economy must retain individual decision-making through the market mechanism. **Cooperative socialism** also *states that capitalism exploits workers, but it asserts that all production decisions in a socialist society must be made by democratic votes of all the employees in an enterprise or by a plan democratically voted on by everyone in a local, state, national, or global society.* The early formulation and later elaboration of these views are found in the rest of this chapter.

As we saw in Chapter 8, classical liberalism most generally functioned as an ideology justifying the new capitalist order and its many economically oppressive laws. In order for classical liberalism to function in this manner, however, people had to accept without question the institution of private ownership of capital.

There were many classical liberals who did not accept the private ownership of the means of production. Particularly influential among these liberals was Thomas Hodgskin (1787–1869), who received a naval disability pension that enabled him to devote most of his time to writing. In 1825, Hodgskin wrote a book entitled *Labour Defended Against the Claims of Capital,* in which he attempted to refute the principal intellectual justification for the private ownership of capital, the argument that capital is productive.

Hodgskin's refutation of the notion that capital was productive showed that the production usually attributed to capital was actually the production of interdependent workers. If we observe, for example, a fisherman catching fish with the aid of a net, then it appears to the conservative defender of capitalism that part of the fish are caught by the labor of the fisherman and part are caught by aid of the net. Therefore, it appears that the net is productive and that the capitalist owner of the net deserves a profit due to the productivity of his net.

The real productivity, said Hodgskin, is that of interdependent workers. The fisherman was able to catch so many fish because other workers are making nets. The fish are caught through the joint labors of both the fisherman and the net makers. But since the net-making laborers are not present at the point at which the catch takes place, it may appear that their share of the productive endeavor of fishing is actually performed by the product they have created—the net. Thus, in capitalism it may appear that a worker (such as a fisherman) depends on the productivity of capital (such as a net) and hence depends on the capitalists (such as the capitalist owner of the net). This appearance is false. The worker depends solely on the coexisting labor performed by other workers (such as those who produce the nets).

WILLIAM THOMPSON AND THE REJECTION OF CLASSICAL LIBERALISM

Although Hodgskin accepted classical views of the usefulness of the market, most socialists rejected many of the individualistic tenets of classical liberalism as well as the notion that the market should allocate resources in a socialist society. Perhaps the most influential of the early socialists in this regard was William Thompson (1775–1833). Writing in the 1820s, he argued that the individualistic pursuit of wealth within a competitive market, whether that market is in a capitalist or a socialist society, led inevitably to many evils (see Thompson, p. 258).

First, he argued that capitalism forced every worker to compete with all others and encouraged selfishness. The second evil inherent in the individualistic pursuit of wealth even in a market socialist economy was the systematic oppression of women because men followed the ethic of capitalism to give themselves all power in the family. The third evil of market competition is that it causes an unstable economy. In addition, market competition retarded the advance and dissemination of knowledge by making the acquisition of knowledge subsidiary to greed and personal gain.

As an alternative to market capitalism, Thompson advocated a publicly owned economy with comprehensive planning. Thompson's description of a planned, cooperative, socialist society was one of the earliest and the most fully elaborated in the history of socialist ideas.

THE PATERNALISTIC SOCIALISM OF ROBERT OWEN

The most important of the early organizers of a socialist movement to transform capitalism was Robert Owen. Born in 1771, Owen served as a draper's apprentice from the age of ten. At twenty, he was the manager of a large mill. Wise business decisions and good luck soon resulted in the acquisition of a considerable fortune. Owen was a perfect example of a benevolent autocrat. His factory at New Lanark became known throughout all England because he insisted on decent working conditions, livable wages, and education for working-class children. His workers received "affectionate tutelage" from him, and he thought of himself as their trustee and steward.

The paternalistic attitude did not interfere with Owen's very strict organizational discipline in his factory. Owen described one of his methods of maintaining discipline thus:

> That which I found to be the most efficient check upon inferior conduct was the contrivance of a silent monitor for each one employed in the establishment. This consisted of a four-sided piece of wood, about two inches long and one broad, each side colored—one side black, another blue, the third yellow, and the fourth white, tapered at the top, and finished with wire eyes, to hang upon a hook with either side to show front. One of these was suspended in a conspicuous place near to each of the persons employed, and the color at the front told the conduct of the individual during the preceding day, to four degrees of comparison. Bad, denoted by black and No. 4; indifferent by blue, and No. 3; good by yellow, and No. 2; and excellent by white, and No. 1. Then books of character were provided, for each department, in which the name of each one employed in it was inserted in the front of succeeding columns, which sufficed to mark by the number of daily conduct, day by day, for two months; and these books were changed six times a year, and were preserved; by which arrangement I had the conduct of each registered to four degrees of comparison during every day of the week, Sundays excepted, for every year they remained in my employment (quoted in Beer, p. 111).

So in his life and deeds, Owen, like other capitalists of his era, strove to maximize his profits. He believed his competitors' harsh treatment of their workers was stupid and shortsighted, and he based his life on the assumption that the Christian paternalist ethic was compatible with the capitalistic system at least at the factory level. In his own words, "My time, from early to late, and my mind, were continually occupied in devising measures and directing their execution, to improve the condition of the people, and to advance at the same time the works and the machinery as a manufacturing establishment" (quoted in Beer, p. 112).

Although Owen's life and actions did not differentiate him from many of the conservative Tory radicals (as aristocratic critics of capitalism were called) of his time, some of his ideas did. He did not believe that any society in which one class was elevated to a position of power and used this power to exploit the lower classes could ultimately become a truly good society. Private ownership of the means of production (factories, machinery, tools) was the social institution by which one small class in the existing economic system gained immense power over the mass of farmers and workers. The profit motive was the force that drove this small class to use its power to exploit the workers and farmers in order to gain profits.

Owen believed that in an ideal society the people could most effectively control nature because they would reap the greatest collective benefit if they cooperated. This cooperation should take the form of self-governing industrial and agricultural communities. In such communities, private ownership of the means of production would be abolished and the selfish quest for profits eliminated. He maintained that only when such a society was established would it be true that:

> One portion of mankind will not, as now, be trained and placed to oppress, by force or fraud, another portion, to the great disadvantage of both; neither will one portion be trained in idleness, to live in luxury on the industry of those whom they oppress, while the latter are made to labor daily and to live in poverty. Nor yet will some be trained to force falsehood into the human mind and be paid extravagantly for so doing while other parties are prevented from teaching the truth, or severely punished if they make the attempt (Owen, pp. 47–48).

There was something in these writings that differed very radically from his description of the way in which he ran his own factory at New Lanark. In the ideal society, for Owen, the paternalism of the traditional Christian ethic would be expressed as a brotherhood of equals, a considerable shift from the parent-child type of subordination expressed in the medieval and Tory radical versions of the Christian paternalist ethic.

The feudal version of that ethic accepted a hierarchical society. In this version those at the top lived lavishly (by the standard of the day, at least), and they did so by exploiting those at the bottom. Chaucer's parson's description of the medieval view is apt: "God has ordained that some folk should be more high in estate and degree and some folk more low, and that everyone should be served in his estate and his degree" (Hammond and Hammond, p. 215). This traditional feudal ethic seemed to most capitalists to be incompatible with the capitalist order, and it was gradually replaced by the new individualist philosophy of classical liberalism.

Classical liberalism, however, was a two-edged sword. Although this ideology was used to justify the new capitalist order, its individualistic assumptions were very radical at the time. If the old feudal aristocracy had no inherent superiority over the middle class and if any member of the middle class was to be freed of the old restraints, and if individuals should be the best judge of their own affairs, then how could one stop short of asserting the same rights and advantages for the lowest classes? The ideal that each individual ought, in some abstract way, to be considered as important as any other individual was radical indeed.

If individualism seemed to imply equality in theory, it certainly did not lead to it in practice. The rugged battle for more profits led not only to the social misery described earlier but also to a new class division of society that was sharply defined and as exploitative in nature as the medieval class structure. Membership in the higher class of the new system depended not on genealogy but on ownership. Capitalists derived their income and their power from ownership of the means of production.

Socialism, then, was a protest against the inequality of capitalism and the social evils resulting from that inequality. The inequality itself, in the opinion of socialists from the earliest times to the present, resulted inevitably from the institution of private property in the means of production. Hence, socialism asserted as its most important idea that social justice demanded the abolition of private ownership of capital.

Intellectually, socialism was a wedding of the liberal notion of the equality of all human beings to the notion inherent in the traditional Christian paternalist ethic that every man should be his brother's keeper. Incorporating the **egalitarian,** *belief in the equal social, political and economic rights for all people*, elements of classical liberalism into the traditional Christian ethic made this a utopian ethic, in comparison with which existing society was criticized. Without this egalitarian element the Christian ethic served well as an ideological justification of the hierarchical class system of the Middle Ages and was sometimes used to defend the capitalist system, particularly in the late nineteenth and twentieth centuries.

OTHER IMPORTANT PRE-MARXIST SOCIALISTS

Gerrard Winstanley

When Owen asserted that in the ideal society private property and acquisitive profit seeking would be eliminated, he became part of a socialist tradition that was already firmly established. One of the first voices of socialist protest against capitalist property relations was that of Gerrard Winstanley (1609–1676), a cloth merchant who had been bankrupted in the depression of 1643. He blamed his own misfortune as well as that of others on the "cheating art of buying and selling" (quoted in McDonald, p. 63). In 1649 he led a strange band of followers from London to Saint George's Hill, Surrey. There they occupied unused crown lands, which they cultivated in common and, in general, shared in a communal existence.

In the same year Winstanley published *The True Levellers Standard Advanced,* in which he rebuked "the powers of England" and "the powers of the world" for their failure to realize that "the great creator . . . made the Earth a common treasury for beasts and man." He asserted that all who derived their incomes in part or in full from property ownership were violating God's commandment "Thou shalt not steal." "You pharaohs, you have rich clothing and full bellies, you have your honors and your ease; but know the day of judgment is begun and that it will reach you ere long. The poor people you oppress shall be the saviors of the land" (McDonald, p. 63).

Gracchus Babeuf

Throughout the eighteenth and nineteenth centuries, a large number of writers argued that private property was the source of the inequities and exploitation that existed in the capitalist economy. In this chapter we can mention only a few of the better known among them. One of the most interesting was the Frenchman, Gracchus Babeuf (1760–1797). Babeuf argued that nature had made all persons equal in rights and needs. Therefore, the inequalities of wealth and power that had developed should be redressed by society. Unfortunately, most societies did the opposite: they set up a coercive mechanism to protect the interests of the property holders and the wealthy. For Babeuf, the presence of inequality meant, of necessity, the presence of injustice. Capitalist commerce existed, he said, "for the purpose of pumping the sweat and blood of more or less everybody, in order to form lakes of gold for the benefit of the few" (Gray, p. 105). The workers who created the wealth of society received the least in return; and unless private property was eliminated, the inequalities in society could never be redressed.

Babeuf led the extreme left wing of the French revolutionary movement. After the fall of Maximilien Robespierre in 1794 he masterminded a conspiracy to destroy the French government and replace it with one dedicated to equality and brotherhood. The plot was betrayed and its leaders were arrested. Babeuf and his lieutenant, Augustin Darthé, were executed on February 24, 1797.

Babeuf is important in the socialist tradition because he was the first to advance the notion that if an egalitarian socialist state is to be achieved, the existing government must be toppled by force. The issue of whether socialism can be achieved peacefully has divided socialists since Babeuf's time. Babeuf also believed that if his revolt were successful, a period of dictatorship would be necessary during the transition from capitalism to a communist democracy to root out and destroy the surviving remnants of the capitalist system. Thus, in several important ways Babeuf was a precursor of the twentieth century Russian Bolsheviks.

William Godwin

Other important ideas in the socialist critique of capitalism can be seen in the writings of the Englishman William Godwin (1756–1836). While the classical liberals were bemoaning the natural laziness and depravity of the lower classes, Godwin argued that the defects of the working class were attributable to corrupt and unjust social institutions. The capitalist society, in Godwin's opinion, made fraud and robbery inevitable: "If every man could with perfect facility obtain the necessities of life . . . temptation would lose its power" (quoted in Gray, p. 119). Men could not always obtain these necessities because the laws of private property created such great inequality in society. Justice demanded that capitalist property relations be abolished and that property belonged to that person whom it would benefit most:

> To whom does any article of property, suppose a loaf of bread, justly belong? To him who most wants it, or to whom the possession of it will be most beneficial. Here are six men famished with hunger, and the loaf is, absolutely considered, capable of satisfying the cravings of them all. Who is it that has a reasonable claim to benefit by the qualities with which the loaf is endowed? They are all brothers perhaps, and the law of primogeniture bestows it exclusively to the eldest. But does justice confirm this reward? The laws of different countries dispose of property in a thousand different ways; but there can be but one way which is most conformable to reason (quoted in Gray, p. 131).

That one way, of course, must be based on equality of all human beings. To whom could the poor turn to correct the injustices of the system? In Godwin's opinion, it most certainly would not be the government. With economic power went political power. The rich were "directly or indirectly the legislators of the state; and of consequence are perpetually reducing oppression into a system." The law, then, is the means by which the rich oppress the poor, for "legislation is in almost every country grossly the favorer of the rich against the poor."

These two ideas of Godwin's were to be voiced again and again by nineteenth-century socialists: (1) Capitalist social and economic institutions, particularly private property relations, were the causes of the evils and suffering within the system; and (2) government in a capitalist system would never redress these evils because it was controlled by the capitalist class. Godwin, however, had an answer to this seemingly impossible situation. He believed human reason would save society. Once people become educated about the evils of the situation, they would reason together and arrive at the only rational solution. As Godwin saw it, this solution entailed the abolition of government, the abolition of laws, and the abolition of private property. For this radical social transformation Godwin believed socialists could rely primarily on education and reason. Most subsequent socialists argued that education and reason alone were insufficient. Education, they believed, should be only a part of the larger objective of creating a mass socialist movement. The importance of education and intellectual persuasion in attaining socialist ends has remained a much-debated issue to this day.

Henri de Saint-Simon

Other important socialist ideas were advanced by Henri de Saint-Simon (1760–1825), who was actually closer to the Tory radicals than the socialists in many ways. He came from an impoverished family of nobility, and his writings show an aristocrat's disdain for the antisocial egoism of the rich capitalists.

He also condemned the idle rich, who lived off the labor of the poor but contributed nothing to society's well-being:

> Suppose that France preserves all the men of genius that she possesses in the sciences, fine arts and professions, but has the misfortune to lose in the same day Monsieur the King's brother [and all of the other members of the royal household]. . . . Suppose that France loses at the same time all of the great officers of the royal household, all the ministers . . . all the councilors of state, all the chief magistrates, marshals, cardinals, archbishops, bishops, vicars-general and canons, all the prefects and sub prefects, all the civil servants, and judges, and, in addition, ten thousand of the richest proprietors who live in the style of nobles. This mischance would certainly distress the French, because they are kindhearted, and could not see with indifference the sudden disappearance of such a large number of their compatriots. But this loss of thirty thousand individuals . . . would result in no political evil for the state (quoted in Markham, ed., pp. 72–73).

Saint-Simon was the first to emphasize the efficiency of huge industrial undertakings and argued that the government should actively intervene in production, distribution, and commerce in the interest of promoting the welfare of the masses. He sanctioned both private property and its privileges as long as they were used to promote the welfare of the masses.

Many of his followers were more radical. They wrote endless pamphlets and books exposing abuses of capitalism, attacking private property and inheritance, denouncing exploitation, and advocating government ownership and control of economic production in the interest of the general welfare. It was from Saint-Simon and his followers that socialism inherited the idea of the necessity of government administration of production and distribution in a socialist economy.

Charles Fourier

There were many other important socialists in the first half of the nineteenth century. The Frenchman Charles Fourier (1772–1837) popularized the idea of cooperatives (or phalanxes, as he called them). He attempted to change society by encouraging the formation of phalanxes. His failure proved to many socialists that capitalism could not be reformed by the mere setting of examples. He was also one of the first socialists to predict that competition among capitalists would lead inevitably to monopoly:

> Among the influences tending to restrict man's industrial rights, I will mention a formation of privileged corporations which, monopolizing a given branch of industry, arbitrarily close the doors of labour against whomsoever they please. . . . Extremes meet, and the greater the extent to which anarchical competition is carried, the nearer the approach to universal monopoly, which is the opposite excess. . . . Monopolies . . . operating in conjunction with the great landed interest, will reduce the middle and labouring classes to a state of commercial vassalage. . . . The small operators will be reduced to the position of mere agents, working for the mercantile coalition (quoted in Coontz, p. 54).

Fourier believed that in a capitalist economy only one-third of the people really did socially useful work. The other two-thirds were directed by the corruption and distortion caused by the market system into useless occupations or were useless, wealthy parasites. He divided these wastes into four categories:

> First Waste: Useless or destructive labour. (1) the army (2) the idle rich (3) ne'er-do-wells (4) sharpers (5) prostitutes (6) magistrates (7) police (8) lawyers (9) philosophical cranks (10) bureaucrats (11) spies (12) priests and clergymen.
>
> Second Waste: Misdirected work, since society makes it repellent, and not a vehicle of man's personality, attractive to him. (a) Deflection of the passions into greed and morbidity, instead of being utilized as society's motors. (b) Scale of production too small to utilize labour properly. (c) No co-operation. (d) No control of production. (e) No adjustment of supply to demand, except by the mechanism of the "blind" market. (f) The family: this economic and educational unit is absurdly small.
>
> Third Waste: Commerce dominated by middlemen. It takes a hundred men to do what society, with warehouses, distributed according to need, could do with one. A hundred men sit at counters, wasting hours waiting for someone to enter, a hundred people write inventories, etc., competitively. These hundred wasted merchants eat without producing.
>
> Fourth Waste: Wage labour in indirect servitude; cost of class antagonisms. Since class interests are opposed, the costs of keeping men divided are greater than the gains in making them co-operate (quoted in Coontz, p. 55).

Most socialists agreed that capitalism was irrational and wasteful and led to extreme inequalities, and therefore was unjust and immoral. They disagreed, however, on the tactics they should use to achieve socialism. Many famous socialists, such as Louis Blanc (1811–1882), believed that the government could be used as an instrument of reform and that socialism could be achieved through gradual, peaceful, piecemeal reform. Auguste Blanchqui (1805–1881), a pupil of Babeuf, based his ideas on the assumption that capitalism involved a constant class war between capitalists and workers. He believed that as long as capitalists occupied the position of power that ownership of capital gave them, they would exploit the workers, and the government and laws would be weapons used in this exploitation. He, therefore, saw no hope of achieving socialism through gradual political reform. Revolution was, for him, the only answer.

Pierre-Joseph Proudhon

Pierre-Joseph Proudhon (1809–1865), in his well-known book *What Is Property?* answered the question posed in the title with a slogan that made him famous: "Property is theft." He believed property was "the mother of tyranny." The primary purpose of the state was the enforcement of property rights. Because property rights were simply sets of special privileges for the few and general restrictions and prohibitions for the masses, they involved coercion, of necessity, in their establishment and continued enforcement. Hence, the primary function of the state was to coerce.

"Every state is a tyranny," declared Proudhon. The state was the coercive arm of the ruling class, and Proudhon advocated resistance rather than servitude: "Whoever lays a hand on me to govern me is a usurper and a tyrant. I declare him to be my enemy." There could be no justice until property relations were abolished and the state was made unnecessary:

> To be governed is to be watched over, inspected, spied on, directed, legislated, regimented, closed in, indoctrinated, preached at, controlled, assessed, evaluated, censored, commanded;

all by creatures that have neither the right, nor wisdom nor virtue. . . . To be governed means that at every move, operation, or transaction one is noted, registered, entered in a census, taxed, stamped, priced, assessed, patented, licensed, authorized, recommended, admonished, prevented, reformed, set right, corrected. Government means to be subjected to tribute, trained, ransomed, exploited, monopolized, extorted, pressured, mystified, robbed; all in the name of public utility and the general good. Then, at the first sign of resistance or word of complaint, one is repressed, fined, despised, vexed, pursued, hustled, beaten up, garroted, imprisoned, shot, machine-gunned, judged, sentenced, deported, sacrificed, sold, betrayed, and to cap it all ridiculed, mocked, outraged, and dishonored. That is government, that is its justice and its morality! . . . O human personality! How can it be that you have cowered in such subjection for sixty centuries? (quoted in Guerin, pp. 15–16).

Property rights were not only the source of tyranny and coercion, but also the source of economic inequality. Whereas the amount of labor expended determined how much was produced in a capitalist society, ownership of property determined how that produce was divided. It was divided in such a way that those who produced received almost nothing of what they produced, whereas those who owned property used the laws of private ownership to "legally steal" from the workers. Proudhon's ideal state rejected not only capitalist property relations but industrialization as well. Like Thomas Jefferson, Proudhon envisioned a golden age of small-scale agriculture and handicraft production, in which each farmer and worker owned his or her own capital and no one lived through property ownership alone.

The list could be continued, but we have included most of the important pre-Marxist socialist ideas and have introduced some of the most famous socialist thinkers. Unquestionably the most influential socialist thinker was Karl Marx, and it is to a summary of his ideas that we turn in a later chapter.

SUMMARY

The workers bore the cost of industrialization. The new factory system reduced most of them to poor, unhealthy, dehumanized wretches. Classical liberalism was generally not only impervious to their plight but even taught that the desire to improve the conditions of the poor was doomed to failure.

There were, however, a few exceptions among the classical liberals, the most outstanding of whom was Thomas Hodgskin. Hodgskin argued that capital was unproductive and the profits represented an unfair, coercive extraction by a parasitic elite from the produce of the producers, the working people. He believed that the invisible hand of the competitive market system could function effectively only in a market socialist economy.

William Thompson argued that market competition, even under its very best form, market socialism, contained several inherent evils that could be eliminated only in a planned, cooperative, socialist economy. Robert Owen was a wealthy capitalist who espoused and helped build a movement for cooperative socialism. The ideas of several other socialists were briefly discussed in this chapter. All of them protested the inequalities of capitalism. They believed that by eliminating the capitalists' method of robbing workers—private ownership of capital—they could create an industrial society in which every man and woman was treated with dignity and in which the fruits of production were reasonably and equitably divided.

SUGGESTED READINGS

The classic history of socialist views is by G.D.H. Cole, *History of Socialist Thought* (1953). This history by Cole is in five volumes from the French Revolution to World War II, but the five volumes are fairly short, beautifully written and interesting, and one can choose a volume by date.

KEY TERMS

individualistic socialism   egalitarian
cooperative socialism   socialism

REVIEW QUESTIONS

Comprehend the evolution of socialist thought.
1. Explain how socialists claimed that the existence of private property affected society.
2. What are two early divisions of socialist thought?
3. According to Hodgskin, what is the real source of productivity in capitalism? Explain.
4. According to Thompson, what are the inherent evils created by any competitive market system? What alternative to capitalism did he suggest?
5. List the major socialist thinkers before Karl Marx, and briefly explain their contributions to socialist thought.
6. According to Owen, if individualism seemed to imply equality why did it not lead to equality in practice, in other words, why does a hierarchical society persist?
7. Goodwin introduced two key ideas that were often repeated and used in the nineteenth century. Explain why a government in a capitalist society would never address the problems of capitalism.
8. List and explain the two main methods for achieving socialism.

Compare and contrast the basic elements of socialism and capitalism.
9. How did the ideals of socialism conflict with the major tenets of classical liberalism?
10. Explain how capitalists exploited the working class.
11. Compare and contrast the major tenets of capitalism and classical liberalism with the fundamental ideas present in socialism. Which side do you find most appealing?
12. Does socialism mark the re-emergence of Christian Paternalism? Why or why not?
13. Pick three people mentioned in this chapter whose ideas are most appealing to you and provide a brief summary of their thoughts. In addition, explain why you picked these particular people/ideas.

CHAPTER 10

Marx
Critique and Alternative to Capitalism

Karl Marx (1818–1883) has been the most influential of all socialists. His writings have had, and continue to have, a profound impact on socialist thought. Although he worked in close collaboration with Friedrich Engels (1820–1895) and was unquestionably deeply influenced by him, Marx was the intellectual leader in most matters of political economy, so no attempt is made in this chapter to distinguish Engels's separate contributions.

LEARNING OBJECTIVES

After reading this chapter, you should be able to:

- Understand capitalism from a Marxist perspective.
- Explain how Marx saw society moving from capitalism to socialism.

HISTORICAL MATERIALISM

Marx believed that most of the late eighteenth and early nineteenth century socialists were humanitarians who were rightly indignant about the harsh exploitation that accompanied early capitalism. Despite his admiration for many of them, he gave to them the derisive label "utopian socialists." He believed most of them to be **utopians**, *unpractical social reformers with a vision of social and political perfection*, who hoped to transform society by appealing to the rationality and moral sensibilities of the educated class.

In Marx's view, educated men were usually members of the capitalist class, and thus they owed their position, prosperity, and superior knowledge and education to the privileges inherent in the capitalist system. Therefore, they would generally do everything within their power to preserve that system. The few heretics and humanitarians among them would certainly never constitute the power base from which a transition from capitalism to socialism could be effected.

Yet Marx had an undying faith that such a social and economic transition would occur. This faith was not the result of his belief in the rationality and humanity of people, but rather was based on an analysis of capitalism itself. He concluded that internal contradictions and antagonisms within the capitalist system would eventually destroy it.

Marx based his study of capitalist society on a historical review of previous economic systems.

When he looked at the mass of ideas, laws, religious beliefs, mores, moral codes, and economic and social institutions that were present in all social systems, he tried to simplify the complex cause-and-effect relationships among these many facets of such systems. Such a simplification, he believed, would enable him to focus his attention on the relationships that were most fundamental in determining a social system's overall direction of movement and change.

Marx's method, called **historical materialism**, was *an analytical approach that saw each social, political, and economic institution and each intellectual tradition or ideology as related in a complex web of cause-and-effect to all the others in that particular social-economic system.* He also believed that in order to unravel all of these tangled relationships, it is best to begin with the economic system or mode of production. It is part of the tangled web, but one must begin somewhere and this starting point provides the best key to that web.

To provide a framework for analysis, Marx divided society into a base, which he called "the mode of production," and what he called the "ideological superstructure." The **ideological superstructure** *includes all of our ideas, ideologies and traditions, plus all of the institutions that spread those ideas, such as churches, schools, and the media of communication.*

The **mode of production** *consists of two elements: (1) the forces of production and (2) the relations of production.* The **forces of production** *include tools, factories, and equipment; the labor force and its level of knowledge; natural resources; and the general level of technology.* The **relations of production** were *the social relationships among people, particularly the relationship of people to the means of production.* When he referred to the relations of production, Marx meant the class structure of society, the most important single aspect of the mode of production. In each society that is divided into classes, one class controls the means of production, while another class does all the work. For example, under capitalism some people own the means of production and receive the profits of production—these people are called capitalists. Some people labor using the means of production, but do not receive the profits from production; they only receive wages—these people are called employees or workers.

The importance of the mode of production and the class antagonisms it engendered have been summarized by Marx in a famous passage. First, he says that when human beings produce things, "they enter into definite relations that are indispensable . . ." (Marx, 1970, pp. 20–21). Next he says that "these relations of production correspond to a definite stage of development of . . . production. The sum total of these relations of production constitutes the economic structure of society . . . " (Marx, ibid.). Finally, he claims that this must be our starting point because the economic structure constitutes "the real foundation, on which rise legal and political superstructures and to which correspond definite forms of social consciousness. The mode of production in material life determines the general character of the social, political, and spiritual process of life" (Marx, ibid.).

After exploring the relationship between the economic process and the political and ideological processes in class-divided societies, Marx turns to the question of how change and evolution occur. The antagonisms between social classes were, for Marx, the propelling force in history. "The history of all hitherto existing society is the history of class struggles," he proclaimed (Marx and Engels, 1848, p. 13). He writes:

> At a certain stage of their development, the material forces of production in society come into conflict with the existing relations of production, or—what is but a legal expression for the same thing—with the property relations within which they had been at work before. From forms of development of the forces of production the relations turn into their fetters. Then comes the period of social revolution. With the change of economic foundation the entire immense superstructure is more or less rapidly transformed. In considering such transformation

a distinction should always be made between the material transformation of the economic conditions of production which can be determined with the precision of natural science and the legal, political, religious, aesthetic or philosophic—in short ideological forms in which men become conscious of this conflict and fight it out (Marx, 1970, pp. 20–21).

Marx identified four separate economic systems, or modes of production, through which the European civilization had evolved: (1) early communal, (2) slave, (3) feudal, and (4) capitalist. In any one of these economic systems there was a unique mode of production that included forces of production as well as a particular class structure, or relations of production. Increasing demands for more production inevitably led to changes in the forces of production, yet the relationships between classes remained fixed and were fiercely defended. Therefore, there were conflicts, tensions, and contradictions between the changing forces of production and the fixed social relations (and vested interests) of production. These conflicts and contradictions grew in intensity and importance until a series of violent social eruptions destroyed the old system and created a new system. The new system would have new class relationships compatible (for a time at least) with the changed forces of production.

One example of these cataclysmic changes in the relations between classes and every other economic relationship would be the fall of the Roman Empire when slavery disappeared and feudalism began. Another such revolutionary change was the end of slavery in the southern United States and its eventual replacement by capitalism. The British Revolution of 1648 and the French Revolution of 1789 also marked such cataclysmic changes when the old class relationships of feudalism were violently replaced by new capitalist relationships.

In each mode of production, the contradictions that developed between the forces of production and the relations of production showed themselves in the form of a class struggle. The struggle raged between the class that controlled the means of production and received most of the benefit and privilege of the system (such as the Roman slaveholders) and the much larger class they controlled and exploited (such as the Roman slaves). In all economic systems prior to capitalism, this class struggle had destroyed one system only to create a new system based on exploitation of the masses by a new ruling class. Thus, it marked the beginning of a new class struggle.

Capitalism, however, was, in Marx's opinion, the last mode of production that would be based on the existence of antagonistic classes. The capitalist class, which ruled by virtue of ownership of the means of production, would be overthrown by the working class, which would establish a classless society in which the means of production were owned in common by all.

Before we can understand Marx's views on the ways in which capitalism tended to create the seeds of socialism, however, we must understand his conception of capitalism itself. Capitalism is an economic system in which resources are allocated by, and income distribution is determined within, the market. Marx called this a "commodity-producing society." In addition to this, capitalism is characterized by a particular class structure.

THE CLASS STRUCTURE OF CAPITALISM

Marx believed that in every historical setting and within every cultural or national boundary in which capitalism had existed, it was characterized by the existence of four classes of people: the capitalists, the small shopkeepers and independent craftsmen or professional people, the workers, and a poverty-stricken class that generally owned little or no property and whose members for a variety of reasons could not work. In some settings, capitalism had other classes as well. In the period of early capitalism, for example, by the side of these four classes were peasants and nobility which were the remains of the two main class characteristics of feudalism. But the above-mentioned four classes were always characteristic of capitalism.

Of the four, the working class and the capitalist class were by far the most important. In most capitalist settings, and always in well-developed capitalist economies, the working class constituted the majority of the population and created or produced nearly all of the commodities. The capitalist class had the bulk of economic and political power in a capitalist society.

A capitalist class could not exist without a class of wage laborers. Working for wages, or wage labor, characterized the working class in capitalism. Wage labor came into existence in the sixteenth to eighteenth centuries when large numbers of peasants were pushed off the land by landlords who took over the peasants' land and the formerly common lands. Peasants were thus forced to migrate to cities, where they found a commercial market-oriented economy. The peasants could no longer sell the commodities they produced in order to acquire the commodities necessary to sustain their lives because they had no access to the land or to means of production.

Workers in the city had to buy commodities in order to live, however, and they could not buy commodities without selling something first so as to acquire money for purchases. Such workers had but one salable thing, a body or capacity to produce. A worker could not sell his or her body once and for all, or we would have had a slave economy and not a capitalist one. In capitalism, workers recurrently sold their **labor power**, or *one's capacity to work for a definite period of time, say in a typical working day*. For example, they "hired out" by the hour, the day, or the week. The wage was the price workers received for selling control of themselves for this period of time. Therefore, the defining characteristic of the working class of capitalism was that it was composed of wage laborers who had to sell their labor power as a commodity in order to survive.

The class that owned the means of production, of course, was the capitalist class. Capitalists got their initial capital in many ways. Marx listed the important forms of that initial accumulation of capital as the enclosure movement and the dislocation of the feudal agrarian population, the great price inflation, monopolies of trade, colonies, "the extirpation, enslavement and entombment in mines of the aboriginal population, the beginning of the conquest and looting of the East Indies, [and] the turning of Africa into a warren for the commercial hunting of black skins" (ibid., p. 751).

The capitalist class owned the machines and materials necessary for production. They then bought labor power as a commodity on the market. They directed the laborers, whose labor power they had purchased, to produce. The laborers produced commodities that had some given magnitude of value. These commodities were owned by the capitalists, of course, who then sold the commodities. The value that the laborers had produced was generally sufficient for the capitalist to pay the laborers their wages, to pay for raw materials used, to pay for the wear and tear of the machines and tools used, or to acquire new machines and tools. After these expenses, there was enough to leave a surplus for the capitalist. Capitalists received the surplus purely as a result of their ownership of property.

Not all of the surplus, however, was profit. The capitalist might have borrowed funds to expand his capital, or he might have rented the land on which his factory was constructed. For the capitalist, the interest he paid on his debt and the rent he paid on the land were both expenses which he deducted, along with his other expenses, from the value his laborers had created in order to arrive at his profit. The persons who received this interest and rent were also, in Marx's view, receiving income purely from ownership. Thus, the surplus value created by workers, in excess of the value of their own wages and the materials and tools used up in production, went to profit, interest, and rent. All three of these latter forms of income were derived from ownership. Therefore, they were all capitalist income. Ownership of money, land, or tools and machinery could thus all become capital under the right circumstances, and the return from owning capital could take the form of interest, rent, or profit.

In every capitalist economy, there was another social class that stood between the capitalists and the wage laborers. This was the class of small shopkeepers, independent craftsmen, and professionals or other independent proprietors. This class had features resembling both capitalists and workers. They owned their own means of production and did much (and sometimes all) of the work in creating or selling their commodities. Most frequently they themselves, like wage laborers, had to work, but they also, like capitalists, hired wage laborers to assist them. Included in this class would be most doctors, lawyers, independent accountants, barbers, and many owners of such small businesses as hamburger stands, dry cleaners, repair garages, small retail shops, and the like. This class has always been much smaller than the working class and much larger than the capitalist class. In some circumstances, the interests of this class might be very close to those of the capitalist class, whereas in other circumstances their interests might be closer to those of the working class.

Finally, the last class in capitalism was the poorest class. It included people who received little or no income from either owning or working. Included in this class were two distinctly different groups. First, there were those who could not work for a variety of reasons, such as mental, physical, or emotional handicaps or problems; people who were too young or too old to work and had no one to support them. There were also people such as single parents of very small children whose necessary activities left no time for wage labor.

Another group of the poor were people who were able and willing to work, but for whom capitalism did not provide enough jobs. Throughout the history of capitalism there have always been millions of such involuntarily unemployed people. They have generally performed two very important economic functions. First, they have weakened the bargaining power of employed laborers in their wage negotiations, since if employed workers demanded too much, they could easily be replaced. Second, capitalism has always been an unstable economy. It has experienced alternative periods of prosperity and depression. The involuntarily unemployed have constituted a reserve of individuals who could be used in times of prosperity when the economy was growing and needed more workers, and could be discarded when recession or depression set in and fewer workers were needed. Thus, the size of this lowest or poorest class in capitalism has always varied in accordance with general business conditions.

After examining the sources of income among all four classes, Marx concluded that interest, rent, and profit were not the only forms taken by the surplus created by the working class. Taxes also came from this surplus. Whether the taxes were collected from wage earners or from the recipients of interest, rent, and profits, they represented a claim on the product of labor and were hence a part of the surplus value created by workers, but not received by workers. Thus, we see that two of the classes in capitalism, the highest and the lowest, did not contribute to the production of commodities but lived off the surplus created by wage laborers.

Within the context of Marx's theory, it is interesting to note that whenever workers become angry or frustrated by their support of unproductive consumers, it is, of course, much more conducive to the peace and stability of capitalism if all of their anger and frustration is turned against those living in dire poverty, the unemployed and unemployable, rather than against those living in extravagant luxury, the capitalists. It is not surprising that conservatives generally protest the parasitic nature of the very poor and the powerless, while critics who have been influenced by Marx protest the parasitic nature of the wealthy and the powerful. In Marx's view, however, both classes were integral parts of capitalism and would continue to exist as long as capitalism itself existed. Thus, the market allocation of productive labor and natural resources, together with the four-level class structure, constituted the defining features of capitalism for Marx.

THE LABOR THEORY OF VALUE AND SURPLUS VALUE

Because for Marx the capitalist mode of production was based on the opposition of labor and capital, he began by analyzing the capital-labor relationship. This relationship was essentially one of exchange. The worker sold his labor power to the capitalist for money, with which the worker bought the necessities of life. Thus, this exchange relation was obviously merely a special case of the general problem of exchange values within a capitalist market economy. Marx therefore began Volume I of *Capital* (1867) with a section entitled "Commodities," in which he defined commodities as objects that are usually intended for exchange rather than for the direct personal use of the producer. He then attempted to analyze the basic determinant of the exchange value of commodities. In other words, he analyzed the ratio in which commodities could be exchanged for other commodities, as opposed to use value, which was a measure of the usefulness of commodities to their possessor.

Like Adam Smith, David Ricardo (1772–1823), and most of the pre-Marxist classical economists, Marx believed *the exchange value of a commodity was determined by the amount of labor time necessary for its production*. His theory is therefore usually called the **labor theory of value**. He recognized that laborers differed in abilities, training, and motivation, but he believed skilled labor could be calculated as a multiple of unskilled labor. Thus, all labor time could be reduced to a common denominator.

Marx began by describing how the capitalist buys the means of production and the labor power. Then when the laborers complete the production process, the capitalist sells the commodities for more money. Thus, the amount of money at the end of the production process is greater than at the start. This difference is what Marx called surplus value. He considered it the source of capitalist profits.

Surplus value originated in the fact that capitalists bought one commodity—labor power—and sold a different commodity—what labor produced in the production process. Profits were made because the value of labor power was less than the value of the commodities produced with the labor power. The value of labor power was "determined, as in the case of every other commodity, by the labor time necessary" for its maintenance and reproduction, which meant that "the value of labor power . . . [was] the value of the means of subsistence necessary for the maintenance of the laborer at a socially defined standard of living" (Marx, 1961, Vol. 1, pp. 170–171). The fact was that *the average length of the working day exceeded the time necessary for a laborer to produce the value equivalent of his subsistence wage, which enabled the capitalist to appropriate the surplus produced over and above this subsistence*. Marx called this process the **exploitation** of workers by capitalists. If the worker works for eight hours but uses only six hours to produce the value of his wage goods, then that worker is exploited because he works two surplus hours for the capitalist.

ARGUMENTS ABOUT THE JUSTIFICATION OF PROFITS

During Marx's time (and, indeed, right up to the present) the dominant economic ideology of capitalism justified colossal incomes from ownership as being the fruits of high moral character. In capitalism, the ideologists argued, workers earned wages because of, or in payment for, the strain of producing. On the other hand, because it has always been extraordinarily difficult (very nearly impossible) for a noncapitalist to save enough to become a capitalist, the ideologists argued that whenever anyone did become a capitalist, he or she must have undergone strain and sacrifices that were much more severe than the mere strain of productively creating things that were socially needed. Therefore, the capitalists' profit, rent, and interest were earned because of, or in payment for, the strains and sacrifices of their abstinence.

There were many arguments by which Marx refuted the ideologists' apologetic views on profit. First, the abstinence and strain that were necessary for one to become a capitalist involved no contribution to society. For example, if a person saved all his life in order to buy a factory, he saved only for himself. He had not, in so doing, done any of the work necessary to construct the factory. All the work had been done by working people. Rather, the extent of his stress and strain merely reflected the fact that in any class-divided society there had to be significant barriers to entrance into the ruling class. If it had been relatively easy for anyone to become a capitalist, then everyone would have become a capitalist. There would have been no workers. Nothing would have been produced and everyone would have starved. There had been in history, and were in Marx's time, numerous socioeconomic systems that operated effectively without the abstinence of capitalists—in fact, without capitalists at all. But there had never been, and there never would be, a society without working people creating needed products.

Second, if sacrifice and abstinence could justify capitalists' income, then they could similarly justify the wealth, power, and income of any ruling class in any society. For example, in the American South prior to the Civil War, the economic system was one of commercial slavery. Slaves were very expensive, and most southern whites did not own slaves. Slave owners, of course, enjoyed great wealth and lavish incomes from the surplus their slaves produced over the costs of their maintenance. For a non-slave owner to become a slave owner was very difficult. It required extreme strain and abstinence. It was clear that according to this ideology the surplus that these owners extracted from the sweat and toil of their slaves was merely the just reward for the owners' strain and abstinence.

Third, the majority of capitalists inherited their ownership of capital. Not only did they not strain and abstain, but most of them lived lives of luxury. For those who had not inherited their wealth, most became capitalists not because they had produced and abstained, but through some combination of ruthlessness, shrewdness, chicanery, and luck. Marx detailed the piracy, slave trading, and colonial plundering in the early process of building capitalist fortunes.

ALIENATION

Capitalism, in Marx's view, simultaneously increased society's capacity to produce while systematically rendering this increased productive capacity less serviceable in fulfilling some of the most basic of human needs. More production certainly made possible a more adequate fulfillment of the basic needs for food, shelter, and clothing. Because of the extreme inequalities in the distribution of wealth and income, however, millions of workers in the capitalist system of Marx's time suffered from extreme material poverty and deprivation.

Marx, however, did not base his critique on poverty alone. Although Marx was appalled by the inequities of capitalism and the material deprivation and suffering of the working class, he was well aware that with the increasing productivity of the capitalist system it would become possible for workers to win higher wages in their struggles with capitalists. If they did win such increases, they would be able to buy more useful commodities. The most fundamental evil of capitalism was not, Marx insisted, the material deprivation of workers. Rather, it was to be found in the fact that capitalism systematically prevented individuals from achieving their potential as human beings. It diminished their capacity to give and receive love, and it thwarted the development of their biological, emotional, aesthetic, and intellectual potential. In other words, capitalism severely crippled human beings by preventing their development.

This crippling effect could not, moreover, be overcome within a capitalist system. The forces that increased social productivity could only be utilized in capitalism through the very methods that degraded workers. This was because the technological improvements were always introduced for one purpose and only one purpose: to increase profit. Profit was the source of capitalists' wealth; profit could only be increased by extending and solidifying the control of the capitalists over the work process. Yet it was the control of capital over nearly all processes of human creativity that was the source of the degradation of workers in capitalism. Marx concluded that the "accumulation of wealth at one pole is, therefore, at the same time accumulation of misery, agony of toil, slavery, ignorance, brutality, [and] mental degradation at the opposite pole" (ibid., p. 646).

The social nature of the work process was, for Marx, extremely important. It was through social cooperation in transforming nature into useful things that human beings achieved their sociality, and developed their potential as individual human beings. If that production were a cooperative venture among social equals, it would develop bonds of affection, love, and mutual affirmation among people. Moreover, such creative endeavor was the source of human aesthetic development. It is significant that when ancient people spoke of the "arts" they were referring to various productive skills. Moreover, the creation and use of tools have always been involved in the advancement of human knowledge and scientific understanding.

The production process, however, had exactly the opposite set of effects on workers in a capitalist system. In feudalism the exploitative class structure had severely limited human development. Yet because these exploitative social relations were also personal and paternalistic, not all of the human developmental potential of the work process was stunted or thwarted. Work in feudalism was more than merely a means of making a livable wage for the worker while he created wealth for his overlord. This changed with capitalism, when, in Marx's opinion:

> . . . the bourgeoisie, wherever it has got the upper hand, has put an end to all feudal patri-archal, idyllic relations. It has pitilessly torn asunder the motley feudal ties that bound man to his "natural superiors," and has left remaining no other nexus between man and man than naked self-interest, than callous "cash payment." It has drowned the most heavenly ecstasies of religious fervor, of chivalrous enthusiasm, of philistine sentimentalism, in the icy water of egotistical calculation. It has resolved personal worth into exchange value (Marx and Engels, p. 15).

In a capitalist society the market separated and isolated "exchange value," or money price, from the qualities that shaped a person's relations with things, as well as with other human beings. This was especially true in the work process. To the capitalist, wages were merely another expense of production to be added to the costs of raw materials and machinery in the profit calculation. Labor became a mere commodity to be bought if a profit could be made on the purchase. Whether the laborer could sell his labor power was completely beyond his control. It depended on the cold and totally impersonal conditions of the market. The product of this labor was likewise totally outside of the laborer's life, being the property of the capitalist.

Marx used the term "alienation" to describe the condition of individuals in this situation. They felt alienated or divorced from their work, from their institutional and cultural environment, and from their fellow humans. The conditions of work, the object produced, and indeed the very possibility of working were determined by the numerically small class of capitalists and their profit calculations, not by human needs or aspirations. The effects of this alienation can best be summarized in Marx's own words:

What, then, constitutes the alienation of labour? First, the fact that labour is external to the worker, i.e., it does not belong to his essential being; that in his work, therefore, he does not affirm himself but denies himself, does not feel content but unhappy, does not develop freely his physical and mental energy but mortifies his body and ruins his mind. The worker therefore only feels himself outside his work, and in his work feels outside himself. He is at home when he is not working, and when he is working he is not at home. His labour is therefore not voluntary but coerced; it is forced labour. It is therefore not the satisfaction of a need; it is merely a means to satisfy needs external to it. Its alien character emerges clearly in the fact that as soon as no physical or other compulsion exists, labour is shunned like the plague. External labour, labour in which man alienates himself, is a labour of self-sacrifice, or mortification. Lastly, the external character of labour for the worker appears in the fact that it is not his own, but someone else's, that it does not belong to him, that in it he belongs, not to himself, but to another. . . . As a result, therefore, man (the worker) no longer feels himself to be freely active in any but his animal functions—eating, drinking, procreating, or at most in his dwelling and in dressing up, etc.; and in his human functions he no longer feels himself to be anything but an animal. What is animal becomes human and what is human becomes animal (Marx, 1959, p. 69).

It was this degradation and total dehumanization of the working class, thwarting man's personal development and making an alien market commodity of man's life-sustaining activities that Marx most thoroughly condemned in the capitalist system. His moral critique thus went far beyond those of most of his socialist precursors.

His faith in the possibility of a better future for the working class, however, was not based on the hope that ever-increasing numbers of people would share his moral indignation and therefore attempt to reform the system. Rather, he believed the capitalist mode of production and the class conflict inherent in it would lead to the destruction of capitalism. Capitalism, like all previous modes of production in which class conflicts were present, would destroy itself. Thus, Marx's belief in a better future was based on the scientific analyses in his labor theory of value, in his evolutionary theory of historical materialism, and in his analysis of why capitalism is always subject to a cycle of boom and bust.

ECONOMIC CRISES

Marx was the first major economist to treat economic crises seriously as a basic, integral part of his economics. He described an approximately ten-year cycle of boom and bust in England and wrote extensively of its tragic consequences for human beings in the economy. He wrote parts of several theories, but he never synthesized them. He intended to write a fifth volume of his book, *Capital*, on economic crises, presenting a systematic and unified theory but he only had time in his life to finish three volumes (and the last two were not completed by him, but by Engels).

Marx wrote very clearly about the historical prerequisites for the economic cycle of boom and bust, which did not exist in feudalism, but was always present in capitalism. There were three prerequisites for the modern business cycle. First, in feudalism each manor was self-sufficient, but crises and recession can only come when there is a market and exchange. A self-sufficient manor cannot have a crisis in which there is insufficient demand to buy all the goods and services on the market. Only a market can have a crisis of exchange. Capitalism has such a market in which people live and die by exchange—that is the only reason anything is produced.

Second, there must be money as the medium of exchange and store of value. In a barter economy, a person brings a goat to market to exchange for other things. The goat is a supply of goods, but it also represents demand (the ability to trade) for other goods. In a barter economy, there can be too much of one thing and too little of another, but in the **aggregate** (*the entire economy comprised of all the buyers and all the sellers*) supply must equal the aggregate demand for they are the same thing. In a capitalist economy with money, people can sell something, but then hide the money away and not buy anything with it. It is possible under a capitalist money economy to have money leak out of circulation (or a slower circulation of money, which is the same thing). If there is less money in circulation—or slower circulation of money—then there may be insufficient monetary demand for goods. That happens under capitalism, but could not happen with occasional barter as under feudalism.

Third, not only must there be market exchange and the use of money, there must also be production for profit. In feudalism a manor calculates its needs and that is all that it produces so there can be no crisis of overproduction, no excess of aggregate supply over demand. Under capitalism, production is for profit and the enterprise tries to produce more and more to expand its profits. But if profits decline, then the capitalist enterprise cuts back production and fires workers. Business is not for charity, but for profit, so lack of profit spells crisis.

Why do profits ever decline? Marx discusses several theories, including theories about the cost of production as well as theories about the demand for goods and services. On the cost side, Marx points to the fact that raw materials prices almost always rise faster than the prices of final goods. This tends to lower the profit on most final goods in every expansion. Low profit leads to less investment, which causes a recession or depression. Another negative factor discussed by Marx is the rise of the interest rate in each expansion. This also eventually tends to lower profits as it becomes more expensive to borrow money to buy more capital.

Marx also discusses the cost theory that high wages cut into profits. He says, however, that this theory applies only in a few exceptional circumstances, so it is not the usual cause of contractions. He mentions the exceptional situation of the U.S. railroad boom of the mid-nineteenth century. Another example might be war time when governments have an apparently limitless appetite for war materials. In all normal peacetime expansions, wages do not rise faster than prices, so they are not a negative cost factor according to Marx.

On the demand side, Marx emphasizes that wages rise more slowly than output in every expansion. Since wages rise more slowly than profits, this means that in Marx's terms the rate of exploitation rises. This is not only a problem for workers, it is also a problem for the economy according to Marx. Why should a lower ratio of wages to output or to profits be a problem? On the average, all wages go into consumption of goods and services. But profits go to the rich, so in Marx's view the higher profits are mostly not spent for consumer goods. So when income shifts to the rich, the spending for consumption is reduced relative to the total output. A decline in overall demand means less sales and profits.

Thus, Marx emphasizes two sets of facts. First, consumption is limited by the relationships between the classes, so increases in consumption rise at a slower and slower rate in the expansion. Second, the costs of raw materials and of interest payments keep rising in every expansion. Therefore, profits are assailed from both sides and must decline. This profit decline leads to less investment. Less investment causes a crisis of overproduction of goods that cannot be sold. Thus do recessions and depressions begin.

ECONOMIC CONCENTRATION

According to Marx, economic concentration, the concentration of economic power in a few giant corporations in each sector, was the result of two forces. First, competition among capitalists tended to create a situation in which the strong either crushed or absorbed the weak. "Here competition rages in direct proportion to the number, and in inverse proportion to the magnitudes, of the antagonistic capitals. It always ends in the ruin of many small capitalists, whose capitals partly pass into the hands of their conquerors, partly vanish" (ibid., p. 626).

Second, as technology improved there was "an increase in the minimum amount of . . . capital necessary to carry on a business under its normal conditions. In order to remain competitive, a firm would constantly have to increase the productivity of its laborers. The productiveness of labor . . . [depended] on the scale of production" (ibid., p. 626). Thus, changing technology as well as competition among capitalists created an inexorable movement of the capitalist system toward larger and larger firms owned by fewer and fewer capitalists. In this way the gulf between the small class of wealthy capitalists and the great majority of society, the workers, would continually widen.

THE CAPITALIST STATE

By the "state" Marx meant something more than simply any government: "We may speak of a state where a special public power of coercion exists which, in the form of an armed organization, stands over and above the population" (Hook, p. 256). Many socialists believed that the state was an impartial arbiter in the affairs of society. Those socialists had faith that socialism could be obtained by moral and intellectual appeals to the state. Marx rejected this idea. "Political power," he declared in *The Communist Manifesto* (1848), " . . . is merely the organized power of one class for oppressing another." During each period of history, or for each mode of production, the state is the coercive instrument of the ruling class that enforces laws desired by that class.

Thus the state is simply a dictatorship of the ruling class over the remainder of society. Friedrich Engels summarized the Marxist argument:

> Former society, moving in class antagonisms, had need of the state, that is, an organization of the exploiting class at each period for the maintenance of external conditions of production; that is, therefore, for the forcible holding down of the exploited class in the conditions of oppression (slavery, . . . serfdom, wage labor) determined by the existing mode of production. The state was the official representative of society as a whole, its embodiment in a visible corporation; but it was this only in so far as it was the state of that class which itself, in its epoch, represented society as a whole; in ancient times, the state of the slave-owning citizens; in the Middle Ages, of the feudal nobility; in our epoch, of the bourgeoisie (Engels, p. 295).

In the capitalist system this dictatorial government has two functions. First, it has the traditional function of enforcing the dictatorship of the capitalists over the rest of society. The state achieves this primarily by enforcing property rights, the source of the capitalists' economic power. It also serves in innumerable other ways, for example, jailing or harassing critics of capitalism, fighting wars to extend capitalists' markets, and providing roads, railroads, canals, postal service, and hundreds of other prerequisites for profitable commerce.

Second, the government acts as the arbiter of rivalries among capitalists. Each capitalist is interested only in his own profits, and therefore it is inevitable that the interests of capitalists will clash. If not resolved, many of these clashes would threaten the very existence of the system. Thus, the government intervenes, and in doing so it protects the viability of the capitalist system. This is why it is sometimes possible to observe the government acting in a way that is contrary to the interests of some of the capitalists. But the government never acts in a way that is contrary to the interests of all capitalists as a class.

For these reasons Marx rejected the notion that socialists could rely on the government for help in bringing about the transition from capitalism to socialism. The establishment of socialism, in Marx's opinion, would require a revolution.

THE SOCIALIST REVOLUTION

In his overall view of capitalism, Marx saw the process of capital accumulation as inevitably involving several steps. Business cycles or crises would occur regularly and with increasing severity as the capitalist economy developed. There would be a long-run tendency for the rate of profit to fall, and this would exacerbate the other problems of capitalism. Industrial power would become increasingly concentrated in fewer and fewer giant firms that were monopolistic and oligopolistic (an **oligopoly** is *a market characterized by a very few firms*), and wealth would become concentrated in the hands of fewer and fewer capitalists. The plight of the laborer would steadily deteriorate.

Given these increasingly bad conditions, the system could not be perpetuated. Eventually life under capitalism would become so intolerable that workers would revolt, overthrow the whole system, and create a more rational socialist economy:

> Along with the constantly diminishing number of magnates of capital, who usurp and monopolize all advantages of this process of transformation, grows the mass of misery, oppression, slavery, degradation, exploitation; but with this too grows the revolt of the working class, a class always increasing in numbers, and disciplined, united, organized by the very mechanism of the process of capitalist production itself. The monopoly of capital becomes a fetter upon the mode of production, which has sprung up and flourished along with, and under it. Centralization of the means of production and socialization of labour at last reach a point where they become incompatible with their capitalist integument. This integument is burst asunder. The knell of capitalist private property sounds. The expropriators are expropriated (Marx, 1961, Vol. 1, p. 763).

SUMMARY

Karl Marx, one of the most influential of all socialists, based his economic analysis on a theory of history called historical materialism. Most social and political institutions, he believed, were significantly shaped by the economic base of society, called the mode of production. Over time, conflicts developed between the forces of production and the relations of production. The working out of these conflicts was the most important element in the historical evolution of society. Marx's economic writings were aimed at understanding the conflicts between the class system (or private property system) of capitalism and the methods of production of that system. He also discussed the replacement of capitalism by a classless, socialist society.

SUGGESTED READINGS

The best place to start in understanding Marxism is the pamphlet by Marx and Engels, called *The Communist Manifesto*. It was written during a revolution and breathes fire. For a book on the modern tradition of detailed economics that has descended from Marx, see Paul Sweezy, *The Theory of Capitalist Development* (1941). For a book on the views of contemporary Marxists, see Howard Sherman, *Reinventing Marxism* (1995).

KEY TERMS

aggregate	labor theory of value
exploitation	mode of production
forces of production	oligopoly
historical materialism	relations of production
ideological superstructure	utopians
labor power	

REVIEW QUESTIONS

Understand capitalism from a Marxist perspective.

1. What is "historical materialism"? How did Marx used this method to analyze society?
2. Explain the concept of a mode of production. What are the four modes of production Europe experienced?
3. What did all four modes of production have in common? How was socialism different in Marx's mind?
4. Name the four classes present in any capitalist system and explain their respective roles in society.
5. What four classes of people existed in a capitalist society? What characteristics does each class possess?
6. List and describe the two important functions served by the unemployed and explain why they are important to capitalism.
7. What is surplus? How does the owner of the means of production calculate his profit?
8. Describe the source of income for each of the four main classes under capitalism as described by Marx. From what are interest, rents, profits, and taxes derived?
9. Explain the labor theory of value and labor as the source of surplus.
10. Explain how Marx sees workers being exploited.
11. How does capitalism alienate the worker in society? How does it affect the worker?
12. What is the present justification for allowing the existence of profits for the owners of capital? Why does Marx refute this argument?
13. Why is Marx concerned about labor being treated just like any other commodity? What impact does it have on the social nature of work?

Explain how Marx saw society moving from capitalism to socialism.

14. What role do economic crises play in the business cycle? What prerequisites are necessary for the modern business cycle and why are they only possible under a capitalist system?
15. What will eventually happen to the capitalist mode of production if class conflict continues?
16. Why would profits ever decline and cause the downturn in a business cycle? How do workers get shorted no matter what stage of the business cycle the economy is in?
17. Which factors about the economy inevitably lead to economic concentration?
18. According to Marx, could the "state" be a catalyst for the transition from capitalism to socialism? Explain how the transition will occur if not by the state.

CHAPTER 11

Rise of Corporate Capitalism in the United States, 1865–1900

After the Civil War ended slavery in 1865, capitalism became the dominant system throughout the United States. Businesses grew quickly and some became giants and many major industries were dominated by firms with monopoly power. The organization of firms changed from one-person ownership to corporations, allowing a great deal of capital to come together in an efficient manner with less risk to investors. Women struggled hard and gained many new rights, but could not yet vote. African-Americans were held back and limited to sharecropping and poverty in the South. In the 1890s, the United States started its first colonial ventures in the Philippines, Puerto Rico, and Cuba.

LEARNING OBJECTIVES

After reading this chapter, you should be able to:

- Explain the reasons for the progression from a world of small competitive businesses to a climate controlled by monopolistic giants.
- Identify the questionable behavior of the entrepreneurs of this age and explain how industrial warfare affected the political and social atmosphere.
- Explain the role of women and African-Americans, conditions for workers, and the environmental impact during this period of time.
- Describe the changing relationship with Britain during this period and the move toward colonialism.

THE U.S. INDUSTRIAL REVOLUTION, 1865–1900

In the period after the Civil War, the United States changed from a relatively backward, rural, agricultural country to an urban, industrialized country with some very large businesses organized as corporations. U.S. firms made major industrial innovations and industry expanded in every geographical area, though far more slowly in the South than in the North. In many industries, large firms gained a high degree of monopoly power.

The number of miles of railway jumped from 47,000 in 1860 to 237,000 in 1900. This included the first intercontinental railroad in 1869, with a telegraph line running right next to the railroad tracks. After that, goods and people could cross the United States in a week. This achievement was in stark contrast to the six months to a year by wagon or around the southern tip of South America. The fact that the train could give a relatively pleasant trip in one week from coast to coast was an incredible change. In addition, the completed telegraph line meant instantaneous messages from coast to coast. The stage was now set for the expansion of nationwide firms.

The expansion was driven by private investment and aided by extensive government subsidies. **Gross private investment**, *the total dollar amount of spending for plants, equipment and other items in one year*, rose from less than $15 billion in the decade 1849–1858 to $28 billion in the decade 1889–1898. Production in the earlier period had been on a very small scale, often in the home, and much of it in the rural areas. Now production was in larger and larger units, shifted from home to factory, and from countryside to city. In the period from 1859 to 1899, agricultural production fell from 56 percent to 38 percent of gross domestic product. At the same time, manufacturing rose from 32 percent to 53 percent of gross domestic product. Together, these changes mark the end of an underdeveloped capitalism and the emergence of a new, major capitalist power.

RISE OF MONOPOLY, 1865–1900

The post-Civil War period not only saw the emergence and rapid expansion of industry under capitalist institutions, it also saw the change of the form of capitalism—from individual entrepreneurs to corporations and the rise of monopoly power. Most large firms decided to organize as corporations, and corporations produced the majority of manufacturing output by 1902. A corporation is defined as an enterprise that is owned by many investors, each owning a share of its assets. This form of business organization allowed a large number of investors to invest money into an enterprise. Moreover, the law said that creditors may sue the corporation, but investors have no personal liability for corporate debts.

Larger size meant more concentration of production and sales in a few firms. By 1902 just one or two firms accounted for more than half the production in seventy-eight U.S. industries. These giant firms had monopoly power, which means that they could manipulate prices usually by manipulating their supply. The one hundred largest firms had one-half of all manufacturing assets (see DuBoff, 1989).

What caused this change from small, often rural, and competitive firms to giant firms with monopoly power? First, the new technology in transportation and communication allowed nationwide firms. Second, new technology meant cheaper production by larger firms. Not only could costs be cut by better machinery, but the large size also meant groups of workers could specialize. Third, larger size enhanced a firm's ability to borrow at lower rates. Fourth, giant firms could have more power over government in any deal with government as well as subsidies from government. Finally, it was not just size that counted, but monopoly power in an area of industry, which allowed higher prices and higher profits. For example, Standard Oil either destroyed its competitors, sometimes by artificially low prices or by control of oil pipelines or railroads, or merged with them. Once the firm had enough power, it raised prices and made enormous fortunes for John D. Rockefeller and his associates.

Legal developments also propelled monopoly. At first, competing firms used informal agreements on price, then formal agreements on price, then trust agreements, in which the trust often owned the stock of several firms and the trust set the price for all. A **trust** is *a combination of firms or corporations with the goal of reducing competition and controlling prices*. These are all examples of **collusion** which is *a secret agreement between two or more parties, usually for fraudulent, deceitful or illegal purposes*. Legislation, such as the Sherman Antitrust Act of 1890, eventually made each of these illegal. One large loophole, however, was left. The law allowed a single firm to set its prices as it wished. The law also allowed firms to combine with each other into one firm. Many firms combined into one giant firm which could then use monopoly power to set prices. In the period from 1895 to 1905 mergers between firms hit a peak. In one industry after another, a large number of competitors combined into one firm. In the oil industry, at one time Standard Oil owned 95 percent of refineries. United States Steel had 85 percent of steel production. The courts tended to punish certain anticompetitive business practices, but did nothing against pure size.

BANKING CORPORATIONS

Bankers came to be part of some corporate boards from 1840 to 1860, as discussed in Chapter 5. After the Civil War, corporations needed more and more money to run larger scale enterprises; so more bankers joined corporate boards. Banks also became very close partners, with much influence over governments to whom they loaned money. For example, even the federal government borrowed money from banks to pay for wars. A coalition of government and banks financed the railroads and the canals. The U.S. government used banks to penetrate new foreign areas, such as China, by offering loans. In turn, the banks used government to protect themselves. In the state governments, U.S. banks bought legislators. For example, when Maryland stopped interest payments on its debt, bankers bought the "worthless" bonds and then bribed legislators to reinstate the bonds.

From 1865 to 1900 was the period of the so-called robber barons: John D. Rockefeller (1839–1937) in oil; J.P. Morgan (1837–1913) in banking; . Cornelius Vanderbilt (1794–1877) in railroads; Andrew Carnegie (1835–1919) in steel. The rule of the robber barons was that anything goes—all is fair in love, war, and business. Each of the robber barons worked closely with a big bank or a group of banks. In the early twentieth century, there were only six big banking groups. Each controlled many corporations and worked with one of the robber barons. Thus, the J.P. Morgan banks helped create the monopoly called U.S. Steel. The Morgan banks also helped create a world shipping trust. Under the robber barons and the bank groups, the railroads gave preferences to big customers, such as oil, and usually they were owned by the same group. Thus Rockefeller was able to ship oil much cheaper than his competitors. The robber barons and their bankers reacted violently against unions. In the steel strike of 1892 in the town of Homestead, Pennsylvania, and in the railroad strike of 1894, the strikes were crushed when the robber barons got the government to use police and soldiers.

THE ROBBER BARONS AND INDUSTRIAL WARFARE

Examples of the industrial warfare between competing corporations at this time have filled many books (see, e.g., Josephson). In the oil industry, for example, John D. Rockefeller and Henry M. Flagler (1830–1913) shipped so much oil that they were able to demand large concessions from the railroads. With this cost advantage they could undersell competitors. Their company, which was incorporated in 1870 under the name of Standard Oil Company of Ohio, was able to force many competitors to the wall and thus achieve regional monopolies, at which point the price could be substantially increased without fear of competition.

After securing large rebates on transport costs, Standard Oil's share in the petroleum industry quickly increased from 10 to 20 percent. But the company did not stop there. Next it succeeded in forcing the railroads to give it rebates on its competitors' shipments as well as "all data relating to shipper, buyer, product, price and terms of payment," a scheme that "provided Rockefeller and his associates with rebates on all their own shipments, rebates on all shipments by their competitors, and in addition a complete spy system on their competitors" (Dillard, p. 410). With this power Rockefeller was able to smash most of his competitors. By 1879, only nine years after incorporation, Standard Oil controlled between 90 and 95 percent of the nation's output of refined petroleum. A sympathetic biographer of Rockefeller has written, "Of all the devices for the extinction of competition, this was the cruelest and most deadly yet conceived by any group of American industrialists" (Nevins, p. 325).

Competition among the railroad magnates was particularly intense. Rate wars were common, forcing weaker competitors out of business and giving stronger competitors monopoly power over large regions. The battles sometimes were so brutal that locomotives were crashed into each other and trucks were destroyed. The railroads also extorted money from towns along proposed railroad lines. A member of the California Constitutional Convention of 1878 described a technique:

> They start out their railroad track and survey their line near a thriving village. They go to the most prominent citizens of that village and say, "If you will give us so many thousand dollars we will run through here; if you do not we will run by." And in every instance where the subsidy was not granted this course was taken and the effect was just as they said, to kill off the little town (quoted in Josephson, pp. 84–85).

According to the same report, the railroad " . . . blackmailed Los Angeles County for $230,000 as a condition of doing that which the law compelled them to do." The railroads also manipulated connections with politicians to get government handouts of public lands. It is estimated that these giveaways amounted to 158,293,000 acres—a greater land area than that of some countries. The railroads were certainly not in favor of a laissez-faire policy in practice.

The great entrepreneurs of that age were definitely not men of estimable social conscience. Many founded their fortunes during the Civil War. When shortages of supplies became desperate, they received high prices for selling to the army "shoddy blankets, so many doctored horses, and useless rifles, [and] . . . stores of sickening beef." In order to eliminate their competitors, they did not hesitate to use hired thugs, kidnapping, and dynamite. Likewise, they stopped at nothing as they milked the public of millions of dollars through stock frauds, schemes, and swindles. Some of these actions were legal and some were not, but the dominant mood of these capitalist entrepreneurs was expressed by Cornelius Vanderbilt, who, when cautioned about the questionable legality of a desired course of action, exclaimed, "What do I care about the law? Hain't I got the power?" Much the same idea was expressed by his son William H. Vanderbilt during a public outcry against one of his policy decisions: "The public be damned. I am working for my stockholders." (These quotations are all cited in Josephson, pp. 67, 72).

BUSINESS COLLUSION AND GOVERNMENT REGULATION

After a few years of cutthroat type of competition, most of the remaining business firms were battle-tested giants. Trusts and mergers were the consequence of the earlier competition. Whereas competition was the road to large profits before 1880, after that date it became obvious that collusion would be more beneficial for the remaining firms. In that way they could exercise monopolistic power for their mutual benefit. As the turn of the century neared, the classical liberal vision of many small competing firms was quite different from the reality of massive corporations acting cooperatively to maximize their joint profits.

With the rise of big corporations there was a parallel growth of grassroots opposition to these companies and their blatant disregard for the public welfare. By **grassroots** we mean *groups of people organized at the local level rather than organized by traditional or existing power structures.*

The antagonism became so widespread and intense that in the presidential campaign of 1888 both the Democrats and Republicans advocated federal laws to curb the abuses of big corporations.

After the 1888 election, both parties became extremely reluctant to take any such action. Many of the most important Republicans controlled the very corporations they had promised to curb, and the Democrats were only slightly less involved with big business. Only when public pressure reached incredible heights did Congress respond, in December 1889, by passing the Sherman Antitrust Act. The act, an obvious concession to aroused public opinion, passed both houses of Congress with only a single dissenting vote. But the wording of the law was so weak and vague that it appeared to be designed to ensure that it would be ineffective. Another proposal, which recommended meaningful punishment of firms that violated the law, was overwhelmingly defeated.

The Sherman Act prohibited "every contract, combination in the form of a trust or otherwise, or conspiracy, in restraint of trade or commerce among the several states or with foreign nations." It also declared that any person who attempted "to monopolize, or combine or conspire with any other person . . . to monopolize any part of the trade or commerce among the several states, or with foreign nations" was guilty of a misdemeanor.

The primary effect of the Sherman Act, as a result of court rulings over the next few decades, was not to prevent business monopoly, but to weaken labor unions. What had begun as a concession to the public's hatred of abuses by big business became an anti-labor law. What caused this amazing twist in the law? The weak antitrust laws were interpreted by the courts in such ways that they applied to very few businesses. The courts held that size alone did not mean monopoly and even control of 90 percent of an industry did not show any attempt to monopolize. Only in cases of outrageous criminal behavior against competitors did the courts see any restraint of trade.

On the other hand, the courts ruled that many union strikes constituted constraints against trade. On this basis, the government arrested numerous union leaders and broke up many unions. When workers struck against the railroads in the 1890s, the federal government used soldiers to break the strike. Their excuse was that the railroads carried the mail, so the strikers were violating federal law by interfering with the mail. They sent the head of the union, Eugene V. Debs (1855–1926), to prison. They broke this union, which was the first and last unified railroad union, completely and forever.

While President William McKinley was in office (1897–1901), there were only five cases initiated under the Sherman Act, despite the fact that 146 major industrial combinations were formed between 1899 and 1901 alone. One of these was the massive United States Steel Corporation. In 1901, U.S. Steel controlled or acquired 785 plants worth $1,370,000,000, which would be many times that amount in today's dollars.

Competition among the railroads had been so destructive that the railroads themselves were the leading advocates of extended federal regulation. Staggeringly high profits, graft, corruption, and discriminatory practices on the part of the nation's railroads led to the establishment of the first federal government regulatory agency. The Interstate Commerce Act of 1887 established the Interstate Commerce Commission (ICC), which was designed to regulate the railroads in order to protect the public interest. A few years after the passage of the Interstate Commerce Act, U.S. Attorney General Richard Olney (1835–1917) wrote a letter to a railroad president that read, in part, "The [ICC] . . . is, or can be made, of great use to the railroads. It satisfies the popular clamor for a government supervision of railroads, at the same time that supervision is almost entirely nominal. Further, the older such a commission gets to be, the more inclined it will be found to take the business and railroad view of things" (quoted in McConnell, p. 197).

The attorney general's prediction has certainly been borne out by the facts. In the years since the establishment of the ICC, many other federal regulatory agencies have been established. The

Federal Communications Commission (FCC), the Civil Aeronautics Board (CAB), and the Securities and Exchange Commission (SEC) were among the federal agencies that joined the ICC as "protectors" of the public interest. Most serious students of government regulation would agree that "the outstanding political fact about the . . . regulatory commissions is that they have in general become promoters and protectors of the industries they have been established to regulate" (ibid., p. 199). The agencies help the industries make extraordinary profits at the expense of the public.

Many oligopolistic industries seemed unable to cooperate and act collectively as a monopoly. There is a considerable body of evidence indicating that these industries turned to the government and to federal regulatory agencies as a means of achieving this monopolistic coordination (see Kolko). Regulatory agencies have generally performed this function very effectively.

WOMEN AFTER THE CIVIL WAR, 1865–1900

The Civil War and the rise of corporate capitalism had an immense effect on society. In 1865, most women were still on farms, but were slowly moving into cities and into industry. Most women were uneducated and there was a long fight for free, public education. There was also the notion that women ought to have a segregated education, separate from men. Eventually, schools were set up that were free and were coeducational. For the first time, teaching became respectable for women and women began to take over primary school teaching from men. Because of discrimination against women, the salary of primary school teachers dropped relative to other professions. Women teachers had to be unmarried in most places and were fired if they married. Women were not admitted to most universities and there were few women's colleges. Even as late as 1960, when this author interviewed for a job at Princeton, I was told that one of the best features of Princeton was that it had no women as students and certainly no women faculty.

A few rich women did not work except to direct servants. Rich women were not supposed to do anything but look decorative, so they wore corsets that did not allow much movement and sometimes caused fainting. Most women were not rich and worked on the farm or in factories in addition to their work in the home. Women in the factories received much lower wages than men.

There was resistance to women entering professions, except prostitution. For example, in 1872 Illinois prohibited women from becoming lawyers and the U.S. Supreme Court (filled with conservatives representing industrialists or landowners) upheld this law. By 1890, women were still only 17 percent of the paid labor force. Most unions discriminated against women, but the short-lived Knights of Labor invited them and they joined in large numbers.

In the 1890s a few women joined the American Federation of Labor (AFL), but received little support. The head of the AFL, Samuel Gompers (1850–1924), was antiwomen, anti-African-American, and anti-Asian. Middle class women worked hard in reform organizations, including the Women's Christian Temperance Union, which supported many reforms besides nonalcoholic drinking.

One problem for the women's movement after the Civil War came when the Thirteenth, Fourteenth, and Fifteenth amendments to the U.S. Constitution were passed. These amendments gave civil rights and the right to vote to African-American men. Women, however, were not included in these amendments, so women, including former slave women, did not get the right to vote. Women, who had worked so hard in the abolitionist movement in solidarity with white and African-American men, were infuriated. They formed their own movement to work for equal rights for women and for the vote for women. The women's movement for a long time tended to consist of liberal, middle-class, white women, having little or nothing to do with African-Americans.

Women had been left out of the amendments as a tactical move to get them passed in spite of prejudice. At this point, many women leaders not only split from their former friends in the abolitionist movement, but some of the women's leaders used racism as an argument for votes for women, claiming that the right to vote for white women would offset the ignorant votes of the former slaves. Not until the 1960s did the women's movement and the African-American movement get back into close alliance as a result of new battles.

It required a long, hard fight from 1848 to 1920 to get the vote for women. In that period, the women's movement concentrated only on the vote. Oddly, the first U.S. territory to give women the right to vote was the rural, agricultural area of Wyoming in 1869. Wyoming, still not a state, offered the vote to attract women as settlers. When Wyoming finally became a state in 1890, it was the first to allow women to vote.

SHARECROPPING AND RACISM AGAINST AFRICAN AMERICANS

After the Civil War, the freed slaves received no land, so land ownership was still concentrated in a small class of former slave owners. The ex-slaves did not want to work on their master's plantations, but wanted their own land and independence. This new landlord class did not think in terms of employing free workers to farm their large lands. The landowners did not have the heavy equipment or technology for large-scale farming and they no longer had the extremely cheap labor. What suited their relatively limited resources was to lease out their land to a class of subordinate farmers, mostly ex-slaves, but also many poor whites. Although the slaves had been given their freedom, they were given no land and no money, so they were in a very poor bargaining position. They needed money to lease the land, money for equipment, and money for food until the crop was harvested.

In return for the land, the **sharecropper**, *a tenant farmer who pays a share of his crop as rent, had to share half of his or her crop with the landlord.* Usually, when half the crop was given to the landlord, the remaining half was far from enough to pay for food for the farm family for a year, plus necessary fertilizer, equipment and seeds for the year. They had to renew the lease on bad terms once again, usually about 50 percent of the crop. But they also had to borrow money during the year, either from the landlord or from a moneylender. Therefore, as the system continued, the sharecroppers became deeper in debt each year. Just as in feudalism, they owed a payment in goods to the landlord. In sharecropping, however, they might also owe money for interest to the moneylender. The system was better than slavery or serfdom, but resembled them in that the sharecropper was clearly subordinate to the landlord and the moneylender. The subordination was economic, legal, social, and political.

The economic subordination, as explained already, consisted of having no land but what they leased, paying half their crop for the lease, and heavier and heavier debts. The legal subordination consisted of the fact that the law not only held sharecropping and high rates of interest for loans to be legal, but also held that it was illegal to leave the state without paying all debts. If a sharecropper was caught trying to leave the state while owing money, he or she could be imprisoned. Moreover, it was held to be perfectly legal to use the prisoners in chain gangs, in which people were chained together, to go to various government work projects. The state even sent out prisoners in chains to do jobs for private businesses for which the state was paid so the result was the same as slave labor for many ex-slaves.

The sharecroppers clung to the lowest rung of society. They seldom received any education. They had no participation in any community decision making, and they certainly were not invited to white churches. Most important, during the whole period of sharecropping, from the Civil War to World War II, there was an all-pervasive racism. This racist prejudice and discrimination that existed under slavery, continued under sharecropping. Racism continued because it was very useful to the landlords, merchants, and moneylenders, since it reinforced their economic and political power.

The story of political power and its relation to racism is amazing and unpleasant. The Thirteenth Amendment to the Constitution ended slavery, the Fourteenth gave civil rights to everyone, and the Fifteenth gave the right to vote to black males. With these three amendments and with the protection of federal soldiers, the former slaves participated in the democratic process after the Civil War. They voted, elected candidates, and participated in the then radical Republican Party. But in 1876, there was a close and contested presidential election between the Democrat, Rutherford B. Hayes, and the Republican, Samuel J. Tilden. A compromise was reached behind the scenes of power by which the Republicans got the presidency, but the Democrats got the South. Federal troops were withdrawn. Immediately, the South was terrorized by the Ku Klux Klan, who tortured, murdered, and raped African-Americans. Eventually, the number of African-Americans willing or able to vote or participate in politics dwindled away to a tiny few. The terrorism against the African-Americans in the South was carried out by various gangs and organizations, but it was helped by the police and supported by the many in the white elite.

In the 1880s and 1890s, poor whites and poor African-Americans got together in the Populist Party and started to make big gains in the South. Feeling threatened, the ruling elite deliberately increased the amount of racist propaganda to split the races apart in the Populist Party. Laws were also passed to segregate every public place, though segregation had not legally existed after the Civil War. Laws were also passed to force voters to pay a poll tax, read and explain the Constitution, and other obstacles to voting. It was said that these laws would prevent African-Americans from voting so that all whites would have the political power. Bur a great many poor and illiterate whites were also prevented from voting. Thus the landlords, moneylenders, and merchants kept their power over the sharecroppers.

One result of this political-economic system was the stagnation of technology. The relationships of sharecropping held back technological progress as well as further investment of capital in agriculture for many decades until after World War II. If the sharecropper was foolish enough to invest in better equipment and technology to produce a larger crop, then the next year the percentage going to the landlord would be raised. If the sharecropper refused to pay, the family was forced off the land. Of course, usually the sharecropper had no opportunity to invest in improving the land or equipment because the sharecropper did not have idle cash, but mounting debts. Wise tenants worried about the current crop, not about long run development.

The landlord would continue to own the land, so one might expect that the landlord would be interested in long-run improvements. But the landlord only got half the benefit from improved productivity, so landlords in this situation had much less incentive to invest in improvements than ordinary capitalist enterprises. To be enticing, the investment would have to improve the output by at least twice its cost.

Finally, since the sharecropper was deeply in debt, and since the contract was for only one year, the sharecropper had no margin for experimentation. Therefore, sharecroppers stuck to production of cotton. But in addition to harming the land, the limitation to cotton production meant that much new technology had no application to their farms.

RACISM AGAINST OTHER GROUPS

In the American Southwest, Mexican-Americans faced vicious racial discrimination of many kinds. Asian Americans faced intense discrimination, with frequent campaigns against them in California. White labor attacked Asian-Americans on the grounds that they took jobs from whites.

During World War II, Japanese on the West Coast were put into concentration camps as enemy aliens. This hysterical discrimination applied even to those Japanese-Americans who had been here for generations. Jews faced discrimination in education, where they were not admitted to some medical schools, not allowed in any major law firm, excluded from elite society, and were harmed in their businesses. In the Civil War, General Ulysses S. Grant refused to allow Jewish soldiers in his part of the Union army. From the Civil War to World War II, the J.P. Morgan bank never admitted a Jewish partner, even though some Jews ran their own banks.

In the ideological conflict, all of these groups were labeled with false and cruel stereotypes. Such stereotypes drastically narrowed job opportunities. Stereotypes are prejudices that prevent people from seeing reality and maintain a certain image of a group regardless of reality. For example, it was assumed that African-Americans were good for only manual labor. When the federal occupation of the South allowed real elections, however, a large number of African-Americans were elected to various offices and some served with distinction in the U.S. Congress.

In addition, there was a very high percentage of immigrants, who were often 40 percent of many big cities. Although physically the same as the white majority, members of the immigrant groups were often treated to the same types of discrimination and stereotyping as minorities. For example, the Irish were said to be loud and stupid. When one subtracted all of the minorities, all of the immigrants, and all of the women, the supposed superior white, male, long-time citizens, were a small minority. A small minority of white men voted and controlled almost all political power in the period from the Civil War until 1900.

UNIONS, 1865–1900

After the Civil War, U.S. capitalism expanded rapidly into the South and the West, industry became large-scale, and enterprises with large numbers of employees became commonplace. At the same time, working and living conditions for many people were miserable. For example, in New York City in the 1860s thousands of pre-adolescent girls and boys worked from 6:00 AM until midnight and were paid only three dollars a week. These conditions led to the spread of local unions, national unions composed of many local unions, and national federations composed of many national unions.

The Knights of Labor was a militant federation in the 1870s. The Knights of Labor expanded rapidly because of a major depression in 1873, combined with much police brutality toward strikers. After one strike in which police killed twenty men, women, and children, the *New York Tribune* applauded the police for attacking the strikers: "These brutal creatures can understand no other reasoning than that of force and enough of it to be remembered among them for generations" (quoted in Boyer and Morais, 1970, p. 69). Anyone could join the Knights, so the middle-class character of its leadership and much of its membership eventually turned it to the advocacy of currency reform and opposition to all strikes, which led to a rapid decline in membership.

The American Federation of Labor (AFL) was formed in the 1880s. At first it was quite militant and socialist-oriented. The preface to its first constitution stated: "A struggle is going on in the nations of the world between the oppressors and oppressed of all countries, a struggle between capital and labor which must grow in intensity from year to year and work disastrous results to the toiling millions of all nations if not combined for mutual protection and benefit" (quoted in Boyer and Morais, 1970, p. 90). But the AFL soon gave up the struggle between capital and labor. It became a "business union," which meant that it tried to win incremental wage increases, it paid no attention to larger issues, it had highly paid leaders with no militancy, and it tried hard to compromise with business.

The biggest and bloodiest strikes of this period were fought by unions that were independent of the AFL. For example, the American Railway Union struck the railroads in 1894, but was defeated with violence when the U.S. Army came in to move the trains on the excuse of "protecting the mail."

ENVIRONMENT, 1840–1900

In this period, industry grew rapidly, but there were very few environmental laws to restrain practices that harmed the environment. Since the side effects of business that harmed the environment did not lower profits, they were ignored by corporations. The land was harmed by mining and oil drilling with no worry about pollution. The tightly integrated ecology of plants and animals was harmed by cutting down forests and by killing whole species. The air was polluted by vast numbers of smoke-belching factories. Places like Pittsburgh became very unhealthy places to live. The lakes and rivers were contaminated by waste.

There was only a small environmental movement. The movement argued in favor of national parks against considerable resistance from businesses that wanted to use the areas to make profits. John Muir (1838–1914) spent his whole life working for the environment and started the modern environmental movement with his founding of the Sierra Club in 1892.

GOVERNMENT AND ECONOMIC DEVELOPMENT, 1865–1940

Chapter 6 discussed the fact that the U.S. government was generally dominated by the Southern slave owners until the election of Abraham Lincoln in 1860. We saw that the South then seceded from the United States and was defeated in a long and bloody war. The influence of Southern slave owners on the national government completely disappeared after the Civil War. In the South, however, the influence of the new class of landlords and money lenders continued to be supreme in that area. African-American sharecroppers and other poor farmers had almost no influence in the South after 1876, when the federal troops withdrew from the South.

The federal government was most strongly influenced by business interests, who spent money to pay lobbyists, to bribe legislators, and even to bribe the executive branch. Of course, many of the bribes were more subtle than direct exchange of money for a favor, consisting of campaign contributions. Only rarely, as in the farmer's protest votes of the populist period of the 1890s, did farmers and workers have some influence.

As a result, in this period government helped business as much as it could and often boasted about it. One senator was said to have given a speech to rich industrialists in which he said: you give us the money to get elected and we give you the laws and subsidies you need. Even when popular pressure forced the passage of an antimonopoly law in 1890, it was so filled with loopholes as to have little effect. Government was also used to attack anyone with thoughts that were considered dangerous. College professors who advocated Darwin's theory of evolution were fired by many colleges in the late nineteenth century. Any college professor who was critical of business might also be fired.

THE UNITED STATES AND COLONIALISM, 1865–1900

Before the Civil War, the U.S. economy was much weaker than the British, so it remained in a neocolonial relation to England. The term "neocolonial" means a pattern where the stronger country sells mostly finished goods to the weaker country, while the weaker country sells only raw materials and agricultural goods to the stronger country. It also means that the stronger country invests in the weaker one, while receiving profits and interest that are larger than the annual new investment.

England established the largest colonial empire because it reached the stage of industrial capitalism first, so it had the greatest economic strength. As each European power became an industrial capitalist nation, each tried to catch up with the British in the extent of their colonies, but none ever succeeded, though they fought wars to do so.

After the Civil War, U.S. industry grew rapidly and the relationship with England began to change. Eventually, the U.S. economy began to compare in strength to the British and the two were on a more equal basis. For example, before the Civil War, the U.S. economy slavishly followed every boom and bust of the British economy with a short time lag. After the Civil War, the U.S. and British economies still moved together, but they each played the leader at different times.

As the U.S. economy became stronger, it followed the European example by trying to get its own colonies. It did expand to the Pacific by a war with Mexico in the 1840s, but it was too late to get many external colonies by the time it was strong enough to do it. In 1898, when the United States defeated Spain, Cuba became formally independent, but was a neocolony of the United States. The U.S. Army also took over the Spanish colony of the Philippines against fierce Filipino resistance. Another Spanish colony, Puerto Rico remained a colony of the United States until acquiring commonwealth status in 1952. (Two other U.S. territories—Alaska, purchased in 1867, and Hawaii, annexed in 1898—were eventually incorporated into the United States.) Most important, however, was the fact that, as the Latin American countries liberated themselves from Spain and Portugal, the United States declared that other powers must stay out of Latin America while U.S. influence moved into Latin America.

The United States had to settle for the Philippines, part of Panama, Puerto Rico, and a base in Cuba. When the Latin American countries gained their freedom from Spain and Portugal, however, corporations from the United States moved in to dominate their economies in most cases. The United States then told the European powers to keep their hands off Latin America while U.S. domination slowly became stronger and stronger.

SUMMARY

In the period after the Civil War, the United States had an industrial revolution, which had only barely begun before the war. Industry spread from the Northeast throughout the Midwest and the West, but very little penetrated the South because of its leftover heritage from slavery. In addition to industrial growth, cities grew and people moved from the countryside to cities.

Firms grew very fast and some became giants. Many industries had only a few very large firms in control of a majority of sales so there was a growth of monopoly power. The organization of firms changed from one-person ownership to corporations, thus allowing a great deal of capital to come together in an efficient manner with less risk to investors (since creditors could only take corporate assets, not the assets of individual investors). Women struggled hard and gained many new rights, but could not yet vote. African-Americans were held back and limited to sharecropping and poverty in the South. In the 1890s, the United States started its first colonial ventures in the Philippines, Puerto Rico, and Cuba. On a global scale, this was the period when the European powers completed the spread of their empires over most of the world.

SUGGESTED READINGS

Several of the best suggested readings for this chapter are the same as they were for Chapter 5, including DuBoff, Deckard, Flexner, Reich, Zinn, Ambrose, Chernow, Foster, Foner, and Boyer and Morais.

By far the best book to start reading on the sharecropping period is Roger Ransom and Richard Sutch, *One Kind of Freedom: The Economic Consequences of Emancipation* (1977). A book that is powerful and wonderful to read on the peculiar twists in the politics of racism in the South after the Civil War is by C. Vann Woodward, *The Strange Career of Jim Crow* (1974). An excellent general history of the reconstruction period is Eric Foner (1988).

KEY TERMS

collusion   sharecropper
grassroots   trust
gross private investment

REVIEW QUESTIONS

Explain the reasons for the progression from a world of small competitive businesses to a climate controlled by monopolistic giants.
 1. List and explain three to four reasons for the shift from an agricultural based state to a capitalist one. How did the use of railroads affect national economic growth?
 2. How did the larger size of firms help to increase productivity?
 3. What factors in the economic, social, and political atmosphere were conducive to the formation of monopolies? Give at least three examples from the reading.

Identify the questionable behavior of the entrepreneurs of this age and explain how industrial warfare affected the political and social atmosphere.
 4. Name a few methods used by the robber barons to create monopolies (industrial warfare). How did railroads have an effect on the growth of cities? How did they abuse this power?
 5. Describe the relationship of many of the large banks and the robber barons. Describe the relationship of many of the large banks and the government.
 6. How did government regulation actually help business achieve greater profits? Which group did the Sherman Antitrust Act have the biggest effect on? Explain.
 7. Explain how industrial warfare affected the political and social atmosphere of the time.

Explain the role of women and African-Americans, conditions for workers, and the environmental impact during this period of time.
 8. Explain the economic, social, and political situation most African-Americans were in after being freed from slavery
 9. How were worker strikes usually resolved? Through negotiation or other means? Which group in society was behind this?
 10. How did women's roles change during this period? Why did this lead to a greater interest in equal rights?
 11. Did African-Americans receive any compensation from the government after being freed

for their years of oppression? What job(s) were they forced to work in? Name two other minority groups and explain how they were also discriminated against.

12. How did the system of sharecropping inhibit the growth of technology? How did it strip the incentives from both landowners and sharecroppers?

13. How did entrepreneurs treat the environment? Why was there no incentive or government regulation designed to protect it?

Describe the changing relationship with Britain during this period and the move toward colonialism.

14. Before the late 1800s, what would happen to the U.S. economy if Britain's economy went into a recession?

15. As the U.S. economy became stronger, what part of the world did it began to exert its influence upon through colonialism?

APPENDIX 11.1
SOCIALIST CRITIQUE OF CORPORATE CAPITALISM, 1865–1900

After the death of Marx in 1883, the socialist movement continued to spread across Western Europe. The strongest socialist party was the German Social Democrats. The leader of the Social Democrats and the head of its centrist faction was Karl Kautsky (1854–1938). He wrote on every subject from women's issues to colonialism. In every case he expanded on Marx and gave a more systematic view of the Marxist position. He argued that socialists should try to get a majority and he thought it possible because the party's votes were rapidly rising in Germany. As soon as they had a majority in parliament, they should change the economic system to socialism. His vision of socialism was ownership of the whole economy by the public rather than by private capitalists. He considered private capitalists organized in corporate capitalism to be robbers who take money away from the workers in the form of profits. He was opposed to colonialism by Germany or anybody else.

The rightwing faction of the German Social Democrats was led by Eduard Bernstein (1850–1932). Bernstein became famous by arguing that any dramatic, revolutionary change to socialism is impossible and arguing in favor of what he called evolutionary socialism. By evolutionary socialism he meant that the party should work for very small reforms one after the other (see Bernstein, 1961 [1899]). After a very long time, the small reforms would add up to socialism. The important thing was to be on the right road in a realistic manner, even if it took hundreds of years to arrive at full socialism.

One of the best-known leaders of the leftwing of the German Social Democrats was Rosa Luxemburg (c.1870–1919). She was from a Jewish family in Poland at a time when Germans did not like Jews or Poles. She became very prominent and influential, even though there were also German male leaders on the left as well. She argued for a socialist revolution with fiery rhetoric. She was most famous for her theory that the imperialist powers of Europe were taking over the rest of the world as colonies (see Luxemburg, 1964 [1898]). She went beyond other current theories of imperialism because she argued that this colonial expansionism was driven by the need for markets. The home market of each imperialist country was limited because the wages of workers were very limited, so their consuming power was also limited. Each new colony gave the imperialist power a new market for selling its goods, while getting cheap raw materials from the conquered colony.

But when all the world was conquered by the leading capitalist nations, there would be no more new markets. At that point capitalist profits would decline, permanent depression would ensue, and there would be a socialist revolution.

These issues were debated throughout the twentieth century and led to many fights between parties and between factions of parties—as will be seen in later chapters. The books by Luxemburg (1964) and Bernstein (1961) still make exciting reading.

CHAPTER 12

Neoclassical Economics
Defense of Corporate Capitalism

The period from the mid-1840s to the early 1870s has been called the golden age of competitive capitalism (Dillard, p. 363). These were years of rapid economic expansion throughout continental Europe and especially in England. They were also years in which many individual capitalist enterprises were replaced by corporations that grew to be giants by the end of the century. Industry in the United States began growing by the 1840s, and then grew very rapidly after the Civil War. The merger movement produced the first giant U.S. corporations by the end of the century. Both in Europe and the United States, the distribution of income among individuals also grew more unequal, with a small group of very rich families, a significant middle class, and a large number of laborers working for very low wages.

LEARNING OBJECTIVES

After reading this chapter, you should be able to:

- Summarize neoclassical ideology with respect to production, consumption, and government intervention.
- List and explain the five modifications made to neoclassical thought by subsequent generations.
- Articulate the major tenets of the new Christian paternalist ethic.
- Explain the concept of social Darwinism.

REEMERGENCE OF THE CLASSICAL LIBERAL IDEOLOGY

With the immense concentration of economic power in the hands of a small number of giant firms and a small percentage of the population, it would seem that the classical liberal ideology of capitalism would have been abandoned. Classical liberalism, as developed by Adam Smith and refined by such well-known classical economists as David Ricardo, Nassau Senior (1790–1864), and Jean-Baptiste Say (1767–1832), was based on an analysis of an economy composed of many small enterprises. In such an economy, no individual enterprise could exercise a significant influence on the market price or on the total amount sold in the market. The actions of any firm were dictated to it by consumer tastes through demand in the market, and by the competition of innumerable other small firms, each vying for the consumer's dollars.

As wide as the gulf between classical economic theory and late nineteenth-century economic reality seems to have been, classical liberalism did not fall by the wayside in this later period. Rather, it was combined with Benthamite utilitarianism and refurbished within an elaborate framework of algebra and calculus. This resurgence of the classical liberalism was accomplished by a new school of economic thinkers known as neoclassical economists.

THE NEOCLASSICAL THEORY OF UTILITY AND CONSUMPTION

During the early 1870s, at precisely the time when the drive toward the economic concentration of corporate capitalism was taking place, three very famous economics texts were published. William Stanley Jevons (1835–1882) published *The Theory of Political Economy* in 1871 in English. Carl Menger (1840–1921) published *Foundations of Economic Science* in 1871 in German. Léon Walras (1834–1910) published *Elements of Political Economy* in 1874 in French. Although there were many differences among the analyses of these men, the similarities in both approach and content of these books were striking.

Their theories pictured an economy composed of large numbers of small producers and consumers, each having insufficient power to influence the market significantly. The business firms hired or bought factors of production. Firms utilized the factors in the production process in such a way that their profits were maximized. Prices of the final products and factors of production were taken by the firms as given by the market and beyond their control. The firms could control only the productive process chosen and the amount produced.

Households likewise sold their land and capital, as well as their labor, at prices determined in the market and used the receipts (their incomes) to buy goods and services. Consumers divided their income among the various commodities they wished to purchase in a way that maximized the utility they received from these commodities.

Commodities were the ultimate source of *pleasure* or **utility**, and the utility they yielded was assumed to be quantifiable. Jevons wrote, "A unit of pleasure or pain is difficult even to conceive; but it is the amount of these feelings which is continually prompting us to buying and selling, borrowing and lending, laboring and resting, producing and consuming; and it is from the quantitative effects of the feelings that we must estimate their comparative amounts" (Jevons, p. 11). Walras was less ambiguous in arguing that utility was quantifiable: "I shall, therefore, assume the existence of a standard measure of intensity of wants or intensive utility, which is applicable not only to similar units of the same kind of wealth but also to different units of various kinds of wealth" (Walras, p. 117).

These economists, having assumed quantifiable magnitudes with which to work, next set up general mathematical formulas purporting to show a functional relationship between the utility a consumer received and the amounts of the various commodities he or she consumed. The problem then was to show how the consumer could get the maximum utility, given his or her income and the commodity prices prevailing in the market.

Consumers maximized utility when the increase in utility derived from the last unit consumed, expressed as a ratio over the price of that commodity, was an equal proportion for all commodities. In other words, the last dollar spent on a commodity should yield the same increase in the utility derived by the consumer as the last dollar spent on any other commodity. Jevons explained the same thing in a different way, stating that the consumer maximized utility because he or she "procures such quantities of commodities that the final degrees of utility of any pair of commodities are inversely as the ratios of exchange [prices] of the commodities" (Jevons, p. 139).

Suppose there was a free market in which consumers could freely exchange their incomes for commodities. They would be led by their self-interest to maximize utility. Therefore, it was concluded that consumers distributed their income among purchases of commodities in such a way that the welfare of all would be maximized, given the existing distribution of wealth and income.

THE NEOCLASSICAL THEORY OF PRODUCTION

In neoclassical production theory, the analysis of the firm, or producers, was perfectly symmetrical with the analysis of consumer behavior. In order to maximize profits, the firm would operate at its highest efficiency and hence produce at the lowest possible cost. It purchased factors of production (such as labor) until the amount added to production by the last unit of each factor of production, expressed as a ratio over the price of the factor, was an equal proportion for all factors. The last dollar spent on each factor should yield the same increase in production from all factors. In a free market, firms would always attempt to maximize efficiency in order to maximize profits. Therefore, this condition would always hold. Thus, the factors of production would all be used in such a way that no possible reorganization of production (given the existing technology) could result in a more efficient use of the factors of production.

LAISSEZ-FAIRE

The neoclassical economists gave a very elaborate and analytic defense of Adam Smith's notion of the invisible hand of market competition and the economic policy of laissez-faire. They showed that in a competitive market economy made up of innumerable small producers and consumers, the market would guide the consumers in such a way that they would end up with an optimal mix of commodities, given their income and wealth. Factors of production would be used in the most efficient way possible. Moreover, commodities would be produced in amounts that would maximize the value of society's production. This optimal result depended, however, on a minimum of interference by government in the processes of the free market.

They recognized that this result was optimal if one accepted the existing distribution of income. Some (particularly the American economist John Bates Clark [1847–1938]) tried to defend the distribution of income in a free-market economy. They argued that the principles of profit maximization would lead to a situation in which each category of productive factors would be paid an amount equal to the value of its marginal contribution to the productive process. This seemed to them a model of distributive justice, with each unit of the productive factors being paid an amount equal to what it produced. Critics were quick to point out, however, that units of productive factors were not people (at least as far as land, natural resources, and capital were concerned). In order for such a system to be fair, these critics insisted, an equitable distribution of ownership of the factors of production would be necessary.

In the 1890s, Alfred Marshall (1842–1924) synthesized all of the different currents in neoclassical economics into a masterful analysis. It did not change the principles of the three founders of neoclassical economics, but it did state the whole argument very clearly in a unified way. He particularly emphasized that one must consider both supply and demand and showed how they fit together. His book, *Principles of Economics* (1890) was so clear and systematic that it became the leading textbook in economics for the next three decades.

In spite of much criticism of its basic approach, the neoclassical economists did succeed in erecting an impressive intellectual defense of the classical liberal policy of laissez-faire. They did it by creating a giant chasm between economic theory and economic reality. From the 1870s until today, many economists in the neoclassical tradition have abandoned any real concern with existing economic institutions and problems. Instead, many of them focus on mathematical model building and constructing endless variations on esoteric trivia.

SUBSEQUENT MODIFICATIONS OF NEOCLASSICAL THEORY

Some economists in the second and third generations of neoclassical analysis recognized the need to make the theory more realistic. The economic system was not characterized by "perfect competition." The principal admitted weaknesses were as follows:

1. Some buyers and sellers were large enough to affect prices; moreover, the economics of large-scale production seemed to make this inevitable.
2. Some commodities should be "consumed socially," and their production and sale might never be profitable in a laissez-faire capitalist economy, even though they might be deemed highly desirable by most citizens (e.g., roads, schools, or armies).
3. The costs to the producer of a commodity (such as automobiles) might differ significantly from the social costs (such as smog) of producing that commodity. In such a case it was possible that for society as a whole the costs of production might exceed the benefits of production for the commodity, even though the producer still profited from making and selling it. For example, consider the poisoning of the water and air by producers making profits but doing little or nothing about the pollution, even though its side effects could endanger human life itself.
4. An unrestrained free-market capitalist system appeared to be quite unstable. Capitalism was subject to recurring depressions that incurred enormous social waste.
5. The free-market, capitalist economy always resulted in massive inequalities of income. Those at the bottom of the income distribution were unable to live even at a subsistence standard. Those at the top enjoyed colossal incomes, often hundreds of times higher than an ordinary person would spend on consumption.

It was generally agreed that such flaws did exist and did disrupt the otherwise beneficial workings of the capitalist system. These problems, however, could be corrected only by some amount of government intervention in the market system. Government antitrust actions, it was argued, could force giant firms to act as if they were competitive, and something called "workable competition" could be achieved.

Roads, schools, armies, and other socially consumed commodities could be provided by the government. Extensive systems of special taxes and subsidies could be used to equate private and social costs in cases where they differed. It was also believed, especially after the Great Depression of the 1930s, that through wise use of fiscal and monetary policy the government could eliminate the instability of the system. (This is discussed in detail in Part II of this book.) Finally, through taxes and welfare programs the government could mitigate the unacceptable extremes of the income distribution. (This is discussed in detail in Part III of this book.)

The flaws in the system were thus seen as minor and ephemeral. An enlightened government could correct them and free the invisible hand once again to create the best of all possible worlds. There did develop, however, an inability to agree on the extent and significance of the flaws. Those who believe them to be fairly widespread and quite significant have, during the course of the twentieth century and into the twenty-first, become known as liberals. They have sometimes advocated fairly extensive government intervention in the economic system. Yet most liberal neoclassical economists have continued to use neoclassical economic theory as an ideology to defend the private-ownership, capitalist market economic system.

Economists who see the flaws as minor and unimportant continue to advocate a minimum of government intervention in the market economy. Despite the fact that the laissez-faire policies advocated by these economists have been much closer to those advocated by the nineteenth-century classical liberals, they became known in the twentieth century as conservatives. Both liberals and conservatives, as we have described them here, have used neoclassical economic theory to justify the capitalist system. They differ as to whether it should be reformed.

LAISSEZ-FAIRE AND THE SOCIAL DARWINISTS

Before we leave the topic of late nineteenth- and early twentieth-century advocates of laissez-faire capitalism, a brief discussion of social Darwinism is necessary. Social Darwinists believed that the government should allow capitalists to compete freely in the marketplace with a minimum of government restrictions and, in general, favored as little government intervention as possible in all spheres of life. Therefore, many people have imagined their defense of laissez-faire capitalism to be similar to that of the neoclassical economists. This is not so. The social Darwinists' policy recommendations were based on a substantially different theoretical framework.

The social Darwinists took Charles Darwin's theory of evolution and extended it to a theory of social evolution (in a manner that Darwin himself strongly disapproved of, it may be added). Competition, they believed, was a **teleological** process, where *events are guided by natural and mechanical forces, towards a final outcome in which each succeeding generation was superior to the preceding one*. This upward progress was made possible because those least fit to survive did not succeed in maintaining themselves and procreating. Greater ability to survive was equated with a biological as well as a moral superiority.

Herbert Spencer (1820–1903), the father of social Darwinism, based his evolutionary as well as his moral theory on what he called the law of conduct and consequence. He believed survival of the human species could be ensured only if society distributed its benefits in proportion to a person's merit, measured by his or her power to be self-sustaining. One ought to reap the benefits or suffer the evil results of one's own actions. Thus, the people most adapted to their environment would prosper, and those least adapted would be weeded out, assuming that the laws of conduct and consequence were observed. If the government, wishing to mitigate inequalities of wealth and income in society, took "from him who . . . prospered to give to him who . . . [had] not, it [violated] its duty towards the one to do more than its duty towards the other" (quoted in Fine, p. 38). This type of action slowed social progress and could, if carried to excess, destroy the human species. Survival and progress could be ensured only if the weak were weeded out and destroyed by the impersonal forces of social evolution.

In Spencer's opinion, "The poverty of the incapable, the distresses that come upon the imprudent, the starvation of the idle and those shouldering aside of the weak by the strong . . . are the decrees of a large, far-seeing benevolence" (ibid., p. 38). Spencer categorically opposed any action by the government that interfered with trade, commerce, production, or the distribution of wealth or income. He rejected welfare payments of any kind, attempts to decrease the economic insecurity of workers, and government provision of schools, parks, or libraries as detrimental to human progress. His laissez-faire was thus much more extreme than that of the classical economists or most of the conservative neoclassical economists.

Social Darwinists accepted the large monopolistic and oligopolistic industries as the beneficent result of evolution. Neoclassical economists, if they did not simply define away or ignore the concentrations of economic power, believed government should attempt to create a more competitive and atomistic market situation. In this very important respect the two theories were thus quite antagonistic.

LAISSEZ-FAIRE AND THE IDEOLOGY OF BUSINESSMEN

Most businessmen, however, were not very concerned with intellectual inconsistency. They feared radical and socialist reformers who wanted to use the government as a means of achieving greater equality, and they welcomed any theory that concluded that the government should not intervene in the economic process. Even though they themselves used the government to promote their own interests (through special tariffs, tax concessions, land grants, and a host of other special privileges), they relied on laissez-faire arguments when threatened with any social reform that might erode their status, wealth, or income. Thus, in the ordinary businessman's ideology of the late nineteenth and early twentieth centuries, there was a general attempt to combine neoclassical economics and social Darwinism.

In this ideology, the accumulation of wealth was considered visible proof of evolutionary superiority, whereas poverty was believed to be evidence of evolutionary inferiority. Success, asserted writer Benjamin Woods, was "nothing more or less than doing thoroughly what others did indifferently." Andrew Carnegie equated success with "honest work, ability and concentration"; another businessman argued that "wealth has always been the natural sequence to industry, temperance, and perseverance, and it will always so continue." At the same time, S.C.T. Dodd, solicitor for Standard Oil, maintained that poverty existed "because nature or the devil has made some men weak and imbecile and others lazy and worthless, and neither man nor God can do much for one who will do nothing for himself." (These quotations are all cited in Fine, p. 98.) The beneficial results of competition in neoclassical economic theory seemed to reinforce reliance on the "survival of the fittest" in the "struggle for survival." "Competition in economics," asserted Richard R. Bowker, "is the same as the law of . . . 'natural selection' in nature" (ibid., p. 100).

Although some businessmen and their spokesmen were trying to perpetuate the laissez-faire conclusions of the classical liberal ideology of capitalism, many defenders of the capitalist system believed that in the new age of mass production (with gigantic concentrations of wealth and power in the hands of so few corporations and capitalists) the older, individualistic, laissez-faire ideology was no longer appropriate. The late nineteenth century witnessed a rebirth of the older paternalistic ethic. In the next section we examine a new ideology of capitalism that was based, in many essential respects, on a new version of the Christian paternalist ethic.

A NEW CHRISTIAN PATERNALIST ETHIC

The distance separating the neoclassical liberal ideology of capitalism and economic reality impressed itself on the minds of many academicians and businessmen. The result was a new ideology for the new age of corporate capitalism. Just as the new industrial and financial entrepreneurs ("robber barons") came to resemble the feudal barons, so the new ideology resembled the feudal version of the Christian paternalist ethic. It emphasized the natural superiority of a small elite, the new industrial and financial magnates, and the paternalistic functions of that elite in caring for the masses.

The new ideology reflected the fact that many of the wealthy capitalists of the era were becoming something of folk heroes among the general public. The last two decades of the nineteenth century and the first three of the twentieth were an age during which businessmen became the most admired social group. The success of businessmen was viewed as evidence that they possessed virtues superior to those of the ordinary person. This version of success was the theme of the biographies of William Makepeace Thackeray (1811–1863) and the novels of Horatio Alger (1832–1899). These men and other writers created a cult of success that viewed the increase of industrial concentration as proof of Darwinian superiority on the part of the industrialists, glorified the self-made individual, and kept the rags-to-riches myth constantly in the public mind.

The veneration of businessmen, added to the strong rejection of destructive competition by both businessmen and the general public led to a new conservative version of the Christian paternalist ethic, which resembled the philosophy of the Tory radicals of the late eighteenth and early nineteenth centuries. The unfortunate plight of the poor received prominent mention in the new writings. This problem, as well as that of economic instability, could best be solved, according to the new ideology, by encouraging cooperation among the leaders of the giant corporations. Competition was viewed as antisocial. Through cooperation, business cycles could be eliminated and the plight of the poor improved.

This new version of the Christian paternalist ethic received the support of Pope Leo XIII (1810–1903). Between 1878 and 1901, the pope sought to analyze the problems of corporate capitalism and to suggest remedies in a series of **encyclicals** or *letters from the pope intended for wide circulation*. In *Rerum Novarum* (1891) he argued that "a remedy must be found . . . or the misery and wretchedness which press so heavily at this moment on the large majority of the very poor." He continued with a condemnation of unrestrained laissez-faire competition:

> Working men have been given over, isolated and defenseless, to the callousness of employers and the greed of unrestrained competition. The evil has been increased by rapacious usury . . . still practiced by avaricious and grasping men. And to this must be added the custom of working by contract, and the concentration of so many branches of trade in the hands of a few individuals, so that a small number of very rich men have been able to lay upon the masses of the poor a yoke little better than slavery itself (quoted in Fusfeld, p. 86).

This passage, which sounds so socialist in tone and content, was followed by a strong condemnation of socialism and a defense of private property. The pope hoped the problems could be corrected by rejection of competition and a return to the Christian virtues of love and brotherhood, with the leaders of business and industry leading the way to a new Christian paternalism within the context of a private property capitalist system.

Although this ideology began in Europe, it thrived in the United States. U.S. society had an atmosphere that admired the successful businessman and was extremely weary of destructive competition. The view of many American industrial and financial magnates was expressed by Andrew Carnegie, one of the most successful of the magnates:

> Not evil, but good, has come to the race from the accumulation of wealth by those who have the ability and energy that produce it. . . . We have the true antidote for the temporary unequal distribution of wealth, the reconciliation of the rich and the poor—a reign of harmony—another ideal, differing, indeed, from that of the Communist in requiring only further evolution of existing conditions, not the total overthrow of our civilization. . . . Under its sway we shall have an ideal state, in which the surplus wealth of the few will become in the best sense, the property of the many, because administered for the common good, this wealth passing through the hands of the few can be made a more potent force for the elevation of our race than if it were distributed in sums to the people themselves (Carnegie, pp. 3, 5, 6).

Carnegie argued, and many businessmen and their spokesmen agreed, that the millionaire would be "a trustee for the poor, entrusted for a season with a great part of the increased wealth of the community, but administering it for the community far better than it could or would have done for itself" (Kennedy, p. xii).

The Right Reverend William Lawrence (1850–1941), the Episcopal Bishop of Massachusetts, gave the new elitist view the sanction of religion: "In the long run, it is only to the man of morality that wealth comes. . . . Godliness is in league with riches." Railroad president George F. Baer (1842–1914) had the same idea in mind when he tried to assure railroad workers that "the rights and the interests of the laboring man will be protected and cared for, not by the labor agitators, but by the Christian men to whom God, in his infinite wisdom, has given control of the property interests of the country" (ibid.).

SIMON PATTEN'S ECONOMIC BASIS FOR THE NEW ETHIC

Perhaps the most influential academic spokesman for the new corporate ideology was Dr. Simon N. Patten (1852–1922), professor of economics at the University of Pennsylvania from 1888 to 1917 and one of the founders of the American Economic Association (see Hunt, 1970, pp. 38–55). In keeping with the paternalistic element of the new ideology, Patten denounced the poverty and economic exploitation of his era. The following passage could almost have been written by a Marxist of that era:

> There have flowed then, side by side, two streams of life, one bearing the working poor, who perpetuate themselves through qualities generated by the stress and mutual dependence of the primitive world, and the other bearing aristocracies, who dominate by means of the laws and traditions giving them control of the social surplus (Patten, 1907, p. 39).

In the same vein, fifteen years later, he wrote:

> The glow of Fifth Avenue is but the reflection of a distant hell into which unwilling victims are cast. Some resource is misused, some town degraded, to create the flow of funds on which our magnates thrive. From Pennsylvania, rich in resources, trains go loaded and come back empty. For the better half no return is made except in literary times designed to convince the recipients that exploitation is not robbery. . . . But Nature revolts! Never does the rising sun see children yanked from bed to increase the great Strauss dividends, nor the veteran cripples of the steel mill tramping in their beggar garb, but that it shrivels, reddens, and would strike but for the sight of happier regions beyond (ibid., 1922, p. 226).

This poverty and exploitation were, in Patten's opinion, the last remnants of an earlier age characterized by scarcity. In the economy of scarcity, capitalists competed aggressively with each other, with the result that laborers as well as the general public suffered. The fierce competition of the robber barons, however, had marked a watershed in history. The merger movement that followed this competition was the beginning of a new era, an era of plenty rather than scarcity. Capitalists were becoming socialized. They were putting the public welfare ahead of their pursuit of profits, and in doing this they eschewed competition, recognizing that the public welfare could best be promoted by cooperation. (Of course we have seen that capitalists cooperated with each other mostly to squeeze more profit from the public.)

Evidence that the conditions of economic prosperity at the turn of the century were socializing capitalists could be seen in the fact that "hospitals . . . [were] established, schools . . . [were] made free, colleges . . . [were] endowed, museums, libraries, and art galleries . . . [received] liberal support, church funds . . . [grew] and missions . . . [were] formed at home and abroad" (Ibid., 1902, p. 170). On almost every policy issue of his day, Patten took a strongly pro-industrial capitalist position. He viewed the late nineteenth-century captains of industry as a paternally beneficent elite:

> The growth of large-scale capitalism has resulted in the elimination of the unsocial capitalist and the increasing control of each industry by the socialized groups. . . . At bottom altruistic sentiment is the feeling of a capitalist expressing himself in sympathy for the laborer. This desire of upper class men to improve the conditions of lower classes is a radically different phenomenon from the pressure exerted by the lower classes for their own betterment. The lower class movement stands for the control of the state by themselves in their own interests. The upper class movement directs itself against the bad environmental conditions preventing the expression of character (ibid., 1924, p. 292).

Patten believed competition should be discouraged by taxing competitive firms and exempting trusts and monopolies from these taxes. This would benefit all society by eliminating the extensive waste created by competition. In *The Stability of Prices*, he argued that competition was largely responsible for the economic instability of the late nineteenth century. When the movement toward trusts and monopolies had been completed, production would be controlled and planned in such a way that this instability would be eliminated.

Patten's paternalistic ideology was, like the liberal ideology of capitalism, ultimately a plea for a minimum of government interference with the actions of businessmen. The government was to interfere in the economy only by encouraging trusts and monopolies and discouraging competition. In Patten's scheme, all important social and economic reforms were to be carried out voluntarily by the socialized capitalists in a system of cooperative corporate collectivism.

SUMMARY

In the late nineteenth century, capitalism was characterized by the growth of giant corporations. Control of most of the important industries became more and more concentrated. Accompanying this concentration of industry was an equally striking concentration of income in the hands of a small percentage of the population.

The classical liberal ideology used an analysis based on an economy with many small, relatively powerless enterprises. In light of the facts of the corporate economy discussed above, it would appear that it would have had to be abandoned. The gulf that separated the theory from reality had widened into a giant chasm. But the idea that the market economy channeled acquisitive profit seeking into socially benevolent practices was simply an elegant apologia for unrestrained profit-making activity.

Using new arguments, the classical liberal ideology of capitalism was assiduously disseminated in a new school of neoclassical economics. An elaborate deductive theory permitted the neoclassical economists to defend the classical policy prescription of laissez-faire. Conservative neoclassical economists assigned to the government only the tasks that would directly or indirectly promote business profits. Liberal neoclassical economists also believed the government should enter a limited number of other areas in which the operation of the free market did not maximize the social welfare. Whether in the hands of the conservative or the liberal faction, neoclassical economics remained essentially an ideological defense for the status quo.

Social Darwinist ideology and the ideology of most businessmen defended many of the neoclassical economists' conclusions. They did so, however, on entirely different grounds. They accepted the fact that corporate power, personal wealth, and personal income were highly concentrated. This, they believed, was evidence of the evolutionary superiority of the wealthy and, as such, was socially beneficial.

During this period, however, many ideologists of capitalism rejected classical liberalism because of its unrealistic assumptions. These thinkers created a new version of the Christian paternalist ethic that pictured capitalists as beneficent, fatherly protectors of the public welfare. This new ethic was to become particularly influential in the social and economic legislation of the early New Deal in the 1930s.

SUGGESTED READINGS

The best critical explanation and critique of the rise of neoclassical economics is by John Henry, *The Making of Neoclassical Economics* (1990). The views of Alfred Marshall and the second generation of neoclassical economists are discussed in detail in E.K. Hunt, *History of Economic Thought* (2002).

KEY TERMS

encyclical
teleological
utility

REVIEW QUESTIONS

Summarize neoclassical ideology with respect to production, consumption, and government intervention.
1. What is the difference between competitive and corporate capitalism?
2. Explain the theory of consumer utility. Do you see any problems with quantifying pleasure? How does this theory relate to businesses?
3. Exactly how much pleasure or utility do you receive from eating a banana? A second banana?
4. How was the neoclassical view of the economy, i.e. small firms with no pricing power, inconsistent with reality?

List and explain the five modifications made to neoclassical thought by subsequent generations.
5. Discuss what problems each of the five modifications means to a competitive market outcome.

Explain the concept of social Darwinism and its relationship to laissez-faire policies.
6. Compare and contrast laissez-faire to social Darwinism. Specifically, how did these two views support the existence of income inequality? Why were some people poor while others were rich?
7. Why was the idea of laissez-faire championed by the business elite? What special privileges did the government already give to these businessmen?
8. Does the present government of the United States have a laissez-faire policy?

Articulate the major ideas of the new Christian paternalist ethic.

9. How did the new Christian paternalistic ethic support the wealthy capitalists? How did it differ from the feudalistic version?

10. According to Patten, why is competition harmful?

APPENDIX 12.1
THE NEW PATERNALISM AND THE NEW DEAL

Patten's version of the new ideology of corporate capitalism was to be very important histori-cally. During the Great Depression, two of Patten's students and devotees, Rexford Guy Tugwell (1891–1979) and Frances Perkins (1882–1965), had influential positions as members of Franklin D. Roosevelt's original cabinet. (For a more complete discussion of the material covered in this section, see Hunt, 1971, pp. 180–192.) Tugwell had asserted that Patten's views "were the greatest single influence on my thought. Neither Veblen nor Dewey found their orientation to the future as completely and instinctively as did Patten. The magnificence of his conceptions and the basic rightness of his vision become clearer as time passes. I am eternally grateful to him." (quoted in Cruelly, p. 408). Perkins believed her former teacher to be "one of the greatest men America has ever produced" (quoted in Schlesinger, 1965, p. 229).

Through these two former students, Patten exerted a considerable influence on the economic policies of the early phase of the New Deal. His ideas helped create the intellectual basis of the National Industrial Recovery Act (NIRA) of 1933 (ibid., p. 98). Patten was not, of course, the only source of these ideas. During World War I, the War Industries Board had generated enthusiasm for corporate rate collectivism. Throughout the 1920s, trade associations prospered and the doctrine of business self-government gained many adherents in the business world. In 1922, Franklin Roosevelt was president of one such association, the American Construction Council. However, Patten's teachings were unquestionably influential. His protégés Tugwell and Perkins were both instrumental in the actual framing of the NIRA.

The NIRA proclaimed the intent of Congress "to promote the organization of industry for the purpose of cooperative action among trade groups" (quoted in ibid., pp. 98–99). The bill contained sections providing for codes of fair competition that permitted and even encouraged cooperative price fixing and market sharing and for virtually complete exemption from antitrust laws. Section 7A was designed to promote labor organization but was so diluted that very often it promoted the formation of company unions. "If it [the NIRA] worked," Tugwell thought, "each industry would end with a government of its own under which it could promote its fundamental purpose ('production rather than competition')." The NIRA could have been administered, Tugwell later wrote, "so that a 'great collectivism' would have channeled American energy into a disciplined national effort to establish a secure basis for well-being" (ibid., p. 108).

In explaining the bill to the National Association of Manufacturers, General Hugh S. Johnson (1882–1942), the first head of the National Recovery Administration (NRA), declared that "NRA is exactly what industry organized in trade associations make it." He further asserted that before the NRA, the trade associations had about as much effectiveness as an "Old Ladies' Knitting Society; now I am talking to a cluster of formerly emasculated trade associations about a law which proposes for the first time to give them power" (quoted in ibid., p. 110).

Most of the economics literature that appeared in 1934 recognized that the early New Deal reforms had not significantly extended government control over business. On the contrary, it had given voluntary trade associations the support of the government in forcing the controls of trade associations on all industry (see Rogin, pp. 338, 346, 349–355).

This experiment in business self-government proved disastrous. The distinguished historian Arthur M. Schlesinger, Jr. (1917–2007), assessed the success of this phase of the early New Deal. With Schlesinger we concur:

> And the result of business self-government? Restriction on production, chiseling of labor and of 7A, squeezing out of small business, savage personal criticism of the President, and the general tendency to trample down everyone in the rush for profits. Experience was teaching Roosevelt what instinct and doctrine had taught Jefferson and Jackson; that to reform capitalism you must fight the capitalists tooth and nail (Schlesinger, 1959, pp. 30–31).

The early New Deal philosophy underlying the NIRA was very quickly abandoned. The NIRA was declared unconstitutional by the Supreme Court. The new paternalistic ideology of capitalism, however, was to receive more elaborate statements after World War II.

CHAPTER 13

Veblen
Critique of Corporate Capitalism

In the late nineteenth century the potential profits made possible by mass production and nationwide markets led to intense industrial warfare. Through the crushing of competitors, and not infrequently the swindling of the general public, a handful of giant corporations came to dominate the American economy. The passage of the Sherman Antitrust Act and the establishment of various government regulatory agencies were aimed at controlling these giant corporations. In practice, however, government tended to aid these giants in consolidating and stabilizing their massive empires.

Thorstein Veblen's writings best reflect and describe the effects of this collusion of government and big business on the welfare of the general public. Veblen (1857–1929) stressed the distinction between **industry** (which *produces needed articles for human well-being*) and **business** (which *produces profits for the wealthy absentee owners and often sabotages industry*). He analyzed imperialism, militarism, and the general "chronic misery" caused by **emulative consumption**, *trying to equal or surpass the consumption of someone else,* sometimes known as "keeping up with the Joneses," in an acquisitive, competitive, capitalist society. The depth of many of Veblen's insights is unmatched in American intellectual history.

LEARNING OBJECTIVES

After reading this chapter, you should be able to:

- Describe and explain Veblen's view on the structure of capitalism.
- Understand Veblen's explanation of the role of government in capitalism.
- Explain Veblen's views on capitalist imperialism.
- Explain the concept of conspicuous consumption and how it was used by the leisure class to stay in power.

VEBLEN ON THE NEW STRUCTURE OF CAPITALISM

Chapter 11 discussed the early development of corporate capitalism and the greedy behavior of the robber barons. In its initial stages, the process of industrialization in the United States after the Civil War involved competition among industrial and financial capitalists that was unique in its ferocity. From 1860 until the early 1880s the strongest and shrewdest businessmen built great

143

empires with the fruits of economic conquest. The great improvements in transportation that occurred during this period, the rise of standardization in parts and finished products, and the increased efficiency in large-scale mass production created the possibility of nationwide markets. Giant corporations controlled markets by growth, collusion, or merger.

The huge size and collusion of the businesses in sectors where a few firms comprised most of the industry seemed to go unnoticed by neoclassical economists. They continued to frame their analyses in terms of innumerable small, competing business firms. Neoclassical economists also continued to accept the classical economists' view that as long as free competition prevails, the economy will tend toward full utilization of its productive capacity and full employment will be more or less continuous. During the second half of the nineteenth century, however, economic depressions became more frequent and more severe. During the second half of the century, there were depressions in the United States in 1854, 1857, 1873, 1884, and 1893.

Chapter 11 also showed that during the late nineteenth and early twentieth centuries, capitalism underwent an important and fundamental transformation. Although the foundations of the system—the laws of private property, the basic class structure, and the processes of commodity production and allocation through the market—remained unchanged, the era of small business as the dominant type of firm was ended and the main focus was on the large corporation with monopoly power.

From the standpoint of the giant corporations, their growth depended on organizational skills, cunning, business acumen, ruthlessness, and no small amount of luck. From the standpoint of society, however, the fortune of any particular capitalist was irrelevant. Accumulation was a relentless process that had momentum and patterns of development that were quite independent of the actions of any particular capitalist. Thus the late nineteenth century saw the accumulation process rationalized, regularized, and institutionalized in the form of the large corporation. Because of this structural change, a new managerial class became increasingly important.

Although the social, political, and economic dominance of the capitalist class remained unchanged, the institutionalization of the accumulation process within large corporations permitted the majority of capitalists to perpetuate their status through passive absentee ownership of corporate stock. A minority of capitalists engaged in managerial functions and acted as a kind of executive committee to protect the interests of the entire capitalist class. This committee performed its function by "managing the managers" of the new corporate structure. Meanwhile, some capitalists simply enjoyed lavish incomes derived from ownership alone.

In spite of these changes in economic organization and behavior, most economists clung to the model of an economy composed exclusively of millions of small businesses and ignored the structural changes. The economic writings that most completely reflected and described the institutional and cultural transformation of this period were those of Thorstein Veblen (1857–1929). Veblen was probably the most significant, original, and profound social theorist in American history.

Veblen taught at the University of Chicago and at Stanford University, and he was controversial at both institutions. He was attacked at Stanford for his opposition to U. S. participation in World War I. He wrote prolifically, publishing ten important books and innumerable articles and reviews in journals and periodicals. His great genius and unusual writing style make all of his works enormously enjoyable and intellectually valuable.

THE ANTAGONISTIC DICHOTOMY OF CAPITALISM

Veblen believed that there were two generally antagonistic clusters of behavioral traits. These traits were manifested in different historical eras through the social institutions and modes of behavior peculiar to those eras. Central to one of the clusters was Veblen's notion of the "**instinct of workman-ship**." The instinct of workmanship *stressed cooperation rather than competition, individual equality and independence rather than pervasive relations of subordination, logical social interrelationships rather than ceremonial role playing, and peaceable rather than predatory dispositions generally.* Associated with workmanship were traits that Veblen referred to as the "parental instinct" and the "instinct of idle curiosity." These traits were responsible for the advances that had been made in productivity and in the expansion of human mastery over nature. They were also responsible for the degree to which the human needs for affection, cooperation, and creativity were fulfilled.

Central to the other cluster was his notion of the instinct to exploit, or the "**predatory instinct**" which is *the admiration of predatory skills, acceptance of the hierarchy of subordination, and the widespread substitution of myth and ceremony for knowledge.* Associated with the exploitative or the predatory instinct were human conflict, subjugation, and sexual, racial, and class exploitation. Social institutions and habitual behavior often hid the true nature of exploitation and predatory behavior behind facades that Veblen referred to as "sportsmanship" and "ceremonialism."

The opposition of these two sets of behavioral traits led to social conflict. Veblen was primarily interested in analyzing the capitalist system of his era within the context of this social theory. Just as Marx in the mid-nineteenth century had taken England as the prototype of capitalist society, Veblen, writing during the last decade of the nineteenth and first quarter of the twentieth centuries, took the United States as his prototype. The central question for him was how these two antagonistic clusters of behavioral traits were manifested in and through the institutions of capitalism.

The question could be approached from several vantage points and Veblen used at least three. From a social psychological point of view, he pointed out individuals and classes whose behavior was dominated by the propensity to exploit, or the predatory instinct. On the opposite side, he investigated those whose behavior was dominated by the instinct of workmanship, the parental bent, and the development of idle curiosity. From the standpoint of economics, Veblen saw the same dichotomy. On one side were the forces that he referred to as "business" which he defined as grubbing for profit. On the other side were the forces that he referred to as "industry" which he defined as production of socially useful commodities. From the standpoint of sociology, the dichotomy was manifested in similar differences. On the one side was the "ceremonialism" and "sportsmanship" characteristic of the "leisure class." On the other side was the more creative and cooperative behavior characteristic of the "common man."

Each of these three levels of analysis tended to merge with the other two, for Veblen was in fact analyzing a society that was mainly constituted of two major classes. One class was the capitalists, whom he variously referred to as the "vested interest," the "absentee owners," the "leisure class," or the "captains of industry." The other class was the productive or working class, whom he variously referred to as the "engineers," the "workmen," and the "common man."

PRIVATE PROPERTY, CLASS-DIVIDED SOCIETY, AND CAPITALISM

At the foundation of this class structure was the institution of private property. In the earliest stages of human society, low productivity made a predominance of the instinct of workmanship a social prerequisite for survival. During this period, "The habits of life of the race were still perforce of a peaceful and industrial character, rather than contentious and destructive" (Veblen, 1964b, p. 86). During this early period, "before a predacious life became possible" and while society was still dominated by the instinct of workmanship, "Efficiency [or] serviceability commends itself, and inefficiency or futility is odious" (ibid., pp. 87, 89). In this type of society, property was social and not private.

Only after production became substantially more efficient and technical knowledge and tools were socially accumulated did predatory exploitation become possible. Distinctions likely to cause resentment among different members of society also became possible only at that point. With greater productivity, it became possible to live by brute seizure and predatory exploitation. "But seizure and forcible retention very shortly gain the legitimation of usage, and the resultant tenure becomes inviolable through habitation" (ibid., p. 43). In other words, private property came into existence.

Private property had its origins in brute force and was perpetuated both by force and by institutional and ideological legitimization. Class-divided societies inevitably came with the development of private property: "Where this tenure by prowess prevails, the population falls into two economic classes: those engaged in industrial employments, and those engaged in such non-industrial pursuits as war, government, sports, and religious observances" (ibid.).

Private property and the predatory instinct led to the predatory, class-divided societies of the slave and feudal eras. Capitalism was the outgrowth of feudalism in Western Europe. Whereas the predatory instinct totally dominated society in slavery and feudalism, in capitalism there had occurred an important, profound growth of the instinct of workmanship. Capitalism—or as Veblen sometimes referred to capitalism, "the regime of absentee ownership and hired labor"—had begun as a "quasi-peaceable" society in which the forces of workmanship had originally developed very rapidly. With the passage of time, however, the forces of workmanship and the predatory forces of exploitation had become locked in a struggle. This antagonism was expressed by Veblen as a conflict between "business" and "industry," or between "salesmanship" and "workmanship."

These two social forces were embodied in entirely different classes of people in capitalism. "The interest and attention of the two typical . . . classes . . . part company and enter on a course of progressive differentiation along two divergent lines" (ibid., 1964c, pp. 187–188). The first class embodied the instinct of workmanship or industry:

> The workman, laborers, operatives, technologists—whatever term may best designate that general category of human material through which the community's technological proficiency functions directly to an industrial effect—those who have to work, whereby they get their livelihood and their interest as well as the discipline of their workday life converges, in effect, on a technological apprehension of material facts (ibid., p. 188).

The second class embodied the predatory instinct, the business viewpoint, and salesmanship:

> These owners, investors, masters, employers, undertakers, businessmen, have to do with the negotiating of advantageous bargains. . . . The training afforded by these occupations and requisite to their effectual pursuit runs in terms of pecuniary management and insight, pecuniary gain, price, price-cost, price-profit, and priceloss; . . . that is to say in terms of the self-regarding propensities and sentiments (ibid., pp. 189–190).

While the essence of success for laborers involved workmanship or productive creativity, the essence of success for owners and businessmen involved exploitative advantage over others. Profit making, or business, created behavior that was totally removed from industry or workmanship. Increasingly, owners had less and less to do in the direction of production, which became entrusted to a "professional class of 'efficiency engineers'"(ibid., p. 22). But the concern of this new managerial class of efficiency engineers was never with productivity itself or with serviceability to the community at large. "The work of the efficiency engineers . . . [is] always done in the service of business . . . in terms of price and profits" (ibid., p. 224).

The nature of the control of business over industry was described by Veblen in one term: **sabotage**. Business sabotaged industry for the sake of profit. For Veblen, sabotage was defined as *"a conscientious withdrawal of efficiency."* For business owners, "a reasonable profit always means, in effect, the largest obtainable profit" (ibid., 1965a, pp. 1, 13). The problem in capitalism was that large-scale industry and the forces of workmanship were always increasing the quantity of output that could be produced with a given quantity of resources and workers. But given the existing, extremely unequal distribution of income, this added output could only be sold if prices were reduced substantially. Generally, the necessary price reductions were so great that selling a larger quantity at lower prices was less profitable than selling a lesser quantity at higher prices. Therefore, in modern capitalism:

> [there] is an ever increasing withdrawal of efficiency. The industrial plant is increasingly running idle or half idle, running increasingly short of its productive capacity. Workmen are being laid off. . . . And all the while these people are in great need of all sorts of goods and services which these idle plants and idle workmen are fit to produce. But for reasons of business expediency it is impossible to let these idle plants and idle workmen go to work—that is to say for reasons of insufficient profit to the business men interested, or in other words, for the reasons of insufficient income to the vested interests (ibid., 1965a, p. 12).

The normal state of modern capitalism, Veblen believed, was one of recurring depressions: "It may, therefore, be said, on the basis of this view, that chronic depression, more or less pronounced, is normal to business under the fully developed regimen of the machine industry" (ibid., 1965b, p. 234). Moreover, throughout the business cycle and at all times, capitalism necessarily involved a continuous class struggle between owners and workers:

> In the negotiations between owners and workmen there is little use for the ordinary blandishments of salesmanship. . . . And the bargaining between them therefore settles down without much circumlocution into a competitive use of unemployment, privation, restriction of work and output, strikes, shutdowns and lockouts, espionage, maneuvers, pickets, and similar maneuvers of mutual derangement, with a large recourse to menacing language and threats of mutual sabotage. The colloquial word for it is "labor troubles." The business relations between the two parties are of the nature of hostilities, suspended or active, conducted in terms of mutual sabotage; which will on occasion shift from the footing of such obstruction and disallowance as is wholly within the law and custom of business, from the footing of legitimate sabotage in the way of passive resistance and withholding of efficiency, to that illegitimate phase of sabotage that runs into violent offenses against person and property. The negotiations . . . have come to be spoken of habitually in terms of conflict, armed forces, and warlike strategy. It is a conflict of hostile forces which is conducted on the avowed strategic principle that either party stands to gain at the cost of the other (ibid., 1964a, pp. 406–407).

GOVERNMENT AND THE CLASS STRUGGLE

The ultimate power in the capitalist system was in the hands of the owners because they controlled the government, which was the institutionally legitimized means of physical coercion in any society. As such, the government existed to protect the existing social order and class structure. This meant that in capitalist society the primary duty of government was the enforcement of private property laws and the protection of the privileges associated with ownership. Veblen repeatedly insisted that: "modern politics is business politics. . . . This is true both of foreign and domestic policy. Legislation, police surveillance, the administration of justice, the military and diplomatic service, all are chiefly concerned with business relations, pecuniary interests, and they have little more than an incidental bearing on other human interests" (ibid., 1965b, p. 269).

The first principle of a capitalist government was that the "natural freedom of the individual must not traverse the prescriptive rights of property. Property rights . . . have the indefeasibility which attaches to natural rights." The principal freedom of capitalism was the freedom to buy and sell. The laissez-faire philosophy dictated that "so long as there is no overt attempt on life . . . or the liberty to buy and sell, the law cannot intervene, unless it be in a precautionary way to prevent prospective violation of . . . property rights." Above all else, therefore, a "constitutional government is a business government." (These quotations are all found in Veblen, 1965b, pp. 272, 278, 285).

Thus, in the ceaseless class struggle between workers and absentee owners, the owners have nearly always prevailed. Government, as the institutionally legitimized means of physical coercion or enforcement of the law, was firmly in their hands. Since workers greatly outnumbered owners, the maintenance of the owners' supremacy, the maintenance of the existing class structure of capitalism, depended on the absentee owner being in control of the government. At any point in the class struggle when the workers of a particular industry appeared to be getting the upper hand, the government was called in.

Whenever private property rights were threatened in any way, the property-owning class responded by force of arms. Property rights were the basis of this class's power and of its "free income," and it would protect them at any cost: "And it is well known, and also it is right and good by law and custom, that when recourse is had to arms the common man pays the cost. He pays it in lost labor, anxiety, privation, blood, and wounds" (Veblen, 1964b, p. 413).

CAPITALIST IMPERIALISM

During the last quarter of the nineteenth century and the early twentieth century, aggressive, imperialist expansion was one of the dominant features of industrial capitalism. **Imperialism** is *a policy of acquiring dependent territories or extending a country's influence through foreign trade.* Veblen also wrote extensively on this topic. He believed that the quest for profits knew no national boundaries. The absentee owners of business saw rich possibilities for profits in different areas of the world if those areas could be brought under the domination of capitalist countries or domestic governments that approved of foreigners extracting profits from their countries.

The absentee owners' success in getting the population to believe that everyone's interest was identical to the corporations' interest extended into the realm of patriotism. Patriotism was a nationalist sentiment that could be used to gain support for the government's aggressive, imperialist policies on behalf of business interests. "Imperialism is dynastic politics under a new name," Veblen wrote, "carried on for the benefit of absentee owners" (Veblen, 1964a, p. 35). He was convinced that there was "a growing need for such national aids to business." Continuous economic expansion was necessary to maintain high profits.

However, the profits that imperialism brought to the absentee owners were not, in Veblen's opinion, its most important feature. Imperialism was a conservative force of the utmost social importance. With the development of the techniques of machine production, human productivity expanded rapidly during the capitalist era. Along with the growth of productivity was the growth of the instinct of workmanship and its related social traits.

As workmanship and its attendant traits became dominant in the culture, the social basis of absentee ownership and predatory business practices became endangered. Remember that the ethos of workmanship stressed cooperation rather than competition, individual equality and independence rather than pervasive relations of subordination, logical social interrelationships rather than ceremonial role playing, and peaceable rather than predatory dispositions generally. Thus, the traits associated with workmanship were subversive to the very foundation of the existing class structure. The absentee owners had to find some means to counteract the subversive effects of workmanship, cooperation, individual independence, and the quest for a peaceable brotherhood.

For this important task the absentee owners turned to imperialism. This social role of imperialism was so central to Veblen's view of the functioning of capitalism that we quote him at length:

> The largest and most promising factor of cultural discipline—most promising as a corrective of iconoclastic vagaries—over which business principles rule is national politics. . . . Business interests urge an aggressive national policy and business men direct it. Such a policy is warlike as well as patriotic. The direct cultural value of a warlike business policy is unequivocal. It makes for a conservative animus on the part of the populace. During war time . . . under martial law, civil rights are in abeyance; and the more warfare and armament the more abeyance. Military training is a training in ceremonial precedence, arbitrary command, and unquestioning obedience. A military organization is essentially a servile organization. Insubordination is the deadly sin. The more consistent and the more comprehensive this military training, the more effectually will the members of the community be trained into habits of subordination and away from the growing propensity to make light of personal authority that is the chief infirmity of democracy. This applies first and most decidedly, of course, to the soldiery, but it applies only in a less degree to the rest of the population. They learn to think in warlike terms of rank, authority, and subordination, and so grow progressively more patient of encroachments upon their civil rights. . . . The disciplinary effects of warlike pursuits . . . direct the popular interest to other noble, institutionally less hazardous matters than the unequal distribution of wealth or creature comforts. Warlike and patriotic preoccupations fortify the barbarian virtues of subordination and prescriptive authority. Habituation to a warlike, predatory scheme of life is the strongest disciplinary factor that can be brought to counteract the vulgarization of modern life wrought by peaceful industry and the machine process, and to rehabilitate the decaying sense of status and differential dignity. Warfare, with the stress on a military organization, has always proved an effective school in barbarian methods of thought.
>
>   In this direction, evidently, lies the hope of a corrective for "social unrest" and similar disorders of civilized life. There can, indeed, be no serious question but that a consistent return to the ancient virtues of allegiance, piety, servility, graded dignity, class prerogative, and prescriptive authority would greatly conduce to popular content and to the facile management of affairs. Such is the promise held out by a strenuous national policy (ibid., 1965b, pp. 391–393).

THE SOCIAL MORES OF PECUNIARY CULTURE

Where the instinct of workmanship held sway, the social tendency was toward the advancement of knowledge, cooperation, equality, and mutual aid. But the class division of capitalism depended on the continued social prominence of the traits associated with predatory exploit—the admiration of predatory skills, acquiescence in the hierarchy of subordination, and the widespread substitution of myth and ceremony for knowledge. The free and unearned income of the absentee owners ultimately depended on the cultural and social domination of the mores of the predatory or (what in capitalism amounted to the same thing) the **pecuniary** (*concerning money*) or business aspects of the culture.

When the predatory instinct dominated society, the prevailing mores were those of the leisure class, which constituted the ruling element of society. Veblen believed that "the emergence of a leisure class coincides with the beginning of ownership. . . . They are but different aspects of the same general facts of social structure." In all class-divided societies there had always been a fundamentally significant differentiation between the occupations of the leisure class and those of the common people. "Under this ancient distinction" he wrote, "the worthy employments are those which may be classed as exploit; unworthy are those necessary everyday employments into which no appreciable element of exploit enters" (ibid., 1965a, pp. 8, 22).

Under capitalism there came to be a hierarchy of occupations ranging from the most honorific—absentee ownership—to the most vulgar and repulsive—creative labor:

> Employments fall into a hierarchical gradation of reputability. Those which have to do immediately with ownership on a large scale are the most reputable. . . . Next to these in good repute come those employments that are immediately subservient to ownership and financing, such as banking and law. Banking employments also carry a suggestion of large ownership, and this fact is doubtless accountable for a share of the prestige that attaches to the business. The profession of law does not imply large ownership; but since no taint of usefulness, for other than competitive purpose, attaches to the lawyer's trade, it grades high in the conventional scheme. The lawyer is exclusively occupied with the details of preda- tory fraud either in achieving or in checkmating chicane, and success in the profession is therefore accepted as marking a large endowment of that barbarian astuteness which has always commanded men's respect and fear. . . . Manual labour, or even the work of directing mechanical processes, is of course on a precarious footing as regards respectability (ibid., pp. 231–232).

But wealthy absentee owners usually lived in large cities and spent most of their time with lawyers, accountants, stockbrokers, and other advisors, buying and selling stocks and bonds, manipulating financial deals, and generally engineering schemes of sabotage and fraud. There- fore, whereas the predatory virtues in more barbarian cultures were so obvious and immediate as to easily incite the admiration of the populace, the predatory virtues in a capitalist society were largely hidden from view and could not so readily incite admiration. Therefore, capitalists had to conspicuously display their prowess.

Most of *The Theory of the Leisure Class*, first published in 1899, was devoted to a detailed description of how the leisure class displayed its predatory prowess through **conspicuous con- sumption**, *buying things to show off,* and the conspicuous use of leisure. For Veblen, conspicuous consumption often coincided with conspicuous waste. The housing of the rich, for example, "is more ornate, more conspicuously wasteful in its architecture and decoration, than the dwelling houses of the congregation" (ibid., p. 120). It was always necessary for the rich to have expensive, ornate, and largely useless—but above all expensive—paraphernalia prominently displayed. For the wealthy, the more useless and expensive a thing was, the more it was prized as an article of conspicuous consumption. Anything that was useful and affordable to common people was thought to be vulgar and tasteless.

The beauty and elaborate dressing and display of one's wife were essential for a substantial citizen of good taste. Innumerable servants were indicators that a wife had to do none of the vulgar work of an ordinary housewife and that she was herself primarily an ostentatious trophy of beauty and uselessness that added to the esteem of her husband. Villas on the sea, yachts, and elaborate mountain chateaus, all of which were rarely used but prominently visible, were essential for respectability.

Veblen had much more in mind in describing the conspicuous consumption of the rich than merely giving an amusing anecdotal account. Pecuniary culture was above all else a culture of **invidious distinction** meaning *differences that give rise to envy*. When an individual's personal worth was measured primarily in a pecuniary system of invidious distinction, one of the most powerful forces in society was emulation, which was the most important guarantor of social, economic, and political conservatism.

If the majority of working people came to realize that capitalists contributed nothing to the production process, that the capitalists' business and pecuniary activities were the cause of depressions and other malfunctions in the industrial system, that the disproportionately large share of wealth and income going to the capitalists caused the impoverishment of the majority of society, that the degradation of the work process was the result of the prevailing predatory ethos of capitalists, if the workers came to realize these facts, then they would surely free the industrial system from the oppressive and archaic fetters of the laws, governments, and institutions of the pecuniary business culture. There would be a revolutionary overthrow of capitalism.

The capitalists relied on two principal means of cultural discipline and social control. The first, as we have seen, was patriotism, nationalism, militarism, and imperialism. The second means of emotionally and ideologically controlling the population was through emulative consumption (or "consumerism," as this phenomenon later came to be called). Again the importance of this phenomenon in Veblen's total theory was so great that we again quote him at length:

> A certain standard of wealth . . . and of prowess . . . is a necessary condition of reputability, and anything in excess of this normal amount is meritorious.
>
> Those members of the community who fall short of this somewhat indefinite, normal degree of prowess or property suffer in the esteem of their fellowmen; and consequently they suffer also in their own esteem, since the usual basis of self-respect is the respect accorded by one's neighbors. Only individuals with an aberrant temperament can in the long run retain their self-esteem in the face of the disesteem of their fellows. . . .
>
> So soon as the possession of property becomes the basis of popular esteem, therefore, it becomes also a requisite to that complacency which we call self-respect. In any community . . . it is necessary, in order to have this own peace of mind, that an individual should possess as large a portion of goods as others with whom he is accustomed to class himself, and it is extremely gratifying to possess something more than others. But as fast as a person makes new acquisitions, and becomes accustomed to the resulting new standard of wealth, the new standard forthwith ceases to afford appreciably greater satisfaction than the earlier standard did. The tendency in any case is constantly to make the present pecuniary standard the point of departure for a fresh increase of wealth; and this in turn gives rise to a new standard of sufficiency and a new pecuniary classification of one's self as compared with one's neighbors. So far as concerns the present question, the end sought by accumulation is to rank high in comparison with the rest of the community in point of pecuniary strength. So long as the comparison is distinctly unfavorable to himself, the normal average individual will live in chronic dissatisfaction with his present lot; and when he has reached what may be called the normal pecuniary standard of the community, or of his class in the community, this chronic dissatisfaction will give place to a restless straining to place a wider and

ever-widening pecuniary interval between himself and this average standard. The invidious comparison can never become so favorable to the individual making it that he would
not gladly rate himself still higher relative to his competitors in the struggle for pecuniary
reputability (ibid., pp. 30–32).

When people were caught on this treadmill of emulative consumption, or consumerism, they led
a life of "chronic dissatisfaction," regardless of the amount of income they received. The misery
of workers, in Veblen's view, arose predominantly from material deprivation only in that part of
the working class that lived in abject poverty. For the remainder of the working class, the misery
was caused by both the social degradation of labor and the "chronic dissatisfaction" associated
with emulative consumption. The misery of the materially advantaged workers was spiritual. But
Veblen insisted that this misery "is . . . none the less real and cogent for its being of a spiritual kind.
Indeed it is all the more substantial and irremediable on that account" (ibid., 1964c, p. 95).

It seemed hopeless because the workers' response to the misery furthered and perpetuated
the misery, the reaction being to believe that they would be happy if they acquired more and
consumed more. So the workers went into debt, depended more and more heavily on moving up
in their jobs and securing more income, and ultimately were convinced that their only possibility
for transcending their chronic dissatisfaction was to please their employers and never do or say
anything disruptive or radical.

Such a treadmill was endless, however. The harder one tried to overcome one's chronic dissatisfaction and misery, the more dissatisfied and miserable one became. In a system of invidious
social ranking and conspicuous consumption, workers rarely blamed the "system," the "vested
interest," or the "absentee owners" for their plight. They generally blamed themselves, resulting in a further decline in self-esteem and self-confidence and a tighter clinging to the values of
pecuniary culture.

Veblen hoped that the more secure elements of the working class, in whom the instinct of
workmanship was most highly developed, might someday transform capitalism. He envisioned
a better society in which absentee ownership would be a thing of the past, in which there would
no longer be a business class to subvert industry, and in which production would reflect the needs
of all people rather than being controlled solely by the profits, and greed, of a tiny minority. But
his social theory showed that capitalism systematically created an overwhelming conservative
prejudice in most people and that, therefore, this transformation of capitalism would certainly be
a profoundly difficult task.

SUMMARY

In the late nineteenth century the potential profits made possible by mass production and nationwide markets led to intense industrial warfare. Through the crushing of competitors, and not
infrequently the swindling of the general public, a handful of giant corporations came to dominate
the American economy. The passage of the Sherman Antitrust Act and the establishment of various
government regulatory agencies were ostensibly aimed at controlling these giant corporations. In
practice, however, government tended to aid these giants in consolidating and stabilizing their
massive empires.

Thorstein Veblen's writings best reflect and describe the effects of this collusion of government
and big business on the welfare of the general public. Veblen stressed the distinction between
industry (which produces needed articles for human well-being) and business (which produces
profits for the wealthy absentee owners and often sabotages industry). He analyzed imperialism,

militarism, and the general "chronic misery" caused by emulative consumption in an acquisitive, competitive, capitalist society.

SUGGESTED READINGS

Some very interesting books describing the struggle among industrial corporations in this period are: Matthew Josephson, *The Robber Barons* (1962); Gabriel Kolko, *The Triumph of Conservatism* (1963); and Allan Nevins, *John D. Rockefeller, The Heroic Age of American Enterprise* (1940). All of the books of Thorstein Veblen are interesting; the most important ones are: *Absentee Ownership and Business Enterprise in Recent Times* (1964a); *The Engineers and the Price System* (1965a); *The Theory of Business Enterprise* (1965b); and *The Theory of the Leisure Class* (1965c).

KEY TERMS

business	instinct of workmanship
conspicuous consumption	invidious distinction
emulative consumption	pecuniary
imperialism	predatory instinct
industry	sabotage

REVIEW QUESTIONS

Describe and explain Veblen's view on the structure of capitalism.
1. What were economic conditions like in Veblen's time, and how did this environment affect his view of the world?
2. What are the two basic clusters or behavioral traits that form the basis of Veblen's analysis? Describe the characteristics and outcomes associated with each trait.
3. Explain what Veblen means by the antagonistic dichotomy of capitalism.
4. How did private property cause society to be divided?
5. Explain how productivity gives rise to exploitation. Which behavior raises productivity and why?
6. Explain how Veblen distinguishes "business" from "industry" and distinguishes "salesmanship" and "workmanship." What is the result of conflict between business and industry and salesmanship and workmanship?
7. How does Veblen see sabotage as a tool for business to maintain profit? What happens to efficiency and use of available productive capacity?
8. According to Veblen, what caused business cycles and fluctuations?

Understand Veblen's explanation of the role of government in capitalism.
9. In a capitalist system, who has the legal right to enforce the laws?
10. How does the capitalist class "control" government and use it to perpetuate their power?

Explain Veblen's views on capitalist imperialism.
11. How did Veblen view capitalist imperialism? Why is expanding markets important to capitalism?
12. What common sentiments to gain public support for imperialism? How does this work?
13. Who did imperialism actually benefit? Explain.

Explain the concept of conspicuous consumption and how it was used by the leisure class to stay in power.

14. Society views the rich with a certain level of admiration. What must the wealthy elite to do to retain this? What forces put pressure on the leisure class?

15. The capitalists relied on two principal means of cultural discipline and social control. Explain each. How did they result in "chronic dissatisfaction" among other things for the working class?

16. What is conspicuous consumption? How does it tie into the consumerism we see today?

CHAPTER 14

Growth and Depression in the United States, 1900–1940

The period from 1900 to 1940 began with rapid economic growth, but this was interrupted for most countries by World War I. The United States actually grew during World War I, then experienced spectacular growth in the 1920s. This was followed by a decade of depression in the United States and most of the capitalist world, ended only by World War II in 1940.

LEARNING OBJECTIVES

After reading this chapter, you should be able to:

- Discuss growth in the United States from 1900 to 1920.
- Describe the impact of the Great Depression on the United States.
- Explain what is happening with the status of women, unions, and non-white groups in the period.
- Explain U.S. colonialism and its relationship to wars fought in the early twentieth century.

SPECTACULAR GROWTH, 1900–1929

In the early twentieth century, as the economy grew, so too did the power of corporations. Corporate income was 53 percent of all business income in 1929 and rose to over 60 percent by 1980. **Retained earnings**, *profits not distributed to shareholders,* and allowances for **depreciation**, *decrease in the value of plants and equipment over time,* became important components of corporate savings. The ratio of corporate saving to all private income rose from 5 percent in the 1920s to 12 percent in the 1980s.

Corporations were profitable and mostly unregulated with few taxes. This enabled corporations to grow even larger and they began to combine. The second great merger wave lasted from 1916 to 1929. The first merger wave had been *mostly mergers with competitors on the same level,* so they were called **horizontal mergers**. This form of merger, however, was now made illegal by congressional action and court interpretation. The second wave of mergers were *mergers of firms along the upward production path from the raw materials to the factory to the wholesale and retail sales places,* so they were called **vertical mergers**.

Although the period from the Civil War to 1900 was one of rapid economic expansion in the United States, these accomplishments were dwarfed by the growth that occurred in the first two decades of the twentieth century. Growth of output was slowed by a financial panic in 1907, but

Table 14.1

Production Increases, 1899–1927

Industry	Percentage Increase
Chemicals	231
Leather and products	321
Textiles and products	449
Food products	551
Machinery	562
Paper and printing	614
Steel and products	780
Transportation and equipment	969

then took off strongly after World War I gave production a boost through government demand. The 1920s showed rapid growth, interrupted by short recessions. It has been estimated that U.S. wealth (the market values of all economic assets) reached $86 billion by 1900; in 1929, it stood at $361 billion (data in Huberman, p. 254). The figures above show the huge increase in several key industries.

This spectacular growth gave the United States a huge edge over all other countries in manufacturing output. The American prosperity of the 1920s was based on high and rising levels of output, though there were recessions in 1923 and 1927. Output increased by 62 percent from 1914 to 1929. Only 3.2 percent of the labor force was unemployed in 1929, and labor productivity rose during that decade at least as fast as wages. Between 1921 and 1929, total automobile registrations increased from less than 11 million to more than 26 million; consumers spent tens of millions of dollars on radios, refrigerators, and other electric appliances that had not been available before. American manufacturing seemed to most people a permanent cornucopia destined to create affluence for all.

This leadership in manufacturing was associated with financial leadership in the world economy. The American economic empire began to rival that of England. By 1930 American businessmen owned large investments around the world.

OMINOUS SIGNS IN THE 1920s

The rapid growth in the 1920s included some ominous signs. One basic problem was increasing inequality. The United States was rapidly becoming a country with a small percentage of rich people and a very large percentage of poor people. There was persistent poverty of 15 percent or more of the population. The problem of poverty is not only a human problem for all those whose lives are impacted by poverty, but is also a problem for the whole economy. A small income means a small consumer demand for many products.

The monopoly power of many businesses caused high prices and smaller amounts of output, tending to make every downturn worse. The giant firms keep their prices high to maintain profits and at the same time, millions of small firms have to lower prices because of the attempt to compete with the giants. When the economy moves into a recession, thousands of small firms tend to go bankrupt which in turn lowers output even more. Finally, the 1920s witnessed a huge growth

Table 14.2

U. S. Investments Abroad In 1930

	Amount in Millions of Dollars
Canada	$3,942
Europe	4,929
Mexico and Central America	1,000
South America	3,042
West Indies	1,233
Africa	118
Asia	1,023
Oceania	419

in consumer and corporate debt, which made the economy very vulnerable to catastrophe in the case of a recession.

Earlier periods had also seen instability. In spite of overall rapid growth, there were major depressions in the 1870s and in the 1890s. In these depressions, it suddenly appeared to be the case that the economy was running backward. Production fell. Vast numbers of workers were unemployed. As income dropped, demand for goods dropped precipitously. People thought each depression would never end.

On the other hand, a long prosperity always gave rise to the notion that prosperity would last forever. This was true before the 1873 and 1893 depressions and was especially true in the 1920s. In 1929, on the eve of the Great Depression, many economists said depressions were a thing of the past. Investors and economists had the same unreal hopes in the 1990s, when it was thought that the boom in the economy and in the stock market prices would go on forever. After a depression begins, the extreme optimism turns to extreme pessimism. The decline in stock market prices does not cause contractions in production, but it does make them worse.

THE GREAT DEPRESSION

The era of rapid growth and economic abundance of the 1920s came to a halt on October 24, 1929. On that "Black Thursday" the New York Stock Exchange saw security values begin a downward fall that was to destroy all faith in business. Their confidence undermined, businessmen cut back production and investment. This decreased national income and employment, which, in turn, worsened business confidence even more. Before the process came to an end, thousands of corporations had gone bankrupt, millions of people were unemployed, and one of the worst national catastrophes in history was underway.

The **Great Depression** was *a worldwide economic downturn that started in 1929.* Between 1929 and 1932 there were over 85,000 business failures and more than 5,000 banks suspended operations. Stock values on the New York Stock Exchange fell from $87 billion to $19 billion. Unemployment rose to 12 million, with nearly one-fourth of the labor force having no means of sustaining themselves. There was no unemployment compensation, so unemployed workers starved, stole, went to private charities, begged, or went to city soup kitchens to meet their material needs. Not only did many corporations go bankrupt, but many banks also closed their doors. There was no insurance on bank accounts, so millions lost their savings when banks failed. Each of these aspects reinforced the others and made the depression worse. Farm income fell by more than half, and manufacturing output decreased by almost 50 percent (Hacker, pp. 300–301).

America plunged from being the world's most prosperous country to one in which tens of millions lived in desperate poverty. Particularly hard hit were the African-Americans and other minority groups. The proportion of African-Americans among the unemployed was from 60 to 400 percent higher than the proportion of African-Americans in the general population (Chandler, pp. 40–41). Certain geographic areas suffered more than others. Congressman George Huddleston of Alabama reported in January 1932:

> We have about 108,000 wage and salary workers in my district. Of that number, it is my belief that not exceeding 8,000 have their normal incomes. At least 25,000 men are altogether without work. Some of them have not had a stroke of work for more than 12 months, maybe 60,000 or 75,000 are working one to five days a week, and practically all have had serious cuts in their wages and many of them do not average over $1.50 a day (U.S. Congress, p. 239).

Many cities reported that they could give relief payments for only a very short time, often one week, before people were forced to their own devices to subsist. The executive director of the Welfare Council of New York City described the plight of the unemployed:

> When the breadwinner is out of a job he usually exhausts his savings if he has any. Then, if he has an insurance policy, he probably borrows to the limit of its cash value. He borrows from his friends and from his relatives until they can stand the burden no longer. He gets credit from the corner grocery store and the butcher shop, and the landlord forgoes collecting the rent until interest and taxes have to be paid and something has to be done. All of these resources are finally exhausted over a period of time, and it becomes necessary for these people, who have never before been in want, to ask for assistance. The specter of starvation faces millions of people who have never before known what it was to be out of a job for any considerable period of time and who certainly have never known what it was to be absolutely up against it (Quoted in Chandler, pp. 41–42).

The despair of millions of people is best suggested by a 1932 report describing the unloading of garbage in the Chicago city garbage dumps: "Around the truck which was unloading garbage and other refuse were about 35 men, women and children. As soon as the truck pulled away from the pile all of them started digging with sticks, some with their hands, grabbing bits of food and vegetables" (quoted in Huberman, p. 260).

U.S. politics was changed forever by the Great Depression. Before the Great Depression, labor laws were antiunion, minimum wage laws were held to be unconstitutional, and business was largely unregulated. All of this changed. When the Depression started, the Republicans were in power, so the Democrats claimed they would cure the Depression. Overnight the Democrats came to be considered the party of the middle and poor income groups. The Democrats appealed to the majority interests with their propaganda and, to some extent, with their extensive reforms. They did not cure the Depression, but they did accomplish a great many other things for ordinary people in what was called the **New Deal**. The New Deal was *a series of progressive programs and reforms initiated during the period 1933–1937 under President Franklin D. Roosevelt designed to take the United States out of the Depression.* These reforms could only have emerged from the political upheaval caused by a great catastrophe. Social safety nets created by the New Deal included unemployment compensation and Social Security. Laws were passed to set minimum wages and maximum hours. Labor unions were recognized and made legal, with mandatory elections by the employees to determine their representatives when it was requested.

It was not until the 1930s that there were strong regulations put on the banks and the stock market, as a result of the Great Depression. Banks and the stock market were now more closely regulated as part of the New Deal legislation. It should be noted that throughout the nineteenth century the United States had no central bank. There were monetary panics and **runs on the banks**, a situation where *many of the banks' depositors on hearing a rumor or report that the bank was in trouble would come in to withdraw all their money*. This had occurred every ten years or so. A few large bankers would sometimes step in to restore monetary stability, sometimes successfully, but often not. In the monetary panic of 1907, J.P. Morgan used his immense wealth and banking power to help restore stability to the banks and the stock market while getting richer himself by the maneuvers.

After 1907, there were calls for a central bank, which finally led to the Federal Reserve in 1913. But the Federal Reserve had only limited powers to aid banks in distress and to manipulate the interest rate. Moreover, the Federal Reserve was, by law, a curious combination of bankers' and public interests—and still is. Although the central board is appointed by the President of the United States (with bankers' influence), the regional reserve banks are mostly appointed by bankers. For example, the New York Federal Reserve, usually the most important, was totally dominated by J.P. Morgan for many years.

The U.S. economy had changed in the 1930s from unregulated capitalism to regulated capitalism. In other words, the United States changed from fend-for-yourself capitalism to a mixed economy, with government providing a social safety net to the elderly, the unemployed, and the infirm.

STATUS OF WOMEN, 1900–1940

Because it was said that women were weaker and had to be protected, some protective laws for workers were passed only for women, not men. For a long time, the Supreme Court, which was dominated by conservative justices, held that minimum wage and maximum hour laws were unconstitutional. However, the Court made exceptions for women workers. Many unions argued that the laws should be applied to men as well as women.

Some were very good laws, such as maximum hour laws. Some "protective" laws, however, prohibited women from taking some good jobs, and in a sense protected men from competing with women for certain jobs. An example was the law in many states that women could not be bartenders. The argument was that bartending would tend to degrade women, yet women were allowed to be the more lowly paid bar girls.

Quite a few women joined the Socialist Party in the years 1900 to 1912, when the party grew rapidly to about 10 percent of the U.S. electorate. While there was some prejudice against women even in the Socialist Party, the party did firmly support the right of women to vote, so there was some alliance between the growing women's movement and the growing socialist movement with many people participating in both.

For decades the women's movement in the whole United States had proceeded very quietly and respectably so as not to antagonize men, but they achieved little. Then in the short period from 1914 to 1920, by taking advantage of the need for women to support World War I, the movement gained force, focusing mainly on the goal of passing a constitutional amendment that would give women the right to vote. To achieve this, some women practiced very militant tactics, which often landed them in jail. However, all of the movement's efforts paid off with the passage of the Nineteenth Amendment in 1920.

One area of the country that never supported the constitutional amendment was the South. The South combined prejudice against African-Americans with prejudice against women. Both prejudices had their ideological roots in the institutions of slavery, but carried over into the still mainly rural and poor South until the 1960s. Southern white, elite men wanted to keep power in their hands, as opposed to African-Americans, women, or any lower income person. The Southern elite claimed to put women on a pedestal, but it was a lonely pedestal. Women were isolated from society in the home, separated from politics, and usually denied much education. Because of its tight control by high-income, white males, no Southern state ratified the amendment until long after it was passed.

Outside the South, women's right to vote was also opposed vehemently by the liquor industry because the industry was afraid that women would vote against liquor, as many did in the Prohibition era. Opposition to women's right to vote also came from the Catholic Church, which felt that women in public positions would violate the proper subordinate place of women. Women's right to vote was strongly opposed by big city bosses, who felt they had men under their control, but that women added an uncertain factor. Finally, much of big business opposed women's right to vote because prejudice was profitable. Prejudice allowed business to keep paying women very low wages, which produced higher profits. By maintaining sexist prejudice among men and women employees, corporations were able to divide the two groups and thus continue to rule over wage bargaining.

The women's movement had over two million active members by the time the voting amendment was passed in 1920, but by 1924 there was almost no movement. Why? Mostly because the coalition was around one issue, the vote, so it fell apart when that issue was won. However, there were also some further gains in the 1920s, as politicians grew more afraid of women.

The Great Depression hurt both men and women employees by low wages and massive unemployment. As men worried about their own jobs, some men said women did not need to work, so they should be fired before men and get lower wages than men if they worked. In reality, most women had to work—and still do—just to keep their families out of poverty. Many husbands of married women have wages too low to support a family, while single women need the wages just to support themselves.

As families moved to the cities, women became more integrated in society outside the home. In 1890, women were only 18 percent of the paid labor force. By 1940, they were 25 percent of the paid labor force though most women continued to work many unpaid hours at home. In 1890, women had only 17 percent of all Bachelor's degrees from college, but that rose to 41 percent in 1940.

UNIONS, 1900–1940

In the early 1900s, the Western Federation of Miners struck against miserable conditions in the Colorado mines owned by Rockefeller. The union was defeated by the state militia, who used machine guns on some miners' camps, killing men, women, and children. In 1912 there was a strike by women and children against long hours, low pay and notoriously bad working conditions in the textile mills of Lawrence, Massachusetts. The strike turned into a long, hard battle. The women strikers sang the song *Bread and Roses*, asking for both higher wages and respect. Although they lost, they did make the miserable working conditions known to most of the country in a series of sympathetic protests covered by the media.

In the Great Depression, wages fell by one-third and one of every four workers was unemployed. The AFL did nothing to help the unemployed and it even opposed unemployment compensation as an un-American proposal. Again, independent unions led some militant strikes. One example was the strike of the International Longshoreman's Union on the West Coast in 1934. When the union first tried to bargain with the employers, the employers simply fired all the union leaders. Eventually, about thirty-five thousand maritime workers were out on strike, the center of the strike being the Embarcadero at the port of San Francisco. On July 3, 1934, the police decided to break the mass picket lines to allow **scabs** (*replacement workers*) to work. One reporter wrote: "The police opened fire with revolvers and riot guns. Clouds of tear gas swept the picket lines and sent the men choking in defeat. . . . Squads of police who looked like Martian monsters in their special helmets and gas masks led the way, flinging gas bombs ahead of them" (quoted in Boyer and Morais, 1970, p. 285). But this was only the beginning. The pickets returned on July 5 (known as Bloody Thursday), and they were joined by many young people from the high schools and colleges as well as by hundreds of other unions' members. The police charged, using vomiting gas, revolvers with live ammunition, and riot guns. Hundreds were badly wounded, and two workers were killed.

The pickets finally were driven away and the employers thought they had won. But many union locals, as well as the county Labor Council, called for a general strike. In spite of a telegram from the president of the AFL forbidding any strike, the workers of San Francisco launched a general strike to support the maritime workers and in protest against the killings by the police. The general strike was amazingly successful: "The paralysis was effective beyond all expectation. To all intents and purposes industry was at a complete standstill. The great factories were empty and deserted. No streetcars were running. Virtually all stores were closed. The giant apparatus of commerce was a lifeless, helpless hulk" (newspaper report, quoted in Boyer and Morais, 1970, p. 287).

During the general strike, labor allowed emergency food and medical supplies into the city, but nothing else. Thousands of troops moved into the city, but there was no violence. Labor simply refused to go to work. The general strike lasted until July 19, when the local AFL officials, refusing to hold a roll-call vote of the central labor council, announced that a majority of the council had called off the strike. The employers, worried about another strike, raised the wages of the maritime workers to ninety-five cents an hour.

In 1935 John L. Lewis (1880–1969), head of the United Mine Workers, led an exodus of the most militant unions out of the AFL to form a new federation, the Congress of Industrial Organizations (CIO). The CIO engaged in many strikes, used many socialists and communists as organizers, fought the employers tooth and nail, and spread very rapidly. The CIO supported Franklin Roosevelt and the New Deal, which legalized unions (forcing elections when enough workers petitioned). Because of labor militancy and a supportive government, unions grew from 11 percent of all employees in 1930 to 32 percent in 1950.

ENVIRONMENT, 1900–1940

In this period, there were very few government regulations, and little was done for the environment. One exception on the environment was President Theodore Roosevelt. In the early 1900s, Roosevelt was the first president to make environment a top priority and created the National Park System. President Franklin Roosevelt used unemployed workers on many conservation projects in the 1930s. Nevertheless, until the 1960s the growing capitalist manufacturing met few environmental regulations.

RACISM, 1900–1940

The period of sharecropping lasted from the Civil War to World War II. It was very difficult for sharecroppers to organize. They lived on isolated farms, far from each other. That isolation makes organizing very different from organizing a manufacturing plant with large numbers of workers and a variety of skills and techniques. Another obstacle to organizing was that African Americans were often illiterate or had very little education because the Southern schools were all segregated, with little or no resources put into African-American schools. Moreover, they had no equipment for quick communication, no vehicles for quick transportation, and no money for political purposes.

On the world stage in this period, the worst racism was against Jews. In the 1930s and during World War II, fascist Germany put all Jews in concentration camps, tortured them, and killed millions in the largest genocide of the twentieth century. In the United States, the business elite were just as prejudiced against Jews as the least educated white, male workers and some of that elite actively encouraged prejudice. For example, both Henry Ford (1863–1947) and J.P. Morgan were violently anti-Jewish and certainly never considered African-Americans, Mexican-Americans, or Asians as anything but inferiors who should be their servants. Henry Ford edited a newsletter that often praised Adolf Hitler and was filled with anti-Jewish prejudice.

FASCISM

While the U.S. government became more liberal and tolerant in the 1930s, great intolerance and extreme reactionary views became dominant in Germany, Italy, and Japan, among others. The political-economic system they evolved may generally be called fascism. To understand U.S. history after 1940, it is necessary to detour and take a look at **fascism**. Fascism is *a system of government led by a dictator having complete power and forcibly suppressing opposition and criticism and emphasizing an aggressive nationalism and racism.* Fascism in Italy and Germany in the 1930s carried the pattern of entanglement and cooperation between business and government to an extreme. The heads of the fascist (Nazi) party in Germany became heads of many large corporations. These corporations were guaranteed to get all of the government's business.

In addition to its merger of business and government, fascism also had a practice and ideology of racism and sexism. Women were told to stay in "the kitchen, the church, and care of children." Anti-Jewish views were a principal feature of German fascism. At first, Jews were harassed, then herded into concentration camps, and then killed—six million of them.

Anti-Jewish ideology was used by Hitler to come to power by blaming all of Germany's troubles on the Jews. Hitler's standard speech to German workers claimed that their troubles were all due to the Jewish bankers, who controlled finance and ruined the economy. Yet Hitler's standard speech to the German bankers claimed that all of the labor organizers were Jews, who were causing all of the problems of German bankers.

It is very revealing that U.S. business leaders were very friendly toward fascism in Germany, Italy, and Japan. For example, Henry Ford wrote favorably about Hitler and the institutions of German fascism. J.P. Morgan's bank worked with the Italian fascist leader, Benito Mussolini, giving him loans, advice, and quite a bit of propaganda to improve his public relations. The J.P. Morgan Company also had close ties with militarist Japan and provided it with many loans. When Japan invaded Manchuria, an act of unprovoked aggression, the top J.P. Morgan partner secretly wrote an article defending Japan. The Japanese government changed a few words, and then released the statement as its own to the U.S. media.

COLONIALISM, 1900–1940

U.S. corporations moved into Latin America in the nineteenth century and have been there ever since. In some cases, the U.S. and local military aided these corporate efforts. In Nicaragua throughout most of the period from 1912 to 1933, for instance, the U.S. Marines helped U.S. corporations and the U.S. government to collect debts, to manage Nicaragua's tariff collections, and to quell left-wing rebellion.

The pattern of production and trade between the United States and Latin America makes them fall into the classic picture of neocolonial countries. What was this pattern? First, U.S. corporations owned most of the industry and mining, as well as much profitable agriculture. Profits coming back to the United States were greater each year than the investment flowing into Latin America. Second, raw materials and agricultural goods were exported by Latin America, while most finished goods were imported from the United States.

The pattern of production and trade was reinforced by the pattern of investment. The U.S. corporations invested in the agricultural and mining sectors of Latin America with emphasis on extraction of oil and other raw material exports. Areas of attention by U.S. corporations included copper in Chile and cotton, bananas, and coffee throughout much of Central America. There was very little investment in manufacturing. The profits of the agricultural and extractive corporations were shipped back to the United States. Some of the food and raw materials produced were also shipped to the parent corporations in the United States at low prices to be made into finished goods and sold at high prices. Again, this pattern of investment characterized all of the colonizing powers in the late nineteenth and early twentieth centuries.

Why were the colonizing powers, including the United States, so eager to gain colonies? First, their conquering armies grabbed gold and silver if there was any. Then they made huge profits in agriculture, mining, and oil extraction with cheap labor. When these treasures and profits were returned to the colonizing country, they helped with the process of accumulating capital for industry owned by U.S. corporations.

It has often been pointed out that it takes more money to conquer and hold a colony than can be extracted from it. Most people in the colonizing country do not gain, but often lose from the colonizing from the expense of maintaining armies to the loss of the lives of their soldiers. But those corporations that control the economy and trade of a colony usually make extremely high profits. This was true in the nineteenth century and remains true today. For example, colonizing India and holding it cost England a lot of money and lives but some British companies made fabulous fortunes in India. The colonies helped capitalist corporations to grow faster and create more economic advance in the imperial country, while the outward flow of profits held back the growth of the colonial economies.

Italy, Germany, and Japan came relatively late to industrialization, so in the nineteenth century they lacked the power for gaining a large empire at the time when Britain and France had already gathered empires. In the period from 1900 to 1940, many wars were fought to subordinate other countries and make them colonies. But there were also wars between the imperialist countries, which were always rivals for new territory. Germany had increasing economic power and was resentful that England had an empire that was much larger than England's economic strength compared with German economic strength by 1914. One reason for World War I was the clash of these two rivals, with England wanting to keep the status quo with its large empire, while Germany needed war to gain a large empire in keeping with its new economic power.

ECONOMIC INSTITUTIONS AND WAR

Let us remember from earlier chapters the nature of war in different historical periods. In the early communal period, there were a few individual fights over hunting grounds, but no sustained warfare because there was no wealth to fight about. In the ancient empires built on slavery, there was war to take the wealth of cities, to conquer new land for plantations, and to take more slaves. In the feudal period, lords fought over who controlled various villages of serfs, both for wealth and for military power.

In the period of capitalism, the underlying mechanism for war has been the expansionist drive of corporations and their governments to take over colonies or later, neocolonies. Colonies and neo-colonies are sources of markets, cheap labor, cheap raw materials, and profitable investments. In the period from 1776 to 1940, there were wars between a colonizing country and a weaker country, in which the object was to take over the weak country as a colony. But there were also wars that were between rivals for empire.

SUMMARY

The period from 1900 to 1940 began with rapid economic growth, but this was interrupted for most countries by World War I. The United States actually grew during World War I, then had spectacular growth in the 1920s. This was followed by a decade of depression in the United States and most of the capitalist world, ended only by World War II.

Discrimination against women continued unabated in most respects, even though women got the vote in most advanced capitalist countries. Discrimination continued in the United States against African-Americans, Latino-Americans and other groups. Fascist countries committed genocide against the Jews. Industrialization and environmental deterioration proceeded merrily along their way with little regulation.

Almost all of the less developed countries were held in colonial or neocolonial dependence by the European powers, the United States, and Japan. Fights over who was to get what empire were one cause leading to World Wars I and II. Another reason for war was that fascist combinations of big business and government in some countries were militarist and gained huge empires until they were defeated in World War II.

SUGGESTED READINGS

Once again, excellent readings are DuBoff on economic history, Deckard on gender discrimination, Flexner on the women's suffrage struggle, Reich on the history of racism, Foster on environment, and Philip Foner as well as Boyer and Morais on unions.

KEY TERMS

depreciation   retained earnings
fascism   run on the bank
Great Depression   scabs
horizontal mergers   vertical mergers
New Deal

REVIEW QUESTIONS

Discuss growth in the United States from 1900 to 1920.

1. Give examples of how output in the United States grew from 1900 to 1920.
2. What were some problems in the 1920s that were to later be recognized as warnings of the Great Depression?

Describe the impact of the Great Depression on the United States.

3. What is the Great Depression? Why isn't it called the Great Recession?
4. What were some economic impacts of the Great Depression for workers? For businesses?
5. Why was unemployment such a dire situation for some workers in the Great Depression?
6. Why was a "run on a bank" such a catastrophic event during this period of time?
7. What is the New Deal? What are some examples of programs initiated during the New Deal?
8. How do you think the programs stemming from the New Deal kept future recessions from turning into major depressions?

Explain what is happening with the status of women, unions, and non-white groups in the period.

9. What are some examples of positive protections for women workers in this period? Some not so positive "protections?"
10. Why was the South resistant to giving women and former slaves the right to vote?
11. What were some examples of union activity and their outcomes? What were unions trying to achieve?
12. What is fascism? How did this affect certain groups of people? Give examples.

Explain U.S. colonialism and its relationship to wars fought in the early twentieth century.

13. What is the reason for a country to hold colonies? How are profits generated from holding colonies?
14. How were the holding of colonies related to World War I?

APPENDIX 14.1
SOCIALISM, 1900–1940

From 1900 until World War I (1914–1918) socialist parties grew around the world. From a small start in 1900, the Socialist Party of the United States grew to 10 percent of the vote in 1912. Each year, the socialist parties of the world had an international congress. One major topic every year was the possibility of war and what to do about it. They all agreed that a war between the capitalist powers would be a war of clashing imperialisms and that socialists should oppose it.

Yet when war broke out in 1914, the socialists split over what to do about it. Most of the socialist parties joined their governments and declared that they were fighting purely defensive wars. The radical socialists, such as Rosa Luxemburg of Germany and V.I. Lenin (1870–1924) of Russia, urged all out opposition by any possible means, including general strikes or revolutions. These opponents of war soon created left-wing socialist parties in every major country.

In Russia, the left-wing socialist party led by Lenin made a successful revolution in 1917 and they made peace with Germany in 1918. Eventually, the party was renamed the Communist Party and the Russian empire was renamed the Union of Soviet Socialist Republics. Each city elected a council and all of the councils elected representatives to a national council. The Russian word for council is Soviet. All Soviet industry became public property. There was no more private capitalism in the Soviet Union. All industry was planned in one central plan approve by the government. The government itself became a dictatorship when all parties other than the Communist Party were banned in the midst of the civil war in which the Communists had to fight for survival.

After World War I, most countries had both Socialist and Communist parties. The Socialists supported a very gradual approach to socialism through democratic legislation, while the Communists wanted immediate and complete socialism by legislation or—if that was prevented by the ruling classes—by revolution.

In 1929, there was a world wide depression, including all capitalist countries. Since the Soviet economy was planned and did not rely on private profit, it did not decline, but actually rose at a very rapid rate through out the 1930s. The population of Soviet cities tripled and in a decade, they went from being a poor, mainly agricultural country to a mainly industrial country. This made the Soviet model very attractive, especially to poor, agricultural countries.

In China a Communist Party was formed, based partly on industrial workers and partly on poor peasants. At first the Communists had a coalition with the Nationalist Party, which represented the landlords and capitalists of China. In 1927, the Nationalists slaughtered hundreds of thousands of Communists in the cities, so the Communists retreated to bases in the countryside.

In the United States a majority of the Socialist Party opposed World War I and U.S. participation. The Socialist leader, Eugene Debs, was put in prison for his opposition to the war. In 1920, Debs ran for president from prison and he got over 10 percent of the vote as a socialist! But in the 1920s the Socialist Party split in a right-wing socialist party called Socialist and a left-wing socialist party called Communist.

Both the Socialist and Communist parties remained weak during the affluent 1920s, but both became very strong in the 1930s. Moreover, in the Great Depression of the 1930s the Democratic Party swung to the left and took an enormous majority of the votes under the leadership of President Franklin Roosevelt. The trade unions tripled and many unions were run by Socialists or Communists. The Socialists and Communists supported many of Roosevelt's reforms, though they criticized him for not moving fast enough.

SUGGESTED READINGS ON SOCIALISM

G.D.H. Cole's five volumes (1953) are the best source on the traditional socialist parties in Europe. The quick rise and remarkable strength of the Socialist party of the United States in the early twentieth century are described with enthusiasm and clarity by Ira Kipnis in *The American Socialist Movement, 1897–1912* (1952). The history of the Communist parties is told in the excellent and readable book by Fernando Claudin, *The Communist Movement* (1975).

CHAPTER 15

Keynesian Economics and the Great Depression

The previous chapter showed that there was very rapid growth in the United States in the 1920s followed by a spectacular decline and depression in the 1930s. What happened to reduce the output of goods and services so drastically? Natural resources were still as plentiful as ever. The nation still had as many factories, tools, and machines. The people had the same skills and wanted to put them to work. Yet millions of workers and their families begged, borrowed, stole, and lined up for a pittance from charity, while thousands of factories stood idle or operated far below capacity.

The explanation lay within the institutions of the capitalist market system. Factories could have been opened and people put to work, but they were not because it was not profitable for businessmen to do so. In a capitalist economy, production decisions are based primarily on the criterion of profits, not on people's needs. While the capitalist world was suffering what was perhaps its most severe depression, the Soviet economy—which claimed to be socialist—was experiencing rapid growth. As a result, the socialist cause gained many enthusiasts in the 1930s. When the Great Depression struck, it was a traumatic shock to many Americans who had come to believe their country was destined to achieve unparalleled and unending increases in material prosperity.

LEARNING OBJECTIVES

After reading this chapter, you should be able to:

- Describe Keynes' basic explanation of the boom and bust cycle of a capitalist market economy.
- Explain how the government can act to stabilize the economy.

HOW KEYNES DOUBLED THE SIZE OF ECONOMICS

The capitalist economic system seemed to be on the verge of total collapse. Drastic countermeasures were essential, but before the system could be saved, the problems had to be better understood. To that task came one of the most brilliant economists of the twentieth century: John Maynard Keynes (1883–1946). In his famous book, *The General Theory of Employment, Interest and Money* (1936), Keynes attempted to show what had happened to capitalism so that it could be reformed and thus preserved.

In order to understand the business cycle of boom and bust that causes depressions, Keynes invented a whole new area of economics. Before Keynes, economics students learned only microeconomics. After Keynes, students learned both micro- and macroeconomics. What is microeconomics and macroeconomics and why did Keynes have to invent macroeconomics? **Microeconomics** is *the study of individual firms, individual employees, and individual consumers.* **Macroeconomics** studies *the economy as a whole, the aggregate growth of the economy, and the aggregate amount of unemployment.* Before Keynes, economists considered it important only to teach the theory of individual consumers, employees, and firms.

Even in the midst of the Great Depression, they argued that aggregate economics was unnecessary because every good economist knew that there was automatically full employment and therefore growth at the highest possible rate. This remarkable view was based on Say's law written by Jean-Baptiste Say in 1800. **Say's law** claims that *any amount of output supplied to the market will always generate an equal amount of demand.* The reasoning is that output always generates income in terms of wages and profits. This income will then be used to buy other goods, since it is irrational for people to hoard money for no purpose. There may be a brief lack of demand in one industry until capital moves to another industry. There may also be a brief lack of demand in the aggregate economy if there is an external shock, such as a flood. But there can be no aggregate lack of demand for any considerable period. Economists argued that "in the long run" the economy as a whole must be in equilibrium at full employment. Keynes noted that "in the long run we are all dead!"

Keynes, in his famous book cited above, begins by an attack on Say's law that is systematic and detailed. Keynes's main point is that Say and the neoclassical economists speak as if the present economy is a real or barter economy, but the fact is that money is used for transactions. In fact, money is used not only as a **medium of exchange** or as *payment for goods and services;* money is also used to keep in reserve for emergencies or to hold back for speculative purposes. If the outlook for profit is poor, then firms and individuals have a rational reason for hoarding savings until there is a better opportunity to invest.

For more systematic analysis, Keynes divides spending into four great flows: consumer spending, business spending on plant and equipment, government spending, and spending on U.S. exports by foreigners. Keynes examined what income in the form of money is spent and goes back into the economy and what income "leaks out" of circulation or is kept in reserve and not spent.

In the purely private domestic economy (leaving out government and foreign trade) Keynes points out that people receiving income may spend it for consumption of goods and services or may save it. It appears that the savings must all leak out of circulation and not be part of demand. Actually, however, Keynes emphasizes that some of savings goes into business investment, that is, spending for plant and equipment. If all of the savings goes into this investment spending, then there is equality between the output supplied to the market at present prices and the output demanded (income spent) in the market at present prices.

If the saving out of income is much greater than the amount going into investment, then some income is not spent or is held for some rational reason, such as a reserve or worry about future possible losses. If this means insufficient money going into demand, then the lack of demand may cause a recession. In other words, at present prices the amount of consumer demand plus investment demand is less than output supplied, there are losses rather than profits. Business losses lead to production cutbacks and unemployment.

On the other hand, if the investment spending is greater than available savings out of income, this may cause price inflation. The reason for price inflation is that consumer spending plus business investment spending create demand that is greater than the available supply at present prices. Therefore, prices will rise.

When the whole economy is considered, behavior of government must be included. Federal, state, and local governments spend money, which is part of aggregate demand for output. On the other hand, there is some leakage out of circulation into taxes. Taxes take away money that might otherwise have been spent.

Finally, a complete analysis of the economy must include foreign trade. Exports bring in money from foreigners so exports also boost demand. On the other hand, imports mean the payment of money by our citizens to foreigners, so imports reduce aggregate demand.

Keynes considers how these four flows—consumption, investment, government, and exports— may fluctuate, focusing first on consumer demand. His most important finding is that consumer demand rises as income rises, but usually rises more slowly. The reason is that at low levels of income, people are forced to spend their whole income on necessities. As income rises, however, people increase their spending above the bare minimum, but they also have the freedom to save more money. In an expansion, excessive saving may cause lack of demand. Lack of demand is one very important factor affecting profit and profit behavior affects investment. A falling percentage of consumption out of income may tend to depress the economy through its influence on investment.

From Keynes' analysis, it follows that private sector behavior may lead to a recession as there is insufficient demand for aggregate output. He therefore advocates an active government policy to prevent recessions. The government may spend more money on projects such as schools or hospitals, which put people to work and generate more income.

Keynes makes the point that constructive government expenditures, such as health and education, are the preferable type of expenditure. However, wasteful expenditures such as for war may also expand demand. He makes the point in an amusing and dramatic way:

> Ancient Egypt was doubly fortunate, and doubtless owed to this its fabled wealth, in that it possessed two activities, namely, pyramid building as well as the search for precious metals, the fruits of which, since they could not serve the needs of many by being consumed, did not stale with abundance. The Middle Ages built cathedrals and sang dirges. Two pyramids, two masses for the dead, are twice as good as one; but not so two railways from London to York (Keynes, p. 131).

Keynes also shows how private enterprise may be added to the policy picture if that is politically necessary:

> If the Treasury were to fill old bottles with banknotes, bury them at suitable depths in disused coalmines which are then filled up to the surface with town rubbish, and leave it to private enterprise on well tried principles of laissezfaire to dig the notes up again . . . there need be no unemployment. . . . It would indeed be more sensible to build houses and the like; but if there are political and practical difficulties in the way of this, the above would be better than nothing" (ibid., p. 129).

Keynes further considers the possibility that the government may lower taxes on the middle class and the poor, who have incentive to spend all of their remaining money to demand goods and services. Moreover, Keynes considers the possibility that the government may use monetary policy to encourage investment through low interest rates.

The Great Depression dragged on for ten years. It ended only when the government began to spend enormous amounts of money on the military during World War II. The fact that government spending could end a severe depression impressed economists. Most economists declared themselves to be Keynesians and some sort of Keynesian policies were dominant in the United States for at least two decades. Keynes set the framework for modern macroeconomics. This brief chapter merely introduced his ideas. Many of Keynes' ideas as well as those of other contributors to macroeconomics will be discussed in detail in Part III.

SUMMARY

The severity of the Great Depression of the 1930s caused many economists to become dissatisfied with the orthodox neoclassical economists' view that unemployment was merely a short run adjustment to a temporary disequilibrium situation. Keynes's new idea that there is a real problem requiring real remedies was rapidly accepted by most important economists. Keynesian economists thought that World War II proved that massive government intervention in the market economy could create full employment.

Keynes rejected Say's law that demand always adjusts to supply. He showed that there is no automatic adjustment after a shock to immediate equilibrium. He showed that there can be long-lasting unemployment under certain conditions. He explained how aggregate demand can be insufficient to buy aggregate supply at present prices.

The new area of macroeconomics, invented by Keynes, was taught all over the globe. National income accounts also made use of Keynes' division of spending into consumer spending, investment spending, government spending, and net export spending. Keynesian economics was dominant in the United States after World War II for about twenty-five years. Then a more conservative macroeconomics based on neoclassical economics came back into dominance. All of this will be investigated in detail in Part III of this book.

SUGGESTED READING

An excellent book giving Keynes in clear language in the spirit of that day is Alvin Hansen, *A Guide to Keynes* (1953).

KEY TERMS

macroeconomics	microeconomics
medium of exchange	Say's law

REVIEW QUESTIONS

Describe Keynes's basic explanation of the boom and bust cycle of a capitalist market economy.

1. What is macroeconomics?
2. State Say's law and then explain what it means in your own words.
3. How does the use of money in the economy create the possibility that Say's law may not hold?
4. What are the two main things people can do with their income (money)?

5. What are the components of spending?
6. How does income (money) "leak" out of circulation? In what way do savings enter back into circulation?
7. What happens when there is not enough demand for the amount of goods produced?

Explain how the government can act to stabilize the economy.

8. How can the government offset a lack of private demand? How does this help prevent a recession?
9. How could lower taxes, especially for middle and low income households, help the economy?

CHAPTER 16

The United States and Global Capitalism, 1940–2006

Global capitalism is the *latest stage of capitalism in which capitalist institutions dominate most of the world and global corporations are found in every country.* The United States now has vital connections to every aspect of the global economy, military bases throughout the world, economic domination of many countries, and outright occupation of some other countries. The focus of this chapter is on the United States and its relationship to global capitalism.

LEARNING OBJECTIVES

After reading this chapter, you should be able to:

- Describe how the United States emerged as a superpower at the end of World War II.
- Compare and contrast the defining features and events of the "long boom," the "long slow down," and the "boom and bust" of 1990 to 2004.
- Describe the emergence of global capitalism.
- Discuss the debates about the role of the government in capitalism.
- Compare and contrast criticisms of globalization.

FROM U.S. POWER TO U.S. SUPERPOWER

World War II lasted from 1939 to 1945, destroying entire cities and killing over 50 million people. The economies of much of the world were devastated. The United States escaped the physical devastation of that war. The U.S. economy quickly recovered from the Great Depression and grew at a fast pace during World War II. By 1950, the U.S. economy was producing 80 percent of the world's manufactured goods. As other economies recovered slowly from the war, they needed financing and goods from the United States both for consumer survival and to rebuild industry. Providing both the financing and the manufactured goods, the United States emerged from World War II as the greatest economic and military power.

The closest contender was the Soviet Union, whose economy was badly hurt by the war, losing perhaps a third of its housing and industry to the German invasion and suffering more than 20 million deaths. There was an economic and ideological conflict called the Cold War between the United States and Soviet bloc countries from 1945 until the end of the Soviet Union in 1990. The Soviet demise left the United States as the sole superpower.

THE LONG BOOM IN THE UNITED STATES: 1945–1970

To explain how the United States became the sole superpower, this chapter begins with a look at the great U.S. boom or economic expansion from 1945 to 1970. Some U.S. capitalists became fabulously rich in a long upward trend of gross domestic product (GDP) from the end of World War II in 1945 to about 1970. Workers' incomes increased as well. In that period, the United States had short recessions and long, strong expansions. **Real wages**, *the actual purchasing power of the money made from employment or the value of the dollars earned after adjusting for inflation*, rose from year to year. Profits rose in most years. The U.S. economy dominated trade because other countries were devastated by the war. Money flowed into the U.S. economy and exports poured out. U.S. exports were profitable, and the percentage of production exported out of the United States kept growing. U.S. corporations also made large, profitable investments abroad. The U.S. government and U.S. banks made vast loans abroad, so most other countries were in debt to them.

Many of the brightest people from all over the world immigrated to the United States to make their fortunes, causing technological progress to accelerate. The U.S. economy alone had money for large research projects, so its technology led all others by a substantial margin. The average unemployment rate was relatively low. In short, the period from 1945 to 1970 was a long-run boom, often referred to as a "golden age."

THE LONG SLOWDOWN IN THE UNITED STATES: 1970–1990

There was, however, a long period of relative stagnation from about 1970 to 1990 with weaker expansions and longer, deeper recessions. Compared with the averages for 1945 to 1970, the rate of growth of GDP fell, while the rate of unemployment rose. From 1947 to 1970, the U.S. GDP grew 3.7 percent a year. By contrast, the period from 1970 to 1990 witnessed only 2.5 percent growth of GDP per year. The average amount of annual net investment also declined. While fixed investment grew 3.5 percent a year in the earlier period (1947–1970), it grew only 2.8 percent per year in the latter period (1970–1990). Real wages were stagnant and actually fell in the thirty years between 1973 and 2003.

Why did the great boom of the 1950s and 1960s turn into the great stagnation of the 1970s and 1980s? First, the rest of the world rose from devastation to become strong again, and the corporations of Japan and many European countries began to compete effectively with, and in some cases outcompeted, the U.S. corporations. Foreign competitors grabbed away at U.S. markets, and the U.S. share of global industry fell. Second, the boom of the early post–World War II years was helped by pent-up U.S. demand in the form of savings that could not be spent in the war years. When this demand was unleashed at the end of the war, it gave a strong initial push to the economy, and then the effect eventually dwindled away. Third, the United States started out with a technological advantage, but other capitalist countries soon caught up.

U.S. BOOM AND BUST: 1990–2004

In the 1990s, U.S. technology spurted ahead, and the U.S. economy had an unusually long expansion. It outcompeted all of its rivals in many areas and again looked like a superpower. The U.S. economy grew especially rapidly for four or five years in the late 1990s. However, real wages also hardly rose until 1995 and then made some gains for a few years in the late 1990s. Since the stock market grew very rapidly in the 1990s, profits from investing in stocks greatly outstripped wage growth for the whole period, so income distribution became more unequal. Even in the 1990s, the U.S. economy was not anywhere near as dominant as in the 1950s.

Some economists predicted the boom of the 1990s would go on forever. In the early 2000s, however, there was a recession plus a **stock market bubble**, when *the price of a share of stock is not supported by economic fundamentals*, which burst, generating three years of general stock market decline. The recession meant rising unemployment and lower real wages. The U.S. recession and stock market decline influenced the rest of the world, and there ensued recession and stock declines all over the world. The reality of global capitalism is that both boom and bust are transmitted worldwide in an instant.

EMERGENCE OF GLOBAL CAPITALISM, 1970–2004

What is **global capitalism**? Most countries are predominately capitalist or moving that way quickly, although some are in a less-developed stage. **Globalization**, broadly speaking, is *the process of growing interdependence among countries*. For the purposes of this book, globalization refers to the process by which the world is moving toward a fully global capitalism.

The economy of the entire world is held together in a tighter and tighter network consisting of thousands of economic connections. Why has the world become such a tight, closely knit economic unit even while individual nations persist and are important? For centuries, communication and transportation have been improving. Since the information revolution of the 1990s, communication is instantaneous around the globe. People and goods can be transported around the world in many hours rather than many months. In the time it takes to make a few keystrokes, billions of dollars can be moved from one continent to another.

Although some of the changes in the global economic network began hundreds of years ago, many changes accelerated in the early 1970s, so the stage of global capitalism may be dated in one sense from about 1970. More important than communication and transportation improvements, the institutions of capitalism and its ideology have spread into every nook and cranny of the world. While some aspects of global capitalism began to emerge clearly in the 1970s and 1980s, full global capitalism did not become a reality until the 1990s. Only after the Soviet Union, China, and Eastern Europe turned toward more extensive use of markets and capitalism was the globe fully dominated by capitalism.

One indicator of the magnitude of global capitalism is that by the year 2000, the total movement of money across borders every single day amounted to $1.5 trillion. Another indicator of the growth of global capitalism in this period is that in 1982 the flow of **foreign direct investment**, *an investment that gives the investor a controlling interest in a foreign company*, across borders amounted to $57 billion for the whole global economy. By 2000, the flow of foreign direct investment across borders amounted to $1,271 billion—an incredible increase of over twenty times! (These data and data on the whole international financial scene are found in Burton and Nesiba, 2004.)

SURPLUS TO DEFICIT IN GLOBAL TRADE, UNITED STATES:
1970–2004

Earlier sections of this chapter examined the domestic changes in the United States beginning around 1970. In addition, there were international changes in trade, finance, and investment. These international changes show the important impact of the new global economy.

For about a hundred years, from 1870 to 1970, the U.S. economy sold more goods and services abroad, or exported, than it bought or imported. It is called a **trade surplus** *when exports exceed* *imports*. Therefore, money in the form of payments for the exports flowed into the United States. Until 1970, the United States had a trade surplus and an inflow of money sometimes called a favorable balance of trade. After 1970, for the first time in a century, the United States was buying more goods abroad than it sold. It moved from a trade surplus to a **trade deficit**, *when imports exceed exports*, and money was flowing out of the United States in payments to foreign countries for imports. Since 1970, the unfavorable trade balance and trade deficit has grown.

The U.S. trade deficit has become an important issue because trade has become a bigger part of the U.S. economy. In fact, the ratio of U.S. trade (exports plus imports) to GDP was still only 5 percent in 1950–54. But then it began to rise and was 11 percent by 1980–84. It is clear that the U.S. economy had became more dependent on its international trade by the end of the 1980s, and this trend continued throughout the 1990s and early twenty-first century.

Some of the U.S. trade deficit is due to the great amount of consumer and military goods and services purchased abroad. Some is due to competition from the growth of technology and industry in Europe and Asia. Some is due to new **free trade zones**, where *countries agree to lower barriers to trade such as tariffs and quotas*, which leave out the United States. The U.S. free trade zone includes only Canada and Mexico. The European Union established a free trade zone in all of Europe. Eastern Asia now has its own free trade area covering China, Japan, and all of Southeast Asia.

CREDITOR TO DEBTOR, UNITED STATES: 1970–2004

The changes in the international balance of trade affected the U.S. international financial situation. Instead of money flowing into the United States because of a trade surplus, money started flowing out of the United States because of a trade deficit after 1970. A country must find some way to pay for its trade deficit. In order to pay for a trade deficit when a country is spending more than it is making, a country often borrows money and goes into debt. After World War II until 1970, the United States was a creditor nation lending money to other countries. As a **creditor nation**, *other countries owed more money to the United States than the United States owed to foreign countries*.

After 1970, the United States became a net debtor. As a **debtor nation**, *the United States owes more money to foreign countries than foreign countries owe to the United States*. The United States is now the largest debtor among all nations. In addition to **private debt**, *how much business and households owe*, the U.S. government has been spending vast sums abroad for military purposes. For this reason, in recent decades the U.S. Treasury has had to borrow money abroad by selling bonds to foreign citizens. For the first time in a hundred years, foreigners now own more of the U.S. national debt than Americans. The United States is again a net debtor, as it was in its early days when it was a neocolony of England. The large debt also puts the United States in some economic danger. For example, China owns quite a bit of the U.S. national debt, and if China should decide to shift its bondholding rapidly from the United States to the European Union, it would disrupt the U.S. economy to some extent.

There were also changes about this time in U.S. international investment. From 1914 until recently, U.S. corporations invested more abroad than foreigners did here. U.S. investment abroad was 7 percent of all U.S. investment in 1929 but rose to 30 percent by 1987. Since the 1970s, however, the amount of foreign investment in the United States has been growing rapidly. By 2003, total foreign investment in the United States was $2.3 trillion more than U.S. investment abroad (National Bureau of Economic Research, 2004). While the United States remains the largest single investor overall, Japan and Europe have been gaining since the 1970s. The United States is still the only military superpower. In the economic race the United States is still the largest single economy, but Europe and Asia are closing the gap.

GOVERNMENT POWER AND LIMITS UNDER GLOBAL CAPITALISM

Conservatives argue that, in general, the government should spend as little as possible so that the private economy will use all resources efficiently. This broad statement by conservatives that the government should be relatively small is often reversed by major exceptions to that policy. The most important single exception is military spending. Conservatives also argue for expenditure on police and prisons because these institutions defend private property. Liberals argue that it is also important to spend money on education, health care, roads, and other social necessities. Thus, one vital political issue is how the government should spend money.

Throughout U.S. history, government spending was usually low in peacetime. For example, the federal government spent only 1 percent of the GDP in 1929. In wartime, however, the amount going to government spending rose drastically. Government spending rose to 40 percent of the GDP in World War II. After the war, military spending was at first reduced, but then there was the Cold War, which included propaganda, economic pressure, and some military adventures between the United States and the Soviet Union. Both sides used the Cold War as a rationalization for increasing military spending. The percentage of military spending out of GDP in the United States continued to increase until the end of the Cold War in 1990. The percentage of military spending then fell for a while. Under the second President Bush, however, it rose again, partly to cover the occupation of Afghanistan and Iraq. Since the election in 2000, under a conservative U.S. government, there has been a strong tendency to spend more on the category of military equipment but less on social services and unemployment compensation.

The other issue often debated is the total of government spending versus taxes. The last thirty years have often witnessed extremely large budget deficits. A **budget deficit** means that *government spends more than it takes in taxes and fees in a year*. How does the government spend more than it takes in? *The government borrows money by selling government-issued bonds to investors both in the United States* (**internal debt**) *and in foreign countries* (**external debt**). A **budget surplus** means that *the government takes in more money than it spends in a year*. The **government debt** is *the sum of accumulated surpluses and the accumulated deficits over time*.

People often assume that debt is bad because they know that debts by individuals are sometimes bad. If I continue to spend well over my income, I go bankrupt. Governments do not go bankrupt because they can always issue more money so they can pay off any internal debt that is owed. Of course, paying off a debt by issuing new money tends to be inflationary, and creditors abroad want real assets, not inflated paper money. The negative effect of a big unpaid government debt is that government debt means paying interest. Interest payments come from the average taxpayer and go to the relatively affluent bondholders, causing redistribution of income within the United States. However, in recent years, foreigners purchased a growing share of the outstanding government debt, so some of U.S. income goes to foreign citizens.

Deficit spending by the government tends to stimulate the economy. For example, the large military spending by President Roosevelt during World War II brought the economy out of the Great Depression. Quite a different problem results from deficit spending if the economy is already at full employment and the government stimulates it further. For example, during each U.S. war, the government spent more than its tax revenues and the result was inflation in each war. Sometimes **price controls**, that is, *limits placed on the price of goods by the government,* have prevented actual inflation, but the inflationary pressure eventually caused problems.

COLONIALISM TO NEOCOLONIALISM, 1945–2004

Under colonialism, European capitalist countries took over much of the world, including North and South America, Africa, and Asia except for Japan. Colonialism was described as forceful occupation of another country, extraction of its treasures, and extraction of continuing profits. The authors have earlier showed that the imperial country invested mostly in the raw materials of the colonial country, limited the colonial exports to agricultural and raw material commodities, and sold finished goods to the colonial country at a high profit. This period of colonial occupation and exploitation lasted until the end of World War II.

During World War II and in the decades following it the colonial peoples heard much about freedom and equality from the antifascist coalition that won the war. When the war was over, the colonial peoples each asked for their independence. If it was not granted, they each eventually revolted and took independence at gunpoint. The freeing of the colonies began in 1945 and was mostly over by about 1970.

When a former colony became legally free, it often remained dominated both economically and politically by the major capitalist powers. Moreover, the economic pattern of the former colony often remained the same for a long time. The neocolonial countries are those that are formally free but have the same old economic pattern. Foreign corporations own their natural resources; they export food and cheap raw materials; they import expensive finished goods. While those features are still true of many neocolonial countries, what has changed in a large number of neocolonial countries is that global corporations have now built and own a large amount of industry, making use of the cheap labor supply. This has greatly increased the flow of profits out of those countries. One cause of the underdevelopment of many neocolonial countries is that the flow of profits and interest out of these countries is greater that the flow of investment into them. For example, for many decades, U.S. corporations have invested only about half as much each year in Latin America as they have extracted in profits and interest from their accumulated investments.

In the global economy, the big global corporations are strong in many countries, and they often dominate the neocolonial countries by sheer economic power. Only in a few cases does economic power by itself fail to get the neocolonial countries to follow the policies that are most profitable to the global corporations. For example, the United States has military bases in many neocolonial countries but seldom has to resort to military force to keep profits flowing smoothly from the neocolonial countries to the United States. In Iraq, the United States was unable by economic coercion alone to change policies it did not approve. It was therefore forced to launch an invasion and act as a colonial occupier with large expenses in money and in killed and wounded U.S. soldiers.

Although they benefit either way, global corporations prefer peaceful domination to the expense and inconvenience of military force. In terms of costs and benefits, the expenses of the U.S. occupation of Iraq were borne by the U.S. taxpayer and by the U.S. soldier. Some U.S. corporations make large profits from occupied countries, such as Iraq. For example, there is the lucrative work done by corporations that received a very profitable contract with no other bidders allowed. There are also the oil companies who want the oil of Iraq. This is the usual pattern of all colonial and neocolonial wars and occupations—the common people bear the costs while the global corporations reap large profits.

U.S. economist John Kenneth Galbraith wrote: "Corporate power is the driving force of U.S. foreign policy—and the slaughter in Iraq." (Galbraith, 2004). Normally, capitalist governments aid corporations to penetrate a country peacefully, while holding military force in reserve as a threat. The most successful capitalist empire would make the rest of the world its neocolony, not its colony. The military occupation of Iraq and Afghanistan in 2003 was an anomaly, showing an ineffective foreign policy.

INTERNATIONAL GOVERNMENTAL ORGANIZATIONS, 1945–2004

U.S. power is exerted not only by armies but to some degree through domination of some international organizations that have become more important in the period of global capitalism. After World War II, the United Nations was formed to stop wars. It has complete power in the world on paper, but it requires agreement of five big powers and it is actually helpless without their agreement. Many of its subsidiary organizations are important, such as the United Nation's International Children's Emergency Fund (UNICEF), which helps the world's children. There is also the International Labor Organization (ILO), which attempts to improve the conditions of labor. Under pressure of the global corporations, globalization has been leading toward completely free movement of international trade and capital flow. There is, however, not the same freedom for labor to move across international borders (except within the European Union). Even if the new free trade treaties were good ones, there is no world government to enforce laws such as worker safety or minimum wages or antimonopoly.

Outside the United Nations are the World Bank and the International Monetary Fund (IMF), designed to support monetary systems when they are in trouble and to help give a financial start to underdeveloped countries. Under control of the United States and England, the IMF was formed at Bretton Woods in New Hampshire in 1944. It was designed by the great liberal economist John Maynard Keynes to be lender of last resort to stop recessions and monetary panics. Considered at first by global bankers to be too liberal, it very slowly became a conservative organization, making countries safe for the interests of global banks. The IMF does give emergency help to countries in monetary trouble, and some of its projects have been constructive.

The IMF demands, however, that the countries accept conditions, referred to as structural adjustment policies (SAPs), that many people feel harm development of that country. The first condition is to reduce government's services to its people in order to save money and reduce debt. These cuts in services have included health care, fuel and food subsidies, and even anti-AIDS money. The reductions in services hurt people directly, but they also hurt the economy because they remove the stimulus from that government spending. The second condition for an IMF loan is that the borrower must privatize many state agencies. A change from public to private ownership often leads to enormous disruption. It also leads to more profits for a few corporations but fewer services for many people. The third IMF condition is complete freedom for capital to flow in and out of the borrower country. Huge flows of capital can easily disrupt a whole economy and have often done so.

Joseph Stiglitz, who was head of the Council of Economic Advisors under President Clinton and was later president of the World Bank, says he discovered that in international organizations, "especially at the IMF . . . decisions were made on the basis of . . . ideology and bad economics, dogma that sometimes seemed to be thinly veiled special interests" (Stiglitz, 2002, p. xiii). The harmful conditions imposed on countries by the IMF were designed to help those outside groups that wished to invest in these countries, not to help the people of those countries. Many critics argue that these conditions by the IMF mean that such international agencies cause more harm than good.

The World Bank is supposed to help the biggest problem—world poverty. The extent of world poverty may be seen in the fact that 1.2 billion people live on less than one dollar a day. But the World Bank and the IMF have accomplished very little. One reason for the failure of globalization to help people has been that the policies of international organizations have been set by "commercial and financial interests and mind-sets" (Stiglitz, p. 224). This is not a conspiracy, but happens naturally, because they are international institutions of capitalism.

CRITICS OF GLOBALIZATION

At the beginning of the twenty-first century, there are many critics of globalization. Some fought to stop globalization—but what does that mean? How can anyone stop better communications, better transportation, or building new plants around the world? Why stop the improvements in technology and the ability to move or communicate? People resisting globalization in this sense were trying to do the impossible for no good reason.

Even if critics accept technological improvement as a positive development, they still see problems in globalization. The globalization process has meant that giant corporations exercise economic and political control to varying degrees around the world. Global corporations effectively lowered wages in the United States and Europe by outsourcing jobs to areas of cheap labor. The global corporations attempt to keep the wages of the poor, underdeveloped countries as low as possible. In other words, they have extracted enormous profits from the global industrial revolution and yet they have kept employees from sharing much of the output of higher production. Moreover, there have also been disastrous environmental effects in some areas.

A very different kind of resistance to globalization has arisen from these problems. Organizers have attempted to build a movement dedicated to stopping environmental destruction, fighting for democratic rights in each country, and getting a share of the global gains for employees in all countries. One interesting support for this movement has come from trade union organizations, which have turned some attention from national organizing to international organizing.

SUMMARY

This chapter very briefly sketched the main lines of the transition of the United States from a relatively isolated country as late as 1940 to a superpower today. The United States now has vital connections to every aspect of the global economy, military bases throughout the world, economic domination of many countries, and outright occupation of some other countries. Globalization, or global capitalism, may be defined as the domination of the world economy by the major corporations, technology that makes the world a small place, and conservative policies imposed by the giant corporations as well as by the governments and the international organizations controlled by them. Future chapters spell out the consequences of this regime for the U.S. population.

In more general terms, one conclusion is that the era of global capitalism is here, but the basic system is still capitalism, and individual nations still exist and have some influence. The United States is a superpower militarily and economically. The United States is the only superpower, but its economic strength is rising more slowly than that of Europe and Asia, so it is less dominant than it was in the 1960s.

SUMMARY OF STAGES IN U.S. CAPITALISM

It is clear that U.S. capitalist institutions have changed and evolved. The story to this point has shown roughly three stages in U.S. capitalism. The first stage was industrial capitalism from about 1840 to about 1870, with unregulated companies owned and run by individuals. The second stage was corporate capitalism, from roughly 1870 to 1970. It had corporations instead of individuals running industry. It had giant firms. And it had highly concentrated ownership, with just three or four large firms in each industry, a hundred giant firms owning most of all U.S. industry, and only 1 percent of individuals owning most stock. The third stage is global capitalism, of which the United States is only one part, but an important part. It characterizes the period from 1970 to the present. Evolution of an economy within a given economic system is mostly continuous with gradual changes, though there are ups and downs, so this division is somewhat arbitrary—it is only meant to be a sign post for the reader.

SUGGESTED READINGS

Once again, an excellent source on U.S. economic history is Richard DuBoff's *Accumulation and Power: An Economic History of the United States* (1989). An excellent source on social history is Howard Zinn's *A People's History of the United States* (1999). The fascinating story of the clash of conflicting economic policies, their role in globalization, and the meaning of globalization for the world is told beautifully in Robert Pollin's *Contours of Descent: U.S. Economic Fractures and the Landscape of Global Austerity* (2004).

International organizations are explained and criticized in clear prose by an insider in Joseph Stiglitz's *Globalization and Its Discontents* (2002). An interesting collection on imperialism is contained in the whole issue of *Monthly Review,* July–August, 2003. A new Asian trade agreement is described by Evelyn Iritani in a November 30, 2004 article in the *Los Angeles Times* (p. C1) titled, "New Trade Pact Could Cut Clout of U.S. in Asia."

KEY TERMS

budget surplus	government debt
creditor nation	internal debt
debtor nation	price controls
deficit	private debt
external debt	real wages
foreign direct investment	stock market bubble
free trade zones	trade deficit
global capitalism	trade surplus
globalization	

REVIEW QUESTIONS

Describe how the United States emerged as a superpower at the end of World War II.
1. What country is a superpower today? What does that mean?
2. Explain why the United States was an economic superpower after World War II. Compare and contrast the defining features and events of the "long boom," the "long slow down," and the "boom and bust" of 1990 to 2004.
3. State some characteristics and explanations for the long boom of the post–World War II period. Specifically, what factors made this period unique?
4. Why did the economy slow down starting in the 1970s? Give some examples.
5. What is cited as the key driver of the boom of the 1990s? What happened?
6. What happened to real wages in the three periods? As part of your answer, define the term *real wages* and explain why it is such an important measure. Describe the emergence of global capitalism.
7. What is generally meant by *globalization*? Is it something new? Explain.
8. Discuss some of the reasons for the rapid increase in globalization in the last part of the twentieth century.
9. What is some evidence of the increase in globalization?
10. What is a trade deficit? A trade surplus? What is the explanation for the United States going from a trade surplus to a trade deficit?

11. Explain the relationship of the trade deficit or surplus to whether a country is a net borrower or lender.

12. What are some of the effects of the United States being a net debtor nation? Some people argue we should worry and others argue we should not worry about the United States being a net debtor. What do you think and why? Discuss the debates about the role of the government in capitalism.

13. Governments are also players in the economy. What is the main source of funds for the U.S. government? What happens if the government spends more than it takes in?

14. How does the government raise money if there is insufficient tax revenue to cover spending?

15. What is the difference between internal and external debt? Why is external debt such a concern? Compare and contrast criticisms of globalization.

16. What is neocolonialism? What are the examples of neocolonialism over the 1945–2004 period?

17. Name two international organizations and discuss what they do.

18. What are some of the concerns about powerful global corporations, especially in smaller developing countries?

APPENDIX 16.1
HOW WAR HAS CHANGED

Wars are shaped by human relationships. Therefore, they reflect certain types of political-economic institutions. This book has shown how institutions shape wars. Chapter 2 discussed how early communal societies had skirmishes over hunting grounds. Chapter 3 emphasized that slave societies warred for land and slaves. Chapter 4 revealed that feudal lords warred over land and serfs. Appendix 16.1 discusses further the evolution of war in a global context.

LEARNING OBJECTIVES FOR APPENDIX 16.1

After reading this appendix, you should be able to:

- Compare and contrast the nature of war over time.
- Explain the relationship of neocolonialism and war.

U.S. wars changed as the society changed. The Revolutionary War was a war of liberation of the United States from British colonialism. The War of 1812 was a war in which the United States defended itself against a British attempt to again make a colony of the United States. The 1845 war against Mexico was naked aggression to take over Mexican lands in order to extend U.S. slavery to the new Western lands. The U.S. Civil War was the crucial and bloody event deciding whether slavery or capitalism would dominate the economy of the United States.

After the Civil War, the rapidly industrializing capitalist country pursued the usual motivations of capitalist countries. As the United States evolved, the different stages of capitalism and technology produced many changes in the nature of war. In 1898, the United States fought a rival imperial country, Spain. Spain was much weaker and was easily defeated, so the United States took over its colonies of Puerto Rico, Cuba (dominated by treaty but not occupied except at Guantánamo), and the Philippines (after a long, bloody colonial war against the native people). World War I involved the

United States, England, and France against Germany and Austria, which resulted in a change in who owned what colonies and a change in the power relationships of different countries in Europe.

World War II was the fight of the fascist, capitalist powers (Germany, Italy, and Japan) versus the liberal capitalist powers and the Soviet Union over who would control the world. It was the bloodiest war in human history and ended with U.S. atomic bombs destroying Hiroshima and Nagasaki. Two good results were that fascism, a system of dictatorship, racism, and sexism, was stopped and that no more nuclear bombs have ever been used in war.

One bad result was the emergence of the Soviet Union and the United States as rival superpowers with opposing ideologies, economic systems, and global interests. During the 45-year Cold War, there were two "hot wars," Korea and Vietnam. Vietnam was not just a clash of the two giants but also involved the attempt of the Vietnamese people to free themselves from the colonial domination of France and then the United States.

Since capitalism matured in the nineteenth century, large capitalist powers have fought colonial wars to extend their colonial holdings, to defend them against rivals, and to hold them against wars of liberation by the colonial countries. It was shown in this book that the motivation for colonialism changed from land and slaves or serfs to extremely profitable investment and control of trade during capitalism. This background for wars changed to a considerable degree when the colonies achieved formal independence from 1945 to about 1970.

As shown in this chapter, the end of colonialism brought a new system of neocolonialism in which advanced capitalist countries dominate weaker capitalist countries through investment, unequal trade, and threat of military power. Usually, no actual war is necessary. However, in addition to neocolonialism, there are impulses toward war from the military, from military systems producers, and from particular corporations. If the world is lucky, neocolonial dominance will continue to be mostly determined by peaceful economic coercion rather than war.

REVIEW QUESTIONS FOR APPENDIX 16.1

Compare and contrast the nature of war over time.
1. How do wars and the reasons for war differ over time? Give examples.
2. What is the difference between a "hot war" and a "cold war"? How is a cold war waged?

Explain the relationship of neocolonialism and war.
3. Is military power necessary to maintain a neocolony? Explain.
4. What methods are used to control neocolonies?

APPENDIX 16.2
SOCIALIST CRITIQUE OF GLOBAL CAPITALISM

Appendix 16.2 briefly explores the evolution and varieties of socialist thought since World War II.

LEARNING OBJECTIVES FOR APPENDIX 16.2

After reading this appendix, you should be able to:

- Discuss the different faces of socialism.
- Explain the difference between Marxism and Soviet Marxism.
- Name current "flavors" of socialist thought.

In World War II, one side was made up of the fascist powers Germany, Italy, and Japan. Their fascism meant a capitalist economy plus a political dictatorship. On the other side were the capitalist democracies consisting of the United States, United Kingdom, and France plus the Soviet Union and China. In many countries conquered by the fascists, such as France and Vietnam, the resistance was led by the communists, often with help from the socialists. At the end of the war, the communists were very popular in many countries. Elections in Western Europe produced majorities of socialists and communists in many countries. England had a socialist government led by the Labor Party.

When India became independent of England, its newly elected government called itself socialist. In China, the communists and nationalists fought a civil war, and the communists won in 1948. By 1948, one-third of the world was ruled by communist parties, while communists and socialists were strong in many countries of Asia, Africa, Latin America, and Western Europe. In 1948, there was also a significant leftwing party in the United States called the Progressive Party. It appeared that various parties claiming to be socialist would take over control and end capitalism.

But the U.S. government and its allies launched an aggressive campaign that included massive propaganda, economic coercion, and wars in Korea and Vietnam. The Cold War protagonists were the United States and the Soviet Union and their allied governments, but there were also internal battles in many countries between interests advocating capitalism and those advocating socialism. The Cold War lasted until about 1990, when the communist governments of the Soviet Union and Eastern Europe were all overturned in counterrevolutions that returned them to capitalism.

During the history of the Soviet Union from 1917 to 1990, its official view was called Marxism. It is unclear, however, whether Karl Marx would have recognized this so-called Marxism, and it is perfectly clear that Marx would have gone to prison in the Soviet Union for his views. What were the views of Soviet Marxism? The Soviets argued that all history was dominated by economic factors. As technology and the economy moved inexorably forward, there must be a slow evolution and sometimes revolutions from primitive societies to the modern Soviet economy. The Soviet type of economy was said to be inevitable as socialism replaced capitalism. Workers are exploited under capitalism but are not exploited in the Soviet system in which there are no capitalists and all profits go to a workers' government, which uses them for the people's needs. Because all parties representing capitalists are banned, it was argued that the one-party dictatorship of the Communist Party represented all of the people and is therefore the most democratic government on Earth.

These views were challenged by Marxist scholars all over the world. Most modern Marxists argue that nothing is inevitable. Modern Marxists argue that socialism means both political and economic democracy. Socialism is desirable, but its achievement depends on the actions of millions of individuals under certain circumstances. Most modern Marxists advocated democratic socialism and consider that the Soviet Union was neither democratic nor socialist. They argue that socialism means the democratic control of the economy and that cannot happen without political democracy.

In the United States, the old socialist and communist parties almost disappeared by the 1960s. There were, however, three new movements that produced progressive political activity and progressive social science. First, there was the Civil Rights movement, which attempted to gain equality for African Americans. There were allied movements for the rights of Latino Americans, Native Americans (erroneously called Indians because Columbus thought he had landed in India), all religious minorities, and all other ethnic minorities. Second, there was a movement for the liberation of women from all of the discrimination they had faced for so long. Third, there was a movement against the Vietnam War, led mostly by students and young people previously in no political organization.

These three movements achieved many victories and changed the way many in the United States thought about issues. They defeated an incumbent president for his support of the Vietnam War, they produced formal equality for minorities (but not economic equality), and they produced formal equality for women (but not economic equality). The movements also profoundly changed U.S. social sciences and humanities, producing progressive movements in anthropology, economics, sociology, political science, history, philosophy, and many other areas. There was the creation of new areas of formal study, such as women's studies, environmental studies, and ethnic studies. In economics, the progressive economic movement combined the progressive post-Keynesians who evolved from Keynes, the radical institutionalists who evolved from Veblen, and the radical non–Soviet Marxists.

REVIEW QUESTIONS FOR APPENDIX 16.2

Discuss the different faces of socialism.
1. Describe the evolution of communism from the socialist movements in the post–World War II period.
2. How is communism like socialism, and how is it different?
3. Explain how communism is viewed and treated in the United States.

Explain the difference between Marxism and Soviet Marxism.
4. Explain how Marxist scholars argue that Marxism and Soviet Marxism are different.

Name current "flavors" of socialist thought.
5. Describe social movements of the late twentieth century and their impact on the United States.

PART II

MICROECONOMICS: PRICES, PROFITS, AND POVERTY

PART II, SECTION 1

INTRODUCTION

CHAPTER 17

Robinson Crusoe
Two Perspectives on Microeconomics

This chapter begins with a discussion of two sharply conflicting perspectives: traditional, neoclassical economics and progressive political economy. It then provides a brief road map that shows where the rest of the book will go. Finally, for an amusing example of the differences between these perspectives, we present two different views on Robinson Crusoe's interesting island economy.

LEARNING OBJECTIVES

After reading this chapter, you should be able to:

- Explain the key differences between neoclassical economics and progressive political economy.
- Describe how the different models or views of neoclassical economists and progressive political economy lead to different policies in dealing with social issues.
- Compare and contrast the two views in the case of a hypothetical "Robinson Crusoe" economy.

TWO DIFFERENT LENSES TO VIEW THE WORLD

An important feature of this book is that we provide two different lenses through which to examine the actual working of today's capitalist system. The first lens is that of traditional or neoclassical economic theory. As you will see in Sections 4 and 5 of Part II, **neoclassical economics** *asserts a basic policy conclusion that free-market capitalism works well as long as government does not intervene in the economy.* The government should not try to increase equality, cure poverty, or provide free health care or free higher education. Government should not intervene in the economy on behalf of women or subordinated groups but should let competitive markets work to eventually cure all problems. This lens is a conservative way of looking at economics. Most neoclassical economists are conservative. There are neoclassical liberals, but their liberal views on issues such as free public education and universal health care are always contrary to the basic neoclassical view that market prices should allocate all goods and services.

The second lens comes from a perspective that rejects neoclassical economic analysis. This perspective is familiar to you because of the ideas of economists such as Thorstein Veblen, Karl

Marx, and John Maynard Keynes, studied earlier in Part I. We call the perspective that combines the common features of nontraditional economists progressive political economy. **Progressive political economists** *do not believe that the existing market system is perfect. They analyze it in order to see how to change it so as to improve it in the interest of better social outcomes.* While the neoclassical analysis is used by almost all conservative economists and some liberals, progressive political economy analysis is used by many liberals and all radicals. When liberals and radicals differ, both views are discussed.

What are some of the highlights of the specific differences? First, the basic unit of analysis for traditional or neoclassical economics is the individual. Neoclassical economists make assumptions about the behavior of individuals, such as that everyone makes rational decisions or choices. They assume that those choices are made in the individual's own best self-interest. From the assumption that people make rational decisions on the basis of what they think is best for them, neoclassical economists then deduce how individuals as members of households or owners of businesses make decisions about consumption and production.

The basic unit of analysis for progressive political economics is the relationships between groups in the economy. The economy includes not only the technological basis to produce what society needs to provision itself but also the relationships of consensus or conflict between the groups in that production process. For example, in a society based on slavery, there are conflicts between slaves and masters. In a society based on capitalism, there are relations between the dominant group, the capitalist owners of business, and the largest single group—the employees. According to progressive economists, the relationships between owners and employees often involve conflicts. These relationships are explored in detail.

Second, most neoclassical economists analyze the economic sphere in isolation from the rest of society. The analysis focuses on market activity. Nonmarket activities and transactions, such as household activities and childcare, and the impact of culture and norms on choices and opportunities are not part of the picture. Progressive political economists believe that society evolves as described in Part I, and they focus on the context in which individuals make their decisions. Each succeeding society in the evolutionary process has a new and unique set of norms and institutions. For example, the labor market in the period of slavery had economic and political laws about buying and selling people. The labor market under capitalism has quite different laws about buying and selling labor services for a given length of time. Slaves were sold by their owners, whereas free workers normally sell their own services. Thus, one set of conditions and behaviors is acceptable and common in feudalism or slavery, but a quite different set holds for modern capitalism. Progressives believe that economics and choices are embedded in a social and political context. For example, spending decisions in the family are influenced by social ideas about men and women. Public health care is influenced by the political power of legislators to obtain funding, while the rich can pay high amounts of money for their own private doctors.

Third, conservative economists, such as Milton Friedman, claim that they champion the rights of the individual. It is true that neoclassical economists do emphasize the right of all individuals to spend their money to buy whatever they want. They also emphasize the right of capitalist investors to invest in whatever they want. They argue that capitalists should have the right to hire and fire employees any time, just as employees should have the right to quit at any time. They argue that there should be no taxes on investment income because such taxation interferes with individual rights within a free market.

Progressives point out that even if people have the right to buy the goods and services they want, many things cost too much for most people to buy. Therefore, this type of freedom is not really freedom for everybody but freedom only for the rich. In the name of freedom for individuals to spend freely, conservatives fight against many types of government spending, except for military spending, that requires taxes from the earnings of individuals because it reduces spending by individuals. Progressives question the security of individuals if corporations do not have to follow safety laws and if disabled or retired employees have no public health care or social security. How free is the average worker if there are no free lunches for poor children and no unemployment compensation? How can one support individual rights but oppose social security for elderly individuals, many of whom would otherwise be living in poverty?

Part III reveals that neoclassical economists believe that the aggregate economy tends to be in balance except when there is an external shock, after which it recovers automatically and rapidly. Progressive economists believe that the capitalist economic system generates cycles of boom and bust. These cycles lead to instability and insecurity for many individuals. Progressives consider how the economy could be changed to eliminate cycles of boom and bust.

We have listed only a few main points of the neoclassical and the progressive views. These two lenses, through which two sets of economists see the world, are explained in detail in the rest of the book. Most economists do not fall at either extreme of the two views but somewhere in between.

ROBINSON CRUSOE

Robinson Crusoe was a fictitious character in a novel called *Robinson Crusoe*, written by Daniel Defoe and initially published in 1719. Crusoe is shipwrecked on an island. No one else is on the island when he lands. Crusoe decides for himself what crops to plant and what technology to use on the basis of the resources of the island. This island economy metaphor was and is still used as a model by many classical and neoclassical economists. One famous example of its use by economists is its presentation as a model by the famous conservative economist Milton Friedman in his popular book *Capitalism and Freedom* (1967).

Friedman supposes that there are millions of households, each on a separate island as Robinson Crusoe was, and that they freely decide to exchange goods with each other. His story assumes that every household is an independent producer. The model assumes that exchanges are freely pursued with other independent producers with no coercion and no government. Friedman calls these producers "a collection of Robinson Crusoes, as it were. Each household uses the resources it controls to produce goods and services that it exchanges for goods and services produced by other households, on terms mutually acceptable to the two parties to the bargain" (p. 12).

Friedman tells us that this economy of exchange by millions of Robinson Crusoes is just the way that capitalism works. Under capitalism, there is voluntary coordination among all producers through market exchange from which everyone benefits. According to Friedman, "Voluntary cooperation rests on the elementary . . . proposition that both parties to an economic transaction benefit from it, provided the transaction is bilaterally voluntary and informed. Exchange can therefore bring about coordination without coercion" (p. 12). Friedman assumes that both parties benefit and that there is no coercion in a market system. He notes that many critics attack this argument. Instead of giving us the contrary arguments and refuting them, however, he merely illustrates how his assumptions apply in the hypothetical, idealized form of capitalism in which everybody is a Robinson Crusoe and lord of their own island.

Although Friedman admits that his model in which a number of Robinson Crusoes voluntarily engage in exchange is unreal, he assures us that the situation in the ideal form, market capitalism, is the same as in the imaginary model. This view of capitalism is held by most neoclassical economists, though usually less clearly stated. Friedman writes: "Despite the important role of enterprises and of money in our actual economy, and despite the numerous and complex problems they raise, the central characteristic of the market technique of achieving coordination is fully displayed in the simple exchange economy that contains neither enterprises nor money" (p. 13).

The problem is that such is not capitalism in the real world. It is a fictitious and imaginary economy used by Friedman and other neoclassical theorists to try to understand the real world. Even Friedman admits that this assumed Robinson Crusoe capitalist economy is not true and cannot be true under present conditions. Actually, under present complex technological and global circumstances, capitalism must use large-scale enterprises instead of producing everything by the capitalist's own labor. Moreover, each separate producer cannot just barter its goods for others but must sell goods for money and buy other goods with money, which adds many more complications. Thus, in the real world, capitalist enterprises must hire workers. Capitalists produce only for profit made from employing workers. Firms sell the product for money, not for the use of those who produce it. Most twenty-first-century Americans have little choice but to seek employment and perform wage labor in order to earn a living.

In the ideal, hypothetical capitalist economy, all resources go to their most productive uses, and all goods and services are allocated efficiently. In Friedman's ideal world of millions of individual Robinson Crusoes, everyone has resources and can decide voluntarily whether to exchange with others. "As in that simple model, so in the complex enterprise and money-exchange economy, co-operation is strictly individual and voluntary" (p. 13). But critics point out several problems with the model. For example, employees in the real world are not the same as independent producers. Yet Friedman alleges: "The employee is protected from coercion by the employer because of other employers for whom he can work . . ." (pp. 14–15). This notion that employees are completely free to do as they please is the most important false assumption of conservative economics. Why is it false?

That there is an economic category termed "workers" or "labor" is determined by the reality that workers do not control the physical means of production. Workers are required to sell their skills for a price (wage) in order to survive. Workers must take available jobs at any company offering them because unemployment is a reality. Unemployment means increased coercion in the job market. In the real world, enormous enterprises with enormous resources face individual workers with almost no resources. An individual worker does not have power equal to that of IBM or General Motors. Thus, the employment relationship is inherently an unequal one. If there is any unemployment, and there always is under capitalism (except in rare exceptions such as during World War II), then a worker faces the choice of working for a capitalist at the wage offered or being unemployed. If it is a pure, unregulated market economy with no unemployment insurance, then the unemployed must starve.

The flaw in Friedman's argument may be seen not only in the labor market between employers and employees but also in the commodity market between consumers and firms. Friedman claims that capitalism ". . . is, in political terms, a system of proportional representation. Each man can vote, as it were, for the color of tie he wants and get it; he does not have to see what color the majority wants and then, if he is in the minority, submit" (p. 13). In other words, according to Friedman, people can spend their money any way they like. Consumers are free to spend on black shoes or brown shoes. The market will produce just exactly what consumers want according to the number of dollars spent by each person.

Consumers voting with their dollars might make some sense if we all had the same amount of wealth to start with, but we do not. It has been calculated that the richest man in the United States has wealth equal to the poorest 40 million. The richest 226 individuals in the world have wealth equal to that of the poorest 2.5 billion (see Sherman, 1995, Chapter 6). In this system of monetary "proportional representation," the richest man in the United States has 40 million times the votes of each of the 40 million poorest Americans on average. Surely, that is not an equal degree of freedom, and it is not the same as political proportional representation in which each person has one vote. Rather, it is an economic and political oligarchy in which some have almost anything they want while others have insufficient food, inadequate clothes, and miserable slum housing or are homeless. In theory, everyone has the power to choose among various commodities, but the crucial point is that one's spending depends on how much income one has.

ROAD MAP TO PART II

Part I of this book provided an introduction to economic history and thought. It gave the reader a sense of how contemporary economic theory fits into this broader intellectual tradition. Part II discusses microeconomics. Microeconomics is the study of how individual consumers, individual firms, and individual workers make decisions about production and consumption. The interplay of firms and households within capitalism determines how output and income is divided among people—a key issue of microeconomics. Microeconomics deals mainly with how prices are determined in the market and how profits are determined for business. Microeconomics also explores the distribution of income and poverty. The first two sections of Part II deal with progressive microeconomics. The last two sections deal with neoclassical microeconomics. Instructors and general readers may choose what approach or approaches to read.

SUMMARY

The authors use two main lenses through which to examine and evaluate the world. These views are the traditional or neoclassical perspective and the critical or progressive political economy perspective. The traditional view builds on the work of the classical economists, such as Adam Smith, and the neoclassical economists, such as Alfred Marshall. This approach makes assumptions about how the world works and then uses deductive logic to reach conclusions. Policies based on these conclusions often advocate unregulated market capitalism and oppose government intervention. The progressive perspective builds on the work of Karl Marx, Thorstein Veblen, and John Maynard Keynes. This perspective is often critical of traditional analysis. Progressive activists often advocate policies that help ordinary working people, the middle class, and the poor. These policies often involve more democratic public involvement in the economy.

The story of Robinson Crusoe is a useful metaphor for the neoclassical view of the world. It sees the economy as a collection of autonomous producers and consumers engaging in mutually beneficial exchange. The actors in this mythical world work for themselves, experience no coercion, and live in a world with no government. Progressives see the Robinson Crusoe story as a biased and incomplete metaphor. Progressives assert that the study of economics must begin with an understanding of the actual economic institutions of modern capitalism.

The study of economics today is divided into microeconomics and macroeconomics. Microeconomics is the study of how individual consumers, firms, and workers make decisions about production, distribution, and consumption. Macroeconomics is the study of how the economy as a whole behaves with respect to growth, unemployment, inflation, and business cycles.

SUGGESTED READINGS

Milton Friedman, *Capitalism and Freedom* (1982 [1957]), provides an accessible introduction to the neoclassical view of the world, while an accessible introduction to the progressive view of the world is presented in Howard Sherman, *How Society Makes Itself* (2006). Part I of this book spelled out the views of the economists in each of these camps.

KEY TERMS

neoclassical economics
progressive political economists

REVIEW QUESTIONS

Explain the key differences between neoclassical economics and progressive political economy.

1. What are the two key assumptions that neoclassical economists make about individuals? What are those assumptions used for?
2. What do progressive political economists claim is a key factor for individuals making decisions? Give an example.
3. Neoclassical economists talk about how individuals are free to spend their dollars in the market. What does this mean? What problems do progressive political economists see with this "freedom"?
4. What is the difference between microeconomics and macroeconomics?

Describe how the different models or views of neoclassical economists and progressive political economy lead to different policies in dealing with social issues.

5. What role should the government play according to neoclassical economists? According to progressive political economists?
6. Should the government do much spending in the economy according to neoclassical economists? Why or why not?
7. What types of spending does each group think the government should do in the economy?
8. What do the neoclassical economists have to say about taxes? How do taxes interfere with the individual?

Compare and contrast the two views in the case of a hypothetical "Robinson Crusoe" economy.

9. Briefly describe the Robinson Crusoe metaphor underpinning the traditional economics perspective.
10. What happens if transactions are not voluntary? Can you give an example of a transaction that might not be voluntary?
11. What shortcomings do critical economists see in the neoclassical use of the Robinson Crusoe metaphor?
12. How does relative power enter into transactions between employers and employees?
13. What is meant by consumers "voting with their dollars"? Does everyone have an equal vote? Why or why not?

PART II, SECTION 2

ELEMENTS OF PROGRESSIVE MICROECONOMICS

CHAPTER 18

The Two Americas
Inequality, Class, and Conflict

Part I followed the evolution of economic systems from the earliest hunter-gatherer societies to contemporary capitalism. While capitalism as an economic system has clearly led the way for unprecedented growth in the production of goods and services, it has not done so well in the distribution of the income and wealth that comes from production for the market. It is the core objective of this chapter to describe some of the outcomes of capitalism by focusing on the extent of income and wealth inequality that characterize life in the United States. Some people refer to today's state of growing inequality as the "Two Americas." By the end of this chapter, the reader will have a more concrete understanding of what this phrase means.

LEARNING OBJECTIVES

After reading this chapter, you should be able to:

- Describe the sources of income and purchasing power for households.
- Compare and contrast relevant statistics on income and wealth for the United States.
- Define class and explain how the definition ties into the sources of income to households.

INEQUALITY: INCOME

The degree of inequality in economic outcomes and the purchasing power of households in a particular economy are frequently measured on the basis two criteria: income and wealth. Wealth and wealth inequality are discussed in the next section. **Income** is *the stream of receipts from work or property generated by an individual or household over a time period.* If a person earns $25,000 a year from working at a job, these wages are his or her income. Most income for households is earned through involvement in the production of goods and services in the economy in the form of wages and salaries (employee income) and from profits, interest, and rent (income from property). Other sources of income that do not come from production include government programs (transfers) such as Social Security, disability insurance, and welfare programs, to name a few.

As can clearly be seen in Table 18.1, the majority of income in the United States comes from wages and salaries. Personal income (before taxes), which includes wages and salaries, profits, interest, rent, and government transfers, totaled $10,891.2 billion in the year 2006. Wages and salaries were $7,485.9 billion, or almost 69 percent of personal income. Profits were $1,015.1 billion, or about 9.3 percent

194

94

Table 18.1

Personal Income to U.S. Households (billions of dollars)

	2005	2006
Employee compensation	7,030.3	7,485.9
Profit (proprietor's income**)**	970.7	1,015.1
Rent	72.8	77.4
Interest (receipts on assets)	1,519.4	1,656.3
Government transfers	1,526.6	1,602.2
TOTAL: Personal income (before taxes)	10,239.2	10,891.2

Source: Bureau of Economic Analysis, National Economic Account, National Income and Product Accounts Table, http://www.bea.gov/national/nipaweb/TableView.asp#Mid.

of personal income; interest was $1,656.3 billion, or 15.2 percent of personal income; rent was $77.4 billion, or 7.1 percent of personal income; and government transfers were $1,602.2 billion, or 14.7 percent of personal income in the year 2006. Table 18.1 also shows figures for 2005. Although the numbers are somewhat different, the percentages for each source of income are comparable.

There are many ways to examine the distribution of income to households. We can look at distribution of income by different social groupings, such as by ethnicity, gender, or age (the focus in Chapter 22). We can also look at the overall distribution of income by breaking the population into five equal-sized groups called quintiles. Table 18.2 shows the shares of total household income by quintiles. The lowest quintile (one-fifth of U.S. households) took in only 3.4 percent of total income in 2005. The highest quintile took in 50.4 percent of total income. Putting it another way, 20 percent of households took in over 50 percent of the income generated in 2005, while 20 percent took in less than 4 percent of income generated. As you can see from Table 18.2, the share of total income going to the lowest 20 percent of households has decreased, and the share of income going to the highest 20 percent of households has increased since 1975. For example, in 1975, the highest quintile received 43.6 percent of income compared to 50.4 percent in 2005.

How does the United States compare with other countries with respect to distribution of income? A measure commonly used to compare income distribution between countries is the Gini coefficient. It was developed by an Italian statistician named Corrado Gini early in the twentieth century. The **Gini coefficient** is *a calculation of income inequality that falls between zero and one.* A Gini coefficient of zero would mean income is distributed perfectly equally among the population. For example, if the population of a country is divided into quintiles, each quintile receives an equal proportion of income generated. The closer the number gets to one, the more unequal the distribution of income. Looking at Table 18.3, in the year 2000, the Gini coefficient for the United States was 0.408. Compare that statistic to India with a Gini of 0.368, Denmark at 0.247. Clearly, the United States does not fare well in comparison to other countries using this measure.

Table 18.3 also compares the share of income going to the lowest quintile (or 20 percent) of the population and the highest quintile for several countries. Next to each country is the year the data was collected, so comparisons between countries must be used with care. In fact, all statistics must be used with care. In this table, the column reporting income for the lowest quintile of the population, the share going to poorest 20 percent of the population in the United States, is in about the middle of the countries listed. It is interesting to note, however, that the share of income going to India's poorest quintile is higher than the share going to the poorest quintile in the United States.

Table 18.2

Distribution of Household Income: Shares by Quintiles

	2005	1995	1985	1975
Lowest Quintile	3.4%	3.7%	3.9%	4.3%
Second Quintile	8.6	9.1	9.8	10.4
Third Quintile	14.6	15.2	16.2	17.0
Fourth Quintile	23.0	23.3	24.4	24.7
Highest Quintile	50.4	48.7	45.6	43.6

Source: U.S. Census Bureau, Selected Measures of Household Income Dispersion: 1975 to 2005, http://www.census.gov/hhes/www/income/histinc/p60n0231_tablea3.pdf.

Table 18.3

Gini Coefficients and Share of Income for Selected Countries

Country (year)	Gini Coefficient	Share of Income to Lowest Quintile (%)	Share of Income to Highest Quintile (%)
Denmark (1997)	0.247	8.3	35.8
Sweden (2000)	0.250	9.1	36.6
Germany (2000)	0.283	8.5	36.9
Australia (1994)	0.352	5.9	41.3
India (2004–05)	0.368	9.5	36.5
Russian Federation (2002)	0.399	6.1	46.6
United States (2000)	0.408	5.4	45.8
Argentina (2004)	0.513	3.1	55.4
Haiti (2001)	0.592	2.4	63.4
Bolivia (2002)	0.601	1.5	63.0

Source: The World Bank, 2007 World Development Indicators, July 1, 2007, http://siteresources.worldbank.org/DATASTATISTICS/Resources/table2_7.pdf.

Not only is there inequality in America, but this richest of all countries also has a large amount of outright poverty. According to the U.S. Census Bureau, the average poverty threshold for unrelated individuals in 2005 was an income of $9,973, and for a family of three, the poverty-level income was $15,577. In 2005, 12.6 percent of the U.S. population lived in poverty, according to the official government data. Nearly 11 percent of families lived below the poverty level. For female-headed households, the numbers are even worse. In 2005, a little over 31 percent of female-headed households lived below the poverty threshold. Even more surprising is the number of working people who live below the poverty threshold. Just over 11 percent of people living below the poverty-level income worked year-round, full-time jobs.

The average weekly wage in 1973 was $502. By 1998, the average weekly wage had dropped to $442. (These figures were derived after removing inflation; that is, they are calculated in 1997 dollars.) While workers' wages declined, aggregate U.S. production actually rose by 32.8 percent in the same period. While ordinary production-line workers suffered in this period from declining real-wage rates, corporate executive officers (CEOs) did very well. The salaries of CEOs rose

Table 18.4

Poverty Status in the United States

	2005	1995	1985	1975
All people	12.6%	13.8%	14.0%	12.3%
All families	10.8	12.3	12.6	10.9
Female-headed households	31.1	36.5	37.6	37.5
Workers as percentage of all poor people: worked year round, full time	11.4	10.5	9.3	7.7 (1978)

Source: U.S. Census Bureau, Historical Poverty Tables Current Population Survey various years. http://www.census.gov/hhes/www/poverty/histpov/histpovtb.html

from being 41 times the average wage in 1960 to 326 times the average wage in 1997 and to 500 times the average wage in 2002. The one thing that ordinary workers were able to increase was their debt. The debt of the average household rose from 29.5 percent of personal income in 1949 to 84.8 percent of personal income in 1997.

It is worth stressing that the members of the richest 1 percent—from millionaires to billionaires—make most of their income from property ownership, mainly from ownership of corporations. The only apparent exception is the salary of CEOs, but these enormous salaries are actually corporate profits for the most part. Corporations also often give CEOs the option to buy stock at very favorable prices.

On the other hand, the income of the bottom 90 percent comes primarily from wages and salaries, plus government transfers for things such as unemployment compensation. The bottom 90 percent, however, receive only negligible amounts of property income.

What is the source of corporate profits? If we examine what the income of the average employee can buy, we see it is far below the amount of product the employee produces. The average employee produces a surplus above his or her wages. This surplus is what constitutes corporate profits. Picture how much profit General Motors would make if it had no workers. The answer is zero. Moreover, being a rational corporation, General Motors hires men and women only if it expects to make a profit from them. If it does not look profitable to use all of the employees that General Motors has, it immediately fires those it thinks will not produce profits for the corporation. Multiply the number of employees by the surplus that each employee produces each day and you have the daily profit—no mystery! Actually, it is more precise to say that the surplus is produced by all the employees working together, since modern labor is not done by isolated individuals.

It does not matter whether an employee's wage is high or low. Employees must produce a profit for the corporation or they are fired. It is clear if we look at women in a sweatshop producing high-priced clothing for extremely low wages that this process produces a surplus that becomes a high rate of profit. However, a woman working as a computer engineer for IBM at $100,000 a year (a long way above the average wage) also produces a surplus for the company. If she does not produce far more product than the $100,000 she is paid, she too will be fired. It is quite common that this computer engineer is paid $100,000 but produces a product worth $200,000 a year, thus producing a surplus of $100,000 a year for IBM. The computer engineer and the sweatshop worker have something in common that neither would suspect: both create profit for a corporation. Of course, one has a comfortable life and one has a miserable life, so their views will be very different.

For this reason, there may be conflicts over the amount of wages and the quality of working conditions at any wage level. There have been bitter strikes by women producing clothing for a tiny wage under terrible conditions. But there are also conflicts by highly paid computer engineers against a corporation. There have also been struggles by highly compensated professional athletes against owners of sports franchises.

The end result is always determined by the comparative power of the employees and the employers, expressed in conflicts under given economic conditions of supply and demand. For example, if millions of workers are unemployed, then it is possible for a corporation to cut the wages of those who are employed because of the implicit competition for jobs by the unemployed. The wages of employees are determined, in part, by their power and courage under given economic conditions, not by some impersonal and implacable economic principle that holds at all times in all places.

INEQUALITY: WEALTH

Wealth or net worth refers to *the accumulated assets minus liabilities held by a particular household or individual.* An example makes this definition clearer. Assume an individual's possessions consist of a car worth $5,000, furniture worth $1,000, and other personal assets worth $1,000. At the same time, he owes $5,000 in student loans. We would say this person has a positive net worth of $2,000. As you might expect, many college students have a negative net worth.

Wealth signifies ownership of financial resources and the opportunity to secure the "good life." Wealth enables members of households to pursue opportunities for education, home ownership, comfort, and the ability to weather shocks such as a job loss or a sudden medical bill. Wealth inequality is even more extreme than income inequality. Wealth inequality probably means low income in the past and the lack of any rich relative to leave you some money or other assets. Inability to save out of income means you cannot buy assets and build wealth.

Again dividing the population into quintiles, the lowest income quintile had median net worth of $7,396 in the year 2000. Not counting home equity of those who owned homes, the net worth of the lowest quintile was $1,025. The highest income quintile had $185,500 in median net worth and, not counting equity in their homes, still had net worth of $98,510. In 2000, 9.1 percent of families did not even have a checking account, only 52.2 percent had retirement accounts, 21.3 percent owned stocks, and only 3 percent of families owned bonds. On the other side, according to the Federal Reserve's Flow of Funds Accounts, borrowing by households rose from $330.5 in 1995 to $771.1 in 2002 and personal savings by households dropped from $250.9 in 1995 to $183.2 in 2002 (in billions of dollars).

We saw that corporate stock is mostly held by a tiny percentage of the American people. In 2003, 58 percent of all corporate stock was held by the top 1 percent of households. This is an enormous increase in a little over a decade. In 1991, the top 1 percent owned "only" 39 percent of all corporate stock. Thus, the percentage of corporate stock held by the richest 1 percent rose at a very rapid pace, while the percentage of holdings of every lower income group fell dramatically. These findings are from official tax data analyzed by the Congressional Budget Office (see Johnston, 2006).

CLASS

There is a myth that no conflict exists among classes in the United States and that almost every American is "middle class." Yet every day in the media, there is widespread discussion of conflict among classes—though the classes are called by names other than "upper," "middle," and "low." Most liberals describe the class warfare carried out by corporations and their rich owners against their employees by pushing wages lower, against consumers by pushing prices higher, and against public interests in many ways, such as by poisoning the environment. Many conservatives claim there is no conflict between corporations and their employees, consumers, or the public. They do spend a lot of time describing an alleged conflict between what they call the "liberal, intellectual (effhead) elite" and "us common people."

Table 18.5

Median Net Worth by Income Quintile in 2000: All Households

	Total	Excluding Home Equity
Lowest Quintile	$7,396	$1,025
Second Quintile	$26,950	$6,349
Third Quintile	$44,400	$12,333
Fourth Quintile	$78,001	$26,998
Highest Quintile	$185,500	$98,510

Source: U.S. Census Bureau, Net Worth and Asset Ownership of Households, Current Population Reports, May 2003.

The concept of class is seldom, if ever, considered by most Americans. If they think of class at all, most say, "I am in the middle class." But middle class is fuzzy and undefined, so it is not much help for any kind of analysis. What is needed is a definition that can be a sharp tool of analysis among different groups of people. For that purpose, **class** is defined to mean *a group of people who obtain their income in a way that distinguishes them from other groups and shows their relationship to other groups in the economic process.* This definition clearly ties into earlier discussions about sources of income to households from involvement in production of goods and services.

Every complex society thus far in history has maintained class systems. In the U.S. South before the Civil War, for example, there were slaves and slave owners. Slaves were forced to provide labor but had no rights, legal or otherwise, to any part of the final product. The slave owners, who owned the final product, hired supervisors to manage the slaves for optimum profit. The Old South also had a class of free farmers, a class of merchants, and a class of free craftspeople. Notice that what is important is the relation of each class to the economy, not their level of income. A merchant is someone who buys and sells goods. He or she may have high income or low income, but he or she is still a merchant.

What are the classes in the United States today? The largest class, larger than all the rest combined no matter how you define it, is the employee class, people who work for wages and salaries. Clearly, employees get most of their income by working for the owners of businesses. Some are very poor because their wages for full-time work are low or because they cannot get enough hours of work. Others may be basketball players who make a million dollars a year. Basketball players are still employees, have conflict with their bosses over who should receive the box-office receipts and television revenues, and sometimes go on strike.

Some of the literature on class calls employees "workers." In the nineteenth century, almost all employees were industrial workers or farm workers. Professionals, such as lawyers, were usually independent and were not employed by anyone else but were their own bosses. Today, even lawyers are often employed by a firm or agency. The term *employee* today applies to intellectual workers and professionals, such as lawyers and college professors. A college professor performs labor and is employed by a college just as a gardener performs labor and is employed by a college. A gardener may be called a "worker" while a professor is called an "employee," but they are in the same economic relationship with the college. This book uses *worker* and *employee* to mean the same thing: a person hired by someone else to provide labor services.

On the other side of the line from employees and workers are the employers who own the business. They may own all of a small business, part of a partnership, or stock in a corporation. They get most of their money from the profits of the business. Since higher wages to employees reduce profits for the business owner, the employees and employers are always in a tug-of-war: firm owners want higher profits and employees want higher wages and more benefits.

Of course, if the class situation were that simple, we would all be perfectly clear about it. But it is not simple. Many employees also own some stock, whether directly or indirectly through pension plans, which means they are also part-owners of a business. Typically, employee stock ownership amounts to relatively little income. Many owners of business also are employed. Usually, they work as managers. The top managers own most of the corporate stock, and the wealthiest owners of stock constitute most of the top managers by income.

Among the employee class are both very low-paid and very high-paid workers. As we learned earlier, the top managers have incomes hundreds of times the income of the average worker. Yet the very richest draw most of their income from corporate profits that dwarf their incomes as managers. There are groups or classes that fall between the very low-paid and very high-paid workers; for example, middle managers may make significantly more than the average employee, and lower level managers may make little more than the average employee. Both lower and middle managers give orders to employees, but they must also take orders from higher management. Moreover, like the average employee, lower and middle managers can be fired. They are literally in the middle not only in income but also in power and job security.

Among employees is also a group or class of professionals. Professionals range from low-paid teachers and nurses to very high-paid engineers. High-paid professionals often are in a position to give orders to many other employees, but they also must take orders from those above them. Moreover, high-paid professionals can be fired, as many were in the last recession. Even high-paid professionals, like many managers, are in the middle in various ways.

Individual businesspeople who run small businesses are also in the middle to some extent. The smallest ones have no employees. Even with a few employees and a middle-level income, their interests are similar to those of big business only in the preservation of an economy based on private business. They differ in many ways from big business, however, because most operate on the thin edge between survival and bankruptcy. They have no reserves, and their own salaries are an important part of expenses.

SUMMARY

While traditional theory begins with abstract assumptions to study the economy, most progressive economists believe we should begin with known facts about the economy and economic outcomes. Thus, this chapter began with evidence of the unequal distribution of income in the United States. It then examined the class relationships underpinning that inequality. In the United States today, there is extreme inequality between individuals in terms of both income and wealth. We saw that income and wealth tend to be concentrated within a small group and that the average citizen is now going deeper into debt each year.

SUGGESTED READINGS

The best book on class is Eric Olin Wright's *Class* (1985).

The data on individual inequality (all from government agencies) are reported in clear, simple language by Chuck Collins, Betsy Leondar-Wright, and Holly Sklar in their book *Shifting Fortunes: The Perils of the Growing American Wealth Gap* (1999). Similarly, Chuck Collins and

Felice Yeskel's book, *Economic Apartheid in America* (2000) examines the recent trends in income and wealth inequality, their causes, and possible solutions. In August of 2006, The Center on Budget and Policy Priorities reported that, "The number of uninsured Americans reached an all-time high in 2005." The number of uninsured Americans rose to 46.6 million or 15.9 percent of the population. Since 1981 the center has been informing public debates with its research and analysis of state and federal budgeting decisions. It has a special interest in understanding how these policies influence the welfare of low-income families and individuals. They are on the web at http://www.cbpp.org/

KEY WORDS

class	income
Gini coefficient	wealth

REVIEW QUESTIONS

Describe the sources of income and purchasing power for households.
1. What is the difference between income and wealth?
2. Personal income can be broken down into five sources or categories. What are these categories and what percentage of personal income comes from each of these sources?
3. Which sources of income are generated from work and which from the ownership of assets?

Compare and contrast relevant statistics on income and wealth for the United States.
4. Use Table 18.2 to describe how the distribution of income has changed in the United States over the last three decades. Has inequality increased or decreased? How do you know?
5. How does the distribution of income in the United State compare with other countries?
6. What is a Gini coefficient? What would it mean if the Gini coefficient were equal to zero? What if it were equal to one?
7. Which counties in the world have a more equal distribution of income than the United States? Which countries have a more unequal distribution of income?
8. What is the poverty threshold for a family of three in the United States in 2005? What percentage of the population have income below this level?
9. One percent of households own what share of total stock market value?
10. Use Table 18.5 to compute the ratio of net worth for the highest income quintile with that of the lowest income quintile. Given the other evidence in this chapter, do you suspect that this ratio has increased or decreased over the last 30 years?
11. What has caused the increases in income and wealth inequality over the last three decades?

Define class and explain how the definition ties into the sources of income to households.
12. What do the authors mean by class? What is the largest class?
13. Which is more important in determining class: the level of income a person earns, or their relationship to the ownership of capital?

CHAPTER 19

Inequality, Exploitation, and Economic Institutions

Capitalism is a system in which capitalists own enterprises, hire employees to make a profit, own the product, and sell the product for a profit. Employees are fired if they do not make a profit for the capitalist enterprise. The employee's labor time (whether a day or a month) is divided into the necessary labor time to produce a product equal in value to the employee's compensation and the surplus labor time that is used to produce a profit for the employer. People are exploited when part of their day's labor is taken from them without pay. The surplus labor time of American employees is taken from them without pay. In this sense, all American employees of capitalist firms are exploited.

LEARNING OBJECTIVES

After reading this chapter, you should be able to:

- Define and describe surplus labor.
- Discuss what constitutes exploitation and how exploitation occurs in various economic systems over time, including in contemporary capitalism.
- Define and use measures of exploitation.
- List and discuss the sources of conflict between employers and employees and the rate of exploitation.
- Give a brief overview of the history of labor conflicts.

EMPLOYEE COMPENSATION AND CORPORATE PROFIT

Meet Lisa. She just graduated college and took a job to earn money. She works as a copy editor for a publisher. She works hard at a computer all day, editing book manuscripts. Her job requires applying all she learned in four years of studying English. However, her check looks very small compared with what she produces for the employer.

Lisa is not paid an amount equal to what she produces. If she were, the employer would make no profit. No profit, no employment: Lisa would be fired. The only employer who will hire her with no profit is perhaps her favorite aunt. Every other employer expects Lisa to produce more than her wage. Under our economic system, a business does not last long unless every employee works for compensation less than the value of what she produces. That additional value produced by employees, above the amount of their wages and salaries, is a large profit when taken all together. The average employee's compensation is far less than the profit levels of the company owners, and therein lies the basic cause of inequality.

PUTTING NUMBERS ON A RAW DEAL

To illustrate further the disparity between workers' wages and companies' profits, suppose Lisa is paid a wage of $10 an hour, or $80 for an eight-hour day. Suppose that in an eight-hour day, she produces copy editing that adds $160 to the price of the books sold in the market. The publisher thus makes $80 profit from Lisa every day. That is $400 profit a week, or $20,800 a year. Similarly, meet Paul, who is a high-paid programmer making a salary of $78,000 a year, or $300 a day for a five-day week, working for a large software firm. When the programs he has produced in one day are sold, suppose their value is $600. The company makes $300 profit a day, or $78,000 a year, from Paul's labor. If Paul knew these figures, he might say, "I've been robbed." Of course, his employer will say it just pays the market price of Paul's power to labor, so it is perfectly legal under our economic institutions. Still, it is a raw deal for Paul, but a great deal for the software firm.

ARE LISA AND PAUL EXPLOITED?

The popular idea of economic exploitation is that people work long hours in bad conditions for low wages. About 15 percent of all Americans live in poverty. Millions of those people work full time at difficult or unpleasant jobs, but the jobs are so poorly paid that they are still below the poverty level. The minimum wage is only $5.85, so a full-time worker making minimum wage is still in poverty. That is exploitation. The federal minimum wage is scheduled to increase to $6.55 an hour on July 24, 2008 and to $7.25 an hour on July 24, 2009. These increases will not eliminate exploitation.

The technical definition of exploitation by progressive economists is precise. **Exploitation** *means that one group or class appropriates the labor of another group or class without paying the market price for all the commodities produced by that labor.* As shown earlier, under our present capitalist economic system, a business owns the entire product of an employee's labor. The employee gets only a fixed wage or salary. That wage or salary must be lower than the value of the product produced by the employee or the system does not work.

In the case of Lisa, we saw that her wage is $80 for an eight-hour day, while the employer's profit is also $80 a day from her labor. The amount of wages just equals the amount of profit, so her working day is divided equally between producing these two amounts. Thus, she works four hours a day to produce the amount of product necessary to pay her wages. But she also works four hours a day to produce a surplus that goes to the employer's profits. We call the four *hours worked to produce an amount of output equal to the value of her wages* the **necessary labor** time. We call *the amount produced for the company's profits* the **surplus labor** time.

What about Paul? His salary of $78,000 a year, or $300 a day, is far above that of the average worker. The software company's profit from his labor is also $300 a day, or $78,000 a year. Each day, Paul spends four hours of necessary labor producing an amount equal in value to his salary, but he also spends four hours of labor each day producing a surplus that becomes profit for his employer. Therefore, although Paul may live above the average living standard, he is still exploited according to the technical definition of exploitation. Whether you are exploited or not does not depend on the absolute level of your wage or salary. It only depends on whether or not you produce a surplus creating profit for a firm.

To measure exploitation, we use the rate of exploitation. Progressive economists define the **rate of exploitation** as *the ratio of surplus hours to necessary hours*, or the ratio of profit to employee compensation. In Lisa's case, we found that there are four hours of necessary labor per day to produce an amount of value equal to her wages. We also found that the surplus labor going to produce profits is four hours. Therefore, the rate of exploitation of Lisa is 1. In the case of Paul, we calculated that he expends four hours on necessary labor to produce his salary but also gives four hours of surplus labor to creating profits.

We look later at how and why exploitation happens and what might be realistic numbers for it. First, however, to clarify further the concept of exploitation, let us turn to the evolution of exploitative relationships during the course of history.

EXPLOITATION IN PREHISTORIC COMMUNAL SOCIETY

We find no exploitation in prehistoric communal societies. The economic unit consisted of the extended family, and the whole family worked together to hunt and gather food. There was some division of labor between groups of men and women, but all worked together with the group. No matter which group brought in the food, the food was shared by everyone. Since there were no ruling classes and no separate working classes, there was no group to be exploited and no group to do the exploiting.

EXPLOITATION IN A SLAVE SOCIETY

In the ancient slave societies of Greece and Rome as well as in the slave society of the U.S. South before the Civil War, the main economic institution was slavery. The main economic unit was the plantation. Every plantation had a small class of owners and masters plus a large class of slaves. The slaves worked a very long day. In ancient Rome, most slave plantations produced some commodities for the market, but most of their production was used on the plantation itself. Thus, the slaves produced food, clothing, and shelter for themselves. Because of the low level of technology, the necessary labor to produce a bare subsistence for themselves was perhaps eight hours on an optimistic estimate. In addition, the slaves were forced to work at least four more hours to produce a surplus for the masters. That surplus was used to provide luxurious living for the master's family, to pay the overseers, and to spend in the market. The rate of exploitation was at least four hours surplus to eight hours necessary labor. Thus, the rate was 0.5.

The slave owners would have liked a higher rate of exploitation, but if the slaves were given less subsistence or were forced to work many more hours, then the death rate of them would have risen. In both Rome and the old U.S. South, the life expectancy of the slave was already far lower than that of the masters. If life expectancy of the slave declined much lower, it would not have been profitable to buy slaves. Moreover, if the exploitation became intolerable, the slaves revolted. Even at this "low" rate of exploitation, each major slaveholder owned thousands of slaves, so the total profit was very large.

EXPLOITATION AND SERFDOM

Feudal society used a labor system known as serfdom. The serf was bound to the land of the manor. The serf had to work for the lord of the manor some number of days a year and hours a day. This system was enforced by tradition and by armed coercion from knights and men-at-arms. Most days of the year, the serf worked primarily for the feudal lord. Some days of the year, the serf worked for herself or himself. We take an average of the necessary labor and surplus labor done each day of the year to see how much necessary labor time and how much surplus labor time is typical for the whole year.

The level of technology had not changed too much from the most prosperous period of Roman slavery. Therefore, we can assume that on the average, the serfs, like slaves, worked eight hours a day for himself or herself in necessary labor to create their food, clothing, and shelter. In addition, the serfs were forced to work an average of four more hours a day to create castles and luxury goods for the lords and all of their many armed retainers. The labor included the labor of the men in the fields and of the women in the manor house. Each serf, male and female, was exploited economically. On the average, the rate of economic exploitation was four hours surplus to eight hours necessary labor. By these estimates, the rate of exploitation was 0.5. The feudal lords sometimes tried to enforce a higher rate of exploitation. The result, however, was either that the serfs began dying of disease or malnutrition or the serfs revolted.

EXPLOITATION AND CAPITALISM

What is the definition of capitalism? Capitalism is an economic system with the following features. First, a small class called capitalists owns the capital or means of production (equipment and industrial or commercial buildings). Second, capitalists hire employees for money per hour (wage) or per month (salary). Third, capitalists own the product or output of employees. Fourth, capitalists try to maximize profit and hire no workers unless they expect to make a profit from them.

Employees under capitalism normally work some hours of necessary labor to produce products equal to their own compensation. But they also work some hours of surplus labor to produce the profit of the capitalist business. In other words, an employee receives in wages or salary only part of the value of the product produced in the day's labor.

Now suppose that the directors of a corporation appoint a saintly woman with great compassion to be the corporate executive officer (CEO). This saintly woman does not want to exploit anyone, so she pays each employee a wage or salary equal to the value of the product produced by that employee. The result is that there is no margin for profit. What will happen when there are no profits? Most likely, the directors will fire her and put in another CEO who will lower the wages back to the market value of employees, far below the amount they produce. If the directors are also saintly and take no action, then eventually the thousands of stockholders will vote to fire the saintly directors. The new directors will hire a new CEO to lower the wages and salaries back to market value. If the corporation takes no action against the saintly CEO, but continues to pay wages and salaries equal to the whole product and leaving no profits, the corporation will fall behind its competitors and start losing money. Finally, it will go bankrupt and vanish.

Even without the intent to exploit, it is impossible to stop exploitation within this economic system. The economic institutions of capitalism cause exploitation even when run by ordinary men and women executives who merely follow the dictates of market competition. Of course, corporate scandals of recent decades have shown that some CEOs are crooks who will try to take even more profit than the institutions normally allow. Such crime, however, does not change the normal exploitation under legally operating businesses.

WHAT IS THE DEGREE OF EXPLOITATION IN AMERICA?

About 70 percent of labor time goes to necessary labor to produce employee compensation. This is the official ratio of all employee compensation to all national income in 2005, according to the

Bureau of Economic Analysis, United States Department of Commerce (found at http://www. bea.gov/). The remaining 30 percent of labor time goes to surplus labor used to produce a surplus going to profits, rent, and interest in the nation as a whole (ratio of all property income to all national income). The 30 percent of national income going to employee compensation divided by the number of employee hours a day translates to about two and a half hours of surplus labor every day and five and a half hours of necessary labor a day.

Many progressive economists believe that the surplus is much larger than the official 30 percent of the national product. There are many biases involved in the data. For example, the tax information on business has many loopholes to allow less profit to be reported. It is also easier for profit recipients than for recipients of ordinary employee compensation to stretch the law or lie. Some progressive economists argue that the surplus could be as high as four hours a day. In that case, the day is divided into four hours necessary and four hours surplus. As a compromise estimate that is easy to understand, we can say that there are at least three hours of surplus labor a day and five hours of necessary labor a day for the average worker in the United States as of 2006. If for all companies in the United States, the ratio of surplus labor to necessary labor averages about 3 divided by 5, then the rate of exploitation is about 0.60.

CAUSES OF CONFLICT

In Figure 19.1, the employee's day is divided between producing employee compensation and producing a surplus (profits). Let's assume that, on average, five labor hours go to compensation of employees, while three hours go to the employer's surplus, which becomes profit.

Three sources of conflict occur over this division. First, there are conflicts over wages and salaries. If employee compensation rises, then necessary labor increases and profits decrease as long as the total number of hours remains unchanged.

The second type of conflict is the total number of hours in the workday. If employee compensation stays the same, then longer hours mean more surplus labor going to profit. In the factories of the late nineteenth century, employees often worked 12 hours or more a day. In the early twentieth century, union-backed workers fought—through massive demonstrations and bloody confrontations with police and even the National Guard—for a shorter workday. In the 1930s, a liberal Democratic congress passed a law that prohibited workdays of longer than eight hours except at higher overtime rates of pay. The struggles continue even today as employers try to find loopholes in the law to force employees to work longer hours at the same pay.

Finally, even if employee compensation and the total number of hours are fixed, employers can still try to get employees to work harder and faster, that is, with greater intensity. Greater intensity of labor in the same number of hours would also raise the surplus and profits. We examine the struggle over intensity of labor in more detail later.

WHAT DETERMINES THE RATE OF EXPLOITATION?

Under the economic institutions of capitalism, employees do not receive payment for all they produce. Some goes to a surplus, which is used to create fortunes in profit. We saw that this source of great inequality is not caused by evil people but by the operation of capitalist economic institutions, which drive into bankruptcy any firm that does not appropriate a large surplus from its employees. We also saw that three main areas of conflict arise from the division of necessary and surplus labor: the total hours of work, the rate of employee compensation, and the intensity of labor.

The next obvious question is, what determines the exact division of the product between

Figure 19.1 **Necessary and Surplus Labor Time**

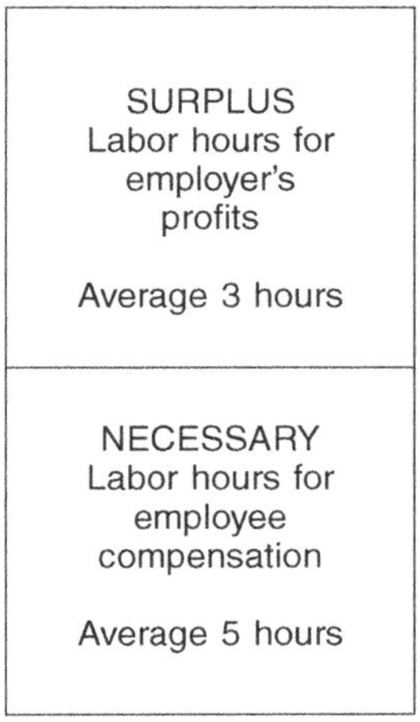

```
┌─────────────────────────────┐
│                             │
│          SURPLUS            │
│       Labor hours for       │
│         employer's          │
│           profits           │
│                             │
│       Average 3 hours       │
│                             │
├─────────────────────────────┤
│                             │
│         NECESSARY           │
│       Labor hours for       │
│          employee           │
│        compensation         │
│                             │
│       Average 5 hours       │
│                             │
└─────────────────────────────┘
```

employees and capitalist owners—that is, what determines the rate of exploitation? The basic answer is that the division of the product is determined by conflict between employees and capitalist owners. These conflicts, however, take place under certain objective conditions, which we identify and discuss next.

Ceilings and Floors

Before examining the three issues of conflict, it is worth noting that there is a ceiling and a floor to compensation in each society. In the capitalist economy, the **wage ceiling** is *the total amount produced by the employee above which the employee's compensation may not rise*. If an employee works an eight-hour day and produces a hundred hats, then there will be no profit if the employee is paid the equivalent of a hundred hats a day. Some early writers, such as the American neoclassical economist John Bates Clark (1847–1938), claimed that employees were paid an amount equal to what they produced, but that seems counter-intuitive. If all employees got the full amount of what they produce in compensation, then all firms would go bankrupt and there would be no capitalist system.

At the other extreme, other early writers, such as Thomas Malthus (1766–1834) said that employees would never be paid more than the lowest possible wage floor. The **wage floor** is *that compensation level below which an employee knows that she cannot provide necessary food, clothing, and shelter for her family*. Wages below the wage floor are subsistence wages. If capitalists attempt to pay below the wage floor to the average employee, then strikes, political upheavals, and in some countries, revolutions will occur. For example, employee compensation dropped by more than a third during the Great Depression. The result was political upheaval, a whole new labor federation, and major economic reforms. What is the actual level of compensation at the present time? It is well above subsistence for most employees, though approximately 15 percent of Americans live in poverty.

Conflict over Labor Compensation

Between the wage ceiling of the whole-product value and the wage floor of mere subsistence, how are wages and salaries determined? The most important factor determining employee compensation is the bargaining or battling between capital and labor. What is the bargaining strength of employees, individually and in unions? What is the bargaining strength of business, from a store on the corner to a giant corporation? Compensation is not determined in a technical fashion by some line on a graph but by the strength of two groups or classes bargaining and sometimes fighting with each other.

The power of employees depends in part on the power of their labor unions. This power is reflected in the percentage of employees who are unionized. Overall, unionization has fallen from about 35 percent in 1955 to about 13 percent today. Just as the power of employees is expressed in unionization, the power of business is expressed by monopoly (the only seller) power. When *a market is characterized by a single buyer,* we refer to it as a **monopsony**. In the labor market, this means there would be only one purchaser of labor power. A pure example would be a mining operation where everyone in the town works for the mine. In some towns, a large corporation may be the only large employer. Such a position gives them a great deal of power over wages and salaries, since workers have few options if they want to remain in their hometown. Giant corporations also have great power over prices of their goods and services. When prices go higher, the purchasing power of wages, the real wage, declines.

What are the key factors that affect the conflict between employees and capitalist employers? First, a major factor affecting the conflict between capital and labor over compensation is whether there is full employment or some degree of unemployment in the overall economy. The only reason that employers hire anyone is that they think there is enough market demand to make a profit from what is sold. If the demand for some product doubles, then more employees must be hired. If there is a depression and little demand for a product, then employees will be fired.

Second, the power of employees to ask for decent wages is affected by the employee's safety net in the event of unemployment. The safety net includes the level of unemployment benefits. The safety net also includes welfare benefits not only in money but especially in health care guarantees. How good these benefits are depends in part on the political clout of the labor movement. The political struggle between capital and labor affects these benefits.

Third, the struggle over wages and salaries is affected by some noneconomic institutions. These institutions include the pro-labor or pro-corporation attitude of Congress, the president, the print and broadcast media, and the churches. Finally, even international issues, such as the cost of wars and the struggle over oil, can affect the struggle over wages and salaries versus profits.

CONFLICT OVER INTENSITY OF LABOR

When a corporation buys a machine, it knows just what the machine can produce in an hour, but it is different with employees or human beings. The productivity of labor per hour is not a predetermined speed but a variable. The speed with which labor works is dependent on the strength and motivation of employees versus the strength of capitalists. As in the battle over wages and salaries, their strength is affected by government action, media views, and international events.

Capitalists are aware that how much the worker produces depends partly on effort expended. The **intensity of labor** refers to *the effort an employee exerts each hour.* Even if a contract is signed for wages and hours, that still leaves the intensity of labor each hour on the job as something that will be decided by conflict. In some circumstances, the conflict may be very peaceful, and some normal standard may emerge as more or less acceptable to all parties. At other times and places, conflict over the intensity of labor may escalate to any level. The clearest understanding of battles over the intensity of labor may be seen in Charlie Chaplin's film

Modern Times. No one who has seen that film can ever forget Charlie working on the assembly line and trying to keep up with his job, but the assembly line moves faster and faster. Charlie has to keep moving further and further along the conveyor belt until finally he reaches the end and is about to be sucked into it.

In each enterprise, the average intensity of labor is determined by capitalist attempts to increase intensity and employees' resistance to speed-up. The success of capitalist speed-up depends on many of the same factors that determine wages. If there is a weak union and high unemployment (so that workers feel threatened by job loss), then it is possible to intensify labor expenditure per hour. If there is a strong union and full employment, workers may successfully resist speed-up.

THREE LEVELS OF CONFLICT

The number of hours to be worked, the compensation to be paid, and the intensity of labor are bargained or battled for at three levels. First, there is conflict at the economic level in each enterprise. Second, there is a fight at the legal and political level over what laws will govern labor relations and how the laws are to be interpreted and applied. Third, in the media, churches, and education system, there is conflict between favorable and unfavorable views of the labor movement and of the giant corporations.

The conflict over exploitation in the legal and political sphere generated many ferocious battles. In the 1920s, there were battles over laws prohibiting child labor, with the Catholic Church saying that it would destroy the family if children were not permitted to work. A constitutional amendment against child labor was defeated at that time. Many laws have been passed by Republicans to limit union activity, which raises the rate of exploitation.

There is a continuing battle of ideas over exploitation in the universities, the media, and the churches. In economics departments of colleges and universities, neoclassical economics is the dominant view. In the neoclassical view, there is no such thing as exploitation because every factor in production, including labor, is paid exactly at its market price and receives an amount equal to the value that it has added to the product. The media portray most strikes as an attempt by greedy men to make huge wages and usually emphasize how the strike is hurting consumers. The media very seldom portray the low wages and bad working conditions that lead to strikes, nor do they spotlight the suffering of working families during the strike. The media are often controlled by giant corporations. This antilabor portrayal helps weaken unions and raise the rate of exploitation. Conservative churches have recently become more active politically. They help elect conservative legislators, who pass anti-union laws.

HISTORY OF LABOR CONFLICTS

In America, organizations such as the American Civil Liberties Union (ACLU) represent women and minorities fighting inequality. Other organizations, usually trade unions, represent employees fighting inequality. Part I of this book portrayed the often violent history of conflict between labor and big business from 1776 to 1940. This section gives an overview of the dramatic events from 1940 to the present.

Remember that after a century of confrontation, the Democratic administration of Franklin Roosevelt in the 1930s finally recognized the right of unions to exist and spelled out a legal procedure to guarantee free elections within enterprises when employees demand them. In this framework, unions grew rapidly during the full employment of World War II and the economic boom of the

1940s and 1950s. Peak union strength as a percentage of the labor force was achieved in the mid-1950s. Since then, however, union membership has declined for several reasons.

In the late 1940s and 1950s, unions came under attack by government. Laws restricting union activity, particularly the Taft-Hartley Act of 1946, were passed. The **Taft-Hartley Act** (or Labor-Management Relations Act) was passed over President Truman's veto. It greatly restricted the activities and power of unions. In the 1950s, Senator Joseph McCarthy and his supporters incited a witch hunt against alleged communists (hence the term "McCarthyism" to mean an attack on liberals and unionists). The Republican supporters of McCarthy generated public hysteria about communism, even though only a small number of communists lived in the United States. Most of the people attacked were militant trade unionists. Alleged communist ideas were only an excuse for conservative state and federal governments to attack liberals and unions.

Unions were growing and confident until then, but many lost confidence and ceased growth under the concerted attack of corporations and government. In the face of such harassment and of the dominant ideology that considered any militant defense of labor to be communist and evil, the Congress of Industrial Organizations (CIO) became very worried and divided. The CIO tossed out its ten most militant unions in 1949 in part because of allegations that some members of those unions were communists. The previously liberal CIO then merged with the conservative American Federation of Labor (AFL) in 1953. The new AFL-CIO compromised with big business and received some gains for its workers in return for pledges not to strike.

A long-range problem also became apparent at about this time: global capitalism has had a devastating affect on U.S. trade unions. Unions were established mainly in the manufacturing industries. Since the 1950s, the U.S. manufacturing sector has declined. It has been replaced by service sector jobs. Manufacturing often comprised huge factories with ten thousand or more workers who were relatively easy to organize. Service workers, such as restaurant employees and office secretaries, on the other hand, are scattered throughout a given region, so they are much harder to organize. As U.S. manufacturing jobs migrate overseas, new jobs are mostly in the low-paying service sector. Thus, unions were weakened by the shift from manufacturing to services, by antilabor laws, by government and corporate attack, and by the lack of militancy. Union membership fell from 36 percent of all nonagricultural workers in 1955 to only 13 percent in 2003. This decline drastically reduced the bargaining power and political influence of labor. One effect of the union decline is that real wages stagnated or fell from the 1970s to the present.

The decline in union strength does not mean there are no more conflicts between labor and capital, only that labor's position is weakened. For example, in 2004, the three largest grocery store chains in California tried to end all health benefits for their employees. Their employees went on strike. The strike lasted many months and caused great hardships for the employees and their families. Eventually, the strike was settled with a large decline in benefits for the employees, though they did retain some health benefits. New employees would get no benefits.

The weakness of unions in the political arena is a large reason for the rise in Republican power in politics. It also makes it very difficult to obtain universal health care, because unions are a principal supporter of universal health care.

Unions are making strenuous efforts to reverse the decline. In 2005, the AFL-CIO split over how best to resuscitate and expand the unions. Some favored more emphasis on union organizing and membership drives, while others argued for the need to focus on political campaigns to get a more friendly congress and president. It is too soon to know how this split will work out and whether it will help or hurt the unions. Even the name of the new federation is unclear at this time, but it will be an exciting new stage in union history.

SUMMARY

Capitalism is a system in which capitalists own enterprises, hire employees to make a profit, own the product, and sell the product for a profit. Employees are fired if they do not make a profit for the capitalist enterprise. The employee's labor time (whether a day or a month) is divided into the necessary labor time to produce a product equal in value to the employee's compensation and the surplus labor time used to produce a profit for the employer. Workers are exploited when part of their day's labor is taken from them without pay. The surplus labor time of American employees is taken from them without pay. In this way, all American employees of capitalist firms are exploited.

SUGGESTED READINGS

By far the best way to learn about labor strife and its relations to race and gender is to see the wonderful movie called *Salt of the Earth*, about the exploitation of Latino mine workers and their wives in a dramatic struggle with the employer and the police. Mentioned earlier was the funny but hard-hitting movie by Charlie Chaplin, called *Modern Times*.

An exciting book to read on labor history is Richard O. Boyer and Herbert Morais's *Labor's Untold Story* (1970). The July–August 2006 issue of *Monthly Review* presents *Aspects of Class in the United States*, a collection of excellent articles on class.

KEY TERMS

exploitation	surplus labor
intensity of labor	Taft-Hartley Act
monopsony	wage ceiling
necessary labor	wage floor
rate of exploitation	

REVIEW QUESTIONS

Define and describe surplus labor.
1. What is surplus labor? Give an example.
2. How is surplus labor different from necessary labor?
3. Explain how surplus labor relates to profits for the employer.

Discuss what constitutes exploitation and how exploitation occurs in various economic systems over time, including in contemporary capitalism.
4. What is exploitation as discussed in this chapter? Does an employee need to be making low wages to be exploited?
5. Does exploitation depend on the absolute value of your wage or salary? Why or why not?
6. Why does exploitation necessarily occur in a capitalist economy? What happens to the employer if there is no surplus labor? To the employee?
7. Was there exploitation in the prehistoric communal society? Why or why not?
8. What put a limit on the rate of exploitation in a slave economy?

212 MICROECONOMICS: PRICES, PROFITS, AND POVERTY, SECTION 2

Define and use measures of exploitation.

9. Assume an employee works five hours producing an amount of product equal in value to her wage and then spends another three hours producing an amount of product over and above the value of her salary. What are the number of hours of necessary labor? Surplus labor? What is the rate of exploitation? Explain in words what the numbers mean.
10. What does a rate of exploitation mean?
11. If you were an employer, would you want a high or low rate of exploitation? Explain.

List and discuss the sources of conflict between employers and employees and the rate of exploitation.

12. Explain why employers and employees bargain or struggle over necessary and surplus labor. What are the three main sources of conflict?
13. If an employee's compensation rises, what happens to necessary labor? Profits for the employer?
14. Even if employee compensation rises and the number of hours of work remains unchanged, why might an employer still make the same amount of profit or even increase profits?
15. Why can't an employee be paid below a wage floor? Why wouldn't an employer pay above a wage ceiling?

Give a brief overview of the history of labor conflicts.

16. What factors would give employers power as they bargain with employees over compensation, hours, and effort? Explain.
17. What factors would give employees power as they bargain with employers over compensation, hours, and effort? Explain.
18. When was union membership at its highest level? Why?
19. What has happened to union membership since the 1950s? Why?

CHAPTER 20

Prices, Profits, and Exploitation

The labor theory of value is a theory of prices, profits, and exploitation of employees. This chapter applies the labor theory of value to the simple economy of America's Old West to illustrate that it is easy to understand. Next, this chapter looks at the complexities of the labor theory of value under capitalism, in which prices are measured in dollars. The criticisms of the labor theory of value and the alternatives to it are presented in Appendix 20.1.

LEARNING OBJECTIVES

After reading this chapter, you should be able to:

- Explain how the relative value of products is determined by the amount of labor in a simple economy.
- Explain how the relative value of products is determined by the amount of labor in a capitalist market economy.
- Show how employers take part of the employee's product as profit in market capitalism.
- Discuss the ways in which labor is unlike other commodities bought and sold in the market.

MARKETS AND PRICES: THE WILD WEST

Markets and prices have not always existed. In prehistoric communal societies, there were no markets and no prices. People helped their extended family and gave them what they needed while receiving what they needed in return. As late as the thirteenth century in feudal Europe, each manor was mostly self-sufficient. On the rare occasion fairs were held, people exchanged goods by barter. In a barter system, no money is exchanged. One product is simply exchanged for another—for example, I might trade my pig for your salt. As the volume of trade increased, barter became inconvenient, and people started to pay with small pieces of metal. Only slowly, over the fifteenth to the eighteenth centuries, did markets mature and become more permanent in Western Europe.

How are prices formed in the market place? As discussed in detail in Part I, Adam Smith, David Ricardo, and Karl Marx all contributed to the explanation of how prices are determined by the labor theory of value. The theory argues that only labor creates value. To see what this means, let us take an example of a simple economy, similar to some examples used by Adam Smith.

Table 20.1

Pigs and Chickens

Commodity	Hours of Labor	Relative Value
Pigs	10 hours per pig	1 pig to 2 chickens
Chickens	5 hours per chicken	1 chicken to half a pig

PRICES ON THE WESTERN FRONTIER

On the western frontier of the United States in the early nineteenth century, most people lived on farms with no one else but the immediate family. The farms were fairly self-sufficient, so there was little exchange. What exchange took place was conducted by bartering. Suppose a woman on one farm had some extra chickens but no pigs. Suppose a woman on the next farm had some extra pigs but no chickens. They might then exchange one for the other. The question for economists is, at what rate would they exchange? How many pigs for one chicken, or how many chickens for one pig?

The answer depends on how much work it took the woman to produce a pig or a chicken. The labor to produce a pig is not just taking it to the butcher, but raising it, feeding it, making equipment and sheds to care for it, plus any other labor that was part of the total labor necessary to produce, on the average, one pig with the existing technology. The same was true for chickens. The woman did not just go out and catch one but had to do all of the labor necessary to raise and feed it. It is not just the latest labor but all labor in the production process that counts.

Suppose that, on average, it took four hours of labor, counting everything that went into it, to produce a chicken. Suppose it took eight hours of labor to produce a pig. The two women would compare how much work it took to produce each of the two products. After negotiating, they would end up exchanging at a ratio that more or less reflected how much work each person did. They would exchange, on average, one pig for two chickens. Table 20.1 summarizes this exchange.

In summary, the value of each commodity in the simple farming society on the western frontier was determined by how much work or labor was put into each product. The typical exchange did not involve money, prices, or a permanent market. It was usually just two people exchanging by barter. This story illustrates the simplest version of the labor theory of value. In a modern capitalist society, the process is quite different and far more complex.

PRICES UNDER CAPITALISM

The previous section showed the relative value, or *price*, of two goods in a simple society similar to the Old West. In that society, the ratio at which pigs and chickens were exchanged was determined by the average amount of labor that went into producing each of them. That ratio still holds under capitalism unless the technology changes so as to change the ratio of labor to produce pigs versus chickens. A first glance tells us that a corporation producing chickens could exchange with a corporation producing pigs according to the labor that went into each of them.

In that limited sense, the labor theory does tell us something about prices under capitalism. But that is only the beginning of the story. Some important features of capitalism change the way the relative values, the price of one good in terms of the other good, are determined. First, a simple society can use barter, but a highly complex society like ours makes barter impossible. If you are a pig producer, you cannot walk around with a pig in your pocket to buy things. Money is needed to grease the wheels of exchange. In our monetary economy, the corporation pays money for raw materials, including pigs and feed for pigs. It also pays money for employees' labor time, for equipment, and for buildings to house the pigs or chickens. After the corporation produces a commodity, it sells it in the market for money. Some of the money goes to profit. The rest of the money goes to repeat the process of buying labor power and other production necessities.

The institutions of capitalism include a monetary system that allows the corporation to buy or sell anywhere in the world rather than barter within a small area. Prices are measured in terms of money instead of the value of one good to another—a pig to how many chickens. An even more dramatic change from the Old West is that the owners of the corporation do not provide the labor, as was done by the farm owners in the earliest frontier days. The corporation hires employees to do the labor at some wage or salary (money). In the simple economy of the Old West, neighbors exchanged products according to the labor value of each, but neither made a profit. How does the corporation buy labor power (*the employee's ability to labor for some hours*), raw materials, and capital in the market, then sell the resulting product at a profit?

The question seems mysterious only until we examine the capitalist market process more concretely. Remember the basic labor relationship of capitalism and how it differs from the simple society of the Old West. In the Old West, each farmer produced his or her own product by himself or herself. A large corporation, on the other hand, hires thousands of employees. The corporation does not hire for charity. It hires new employees only when it thinks that each additional employee will increase its profit. The question is, how do employees make profit for a corporation?

In Chapter 19, the examples showed that under the institutions of capitalism, employees are hired for a given time at a given level of compensation. The employees then labor for part of the day doing necessary labor to produce an amount equal to their wages or salaries. But the employee must continue working to the end of the working day in order to produce a surplus.

Let us see how the labor theory of value explains this process in an actual example. The labor theory of value stresses that the labor put into raising the pig is of several types. There is the labor of the farm workers. There is also the labor that went into what the farm workers need for their work, including raw materials, equipment, and buildings. The farmer buys feed for the pigs at a price reflecting the labor that went into producing that feed. The farmer buys equipment used in taking care of the pigs at a price reflecting the labor that went into producing that equipment. Finally, the farmer buys buildings to house the pigs at a price reflecting the labor that went into producing the buildings.

Suppose the farmer can buy a pound of feed at $1. Suppose each worker used up 15 pounds of feed a day, costing $15. In addition, the farmer must spend $5 a day per worker on replacement of used-up equipment and buildings. The farmer's total material costs per worker (including raw materials, equipment, and building costs) come to $20 a day.

The price of the commodity, in this case, pigs, is determined by supply and demand in product markets. The price of the employee's labor that produced the pig is also determined by supply and demand in labor markets. The difference between labor costs and the market price at which the pig can be sold is called the **surplus**. The surplus is *the amount above costs that goes as profit to the owners of industry*. The surplus can be calculated in three ways: first, it is the amount of labor expended beyond that which covers their compensation. Second, it is the amount of product produced by this surplus labor. Third, it is the amount of money received for that surplus product. (Note: This economic definition of the surplus is distinct from the anthropologist's definition of surplus we used in Part I of this text.)

Table 20.2

Price of Pigs

Material Cost, Including Equipment and Buildings	Necessary Labor Cost	Surplus Labor Cost	Price
$20	+ $40	+ $40	= $100
2 hours	+ 4 hours	+ 4 hours	= 10 hours

Let us continue with the pig example. Suppose each farm worker gets $10 an hour and works an eight-hour day—$80 a day. Suppose the price of pigs in the market is $100. The farm workers only need to work four hours a day, the necessary labor, to produce a value of pigs equal to their wages for four hours ($40). They must also work another four hours a day at surplus labor, so the surplus is $40. The total costs are the material costs ($20) plus the necessary labor costs ($40), or a total of $60 in costs per pig. The price is the costs ($60) plus the profit ($40), or $100. Table 20.2 shows these relationships.

Remember that the rate of exploitation is defined as the ratio of surplus labor to necessary labor. In Table 20.2, the figures show that the rate of exploitation of farm workers is $40 divided by $40, or 100 percent. While employees are interested in the rate of exploitation, corporations are interested in the rate of profit on their investment. Here we may calculate the rate of profit per worker per day. Our example shows the daily expenditure for the necessary labor of each employee, or in other words, the employee's compensation. The necessary employee compensation is $40. The surplus or profit per day for each employee is also $40. The material costs (including raw materials, equipment and buildings used up) are $20 a day. The total cost per pig associated with each worker is $60.

In this simple case, the **rate of profit per worker** *equals the profit* ($40) *divided by the costs to the corporation for this worker and her used-up material goods* ($60) The rate of profit on each employee for each pig is simply $40/$60. This is a profit rate of two-thirds, or 66.6 percent.

WHAT DETERMINES THE LEVEL OF EMPLOYEE COMPENSATION?

Most progressive economists agree that there is a surplus going out of the pockets of employees into the treasury of the corporation. The question is how the corporation can get away with this surplus year after year. The answer lies in the relationship between employees and business.

Many early advocates of the labor theory had a simple answer. Labor power is defined as one's capacity to work for a definite period of time, say in a typical working day. It is called labor power because we do not sell our bodies to employers. We sell our power or ability to labor, or labor power. Early labor theory advocates argued that labor power is just another commodity and its price is determined like all other commodities.

In this view, the price (the wage or salary) of an employee's labor power must equal the labor that is put into producing the employee. What does that mean? The labor of producing the employee's food, clothing, and shelter is considered to be the labor of producing the employee.

This view implies that the profit (or surplus) of the corporation comes from the difference between the labor expended on what the employee produces minus the labor that goes to the employee's food, clothing, and shelter. The whole argument can be reduced to three simple statements.

1. In the long run, when supply equals demand, the price of every commodity must equal the labor time put into it.
2. Human labor power (the capacity to work) is a commodity under capitalism and sold in the market. Like all other commodities, it is bought and sold at its long-run value. The value of the worker's labor power is the amount of labor time necessary to produce the worker.
3. Capitalists extract from workers their labor for a given number of hours. Those hours worked may number, and usually do under capitalism, far more than the hours required to produce the value of the worker's labor power (wages or salary). The difference between the value of the worker (wages or salary) and the value of the product (price) is the surplus value (or profit) going to the capitalist.

This argument is very formal and a technological one in which labor power is the same as any other input or commodity used in production. This view is too simplistic because labor power is not like other commodities. Commodities under capitalism (1) are produced by the capitalist firm, (2) are sold by the capitalist firm, and (3) have clearly defined usefulness. An employee and his or her labor power (1) is *not* produced by a capitalist firm, (2) is *not* sold by a capitalist firm, and (3) can produce a varying amount of output in a day—in other words, the employee's usefulness may not always be clearly defined.

In the view of most modern progressive economists, the wage or salary does not depend merely on technology. Rather, the understanding of wages and salaries should be firmly rooted in institutions and human relations. Labor power is different from the usual capitalist commodity in some very important respects. It is true that labor power is similar to the usual capitalist commodity in that it is bought and sold in a market. When it cannot be sold, employees are unemployed. Yet we noted earlier that labor power differs from most things called commodities in three ways. Let us now clarify those three points. First, in a pure capitalist system, commodities are produced by capitalists. Employees are not produced by a capitalist assembly line. Employees are not produced in a factory like other commodities. Most of the labor going into the production of an employee is the unpaid love and care of a family and the paid labor of teachers at all levels of education.

Second, all other commodities are sold by capitalist businesses in market exchanges governed by impersonal supply and demand. Not only is the employee's capacity to work (or labor power) not produced by business, it is not sold by business. The employee's labor power is sold by the employee. Of course, once a corporation buys labor power, it may sell the services of the employee, such as the sale by a plumbing company of the service of a plumber.

Third, in the case of other commodities, there is no need for the seller to be present when the commodity is used or consumed. If one buys a robot, then the seller need not be present when it is used. Moreover, we know exactly how much the robot can produce per hour. The employee, however, must be present when his or her labor power is used. Therefore, the employee may or may not agree to a certain speed of production. A machine, such as a robot, has a specific, technologically given maximum speed. The intensity of labor by employees, however, depends not only on their ability but also on their conscious attitudes, family background, union membership, and many other factors.

For all of these reasons, it is not the case that the price of labor power (wages or salaries) is automatically determined. Labor power cannot be viewed as a separate commodity with a certain value given exactly by technology. Rather, the employee's labor power must be viewed as a relationship with the employer, which may be harmonious or hostile.

MODERN PROGRESSIVE VIEW OF COMPENSATION AND SURPLUS

Many modern progressive economists agree that one can conceptualize the price of a product as the amount of labor expended by all the employees who produced the raw materials, equipment, and buildings. They also agree that the employees produce an amount of product necessary to pay their wage or salary and a surplus that goes to profit.

Modern progressives recognize, however, that there is no simple, mechanical equation to calculate employee compensation and business profits. The division of the product between wages or salary and profit depends on the bargaining power of each group. There are conflicts between employees and employers over the number of hours to be worked, the working conditions, the intensity of labor, and the rate of pay per hour or per month. These conflicts happen within enterprises and sometime include strikes. The conflicts also occur in the wider arena of ideological fights in the media and in the government over laws regulating work. Chapter 19 discussed the recent history of conflict between employees and capitalist corporations. It also explained that the result of a conflict depends not only on the strength of each party but also on the surrounding conditions and institutional structures. For example, the level of employment and compensation of labor may be affected by the lack of demand in a recession or the full employment of a war (such as the World War II).

In addition, Chapter 19 showed that any theory about employee compensation must consider the effects of monopoly power by business, government regulations and spending, the unemployment rate, and the international trade and finance situation, among other factors. When all of these factors are incorporated into a labor theory of prices, the theory becomes more realistic, but it also becomes more complex. No specific wages, prices, or profits can be predicted if all of these factors are added. Only a range for wages, prices, and profits, depending on the strength of contending parties under certain conditions of supply and demand, can be predicted. Even with all of these modifications, the labor theory of value creates a clear framework for understanding exploitation through the conflict between capitalist employers and employees under given economic circumstances.

SUMMARY

From its consideration of the productive process in a competitive capitalist market, the labor theory of value concludes that in the long run, when supply equals demand, the price of every commodity must equal the labor time put into it. In a capitalist economy, the total labor time is composed of three parts. First there are the hours of labor that go to produce the amount of product going to the wages and salaries paid to employees. Second, there are the hours of labor to produce the amount of product taken by the capitalist as profit. Third, there are the hours of labor that were previously expended producing raw materials that are used up, as well as buildings and equipment that have depreciated during the production process.

If anyone tries to sell for a price greater than the labor time put into it, then others will be able to undersell that individual and still make the average profit. If anyone tries to sell under that price, he or she will not be able to make the average rate of profit. This simple theory, that the long-run price of a commodity equals the total labor time put into it, becomes far more complicated when all the aspects of our complex economy are considered.

Progressive economists agree that most employees are exploited. Progressive economists agree with Adam Smith that under certain conditions, the prices in a simple precapitalist society such as the Old West are determined by the amount of labor expended. Some progressive economists use the labor theory of value to understand the process of exploitation present in capitalism. The modern version of this theory says that an employee expends a certain amount of labor in the production process. For some hours a day, the employee produces an amount of value equal to the amount necessary to pay wages or salaries. Employees work surplus hours beyond the level of their own compensation to produce a profit for the capitalist business. The same is true even if employees are paid some flat amount for a month or a year; their working time is still divided into the necessary labor to produce compensation and the surplus labor necessary to produce profits.

Some progressive economists, however, strongly criticize the labor theory of value. They agree that there is exploitation of employees by capitalist enterprises, but they disagree on price theories. These criticisms and disagreements are discussed in Appendix 20.1.

SUGGESTED READINGS

For a more complete and detailed discussion of Karl Marx's view of the labor theory of value, a clear and non-mathematical presentation is provided in Chapter 9 of E. K. Hunt's *History of Economic Thought: A Critical Perspective* (2002). Instructors may also examine an excellent article on the struggle over the intensity of labor in an enterprise and its importance to the labor theory of value by Herbert Gintis and Samuel Bowles (1981) "Structure and Practice in the Labour Theory of Value," *Review of Radical Political Economics*, vol. 12, no. 4, pp. 1–26.

KEY TERMS

rate of profit
surplus

REVIEW QUESTIONS

Explain how the relative value of products is determined by the amount of labor in a simple economy.
1. What is meant by the term *relative value*? What does it measure?
2. Explain how the number of chickens could be the "price" of a pig in the simple economy.
3. How does the example in this chapter use the amount of labor used to produce a product to determine the relative value of one product in terms of another product, such as the value of pigs in terms of chickens? What types of labor go into producing the product?
4. How does the use of term "surplus" in this chapter differ from its use in Chapter 2?

Explain how the relative value of products is determined by the amount of labor in a capitalist market economy.
5. State the key factors that make the analysis of the labor theory of value more complex in a capitalist market economy. Explain.
6. How do prices in an advanced economy help measure the relative value of two different commodities? How are the prices of various goods measured in an advanced market economy?
7. Explain how money helps facilitate trade and enables economies to grow.

8. How is labor input into a product measured in a capitalist market economy? Explain using an example.

9. What does the labor theory of value assume about other inputs such as, in the example of the pigs, feed or machinery? In other words, how is the labor measured for inputs other than employees?

Show how employers take part of the employee's product as profit in market capitalism.

10. What is necessary labor?

11. What is the surplus created in the production of a product? Explain how this surplus is created.

12. How does surplus translate into profits for business owners in a capitalist market economy?

13. Assume the price of a quart of yogurt is $5 in the market. A firm employs one worker, and she earns $6 an hour for an eight-hour day. Other inputs to produce a quart of yogurt come to $2 per quart. Each day, the firm produces and sells 20 quarts of yogurt. Calculate the surplus value and rate of profit per worker.

Discuss the ways in which labor is unlike other commodities bought and sold in the market.

14. Use the concept of labor power to explain how working for an employer in a capitalist market economy is not the same as slavery.

15. How can labor power be treated as just another commodity, such as cheese, in the market?

16. What are some criticisms of this idea of labor power as a commodity? How is labor power *not* like other commodities?

17. Why do employers try to keep wages and other employee compensation low? Explain the impact on business owners if the cost of labor rises.

18. Why do workers struggle to raise wages and other employee compensation? According to the labor theory of value, what are they bargaining over?

19. What are some of the ways that the conflict between employers and employees over surplus product is manifested?

APPENDIX 20.1
REJECTION OF LABOR THEORY AND CONSIDERATION
OF ALTERNATIVE THEORIES

This appendix explains why some progressive economists reject the labor theory of value and accept alternative theories of exploitation.

LEARNING OBJECTIVES FOR APPENDIX 20.1

After reading this chapter, you should be able to:

• Explain how the labor theory of value has been criticized and defended and how some reject it and use other theories to explain exploitation.

TRANSFORMATION FROM LABOR HOURS TO PRICES

Many progressive economists believe that the labor theory of value, along with conflict between labor and business in determining wages, describes the process by which employees are exploited and profit is made by employers. Many progressives, however, argue that the labor theory does not provide a logical and acceptable explanation of prices. In fact, its main inventor, Karl Marx, focused on the problem of exploitation and was not much interested in relative prices of oranges and apples.

Those who reject the labor theory as a theory of prices have several arguments. The most famous is called the **transformation problem**. *How can values given in labor hours be transformed into prices in money terms under capitalism?* Since the issue is how to transform labor hours into prices in the analysis of the economy, the term "transformation problem" provides a reasonable name.

The main allegation is that the rate of profit and the rate of exploitation cannot behave consistently with each other under the labor theory of value. Remember that the *rate of exploitation* is profit to employee compensation. Remember that the rate of profit is profit to total costs. Costs include not only employee compensation but also the price of all material goods, including buildings, equipment, and raw materials. Suppose the simplest case in which the rate of exploitation is the same in every industry. Under the labor theory, the same labor payments will generate the same profit if all industries have the same rate of exploitation.

Under pure competition, the rate of profit must be equalized in all industries. If profit is less in one industry than another, then capitalists move their money to the more profitable industry. This reduces supply in the industry with lower profits. Therefore, prices may rise in that industry because there is less supply (assuming demand does not change). Eventually, prices and profits both must rise in that industry. In short, competition must force an equal rate of profit in all industries. Thus, if the rate of exploitation is the same in all industries, the rate of profit must also be the same in all industries.

That, however, is never actually the case, and critics point out that the rate of profit could not be the same in all industries. The profit rate is based not only on labor costs but on all material costs as well, including used-up raw materials, equipment, and buildings. The profit rate will be equal in all industries only if the ratio of labor costs to material costs is the same in all industries. But, in truth, the amount of material costs per employee differs in every industry. If the material costs are different in every industry, then the same profit will be divided by different total costs in each industry. In that case, the rate of profit will be different in every industry.

We now have two conflicting statements. On the one hand, competition makes the profit rate the same in all industries. On the other hand, employees use different amounts of material goods per day in every industry. If profit comes only from the exploitation of labor, then similar rates of exploitation must produce different rates of profit in every industry. So profit is expected to be the same in every industry, but profit is expected to be different in every industry.

SOLUTIONS AND ALTERNATIVE THEORIES

There have been many ingenious attempts to solve this dilemma, but the claim is that it is logically impossible to solve it under the labor theory of value. In the last hundred years, many solutions have been presented and all have been criticized. This issue remains a great controversy among those interested in proving exploitation with a price theory. But the great controversy is not as important as it sounds. In the first place, all progressive economists still agree that some type of exploitation exists within capitalist institutions. The argument is only over what is the best price theory. In the second place, progressive economists who reject the labor theory have offered two other price theories within which they explain exploitation.

Some economists argue that the neoclassical theory of prices itself can be used to prove exploitation. The neoclassical approach was presented briefly in Part I, and it is spelled out fully in Chapters 29, 30, and 31. The use of neoclassical theory to explain exploitation appears in the works of John Roemer (see, e.g., Roemer, 1982).

The theory of exploitation based on neoclassical theory is rejected by most neoclassical economists as an erroneous conclusion from their assumptions. The criticisms of neoclassical economics are also discussed in chapters 29, 30, and 31. Therefore, no further discussion of the neoclassical theory and its relevance to exploitation is presented here

In addition to the labor theory of value and neoclassical theory, many progressive economists use a third theory to explain the details of exploitation. This theory was developed by Pierro Sraffa, using some propositions first stated by David Ricardo. It does not use labor hours but only the price of commodities. Progressive economists following this price theory also conclude that all employees are exploited. Sraffa's theory is as full and elaborate as the neoclassical and labor theories, so there is no room to present it here.

E. K. Hunt's book, *History of Economic Thought* (2002), provides a clear explanation of Sraffa's theory of prices. For a model based on Sraffa and showing exploitation, see the very clear exposition in Robin Hahnel, *The ABCs of Political Economy: A Modern Approach* (2002).

SUMMARY OF APPENDIX 20.1

Some progressive economists reject the labor theory of value, mainly because they claim that it cannot solve the transformation problem. Some substitute Sraffian price theory. A small number substitute the neoclassical theory of value. Still others are skeptical of all price theories because they require so many unreal assumptions. Nevertheless, all progressive economists agree that employees are exploited even though they use different price theories to explain the details of exploitation. All agree that it is the institutions of capitalism that cause exploitation.

KEY TERM FOR APPENDIX 20.1

transformation problem

REVIEW QUESTIONS FOR APPENDIX 20.1

Explain how the labor theory of value has been criticized and defended and how some reject it and use other theories to explain exploitation.
1. What is the transformation problem?
2. Explain why the rate of profit and the rate of exploitation are considered to be inconsistent by some economists. As part of your explanation, define the rate of profit and the rate of exploitation.
3. What is an alternative theory, besides the labor theory of value and the neoclassical model, used in attempting to explain exploitation?

CHAPTER 21

Market Power and Global Corporations

The world of numerous, small, competitive capitalist enterprises that Adam Smith thought would produce the best possible economic system is gone forever. The modern capitalist world is characterized by the domination of giant global corporations. Chapter 20 explained how the basic capitalist institutions led to employees being exploited even under pure competition. With strong market power, the inequality and exploitation continues, but some more unpleasant economic aspects may be added, as shown in this chapter.

This chapter examines the evolution of American business from small firms to giant domestic corporations to global corporations. It then answers the question why market power has increased over time and spread throughout the world. Next, it examines how market power unfavorably affects the environment, increases inequality, influences the government, and contributes to instability in the economy. Finally, the chapter considers the different policy decisions on issues involving market power.

LEARNING OBJECTIVES

After reading this chapter, you should be able to:

- Describe how corporations grow in size, and cite data documenting their growth.
- Explain reasons behind the capitalistic tendency toward large firms with market power.
- Describe the impact of firms with market power on economic outcomes.
- Compare and contrast policies and policy debates about regulating the monopoly power of businesses.

THE TREND OF CONCENTRATION

Market power means that *an individual firm can influence or manipulate prices or output in the market*. In a purely competitive economy, each competing business unit would be one of many so that its actions taken alone could *not* influence the quality and/or quantity of goods or the price in the market. In the U.S. economy during the early nineteenth century, many small farms and small businesses produced most of the output. There were no giant corporations dominating an entire industry (though there were many local monopolies). As late as 1860, there were still no incorporated business firms in many of the major urban industrial centers. Since that time, the picture has changed drastically.

The size of corporations rose rapidly in the post–Civil War period. By 1900, the share of manufactured goods produced by corporations grew to two-thirds of total output. Some of the big corporations developed by virtue of rapid internal growth. Others arose through mergers of formerly independent firms. Mergers have come in waves. The first massive merger movement lasted from the early 1890s to the outbreak of World War I. It was characterized by **horizontal mergers**, in which *a big corporation absorbed other corporations that were its direct competitors*. The result of such mergers was that industries were dominated by fewer and much larger corporations. The second merger wave came in the 1920s. It was characterized by **vertical mergers**, *occurring between firms producing goods in sequence*, as when a giant corporation absorbs its suppliers or absorbs the firms to which it sells its output.

THE THIRD WAVE

The 1960s witnessed a third and unique wave of mergers. Most of these were **conglomerate mergers** in which *a giant corporation absorbs other corporations that have no relation to its primary product line*. The aim is simply to establish a colossal corporate empire that gives its owners immense economic and political power. From 1950 through 1959, corporate mergers averaged 540 a year. From 1960 through 1967, the average was 1,100 a year. In 1968 alone, there were 2,655 mergers. From 1948 through 1953, conglomerate mergers accounted for 59 percent of total mergers. From 1960 through 1965, they comprised 72 percent of the total. In 1968, conglomerate mergers accounted for 84 percent of all mergers.

The enormous size and power of the one hundred largest conglomerates may be seen in the data on how many large firms in each separate industry are under their control. "In more than half of the 1,014 product classes in manufacturing as a whole, at least one of the 100 largest was among the 4 largest producers, and in 31 percent at least 2 came from the 100 largest. It is thus obvious that the 100 largest companies are not limited in their operations to only a few large-scale industries but rather are broadly represented among the largest producers of manufacturing products throughout most of the wide spectrum of U.S. industry" (Blair, 1972, pp. 53–54).

The strongly pro-business, laissez-faire attitude that characterized the Reagan administration led to a mushrooming of mergers and corporate buyouts of other corporations. All evidence points to the 1980s as being, perhaps, the most dramatically rapid increase in industrial concentration in American history to that date. These mergers left many small industrial enterprises, but a few hundred corporate giants hold most of the wealth and do most of the producing. Data reveal the extremely high concentration of corporate assets in a comparatively few firms. At the bottom, a large number of small corporations held a minuscule portion of total corporate assets. To make these statements precise for the end of the third wave, this section looks at the data on all U.S. corporations for 1984 (all data come from the U.S. Internal Revenue Service, Statistics of Income Corporation Income Tax Returns, July 1983–June 1984, Washington, DC: GPO, 1987).

At the top, 3,663 giant corporations with over $250,000,000 in assets constituted only one-tenth of one percent of all corporations. Yet these few held 75 percent of all corporate assets. The fact that just 3,663 U.S. corporations held well over $8 trillion in assets is incredible. Such an amount was more than the total value of all western European assets. Among those 3,663 corporations, there was even a greater concentration within just the top 200 or 300 corporations. At the bottom, the smallest corporations, those with under $100,000 in assets, constituted 56 percent of all corporations, or 1,773,000 corporations. They held only one-half of one percent of corporate assets.

THE FOURTH WAVE

In the United States, the lifetime of the average business is only two years. Many businesses start with high hopes and end with losses in a remarkably short time. During every economic expansion, hundreds of thousands of new businesses come into being, but about the same number go bankrupt or simply go out of business in every recession. While most enterprises remain small, some grow to enormous size, often through mergers. The boom of the 1950s and 1960s, like all boom periods, inspired many business mergers. These mergers happen because conditions look very profitable for giant enterprises. The third wave of mergers occurred from 1953 to 1969. Remember that the first wave of mergers in the beginning of the twentieth century consisted mostly of mergers among competitors (called horizontal mergers). The second wave, mainly in the 1920s, consisted of mergers of manufacturers with suppliers and sales outlets (called vertical mergers). The third wave, which occurred in the 1950s and 1960s, consisted mostly of mergers of many types of businesses with little relation to each other (called conglomerate mergers).

One reason for conglomerate mergers was that antitrust laws made illegal the horizontal and vertical mergers (when the laws were enforced, which was seldom during this period). The laws, however, said nothing about conglomerate mergers because it was assumed that conglomerate mergers had no effect on competition.

International mergers between corporations in different countries constitute a fourth wave, which may be called **global mergers**. Global mergers reached an all-time high toward the end of the expansion of the 1990s. In 1985, there were 1,923 mergers among corporations in the world, estimated at $165.8 billion in value. In 1999, there were 9,946 mergers among corporations in the world, estimated at $2.4 trillion in value! The most striking thing about the global merger wave was the enormous size of the corporations involved in the mergers. According to CNNMoney.com in the first seven months of 2007, the Top 25 mergers alone consisted of deals worth over $699 billion. The two largest deals were each worth almost $100 billion.

In addition to mergers, the late 1990s saw growth by foreign direct investment. In 1999, the European Union (EU) countries made two-thirds of all new foreign investments in the global economy. Also, for the first time since the World War II, the European Union invested more than the United States invested in underdeveloped countries. The European Union has surpassed the United States in the annual amount of direct foreign investment. The shifts of economic strength among countries and geographical areas of the world are a source of insecurity for corporations.

Although the European Union is expanding faster, the United States is still increasing the percentage of its investments and profits that come from abroad. In 1997, U.S. corporate investments abroad provided 5.4 percent of all private sector gross production, 16 percent of all exports, and 26 percent of all imports. In 1997, total U.S. investment overseas amounted to over $3 trillion. However, by 2000, investment by foreigners in the United States amounted to over $6 trillion. Investment by foreigners accounted for 22 percent of all investment in U.S. businesses and residences.

All of the old arguments about control by giant firms in each country are now replaced by new arguments about the control by the global firms in the global economy. The large firms have become global corporations with branches in every country. The branches may focus on manufacturing commodities in one country or on selling the commodities in another country, or they may do both. Now there is increasing concentration of economic power in the global context. In other words, a relatively small number of corporations have an increasing share of the world economy. This gives them power in every country. One use of their power is to get laws passed—such as more tax breaks—that help them to make still more profits.

Some degree of market power on the world market does not mean an end to competition.

Huge corporations compete against each other with ferocity, using all kinds of methods to gain market share. They usually do not compete by offering lower prices, however. Instead, they do more advertising, claim higher quality, and provide additional services. Moreover, they all agree on supporting laws to protect global capitalism. There is no international agency with the power to control global monopolies, so the power of these firms continues to grow.

THE REASONS FOR MARKET POWER

One fundamental cause of the emergence of the giant corporation is the **economies of scale**. This refers to the notion that *average total costs (or per unit costs) fall as output increases*. Economies of scale can be briefly summarized by the idea that "bigger is better" when it comes to production. Cost savings can be derived from large-scale production using more specialized machinery, more specialized workers, and mass-production assembly lines to turn out cheaper goods. Small firms are driven out of business by the cheap goods produced through large-scale applications of technology. The large firms gain market power by selling at a lower price while making more profit.

In addition to improved technology based on the economies of scale, there is another reason for the greater profitability of some huge firms. The firms grow internally or via merger far beyond the technologically necessary minimum to exploit economies of scale in production because they wish to exercise monopoly power over their market. With small competitors eliminated or dominated, the few remaining giant firms can restrict output and set higher prices or make higher rates of profit.

The giant firms attempt to eliminate risk and uncertainty not only by controlling their own industry's output but also by (1) buying out raw material suppliers, (2) buying out dealers and outlets for the finished product, (3) using vast nationwide advertising, and (4) linking up with banks and other financial sources. With these motivations, there is no clear upper limit to desirable size. The motto seems to be "the bigger the better."

PRICES AND PROFIT MAXIMIZATION

What is the effect of monopoly on the prices of goods and services? The essence of the monopolist's position is the ability to keep competitors out of the market by means of greater efficiency, control of natural or financial resources, control of patents, or other legal or illegal methods. Prices may be as high as the consumers will bear, and there is no competitive mechanism to bring the higher profit back down to the average rate of profit in industry as a whole. The number of **perfect monopolies**, *only one firm in the market or industry*, in the U.S. economy is rather small.

The quests for greater size, for control over dealers and outlets, for nationwide markets, and for more political influence are all motivated by the general desire for more profits and more economic, social, and political power. But as one or two firms in a given industry gain more power, there is a tendency for others to follow suit. In this way, the firms in an industry must constantly expand in order to remain competitive. Moreover, when a few firms succeed in destroying most of their rivals, as they did in the U.S. automobile industry between 1910 and 1960, and thereby succeed in earning above-average profits, the markets are most generally attacked by their foreign competitors. Just as General Motors, Ford, and Chrysler were succeeding in gaining control of the American automobile market in the 1960s, the German, Japanese, and other foreign competitors began to make important inroads in the market that continue today.

One of the great advantages of size is the diversification of risk and the ability to sustain temporary losses in some plants or take other actions that are not necessarily dictated by the short-run quest for maximum profits. This flexibility makes possible the calculated pursuit of maximum long-run profits. Large corporations can afford to sacrifice short-run profits to ensure the security of their market control, to spur company growth, and to follow any other short-run policy that seems advantageous in the long run. Thus, prices are not always set as high as the market will bear. It could be said that management maximizes a multiple set of objectives.

INDUSTRIAL CONCENTRATION AND WASTE

To some extent, large firms are more efficient because of economies of scale. Production cannot reach optimum efficiency below a certain quantity of output. The fact that large firms account for most U.S. output means that most of the economy is able to produce at lower costs than ever before. Studies of cost data reveal the possibility of high efficiency at a fairly constant level beyond the necessary minimum scale of production. Of course, because the large firms also have disproportionately larger research facilities and control a large percentage of all unexpired patents, they have the greatest potential for increasing efficiency. Moreover, many investment projects require resources beyond the means of small firms.

But the large, entrenched firm stands to lose most from the obsolescence of present machinery and from product improvements—a longer-lasting light bulb, for example—that reduce the number of units the customer needs to buy. Therefore, if the large firm faces no serious competitive pressure for improvement, it may develop and patent, but not use, important inventions. Thus, monopoly power has a paradoxical effect on innovation. Giant firms have a rapid rate of technological progress but often retain a large amount of technologically obsolete equipment.

The existence of economic concentration may also increase the severity and possibly the number of recessions because of (1) its destabilizing effects on remaining small businesses and (2) its lowering of workers' ability to consume. This is another reason the net effect of monopoly seems to be a reduction in the rate of economic growth. On the other hand, breaking up large firms into smaller units would probably not increase economic growth. Reducing the American economy to small firms would certainly cause a major decrease in economic efficiency because of the loss of economies of scale and most likely would have a negative effect on investment. It is impossible to go backward to a competitive small-business economy.

The rate of growth (and waste) under monopoly is also affected by the greatly expanded marketing efforts. Once relatively unimportant, marketing is now a key feature in many markets. The impact of advertising and related expenditures on the economy is not to be underestimated. The influence of advertising on social norms and what consumers "want" continues to grow. In an economic system in which competition is fierce and relentless, advertising becomes the principal weapon of the competitive struggle.

Relatively large firms are in a position to exercise a powerful influence on the market by establishing and maintaining a pronounced difference between their products and those of their competitors. This differentiation is sought chiefly by means of advertising, trademarks, brand names, distinctive packaging, and product variation. If successful, it leads to a condition in which consumers believe that slightly different products can no longer serve as substitutes for each other. Some economists argue that advertising involves a waste of resources, a continual drain on the consumer's income, and a systematic destruction of the consumer's freedom of choice between genuine alternatives. The economic importance of advertising lies partly in its causing a reallocation of consumers' expenditures among different commodities. The function of advertising, perhaps its dominant function today, is to wage a relentless war on behalf of the producers and sellers of consumer goods against saving and in favor of consumption.

By creating demand for a product, advertising encourages investment in plant and equipment that might otherwise not take place. However, many research and development programs, which constitute a multibillion-dollar effort in the United States, are more closely related to the production of salable goods and marketing than to their much-touted mission of advancing science and technology. Actually, much of the "newness" with which the consumer is systematically bombarded is either fraudulent or related trivially, and in many cases even negatively, to the function and serviceability of the product. Moreover, other products are introduced that are indeed new in design and appearance but serve essentially the same purposes as old products they are intended to replace. The extent of the difference can vary from a simple modification in packaging to the far-reaching and enormously expensive annual changes in automobile models.

Another aspect of advertising and market power is pollution. In the competitive model, economists argue that consumer preference dictates what is produced, and therefore pollution is merely an unfortunate by-product of the demands of the public. The unfortunate by-products of public preference could be handled by public action to beautify the environment. When firms have market power such as in monopolies, the argument is that consumer preference is manipulated toward whatever products are most profitable to produce. Therefore, "environmental damage becomes a normal consequence of the conflict between the goals of the producing firm and those of the public" (Galbraith, 1967, p. 477).

REGULATORY AGENCIES

The debate over the impact of large firms with market power and monopolies continues today. In policy terms, the conservative position on mergers and monopoly power is that large size does no harm. In fact, there are cases in which large size and/or monopolies may even be the best outcome. For example, imagine what would happen if many firms built dams and ran multiple sets of wires to supply electricity. The duplication of services would increase costs, yet most likely result in inferior service for the customers. If capitalist markets result in larger firms, it is simply because those firms are the most efficient,. Therefore, nothing should be done about firms with market power and monopolies. This conservative position, that nothing should be done about monopoly, was dominant in the nineteenth century, so nothing was done about monopoly until the 1890s.

The liberal position is that giant corporations have market power. Firms with market power tend to promote higher prices and less output. Therefore, giant firms should be broken into smaller, more competitive firms. But conservatives argue that the smaller units will be less efficient. They claim that the firms merged for efficiency in the first place, so smaller size would mean less efficiency.

In answer to conservatives, some liberals have argued that the giant firms could be left large and efficient but should be regulated by government agencies to see that they behave in a competitive manner. The agencies regulate prices and profits. Conservatives claim that regulations reduce competition and efficiency. The position of strongly anticorporation economists is that state, local, and federal governments should take over firms that used their giant size and monopoly power to make immense profits. These anticorporate economists argued that the public should run the monopoly firms for the public interest (as the post office is run). Some anticorporate economists also argued that employees should participate in running the firm.

Since the late nineteenth century, the U.S. government established many regulatory agencies, such as the Interstate Commerce Commission, supposedly designed to protect consumer and environmental interests. Telephone and electric companies are given monopolies, but public agencies are placed above them to regulate their profits. Such commissions are often dominated by those whose interests they are supposed to regulate, and they often neglect the public interest. When the public does not give them careful attention, the public utilities commissions usually grant most price increases desired by the regulated companies. This phenomenon is referred to as **regulatory capture**. It *occurs when a government regulatory agency, which is supposed to be act in the public interest, becomes dominated by the industry it is assigned to regulate and acts in its interest.*

ANTITRUST LAWS

Four major laws were designed to decrease monopoly power. The first, the **Sherman Antitrust Act of 1890**, *forbade any contract, combination, or conspiracy to restrain trade.* In fact, it forbade any agreement not to compete, regardless of how the agreement was achieved. It also forbade monopolies or attempts to monopolize. The **Clayton Act of 1914** *forbade corporations to engage in price discrimination*—that is, to force some customers to pay more than others. *It also prohibited interlocking directorates where this would lead to a substantial reduction of competition.* The **Federal Trade Commission Act of 1914** *outlawed unfair methods of competition and established the FTC to investigate the methods of competition used by business firms.* Finally, the **Celler-Kefauver Act of 1950** *forbade the purchase of either the stock of a competing corporation (which had already been illegal) or the assets of competing corporations* (hitherto a big loophole in the laws).

The antitrust laws were supposed to limit the concentration of economic power among corporations. Yet, as one observer has written, "The fact that after the passage of the Sherman Act the country witnessed a spectacular merger movement, another wave after the passage of the Clayton Act (1914), and again after the Celler-Kefauver Act, indicates that the laws have been ineffective in 'limiting the concentration of control'" (Dowd, 1965, p. 49). For the first two decades after the passage of the Sherman Act, the antitrust laws were used almost exclusively to break the power of labor unions to strike against employers.

Why, then, are a few corporations occasionally convicted for violations of which virtually all corporations are guilty? In these cases, the government uses the antitrust laws to act as arbiter in the irreconcilable conflicts among various corporations. Antitrust convictions are generally mild, punitive actions, taken when the government decides which group of corporations should be supported in a particular conflict of interest. This use of antitrust laws was most apparent recently when the U.S. government acted against certain conglomerate mergers in which "young newcomers" tried to take over old, established corporations.

SUMMARY

In several waves of mergers since the late 1890s, the American economy has been converted from one of numerous small, competitive industrial enterprises to one dominated by giant corporations. In some industries, three or four corporations together make the output, investment, and pricing decisions. All small businesses together produce a small percentage of total output and receive an even smaller percentage of profits. The high degree of concentration increases instability and unemployment in at least two ways. First, driven to the wall, small businesses reduce employment and sometimes set off depressions; they may also go bankrupt, thus worsening the depression. Second, the giant corporations keep their own prices and profits high by restricting the supply of output and further reducing employment.

Giant firms increase their prices rapidly during prosperity, causing inflation by pushing profits up through the use of monopoly power over the market. Since the 1950s, they have even had the power to continue to raise prices during recessions (though more slowly than during expansions). The giant firms also mount enormous advertising campaigns, wasting vast resources in an attempt to prove that their products are better than others. Finally, the giant firms contribute pollution to the air, land, and sea; it is simply not profitable to spend their money on purifying devices for their industrial processes or for their consumer products, such as cars.

SUGGESTED READINGS

A very clear discussion of the data on monopoly power is presented in John M. Blair, *Economic Concentration* (1972). The relation of monopoly to private waste and government waste is explored in the beautifully written classic by Paul Sweezy and Paul Baran, *Monopoly Capital* (1966). The founder of much of the field of industrial organization and monopoly power was Joe Bain (see, e.g., 1948). Early development of the corporation was discussed in Richard Barber (1970).

KEY TERMS

Celler-Kefauver Act of 1950

Clayton Act of 1914

conglomerate mergers

economies of scale

Federal Trade Commission
   Act of 1914

global mergers

horizontal mergers

market power

perfect monopolies

regulatory capture

Sherman Antitrust Act of 1890

vertical mergers

REVIEW QUESTIONS

Describe how corporations grow in size and cite data documenting their growth.
1. What is the difference between a horizontal merger and a vertical merger?
2. The "third wave" of mergers consisted primarily of conglomerate mergers. Explain how conglomerate mergers are different from horizontal or vertical mergers.
3. Policymakers often worry less about conglomerates and market power and more about firms whose business is concentrated in a single industry. Why? What concerns are there about large conglomerates?
4. What are the concerns about the concentration and size of businesses in the global market?
5. Does a global corporation have a perfect monopoly with no competition? Explain.

Explain reasons behind the capitalistic tendency toward large firms with market power.
6. What are economies of scale? Give an example of how the cost per unit of production could be cheaper when many units rather than just a few are produced.
7. How can a firm attempting to capture all possible economies of scale end up having market power in that industry?

Describe the impact of firms with market power on economic outcomes.
8. What does it mean when economists say that a firm has market power? How does the position of a firm with market power differ from that of a firm in a perfectly competitive market?

9. Why might large firms with little competition in their market become less efficient?

10. What are the debates about the impact of advertising on businesses? on consumers? on the larger economy?

Understand some of the policies and policy debates about regulating the monopoly power of businesses.

11. What are some of the debates about regulating monopolies? What is the logic behind the arguments of the different points of view?

12. What are some key pieces of legislation aimed at controlling the impact of monopolies?

PART II, SECTION 3

APPLICATIONS OF PROGRESSIVE MICROECONOMICS

CHAPTER 22

===

Economics of Racial and Gender Discrimination

In Chapter 18, we looked at various measures of inequality in the United States. Chapters 19, 20, and 21 examined various ways that progressive economists view how capitalism generates inequality of economic outcomes. This chapter turns to another facet of inequality: the role of differences and "-*ism*s," such as racism and sexism, in economic opportunities and outcomes.

LEARNING OBJECTIVES

After reading this chapter, you should be able to:

- Explain how membership in either the dominant social and economic group or subordinate group impacts economic opportunities and outcomes.
- Describe how the -*ism*s, such as racism, sexism, and classism, are developed and maintained.
- Discuss how exploiting differences can benefit the dominant group in the economy.

DISCRIMINATION: DIFFERENCES MATTER

Most students believe that success and the good life in the United States are based on hard work by individuals and that deserving individuals will earn economic and social rewards. We come into the world without prejudice, but the people around us teach us to accept stereotypes and discrimination. We come into a world where a dominant social and economic group has greater access to resources and the power to build a better life than the people who are not members of the dominant group. People are oppressed or privileged on the basis of their group membership. The dominant group protects its privileged status by creating the illusion that their status is natural and normal. If you are "different" from the dominant group, you do not have the same access to resources to build a good life.

A political function of exploiting differences between groups of people is to find a scapegoat for problems. Hitler told German workers that Jewish bankers were responsible for unemployment, and he told the middle class that Jewish communists were to blame for all the agitation leading to war. Racism is a particularly handy tool of colonialism: Hindu against Muslim, Jew against Arab, Protestant against Catholic, black against Hindu. And America is quite willing to use the same tactic: Vietnamese against Cambodian, Shiite against Sunni.

Moreover, "inferiority," whether it is supposed to be inherited or acquired, is still given as a reason for lack of development in poor countries where colonialism is the real reason for lack of development.

A **stereotype** is a *standardized, oversimplified image of a particular group*. **Prejudice** is *subjective dislike of a person or a group (usually based on stereotypes)*. Individuals can be prejudiced, institutions can be built on prejudice, and society can be prejudiced. **Discrimination** is *the adverse treatment of an individual based on group membership instead of individual productivity*. Based on prejudice and stereotypes, one group claims another group is inferior in order to justify profit-making activity and discrimination against the members of that group. For example, the white colonists in America declared that Native Americans were inferior, and on that "justification," the colonists stole their land and almost eliminated the Native American population. Today, Native Americans have a median income only one-third the national average, over one-half of the Native American population lives below the official poverty line, and unemployment on Native American reservations ranges between 20 and 90 percent.

Ironically, each succeeding wave of settlers was met with prejudice directed at them by those already living in America. Chinese and Japanese immigrants faced a combination of nationalism and prejudice. During World War II, Americans of Japanese ancestry on the West Coast were confined to concentration camps. (German Americans were never imprisoned.) Prejudice also supports discrimination against Latino Americans, most of whom came from Mexico and Puerto Rico. Both groups were incorporated into the United States through imperialist expansion, one group in the war against Mexico and the other in the war against Spain.

Religious bigotry drives another form of discrimination. In Europe, Protestants and Catholics killed each other for centuries. Much worse, of course, is the centuries-old oppression of the Jews, who were forcibly converted, limited to certain occupations, often taxed to bankruptcy, and periodically massacred. In the late nineteenth and early twentieth centuries, it appeared that anti-Jewish sentiment was finally dying away, and it has never been as severe in America as in some other countries, although it is certainly present. In the 1930s, just as the Jews began to feel secure in most countries, Hitler's fascism unleashed the worst atrocity in the history of humankind. More than 6 million Jewish men, women, and children were tortured, gassed, and burned to death during the Holocaust. In addition, 5,000 to 15,000 gay men were killed in German concentration camps because of their sexual orientation.

THE IDEOLOGY OF *-ISM*S

Racism, sexism, classism, anti-Semitism—all of these *-isms* are examples of *subordination of members of targeted groups by members of dominant groups with relatively more economic and social power*. They are based on systematic ideologies that claim one group is innately superior to others. These extreme forms of prejudice are difficult to reverse. There is also similar prejudice and discrimination against gays, lesbians, senior citizens, and the handicapped.

Since prejudice can distort evidence, objective evidence can rarely change prejudice. White slave owners, the dominant social and political group in the pre–Civil War South, claimed that African Americans were biologically inferior. According to the stereotype, African Americans were stupid and lazy, shuffled their feet when they walked, and liked to sing and dance (to celebrate their happy life as slaves). Dr. William Shockley, a white male physicist, claimed in 1973 that "a one-point increase in average 'genetic' IQ occurs for each 1% of Caucasian ancestry, with diminishing returns as 100 IQ is reaches." (National Academy of Sciences Annual Meeting, 1971, p. 1390.) Yet anthropologists and psychologists have demonstrated repeatedly that IQ scores are dependent on socioeconomic status and cultural background (because of the way the tests are designed) and are thus not true measures of intelligence.

Such unscientific stereotypes are common in everyday thinking and strongly affect and harm African Americans in occupational and professional roles. The following incident illustrates the awful power of prejudiced stereotypes:

> A young Negro lawyer recently recalled his first case, in which he was called upon to defend a burglar. The thief, white, appeared before the judge dressed as he had been when apprehended by the police, in dirty work clothes, his hair mussed, an unshaven face. The lawyer . . . was neatly dressed in a business suit, was well-shaven, and was carrying a briefcase. The judge looked at both men and asked, unjokingly, "Which man is the lawyer?" (quoted in Epstein, 1971, p. 180n).

How much attention do you imagine the judge paid to the African American lawyer's arguments?

Just as the ideology of racism relies on stereotypes of ethnic groups, the ideology of sexism relies on stereotypes of women. One stereotype of women is that they are all sentimental and impulsive, emotional and foolish, not hard-headed, not stable, and definitely not logical, as in the stereotype of men. For example, former Vice President Spiro Agnew (who was forced to resign because of his criminal activity) said: "Three things have been difficult to tame: the ocean, fools, and women. We may soon be able to tame the ocean; fools and women will take a little longer" (quoted in Amundsen, 1971, p. 114).

Adolf Hitler carried anti-Semitism to its ultimate point in the 1930s, when he proclaimed that white, male, non-Jewish Germans (called Aryans) were a master race, superior to all other groups. He created a stereotype, or ideal picture, of all Aryans as big, strong, blond, and of superior intelligence—even though Hitler himself was none of these. His stereotypic Jew was small, dark, greedy, and cowardly. His stereotype of all other peoples was likewise physically weak and mentally inferior. In his stereotype, all women were stupid and good for nothing but sex and childbearing. Such stereotypes were far more than harmless nonsense. On this basis of this prejudice, Hitler killed millions of Jews and Russians, and enslaved millions of people, many of whom were women.

DISCRIMINATION AGAINST AFRICAN AMERICANS

Part I discussed the enslavement of Africans throughout three centuries and the inhumane conditions under which they were brought to the Americas for trade. Africans were enslaved not in the name of white Christian domination, as was Hitler's killing of the Jews and other "inferior" people. The dominant white culture in the American colonies believed it was the white man's burden to bring civilization and the true faith to the black man. Despite the difference in intentions, the result was still one of subordination of blacks. African Americans today constitute one of the largest nonwhite groups in the United States—and one of the most oppressed. Blacks continue to be overrepresented in rates of poverty, unemployment, and incarceration. These continuing problems are rooted in the specific history of African Americans in the United States.

It was not until World War II that a great many African American sharecroppers moved out of agriculture into the war production industries or into the army. After the war, more Northern capital moved into the South, creating employment in manufacturing in the cities. Only then did sharecropping finally die away and the South become fully capitalist. The process of industrializing

Table 22.1

Median Household Income by Race and Hispanic Origin of Householder
(current year dollars)

	2005	1995	1985	1975
All	$46,326	$34,076	$23,618	$11,800
White, not Hispanic	50,784	37,178	25,468	12,433
Hispanic	35,967	22,860	17,465	8,865
Black	30,954	22,393	14,819	7,408
Asian	61,048	40,614	—	—

Source: U.S. Census Bureau, Table H-5. Race and Hispanic Origin of Householder—Households by Median and Mean Income: 1967 to 2006. http://www.census.gov/hhes/www/income/histinc/h05.html.

the South, however, took decades. The South still witnessed lynching, segregation, and resistance to change in the 1950s and later.

Employers can benefit from a certain degree of prejudice among their employees. If white employees are prejudiced against African American employees, then it is difficult to build a strong union or a sense of solidarity among the workforce. Any strike activity supported by one group may be opposed by the other group. During many strikes in the South, one group was actually used to break the strike of another group.

As a result, the South continued to have the fewest unions and the lowest wages in the nation. But the same divisions among employees existed in the North. Prejudice also reduced wages of both whites and nonwhites in the North, though to a lesser degree than in the South.

While both whites and nonwhites were hurt by racial and ethnic divisions, the lowest wages still went to nonwhites. Moreover, nonwhites were the first fired and the last hired. Economic discrimination still is a major cause of inequality for African Americans. It is true that equal employment, fair housing, and fair lending laws have made overt discrimination illegal, so those battles has been won. But informal discrimination, which is difficult to prove, continues. African Americans and Latino Americans still have lower household income, higher unemployment rates, less access to housing and home mortgages, poorer schools in segregated neighborhoods, and less access to health care than do whites.

Median income for all households in 2005 was $46,236. But looking at income in the aggregate hides some interesting facts. In addition to median income for all households over time, Table 22.1 presents data on median income by ethnicity. In 2005, median household income for white, not Hispanic, households was $50,784, which is well above the aggregate median income. Median income for black households was $30,954, which is clearly well below aggregate median income. Median income for Hispanic households was $35,967, and for Asian households, $61,048.

A large amount of data is available on unequal economic outcomes, but some of the most dramatic describes differences in the median wealth of various groups. Looking at Table 22.2 for the year 2000, African American median wealth was only $7,500, while Hispanic median wealth was $9,750. White median wealth was $79,400. Among white, non-Hispanic families, 24.5 percent owned stocks, while only 11 percent of nonwhite families owned stock. While 94.9 percent of white families had a checking account, only 78.2 percent of nonwhite families had a checking account.

Table 22.2

Median Net Worth by Income Quintile in 2000: All Households

Median Net Worth by Race (in 2000 dollars)	Total	Excluding Home Equity
All Households	$55,000	$13,473
White, not Hispanic	79,400	22,566
Hispanic	9,750	1,850
Black	7,500	1,166

Source: U.S. Census Bureau, Net Worth and Asset Ownership of Households: 1998 and 2000, Current Population Reports, Issued May 2003, pp. 70–88. http://www.census.gov/prod/2003pubs/p70-88.pdf.

What is the impact of globalization on racial discrimination? Because of improved communications and movement of people around the world competing for jobs, people of various cultures have learned more about each other, which tends to decrease prejudice. Global corporations, however, have increased the level of competition among workers of different groups and countries. As a result, many groups blame job loss on other groups, which tends to increase prejudice. In the United States, for example, some white male workers now vote for conservatives, because they view liberals as the friends of nonwhites who are the perceived cause of their job losses.

WHO BENEFITS FROM RACISM?

Why does racism persist? One answer is that it benefits some groups. Conservative economists argue that no one benefits from discrimination, that it is merely a matter of irrational and inexplicable tastes or preferences. Conservatives emphasize that discrimination by business is irrational because profits are lost as a result. They argue that if there is discrimination in other areas of the economy, then each capitalist is presented with a supply of qualified African Americans willing to work for wages below the going wages. Since the capitalist can purchase these workers' time at lower wages, profits can be increased by doing so. Therefore, capitalists who are willing to hire African Americans (below the going wage) will make more profits, whereas those who refuse to hire African Americans at any wage will lose profits. Thus, the conservative Milton Friedman (1982) claims,

> a businessman or an entrepreneur who expresses preferences in his business activities that are not related to productive efficiency is in effect imposing higher costs on himself than are other individuals who do not have such preferences. Hence, in a free market they will tend to drive him out (Friedman, p. 108).

The conservative economists conclude that the capitalists who discriminate do so for irrational reasons and lose money because of the discrimination. They further argue that under pure competition, capitalists who discriminate will eventually be put out of business because of their higher costs per unit. Thus, competition will tend to end discrimination and push African American wages ever closer to white wage levels.

Most liberal economists seem to agree with most of these premises. They argue, however, that the U.S. economy is characterized by a high degree of monopoly rather than by pure competition.

By the exercise of monopoly power in the labor market and in the commodity market, firms can hold down all wages and pass on to consumers some of the cost of discrimination. In other words, although the liberals agree with the conservatives that racism is an inexplicable attitude, they contend that it costs the capitalist only a little to indulge his or her strange preference. Therefore, they believe it might be a long time, if ever, before capitalism ends discrimination, and so they support the passage of legislation to end discrimination.

Progressives, on the other hand, do not believe that capitalists lose money from discrimination or that their attitudes are inexplicable. How could discrimination continue for such a long time if capitalists lose from it? Capitalists gain in many ways from racist discrimination and hence have an interest in continuing it. They gain because (1) racist prejudice divides workers, making unions weaker and resulting in lower wages for all workers; (2) the same division makes capitalist politicians safer from attacks by labor; (3) racist discrimination makes it easy to keep African Americans as an unemployed reservoir of cheap labor for boom times; (4) racism provides white politicians with a scapegoat for many social problems; and (5) racism helps inspire soldiers when they are supposed to go to war in other countries. As a result, white capitalists as a whole benefit from racism, although white workers as a whole lose from racism (Reich, 1988).

In the pre–Civil War South, prejudice was a useful justification for slavery, alleviating guilty consciences on the part of slave owners, promoting an easier acceptance of their lot among slaves, and preventing Northerners from interfering. Racism declared that slavery was divinely ordained by God as a benefit to the "inferior" black. Its first function was to justify economic exploitation. This function of racism continues today, when apologists contend that African American and Latino employees are poorly paid only because they are inferior workers. More important, to the extent that white workers believe the racist ideology, unions are weakened by excluding African American workers—or by accepting them reluctantly and preventing them from having equal power. White and black workers have frequently broken each other's strikes in the past, though they are now learning to work together. In the areas of strongest racism and weakest unions, such as the South, black workers' wages are very low, but white workers' wages are almost as low. For this reason, one liberal economist has concluded, "Far from being indifferent to the existence of discriminatory attitudes on the part of workers, the capitalist gains from them and may find it profitable to invest in their creation" (Morris Silver, quoted in Franklin and Resnick, 1973, p. 23).

Another reason that racism is profitable to capitalists is its provision of a handy but disposable labor force. If an employer has ten black and ten white workers, and must fire half for a couple of months, which will he fire? If "he is rational and seeks to minimize his labor turnover costs, he will lay off his ten black workers on the assumption that they will be unlikely to get permanent or better jobs elsewhere because of the discriminatory practices of other employers" (ibid., p. 20). Thus, the capitalist can (and does) fire African American workers in each recession, easily hiring them back in times of expansion. He or she also gains by not having to pay the fringe benefits due employees who stay on the job for a longer time.

Because racism is rooted in the interests of those who control the system, the dominant group, individuals who are not part of the dominant group can move up, but it is very difficult for the group as a whole to move up relative to the dominant group. Legal reforms have brought legal equality to all groups. However, equal opportunity laws have not ended the power of corporations to make use of racism to gain more profits. Therefore, economic discrimination against African Americans (and most others who are not members of the dominant group) remains a fact.

DISCRIMINATION AGAINST WOMEN

Sexism is the systematic subordination of women by members of a dominant group, men, with relatively more economic and social power. A theory of male supremacy is an ideology that serves to justify discrimination against women, who are the majority of Americans. Although sexism is similar in pattern to racism, it is more pervasive, more deeply ingrained in people, and harder to combat. Clearly, the African American woman is held to be doubly "inferior" and suffers the most discrimination.

After World War II, men immediately took some jobs back from women. Starting in the late 1940s, as the U.S. economy continued to grow, there were large increases in the number of women working for wages. There were also considerable increases in women's wages. Finally, there was a 40 percent rise in the number of women who were members of unions. Because of the change in their work situation, many women came to recognize that they were qualified workers who could make an important contribution to society.

Then in the 1950s, the Cold War brought repression of unions, with no more gains by women. Moreover, media views and "expert" views by male psychologists became much more conservative. Some claimed that women worked for wages only out of envy, that they did not need the money, and that they could and should stay home. Women were taking jobs from the men who really needed the work. The media and the school system promoted this view. In reality, most women worked because they were forced to do so. Many women workers were single and were often single mothers. Many other women worked for wages because their husbands' wages were below the poverty line.

Women's wages were only 65 percent of men's wages in 1950. After twenty years of struggling for higher wages, women instead saw their wages fall by 1970 to only 59 percent of men's wages. Why did this decline occur? During those two decades, many new women had entered the labor market with no experience in union organization. At the same time, there was an onslaught of sexist ideology and discrimination against women. As a result, almost all of the new women employees were kept out of high-paying occupations and were forced into low-paying ones, such as teaching. Those low-paid occupations were seen as the proper place for women. Even within those occupations, men received higher wages than women. Thus, women received lower wages partly because they were pushed into the lowest paying occupations but also because they were paid the lowest salaries within those occupations. By 1970, women workers were far more segregated by occupation than any other group of workers. Even in areas such as teaching that were considered "women's work," the top jobs went to men. For example, 55 percent of all school principals in 1928 were women, but the percentage steadily fell. In 1968, only 22 percent of all principals were women.

Because of all of these problems, women fought for a new amendment to the U.S. Constitution, called the Equal Rights Amendment, which would give every person equal rights regardless of gender. Big businesses opposed it because of the fear that they would have to raise the pay of all women workers who were paid less than men for performing the same job. Since this practice accounted for a significant percentage of all corporate profits, corporations fought hard against it and used a great deal of money in that fight (see Deckard, 1983). The Equal Rights Amendment finally passed Congress. Then, however, many state legislators, who initially supported it, had to bow to the business interests that gave them large contributions. Thus, the Equal Rights Amendment failed to be ratified by the requisite number of states.

At the beginning of the twentieth century, only a small percentage of women held paying jobs outside the home. Against many obstacles, women are now, at the beginning of the twenty-first century, a very large part of the labor market and account for an increasing percentage of union members. Also overcoming many obstacles, women went from a small percentage of all those earning bachelor degrees at universities to a majority, though they still lag far behind in the number of doctorates in most fields. Women's salaries rose relative to those of men. Women now have more high-paying jobs as doctors, lawyers, college professors, and even elected officials.

What is the impact of the global economy on women? Instant communication has improved the ties of women to other women around the world, so it has helped strengthen the international women's movement. Better knowledge of other countries has also given impetus to the women's movement in those countries with extreme discrimination because of the contrast with the news about other countries.

At the same time, the movement of jobs to areas of cheap labor outside of the United States and other advanced capitalist countries has badly hurt women in the advanced countries. In less developed countries, however, the increase in manufacturing jobs has not greatly raised the extremely low wages, because corporations have done all in their power to keep wages as low as possible. Moreover, the work conditions are not good. In these less developed countries, corporations have often tried to change the way of life of women in order to make these women come to work exactly on time, work at high intensity for long hours, and never go on strike. The situation is complex and is different in each country.

WHO BENEFITS FROM SEXISM?

As in the case of racism, conservative economists argue that capitalists actually lose by discriminating against qualified women. Such discrimination, they say, means paying men for a job that women could do equally well for less pay. In the words of economist Barbara Bergmann (1973):

> We come . . . to the allegation, usually made by radicals out to discredit capitalism, that women's subjection is all a capitalist plot. Who benefits financially from maintenance of the status quo? The most obvious beneficiaries of prejudice against women are male workers in those occupations in which women are not allowed to compete. . . . It is not the male workers or their wives who do the discriminating, however. The employers of the male workers (almost entirely males themselves) are the ones who do the actual discriminating, although of course they are cheered on in their discriminatory ways by their male employees. The employers actually tend to lose financially since profits are lowered when cheap female help is spurned in favor of high-priced male help (p. 14).

In Bergmann's view, it is not the capitalist employers, but only the male employees, who gain from discrimination. The poor capitalists, who are actually responsible for the discrimination, lose by it. But why do capitalists in business for profits systematically choose to lose money? She says they lose financially but gain psychologically: "It feels so good to have women in their place." Neither she nor anyone else with this view answers the obvious question: If it causes financial losses (even small ones), why hasn't such discrimination tended to decline and disappear under capitalism?

From a progressive perspective, capitalists do not merely gain psychologically while incurring losses from sex discrimination. On the contrary, capitalists gain from sexism both in power and in profits. Moreover, all employees, men as well as women, lose from sexist attitudes.

How do capitalists make profit from sexism? Obviously, they use it as an excuse to pay women lower wages. More important, sexist prejudice divides men and women employees, making it more difficult to organize strong unions. The prejudice of union men is apparent in the fact that women constitute a smaller percent of all union executive board members than they do of all union members. Union men have often paid for their prejudices in broken unions and lower wages. This situation in unions is now changing dramatically for the better. For example, the new union federation that started in 2005 began with a woman as president.

Although discrimination has greatly diminished in unions, it still exists throughout the economy. Women continue to be paid lower wages than men for comparable work. Occupations in which women predominate have far lower wages than other occupations with the same level of education. In most cases, occupations requiring the highest education offer the highest wages for the average worker. But in an occupation such as librarian, in which women predominate, the wages are much lower than the required education level might predict.

In addition to weak unions, another reason for low wages in the predominantly female occupations is that women have few other economic options. To the extent that women are systematically excluded from some occupations, they are pushed into the lower paying occupations. Such segregation causes overcrowding or oversupply in the areas where women are "allowed" to work, thereby lowering wages in these jobs.

The glorification of housework can also be profitable. In the words of one male advertiser of a few decades back, "Properly manipulated . . . American housewives can be given the sense of identity, purpose, creativity, the self-realization, even the sexual joy they lack, by the buying of things" (quoted in Friedan, 1963, p. 199). Thus, advertisers use the sexist ideology to instill "consumerism" in women. The sexist image of the good woman shows her in the kitchen surrounded by the very latest gadgets, using the best cake mix, and made up with miracle cosmetics. Commercials imply that she is a failure if her floors are not the shiniest and her laundry is not the whitest in the neighborhood. This image helps business sell billions of dollars of useless (or even harmful) goods. It also causes stress for women who work full time and then are expected to work a second shift at home in an attempt to create environments like those depicted in television shows and commercials.

Sexism is also profitable because women's unpaid work in the home is crucial to provision of the needed supply of labor. Housework is equivalent to about one-fourth of the GDP, though it is not counted in the GDP. If business had to pay women in full to raise and clean and cook for the labor force, profits would be seriously reduced. The labor of women as housewives is vital to industry; there would be no labor force without it, and yet it goes unpaid. Furthermore, women in the family are profitable to capitalism not only through their unpaid material labor but, perhaps even more so, in the psychological jobs that women (under sexist conditioning) do in the family.

The woman in the sexist family helps provide "good" workers: "A woman is judged as a wife and mother . . . according to her ability to maintain stability in her family and to help her family 'adjust' to harsh realities. She therefore transmits the values of hard work and conformity to each generation of workers. It is she who forces her children to stay in school and 'behave' or who urges her husband not to risk his job by standing up to the boss or going on strike" (McAfee and Wood, 1972, p. 156). Moreover, as a result of their dependent role in the sexist family, women themselves are socialized to be passive, submissive, and docile as workers.

The last, but not the least, important profit to capitalism from sexism comes in its increased support for political stability. Much like racism, sexism is also used as a political divide-and-rule tactic. White politicians frequently blame urban problems on African Americans. During the Nixon administration, Secretary of the Treasury George Schultz blamed unemployment (and accompanying pressure for low wages) on the increased number of women workers entering the labor force.

Thus, some conservative politicians try to make women a scapegoat for men's problems so that men do not see in women their natural ally against a system that oppresses them both.

SUMMARY

Discrimination on the basis of ethnicity, religion, race, gender, and sexual orientation exist in America today. The well-documented oppression of African Americans and Latino Americans is particularly severe in housing, education, jobs, and health care. The prejudice against African Americans originated as an apology for slavery, but it continues as an apology for low wages, poor housing, and limited employment opportunities.

Women continue to suffer from fewer educational opportunities, fewer job opportunities, lower pay for comparable jobs, and a sexist ideology that says they are inferior. The ideology and discriminatory patterns continue to be supported, in part, because some important business interests find them very profitable.

Women as well as African Americans, Latino Americans, and other members of the nondominant group have organized liberation movements. They have achieved some important reforms under capitalism. Their attempt at greater economic equality, however, is blocked by the power of right-wing groups backed by those with money and power who benefit from discrimination.

SUGGESTED READINGS

An excellent and comprehensive book on the history of sexist discrimination and the movement against it is Barbara Sinclair Deckard's *The Women's Movement: Political, Socioeconomic, and Psychological Issues* (1983). The most thorough study of racism against African Americans is Michael Reich's *Racial Inequality, Economic Theory, and Class Conflict, Princeton University Press* (1980). The best history of discrimination against Latino Americans is by Mario Barera, *Race and Class in the Southwest* (1980).

The story of discrimination against African Americans is brought up to date in a passionate book by Manning Marable, *Black Liberation in Conservative America* (1997). A book relating discrimination against women to the understanding of class is Johanna Brenner's *Women and the Politics of Class* (2000).

KEY WORDS

discrimination	prejudice
*-ism*s	stereotype

REVIEW QUESTIONS

Explain how membership in either the dominant social and economic group or nondominant group impacts economic opportunities and outcomes.

1. Why do members of dominant social groups have greater opportunities? Give two specific examples of this phenomenon.
2. How does a dominant group protect its status?
3. Give a contemporary example of one group using another group as a scapegoat for a social problem.
4. Define and explain what is meant by stereotype, prejudice, and discrimination.

Describe how the -*ism*s, such as racism, sexism, and classism, are developed and maintained.

5. What are "–isms"? What do they share in common?
6. What are the different ideas that reinforce the discrimination of African Americans?
7. List two stereotypes each about African Americans, women, and the poor. What is a shared shortcoming of all of these stereotypes?
8. Briefly recount the differences in median incomes among whites, blacks, Hispanics, and Asians. Briefly describe the differences in median wealth for these same groups. Draw on Tables 22.1 and 22.2 as necessary.
9. How has globalization both positively and negatively impacted the degree of discrimination that exists?

Discuss how exploiting differences can benefit the dominant group in the economy.

10. Who benefits from racism and sexism?
11. According to progressives, what are the ways in which capitalists benefit from racist discrimination? How does this view differ from the conservative economics perspective?
12. Give an example of how racism is used to create a disposable labor force.
13. According to progressives, how do capitalists gain through sexism? What would a conservative economist say in response?
14. How can the glorification of housework be profitable for capitalists?

CHAPTER 23

Environmental Devastation

This chapter begins with a summary of the problems of environmental destruction. It then looks at why this destruction exists and the debates about what might be done to end it. The contemporary debate over climate change is used to illustrate the fundamental differences among conservative, liberal, and progressive economists on environmental issues.

LEARNING OBJECTIVES

After reading this chapter, you should be able to:

- Describe types of pollution resulting from production and consumption.
- Explain the overarching reason that firms in capitalist market economies may not actively seek to reduce the pollution from production.
- Compare and contrast the policy recommendations of conservatives, liberals, and progressives.

ENVIRONMENTAL PROBLEMS AND CAPITALISM

One poetic observer writes, "America was once a paradise of timberland and streams, but it is dying because of the greed and money lust of a thousand little kings who slashed the timber all to hell and would not be controlled" (Bell, 1970, p. 3). Environmental destruction, however, is not just a matter for poets and of far-off forests. Consider the environment in Los Angeles. Anyone flying to Los Angeles will notice a large, brownish cloud covering much of southern California. This cloud, called smog, does not merely look bad and cut visibility, it is also a menace to the health of the public. Ironically, many people came to southern California in the 1930s and 1940s because they had respiratory problems, and it was a place where the air was crystal clear, warm, dry, and healthy. It seems almost incredible that in such a short time it could become a place where a few minutes of outside work in the afternoon are exhausting and the air itself causes thousands of respiratory diseases among children.

Let us list systematically the major forms of pollution. First, there are visible objects such as cans and wastepaper and smoke. Businesses spew billions of tons of pollutants into the air and water and land every year. Visible pollutants include about 150 million tons of smoke and fumes that blacken the skies and poison the air, millions of tons of waste-paper products, and millions of tons of mill tailings. Pollution is not a new phenomenon, but it has increased with economic growth. It is a particular problem in low-income areas that get much of the smoke and act as dumping grounds for garbage and other toxins.

A second form of pollution is organic waste. Organic waste comes from fire, detergents, and fertilizers; human and animal wastes; and materials such as nitrates and phosphates that lead to rapid growth of algae. Altogether, many trillion gallons of heated and polluted liquids are dumped into our streams, rivers, and lakes each year. The amount has been rapidly increasing in recent years. When the organic wastes and algae cause exhaustion of the oxygen in the water, other life is unable to survive, and septic decay by anaerobic bacteria causes terrible odors and serves as an incubator for many diseases.

A third pollutant is local air pollution, including smoke, carbon monoxide from automobile exhaust, nitrogen and sulfur oxides, and photochemical smog produced by hydrocarbons reacting chemically in the air. Automobiles are the worst offenders, producing many million tons of pollutants a year. Industry and power plants produce many more million tons. Altogether, all sources in the U.S. economy introduce millions of tons of carbon monoxide, sulfur oxides, nitrogen oxides, hydrocarbons, and particular matter into the air each year. This pollution causes property damage, local weather changes, lung disease, and many other diseases. In some temporary emergency situations, caused by local air inversions, even deaths have been caused by pollution.

Fourth, there is worldwide atmospheric pollution, including carbon dioxide and dust clouds that may affect the climate. Increasing carbon dioxide in the atmosphere traps heat and warms the earth, while dust reflects the sun's rays and tends to cool the earth. If either trend becomes dominant, our climate will change drastically.

The unanimous report of a United Nations panel of experts from many countries found that global warming, if unchecked, would mean large rises in water levels, flooding sea coasts, and drastic weather fluctuations and long-run changes. Even if the world stops all further damage to the atmosphere, it will not return to normal for at least 150 years. But it is possible to greatly reduce harmful emissions in a short time. For example, 39 percent of the harmful emissions of carbon dioxide, the main villain, come from coal-burning to create electricity in the global economy. Changing this power generation to alternative fuels would make an incredible difference. But the changes needed are very progressive, so they must overcome resistance by profit-making corporations and by vested interests controlling governments. One article detailing this report is insightfully titled "Game over on global warming? Action would have to be radical—but climate change can be slowed" (Zarembo, 2007).

Fifth, persistent poisonous materials, including DDT and heavy metals (lead, mercury, and cadmium), threaten health. DDT remains in each animal until it is eaten by another, right up the food chain to humans, causing various health effects. The heavy metals tend to attack the central nervous system of animals.

A sixth form of pollution is stray energy from sonic booms to radioactivity. Of increasing concern is that nuclear power plants produce heat, atomic contamination, and radioactive fallout. Radioactivity not only has a direct, harmful effect on the exposed body but also carries over through genetic defects to the next generation. Nuclear accidents such as the one at the Three Mile Island plant in Pennsylvania in 1979 and the one at Chernobyl in 1986 can spread radioactivity over an enormous area in a short time. In addition, no one has yet devised a good way to eliminate the increasing piles of radioactive waste, which remain dangerous for thousands of years.

WHAT TO DO ABOUT POLLUTION

Pollution is associated with the production and consumption of the goods and services that society wants and needs. How do we balance the needs and wants of society against the damage to the environment that also sustains us? Policy prescriptions tend to be associated with a general political/economic outlook—conservative, liberal, and progressive.

The Conservative View

Some conservatives deny that the picture is as grim as we painted it. They acknowledge that there are some environmental problems but give them a low priority. Production and profits come first. The conservative economists who do take the problem seriously begin with Adam Smith's analysis. The "invisible hand" of competitive private enterprise will balance all costs and benefits to consumers and producers and will finally give the optimal social result. They do acknowledge that, to some extent, the market does not seem to be working well enough to prevent pollution.

The reason that Adam Smith's reasoning may not work well with respect to pollution is that some costs—like pollution—are costs to all of society but not costs to individual firms. Moreover, the benefits of nonpollution go to all of society rather than just to individual firms. Thus, the costs of pollution do not lower their profits, nor do the benefits of nonpollution raise the profits of individual firms. Since the decisions of individual firms are determined by their expected profits, they ignore the existence of the pollution they create.

Since the problem is that the costs of pollution may not affect the individual firm in a competitive market, the logical solution for conservatives is to control pollution through markets. One market approach is to make air and water into private property. Then we could have competition between those who wish to buy air to pollute and those who wish to buy air to breathe. The idea is grounded in the incentives associated with taking more care of something you own. The "tragedy of the commons" says that if something is used by everyone with no control over access to the natural resource, everyone will try to use as much as possible as fast as possible. The reasoning is that as the owner of a natural resource, you will try to take care of it so you can earn profits over the long-run.

Another suggestion is that the government could auction off the "right to pollute." Policymakers would determine the tolerable amount of pollution in an area and then divide up that quantity between the firms creating the pollution. If some firms were not using all their allowable pollution on their permit, they could sell the unused portion to firms that were polluting more than their allotment. Another strategy is that firms could pay for pollution damage through fines or taxes, or we could all pay firms not to pollute by giving them subsidies from local governments to use cleaner production methods.

The Liberal View

Liberals argue that the problem is much broader than the conservatives tend to acknowledge. Like conservatives, liberals argue that the costs of pollution are external to private accounting of costs of production by the individual firm. Liberals also point out that many of the benefits of nonpollution of air and water are collective or public goods by nature. Because they are public goods, there is no way to divide up clean air for sale to some people but not to others. Liberals conclude that private enterprise cannot solve this problem by tinkering with new property rights in air and water but that the government must exercise its power to stop pollution. For example, Samuelson says: "Is reliance on spontaneous business efforts futile in the solution of a problem like this? Experience gives a pessimistic answer. Since no one profit maker has the incentive, or, indeed, the power to solve problems involving 'externalities,' here is a clear case for some kind of public intervention" (Samuelson, 1973, pp. 816–817). Liberals advocate various laws to control the polluters (see Freeman, Haveman, and Kneese, 1973).

Power and Pollution: A Critique of the Liberal View

Liberals assert that the government can pass and enforce laws controlling pollution while preserving capitalism. They fail to see that the "right to pollute" is deeply embedded in our present economic system and that efforts to control pollution will meet fierce opposition. A corporate manager must focus on the bottom line of profit. Therefore, corporations usually oppose environmental regulations that would have a negative impact on their profits. The natural resistance of businesspeople to pollution controls tends to be passed along to the government. A delicate balance must be maintained—politicians must say enough about the environment to get elected by a public that demands pollution controls, and yet they must also be careful that few such controls are put into effect or they will antagonize the businesspeople who give them their campaign funds.

Some politicians admit that clean air is less important than continued profit making in the automobile industry because clean air is not important to the U.S. economy. Indeed, the automobile and related industries are very important interests in our economy. When we add together automobile production, gasoline and oil production, highway building and maintenance, plus automobile parts and accessories production, we arrive at a large percentage of gross domestic product. When we ask why there is not more public investment in rapid transit systems or more public research into alternatives to the internal combustion engine, the answer seems to be the political-economic power of the automobile, gasoline, and highway industries. In fact, private opposition and political constraints helped to reduce rides on public transit from 23 billion in 1945 to only 8 billion a year in 1967. A recent documentary, *Taken for a Ride* (by Jim Klein and Martha Olson, New Day Films, 1996) "reveals the tragic and little known story of an auto and oil industry campaign, led by General Motors, to buy and dismantle streetcar lines."

Lobbyists from the American Road Builders Association, the Associated General Contractors of America, the National Highway Users Conference, the American Trucking Association, the American Association of State Highway Officials, the American Automobile Association, as well as representatives of many individual firms have so far been able to prevent much use of the immense highway funds for public transit. The same lobbyists have also been successful in preserving the oil depletion tax loophole.

In addition to preventing the passage of pollution-control laws (or better rapid transit or research for better cars), the same forces have prevented effective use of the laws that have been passed. For example, there are antipollution boards in many states, but most of them are dominated by the very polluting firms they are supposed to control. In the 1970s, the Federal Power Commission was found to be similarly controlled by the gas and electric power interests.

Since automobiles are the most important source of smog, we would expect many legal procedures to force the automobile companies to institute controls. Their tremendous power, however, has been used to reduce the impact of law enforcement. For example, "Throughout 1969, the Department of Justice in Washington held a secret hearing to discuss with industry lawyers its charge that automobile manufacturers have conspired to stifle the introduction of smog-control devices on automobiles. On September 11, the department announced that it had entered into a consent decree allowing the companies to escape federal sanctions by promising that they would not conspire any more" (Bell, 1970, p. 269). Furthermore, in the general atmosphere of big business influence, it was easy for the automobile companies to exert pressure on the Environmental Protection Agency. As a result, the EPA postponed the enforcement of the standards set by the Clean Air Act passed by Congress. Finally, the automobile lobby forced Congress itself to postpone enforcement of the Clean Air Act.

Even if the laws are enforced, the existence of the capitalist system brings about a clash between environmental and economic interests. For example, under the Clean Air Act, a cement factory in the little town of San Juan Batista, California, was found guilty of terrible pollution of the air. The company admitted this but said that it will "cost too much"—that is, it will lower profits—to install the proper purification machinery. The entire cement factory closed and moved elsewhere. In this way, the burden of environmental protection is made to fall on local workers and on the local populations and governments. Similar threats can be utilized at the national level. Already, many small countries have capitulated to the demands of polluters rather than lose business and jobs to other countries. Even the United States is not immune. Since the environmental protection laws were tightened, many of the most powerful U.S.-based multinational corporations moved or threatened to move whole enterprises to less well-protected countries.

At present, the big corporations have launched a well-financed drive to modify or end antipollution and safety regulations in many industries. The corporations (and many economists) argue that they are forced to spend a great deal of money for safety and to reduce pollution, so these laws are a major cause of reduced investment, lowered growth, and raised prices. On the other hand, the ecology movement points out that the lack of stricter safety and pollution laws has resulted in the loss of lives.

THE REVIVAL OF MALTHUSIANISM

In the late 1700s, Reverend Thomas Robert Malthus studied population and poverty. In *An Essay on the Principle of Population,* published in 1798, he proposed that human population increases geometrically—2, 4, 8, 16, . . . , *n*. He also proposed that production could increase only arithmetically—1, 2, 3, 4, . . . , *n*—because of our limited land and resources. From these assumptions, he concluded that poverty occurs because the number of people grows faster than the ability of an economy to produce the goods they need to survive. The only alternatives are to abstain from sex altogether or to wait until famine and disease remove the excess population. What Malthus overlooked was advancements in technology that allow us to produce more per input. He also overlooked that after industrialization, more educated and sophisticated men and women would decide to have fewer children per family by practicing birth control. Therefore, instead of ever-decreasing product per person, developed countries have experienced growing per-capita production.

In recent years, many conservatives, some liberals, and even some progressives brought back to life the old **Malthusian argument**. They conclude that *rising population and rising production together doom us to ecological catastrophe and to eventual poverty as our resources are depleted.* The only way out, they tell us, is to have a zero population growth and a zero rate of economic growth under capitalism. Partly, they are concerned with the very real problems inherent in growth in capitalism. It is not true, however, that nothing can be done or that limiting growth and population are the only or even the best answers. In the first place, the link between pollution and GDP growth is not a simple one-to-one relationship. If we spend $10 to go to the movies, the accountants record $10 GDP growth, but very little pollution was created. If, on the other hand, we spend $10 for gas for pleasure driving, a great deal of pollution was created.

The problem is not merely that some economic growth involves much more pollution than other growth; it is also that much of this spending is on unnecessary or even harmful goods that could be eliminated without reducing food, clothing, and shelter. Furthermore, some activities should grow—for example, services to combat pollution—even though they will be treated as GDP growth by the accountants.

In the second place, no-growth policies cannot be considered apart from income redistribution policies. Under the present capitalist system, poor people rightly suspect that "no growth" means they would be frozen into poverty forever.

In the third place, international redistribution must be considered. At United Nations conferences, when affluent American delegates argue for no-growth policies, the poor countries conclude that this means that their whole countries would be doomed to poverty for all time. Moreover, when birth control is advocated by the U.S. government for these countries, they are rightly suspicious of nationalist and racist motives for reducing their populations but not the U.S. population. It is also a fact that the best way to introduce birth control and reduce population growth is to achieve an urban and industrialized society, since people then have the knowledge of birth control and the desire to limit the number of children they have.

In the fourth place, the proponents of no-growth never consider whether a different political-economic system could achieve less pollution with the same growth. We have seen that although some pollution is caused by any massive economic growth under present technology, it is capitalist drive for profits that causes many additional problems. It is a government dominated by capitalist economic power that is slow to legislate and slow to enforce pollution controls. It is a capitalist system that cannot guarantee workers other jobs when some jobs are eliminated because of pollution effects. It is capitalist systems that cannot willingly redistribute to poor people and poor countries the existing goods and services. It is the capitalist system that makes poor people and poor countries suspicious of birth control—though birth control would make very good sense under a nonprofit-oriented system. Finally, it is impossible to conceive of a no-growth rule imposed on capitalism. How could private enterprises exist if they are prevented from growing?

The Progressive View

Progressives agree that some pollution is likely in any highly industrialized, densely populated economy. For the reasons discussed previously, progressives argue that a large part of pollution in the United States is due to the capitalist economic system. "Look at the values which galvanize energies and allocate resources in the business system: pursuit of money, enrichment of self, the exploitation of man—and of nature—to generate still more money. Is it surprising that a system seeking to turn everything into gold ends up turning everything into garbage?" (Editors of Ramparts, 1970, p. ix).

Progressives argue that the solution is a new economic system in which the people decide democratically how to run it rather than the decisions being made by a few corporate elites. Note that this is a classic definition of "socialism." Under a democratically run socialist economy, the national income would be shared much more equally than today, so most people could live better at any level of GDP than under our present system of unequal distribution. Under a democratically run socialist economy, there would be no private enterprises to push frantically for more growth to make more profits.

Climate Change

The environmental problem currently receiving the most press is that of global warming, or as scientists increasingly refer to it, climate change. In short, **climate change** *refers to variations in the Earth's prevailing weather conditions over time.* These changes can be caused by natural processes, such as changes in the intensity of sunlight or volcanic activity, as well as by human activity. The most important human cause of climate change is the increased emission of pollution into the atmosphere. These pollutants cause a **greenhouse effect**. *Just as a florist's greenhouse uses glass panels to let in light and keep in heat, greenhouse gases, such as carbon dioxide, allow in light and trap heat in the Earth's atmosphere.*

The greenhouse effect causes the earth to heat up in particular places and may cause weather patterns to change. As a result, some places become warmer, while others turn cooler. Some geographic areas will receive increased rainfall, while others become deserts. Some scenarios show increased warming on average to melt large portions of the polar ice caps. This would increase sea levels around the world and inundate low-lying coastal areas—locations where hundreds of millions of people live. Estimates on the loss of life and economic costs of relocation vary widely.

On October 12, 2007, MSNBC reported that former United States Vice President, Al Gore, and the United Nations' Intergovernmental Panel on Climate Change were awarded the Nobel Peace Prize. The Nobel citation notes that the award was given to Gore for a variety of reasons. "His strong commitment, reflected in political activity, lectures, films and books, has strengthened the struggle against climate change. . . . He is probably the single individual who has done most to create greater worldwide understanding of the measures that need to be adopted." The Panel was noted for 20 years of reports that have "created an ever-broader informed consensus about the connection between human activities and global warming."

Despite the widespread recognition of this problem by scientists and social scientists, particularly by those outside of the United States, deep divisions remain related to how best to go about lowering greenhouse gasses. As this chapter has described, economists of different political economic worldviews have very different perceptions about the environment and therefore different prescriptions for how best to address problems of pollution. This general view applies also to the specific case of climate change.

As we've seen earlier in this chapter, there are at least three perspectives on this issue. Neoclassical conservatives are the least concerned about the problem and believe that technological development and economic growth will allow us to avert any major crisis. Neoclassical liberals recognize that a problem exists, but that it can be managed by fairly traditional tax-based or market-based solutions. Progressives see the problem as rooted in the economic relations of capitalism. If markets caused the problem, they are unlikely to serve as a solution. Each of these three perspectives is discussed in turn.

Neoclassical conservative or traditional economists are the most optimistic about climate change. They tend to see the capitalistic system that dominates the global economy as robust and self-correcting. In fact, they generally see unbridled capitalism on a global scale as being an ideal. Many of these economists would argue that freer trade and higher rates of growth as leading to technological advances. These advances, in turn, will allow us to have more economic output and a cleaner environment at the same time. In short, free trade, higher incomes, and technological progress can save us.

Neoclassical conservatives tend to characterize the economy as stable and self-equilibrating. They see the natural systems of the earth in the same way. They also doubt the degree to which humans have been a cause of the climate change phenomenon. If they do believe that humans created the problem, they also believe that the earth itself will be able to adjust to these changes. Thus, as might be expected, they view the threat of global warming as minor, regard its dire ecological implications as inflated, and see little or no need for governmental action. Other conservatives argue that even if climate change has human causes, the costs of addressing the issue would be far higher than the costs. Thus, there is no reason to take aggressive action. Doing so would make the situation worse.

An excellent example of this last perspective is from a July 2, 2006 opinion piece written by

Bjorn Lomborg in *The Observer.* He asserts that, "Some options will always be better than others. If we know which causes produce the greatest social benefits, then it is reasonable to propose the money goes to those causes." His opinion piece goes on to argue that spending public funds on HIV/AIDS, providing food and dietary supplements to the world's hungry, and encouraging greater trade liberalization would each have bigger positive impacts on the world than spending funds reducing greenhouse emissions. In short, spending scarce resources to reduce carbon emissions is inefficient. We would get higher returns from investments by addressing other social problems.

Neoclassical liberal economists have a more nuanced and more contentious approach to climate change. They agree that it is important issue. However, they vigorously disagree about how best to confront it. The two dominant liberal approaches to limiting greenhouse emissions are to (1) implement a carbon tax, or to (2) set a strict limit on carbon emissions and then allow polluters to sell unused "rights to pollute" at a profit.

A **carbon tax** is a *type of pollution tax on energy sources, such as coal or gasoline, that varies in proportion to the amount of carbon dioxide their use emits into the atmosphere.* As you will learn more formally in Chapter 35, when a market transaction adversely affects a third party, the market outcome can be improved by imposing a tax which pushes up the market price of that good, thereby reducing its quantity demanded. In short, taxing a good discourages its use and encourages substitution to cleaner energy alternatives. This is the objective of a carbon tax.

A more complicated and less easily understood liberal approach to limiting greenhouse emissions is a carbon cap-and-trade system. A **cap-and-trade or emissions trading system** is *an administrative process by which emissions are limited, but polluters are required to buy and sell pollution permits.* The intent is that market incentives can be used to encourage conservation and emission reduction.

This system would establish a limit on the amount of a pollutant, such as carbon dioxide, that can be discharged into the atmosphere. In addition, credits—pollution permits—would be issued to power companies. If a company wanted to increase its emissions, it would need to buy a permit from a firm that has reduced its emissions and has a permit for sale. A market incentive—the profit gained from selling a permit—gives firms a financial reason to pursue ways in which to reduce their carbon discharges. In addition, those firms that can most cheaply reduce their emissions are the ones who will do so. This ensures that emissions are reduced by those best able to do and therefore the total cost of pollution reduction is decreased.

One can debate which of these two neoclassical liberal approaches is best. John Cranford writing in *CQ Weekly* (November 10, 2007) argues that a carbon tax would be "simpler and easier to administer." In addition, it would be "transparent to businesses and consumers, and thus easier to plan for." It would also generate revenue "that could be used to mitigate adverse consequences to the economy as a whole and to low-income consumers of energy, in particular." Others point out that a cap-and-trade system tends to maintain the status quo by allowing high volume polluters to remain high volume polluters. In contrast, a carbon tax would fall most heavily on those who pollute the most.

Progressive economists, as the earlier section of this chapter suggests, see climate change as rooted in a corporate-led, market-driven economic system that ruthlessly pursues profits, faithfully encourages consumerism, and that demonstrates little regard for the natural environment. Since progressives see capitalism as the source of the problem, they are directly at odds with the conservatives who see capitalism as the planet's potential savior. Similarly, progressives are skeptical of the plans advanced by neoclassical liberals that advocate market-based tax systems, let alone market-based trading systems of pollution permits. What is needed from the progressive perspective is a fundamentally different economic system designed to meet the needs of all human beings as well as to protect the natural systems upon which all human life depends.

SUMMARY

There are various kinds of economic waste: military production, monopoly misallocation, most advertising and sales expenses, planned obsolescence, lack of conservation. Environmental destruction and pollution may be regarded as a kind of waste of resources. There is pollution of land, air, and water, with eleven types of environmental destruction spelled out at the beginning of this chapter.

Extreme conservatives argue that nonpollution (such as clean air) could be given a price and bought and sold in the market, thus automatically solving the problem. Liberals believe that conservative approach is insufficient and that legal controls are needed to prevent pollution by private enterprise. Progressives do not believe controls will work under capitalism. It appears to them that a change from capitalism to a different set of institutions is a necessary condition for an end to waste and pollution.

SUGGESTED READINGS

A good, brief, and popular book is John Bellamy Foster's *The Vulnerable Planet: A Short Economic History of the Environment* (1984). A good, lengthy, popularly written book is Jared Diamond's *Collapse* (2004) In particular, the final three chapters of the book, Chapters 14–16 discuss the lessons learned from pervious ecological disasters and how we might, yet, avert our own. Al Gore's influential and Academy Award winning movie, *An Inconvenient Truth,* opened in 2006. The movie summarizes the state of scientific knowledge about climate change as well as its political economic implications.

KEY TERMS

cap-and-trade or emissions trading system   greenhouse effect
carbon tax   Malthusian argument
climate change

REVIEW QUESTIONS

Describe types of pollution resulting from production and consumption.
1. List different types of pollution and their impact on the environment.
2. Do the different types of pollution affect only the area immediately surrounding the source of the pollution? Explain using examples.
3. Are the effects of some types of pollution always immediately apparent? Why or why not? Give an example.

Explain the overarching reason that firms in capitalist market economies may not actively seek to reduce the pollution from production.
4. Explain how firms can pass on the costs of pollution to the public.
5. What are some ways the public "pays" for the costs associated with pollution from nearby plants or factories?
6. If firms are not paying all costs associated with the production of a product, how do you think that will affect the price of that product in the market and the consumption of that product?

Compare and contrast the policy recommendations of conservatives, liberals, and progressives.

7. What is the implied assumption about how people behave in the "tragedy of the commons"? Do you think this is always the way people behave? How might different institutions and incentives work into your answer?

8. Describe the market solutions to pollution. What are some possible problems with the solutions?

9. According to liberals, why does the Environmental Protection Agency exist? How does it fit into their policy suggestions about pollution?

10. What are problems that might be associated with regulation of polluting firms?

11. How do conflicts of interest of profit-maximizing business and governmental regulators affect pollution laws and their enforcement? Give an example.

12. Why is a no-growth policy to pollution not feasible? Give some specific examples to support your argument.

13. What do progressives suggest is the solution to pollution?

14. What do you think would be an effective policy to control pollution? How would you support your argument?

15. Climate change provides an engaging example of an issue where neoclassical conservatives, neoclassical liberals, and progressives have far different perceptions of the problem and proposed solutions. Briefly describe these three different perspectives.

16. Explain the advantages and disadvantages of a carbon tax and an emissions cap-and-trading system. Which do you think is better? Why?

CHAPTER 24

Government and Inequality

Chapter 18 discussed different aspects of inequality in the United States. This chapter discusses how that inequality affects the government. It explores the degree to which economic power gives disproportionate political power to a relatively small number of people. Finally, the chapter discusses how the government affects economic inequality through taxation, welfare, antitrust laws, media, and education.

LEARNING OBJECTIVES

After reading this chapter, you should be able to:

- Explain the difference between formal democracy and effective democracy.
- Discuss how economic power leads to political power.
- Explain how differences in economic power impact policy decisions.
- Describe how policy decisions that create opportunities for one group of people can lead to lack of opportunities for other groups of people.

HOW ECONOMIC INEQUALITY PRODUCES POLITICAL INEQUALITY

In spite of our formal political democracy, a **democracy**, meaning *rule by the people* in which the legal institutions of democracy, such as elections, are in place, money still has power in politics. It should be no surprise that many writers allege that people with economic power dominate American politics. While he was president of the United States, Woodrow Wilson wrote: "Suppose you go to Washington and try to get at your Government. You will always find that while you are politely listened to, the men really consulted are the men who have the biggest stake—the big bankers, the big manufacturers, big masters of commerce, heads of railroad corporations and of steamship corporations. . . . The masters of the Government of the United States are the combined capitalists and manufacturers of the United States" (Wilson, 1914, pp. 57–58).

How far can Wilson's hypothesis be substantiated by the facts? First, **government** is defined as *institutions that regulate and implement policies on behalf of the state in domestic and global settings*. Who dominates American politics? Suppose the few very rich who control American corporations also control American politics. Chapter 18 showed that over 95 percent of Americans are employees, with interests contrary to the rich and the big corporations. It is also the case that

America has free elections in which all those employees can vote. If the government is controlled by the 1 percent who have most of the economic power, then there seems to be a mystery. With democratic elections, how can the government end up being controlled by the 1 percent of the most elite in money terms? Given formal democracy and capitalism, exactly how does economic inequality tend to be translated into political power?

The first argument is simply that the degree of political participation tends to vary with class background. "The average citizen has little interest in public affairs, and he expends his energy on the daily round of life: eating, working, family talk, looking at the comics, sex, sleeping" (ibid., p. 165). Higher income households, especially the top 1 percent of earners who own most of the corporations and financial assets, have a high level of voting, a high level of political contributions, a high attendance at political meetings, and a high level of working for the candidate of their choice. Middle- and high-income employees and households vote and participate in all these ways, but at a considerably lower level. Lower income employees and low-income households, people on welfare, and the unemployed often do not vote or participate at all. Why participate if you think it will have no effect and you have little spare time and no extra money?

All in all, in most presidential elections, only about half of all eligible Americans vote, and much fewer vote in nonpresidential and local elections. It should be noted that 59 percent of those eligible voted in the hotly contested election of 2004. Of those who do not vote, most are poorly paid, minorities, and/or unemployed. In most elections, only the higher income part of the population needs to be persuaded how to vote.

Contributions by the wealthy and the corporations are a major factor moving politicians and parties toward the conservative ideas of preserving the economic system as it is. It was noted that every election season now witnesses the spending of billions of dollars for political propaganda by the two major parties. Republicans usually spend more than Democrats, and corporations spend many times what unions spend. Finally, if any candidates are elected who oppose some corporate policy goals, they are subject to thousands of lobbyists hired to promote the corporate agenda.

HOW RACE AND GENDER AFFECT THE GOVERNMENT

A precise notion of how race, gender, and class differences affect U.S. politics can be seen in the voting patterns of the 2004 presidential election between the more liberal John Kerry and the more conservative George W. Bush. The data are for those who actually voted according to exit polls (see Perry, 2004). Because of their different conditioning by family, church, intense advertising and media, education, and life style, men and women voted somewhat differently on the average. Men voted 53 percent for Bush and 46 for Kerry, whereas women voted 49 percent for Bush and 50 percent for Kerry. A higher percentage of women than men voted for Kerry because Kerry was perceived as a better candidate on women's issues.

Whites voted 57 percent for Bush and 43 percent for Kerry. Latinos voted 45 percent for Bush and 54 percent for Kerry. Asians voted 34 percent for Bush and 64 percent for Kerry. African Americans voted 14 percent for Bush and 86 percent for Kerry (Perry, 2004). These numbers show that Bush received a majority of white votes, but Kerry received more votes from minorities because Kerry was perceived to be friendlier toward minorities.

Finally, in terms of class differences as reflected to some degree in income, there were five groups in the exit polls: below $20,000; $20,000 to $40,000; $40,000 to $60,000; $60,000 to $75,000; and over $75,000. The percentages voting for Bush were 46, 47, 51, 53, and 57 percent respectively. Bush's vote rose steadily from the lowest income group to the highest. Kerry's percentage of the vote in each income group was 51, 52, 48, 46, and 45 percent. Kerry's vote percentage fell from the lowest to the highest income group (Perry, 2004). Obviously, Bush was perceived as more of a friend of the rich, while Kerry was perceived as more of a friend of the poor. The perceptions were the result of life experience plus all of the conditioning mentioned previously.

ECONOMIC POWER AND THE PRESIDENT

There is no great mystery about how economic power gains influence over the president. The cost of campaigning escalates every presidential campaign year, and campaign costs are now in the billions of dollars. Big contributors need not spell out to presidents and their money raisers what they want—their wishes are known and usually followed. Lobbyists for the big donors may not be able to dictate outcomes in every case, but they do have much more access to the president or top officials than do ordinary citizens.

Often, a feedback is mechanism at work. A feedback mechanism is the process by which the president is elected by economic power and then appoints economically powerful people to positions from which they can further extend and defend their influence. For example, in return for the money donated to the Republican Party, President George W. Bush appointed mostly millionaire businesspersons or their functionaries to his cabinet and appointed friends of business to head many government agencies. Obviously, these powerful positions are desirable and used in furthering the interests of individual businesspersons and of all business.

In later sections, we look at how the political feedback mechanism causes presidential bias in favor of big business, such as tax cuts for businesses and the wealthy, increases in military spending, and cuts in spending for social services for the middle class and the poor. More direct feedback mechanisms to influence the political process itself include the use of police to stop demonstrations, use of the CIA and FBI to attack anyone opposed to the administration's policy, and use of the president's prestige in television and press announcements to promote big-business politics.

CONGRESS AND ECONOMIC POWER

Congress is not immune to the lure of economic power. Members of Congress need money to be elected and reelected. They need money to pay for television, direct mail, internet, and other forms of advertising, travel expenses, and many other basic necessities of political life. Lincoln is said to have spent only 26 cents on his campaign, but the amount of money needed for a campaign has certainly escalated ever since. Now campaigns costing hundreds of thousands of dollars are common. Millions of dollars are spent in many campaigns for the House of Representatives. All Senate races involve millions. While unions make some political contributions, corporations normally outspend them more than ten to one. Where direct contributions are banned, contributions are made through committees generally called political action committees, or PACs.

Members of Congress are also indirectly affected by economic power through the strong influence of the president. Furthermore, big business can threaten to open or close plants in a particular congressional district. Businesses can give a Congress member free time on the radio or television or a free plane ride. In addition, there are about five thousand full-time lobbyists in Washington, about ten for each representative (and many are former members of Congress). The two largest lobbies are the oil interests (with corporate income of billions of dollars because of tax loopholes) and the military armaments industry.

On a large number of issues, the American government follows the wishes of a few very wealthy capitalists and big businesses rather than the wishes of the majority of the American people. The reason, of course, is the money contributed to Congress and the president. For example, in January 2006, 55 percent of Americans said the Iraq war was a mistake and we should get out. Nevertheless, the president, the Republicans in Congress, and most of the Democrats in Congress refused to get out. Sixty-five percent of Americans want the American government to run a universal, national health care system and are willing to pay for it, but Congress refuses to pass it. Eighty-five percent of Americans are in favor of raising the minimum wage. Sixty percent of Americans want to repeal all of the tax cuts that Bush and Congress passed for the rich. Sixty-six percent of Americans want to lower deficits by cutting military spending, not domestic spending (all data from Ivins, 2006).

As a result of the pressures to elect people sympathetic to the upper-income members of the capitalist class (mostly white, male, Anglo-Saxon Protestants), they hold a disproportionate percentage of the top political positions. Between 1789 and 1932, the fathers of U.S. presidents and vice presidents were 38 percent farm owners and only 4 percent wage earners or salaried workers. Similarly, from 1947 to 1951, the fathers of U.S. senators were 22 percent professionals, 33 percent proprietors and officials, 40 percent business owners, and only 4 percent wage earners or salaried workers. This general pattern, with few wage employees in Congress, has continued to the present.

Of course, no serious critic would state the thesis of big-business control of government as if it were total. There are many qualifications. For example, although most members of Congress are rich, white males, the influence of wealth in Congress is much less than it is in the cabinet and in other executive offices. Similarly, in state and local governments, the influence of the wealthy is strong, but certainly they do not have exclusive control. Moreover, even among the members of the capitalist class in high positions, there are many differences of opinion, mistakes in perceiving their own interests, and conflicts of interest between different business groups. Thus, the rule of the capitalist class is by no means monolithic; it rules through shifting coalitions as reflected in the Democratic and Republican parties. Finally, other interests and groups, including industrial workers, intellectual workers, and professional employees, can sometimes organize sufficiently to overcome the power of money by pure weight of numbers. The working class can sometimes exert pressure, elect a few representatives, and sometimes even prevail on particular issues.

HOW THE GOVERNMENT AFFECTS INEQUALITY

Taxation

Government spending and taxes directly affect income distribution. Taxes take about one-third of the gross domestic product in order to support local, state, and federal government. Taxes are controlled by governments at the local, state, and national (federal) levels. The most important kinds of taxes are income taxes (at the federal, state, and sometimes local levels), property taxes (at the state and local levels), sales taxes (at the state and local levels), and excise taxes (at all levels). There are a number of other taxes as well.

Progressive taxes occur *if, as income increases by a certain percentage, the tax increases by an even larger percentage.* Traditionally, the federal income tax has been given as the prime example of a progressive tax. At one time, the nominal, or apparent, percentage taxation for extra income was as high as 90 percent for the very rich (although as we shall see, the rich never pay as high a rate as the Internal Revenue Service tax schedule would suggest).

Proportional taxes occur *if the percentage or proportion of income paid to taxes stays the same as income changes.* If I make $4,000, I pay 10 percent of that amount in taxes, and if I make

$400,000, I pay 10 percent of that amount in taxes. **Regressive taxes** occur *if, as income increases by a certain percentage, taxes increase by a lesser percentage.*

The official IRS tables grossly understate the inequity of the federal income tax system. It would certainly seem unfair that the well-paid worker earning $50,000 per year pays the same amount in taxes as the multibillionaire whose annual income exceeds $1 billion. In practice, rich taxpayers find many loopholes that allow them to pay much lower tax rates. For example, in 1957, the highest tax rate had risen to an apparently confiscatory 91 percent, and yet that category of taxpayers paid only 52 percent of income in taxes to the government (Kolko, 1963, Chapter 2). In 1969, the tax rate paid by all taxpayers with incomes reported over $1 million was only 34 percent, and because they are not required to report all of it, the rate was actually only 20 percent (Gurley, 1967, p. 11). While we do not have similar studies showing just how much billionaire capitalists actually pay under the current tax law, we do know that tax loopholes will suffice to make working people pay much higher taxes as a percentage of their incomes than are paid by wealthy capitalists.

One example of a loophole is the tax-free bond. The interest on federal bonds cannot be taxed by states, and the interest on municipal bonds cannot be taxed by states or by the federal government. In order to make a significant amount of money from bonds, a very large investment is necessary, and many bonds are sold in large lots that only the rich can afford. Other loopholes include dividend exclusion, depreciation allowances, and depletion allowances (especially gas and oil).

Important to the perpetuation of income inequality in the United States is the fact that the federal income tax amounts to only 40 percent of all taxes and is the only tax that is progressive to even a slight extent. The other 60 percent of taxes are mainly regressive, according to some observers, in that they fall more heavily on the lower income groups. "We might tentatively conclude that taxes other than individual income taxes do not reduce, and probably increase, income inequality" (Ackerman, 1971, p. 24). Most of the regressive taxes are state and local, such as the sales tax and the property tax. In terms of percentages, these taxes fall much more heavily on low- and middle-income groups than on the rich. For example, a tax on gasoline or telephone service is spread quite equally among the population; therefore, these taxes take a much higher percentage of a poor person's income. A number of studies have shown that the burden of state and local taxes is definitely regressive. The lower one's income, the higher the rate at which one pays these state and local taxes (Cantor, 1976). In addition, a large amount of taxes are paid in the form of compulsory contributions by all employees to the social security system. These taxes are highly regressive because there is a threshold beyond which no more tax is paid. After the rich person receives income above the point at which the maximum tax is incurred ($97,500 in 2007), the remainder of his or her income is free of Social Security tax. What this means is that someone making an annual income of $97,500 and someone else making $9,750,000 pay the same dollar amount in Social Security tax.

The U.S. income tax has been called progressive because the rates are supposed to rise as the level of income rises. After all the loopholes for the rich, taxes are no longer progressive as they once were. A succession of conservative presidents and congresses have made them fairly flat. Thus, in 2005, middle-income people earning from $50,000 to $75,000 per year paid an actual tax rate of 17 percent. After that, the rate went up very slowly and was only 4 percent higher in the top class. So the rich with incomes of over $1,000,000 paid only 22 percent. The data is from the Internal Revenue Service (see Havemann, 2006, p. A6). As a result of these loopholes, some startling statistics have appeared. In 1965, a certain taxpayer had an income of $20 million but paid no taxes. In 1974, some 3,302 people earning more than $50,000 paid no federal taxes—and that included five people with incomes over $1 million in that single year. It has been estimated that the total loss of government revenue from all loopholes in the income tax laws is about $77 billion a year (Lechman and Okner, 1972, pp. 13–40).

The real windfall for corporations came with the Reagan tax cuts of 1981. These cuts contained two provisions by which large corporations could escape federal taxes. First, they were given an accelerated depreciation schedule. Second, they were given "tax leasing" provisions. The notorious tax leasing law allows corporations whose tax breaks exceed their profits to sell those tax breaks to other firms. This has resulted in a situation in which hundreds of firms make profits ranging into the millions of dollars and pay absolutely no federal taxes. Even worse, many of them not only pay no taxes but receive tax refunds after paying no taxes. For example, in 1981, General Electric Company bought so many tax breaks that it paid absolutely no taxes on its profit of $2.55 billion and received an approximately $100 million tax refund for its previous year's taxes. By 1986, the average tax rate actually paid by corporations was estimated to be less than 10 percent, and the economy was rapidly moving toward a state in which corporations do not pay taxes. It is not hard to see why the corporate PACs have had such enthusiasm for Reagan, Bush, and their political supporters.

It matters very much who pays the taxes. The corporations and the rich have enormous tax breaks. For example, a bill passed in October 2004 gave an astonishing list of tax cuts and tax breaks to corporations amounting to $137 billion (for details, see Andrews, 2004). The U.S. Senate voted 69 to 17 in favor of the corporate tax breaks, showing the strength of the friends of vested interests when it really matters for profits. On the other hand, the middle class and the poor have very few tax breaks and must pay a large percentage of their income in taxes. The reason for this difference is that few tax breaks are available to those earning wages and salaries, but a great many tax breaks are available to anyone receiving profit income.

When all kinds of taxes—federal, state, and local—are added together, the proportionate burden on the poor seems to be actually larger than on the rich. Although the rich pay a larger total dollar amount of taxes, the percentage of their incomes going to taxes is actually less than the percentage of poor families' income going to taxes (see Pechman, 1969, pp. 113–137). In conclusion, the whole tax system redistributes little, if any, income from the rich to the poor. In recent years, it has redistributed income in the opposite direction, that is, from the poor and the middle class to the wealthy.

Welfare

Some policymakers assert that absolute poverty is the only income problem left, ignoring the fact that extreme inequality of income creates a relative, or social, poverty as well. They argue that because a growing number of people are receiving welfare payments, the poverty problem will be solved. But poverty is not defined simply as an absolute income level of less than a particular dollar amount; it is relative to the society in which a person lives. The average worker in India makes about $500 per year. A person earning $3,000 per year in that country might be considered wealthy. But there can be no doubt that an American family living on that income can afford neither the cultural nor the physical necessities of life. Even if a person earns $3,000, in a society as affluent as the United States, that person is living in relative poverty. Therefore, others argue that "brutalizing and degrading poverty will exist as long as extreme income inequality exists" (Edwards, 1972, p. 244).

Because taxation does not significantly redistribute income, the question is whether welfare programs have a significant effect in mitigating the effects of poverty. In the first place, expenditures for welfare are relatively small. Even if we include all public aid, unemployment payments, workers' compensation, health and medical programs, public housing, and educational aid to low-income students, this is still a tiny and declining part of the U.S. budget. These payments do help the poor somewhat, but the effect is small. The payments do virtually nothing to alter the relative positions of the poorest or the richest segments of society. Therefore, although it could improve the lot of a few people in absolute terms, it does not change things in relative terms.

What has been the historical trend of welfare payments? In 1938, welfare payments were 6.7 percent of personal income; in 1950, welfare was down to 3.9 percent; in 1960, it was down a little more, to 3.3 percent. In 1968 it was 3.8 percent, whereas in the 1980s, the figure fluctuated between 4 and 5 percent. In the long period of Republican control in the 1990s and 2000s up to 2006, the welfare percentage declined again. Moreover, the poor help pay for welfare, so the net amount received is even less. It is estimated that the poorest 40 percent of the population paid taxes that financed about 25 percent of all welfare payments. Thus, nearly one-quarter of all welfare payments represents money taken from some poor people and then given to others who are poorer. It is no wonder, then, that our tax and welfare systems have not resulted in any significant redistribution of income.

Interestingly, this pattern of small effects and no significant reductions in income inequality over many decades also holds true for the capitalist countries of Western Europe. Even in Denmark and Sweden, where taxation and welfare programs are supposed to be extremely progressive, recent studies have shown little change in income distribution (after taxes and welfare) for several decades. A U.N. report reveals that for all Western Europe, "the general pattern of income distribution, by size of income, for the great majority of households, is only slightly affected by government action" (U.N. Economic Commission of Europe, 1957, pp. 1–15).

The problem is that the social and economic conditions of a private enterprise economy lead to a psychology in which one works only if one has to work. Thus, only by offering extremely unequal incomes for differing amounts of work performed can work incentives be maintained under this system. It would take very different institutions with very different education and propaganda to change this psychology. Therefore, U.S. welfare programs are very carefully designed to assist those who do not work—children, the old, the blind. Very little welfare income goes to those who work hard but are paid low wages (who constitute about half of the poverty group) because that might lower their "incentive." A few programs give the low-paid worker minimum health and education so that he or she is able to work, but these programs are very careful to avoid providing any food, clothing, or shelter. This philosophy of welfare leads to extreme degradation of welfare recipients.

Education and Inequality

Government-subsidized education is often thought to decrease the inequality of incomes. The government gives free education to all, goes the argument, so anyone can improve his or her station in life by going to school for a longer period. Clearly, there is a significant positive correlation between amount of education and level of income. Over the years, a number of studies have shown that on average the more education a person has, the higher will be his or her income. In large part, however, more and better schooling is the effect of having a higher income (and to some extent, individuals from high-income families may get high-income jobs merely because their parents own the business in which they work).

Children of richer parents receive more schooling largely because their parents can afford to help them in school longer than poor parents can. They can pay high tuitions in private schools that admit students even with low grade averages. Even in the public universities, where the tuition may be much lower or nonexistent, there are still living expenses. Many students must drop out of college or are unable to enroll simply because they have no money on which to live while in school.

Furthermore, children of richer families have a better chance to do well in school and to learn more. Opportunities and encouragement provided in the home and community are much more likely to produce highly motivated children who know how to study. Cultural background is very important in the performances on IQ tests and college entrance examinations. These examinations, which purport to test general ability, in reality are designed to conform to the middle-class, white, urban experience. A student from a poor or rural background will lack the necessary cultural references to understand the questions or have any intuition of the answers. This bias has been proved again and again, but the tests are still used. They determine which "track" (discussed below) an elementary student is put into, and they determine who enters college. Thus, it is no surprise that only 7 percent of all college students come from the poorest 25 percent of all families.

Another condition that hurts students from poor families and helps those from richer families is that schools in different areas receive very different amounts of money. Inner-city schools in minority areas often are given less money per student and almost always attract less competent teachers. Suburban township schools are apt to receive more money per student and attract better teachers.

Students in elementary and high schools are often put into different tracks. One track is vocational training. Another track, college preparation, prepares students, generally from upper-middle-class and richer families, for college, so that they can move into high-income jobs. In elementary schools, it is often called ability grouping. However, the degree of ability is determined by IQ tests that are not objective measures of innate intelligence but, as noted previously, discriminate on the basis of class background.

Within some high schools, counselors push the poor and the minority groups into vocational training and the more affluent students into college preparation. Within other high schools, such pushing is hardly necessary because of the vast differences among schools. Schools in the low-income areas sometimes provide only basic, or vocational, training. Schools in the wealthiest areas give only college preparation. These different tracks are enforced both formally by the tests given and informally by counselors and teachers. One investigation in New York showed that middle-class white children were usually offered voluntary classes in how to pass college examinations, but in Harlem, even seeing the old tests was "against the rules" (Howe and Pautner, 1972, p. 234).

We may conclude with certainty that our educational system does not reduce inequality from generation to generation. On the contrary, the richer students have more opportunities to obtain a good elementary and high school education, to be accepted into college, to remain in college, and therefore to be hired for a higher-income job after college—and then to send their own children to college. Thus, the educational system seems to transmit inequality from one generation to the next.

Government and Business

In the United States, the Industrial Revolution commenced after the Civil War. During more than a century of American industrial capitalism, the relationship between government and big business is seen by some observers as often being contradictory because many government programs and legislative acts have been designed to promote big business, whereas some laws, particularly antitrust legislation, have ostensibly been designed to curb the size and power of big business.

Thurman Arnold, former "trust-busting" head of the federal government's antitrust division, believes that these contradictory policies and laws have stemmed from "a continuous conflict between opposing ideals in American economic thinking" (Arnold, 1969, p. 151). The power of "economic thinking," taken alone, explains very little, however. A more realistic explanation of these seeming contradictions would be based on the two broadest objectives of government in its dealings with big business.

First, the government has been committed to the maintenance of the capitalist system and the promotion of the interests of big business. This commitment has generally dominated the relationship between government and business. The interests of various capitalists and business firms, however, are not always mutually compatible. Many conflicts are so intense that, if left unresolved, they could eventually threaten the very existence of the capitalist system. Government's second objective, therefore, is to act as the arbiter or referee in these rivalries and to resolve the difficulties before they become so extremely serious.

The antitrust laws gave the federal government a measure of power to enforce its function as arbiter. Interpreted in this way, the government's policy toward business has not been contradictory. Nor has this policy been designed, as many liberals believe, to curb the immense power of giant corporations. Rather, it has always attempted to promote the general interests of all capitalists and all businesses. Sometimes the individual interests of capitalists have coincided—as, for example, in the late-nineteenth-century attempt to crush labor unions. But in instances of industrial or commercial rivalry between two giant corporate empires, the interests have been in conflict. In such cases, the general interests of all capitalists would depend on at least partial restriction of one or both of the rivals.

American industrialization was aided significantly by the intimate association of government and business. Big business was supported by protective tariffs, which began with the Morrill Tariff of 1861 and were expanded significantly in 1890, 1894, and 1897. The protection from foreign competition thus afforded large corporations removed all restraints on their use of domestic monopoly powers to charge high prices. The due process clause of the Fourteenth Amendment was intended to give equal rights to blacks. In the late nineteenth century, however, it was interpreted to prohibit state regulation of corporations (who were considered legal "persons"). The courts denied state governments the right to interfere in any way with even the most abusive, malicious, and socially deleterious corporate behavior.

The railroad magnates were among the most important entrepreneurs in the American Industrial Revolution. Through bribery, chicanery, and fraud, they amassed great personal fortunes. Building railroads was never more than the vehicle from which they launched their financial schemes. The federal government responded by generously giving federal lands to the railroads. Between 1850 and 1871, the railroads were handed 130 million acres of land, an area as large as all the New England states plus Pennsylvania and New York. During the same period, state governments gave the railroads another 49 million acres. All this, and yet some economic historians still refer to the second half of the nineteenth century as an age in which government stayed out of business affairs!

Toward the end of the nineteenth century, the relationship between the federal government and big business became a symbiosis in which the government governed in ways big business wanted it to govern and big business furnished the money, organization, and power structure through which politicians could come to power in the federal government.

In addition, federal, state, and local governments buy one-quarter to one-third of our national product. Corporations selling to government earn much higher than average profit rates. The largest single government purchase is of military supplies, where the most spectacular profits are made. Through this mechanism, government-purchasing policies tend to shift income to the corporations and to their rich stockholders. Government spending is analyzed in detail in Part III.

LEGAL INSTITUTIONS AND INEQUALITY

Government continues to play its traditional role of protector of private property. People who are poor and desperate often violate the laws of private property. As our society has acquired a permanent group of people living in poverty, government has replied to crime not by raising low incomes but mostly by increasing the severity of punishment. Over 2 million people in the United States are in prison, the largest number per capita in the entire world. In 2003, one in every seventy-five U.S. males was in prison. Those in prison included one in ten of all African American males between the ages of 20 to 34. Most prisoners are poor.

Governments make many changes in the economy directly by changing the laws. Chapter 7 described the first period of U.S. law a precapitalist period. It showed how precapitalist law evolved into the second period of laws, which benefit industrial capital. There were also programs put into law during the 1930s to give some benefits to the poor and middle-income employees to keep them happy with industrial capitalism. Starting in the 1930s, during the Great Depression and throughout World War II, there was a great increase in the power of government over the economy. At first, this meant the creation of many programs to help the average person. These included unemployment compensation, social security insurance for old age, minimum wages, maximum hours, and eventually workers' compensation for injuries on the job, plus Medicare. After World War II and during the 1950s, however, the law came to include antilabor laws and political oppression. Government also makes labor laws governing the relationship between capital and labor. After the end of World War II, labor laws were changed. These changes, especially the 1947 Taft-Hartley Act, provide more power for corporations and make it far more difficult for unions to organize. Although other factors were also important, the legal changes were one of the major factors that caused the percentage of workers in unions to steadily decline since that time.

After a reduction of constructive government programs during the 1950s, there was another wave of improved programs during the 1960s. The reform programs of the 1930s were known as the New Deal. The reform programs of the 1960s were known as the Great Society. Both waves resulted from massive progressive movements of the population and their elected representatives. The Great Society especially focused on the war on poverty, including the expansion of Medicare and other entitlement programs. These reforms did not succeed in eliminating poverty because they were never expanded enough. They did, however, succeed in sharply reducing poverty for the elderly. The programs did bring down the overall poverty rate for a while, but it has risen again since then (see Collins and Yeskel, 2000).

New legal problems also emerged under global capitalism. This new economic stage was reflected in the law. This period, particularly from the 1970s to the present, witnessed the relative decline in the powers of individual nations and the rise in power of the global corporations and global agencies. Legal disputes centered more and more on the use of the new technology, such as the World Wide Web.

How is it possible to avoid pirating of songs and movies on the Internet? What are the rights of individuals to free speech the Internet? The new technology produced many new types of intellectual property, not foreseen in earlier law. Each of these legal issues over worldwide rights to new kinds of commodities meant disputes about billions of dollars. The point that new technology leads to new organization of the economy and new laws has been driven home more dramatically than ever before.

CRIMINAL LAW AND INEQUALITY

Criminal laws protect capitalist institutions against those who would violate private property or contract rights. Criminal laws are enforced by the government through prison sentences and sometimes executions. Under capitalism, if a man or woman steals a loaf of bread, he or she is guilty, regardless of the need of the person or of his or her family. Early communal societies, some of which lasted 100,000 years, allowed anyone to take food they needed without paying. In the prehistoric communes, anyone would be thought criminal who would prevent a starving man or woman from taking whatever he or she needed to stay alive. Under the legal institutions of capitalism, a hospital may turn away a sick person who has no money. There are now many proposals for a universal health care system in the United States. Under a system of universal health care, it would be a crime for a hospital to refuse care to anyone. Refusal of bread to a starving person or health care to an ill person is the logical legal consequence of a process built on our present system of private property.

The effects of differences in economic status stand out very clearly in law enforcement practices. Inequality in the legal process is caused by economic inequality. The actual inequality, however, is mostly concealed in the formal equality under the law. Both the unemployed worker and the billionaire have the same formal rights under the law, but the actual treatment is very different. Crimes committed by the poor are usually punished with much harsher sentences than are crimes by white-collar or more affluent citizens. The report of the President's Crime Commission concluded that "the poor are arrested more often, convicted more frequently, sentenced more harshly, rehabilitated less successfully than the rest of society" (President's Commission on Law Enforcement and the Administration of Justice, 1968, p. 87). This 1968 statement remains true according to every investigation (e.g., Reiman, 1999). The extremely rich executive officers of Enron, who took billions of dollars through illegal schemes, used every trick by many highly paid lawyers to fight against their punishment.

The vast majority of the low-income victims of the legal process lack the financial resources to hire a good lawyer or to post bail. Therefore, most (70 percent of all those arrested in the United States) are forced to plead guilty in order to avoid lengthy detention before their case comes to trial. Thus, in order to avoid a long pretrial time in jail and the probability of a long jail sentence, they settle with the prosecutor for a shorter jail sentence even if they are innocent. Furthermore, the poor are more likely than the rich to have a high bail set because they are not "respectable" citizens and have no economic stake to keep them from fleeing prosecution.

REPRESSION AND INEQUALITY

The Cold War of the 1950s led to repression in both the Soviet Union and the United States. In the name of patriotism, Soviet hardliners attacked all reformers and other opponents as agents or supporters of the United States. Using this excuse, the hardliners caused large numbers of Soviet citizens to lose their jobs or be sent to prison. Repression was at its most severe until the death of Stalin in 1952. During Stalin's era, there were many political executions, but after his death, there were no more clearly political executions and only a few questionable cases. Nevertheless, many thousands were deprived of employment, no freedom of speech was allowed, and the secret police held most of the power without any free elections. Repression continued throughout the Cold War.

In the name of patriotism, hardline American conservatives in the 1950s used repression against all reformers and almost anyone charged with being militant in favor of peace or equality. Many Americans lost their jobs and some went to prison for advocating peace with the Soviet Union or changes in the U.S. economic system, reforms that were designed to increase equality. In 1953, in the midst of the hysteria throughout the government and the media, two people, Ethel and Julius Rosenberg, were executed for passing military secrets to an enemy; no one in American history had ever before been executed for this crime in peacetime. The severest repression was in the 1950s, but it continued throughout the Cold War. Much of the organized witch-hunting (searching for Communists) in America was done by the Un-American Activities Committee of the U.S. House of Representatives and by the Internal Security Committee of the U.S. Senate, chaired by Senator Joseph McCarthy. Because of his activities, the whole repressive behavior of this period is called McCarthyism.

Although defense of inequality was always the underlying reason for the government's pursuit of those on the political left, espionage or "subversion" was almost always the official charge. The government's attempt to defend inequality is most clearly shown in the fact that most of the attacks centered on trade unions, which are the strongest defenders of equality and critics of inequality in America (as shown in the next section). There were also attacks on college professors who had unpopular and antiestablishment views, Hollywood stars who opposed the Korean War, and "subversives" in the U.S. Army.

It is difficult to grasp the witch-hunting atmosphere of the 1950s without examples in every area of American life. But limited space allows examples from only one area, so let us examine the repression in the U.S. Army. In 1953, Senator McCarthy investigated subversion within the U.S. Army and tried to show that the Army leaders were "soft on communism." A week after the Army–McCarthy hearings started to be broadcast on national television, the Army passed a new regulation requiring an anti-Communist oath of all soldiers. The oath said that "I am not and never have been a member of the Communist Party." The same oath also required the soldier to say that he had not been a member of any of five hundred other organizations that the government claimed were sympathetic to communism! There was never any evidence offered in a court to show that any of the other five hundred organizations had ever violated any law.

Repression is not merely a historical oddity but exists at present in the context of the Iraq War. The Bush administration claims the right to eavesdrop on any phone or e-mail conversation in the United States and abroad. The Bush administration claims the right to hold without trial anyone designated an "enemy combatant," whether foreign citizen or American citizen. The Bush administration claims the right to use torture to extract information. Many cases of torture in American prison camps in Iraq have been revealed through official reports. The United States Senate voted 91 to 9 in October 2005 to prohibit torture (see Blummer, 2005). When President Bush signed the bill prohibiting torture, he still claimed in the official statement at the time that he could use torture "when necessary."

THE MEDIA AND INEQUALITY

Unequal political power is also achieved through control of the news media. Even if the average employee had an interest in politics, he or she "would have great difficulty getting accurate information" (Irish and Prothro, 1964, p. 42). Since that statement was made in 1964, the amount of political news in the media has declined even further, and the control of the media by a few corporations has increased.

If the quantity of political news is deplorable, its quality is abysmal or worse. The first problem is that only one view is available to most people because of increasing concentration of newspaper ownership. In 1910, some 57 percent of American cities had competing daily papers, whereas in 1960, only 4 percent had competing dailies, and it was less than 2 percent by 2006. Furthermore, news media tend to have a conservative bias because (1) they do not want to offend any powerful interests, (2) they especially do not want to offend major advertisers, all of whom are big businesses, and (3) most important, it is natural for the business tycoons in control of the media to share the opinions of most other businesspeople, so they bias the news in that direction.

Economic power also worsens the substantial inequality of political power available to different pressure groups. In addition to control of the press and television, advertising by big business paints a particular picture of life. Its message is that we live in a lovely country, material luxuries represent the ultimate goal, and everyone can have these material luxuries. A certain percentage of business advertising is devoted to specifically political issues. Yet the government permits all business advertising to be counted as a cost, which can be deducted from income when taxes are computed. Of course, labor unions are not allowed this tax deduction for political advertising.

The media tend to convince people, because of the emphasis in most of the stories that they write, that nothing can be achieved by participation in politics because it is all corrupt. If most people are convinced that nothing can change, how can change ever occur? If everyone believed the media all of the time, then inequality would never be reduced. In reality, however, crises lead to protest regardless of the media, and protest leads to political change. If the media cannot be changed, then only traumatic experience in crises can convince people that basic institutional change is desirable. It is important to remember that reforms do happen and revolutionary change has occurred. For example, this book is a story of enormous change from one alternative society to another in a number of cases.

The paradox of modern U.S. democracy is that improved communications technology is available to most people, yet most people seem to have less knowledge of politics and society. Every poll on major issues shows appalling ignorance of basic facts. One reason is the increasing concentration of ownership of the media. The information media are owned and controlled by a few large corporations. The interest of these large corporations is to provide sensationalism in order to attract listeners or viewers; they have little or no interest in educating people about politics or economics. For instance, the Fox News network is owned by a small group of very rich conservatives. As a result, most people who primarily relied on Fox for their news thought that Iraq had weapons of mass destruction long after official reports had disproved this myth. In spite of the reports exposing these myths, a large majority of self-identified Bush voters polled believed that Saddam Hussein provided "substantial support" to Al Qaeda, and 47 percent believed that Iraq had weapons of mass destruction before the U.S. invasion (see Wirzbicki, 2004).

If there is an internal crisis, such as a major depression, or if there is a foreign crisis, such as a war, can the influence of the media be overridden by people's experiences? During the Great Depression, everyone saw its effects, so a broad progressive movement arose despite conservative media views. During the Vietnam War, the media tended to downplay the negative impacts of the war. Many people, however, lost family members or friends to that war, and many questioned the reasons for U.S. involvement in it, so an antiwar movement spread rapidly.

Although the media have incredible power, it is good to remember that the media themselves emerge from certain political-economic institutions. Institutions result from struggles by groups of people. Human struggle, therefore, can change the media in the long run. To make the point dramatically, consider that the only media existing in medieval Europe were the Catholic Church and all of its priests. Thus, the media influence people in every society, but it is also true that people sometimes change the basic institutions, which change the media.

The media do not conspire to be antidemocratic and pro-business, but they are driven by profits, which are driven by advertising. Since corporate giants own the media, their prime concern is making profits from the media by sensational stories. The corporate owners of the media, however, are also interested in favorable treatment of their businesses and the political objectives of those businesses. Those who benefit from the present economic institutions are the ones who strongly defend them. If they own the media, they use it to support the present institutions. The media get rich at the expense of democracy.

Increasing concentration of media ownership means that the media are controlled by fewer and fewer corporations (the entire historical trend is mapped in detailed data in McChesney, 1999). In 2003, the Federal Communications Commission (FCC) passed new rules allowing more concentration of ownership by one firm, both in the percentage of television outlets controlled and in the ownership of other media (newspapers and radio) in the same market. Hundreds of thousands of people complained, but the FCC held to that decision under pressure from media giants.

Why worry about concentration of ownership of the media? There is a myth that the Internet will set us free. The Internet is mostly unregulated, free-market capitalism. The judicial system has interpreted the First Amendment to mean that the corporations can do as they please on the Internet, selling it or putting ads all over it. Everyone has the formal freedom to use it, but it costs money. Those with money can use the Internet and gain access to all of its power. The poor find it more difficult to afford computers or Internet service and therefore have limited or no access to the Internet.

The interpretation of the First Amendment to the United States Constitution has changed in the last three decades. Part of its original purpose was to protect the free speech of critics of the government. Now it is used to defend corporate giants and the wealthy. It has been accepted by the courts that the wealthy can make campaign contributions of as much money as they wish as a right of free speech. It has also been argued, as a right of free speech, that the government should not regulate the ownership of radio and television stations. The courts have presumed that freedom of speech is compatible with any degree of concentration in the media. These new uses of the First Amendment are contrary to case law before the 1970s, but the new interpretation of speech rights as money rights is consistent with the emergence of global capitalism. The argument for protection of money rights under the First Amendment assumes that government is the only problem for free speech, while giant corporations are no problem.

HEALTH CARE AND INEQUALITY

The U.S. health care system reflects an unequal society. The rich receive very good health care, but most people receive mediocre health care, and a large number of people receive no health care. Health care for everyone has been held back in part by the vested interests of the insurance companies. In addition, many wealthy people do not want to pay taxes toward universal health care. As an example of the power of American vested interests in the age of global capitalism, the United States spends the highest proportion of gross domestic product of any country in the world on health care—14 percent of GDP. Yet over 40 million U.S. citizens, or 17 percent of the population, have no health care benefits at all (see Navarro, 1993).

Why is the health care system so inadequate for most people? The problem is that most people have very little political power, while those with power have very little interest in extending health care to everyone. The people without health care are typically poorly paid employees and the unemployed, who have little economic or political power. Those who have immense economic power do not need public health care and resent paying taxes to maintain it. Rather than having a universal publicly owned health care system, much of the health care industry in the United States is directly controlled by giant corporations, including the insurance companies. These very large corporations make enormous profits from health care and want to keep it that way (data on the health care industry is discussed in detail in Navarro [1993]).

SUMMARY

The economic power of a comparatively few corporations and individuals, examined in previous chapters, was shown here to result in a disproportionate degree of political power for this group. Some critics say that America has the best government that money can buy. This is not an accident but a perfectly natural result of their control over the press, television and radio, advertising, financing for political campaigns and for lobbying, foundations, and the many other avenues of control open to those with wealth.

Because of this natural influence of wealth (not a conspiracy), government policies do not decrease inequality in the American economy. In fact, after considering only the policies that are supposed to reduce inequality (such as taxation and education), we may conclude that many of the policies actually increase the degree of inequality. If we considered all government policies, the net effect would undoubtedly have been a substantial increase in inequality. Given the present sources of political power, it appears very doubtful that the government will ever take actions that will substantially reduce poverty and inequality.

SUGGESTED READINGS

The best single survey of radical political analysis is Albert Szymanski's *The Capitalist State and the Politics of Class* (1979). The socioeconomic role of education is explained in a potent fashion in Samuel Bowles and Herbert Gintis's *Schooling in Capitalist America* (1978). An excellent book on the economic bases of Congress is Philip M. Stern's *The Best Congress Money Can Buy* (1988). An outstanding book on our low voting turnout is Frances Fox Piven and Richard A. Cloward's *Why Americans Don't Vote* (1988). The history of the labor movement is detailed in Richard Boyer and Herbert Morais's *Labor's Untold Story* (1970).

The best discussion of the U.S. criminal law process is contained in Jeffrey Reiman's *The Rich Get Richer and the Poor Get Prison,* 8th edition (2006). An entire July–August 2001 issue of the journal *Monthly Review* "Prisons and Executions: The US Model" reveals that United States incarcerates five to eight times more of its people per capita than do Western European nations. The evolution of the legal system is detailed in Anthony Chase's 1997 book titled *The American Legal System: The Evolution of the American Legal System.* Jay Feinman's release from *Unmaking Law: The Conservative Campaign to Roll Back the Common Law* (2004) explains how conservative lawyers have protected the wealthy by emphasizing property rights and freedom of contract as legal absolutes.

All of the facts about the diseased condition of American health care used in this chapter come from the excellent but brief book by Vincente Navarro's *Dangerous to Your Health* (1993). Another excellent book on health care is Kant Patel and Mark Rushefsky's *Health Care and Politics and Policy in America* (2006).

The role of the media and its relation to global capitalism is told in a startling way, but with full documentation, in Robert McChesney's *Rich Media, Poor Democracy: Communication Politics in Dubious Times* (1999). The myth of the intellectual elite controlling everything is exposed in an important but delightful and humorous book about political ideology by Thomas Frank, *What's the Matter with Kansas?* (2004).

KEY WORDS

democracy
government
progressive taxes

proportional taxes
regressive taxes

REVIEW QUESTIONS

Explain the difference between formal democracy and effective democracy.
1. What is formal democracy, and what is effective democracy?
2. Give some examples of why people may not participate in democratic processes such as elections or running for office in the United States.
3. Give examples of how race and gender affect election participation and outcomes. What are the links to levels of income? How do those links affect the examples you chose?

Discuss how economic power leads to political power.
4. What is the feedback mechanism discussed in the section "Economic Power and the President"? Explain how it furthers the interests of the group in power.
5. What are the most important interest groups that influence the American government?
6. What are the mechanisms through which wealthy individuals and large corporations influence the political system?

Explain how differences in economic power impact policy decisions.
7. Discuss an example of Congress's disregard for the wishes of the majority of the population.
8. How does lobbying work? How can economic power impact lobbying?

Analyze how policy decisions that create opportunities for one group of people can lead to lack of opportunities for other groups of people.
9. Distinguish between progressive, regressive, and proportional or flat taxes. Explain how regressive taxes impact low-income taxpayers more heavily than do progressive taxes.
10. What are the incentives for high-income taxpayers to retain the current federal income tax structure? Explain how high-income taxpayers (individuals and businesses) work to retain the current structure.
11. Explain the difference between relative poverty and absolute poverty. Why is relative poverty so important?
12. What are the arguments for policies that support the income of low-wage workers in addition to policies that support people who cannot work?
13. Why do some school districts struggle to get supplies and retain teachers while other school districts have the latest technology, the newest books, and the best teachers?
14. How do economic differences lead to treating students differently in different school districts? What does this inequity mean for breaking (or perpetuating) the cycle of poverty? What does it mean for maintaining economic advantages for some groups?

15. One of the roles of the government is as a referee or arbiter between businesses and between businesses and labor. How can economic power influence the decisions of the referee? Give examples.

16. Why must government enforce private property rights? In certain circumstances, how can enforcing private property rights lead to ethical and moral concerns? Give examples.

17. Explain how the increasing concentration of ownership of media outlets impacts political decisions.

APPENDIX 24.1
A CASE STUDY

This appendix presents a case study of political repression. Although the name of the soldier is fictitious, the story is true.

LEARNING OBJECTIVES FOR APPENDIX 24.1

After reading this appendix, you should be able to:

• Discuss a case study of repression during the McCarthy era.

THE STORY

The following events took place during the McCarthy era. In the Army, individual soldiers who refused to sign the loyalty oath were investigated, given hearings, and then discharged as Undesirable. In one case, "Private Jones" was drafted and told to sign the Oath. Private Jones had just graduated law school, where he was taught that such oaths violated his right of free speech as guaranteed by the First Amendment to the Constitution. The form he was asked to sign provided an option to exercise the constitutional right not to sign the Oath. The soldier could just put an X in the box for that alternative. After a few minutes during which Jones admits that he feared the consequences of not signing as well as cowardice for hesitating in his resistance, he put an X in the box indicating he claimed his constitutional right not to sign the Oath.

After many months in the Army, Jones was suddenly given a list of twenty-one extraordinary charges. Every charge against Jones took the form: "An informant says that Private Jones. . . ." The Army never put any of the informants on the witness stand to hear from them. Therefore, they could not be cross examined, so Jones could not prove the information false. Even the names of the informants were kept secret, so the Army merely alleged what the informants had said.

The Army claimed that it had the right to discharge, at its discretion, any soldier with whom it was not fully satisfied. The Army's charges against Jones were not criminal but a mixture of rumors that he supported unpopular ideas. In effect, Jones was asked to prove that he had never uttered a single word against the Army or made any criticism of the government that might be considered disloyal. One cannot prove such a general negative statement.

The first specific charge was that Jones had refused to sign the Anti-Communist Oath, even though the Army agreed that it was his constitutional right to decline. Another charge was that he had refused to sign the Oath a second time when they invited him, as a law school graduate, to join the Judge Advocate General Department. This Oath had far more detailed questions than the ordinary Oath. The question that struck Jones as most fascinating in the second Oath was, "Has your mother-in-law ever been a member of the Communist Party?"

Another charge alleged that Jones had been a delegate to the convention of the Independent Progressive Party in New York City. Jones had never been in New York in his life, and the Independent Progressive Party was actually a California-based party that had never met in New York. Jones's lawyer was not allowed to question the informant who made this false statement.

Another charge was that Jones had written a letter published in the student newspaper at the University of California–Los Angeles advocating an antiwar demonstration. Still another charge alleged that he wrote a letter to a Chicago labor newspaper advocating proportional representation in the election of Chicago aldermen. Jones's article showed that the Republicans had taken a large percentage of the vote but had elected only a few aldermen. So Jones concluded that proportional representation would be a much fairer electoral system. The Army said this was a Communist view.

Most charges were supported by only one informant. However, one charge included two informants. It read: "At the University of Chicago Law School one informant says that Jones is a radical, but not so radical as to be a Communist (a second informant says that the first informant signed a petition in favor of pardoning the Rosenbergs)." Jones is not sure if the statement in parentheses was intended to imply that he was more radical than the first informant said or was intended to condemn Jones by virtue of his knowing the first informant.

Finally, one charge was that Jones had been invited to the home of a man in Berkeley, California, "whose mother often had Negroes to her home." Why did it jeopardize U.S. security to have "Negroes" to one's home? The point of course is that the Army was attempting to intimidate Mr. Jones.

Some men in the Army had even more extraordinary charges against them. One soldier was charged with advocating recognition of China. The most extraordinary, however, was the charge that a soldier "intimately knew" Mrs. Smith, who was said to be "a Communist in the Peace movement, who was now lying low." In fact, Mrs. Smith was the soldier's mother-in-law and she had died eight years before he met his wife. Thus, she was lying very low.

After 21 months in the Army, Jones was suddenly given an Undesirable Discharge, and denied all GI benefits. Jones joined a class action lawsuit against the Army, which after eight years went to the Supreme Court. The Supreme Court upheld the suit. Jones was eventually given a general discharge under honorable conditions and received all of his GI rights. For eight years, Jones requested education benefits and was refused. Finally, he was paid. The money was not much, but it was a victory against McCarthyism. Since McCarthyism defended inequality, Jones felt it was a victory against inequality.

CHAPTER 25

Economic Democracy

The world today is dominated by global capitalism, but as economic evolution continues, that balance may change. Many attempts have been made to strengthen both political and economic democracy. This chapter examines some of these attempts.

LEARNING OBJECTIVES

After reading this chapter, you should be able to:

- Describe the formal structures of democracy.
- Distinguish between formal and effective political democracy.
- Discuss characteristics and examples of economic democracy.

EVOLUTION OF DEMOCRATIC INSTITUTIONS

Before discussing the present state of democracy, it is useful to look at the evolution of democratic institutions as one thread in the evolution of society. Chapters 1 and 2 showed that in the earliest societies, the economic and political unit was the extended family, usually of twenty-five to thirty-five people. In such a society, decision making was usually done at a meeting of all of the adults. It was often by consensus guided strongly by tradition. Chapter 3 showed that most slave societies were empires ruled by emperors with no effective democracy. A few Greek cities, however, did use democratic forms of government. As a result of many sharp struggles, monarchy was overthrown and all "citizens" could vote. Citizens, however, did not include the large number of foreigners who were permanent residents. Citizens did not include the large part of the population who were slaves. Citizens did not include women.

Ancient Athens is an example where the legal structures of democracy, including free speech and voting, were present but where many people were excluded from participating in the structures. This example was followed by the U.S. South before the Civil War, which also claimed to be a democracy but excluded all slaves and all women from participating in government. The real economic and political power in ancient Athens and in the pre–Civil War South was exclusively with the slave owners. It was normal in ancient Athens for wealthy citizens to buy the votes of other citizens.

Chapter 4 showed that under feudalism, there was very little democracy. The lord governed the serfs both as political ruler and as economic manager. There was some democracy when the peasants had to make collective decisions among themselves. The lords also sometimes asked the king for greater rights for themselves, but their democratic requests did not extend to the peasants.

Two revolutions—the British Revolution of 1648 and the French Revolution of 1789—swept away the final remnants of feudalism in those countries and initiated a capitalist economy with a limited democratic political process. From 1789 to the present, there has been a slow tendency, with some backward steps at times (as in the period of fascism), toward an increase in the forms of democracy. At the expense of long and bitter struggles, barriers were removed for voting by those without property, by minorities, and by women. There is no space to follow this process all over the world, so it is examined here only for the United States, which was one of the leaders in this process.

POLITICAL DEMOCRACY IN THE UNITED STATES

In the United States, the revolution of 1776 tossed out British colonial rule in which the ultimate power rested with British colonial governors. The new U.S. government initiated a political process that produced an elected president and legislature, but no king. Like ancient Athens, the United States had all the mechanisms or forms of democracy but excluded large groups of people from the process. In the period after the U.S. revolution, people without property were excluded from the political process in many states, slaves were excluded in the southern states, and women were excluded in all states. It required many battles until, in the 1840s, white men without property could vote in all states. It took a century of struggle from the 1820s to the 1920s before women could vote and participate. It took a Civil War for the slaves to be emancipated and given the vote. Additional obstacles kept the former slaves from participating fully in voting for almost a hundred years. Finally, the Civil Rights movement of the 1950s and 1960s demolished the remaining obstacles to the political procedures of voting for African Americans.

Every American schoolchild knows some of that history and is told that "we have democracy" now. There are only a few remaining undemocratic structures or mechanisms, such as the electoral college, a system that in 2000 gave the presidency to George W. Bush even though Al Gore received more votes. Nevertheless, the United States does have most of the forms of democracy in the sense that almost all adults can vote and most people can freely express their political opinions because of the rights to free speech and a free press. Remember that **formal political democracy** means that *a country has all the mechanisms and forms of democracy. All can vote and all can speak their minds.* A country with formal democracy, however, may not have a fully effective political democracy where effective is defined to mean that everyone can really participate on fairly equal terms. **Effective political democracy** means *that a country not only has all of the mechanisms and forms of democracy, but is also characterized by a situation in which all citizens have a significant amount of power and no group with wealth or military control has disproportionate power.* There may be formal political democracy, yet it would not be effective political democracy if most of the power is controlled by a small group with disproportionately vast wealth.

Suppose there is a town with 10,001 adults, all of whom can vote and all can say what they please. They elect a city government with their votes, so there is formal democracy. Ten thousand adults, however, are very poor, while one man is a billionaire. The billionaire owns all of the businesses in town, including the local newspaper, radio station, and television station. The billionaire gives much money to candidates he wants and none to others. In the newspaper, radio, and television, he carries stories and editorials favorable to the candidates he wants and against the other candidates. His candidates always win. This town has a formal democracy, but little or no effective democracy.

There are still obstacles to a fully effective democracy in the United States. Because there is some democracy, but it is limited, it is more precise to speak of the degree of effective democracy rather than just saying there is or is not democracy.

THE DEGREE OF EFFECTIVE DEMOCRACY

There are two main kinds of problems for American democracy that reduce its degree of completeness and effectiveness. First, the economic power of a relatively small number of wealthy people and giant corporations prevents political equality in participation and in influence. Second, the formal democratic process applies only to the political sphere of legislatures and the executive branch. Formal democracy does not extend to the economic sphere. For example, most chief executive officers of corporations are elected only by the stockholders. However, employees, consumers, and the public have no say in the matter.

Let us examine the first problem, how economic power limits political democracy. The problem of economic influence must be thoroughly distinguished from that of dictatorship. Germany in the 1930s had a dictatorship (fascism) that abolished most formal democratic rights. The United States in the 1950s had a considerable degree of repression (McCarthyism) that greatly reduced democratic rights. But the question here is, what restricts democracy under capitalist institutions when all formal rights are granted?

The United States has full formal democracy but severe limits on effective democracy. Effective democracy requires a high level of participation, which is lacking. All in all, in most presidential elections, only about one-half of all eligible Americans vote and much fewer vote in nonpresidential and local elections. For example, in the American presidential election of 2000, only half the eligible voters actually voted. Most of the nonvoters were in the lower income half of the nation, including a large part of the middle class and most of the poor. Therefore, the election process was very strongly biased toward the interests of the more affluent voters. Moreover, the two main parties spent a total of $3 billion in 2000, and the political action committees spent a lot more. In brief, money rules, and effective democracy is very limited. By what mechanisms does this happen?

First of all, begin with the fact that the main political parties spend enormous sums. Where does this vast river of political spending come from? The answer is that all of the large contributions come from the wealthy and, by indirect means, from the big corporations. Note that labor unions contribute less than a tenth of what corporations do.

Second, lobbying has the reputation of being the main cause of bribery, corruption, and distortion of the democratic process. In spite of dramatic examples, lobbying plays a relatively minor role compared with other mechanisms. However, lobbying is the bridge between the legislator and a corporation or organization that supplies money or supporters or even writes a bill for a legislator.

Third, corporate culture tries to condition every professional and other employee to its own view of the world through a pervasive atmosphere of loyalty and common interests with the corporation. This pervasive influence every working day is one reason most people never question whether any other way of life, let alone a different economic system, is possible.

Fourth, our views are shaped in part by the educational system, but the educational system is shaped to some extent by the money contributions of wealthy individuals and corporations to private and public colleges. In public colleges, it is also shaped by political influence, which reflects economic influence. Many of the big donors sit on boards that rule the colleges and universities. Education prepares an educated workforce for the economy and is a road to upward mobility for some people. The percentage of students going to college, however, increases with family income. Thus, the degree of inequality is reproduced from generation to generation.

Fifth, religion helps shape some people. Big donors naturally have influence over church policy. Churches in turn influence the minds of both children and adults. Because of the influence of wealthy donors and the church's own interests, the bias is usually strongly in favor of the existing economic system. Some religious groups are openly in favor of very conservative, right-wing ideas and candidates, as they believe their religion demands. Yet some religious leaders take courageous stands in favor of the poor and oppressed, as they believe their religion demands.

Sixth, the media have a powerful effect on people's minds. The paradox of modern U.S. democracy is that in spite of advanced communications technology available to most people, people seem to have limited knowledge of politics and society. Every poll on major issues shows appalling ignorance of basic facts. One reason is the increasing concentration of ownership of the media. The information media are owned and controlled by a few large corporations. The interest of these large corporations is to attract listeners. They have little or no interest in educating people about the facts of political and economic life. In addition, most of the media are owned by a few giant corporations. In the last 20 years this ownership has become increasingly concentrated. In conformity with the corporate interests that provide their bread and butter, the media convey the message that there is no alternative to the present economic system while at the same time imply that it is useless to vote because all politicians are corrupt.

Seventh, as income declines, so does political participation. As we said in Chapter 24, as household income rises so does a household's likelihood of voting, making political contributions, and actively participating in the political process.

As a result of all of these mechanisms, most elected officials are happy to do the bidding of the rich. A disproportionate number of the rich themselves are elected. For example, a quarter of the U.S. Senate are millionaires. Given the composition of the elected politicians and the powerful forces that affect them, it is not surprising that governments do as the rich desire to a large degree. The government gives tax breaks to the rich, gives harsh sentences to the poor who take private property, protect environmental polluters, and give lucrative contracts for military spending or for rebuilding conquered nations. For example, before the war with Iraq, deals were made in secret with no competition with some firms (one of which had been led by Vice President Cheney). These contracts were to do various construction jobs in Iraq after the war at high rates of profit that were guaranteed in the contract.

Many politicians follow corporate interests most of the time, but they have their own autonomous interests as well. If a political position is very unpopular, a politician may be forced to oppose it even if all of his or her money comes from those in favor of it.

STRUGGLES FOR ECONOMIC DEMOCRACY

The previous sections showed that a long struggle finally resulted in almost complete formal political democracy in the United States (and in most of the capitalist world). In practice, however, this has meant an ongoing struggle among groups in which the corporate elite, who control the economy, often win the important battles due to their economic power. It was shown that their power is not absolute but is very strong.

In addition to the problem of the exercise of economic power over the political process, there is also the related question of having a democratic process of decision making within business enterprises as well as in politics. Chapters 7 and 8 showed that under capitalism a relatively small elite control the economy by their private ownership and control of businesses. Most people are employees who can be hired and fired, promoted or demoted, and told what work to do, with no say in the matter. In brief, the owners and the managers may act as dictators in the workplace.

Economic democracy means that the *people rule the economy, not just politics*. Economic democracy may be achieved through many types of institutions and processes. The following discussion investigates the ways in which economic democracy has been extended in some times and some places in the United States. The rest of the world has seen much greater and more successful movements for economic democracy, but there is room here to examine only one country on this point, so the focus is on the United States.

COOPERATIVE FORMS OF ECONOMIC DEMOCRACY

One form of economic democracy is the voluntary cooperation of many people in forming an enterprise to be governed by its members rather than just by the stockholders. Some examples are consumer-organized cooperatives, business-organized cooperatives, and worker-organized cooperatives. By 2004, about 10 percent of all workers were employed by cooperatives of all kinds and by other nonprofit enterprises. There are large health organizations, such as Kaiser, that are nonprofit. The focus here, however, is on democratically run enterprises, beginning with cooperatives.

Consumers have organized many groups to buy goods at low wholesale prices and then resell them to their members without a profit. Consumer cooperatives are not inherently capitalist institutions because there are no private owners and there is no private profit. Rather, a cooperative is formed by many people, and each person usually has one vote in the cooperative. In this way, consumers organize themselves democratically to buy and market some goods. One type of consumer cooperative is subscriber-controlled radio stations, such as KPFK in Los Angeles, California and KCSD in Sioux Falls, South Dakota. To a large extent, National Public Radio (NPR) and the Public Broadcasting System (PBS) for television are financed by their subscribers—though other types of financing also play a major role, as discussed later.

Another type of cooperative is the condominium association. The most common type of governance for condominium associations, especially in large buildings, is a structure in which the apartment owners each cast one vote for a board of directors. The board then selects a property management enterprise to provide professional management. The management company collects the monthly fees and does all day-to-day direction and decision making. Few homeowners see this as a democratically run enterprise, but only as a useful way to own an apartment without worrying about building management. While most condominiums are bought by relatively affluent citizens, there are also some nonprofit enterprises providing housing to the poor.

Some groups of small businesses organize themselves into cooperatives to get the advantages of size. For example, there are cooperatives of chicken farmers to market chickens and cooperatives of grocery stores to facilitate the retail sale of food.

There are many cooperatives designed to raise enough money for various projects. This has led to credit unions, which collect savings and make loans. In the United States, over 79 million people belong to cooperative credit unions. In addition, employees often get together to provide insurance for the group. Some of these small insurance activities have grown into giant corporations.

Besides consumer and financial cooperatives, there are also many producer cooperatives. In a producer cooperative, each employee is also an owner. The employee owns a share of the enterprise. In fact, all stock in the enterprise is owned by its employees. In most **cooperative enterprises**, *each employee/owner has one vote on how to run the enterprise*. No one may have more than one vote, no matter how much of its stock they own. They democratically elect a board of directors. The board of directors appoints a manager for day-to-day decisions.

There are a considerable number of such enterprises in the United States in which the employees own all of the stock and therefore control the enterprise through a board of directors. Who gets the profit in these employee-owned enterprises? The profit is reinvested or is distributed among the employees. Of course, if all employees get both wages and profits, there is very little difference between the two streams of income. As far as employees are concerned, they perceive little or no difference between the two types of income. The legal differences and the tax differences, however, may be considerable.

There are a wide variety of forms of employee-based cooperatives. One example is the Denver Yellow Cab Company. This company was originally privately owned. It was bought out by its employees, and they designed their structure to be based on one vote by one driver. Each driver collected his or her own fares but contributed a certain percentage to the company for operating expenses. Any profit at the end of the year could be paid out to every member. Otherwise, profit might be reinvested for expansion purposes. This employee-owned firm began and continued as a quite profitable enterprise.

In the meat-packing industry, the Rath Packing Company was on the edge of bankruptcy when it was taken over by its workers. They did this to protect two thousand jobs. Of course, after they took over, it was still on the edge of bankruptcy. This is often the case with such takeovers, and the companies often remain in great financial difficulty. The Denver Yellow Cab Company was unusual in that it was profitable. The cab drivers wanted independence and democratic procedures. The drivers achieved this independence by risking their own money plus a large bank loan.

In the 1960s, partly for job protection but partly to achieve more democracy, about twenty cooperatives were formed by forestry workers in Oregon and adjoining states. The employees in the cooperatives received certain wage levels plus fringe benefits plus year-end profit bonuses. Also formed were many cooperatives in the plywood manufacturing industry. These cooperatives owned the whole enterprise, and every worker got an equal vote as well as equal pay per hour of work.

Another quite different type of cooperative is the Employee Stock Ownership Plan (ESOP). In an ESOP, employees take over a firm through a very particular type of corporation, set up by Congress. Employees in the ESOP own the corporation through their ownership of stock, so it remains very similar to an ordinary capitalist institution. Some important ESOPs have been Avis Rental Car Company and United Airlines.

Under the legal rules, it is possible to make an ESOP very similar to a workers' cooperative, except for the difference made by leaving control tied to the amount of stock ownership. Other ESOPs are clearly far from workers' cooperatives. Basically, some enterprises manage to sell most of the stock to employees but retain control of all decisions. One way to do this is to put all the employee stock in to a trust, and then management controls it.

Several arguments have been given in favor of employee cooperatives. First, they increase democracy over firms run by private owners. Second, cooperatives result in more equality of income in the society. Third, cooperative ownership results in more incentive for the individual professional worker or manual worker.

On the other hand, many controversial issues have been encountered. After a workers' cooperative is formed, are unions needed any more? If employees become rebellious against their own elected management, should strikes be allowed? How much financing can a cooperative get from the banks? Does bank interference reduce democracy? In more general terms, can cooperatives be maintained when the rest of the society is capitalist? Should the whole society be run by workers' cooperatives? Should wages be equal for all workers in a workers' cooperative, or should wages differ by skill or by performance? Should individual groups of workers on the shop floor be allowed independence? These are difficult questions. To their credit, many cooperatively managed firms raise these questions and debate them among the employee/owners.

THE PUBLIC ROAD TO ECONOMIC DEMOCRACY

In addition to employee ownership, control may also be exercised by the representatives of democratically elected bodies, as is the case for publicly owned universities. Some of the media are run through democratic ownership of various types. Many writers argue that the media are a likely place for democratic control for two main reasons. First, there can be no effective political democracy without a media free of control by giant corporations. Second, the media are highly concentrated in ownership by a relatively few corporations, so democratic control of some media will reduce income inequality as well as inequality of power.

There is a myth that the private ownership of the media is "natural" in some sense and there is no alternative. This myth may be shown to be false by considering American media of the 1930s. At that time, public radio broadcasting predominated. Many stations were nonprofit and run by universities. In the 1930s, many educators tried to establish a nonprofit and noncommercial radio broadcasting system. There were over a hundred broadcasting stations established by universities. Thus, educators were the pioneers in radio broadcasting. In the early 1930s, only the name of a private advertiser was mentioned. It was unthinkable in America in the 1930s that anyone would sit through a commercial advertisement!

Many of the universities that owned radio stations were public universities whose leaders were appointed by democratically elected governors and legislators. Private industry at first thought that radio would be unprofitable. How could one make a profit by broadcasting when no one had to pay for the broadcasts? There was a long fight for public radio and against private radio. Private radio broadcasting—and later private television broadcasting—were seen as antidemocratic by most educators because a few corporations would control the flow of information.

The U.S. Public Broadcasting System (PBS) and the National Public Radio (NPR) system are publicly owned institutions that have made major contributions to the development of radio and television broadcasting. Part of their revenue comes from the public treasury by law and part comes from individual subscribers, as in a cooperative. This structure illustrates the very important point that public and cooperative control need not be mutually exclusive but can be mixed in different percentages in different industries and at different times.

The lack of possibility for competition is true of cable television suppliers. A natural lack of competition if there is to be efficiency is also true, to some extent, of telephone lines. (Of course technology, in the form of satellite television and mobile phones, has over time challenged even these traditional sources of monopoly power.) Since cable television and phone companies were natural monopolies, to leave them to a single private firm without regulation is to ask to be exploited by monopoly prices. The monopolies can be regulated. The regulators, however, are often bribed in various ways to do as the corporations say. Therefore, according to its advocates, public ownership by the city or other local government entity is the best way to ensure efficiency and low cost.

At the regional or state level, an interesting example is in North Dakota. In that state, during the period of control by the populist movement of angry farmers in the late nineteenth and early twentieth centuries, it was decided that control of the financial system was too important to leave to private, capitalist enterprise. Farmers and small business needed loans with low interest rates, and the banks were unwilling to provide them. The state of North Dakota set up the Bank of North Dakota, which was wholly state owned and state controlled. It still exists today and continues "to encourage and promote agriculture, commerce and industry" in North Dakota.

At the national level, the delivery of much of the mail is done by the U.S. Postal Service (USPS). The democratically elected U.S. government owns and controls the USPS. It sells its services to anyone who pays for it. It is a **public enterprise**—*under government ownership*—that is, under democratic control of all American voters through their representatives. Various businesses would like to take over the USPS as a private enterprise, making large profits. The private profit would be made from what customers would pay in higher prices and what postal employees would have taken from them through lower wages. There has been a long struggle by postal employees and consumers to defend the USPS against those who would take it over for profit reasons.

Another example at the national level is one in which democracy lost. The nuclear energy industry was developed by the U.S. government, which poured huge amounts of money into its research to build an atomic bomb during World War II. After the war, the government poured more money into developing the peaceful use of nuclear energy. Once the government had gone to the enormous expenditure of research and construction of a nuclear industry, it was not maintained under the democratic control of the public. Instead, this rich bonanza was given away for free or very low prices to private entrepreneurs, who expected to make large profits from it.

At the global level, some reformers have advocated ownership of the international airlines by an international, democratically governed agency. It is argued that one integrated global airline would be much more efficient and provide better service. The airlines are presently in economic trouble, so they might be bought cheaply.

One problem with any global regulation or ownership is that there is no democratic global government. The United Nations is both weak and largely undemocratic in structure. There was a very slow evolution toward a global government in the twentieth century. After World War I, the League of Nations was formed, but it had very limited powers. Also, some countries, such as the United States, refused to join it. After World War II, the United Nations was established.

The United Nations is much stronger than the League in theory, but it is far from democratic. The power to police the global community is mostly held by just five nations. Those five often disagree, so it is weak as well as undemocratic. Many people, including Albert Einstein, began, immediately after the United Nations was organized, to advocate making the United Nations into a strong and democratic global government, but that has not happened so far.

ALTERNATIVES IN THE ENERGY INDUSTRY

There are dramatically different types of enterprises in the electric power industry, so it is a good place to contrast them. There are (1) private profit-making corporations, (2) cooperative enterprises, and (3) publicly owned enterprises.

What exactly are these forms of enterprise that have developed in the power industry? First, there are investor-owned, profit-making corporations. In almost every state, usually just one of two massive corporations control most of the energy, with a high level of monopoly or oligopoly power. Monopoly applies to one supplier, while oligopoly applies to a few suppliers. Second, many cities have publicly owned electric power companies, operating as agencies of a democratically elected city government. Third, in the rural areas of most states, there are cooperatives among the rural people, supplying power to all of the farms and rural areas. These are mainly consumer cooperatives, owned by those who buy the power, but some cooperatives in rural areas also produce and transmit electricity.

All three types of enterprise operate in an environment quite different from any picture of competition painted by most textbooks. Almost all public utilities, such as water, gas, and electricity, are natural monopolies. It makes no sense to have more than one supplier in a particular area. The reason that only one supplier can be efficient is that the cost of infrastructure and initial investment is enormous. The cost per unit of water or electricity is much less if there is only one supplier. For example, the water company supplies water through certain pipes. It would be ridiculous for a competitor to lay down additional water pipes to serve the same areas.

Private Profit-Making Corporations in the Electric Industry

Energy companies must own some huge source of power, then build lines to deliver it. For example, California has just two extremely large private energy companies, supplying mostly different parts of the state.

These two main suppliers of California electricity have no competitors in their areas, so they each have a very high degree of monopoly power. They are not democratically owned by the community or by consumers or by employees. They make profits from their monopoly position. They send these profits to a holding company, owned by investors.

Some of the privately owned firms are in states with little or no regulation of the energy industry because of the local political muscle of the giant corporations that inhabit the industry. Some states do have public boards that regulate these giant corporations with oligopoly power. The boards are supposed to ensure that the corporations perform reasonably well in bringing electricity to the state. They are also supposed to see that the prices and profits of the monopoly or oligopoly corporations remain in a reasonable range according to legislated standards.

The problem is that the regulators are almost always ex-employees of the corporations and hope for favors or better jobs from the corporations. Therefore, the state boards of regulators almost always give the corporations whatever they want. Thus, the corporations find ways to get around the law. If the law says that their profits must be in a reasonable range, they manage to show extremely high costs that greatly reduce the reported profits. These costs are often manipulated in ways that are controversial or semi-legal or illegal.

The giant energy corporations also have a culture of greed. The executives are under heavy pressure from stockholders to produce high profits. The executives also compete among themselves for the highest income, so they may consider a mere $100 million income far too small. As a result, many of them have been caught making more profits by illegal means. Enron Corporation's 2001 failure caused by corruption and fraud serves as an excellent recent example.

Publicly Owned Corporations in the Electric Power Industry

A very important area of democratic ownership is the public utilities sector. There were many fierce battles in the early-twentieth-century United States, with reformers and unions on one side and big business on the other side. As a result of that struggle for reform, many towns and cities decided that they should own the public utilities that they used.

One example of the many publicly owned utilities is the Los Angeles Department of Water and Power (LADWP). This agency sells all of the water and electricity in Los Angeles. Customers pay according to their use. The record shows that it is very efficient and more successful than private firms in terms of production and profits. All profits go to the city of Los Angeles and reduce the need for taxation.

It should be stressed that it is not just big cities that manage their affairs this way. Even out on the Great Plains, the Nebraska Public Power District is a public corporation owned by the state. Through collective ownership and a democratically elected board, the citizens of the Cornhusker State enjoy reliable service and some of the lowest electrical utility rates in the country.

The record of California's profit-making electric corporations contrasts strongly with that of the LADWP. In the early twenty-first century, the private energy firms of California were involved in a crisis. The firms convinced the state government that little or no regulation was needed. So even the mild and ineffective regulation was mostly removed. The resulting crisis included manipulation of prices to make vast extra profits. The crisis centered around exaggerated shortages to make even more profits. After extracting as much profit as possible, the firms sent much of their earnings out of state to an investor-owned holding company. They then had no money left to expand the electric power generation. Formally, since they had sent the profits out of state, they threatened to go bankrupt in order to get more money as a subsidy from California. All of these charges were confirmed by the state's investigation. But only some of the money was returned to the state.

During this crisis, the LADWP went about its business serenely with no problems. Thus, the LADWP has proven itself to be more efficient than the private, profit-making firms. At the same time that it makes high revenues, it is able to charge lower prices because it is nonprofit and publicly owned.

Cooperative Ownership in the Electric Industry

In the 1930s during the Great Depression, over 90 percent of farm and rural homes had no electricity. The Democratic administration of President Roosevelt decided to help rural electrification. In 1935, it passed a law to loan to the rural inhabitants money at reasonable rates to start companies that would build lines and buy electricity for them. The loan program continues to this day and is called the Rural Electrification System under the Agriculture Department. The program was very successful, and many rural people hung a portrait of Roosevelt on their walls. The low-cost loans enabled the farmers to form companies that would provide electricity and would be able to perform as well as investor-owned private corporations because the corporations received large subsidies, mostly in the form of tax breaks.

Rural people responded with enthusiasm. They formed cooperatives to buy electricity. Under federal law, each cooperative must follow two rules. First, it must be nonprofit, so any revenue beyond operating costs must be returned to the consumers of the electricity. This policy contrasts strongly with investor-owned corporations, which will not undertake to bring electricity anywhere unless it makes them a large profit.

Under the federal law, the second rule defining a cooperative is that it must be democratic, with governance by free elections. According to the National Rural Electric Cooperative Association (NRECA) in 2007, there are over 900 rural electric cooperatives, located in 47 states, serving over 40 million customers. The people who receive electricity from them are their owners. Each person gets one vote. They hold elections to elect the governing board of each cooperative. Then the boards elect representatives to go to a national convention to elect the members of a national organization representing all of the rural electric cooperatives in the United States. It speaks to the U.S. Congress as the duly elected representative of all the members of the rural electric cooperatives.

The organization is named the National Rural Electric Cooperative Association. It is the largest cooperative in the United States. All of its activities are nonprofit, and it is democratically elected by those who consume electricity from it.

Each year, the National Rural Electric Cooperative Association must ask Congress for the loans it needs to compete with private, profit-making electric corporations. The profit-making electric corporations have large subsidies from the government. The National Rural Electricity Cooperative Association also helps farmers with suggestions about the best technology to use. It has survived and brought electricity to the rural areas at affordable rates.

The electric cooperatives buy their electricity from three sources. Some of it is bought from the private, profit-making corporations. Some of it is bought from government-owned agencies, such as the Tennessee Valley Authority. Some of it is bought from cooperatives that produce electricity and transmit it. These producing cooperatives were all aided the their creation by the existing consumer cooperatives, so they operate by the same rules of democracy and nonprofit production.

ECONOMIC DEMOCRACY IN HEALTH CARE AND EDUCATION

In American education, elementary school is public and free. Secondary school is public and free. Students must go to school, but they are also free to choose a private school if they wish. There are public universities in most states, so there is also economic democracy at that level. Public universities used to be free, but conservative lawmakers have been adding fees, so they are now less equal and more difficult for lower-income students to attend. Most graduate programs cost a lot of money, even in public universities. Although some economic democracy exists at the university level, lower-income students must overcome a great deal of inequality and numerous obstacles in order to gain higher education. There is a movement to make all public higher education available to every qualified student and completely free. Conservatives argue that all education should be left to market supply and demand. Liberals argue that free education not only benefits the student but is a very profitable investment for society because it provides a much larger pool of educated specialists.

Most health care in the United States is provided through profit-making insurance companies. It is an undemocratic system that leaves over 45 million people without health insurance, but it costs a higher percentage of gross domestic product than in any other country. Medicare, a health care system supplied by the democratically elected government to older citizens, provides a degree of economic democracy in that sector of the health care industry.

Canada has economic democracy in all of its health care, as do most other industrialized countries. All Canadians receive free health care from a system funded by their democratically elected government. This system increases both democracy and equality. It also reduces the number of sick days the average employee takes off from work.

In health, education, and many other sectors, a careful look reveals an emerging embryo of what may be a new, democratic economic system. If historical experience is any guide, however, the elite will resist such changes, and an equal system will be won, if it is, only by a long struggle.

SUMMARY

This chapter explained how a political system may be democratic in form but not actually or effectively democratic. Economic democracy was defined, and its various forms were discussed. These forms of economic democracy include cooperatives and public enterprises in a democratic country. The arguments for and against economic democracy were discussed. Economic democracy in health care and education was briefly discussed.

SUGGESTED READINGS

The fascinating story of early broadcasting and university participation in it is described in depth in McChesney's *Rich Media, Poor Democracies* (1999). The relationship of democratic political institutions to capitalist economic institutions is best described in Bowles and Gintis's *Democracy and Capitalism* (1986). A powerful and clear argument for a change to more democratic economic institutions is given in David Schweickart's *There Is an Alternative* (2002).

The development of employees' cooperatives is told with excellent scholarship in Christopher Gunn's *Workers' Self-Management in the United States* (1984). Gunn followed up with a book covering nonprofit enterprises as well as cooperatives, *Third Sector Development: Making Up for the Market* (2004). The vehement arguments for and against a system of cooperative enterprises are presented clearly in Robin Hahnel's *Economic Justice and Democracy: From Competition to Cooperation* (2005).

A good, scholarly book on public ownership is Yair Aharoni's *Evolution and Management of State Owned Enterprises* (1986).

KEY WORDS

cooperative enterprise
economic democracy

effective political democracy
formal political democracy

REVIEW QUESTIONS

Describe the formal structures of democracy.
1. What is the definition of democracy? Give examples of the formal structures and institutions of democracy.
2. How can you have a formal democratic structure in place that is not really democratic? Give historical examples and explain.

Distinguish between formal and effective political democracy.
3. Can you have an effective democracy without the structures of democracy? Can you have a formal democracy without having an effective democracy? Explain.
4. What are some barriers to effective democracy?
5. What are some possible conflicts of interest in how the media presents news and events? How could these conflicts create bias in reporting? What policies would you recommend to attempt to stop biased reporting?
6. "It's not what you know, it's who you know." How could this statement apply to elections?
7. What is the relationship of income to percentage of voter turnouts and political participation? What might be some reasons? What would you suggest to increase voter participation at lower income levels?
8. Does big business have total control of elected officials and policies? Support your argument.

Discuss characteristics and examples of economic democracy.
9. What is the authors' definition of economic democracy? What does that mean?
10. What is a cooperative enterprise? Give examples. In what way is a cooperative enterprise democratic?

Could a cooperative enterprise be operated in a way that was nondemocratic? Explain.

11. What is an ESOP? Give examples.
12. What are the arguments for and against cooperative enterprises?
13. What are the arguments for and against public enterprises?
14. What is a natural monopoly? Give examples of how policymakers deal with businesses that are natural monopolies.

PART II, SECTION 4

ELEMENTS OF NEOCLASSICAL ECONOMICS

CHAPTER 26

Scarcity and Choice
Neoclassical View

Chapters 26 through 35 discuss neoclassical or traditional economics. Each chapter begins with a simple exposition of the key theories or framework and assumptions of neoclassical economics. Next, a progressive criticism of the neoclassical framework and assumptions is presented. Finally, appendices provide a detailed technical explanation of the neoclassical view.

This structure allows the instructor to choose among three strategies. Since many of these topics have all been covered already from a progressive view, the instructor may wish to avoid repetition by eliminating all of these chapters from the course. Second, the instructor may wish to briefly present the neoclassical view and progressive criticism by assigning the chapter, but not the appendix. Third, the instructor may wish to present a fuller discussion of neoclassical economics by assigning both chapters and appendices.

LEARNING OBJECTIVES

After reading this chapter, you should be able to:

- Explain the concept of scarcity and how people make choices according to neoclassical analysis.
- Describe how the production possibilities curve captures production choices in a society.
- Describe what progressive economists see as the primary shortcomings of the neoclassical scarcity perspective.

NEOCLASSICAL VIEW OF SCARCITY AND CHOICE

Neoclassical economists begin with an isolated individual, such as Robinson Crusoe, or a bunch of individuals, such as twenty individuals like Crusoe, each living on his own island. The islands have limited **resources**, that is, *assets needed for production and development,* and each Crusoe must choose which resources to use in order to satisfy his needs. The Crusoes may trade with each other from island to island. The analysis assumes certain things about the psychology of every individual (or Crusoe) and assumes those characteristics will exist in every society. The first assumption is that human beings make rational choices by weighing the costs and benefits of a decision. The second assumption is that human beings make decisions in their own best self-interest.

286

Neoclassical economics also assumes that there is *never enough production to satisfy the wants and desires of all individuals which results in* **scarcity**. Note the deliberate use of the phrase *wants and desires*. Wants and desires are very different from what people actually *need* to survive. If our wants and desires are unlimited, there is a problem in any society, whether feudalism or capitalism, to produce as much as possible to overcome the scarcity of commodities compared with human desire. Imagine producing enough to satisfy the wants and desires of every human being on earth! Clearly that is impossible if we assume people always desire more and more things. If there is not enough production to meet unlimited desires, then some serious decisions or choices must be made.

Based on the existence of scarcity, the central economic problem is **choice**. *The producer, such as Robinson Crusoe, must choose what raw materials and* **technology** *to use; by that, we mean the existing levels of knowledge, techniques, and types of tools available for the production of goods and services.* The consumer, such as Robinson Crusoe, must decide which goods he or she wants most to consume. If Crusoe prefers potatoes to tomatoes, he should produce more potatoes and fewer tomatoes. We know that societies are made up of many individuals or Crusoes, all living on the same island. How do the many individuals coordinate their production and consumption choices? That is what economics is all about!

Choice, Scarcity, and the Production Possibilities Curve

One way to illustrate the neoclassical view of scarcity and choice is illustrated in the production possibilities curve (PPC). Graphs are nothing more than a snapshot of the relationship between two variables at a point in time. In the case of the PPC, it is a graph that demonstrates the maximum possible production of two different goods with fixed resources and technology. A typical PPC is shown in Figure 26.1. Again, the graph represents the assumption of fixed resources (including capital and labor) and fixed technology. To make things simple, the PPC examines the production of only two goods produced in this society, in this case, food and health care. The amount of food produced is measured along the horizontal axis. The amount of health care produced is measured along the vertical axis.

The curve shows all the points at which a combination of food and health care can be produced if all resources are fully employed. The curve is thus a production frontier showing the maximum possible production of different combinations of food and health care. At point A, only food is produced. At point B on the vertical axis, only health care is produced.

At both extremes, point A and point B, the resources are being pushed to capacity to produce only food or only health care. In between those two points, somewhat less is produced of either food or health care. The PPC shows a trade-off between food and health care. If resources and technology are fixed, in order produce more food, we must take resources away from the production of health care. As revealed in the PPC, a decision to produce more food means less health care can be produced. A decision to produce more health care means less food. In a society producing many things, higher production of one good generally means lower production of others if we assume resources are fixed and that we are using all available resources.

Choice comes into the picture because somehow individuals comprising a society must decide which combination of health care and food it desires. Remember, if society decides it wants more food, it must give up some health care. If society decides it wants more health care, it must give up some food. Of course, the PPC shows the relationship of the production of two different goods with fixed resources and technology. If there are increased resources or improved technology, it would be possible to produce more of both goods.

Figure 26.1 **Production Possibilities Curve**

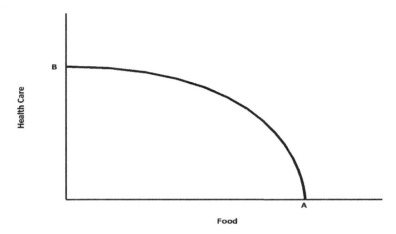

At point A, only food is produced. At point B, only health care is produced.

 We still haven't figured out how society decides where on the PPC to operate. The PPC illustrates possible choices, but the actual choice is determined by society's preferences at a particular point in time. In a market society, the most important criterion is what individual consumers want. For example, if society can make either good A or good B, but consumers want more of good A, more A will be produced and less B will be produced. How do producers know which good to produce? By looking at the price consumers are willing to pay and the number of goods left on the shelf. If consumers are willing to pay a high price for good A, producers are more likely to make a profit and will produce that good. We look more at how the market provides and responds to price signals throughout Chapters 27 to 35.

PROGRESSIVE CRITICISM OF NEOCLASSICAL VIEW OF SCARCITY AND CHOICE

The progressive criticism of the neoclassical concepts of scarcity and choice is presented here. To start with isolated individuals would be proper in the case of a man living alone on an island, but progressive economists stress that we do not live alone on separate islands. We live in a highly complex society in which every individual is closely tied to every other individual within the context of social and cultural norms, laws, and relationships. Few decisions are made in isolation. The current social and cultural norms and laws create a context in which individuals make their decisions. People often make decisions based on reasons other than self-interest, and sometimes those choices are made without carefully weighing the costs and benefits of a decision.

 Neoclassical economics says that we live in a world of scarcity, where resources are limited and where producing more for society is the economic problem. But this notion is based on assumptions about our behavior. It does not deal with the reality of social and economic **institutions** within which we live, meaning the *structured systems, habits, or processes that influence human behavior*. In particular, we live within capitalism. Under capitalist economic institutions in peacetime, there is no problem of scarcity. For consumers, there are plenty of products available to meet any whim. The problem is not a lack of goods to meet our desires, as it was in the prehistoric times of hunters, who might not find meat for a long time and sometimes starved. There are goods to meet our desires, but the problem is money. No money, no consumption.

Ask a top corporate executive what the corporation's biggest problem is. Is it a scarcity of workers? No, not if the corporation can pay wages. Is it a lack of raw materials? No, not if the corporation has money. The biggest corporate problem in the capitalist economy of the United States is how to sell all the goods and services it can produce. If it produces automobiles, it needs enough consumers to buy that brand of automobile. The problem is that most of the time, the automobile corporations of the world can produce far more cars than people have the money to buy. The problem is not a scarcity of cars. The problem is too many cars for the capitalist market economy. This situation is emphasized dramatically whenever General Motors fires fifty thousand employees because there are too many cars on the market for the money that consumers have to spend.

As in the problem of scarcity, neoclassical economists look at the problem of choice in terms suited to an isolated farmer on an island. The farmer asks himself, as we saw earlier, what foods do I desire, and what ways will I use to produce this mix of products? The reality of capitalist economic institutions, however, is very different. Most people are not isolated farmers but are employees of some business. Many workers are unemployed, but that is usually not a voluntary choice; most are fired or laid off with no chance to negotiate a lower wage. A woman may be the best worker around, but she is still fired when General Motors wants to fire thousands of workers. When the economy recovers and firms start hiring again, the same woman worker must grab the first job available to feed her family. Often, she cannot pick and choose between different jobs.

Progressive Criticism of PPC

Neoclassical economists use the PPC to argue that everything produced creates a trade-off. This argument rests on the assumption that the economy is producing on the PPC and not producing a combination of goods underneath the PPC. The argument is that a market economy and competition and the assumption that consumers always prefer more and more goods drives the economy to produce efficiently and on the frontier. Previous chapters demonstrated less than optimal performance of the American economy in some areas, such as environmental destruction and global warming. Moreover, earlier chapters pointed out that the economy is not purely competitive but is dominated by giant corporations, so there is no reason to expect it to behave like an ideal competitive economy might behave.

In fact, the economy is not always on the production frontier represented by the PPC. In Part III, we shall see in detail that the economy often has unemployed human and material resources. In reality, capitalist economies are often far below the PPC. If the economy is below the PPC, we can produce more of everything! If the economy can be reformed to move from below the PPC to a point on the PPC, there can be more of both health care and food.

SUMMARY

According to the neoclassical perspective, the following conclusions are reached.

1. Economics can best be understood in terms of the psychology of individuals. The psychology that determines how we make choices is timeless and unchanging.
2. The presence of scarcity implies that our wants and desires exceed our ability to produce. Scarcity means that individuals and enterprises must always be deciding which scarce resource to use and how to allocate the output.

3. Everyone makes choices: consumers and producers all make choices about what to produce, how to produce it, and what to consume.

4. Progressive economists reject the neoclassical focus on scarcity and isolated individuals for two main reasons. First, analysis should not start from the behavior of isolated individuals but from the behavior of people living in particular social and economic institutions. Second, under modern capitalist business institutions, the problem is not scarcity of labor and raw materials but the existence of more than it can sell under given conditions of what people have to spend.

KEY TERMS

choice   resources
institutions   scarcity

REVIEW QUESTIONS

Explain the concept of scarcity and how people make choices according to neoclassical analysis.

1. List the underlying assumptions that neoclassical economist make about people.
2. Explain the foundation of neoclassical analysis. What are two key assumptions made about people and how they make decisions?
3. What creates scarcity, according to neoclassical analysis? Explain the difference between what people need and what people want and desire and how this difference creates scarcity.

Describe how the production possibilities curve captures production choices in a society.

4. Explain what the production possibilities curve (PPC) demonstrates. What assumptions are made when creating a PPC?
5. What does it mean if a society is producing on the frontier or directly on the PPC?
6. If a society is producing on the frontier, what happens if society decides it wants more of one of the goods being produced?
7. Is it *always* impossible to produce more of one good without giving up some of the other good? Why or why not?

Describe what progressive economists see as the primary shortcomings of the neoclassical scarcity perspective.

8. What is the progressive criticism of the analysis of the economy, starting with isolated individuals? What is the critique of the assumptions about individuals and how individuals make decisions? What is the progressive alternative?
9. Why is the context in which individuals make decisions important? How do social and cultural norms play into how individuals make decisions? Give an example of how a social norm may influence an economic decision.
10. What is the progressive criticism of the neoclassical notion of scarcity? Give a specific example. What is the progressive alternative?
11. A progressive economist would claim we should not assume a market economy is always producing on the PPC. Explain. What does this mean about the decision to produce additional amounts of one good? Both goods?
12. Progressive economists claim the types of choices different people make are very different from the simple choices presented in the overview of neoclassical choice. Explain.

APPENDIX 26.1
MORE ON THE PRODUCTION POSSIBILITY CURVE

Earlier in the chapter, we introduced a production possibility curve (PPC) demonstrating the production of food and health care. This section goes into more detail about the PPC and how it can be used to illustrate important concepts in traditional economic analysis.

LEARNING OBJECTIVES FOR APPENDIX 26.1

After reading this chapter, you should be able to:

- List the assumptions behind the PPC.
- Use the PPC to illustrate scarcity, choice, constant opportunity costs, and the law of increasing opportunity cost.
- Explain why and how changes in technology, resources, and institutions influence the PPC.

THE SIMPLEST, LINEAR PPC FOR INDIVIDUALS

The **production possibilities curve** (**PPC**) is a *curve that shows the production combinations available to an economy given finite inputs and technology.* This model is used to illustrate some of the most important concepts in economics, including scarcity, choice, and opportunity costs. Earlier in this chapter, we discussed scarcity and choice. Now we also introduce opportunity costs. Every decision involves an opportunity cost. An **opportunity cost** is *the value of what you are giving up when you make the choice to do something else.* It is the value of next best thing you could be doing.

We begin our development of the PPC with a simple linear model before we develop a more realistic nonlinear model. The first step toward building this model is to assume that resources are fixed and wants and desires are unlimited. As was noted in the previous section of this chapter, if we are on the frontier or on the PPC, and if we want more of one thing, we must shift existing resources away from the production of the other good. From this starting point, it follows that every choice we make means giving up something else. In other words, there is an opportunity cost. If we decide we want more of A, we give up some B.

LINEAR OPPORTUNITY COSTS

Okay, you are having a hard time finding a summer job when you read about Student Painters, a company that employs college students to paint houses in the summer. You apply and accept the job. Since you show an aptitude for management, you are hired as a crew chief. Your job is to find houses that need painting. You then bid on the jobs, and if successful, buy paint and make sure your work team does a good job. About midsummer, your reputation for managing a quality painting crew has spread so far and wide that you have more than enough jobs to finish the summer. In fact, you have so many potential jobs lined up that you can choose between painting several small houses, a few large ones, or some of each.

Large houses usually take twice as much time to paint as small houses. Given the size of your crew and the time left before you have to return to school, you calculate that you could paint either twenty small houses or ten large houses. You could also paint different combinations of

Table 26.1

House Painting Possibilities

Small houses	20	18	16	14	12	10	8	6	4	2	0
Large houses	0	1	2	3	4	5	6	7	8	9	10

the two—ten small houses and five large houses, eighteen small houses and one large house, Remember that an opportunity cost is the value of the best-foregone alternative. A **marginal cost** is *simply the additional cost of producing an additional item.* In the house example, the marginal opportunity cost of painting *one* additional large house is the number of small houses you do not paint. The marginal opportunity cost of painting one additional small house is the number of large houses you do not paint.

In our example, every large house you paint means that you have to forego painting two small houses. The marginal opportunity cost of painting a large house is two small houses. Looking at it from the perspective of small houses, the marginal opportunity cost of painting one small house is one-half of a large house. This relationship or trade-off between painting large or small houses holds true anywhere along the linear PPC. Economists would say this relationship is characterized by constant marginal opportunity costs. Stated more generally, *as the production of one good increases, the additional amount of another good that must be given up remains the same.*

In short, the PPC helps us see that the choices involve **trade-offs**. *To get one additional thing, something else must be given up.* A few calculations result in the information in Table 26.1, which is illustrated in the PPC in Figure 26.2.

The intercepts of the PPC show the maximum number of each product that can be produced if all resources are devoted to the production of that item. In this case, a maximum of ten large houses or twenty small houses can be painted. Since painting a large house means that two small houses cannot be painted, the opportunity cost of each large house is two small houses, and the slope of the PPC is −0.5.

Several things about Figure 26.2 are worth noting and remembering:

- The table and graph assume that resources, institutions, and technology are fixed. By resources, we typically mean land, labor, capital, and time used in production, or more specifically, the number of workers, tools (brushes and ladders), and hours needed to complete the job. Institutions refers to the structured systems, habits, or processes that influence the production process. Examples include the manner in which labor is hired, the length of a typical workweek, and the minimum wage rate. Finally, technology refers to the existing level of knowledge, techniques, and types of tools available for the production of goods and services.
- We also assume that the trade-off is only between two things: big houses and small houses.
- The intercepts of a PPC show the maximum amount of production of each product assuming that all inputs are fully utilized and sustainable. In this case, the horizontal intercept gives the number of small houses that can be painted (20) if no large houses are painted. The vertical intercept gives the number of large houses (10) that can be painted if no small houses are painted.
- The slope of a PPC represents the marginal opportunity cost of choosing one option over the

Figure 26.2   **House Painting Production Possibilities Curve**

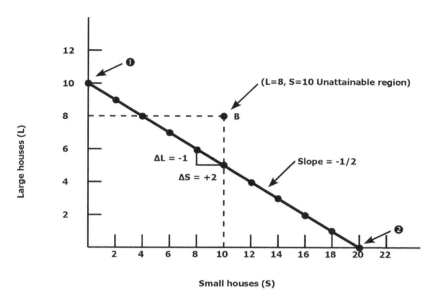

1. If no small houses are painted, ten large houses can be painted.
2. If no large houses can be painted, twenty small houses can be painted.
The intercepts of PPC show the maximum number of each product that can be produced if all the resources are devoted to the production of that item. In this case, a maximum of ten large houses or twenty small houses can be painted. Since painting a large house means that two small houses cannot be painted, the opportunity cost of each large house is two small houses, and the slope of the PPC is –0.5.

other. In this case, the slope is –0.5 because every small house (S) you paint means giving up the opportunity to paint one-half of a large house (L). This can be calculated as $\delta L/\delta S = -1/+2 = -0.5$. If the PPC were drawn with small houses on the vertical axis, the slope would be –2.0. Notice that –2.0 is the reciprocal of –0.5. Since this ratio stays the same along the line, we know that this production relationship is characterized by constant marginal opportunity costs.

• Points on the PPC are said to be efficient because they represent the maximum number of houses that can be painted given our resources, institutions, and technology. You could decide to paint any combination of houses on or inside the PPC, but operating inside the PPC would indicate that you are not working up to your capabilities—due perhaps to a sudden case of laziness, bad management, or some other kind of inefficiency. All points inside the PPC are attainable but inefficient.

• *Points on and inside of the PPC comprise the attainable combination* of houses. The **unattainable region** is *comprised of points outside of the PPC.* For example, the point representing eight large houses and ten small houses is unattainable given current resources, institutions, and technology. *The only way to operate at these points is through a positive change in our resources, technology, or institutions. Clearly, with more workers or tools, a new technological breakthrough, or an improved organization of work, the painting process production possibilities would expand.*

The data and PPC show the painting opportunities available, but they do not reveal which combination of large and small houses should be selected. How do you make this choice? That depends on your preferences, and those are determined elsewhere. Obviously, if you can make more profits from painting large houses than from painting small houses, you would select the large houses. If you like variety, you might select some of each if you make the same profits from painting two small houses as you make from painting one large house. However, without further information, the PPC does not help you in deciding what choice to make. It only illustrates the "menu" of available choices and the fact that every choice involves opportunity costs. We will find out later that one of the most important choices that society can make is deciding where to operate on its PPC.

CHANGING THE SLOPE OF THE PPC

The PPC drawn in Figure 26.2 was based on hypothetical data consistent with our assumptions that you could paint two small houses for every large house. Suppose that, upon further reflection, you conclude that you could actually paint thirty small houses this summer if you spent all of your time painting small houses. If you could still paint only ten large houses this summer, the horizontal intercept would change from twenty to thirty, and the PPC would look like the one in Figure 26.3.

Two things should be apparent from the PPC in Figure 26.3 compared to the one in Figure 26.2. First, the opportunity cost of one large house has increased from two small houses to three small houses. The result is that the slope of the PPC has changed from −0.5 to −0.33. Second, the **attainable region** has expanded, and it is now possible to paint more houses. For example, the point $(S = 6, L = 8)$ is on the new PPC but was previously unattainable.

The slope of the PPC will change if the intercept of one of the axes changes. In this case, it is assumed that if all resources are devoted to painting small houses, thirty houses could be painted. If it is still possible to paint a maximum of ten large houses, the slope of the PPC will change from −0.5 to −0.33, so the new PPC is less steep than the old PPC.

Shifting the PPC

Several factors can shift the entire PPC. Three of the most important shift factors are changes in the amount of available inputs, changes in technology, and improvements in existing economic institutions. Again remember, by **inputs**, we mean land, labor, capital, and time. *Technology* refers to the way in which the work is done or the tools used to do it. *Institutions* refers to other factors such as the organization of work or the incentives given to the employees; it can even involve issues such as racism or sexism. An example will make this clearer.

Suppose that after seeing how many houses need painting, you decided to hire another work crew. This would increase the number of both large and small houses you could paint and would shift the entire PPC outward. The same thing would happen if there were a technological advance. Let's say you were able to get hold of a new kind of paint that required only one coat instead of two, or perhaps a spray gun to use instead of brushes. Similarly, a positive change in institutions, such as a new incentive pay system for your paint crew would increase their interest in working harder and doing higher-quality work.

All three of these changes would result in a parallel outward shift in the PPC and an increase in the attainable region. Notice, however, that none of these events would change the slope of the PPC. We presume that the increased output would affect large house painting and small house painting equally. The effect of an improvement in available resources, technology, or institutions is shown in Figure 26.4.

Figure 26.3 **Linear Production Possibilities Curve**

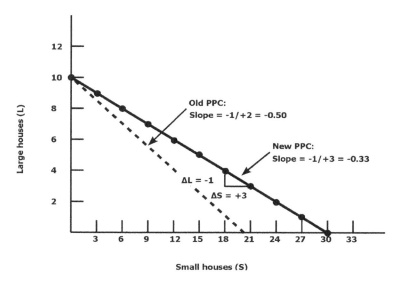

The slope of the PPC will change if the intercept of one of the axes changes. In this case, it is assumed that if all the resources are devoted to painting small houses, thirty houses could be painted. If it is still possible to paint a maximum of ten large houses, the slope of the PPC will change from –0.5 to –0.33, so the new PPC is less steep than the old PPC.

Figure 26.4 **Shifting the Production Possibilities Curve**

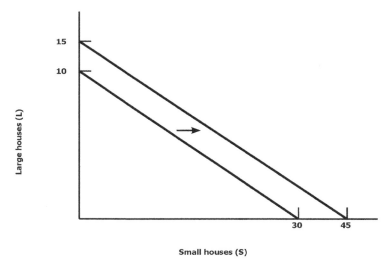

An increase in technology or available resources will expand production possibilities and result in a parallel outward shift in the PPC. In this case, available resources have increased by 50 percent, so it is possible to paint fifteen large houses, forty-five small houses, or any combination on the PPC that passes through these points. A decrease in available resources would cause the PPC to shift inward.

An increase in available resources, technology, or institutions will expand production possibilities and result in a parallel outward shift in the PPC. In this case, available resources have increased by 50 percent, so it is possible to paint fifteen large houses, forty-five small houses, or any combination on the PPC that passes through these points. A decrease in any of these three variables would cause the PPC to shift inward.

NONLINEAR OPPORTUNITY COSTS

Our story about Student Painters was a bit contrived. It was meant only to introduce some of the key points behind PPC analysis—opportunity cost, choice, and scarcity. In the real world, the PPC is most often nonlinear because of an important economic law, the law of increasing marginal opportunity costs. Stated simply, the **law of increasing opportunity costs** says that as *production of one good increases, the opportunity cost of producing the other product must eventually rise*. This occurs because resources are finite, and some factors have a comparative advantage in the production of a particular good. **Comparative advantage** means that *some inputs are better suited for producing some goods than for producing other goods*. The classic illustration of the law of increasing costs is the guns and butter example.

Suppose that society can produce only two kinds of goods, defense goods (Guns = G) and consumer goods (Butter = B). Suppose further, that if all available resources and technology are fully employed, 150 units of butter or 50 units of guns can be produced. Other combinations of guns and butter are possible; however, if the law of increasing costs holds, the resulting PPC is bowed out from the origin or concave with respect to the origin, as shown in Table 26.2 and Figure 26.5.

The concave shape of the nonlinear PPC illustrates the law of increasing marginal opportunity costs. Moving from point a to point b represents a reduction in gun production by ten units and a fifty-unit increase in butter production. Thus, the opportunity cost of the first fifty units of butter is ten guns, or 50B = 10G, which can be written as 1B = 0.2G. However, as butter production increases, the opportunity cost of butter rises. Moving from point b to point c again represents a sacrifice of ten units of guns, but results in only forty additional units of butter. The opportunity cost of butter has risen to 1B = 0.25G.

The hypothetical data in Table 26.2 and Figure 26.5 reflects increasing marginal opportunity costs. However, more important than the actual numbers is the reasoning behind the numbers. It goes something like this. Begin at point a where production is fifty guns and no butter (G = 50, B = 0). There is a pretty good chance we would all starve at point a, so let's take some resources out of gun production and put them into the butter industry. Focusing on labor, would you want to give up your best gun makers to now make butter, or would you want to use workers who were not so good at producing guns? Clearly we would want to give up workers who were not so productive in gun making. Let's also assume that the workers who are not so good at making guns, are very talented when it comes to making butter. According to our table, cutting gun production by just ten units will free enough resources to enable the production of fifty units of butter. Thus, the opportunity cost of the first fifty units of butter (50B) is ten units of guns (10G). On average (10G/50B) then, the opportunity cost of each of the first fifty units of butter is 0.2 units of guns, or 1B = 0.2G.

Now suppose that society decides that fifty units of butter is not enough to feed everyone, so the decision is made to reduce gun production by another ten units. How much more butter can be produced? The table shows point b with 30G and 90B. This means that the opportunity cost of the next 40 units of B is 10G, or 40B = 10G, which means that 1B = 0.25G. Rather than giv-

Table 26.2

Guns and Butter Possibilities

Point	a	b	c	d	e	f
Guns	50.00	40.00	30.00	20.00	10.00	0.00
Butter	0.00	50.00	90.00	120.00	140.00	150.00
Opportunity cost of one unit of butter in terms of guns	n/a	0.20	0.25	0.33	0.50	1.00
Opportunity cost of one unit of guns in terms of butter	n/a	5.00	4.00	3.00	2.00	1.00

Figure 26.5   **The Law of Increasing Costs: Guns and Butter PPC**

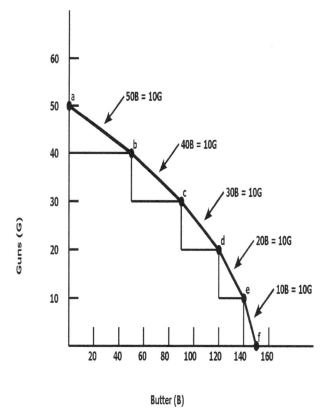

The concave shape of the nonlinear PPC illustrates the law of increasing opportunity costs. Moving from point a to point b represents a reduction in gun production by ten units and a fifty-unit increase in butter production. Thus, the opportunity cost of the first fifty units of butter is ten guns, or 50B = 10G, which can be written as 1B = 0.2G. As butter production increases, however, the opportunity cost of butter rises. Moving from point b to point c again represents a sacrifice of ten units of guns, but results in only forty additional units of butter. Thus, the opportunity cost of butter has risen to 1B = 0.25G.

ing up 0.2G to get 1B, we now have to give up 0.25G to get 1B. In order to add more workers to making butter, we take more workers away from producing guns. The new workers we just took out of producing guns were more skilled at gun making than the first group and maybe not so good at producing butter as the first group. Are you still with me? We just illustrated increasing marginal opportunity costs: as the production of one good rises, an increasing amount of the other good must be given up. In this case, the opportunity cost of butter production rose from 0.20G for each of the first fifty units of butter to 0.25G for each of the next forty units. Why is this likely to occur? The answer is a key aspect of traditional economic reasoning—imperfect substitution of resources.

Clearly, the substitution of resources from gun production to butter production is characterized by less than perfect substitution in inputs. The result is that producing more butter results in the loss of more and more guns. In economic terms, the marginal opportunity cost of butter production increases. The law of increasing marginal opportunity costs applies to all production processes *given our assumptions*. To ensure that you understand this concept, confirm that this relationship continues to exist even if we move in the other direction from point b to point a.

CHANGING THE SLOPE AND INTERCEPTS OF THE PPC

As with the linear PPC in Figure 26.2, the intercepts of the nonlinear PPC in Figure 26.5 show how much can be produced if all resources are devoted to the production of only one of the goods, and the slope shows the opportunity cost of production. The PPC will shift if there is a change in technology, a positive change in institutions, or an increase in available resources.

As shown in Figure 26.6, additional resources, improved institutions, or an increase in technology that has an equal effect on the production of both goods will result in a parallel outward shift of the PPC. This expands the attainable region and means that society can have more of both goods.

The PPC will shift when there is a positive change in resources, institutions, or technology. Figure 26.5 illustrates what happens if there is an increase in resources that affects the production of *both* guns and butter: there is an outward shift and an expansion of the attainable region. An increase in resources that affects only gun production would raise the intercept on the gun axis and change the slope of the PPC. The opportunity cost of butter production is now greater because more guns are lost for each unit of butter that is produced.

Figure 26.7 shows what happens if there is a technological change, a positive change in institutions, or an increase in resources that affects the production of only one good, guns in this case. The guns intercept increases, but there is no change in the butter intercept. In this case, the guns intercept rises from fifty to sixty, so the PPC becomes steeper over its entire range. The result is that the opportunity cost of butter production rises because more guns must be given up for every unit of butter that is produced. Had butter technology increased or the number of cows increased, the intercept on the butter axis would have expanded and the opportunity cost of guns would have increased.

SUMMARY OF APPENDIX 26.1

According to the neoclassical perspective, the following conclusions are reached:

1. The presence of scarcity means that our wants and needs exceed our ability to produce. The PPC illustrates this notion and shows the maximum amount of two goods that can be produced given our resources, technology, and institutions.

Figure 26.6   **Changing the Slope and Shifting the PPC**

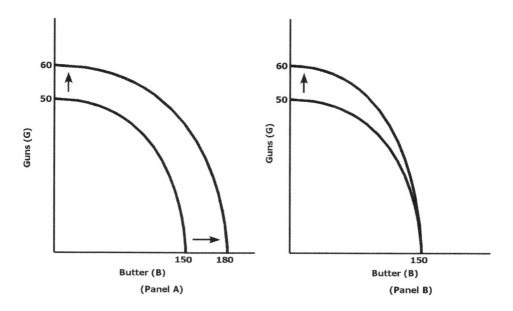

The PPC will shift when there is an increase in resources or technology. Panel (A) illustrates what happens when an increase in resources or technology affects the production of both guns and butter: there is a parallel outward shift and an expansion of the feasible region. An increase in resources or technology that affects only gun production raises the intercept on the gun axis and changes the slope of the PPC, as shown in panel (B). The opportunity cost of butter production is now greater because more guns are lost for each unit of butter that is produced.

2. A linear PPC illustrates the idea of constant marginal opportunity costs. The shape of a concave PPC is caused by imperfect substitution and characterized by the law of increasing marginal opportunity costs. The slope of either a linear or nonlinear PPC defines the opportunity cost of producing one good in terms of another.

3. The intercepts of the PPC show how much of either good can be produced if all resources are devoted to a single product. Points on the PPC are efficient and attainable given our assumptions; points inside the PPC are attainable but inefficient; points outside the PPC are unattainable. The PPC will shift outward if there are more resources, technological advances, or institutional improvements. An outward shift in the PPC represents an increase in economic output.

4. The PPC can be used to illustrate trade-offs not only at any point in time but also over time. Countries that forgo the production of some consumption goods in order to produce more investment goods can be expected to grow more rapidly over time. This is because the production of investment goods increases resources and improves technology. An increase in resources and/or an improvement in technology will cause the PPC to shift rightward.

Figure 26.7 **Economic Growth and the PPC**

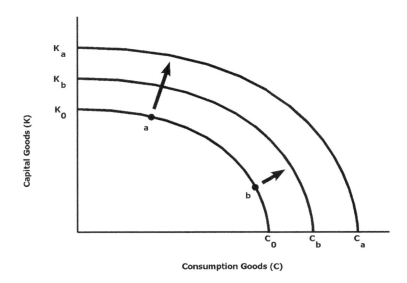

Consumption Goods (C)

One factor that influences economic growth is how current production is split between capital goods (K) and consumption goods (C). If the current PPC passes through (K_0, C_0) and society chooses to produce at point a, the future generation will enjoy the PPC passing through (K_a, C_a); if current production is at point b, the future generation will have less production possibilities, as illustrated by the PPC passing through (K_b, C_b). This is because point a represents more capital goods than point b. At point a, the current generation is sacrificing more current consumption, whereas at point b, the current generation is better off, but future economic growth will be slower.

KEY TERMS FOR APPENDIX 26.1

attainable region

comparative advantage

constant marginal opportunity costs

institutions

law of increasing marginal opportunity costs

marginal cost

opportunity cost

production possibilities curve (PPC)

resources/inputs

technology

trade-offs

unattainable region

REVIEW QUESTIONS FOR APPENDIX 26.1

List the assumptions behind the PPC.
1. What do we assume about inputs, institutions, and technology in building the PPC?
2. What does the PPC represent?
3. What is an opportunity cost? Give an example of an opportunity cost involved in a decision you made today.
4. What does marginal cost mean? Create an example of a marginal cost.
5. When you decide to produce more of one good on the PPC, what is the "cost"? Explain.

Use the PPC to illustrate scarcity, choice, constant opportunity costs, and the law of increasing marginal opportunity cost.

6. Draw a PPC diagram and illustrate the attainable region and unattainable region. Label a combination of goods representing efficient production.

7. Why are typical textbook PPCs bowed outward?

8. What does it mean when PPCs are illustrated with a straight line?

9. Draw a linear PPC. Label two points on this diagram and explain how these points are consistent with the idea of constant marginal opportunity costs.

10. Draw a concave PPC. Label two points on this diagram and how these points are consistent with the law of increasing opportunity costs.

11. Draw a linear PPC like that illustrating the work of Student Painters. On the vertical axis, label large houses, and on the horizontal axis, put small houses. Assume that the company begins using a special kind of scaffolding for painting big houses. However, setting it up takes time, so it is not useful for painting small houses. How will the firm's PPC be affected by this new resource?

12. In the 1980s, rates of growth in Japan were higher than in the United States. One argument given for the stronger growth in Japan was higher levels of investment. Draw a PPC for both the United States and Japan. On the axes, label the goods as investment goods and consumption goods. Use these two diagrams to explain why Japan experienced faster growth than did the United States.

Explain why and how changes in technology, resources, and institutions influence the PPC.

13. What would cause a parallel shift in a PPC? What would cause a change in its slope?

14. Give an example of how a change in technology might have an effect on the production of one good and not the other, and illustrate this situation with a PPC. What changed in the graph?

15. What kind of institutional changes could cause an increase in production even though no other inputs increased and no technology changed?

16. Assume a hurricane devastated an island economy that produced only coconuts and bamboo. Demonstrate this event on the island's PPC.

CHAPTER 27

Simple Analytics of Supply and Demand

This chapter discusses the relatively noncontroversial issue of the everyday workings of supply and demand in an idealized capitalist marketplace. Neoclassical economists use supply and demand analysis for labor markets to determine wage rates, supply and demand for money to determine interest rates, supply and demand for foreign currencies to determine exchange rate, just to name a few. Similarly, many progressive critiques are difficult to understand if one does not first understand the neoclassical model of supply and demand. Therefore, make sure you master the material in this chapter before moving on. The limitations and criticisms of supply and demand analysis are discussed toward the end of the chapter.

LEARNING OBJECTIVES

After reading this chapter, you should be able to:

- Define and explain the basics of supply and demand analysis.
- Understand the context in which the supply and demand model is developed.
- Explain progressive critiques of supply and demand analysis.

THE MARKET SYSTEM AND INDIVIDUAL MARKETS

It is important to begin by distinguishing a particular market from the market system (often just called "the market"). Historically, a market was an area, usually near the center of a village or town, where buyers and sellers would meet and exchange goods. Later, any place where a merchant regularly sold commodities was referred to as a market. Today, the word "market" sometimes refers to a grocery store, but it is more generally used as an abstract concept among economists. In this text, market refers to the *process* through which buyers and sellers exchange money for goods and services. We speak of the stock market, the labor market, or the automobile market when we are specifically referring to the buying and selling of stocks, labor services, or automobiles. We speak of the market or the market system when we mean monetary exchange and price determination in general. It is obvious that any modern market system that successfully facilitates exchange must contain complex systems of customs and traditions, laws and agencies of law enforcement, as well as the infrastructure in which and through which exchange takes place.

In this part of the book, we ignore the physical settings and institutional processes of markets as well as many of the customs and laws that enable markets to function. Instead, we concentrate on exchange (buying and selling) and the determination of price at a more abstract level. This abstraction allows economists, businesspeople, or journalists to talk about market exchange processes in a more general way.

A market is a two-sided phenomenon, with both buyers and sellers. (In this chapter, we ignore any beneficial or adverse affects transactions may have on others besides the buyer and seller.) Buyers have money they wish to exchange for goods and services, and sellers have goods and services they wish to exchange for money. The amount of a good that buyers would like to purchase at any given price is called the demand for that good. Similarly, the amount of the good that sellers would like to sell at any given price is called the supply of the good.

It should be stressed that demand is not simply related to need or desire. A penniless child longingly gazing through the window of a candy store adds nothing to the market demand for candy. Similarly, in the Great Depression of the 1930s, millions of people went hungry while tons of wheat and thousands of cattle and sheep were destroyed and wasted because of the lack of any market demand for these products. The problem, of course, was that, like the child at the candy store, the unemployed millions had no money to exchange for the food they needed.

Supply, Demand, and Prices

Restated more formally, the definitions of demand and supply are as follows: **demand** for a good is *the quantity of that good buyers would be willing and able to purchase during a given period, at various price levels, holding all other things constant.* Obviously, demand must be expressed in terms of a given period if it is to have any meaning. The number of automobiles people wish to purchase is certainly very different over the course of a week than over a year. Moreover, a given price must be specified. Clearly, the number of Ford Explorers people would like to buy will be very different if the price is $500 than if it is $50,000. The lower the price, the more of them people will want to buy.

The definition of supply is very similar to that of demand. **Supply** of a good is *the quantity of the good sellers would like to sell during a given period, at various prices, holding all other things constant.* In most circumstances, firms are willing to increase the quantity they produce if the market price increases.

If the reactions of buyers and sellers at different prices are considered, it becomes possible to define a demand schedule and a supply schedule. A **demand schedule** *relates various prices of that good with the amounts of that good people would like to buy at each of the various prices (given the incomes and preferences of the buyers).* If people in a particular state or region of the United States were polled in order to determine the number of Ford Explorers they would like to buy at various prices, the results might be similar to those given in Table 27.1.

At a price of $35,000, only 35,000 Ford Explorers will be purchased. If the price fell to $15,000, then the quantity demanded would increase to 55,000 Ford Explorers. The information contained in this demand schedule is illustrated in Figure 27.1 as a demand curve. This **demand curve**, D, *illustrates graphically the relationship between prices and the quantity demanded.* It can be used to ascertain the quantity of Explorers buyers would be willing and able to purchase at any given price.

Why does the demand curve usually have a downward slope? Because the **law of demand** says *there is an inverse relationship between price and quantity demanded.* The law of demand says that as the price of a good falls, the quantity demanded increases, ceteris paribus (holding everything else constant). Similarly, as the price of a good rises, the quantity demanded of the good decreases, ceteris paribus.

Table 27.1

Quantity Demanded of Ford Explorers at Various Prices

Price	Quantity Demanded Per Month
$35,000	35,000
$30,000	40,000
$25,000	45,000
$20,000	50,000
$15,000	55,000

Figure 27.1   **Demand Curve for Ford Explorers**

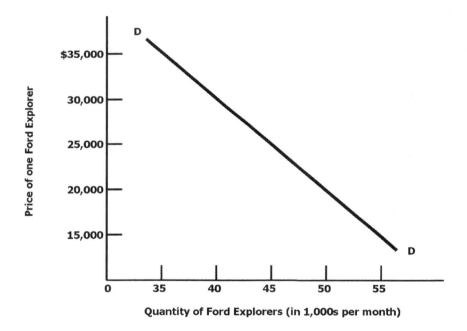

At higher prices, the quantity demanded is smaller both because other goods or substitutes appear relatively more attractive and because people simply do not have enough income to buy at those higher prices. As prices decline, the quantity demanded increases both because people can afford more and because these goods are now relatively cheaper compared to other alternatives than they were before.

In a similar manner, a **supply schedule** *expresses the number of Ford Explorers (amount of a good) the Ford Motor Company (the seller) would desire to sell at various prices.* Table 27.2 summarizes this hypothetical information.

Table 27.2

Number of Ford Explorers Supplied at Various Prices

Price	Quantity Supplied Per Month
$35,000	55,000
$30,000	50,000
$25,000	45,000
$20,000	40,000
$15,000	35,000

Figure 27.2 **Supply of Ford Explorers**

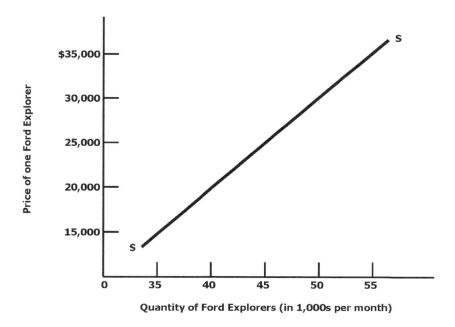

In this case, if the market price were $15,000, Ford would be willing to produce only 35,000 Explorers. However, if the price increased to $35,000, Ford would be willing to increase its quantity supplied to 55,000 of these vehicles. In Figure 27.2, this same information is expressed graphically in the form of a **supply curve**, *demonstrating the quantities sellers would like to sell at various prices.*

Why does the supply curve usually slope upward? Because the **law of supply** declares that *a positive relationship exists between price and the quantity supplied of any good. The law of supply says that as price increases, the quantity supplied of goods increases, all other things being equal. Similarly, as the price of a good falls, its quantity supplied falls, ceteris paribus.* Ford is in business for profit. At higher prices (assuming input prices do not change), it can

Figure 27.3 **Supply and Demand of Ford Explorers**

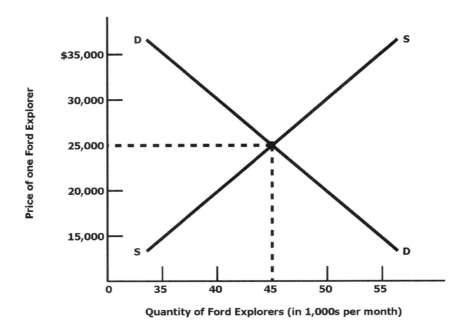

make more profit, so it is willing to increase the quantity supplied of Explorers only when prices are higher.

Market prices are determined jointly by the forces of both supply and demand. Sellers wish to exchange products for money, and buyers wish to exchange money for products. When a particular price is established, a specific quantity will be offered for sale and a specific quantity will be demanded. If these two quantities are equal, both sellers and buyers may conduct transactions in the desired quantities. For example, in Figure 27.3, the demand curve for Explorers in Figure 27.1 is superimposed on the supply curve used in Figure 27.2. It is clear that if a price of $25,000 is established, the point at which the curves intersect indicates that buyers and sellers want to buy and sell 45,000 Explorers.

When the quantity supplied and the quantity demanded for a particular good are equal at a particular price, the market is said to be in equilibrium. At equilibrium price, everyone is able to buy or sell all that they choose to buy or sell within their budget.

Many more technical details on supply and demand are found in appendices 27.1 and 27.2. These appendices are useful for all students, but they are essential for students going on to other courses in economics.

PROGRESSIVE CRITICISMS OF SUPPLY AND DEMAND ANALYSIS

Most traditional and progressive economists agree on the everyday workings of supply and demand in the capitalist market for goods and services. But progressives point out many limitations that make it far less useful than it at first appears. First of all, this is only a chapter on the simple mechanics of supply and demand, assuming a perfect capitalist system in which prices move freely to adjust supply and demand, and there are many buyers and many sellers in the market. There are also strong disagreements between neoclassical and progressive economists over what determines supply and what determines demand. Sometimes the government intervenes in the workings of markets, and that may be good or bad, but it certainly changes the results from what they would have been if the markets were left alone.

In addition to government controls, the economy itself is far from a perfect capitalist market system. For example, a pure capitalist competitive system would have thousands of small firms in every industry, with no single firm having any control over the market. A perfectly working capitalist market requires that every individual and every firm have perfect knowledge of what is going on and the ability to enter and exit markets easily. In fact, in most industries in the United States, production is concentrated in just a few firms with great market power. Information is not perfect. Consumers and enterprises have very poor knowledge of many facts, and the same information is not easily available to everyone. In most markets, business owners can not easily move from one industry to another. Therefore, the prices in most industries are very far from the results that supply and demand in a perfectly competitive market would predict. Only agriculture still has tens of thousands of firms, but agricultural prices are often determined by government subsidies and controls.

We used the example of the Ford Explorer because it is a well-known commodity on the market that most people have seen and can picture. It is actually, however, a poor example of the mechanics of supply and demand because it is definitely not the product of a perfectly competitive industry. There are only a relatively small number of automobile producers who control most of the supply of SUVs. Ford is one of the giants, so it has a certain degree of power to manipulate prices differently than a firm in an imaginary competitive industry. Moreover, all buyers of automobiles know that their knowledge is limited. In such an industry, the price of the Ford Explorer is far different than it would be under pure and perfect competition. Why did we not choose a famous product from some industry that has pure and perfect competition? There are none!

The final problem with the traditional analysis is that nobody has ever seen a supply or demand curve outside of a book. All that we actually see are a series of prices at different dates, accompanied by a series of quantities sold at those dates. We could graph those points, but if we ran a line through all of them, it would wander all over the page. Is that line supply, or is it demand? Or did demand stay the same while the supply curve shifted each time? Or did supply remain the same while the demand curve shifted each time?

In the real world, it is often difficult to determine whether it was a change in demand or a change in supply that caused price and quantity to change. Students must remember that supply and demand is simply one lens through which we view the world and attempt to understand, explain, and make predictions. Don't confuse the supply and demand lens with the real world itself. Always remember that supply and demand curves are imaginary constructions that some economists think may be useful to understand how prices of goods and services are determined. Others use different approaches.

SUMMARY

This chapter is important for neoclassical analysis (and also for the analysis of many progressive economists). Thumb through any economics textbook, and you will find supply and demand graphs in almost all of the traditional economics chapters. Similarly, many progressive critiques are difficult to understand without first understanding the neoclassical model of supply and demand. Therefore, make sure you have mastered the material in this chapter before moving on. The key points to remember are as follows:

- The law of demand states that people will buy less of a product at higher prices and more at lower products, holding everything else constant. The demand curve slopes downward.
- A change in price results in movement along a demand curve; a change in any other relevant factors causes the demand curve to shift. The main factors that shift the demand curve are income, tastes, and prices of other goods. An increase in demand tends to raise price and the quantity supplied; a decrease in demand tends to lower price and the quantity supplied (see Appendix 27.1).
- The law of supply states that, in the short run, firms will offer more of a product at higher prices and less at lower prices, holding everything else constant. The short-run supply curve slopes upward.
- A change in price results in movement along a given supply curve; a change in other relevant factors causes the supply curve to shift. The main factors that shift the supply curve are costs of production related to input costs. An increase in supply tends to decrease price and raise the quantity demanded; a decrease in supply tends to raise price and lower the quantity demanded (see Appendix 27.1).
- The intersection of the supply and demand curve is the point of equilibrium. Equilibrium represents the price at which quantity demanded equals quantity supplied. The market will stay in equilibrium until disturbed by an outside influence.

The key points about the critique of supply and demand analysis are as follows:

- Demand and supply curves are a theoretical construction that cannot be proven because it is sometimes impossible to identify which changes are due to supply and which to demand.
- Controversy has raged over what determines supply and demand curves.
- The analysis applies precisely only to an economy of pure and perfect competition, which does not exist. Analyses of prices in impure and imperfect competition are far more complex and controversial, as seen in Chapters 32, 33, and 34. Does this mean supply and demand analysis is worthless? No, the concept of supply and demand is useful to economists in analyzing some types of problems if it is handled with great care.

KEY TERMS

demand	law of supply
demand curve	supply
demand schedule	supply curve
law of demand	supply schedule

REVIEW QUESTIONS

Define and explain the basics of supply and demand analysis.
1. Explain what is meant by referring to the market as a "process."
2. State the law of demand. State the law of supply. What is meant by the phrase ". . . holding all other things constant"?
3. What is equilibrium? Why is it significant? Does it ever change?

Understand the context in which the supply and demand model is developed.

4. Explain why the focus of supply and demand analysis is strictly limited to exchange?
5. Does the demand curve in the supply and demand model capture all the people who want or desire a good? Why or why not?

Explain progressive critiques of supply and demand analysis.

6. What happens to supply and demand analysis if the government intervenes in the market?
7. Are there many real world examples of perfectly competitive markets? What might that mean for supply and demand analysis? Give an example.

APPENDIX 27.1
EQUILIBRIUM

The appendix puts supply together with demand to demonstrate how prices are determined in the market, what happens if the market is not in equilibrium, and how prices change in the market.

LEARNING OBJECTIVES FOR APPENDIX 27.1

After reading this appendix, you should be able to:

- Define equilibrium price and quantity and explain what it means.
- Understand and describe what happens when a market is not in equilibrium.
- Explain how equilibrium changes in the market.

EQUILIBRIUM

When the quantity supplied and the quantity demanded for a particular good are equal at a particular price, the market is said to be in **equilibrium**. At equilibrium price, everyone is able to buy or sell all that they choose to buy or sell within their budget. However, this is not true at prices above or below equilibrium price.

Imagine for a moment that *a price higher than the equilibrium price is established*. In this case, the market will experience **excess supply**, or *surplus, which means the quantity supplied will exceed the quantity demanded*. In Figure 27.4, if the price of Explorers is set at $30,000, an excess supply exists. Ford would like to sell 50,000 Explorers at that price, but buyers would like to buy only 40,000. There is an excess supply of 10,000 Explorers.

In many markets, there is a tendency for the forces of supply and demand to cause price changes that will eliminate excess supply. In the situation illustrated in Figure 27.4, thousands of Explorer

Figure 27.4 **Excess Supply of Ford Explorers**

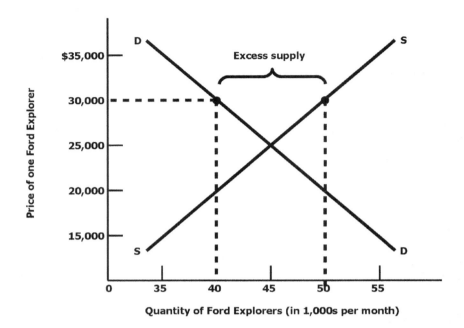

Quantity of Ford Explorers (in 1,000s per month)

dealers will find that at the established price of $30,000, they are unable to sell the quantity of vehicles they had anticipated. As unwanted inventories of unsold cars accumulate, the dealers cut back on or eliminate entirely their orders with the Ford Motor Company. With production geared for the 50,000 cars per month that the manufacturer had hoped to sell in this particular region, it is not long before unwanted inventories fill the parking lots up at the factory.

In order to reduce these inventories and stimulate sales, the manufacturer may reduce the price, which definitely would improve the imbalance between the quantity supplied and the quantity demanded. As long as the price remains above $25,000, however, the excess supply will persist, and the motive to cut the price further will continue to exist. Only at the equilibrium price of $25,000 will excess supply disappear and the market be cleared.

What would happen if *the price established was below the equilibrium price* of $25,000? At any price below $25,000, we would have **excess demand**, or *a shortage, where the quantity demanded exceeds the quantity supplied.* For instance, take a look at Figure 27.5.

At a price of $20,000, buyers wish to purchase 50,000 Explorers, but producers wish to sell only 40,000 Explorers. Therefore, there is an excess demand of 10,000 vehicles. Dealers would find long lines of customers waiting to buy the few available cars. Orders sent to Ford would go largely unfilled because these orders would far exceed the number of Explorers being produced.

Under these conditions, it would be obvious to the dealers and the manufacturer that more cars could be sold at higher prices. The search for unavailable Explorers would lead buyers to bid up the price they are willing to pay for one of these vehicles. As the price is raised, the amount of excess demand declines. Yet at any price below $25,000, there will continue to be some excess

Figure 27.5   **Excess Demand for Ford Explorers**

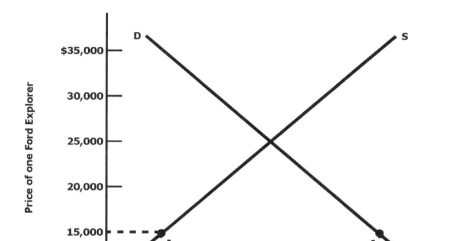

Quantity of Ford Explorers (in 1,000s per month)

demand. There will continue to be an upward pressure on the price until it reaches the equilibrium level of $25,000.

Note under conditions of excess supply, sellers were frustrated, experienced rising inventories, and therefore had an incentive to lower their prices to sell more vehicles. Under conditions of excess demand, it is the buyers who are frustrated. They find that at the established price, vehicles are simply unavailable. Therefore, buyers have an incentive to bid up the price. In either case, the pressures of the market system encourage a movement toward the equilibrium price and quantity.

However, the rate at which price changes can bring any particular market into equilibrium varies greatly among markets. In some markets, sellers are very sensitive to unwanted changes in inventories, so adjustments in price occur very quickly. The New York Stock Exchange (NYSE) is highly sensitive to minute-by-minute fluctuations in supply and demand. Frequent price changes serve to keep the market near equilibrium at all times.

At the other extreme, what is for most people the most important of all markets—the labor market—may remain for years in a situation of disequilibrium. With only a few exceptions (mostly in time of war), this market has had a persistent excess supply, which means, of course, involuntary unemployment for some people.

There are also many cases in which control over supply or demand gives an individual or group of individuals the power to fix prices. In this case, excess supply or demand may not lead to price changes if those changes are not in the best interest of the price fixer. We examine this fact and its implications in Chapters 33 and 34 when we examine market under conditions of imperfect competition.

CHANGES IN QUANTITY DEMANDED VERSUS CHANGES IN DEMAND

Economists distinguish between two kinds of changes with regard to the demand curve. To follow what economists are talking about, students must keep two key concepts straight. They sound similar but mean entirely different things.

We already established that the law of demand shows that, in general, there is an inverse relationship between the price of a good and the quantity demanded of that good. There is movement along the curve, or **change in quantity demanded**, when *a change in price causes the quantity demanded for a good to change*. For instance, when the price increases, quantity demanded decreases. When the price falls, quantity demanded increases. In both of these cases, demand—the entire schedule of price and quantity demanded pairings—did not change. The only thing that can cause movement along the demand curve, or a change in quantity demanded, is the change in the price of that good.

If anything other than the price of the good changes, there is a **change in demand**. A change in demand refers to a situation in which *the entire demand schedule or line shifts either out (to the right) or in (to the left)*. There are three main factors that can change the demand for a particular commodity: (1) changes in tastes or preferences, (2) changes in the price of a related good, and/or (3) changes in consumers' available income.

Suppose there is change in preferences, with consumer preference changing from small, fuel-efficient cars to large, gas-guzzling ones like the Explorer. What happens to the demand schedule? At any given price, more will be demanded. This shift to the right in demand is illustrated in Figure 27.6. The old demand curve, D_1, is replaced by a new and higher demand curve, D_2.

A second shift factor for demand is the price of related goods. Imagine a significant decrease in gasoline prices. This too would likely encourage consumers to be less concerned about fuel economy. Thus, demand for Ford Explorers would shift out or to the right as a result of the decrease in gas prices.

A third influence on demand is the effect of income. Suppose there was a general increase in the incomes of all people buying Explorers. With the new, higher incomes, individuals would probably buy more Explorers at every possible price. The higher incomes cause a shift to the right in the demand curve. This produces a new demand curve, D_2. At any price, the new demand curve shows that people wish to buy more at that price than they formerly did when line D_1 was the demand curve. This increased demand is the result of the increase in income.

In general, whenever there is a change in any factors that affects demand *other than the price of that good*, the change will be shown as a shift in the demand curve or change in demand.

CHANGES IN SUPPLY

The explanation of shifts in demand and movements along demand curves may be repeated for changes in supply. There is movement along the curve or **change in quantity supplied** when *a change in price causes the quantity supplied for a good to change*. For instance, when the price increases, quantity supplied increases. When the price falls, we say quantity supplied decreases. In both of these cases, supply—the entire schedule of price and quantity supplied pairings—did not change. The only thing that can cause movement along the supply curve or a change in quantity supplied, is the change in the price of that good.

If anything other than the price of the good changes, there is a **change in supply.** A change in supply refers to a situation where *the entire supply schedule or line shifts either out (to the right)*

Figure 27.6 **Increase in Demand for Ford Explorers**

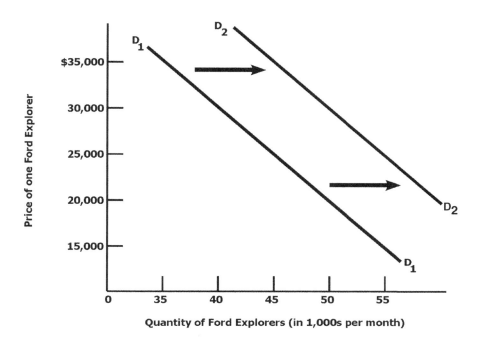

or in *(to the left)*. The student should work through this in Figure 27.7. Consider, for example, the way higher or lower prices per car would cause Ford to move along the supply curve S_1, offering more or fewer Explorers to the consumer market at different prices. But also consider the way lower costs per car such as a lower price of steel per ton might motivate Ford to offer more Explorers at each given price (i.e., a shift from supply curve S_1 to S_2). For now we will assume that anything that lowers the cost of production such as lower input costs (for raw materials or labor) or higher productivity per worker. Lower taxes will shift a supply curve out or to the right. Similarly anything that increases costs of production (higher input costs, lower productivity, higher taxes) will shift the supply curve to the left.

CHANGES IN SUPPLY AND DEMAND

Finally, by putting the changes in supply and demand together, it is possible to explain how prices are forced to change. The effect on the price of Explorers of an increase or decrease in demand (with supply conditions remaining unchanged) is shown in Figure 27.8.

Imagine that the economy is experiencing a period of rising incomes. This will result in an increase in demand for Explorers and can be illustrated and explained as a shift outward or to the right from curve D_1 to D_2. Both descriptions are correct. Either way, the fact is that Ford can sell more Explorers at a higher price. The quantity sold went from 45,000 to 50,000; the price went from $25,000 to $30,000. Of course, there is nothing mysterious about that delightful result for Ford. It happened because it was assumed that demand shifted to Explorers (from Chevrolets or Volkswagens, perhaps) as a result of higher incomes among consumers. In our earlier example

Figure 27.7 **Increase in Supply of Ford Explorers**

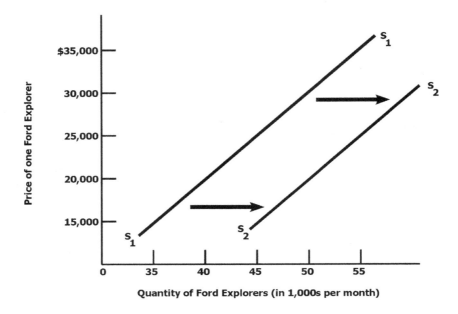

in which Ford could sell more Explorers only at a lower price, it was assumed that there was no shift in demand to Explorers. This is a different case.

Similarly, in Figure 27.8, a decrease in demand for Explorers means a shift to the left from curve D_2 back to D_1. This could have been caused by a change in preferences. Suppose consumers shift demand from Explorers to Honda Civics. Then Ford will sell fewer Explorers at a lower price per car, assuming that the supply curve remains as drawn.

Now, on the other side, consider the changes in the supply of Explorers while the demand remains the same. Consider a case in which the costs of production have fallen because of lower steel prices. Steel costs account for a significant portion of the total production costs. This scenario is illustrated in Figure 27.9. An increase in supply means a shift from curve S_1 to S_2: Ford is offering to supply more Explorers at each price. There is an outward shift in the supply curve. If demand is unchanged, Ford is selling more Explorers by increasing supply, and therefore the market price is lower. Whereas it previously sold 45,000 Explorers at $25,000 each, it now sells 50,000 at only $20,000 each.

A decrease in supply means shifting back from S_2 to S_1. Suppose, for example, that Ford's production costs rise for some reason, perhaps because of higher labor costs. It may then reduce its supply and thereby drive up the price and reduce the quantity demanded of Ford Explorers.

KEY TERMS FOR APPENDIX 27.1

change in demand

change in supply

change in quantity demanded

change in quantity supplied

equilibrium

excess demand

excess supply

Figure 27.8 **Changes in Demand and Price of Ford Explorers**

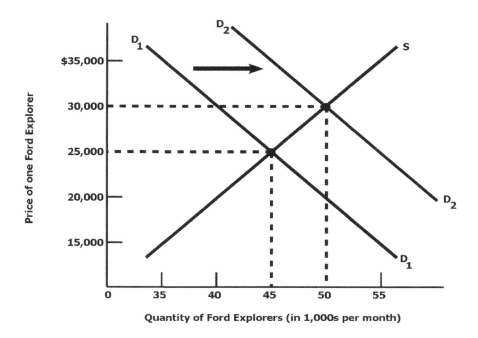

Figure 27.9 **Changes in Supply and Price of Ford Explorers**

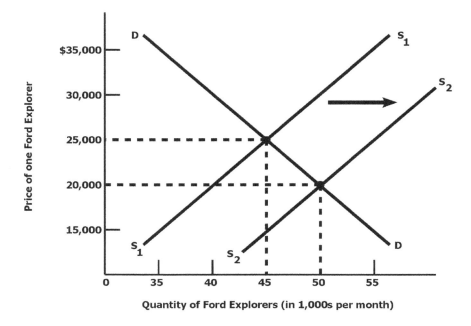

REVIEW QUESTIONS FOR APPENDIX 27.1

Define equilibrium and explain what it means.
1. What is equilibrium? Why is it such an important concept?

Understand and describe what happens when a market is not in equilibrium.
2. Use supply and demand to explain excess supply. What might cause excess supply? Describe the process that eliminates excess supply.
3. Use supply and demand to explain excess demand. What might cause excess demand? Describe the process that eliminates excess demand.

Explain how equilibrium changes in the market.
4. Carefully distinguish between a change in demand and a change in the quantity demanded.
5. What three factors can cause a change in demand? What factor can cause a change in the quantity demanded?
6. Carefully distinguish between a change in supply and a change in the quantity supplied.
7. What factors can cause a change in supply? What causes a change in the quantity supplied?
8. Draw a simple supply and demand curve diagram for coffee. Assume that incomes of consumer are rising. What happens to demand and supply? What happens to equilibrium price and quantity?
9. Assume that for some reason the coffee price in the previous question is above the equilibrium price. What pressures would cause this market to tend toward equilibrium?
10. Assume that the price of coffee is below equilibrium. What pressures would cause this market to tend toward equilibrium?
11. Suppose that the market for wooden Number 2 lead pencils is in equilibrium. Determine how the following shocks will affect the equilibrium price and quantity. Draw a graph to illustrate each of your answers.
    a. Professors begin to require ink on all exams.
    b. The price of lead increases.
    c. School attendance falls.
    d. Legislation restricts lumber harvests.
    e. Pencil makers receive a large wage increase.
    f. The price of ballpoint pens falls.
12. Suppose that the market for PC laptop computers is in equilibrium. Determine how the following shocks will affect the equilibrium price and quantity. Draw a fully labeled demand and supply curve diagram to illustrate each of your answers.
    a. Computers become easier to use.
    b. The price of memory chips falls.
    c. Software prices fall.
    d. All college students are required to own personal computers.
    e. The price of electricity rises substantially.
    f. Doctors warn of health risks from radiation from video terminals.

APPENDIX 27.2
ELASTICITY

Elasticity is a measure of responsiveness: the responsiveness of consumers and producers to a change in the prices of their products, the responsiveness of consumers to a change in income or to the change of prices of other goods. Knowledge of price elasticity is useful in several ways. For example, firms know that when they raise their selling price, the quantity they sell usually falls. The question is how much? What will happen to total revenue? Policymakers often need to compute elasticity as well. For example, a gasoline tax increase may be intended as a conservation measure to reduce gasoline usage, but without knowing how much quantity demanded will fall due to a price increase, it is impossible to determine how much to increase taxes.

LEARNING OBJECTIVES FOR APPENDIX 27.2

After reading and studying this chapter, you should be able to:

- Define and calculate price elasticities of demand and supply and give examples how they are used by businesses and government.
- Show the relationship between price elasticity of demand and total revenue and how this relationship is important to firms and policymakers.
- Define and calculate income elasticity and give examples of how it is used.
- Define and calculate cross-price elasticity and give examples of how it is used.
- Explain the limitations of elasticity (price, income, and cross-price).

ELASTICITY: BASIC CONCEPTS AND COMPUTATIONS

Elasticity is used in several contexts in economics, but the most common usage is the price elasticity of demand. The **price elasticity of demand** tells how much quantity demanded responds to a change in its "own-price." It is defined as *the percentage change in quantity demanded divided by the percentage change in its own-price.* In this appendix, we frequently must distinguish between the price of the good under consideration and the prices of related goods, so we use the term *own-price* when appropriate to avoid confusion. We can get an idea about elasticity by looking at the two demand curves in Figure 27.10 and seeing what happens when own-price falls from $6 to $5.

On the relatively steep demand curve D_1, the quantity demanded rises by only ten units, from forty to fifty units. On the relatively flat demand curve D_2, the quantity demanded doubles from forty to eighty units. Economists would say that demand curve D_1 is inelastic relative to demand curve D_2. The term *inelastic* indicates that a change in price results in a relatively small quantity response. Consumers do not respond much to a change in price. It means the same thing to say that demand curve D_2 is elastic relative to demand curve D_1. D_2 indicates that a change in price results in a relatively larger quantity response along D_2 than along D_1. Consumers on D_2 are very sensitive to a change in the price of that good.

Before we go a word further, we need to dispel a common confusion. Elasticity is not the same thing as slope. It is true that there is less of a change in the quantity demanded along D_1 than along D_2, so it is correct to say that D_1 is inelastic relative to D_2, at least over the region illustrated in Figure 27.10. However, we should not confuse slope with elasticity. Remember that slope is simply the rise over the run. We see in Figure 27.10 that along D_1, as price decreases by one, the quantity increases by ten. Thus, the slope is a negative 1/10. Since it is a straight line, the slope

Figure 27.10 **Elastic and Inelastic Demand Curves**

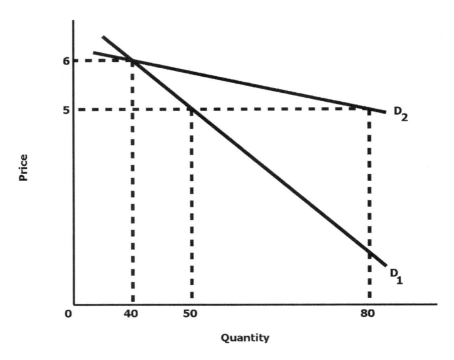

As price falls from $6 to $5, the quantity demanded along demand curve D_1 rises from forty to fifty units; along demand curve D_2, quantity demanded rises a larger amount, from forty to eighty units. This means that D_1 is inelastic relative to demand curve D_2 over this region.

is a negative 1/10 anywhere on that line. You should be able to see that the slope of D_2 is a negative 1/40 for the same reason. In contrast, remember that elasticity is the percentage change in quantity demanded over the percentage change in price. Thus, the elasticity of a straight demand curve, unlike slope, changes everywhere along the curve. This is why we must be able to actually compute elasticity and understand the factors that influence them.

Price Elasticity of Demand

The price elasticity of demand, E_p, is measured as the percentage change in quantity demanded divided by the percentage change in own-price. The changes in the price (denominator) drive the change in quantity demanded (numerator). The formula for the price elasticity of demand is:

$$E_p = \frac{\text{percentage change in quantity demanded}}{\text{percentage change in price}}$$

This equation is of little use if you do not remember how to calculate percentage changes, but that is simple enough to do. The percentage change in a variable is computed as the change in the variable divided by the variable itself. The price elasticity of demand, E_p, is given by the following formula:

$$E_P = \left| \frac{\dfrac{\Delta Q}{Q_0}}{\dfrac{\Delta P}{P_0}} \right|$$

where:

ΔQ = change in quantity (i.e., $Q_1 - Q_2$)
Q_0 = the midpoint between Q_1 and Q_2
ΔP = change in price (i.e., $P_1 - P_2$)
P_0 = the midpoint between P_1 and P_2

We must make some comments about this formula before we are ready to apply it. First, the two vertical bars indicate that we need to take the absolute value of the fraction inside the bars. The absolute value of a negative number eliminates the minus sign but has no effect on a positive number. For example, $|-5| = 5$; $|+5| = 5$. This means that the price elasticity of demand is always a positive number. The reason for working with absolute values is that it is much easier to compare values of positive numbers than values of negative numbers.

Second, we use the midpoints of P and Q because elasticity changes over the demand curve. Price elasticity depends on whether low or high values of P and Q are used in the computation. As we show below, the quantity and price midpoints are found by adding the two points together and dividing by two: $Q_0 = (Q_1 + Q_2)/2$ and $P_0 = (P_1 + P_2)/2$

RANGES OF PRICE ELASTICITY OF DEMAND

Economists use the calculations to find out the price elasticity of demand or responsiveness of consumers to a change in price. We can use the results of the calculations to group elasticity into ranges. Demand is considered **inelastic** if *the price elasticity of demand is less than one*. What this means is that the percentage change in demand is less than the percentage change in price. In plain English, consumers are not responsive to a change in the price of that good. Prices can change a lot but the quantity demanded of that product changes very little.

Demand is considered **elastic** if *the price elasticity of demand is greater than one*. This means that the percentage change in quantity demanded was much larger than the percentage change in the price. Consumers are very sensitive to a change in the price of that good. The third case is if *price elasticity of demand equals one or the percentage change in price is the same as the percentage change in quantity demanded*. This is called **unit elastic**.

Determinants of Price Elasticity of Demand

Several factors influence price elasticity of demand or how sensitive consumers are to a change in price, but perhaps the most important one is the availability of substitutes. For example, gasoline has few good substitutes, because most cars run on gasoline and nothing else. This suggests that the demand for gasoline is probably inelastic because a change in the price of gasoline ordinarily has only a small effect on the quantity of gasoline demanded, at least in the short run. On the other hand, the demand for fast-food hamburgers is relatively elastic. MacDonald's Big Mac, Burger King's Whopper, and Wendy's Dave's Deluxe are comparable products to most people, so if MacDonald's raised the price of a Big Mac, many people would just go down the street for a Whopper.

Other factors influence the elasticity of demand as well. The demand for goods that are considered necessities is usually inelastic. People may grumble at a price hike, but there is little they can do other than pay the price if the good is truly a necessity. Insulin is a good with very inelastic demand. Most diabetics would buy insulin even if the price were to double or quadruple. On the other hand, luxury goods often exhibit elastic demand. Häagen-Dazs ice cream is great stuff, but if the company raises the price too much, you might have to make do with Ben and Jerry's.

The price of the good relative to the size of the consumer's budget can also influence elasticity. For example, an increase in the price of chewing gum from 25¢ a pack to 50¢ a pack would go unnoticed by most people because an extra 25¢ does not mean much if your grocery store bill is $50 per week. But to the 8-year-old on a dollar-a-week allowance, the same price hike would definitely be cause for alarm and probably a lower quantity demanded.

Finally, elasticity varies over time because people can usually find better substitutes in the long run than in the short run. If the price of heating oil rises, there will be only a little decline in the quantity of heating oil demanded in the short run, but over the long run, people will find sweaters more fashionable, insulate their homes, switch to electric heating or natural gas, or even move to smaller houses.

Before going on, we need to qualify much of the foregoing. We just said that the demand for gasoline is inelastic because there are few good substitutes for gasoline. An increase in the price of gasoline from $2.00 to $2.05 a gallon would have very little effect on the quantity demanded for gasoline. But what if the price of gasoline were to suddenly increase to $10 a gallon? The same people would find substitutes rather quickly. Car-pooling would become more popular, as would walking and bicycles. What does this mean? In general, demand is more elastic at high prices than at low prices. Remember that we said that elasticity is not the same thing as slope. Demand for all goods is elastic at higher prices on the demand curve and inelastic at lower prices on the demand curve. There is no single answer to just how high is "high" and how low is "low" when it comes to elasticity.

Let's do some calculations based on the demand curve in Figure 27.11 to show how to use the price elasticity of demand formula. First, let's calculate elasticity as price rises from $6 to $8. When price rises over this region, the quantity demanded falls from two units to one unit. Substituting these values into the previous equation gives:

$$E_P = \left| \frac{\frac{\Delta Q}{Q_0}}{\frac{\Delta P}{P_0}} \right| = \left| \frac{\frac{Q_1 - Q_2}{(Q_1 + Q_2)/2}}{\frac{P_1 - P_2}{(P_1 + P_2)/2}} \right| = \left| \frac{\frac{2-1}{(2+1)/2}}{\frac{6-8}{(6+8)/2}} \right| = \left| \frac{\frac{1}{3/2}}{\frac{-2}{7}} \right| = \left| \left(\frac{2}{3}\right)\left(\frac{7}{2}\right) \right|$$

$= 2.33 > 1.$

The result implies **elastic demand**.

What does this answer mean? As price rises from $6 to $8, the percentage change in the quantity demanded is 2.33 times as large as the percentage change in price. This means that the quantity demanded is highly responsive to price changes.

Look what happens when we calculate the elasticity over a different price range, say as the

Figure 27.11   **Price Elasticity of Demand**

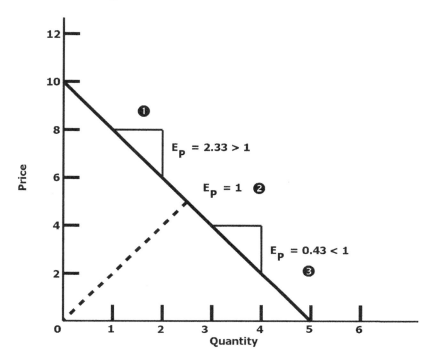

1. High prices = elastic demand
2. Midpoint = unitary elasticity
3. Low prices = inelastic demand
Every linear demand curve has regions of elastic, inelastic, and unitary demand. At high prices, people can almost always find a substitute; this is the region of elastic demand, $E_p > 1$. At low prices, people may not even look for substitutes; this is the region of inelastic demand, $E_p < 1$. The midpoint of the demand curve has unitary elasticity, $E_p = 1$.

price rises from \$2 to \$4. In this case, the quantity demanded falls from four to three units, so the calculations are:

$$E_P = \left| \frac{\dfrac{Q_1 - Q_2}{(Q_1 + Q_2)/2}}{\dfrac{P_1 - P_2}{(P_1 + P_2)/2}} \right| = \left| \frac{\dfrac{4-3}{(4+3)/2}}{\dfrac{2-4}{(2+4)/2}} \right| = \left| \frac{\dfrac{1}{7/2}}{\dfrac{-2}{3}} \right| = \left| \left(\frac{2}{7} \right) \left(\frac{3}{-2} \right) \right| = \frac{6}{14}$$

$= 0.43 < 1$

The result implies **inelastic demand**.

In other words, as price rises from \$2 to \$4, the percentage change in the quantity demanded is less than half as large as the percentage change in price. Remember that when elasticity is less than one, demand is said to be inelastic. This means that the quantity demanded is relatively unresponsive to price changes.

Finally, *the midpoint of a linear demand curve always has an elasticity coefficient equal to one*; this is the point of **unitary elasticity**. This can be verified by calculating the elasticity coefficient as price changes from $4 to $6. As price rises from $4 to $6, the quantity demanded falls from three to two, so the elasticity coefficient is:

$$E_P = \left| \frac{\dfrac{3-2}{2.5}}{\dfrac{4-6}{5}} \right|$$

$= 1.$

The result implies unitary elasticity.

A unitary elasticity coefficient means that the percentage change in quantity demanded is equal to the percentage change in price.

Special Cases

There are three special cases we must examine: vertical demand curves, horizontal demand curves, and nonlinear demand curves.

Vertical Demand Curves

A vertical demand curve means that there is no change in the quantity demanded regardless of the change in price. Demand for this good is considered **perfectly inelastic**. Few goods exhibit this characteristic in the real world, but we can imagine a good with no substitutes at all as having a demand curve that is almost vertical. The demand curve for a diabetic's insulin may be almost vertical. A vertical demand curve is perfectly inelastic and has a zero elasticity because the ΔQ in the numerator of the elasticity equation equals zero. A perfectly inelastic demand curve is shown in panel (a) of Figure 27.12.

Horizontal Demand Curves

An all-purpose good might have a horizontal demand curve. Why? If the good is truly all-purpose, it can be used as a substitute for every other good. In this situation, *even a tiny decline in price would cause people to purchase more of the good to be used as a substitute for some other good.* Are there any examples of all-purpose goods? Perhaps not, but there are goods that are perfect substitutes for some other goods. For example, you should not care whether the wheat you buy is from Farmer Brown or Farmer Smith. Smith's wheat is a perfect substitute for Brown's wheat. If Farmer Smith raised the price of wheat by even a penny, you'd give your business to Farmer Brown. *When the demand curve is perfectly horizontal*, it is said to be **perfectly elastic** and the elasticity approaches infinity. A perfectly elastic demand curve is shown in panel (b) of Figure 27.12.

Nonlinear Demand Curves

Demand curves are often nonlinear, and in such cases it is difficult to calculate elasticity coefficients without calculus. Nevertheless, the general results we have just developed still apply. At relatively high prices, elasticity tends to be high, and at relatively low prices, elasticity tends to be low; and there may be a region of unitary elasticity in between. However, it is possible for nonlinear demand

Figure 27.12 **Special Cases of Demand Elasticity**

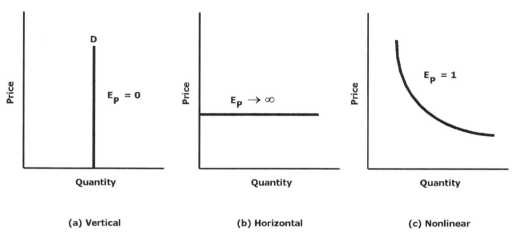

(a) Vertical   **(b) Horizontal**   **(c) Nonlinear**

The demand curve is vertical if there are no substitutes; this results in an elasticity coefficient of 0, as shown in panel (a). The demand curve is horizontal if the good is an all-purpose good or if there are perfect substitutes; this results in an elasticity coefficient that is undefined but approaches infinity. This is shown in panel (b). No set rule governs the elasticity coefficient of a nonlinear demand curve. One possibility is a rectangular hyperbola that has constant unitary elasticity, as shown in panel (c).

curves to have a constant elasticity over the entire curve. This occurs when the demand curve is a rectangular hyperbola. A rectangular hyperbola is shown in panel (c) of Figure 27.12.

Elasticity of Supply

It is also possible to compute the price elasticity of supply. The **price elasticity of supply** *measures the relative responsiveness of the quantity supplied to the change in price.* The formula for supply elasticity is shown here:

Elasticity of Supply = $\dfrac{\text{percentage change in quantity supplied}}{\text{percentage change in price.}}$

We could also write this formula as

$$\frac{\Delta Qs/Qs_0}{\Delta P/P_0}$$

Supply elasticity depends on several factors, but time and technological constraints are probably the most important. In the instantaneous period (the very short run), the supply curve is vertical because all production has already taken place. This means that supply is perfectly price inelastic in the market period. In the short run, the supply curve is upward sloping because firms respond to price increases by raising output. In the long run, elasticity is higher because firms have the ability to build new plants or increase the size of existing facilities.

Figure 27.13 **Supply Elasticity**

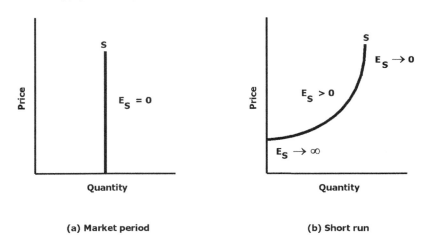

(a) Market period   (b) Short run

Time affects supply elasticity. In the market period, all production has taken place, so there can be no quantity response to a change in price. This gives a zero elasticity of supply. In the short run, elasticity varies depending on plant capacity. If the firm is operating with unused capacity, output can vary considerably with only a small price incentive. As output approaches plant capacity, even a large price change cannot elicit a significant output response because of technical limitations. In the long run, firms can expand capacity and increase output. In general, elasticity is higher in the long run than in the short run.

Figure 27.13 illustrates supply elasticity in the market period and the short run. Quantity is fixed on the vertical market period supply curve, so the ΔQ in the numerator of the equation equals zero. This gives an elasticity of zero as well. The short-run supply curve on the right (panel b) shows that supply elasticity depends on plant capacity. When output is considerably less than capacity, the supply curve is relatively flat, so supply elasticity is very high. As output expands, the supply curve gets steeper and the elasticity coefficient declines until the firm is faced with technical constraints on production. At this point, output cannot expand (in the short run) regardless of the change in price, so the elasticity coefficient approaches zero.

What about a diagram of the long run? As a rule of thumb, economists presume that the longer the time period considered, the more elastic the supply curve. As time increases, the E_s approaches infinity.

Elasticity and Total Revenue

One of the most important applications of elasticity concerns the concept of total revenue. **Total revenue** is *the entire amount of money that a firm receives from selling a product*. It is calculated as the selling price multiplied by the quantity sold, or Total Revenue = Price × Quantity. Firms are vitally interested in their total revenue. If total revenue exceeds the total costs of production, the firm has profits, which can be used for expansion. If total revenue is less than production costs, the firm loses money and may face bankruptcy. As prices change, the quantity sold changes, and this usually changes total revenue. To understand how much total revenue changes, and whether it rises or falls in response to a price change, the firm must understand price elasticity of demand.

Total revenue falls if price is increased when demand is elastic. Why? When demand is elastic, the relative change in quantity demanded is greater than the relative change in price. Price rises a little bit, quantity demanded drops a lot. That means that total revenue, or *PQ*, declines. A price cut, however, will increase total revenue when demand is elastic because the change in quantity demanded is enough to offset the losses from a lower price. In other words, if a business knows that demand for their product is elastic, they will make more money by dropping the price!

The reverse happens when demand is inelastic. The relative change in quantity demanded is less than the relative change in price, so price hikes increase total revenue and price cuts decrease total revenue. If the business owner knows demand for their product is inelastic, they can increase their total revenue by increasing the price since consumers have no other choice but to purchase their product.

Other Kinds of Elasticity

So far, we have discussed only one kind of elasticity, the price elasticity of demand. This may be the most important kind of elasticity, but it is not the only application of the elasticity concept that economists find useful. Three other applications include income elasticity, cross-price elasticity, and the elasticity of supply.

Income elasticity *measures the relative responsiveness of a change in demand to a change in income. It is defined as the percentage change in demand divided by the percentage change in income.*

$$\text{Income Elasticity:} \quad E_Y = \frac{\dfrac{\Delta Q}{Q_0}}{\dfrac{\Delta Y}{Y_0}}$$

% change in quantity demanded
% change in consumer income

where *Y* stands for income and *Q* is the quantity that will be purchased at different income levels. For example, if your income rose from $1,000 to $1,100 per month and you increased your trips to the movie theater from once a month to twice a month, your income elasticity of demand would be:

$$E_Y = \frac{\dfrac{\Delta Q}{Q_0}}{\dfrac{\Delta Y}{Y_0}} = \frac{\dfrac{2-1}{1.5}}{\dfrac{1,100-1,000}{1,050}} = 7$$

We need to make a few comments about this formula. First, unlike the equation for own-price elasticity, there are no absolute value bars. This is because we need to know the sign of the income elasticity coefficient. For example, an increase in income will result in an increase in demand for normal goods, but it will cause a decrease in the demand for inferior goods.

Normal goods are *goods whose consumption increases when income increases.* **Inferior goods** are *goods that people would prefer not to consume and only do so because of their low* *income. As income rises, the quantity demanded of inferior goods falls.* For normal goods, the income elasticity is positive, but what determines whether it is "large" or "small"? One of the main factors is whether the good is considered a luxury or a necessity. A **luxury good** *has an income elasticity of greater than one.* For example, the income elasticity of demand for automobiles has been estimated to be about 1.2; it is almost 6 for airline travel. High-income elasticity is one reason the airline industry offers huge fare discounts during recessions—when people's incomes fall, they cut back on luxuries like vacation air travel. The income elasticity of demand for restaurant meals (almost 2) is considerably higher than the income elasticity of demand for grocery store food, which is under 1. This is probably because most people consider restaurant meals to be luxury items, whereas they view food from the grocery store to be an essential purchase.

A **necessity good** is *a normal good with an income elasticity of demand of less than one.* It may be surprising to learn that the income elasticity of demand for alcoholic beverages is less than 1. This is an apparent indication that people maintain relatively stable consumption of alcoholic beverages despite relatively large changes in income. This suggests that many drinkers consider alcohol essential, or that there are no good substitutes for alcoholic beverages. In short, when consumer incomes increase, the demand for necessities increases. However, demand for luxury goods increases even faster. The same is true in reverse. When incomes fall, the demand for luxury goods falls most rapidly, and the demand for necessities decreases at a slower rate.

Cross-Price Elasticity

Cross-price elasticity *measures the relative responsiveness of the demand for one good to the relative price change of another good.* It is computed by

$$Ex,y = \frac{\text{percentage change in the quantity demanded of good Y}}{\text{percentage change in the price of good X}}$$

As with income elasticity, there are no absolute value bars on the formula for cross-price elasticity. This is to distinguish between complementary and substitute goods. **Complementary goods** are *goods that are typically consumed together and characterized by a positive cross-price elasticity of demand.* For instance, if a decrease in the price of hot dogs causes an increase in the demand for hot dog buns, then these two goods are complements. Similarly, **substitute goods** are *goods that can be used interchangeably and are characterized by a negative cross-price elasticity of demand.* For example, an increase in the price of Coca-Cola would lead to an increase in the demand for Pepsi. In short, cross-price elasticity is positive for substitute goods and negative for complementary goods. A cross-price elasticity coefficient of zero indicates that the two goods are unrelated.

Shortcomings

The four different elasticity notions as explained in this appendix have been shown to theoretically serve as useful analytical tools. However, in the real world of market research, theoretical ideas are plagued by fundamental shortcomings in the data available to researchers. One simple hypothetical example illustrates this problem.

Imagine for a moment that you know that price and quantity sold of a particular brand of DVD player in a particular city for a specific year were as follows:

Year	2006	2007	2008
Price	$ 150	$ 100	$ 75
Quantity	2,000	3,000	4,000

If you were to plot these points in price and quantity space, what would you have? The figure seems to be downward sloping and thus looks like a demand curve. Could it be a downward sloping supply curve? Could it be both?

Unfortunately, what we most likely have are the price and quantity intersections of three different sets of supply and demand curves. This creates what economists call an **identification problem**. *The data available cannot be identified as being on either a single demand or supply curve.* We could *assume* that this is a demand curve and that three supply changes caused the change in price. This assumption would allow us to compute our price elasticity of demand, but it would prevent us from saying anything about the elasticity of supply, since there would be three supply curves. Similarly, we could *assume* that this is a supply curve, but then we would have three different demand curves and be unable to say anything about price elasticity of demand. Either of these solutions is less than satisfying, since, most likely, both demand and supply are moving simultaneously. We lack either the stable supply curve or stable demand curve along which we could compute price elasticity.

This problem is compounded for cross-price elasticity. Instead of just looking at the prices and quantities of one good, like DVD players, we would be looking at two different goods, such as the price of DVD players and the demand for DVDs of the movie *King Kong*. Although elasticity has the theoretical potential to inform and guide management and policy decisions, we must also be wary of the real-world empirical data on which elasticity is calculated.

SUMMARY OF APPENDIX 27.2

The central ideas from this chapter are:

1. The price elasticity of demand is a measure of relative responsiveness of the quantity demanded to a change in own-price. Factors that influence price elasticity of demand are the availability of substitutes, whether the good is a luxury or a necessity, and the price of the good relative to the consumer's income.
2. The formula for computing own-price elasticity is

$$E_p = \frac{\text{percentage change in quantity demanded}}{\text{percentage change in price}}$$

In algebraic terms, this is equal to

$$E_P = \left| \frac{\frac{\Delta Q}{Q_0}}{\frac{\Delta P}{P_0}} \right|$$

where:

$\Delta Q =$ change in quantity (i.e., $Q_1 - Q_2$)
$Q_0 =$ the midpoint between Q_1 and Q_2
$\Delta P =$ change in price (i.e., $P_1 - P_2$)
$P_0 =$ the midpoint between P_1 and P_2

3. If the percentage change in price is less than the percentage change in quantity demanded, price elasticity of demand is greater than one and is elastic. If the percentage change in price is more than the percentage change in quantity demanded, price elasticity of demand is less than one and is inelastic. If the percentage change in price is equal to the percentage change in quantity demanded, price elasticity of demand is equal to one and is unitary elastic.

4. All downward-sloping linear demand curves have elastic, inelastic, and unitary elastic portions. Demand is elastic at high prices, inelastic at low prices, and unitary at the midpoint. Vertical demand curves are perfectly inelastic; horizontal demand curves are perfectly elastic.

5. Supply elasticity is a measure of the relative change in quantity supplied to the change in price. Supply is usually more elastic in the long run than in the short run.
The formula for computing the price elasticity of supply is

$$\frac{\Delta Qs/Qs_0}{\Delta P/P_0} \quad \text{or} \quad \frac{\% \text{ change in quantity supplied}}{\% \text{ change in price}}$$

6. When demand is elastic, an increase in price reduces total revenue and a decrease in price raises total revenue. When demand is inelastic, an increase in price increases total revenue and a decrease in price decreases total revenue. When demand is unitary elastic, a change in price does not change total revenue.

7. Income elasticity is a measure of the percentage change in demand relative to the percentage change in income.

8. The formula for computing income elasticity is

$$\frac{\Delta Q/Q_0}{\Delta Y/Y_0} \quad \text{or} \quad \frac{\% \text{ change in quantity demanded}}{\% \text{ change in consumer income}}$$

9. If demand increases as income rises, then the good in question is normal. If demand falls as income rises, then the good is inferior. Normal goods with income elasticity coefficients of one or more are luxury goods. Normal goods with income elasticities of less than one are necessities.

10. Cross-price elasticity is a measure of how responsive the demand for one good is relative to the change in the price of another good. The coefficient for cross-price elasticity is positive for substitute goods and negative for complementary goods.

11. Elasticities can be useful theoretical notions. However, in the world of market research, generating an elasticity estimate is plagued by a variety of empirical issues, the identification problem being one of the most difficult.

KEY TERMS FOR APPENDIX 27.2

complementary goods

cross-price elasticity

elastic demand

identification problem

income elasticity

inelastic demand

inferior goods

luxury goods

necessity goods

normal goods

perfectly elastic

perfectly inelastic

price elasticity of demand

price elasticity of supply

substitute goods

total revenue

unitary elasticity

REVIEW QUESTIONS FOR APPENDIX 27.2

Understand price elasticities of demand and supply and how they are used.

1. What does the measure of price elasticity try to capture? Why might this measure be useful information?

2. What are the main determinants of price elasticity of demand? What are the main determinants of price elasticity of supply?

3. How is price elasticity of demand calculated? Why do we use absolute values for price elasticity of demand?

4. How is price elasticity of supply calculated?

5. Explain why all downward-sloping linear demand curves have elastic, inelastic, and unitary elastic regions.

6. What is the difference between elasticity and slope?

7. Suppose that the demand schedule is given as:

   i. Q   20   22   24   26   28   30   32   34

   ii. P $70   60   50   40   30   20   10   0

   a. Graph this data and find the vertical intercept. Assume the demand curve is everywhere linear.

   b. Calculate an elasticity coefficient in the inelastic range of the demand curve.

   c. Calculate an elasticity coefficient in the elastic range of the demand curve.

   d. Find the point of unitary elasticity.

   e. Find the point of maximum total revenue. What is the maximum total revenue at that point?

8. Suppose that a supply curve is given as:

   i. Q   30   28   26   24   22   20

   ii. P $60   50   40   30   20   10

   a. Graph this data.

   b. Calculate an elasticity of supply coefficient.

Show the relationship between price elasticity of demand and total revenue and how this relationship is important to firms and policymakers.

9. How are total revenue and price elasticity of demand related?

10. Would a firm planning a price increase be better off if the demand for its product was elastic or inelastic? Explain.

11. As manager of the Eagle Crest Ski Resort and Lodge, you announce an increase in the price of lift tickets from $35 to $50. The number of skiers falls, but your total revenue increases.
    a. What does this say about the elasticity of demand for lift tickets? Should you raise ticket prices even more?
    b. Your friend, an avid skier and economics major—but in no way affiliated with the ski lodge—says she is actually happy that you raised the ticket prices. How could she think such a thing?

12. Use price elasticity to explain the following observations:
    a. The price of gasoline is higher near the freeway than at a gas station two miles off the freeway.
    b. Airline tickets are less expensive if purchased a month before you plan to fly than if purchased one day before you plan to fly.
    c. Prices in grocery stores in low-income areas of town might actually be higher than in a more affluent area of town.

Calculate and explain the use of income elasticity.

13. What is income elasticity? What is it used to measure?
14. Use income elasticity to explain the differences between normal, inferior, luxury, and necessity goods.
15. Look at each of the following pairs and discuss which component has a higher price and income elasticity. Briefly explain your answer.
    a. movies/taxi cabs
    b. tobacco/gasoline
    c. electricity/water
    d. mobile phone service/clothing
    e. intercity busses/doctor's services

Define cross-price elasticity and show how it is used to define necessity and luxury goods.

16. What is a complement and what is a substitute good? Give examples of goods that are complements and goods that are substitutes.
17. What is cross-price elasticity? What is the formula for calculating cross-price elasticity?
18. Using cross-price elasticity, how is it determined whether a good is a complement or substitute?

Explain the limitations of elasticity (demand, supply, income, and cross-price).

19. What are some problems with measuring the various types of elasticities?
20. Explain the "identification problem."

CHAPTER 28

Consumption Theory: Demand

In this chapter, we continue our exploration of neoclassical microeconomics by introducing the traditional approach to consumer decisions. In a sense, you already know the conclusion of this story. It ends with the demand curve that you already mastered in the last two chapters. The primary goal of this chapter is to explain the assumptions underlying the individual demand curve. Knowing the assumptions is important in understanding, predicting, and explaining consumer decision making. Next, the chapter presents a brief critique of utility theory. In the appendix to this chapter, a little algebra is used to demonstrate how the assumptions of consumer theory lead directly to the derivation of a demand curve.

LEARNING OBJECTIVES

After reading this chapter, you should be able to:

- Explain the assumptions made about consumers and households used to build utility theory.
- Define and explain how utility, total utility, and diminishing marginal utility are used to build the demand curve.
- Explain how consumers maximize their utility (joy) within the bounds of their income.
- Discuss the criticisms of the assumptions of neoclassical consumer theory.

THE FOUNDATIONS OF UTILITY ANALYSIS

As we learned in Part I, neoclassical economics arose in the 1870s when British economist William Stanley Jevons (1835–1882), Austrian economist Karl Menger (1841–1921), and French economist Leon Walras (1834–1910), introduced similar theories explaining why consumers behave as they do. These ideas were further refined and popularized by Alfred Marshall (1842–1924). Marshall published a famous *Principles of Political Economy* in 1890 that remained the bible of economics for a whole generation.

All four of these theorists were building on the ideas of a philosopher named Jeremy Bentham. He is often credited as the father of utilitarianism. Bentham (1748–1832) asserted that "nature has placed mankind under the governance of two sovereign masters, pain and pleasure. It is for them alone to point out what we ought to do, as well as to determine what we shall do." In short, Bentham and most traditional economists assume that people pursue pleasure and avoid pain in a quest to maximize their happiness. This philosophical position is one of the five key ideas on which traditional consumer theory rests. The next section briefly lists and then more fully explains each of these five foundational assumptions.

ASSUMPTIONS OF TRADITIONAL CONSUMER THEORY

1. Consumers are rational. They carefully weigh costs and benefits (pain and pleasure) before making their decisions. Consumers possess perfect information about the goods and services they wish to purchase as well as the price of all goods.
2. Pleasure or satisfaction can be expressed in measurable terms of utility (pleasure or joy). **Utility** refers to *the satisfaction derived from consuming a good or service.*
3. Consumers have limited incomes, and resources are scarce.
4. **Diminishing marginal utility** characterizes most consumption situations. *As more units of an item are consumed, beyond some point the marginal utility (the incremental increase in utility) falls.*
5. Despite diminishing marginal utility, more is better. Total utility increases as more units of a good are consumed.

At first glance, you may want to reject these assumptions as unrealistic, since they seem to reduce human decision making down to a mathematical calculation with little room for human passion, impulse, and manipulation by advertisers. Many progressive economists would agree with you. However, in defense of neoclassical economics, all theorizing in any discipline requires abstracting from reality. Human behavior is complex. We have to start somewhere. Neoclassical economists begin by assuming simplified human motives and by isolating individual variables. This simplification is done in an attempt to think clearly about the interrelationships among variables, particularly between price and the amount of a good purchased. To see how this process works, let us examine each of these assumptions in more detail.

Rationality and Perfect Information

Rationality from an economic perspective means that *consumers make purposeful choices based on their own self-interest.* People attempt to make themselves better off, or at least avoid being made any worse off, whenever they make an economic choice. This is not to say that consumers are purely selfish, but cultural, social, ethical, and political influences cannot be factored into an individual's decision-making process in this simple model. Also ruled out are actions unduly influenced by fleeting emotion, addiction, insanity, or immaturity, and otherwise impulsive actions. In short, rationality means that people have clear preferences and act on them in a logical manner. I may prefer a hamburger to a salad, and my wife may prefer a salad to a hamburger. The point is that we each know what we want, and this knowledge is reflected in our purchasing decisions. I order a bacon cheeseburger, she has a Caesar salad, and we both enjoy lunch.

Related to rationality is the notion that consumers possess all the information necessary to make smart consumer decisions. This requires that we assume buyers know what they like, know the quality of the goods offered in the marketplace, and know all of the prices of alternative goods. Now this may sound daunting. However, when you go to the grocery store, do you usually come home with goods that you like? If so, traditional economists would say that you made choices informed by your preferences, based on the prices listed on the store shelves, and based on some knowledge of the characteristics of those goods. Perhaps you learned about these goods from previous experience, a friend's recommendation, or from the information contained in television, radio, and newspaper advertising. In any case, regardless of its shortcomings, the assumption of rationality in a theoretical world of perfect information is one of the foundations on which contemporary demand theory is built.

Utility or Joy

Traditional economists assume that people want to be happy and that it is useful to talk about the pursuit of that happiness in terms of measurable units we call *utils,* or joy. When traditional economists discuss **cardinal utility**, they mean *the idea that the consumer satisfaction (utility or joy) received from a particular good can be numerically measured in countable units.* For instance, one slice of pizza may give me 30 utils, and a second may give me an additional 20 utils. Clearly, economists lack direct knowledge of one utility and have no way to directly measure cardinal utility. In most cases, economists only have access to **ordinal utility**, which is *the idea that consumers can rank consumption bundles but cannot precisely measure the quantity of utility with cardinal numbers.* We might know that a particular consumer prefers pizza to hamburgers and hamburgers to hot dogs. However, in the real world, we cannot measure exactly how much more joy is generated by a slice of pizza than by a hamburger.

Limited Income

The existence of scarcity is one of the key underpinnings of traditional economic theory. People have unlimited wants but limited or "scarce" means to achieve them. We all have preferences, but in the immortal words of the Rolling Stones, "You can't always get what you want." Instead, you buy what your income, previously acquired wealth, and/or credit card limit will allow. In capitalism, people who have income and wealth gained either from inheritance or work are able to buy the goods and services. Those who don't have wealth and income or access to credit don't get to buy goods and services. In the marketplace, a buyer must possess both the willingness and the ability to pay in order to make a purchase. For most of us, our wants far exceed our means.

Diminishing Marginal Utility

When traditional economists talk about utility, they often distinguish between total utility and marginal utility. **Total utility** *refers to the total amount of utility or joy one gets from consuming a good.* Related to this is **marginal utility**, *the change in satisfaction from consuming one more unit of a good.* One of Bentham's key insights, adopted by later theorists, is the idea that most consumption is characterized by diminishing marginal utility. This means that *other things* being equal, as the consumption of any item increases, the additional satisfaction (utility) derived from that item, at some point, declines. To develop this idea, the marginal utility theorists of the late nineteenth century assumed that utility could be measured on a cardinal scale. For example, if you buy a new sweater, you might get a great deal of satisfaction from it, say 100 utils. If you buy a second sweater, you will probably get less additional satisfaction, perhaps only 90 utils; a third sweater will give even less satisfaction, and so on. The point is that additional units of consumption, beyond some point, generate decreasing amounts of additional satisfaction. Even if we cannot exactly measure the changes in utility, we can rank our utility and say that the first sweater brought more joy than the second or third sweater.

At the limit, it is possible that additional units of consumption create **negative marginal utility**,

Table 28.1

Tabular Relationship Between Total and Marginal Utility

Q	TU	MU
0		100
1	100	90
2	190	80
3	270	50
4	320	10
5	330	0
6	330	−10
7	320	

or negative returns. This situation means that *as additional units of a good are consumed, not only does marginal utility decline, it becomes negative. If marginal utility becomes negative, total utility also declines.* Consumption in this range is ruled out by the assumption of rationality. We presume that consumers stop consuming when further consumption of a commodity is expected to make them worse off. Given the existence of obesity and alcohol abuse in America, we can see that this rationality assumption is sometimes violated.

More Is Better

As long as the consumer is not experiencing negative marginal utility, each additional sweater discussed earlier generates declining amounts of additional joy or utility, but total utility continues to increase. This is an important insight. What we are saying is that although marginal utility is declining, total utility continues to increase. However, it is increasing at a decreasing rate. This point is illustrated in Table 28.1 and Figure 28.1.

The Relationship Between Marginal and Total Utility

Imagine you are shopping for sweaters. The first sweater purchased generates 100 utils, the second generates 90, and the third generates 80. After two sweaters have been purchased, 190 units of total pleasure have been created. If a third sweater is purchased, total utils increase to 270. Table 28.1 and Figure 28.1 illustrate this relationship between marginal and total utility more clearly.

As a consumer buys more sweaters, total utility continues to increase, as shown on the left-hand side of the figure. However, it increases at a decreasing rate. This rate of change, the marginal utility, is illustrated on the right-hand pane of the figure. Saying that the rate of increase in total utility declines is another way of saying that marginal utility decreases.

As the number of sweaters purchased increases, the total number of utils (total utility, TU) continues to increase up to five sweaters, then declines. However, the rate of increase declines, the marginal utility diminishes, as more sweaters are purchased. Given this relationship, how many sweaters should this consumer purchase? To answer that question, we must put together the consumer's preferences with his or her income. In short, we will find that consumer will attempt to maximize utility subject to his or her budget constraint. This will occur when the marginal utility per dollar spent on one good is exactly equal to the marginal utility per dollar spent on another good. If you consume any other way, you are giving up some joy.

For those who wish to see more on utility maximization and how utility maximizing takes us

Figure 28.1 **The Graphical Relationship Between Total and Marginal Utility**

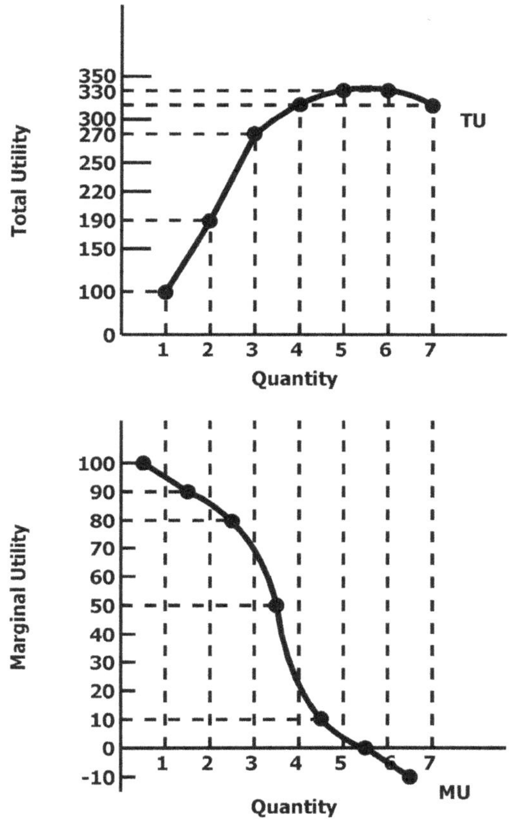

to an individual's demand curve, look at Appendix 28.1. This appendix is very useful for anyone going on to further courses in neoclassical economics.

PROGRESSIVE CRITICISM OF NEOCLASSICAL CONSUMPTION THEORY

There are many progressive criticisms of the neoclassical consumption theory. The theory is not based on any factual data about consumers but assumes that all consumers act in certain ways considered to be rational by the theory. It assumes that consumers have fixed preferences and that they always act in their own best self-interest by calculating the costs and utility or joy of each purchase. People may not always act in rational ways as assumed by the model. A rich man may buy a fur coat for his wife because he wants to show off his wealth, even though they live in Miami where it is usually too hot to wear a fur coat. *This kind of consumer spending merely to show one's high status* is called **conspicuous consumption** by the economist Thorstein Veblen.

The marginal utility theory has also been criticized for its notion that the only big problem of modern society is scarcity. As we saw in detail in Chapter 26, Robinson Crusoe had to worry about scarce food on his island. But the situation is different under the institutions of capitalism.

Many people do not have enough food to eat in America. But, unlike the assumptions of neoclassical consumption theory, the problem of poor people is not that food is scarce in some absolute sense. The problem is that they lack the money to buy food. There is plenty of food, but some people cannot afford it. During recessions, this problem goes beyond the long-term poor and is a problem for many more millions.

Neoclassical consumption theory is not a science in the way that biology and physics are sciences. Neoclassical economists cannot directly measure their basic assumptions about how people act. Yet these assumptions are assumed to be true of any group in any society. Each society has different cultural notions about what is preferable. For example, the French may prefer to eat snails, while other societies find snails unacceptable. People in prehistoric societies sitting in a cave with only certain foods available to them had entirely different notions about consumption preferences than do people in our present society. Rather than being born with certain consumer preferences for this or that, we acquire our preferences through our experiences in society. Our parents, friends, social groups, schools, religion, to name a few, are examples of social institutions that shape many of our consumer preferences.

Advertising also shapes many of our preferences. Advertising tries to convince us that a certain product is necessary to our love life, to our happiness in eating or sleeping, or even to our survival. Most advertising is not informative but convinces us to buy things we do and do not need. It also convinces us that one product is better than another when that is not always true. Movies and television are also advertising of a sort because they teach us to prefer this or that from watching what the media claim is reality. "I must have a swimming pool at my house because television shows every typical house with a swimming pool!" "Television shows houses that are spotlessly clean and that use all kinds of equipment and cleaning fluids. Therefore, I must have the latest equipment and cleaning fluids, no matter how expensive."

The truth about consumer preferences is the exact opposite of the neoclassical assumption that consumers are sovereign and determine what the economy shall produce. In many ways, through advertising and other means, business determines what consumers will prefer. One progressive author suggested that *the theory should change from the sequence of consumer preference to business production to the sequence of business produces and then gets consumers to buy it.* This has been called the **revised sequence** by economist John Kenneth Galbraith.

SUMMARY

Consumers make choices based on pleasure (utility) and pain (cost). They are rational, have all information, act in their own best self-interest, have limited incomes, prefer more rather than less, and the more they consume of an item, the less joy that item brings. From these basic assumptions, predictions are made about how consumers make decisions about what to buy given the limits of their budgets. The only problems are scarcity, limited incomes, and freedom of choice. The criticisms of progressive economists show the limitations of the traditional model of consumer behavior.

KEY TERMS

cardinal utility	ordinal utility
conspicuous consumption	rationality
diminishing marginal utility	revised sequence
marginal utility	total utility
negative marginal utility	utility

REVIEW QUESTIONS

Explain the assumptions made about consumers and households used to build utility theory.

1. List the assumptions that are used to build the traditional model of consumer demand.
2. What does it mean if a person is rational and making rational choices?
3. Why is income limited? Does everyone get to make the same choices? Why or why not?

Define and explain utility, total utility, and diminishing marginal utility.

4. What is the difference between ordinal and cardinal utility?
5. Why is it not possible to precisely measure utility or pleasure?
6. What is the difference between total and marginal utility?
7. What is the explanation for diminishing marginal utility? Give an example of diminishing marginal utility.
8. What happens to total utility even if there is diminishing marginal utility? Even if there is diminishing marginal utility, why is it assumed that people prefer more rather than less?

Explain how consumers maximize their utility (joy) within the bounds of their income.

9. Is it possible to consume goods until their marginal utility goes to zero? Why or why not?
10. What is the utility-maximizing condition? What does that mean in words?

Discuss the criticisms of the assumptions of neoclassical consumer theory.

11. Do people always behave in rational ways? Give an example.
12. What is conspicuous consumption? How is this type of decision not rational?
13. What is the difference between demand and effective demand or the ability to buy a good or service?
14. What factors might affect your preferences for different goods or services?
15. In general, is there scarcity in a capitalist system? Why or why not?
16. Consumer sovereignty says that households ultimately decide what businesses produce. How does advertising compromise the notion that households control what businesses do?

APPENDIX 28.1
UTILITY MAXIMIZATION AND THE DEMAND CURVE

The appendix further develops the neoclassical model of consumer behavior and explains how an individual's demand curve is derived from utility-maximizing behavior.

LEARNING OBJECTIVES FOR APPENDIX 28.1

After reading this appendix, you should be able to:

- Explain the conditions under which utility is maximized.
- Understand and demonstrate how the demand curve is derived.

Table 28.2

Marginal Utility of Apples

Quantity (in Pounds)	Marginal Utility of Apples (in Units of Utility)	Marginal Utility of Apples per Dollar (Price: $1)
1	12	12
2	11	11
3	10	10
4	9	9
5	8	8
6	7	7

MAXIMIZING UTILITY AND THE INDIVIDUAL DEMAND CURVE

Suppose that a consumer can spend income on only three commodities: apples, bread, and cake. It is then possible to determine the quantities of each to be bought in order to maximize utility. Utility will be maximized if the consumer buys the particular quantities of apples, bread, and cake that will leave the marginal utilities divided by the price (utility per dollar spent) the same:

$$\frac{\text{marginal utility of apples}}{\text{price of apples}} = \frac{\text{marginal utility of bread}}{\text{price of bread}} = \frac{\text{marginal utility of cake}}{\text{price of cake}}$$

The equality of these ratios means that utility is maximized when the last dollar spent on apples yields the same utility as the last dollar spent on bread and cake. A numerical example will help explain this principle, relying on Table 28.2.

Table 28.2 shows amounts of apples ranging from one pound to six pounds. The number of units of marginal utility for each pound of apples and the number of units of marginal utility per dollar for each pound of apples can be determined by reading across the table. Apples sell for $1.00 per unit. The same kinds of assumptions are stated for two additional goods, bread and cake, in Table 28.3. Of course, in reality, it is not so clear that each consumer exactly measures or knows how many units of subjective utility are obtained from each additional commodity. (Could you measure *exactly* the relative desire or utility to you of one more apple versus one more loaf of bread?)

Still, the theory does help demonstrate consumer behavior in a rough sort of way. Here, bread is priced at $2 per unit and cake costs $3 per unit. Now imagine that a consumer with an income of $24 buys six pounds of cake for $18, two pounds of bread for $4, and two pounds of apples for $2. The consumer has spent the entire $24 income but has not maximized utility. The ratios of marginal utility to price are not the same for three commodities. The ratios are as follows:

for apples: $\frac{11 \text{ units of utility}}{\$1}$ = 11 units of utility for last dollar

for bread: $\frac{22 \text{ units of utility}}{\$2}$ = 11 units of utility for last dollar

for cake: $\frac{15 \text{ units of utility}}{\$3}$ = 5 units of utility for last dollar

Table 28.3

Marginal Utility of Bread and Cake

Quantity (in Pounds)	Marginal Utility of Bread (in Units of Utility)	Marginal Utility of Bread per Dollar (Price: $2)	Marginal Utility of Cake (in Units of Utility)	Marginal Utility of Cake per Dollar (Price: $3)
1	24	12	30	10
2	22	11	27	9
3	20	10	24	8
4	18	9	21	7
5	16	8	18	6
6	14	7	15	5

The utility received from the last dollar spent on cake (5 units of utility) was considerably smaller than that of the last dollars spent on apples and bread (11 units each). Obviously, this individual's utility could be increased if some purchases were shifted from cake to either apples or bread.

If the consumer gives up three pounds of cake, 54 units of utility would be lost. However, $9 would be regained. This could be spent on apples and/or bread. With this $9, the consumer purchases three more pounds of apples (thereby gaining 27 units of utility) and three more pounds of bread (thereby gaining 54 units of utility). By shifting $9 worth of purchases from cake to apples and bread, the consumer gives up 54 units of utility and gains 81 units.

Obviously, the second bundle of goods has more utility than the first. If the units of utility in the first bundle are added, they total 204 (6 units from cake = 135; 2 units from bread = 46; and 2 units from apples = 23). The total number of units of utility in the second bundle is 231 (3 units from cake = 81; 5 units from bread = 100; and 5 units from apples = 50). The ratios of marginal utility to price for the three goods in the second bundle are as follows:

for apples: $\dfrac{8 \text{ units of utility}}{\$1}$ =   8 units of utility for last dollar

for bread: $\dfrac{16 \text{ units of utility}}{\$2}$ =   8 units of utility for last dollar

for cake: $\dfrac{24 \text{ units of utility}}{\$3}$ =   8 units of utility for last dollar

The utility-maximizing condition holds:

$$\frac{8}{\$1} = \frac{16}{\$2} = \frac{24}{\$3}$$

At this point of utility maximization, purchases cannot be shifted among the commodities any further without losing some utility. You should experiment with such shifts in order to be convinced that this is a maximum. With this information, it is now possible to demonstrate why demand curves slope downward and to the right, or why the quantity demanded increases as the price decreases.

Imagine an initial position at which all consumers are maximizing their utility—that is, they have equated the ratios of their marginal utilities and prices for all the goods. It is then possible to trace the effects of a decrease in price. If the price of one good, say apples, were to decrease, consumers would find that the utility received for the last dollar spent on apples would be higher than that received for the last dollar spent on other goods. Consumers would immediately shift some of their purchases from other goods to apples. Thus, the initial result of a decline in the price of apples is an increased quantity of apples demanded.

What determines exactly how much demand will shift to apples? Exactly how much will the demand for them increase when the price declines? That depends on their marginal utility (the desire for an additional apple) relative to the marginal utility of other goods (the desire for more bread and cake). As consumers buy more and more apples, their desire for an additional one declines because of the law of diminishing marginal utility. At the same time, consumers are buying less of all other goods (less bread and less cake). So the marginal utility of other goods rises; at the margin, their desire for an additional piece of bread or cake is now increased. The process of shifting demand from bread and cake to apples stops when an additional dollar spent for more apples (even at the new lower price) yields just the same marginal utility as that spent for bread or cake (even at their old, unchanged prices).

Consumer Sovereignty and the Dependency Effect

We have just said quite a bit about how people act to maximize utility given a variety of underlying assumptions. The question arises: Do consumer wants come from the consumer, or do advertising executives create them? Traditional economic theory holds that wants do come from within the consumer; that is, that consumer sovereignty ("consumer is king") prevails. Others believe that consumers can be swayed by advertisers to buy things they really do not want. The implications are important.

When you go to the store, you probably have a good idea about what you want to buy—but where did you get that idea? Would you have decided, on your own, that you wanted lights and pumps on your tennis shoes? That you wanted a salad shooter to chop, dice, and spray lettuce, cucumbers, and radishes into the bowl? If advertising induced you to buy something that you would not have bought otherwise, it is not clear that you—or society—actually benefited from the transaction. The result: your "voluntary" transaction did not result in mutual benefit. The seller gained, but you just bought something you were made to believe you really wanted.

REVIEW QUESTIONS FOR APPENDIX 28.1

Explain the conditions under which utility is maximized.

1. Explain what happens if the marginal utility of the last unit consumed divided by the price (bang per buck) is *not* the same. What are you giving up? Why?

Number of Cookies	Total Utility	Marginal Utility
0	0	—
1		20
2	37	
3	51	
4		11
5		8
6		5
7	77	
8		−1

2. Fill in the table above. Is the principle of diminishing marginal utility operative in this case? How do you know?

Understand and demonstrate how the demand curve is derived.

3. Can consumers dictate the prices they pay for products at the store? What can consumers do if the price of a product rises and their income is fixed? What role does the availability of substitutes play here?

4. If the price of a good goes up and throws the utility-maximizing pattern of consumption out of whack, what does utility theory predict the consumer will do?

5. Why does the marginal utility increase if the consumer purchases *less* of a product?

6. Explain how consumers reacting to changes in prices and attempting to keep at a utility-maximizing level of consumption leads to the relationship between price and quantity demanded.

CHAPTER 29

Production Theory
Supply

In this chapter, we continue our exploration of neoclassical microeconomics by introducing the traditional approach to producer decisions. In a sense, you already know the conclusion of this story. It ends with the supply curve that you already mastered earlier. The primary goal of this chapter is to explain the assumptions underlying the individual firm's supply curve. This chapter investigates and analyzes the relationship between the different factors of production. Understanding production and the costs of production (introduced in the next chapter) are important in understanding, predicting, and explaining producer decision making. Next, the chapter presents a brief critique of the neoclassical notion of production. In the appendix to this chapter, a little algebra is used to demonstrate the concepts introduced to explain production.

LEARNING OBJECTIVES

After reading and studying this chapter, you should be able to:

- Describe inputs into production and use the production function to illustrate the relationships among factors of production and technology.
- Explain the difference between production in the short run and production in the long run.
- Describe challenges faced by U.S. businesses as they make production decisions.
- Discuss the critiques of the neoclassical notion of production and factors of production.

THE PRODUCTION FUNCTION

When Henry Ford first started producing automobiles, most of his employees were skilled crafts people. He could not hire workers to just "tighten bolts" on the assembly line because the parts that went into the early Fords were not standardized. It took skill, time, and money to shape individual parts so that everything fit together. But Ford was an innovator. When he convinced his engineers to find a way to produce standardized parts, the wildly successful and inexpensive Model T was born. Ford's mass-production factory system transformed the face of society and the structure of business. He changed the production process from one that employed skilled workers using inexpensive tools and machines to one that combined unskilled workers with expensive and specialized machines. His engineers saw that this was possible, and Ford saw that it would be profitable. Today, human innovations and technological breakthroughs continue to reshape the world of work. Breakthroughs in communications, biotechnology, and other areas are rapidly changing how we work and where we work.

As the first step in analyzing production, we introduce a production function. A **production function** describes *the connection between the factors of production and output*. Traditional economics recognizes four broad categories or factors of production: land (or natural resources), labor, capital, and entrepreneurship. The factors of production are inputs into the production process. The owner of a firm, the entrepreneur, takes his or her idea, uses technology to combine the other factors of production, and produces a good or service to sell in the market. Therefore, a production function is just a statement, a kind of shorthand, of the relationship between the inputs and output. To make the production function manageable, we focus on capital, the plants and equipment used to make goods and services, and labor. Labor consists of the human beings that produce the good or service. Entrepreneurship and natural resources do not appear specifically but are present in the background. In general, the production function is:

(29.1) $$Q = f\,a(K, L)$$

where:
Q = total production of the firm
a = technology used to combine the factors of production
L = labor
K = capital (machinery)

The equation is a shorthand way of saying the output of the firm (Q) is a function (f) of capital (K) and labor (L) that are combined in a particular way (a).

Analysis is divided into production in the short run and production in the long run. The short run and the long run have no time periods attached to them. By definition, the **short run** is *the period of time when at least one of the firm's inputs is fixed*. In general, in the short-run capital and technology are considered fixed. For the purposes of our analysis, labor is considered the only variable input in the short run. The **long run** is *the period of time when a firm can change any or all of it inputs*. For some firms, it may only take days or a few weeks to change technology or bring in and start using new equipment. For other firms, it may take many years to change their capital and technology.

PRODUCTION IN THE SHORT RUN: THE LAW OF DIMINISHING RETURNS

The law of diminishing returns explains why we cannot grow all of the world's food supply in a flower pot. The law of diminishing returns applies to a short-run production function. Remember, the short run is a period of time when at least one input is fixed. In the examples that follow, we assume that all other factors of production and technology are fixed. Therefore, the firm can increase output only by hiring additional workers.

Now we are ready to state the law of diminishing returns. The law of diminishing returns is a statement of how output changes as additional inputs are added in the short run. The **law of diminishing returns** says that *if at least one input is fixed, output will eventually increase at a diminishing rate as additional units of inputs are added*. Does production always exhibit diminishing returns? Diminishing returns occur only after a certain point of production is reached. Notice the word *eventually* in the statement of the law of diminishing returns. Neoclassical economists claim that all production processes will eventually go through a stage of diminishing returns. They argue, however, that most production processes actually go through three stages of production, with diminishing returns occurring in only one stage.

The three stages of production result from the underlying assumption of **production in the short run**, in which *at least one factor of production is fixed, as additional units of variable factors are added*. Output will go through three stages: (1) increasing marginal returns, (2) diminishing marginal returns, and (3) negative marginal returns. Before we go through a numerical example to illustrate the three stages of production, we must make sure we are clear on the definition of the word *marginal*. As we found earlier, economists use marginal to indicate the incremental effect of the next unit, or what happens if "one more" is added. In the context of the production function, *marginal returns* refers to the additional output when one more unit of labor or one more worker is added to production. For example, if a tenth worker is hired and output rises from 1,000 to 1,050 units, the marginal return associated with the tenth worker is 50. The total return from all ten workers is 1,050.

Suppose we have an orchard of orange trees that is ready for harvesting. Unfortunately, the only tools we have are a fixed number of empty bushel baskets. The task is to hire workers to pick the oranges. One worker alone can hardly do the many tasks, which require coordinated effort to be efficient. One worker would be able to pick very few oranges and therefore have low productivity. Remember, productivity is a measure of output per unit of input. In this example, the productivity would be how many oranges are picked per worker. If five workers were hired, they could coordinate their activity, pick many more oranges, and productivity—oranges per worker—would increase. This would be increasing marginal returns. But if a thousand workers were hired, they would hardly fit in the orchard and would only get into each other's way, and they would have very low productivity per worker.

At some point, each additional worker hired would have lower and lower productivity. For a more thorough explanation of this neoclassical view of diminishing marginal returns, see Appendix 29.1. The appendix provides a thorough numerical example and then a thorough graphical example. The appendix is highly recommended for those going on in economics.

PRODUCTION IN THE LONG RUN: RETURNS TO SCALE

Production in the long run is a period of time in which the factors of production are varied; that is, the firm can vary all inputs. The owner can change the amount of capital and land as well as the number of workers. Because all inputs are variable, the law of diminishing returns no longer applies. Economists use the term **returns to scale** to refer to long-run changes in output that occur when the firm proportionally increases all factors of production. Three situations can arise if all factors are increased: (1) constant returns to scale, (2) decreasing returns to scale, and (3) increasing returns to scale.

Constant returns to scale may be the most common situation. *Constant returns to scale occurs if output increases by the same proportion as all inputs.* For example, if doubling all inputs causes output to double, the production process exhibits constant returns to scale. **Decreasing returns to scale** *occurs when output increases by less than inputs.* In this case, doubling input causes output to increase by only 80 percent, for example. Decreasing returns to scale might occur if expansion resulted in a firm so large that management became inefficient. Concern over decreasing returns to scale may be one explanation for the "downsizing" that has characterized American business in the past few decades. For example, some people believe that the Big Three U.S. automobile companies are too large and that they expanded to the point where returns to scale begin to decrease.

Increasing returns to scale *exist when output increases proportionally more than inputs. Doubling inputs causes output to triple.* How can this occur? The idea is that bigger is better, and it is an argument for the economies of mass production. One explanation is that bigger firms can allow employees and management to specialize. For example, suppose that a firm hires new workers for the product design division. This way, workers can do what they do best. Workers with mechanical skills could specialize in maintaining machinery. Other workers could provide new insights to help come up with new products or novel ways of doing things. Some workers could specialize in billing and accounting while others specialize in sales. The result would be that output expanded by a higher proportion than inputs, or increasing returns to scale. Bigger firms may also have better access to financing to purchase the latest technologies and best machinery.

Product and Process Technologies

The mass-production factory system that Henry Ford set up to produce the Model T used relatively expensive capital and relatively inexpensive, unskilled labor. More specifically, **mass production** is *a system of production in quantity using standardized parts, task-specific capital, and unskilled labor.* The capital used in most mass-production processes is task-specific; that is, it can be used for only one kind of production. The advantage of using task-specific capital is that it is possible to employ relatively unskilled workers who need to be trained to use the machinery only once. As Ford was to find out, mass production can be an efficient production technique if the market is large enough to pay for long production runs required of the large capital expenditures. Mass production is an example of exploiting economies of scale.

The Model T represented an innovation in both product and process technology. By **product technology**, we mean *the application of knowledge to create new goods and/or services.* The product technology was the car itself, which was a hugely successful product. **Process technology** is *the application of knowledge for producing products as efficiently as possible.* The process technology of the Model T was the mass-production factory system. The Model T dominated the automobile market for several years, but not forever. As soon as competitors copied the Model T and introduced mass-production factories of their own, Ford's share of the automobile market began to shrink. The response of Ford was another product innovation—a new automobile model. This set the pattern for competition in the automobile industry for the next fifty years: consumers expected and companies offered new cars and new features almost every year.

The Model T story is instructive because it can help explain the evolution of U.S. business in the last half of the twentieth century. The United States vaulted to the lead in the world economic race by the middle of the twentieth century not only because of its early implementation of mass-production techniques. Three other things also contributed: (1) abundant and inexpensive natural resources; (2) a highly educated workforce, the product of a longer history of compulsory high school than any other industrialized nation; and (3) escape from World War II without a bomb being dropped on the manufacturing base. This meant that the United States had a competitive advantage over most other nations in the world until the 1960s or 1970s.

Import Competition

Unfortunately, this competitive advantage could not last forever. The successful competitive strategy that the automobile industry used became a model for corporate behavior in much of the economy. Research and development was directed toward the development of new products. Unfortunately, the profits from new product technology can last only temporarily in today's world because information and technology can move across international boundaries with astonishing speed. The competitive strategy adopted by our trading partners was to copy the products developed in the United States but produce them at lower cost. It was especially easy to copy goods produced with mass-production factory methods because only unskilled workers were needed. All that was necessary was to build factories similar to those in the United States and staff them with lower-paid workers. About the only way for U.S. products to compete with these imports is by lowering U.S. wages, not an enticing thought.

The competitive strategy adopted by Japanese and German firms was somewhat different and has significant implications for the U.S. economy in the years ahead. The Japanese and Germans devoted most of their research and development efforts to process technology and more efficient ways of producing products. Instead of building factories similar to those in the United States and staffing them with low-wage workers, they found ways to produce products using high-skill and high-wage workers. The success of Japanese process technology was nothing short of amazing, at least until Japan fell into a severe recession in the early 1990s. For example, the video camera and recorder technology was invented in the United States, but the Japanese were able to develop a low-cost production process.

PROGRESSIVE CRITICISM OF NEOCLASSICAL PRODUCTION THEORY

We can always say, as a generalization, that putting inputs together with technology produces an output, but the specific meaning of all the terms is different in different societies. For example, the way that businesses are assumed to use inputs to maximize profits assumes that we have a capitalist economic system in which there are private owners maximizing their profits. To reach the neoclassical conclusions about how to maximize profits assumes that there is perfect competition, but that is a false assumption because perfect competition exists nowhere (see Chapters 22, 32, 33, and 34 of this book).

Even if we assume capitalist economic institutions, a certain level of technology, capital, and land, the neoclassical story is still simplistic, especially in the consideration of labor. The problem is that a "labor input" is not a machine, it is a human being. When using a machine, its specification tells us how much it can produce under normal usage that will not immediately destroy it. There are no such specifications for how fast or intensely an employee may work. We can test the maximum a woman worker can lift. But neither men nor women workers always work at their physical maximum, which would quickly tire them out. The question of how fast and how intensely an employee will work is determined in part by the conflict between labor and capitalist employers. To make maximum profit, capitalists would like workers to work at maximum physical output. Although the capitalist often tries to speed up labor, whether manual or intellectual, often employees attempt to resist such health-threatening speed-ups. Considering only labor, and not all the other social constraints, a technologically driven production function is meaningless because it ignores the social conflict that determines just how much labor an employee will do.

The neoclassical production function is stated as if it is an obvious fact of technology. What is lost in this simplifying assumption is that the theory does not take into account social or economic institutions and their impact on technology and technology choices. Technology does not drop from the sky, so it cannot simply be assumed without ignoring the most important problem of how it comes into being and improves. In Part I, we saw that some societies have helped technology improve rapidly, but other societies have institutions that impede technology.

Now we come to the assertion that in the short-run production processes, there are diminishing returns at some level of inputs. Since the so-called law was first stated in the early 1800s, industry has multiplied its output many, many times. What happened? Part of the answer lies in how early classical economists thought about the world. What they could not foresee or failed to take into account was how rapidly technology would change and evolve. Changes in technology overwhelmed diminishing marginal returns. The assumption of diminishing returns to the business, or diminishing product for each additional worker, simply is not true in most of modern industry, whether manufacturing or services.

The focus then turns to the long-run analysis in which the assumption is that all inputs, including technology, are flexible or can be changed. With better capital and technology, the common situation has been increasing returns as the size of production increased. In almost every industry, we see a few firms (sometimes just one) achieve control over most sales, assets, and profits. These few large firms just get larger and larger. They do not show decreasing returns to scale, but increasing returns. For example, a nationwide firm can do nationwide advertising instead of costly targeting of just a few areas. In brief, there is no evidence of decreasing returns as output increases within the firm, the industry, or the whole economy (except for a few very unusual circumstances).

A great many studies show that there are actual constant returns for each additional worker over a very wide range of output. A giant modern factory can, and often does, reduce or increase its labor force by 20 percent and keep the same level of productivity per worker. Moreover, a giant corporation can, and often does, build a whole new factory with the same technology as the previous one so that product per worker remains the same. The giant corporation can also close an entire factory, but the level of output per worker remains just the same in other factories. Similarly, in service areas, such as computer programming, a great many more employees can be hired, or a great many employees can be fired, with no change in the product of the last employee hired.

In modern economies, technology improves rapidly and capital increases rapidly in expansions. When we allow for the more realistic assumption that capital and technology are improving, then it is possible to explain modern industry, which would be inexplicable if we simply believed in the law of diminishing returns or decreasing returns to scale. Why does this completely unrealistic theory stay around, and why is it taught to millions of students? If there is declining productivity for any reason, this very popular and persuasive theory can be used to speculate that the blame is on the employees for their diminishing productivity. In Chapter 31, we shall see that the theory of diminishing productivity for each additional employee is an integral part of the theory that all employees gets exactly what is due to them for the product they have produced. That discussion will further clarify the importance of this theory. Because of what is seen as the extreme biases of the marginal productivity theory against employees, many progressives consider the neoclassical theory of production to be harmful and reject all of it.

SUMMARY

Chapter 29 began the discussion of where the supply curve comes from. The chapter introduced production and factors of production, explained a production function, and described production in the short run and production in the long run. The relationship of increasing the number of inputs and what happens to the level of output was described for both the short run and long run. In the short run, the owners of firms must take into account diminishing marginal returns, and in the long run the owners of firms take into account returns to scale. The neoclassical notion of production was critiqued in the last part of the chapter.

KEY TERMS

constant returns to scale

decreasing returns to scale

increasing returns to scale

law of diminishing returns

long run

mass production

process technology

product technology

production function

production in the long run

production in the short run

returns to scale

REVIEW QUESTIONS

Describe inputs into production and use the production function to illustrate the relationships among factors of production and technology.

1. List the four broad categories of factors of production or inputs to production. How are they represented in a production function?
2. What is the role of technology in production?

Explain the difference between production in the short run and production in the long run.

3. What is the difference between the short-run and long-run? Is there a fixed time period associated with short-run and long-run? Explain why or why not.
4. What happens to output in the short-run as production increases? What inputs are "fixed" and which input is variable in the short-run? How does this explain diminishing marginal productivity?
5. What might happen to output in the long-run as the number of inputs are increased? Are there any fixed inputs in the long-run?

Describe challenges faced by U.S. businesses as they make production decisions.

6. Compare and contrast product technology and process technology.
7. Describe how a competitive advantage can erode over time.

Discuss the critiques of the neoclassical notion of production and factors of production.

8. Compare and contrast the traditional and progressive view of labor as an input into production.
9. What are the issues raised about the traditional treatment of technology in production?

APPENDIX 29.1
THE RELATIONSHIP BETWEEN TOTAL, AVERAGE, AND MARGINAL PRODUCT

Appendix 29.1 further develops the discussion of production in the short run. The key issue is productivity and ways to measure and understand how productivity changes as inputs are added. The key ideas of diminishing and increasing marginal returns are illustrated with some basic algebra and graphing.

LEARNING OBJECTIVES FOR APPENDIX 29.1

After reading and studying this chapter, you should be able to:

Table 29.1

Law of Diminishing Returns

L	Q	MP_L	AP_L
0	0		—
		40	
1	40		40.00
		50	
2	90		45.00
		60	
3	150		50.00
		50	
4	200		50.00
		40	
5	240		48.00
		30	
6	270		45.00
		20	
7	290		41.43
		10	
8	300		37.50
		0	
9	300		33.33
		−10	
10	290		29.00
		−20	
11	270		24.55

Key:
L = Labor
Q = Total Product
MP_L = Marginal Product = $\Delta Q/\Delta L$
AP_L = Average Product = Q/L

- Calculate various measures of productivity and explain what they mean.
- Understand the relationships of the measures of productivity.
- Explain diminishing marginal productivity and how it is measured.

PRODUCTION IN THE SHORT RUN

Productivity is important to the owners of businesses. In this section, we discuss various measures of productivity and how the measures change with increasing and diminishing marginal returns.

Table 29.1 shows how output changes as we hire additional workers. Column 1 lists the number of variable inputs (labor in this example) that is added to the production process. The symbol for labor is *L*. Column 2 measures total product. **Total product** is *the quantity that is produced*, so the symbol for total product is *Q*.

The third column is the **marginal product of labor** (MP_L). *This is the extra output associated with adding one additional unit of the variable input*—one more worker in this case. The notation for marginal product of labor is MP_L. The formula for marginal product of labor is:

(29.2)   Marginal Product of Labor = $MP_L = \Delta Q/\Delta L$

where, as always, the Greek letter delta (Δ) stands for "change in." Notice that the entries in the marginal product column line up between the entries in the first two columns. This is to indicate that marginal product represents the additional or change in output associated with the change in labor inputs. In this case, one worker is added in each line of the table, so the marginal product is just the change in total product. For example, when the fifth worker is added, production rises from 200 to 240. This means that the marginal product of the fifth worker is:

$$MP_5 = \Delta Q/\Delta L = (Q_5 - Q_4)/(L_5 - L_4) = 240 - 200/5 - 4 = 40$$

The fourth column shows the average product per worker. **Average product of labor** *(AP)* is *calculated by dividing total output by the number of variable inputs,* labor in this case:

(29.3)   Average Product of Labor $= AP_1 = Q/L$

For example, when there are five workers, output is 240. The average product of five workers, then, is:

$$AP_5 = 240/5 = 48$$

A key to understanding the production function and law of diminishing returns is the relationship between inputs, total, average, and marginal product. Line 1 of Table 29.1 reveals the obvious: if we do not hire anyone, the oranges go to waste and there is no production. The second line says that if we hire one worker, total output will be 40 bushels of oranges per day. The first worker raised total product from 0 to 40, so the marginal product of the first worker is 40:

$$MP_L = \Delta Q/\Delta L = (40 - 0)/(1 - 0) = 40$$

The average product of the first worker is also 40:

$$AP_L = Q/L = 40/1 = 40$$

It gets more interesting as we add additional workers.

Line 3 shows what happens if we add a second worker. Total product increases from 40 to 90 bushels of oranges per day. This gives a marginal product of 50 bushels and an average product of 45:

$$MP_2 = \Delta Q/\Delta L = (90 - 40)/(1 - 0) = 50$$

$$AP_2 = Q/L = 90/2 = 45$$

Why did both the average product and the marginal product rise when the second worker was added? The two workers combined their skills and specialized in production. Worker specialization is the process of dividing jobs into simple components so that workers can do single tasks more efficiently. In this case, specialization was accomplished when worker 2 climbed on the back of worker 1 to shake the oranges concentrated at the top of the tree.

Specialization continues with the addition of the third worker. Total product rises from 90 to 150, so marginal product increases to 60 bushels per day and average product rises to 50 bushels.

(Maybe worker 3 scurried about gathering those oranges that rolled away from the trees being shaken by worker 2.) When marginal product increases as additional variable inputs are added, the production process is in stage I, the stage of **increasing marginal productivity**. *If the capital stock is fixed, adding additional workers will result in more output per worker because of specialization.* Firms never operate in stage I. Why limit inputs if the next worker will always be more productive than the previous worker?

As workers 4 through 8 are added, total product continues to increase but at a diminishing rate. Why? At some point, it is no longer possible to achieve gains from specialization—how many workers can climb on your back?—but for a while at least, adding workers will increase output, though by smaller and smaller amounts. This is stage II of the production process, the stage of **diminishing marginal productivity**. *In this stage, additional inputs cause output to increase, but at a diminishing rate.*

Marginal product becomes negative when more than nine workers are added, so total product begins to fall. What causes this to happen? There are too many workers for the size of the orchard. Apparently, the workers get in each other's way and hinder production. This is stage III of the production process, the stage of **negative marginal productivity**. *In this stage, additional inputs cause output to decline.* Stage III is rarely if ever observed in the real world because it never pays to operate in this stage of production—why hire more workers if output is going to fall?

Graphical Analysis

The numbers from Table 29.1 are shown graphically in Figure 29.1. The upper curve in the graph is the production function or the total product curve. As labor inputs rise from 0 to 2.5, it becomes steeper; this is stage I of the production function. (The 2.5 on the labor input axis indicates that we are plotting marginal product as the number of workers rises from 2 to 3.) Notice that the marginal product curve is upward sloping in stage I. When the marginal product curve begins to slope downward, the total product curve becomes less steep and production enters stage II. Stage II continues as long as total product rises and marginal product is positive. This occurs when between 2.5 and 8.5 workers are hired. If more than 8.5 workers are employed, marginal product becomes negative and total product begins to fall. This is stage III of the production function.

The Relationship Between Total, Average, and Marginal Product

Figure 29.1 plots the average and marginal product curves. Marginal product represents the output of the next input. This means that as long as the marginal product is positive, total output will be increasing. This occurs in stages I and II of the production function. If marginal product is negative, total product will be decreasing. This occurs in stage III of the production function. This relationship can be summarized by writing:

(29.4) $$\text{If } MP > 0 - > Q \Uparrow$$
$$\text{If } MP < 0 - > Q \Downarrow$$

There is also an important relationship between marginal product and average product in that marginal changes "pull" averages. For example, suppose that your cumulative grade point average after two years in college is 3.0. This is the average product of your study effort. The grade point average you get next semester will be your marginal product. If you get a 3.5 next semester, your cumulative grade point average will rise above 3.0. But if you get a 2.5 next semester, your cumulative grade point average will fall below 3.0. This is the same thing that will happen if the

Figure 29.1   **The Three Stages of Production**

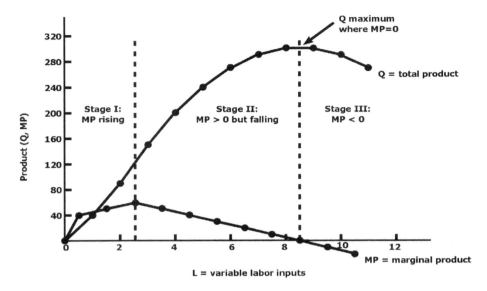

As a variable factor (labor) is added to a fixed factor (capital and land in this example), output will typically go through three stages: (1) increasing marginal product, (2) diminishing marginal product, and (3) decreasing marginal product. These three stages are determined by the shape of the marginal product curve. When the marginal product curve is rising, production is in stage I and the total product curve is getting steeper. When the marginal product curve is positive but declining, total product is increasing but at a diminishing rate so the total product curve is upward sloping but getting less steep. This is stage II of the production function. When marginal product becomes negative, additional inputs cause output to decline, so the total product curve begins to slope downward. This is stage III of the production function.

marginal product of labor is greater than the average product of labor. The average product of labor will rise. On the other hand, if the output of the next worker (marginal product) is less than the output of the average worker (average product), then the average will fall. This explains why the marginal product curve intersects the average product curve at the maximum of the average product curve: When the marginal product curve is above the average product curve, the average product will be rising; when the marginal product curve is below the average product curve, the average product curve will be falling.

(29.5)   If $MP > AP -> AP \Uparrow$
                               If $MP < AP -> AP \Downarrow$
                               $MP = AP$ at maximum AP

Equation 29.5 gives a hint at the most desirable position for society to operate on the production function. This would be at the point of maximum average product. At that point, the output per unit of input is maximized so we are getting the most possible out of our scarce resources. Is this also the position where the firm should operate? Perhaps, but probably not. The firm is interested in maximizing profits—the difference between revenues and costs—but Equation 29.5 says nothing about either revenues or costs, only physical output. To determine revenue, we need to know the selling price of output, and to determine costs, we need to know the wage rate, price of capital, and much more. We bring that information into the analysis in the next few chapters.

Figure 29.2 **Shifting the Production Function**

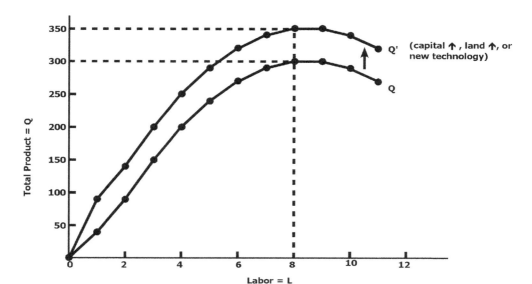

An increase in the stock of capital, land, or a technological advance will increase the output per worker and cause the entire production function to shift upward from Q to Q′. In this case, the production function has shifted so that eight workers can produce 350 instead of 300 units of output. A decrease in capital, land, or technology would shift the production function downward.

SHIFTING THE PRODUCTION FUNCTION

If either of the fixed factors of production (capital or land in this example) increases, or if there is an increase in technology, worker productivity will increase, and the entire production function will shift upward. For example, if the orchard owner bought an additional acre of land, workers would have more trees to harvest and would be more productive because they would pick more oranges. Or if the owner bought a ladder, a capital good, for each worker, they would not have to climb on each other's back and productivity would again increase. The new ladders would also represent an increase in technology because ladder technology was not previously used in the orchard. These events, more land, more capital, or technological advance, will shift the production function upward and increase the output per worker. This is shown in Figure 29.2. A decrease in any of these factors would shift the production function downward and reduce the output per worker. This would be represented as a shift from Q' to Q in Figure 29.2.

CHOOSING PRODUCTION TECHNIQUE: FACTOR SUBSTITUTION

Our discussion of the production function and the law of diminishing marginal productivity side-stepped an important issue. As more workers are added to a fixed stock of capital, the number of workers per machine, the **capital/labor ratio** changes. *This ratio refers to the amount of machinery used in a production process relative to the number of workers.* In the short run, as more workers are added, the numerator is fixed and the denominator increases. More and more workers are using a fixed amount of capital. When alternative capital/labor ratios can be used, managers must choose the optimal capital/labor ratio to operate efficiently.

SUMMARY OF APPENDIX 29.1

We have just been through the economist's rather technical discussion of the production process in the short run, where the assumption is that some inputs are fixed. For simplicity, when building the model, we further assumed that labor is the only variable input in the short run. Based on the assumption that diminishing marginal productivity characterizes production in the short run (when adding more workers to a fixed amount of capital, eventually additions to output will fall), measures of productivity were introduced. The appendix introduced measures of productivity including average product, or output per worker, and marginal product, or additional output for each additional worker. The productivity measures were used to demonstrate increasing and diminishing marginal productivity and the relationship between the productivity measures was discussed.

Although this is an important prelude to our analysis of costs in the next chapter, it may elicit a "So what?" from the business executive. Knowing that all production processes obey the law of diminishing returns is of little solace if you have just lost your market to foreign imports. Business executives know they cannot stand still. The techniques and products that are successful today may not be successful tomorrow. As production changes, managers must be constantly aware of the concepts we have just developed and the possibility of decreasing returns to scale, minimizing costs for a given output target.

KEY TERMS IN APPENDIX 29.1

average product of labor
capital/labor ratio
increasing, diminishing, and negative
    marginal productivity

marginal product of labor
total product

REVIEW QUESTIONS FOR APPENDIX 29.1

Calculate various measures of productivity and explain what they mean.
1. Explain in words what the marginal productivity of labor and average productivity of labor measures and why this is important information for the owner of a business.
2. Why does marginal productivity rise and then fall in the short-run?

Understand the relationships of the measures of productivity.
3. Explain why diminishing marginal productivity eventually causes average productivity to fall.
4. Sketch a graph of marginal productivity and average productivity. Label the point where MP = 0 and AP = 0.

Explain diminishing marginal productivity and how it is measured.
5. Why do the additions to output fall after a certain number of workers in the short-run?
6. When marginal productivity 'increases at a decreasing rate,' what part of the marginal productivity curve are we referring to? What does that mean?

CHAPTER 30

Costs of Production

In this chapter we examine the costs of production. Our goal is to convert the information from the last chapter on neoclassical production theory into a parallel explanation of the costs of production. We will find out that almost all of the important concepts from Chapter 29 are key to the analysis of costs.

LEARNING OBJECTIVES

After reading and studying this chapter, you should be able to:

- Explain the difference between long-run and short-run costs.
- Define and graph fixed, variable, average, and marginal costs.
- Explain the relationship between the costs of production and productivity.
- Calculate and discuss the significance of positive, negative, and zero economic profits.

SHORT-RUN COSTS AND THE PRODUCTION FUNCTION

Here is where we tie costs and productivity together. Costs are directly related to the production function and the law of diminishing returns in the short run. The decision of how much to produce affects the costs of production. If too little is produced, the ability of workers to specialize is limited. The result is that worker productivity is low and the cost of production is high. On the other hand, if the firm tries to produce too much in the short run, it will enter stage III of the production function, and output and productivity declines. To make the correct production decision, the firm must understand the relationship between costs and production.

FIXED, VARIABLE, AND TOTAL COST

Table 30.1 replicates the production function data from Table 29.1 and adds seven additional columns containing cost data. The first three measures of cost are fixed, variable, and total costs. The presence of fixed costs indicates that this analysis relates to the short run. In the long run, everything—including all costs—can vary, so there are no fixed costs.

Fixed costs (FC) are *costs that do not vary with output.* Fixed costs are associated with fixed inputs or inputs that cannot be changed in the short run. One example of a fixed cost is a fire in-

Table 30.1

Costs and Production

(1) L	(2) Q	(3) MP$_L$	(4) AP$_L$	(5) FC	(6) VC	(7) TC	(8) MC	(9) AFC	(10) AVC	(11) ATC
0	0	—	—	$300	0	$300		—	—	—
		40					$10.00			
1	40		40.00	300	400	700		$7.50	$10.00	$17.50
		50					8.00			
2	90		45.00	300	800	1100		3.33	8.89	12.22
		60					6.67			
3	150		50.00	300	1200	1500		2.00	8.00	10.00
		50					8.00			
4	200		50.00	300	1600	1900		1.50	8.00	9.50
		40					10.00			
5	240		48.00	300	2000	2300		1.25	8.33	9.58
		30					13.33			
6	270		45.00	300	2400	2700		1.11	8.89	10.00
		20					20.00			
7	290		41.43	300	2800	3100		1.03	9.66	10.69
		10					40.00			
8	300		37.50	300	3200	3500		1.00	10.67	11.67
		0					NA			
9	300		33.33	300	3600	3900		1.00	12.00	13.00

P$_L$ = Price of Labor = $400.

Key:
L = Variable Inputs (Labor)
Q = Total Product
MP$_L$ = Marginal Product = $\Delta Q / \Delta L$
AP$_L$ = Average Product (of Labor) = Q/L
FC = Fixed Cost
VC = Variable Cost
TC = Total Cost
MC = Marginal Cost = $\Delta TC / \Delta Q = \Delta VC / \Delta Q$
AFC = Average Fixed Cost = FC/Q
AVC = Average Variable Cost = VC/Q
ATC = Average Total Cost = TC/Q

surance premium on real property owned by the firm. Even if the firm closes down and produces nothing, the fire insurance premium must be paid until the contract expires. Other examples of fixed costs include security guard services and existing debt payments. In Table 30.1, fixed costs are assumed to be $300 for all levels of production.

Fixed costs are represented by the horizontal line in Figure 30.1. The intercept of the fixed cost curve is the amount of fixed costs; the slope of the fixed costs curve is zero to reflect that fixed costs do not change as output changes.

Variable costs (VC) are *costs that do change with the level of output*. Variable costs are associated with inputs that change in the short run. For many firms, the most important variable cost is labor. Labor costs increase as production increases because more workers must be hired to increase production. Other variable costs may include the cost of energy, raw materials, and intermediate goods that are used in the production process.

To make our example simple, labor is treated as the only variable cost of production. The cost per worker is $400, so the entries in the VC column are found by multiplying the number of workers

Figure 30.1   **Total, Variable, and Fixed Costs**

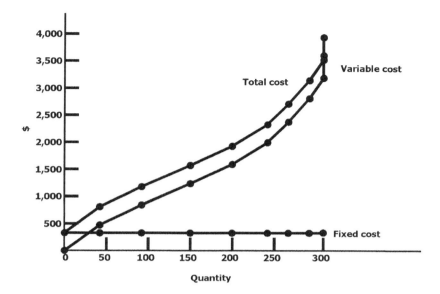

The three kinds of costs are fixed, variable, and total costs. Fixed costs do not vary as output changes and are represented by a horizontal line at the level of fixed costs. The variable cost curve gets its S-shape from the law of diminishing returns. The total cost curve is the vertical summation of the fixed and variable costs curves. Its intercept is equal to fixed costs; it is shaped like the variable cost curve.

In this figure, the dots on the curves represent the contributions of additional workers. For example, the first worker produced forty units of output; this is represented by the dots at Q = 40. The first two workers produced ninety units of output; this is represented by the dots at Q = 90.

(1) by $400. The zero in the first row of Table 30.1 indicates that there are no variable costs when no workers are employed. The intercept of the variable cost curve is always zero.

The S-shape of the variable cost curve in Figure 30.1 is a result of the three stages of production and the law of diminishing returns. The intercept of the variable cost curve is zero because there are no variable costs when no workers are hired. As the first few workers are hired, the variable cost per unit of output changes. This may not make sense at first because each worker is paid the same wage, $400. However, even though the variable cost per worker is always $400, each worker produces a different amount of output than the previous worker, so the variable cost per unit of output changes. The variable cost curve has three stages, just like a typical production function:

- *Increasing marginal returns:* Variable costs rise at a decreasing rate. At very low levels of output, the variable cost curve is relatively steep, but as output expands, it becomes flatter as worker specialization begins to take place. This corresponds to stage I of the production function, the stage of increasing marginal product. The production function gets steeper in stage I as more workers are hired; the variable cost curve gets flatter in stage I as more workers are hired. This should make sense to you. If the next worker is more productive than the previous worker, then the variable cost per unit of output will decline.

- *Diminishing marginal returns:* Variable costs rise at an increasing rate. In the short run, as more workers are hired and production increases, the point is reached when additional workers increase output but to a lesser extent than did the previous additional workers. This is stage II of the production function, the stage of diminishing marginal returns. The variable cost curve begins getting steeper in stage II: The cost per worker is still assumed constant, but each worker produces less than the previous worker, so the variable cost per unit of output begins to increase.
- *Negative marginal returns:* If the firm continues hiring workers, the point will be reached when additional workers actually decrease total product. This is stage III of the production function, the stage of negative marginal product. What happens to the variable cost curve in stage III? If the firm actually did hire enough workers to move into stage III, the variable cost curve would bend backward—an indication that output fell but variable costs continued to rise. This is unlikely in the real world, so the variable cost curve is usually drawn vertically at the maximum level of output.

Total cost (TC) is *found by adding together fixed and variable costs.* That is:

[30.1] $$TC = FC + VC$$

The total cost curve has the same shape as the variable cost curve and the same intercept as the fixed cost curve.

DIRECT AND INDIRECT COSTS

We must emphasize that total costs include all costs of production: not only explicit or direct costs like wages but also implicit or indirect costs like the opportunity cost of foregone alternatives. One important opportunity cost is the lost interest from using funds to acquire new machinery instead of investing the money and earning a return. For example, if you have $1,000,000 in retained profits and decide to use it to build a new plant, you cannot use the $1,000,000 to buy interest-earning financial assets. If the interest rate is 10 percent, this means that the new plant will cost you $1,000,000 plus the lost $100,000 per year that you could have earned by putting your money in an interest-earning financial asset.

In order to account for both explicit and opportunity costs, economists distinguish between accounting and economic profit. **Accounting profit** is *the total revenue received from production and sales (p × q) minus direct or explicit costs like labor, rent, and payments for machinery.* Accounting profit (or loss if costs exceed revenue) is what we read about in the paper when the business section discusses whether or not a firm is earning a profit or incurring a loss. **Economic profit** *starts with the accounting profit and subtracts the indirect or opportunity costs of the owner.* For example, an opportunity cost might be the interest given up when a firm uses its money to buy machinery instead of investing the money. It can also be the next best alternative for the time of the business owner. For every hour the business owner spends working at his or her business, there is some job that would be the next best alternative. Instead of running my firm that produces widgets, I could be working for another factory for a wage. That wage would be my opportunity cost.

A **positive economic profit** means that *the owner is not only earning an accounting profit but is also doing better than her or his next best alternative.* Would this business owner want to do something else? Of course not, because she or he would not be as well off. A **negative economic profit** means that *the owner is not doing as well as the next best alternative.* The accounting profit could even be positive, but the business owner will want to consider other options. A **zero economic**

profit or normal economic profit means that *the owner is doing at least as well as her or his next best alternative*. Will this owner want to leave the business? Absolutely not, since the firm owner will be no better off. In later chapters, the notion of zero economic profit plays an important role in the analysis of the decisions of business owners. If economic profit is negative, the firm owner would be better off pursuing the next best alternative.

AVERAGE AND MARGINAL COSTS

Firms are also concerned about the costs of producing individual units. **Marginal cost (MC)** is *the incremental cost of producing the next unit of output*. It represents the change in total cost associated with producing one more unit of output. It is important to remember that marginal cost is unrelated to fixed costs. Fixed costs do not change in the short run and thus have no influence on the cost of producing the next unit. This means that the change in total cost is equal to the change in variable cost. The formula for marginal cost is:

[30.2] $$MC = \Delta TC/\Delta Q = \Delta VC/\Delta Q$$

If you have a good math background, you will see that the marginal cost curve gives the slope of the total and variable cost curves.

Marginal cost is shown in column 8 of Table 30.1 as well as in Figure 30.2. Like marginal product, the marginal cost data are set between the rows of total cost to show that they represent the change in total cost. A quick inspection of columns 3 and 8 reveals that the marginal cost curve is U-shaped, like an upside-down marginal product curve. Marginal cost starts high and then declines before it rises again. This is the opposite of what happens to the marginal product curve. As marginal productivity is rising, the marginal costs are falling. When marginal productivity begins to fall, marginal costs begin to rise.

Marginal cost intersects average total cost (ATC) at its minimum point. When the first worker is added, output rises from 0 to 40, and total cost rises from $300 to $700. Substituting these values into Equation 30.2 shows that marginal cost is $10.00. But when output increases from 40 to 90, marginal cost falls to $8.00 because of worker specialization. Table 30.1 shows that marginal cost falls to $6.67 when the third worker is added and then begins to rise as production moves into stage II. Marginal cost rises at an increasing rate as more and more workers are added in stage II. Finally, in stage III of the production function, marginal cost will approach infinity if the firm hires and pays additional workers but output falls. The marginal cost in Figure 30.1 becomes vertical as stage II enters stage III.

Average fixed cost (AFC) is *found by dividing fixed costs by total product*:

[30.3] Average Fixed Cost: $AFC = FC/Q$

Fixed costs do not vary with output, but average fixed costs do. This reflects the fact that the more the firm produces, the more fixed costs can be "spread out." As a result, the average fixed cost curve declines steadily, and by progressively smaller amounts, as output increases. For example, if insurance costs $1,000 per year and the firm is able to sell only ten units of output, average fixed costs are $100 per unit, but if sales increase to twenty units per year, average fixed costs are only $50 per unit, and if sales rise to thirty units, average fixed costs are $33.33 per unit. Figure 30.2 illustrates how fixed costs are spread out as output increases.

Figure 30.2 **Average and Marginal Cost Curves**

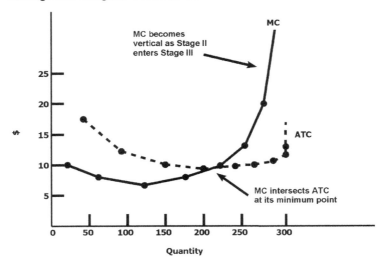

The average total cost and marginal cost curves are U-shaped, a consequence of the three stages of production and the law of diminishing returns. The marginal cost curve intersects the average total cost curve at its minimum point.

Average variable cost (AVC) is *found by dividing variable costs by total product*:

[30.4]   Average Variable Cost: $AVC = VC/Q$

The average variable cost curve is U-shaped as shown in Figure 30.2. At low levels of output, average variable costs are high, but as output increases, worker specialization increases the average product of the workers, which lowers the variable cost per unit of output. The average variable cost curve eventually begins to slope upward after diminishing returns have set in. In other words, as average product begins to fall, average variable costs begin to rise.

There is an important relationship between average and marginal costs. You might have guessed the relationship, given our discussion of average and marginal product in the last chapter. In fact, the relationship between average and marginal product or average and marginal cost holds regardless of the quantities being measured. For example, if the average height of the first ten people in a room is 5'9" and a 6'6" person enters the room, the average height of the people in the room will rise; if the next person who enters is only 5'5", the average height will fall. This example has a direct application to cost theory. Marginal cost represents the cost of producing the next unit, so if marginal cost is less than average variable cost, average variable costs must be declining, and if marginal cost is greater than average variable cost, average variable cost will rise. Finally, the marginal cost curve intersects the average variable cost curve at its minimum point. The importance of this relationship will be apparent in Chapter 32 when we analyze competitive firms.

Average total cost (ATC) is *found by dividing total cost by total output*, and because total cost is equal to fixed cost plus variable cost, the formula for average total cost can be written in different ways:

[30.5]   Average Total Cost: $ATC = TC/Q = (FC + VC)/Q = AFC + AVC$

The average total cost curve is U-shaped like the average variable cost curve. However, the average total cost curve is not quite parallel to the average variable cost curve because total costs include fixed costs as well as variable costs. In fact, the distance between the average total cost curve and the average variable cost curve represents average fixed costs. As output increases from low levels of output, the distance between the two curves decreases as fixed costs are spread out over larger amounts of output. Remember that average fixed costs fall as output rises. The marginal cost curve intersects the average total cost curve at its minimum point.

USING GRAPHS OF COST CURVES

We use diagrams such as the one in Figure 30.2 quite a bit in the next few chapters, so a few comments are in order. First, there is rarely a need to draw the average fixed cost curve. Average fixed cost is the difference between average total cost and average variable cost, so we can get that information—and a less cluttered diagram—by just noting the distance between AVC and ATC. Second, we can calculate total cost and variable cost from their respective average cost curves. For example, consider point a, on the average total cost curve on Figure 30.3. This point corresponds to quantity 90 and average total cost $12.22 from Table 30.1. To find the total cost of producing 90 units of output, all that is necessary is to multiply quantity by the average total cost of production. That is:

[30.6] $TC = ATC \times Q$

In this case, total costs are 90($12.22) = $1,099.80.
Likewise, to find variable costs, multiply average variable costs by quantity:

[30.7] $VC = AVC \times Q$

We know from Table 30.1 that the variable costs at quantity 90 are $8.89, so variable costs are 90($8.89) = $800.10.

Finally, fixed costs are the difference between total costs and variable costs, so fixed costs, indicated by the top shaded rectangle, are $1,099.80 − 800.10 = $299.70 (which differs from the table value of $300 because of rounding).

FACTORS THAT SHIFT COST CURVES

The two most important factors that shift short-run cost curves are (1) changes in technical knowledge that shift the production function and (2) input prices. An advance in technology will increase the amount of production from a given amount of inputs and thus lower the costs of production. For example, the development of automated assembly plants has dramatically reduced the cost of producing personal computers. The result is that the average total, average variable, and marginal cost curves shift downward. Therefore, the price of personal computers is lower. Lower factor prices such as wages, interest, and rent would also cause a downward shift in the average and marginal cost curves. Higher factor prices would shift it upward. Figure 30.4 illustrates the effect of higher costs on the marginal cost curves; the average cost curves have been omitted to simplify the diagram. Notice that higher costs shift the marginal cost curve vertically and toward the vertical axis, not away from it.

What shifts the fixed cost curve? Nothing in the short run because, by assumption, fixed costs are fixed. When fixed costs do change, we enter the long run, the subject of Appendix 30.1.

Figure 30.3 **Finding Total Costs from Average Costs**

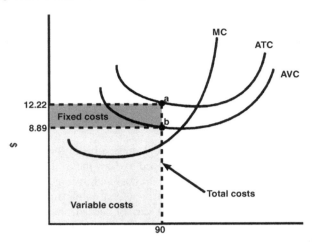

The total cost of producing any quantity can be found by multiplying quantity by average total cost. In this diagram, the average total cost of producing ninety units of output is 90($12.22) = $1,099.80. This is the entire rectangle 0-90-a-$12.22. Variable costs can be found by multiplying average variable cost by quantity. In this case, the variable cost of producing ninety units is 90($8.89) = $800.10. It is usually unnecessary to draw the average fixed costs curve because fixed costs can be found as the difference between total and variable costs. Fixed costs are the difference between total costs and variable costs. This is the top rectangle, $8.89-b-a-$12.22, which is equal to $1,099.80 − 800.10 = $299.70 ≈ $300.

Figure 30.4 **Factor Prices and Marginal Cost**

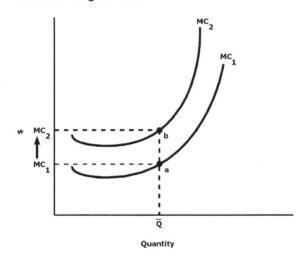

Higher factor prices will shift the marginal cost, average variable cost, and average total cost curves upward. Lower factor prices or advancing technology will shift them downward. This diagram illustrates the effect of higher factor costs on only the marginal cost curve. Notice that higher marginal costs are illustrated by a shift toward the $ axis. This is because the same quantity, Q, can be produced only at a higher cost, MC_2 versus MC_1, if factor costs have risen.

PROGRESSIVE CRITICISM OF NEOCLASSICAL VIEW OF COSTS

The traditional definition of costs is conservative in the sense that it introduces the concept that capitalists deserve to receive a normal profit as a cost of providing capital for production. It is true that physical capital goods are necessary for production. In any society, limited capital goods must be allocated to maximize returns. That allocation is a social cost because it means other areas cannot use those capital goods. It is also true, given a private enterprise system, that capitalist entrepreneurs must be induced with at least a normal profit to get them to furnish their capital. It was argued in earlier chapters, however, that the productivity of capital goods implies neither that the capitalists are productive nor that they deserve their profit. In other words, a progressive economist would argue society might provide capital to itself out of public funds. It would consider provision of capital a cost of production, and it might even calculate rates of profit in each industry to decide where to allocate capital.

SUMMARY

This chapter examined the costs of production.

1. In the short run, firms have both fixed and variable costs. Fixed costs do not vary with output; variable costs do. Total cost is defined as fixed cost plus variable cost. Marginal cost gives the cost of producing one more unit of output. It is computed as the change in variable costs divided by the change in output. In the long run, all costs can vary, so there are no fixed costs.
2. The shape of the cost curves are directly related to productivity.
3. The marginal cost curve intersects both the average variable cost curve and the average total cost curve at their minimum points. The average fixed cost curve declines as output increases.

KEY TERMS

accounting profit   fixed cost (FC)
average fixed cost (AFC)   marginal cost (MC)
average total cost (ATC)   positive, negative, and zero economic profit
average variable cost (AVC)   total cost (TC)
economic profit   variable cost (VC)

REVIEW QUESTIONS

Explain the difference between long-run and short-run costs.
1. What is the difference between the long run and the short run?
2. How do short-run and long-run costs differ? Why?
3. Sketch graphs to illustrate costs in the short run and long run.
4. The text lists three examples of fixed costs—fire insurance premiums, security guard services, and existing debt payments. List and discuss three additional fixed costs for a manufacturing firm.

Define and graph fixed, variable, average, and marginal costs.

5. Explain how and whether each of the following would affect short-run marginal, variable, fixed, and total costs:

   a. wage rate paid to assembly-line workers increases
   b. salary paid to upper management increases
   c. firm is required to implement new environmental controls
   d. price of oil decreases
   e. demand falls, so firm cuts back on production
   f. property taxes rise
   g. demand increases, so firm pays workers overtime

6. Indicate true, false, or uncertain for the following statements, and explain why:

   a. $AVC = ATC$ in the short run.
   b. $AFC + AVC + MC = ATC$.
   c. Average fixed cost falls as production proceeds through stages I and II; it begins to rise in stage III.
   d. Marginal cost intersects the minimum point of the average fixed cost.
   e. $ATC = AVC = AFC$ at $Q = 0$.
   f. In the short run, an increase in factor prices causes the marginal cost to intersect the average total cost at a higher level of output.

Explain the relationship between the costs of production and productivity.

Calculate and explain the significance of positive, negative, and zero economic profits.

7. Explain the difference between accounting and economic profits. What is included in calculating economic profits that is not included in accounting profits?
8. What is the difference between normal (or zero), positive, and negative economic profits?
9. Would a business owner want to stay in business if the economic profit is negative? Explain why or why not.
10. If a business owner is earning a zero or normal economic profit, what does that mean?
11. If a business owner is earning a zero or even negative economic profit, does that mean the accounting profit is negative? Explain.

APPENDIX 30.1
COSTS IN THE LONG RUN

All of the preceding discussions dealt with the short run in which we assumed that there were fixed costs because there were some fixed inputs. In the long run, by definition, there are no fixed costs because there are no fixed inputs. Everything can change. How and why do costs vary in the long run? There are no diminishing returns for the long run because there are no fixed inputs, so the long run must be analyzed separately.

LEARNING OBJECTIVES FOR APPENDIX 30.1

After reading and studying this appendix, you should be able to:

- Explain why there are no fixed costs in the long run.
- Define and graph long-run costs.
- Explain the relationship between the long-run costs of production and productivity (economies and diseconomies of scale).
- Describe how real-world considerations affect the analysis of costs and production decisions in the long run.

PRODUCTION IN THE LONG RUN

Some of the factors that we assumed were fixed in the short run were land, the size of the plant, and the capital stock. The capital stock affects labor productivity and therefore both variable and marginal costs. Suppose that the owners of the firm estimate sales to be a certain level and then build a plant hoping to produce at the minimum point on the average total cost curve. If demand is greater than the anticipated level, the firm will be able to sell more. It may be able to meet the higher demand temporarily by drawing down inventories, but if demand stays high, it will have to hire more workers and increase production. This would cause average costs to rise as production moved beyond the minimum point on the average total cost curve. To remain profitable, the firm would have to raise prices, but this could cut into sales. The alternative would be to build a larger and more efficient plant—which would move the firm to a different set of cost curves. The **long run average costs** (LRAC) is *an "envelope" that contains all of the short-run cost curves representing different plant sizes.* The **optimal plant size** is *the plant that minimizes average total costs in the long run.*

Figure 30.5 shows the relationship between short-run and long-run costs. Each of the small average total cost curves represents the short-run average costs associated with a different plant size. Notice that as the size of the plant increases from ATC_1 to ATC_2, the average cost of production falls. Why is this the case? As the market expands, the firm may be able to use more sophisticated technology and lower the average cost of production. However, if production expands beyond the quantity and the plant size indicated by ATC_3, average costs begin to rise. Why? One possibility, and there are others as well, is that the firm has become so large that management is inefficient and management costs rise.

The long-run average cost curve is constructed by drawing a line tangent to the short-run average costs curves corresponding to different plant sizes. Notice that the long-run average cost curve is not tangent to the minimum points of the short-run average total cost curves. The minimum points have a slope of zero, so connecting these points would result in a series of horizontal lines. The tangency occurs on the downward-sloping portion in the decreasing cost region and the upward-sloping portion of the increasing cost region.

The long-run average total cost curve calls attention to economies and diseconomies of scale, the idea that long-run average total costs depends on the size or the scale of the plant. Where the firm is operating on the long-run average cost curve is important. If production is on the downward-sloping portion (the region between ATC_1 and ATC_3 on Figure 30.5), this firm is showing **economies of scale** because *average costs fall as plant size increases.* Simply put, as output increases in this range, productivity increases. As productivity increases, costs decrease just as in the analysis of costs and productivity in the short run. Economies of scale are associated with the

Figure 30.5 **Long-Run Costs: The Envelope Curve**

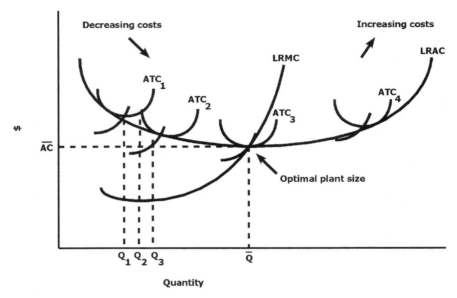

The long-run average cost curve, LRAC, is an "envelope" that holds all of the short-run cost curves representing different plant sizes. The optimal plant size corresponds to the minimum point on the LRAC, $\bar{Q}$. As output expands from zero toward $\bar{Q}$, costs fall because the firm can become more efficient by acquiring more capital. Over this region, the firm is called a decreasing cost firm. After $\bar{Q}$, average costs begin to rise and the firm becomes an increasing cost firm.

long run where all inputs are variable. Economies of scale means that "bigger is better." There can be more specialization of labor and management in larger plants. Firms can get discounts for buying materials in large quantities. Larger firms tend to have access to better financing and can purchase cutting-edge machinery and technologies.

If the firm is operating on the upward-sloping portion (plant size greater than ATC_3), it is showing **diseconomies of scale**. *Average costs will rise if the scale of operation is expanded.* Diseconomies of scale means that productivity is beginning to fall and corresponding costs increase. The plant has become so big that it is becoming inefficient. Management costs tend to soar as it becomes harder to keep control of the production process. The plant size that results in ATC_3 is called the optimal plant size. The long-run average cost curve is tangent to the minimum point of this short-run average total cost curve.

An interesting situation arises at points such as Q_2 in Figure 30.5. This level of production can be produced with the plant indicated by ATC_1, the larger plant suggested by ATC_2, or even an intermediate-sized plant with an average total cost curve between ATC_1 and ATC_2. Which plant should the firm choose? That depends on the firm's forecast of future sales. If the firm expects sales to grow beyond Q_2 in the future, the larger plant is indicated. If Q_2 is expected to be temporary, the smaller plant is probably preferred. However, there are some complications that make this kind of decision especially difficult. If costs fall as output is increased, it may be best to opt for the larger plant to grab market share before a competitor enters the market. However, if you guess wrong and build a plant that is too large, you will be stuck with a costly mistake because it is often hard to find buyers for used factories and machinery.

Figure 30.6 **Long-Run Costs**

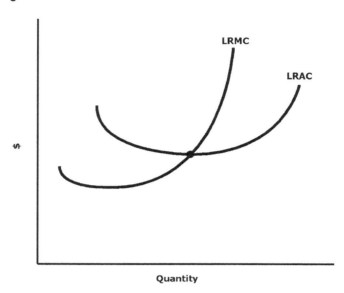

Quantity

The diagram for long-run costs looks like the diagram for short-run costs with one important difference: there is only one average cost curve. This is because all costs can vary in the long run, so there is no difference between average variable cost and average total cost.

Figure 30.5 also shows the long-run marginal cost (LRMC) curve. As you might suspect, long-run marginal cost represents the incremental cost of producing one more unit of output in the long run. Why is the long-run marginal cost shaped as it is? For essentially the same reasons the short-run marginal cost and average total cost have the relationship that they do. When the long-run marginal cost is below long-run average cost, the latter must be falling; when the long-run marginal cost is above the long-run average cost, the latter must be rising. The long-run marginal cost intersects the long-run average cost at its minimum point.

Figure 30.6 distills the most important information from Figure 30.5. The short-run cost curves are eliminated to reduce the clutter. This makes the long-run cost diagram look very much like the short-run diagram but with one noticeable difference. There is only one average cost curve, not two. The reason is that there are no fixed costs in the long run, so average variable cost is the same thing as average total cost. The long-run average cost will be especially important in the next few chapters when we compare different market structures.

SHIFTING LONG-RUN COST CURVES

The same factors that shift short-run cost curves—production technology and factor prices—also shift long-run cost curves. An advance in technology or lower factor prices will lower the long-run average and marginal cost curves. Higher factor costs will shift them upward. Changing technology can also affect costs and optimal plant size. For example, Figure 30.7 illustrates the situation in which a technological advance reduces costs and results in a larger optimal plant size because the new long-run marginal cost curve intersects the long-run average total cost curve at a higher

Figure 30.7 **Changing Long-Run Costs**

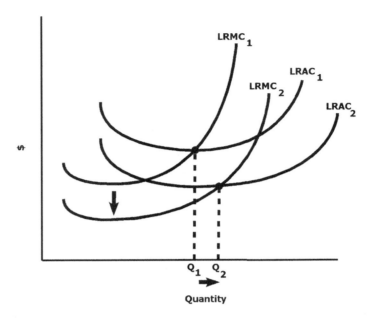

The diagram for long-run costs looks like the diagram for short-run costs with one important difference: there is only one average cost curve. This is because all costs can vary in the long run, so there is no difference between average variable cost and average total cost.

level of output. It is also possible for a technological advance to decrease the optimal plant size. For example, personal computers using desktop publishing software can now produce printed documents much more cheaply than was possible with old-fashioned typesetting equipment.

COSTS IN THE REAL WORLD

Cost and Capacity

Sales fluctuate as the economy goes through cycles, and it is difficult or impossible to forecast sales precisely. One strategy for dealing with sales fluctuations is to produce more than needed for current sales during slack times, store the excess in inventory, then sell out of inventory when sales pick up. The problem with this strategy is that inventories are costly. Money tied up in inventory incurs an opportunity cost of foregone interest.

Another strategy is to build a plant large enough to meet expected peak sales demand. Firms that do so can afford to keep smaller and less costly inventories and still be confident of meeting sales demands during peak periods. The only extra cost they incur is the initial fixed cost of building a plant larger than the optimal size. This strategy is apparently quite common among larger business firms. Nationwide, the capacity utilization rate is typically under 85 percent even during business cycle.

Costs and Competitiveness

Costs and competitiveness are intimately related. The firm that can produce at the lowest cost gains market share at the expense of less efficient firms. In today's world, information and technology move between firms and across international boundaries almost instantaneously. The firm that has a cost advantage today almost certainly will not have it tomorrow unless it is willing and able to make a change. Some of the factors that influence the dynamics of cost advantages are product and process technology, inventory practices, and dynamic considerations.

Product and Process Technology

As we found out in Chapter 29, product technology is the production of a new good, and process technology is a way of producing goods. Both can affect costs and competitiveness. Firms that spend research and development dollars to develop new product technologies may come up with the next big money-maker, but they will enjoy profits only until competitors figure ways to make similar products at lower cost. Perhaps the best recent example is the personal computer market. IBM's introduction of its original personal computer in 1981 was met with immediate success. Almost immediately, there was intense competition from low-cost clones. How could the clone makers offer computers at half the price of IBM machines? Most were produced abroad by low-wage workers, and the clone makers benefited from IBM's research and development without having to pay for it, but these were not the only reasons for the cost advantage. Many of the production facilities in Japan, Korea, and Taiwan used more sophisticated and efficient process technologies than did IBM. Despite a reputation for quality and service, IBM's share of the personal computer market fell steadily throughout the 1980s. The message is clear. Unless you can produce the product at lowest cost, you will lose your market. And the way to produce at lowest cost is to develop efficient process technologies—or pay your workers lower wages.

Inventory Practices

Firms keep two kinds of inventories. One is an inventory of final products ready for sale, and the other is an inventory of intermediate products ready to be used as inputs. Efficient inventory practice is an area on which U.S. firms focus heavily. One example is called "just-in-time" inventory management in which intermediate parts are in stock for less than twenty minutes compared to two weeks or more for the Big Three U.S. automobile manufacturers in the 1980s.

Dynamic Considerations

Many modern production processes follow a pattern whereby the firm invests in a cost-reducing innovation in period I. Lower production costs allow the firm to reap profits in period II. In period III, the cost-reducing innovation becomes available to competitors and profits fall. This story has several important implications to both individual firms and the economy as a whole. For the individual firm, it is clear that there is an incentive to devote resources to cost-reducing technologies but less of an incentive than if these innovations could not be copied. However, what if the cost-producing innovation exhibits decreasing costs? That is, what if costs fall even more as production increases? In this situation, there is an incentive to expand market share perhaps by opening up overseas markets and thus keep forcing down the costs of production. This would keep competitors out of the market and allow the innovating firm to maintain its high profits.

Firms know this, and so do nations. This is why many nations have sought to subsidize investment and research and development in particular industries. If the domestic industry can enter the world market first and gain enough market share, it will be difficult for other firms or nations to enter that market, at least until a new cost-reducing innovation can be found.

SUMMARY OF APPENDIX 30.1

1. The long-run average cost curve is U-shaped. When production takes place on the downward-sloping portion of the average cost curve, the firm is said to exhibit economies of scale and decreasing costs. If production takes place on the upward-sloping portion, the firm is experiencing increasing costs and diseconomies of scale. The minimum point on the average cost curve defines the optimal plant size.
2. Cost considerations are a vitally important component of competitiveness. Successful firms manage inventory effectively and are continually looking for low-cost production technologies.

KEY TERMS FOR APPENDIX 30.1

diseconomies of scale   long-run average costs (LRAC)
economies of scale   optimal plant size

REVIEW QUESTIONS FOR APPENDIX 30.1

Explain why there are no fixed costs in the long run.
1. Are there any fixed inputs in the long run? Why not? What does that mean for costs in the long run?

Define and graph long-run costs.
2. Indicate true, false, or uncertain for the following statements, and explain why:
    a. In the long run, advancing technology makes the optimal plant size smaller.
    b. The long-range average cost envelope curve is tangent to the minimum points of the short-run average total cost curves.

Explain the relationship between the long-run costs of production and productivity (economies and diseconomies of scale).
3. What is happening to the average total costs of production when there are economies of scale? What are explanations for economies of scale?
4. What is happening to the average total costs of production if there are diseconomies of scale? What are explanations for diseconomies of scale?

Describe how real-world considerations affect the analysis of costs and production decisions in the long run.
5. Suppose you fear competition from a low-cost foreign rival. Recognizing that labor costs are your largest cost of production, you decide to announce a 10 percent across-the-board wage reduction. Do you think this action would affect the productivity of labor? Why or why not?

CHAPTER 31

Work and Wages
Neoclassical View of Income Distribution

The traditional theory economists use to explain factor prices and income distribution is marginal productivity theory. It was developed simultaneously by several economists, but John Bates Clark (1847–1938) and Eugene von Böhm-Bawerk (1851–1914) were two of the most important contributors. Marginal productivity theory holds that factor payments such as wages, interest, rents, and profits depend on the productivity of the factor. For example, workers who are more productive receive higher wages than workers who are less productive, fertile land commands a higher rent than barren land. An important implication of this theory was that the payments to the factors of production were "just" in the sense that factor owners "deserve" what they are paid. This idea was crucial to Clark and the other nineteenth-century economists as they developed theories to refute the exploitation arguments of Karl Marx. Marginal productivity theory also seemed to provide a "scientific" argument in support of the existing income distribution because people were being paid in accordance to their productive contributions to society.

LEARNING OBJECTIVES

After reading and studying this chapter, you should be able to:

- Discuss the determinants of the labor demand and labor supply curves.
- Explain the relationship between factor prices and factor productivity.
- Use marginal productivity theory to explain what people earn in the labor market.
- Explain the criticisms of the marginal productivity theory.

THE DEMAND FOR FACTORS OF PRODUCTION

The demand for factors of production is known as **derived demand**. Derived demand means that *the demand for the factors of production are derived or arise from the output or production of goods and services that use the various factors of production.* As firms want to increase or decrease output, the derived demand shows how many inputs they need to use. The focus of this chapter is labor, which is one of the factors of production.

Table 31.1

Marginal Revenue Product and Derived Demand

(1) L	(2) Q	(3) MPP	(4) P	(5) TR	(6) MRP
3	150		$3	$450	
		50			$150
4	200		3	600	
		40			120
5	240		3	720	
		30			90
6	270		3	810	
		20			60
7	290		3	870	
		10			30
8	300		3	900	

Key:
L = Input (Labor)
Q = Total Product
MPP = Marginal Physical Product = $\Delta Q/\Delta L$
P = Selling Price (fixed under pure competition)
TR = Total Revenue
MRP = Marginal Revenue Product = $\Delta TR/\Delta L$ = P(MPP)

Marginal Revenue Product

Table 31.1 provides a numerical example to show how the demand for labor inputs is related to productivity and prices in the output market. Column headings 1, 2, and 3 are repeated from Table 30.1 in which we developed the law of diminishing returns. As before, L stands for labor inputs and Q is total product. The third column shows the marginal product of labor. However, in this table it is labeled MPP instead of MP to emphasize that it is the marginal physical product of labor. The **marginal physical product** of labor is *a measure of the output of labor in terms of goods and services.* It is the addition to output for each additional worker. It is not the monetary value of these goods and services. Column 4 gives the selling price of output, assumed to be $3 regardless of how much is sold. The fixed selling price means that we assume the firm is operating under perfect competition in output markets. We make this assumption throughout this entire chapter. Column 5 shows the total revenue (TR) from selling output. Total revenue is found by multiplying total product (Q) by the selling price. Column 6 shows the monetary value of marginal physical product, the marginal revenue product (MRP). **Marginal revenue product** is *the additional revenue earned from hiring one more worker.*

Firms are more concerned with marginal revenue product than with marginal physical product because their goal is to earn money from the sale of output. Marginal revenue product is found by finding the change in total revenue associated with one more unit of labor. An equivalent definition of marginal revenue product is marginal revenue times the marginal physical product. The formula for marginal revenue product is:

[31.1]   Marginal Revenue Product: $MRP = \Delta TR/\Delta L = \Delta PQ/\Delta L = MR(MPP)$

Marginal revenue is just the selling price under perfect competition, so marginal revenue product can be found by multiplying marginal physical product by the (assumed constant) selling price

Figure 31.1   **Marginal Revenue Product**

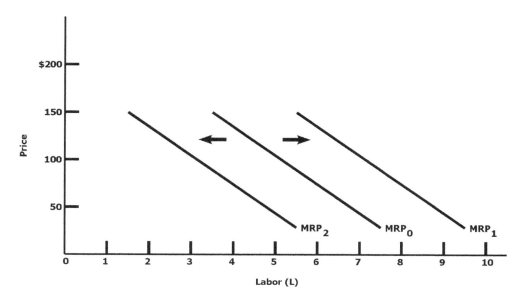

When there is pure competition in the output market, the marginal revenue product (MRP) curve is found by multiplying marginal physical product by the selling price of output. The downward slope is due to diminishing returns. As additional workers are added to a fixed stock of capital, output per worker declines when production is in stage II of the production function. The curve MRP_0 is a plot of the information in column 6 of Table 31.1.

The MRP curve will shift whenever the marginal physical product curve shifts or the selling price of output changes. An increase in marginal physical product or a rise in the output selling price will shift the MRP curve to the right from MRP_0 to MRP_1 A decrease in marginal physical product or a decline in the output selling price will shift the MRP curve to the left from MRP_0 to MRP_2.

in the output market. Because we assume pure competition, it is easiest to calculate marginal revenue product as:

[31.2] $MRP = \Delta TR/\Delta L = P(MPP)$

Slope of the MRP Curve

The marginal revenue product figures from Table 31.1 are graphed in Figure 31.1. The marginal revenue product curve is downward sloping over its whole region because we are using information only from stage II of the production function, the region of diminishing marginal product. The downward slope indicates that the incremental contribution from additional workers declines as more workers are added. What determines whether the marginal revenue product curve is relatively steep or relatively flat? Two things. First, the slope of the marginal revenue product curve depends on the slope of the marginal physical product curve. If the marginal physical product curve is steep, an indication that marginal product falls significantly each time a worker is added, the marginal revenue product curve will be steep as well. Second, the higher the selling price of output, the steeper will be the marginal revenue product curve for a given marginal physical product. For example, in Table 31.1, the selling price is assumed to be $3. The slope of the marginal revenue product curve is −30/1 because marginal revenue falls by $30 every time one worker is added. If the selling price was $5, the total revenue associated with four, five, and six workers would be $1,000, $1,200, and $1,350 respectively. The marginal revenue of adding the fifth worker is $200 (= $1,200 − 1,000) and $150 (= $1,350 − 1,200) when the sixth worker is added. Each worker adds $50 less revenue than the previous worker, so the slope of the marginal revenue curve is −50/1.

Shifting the MRP Curve

Several things can shift the marginal revenue product curve. An increase in the selling price of output will shift the marginal revenue product curve out or to the right because the contribution of each worker would increase. A decrease in selling price will shift it inward to the left. The marginal revenue product curve will also shift any time the marginal physical product curve shifts because of, say, increased worker effort, additional capital to work with, or better technology.

The marginal revenue product curve will shift whenever the marginal physical product curve shifts or the selling price of output changes. An increase in marginal physical product or a rise in the output selling price will shift the marginal revenue product curve to the right from MRP_0 to MRP_1. A decrease in marginal physical product or the output selling price will shift the marginal revenue product curve to the left from MRP_0 to MRP_2.

The Labor Demand Curve

It turns out that the marginal revenue product curve is the firm's labor demand curve. The marginal revenue product curve gives the quantity of workers that are hired at various wage rates, which is the definition of the firm's labor demand curve. This is illustrated on Figure 31.2. Since the marginal revenue product curve is the firm's labor demand curve, the same variables that shift the marginal revenue product curve also shift the labor demand curve—selling prices in the output market, technology, and productivity are among the most important variables. The only thing that results in movement along a factor demand curve is a change in the price of the factor.

THE SUPPLY CURVE FOR LABOR

There is very little difference in the analysis of the demand curves for labor, land, and capital. Unfortunately, the same cannot be said for factor supply curves. The supply of labor, one of the factors of production, is a bit different from the supply of other factors, such as typewriters or coal. The conditions that affect the supply of labor are quite different from those that affect the supply of capital or land. We must look at each factor supply curve separately before we can determine factor prices. This section focuses on the supply of labor.

What affects your decision to offer time and effort to an employer? Money is probably the most important condition for most people. You need money to survive, and most of us would not have enough unless we worked. Unfortunately, the time we spend at work gives us less time to enjoy the income we earn. That is, the decision to work involves a trade-off between income and leisure. This is the key concept behind the labor supply curve.

According to traditional marginal productivity theory, rational behavior involves a trade-off between work and leisure. The reason people work is to earn money to enjoy their leisure. The opportunity cost of working is foregone leisure. The opportunity cost of leisure is forgone income. As the wage rate rises, the opportunity cost of leisure increases because each hour of leisure incurs

Figure 31.2 **Marginal Revenue Product of Labor = Demand Curve for Labor**

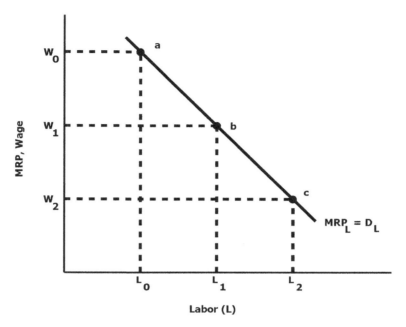

Labor (L)

The marginal revenue product curve is the factor demand curve. As factor prices (wages) fall from W_0 to W_2, the number of workers demanded (hired) rises from L_0 to L_2.

additional lost income. As leisure becomes more expensive, people "buy" less of it and thus work more hours. As the wage rate falls, leisure gets less expensive, so people "buy" more of it and work fewer hours. If the wage rate is too low, people will not work at all.

As shown in Figure 31.3, the labor supply curve is drawn with the wage rate on the vertical axis and the quantity of labor on the horizontal axis. The tradeoff between work and leisure means that the labor supply curve is generally upward sloping, like most supply curves. However, at very high wages, the labor supply curve may exhibit a backward-bending portion. Why? Suppose your wage rate increased a phenomenal amount, say to $1,000 per hour. Would you continue to work 40 hours per week, or would you work fewer hours and spend some of your hard-earned wages on much needed leisure? Many people would choose to work fewer hours and enjoy more leisure. This would cause the labor supply curve to bend backwards at very high wages.

How important is the backward-bending portion of the labor supply curve? Probably not very, though there may be one notable exception. Between 1960 and 1990, the percentage of adult males who held jobs fell from 86 to 76 percent even though the real wage was rising. This suggests a backward-bending labor supply curve for adult males. However, over the same period, the percentage of adult women with jobs rose from 38 percent to 58 percent, so men were probably responding to cultural factors as well as their wage rate. Most economists believe that backward-bending labor supply curves are rare in the real world, so we draw the labor supply curve upward-sloping in this and the next chapter. We also simplify the diagrams a bit by using linear labor supply and demand curves throughout the rest of the chapter. This doesn't change the results in any significant way, and it will make it easier for you to draw the diagrams in your notes as you read along, which, by the way, is strongly advised.

Figure 31.3 **The Labor Supply Curve**

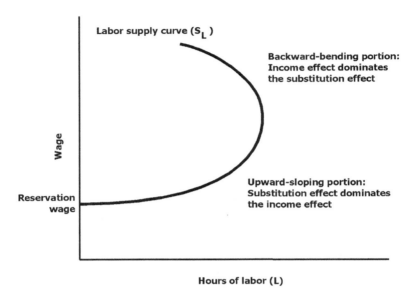

Hours of labor (L)

The labor supply curve, S$_L$, shows the number of hours of work that will be offered at various wage rates. Workers decide how many hours to work by trading off work and leisure. At relatively low wages, the labor supply curve is upward sloping because the substitution effect is more powerful than the income effect. At some very high wage rate, the labor supply curve may become backward bending because the income effect is stronger than the substitution effect. The vertical intercept of the labor supply curve is the minimum wage necessary to attract people into the labor market. Our analysis focuses on the upward-sloping portion of the labor supply curve.

Shifting the Labor Supply Curve

Several factors can cause the labor supply curve to shift. The motivation to work, income taxes, and unemployment compensation are three of the most important. Changes in work effort shift individual labor supply curves. For example, if you are suddenly struck with ambition, you may decide to offer more hours of labor even if there is no change in the wage rate. This would cause your labor supply curve to shift to the right and away from the wage axis. Income taxes can also affect work effort. If you know that your next hour of labor will be subject to a 50 percent tax, you may think twice about putting in overtime. If the tax rate is only 20 percent, the extra time at the office is more enticing. Income tax increases tend to shift the labor supply curve to the left; income tax cuts tend to shift the labor supply curve to the right.

Unemployment compensation reduces the pain of being unemployed and may influence how hard people look for a job. If unemployment compensation is universal and covers 100 percent of lost wages, some people may be inclined to sit at home and watch Oprah instead of looking for a new job; this would shift the labor supply curve to the left. On the other hand, the existence of unemployment compensation may provide a cushion for people as they search for a new job that uses their skills. You would not want to be forced to take a job flipping burgers the day after you were laid off from your public accounting firm, would you?

Few neoclassical economists question whether these factors shift the labor supply curve, but there is debate as to the magnitude of the shifts. Perhaps the most important debate concerns the labor supply response to income taxes. This is potentially very important. If income taxes have a significant effect on work effort, then policymakers must be very careful before raising taxes. If there is a consensus on this issue, it is probably that changes in income taxes have only a small effect on labor supply, and most of that effect is on the decision to work overtime. If correct, this means that income tax changes probably have more effect on the demand side of the economy than on the supply side because taxes affect buying power of consumers.

The Market Labor Supply Curve

A single firm under pure competition is able to hire as many workers as needed at the going wage rate, so the wage lines in Figure 31.3 can be considered the supply of labor facing a single firm. However, if all firms in the entire industry wanted to hire more workers, the wage rate would normally have to rise to induce people to give up leisure in exchange for work. The market labor supply curve is found by adding together the individual labor supply curves for everyone in the particular labor market. Anything that causes an individual labor supply curve to shift will also shift the labor market supply curve. Additionally, the labor market supply curve will shift because of population growth and changes in the labor force participation rate. The labor force participation rate is the ratio of the labor force to the working-age population. The labor force participation rate can change for several reasons. Over the past thirty years, the biggest change has been the large increase in women in the workforce, a fact we documented earlier. Population growth affects the labor supply curve much like increases in the labor force participation rate.

Figure 31.4 illustrates shifts in the labor supply curve. Anything that increases work effort, the number of workers in a particular market, or the labor force participation rate will shift the labor supply curve away from the vertical axis, from S_{L0} to S_{L1} on the diagram. Factors that do the opposite—a decrease in work effort or population, a reduction in the labor force participation rate—will shift the labor supply curve toward the vertical axis (i.e., from S_{L0} to S_{L2}).

The Equilibrium Wage Rate

We can find *the wage rate that clears the labor market*, the **equilibrium wage rate**, by combining the labor demand curve and the labor supply curve. This is done in Figure 31.5. The equilibrium wage rate is the rate at which the quantity of labor demanded is equal to the quantity of labor supplied. The equilibrium wage rate is equal to the marginal revenue product of the last worker hired.

Figure 31.5 also illustrates the effects of shifts in the demand and supply for labor. Suppose the labor market begins at the intersection of D_{L0} and S_{L0} so that the equilibrium wage rate is W_0. An increase in the demand for labor will shift the labor demand curve outward from D_{L0} to D_{L1} and cause the equilibrium wage rate to rise to W_2, assuming that all other factors are held constant. If the labor supply curve shifts outward (S_{L0} to S_{L1}), the wage rate will fall to W_1, assuming again that all other factors are held constant.

Over the long run, the labor supply has grown because of population growth, and we know that labor force participation rates have increased over the past forty years as well. Does this mean that wages have fallen over the same period? Not necessarily. In some markets, the demand for labor has increased faster than the supply of labor, causing wages to rise. This has been true in many markets for skilled labor. On the other hand, when the demand for labor falls relative to supply,

Figure 31.4 **Shifting the Labor Supply Curve**

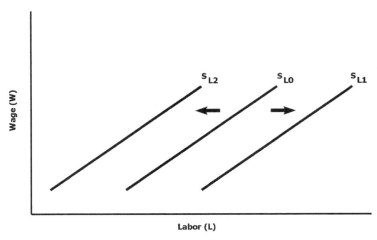

The labor supply curve shifts in response to changes in work effort, population, and labor force participation rates. An increase in the work effort, population growth, or higher labor force participation rates will shift the labor supply curve from S_{L0} to S_{L1} This represents additional hours being offered at every wage rate. If work incentives decrease (perhaps due to higher income taxes), or if the labor force participation rate declines, the labor supply curve will shift from S_{L0} to S_{L2}.

Figure 31.5 **Equilibrium Wages**

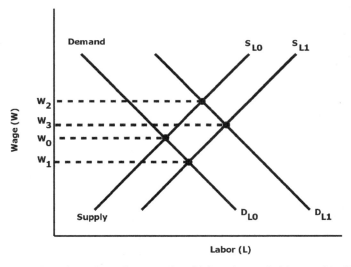

The equilibrium wage rate exists where the quantity of labor demanded is equal to the quantity of labor supplied. If labor demand is initially D_{L0} and the labor supply is initially S_{L0}, the equilibrium wage will be W_0. Other things equal, an increase the supply of labor will cause the wage rate to fall. This is represented by the shift from S_{L0} to S_{L1} and the wage decline from W_0 to W_1 An increase in the demand for labor will raise the equilibrium wage rate. This is illustrated by the shift from D_{L0} to D_{L1} and the wage hike from W_0 to W_2 When both labor supply and labor demand increase, the effect on wages will depend on the relative magnitudes of the shifts. For example, an increase in the wage rate from W_0 to W_3 indicates that labor demand has increased more than labor supply.

the wage rate falls. Many people believe that this is why the wage rate for many unskilled workers has fallen in the past decade.

Does the existence of an equilibrium wage rate imply that there is no unemployment? Perhaps—but it depends on who you ask. Some economists do contend that as long as wages and prices are free to fluctuate, people who are unable to find a job must be voluntarily unemployed because they are unwilling to accept a wage rate that is consistent with their productivity. In this view, the only cause for unemployment would be union or government policies that prevent wages from moving to the equilibrium level. Progressive economists, however, contend that the labor market does not operate quite as efficiently as this model implies and that workers may be unable to find a job even if wages and prices are perfectly flexible.

MARGINAL PRODUCTIVITY AND WAGE DIFFERENTIALS

Why do garbage collectors get higher salaries than game show hosts? Why do teachers get lower salaries than accountants? To start, different occupations earn different wages because there are many different labor markets. The skills required to be a game show host are not directly applicable to the garbage collection profession, so it is not clear that an unemployed game show host could easily find a job in the promising field of urban sanitation. Using the concept of marginal physical product and the revenue generated by the sale of the product the worker makes, it makes sense that the more productive a worker is—in other words, the higher his or her marginal physical product—and the more the product sells for, the more the worker is likely to make.

Marginal productivity theory can be a powerful tool for explaining wage differentials when we consider four additional factors: job attractiveness, human capital, labor mobility, and discrimination.

Job attractiveness. Jobs that involve danger, tedium, or significant physical labor often carry a wage somewhat higher than jobs with otherwise comparable characteristics. For example, off-shore oil workers earn more than onshore oil workers, and the "graveyard" shift typically carries a 10 percent wage premium. More recently, people who worked to disarm the millions of bombs and land mines left after the Desert Storm war earned salaries starting at $100,000 for six months of work. Such wage differentials are called **compensating differentials**. Do compensating differentials violate marginal productivity theory? Not at all. Such jobs attract few people and thus reduce the supply of labor, which increases the wage rate.

Human capital. Why do college graduates typically earn $300,000 more over their lifetime than high school graduates? Why do workers in the United States earn 25 times as much as workers in India? One reason is that U.S. workers have more physical capital (machinery) to work with, but another reason is that U.S. workers typically have more human capital than workers in India. What is **human capital**? *It is the education, training, and experience that increase worker productivity and therefore income.* College graduates earn more income than high school graduates because they possess more skills. The same can be said of workers in the United States relative to workers in India. Workers with more human capital are more productive than workers with less human capital.

Labor mobility. Workers in Alaska receive, on average, incomes that are about 25 percent higher than comparable workers in the lower 48 states. Part of the reason for this differential may be that many people consider jobs in Alaska to be unattractive and thus require a compensating wage differential. But another reason may be that Alaska is so isolated from the lower 48 states that

Alaskan workers do not face competition from lower paid workers. With perfect labor mobility, both between regions and between jobs, wage differentials would not exist. For example, if it were cost-free to move to Alaska, the 25 percent wage differential would cause people to emigrate from the lower 48 states to Alaska. This would reduce wages in Alaska and raise wages in the lower 48 states. Why? The labor supply in Alaska would increase and the labor supply in the lower 48 states would decrease. Emigration would stop when the wages were equal.

Discrimination. It is a sad fact of life, but discrimination exists in most countries. In the United States, for example, women earn only about 70 percent as much as men. Nonwhite males earn only about 60 percent as much as white males in the United States. Does this mean that women are less productive than men, or that nonwhites are less productive than whites? The answer could be affirmative but only if there was no discrimination. Discrimination is one reason cultural minorities earn less than cultural majorities.

There are several kinds of discrimination, and all are costly to society. If all employers suddenly decided that women or nonwhites could not do the job as well as white males, then the labor supply curve—now consisting exclusively of white males—would shift to the left. This would cause the wages paid to white males to rise, and because wages are a cost of production, would result in lower profits for the firms. The effect of discrimination does not stop here. The wages paid to women and nonwhites will decline because there are now fewer employers willing to hire them. Further, the fact that women and nonwhites are paid lower wages than white males is one reason these groups historically change jobs more frequently than white males; it is much easier to quit a crummy job than a good one. Frequent job change is one reason women and nonwhites have such a difficult time building up seniority and moving into upper management. A different kind of discrimination may provide another reason women and nonwhites are rarely seen in upper management. Corporate executives, overwhelmingly white and male, seem resistant to promote women and non-whites, a phenomenon known as the "glass ceiling."

One of the main sources of discrimination against women is the cultural attitude that designates "women's jobs" and "men's jobs." Nursing, child care, and hair styling are considered "women's work" in our society. The effect on male/female wage differentials is obvious. "Women's jobs" are among the lowest paid occupations; "men's jobs" are among the highest paid occupations. This and other issues are evident even today in the difference in earnings between men and women. According to the Current Population Survey, in 2001, women earned 75.1 percent of what a man earns. Women college graduates earned 72.5 percent of what a male college graduate earns. Until these stereotypes can be eliminated, until the glass ceilings can be eliminated, the task of eliminating male/female wage differentials will be difficult.

Not all economists believe that marginal productivity theory is the best or even a reasonable first approximation for explaining factor prices. The demand and supply of labor may depend on social factors as much as or more than on economic calculations. Still, most economists believe that marginal productivity theory is a good starting place for understanding factor prices and income distribution. It is also pretty straightforward—as long as you remember how to apply supply and demand analysis.

PROGRESSIVE CRITICISM OF NEOCLASSICAL DISTRIBUTION THEORY

The neoclassical distribution theory says that every factor of production receives an amount equal to its marginal productivity. Although the modern version of marginal productivity is usually written in very careful language to avoid any direct statement on the fairness of distribution, students are usually persuaded that a "factor," such as an employee, gets paid according to the output she adds in production. Similarly, students are usually led to believe that capitalists get profit according to how much additional product is produced by their efforts. It appears that employees and capitalists both get a fair share of the product produced by their joint activity. Most progressive economists object to the idea that the present capitalist economic system is perfectly fair to everyone. What are their arguments?

In the first place, what exactly does the capitalist do in the production process? A pure capitalist does no labor and produces nothing, but receives income only from ownership of part of a corporation or a noncorporate business. The marginal productivity theory talks about machines helping employees to produce more. Adding more machines adds additional product. Does a machine get paid according to its marginal product? The machine is not a capitalist. A capitalist is not a machine and directly produces nothing.

What do employees produce? Employees may be managers who do managerial labor, professionals who do professional labor, skilled workers (such as carpenters) who do skilled labor, or manual workers who do manual labor. No matter what type of labor they do, employees produce a product. A woman who types on a computer all day produces a product that adds to the total production.

In Chapters 19 and 20, we saw that the employee's day is divided into necessary labor and surplus labor. The necessary labor hours are used to produce the goods that are sold to pay the employee's compensation. The surplus labor done in the rest of the day becomes profit, which is divided among capitalists according to their ownership of the business. Thus, employees are exploited because part of the product does not go to the man or woman producing it, but to the capitalist. The marginal productivity theory hides the fact that some of the product of employees does not go to employees, but to the capitalists who own the corporation. According to the marginal productivity theory, exploitation is impossible (except in illegal activities such as prostitution or hidden sweatshops with involuntary workers), so the system is perfectly fair.

The theory of marginal productivity and the progressive labor theory arrive at completely different conclusions. The neoclassical marginal productivity theory is often used by giant corporations to defend their making $20 billion in three months, as Exxon did in 2006. The corporate executives who use the marginal productivity theory may not call it that and may not even know the theory, but that is what they often say in their defense in a highly simplified and popularized form. On the other hand, the labor theory of exploitation is often used by labor unions when they go on strike for better working conditions, shorter working hours, or higher wages or salaries for employees. Union leaders may have never heard of the labor theory of exploitation, but they often use a popularized form of it when there is a conflict between employee compensation and profits. In politics, conservatives often defend the economic system as fair on the basis of neoclassical theory, while some progressive politicians talk about the system as unfair on the basis of exploitation.

SUMMARY

This chapter covered the following information:

1. The demand for labor is derived from the productivity of labor and the demand for final products. As more workers are added to a fixed stock of capital, the marginal product of labor declines. The marginal revenue product is the demand curve for labor. When there is competition in the output market, marginal revenue product is found by multiplying the marginal physical product of labor by the selling price of output.

2. The main factors that shift the labor demand curve are worker productivity and the selling price of output. Other things equal, an increase in the demand for labor will increase the number of workers that are hired and raise the wage rate.

3. The supply curve of labor depends on the trade-off between work and leisure and is usually upward sloping. As the wage rate increases, the opportunity cost of leisure increases, so people typically offer more hours of labor. However, at very high wage rates, the labor supply curve may be backward bending. The slope of the labor supply curve depends on the relative magnitudes of the income and substitution effects. If the substitution effect is stronger, the labor supply curve is upward sloping. If the income effect is stronger, the labor supply curve is backward bending.

4. The labor supply curve will shift when there are changes in work effort, the labor force participation rate, and population. Other things equal, an increase in the supply of labor will increase the number of workers that are hired and lower the wage rate.

5. Wage differentials can often be explained by factors that shift the labor supply or labor demand curve. Compensating differentials exist in jobs that are unattractive, dangerous, or difficult. Human capital increases worker productivity and the wage rate. Discrimination accounts for some wage differentials. Firms that discriminate face a reduced supply of available workers and thus raise the wage rate for eligible workers.

The neoclassical marginal productivity theory says that every factor of production, such as employees or capitalists, receives an income equal to the marginal product of labor. On the contrary, the progressive exploitation theory says that employees work part of the day to produce their compensation and part of the day to produce capitalist profits.

KEY TERMS

compensating differential
derived demand
equilibrium wage rate

human capital
marginal physical product
marginal revenue product

REVIEW QUESTIONS

Discuss the determinants of the labor demand and labor supply curves.

1. Why is the demand for the factors of production called *derived demand*?
2. Why is the MRP curve downward sloping? What factors cause it to shift? Answer with respect to the MRP for each of the factors of production.
3. Under what conditions is the labor supply curve upward sloping? When is it backward bending? What factors cause the labor supply curve to shift?

Explain the relationship between factor prices and factor productivity.

4. How can marginal productivity theory be used to explain wage differentials? Give specific examples.

Use marginal productivity theory to explain what people earn in the labor market.

5. Using diagrams, illustrate
    a. why offshore oil workers have higher wages than on-shore oil workers.
    b. how human capital raises a worker's wage.

    c. why Alaskan workers have higher wages than workers in the lower 48 states.
    d. why discrimination raises the wage rate for nondiscriminated workers.
6. Ceteris paribus, which of the following would tend to cause the wage rate to increase? Draw diagrams to explain your answers.
    a. an increase in the labor force participation rate
    b. technological advance
    c. higher selling prices for output
    d. additional education

Explain the criticisms of the marginal productivity theory.
7. Compare and contrast marginal productivity theory and progressive labor theory. What are the key differences?
8. How do capitalists use marginal productivity to explain wages of workers and the large profits for the owners?

APPENDIX 31.1
PROFIT MAXIMIZATION AND THE INPUT DECISION

The goal of the firm is to maximize profits. With that in mind, this appendix takes the concepts developed about factor markets and extends the analysis to the decisions of firms on how much of the various inputs or factors of production to use. Since labor is a unique factor input, the analysis begins with the optimal number of workers. Next, the appendix looks at markets for other factors of production, in particular, land and capital.

LEARNING OBJECTIVES FOR APPENDIX 31.1

After reading and studying this appendix, you should be able to:

* Use marginal productivity theory to explain the optimal, profit-maximizing level of inputs.
* Use marginal productivity theory to explain prices of capital and natural resources.
* Explain the concept of economic rent.

HOW MANY WORKERS?

The problem for the firm is to determine the profit-maximizing number of workers to hire. The decision rule for hiring the optimal number of workers (or any variable input) is to hire workers until the marginal revenue product of labor is equal to the marginal cost of labor. In other words, the firm should hire workers until the additional cost of the worker equals the value of the additional output of that worker. Stated formally, the firm should hire workers until:

[31.3] $$MRP_L = MC_L$$

where the L subscripts indicate that the variable input under consideration is labor. This rule holds for all factors of production.

    The marginal cost of labor is the change in total costs associated with hiring one more unit of the variable factor. Marginal costs depend on the state of competition in the input market. In

Figure 31.6 **Net Marginal Revenue Product**

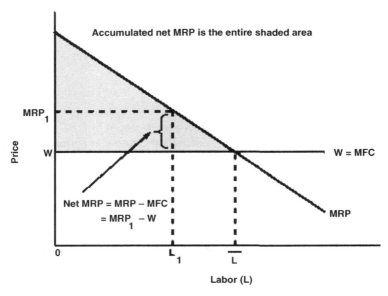

The marginal factor cost of labor is equal to the wage rate if all workers can be hired at the same wage rate. Net marginal revenue product is the difference between marginal revenue product and marginal factor cost of an individual worker; the net marginal revenue product of the L_1 worker is $MRP_1 - W$. Accumulated net marginal product is the entire area between the marginal revenue product curve and the marginal factor cost line. To maximize profits, firms should hire workers until $MRP = W$, or until the net marginal revenue product of the last factor employed is zero.

this appendix, we assume that there is pure competition in the input market as well as the output market. This means that the firm is so small relative to the labor market that it can hire as many workers as needed without having to raise the wage rate. Under these circumstances, the marginal factor cost of labor is the wage rate, so Equation 31.3 can be written as:

[31.4] $$MRP_L = W$$

Why does Equation 31.4 result in the profit-maximizing level of employment? To answer this question, we need to first define the concept net marginal revenue product. Net marginal revenue product is the difference between the marginal revenue product of hiring the next worker and the cost of hiring that worker. In this example, we assume that the only cost associated with hiring the next worker is the wage, so *the area under the marginal revenue product curve above the wage line is what might be called* **accumulated net marginal revenue product**. We must point out that accumulated net marginal revenue is not the same thing as profits; it is only revenue derived from the employment of labor in excess of the amount necessary to pay the workers. Some of this revenue represents profit, but some must also be used to pay for capital and the other factors of production. We elaborate on this idea shortly.

Figure 31.7 uses the information from Table 31.1 to show what happens if the firm does not follow the profit-maximizing strategy of Equation 31.4. Suppose that the wage rate is $75 and the firm chooses to hire a number of workers such that $MRP \neq W$, say $L = 5$. If only five workers

Figure 31.7 **The Optimal Quantity of Labor**

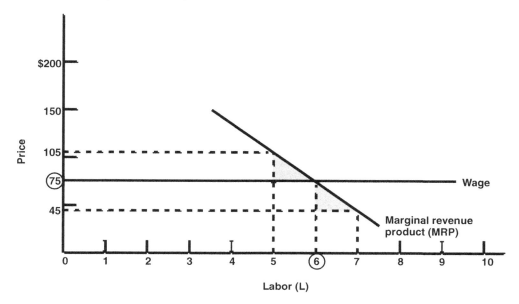

Firms should hire factors until the marginal factor cost (the wage in this example) is equal to the marginal revenue product. In this example, the marginal revenue product of the sixth worker is equal to the wage rate, $75, so six workers should be hired. If only five workers were hired, the marginal revenue product would be greater than the wage rate, $105 > $75, and the firm would be forfeiting net marginal revenue product equal to the shaded triangle above the wage line. If seven workers were hired, the marginal revenue product would be less than the wage rate, $45 < 75, so net marginal revenue product would fall by the amount in the shaded area below the wage line.

are hired, the marginal revenue product of the fifth worker is greater than the wage rate, $105 > $75. (The MRP of the fifth worker is found by taking the midpoint between $120 and $90; this is the MRP of moving between four and six workers.) The net marginal revenue product of the fifth worker is positive, so the fifth worker should be employed. However, the firm is forfeiting the net marginal revenue it could get from hiring the sixth worker. This is the area of the shaded triangle above the wage line. On the other hand, if the firm chooses to hire seven workers, the marginal revenue product of the seventh worker is less than the wage rate ($45 < $75), so the firm loses net marginal revenue product of an amount equal to the area of the shaded triangle below the wage line. The rule is clear: The firm should employ factors until the marginal revenue product of the last unit is just equal to the marginal cost of that unit.

THE MARKETS FOR CAPITAL AND LAND

From the neoclassical perspective, the three main types of resources are labor, capital, and land. Marginal productivity theory can be applied to the markets for capital and land the same way it is applied to labor. The rationale behind the demand curve for capital goods is the same as the rationale behind the demand curve for labor. Firms acquire capital goods because they need them in the production process, and they will keep buying capital goods as long as the marginal revenue product exceeds the marginal factor cost of capital goods.

However, the supply curve for capital is quite different from the supply curve for labor. The supply of capital goods depends on the price of capital goods and the production capacity of the capital goods industry. However, *before* a firm can acquire a capital good, it must have **financial capital**—*money*—so the supply of financial capital puts a constraint on the stock of capital goods. In this sense, savings (sources of funds) represents the supply of financial capital but not necessarily the supply of capital goods. Financial capital becomes capital goods only if the firm believes that the expected return on the capital good is greater than the cost of using the financial capital, the interest rate.

Firms need financial capital before they can buy capital goods, such as a piece of machinery that the firm uses in the production process, and the source of financial capital is savings. Savings can come from many sources, including households (personal saving), business (retained earnings), and the foreign sector (financial capital inflows). Instead of a trade-off between work and leisure in the supply of labor, there is a trade-off between saving and consumption in supplying the financial capital needed to purchase capital goods.

Interest Rates, Saving, and the Capital Stock

Other things equal, higher interest rates increase saving, while lower interest rates decrease saving. Why is the interest rate an important determinant of saving? People need an incentive to postpone current consumption. Paying interest on savings means that more can be consumed in the future, but unless the interest rate is high enough, people will choose to spend all of their income today. How high does the interest rate have to be to induce saving? That depends on the individual, but it must be high enough to cover two factors: time preference and risk. **Time preference** refers to *how people rank current versus future consumption*. If current consumption is valued more highly than future consumption, then a high interest rate will be necessary to induce people to save. If future consumption is valued highly relative to current consumption, then saving will take place at relatively low interest rates.

Risk affects the saving decision because *it is a situation where the outcome of a decision or future is unknown*. If you are afraid that your savings will not be there when you want to withdraw them, you will need a very high interest rate to overcome the risk of loss. On the other hand, if you are confident that your savings will be there in the future, you may be willing to save at a low interest rate. Risk explains why the interest rate on government bonds is usually lower than the interest rate on corporate securities. The chances of the government declaring bankruptcy are exceedingly small, so people are willing to buy government debt at a low interest rate. On the other hand, even Blue Chip companies might go bankrupt, so people need a risk premium to cover the chance of loss; that risk premium takes the form of an interest rate point or two. But wait: Aren't treasury bills and corporate securities investments? No. To economists, **investment** is *the acquisition of plants and machinery and can be undertaken only by firms*. When households "invest" in the stock market or buy bonds, they are actually saving. This money does end up as investment if the financial institution or firm uses the funds for capital acquisition, but the household decision to save is separate from the firm's decision to invest. Households trade off current and future consumption when they decide to save; the firm's investment decision depends on other factors, including the expectation of profits.

One more preliminary point is necessary before we can draw the supply and demand curves for capital. We need to recall the distinction between investment and capital. Investment is a flow and capital is a stock. The process of acquiring capital is investment. Once investment has taken place, the firm has a stock of capital goods. This is an important distinction because the process of investment is often spread out over several years. At any point in time, the stock of capital is fixed.

Figure 31.8   **The Short-Run and Long-Run Supply Curves for Capital**

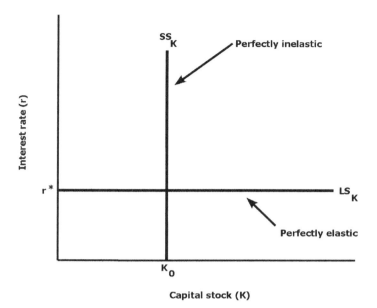

The short-run supply curve for capital, SS_K, is perfectly inelastic because the stock of capital is fixed in the short run. The horizontal intercept of SS_K is the existing stock of capital, K_0. The long-run supply curve for capital, LS_K, is perfectly elastic because households are willing to supply financial capital (savings) at interest rates at or above r^*.

However, in the long run, the supply of capital can be considered infinite because capital goods producers can produce as much capital as industry demands if they have the right price signals.

THE SUPPLY CURVES FOR CAPITAL

The interest rate is the price of capital. Why? When a firm buys a capital good, it ties up money for several years, so it only makes sense to buy a capital good if the return is at least as high as the interest rate that could be earned if the money were spent on a financial asset instead. The return on capital is expressed as a percentage. It is the ratio of additional profits to the cost of capital. This allows firms to compare the return on capital to the interest rate on financial assets. The firm should buy capital as long as the expected return on capital is at least as high as the interest rate.

The long gestation period for capital means that it is best to think of there being two capital supply curves at any point in time. There is a perfectly inelastic short-run supply curve and a perfectly elastic long-run supply curve. These are shown in Figure 31.8. The short-run supply curve for capital goods, SS_K, is a vertical line above the current stock of capital goods, K_0. This curve will shift with changes in the stock of capital goods: an increase in the stock of capital goods will shift it to the right; a decrease will shift it to the left.

The long-run supply curve for capital goods, LS_K, is horizontal to reflect the assumption of a perfectly elastic supply of financial capital in the long run. The vertical intercept of the LS_K is the interest rate, r^*, just high enough to overcome perceptions of risk and time preference and

Figure 31.9 **The Equilibrium Capital Stock**

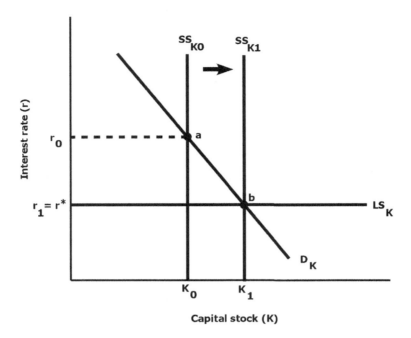

Capital stock (K)

Long-run equilibrium occurs when the long-run capital supply curve (LS_K), the short-run capital supply curve (SS_K), and demand for capital curve (D_K) intersect. In the short run, the capital market operates at the intersection of the short-run capital supply curve and the demand for capital curve. If the market begins at point a with the interest rate r_0 above r^*, households will increase saving because the interest rate is higher than the minimum rate necessary to overcome time preferences. This causes the capital stock to increase and the short-run capital supply curve to move out from SS_{K0} toward SS_{K1} Capital accumulation will continue until the interest rate reaches r^*. This occurs at point b with capital stock K_1 and the simultaneous intersection of SS_{K1}, LS_K, and D_K.

induce saving. At interest rates above r^*, savers will be willing to supply additional savings, so the financial capital necessary to acquire capital goods will be available to firms. At interest rates below r^*, no additional saving and thus no financial capital will be forthcoming, so it will not be possible to increase the stock of capital goods.

The Equilibrium Capital Stock

The capital stock is in equilibrium when the marginal revenue product of capital is equal to the marginal factor cost of capital. The marginal factor cost of capital is the interest rate whether firms borrow or use retained earnings. Firms that borrow to acquire financial capital must pay the interest rate, and firms that use retained earnings incur the opportunity cost of foregone interest they could have earned on an interest-earning financial asset.

When the capital stock is not in equilibrium, there will be adjustments that move it toward equilibrium. This is shown in Figure 31.9, which combines the two capital supply curves from Figure 31.8 with a single capital demand curve. Assume initially that the capital demand curve D_K intersects the short-run capital supply curve SS_{K0} at r_0, an interest rate above r^*. This means that the return on capital is greater than the interest rate required for additional saving. Thus, firms will be willing to offer rates above r^* to borrow money. This will increase the amount of saving. When this money is lent to firms, the short-run capital stock will increase and the short-run capital supply curve will shift to the right. This will continue until the short-run supply curve, SS_{K1}, crosses the capital demand curve at its intersection with the long-run supply curve, LS_K. If the situation were reversed and the market interest rate began below r^*, the capital stock would shrink—firms would not replace worn out machinery—and the short-run supply curve would shift left until long-run equilibrium is restored. Our conclusion: the capital stock is in equilibrium only when the return on capital is equal to r^*.

Some Caveats

Like our discussion of the labor market, this section is meant to be only a brief introduction into marginal productivity theory of capital, but we still need to mention a couple of issues here before proceeding. First, when we drew the demand and supply curves for capital, we were implicitly stating that it was possible to buy capital goods in infinitesimal units. That is only rarely the case. Most often, capital goods are available only in "lumpy" units—you either buy a whole machine or you do not. This means, among other things, that changes in the demand for capital or interest rates may not always result in a change in the amount of capital that is actually purchased. A second problem is that new capital goods are often different from old capital goods. In fact, technological evolution may mean that it is impossible to buy capital goods like your old ones. The new ones may be technologically superior, but they may also be more expensive or require different kinds of labor inputs. Even cheap and highly productive capital goods may not be a good deal if you have to retrain the entire workforce. These and other problems with the marginal productivity theory of capital do not mean that we should reject the analysis entirely, only that we must use it cautiously.

The Market for Land and Natural Resources

When economists use the term *land*, only rarely do they mean the ground we walk on. Most often, they are referring to undeveloped land or natural resources. The markets for undeveloped land and natural resources differ from the markets for labor and capital in an important way. They are in fixed supply. The analysis of both resources is similar, so we use the term *land* when referring to either except where a distinction is necessary.

Goods that are in fixed supply are represented by vertical supply curves like the one shown in Figure 31.10. The vertical axis of Figure 31.10 measures the amount of economic rent that landowners charge for use of their land. **Economic rent** is *a factor payment over and above the payment necessary to bring that factor into production.* Undeveloped land is there for the taking, so no payment is needed to use it unless landowners charge for it. If there is no demand for land, the landowner receives no payment. As demand for land increases, the landowner can charge a higher price, even though there has been no change in the quantity of unimproved land (U).

The earnings of the landowner depend strictly on the level of demand. This is shown in Figure 31.10, where the initial level of demand is D_{U0}. The demand curve intersects the fixed supply curve at point A and results in a rental price of rt_0. The landowner receives rent equal to the shaded area $0Uart_0$. If the population grows and the demand curve shifts out to D_{U1}, the rental price will rise to rt_1 and the landowner will gain the cross-hatched area rt_0abrt_1. The key point is that the landowner did nothing to earn this extra income. Rent increased solely because of population growth.

It is important to distinguish between improved and unimproved land. Land in its natural state

Figure 31.10   **The Price of Unimproved Land**

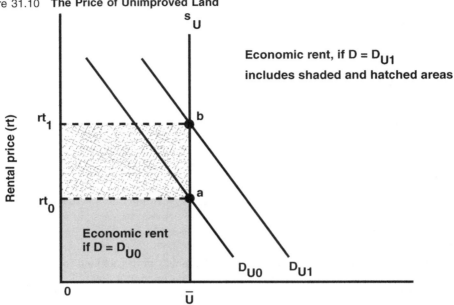

The supply of unimproved land (and natural resources) is fixed so it can be represented by a vertical supply curve. The demand for land determines the rental price that can be charged. When demand is D_{U0}, the landowner receives economic rent equal to the shaded area. An increase in population will increase the demand for land and shift the demand curve out from D_{U0} to D_{U1} This will cause the rental price to rise from rt_0 to rt_1 Here, when demand is D_{U1}, the landowner receives economic rent equal to both shaded and hatched areas. All of this rent is called economic rent because the same quantity of land, U-bar, would be available whether any rent was paid or not.

is in fixed supply, so the payment to the landowner represents pure economic rent. On the other hand, improved land is not available in fixed supply, and higher rents will induce the landowner to increase the quantity supplied of improved land. *The rent on improved land depends on both supply and demand* and is called **marginal productivity rent**, not economic rent.

Finally, even though economists use the term *land* to refer to both land and natural resources, there are times when it is necessary to make a distinction between the two. One situation arises when trying to determine the existing stock of a particular natural resource. Geologists will tell us that there is a fixed amount of oil in the ground, but economists know that much of that oil is too expensive to extract. As the price of oil rises, however, the quantity of available oil will rise. For example, only after OPEC raised the price of oil to $30 per barrel did it make economic sense to search for oil in the Arctic and the Bering Sea. What this means is that the supply curve for many natural resources is only vertical at very high prices or when available technology allows extraction of all resources. Until that point, the supply curve for natural resources is upward sloping.

PROFITS AND THE ADDING UP PROBLEM

Are labor, land, and capital the only three factors of production? They are if you define the categories broadly enough. For example, technology can be included in capital; and human skills and human capital serve to distinguish between different classifications of labor. Still, economists do not agree on how to categorize the work of the manager or entrepreneur. Many economists recognize that there are different kinds of labor and simply lump management into labor. But others believe that entrepreneurial behavior is fundamentally different from other kinds of labor. Not only must entrepreneurs determine how to combine the factors of production in the most efficient manner, but they also take risks when they set up a new business. What is the payment to these risk-taking entrepreneurs? Profit. This is not a trivial concept if you believe that the quest for profit is the most important incentive in market economies.

The term *profit* is not as easy to define as you might think. The simplest definition is probably the residual leftover after all other costs of production have been paid. This definition corresponds to the formula we used earlier: profit equals total revenue minus total costs. Unfortunately, when we try to actually measure profits in the real world, all sorts of complications arise. For example, suppose that total cost is $1 million and total revenue is $1.2 million. This means the firm has earned $200,000 in profits, right? Not necessarily. If the entrepreneur decides to plow that $200,000 back into the firm, profits—at least from the tax accountant's standpoint—go to zero because the "profit" has just become a production expense. From a regulatory standpoint, it is even more difficult to define profit. Utility regulations often permit utility firms to make a "fair return on a fair valuation of capital." But just what is a "fair return"? If we knew that, many of the utility rate battles of the past never would have occurred. The point is that profit is a nebulous concept.

Marginal productivity theory treats profit as another factor payment, the reward to the entrepreneur. However, it is also considered a residual and is calculated after the fact by appealing to an important theorem known as **Euler's theorem**. (Euler is pronounced *oiler*.) The essential result of Euler's theorem is that *factor payments must "add up" to exhaust the value of output.* In other words, if output sells for $1 million, the payments to the factors of production must also be equal to $1 million. Is this always true? Yes—because the payment to the entrepreneur is the residual leftover after all other factors have been paid.

We can see the importance of Euler's theorem by looking at Figure 31.11, which shows the market for labor. As usual, competitive firms hire workers until the marginal revenue product ($MRP = D_L$) of the last worker hired is equal to the wage rate. This means that the total payment is equal to the wage rate, W, times the number of workers hired, L. This is the area 0-L-a-W in the diagram. However, because of diminishing returns, labor's contribution to the production process is greater than 0-L-a-W. Only the last worker hired had a contribution equal to the wage rate; the marginal revenue product of all other workers was higher than the wage rate. Does this mean that those workers have been exploited? No, at least not according to marginal productivity theory. Workers are productive only if they have land and capital to work with, so some of the workers' contribution must be set aside to pay for the other factors of production. The triangle Wab represents that payment. The same arguments apply to the other factors of production. According to Euler's theorem, the area in the triangle Wab is exactly equal to the contribution of all factors of production except labor.

What makes this result interesting (or questionable, depending on your point of view) is that whatever payment is left for the entrepreneur after paying wages, interest, and marginal productivity rents is assumed to be a payment for risk-taking, efficient management, and so on. Thus, an entrepreneur who makes $100,000 "deserves" $100,000 because of efficient management; an entrepreneur who loses $100,000 "deserves" to lose $100,000 because of ineptitude. As we know, not everyone agrees with this view.

Figure 31.11 **The Adding Up Problem**

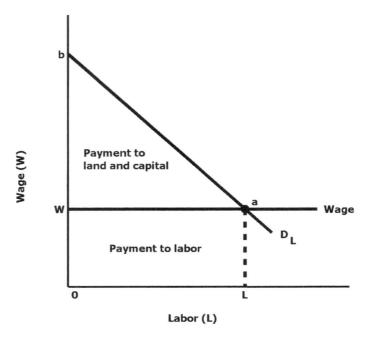

According to Euler's theorem, total factor payments exhaust the revenue earned from selling the product. In this diagram, the wage bill for labor is equal to the area 0-L-a-W. Labor contributes more to the production process only because it has capital and land to work with. The triangle W-a-b represents the contributions of other factors to the productivity of labor. This revenue is needed to pay the other factors of production.

SUMMARY OF APPENDIX 31.1

The acquisition of capital is complex and time consuming, but firms follow the same kind of optimization rules for capital and land as they do for any other factors of production.

1. The demand for labor is derived from the productivity of labor and the demand for final products. The marginal revenue product is the demand curve for labor. When there is competition in the output market, marginal revenue product is found by multiplying the marginal physical product of labor by the selling price of output. Firms hire workers until the marginal revenue product of the last worker hired is equal to the marginal factor cost.
2. The supply of financial capital depends on the supply of household savings. Households will save if the interest rate is above r^*, the rate necessary to cover risk and time preference. Firms must acquire financial capital before they can purchase capital goods.
3. In the short run, the stock of capital goods is fixed, so the supply curve for capital goods is perfectly inelastic. The long-run supply curve for capital is perfectly elastic because financial capital is available if interest rates exceed r^*.
4. The return on capital is the ratio of the change in profits attributable to the new capital

good to the cost of the capital good. Firms acquire capital goods as long as the return on new capital goods is equal to or greater than r^*.

5. If the return on capital is greater than r^*, the short-run capital supply curve will shift out and increase the capital stock; if the return on capital is less than r^*, the short-run capital supply curve will shift in and decrease the capital stock.

6. When factors of production are in fixed supply, they command economic rents. This may be the case with undeveloped land: landowners receive higher rents if the demand for unimproved land increases even though the supply of unimproved land is fixed.

7. Profit is the residual that is paid to the entrepreneur after all factors of production have received their payments. According to marginal productivity theory, profit is the reward entrepreneurs receive for taking risks. Total income is completely exhausted by total factor payments.

KEY TERMS IN APPENDIX 31.1

accumulated net marginal revenue product
economic rent
Euler's theorem
financial capital

investment
marginal productivity rent
risk
time preference

REVIEW QUESTIONS FOR APPENDIX 31.1

Use marginal productivity theory to explain the optimal, profit-maximizing level of inputs.

1. Explain the rationale behind the optimal input rule—that is, that firms should hire factors until MRP = MFC. Draw a diagram to illustrate your answer.

Use marginal productivity theory to explain prices of capital and natural resources.

2. What conditions must hold for the capital market to be in equilibrium? What will happen if the return on capital is less than the rate necessary to overcome risk and time preference? Draw a diagram to illustrate your result.

3. Suppose that the marginal revenue product of capital is greater than r^*, the interest rate necessary to induce saving. However, instead of buying more capital, the firm hires more labor. Would this tend to increase or decrease profits? Why?

Explain the concept of economic rent.

4. Carefully distinguish between marginal productivity rent and economic rent. When does land command economic rent? marginal productivity rent? Draw a diagram to illustrate your answer.

5. Do entrepreneur's "deserve" the money they make? Answer according to marginal productivity theory.

6. Economic rents can be earned on all factors of production, not just unimproved land. Explain whether and why each of the following may command economic rent:
   a. a Beatles reunion concert
   b. Harvard University
   c. a burger flipper at MacDonald's
   d. your college economics professor
   e. your high school history teacher

7. Suppose you bought 100 acres of farmland, installed an irrigation system, and built a farmhouse. You then rented the property for $5,000 per month. Five years later, you have made no improvements on the land and you raise the rent to $7,000 per month. Does the rent increase represent pure economic rent? Explain why or why not.

APPENDIX 31.2
LABOR THEORY OF VALUE VERSUS NEOCLASSICAL MARGINAL PRODUCTIVITY

The progressive view of production theory was stated briefly in this chapter, but this appendix provides a fuller analysis of the progressive labor theory and the neoclassical marginal productivity theory on this point.

LEARNING OBJECTIVES FOR APPENDIX 31.2

After reading and studying this chapter, you should be able to:

- List and explain the differences in the approaches of traditional and progressive economists in explaining labor markets and labor market outcomes.

THE BATTLE OF WAGES AND PROFITS

For about two hundred years, economists have fought ferociously over how to explain wages and profits. What is all the fuss about? There are highly complex mathematical theories supporting the neoclassical marginal utility/marginal product theory, but the radical labor theory showing exploitation has equally complex mathematical theories supporting it. The anger is not over mathematical details. The anger reflects a political and ethical fight over who gets what. Traditional economists claim that every employee gets what he or she deserves from the economy. Progressives, by contrast, claim that a surplus above their wages or salaries is extracted from employees to become the profits of the employers. One theory defends the system as perfect if everything works correctly, while the other theory criticizes the system even if everything works as the textbooks say it should.

In neoclassical economic theory, production is viewed as a process in which three separate and distinct factors of production are combined to produce a variety of outputs. These three factors are called land, labor, and capital. Each factor is said to make a definite, measurable contribution to production. The rewards to the three factors are asserted to be determined by the contributions that each factor makes to the production process. Thus, landlords receive rent for the use of their land, workers receive wages for the use of their labor power, and capitalists receive profits according to the productiveness of their capital.

The labor theory of value begins with a completely different view of the production process. Production is seen as a purely human activity in which humans expand labor on material objects given in nature. The labor theory starts with the fact that, unlike many species of animals, human beings rarely find a natural environment that is immediately acceptable for the satisfaction of their material needs. Subsistence requires the material necessities of food, shelter, and clothing. The enjoyment of pleasures beyond mere subsistence requires other material objects. Nature almost never provides the material prerequisites for human subsistence and pleasure in a directly usable form.

To sustain life, people must transform the natural environment from its unusable state to a state that is serviceable for human needs. This transformation is solely and purely a human activity. The outer crust of the earth existed for untold thousands of years before the appearance of the first human beings. No person is responsible for its existence, nor is anyone responsible for the particular properties of the natural environment, by virtue of which it can be adapted to fulfill people's needs.

People cannot live in a vacuum, nor can they live in the void of outer space. This seemingly obvious statement must be stressed, because distortions and misrepresentations of the labor theory have asserted that the theory ignores the "contributions" of the natural environment. The labor theory begins by taking the earth or natural environment as given independent of any human being or human endeavor. Thus, the land and natural environment are vital to production, but no class of landlords can claim to have provided it in any way. The fact that they own the land and natural resources does not mean that they produced the land.

In traditional theory, production is viewed as a process in which people and resources are co-equal contributors. Thus, some people ought to be paid for nature's contribution. In the labor theory of value, production consists solely of human exertion applied to raw materials in order to transform them into products of human labor that are capable of sustaining life.

The earliest forms of production were very simple and direct. Shelters were made from caves or with trees and branches. Fruits and nuts were picked and gathered, while small animals were killed for food and clothing. From this simple state of affairs, in which life must have been very difficult and precarious, all human progress was based on finding new, more complex methods of producing that would increase human productivity. This meant developing tools with which people could more effectively transform their environment. All human beings of whom we have any direct or indirect knowledge have used tools. Increases in human productivity have been the result of increased knowledge of ways in which the natural environment could be transformed and of increasingly sophisticated and complex tools with which to effect the transformation.

Traditional economic theory defines capital to include tools, machines, factories, and partially processed raw materials. In this view, not only human labor, but also capital, is and always will be a factor of production. Therefore, the owners of capital are said to receive profits because capital is "productive." This assertion confuses material things with human relations.

In the labor theory, on the contrary, factories, tools, machinery, and partly finished raw materials are defined as means of production. (In previous societies, land was the most important means of production, but now it plays a relatively minor role.) The means of production are the physical aspect of capital. But capital in our economy also has a monetary aspect. When a banker loans a billion dollars to a corporation and the corporation uses it to buy the means of production (or physical capital), that billion dollars is not just money, it is financial capital. Both the physical and monetary aspects of capital are important, but they do not sufficiently define capital. For example, if a worker has $10 in money, and if that is not enough to go into business, the money is not "capital." Or if a worker has a tool, such as a lawn mower, that the worker uses for his or her own private purposes, the tool is not capital. So what determines when a tool is capital?

In a capitalist society, there are a particular set of human relationships. One class, called employers (or capitalists), owns the physical and monetary capital. Another class, called employees (or workers), uses the physical capital to produce things. Employees produce both consumer goods and more physical capital. The human relations, codified into laws between employees and employers, determine what we call capital. For example, if an employer hires many employees to cut lawns as a paid service to consumers, then the lawn mowers the employer owns are capital. If the employer spends $10 to repair one of those lawn mowers, that $10 is a capital expenditure.

Of course, the reason that economists study such human relations and argue about definitions of capital or theories of value is ultimately to justify or attack the system of private profit. This is why conservatives insist that private ownership of capital and production based on profit motives is the only way to organize an economic system. Radicals offer the alternative that capital could be owned by a collective group of workers or by all of society through a democratic process. In such a system, profit would be used for collective or social purposes rather than for private purposes.

The marginal utility theory gives students the false idea that there is some inherent difference between items and their utility that determines, in part, the price of hammers versus shoes, for instance. Similarly, in neoclassical production theory, students are told that it is the marginal product of an input that determines its return. Neoclassical economists fail to report that almost no studies are done to determine the marginal product of any input. In terms of labor, the most famous studies involve very narrow, specialized forms of labor such as baseball pitchers. In contrast, the labor theory points out that prices reflect the work that people have expended to produce a good or service. Prices also reflect the way our society is organized into employers and employees rather than in some other system of human relations, such as slavery. Economics is about human relationships, not about inert objects. For radicals, wages are determined not only by the labor embodied but also by power. For some reason, neoclassical economists never talk about how economic or political power can influence how much one is paid. They also rarely, if ever, mention the role that class struggle plays in determining income and wealth distribution.

Just to make life difficult for students, remember that other theories have spoken to this subject. The Sraffian theory, named after Pierro Sraffa, says that both marginal productivity and the labor theory of value are incorrect. Progressive followers of Sraffa do find that exploitation exists and can be best explained by his theory. There are also many institutionalist economists who do not like any of the other three theories mentioned here but believe that the institutions of capitalism lead to exploitation.

REVIEW QUESTIONS

List and explain the differences in the approaches of traditional and progressive economists in explaining labor markets and labor market outcomes.

1. Compare and contrast the debate over "who gets what" according to traditional and progressive analysis.
2. Describe how traditional and progressive analyses think about marginal productivity.

PART II, SECTION 5

NEOCLASSICAL APPROACH TO MARKET STRUCTURE AND MARKET FAILURE

CHAPTER 32

Prices and Profits in Perfect Competition

In this chapter, we discuss the production decisions of the firm in a purely competitive market structure. In Chapter 33, we discuss the prices and profits for a perfect monopoly market, and in Chapter 34 for monopolistically competitive and oligopolistic market structures. At the outset, we should state that very few, if any, firms operate in a situation of pure competition or pure monopoly, so analysis of these situations is not realistic for understanding most pricing procedures. Nearly all businesses in the United States today are in either monopolistically competitive or oligopolistic industries. Yet it remains important to understand pure competition and monopoly. The importance of understanding the analysis of pure competition is largely ideological. Among conservatives, this analysis is depicted either as the actual state of affairs or as the desired or ideal state of affairs. The analysis of monopoly is important because, as we see in the next chapter, even though there are very few actual firms that fit the usual definition of a monopoly, most oligopolistic firms operate to some degree as though they are monopolies.

LEARNING OBJECTIVES

After reading this chapter, you should be able to:

- List and explain the assumptions and characteristics of the four market structures.
- Explain what it means and why firms in a competitive market are "price takers."
- Describe the demand curve facing the individual firm in a competitive market.
- Explain the profit-maximizing level of output for the individual firm in a competitive market.
- Understand criticisms of the competitive market model and its assumptions.

MARKET STRUCTURES AND THE DEGREE OF COMPETITION

A **perfectly competitive market** is one in which four essential conditions are present:

- The industry is made up of a large number of firms and a large number of buyers of the produce they sell.
- Each seller supplies so small a percentage of the market that its actions have virtually no effect on the price at which the industry sells the product. *Each buyer demands so small a percentage of output that the buyer's purchases alone also have virtually no effect on the*

price at which the industry sells the product. That means both the seller and the buyer are **price takers**. Individual firms must take the price as determined in the market.
- It is very easy for new firms to enter the industry or for old firms to leave it.
- Each firm produces a product that is so nearly identical to the product of the other firms that consumers are largely indifferent about which firm within the industry produced the product they buy.

Unlike a firm in a perfectly competitive market operating under the conditions listed above, a **perfect monopoly** exists when *there is only one seller of a product that has no close substitutes.* In a monopolistic industry, one firm is the industry. That means the monopolist can manipulate the price of its product. *A monopolist is a* **price maker**. If the monopolist's position is to be maintained, it must erect barriers that prevent competitors from entering the industry. If it is successful in doing this, the payoff is generally very large.

Between the extremes of pure competition and monopoly, economists make two further classifications. **Monopolistic competition** is *a market structure with elements of perfect competition and monopoly.* Like perfect competition, a monopolistically competitive industry has a large number of sellers. Unlike perfect competition, sellers engage in product differentiation. A product may be differentiated in various ways; for example, one seller packages the product more attractively or gives friendlier service. In any event, some consumers prefer one or another particular seller's product. Product differentiation and brand names create a monopoly over that brand for its producer. For this reason, firms have a degree of control over price. Other firms can enter the industry, but no other firm can produce that brand.

Closer to a monopoly (and often tantamount to it) is an **oligopoly**. *An oligopolistic industry has a few giant sellers, each of which controls a significant share of the market.* Entry into an oligopolistic industry is very difficult, often as difficult as entry into a monopolistic industry. There is generally, but not always, some product differentiation. The most significant feature of an oligopoly is that, because of the interdependence of its members, no firm can make significant changes in price without taking into account the reactions of its competitors.

The analyses of monopolistic competition and oligopoly include, within their definition, nearly all of the business firms in the United States today. We discuss these market structures in Chapter 34. For the remainder of this chapter, we turn our attention to the discussion of pure competition.

DEMAND AND PRICE FOR A PURELY COMPETITIVE FIRM

Looking at the market demand curve for a whole industry, we know that a larger amount can be sold only at a lower price. This is not the case for the single competitive firm. In a purely competitive industry, each firm is so small that whatever quantity it chooses to sell will have a negligible effect on the supply for the entire industry. Therefore, it can sell all that it wishes at the market equilibrium price. The situation for a purely competitive industry and one firm within that industry is demonstrated graphically in Figure 32.1. Figure 32.1(a) shows the supply and demand for coats, which is assumed to be a purely competitive industry. Figure 32.1(b) shows the price curve (or demand curve, since they are the same in this case) for the individual coat-making firm.

The price of a coat ($100) is determined in the industry wide market for coats by the intersection of the industry supply and demand curves. The graph shows that at this price the individual firm can sell any quantity it wishes. It is assumed that the individual firm cannot affect supply for the entire industry and that the market demand is equal to the supply at the prevailing price ($100). Therefore, the firm never experiences any problem in selling all it wishes to sell at this price.

Figure 32.1 **Supply and Demand for Coats**

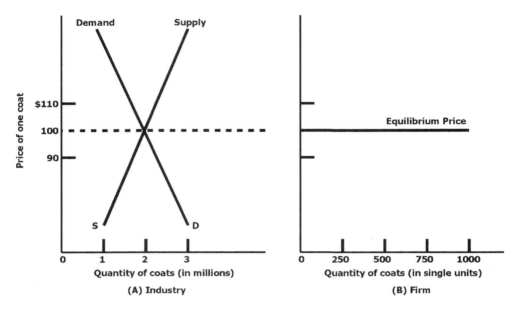

(A) Industry

(B) Firm

As a result, the demand curve for the individual firm's output is a horizontal line at the industry-determined price. The firm sells any quantity it chooses at this price. Let us assume that it decides to raise its price in order to increase its revenue. Because all the firms in a purely competitive industry produce an identical product, no consumer will pay more than $100 for one firm's product when he or she can buy an identical product from a competitor for $100. Similarly, the firm will never sell any quantity at a price below $100. Because it can sell any quantity it chooses at $100, there would be no incentive for it to lower the price. Thus, the firm in a purely competitive industry faces a given price; it cannot vary it upward, and it does not wish to vary it downward. (The situation is very different for a monopoly.)

SUPPLY AND THE COSTS OF PRODUCTION

In this section, we analyze the firm's cost during the short run, when its output is limited to the productive capacity of its current plant and equipment. Over a longer period, the firm could construct a larger plant and install new equipment, thus expanding its scale of operations. For the shorter period considered here, these capital goods are fixed in size and number. Because the amount of a firm's plant and equipment is fixed in the short run, some of its costs must be considered fixed whether it produces nothing or operates at capacity. Fixed costs include the maintenance of plant and equipment, rent, and salaries of watchmen, caretakers, and others. Obviously, if the firm produces more goods, then the average fixed cost will decline because the same cost is spread over, or divided by, more units.

Even during the short run, however, some costs, notably those of labor and material, are variable. The firm can produce more or less of its product by hiring more or fewer workers and using more or less raw materials. Remember from the previous chapter that the average variable cost for a unit of output is obtained by taking the total cost of labor and raw materials and dividing it by the quantity produced.

Figure 32.2   **Average Cost (AC) of Coats**

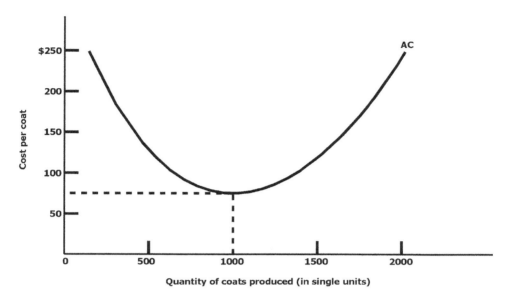

After engineers have calculated the various rates at which the different productive processes will take place, the plant is constructed and equipped in such a way that there is some optimal level of production at which all production processes can be effectively coordinated. Average variable costs are lowest at the optimum level of production but higher both below and above that level. Because average fixed costs fall continuously, the total result is that average cost per unit may fall rapidly at first and continue to fall until the optimal point is achieved, then average cost may slowly rise. This usual short-run behavior of average costs (a U-shaped curve) is illustrated in Figure 32.2.

According to Figure 32.2, the quantity of 1,000 coats is the production level at which all production processes are most effectively coordinated and plant and equipment are most efficiently utilized (the cost is only $75 per coat). At smaller quantities, some equipment is underutilized, and consequently, average costs are higher. At larger quantities, the fixed amount of plant and equipment is being overutilized, and various other bottlenecks and inefficiencies are encountered (diminishing returns). Consequently, average costs are higher. The further a firm moves from the optimally efficient quantity (1,000 coats in this case), the higher its average costs are. This is true whether the firm produces smaller or larger quantities than the optimal amount.

Because it is the basis of the supply curve, marginal cost is even more important than average cost. Marginal cost is defined as follows:

$$\text{Marginal cost} = \frac{\text{Increase in total cost}}{\text{Increase in quantity}}$$

Because we may speak of decrease as well as increase, we may substitute the word *change* for increase in the definition to make it more general.

In Figure 32.3, marginal cost represents the increase in total costs of production attributable to an

Figure 32.3 **Average Cost (AC) and Marginal Cost (MC) of Coats**

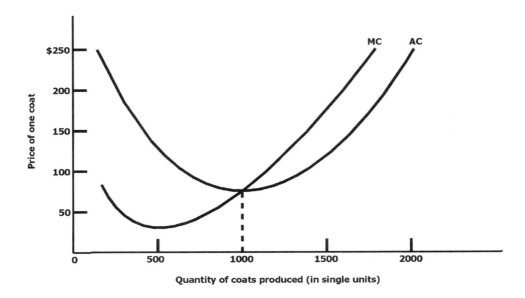

increase in output of one additional coat. If the change in cost of producing one more coat is lower than the average cost of producing the product, then it may be said that the lower marginal cost is pulling the average cost downward. This is similar to the case of a person taking several tests. The last test score pulls the average score up or down, depending on whether it is higher or lower than the average. Thus, it is possible to conclude that as long as the average cost is declining, the marginal cost must be below it. When the average cost is rising, the marginal cost must be above it, pulling it upward. These relations between the average and marginal are illustrated in Figure 32.3.

Notice that at low production levels, those at which each additional coat is produced at less cost, marginal cost is very low (only $25 at 500 coats) and is well below the average cost. But at production beyond the optimal capacity, when the average cost of producing coats is rising, marginal cost rises rapidly to a high level ($150 at 1,500 coats) and goes higher and higher above the average as more coats are produced. These mechanical relations may be summarized as follows: (1) average cost is at its minimum when it is equal to marginal cost; (2) when marginal cost is below average cost, it is pulling average cost downward; (3) when marginal cost is above average cost, it is pulling average cost up.

There is only one other essential point to be made in this discussion of costs. Total costs can be shown quite easily on a graph of per-unit costs. Because the average cost is the total cost divided by the quantity produced, it follows that total cost is given by multiplying the average cost by the quantity produced. In Figure 32.4, total cost is shown as a shaded rectangle.

Taking any quantity (for example, 700 coats in Figure 32.4), we go up the average-cost curve and then over to the cost axis of the graph. Here the average cost per unit required to produce 700 coats is found to be $80. We know that the total cost will equal 700 × $80. But because line 0–700 and line $0–$80 are adjacent sides of a rectangle, their product is equal to the area of the rectangle. Therefore, the shaded rectangle in Figure 32.4 represents the total cost of producing 700 coats: 700 × $80 = $56,000.

Figure 32.4 **Average, Marginal, and Total Costs of Coats**

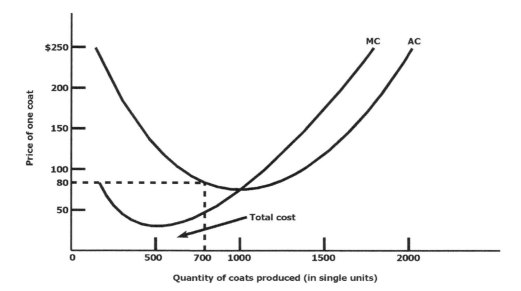

Quantity of coats produced (in single units)

MAXIMUM PROFIT UNDER COMPETITION

In an earlier section, it was shown that once the price of the industry's product is determined, the individual competitive firm faces a demand curve (or a given price) that is a straight, horizontal line. It is further assumed that each firm has the U-shaped short-run average cost curve described earlier. In Figure 32.5, the demand curve has been superimposed on the cost curves in order to present the whole picture for the competitive firm.

In order to understand the firm's reaction to the market price ($100), it is necessary to specify what motivates the firm's owners (or managers). The answer provided by the vast majority of economists, from Adam Smith to the present, is that the one overriding objective of all capitalists, or their managers, is to maximize their profits. We therefore assume that all firm owners seek to maximize profits.

The manager whose cost and revenue curves are pictured in Figure 32.5 will maximize his profits by producing and selling 1,200 coats. At this quantity, the firm's marginal cost is equal to its price. The **rule for maximizing profit under competition** is to *produce the quantity that equates marginal cost and price*. The combined area of the two shaded rectangles in Figure 32.5 is equal to the firm's total income from sales or revenue (because it represents the price times the quantity the firm sells). The area of the lower rectangle is equal to the firm's total cost (because it is the product of the firm's average cost and the quantity produced). The area of the upper rectangle is equal to the firm's profit (because it represents the total revenue minus total costs, which is, by definition, profit).

In order to understand why 1,200 coats is the quantity that maximizes the firm's profit, imagine that the firm produces and sells a smaller quantity of the product. For any quantity below 1,200, the firm's price per unit is higher than its marginal cost. Consequently, if the firm produces and sells an additional coat, this last coat will add more to the firm's profit. As long as the firm is producing fewer than 1,200 coats, it can add to its profit by producing and selling more coats.

Figure 32.5 **Price (or Demand) and Cost of Coats**

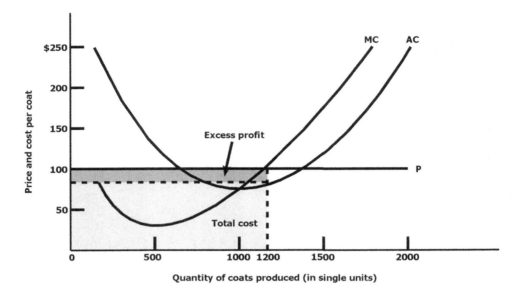

Quantity of coats produced (in single units)

However, imagine that the firm is producing more than 1,200 coats. For any quantity above 1,200, the firm's marginal cost exceeds its price per unit. If the firm were to produce and sell one less coat, the reduction in its costs would exceed the reduction in its revenue. Its profit would therefore increase. As long as the firm continues to sell more than 1,200 coats, it can add to its profit by producing and selling less. It is now easy to see why the competitive firm maximizes its profit by equating its marginal cost and its price.

For any price that prevails in the market, the marginal cost curve will indicate what quantity the firm would like to sell. A line showing the quantities a firm would like to sell at various prices is exactly what we defined a supply curve to be. Therefore, in pure competition, a firm's marginal cost curve is its supply curve. Because the industry is simply the total of the firms within it, the industry's supply curve is the summation of the marginal cost curves of all these firms.

PROGRESSIVE CRITICISM OF THE NEOCLASSICAL VIEW OF PURE COMPETITION

Pure competition requires many conditions to be true. One requirement to fit the neoclassical theory of pure competition is that there should be a very large number of firms, with each firm being so small relative to the market that any action it takes has an insignificant affect on the price. Yet in almost all industries, whether manufacturing or service, we find that only a few large firms have most of the sales, most of the profit, and the power to influence prices.

For example, in software production, there are many small firms, but there is also the supergiant Microsoft. In a purely competitive market, if Microsoft raised its price for Windows by one dollar, it would lose all its customers to competing firms. In reality, there is little that can substitute for Windows, so if Microsoft raises its price by one dollar, it loses very few customers. Thus, it can set prices other than the competitive market price.

You have probably wondered which industries in the contemporary American economy are purely competitive. Only one or two industries (out of many thousands) in the entire American economy present a factual resemblance to the model just worked through. The most obvious choice of a purely competitive market might be from agriculture. Traditionally, in the wheat industry, for example, each farmer produced a homogeneous product, and no farmer produced enough to affect the price significantly. Each would take as given the price determined in the market. Whether all or none of the individual farmer's crop was sold at this price was virtually irrelevant to the determination of price.

Over the past several decades, however, two important changes have occurred in agricultural markets: (1) the government has intervened extensively in the market through various schemes of subsidies and production controls; (2) the agricultural industry (particularly the buyers of grain) has increasingly come under the control of giant corporations that in no way resemble the small, relatively powerless firms pictured in the theory. These two developments have so fundamentally altered the agricultural market that the model of pure competition definitely does not explain or describe it.

If only one or two industries even resemble the model, then a question must be asked: What is the relevance of this analysis to the American economy today? The answer is that the analysis reveals more about the thinking of many economists than it does about the functioning of the economy. The model of pure competition is the basis of the traditional economists' claim that the private enterprise market system results in a situation of optimum production and distributional efficiency. From the analysis just presented, it can be seen that in pure competition each firm, in equilibrium, produces the quantity at which its costs are minimized and its production is most efficient. The firm receives only the socially defined normal rate of profit. No excess profits exist. The consumer is able to purchase the product at the lowest possible price. The theory also claims that every factor of production receives in return the value of what it contributes to production (although the theory says nothing about the inequitable ownership of factors of production that prevails).

The traditional analysis is generally used to show that the free enterprise market economy is the best and most just of all possible worlds. Therefore, the theory of pure competition is studied here primarily to understand the basis of a very important conservative ideology supporting capitalism. The model of pure competition, in its simplest form, also provides analytic tools that can be used to study more realistic cases.

SUMMARY

Orthodox price theory usually distinguishes four different types of market structures within which firms operate: pure competition, monopolistic competition, oligopoly, and monopoly. In this chapter, after defining the four market structures, we focused our attention on pure competition. In perfect competition, the firm has no control over the price it charges for its product. The demand curve of the individual firm in a perfectly competitive market is a single price, a horizontal line, determined by equilibrium price in the market. The firm is one of many firms in the market producing identical goods. When we put the average cost and marginal cost curves of the firm over the demand curve (remember, it's a horizontal line), we can determine the profit-maximizing level of output for the firm. The optimal level of output is where the marginal cost curve intersects the demand curve. Once the output is determined, we can use the average cost curve to determine whether the firm is earning a positive, negative, or normal profit. Progressive criticisms of the competitive market model are centered around the reality that there are few, if any, markets that meet the criteria of a perfectly competitive market. The competitive market model underpins the support for the capitalist market system. The tools used to develop the model are useful for comparing other market structures.

KEY TERMS

monopolistic competition
oligopoly
perfect monopoly
perfectly competitive market

price maker
price taker
rule for maximizing profit under competition

REVIEW QUESTIONS

List and explain the assumptions and characteristics of the four market structures.
1. Explain the significance of each assumption in terms of creating "perfect competition."
2. What assumptions of a perfectly competitive market are violated in each of the other market structures.

Explain what it means and why firms in a competitive market are "price takers."
3. Describe why it takes many firms in a market in order for an individual firm to be price taker.
4. Use a supply and demand graph of a market to demonstrate and explain the price an individual firm "takes."

Describe the demand curve facing the individual firm in a competitive market.
5. Why is the individual firm's product demand curve horizontal? What happens if firms deviate from that price?
6. Why is the assumption of homogenous products important for the horizontal demand curve of individual firms?

Explain the profit-maximizing level of output for the individual firm in a competitive market.
7. Define and describe costs in the short run. Demonstrate their relationships graphically. What happens to MC if labor costs increase?
8. Explain why firms would not produce where MC > MR or where MC < MR.

Understand criticisms of the competitive market model and its assumptions.
9. Why are there so few industries that would be considered perfectly competitive?
10. Why and why not are agricultural markets an example of perfectly competitive markets?

APPENDIX 32.1
LONG-RUN EQUILIBRIUM FOR THE FIRM AND
THE INDUSTRY IN PERFECT COMPETITION

This appendix continues the discussion of firms in a perfectly competitive market by looking at decisions and outcomes for firms the long run when all inputs, and therefore costs, are considered variable.

Figure 32.6 **Competitive Equilibrium in the Coat Market**

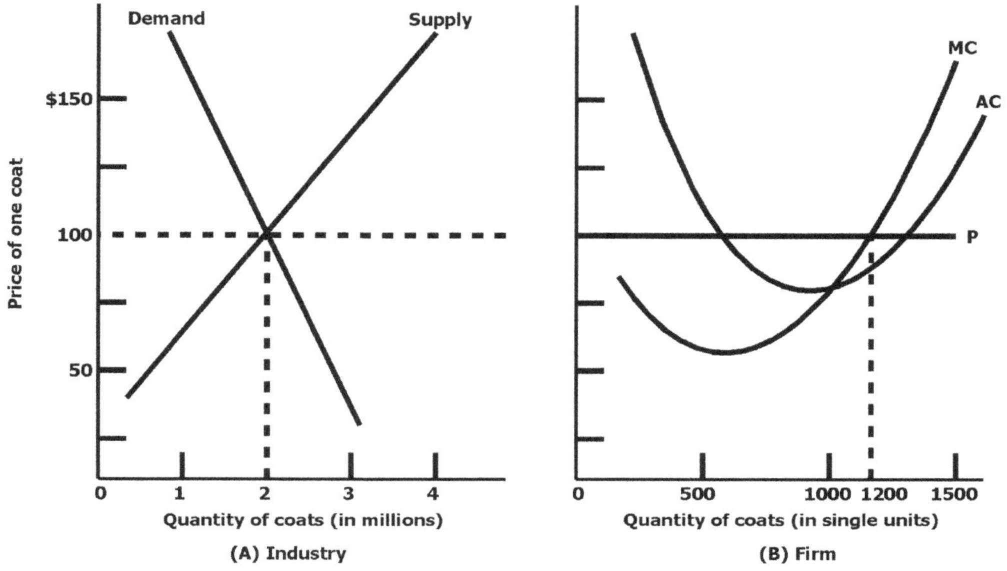

(A) Industry

(B) Firm

LEARNING OBJECTIVES FOR APPENDIX 32.1

After reading this chapter, you should be able to:

- Understand the profit-maximizing level of output in the long run.
- Explain the dynamics of the competitive market that ensure normal profits for all firms in the long run.

COMPETITIVE MARKETS IN THE LONG RUN

In the purely competitive industry, price is determined by the intersection of the industry supply and demand curves. The individual firm adjusts its quantity in order to maximize profit. Figure 32.6 shows an individual firm's cost and revenue curves.

In Figure 32.6, the firm and industry are in short-run, but not long-run, equilibrium. The firm is in short-run equilibrium because it is producing at the point where its price and marginal cost are equal. But the firm is receiving excess profits. In long-run equilibrium, neither the industry nor the firm is making excess profits.

Two points should be made about the firm's excess profits: (1) It is assumed that all firms in an industry have access both to the same technology that this firm is using and to inputs of comparable quality. Therefore, it can be concluded that the cost curves of virtually all firms in the industry are nearly identical to those of the firm pictured in Figure 32.6. (2) It must be remembered that the firm's cost curves include implicit costs covering the next best option for the owners time and money.

Therefore, it must be concluded that the firms in this industry are making excess profits above an average return on capital. Because it is easy to enter a purely competitive industry, capitalists

Figure 32.7 **Change in Equilibrium in the Coat Market**

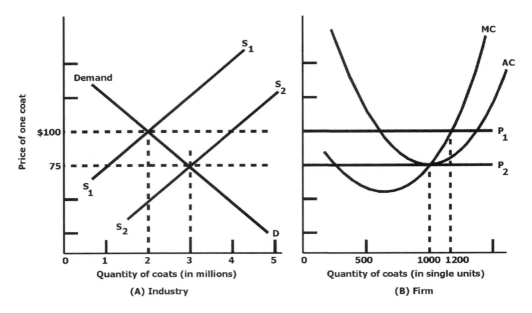

who are making only an average profit in other industries will be attracted to this industry by the lure of excess profits.

An industry is said to be in long-run equilibrium when there is no tendency for firms either to enter or to leave it. The industry pictured in Figure 32.6 is not in long-run equilibrium because it is earning excess profits, so that new firms will be entering it.

As new firms enter, their additional outputs must be added in order to derive the industry's new supply curve. This means that the supply curve will shift to the right. Figure 32.7 illustrates the original situation depicted in Figure 32.6 and also shows what happens as the supply curve shifts to the right (from the original position, S1). When the supply curve shifts, it must ultimately shift to S2. If it stops short of S2, excess profits will continue and more firms will be attracted, shifting the curve farther to the right until it reaches S2.

With the greater supply provided by the new firms entering the industry, all excess profits are eliminated. At the new, lower price of $75, the firm reduces its output from 1,200 to 1,000 coats in order to equate its marginal cost with the new price. This lower output maximizes the firm's profits in the new conditions. At that point, however, it is also true that the firm's average cost is just equal to its price per unit. The decline in price from $100 to $75 has eliminated the firm's excess profits (because its average cost is also $75). With no excess profits, there is no longer any incentive for new firms to enter the industry. The firms within the industry are receiving a normal, or average, rate of return on their capital and labor; therefore, there is no tendency for firms to leave the industry. It can now be said that when the new supply curve results in the establishment of a new price equal to the long-run average cost of each firm, the industry is in long-run equilibrium because the number of firms within the industry has been stabilized.

Thus, when both the individual firms and the purely competitive industry are in long-run equilibrium, the following equality holds for each firm:

Price = marginal cost = average cost

The fact that price equals marginal cost indicates that the firm is satisfied that its profits are maximized by its current level of output. The fact that price equals average cost indicates that there will be no tendency for firms either to enter or to leave the industry (because the average cost includes just an average rate of profit).

SUMMARY OF APPENDIX 32.1

When a perfectly competitive industry is in a long-run equilibrium, firms receive only the socially average (or "normal") rate of profit, costs (which include that normal profit) are minimized, and consumers pay a price for the product that equals the minimum cost of production for the profit. This analysis depicts the ideal state of affairs for traditional economists, and despite that almost no industries meet the criteria defining this market structure, some conservative economists hold that this analysis describes the actual state of affairs in American capitalism.

REVIEW QUESTIONS

Understand the profit-maximizing level of output in the long run.
1. Does earning a normal profit or when economic profit = 0 mean a firm is not earning a profit? Explain.
2. Why can there be excess profits in the short run but not in the long run?

Explain the dynamics of the competitive market that ensure normal profits for all firms in the long run.
3. What assumption(s) of competitive markets is critical for competing away excess profits? Explain.
4. Demonstrate graphically and explain what happens to excess profits in the long run.

CHAPTER 33

Monopoly Power, Prices, and Profits

From the very beginning of the capitalist system, capitalists have understood that they could make very large profits if they "corner the market" for a particular commodity, or in other words, if they could achieve a monopoly. After a firm has achieved a pure monopoly, or complete control over an entire industry, its most important task is to erect barriers that can prevent competitors from entering the industry and taking some of the high profits. From the beginnings of capitalism, firms with monopoly power have sought to use the government to help exclude competitors.

Although it is intuitively obvious that a monopolist can charge higher prices, it is not true that the monopoly firm can simply fix its price at any level it chooses. If that were true, then any monopolist could make such high profits that after a few years the firm might own all the wealth. In fact, monopolists face both cost and revenue constraints.

LEARNING OBJECTIVES

After reading this chapter, you should be able to:

- Explain how monopoly markets differ from competitive markets.
- Understand the production and pricing decisions of a monopolist.
- Explain why monopolies are generally inefficient.

DEMAND AND REVENUE FOR A MONOPOLY

Broadly, the term *monopoly power* includes any firm with significant power over the market including firms in imperfect competition, oligopolies, and perfect monopolies. We saw in Part I that in the mercantilist era, the great trading companies were granted monopolies by their governments. We also saw how the monopoly power of these companies inhibited the growth of industrialization, calling forth the classical liberal cry for a reduction of government interference in the market. With industrialization, however, there came a new and inexorable drive for monopoly power. We saw in previous chapters that the enforcement of antitrust laws and the actions of the numerous government regulatory commissions have consistently aided and abetted the creation and maintenance of monopolies.

In this section, we study the model of **perfect monopoly**. A perfect monopoly exists when *a*

Figure 33.1   **Demand and Average Revenue (AR) from Aluminum**

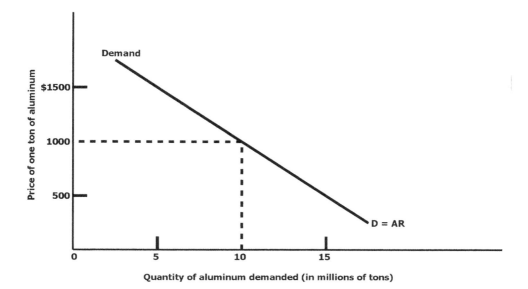

Quantity of aluminum demanded (in millions of tons)

single firm constitutes the entire industry. The firm sells a product for which there are no close substitutes, and potential competitors are prevented in one way or another from entering the industry.

Under competition, the market demand curve for a whole industry slopes down and to the right (because the quantity sold increases only when the price falls). The demand curve for the individual firm in a competitive market is a horizontal line (because the firm's output is so small, it can sell as much as it wishes at the same price). A monopoly firm, by definition, is the only seller of a commodity. The one firm *is* the industry. Therefore, the demand curve for a monopoly firm is exactly like the demand curve for a whole competitive industry. The demand curve for the monopolist slopes down and to the right. Unlike the owner of a competitive firm, who must sell at a given price, the monopolist can therefore choose to sell more goods at a lower price or fewer goods at a higher price (he or she is not a price taker but a price maker).

The market demand curve shows the maximum revenue per unit of the commodity that a monopolist will receive at any particular level of sales. When they view it from this seller's standpoint, economists call the demand curve an average-revenue curve. It shows the average revenue per unit of the commodity sold for any level of sales.

Figure 33.1 shows a demand curve for a monopoly firm. For the purposes of our example, assume it represents demand for aluminum. It can be labeled a demand curve or an average-revenue curve. The curve in Figure 33.1 is labeled D = AR to underscore this equivalence. At $1,000 per ton, consumers wish to purchase 10 million tons. Alternatively, if the monopolist wishes to sell 10 million tons, the $1,000 is the maximum price he can charge.

Assume that the monopolist wishes to know how much total revenue will be increased if sales are increased by one ton. The information the aluminum producer is looking for is what economists call the **marginal revenue**, which is *the change in the total revenue the firm will receive as a result of sale of one additional unit, in this case one more ton of aluminum.* Marginal revenue is defined as follows:

Figure 33.2   **Average Revenue and Marginal Revenue (MR) from Aluminum**

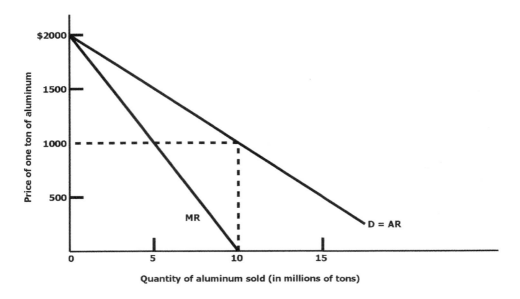

$$\text{Marginal revenue} = \frac{\text{change in total revenue}}{\text{change in quantity sold}}$$

The average and marginal revenue curves of a monopoly are illustrated in Figure 33.2.

Notice that at any quantity of aluminum, the marginal revenue is lower than the average revenue. Whenever the average revenue is decreasing, the marginal revenue must be lower than the average revenue. Again, this is similar to the case of a person taking a series of tests. If the average score declines as more tests are taken, it must mean the marginal score (or the score on the last test taken) is below the average. In fact, it is the lower marginal score that pulls the average score down. Similarly, if the average revenue is decreasing, the marginal revenue must be below it and pulling it down. When 10 million tons of aluminum is sold, marginal revenue is zero. Total revenue can be increased no further. At quantities below (to the left of) 10 million, the marginal revenue is positive.

PROFIT MAXIMIZING FOR A MONOPOLY

In order to see the equilibrium price a monopolist will charge and the quantity the firm will sell, the demand and marginal revenue curves must be superimposed on the cost curves. From the discussion in the previous section, it is known the demand curve will slope downward and to the right and that the marginal-revenue curve will be below it and have a steeper slope. These curves are drawn in Figure 33.3. The profit-maximizing position is reached when the monopolist produces and sells the quantity (6 million tons) at which marginal revenue equals marginal cost. The reason for this is easy to comprehend. Below this level, one additional ton of aluminum brings in more revenue than its additional (or marginal) cost. Above this point, one additional ton of aluminum

Figure 33.3 **Equilibrium for a Monopolist Selling Aluminum**

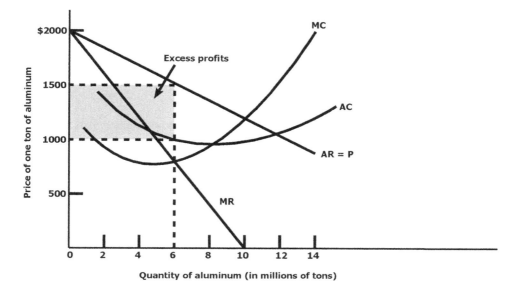

Quantity of aluminum (in millions of tons)

costs more than it brings in. Notice how the monopoly rule differs from the competitive rule that price should equal marginal cost. Because the monopolist has the entire market, the demand curve slopes downward, and therefore the marginal revenue is below the demand. In the competitive case, the firm is so small that the demand curve appears as a horizontal line, a single price. Therefore, the competitive price equals its marginal revenue. Because the monopolist's marginal revenue is lower (and the more general rule is that marginal cost equals marginal revenue), the monopolist chooses to supply less output to the market than would be the case in a competitive industry with similar cost and demand curves.

The demand curve in Figure 33.3 indicates that $1,500 is the maximum price at which 6 million tons can be sold. The shaded area shows the excess profits received at that price. For a monopoly, unlike a purely competitive firm, the making of excess profits is the usual and expected case. Nothing in the short or the long run tends to reduce these excess profits (except for changes in general business conditions as the economy undergoes cyclical fluctuations, a topic examined in Part III).

In addition to the high price monopolists charge and the excess profits they make, they almost never produce at the most efficient level of production. As shown in Figure 33.3, monopolists stop producing before reaching the point at which their average costs are minimized. They do this, of course, because they are interested in maximum profits, not maximum efficiency. Had they produced the quantity that minimized their costs, they would have been forced to sell their product at a much lower price, thus reducing their excess profits. You can now easily see what is meant by the age-old charge that monopolies restrict output and sales in order to increase their excess profits. You can also see why, from the very beginning of the capitalist, private enterprise economic system, most businessmen have tenaciously fought to acquire monopoly power.

PROGRESSIVE CRITICISM OF NEOCLASSICAL VIEW
OF MONOPOLY

To fully understand the theory in this chapter, we require the history and factual description of the market power of monopolies and oligopolies. That history was fully developed in Chapter 21.

SUMMARY

A monopolist is a single seller controlling an entire industry. Because monopolists face no direct competitors, the industry demand curve becomes the average-revenue curve for the monopolist. By producing and selling that level of output at which the monopolist firm's marginal cost is equal to its marginal revenue, it is nearly always the case that its average revenue will exceed its average costs (which already contain a calculation for "normal" profits), and so its profits will exceed the normal rate of profit. The monopolist does not produce efficiently and charges a higher price than would a competitive firm. There are ways in which the government can regulate monopolies, but these regulations do not eliminate excess profits. Moreover, such regulation frequently either has very little impact or even aids the monopolist in securing higher profits.

The technical details of the further modification and complexities of the neoclassical view of monopoly are given in Appendix 33.1.

KEY TERMS

marginal revenue
perfect monopoly

REVIEW QUESTIONS

Explain how monopoly markets differ from competitive markets.
   1. What assumptions of a perfectly competitive market are violated? Explain.
   2. How does demand curve for individual monopolists differ from demand curve for individual firm in a perfectly competitive market? Explain.

Understand the production and pricing decisions of a monopolist.
   3. How is profit maximizing quantity decision the same for a monopoly and for a firm in a perfectly competitive market? How is the pricing decision different? Explain.
   4. How do monopolists maintain their monopoly? How does this violate assumptions of a perfectly competitive market? Explain.

Explain why monopolies are generally inefficient.
   5. Why is output different for a monopolist than for a firm in a perfectly competitive market?
   6. Can a monopolist set both price and quantity? Explain.

APPENDIX 33.1
MODIFICATION OF MONOPOLY ANALYSIS

In the discussion of the market equilibrium for a monopolist, it was assumed both that monopolists took their revenue and cost curves as given and that they maximized profits by equating marginal cost and marginal revenue. These assumptions enabled us to examine only one aspect of the monopolist's ceaseless drive for more excess profits. Monopolists can also increase excess profits by shifting their cost curves downward and their revenue curves upward.

LEARNING OBJECTIVES FOR APPENDIX 33.1

After reading this chapter, you should be able to:

- Describe why and how monopolists increase revenue.
- Explain the sources of a natural monopoly.
- List types of government regulation of monopolies and explain their effectiveness.

MORE ON MONOPOLIES

Shifts in revenue or demand curves can be generated in several ways. The first and most obvious method is through advertising. If monopolists can persuade more consumers that they want or need their product, then they will be able to sell more of it at all prices along the demand curve. In other words, the demand curve will shift out and to the right. We are literally bombarded with advertising as businesses endlessly attempt to convince us to consume ever-increasing amounts of their products.

Another way monopolists can increase the demand for their products is by convincing the government that it should erect and maintain protective tariffs to eliminate foreign competition. Although a firm or a group of firms often manages to achieve a monopoly within national boundaries, only very infrequently can a worldwide monopoly be achieved (however, many American-based multinational firms are working feverishly in that direction). To the extent that consumers are able to buy a close foreign-made substitute for a monopolist's product, the demand for that product is reduced. Protective tariffs can eliminate foreign competition and thereby increase demand for the monopolist's product. Over the past several centuries, business leaders have, generally with considerable success, sought the aid of governments in creating and protecting their firms' domestic monopolies by enacting protective tariffs. Such tariffs increase monopoly revenues at the expense of the consumer, who is forced to pay a higher price for protected products.

Many large business firms are also able to increase the demand for their products through massive sales to the government. The bulk of these sales are connected with military procurement. For many of the largest U.S. corporations, these sales represent from 5 to 100 percent of their total sales. This topic is examined in greater depth in Part III.

There also are many ways business firms can shift their cost curves downward. They can press for government legislation that weakens labor unions. The Taft-Hartley Act of 1947 is an example of very restrictive legislation. They can also work to elevate "cooperative" and "reasonable" people to positions of leadership in unions—people who will not press very hard for wage increases that would disturb the status quo in the wage and profit distribution. They can also get the president to appoint business-leaning "public" people to positions in regulatory agencies. These measures enable large firms to keep their wage costs to a minimum.

Monopolies, in many instances, seek to achieve a monopsonistic position. A **monopsony** exists when *a firm is the only buyer of a particular resource or intermediate product.* Monopsonists can offer a very low price for the resource they are purchasing. Sellers must accept the offer or not sell their resource. Thus, resource costs can be decreased if the firm can achieve monopsonistic buying power, which is no less actively sought than monopolistic selling power.

The immense political power that stems from their economic power permits giant corporations to reduce costs in other ways. The government is often persuaded to allow them to use government-owned facilities for production connected with the armaments they are selling to the government. These facilities are generally used free of charge. When the government has charged rent, it has reimbursed the corporations and given them extra profits on this rent: this is the so-called cost-plus contract. In other words, the government has actually paid the giant corporations to use government-owned facilities free of charge. Such a case was described by a U.S. Senate Committee report on pyramiding missile profits:

> Much of Western Electric's Nike production was done at two government surplus plants, which under the ordinary method of doing business with the government would have been supplied to Western Electric without cost. However, Western Electric instead of having the plants supplied free, rented them from the government. Western Electric included the rentals as part of its overall costs and then charged the government a profit on these costs. The total rentals paid to the government by Western Electric for these plants amounted to over $3,000,000. When added to Western Electric's costs, the rentals generated additional profits to the company of $209,000. In such a situation, there could be little resistance on the part of Western Electric to having the government raise the rent, because as the rent went up, so did Western Electric's profit, since the complete amount of the rent was repaid by the landlord back to the tenant together with a profit (U.S. Congress, 1964).

These are only a few of the ways large monopolistic corporations are constantly striving to use their economic and political power to maximize profits.

WHO ARE THE MONOPOLISTS?

Most introductory economics textbooks identify pure competition and monopoly as the extreme cases along the spectrum of industrial organization. They argue (and we agree) that there are almost no purely competitive industries. Most pure monopolies, they assert, are either local or regional in scope, ranging from the single grocery store in a small village to the single giant real-estate developer in a large city. They maintain that national monopolies are as rare as purely competitive industries. According to these textbooks, monopoly theory is of intellectual interest primarily as an extreme case with little actual or practical applicability at a national level in the American economy.

This view, we believe, is erroneous because it adheres strictly to the definition of monopoly as existing when there is only one seller. It interprets one seller to mean one firm. Admittedly, there are very few national markets in which a single business firm is the only seller. Most important nationwide markets are dominated by a few giant corporations, which are oligopolies. In Chapter 34, however, we shall see that despite some distinct differences between oligopolies (a few firms) and monopolies (a single firm), most oligopolies act as if they were monopolies. We shall argue that our analysis of monopolies applies generally to oligopolies on questions of pricing, output, and the shifting of both revenue and cost curves. If our analysis is correct, so that we can rede-

Figure 33.4   **Ceiling on the Price of Aluminum**

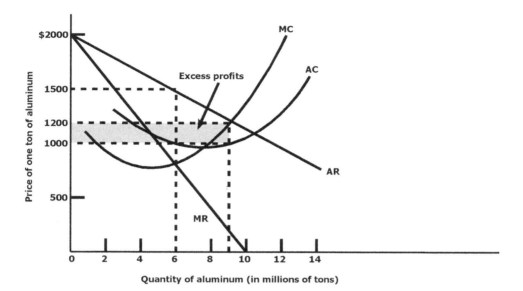

fine monopolies to include industries that behave as if they were a single seller, then monopolies dominate almost all of the important national markets in the United States.

NATURAL MONOPOLIES AND GOVERNMENT REGULATION

There are some industries that economists call **natural monopolies**. *The technology used in these industries creates a cost curve on which the minimum average cost is not reached until a firm is producing a very large quantity.* Generally, before the minimum average cost is reached, a single firm can supply the entire market with the commodity in question. If two firms divided the sales between them, each would produce such a small quantity that its average cost would be much higher than that of a single firm supplying the entire market. In this circumstance, a free market will always lead to one firm's acquiring a monopoly position.

The most common examples of natural monopolies are public utilities such as electric and telephone companies. Because these companies supply a commodity that is a vital necessity for most individuals and most other business firms, they are almost always regulated by the government. This regulation generally takes the form of an imposed price ceiling (although the regulating agencies are often controlled by the monopolies, so the price ceiling is usually high enough to allow considerable excess profits). The governing agency can reduce the monopolist's excess profits by lowering the price it will charge the public, increasing the quantity of the product it will sell, or both. If the government wishes to increase the public welfare and still allow monopolists to choose a profit-maximizing quantity to sell, it will generally attempt to set the price at the level at which monopolists' marginal costs are equal to their average revenue. This type of price ceiling is illustrated in Figure 33.4.

For quantities at which the price ceiling is below the firm's average-revenue curve, that ceiling becomes, in effect, a demand and a marginal-revenue curve for the firm. The reasoning is analogous to that for a firm in pure competition (a horizontal line). The monopolist, unlike the purely competitive firm, however, cannot sell any quantity it wishes at that price. For quantities at which its original demand curve falls below the price ceiling, the maximum price it can charge is determined by its demand curve. In Figure 33.4, for quantities up to 9 million tons, the price ceiling serves as an average-revenue and marginal-revenue curve. At quantities larger than 9 million tons, the firm reverts to its original revenue curves. If the firm is not regulated, it will charge $1,500 and sell 6 million tons. The price ceiling is imposed at the price ($1,200) that will equate the firm's average revenue and its marginal cost (as under competition). The firm then treats the price ceiling as a marginal-revenue curve for quantities up to 9 million tons (where the price ceiling equals the average revenue and the marginal cost). It is then selling more at a lower price and receiving less profit.

Although the welfare of the general public and other business firms is improved by the imposition of the price ceiling, it is obvious that the monopolist firm is still making large excess profits (that is, its average-cost curve is still below its average-revenue curve). As long as monopolists are allowed to choose the quantity they wish to sell, there is no price that will both clear the market (that is, equate supply and demand) and in any way result in better service for the public. For example, if the price ceiling were set at a lower level, the quantity the firm wished to sell would fall short of the quantity the public wished to buy, resulting in a market disequilibrium. If the price ceiling were set at a higher level, the government would merely be returning the monopolist firm closer to its original profit-maximizing position at the expense of the general public's and other business firms' welfare. This happens frequently because of the monopolists' control of the regulatory agencies. Moreover, government-regulated monopolies frequently own the firms that supply them with materials and component parts. Most generally these subsidiary firms are not regulated. The monopolist therefore can direct its subsidiary firm to charge the monopoly firm very high prices. In that way, the excessive profits do not appear on the books of the regulated monopoly firm but appear on the books of its unregulated subsidiary.

KEY TERMS FOR APPENDIX 33.1

monopsony
natural monopoly

REVIEW QUESTIONS

Describe why and how monopolists increase revenue.
1. Explain why monopolists put efforts into maintaining their monopoly.
2. Explain how monopolists lower costs and increase demand.

Explain the sources of a natural monopoly.
3. What are some examples of natural monopolies?
4. How do traditional and progressive economists differ in their analyses of monopolies?

List types of government regulation of monopolies and explain their effectiveness.
5. State examples of great attempts to regulate monopolies.
6. Explain why or why not government regulations are effective. Give examples.

CHAPTER 34

Monopolistic Competition and Oligopoly

The overwhelming majority of firms are in the fields of retailing, wholesaling, and the service industries, and they sell differentiated products. They rely on advertising to promote their brand of product. In a very important sense, the more basic industries (for example, mining, agriculture, banking, transportation, manufacturing, and communications) are the foundation on which the prosperity of the nation depends. Almost all the basic or fundamental industries are in an oligopolistic market structure. Therefore, judged in terms of economic power, oligopoly is an important category of industrial organization. This section examines monopolistic competition and oligopolies and their impact on the economy.

LEARNING OBJECTIVES

After studying this chapter, you should be able to:

- Explain how oligopolies and monopolistic competition differ from competitive markets.
- Understand how brands create a monopoly for a product in monopolistic competition.
- Explain why advertising is so important to firms in monopolistically competitive markets.
- Explain why pricing and output decisions of firms in oligopolistic markets is so different from firms in all the other markets.

Monopolistic competition *exists in an industry composed of many small firms, each producing a slightly differentiated product*. It is like a competitive market in that there are many firms and few barriers to entry. It is like a monopoly market in that the firm is the only producer of that "brand." An example of a monopolistic competitor is the neighborhood gas station, which differs slightly, but only slightly, from its competitors but sells under a particular brand name. The actual differentiation between the gas at the station may be merely in the packaging, the location of a retail store, or the service offered, but in any case it creates a certain amount of consumer loyalty.

Because the firm has legal rights to the brand name and logo, it has a monopoly over that brand even though there may be many products similar to that brand. This means the monopolistic competitor faces a demand curve that slopes downward and to the right. The firm faces the entire demand curve for its brand. Just like a pure monopoly, the monopolistically competitive firm maximizes its profits when it equates marginal cost and marginal revenue. In many cases, if the firm has recently substantially differentiated its product, it may make large, monopolistic excess

Figure 34.1   **Average Revenue Before (A) and After (B) New Firms Enter**

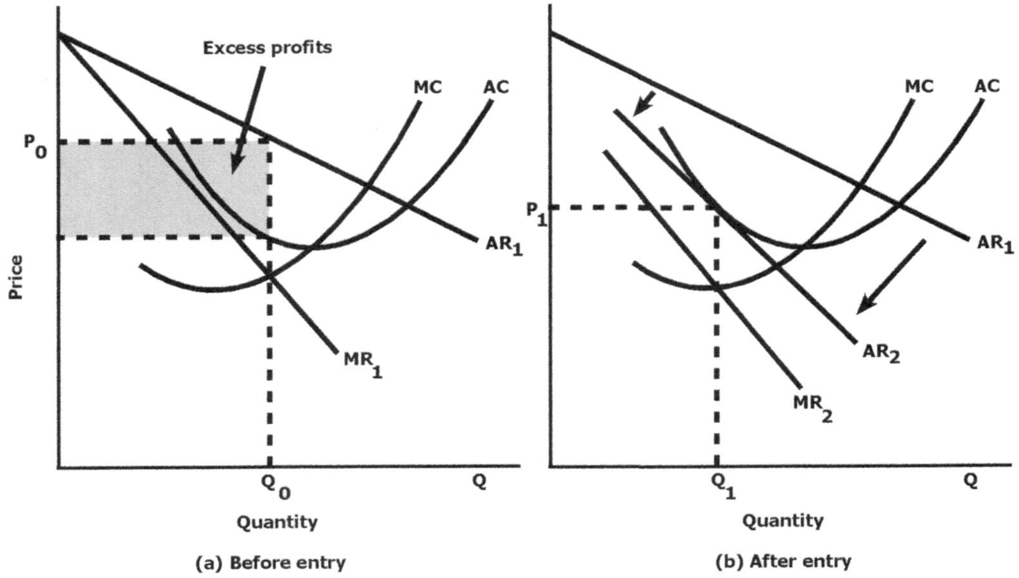

(a) Before entry

(b) After entry

profits. Such a situation is shown in Figure 34.1. If a firm raises its price, it will lose only a portion of its customers to competitors. Many will continue to buy the product at higher prices. If a firm lowers its price, however, it will attract some of its competitors' customers.

A monopolistically competitive market, however, has no significant barriers capable of preventing the entry of new firms. New firms, seeing the excess profits, will begin producing and selling highly similar products and will drain the demand away from the firm pictured in Figure 34.1 (A). As a consequence, the original firm's demand curve will shift back and to the left. As long as excess profits remain, new firms will continue to enter and the average-revenue curve will continue to shift downward and to the left. Therefore, as shown in Figure 34.1 (B), the shift will come to a halt only after the average-revenue curve just touches but does not cross the average-cost curve. At that quantity, the firm's marginal cost is equal to its marginal revenue, and the firm maximizes its profits by producing at this point. It is also the quantity at which the firm's average revenue is equal to its average cost. All of the excess profits have been squeezed out by the entry of new competitors.

Notice, however, that the new equilibrium is always above the minimum point of the firm's average-cost curve. In Figure 34.1 (B), the new demand curve, because it is still not flat as in pure competition, meets the average cost curve above the minimum point. The price is above the minimum cost level, but there are no excess profits because at the actual production level, costs are also higher than the minimum. In other words, the firm in monopolistic competition produces less output at a higher price and higher cost than the purely competitive firm in long-run equilibrium. We can therefore say that, in equilibrium, monopolistically competitive firms incur waste by never producing at their most efficient level. (In fact, only a purely competitive firm can be shown to produce efficiently in a private enterprise economy.)

The only way in which the firm can hope to regain some of its lost excess profits is to convince the public, usually through advertising, that its product is substantially different from (i.e., better than) those of its competitors. But when one firm advertises and attracts new customers, its competitors generally retaliate by competitively advertising their own products. The net result is often that relative distribution of sales returns to the point at which it was before the first firm began to advertise. Now, however, no firm is willing to curtail its advertising for fear of losing its customers to competitors who continue to advertise.

Advertising becomes almost a waste that is locked into the system. We say "almost" a waste because we grant that advertising may occasionally impart useful information. Most advertising, however, is so notorious for its use of half-truths, emotional appeals, brainwashing, and psychological appeals to people's most basic frustrations that few people can tell when any genuinely useful information is being offered. Most of us consciously dismiss advertising as a totally unreliable source of information, even though we may unconsciously be affected by the constant barrage of advertising aggressively directed at each of our senses.

Another waste of monopolistic competition is needless duplication of the same service. For example, how many times have you seen four gas stations on all four corners of the same street crossing? From a social point of view, this is totally inefficient.

We sketched the picture of monopolistic competition, a picture that fairly adequately describes the overwhelming majority of small businesses in a private enterprise economy. Millions of tiny, nearly powerless businesses work feverishly to create or protect some amount of monopolistic excess profits. Millions of competitors try equally hard to take away those excess profits. No competitor is able to sustain the acquisition of excess profits for very long, but each perpetually struggles, worries, competes, connives, and battles in a never-ending war in which there are no victors. Millions of firms almost never produce at the most efficient, lowest-cost level of production.

OLIGOPOLY

If we were to describe America's industrial landscape, we would begin with a vast plain of millions of tiny pebbles, representing all the economically powerless, monopolistically competitive business firms. At the center of this enormous plain would stand a few hundred colossal towers, representing the oligopolistic corporations. These few hundred towers would be so large as to make insignificant the entire plain below them.

An **oligopoly** *exists when a few business firms dominate an industry*. Because there are so few firms, their pricing and output decisions tend to be interdependent. Unlike any of the industrial categories discussed up to this point, an oligopolistic firm does not face a definite, unambiguous demand curve for its product. The amount oligopolists can sell at any price can be substantially affected by their rivals' actions. Furthermore, because the actions of an oligopolistic firm similarly affect its rivals, any time it changes its price, it must assume that other competitors will react in some way to this change. Its rivals' reactions will, in turn, affect the customers' response to its initial price change. All firms must be prepared to respond to any unexpected moves by their competitors. Interconnectedness and mutual interdependence of oligopolistic firms is the outstanding feature of an oligopolistic industry.

How can the effects of competitors' reactions be analyzed? First, their reactions to a price increase and to a price decrease can be differentiated. If a firm raises its price, it will automatically lose many of its customers to its rivals, who sell a highly similar product. Consequently, its action is not likely to provoke a reaction from its rivals. They are happy to acquire new customers.

However, if the firm lowers its price, it will attract its rivals' customers unless the rival firms retaliate. Rather than lose their customers, they are likely to lower their prices by the same amount.

Figure 34.2   **Oligopoly Demand Curves for Ford Explorers**

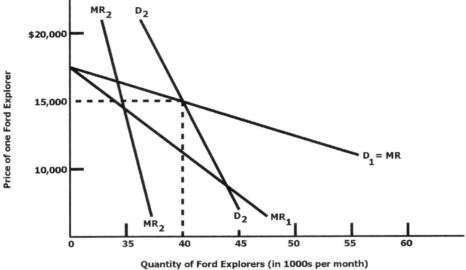

Quantity of Ford Explorers (in 1000s per month)

It might seem that these price changes would cancel each other out, leaving each firm selling the same quantity at a lower price. This is not the case, however. When all the firms lower their prices, they attract new customers. Furthermore, old customers may buy more of the product sold by the industry.

Figure 34.2 provides two demand curves for an oligopolistic firm in an oligopolistic industry: Ford Motor Company (and our old friend, the Ford Explorer). Demand curve D_1D_1 is constructed on the assumption that rivals ignore price changes made by Ford. Demand curve D_2D_2 is constructed on the assumption that rivals follow suit and change their prices by the same amount. For demand curve D_1D_1, marginal-revenue curve MR_1 is constructed. For demand curve D_2D_2, marginal-revenue curve MR_2 is constructed. Demand curves D_1D_1 and D_2D_2 intersect at the price and quantity that prevailed before the price change.

From the discussion of oligopolistic behavior, it is assumed here that, beginning at $15,000, Ford's rivals will not react if it raises its price. Therefore, for all prices above $15,000 (and quantities below 40,000 Explorers sold per month), the curves D_1D_1 and MR_1 are Ford's actual demand and marginal-revenue curves. If Ford lowers its price below $15,000, its rivals will lower their prices accordingly. Thus, for prices below $15,000 (and quantities greater than 40,000 Explorers), the curves D_2D_2 and MR_2 are the firm's actual demand and marginal-revenue curves.

By eliminating the irrelevant sections of the two demand curves, it is possible to construct the firm's actual demand and marginal-revenue curves. In Figure 34.3, these curves are constructed and the firm's cost curves superimposed upon them. Two things should be carefully noted. The demand curve is kinked (where the demand curve abruptly turns down), and the marginal revenue (at 40,000 cars) suddenly falls off into the negative quadrant of the graph.

It is clear from the graph that Ford will lose profits if it changes its price either upward or downward from the initial price of $15,000. It is also clear that it is highly unlikely the revenue curves could ever shift so far downward and to the left that Ford would lower the price it charged.

Figure 34.3   **Kinked Demand Curve for Ford Explorers**

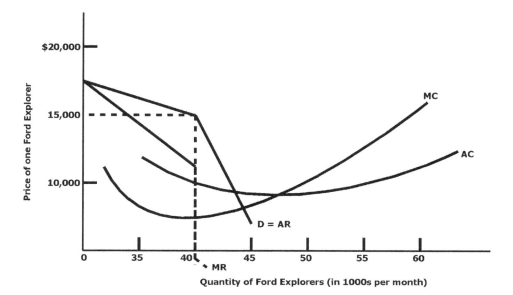

An increase in costs or an increase in the revenue curves would have to be fairly substantial for the firm to raise its price unless business conditions have already led rival firms to raise their prices.

This analysis helps explain the historically observed fact that prices in oligopolistic industries are very stable in the face of small, short-run variations in demand. It also helps explain why, over the longer run, oligopolistic prices almost never fall. Rather, they show a persistent tendency to rise during periods of inflation and remain stable during periods of recession or deflation.

PRICE DETERMINATION IN AN OLIGOPOLY

The simplest and most direct method of oligopolistic pricing occurs when the firms form a cartel. A **cartel** is *a group of firms that acts as a monopoly*. Within a cartel, each firm is treated as if it were merely a separate plant owned by the monopoly.

Figure 34.4 shows that a cartel's price determination is identical to that of a monopoly. The monopolist has a single marginal-cost curve. The cartel's marginal-cost curve is determined by adding together the marginal-cost curves of the various individual oligopolists. The industry price is set at $5,000, and 3 million compact cars is the quantity sold by the industry. Each firm produces the quantity at which its own marginal cost is equal to the industry's marginal cost (and marginal revenue).

Cartels, as such, are illegal in the United States because direct or explicit collusion between businesses is illegal. Yet many oligopolistic industries have found several ways of engaging in covert collusion that enables them to cooperate in such a manner that their pricing and output decisions are tantamount to a formal cartel. Also, explicit collusion is not illegal in other countries. Theory predicts that cartels will eventually break down because there is an incentive to cheat. Once prices are driven up by restricting quantity, the individual producers now have an incentive to increase

Figure 34.4   **Oligopoly Equilibrium in the Compact Car Industry**

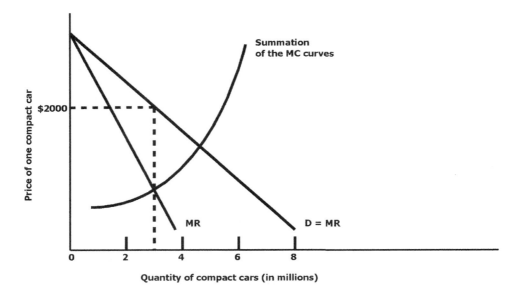

production to take advantage of the higher prices. If each firm in the cartel responds to the price signals, supply in the market increases and the price is driven down.

When explicit collusion is not possible, many oligopolistic industries rely on the price leadership of the dominant firm within the industry. The dominant firm may be either the largest or the most efficient. Sometimes it is both. In this situation, the dominant firm sets the price. The other firms take that price as given in the same way a purely competitive firm accepts the industry price as given. They produce up to the point at which their marginal cost is equal to that price (which they take as their marginal revenue).

In order for the dominant firm to maximize its profits, it must know approximately the marginal costs for the other firms. For some time, U.S. Steel was the price leader in its industry. Figure 34.5 illustrates how price is determined in such an industry. DD is the industry demand curve. The demand curve for U.S. Steel is labeled D_{USS}. The summation of the marginal-cost curves for all firms other than the price leader is also shown.

The demand curve for the price leader (D_{USS}) is computed in the following manner: whatever price the leader (U.S. Steel) selects, it knows the other firms will produce up to the point at which their marginal cost equals that price. U.S. Steel knows, therefore, that the other firms, taken collectively, will produce the quantity (in Figure 34.5, 70 million tons) at which the summation of their marginal-cost curves equals the price it has established. The demand for the leader's output will be the total market demand at that price minus the quantity the other firms sell. In other words, the leader's demand curve at any price will be equal to the difference between the market demand curve and the summation of the other firms' marginal-cost curves.

For example, if the leader establishes a price of $2,000, the other firms will produce all that can be sold at that price (because at that point market demand equals the summation of the marginal-cost curves). At prices below $2,000, the summation of the marginal-cost curves falls successively farther to the left of the demand curve. Therefore, as price declines, the demand remaining for the leader increases.

Figure 34.5 **Price Leadership by U.S. Steel (USS) in an Oligopolistic Industry**

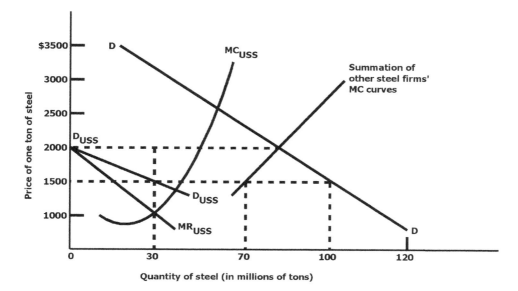

Quantity of steel (in millions of tons)

The marginal revenue (MR_{USS}) is derived from U.S. Steel's demand curve. The leader will maximize its profit by producing the quantity (30 million tons) and establishing the price ($1,500) for the industry. The remainder of the firms will produce, among them, 70 million tons, and the entire industry will produce 100 million tons (equal to U.S. Steel's 30 million plus the others' 70 million).

It should be stressed that the follower firms only very superficially resemble firms in a purely competitive market. Although they take the price that has been established and adjust their output so that their marginal cost is equal to that price, their long-run normal position is one in which they also make monopolistic, excess profits.

OLIGOPOLY OR MONOPOLY?

In Chapter 33, four general classifications of market structures—pure competition, monopolistic competition, oligopoly, and monopoly—were described. We found that there were almost no purely competitive industries. In the preceding section, it was argued that, in their decisions regarding pricing, output, and sales, there is very little difference between oligopolies and monopolies.

Are there other differences of sufficient importance to make the oligopoly category a useful analytical tool? Or would it be better to drop oligopoly and simply refer to all industries that are dominated by a few giant corporations as monopolies?

The principal difference between oligopolistic and monopolistic firms is the rivalry that exists among the former. Although they have found by experience that this rivalry is mutually disastrous when it is extended to competitive pricing, they remain rivals. Their competition is generally confined to advertising, sales promotion, and cost-reduction campaigns, and their actions do not differ substantially from the monopolist's behavior, particularly in attempts to shift revenue curves upward and cost curves downward.

It seems, therefore, that only when the passage of time results in a substantial shift of relative power within an oligopolistic industry are there important differences between a monopoly and oligopoly. During such a situation, a struggle for the industry's price leadership might develop. Such a struggle might result, temporarily, in destructive price competition (or worse). Once a new leader emerges, however, the industry will generally return to the types of policies that make it hardly distinguishable from a monopoly.

The oligopoly category is useful for analyzing temporary situations during which destructive competition takes place. It might also be useful to differentiate between monopolies and oligopolies in analyzing differences between advertising and sales promotion techniques for firms that sell commodities for which there are close substitutes (oligopolistic firms) and for those that sell products for which there are no close substitutes (monopolistic firms).

In almost any other situation or context, the differences between monopolistic and oligopolistic firms are insignificant. In most discussions it is quite appropriate to refer to all giant corporations as monopolistic firms, as is generally done in ordinary conversation. The economist's narrower definition of monopoly, although sometimes helpful, is so restrictive that it eliminates almost all existing business firms. Yet the formal analysis of a monopolist's pricing and output decisions forms the basis for understanding the behavior of most giant corporations.

A perfect example of oligopolists acting as a monopolist was the gasoline shortage of 1978. Although spokespersons for the government and the oil industry continually told the public that the shortage was the result of difficulties in importing sufficient quantities of crude oil, independent investigators soon discovered that the oil companies had curtailed both domestic production of crude oil and the refining of oil. While motorists canceled vacation plans, ran out of gas on the streets and freeways, and endured hours of waiting in long lines at gas stations, the price of gasoline soared from around 70 cents a gallon (to which it had risen in the previously planned "crisis" of 1973) to over $1.00 a gallon, and the oil companies raked in ever higher excess profits. All of this would have been impossible had the oil companies not been able to act as a monopoly.

PROGRESSIVE CRITICISM OF NEOCLASSICAL VIEW OF OLIGOPOLY

Traditional economists see occasional cases of oligopoly. Progressives see oligopoly as the dominant system throughout American industry. See the extensive data in Chapter 21.

SUMMARY

Most American business firms fit into the market structure of monopolistic competition. Our analyses have shown that although these firms generally do not receive excess profits, they incur waste by never producing at their most efficient level and by spending enormous sums of money on competitive advertising.

A comparatively few powerful oligopolistic giants dominate the industrial landscape of American business. Oligopolies generally set prices as if they were monopolies. Large excess profits and inefficiency characterize their operations. The general public's faith that the competitive market of American capitalism automatically results in efficient production is not theoretically or empirically warranted. That faith is a part of the general folklore of our culture by which the status quo of capitalism is ideologically maintained.

KEY TERMS

cartel
monopolistic competition
oligopoly

REVIEW QUESTIONS

Explain how oligopolies and monopolistic competition differ from competitive markets.

1. What conditions for a perfectly competitive market are violated by oligopolies? Monopolistic competition?
2. Compare and contrast oligopolies and monopolistic competition. What is an advantage for a firm operating in each market structure? Disadvantage?

Understand how brands create a monopoly for a product in monopolistic competition.

3. Describe how brand names are legally protected. How does this resemble a monopoly?
4. Explain how product differentiation leads to competing brands.

Explain why advertising is so important to firms in monopolistically competitive markets.

5. Explain the link of advertising and brand names (product differentiation) in maintaining profits for firms in monopolistic competition.
6. Demonstrate graphically what happens to profits if more advertising results in more consumers. Now demonstrate what happens to profit if more advertising raises the costs to the firm.

Explain why pricing and output decisions of firms in oligopolistic markets are so different from firms in all the other markets.

7. Explain why pricing decisions of a firm in an oligopolistic market depend on decisions of other firms. How is this different from decisions of firms in perfectly competitive markets?
8. Compare and contrast explicit and implicit collusion. What are examples of pricing models for explicit and implicit collusion? Explain.

CHAPTER 35

Market Failures
Public Goods, Market Power, and Externalities

After all the discussion earlier about the neoclassical views on market efficiency, it might seem a bit strange that we are about to set out the neoclassical criteria for government involvement in the economy. If markets always worked perfectly, this chapter would be unnecessary because there would be no economic need for government involvement in the economy. Unfortunately, markets do not always achieve the efficient and equitable outcomes described in the textbook. Even if markets were working perfectly, there are still outcomes that might not be desirable by society.

LEARNING OBJECTIVES

After reading and studying this chapter, you should be able to:

- Define and describe different types of market failures.
- Distinguish between private and public goods, and explain why government allocation of public goods is necessary.
- Explain how government policies are used to deal with external costs and benefits.
- Understand the principles of taxation.

MARKET FAILURE AND THE GOVERNMENT

Markets automatically result in optimal outcomes, allocative and technical efficiency and equity, only under the very specific set of conditions that define perfect competition. As we noted in Chapter 32, pure competition exists when there are many sellers, product homogeneity, and easy entry and exit. Perfect competition requires these three conditions plus perfect information. When any of these conditions are absent, there may be a market failure and the door is opened for government involvement. To be clear, **market failure** is *a situation in which market outcomes are not socially optimal or desirable*. Market failure may due to the existence of market power, imperfect information, macroeconomic instability, public goods, or externalities.

Markets characterized by market power (imperfect competition), such as monopolistic competition, oligopoly, and monopoly, represent one kind of market failure. These markets may require government regulation or antitrust policies, as we described in Chapters 33 and 34. Incomplete information can also lead to market failure. For example, if consumers were not aware that a

Häagen-Dazs ice cream bar contains 30 grams of fat or that excessive consumption of high-fat food can lead to heart disease and cancer, then people might eat more ice cream than is good for them. A market failure of this type might be resolved by government-mandated package labeling to warn ice cream lovers of the health risk of fat. Finally, some economists consider macroeconomic fluctuations a form of market failure and call for government policies to address the problems of inflation and unemployment caused by business cycle fluctuations. This is a main subject of macroeconomics, the topic of Part III of this text. This chapter focuses primarily on two other sources of market failure: public goods and externalities.

PUBLIC GOODS

A private good differs from a public good in two important ways. The first difference is that private goods are subject to the **exclusion principle**, and public goods are not. Private property rights can be enforced on a private good. *A person using a private good can exclude others from using it.* Private property rights cannot be enforced on a public good. A person using a public good cannot exclude others from using the same good. I must pay for a cup of espresso before I can drink it. If I do not pay for it, the coffee-shop owner will exclude me from drinking it. You may not have to pay for national defense to receive the benefits. Some of my taxes will be used to pay for defense, but even though you are a starving student earning no income and paying no taxes, you cannot be excluded from receiving the benefits of national defense. National defense is a public good, and espresso is a private good.

The second difference is **rival consumption**. This means *my consumption of a good makes it impossible for you to consume the good as well.* The consumption of public goods is nonrival in the sense that if I consume it, it does not diminish from your ability to consume it as well. National defense is again a good example. If I benefit, it in no way reduces the amount of benefits you receive. On the other hand, once I drink that espresso, it is not available to you. This means that a **public good** is *a good that is not subject to the exclusion principle or rival consumption.* As we will see, free markets are unable to efficiently allocate public goods.

Public goods result in a market failure because there is no way to get people to voluntarily reveal their preferences or pay for public goods. For example, if you want an espresso, you have to pay $2.50. And if many people pay $2.50 for a cup of espresso, the espresso coffee industry will expand and there will be espresso kiosks on every street corner. Public goods like national defense are different. People understand that they will receive the benefits from national defense whether they pay for it or not, so there is no way for the market to determine just how much or what kind of national defense people want. People may vote for candidates who favor strong national defense, but this is an imprecise way to determine which or how many military goods the people want. As a result, military spending decisions are left up to the political process.

EXTERNALITIES

Free markets result in efficiency only when all costs and benefits are reflected in the selling price. Externalities can also interfere with market efficiency. An **externality** *exists whenever the market does not recognize all of the costs or benefits of production or consumption.* There can be both negative and positive externalities. *Costs that are not reflected in price* are called **negative externalities**. *Benefits that are not reflected in price* are called **positive externalities**. Governments are frequently called upon to enact measures so that market prices reflect all costs and benefits. Two ways to solve the problem of externalities are covered in this section. They include the use of taxes

Figure 35.1   **Negative Externalities**

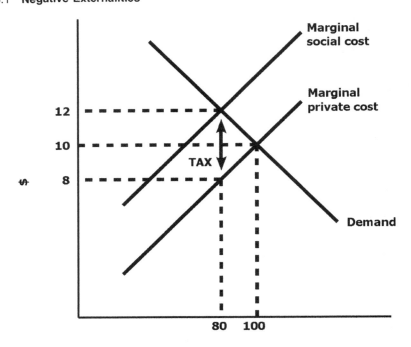

When the production process involves external costs, marginal social costs are greater than marginal private costs. If the market is unregulated, output will be higher than the optimal level and the selling price will be lower than optimal. The optimal level of production can be established by charging a tax equal to the amount of the external cost. In this case, a tax of $4 per unit is levied on each unit sold. The result is that the selling price rises from $10 to $12 and the quantity sold falls from 100 to 80 units. The firm must pay the $4 to the government, so they receive only $8 per unit sold.

or subsidies to internalize externalities and assignment of property rights and the development of a market for the right to pollute.

Negative Externalities

When managers calculate least-cost production methods, they consider both explicit and implicit costs of production. Explicit costs include wages, interest expenses, rents, and other costs that require payment in money. Implicit costs are primarily the opportunity costs of time and foregone alternatives. Both explicit and implicit costs are considered private or internal costs because they are borne by business and counted when setting the selling price of output.

However, many production processes also incur costs that do not need to be paid by the firm or the consumer, and someone has to bear that cost. These are external costs. One common external cost is pollution. When external costs like pollution are not included in the firm's cost calculations, the private cost of production is less than the social cost of production. The result is that, from society's perspective, the selling price is too low and output is too high.

Figure 35.1 shows the market for a product with an external cost. The industry supply curve is the marginal private cost curve. If the industry is unregulated, the market price ($10) and quantity (100) will be determined by the intersection of demand and supply. However, because the supply curve does not include the external costs of pollution, this price is too low and consumption is too high. The vertical distance between the marginal social cost curve and the marginal private cost curve represents the social costs of the externality. The solution to this sort of problem was first suggested by the English economist A. C. Pigou (1877–1959). Pigou showed that efficient resource allocation would be achieved if policymakers imposed a tax equal to the vertical distance between marginal social cost and marginal private cost ($4 in this case) on each unit that is produced. This makes the industry supply curve equal to the marginal social cost curve. The tax would have three effects: (1) the selling price would rise to $12, (2) producers would receive a lower after-tax price, $8 and (3) the quantity demanded would fall to 80 units. Resource allocation would be efficient because marginal social costs would equal marginal social benefit at 80 units of output.

Why don't we just pass a law making it illegal to use polluting production methods or manufacture products that pollute? The simple explanation is that the optimal level of pollution is almost never zero. The cost of getting rid of that last iota of pollution is almost certainly greater than the benefit society receives. Then why don't we pass a law restricting pollution to a certain level? In fact, this is often done, but economists generally believe that taxes are preferable to such quantity restrictions. Why? Emissions taxes provide firms with an incentive to avoid the tax by developing production methods that reduce pollution; quantity restrictions provide no such incentives. If the tax is implemented correctly, firms will design and use nonpolluting production methods whenever the cost of new technology is less than the tax.

Finally, we need to make two additional comments before we go on. First, while it is often clear that marginal social costs differ from marginal private costs, it can be quite difficult to determine just how much they differ. This is important when designing a pollution tax policy. Second, we need to recognize that pollution taxes have some unpleasant side effects, despite that they may result in allocative efficiency. Not only do pollution taxes cause prices to rise but they could force some firms out of the industry and cause unemployment.

Positive Externalities

Not all externalities are negative. In fact, there are many positive externalities. For example, when you go to college, both you and society benefit. You stand to earn a higher income because you are more productive. Society benefits from your higher productivity as well, and there is the additional benefit that you are less likely to resort to a life of crime. You should be willing to pay a price equal to the marginal private benefit you get from the school. If society receives additional benefits, society should subsidize some of the costs of your schooling. This is one reason public education is subsidized in most industrialized nations.

There are many other examples of products with positive externalities. When Intel or Motorola develops the next-generation computer chip, many computer firms benefit, and so do workers who find that there are new job openings in companies that manufacture computers with the new chips. Further, the production techniques used to make the new computer chips will have spinoffs for production methods in the next generation of high-technology products. Recognition of these externalities is the main reason most nations provide huge subsidies for their high-technology industries. In fact, all nations that have semiconductor industries aid their semiconductor producers.

The effect of positive externalities is shown in Figure 35.2, which illustrates the market for schooling. The marginal private benefit curve is the demand curve for education by individuals. The marginal social benefit curve is society's demand curve for education. It is the sum of the marginal

Figure 35.2 **Positive Externalities**

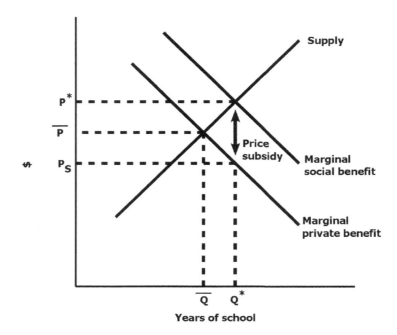

Years of school

When there are positive externalities in consumption, efficient resource allocation requires that prices be subsidized. In this case, the marginal social benefit of education is greater than the marginal private benefit of education because of the positive externality. A subsidy in an amount equal to the distance between the two marginal benefit curves would lower the price paid for education from PBAR to P_S, while the price received by the school would rise to P^*. At Q^*, the marginal social benefit of education is equal to the marginal cost of education, so resource allocation is efficient.

private benefits curve plus the positive externalities of education. In the absence of government intervention many people might not be able to afford an education or only attend school for a few years. This situation is suboptimal because the marginal social benefit of education is greater than the marginal cost (supply price) of education. To achieve optimality, education should be subsidized by an amount equal to the vertical distance between the two marginal benefit curves. This effectively shifts the marginal private benefit curve to the marginal social benefit curve.

Most economists agree that education should be subsidized, but it is never clear how large the subsidy should be because it is so difficult to accurately measure the external benefits of education. There is also ongoing debate among economists as to whether the subsidy should be given to the school district or directly to the students.

PRINCIPLES OF TAXATION: EFFICIENCY VERSUS EQUITY

Just recognizing that market failures may require government intervention does not solve the problem. We also need to determine the extent of government involvement and the best way to raise tax revenues to pay for any needed government spending. Both issues are difficult. Politicians, policymakers, and the public are forever trying to decide how many public goods are needed, how to measure externalities, and how to collect tax revenues to finance these programs. This section looks at the criteria that can be used to design tax programs. The next sections develop the criteria for determining the optimal quantity of a public good and methods for dealing with externalities.

Tax Efficiency

Once a given level of government involvement is decided upon, it is necessary to determine how to raise the funds to finance that spending. This decision involves more than merely determining whether to use progressive, regressive, or proportional taxes. It is also important to use efficient tax collection methods. There are two criteria used to assess the efficiency of the tax collection system. First, the tax should have a minimum effect on economic incentives and activity. For example, many economists believe that income taxes adversely affect the incentive to work because they reduce take-home pay. These economists believe that income taxes are less efficient than sales taxes because sales taxes have little effect on work incentives. You pay sales taxes only when you buy things, not when you work, so there is no disincentive to work longer hours. Second, the cost of collecting the tax revenues should be low. That is, if it is necessary to employ a large team of tax collectors, the tax is inefficient. A tax that is paid voluntarily with 100 percent compliance would be efficient. Many economists believe that income taxes are inferior to most sales taxes according to this criterion.

Tax Equity

A shortcoming of these efficiency criteria is that politicians and the public are just as concerned with equity as efficiency. Sales taxes may be efficient, but they are regressive. Is it "fair" for a rich person to pay a lower portion of his or her income in taxes than a poor person? Is it "fair," even if the poor person is lazy and the rich person is hardworking? Many economists believe that taxes should be based on one of two tax-equity principles: ability to pay or benefits received. According to the **ability-to-pay principle**, *people with higher income should pay proportionately more taxes than poor people because they can afford to.* Progressive income taxes fit this criterion because people in higher income brackets pay a higher portion of their income in taxes. Taxes on luxury goods also fit this criterion. Equal taxes—for example, every person paying the same dollar amount—on every citizen would not fit the ability-to-pay criterion because poor people would find it harder to pay the tax than would rich people. According to the **benefits-received principle**, *people should pay higher taxes if they receive higher benefits from the government programs.* For example, a person with a great deal of property would pay higher taxes to support the police (who presumably would protect the property) than a person with little or no personal property. The trade-off between efficiency and equity is one of the most important issues involving the role of the government in the economy. It is also one of the most difficult. Equity is exceedingly difficult to measure, but many economists would agree that the most efficient taxes, sales taxes and uniform head taxes, tend to be the least equitable.

Earmarked Taxes

Should taxes be tied to specific goods or services? That is, should the revenues from the sale of fishing licenses be used for restocking rivers? Should gasoline taxes be used for highway construction and maintenance? The answer to this question, like so many in economics, can only be, "It depends." Most states do tie fishing and hunting license proceeds to wildlife programs, and most gasoline taxes are used for highway construction. That seems "fair," right? Perhaps. What about property tax revenues? Should they be used to fund projects that benefit only property owners? In many states, property taxes are the main source of revenues for public education, but it would be hard to argue that education benefits property owners more than people who do not own property. What about income taxes? If income tax revenues were used to provide goods that benefited only income tax payers, it would be impossible to fund income redistribution and welfare programs.

It would be impossible to earmark every tax, but it may be appropriate to tie specific taxes to specific benefits in those cases when it is possible. Earmarking reduces the apparent capriciousness of taxes and may increase taxpayer compliance. This may explain why people seem to complain most bitterly about income, sales, and property taxes—none are directly tied to specific benefits. The fact that most federal, state, and local taxes are not earmarked may be one reason there are so many citizen complaints about tax fairness.

Many of the issues in public economics are subject to rather heated debate. It is almost always difficult to accurately measure the impact of externalities or determine the right quantity of a public good to provide, and there are numerous conflicting criteria for determining the best ways to collect tax revenues. These issues probably lie at the core of those jokes so often heard about disagreement among economists but really should be thought of as a strength of economics, not a weakness. The role of economists is to provide policymakers with alternative policies and to understand the consequences of those alternatives. The economists' principles of public finance and taxation serve their intended roles quite well. They are useful for developing alternative policy proposals and for illustrating their consequences to policymakers. It is up to the policymakers to decide which policy to implement. Many technical aspects of the neoclassical approach to market failures are discussed in Appendix 35.1.

PROGRESSIVE CRITICISM OF NEOCLASSICAL VIEW
OF MARKET FAILURE

Neoclassical economists acknowledge that there are some failures of the market to contain harm to the environment in certain cases. Progressive economists see the problem of environmental destruction as pervasive throughout the economy. For example, global warming is not a problem of the failure of a few individual firms caused by some small market imperfections that could be quickly cured by price regulations or voluntary changes. Rather, global warming, like many environmental problems, affects the whole economy. Such externalities throughout the economy do not fit within traditional neoclassical analysis or minor reforms based on that analysis. Rather, environmental destruction represents a failure of the market that must be considered as an integral part of a different kind of economic analysis, such as was discussed in Chapter 23.

Some neoclassical economists also acknowledge the existence of market failure in the form of monopoly power and oligopoly, which prevents the economy from achieving the advantages claimed for competition. They believe that these deviations from pure and perfect competition are fairly minor in most cases, so they have little affect on corporate behavior and can be changed by minor reforms if any are needed. Progressives, on the contrary, see monopoly power and oligopoly as a new stage of capitalism in which the system itself has changed away from pure competition. A progressive economic analysis of monopoly power and oligopoly was discussed in Chapter 21.

Finally, some neoclassical economists acknowledge market failure to provide sufficient public goods. Once again, progressives point out that the whole system of capitalist economic institutions, not just a few small failures, causes the lack of public goods. It is not profitable for private enterprise to produce enormous national parks with high-quality service and maintenance along with free entrance fees (or very low entrance fees). However, a government that is produced under a system of capitalist economic institutions, with overwhelming influence by monied interests, also will refuse to provide sufficient public goods, whether parks or bridge maintenance or sufficient levees at New Orleans. Both economic and political analysis must treat this issue as a systemic problem, as discussed in Chapter 24.

Progressive economic analysis reveals that these three failures (and others) by the market under capitalism are systemic. These market failures could be cured by a democratic economic system and a democratic government based on that system.

SUMMARY

Neoclassical economists laud the self-correcting nature of the market system in general, but many also recognize that there are limited, but important, roles for government intervention. The main ideas from this chapter are as follows:

1. Public goods cannot profitably be efficiently allocated by private markets because there is no mechanism to force people to reveal their preferences. People receive the benefits of public goods whether they pay or not because public good consumption is nonrival and nonexclusive.
2. External costs and benefits are not included in market prices, so many neoclassical economists believe the government should enact measures to internalize externalities. Pollution is an example of an external cost. Technological spillover from research and development is an example of an external benefit. External costs should be taxed and external benefits should be subsidized.
3. Principles of taxation include both efficiency and equity. Efficient taxes should have a minimal effect on economic incentives, and the cost of collecting should be low. Equity principles for taxes includes the ability to pay principle and benefits received principle.

KEY TERMS

ability-to-pay principle
benefits-received principle
exclusion principle
externality
market failure

negative externality
positive externality
public good
rival consumption

REVIEW QUESTIONS

Define and describe different types of market failures.
1. What is the definition of a market failure? Why do they occur?
2. Early in the chapter, it was suggested that there is a market failure if ice cream consumers are not aware of the high fat content of ice cream. Suppose that the government requires all ice cream producers to label the fat content of their ice cream and a stern warning that high-fat diets can lead to heart disease. Some people would ignore the warnings and continue to consume mass quantities of both Ben and Jerry's Cherry Garcia and Häagen-Dazs's macadamia nut ice cream on a regular basis. Does this mean that the labeling did not eliminate the market failure? Why or why not?

Distinguish between private and public goods, and explain why government allocation of public goods is necessary.

3. What are the two main attributes that distinguish public goods from private goods? What conditions must hold for optimal allocation of public goods?
4. Identify the public good attributes of each of the following. Also, explain how (and if) these goods could be efficiently provided by the private sector.
    a. lighthouse
    b. an income redistribution plan
    c. universal health care
    d. snow removal service
    e. cable television
    f. broadcast television
5. The national parks received millions of visitors annually, and there is often a bumper-to-bumper traffic jam on the roads throughout the parks. Do you think this would be true if the national parks were sold to private business? Would you favor such a sale? Why or why not? Can you think of an alternative solution to the crowding problem in the national parks?

Show how government policies are used to deal with external costs and benefits.

6. What policies can be used to internalize externalities? Draw diagrams to illustrate your answer.
7. Suppose that a factory currently dumps waste into the river. Explain how taxes could be used to solve this problem.

Understand the principles of taxation.

8. Define the benefits-received and the ability-to-pay principles of taxation. How do these principles relate to tax efficiency and tax equity? What are earmarked taxes?
9. In many states, property taxes are earmarked for public schools. There is the perennial argument that property owners who do not have children should pay less or even be exempt from property taxes. Explain why this argument may be fallacious.
10. Many states have policies that tuition at public universities is set at a fixed fraction—often 20 or 25 percent—of the state's cost of providing the education. Is this a reasonable program? Why or why not?

APPENDIX 35.1
FURTHER ASPECTS OF NEOCLASSICAL THEORIES OF MARKET FAILURE

This appendix examines the free rider problem that arises in any discussion of public goods and the Coase theorem, which is a property rights–based approach to correcting externalities.

LEARNING OBJECTIVES FOR APPENDIX 35.1

After reading and studying this chapter, you should be able to:

*   Define the free rider problem and why it happens.
*   Describe allocative efficiency and why it breaks down.

- Discuss the problems with government provision and allocation of public goods.
- Define the Coase theorem, and describe how it will solve externalities.
- Discuss the real-world problems in the application of the Coase theorem.

FREE RIDERS

Suppose that in a desperate bid to win votes for reelection, the new president allows people to voluntarily contribute funds for national defense. The average contribution, she argued, should be about $1,500 per person, but you were free to voluntarily contribute as much or as little as you liked. How much would you contribute? Your civic duty might make you inclined to send in the recommended $1,500. But if you are a **free rider**, *a person who receives benefits from public goods without paying for them*, you will recognize that you will receive the benefits of the national defense whether you send in any money or not. National defense is a public good, so no one can exclude you from enjoying the benefits of national defense. Recognition of this fact is a bit unsettling. The self-serving approach may be to decline to contribute to national defense because you will receive benefits whether you contribute or not. Public goods cannot be allocated in the market because there is no incentive for people to voluntarily reveal their preferences or pay even if they do.

Allocative efficiency for a private good requires that *the marginal benefit of the last unit consumed be equal to the marginal cost of production*. Rational consumers are willing to pay a price equal to the marginal benefit they receive from the private good, so the allocative efficiency criterion can be stated as $P = MB = MC$.

Two complications arise when we try to apply this criterion to public goods. First, it is not clear that people will reveal their preferences, but let's skirt this issue for a moment and assume that people do reveal their preferences. The second problem is that everyone receives the same amount of the public good, so the total demand curve for a public good is constructed differently than the market demand curve for private goods.

Efficient allocation of a public good is shown in Figure 35.3. For simplicity, we are assuming that only two people use the public good, person a and person b. Their individual demand curves are illustrated as D_a and D_b. The total demand curve for the public good, D_{a+b}, is found by determining the total price that society would pay for each quantity of a public good, perhaps hours of public radio broadcasts. D_{a+b} is found by vertical addition. Add the price person a would pay for each quantity to the price person b would pay for the same quantity to find the total price that society would pay for every quantity. In this example, person a is willing to pay an annual fee of $40 for 8 hours of daily public radio broadcasts, while person b is willing to pay an annual fee of $80 for 8 hours of daily public radio broadcasts. If a and b are the only two people in society, then the total price that society would be willing to pay for 8 hours of daily public radio is $120. The technique is used to find all points of the total demand curve D_{a+b}. Two things are worth noting about the resulting total demand curve. First, person a would not voluntarily pay for more than 12 hours of radio broadcasts at any price. This means that the total demand curve is identical to person b's demand curve for quantities greater than 12 hours. Second, the upper portion of the total demand curve is steeper than either of the individual demand curves because the change in price is larger relative to the quantity on the total demand curve than it is on either of the individual demand curves.

The optimal quantity of the public good is found where the supply curve intersects the total demand curve. If we assume that the marginal cost of providing public radio is constant, then the supply curve is just the price line, $P = MC$, which is equal to $120 in this example. The optimal number of public radio broadcast hours is 8. Once the optimal quantity of the public good is

Figure 35.3 **Efficient Allocation of a Public Good**

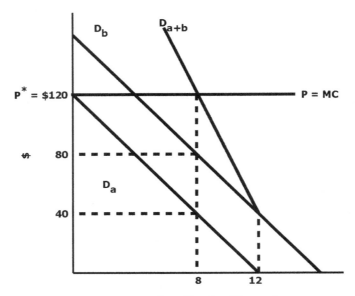

Quantity of public good
(hours of daily public radio broadcasts)

The total demand for a public good is found by vertical addition because each person consumes the same quantity. For every possible quantity, the prices that each individual is willing to pay are added together. The public good in this case is hours of public radio broadcasts. Person a would be willing to pay an annual fee of $40 for 8 hours of daily broadcasts and person b would be willing to pay $80 for the same 8 hours of daily broadcasts. This means that the total demand curve, D_{a+b}, passes through the point ($120, 8).

Allocative efficiency exists when price equals marginal cost. This occurs at the intersection between of the total demand curve, D_{a+b}, and the supply curve, P = MC = $120. The social price of the good, P*, is the total price that all consumers would pay for the fixed quantity. Once the optimal quantity of the public good is found, it is necessary to determine how to finance it. This may entail charging different prices to each consumer.

determined, it is necessary to determine the how to raise the $120 to pay for it. One option is to charge different prices to each person based on their individual demand curves. In this case, person *a* would pay $40 and person *b* would $80. This may seem reasonable because people would be paying a price equal to their marginal benefit of consuming the public good, but it might be politically difficult to implement such a program. Precisely because people are reluctant to reveal their preferences for a public good, it is often necessary to use other criteria, ability to pay, for example, to fund public goods.

Some Real-World Complications

There are a few problems with the scenario we just laid out. First, there are incentives for people to hide their preferences and become free riders. This means that it is virtually impossible to draw true individual demand curves as we did in Figure 35.3. Second, even if we could determine the actual preferences of everyone who benefited from the public good, there could be rather severe political problems when we tried to charge different prices (taxes or user fees) to people who received the same quantity of the public good. What this means, of course, is that it is up to the politicians to decide how much of a public good to provide as well as how to tax people to pay for it. How close the outcome approximates the economist's definition of efficiency is difficult to determine.

Another problem arises when the public good can be provided with a very low or zero marginal cost. For example, once a public radio station is operational, the marginal cost of providing the service to one more listener is zero, so the efficient tax price of listening to the radio should be zero as well. Great—but how do you pay to build the radio station in the first place? If people were required to pay to listen to the radio (perhaps via the purchase of a special box to decode scrambled radio waves), some people would not listen to the radio and the level of radio listening would fall below the optimal level. In this case, the radio station would no longer be a public good because exclusion would be possible. An alternative financing scheme is to use general tax revenues to build and operate the station, but this would divorce the connection between the people who pay the taxes and receive the benefits. Another method—and one that is used with a varying amount of success by public radio stations around the nation—is to rely on voluntary contributions. Those annual fund drives may not be fun to listen to, but they often do work.

Finally, the examples we have used so far were chosen to make the distinction between public and private goods as clear as possible, but in the real world there are many cases in which the distinction between private and public goods is not so clear. Some goods are best classified as quasi-public goods. Two examples of quasi-public goods are parks and education. Both goods could be provided by the private sector because (1) it is possible to exclude people from using them without payment, so people would be forced to reveal their preferences, and (2) consumption is rival because if too many people enroll in school or use the park, the benefits will decline. However, these goods also have attributes like public goods: consumption is, within limits, nonrival because a few more people in the park or classroom would not detract from the benefits enjoyed by others. There are also significant externalities associated with most quasi-public goods. The quasi-public nature of schools and parks explains why they are sometimes provided by the public sector and sometimes provided by the private sector. However, there are inevitable consequences with private allocation of pure public goods.

Property Rights and the Coase Theorem

Another deceptively simple solution to the problem of externalities would be to have the government assign and enforce property rights to internalize the external costs or benefits, and then allow private individuals to bargain among themselves. This is the major result of the Coase theorem, named after the 1991 Economics Nobel Laureate, Ronald Coase. In simplest terms, the **Coase theorem** says that *externalities do not lead to resource misallocation as long as there is a system of well-defined property rights.* Here is how the Coase theorem would be applied. Suppose there are two groups that use the water in a river, the citizens downstream who use it for drinking and bathing, and the producers upstream who use it for paper processing. If the government grants citizens the right to drink clean water, then the effluents from the paper mill would infringe on the citizens' rights to clean water. The paper company will have to stop polluting or buy the right to pollute from the people downstream who are harmed by the pollution. People do not like dirty water, but most would be willing to put up with it if they were paid enough money. How much money would the citizens require? Just enough so that the marginal benefit of the payment was equal to the marginal discomfort and harm of dirty water.

The interesting thing about the Coase theorem is that it does not matter who is assigned the property rights as long as property rights are well defined and voluntary market transactions are allowed to take place. For example, if the government gave the right to pollute to the paper mill, consumers could buy cleaner water by paying the paper mill to pollute less. Such a transaction would make the firm recognize that there is an opportunity cost of destroying clean water. Clean water can be sold to consumers downstream; dirty water cannot. Further, it can be shown that the payment will be equal regardless of who is assigned the property rights. Does this mean that it does not matter whether the firm is given the right to pollute or the consumer is given the right to clean water? Not necessarily. The initial assignment of property rights affects income distribution. If the right to clean water is assigned to consumers, then the firm will lose income when it is forced to pay for the right to pollute; the reverse would happen if the firm is given the right to pollute.

Some economists believe that government intervention is so inherently inefficient that measures designed to ensure efficient operation of market processes are almost always preferable to direct government involvement. This is one reason for the broad appeal of the Coase theorem; however, its practical applicability in the real world has been limited because of transactions costs, which are, literally, *the costs involved in conducting a transaction*. The **transactions costs** associated with the Coase theorem include the difficulty of setting up a mechanism for the two (or more) parties to bargain. For example, suppose that the downstream consumers had previously enjoyed swimming in the clean river for free. Would they be willing to sacrifice free swimming in clean water for $5 per person? For $10? At some price, the paper mill would be forced to close down, but there may be an efficient price such that downstream consumers could afford to build a swimming pool (or tolerate a little pollution) and the paper mill could continue operating and providing jobs. The point is that finding the efficient price can be quite difficult. In these cases, it may be more efficient to resort to pollution taxes or direct controls.

KEY TERMS FOR APPENDIX 35.1

allocative efficiency   free rider
Coase theorem   transactions costs

REVIEW QUESTIONS FOR APPENDIX 35.1

Define the free rider problem and why it happens.
1. Is free riding always something that is "bad"? As part of your answer, define free riding and give examples.
2. What is it about goods that are not subject to the exclusion principle and non-rival consumption that lead to free riding? Explain.

Describe allocative efficiency and why it breaks down.
3. Define allocative efficiency. What are two complications that arise when applying the concept of allocative efficiency?
4. What are some methods that can be used to fund public goods?

Discuss the problems with government provision and allocation of public goods.
5. Is the distinction between public and private goods always clear? Explain and give examples.

Define the Coase theorem, and describe how it will solve externalities.

   6. Explain how application of the Coase theorem would make pollution taxes unnecessary.
   7. Do you think assigning private property rights would get rid of all pollution? Explain.

Discuss the real-world problems in the application of the Coase theorem.

   8. What might be some problems in assigning private property rights?
   9. What are transactions costs and how do they make the application of the Coase theorem more difficult?

PART III

MACROECONOMICS:
GROWTH AND STABILITY

PART III, SECTION 1

AGGREGATE SUPPLY AND DEMAND

CHAPTER 36

History of Business Cycles and Human Misery

What is **macroeconomics**? Macroeconomics is *the part of economics that deals with the behavior of the economy as a whole*. In comparison, **microeconomics**, discussed in Part II, investigates the *behavior of individual consumers, individual business owners, and individual employees (one of the factors of production)*. Macroeconomics is concerned with such problems as the causes of economic depression, inflation, and growth of the whole economy. This chapter deals with the rate of unemployment, how instability and business cycles began, how they spread, and how they effect people.

LEARNING OBJECTIVES

After reading this chapter, you should be able to:

- Discuss how and when business cycles began and how business cycles have spread over the whole world.
- Describe the "costs" of recessions and depressions.
- Give examples of expansions and recessions throughout history and explain the effects that are common to all recessions.

THE UNEMPLOYMENT RATE

In October 2006, just before an election, President George W. Bush boasted that the unemployment rate dropped to 4.3 percent, so the economy was great. Some things he did not say are the following:

1. The American economy is so big that small percentages, like 4 percent, mean millions of people.
2. On average, there are three times as many people unemployed sometime during the year than are unemployed each month. If 4.3 percent were unemployed in October, then 12.9 percent of the labor force was unemployed sometime during the year, for at least a while.
3. According to the U.S. Labor Department definition, if a person is employed even one hour a week, he or she is "employed." For example, if you had a full-time $100,000-

a-year-job, then you were fired but finally found a job at low pay for one hour a week, You would be counted as employed, even if you were desperately seeking a full-time job. Thus, more millions of people face hardships because they have part-time jobs while trying hard to find full-time jobs.

4. If an employee is out of work for a long time and grows too discouraged to look for work any more, that person is *not* considered unemployed. Rather, by the official definition, he or she is no longer in the labor force. For more accurate picture, we should count millions of people more as unemployed.

5. Some students think that everyone who is unemployed must be poor, lazy, and uneducated. But those students are wrong. For example, in the 2001 recession, the city hardest hit was San Jose, California, the heart of the computer industry. A great many high-paid computer engineers lost their jobs.

SPREAD OF THE BUSINESS CYCLE

The **business cycle** is the *cyclical movement of the economy through periods of boom and bust.* All capitalist economies suffer from business cycles. A business cycle is *an* **expansion** *in economic activity (measured by indicators such as increased in output, employment, and profits) followed by a* **contraction***, downward turn in economic activity (including declining production, unemployment, business losses and bankruptcies).* Each business cycle is different, but there are many regularities or similar sequences found in every business cycle. Unemployment tends to be higher during recessions or depressions, though some unemployment remains throughout expansion. A depression is a large downturn in output and employment. A recession is a small downturn in output and employment. Since no one agrees on what is "small" or "large" in this context, the terms are best defined by means of an ancient but accurate old joke: A recession is when the other guy is out of work; a depression is when you are out of work. Whatever the term, it means a lot of human misery.

Precapitalist societies are subject to war and to natural disasters such as floods or droughts. Precapitalist societies, however, never rise and fall because there is not enough demand for all the goods produced at full employment. The signs of the modern cycle of boom and bust arise in each economy as capitalism begins to dominate the production system. The modern business cycle began in England in 1793, in France in 1847, and in Germany in 1857. In the period from 1888 to 1891, it spread further to Russia, Argentina, Brazil, Canada, South Africa, Australia, India, Japan, and China. After 1890, the business cycle assumed a truly international character with regard to all large, cyclical downturns and large, cyclical upturns.

The less developed countries in the early nineteenth century were mainly agricultural and did not have primarily capitalist institutions. Therefore, countries such as China, India, and all of Africa, produced no business cycle of their own. As each of these countries became a colony of the more advanced capitalist countries, however, they also joined the international business cycle. As we shall see in later chapters, they became entrapped in the international business cycles because the colonizers controlled much of their trade, investment, and finance.

HISTORY OF UNEMPLOYMENT IN THE U.S. ECONOMY

Business cycles have occurred regularly in the United States for more than 150 years. The very earliest cycles were clearly tied to events abroad. In its infancy, from 1776 to about 1840, the American economy depended heavily on the export trade to Europe, especially England. During this period, about half of all U.S. exports went to England, while about two-thirds of all U.S. imports came from England. The United States sold mostly raw materials to England, while England sold all kinds of manufactured goods to the United States. If you wanted good dishes or linens or a watch, you usually imported it from England. The American economy was no longer a British colony but remained extremely dependent on England. In the whole first half of the nineteenth century, U.S. depressions followed immediately after the start of British depressions.

The United States prospered with every increase in the flow of ships and goods from Atlantic ports. Whenever this flow was interrupted, distress in the coastal towns persisted until some new stimulus brought a return of strong demand for American goods. Most profits came from foreign commerce. It was in commerce and shipping that the most important capital investment was occurring. Therefore, in the first half of the nineteenth century, a remarkably close correlation existed between the demand for American exports and the health of the American economy as a whole.

European investment also meant much in the American economy. For example, in 1836, when European economic activity declined and American expansion faltered, Europeans sold many of their holdings and withdrew their funds, intensifying the major depression that followed. In the last half of the nineteenth century, foreign influence persisted, but the course of the economy was increasingly shaped by the domestic environment. In the last half of the century, American business cycles were starting to be generated more by internal factors but with heavy influence by foreign economies.

The cyclical pattern of fluctuation characteristic of modern capitalist economies had set in. During the nineteenth century, depressions or recessions began in 1857, 1860, 1865, 1869, 1873, 1882, 1887, 1893, and 1899. The twentieth century witnessed depressions or recessions beginning in 1902, 1907, 1910, 1913, 1918, 1920, 1923, 1926, 1929, 1937, 1948, 1953, 1957, 1960, 1969, 1973, 1980, 1981, 1990, and 2001.

During the period of American industrialization (1870s through 1920s), "millions lived in abject poverty in densely packed slums. . . . They struggled merely to maintain their families above the level of brutal hunger and want for such little pay that their status was a tragic anomaly in light of the prosperity enjoyed by business and industry" (Foster R. Dulles, quoted in Boyer and Morais, p. 34). Output, productivity, and profits all climbed impressively, but the improvement was mostly in expansions, with some ground lost in business contractions.

The last decades of the nineteenth century saw frequent periods of distress and depression. From 1873 to 1879, thousands of small businesses failed, farms were lost to foreclosure, and the accumulated savings of thousands of families disappeared in bank failures. Estimates of unemployment during the long depression that started in 1873 range from 1 to 3 million people. When recovery came in the 1880s, output expanded more rapidly than at any other time in U.S. history, and yet the decade was interrupted by three years of depression. Vigorous expansion did not return to the economy until late in the 1890s. The depression of the early 1890s is generally regarded as the most severe on record prior to the Great Depression of the 1930s. More than 4.5 million employees, or almost 20 percent of the labor force, were unemployed in 1894, and unemployment remained high until 1899.

In the early nineteenth century, most of the people in the U.S. economy were self-employed farmers or craft producers. A cyclical downturn meant they sold less, but they were not unemployed. By the end of the nineteenth century, however, most people in the U.S. economy were employed by capitalists and were paid wages or salaries. A cyclical downturn then became more painful because it was reflected in large-scale unemployment.

World War I brought economic expansion. It was followed, however, by the severe depression of 1920–21, when production fell 20 percent and employment dropped 11 percent within a year.

The rebound out of the 1921 depression was strong, and in spite of the three temporary downturns, the 1920s were growth years. Major advances in productivity took place, and employment was high. Major new industries led the expansion. Automobile production tripled during the decade, making up one-eighth of the value of manufacturing by 1929. The automobile's stimulus to the construction, steel, glass, rubber, oil, retail trade, and service industries led to widespread increases in production. These were boom years for new housing and business construction as well. Radio was a new growth industry, and production of other consumer durables reached record levels.

In October 1929, the stock market collapsed. However, it would be difficult to support a view that the stock market breakdown was the basic cause of the depression of the 1930s. Manufacturing had begun to falter at least three months earlier, and the construction industry had been depressed for almost two years. But the collapse of the stock market was spectacular. Buyers for securities vanished as everyone rushed to sell. Debts that could not be paid encompassed the lenders in the downward spiral of asset values.

The loss of wealth was being matched by the loss of income as prices, sales, and production continued to fall. There were signs that the debacle had ended in early 1931, but instead of beginning to recover, the downward momentum suddenly quickened. By 1933, at least 25 percent of the labor force was unemployed. The homeless, the hungry, and the desperate were never fully counted. The economy improved slightly until 1938, when it took another downward plunge. Full employment was restored only by the all-out spending of World War II.

Since World War II, the American economy has been plagued by instability, although depressions approaching the seriousness of the Great Depression have been avoided. Many small recessions occurred in the 1950s and 1960s, but recessions grew in force from 1970 until 1990. There was a long expansion in the 1990s, followed by a recession in 2001 and a weak recovery since then.

THE MISERY AND WASTE OF UNEMPLOYMENT

In the Great Depression of the 1930s, millions of people were involuntarily unemployed. Many of the unemployed did not have enough money to buy the food, clothing, and shelter they so badly needed. To the degree that this human misery repeats itself in the contraction phase of every business cycle, and to a much lesser degree during expansions, there is a major social problem arising from a seemingly irrational economic situation. It seems irrational because there is great need for goods and services, yet millions of people are no longer employed. The cause of this situation is explored in later chapters, but here the focus is on **social losses** *caused to society by the economic downturn,* business losses, *in which businesses cannot sell their goods at a profit,* and the human suffering of the unemployed and their families.

Losses to Society

Society suffers many types of losses from the contractions that occur during business cycles. Thousands of factories stand idle and millions of employees are unemployed, so society loses an enormous amount of potential output for current consumption. Society also loses because very few new plants and little new equipment are produced. This means there is very little, if any, growth of productive potential for future expansion. For that reason, every recession or depression lowers the long-run rate of growth. Although the overall, long-run U.S. trend has clearly been one of economic growth, the trend rate of growth has been lowered by these losses. Society loses the new inventions that are not discovered because there is less motivation and less money for research and development. Society loses because millions of people are unable to work and to create to the best of their potential. Society loses because millions of people are frustrated and unhappy, and the social atmosphere is poisoned.

Losses to Business

In every contraction, many businesses cannot sell their goods at a profit. The number of bankruptcies skyrockets. The number of new businesses declines drastically. Millions of small businesses are forced out of business, and their owners are often left unemployed. Even a few large corporations go out of business, leaving all of their employees out of work.

Losses to Individual Employees

The greatest scourge of the business cycle, however, is the involuntary unemployment of millions of employees. Every one of these individuals suffers the disruption of a useful life. Heads of families may not be able to maintain the standard of living to which their family is accustomed. The unemployed feel useless; each believes that he or she is a personal failure. There is a measurable increase in mental and physical illness among the unemployed and their families. Increased unemployment is associated with increases in alcoholism, divorce, child abuse, crime, and even suicide.

A study for the Joint Economic Committee has documented the grim facts. A sustained 1-percent increase in unemployment is associated with the following statistically significant percentage increases (Brenner, 1976, p. v):

suicide	4.1 percent
state mental hospital admissions	3.4 percent
state prison admissions	4.0 percent
homicide	5.7 percent
deaths from cirrhosis of the liver	1.9 percent
deaths from cardiovascular diseases	1.9 percent

BOOMS AND BUSTS IN THE TWENTY-FIRST CENTURY

Economic insecurity is not just ancient history but has continued unabated into the twenty-first century. The boom of the 1990s ended in 2001 in a recession during the Bush administration. Production dropped, employment dropped, and income dropped. Moreover, the stock market dropped and millions of small investors lost their savings.

In the recovery from 2001 to 2007 (the present time), output rose at a good pace and corporate profits rose very fast. Those who owned large amounts of corporate stock or bonds made very large increases in income and wealth during the recovery.

Most of the United States, however, is composed of employees, who own little corporate stock and bonds. Employees' wages and salaries stagnated in this period. Their compensation rose in money terms, but inflation rose about as fast. In this weak recovery, instead of people having more and more savings, the average person was in debt by 2005. Instead of poverty declining as it has done in most expansions, the number of working poor increased. Instead of more people with health care, the number of people without health care rose during the recovery, at least up until 2007 at the present writing.

In later chapters of Part III, these impressions are spelled out in numerical data, and the trends are explained.

SUMMARY

In each country in which capitalist economic institutions have become dominant, there are cycles of boom and bust. Since the early nineteenth century, the U.S. economy has been subject to alternating periods of expansion and contraction. The longest depression lasted from 1929 to 1939. In each contraction period, the amount of unemployment rises. The unemployment causes business losses, social losses, and human misery among employees and professionals at all levels of wage and salary income.

KEY WORDS

business cycle
contraction
expansion
macroeconomics
microeconomics
social losses

REVIEW QUESTIONS

Discuss how and when business cycles began and how business cycles have spread over the whole world.

1. What is a business cycle? What is an expansion, and what is a contraction? How are they measured?

2. When and where did the modern business cycle begin?

Describe the "costs" of recessions and depressions.

3. Who loses from recessions and depressions?

4. What do employees lose?

5. What do corporations lose?

6. Does the official unemployment rate tell the whole story about how much unemployment exists?

7. What other points must be considered?

Give examples of expansions and recessions throughout history and explain the effects that are common to all recessions.

8. Were there recessions or expansions in pre-capitalist societies? Explain.
9. What is the largest recession of the twentieth century? What were some of its most significant effects? How did this recession differ from other recessions that followed?

CHAPTER 37

National Income Accounting
How to Map the Circulation of Money and Goods

The U.S. Department of Commerce publishes detailed national income accounts. These accounts report the total flow of money and goods in the nation for a given period of time the same way that private accounting reports the flow of money and goods in a single private enterprise. Many economists have labored to map this circulation of money and goods in the nation just as biologists trace the circulation of blood through the body. Students should not try to memorize every detail of this chapter, but should remember the main paths of income circulation.

LEARNING OBJECTIVES

After reading this chapter, you should be able to:

- Explain the flows of money and goods between business, households, and the government.
- Discuss the relationships of GDP, expenditures, and national income.
- Describe the components of expenditures and national income and explain how each is calculated.

INTRODUCTION

John Maynard Keynes (1883–1946) made his major contributions to aggregate economic concepts (macroeconomics) in the midst of the Great Depression of the 1930s. He wanted to trace the total flow of money and goods in order to learn how it was possible for a nation to have a lack of demand for goods while millions of people were hungry, poorly clothed, and ill-housed. Before 1930, there were no national income accounts in the United States that tracked aggregate economic activity.

The aggregate concepts of Keynes constituted a radical new way of thinking about the economy. Before Keynes, most orthodox academic economists denied the possibility of prolonged aggregate depression or recession. The Great Depression of the 1930s and its toll in lost production and human suffering caused economists to question this assumption. Keynes was one of the economists who thought the economy needed to be viewed in a new way. Keynes, along with others, developed the aggregate concepts as the basis for a whole new aggregate or macroeconomic analysis. These concepts and their measures are now used by the U.S. Department of Commerce. The following discussion is based on their data.

452

Figure 37.1   **Circular Flow of Supply and Demand**

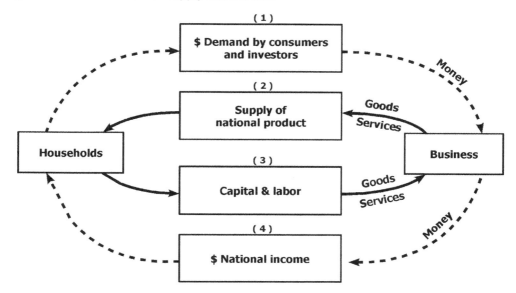

Keynes concentrated on the total or aggregate demand for goods. He found that this demand comes from spending by consumers, investors, and government and through trade with other countries. Spending on goods and services is clearly connected to the production of goods and services. When factors of production such as labor services are supplied by households to business, they are provided payment. Payment must be made by means of money. Money is used to buy the goods and services produced by businesses. This process is the only way to buy goods and services, or have "effective" demand. The concept of **effective demand**, or *demand based on spending of money by consumers and investors*, was Keynes's main analytic tool.

THE CIRCULAR FLOW OF GROSS DOMESTIC PRODUCT

Gross domestic product (GDP) is *the total value of all the finished goods and services produced and sold by a nation during some period of time*, such as a year. Each good or service is valued at its market selling price. The market pricing system thus provides a yardstick by means of which totally different and otherwise unrelated items can be compared and added together.

The flow of production and income in the private domestic sector may be thought of as a **circular flow** of the supply of goods and services in one direction, while demand in the form of money moves in the other direction. The flow is between households and businesses (leaving aside government and foreign trade for now). The four flows involved are illustrated in Figure 37.1.

Figure 37.1 depicts four flows. Two consist of money used for demand of goods and services, while two consist of supply or production of goods and services. This figure indicates how, in flow 1, money spending flows from households to business to buy consumer and investment goods. This spending pays for the goods and services that are in flow 2. Flow 2 is the transfer of products from business to households.

Flow 3 shows the movement of labor services and capital from households to business. Business pays money for these services and for capital in flow 4. Flow 4 shows the flow of money income from business to households.

Figure 37.2 **Circular Flow of Money, Goods, and Services**

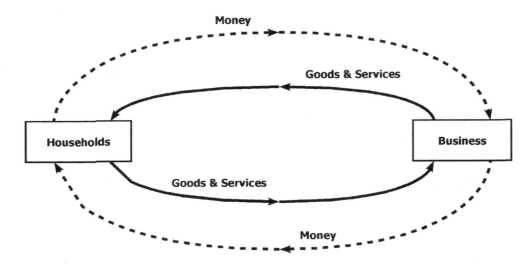

Notice that money moves in one direction around the circuit, while goods and services move in the opposite direction. This circular flow is illustrated in Figure 37.2. If there is no glitch, the supply and demand will flow smoothly and just balance each other in both sets of transactions. All four flows are equal in accounting. They are just different ways of looking at our aggregate economic activity.

By definition, GDP is calculated by either method, that is, expenditures of money or incomes of money, and they must be equal to the same money value. Indeed, the U.S. Department of Commerce, which makes these calculations, always arrives at the same amount by either method (after adjustments and allowing for statistical mistakes).

GDP FROM THE EXPENDITURE SIDE

In Figure 37.1, GDP was shown as *the flow of money for spending*, or **expenditures**. Expenditures are divided into different components. The largest component is consumption spending. **Consumption** means *the money that individuals spend for food, clothing, shelter and everything else they buy*. The next category is investment spending. **Investment** means *all private investment in the United States for fixed capital*. Fixed capital means buildings and equipment.

The third category is **government spending**. *The government receives money from the circular flow mainly by taxing the incomes of labor and profits of business owners. The government returns money to the spending stream by paying its employees for services and buying goods and services from businesses.* The types of goods and services government buys, as well as the uses to which it puts them, are considered in later chapters. The U.S. government is not to any appreciable extent an owner of any instruments of production. Government spending is a very significant part of overall demand. The government not only directly employs about 20 percent of the labor force, it also purchases many goods and services from private companies, which indirectly creates more employment through those companies.

The total flow of money to business in the whole economy also includes money from net exports. **Net exports** is *the difference between what is sold to other countries (exports) and what is purchased from other countries (imports).* Exports bring a flow of dollars into the country in exchange for goods produced at home but sold abroad. Imports result in a flow of dollars out of the country for the purchase of goods produced abroad. If more is exported than imported, the net figure is an addition to the total amount of spending for domestically produced goods and services. But if imports are greater than exports, money flows out of this country. *When exports are greater than imports,* a **trade surplus** results. If *exports are less than imports,* a **trade deficit** results. A trade surplus means that money flows into the country, but a trade deficit means that money flows out of the country.

This process can be captured in the simple statement that the dollar value of all final goods and services produced and sold in one year (GDP) must equal the dollar value of all spending in one year. We can use a simple equation to describe this relationship:

$$\$Gross\ domestic\ product\ (GDP) = \$Consumption\ (C) +$$
$$\$Investment\ (I) + \$Government\ (G) + \$Net\ exports\ (NX).$$

or

$$GDP = C + I + G + NX$$

For the year 2005, in billions of dollars, the U.S. data are:

Gross Domestic Product	$12,487
= Consumption (C)	$8,536
+ Investment (I)	$2,105
+ Government (G)	$2,365
+ Net exports (NX)	($727)

The source of all data in this chapter is the Bureau of Economic Analysis, U.S. Department of Commerce, released March 30, 2006 (see http://bea.gov).

What percentage of the demand for GDP did each component provide? These data show that consumer demand is 69 percent, investment spending is 17 percent, and government spending is 20 percent of the demand for GDP (all figures rounded to nearest whole number). When we add up consumption, investment, and government, the total is 106 percent of GDP. But that presents a mystery. How can these three components be greater than all of GDP? The simple answer is that the negative net exports, a trade deficit, drained 6 percent of GDP. The amount of net exports is negative and is subtracted from the components of expenditures.

Notice that consumer spending is the largest single expenditure. Notice also that net exports are negative, which means that imports were bigger than exports, so money is flowing out of the United States (see Chapter 52 for further discussion). Also note that GDP is "domestic" in the sense that it captures production taking place in the United States. GDP is also "gross" because of how investment spending is calculated. **Gross investment spending** is *spending on all capital equipment including capital that replaces worn-out machinery and plants.* Therefore, gross investment spending includes replacement investment for depreciated capital. By definition, **depreciation** means *the funds set aside to replace the machinery and factory buildings that are used up or eventually worn out in the process of production.* There is more on consumption, investment, and government in later chapters.

CALCULATING GDP FROM THE INCOME OR COST SIDE

After business takes in the revenue from consumption, investment, government spending, and net exports, it pays out most of it. It counts those payments as costs, but they are also incomes to other people or businesses. These payments include wages and salaries to employees; dividends, rent, and interest to capitalist investors; and various taxes to governments at all levels. The Department of Commerce traces this process from GDP through other categories down to personal disposable income and finally down to what is left as saving. Let us examine these categories as they appear in the accounting process.

From GDP to National Income

National income is *the revenues received by all business and households*. It differs from GDP only in that it does include flows from and to the rest of the world. It also differs from GDP because it does not include replacement of depreciated capital. We saw that depreciation means the funds set aside out of investment spending to replace the machinery and factory buildings that are used up or eventually worn out in the process of production. These funds are not paid out to any household, but to other businesses when it is time to replace the worn-out instruments of production. Therefore, depreciation is subtracted from GDP before calculating national income.

What exactly are the types of income that constitute national income? National income is divided into income from labor by employees and income from property by capitalists. All labor income is called *employee compensation* by the Commerce Department. **Employee compensation** consists of *wages, salaries, bonuses, commissions, and fringe benefits*. Remember that:

Labor income (employee compensation) = wages + salaries,
including bonuses, commissions, and fringe benefits.

Property income is defined here to mean *all the income that derives from ownership of various types of property*. First, property income includes the profits of individual proprietors and the profit income of all U.S. corporations. Second, property income includes the rent from land and buildings. Finally, it includes all interest paid on loans to individuals, businesses, and government.

Remember that:

Property income = rent + interest + profit.

Finally, when we put them together:

National income = Labor income + Property income.

The data for the United States in 2005 in billions of dollars shows:

National income	$10,904
= Labor income (employee compensation)	$7,125
+ Property Income	$3,779

The rate of exploitation was defined in Chapter 19 to be property income divided by labor income. In this case, the rate of exploitation for the whole society is equal to $3,779 \div 7,125 = .53$. Thus, the rate of exploitation in the United States in 2005 was 53 percent.

There are two related percentages that are also useful in macroeconomics. The labor share is defined as labor income divided by national income. In this case, the labor share is $7,125 \div 10,904 = .65$. The labor share is 65 percent of national income. The property share is defined to be property income divided by national income. In this case, the property share is $3,779 \div 10.904 = .35$. That makes the property share 35 percent of national income.

For those who like to play with numbers, notice that the property share plus the labor share always add up to 100 percent of national income. Also notice that the rate of exploitation is the property share divided by the labor share. The property share, which is the money that goes to capitalists, always moves the in same direction as the rate of exploitation. The labor share—is the income that goes to employees. The labor share always moves opposite to the rate of exploitation. We have occasion to use these different concepts in the rest of Part III.

Let's look at the details of the surplus or property income. The data for the United States in 2005 in billions of dollars shows:

Property income	$3,779
= Corporate profit	$1,352
+ Proprietor's profit	$939
+ Rental income	$73
+ Interest income	$498
+ Business taxes	$917

Proprietors here are defined as all the individual business owners. Total profit goes to corporations plus proprietors. Business taxes here include mainly sales taxes as well as smaller miscellaneous taxes and fees. All of these taxes on the business income come out of the surplus produced by employees, so they are considered here as part of property income.

From National Income to Disposable Personal Income

What actually goes to individuals is not the same as national income for two reasons: corporate transactions and government transactions. Corporations give out some profits in the form of dividends to individuals. But they also retain some for purposes such as investment. Moreover, corporations pay taxes on their profits to the government.

Government also collects various taxes from employees. For example, the government collects a tax from every employee called the Contribution to Social Security. This tax falls most heavily on poor and middle-class employees because it has a cap on it at some level of income. Therefore, very large salaries to corporate executives are taxed for Social Security at only a tiny percentage of their whole income. Look at the following examples. Suppose the Social Security tax is 5 percent of total income up to $100,000. An employee earning $20,000 pays $1,000, or 5 percent. But suppose the chief executive of the corporation gets $20,000,000 a year in salary. He pays only 5 percent of $100,000, or $5,000. But $5,000 is only 0.025 percent of $20,000,000.

Government also collects taxes on income as a percentage of an individual's whole income. The rate to be paid goes up as income rises to higher levels. Thus, the tax rate on an income of $25,000 might be 10 percent, or $2,500. The tax rate on $1,000,000 might be 20 percent, or $200,000,000.

In later chapters on government, however, we shall see that there are few tax loopholes for the poor, but very large tax loopholes for the rich. A **tax loophole** *is a way that the tax law allows an individual to pay less than the rate for that group.* Therefore, the actual rate paid by an individual earning a very large income may be no higher than that paid by an individual earning a very low income. We investigate loopholes in detail in later chapters.

On the other hand, *government also pays money to people for reasons other than current services to the government.* These payments are called transfer payments from government to household. **Transfer payments** from the government to households include everything from flood relief and hurricane relief to unemployment compensation as well as many subsidies to business and large farmers.

When we subtract the amounts of (1) profits kept by corporations and (2) all kinds of taxes, but add (3) all subsidies, the result is what individual persons have at their disposal. This amount is officially called disposable personal income.

Disposable Personal Income

Finally, people have **disposable personal income**, which is *the amount of money actually at the disposal of individuals and households for spending.* Consumers may now spend for consumption or save out of disposable personal income. If *consumption expenditures are subtracted,* we arrive at **personal savings**. In 2005 in billions of dollars, the result for the United States is striking:

Personal Disposable Income	$9,039
– Consumption (and other personal outlays)	($9,072)
Personal Savings	($34)

In other words, these preliminary data showed that the whole population of the United States in the aggregate went into further debt by $34 billion. Later, revised data issued by the Department of Commerce found that personal saving for the whole year was slightly positive. The revised data did show, however, that there were some quarters where the average person did go into debt rather than saving in both 2005 and 2006. The result is still striking. The revised finding, however, also illustrates the fact that one should never trust preliminary government data too much, since they are often revised.

Personal savings used to be the main source of investment. When personal saving was negative, there was little or nothing going into investment in the aggregate. This has changed. Most investment spending now comes from the profits of corporations and from borrowing by corporations.

SUMMARY

This chapter explained gross domestic product, national income, and disposable personal income. It explained how national income is divided into labor income (employee compensation) and property income. Finally, it explained how disposable personal income leads to savings (though there is sometimes dis-saving or increasing debt).

Appendix 37.1 provides a systematic account of all of the main features of national income accounting, from GDP to saving. Appendix 37.2 discusses the difference between gross domestic product and gross national product, each of which is useful for different purposes.

KEY TERMS

circular flow

consumption

depreciation

disposable personal income

effective demand

employee compensation

expenditures

government spending

gross domestic product

gross investment spending

investment

national income

net exports

personal savings

property income

tax loophole

trade deficit

trade surplus

transfer payment

REVIEW QUESTIONS

Explain the flows of money and goods between businesses and households.

  1. Explain how and why money goes from businesses to households and how and why money goes from households to businesses.
  2. Explain how demand and supply flows between businesses and households.

Discuss the relationships of GDP, expenditures, and national income.

  3. How is GDP measured?
  4. What is national income used for? How does this correspond to expenditures and GDP?

Describe the components of expenditures, GDP, and national income and explain how each is calculated.

  5. What are the components of expenditures? Describe each one in detail. What is the difference between gross and net expenditures?
  6. What are the sources of income from production? What are other sources of income to households?

APPENDIX 37.1
DETAILED, SYSTEMATIC INCOME ACCOUNTS

This appendix takes a detailed look at how the Department of Commerce tracks aggregate economic activity. It introduces the differences between GDP and GNP, or gross national product.

LEARNING OBJECTIVES FOR APPENDIX 37.1

After reading this appendix, you should be able to:

  • Describe how official government agencies track aggregate economic activity in great detail.
  • Explain the difference between GDP, GNP, and national income.

INCOME ACCOUNTS

The Department of Commerce uses five different versions of income: GDP, GNP, national income, personal income, and disposable personal income. We begin with the relation of GDP to GNP. GNP includes U.S. flows to and from the rest of the world. The amounts are shown in billions of dollars for 2005.

GROSS DOMESTIC PRODUCT	12,487
+ Receipts from rest of world	508
− Payments to rest of world	474
= GROSS NATIONAL PRODUCT	12,521

Next we examine the differences between GNP and national income:

GROSS NATIONAL PRODUCT	12,521
− Depreciation (consumption of fixed capital)	1,574
− Statistical discrepancy	43
= NATIONAL INCOME	10,904

Next we look at the relationship between national income and personal income (that part of national income that actually goes to individuals).

NATIONAL INCOME	10,904
− Business taxes (sales tax + miscellaneous)	917
+ Business transfers from government	80
− Deficit from government enterprises	11
+ Personal transfers from government	1,525
− Contributions to Social Security	871
− Corporate profits	1,352
+ Dividends from corporations	512
= PERSONAL INCOME	10,248

Next we see how personal income is related to disposable personal income.

PERSONAL INCOME	10,248
− Personal income taxes	1,210
= DISPOSABLE PERSONAL INCOME	9,039

Finally, disposable personal income is related to personal savings.

DISPOSABLE PERSONAL INCOME	9,039
− Personal outlays (mostly consumption)	9,072
= PERSONAL SAVINGS	−34

Note: The data in this table were the first publication of the 2005 figures by the Department of Commerce. Such data are always being revised, so later versions will differ. For example, the latest revised Department of Commerce figures show that Personal Saving for all of 2005 was a small positive amount instead of the small negative account shown in this table. One quarter of 2005 did have negative personal saving (debt increase) in the latest revised data.

SUMMARY OF APPENDIX 37.1

Gross domestic product was defined to include all of the value of economic activity that takes place domestically, that is, in this country. Gross national product (GNP) includes domestic activity as well as the net flow of payments from abroad, reflecting American economic activity abroad. Thus, GNP is GDP plus the flow of income from rest of world minus the flow of income going to the rest of the world.

REVIEW QUESTIONS FOR APPENDIX 37.1

Describe how official government agencies track aggregate economic activity in great detail.
1. What agency tracks flows of dollars and production?
2. What are some measures listed under national income?

Explain the difference between GDP, GNP, and national income.
3. How is GDP calculated? How is GNP calculated?
4. How is national income calculated from GNP?

APPENDIX 37.2
NET ECONOMIC WELFARE

So far in exploring aggregate measures, we have not discussed whether these measures are an accurate reflection of social welfare. This appendix takes up that discussion.

LEARNING OBJECTIVE FOR APPENDIX 37.2

After reading this appendix, you should be able to:

- Discuss why GDP is not necessarily a reflection of social and individual well-being.

NET ECONOMIC WELFARE

Is GDP a good measure of individual human welfare or social well-being? More and more economists are coming to the conclusion that it is not a good welfare measure. On the one side, there are some goods and services not included in the GDP because they are not given a value in the market. For example, the work of homemakers is not counted in the GDP. Yet many women (*and* some men) work long, hard hours in the home. Estimated in terms of the labor expended, the labor of women and men in the home equals about one-fourth of the official GDP value.

This exclusion of home labor is very inconsistent. Suppose a woman works as a maid for a man who owns a house. That woman's labor is counted in the GDP to the amount of her wage. Yet if she marries the house owner and receives and $300 a week "household allowance," her labor is no longer counted, and GDP is reduced. She is still doing the same work, but now it is not counted in GDP. The reason for this exclusion is the capitalist notion that services have value only if they are bought and sold in the market.

On the other side, many costs to the public are not subtracted from GDP even though they are caused by the private capitalist production of GDP. For example, the production and use of cars and trucks cause air pollution. This pollution costs the public in terms of health, such as eye and respiratory diseases, and even property damage, such as harm to trees and plants. GDP also does not account for nonrenewable resources that are depleted through their use in production. Many economists argue that GDP should be reduced by the amount of this damage. Another cost that is not captured in GDP is the social costs of family breakups or medical catastrophes. If a married couple divorces and sets up separate households, this is reflected in an increase in GDP. Catastrophic illnesses and accidents also raise GDP.

Moreover, a significant portion of GDP is composed of wasteful or harmful goods that reduce or do not increase human welfare. These types of goods should not be included in GDP. For example, cigarettes are part of GDP, but they are harmful. Advertising "service" is part of GDP, but over 90 percent of it is pure propaganda or misinformation. Military spending in the billions of dollars for building and stockpiling bombs and tanks are included in GDP.

Some projects do benefit the public beyond the cost shown in GDP. For example, a dam built by the government to provide water and power is counted in GDP at cost. Yet dams may also produce recreation and beauty.

Therefore, a new measure is needed to replace the official GDP or at least to be used in addition to it. The new measure would equal the GDP but would in addition (1) add household labor, (2) add unpriced benefits (such as recreation from lakes behind dams), (3) subtract unpriced costs (such as pollution from industry and cars), and (4) subtract all harmful and wasteful products. One measure that has been discussed over the last several years is the GPI or Genuine Progress Indicator that attempts to capture the costs and benefits mentioned above.

SUMMARY OF APPENDIX 37.2

GDP may not accurately capture social and individual well-being. Many costs, especially housework and environmental costs, are not measured as part of GDP. Many benefits also are not measured in official GDP accounts.

REVIEW QUESTION FOR APPENDIX 37.2

Discuss why GDP is not necessarily a reflection of social and individual well-being.
  1. What are some "costs" not captured by GDP?
  2. What goods and services are not captured by GDP?

CHAPTER 38

===

Money and Profit
Say's Law and Institutionalist Criticism

According to the theory known as Say's law, the capitalist economy runs smoothly. Production (GDP) and the demand for goods and services (expenditures) are equal. There is never a long-term lack of demand for the total goods produced by society. This happens as long as the government does not intervene in the economy—laissez faire. According to progressive critics, this theory may apply under some earlier economic institutions, but it is not true with capitalist economic institutions. Progressives argue that we frequently witness recessions based on the lack of demand for the total goods and services produced in the country.

LEARNING OBJECTIVES

After reading this chapter, you should be able to:

- Explain Say's law and discuss the arguments supporting it.
- Explain the relationship of business cycles and Say's law.
- Describe how Say's law informs policy decisions about the economy.
- Discuss why Say's law is true in many precapitalist societies but not in capitalism as we see it today.

THE CONSERVATIVE VIEW OF J.B. SAY

J.B. Say (1767–1832) claimed that the internal workings of market capitalism produce an economy without any booms or busts or price inflation that the market would not correct quickly if left alone. He claimed that unemployment and inflation are caused by factors external to the economy and are not due to how the economy itself operates. Any job losses are always minor and temporary. The capitalist economy, if left alone, will always return to full employment and stable prices in a short time. Since the economy will automatically correct any problems, the government should keep out of the economy.

Say's law states that *the supply of goods and services calls forth its own demand.* In other words, there can never be excess production above demand for any length of time because demand always rises to equal supply. Say argues that the production of output leads to income for its producers. This income must lead to an equal amount of demand or expenditures. Thus, there can never be a lack of demand in the aggregate. For example, suppose the United States produced $10 trillion of goods and services in 2001. According to Say's law, this means that firms paid out $10 trillion in income to employees and owners of property. These people will then spend the $10 trillion to buy all kinds of goods and services. As a result, the supply of $10 trillion of goods and services will be equaled by a demand of $10 trillion of money from income.

In its most rigid form, Say's law states that aggregate demand must always equal aggregate supply at any level of supply. **Aggregate supply** is *the total output that business produces and plans to sell at a given price level.* **Aggregate demand** is *the total dollar amount of goods that consumers, investors, foreigners, and governments plan to buy at a given price level.* If full employment produces a certain level of supply, demand will rise to equal that level. Say's law does not state that aggregate supply and aggregate demand are "identical" or are equal by definition. Rather, Say's law says that an increase of supply, through various automatic processes including an increase in income, creates an increase in demand. Say's law does not state an instantaneous adjustment but a process leading to equilibrium.

The interesting question is what process makes aggregate supply and aggregate demand come to be equal. Suppose when all employees are fully employed, firms produce $10 trillion of goods and services. In order to produce $10 trillion of goods and services, producers must pay $10 trillion to the inputs used in production. This includes payment to property owners and payment to employees. The assumption is that people have no reason to hold money except for the purpose of buying goods and services. Therefore, people who receive $10 trillion of income will always automatically spend the $10 trillion for goods and services. In this way, the economy behaves so as to bring itself to equilibrium of supply and demand at full employment. The term **equilibrium** means that the *quantity supplied and quantity demanded come to be equal at some point.*

Aside from a few dissenters, whole generations of economists believed Say's law. In the period from Say's statement of the law in 1800 until the 1930s, almost all classical and neoclassical economists assumed that Say's law was true. They refused to accept the possibility that there could be involuntary unemployment or an excessive supply of goods and services, except temporarily. Furthermore, they never challenged the assumption that the total of all commodities could always be sold at prices equal to their full, long-run costs. They admitted only the possibility of temporary, accidental maladjustments in one or a few industries.

Maladjustments in the economy were sure to be corrected as soon as competition could force capitalists to switch their investments from one industry to another. In a typical statement, Ricardo argued, "Too much of a particular commodity may be produced, of which there may be said to be such a glut in the market as not to repay the capital expended on it; but this cannot be the case with all commodities" (Ricardo, 1962 [1817], p. 276). The kernel of truth in Say's law is that every purchase constitutes a sale, and every sale means some money income is paid to someone to produce it. Remember, if $10 trillion of goods and services is produced, then firms must pay out $10 trillion to produce it. Then $10 trillion of payments by firms becomes $10 trillion of income to the population.

Say's law assumes that the $10 trillion of income will be used to demand goods and services equal to $10 trillion. Ricardo phrased the case for Say's law in this way: "No man produces but with a view to consume or sell, and he never sells but with an intention to purchase some other commodity which may be useful to him or which may contribute to future production" (Ricardo, 1962 [1817], p. 273). In other words, when people receive an income from selling things, they will always use their income to purchase consumer goods or to purchase investment goods for a business.

Figure 38.1   **Circular Flow of Money**

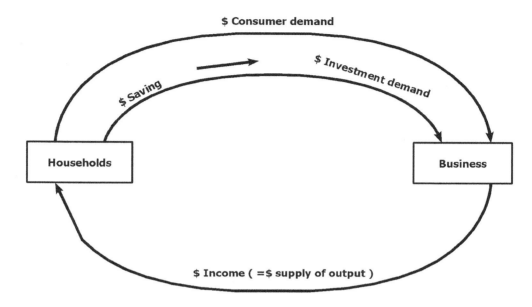

A DIAGRAM OF SAY'S LAW

Before spelling out the progressive view, let us examine Say's law in a graph. Leaving aside government and foreign trade for the moment, the essentials of Say's view of the economy can be portrayed in a very simple diagram (Figure 38.1).

This figure shows one important truth lodged in what Say claimed. It is true that output, which is supplied to the market and sold there, generates income. The capitalist pays out wage and salary income, rental income, and interest income, while the residual from sales is called profit income. These incomes all go to households (if we assume that corporations pay out all profits to stockholders). The households use all the money for consumption or savings. The money saved is then assumed by Say's law to be spent on purchase of investment goods, that is, buildings and equipment.

Examples of Say's Law Given by Its Defenders

Some conservative economists have used Robinson Crusoe on his island as an example of this automatic process of equilibrium. Note that Crusoe is alone on his island (before Friday comes). Robinson has a certain amount of raw materials and tools as well as his own ability to labor. Each year, he figures out how much he can produce. He also decides how to divide the production into consumption and saving. If he is going to produce a hundred pounds of some food, he must decide how much to eat. The rest will be savings.

The saved food, in the form of seeds, will be planted. The amount planted is his investment for the next year. He may cut down ten trees and use six for burning to keep warm. The other four are saved. Say's law assumes that these four saved tree trunks are used productively, such as for building a house. Robinson's production is always used to consume or to invest. Of course,

Robinson Crusoe has a very simple precapitalist economy that does not follow the laws of capitalist enterprise.

In this example, saving is defined as the goods that are not consumed. It is assumed that all saving is automatically used to invest in business, such as the saved logs that Crusoe uses to build a new storage facility. All income is either spent for consumption or saved. Demand for consumer goods plus demand for investment goods must equal the total amount that is supplied to the market. Supply equals demand. The reason is that all of the income from supplying goods to the market is spent as demand in the market.

Evolutionary Criticism of Say's Law

Under capitalism, we live in an economy in which everything is bought and sold with money. Most exchange of goods and services is done in the market place. Private production is guided by the expectation of profits. For progressives, who base their argument on economic institutions, the institutional features—money, markets, and profits—are the basis for understanding the progression of boom and bust in the economy.

In the progressive view, the business cycle of boom and bust is caused by the imbalance of aggregate supply and aggregate demand. Because Say's law predicts that the economy will always return to full employment equilibrium where production equals demand, the argument implies that there can be no long-term recessions or depressions in modern private enterprise economies.

The reasoning is simple. Suppose that all enterprises in the United States double their production in just one year. Does this mean that there will be too many goods and services in the market for the existing demand? Will the supply of goods and services be double the demand for goods and services? When firms double their production, the conservative economists argue, they must pay out double the income to those who supply labor, raw materials, equipment, and buildings. The income paid out to everyone in the production process will double when supply doubles. With this higher income, people want more goods. Spending will double as all of the new income is spent. Demand will rise to equal the supply. Therefore, no matter how much workers produce at full employment, there will be an equal amount of demand. Assuming that the number of workers doubles, the income from production doubles, and the demand for goods and services also doubles.

Suppose there is suddenly a vast increase in farm production, temporarily creating too much supply and causing workers to be fired. The farms have paid out a lot more money to produce the new supply of agricultural goods. This increase in income will soon be used to buy the goods supplied to the market. Then the farms will need to hire employees back to produce more goods. Full employment will be restored. Since the market will automatically restore full employment, the government should do nothing if there is unemployment. Say's law is not merely an academic argument about the economy but an argument for a policy that the government should do nothing about aggregate economic problems.

Yet observation reveals that capitalist economies have never been without periodic depressions. Sometimes the aggregate supply of goods and services is either too small or too great in terms of the aggregate demand for goods. Depressions and recessions occur when the aggregate demand, in money terms, is insufficient to purchase the aggregate supply. What causes such imbalances? Say's law argues that each of these downturns is caused by accidents external to the economic system. But why do they keep occurring under capitalist economic institutions?

We shall see that Say's law is indeed true for certain earlier types of economies. These economies could not have less aggregate demand than supply because production was for the use of self-contained feudal manors with little external trade and little use of money. The feudal lord simply planned how much to produce according to his or her best estimate of how much the manor would need this year. It had nothing to do with sale for money in the market place.

Under capitalism, however, the economy has changed in ways that allow demand to fall short of supply. By ignoring these evolutionary changes in economic institutions, the classical economists, such as Say and Ricardo, built an analytic model that fit a simple precapitalist economy, such as feudal Europe. The model did not, however, fit modern capitalism. The basic progressive criticism is that Say's law ignores the evolution from feudal economic institutions to capitalist economic institutions.

J.B. Say versus Wesley Mitchell

We live in an economy where everything is bought and sold using money. Most exchange of goods and services is done in the market place. All private production is guided by the expectation of profits. This is the background that helps explain the strange progression of boom and bust in the economy. Notice that this is very different from the view of the defenders of Say's law. The defenders use an analogy of an economy like that of Robinson Crusoe, in which there is no money, no exchange with other economic units, and production only for his own use.

Progressives argue that the business cycle of boom and bust is most often caused by the imbalance of aggregate supply and aggregate demand, not by external shocks or accidents. Sometimes the aggregate supply of produced goods is either too small or too great in terms of the aggregate demand for goods. Depressions occur when the aggregate demand, in money terms, is insufficient to purchase the aggregate supply. What causes such imbalances?

Progressive economists, such as Wesley Mitchell, believe that the science of economics should not be based on voluntary preferences by individuals with no consideration of the society in which they live. Rather, economics should trace the evolution of institutions, such as exchange in the market. The market did not always exist, but now it does exist as a foundation of capitalism. Similarly, economists should examine the history of economic systems to understand that money did not exist at one time, but now it does. Finally, it should see how our capitalist society evolved from earlier ones that did not produce for profit.

Wesley Mitchell applied the progressive views of economic institutions to the critique of Say's law. He seldom mentioned Say. He did, however, show that capitalist economies often do not produce equilibrium but do produce a business cycle with booms and busts. Recessions and depressions are caused by the basic institutions of capitalism.

In precapitalist systems, there was never a problem of lack of demand, though many other problems existed. Under capitalism, however, demand is effective only if desire is backed by money. Only demand backed by money is effective in inducing a capitalist to produce and to hire more workers. The poor may desire more food, but that is not an effective demand unless they have the money to buy the food.

THE CAPITALIST SYSTEM

Remember exactly what is meant by capitalism? One group of individuals, the capitalists, owns the means of production. The means of production, such as factories and equipment, are called capital goods. The capitalists hire other individuals who own nothing productive but their power to labor. The product of the employees' labor is owned by the capitalists. The capitalists sell the product in the marketplace for money. The capitalists will produce only so long as they expect to make a profit in the market above and beyond all their expenses.

It is this system that creates the possibility of a cycle of boom and bust with episodes of massive unemployment. Previous economic systems, such as slavery or feudalism, did have unemployment at times, but only rarely and usually as a result of some natural catastrophe such as a flood or an epidemic—an external shock. Only modern capitalism shows a systematic business cycle with periodic mass unemployment caused by declining profits and a lack of effective demand. We must examine these differences from previous systems in some detail if we are to understand the nature of the present business cycle.

PRODUCTION FOR THE MARKET

Capitalist economic institutions were fully developed in England by the end of the eighteenth century. In the nineteenth century, most British production was directed solely toward sale on the market. This was hardly ever true of earlier societies. In prehistoric communal societies, almost all productive activity was directed at the collection of food by gathering or hunting. These activities were necessarily carried out by the collective unit of all the males or females of the tribe. Even at a somewhat higher economic state, production was still for use, not for sale. None of the native tribes of the Americas, not even the Aztecs, bought or sold land or produced crops to sell for a profit to others. All over the world for thousands of years, almost all economic systems, whether tribal or feudal, were based on relatively self-sufficient agricultural units.

In the Roman Empire, there was a great deal of trade, but most of it was in luxury goods. This trade therefore did not affect the self-sufficiency of the basic agricultural unit, the slave-run plantation. The slave plantation produced all of its own food, clothing, and shelter. Only a small part of its produce was sold in the market, so if there was no market demand, it was no great problem. The same was true of feudal England. Both the lord's estate and the serf's small holding were planned to be self-sufficient. If there happened to be a surplus from the feudal estate, then it might be marketed in return for foreign luxury items to be used by the lord of the estate. Finding a market, however, was not a matter of life and death for the economic unit. If the surplus found no market, the manor was still supplied with its necessities for that year and it could and would continue the process of production for the next year's needs.

Such economically self-sufficient societies could be disturbed only by the catastrophes that were more or less external to the economy. There were natural disasters such as droughts, plagues, and floods. There were wars that destroyed crops and thousands of peasant lives. There were also massive peasant revolts, in which the lords slaughtered thousands of peasants, including not just men but also all of the women and children in each village. All of these disasters could cause reduced production.

The feudal type of economy could not conceivably face the problem of lack of effective money demand for all commodities. The reason was that the economic unit directly consumed most of the products of its own land and could do without trade altogether. During the period of transition from feudalism to capitalism in England of the sixteenth, seventeenth, and eighteenth centuries, most people still lived on the land and consumed their own products. As time went on, however, more and more products, both agricultural and industrial, were delivered to the marketplace. By the end of the eighteenth century, the private enterprise system of production for the market embraced most economic activity. Suppose a factory produced shoes. The shoes had to be sold in order for the capitalist to pay wages to the employees. Sales were also necessary to get the money to replace and expand the plant and equipment of the business.

In the United States, the transformation to a market economy took place in the nineteenth century. As described in Part I of this book, the United States in 1800 was mostly a land of self-sufficient farms. By 1900, it had become a land of factories that had to sell their goods on the market in order to continue production. If millions of consumers do not buy enough automobiles, the automobile worker loses his or her job.

Under capitalism, the sale in the market of privately produced goods and services generates income. Decisions to purchase are made by millions of households and corporations. The total of these purchasing decisions comprises the total, or aggregate, demand. In previous economic systems, the self-sufficient economic unit, the farmer or craftsman produced a trickle of hand-made items for known customers. When almost all that was produced by the economic unit was consumed by it, supply had to equal demand. Under capitalism, however, the goods and services must be sold in the market for production to continue. Production for the market is the first pre-condition for a business cycle.

MONEY

Another institutional condition that opens up the possibility of a lack of aggregate demand is the regular use of money in exchange. The monetary system takes the place of the barter system of exchanging one good for another good. Use of money in the market exchange is a second necessary condition for the emergence of business cycles. Barter means exchanging one commodity, such as a pig, for another, such as a cow. Money replaced the barter system because money is much more convenient to use.

What precisely are the functions of money in the modern economy? Each use of money is quite complex, and people are often confused about money. Traditionally, money is said to have four functions:

1. Money is the unit of accounting, or the standard of value, that serves as a measuring stick for everything else. All contracts are drawn up in money terms, with so much money to be paid for a certain product at a certain time. We think of a coat or a table as being worth so many dollars.
2. Money is the medium of exchange, or actual intermediary, between commodities (including goods and services). Under barter, one commodity is exchanged for another commodity. In the monetary economy, a commodity is exchanged for money. Then the money may be exchanged for another commodity.
3. Money is a store of value. When money is received as an income, it need not be spent immediately. Instead, if it is in a nonperishable form such as gold, it may be buried or stored away and hoarded until the possessor chooses to use it. In the modern world, money is deposited in a bank account, which is completely nonperishable. The money may even grow by earning interest while it is on deposit.
4. Money is a standard of deferred payment, or a unit of accounting for future payments on debts. In other words, I may buy something from you now and promise to pay for it later. My promise is always in terms of so many units of money, not, for example, in so many pairs of shoes. In the United States, paper money is a legal tender (or legally acceptable unit) for the payment of any debt.

The Abuses of Money

Money does not serve its four functions equally well under all conditions. Imagine that there is a catastrophic inflation, with prices doubling every hour, so that the value of money falls by half each hour. Money then functions badly as a unit of accounting because the same product sells at such rapidly changing prices that neither consumers nor sellers can keep track of them. Money obviously also loses its function as a store of value, since the value keeps changing in rapid inflation. This situation actually happened in Germany after World War I. The price of a loaf of bread started at, say, $0.50. But after an hour, it became $1. After another hour, it became $2. Pretty soon, the workers in each factory demanded to be paid every hour. They would then take a wagon load of money and run down to the bakery to buy a loaf of bread.

With rapid inflation, money is also a poor medium of exchange. People may refuse to accept it at all because its buying power is so uncertain. The buying power of money may diminish further before you can spend it. In post World War I Germany, when the workers ran down to the bakery with millions of marks to buy a loaf of bread, the bakers finally stopped accepting money at any price. The bakers knew that by the time they spent the money, it would buy far less.

Eventually, under these circumstances, the bakers require the workers to give them goods instead of money. The money becomes worthless. The workers in a shoe factory must get their wages in pairs of shoes. They can then use the shoes to exchange for bread. The money system disappears and the economy goes back to the barter system. A reversion to the bartering system occurred not only in the galloping inflations of Germany but also in Russia and later in China.

With rapid inflation, money is also a very bad store of value. The money that was hoarded away now will buy very much less in the future. In the great inflations of Germany, Russia, and China, millions of people lost their savings when money became useless pieces of paper that could buy nothing. Instead of keeping money, everyone rushes to buy goods or real property that will be worth increasingly more units of money so long as the as the inflation continues. Anyone with cash savings in paper money, bank accounts, or government bonds is badly hurt. It may happen that no one will put money in banks or buy government bonds, no matter what is the interest rate.

In Chapter 50, we shall see that inflation usually results from a huge amount of excess demand. For example, in World War II, governments spent vast sums of money to buy military goods. Still, they wanted more, so they offered even more money. But nothing more could be produced. Therefore, the additional spending simply resulted in pressure to increase prices, not in more goods and services. It is impossible to make additional goods and services if the economy is already at full employment of labor and full use of productive facilities. The details on these examples are given in Chapter 50.

Finally, with rapid inflation, money cannot function as a standard of deferred payment because the standard itself keeps changing. Suppose someone lends $100 today. But suppose when it is paid back in a year, it will buy only $2 worth of goods in terms of the present prices. Then the lender is very badly hurt. Therefore, no one wants to make loans. When people refuse to accept money because they have lost confidence in it, economic activity falls to the level that can be maintained only by barter, that is, exchange of one good for another.

The use of money brought many new complications onto the economic scene. The modern capitalist economy requires continuous use of money as the go-between in market exchange. In a barter economy, it is impossible for one commodity to be brought to market in larger supply than there is demand. There may be a mismatch of particular supplies and demands, but there can be no lack of aggregate demand. For example, those who bring cows to market may find more shoes and fewer coats produced than they desire. They would rather "spend" their cows for fewer shoes and more coats than are available. The excess supply of shoes, however, is balanced by the excess demand for coats. The result is only a temporary unemployment of shoe producers.

The problem in a capitalist economy is not necessarily lack of money in the economy in the aggregate or overall. While there are people who wish to buy but may have no money, there are also people who have money but may not wish to spend it at present. We noted earlier that savings is all the money that is not spent for consumption. It may be invested in equipment and buildings, or it may be stored away somewhere. The problem for aggregate demand is that the money not spent for consumption or for investment, but left idle, is not part of aggregate demand. The chain of circulation may then be broken at any point at which the flow of money is slowed, stopped, or withdrawn from the system. In that case, the reduction of the flow of money, like the reduction of the volume of water flowing in a stream, causes a slowdown in the movement of products being purchased.

In one sense, it is basically true that goods and services exchange for other goods and services and money is just a go-between or necessary bridge. But that bridge makes all the difference in the world. If the monetary bridge is absent, finished commodities may pile up in warehouses while potential consumers are unable or unwilling to buy them. Only money can make a possible consumer into an actual buyer in the capitalist system. An excess of supply in this economic system does not mean that everyone is fully satisfied, just that they have no money or desire to buy more commodities.

The use of credit intensifies money problems. If Brown owes Smith, and Smith owes Johnson, and Johnson owes Martin, a break anywhere along this chain of credit circulation may be disastrous for all of the later parties in the chain. If one creditor in the chain is a bank, then that bank goes bankrupt, its fall will hurt all of its depositors. This does not, of course, explain why the chain should ever break in the first place, but it does explain why one break or hesitation in one sector can be so harmful to the whole economy.

When money and credit institutions become the usual way of doing business, the business cycle of boom and bust becomes a more likely possibility. Does this mean that money and credit institutions are sufficient to explain the business cycle? Actually, money and credit existed in ancient Rome and in the sixteenth to eighteenth centuries in Western Europe. Yet the financial disturbances of those times were not the same phenomena as the modern type of business cycle.

In the eighteenth century, financial crises resulted from the bursting of the South Sea stock speculation "bubble" in 1720, the aftermath of the Seven Years' War in 1763, and the disturbances caused by the American Revolution in 1776. These panics were, however, unlike the modern business cycle. These early financial panics originated in causes external to the economy, unlike modern business cycles. Moreover, these panics resulted in only limited depressions in a few trades for brief and random periods, whereas the modern business cycle engulfs the whole economy for a significant length of time. The first truly general industrial depression of the modern type appeared in 1793 in England (see Mitchell and Thorp, 1926).

In brief, there is evidence of a long period of extensive use of money and credit with only temporary and externally caused financial panics. Conversely, in the nineteenth, twentieth, and twenty-first centuries, there have been many recessions that did not produce financial panics. It appears that the regular use of money and credit is a necessary prerequisite of the business cycle but not a sufficient explanation of business cycles.

PRODUCTION FOR PRIVATE PROFIT

This chapter examined two conditions, production for the market and regular use of money, that must be present if business cycles are to occur. In business recessions, demand falls, industry is reduced, and unemployment rises. But one more macroeconomic institution is necessary before a business recession can occur. It is the existence of private ownership of production facilities and production for private profit.

Even in an economy characterized by exchange in the market through the medium of money, supply and demand may be kept in balance or brought back into balance if production is not for private profit. Nothing done by government agencies, from the post office to the building of levees for New Orleans, is determined by private profit. Of course, private contractors work for the government for profits, often very large profits, and constantly lobby the government to spend more. But suppose there are no large private corporations and no business lobbyists. Then government spending would be determined by voters according to their view of human needs. Therefore, a whole economy run democratically by the public might not be subject to business cycles.

We saw in Part I that many types of society did not have private profits and did not have the business cycle. Business cycles of boom and bust are found only in countries in which the economy is primarily run by private business. Private business is motivated by profit. No profit, no production. In an economy based on private ownership of individual competing units, the sum of decisions to produce may not equal the sum of decisions by other individuals and businesses to spend. In other words, consumption and investment spending may not be enough to buy the whole output. No one plans a private economy. Every firm makes its own decisions.

If the sum of the outputs produced at present prices is greater than the sum of the demand expressed in money, then there is not enough revenue to cover the costs of production and also yield a profit for the private entrepreneur. This criterion is decisive because if the private entrepreneur can make no profit, the firm will not continue production. If no profit is expected, machinery will stand idle, and all of the employees in that business will be unemployed.

SUMMARY

This chapter uses Say's law as a starting point for examining business cycles in capitalist economies. After discussing the nature and implications of Say' law, an alternative construction of the relationship of production and consumption is introduced based on the basic institutions of a modern capitalist economy. Key points are:

1. J. B. Say states that aggregate demand automatically adjusts to aggregate supply at the level of full employment.
2. Say's law was true of earlier societies in which production was for self-sufficient isolated units and profit was not the main motive of production. Production was just for the lord's manor or the serf's family. The little exchange that existed under feudalism was by barter, not money. Say's law ignores the fact that capitalist economies are different from feudal societies.
3. Cycles of boom and bust do exist in capitalist economies in which (a) production is for the market, (b) exchange operates by means of money and credit, and (c) the aim of production is private profit.
4. Despite its impressive long-run growth, the American economy has been plagued by instability. In human terms, the loss of income and jobs leads to feelings of failure, helplessness, and isolation from society and other people. The result for Americans in these recessions is an increase of physical and mental disease, crime, divorce, and even suicide.

KEY WORDS

aggregate demand	equilibrium
aggregate supply	Say's law

REVIEW QUESTIONS

Explain Say's law and discuss the arguments supporting it.

1. What does Say's law mean? Why can't there ever be a lack of demand in the aggregate?
2. Describe the process that keeps aggregate supply and demand equal.

Explain the relationship of business cycles and Say's law.

3. What are three main characteristics of the capitalist economy that make possible cycles of boom and bust?
4. How do these cycles violate Say's law? What would a conservative economist say about how the economy readjusts? Why?

Describe how Say's law informs policy decisions about the economy.

5. If Say's law holds, should the government try to smooth the effects of a boom and bust? Why or why not?
7. How is the economy different today from feudalist society that leads to boom and bust?

Discuss why Say's law is true in many precapitalist societies but not in capitalism as we see it today.

6. Did cycles of boom and bust exist under feudalism? Why or why not?

List and describe the four functions of money.

8. What are the four functions of money? Does it serve all functions equally well? Explain.
9. How does the use of credit complicate business cycles?

CHAPTER 39

Neoclassical View of Aggregate Supply and Demand

Modern neoclassical economists use a very different and far more complex theory of aggregate supply and demand than the old classical approach used by J. B. Say. This chapter provides a simplified overview of the macroeconomy as modeled by many mainstream economists.

LEARNING OBJECTIVES

After reading this chapter, you should be able to:

- Name the three markets that comprise the macroeconomy and explain how traditional economists come to the conclusion that all three markets tend to be in equilibrium.
- Give a brief history of the evolution of the current traditional economic models of the macroeconomy.

THE CONCEPTS OF AGGREGATE SUPPLY AND DEMAND

Traditional neoclassical economics employ arguments that support Say's law. Say's law leads to the conclusion that the economy as a whole tends toward equilibrium of aggregate demand and aggregate supply at full employment. The arguments for the tendency toward aggregate **equilibrium** rest on a particular view of the *concepts of supply and demand in which they come to be equal at some point.*

When looking at an individual product, economists think of a quantity demanded that declines as the price rises. This happens because consumers find the product relatively less attractive as its price goes up. This view of demand is combined with a view of supply wherein the quantity supplied rises when prices rise. Quantity supplied rises because capitalists are willing to supply more at higher prices, assuming no increase in costs, since they then expect a higher profit.

Suppose we begin in the market at a very high price. Suppose at this high price, there is a big supply but not enough demand. The model predicts that competition will force prices down. Put simply, as prices adjust or fall, the quantity supplied will fall and the quantity demanded will rise until an equilibrium is reached.

Although these arguments were first used for individual markets, neoclassical economists use a similar analysis to look at the three main markets that comprise market capitalism: the market for goods and services, financial markets, and labor markets. If prices are left alone to freely move, then all three markets will be in equilibrium. If there is a shock to any of these markets, prices

Figure 39.1   **Neoclassical View of Aggregate Supply, Demand, and Prices**

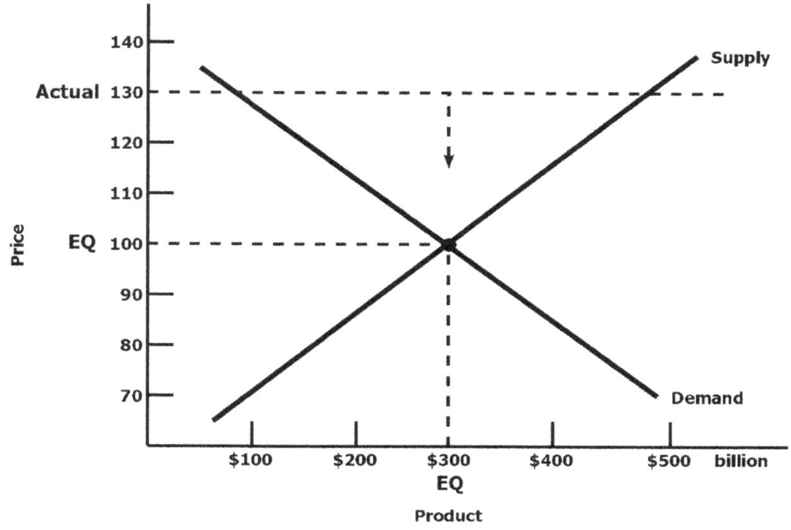

This figure shows the equilibrium of aggregate supply and demand at full employment.

will quickly adjust so that quantity supplied equals quantity demanded in all three markets. If all three markets are in equilibrium, the aggregate economy is in equilibrium and a full-employment level of output is reached.

EQUILIBRIUM OF SUPPLY AND DEMAND FOR ALL GOODS AND SERVICES

Suppose that the economy is operating at the full-employment level of output. Now suppose that for some reason there is a temporary lack of demand for all goods and services. In the neoclassical view, this lack of demand will cause a decrease in the price level. At the lower price level, consumers will have a greater demand for goods and services. Thus, demand will rise to meet the supply. As a result, equilibrium of supply and demand will be at the full-employment level of supply.

Figure 39.1 illustrates the assumption that the existing price is above the equilibrium level. In that case, we see that there is a gap between the supply and the demand. The aggregate demand is too small to purchase the aggregate supply at the existing price. But the graph also shows an arrow pointing down from the existing price level toward the equilibrium price level.

The reason for the falling price is that capitalists are unable to sell all of their goods at the existing price. Therefore, they lower their prices to attract more customers. As the price declines, the quantity demanded increases, while the quantity supplied decreases. Finally, equilibrium of quantity supplied and demanded is reached at the lower price level. Capitalists can then sell all of the goods that they are producing at the going price, so there can be no overproduction. If there is insufficient demand, prices will decline until equilibrium—a point at which all supply is bought. In other words, the price level will adjust to clear markets.

Figure 39.2   **Neoclassical View of Savings, Investment, and Interest Rates**

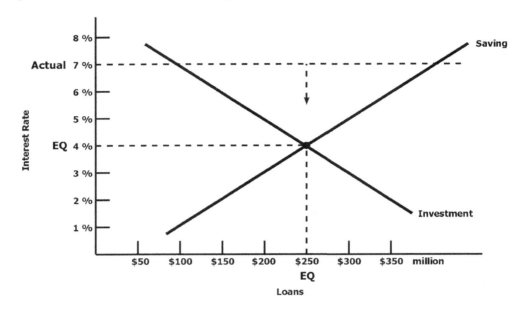

EQUILIBRIUM OF SUPPLY AND DEMAND FOR SAVINGS AND INVESTMENT

A second neoclassical argument claims that any income not used for consumption spending will always be invested. What households do not consume is called savings. These savings are the source of loans. Assume that all money that businesses use to buy plants and equipment business is borrowed. The price of loans is the interest rate. If there is a not enough investment spending to soak up all savings available for loans at the present interest rate, then competition among lenders will cause the interest rate to decline. The interest rate will fall until a new equilibrium is reached. At that point, all savings will be invested, thus preventing hoarding.

The argument is illustrated in Figure 39.2. This picture shows that the existing interest rate is too high for all savings to be lent to investors. The arrow shows the downward pressure on interest rates caused by competition. As the interest rate goes down, we see that investment goes up because it costs less to borrow. At the same time, the falling interest rate means that people have less incentive to save, so they will consume more of their income. All savings at the equilibrium interest rate is used by businesses to by capital. Thus, all income is spent on either consumption or investment. Since all income is spent and there is no hoarding, aggregate supply must equal aggregate demand.

EQUILIBRIUM OF SUPPLY AND DEMAND FOR LABOR

Suppose that for some reason there are too many workers seeking work at the present wage. Then there is more quantity of labor supplied than employers are demanding. There is then temporary unemployment. But neoclassical economists believe that this oversupply of workers will be cured as competition among workers forces the wage to drop. At lower wages, an equilibrium will be reached at which all workers will find jobs at the going wage rate.

Figure 39.3 **Neoclassical View of Labor Supply, Labor Demand, and Wages**

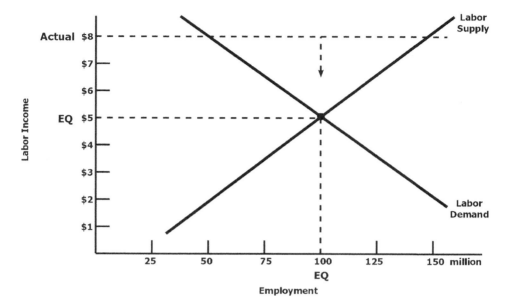

Figure 39.3 illustrates the neoclassical view of employment and wages. At a high wage level, more workers will be attracted to the labor market to find jobs. But if that wage level is too high, employers will reduce the number of jobs they are willing to offer. Therefore, Figure 39.3 shows a temporary unemployment gap at the existing wage. Wages are pushed down, however, by the competition among workers for the small number of jobs. As the wage level declines, fewer workers go into the job market. Yet at the lower wage level, employers are offering more jobs. There will therefore be an equilibrium of supply and demand for labor at full employment. In other words, all workers who want jobs at the equilibrium wage will find jobs offered at that wage.

EVOLUTION OF NEOCLASSICAL VIEW OF THE MACROECONOMY

As discussed in Chapter 38, in 1800, J.B. Say stated his law that aggregate demand automatically adjusts to aggregate supply. Therefore, lack of aggregate demand can never cause a recession. Aggregate supply and demand will always move together smoothly, aside from **outside shocks**, that is, *disturbances or disruptions to the economy that do not originate from the workings of markets.* Examples include such things as floods, wars, or the actions of monopolies or cartels to manipulate output and prices. This view was strongly supported by David Ricardo and almost all other classical economists. Chapter 18 also explained the criticism of Say's law by non-neoclassical economists, such as Wesley Mitchell. The opponents showed that Say's law might be true under precapitalist economic institutions but is false under capitalist economic institutions. When neoclassical economics became dominant, they supported Say's law. It did not rely on the classical arguments, however, but arrived at the same conclusion with new arguments. These arguments began in words but became increasingly complex and mathematical over time.

As we shall see in Chapter 40, the arguments were criticized and opposed by Keynesian economics from the 1930s onward. Keynesian economics was dominant in the 1940s and 1950s, though a few neoclassical economists continued to present the three arguments for Say's law, discussed in this chapter. By the 1950s, some neoclassical economists, such as Milton Friedman, restated Say's law in a new form. They emphasized that most recessions result from the monetary mistakes of the government. If the government did not make such mistakes, most recessions would never occur. Therefore, they advocated that the government take no action to cure unemployment, no matter how severe it is. Details of this approach, called monetarism, are presented in Chapter 51 on monetary policy.

Other neoclassical economists, such as Nobel Laureate Robert Lucas, have new, very complex models to show how a cyclical downturn may result from any outside shock. Lucas, however, calls his model an "equilibrium" model (see Lucas, 1975; also Lucas, 1986). In other words, he assumes that the capitalist economy is normally at equilibrium if there is no outside shock to the system. That is, there are no internal dynamics leading to a business cycle in Lucas's model. If there were no outside shocks, the Lucas' model comes to a similar conclusion as Say—the economy will adjust to keep all markets in equilibrium.

Most neoclassical economists at the present day reach a similar conclusion by various means that aggregate supply and aggregate demand will not show a cyclical pattern of boom and bust if there are no outside shocks. They reach this conclusion partly because of the way that they approach the problem. Neoclassical economists begin their analysis with the preferences of individuals regarding work and consuming activities. Lucas and other neoclassical economists ordinarily assume that all economic activities are voluntary. Because Lucas begins his analysis of unemployment with voluntary preferences by individuals to be employed or not to be employed, it must be the case that all unemployment is voluntary.

As an example, if an outside shock, such as a tsunami, reduces production, then employers will only be willing to hire people at lower wages and salaries. Employees must then decide voluntarily whether to continue working at lower compensation or to be unemployed for a while. This argument makes it difficult for Lucas to explain why hundreds of thousands of employees decide at the same time to choose to be unemployed. Long-term, large-scale unemployment seems hard to explain on neoclassical premises. Thus, Robert Lucas writes: "To explain why people allocate time to . . . unemployment, we need to know why they prefer it to all other activities" (Lucas, 1975, p. 38).

For Lucas and other conservative neoclassical economists, individual unemployment is the result of a voluntary decision, like all other decisions. Therefore, modern conservatives advocate the same policy as Say with respect to unemployment. They are in favor of letting the economy automatically correct itself. They argue, as we shall see in Chapter 48, that government should take no action to increase demand. They favor reduction of the government role in the macroeconomy largely on this basis.

We shall see that they favor no government policies to correct unemployment by spending or taxation. In addition, monetary policy should not actively promote demand but only keep enough money in circulation to handle the volume of transactions. They do acknowledge that lack of demand in one industry may force employees to move to another industry. Therefore, they may consistently advocate policies—for example, job retraining—to help such temporarily unemployed employees to move to another job. Conservative economists do not deny temporary unemployment in one industry. They only deny general unemployment for some length of time in all industries at once.

SUMMARY

Traditional neoclassical economists present arguments to prove that the aggregate economy is always at equilibrium if there is no outside shock, such as a war or a tsunami. The first argument concerns the aggregate supply and demand for goods and services. If there is lack of demand for goods and services, prices will fall until there is equilibrium of aggregate supply and aggregate demand for goods and services. The second argument concerns the aggregate supply and aggregate demand of the use of savings in investment. If there is an excess of savings that cannot be invested, then the interest rate will fall until there is an equilibrium between saving and investment in the loan market. The third argument concerns the aggregate supply and demand for the labor of all employees. If there is lack of demand for employees, then wages and salaries will drop until an equilibrium is reached between supply and demand for labor.

Traditional neoclassical economics contends that there is never any long-lasting deficiency of aggregate demand and that there is never any involuntary unemployment. It claims that all unemployment is due to the preferences and voluntary actions of the unemployed.

KEY TERMS

equilibrium
outside shock

REVIEW QUESTIONS

Name the three markets that comprise the macroeconomy and explain how traditional economists come to the conclusion that all three markets tend to be in equilibrium.
1. Which neoclassical argument claims that prices and output react in a certain way to outside shocks so as to lead back to equilibrium?
2. Which neoclassical argument claims that employee compensation and number of employees hired react in a certain way to outside shocks so as to lead back to equilibrium?
3. Which neoclassical argument claims that money and interest rates react in a certain way to outside shocks so as to lead back to equilibrium?
4. Do these three arguments support or oppose Say's law?

Give a brief history of the evolution of the current traditional economic models of the macroeconomy.
5. Who was Wesley Mitchell? What was his argument against Say's law?
6. What is the neoclassical response to Keynes' vision of business cycles?

APPENDIX 39.1
BLAMING THE VICTIM

This appendix explains why progressive economists consider blaming the victims of the system for their unemployment to be generally unjustified.

LEARNING OBJECTIVES FOR APPENDIX 39.1

After reading this appendix, you should be able to:

• Compare and contrast the traditional and progressive views of unemployment in the macroeconomy.

CHOICE?

Conservative economists have always tended to blame the unemployed for unemployment. Some conservative politicians claim that anyone who really wants a job can get one. Using Say's law, conservative economists for many decades proved to their satisfaction that a general depression is impossible, so involuntary unemployment on a large scale is impossible. They admitted only frictional unemployment. Frictional unemployment means temporary unemployment in a few depressed industries until workers can move to other industries that are booming.

On the basis of these arguments, conservative economists concluded that all unemployed (beyond the frictional unemployed) must be unwilling to work at the prevailing wage. The unemployed must, according to these economists, all be people who voluntarily leave their jobs to look for easier or better-paying jobs elsewhere. Imagine arguing this notion during the 1930s when official unemployment was over 25 percent. Imagine arguing that employees voluntarily quit their jobs in any recession. Do all workers periodically get fits of laziness or greed? Are millions only pretending to be unhappy when out of a job and living on a thin handout from the government?

This argument leads conservative economists to the conclusion that all workers would be fully employed if only they would accept lower wages. For example, one argument is that when demand declines, workers are faced with a choice. They can agree to continue working at a lower wage or voluntarily quit their present jobs and go hunting for a better one. It is assumed that many workers are ignorant of the true facts of the job market. Therefore, workers spend many months hopping around looking for nonexistent jobs at their old wages. Meanwhile, these millions of ill-informed workers may be considered voluntarily unemployed or frictionally unemployed. Some conservatives have even described the unemployed as "employed" in acquiring information.

REVIEW QUESTIONS FOR APPENDIX 39.1

Compare and contrast the traditional and progressive views of unemployment in the macroeconomy.

1. What is the traditional view of involuntary unemployment?
2. How would conservative economists explain the high unemployment rates of the Great Depression? How would progressive economists?

CHAPTER 40

Keynesian View of Aggregate Supply and Demand

This chapter explains the progressive view of aggregate supply and demand. It is primarily based on the work of John Maynard Keynes. Contrary to Say's law and the traditional neoclassical arguments, there may be a lack of effective demand in the whole economy. This means that in the aggregate, output and income may, or more importantly, may not, equal expenditures.

LEARNING OBJECTIVES

After reading this chapter, you should be able to:

- Explain and give examples of how a progressive view of aggregate supply and demand is completely different from the traditional view.
- Discuss how Keynes refuted Say's law.
- Describe how Keynes built an entirely new view of aggregate supply and demand in which an economy may not automatically recover from a recession in a short time.

KEYNES'S PROGRESSIVE VIEW

John Maynard Keynes (1883–1946) is perhaps the most important economist of the twentieth century. His background does not appear to be that of a radical or an earth-shaker. His father was a prominent and respected English economist. Keynes was educated in the best British schools and later worked for His Majesty's Civil Service and then headed the Bank of England. He edited the *Economic Journal*, Britain's most important economics journal at the time. He wrote careful treatises on Indian finances, formal logic, and on the general problems of money. Keynes was always considered part of the elite in cultural, governmental, and financial circles. However, Keynes also showed a critical mind in political economy. Most famous was his devastating analysis of the terms of the peace imposed on Germany in World War I, called *The Economic Consequences of the Peace*.

In 1936, Keynes rocked the economics establishment both in England and the United States. In his most famous book, *The General Theory of Employment, Money, and Interest*, he demolished Say's law and automatic full employment. Say's law had been attacked by nontraditional economists as Malthus and Marx. Keynes, however, was the first establishment economist to attack it in detail using the academic tools of the classical and neoclassical economists. Writing

Figure 40.1   **J. M. Keynes's View of the Macroeconomy**

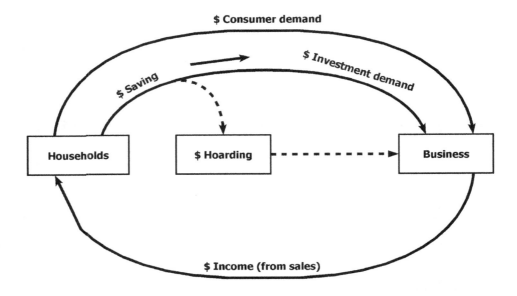

in the depths of the Great Depression, he challenged Say's law and proved that the equilibrium level of the economy might be either at a point of heavy unemployment or at a point of overly full employment and inflation.

RELATIONS OF AGGREGATE SUPPLY AND DEMAND

Aggregate supply is defined by Keynes as the total output that is produced and offered for sale at a given price level by all economic units. Aggregate demand is defined as the total dollar amount of money spent on goods and services by consumers, investors, government, and net spending by foreigners at a given price level. When there is not enough effective demand at present prices, Keynes points out that people may still have the desire for all of this supply and more. The problem is that in a monetary, capitalist economy, the people's desire by itself counts for nothing. What counts is that people must have desire plus money. *When someone has both desire and money*, Keynes calls it **effective demand**. Keynes says that there is often a lack of effective demand.

KEYNESIAN VIEW OF CIRCULAR FLOW OF SUPPLY AND DEMAND

If we think of effective demand as a flowing river, the question is whether the flow of income all goes into the channel called spending or remains in a stagnant pool. The problem of the lack of effective demand, as seen by Keynes, is illustrated in its simplest form in Figure 40.1. This is the same figure we saw in Chapter 38 illustrating the relationship of income and expenditures as described by Say's law. However, there is one important difference. Some of the income earned by households is not spent. Some of the money flows out of the main channel and is held by households and/or business and not spent on consumption goods or new plants and equipment. It is called a **leakage** when *some money income is not spent on consumption or investment*.

Figure 40.2 **Lack of Effective Demand**

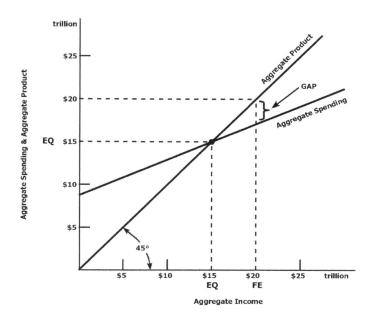

THE LACK OF EFFECTIVE DEMAND

The Keynesian picture of the economic world begins with a simple graph showing that spending may rise more slowly than income. The slower rise of income leaves a gap between aggregate demand and supply. This gap means that there will be a lack of effective demand for some part of the available goods and services. This gap is illustrated in Figure 40.2.

Figure 40.2 shows us the relationship of three aggregate variables: output or GDP, income, and expenditures. Before Keynes, there were no such aggregate measures in mainstream economics. Mainstream economists dealt only with individual incomes of people such as Tom, Dick, and Harriet. Keynes and some of his contemporaries developed the aggregate measures in the 1930s and showed how they are related. This was the beginning of the macroeconomics you are studying today.

The horizontal axis of the figure shows aggregate income. By aggregate, we mean, in the case of the United States, the national income. Remember that national or aggregate income includes wages, salaries, profits, rent, and interest income. On the 45-degree line is shown the path of aggregate product or GDP. This includes goods and services for consumers, investors, government, and foreign buyers.

Why is this aggregate product shown at a 45-degree angle from the aggregate income? The simple answer to this mystery is that the aggregate product of the whole economy is just the same as the aggregate income. They are two sides of the same coin. They are two different ways of looking at the same thing. The amount of product produced gives the amount for which there are payments of income to various people and corporations.

This imaginary, purely illustrative graph is in trillions of dollars. When the aggregate product is $5 trillion, then the aggregate income is $5 trillion. When the aggregate product is $10 trillion, then the aggregate income is $10 trillion. Therefore, the line of dots showing where these two meet is a straight line going up at 45 degrees.

Now we come to the more interesting part of the figure. The line showing aggregate spending rises as GDP and income rise, but it rises more slowly. Remember that aggregate spending is composed of consumer plus investor plus government plus net foreign spending. At the level of $15 trillion product, the spending line crosses the product line. At this point, the two aggregates are in equilibrium, shown by the symbol EQ.

But Keynes asked the disturbing question, Suppose the aggregate product (or income) rises? Will spending always rise by the same amount? Keynes's answer was no. In the figure, the amount of product produced at full employment (EQ) is $15 trillion. This is above the spending level, which is below $15 trillion. In this scenario, at full employment, there is a gap between the product offered in the market at its going price and the amount of spending that is done in the aggregate.

As output and income rise above $10 trillion, spending slows. According to Keynes, some of the money taken in as income leaks out of circulation, or at least it temporarily stops moving. Spending sits still like some stagnant lake without circulation.

What are the reasons that spending usually rises more slowly than income? Keynes mentioned that at higher levels of income, consumers may find they already have most of their immediate needs for consumer goods. Therefore, they do not spend all of their money on consumption. There are a number of other reasons, which are explored in detail in separate chapters on consumer, investor, government, and net foreign spending.

At any rate, such leakage does occur, so spending rises more slowly than income or product. What happens if there is a gap between them with spending below product offered in the market? The result is that millions of automobiles, television sets, and other items cannot be sold. When products cannot be sold at a price that is equal to or greater than their costs, there will be no profit and may even be losses. If corporations cannot sell all of their millions of products at the going price, then they fire employees. A recession may result as firms cut production and lay off employees. The reason is that, in the aggregate, people and businesses are not spending enough to buy all of production at present prices.

This gap between aggregate spending and aggregate product at present prices is not possible according to Say's law. Remember that Say's law claims that any level of production and income always generates an equal demand, except for a short time after an outside shock. Until Keynes introduces his ideas, traditional economists defended Say's law.

Nowadays, they still defend it, at least in the long run. This difference is the basic difference between Keynesian economists who see leakages from circulation and the possibility of disequilibrium and traditional economists who see no leakages and equilibrium between expenditures and output except for external shocks.

In the Keynesian view, aggregate demand or expenditures may be below aggregate supply or output. In the traditional view, aggregate demand will always equal aggregate supply except for temporary differences caused by outside shocks. Keynesians think that people, in the aggregate, may lack the money (effective demand) to buy what they desire. In the traditional view, this cannot happen except as a result of outside shocks. The Keynesian view explains the internal causes of recessions and unemployment. On the contrary, the traditional view denies that there are any internal causes of recessions.

KEYNESIAN VIEW OF INFLATION

Figure 40.2 is often called the **Keynesian cross**. *It shows the situation if there is unemployment. It can also be used, however, to illustrate the opposite problem of inflation.* Inflation arises whenever aggregate spending is higher than aggregate production.

Figure 40.3 **Excess Effective Demand**

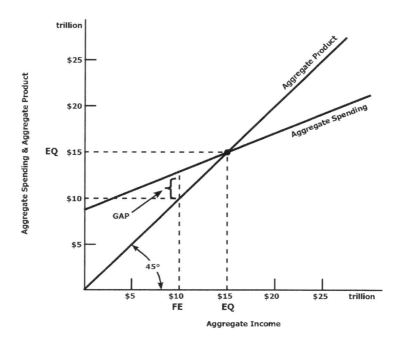

There can be many causes of inflation. The most important has been war. There was inflation in the Revolutionary War, the Civil War, World Wars I and II, and the Vietnam War. The basic reason for inflation in wartime is that the government wants as much military goods and services as it can get. It tries to buy more military goods and services than the economy can produce. This causes prices to rise. This Keynesian view of the problem of inflation is illustrated in Figure 40.3.

As in the preceding figure, Figure 40.3 shows aggregate product rising along a 45-degree line as aggregate income rises. The two always must move together by definition. On the other hand, the figure shows that aggregate spending rises more slowly than product. At a low level of production and income, spending will usually be above product and income.

How can aggregate spending be higher than aggregate income? People and corporations may borrow to spend more than their income. In a wartime situation, the government spends more than its income by borrowing money from creditors or by printing money. In Figure 40.3, if all employees are fully employed, it is possible to produce $10 trillion worth of products. At the $10 trillion level of income and production, however, the government is trying to spend so much that aggregate spending is more than $10 trillion. Since more money is being spent than there are products at the present level of prices, something must give.

If we assume the economy is truly at full employment, than the aggregate product cannot rise. It is impossible to reach the equilibrium level of product and spending (at $15 trillion) by raising production. One thing that must happen under this pressure is that prices rise. At the higher level of product prices, the gap may be ended. The total value of the product may rise to equal the spending at $15 trillion. Notice that there is no increase of production. Only prices are higher, so there has been inflation.

In the Keynesian view, it is possible that the supply of product may be below the demand expressed in spending, in which case the result is inflation. It is also possible that the supply of product may be above the spending demand for product, thus causing recession.

DEBATE BETWEEN TRADITIONAL AND KEYNESIAN ECONOMISTS

Neoclassical economists believe that demand rises to meet supply at full employment. This equilibrium is upset only if there is an outside shock that disturbs the market. Therefore, they believe that government should do nothing at all about unemployment because the market will automatically restore full employment.

Keynesians point out that the facts are contrary to this theory. There were very long and deep depressions in the 1890s and 1930s. There have also been more than 30 recessions lasting one year or more. Keynesians believe that there is no quick, automatic recovery from widespread unemployment. Even if the economy, left alone, eventually readjusts from a recession and widespread unemployment, Keynes would claim that the costs to households in lost income, to businesses in lost profit, and to society in lost production are just too high to wait. This high cost of waiting creates a role for the government to take appropriate action to help the economy readjust to full employment output.

Conservative economists offer the following explanations for why the market will return to equilibrium at full employment from a recession. All three explanations are based on the role of prices in different markets. Suppose that effective demand falls far short of the supply of goods and services offered in the market. Traditional economists argue that prices will drop. The lower prices will cause a reduction of production and encouragement for spending. More spending will induce more production and more employment. Thus, equilibrium will be restored at full employment.

But Keynesians reply that claiming lower prices will cure a lack of demand is incorrect. Keynesians argue that if demand declines and prices also decline, the lower prices will do as much harm as good toward ending the recession. Lower prices may help consumers to buy more, but only if consumers have the same income as before the recession. In a recession, the lower prices mean that, in the aggregate economy, business has less revenue, so there is less income going to households. If households have less income, they cannot buy as much. Instead of curing a recession, lower prices can be part of a downward spiral of lower prices and lower demand.

Consider the second traditional argument. Suppose the demand for labor declines and there is unemployment. Conservatives argue that wages and salaries will also decline. If effective demand remains constant, lower wages and salaries mean that the costs of production to a company go down and its profits rise. Then there is incentive for employers to hire more employees until full employment is reached. Keynesians, on the contrary, point out that traditional economists are considering only the individual firm and its wage and salary costs. They neglect the aggregate effect of falling wages and salaries. In the aggregate, falling wages and salaries mean less purchasing power. If there is less purchasing power, there is less demand for goods and services. Therefore, reduced wages may make the crisis worse, not better.

Third, suppose there is insufficient new investment to utilize all savings. Then some savings are not spent on new buildings and equipment. When the savings are not invested in the form of equipment and buildings, what happens to them? The money may be used for purely speculative purchases of stock or land. These speculative purchases do not add to the aggregate demand for new goods and services. If the funds are not used for speculation, then they are just held as idle funds.

Conservative economists believe that the interest rate will be forced to fall because there is not enough demand for loans to use all of the idle funds. When the interest rate falls, there may be more loans from financial institutions to businesses. Business can borrow at a lower interest rate and increase its rate of profit. Therefore, business borrows more and invests more until investment equals the amount saved at the full-employment level of output.

Keynesians disagree because falling demand for goods and services reduces the profit expected from investment. In fact, expected profit in a recession is usually negative. Since the profit outlook is negative, even very low interest rates may not entice corporations to borrow money and invest more in new buildings and equipment. In other words, in a recession, there may be a lot of idle money that is not being loaned out to businesses to make investments. Furthermore, interest rates are a small part of costs for most firms. The most important issue is whether there is plenty of demand for their product with a high expectation of profits. If expectations of profit are high, they will invest regardless of the interest rate. If expectations of profit are low, they will not invest regardless of low interest rates. When the economy rises again, there will be more demand for loans, so interest rates will rise again.

Notice that in all three areas, the market for commodities, the market for labor, and the market for loans, conservative economists believe that prices, wages, and interest rates will adjust to any lack of demand. Thus, the market will recover automatically without any government action. Keynesians, on the contrary, believe that the downward adjustment of prices, wages, and interest rates will not cause a return to full employment equilibrium. Lower prices mean lower profits for business, lower wages and salaries mean less demand for goods and services, while interest rates cannot fall below zero. The movements of these three kinds of prices do not solve the problem of negative expected profit rates. In all three markets, no adjustment back to a full-employment level of demand occurs in any automatic way from a low level of demand in a recession. Therefore, in Keynes's view, the government must take decisive action to cause an economic recovery. Otherwise, the economy may fall to a low-level equilibrium and remain at a very low level for years.

THE KEYNESIAN FRAMEWORK AND MACROECONOMICS

The most basic part of the Keynesian framework for macroeconomics is the concept that if there is equilibrium, the gross domestic product (GDP) equals consumer spending (C) plus investment spending (I) plus government spending (G) plus net export spending (NX). So we can say

$$GDP = C + I + G + NX$$

This simple concept of the aggregates that add up to GDP is so useful that all progressive and conservative economists use it. The Department of Commerce uses it to define its national income accounts. We use it and have four separate chapters on consumption spending, investment spending, government spending, and net foreign spending. This concept and many other Keynesian concepts will pop up throughout our discussion of growth and instability. In each case, we shall also consider the opposing neoclassical concepts.

Keynes gave much time in his work to the four great pillars of GDP from its spending or expenditure side. Remember the components of expenditures are consumer, business, government, and foreign spending. While these components of aggregate expenditures are important, one must still pay close attention to the division of income between employees and employer capitalists. Figure 40.4 illustrates both the spending side of output and the income division of output.

Figure 40.4 shows not only the spending and income sides of GDP but also how they are related. Income is divided into two types: labor income, including wages and salaries, and property

Figure 40.4 **Demand by Capitalists and Demand by Employees**

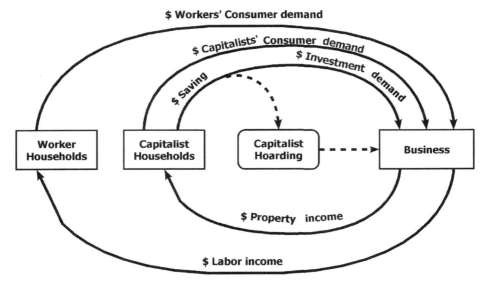

income, including rent, interest, and profit. Labor income goes to employee households. Property income goes to capitalist households.

On the spending side, the division in income for employee households and capitalist households generates different spending patterns. Most employees do not have vast incomes, so they are forced to spend most or all of their income. Remember that in 2005, saving was negative by half a percent, so on the average, all households spent 100.5 percent of their income.

Figure 40.4 also illustrates the very different spending pattern of capitalist households. These households do a high level of consumer spending, but they tend to have money left over for savings. Remember that savings is defined as all income minus consumption. They then use part of their savings for investment. But they may have still more money after investment because the situation looks unsafe for putting all of their savings into investment. In that case, they hold some money in the form of cash kept in banks.

Finally, Figure 40.4 shows how funds may flow back into circulation. In the figure, an arrow goes from cash holdings to business. This depicts the flow of money out of the savings of capitalists into the hands of business as soon as the situation looks profitable. For example, in the present expansion, this new flow of investment began very slowly in 2002 and 2003, when profit prospects still looked very risky. Since then, the expansion of business profits led to the flow of money from capitalist savings out of cash hoards and into business investment.

SUMMARY

The previous chapter explained there are three traditional arguments claiming there is always full-employment equilibrium of supply and demand, savings and investment, and labor supply and labor demand. In this chapter, we saw that Keynesians argue against each of these three arguments.

First, if demand for goods and services declines, neoclassical economists argue, prices will decline. The result of falling prices is that demand again rises to the equilibrium full-employment level. Keynesians answer that when wages fall in the whole economy, the result is that millions of employees have less money, so consumer demand drops. The drop in consumer demand prevents any recovery to full employment.

Second, if demand for goods and services declines, then employment declines and unemployment rises. Neoclassical economists argue that falling demand for labor will lower the price of labor; that is, wages and salaries go down. But when the wage rate falls, it is profitable to hire more workers, so employment goes back to equilibrium at the lower wage. Keynesians argue that lower wages cause less consumer demand, so there will be no automatic recovery to full employment.

Third, if the demand for goods and services drops, investment spending drops. Conservatives argue that lower investment means less demand for loans from bankers. The lower demand for loans must cause the interest rate to fall. But lower interest rates will encourage investment, so it will rise back to equilibrium with savings. The total consumer demand and investment demand will then equal all supply, so the economy comes back to full-employment equilibrium. Keynesians counter this third argument by pointing out that investment is determined by the expectation of profits. If expected profits from an investment are below zero, then no one will invest. Interest is only one cost affecting profits. If total profits declines, then investment will continue to decline no matter how low the interest rate falls.

KEY TERMS

effective demand   leakage
Keynesian cross

REVIEW QUESTIONS

Explain and give examples of how a progressive view of aggregate supply and demand is completely different from the traditional view.
   1. What is "effective demand" according to Keynes? How can there be a lack of effective demand?
   2. Can aggregate demand suffer from "leakages" according to the traditional view? Explain.

Discuss how Keynes refuted Say's law.
   3. How did Keynes explain that aggregate production and aggregate spending might not be equal? What happens if aggregate production is greater than aggregate spending?
   4. Why does aggregate spending rise more slowly than income?

Describe how Keynes built an entirely new view of aggregate supply and demand in which an economy may not automatically recover from a recession.
   5. How do Keynesians counter the neoclassical argument that, in a recession, falling prices will restore demand for goods to the full employment equilibrium point?
   6. How do Keynesians counter the neoclassical argument that. in a recession, falling wages and salaries will restore demand for labor to the full employment equilibrium point?
   7. How do Keynesians counter the neoclassical argument that in a recession, falling interest rates will restore demand for loans for new investment to the full employment equilibrium point?
   8. How does Keynes explain inflation?

APPENDIX 40.1
MARX, MITCHELL, AND THE KEYNESIAN REVOLUTION

In 1800, J.B. Say formulated the law that aggregate demand always follows aggregate supply. Whatever is produced at full employment and is supplied to the market will be demanded and bought at the market equilibrium price. Say's law was accepted by almost all of the classical economists of the early nineteenth century, from David Ricardo to John Stuart Mill. It was only economists outside of the ruling establishment who criticized Say's law. This appendix presents critiques of Say's law by critics of classical economic theory.

LEARNING OBJECTIVES FOR APPENDIX 40.1

After reading this appendix, you should be able to:

- Compare and contrast the arguments of critiques of classical economics and Say's law.

KARL MARX

In the mid-nineteenth century, Karl Marx gave a very long and detailed analysis of Say's economics. Marx showed that Say discussed how the economy operated under precapitalist systems. Marx showed that the economic institutions of capitalism make economic recessions and depressions possible and likely to happen. In feudal Europe, the lord and the serfs had farms that they tried to keep self-sufficient so the lord could feed his family and retainers while the serf could feed his or her family. Under present-day capitalism, however, income comes from selling goods and services in the market. Self-sufficient farmers had nothing to sell, and they did not have to worry about demand. Modern capitalists cannot stay in business unless there is sufficient demand in the market for their product.

Second, Marx pointed out that feudal lords and serfs were not concerned with profit, since they did not sell their goods. Capitalists produce only so long as they expect to make a profit but will fire workers if no profit is in sight. Finally, Marx emphasized that isolated, self-sufficient feudal manors had no need for money. Every product under capitalism must be sold, often at great distances, and this complex transaction cannot be accomplished without money. Where money is received for goods, it may or may not be spent again for something else. If the money is not spent, then there is no effective demand for goods, and a recession is the result.

WESLEY MITCHELL

From the 1870s to the 1930s, the dominant school of economics was the neoclassical school, described in Chapter 39. Neoclassical economists agreed with Say's law and therefore argued that the economic system usually operates smoothly. Demand usually equals supply, and any disequilibrium situation must lead through competition and flexible prices back to equilibrium. Outside shocks may cause short disruptions in the economy, but there will soon be a recovery from recession back to equilibrium at full employment.

Wesley Mitchell was an institutionalist writing in the early twentieth century. His view was that basic economic institutions determine the performance of an economy. With far more detail than Marx, and using the latest findings of economic history, Mitchell showed that there were no modern-type business cycles in the feudal period. He demonstrated that the booms and busts of the business cycle occur only under capitalism. He showed how each stage of the capitalist business cycle leads to the next stage. Recovery from recession leads to a strong prosperity, which eventually ends in another recession.

Mitchell emphasized that we no longer have an economy based on barter of one good for another, but we now have a monetary economy. In a monetary economy, the circulation of goods and services may always go awry, so the possibility of recession always lurks just offstage.

THE KEYNESIAN REVOLUTION

In the 1930s, everyone knew that a quarter of all workers were unemployed, many factories had closed their doors, and there was insufficient demand to buy all the goods and services on the market. Yet in their classrooms, neoclassical economists in England and the United States continued to claim that depression was temporary and the market would soon restore full employment. Actually, full employment was not restored for ten long years until government demand for military goods solved the problem in the Second World War.

Many governments and many economists, who had ignored Marx and Mitchell, were ready for some new viewpoint that would explain and help get them out of the Great Depression. This was the background for the Keynesian revolution in economic thought. Keynes convinced a whole generation of younger economists that the old, neoclassical view of the economy as a whole was totally wrong. Using the language of mainstream economics, Keynes meticulously tore Say's law and the economics that supported it into little pieces. As this chapter has shown, he destroyed each of the three neoclassical arguments for Say's law. He liberated mainstream economists to think about the reality of an economy with bouts of unemployment and depression that could last for many years.

Like Marx and Mitchell, Keynes emphasized that the modern capitalist economy is a monetary economy. The classical economists thought of money as a mere neutral go-between used to exchange commodities. Keynes showed that the circulation of money could slow up, so there might not be enough money in circulation to buy goods and services. He built a whole theory about how the circulation of good and money works, discussed in this chapter. With this viewpoint, he explained why the capitalist world was in a long, deep depression. He showed why expansions often lead to depressions.

This new view of the economy led to the economic theories called macroeconomics, which you are now studying. Before Keynes, there was only microeconomics, the study of individual consumers and firms. Since the Keynesian revolution, every textbook of the whole of economics contains both microeconomics and macroeconomics.

Marx thought that capitalism must always be plagued with booms and busts, including deep depressions. Keynes, however, believed that certain reforms and government policies could prevent or reduce the severity of recessions and depressions. Keynes convinced many governments to try his approach. In the United States, Keynesian policies were used first in a full program by President John F. Kennedy.

In the 1940s and 1950s, the Keynesian revolution swept everything before it. Classical voices were few, and discussion of Keynesian remedies became dominant. The viewpoint of most economists and the government was mildly conservative to mildly liberal Keynesians. They embraced a synthesis of Keynesian macroeconomics plus classical microeconomics. They believed that in the short-run, there was sometimes a brief period of failure to reach full-employment equilibrium in the macroeconomy. Unemployment could be addressed by the government through measures suggested by Keynes. When equilibrium was restored in the economy, all the laws of economics proposed by classical economics would produce all the excellent results promised by classical economics.

In the 1960s and 1970s, however, there was a new situation combining both inflation and unemployment. The traditional measures and models that had been called Keynesian could not explain or solve this economic situation. Therefore, the Keynesian consensus split asunder. Some economists went back to the earlier classical view of Say's law. Everything would be solved if the government kept its hands off the economy, except for the most minimal measures, and let the free market bring about equilibrium at full employment. This view became dominant under many different names and many different complex models of the economy. The basics of this view remain dominant today, though there continue to be technical innovations in its details. Its attitude on many specific issues are discussed throughout the rest of Part III of this book.

On the other hand, many nontraditional economists, including post-Keynesians, institutionalists, and Marxists, built on the more militant parts of Keynes's work. Many of them used his framework to come to conclusions completely opposite to the neoclassical conclusions. They argue that it is perfectly possible to have unemployment last a long time, as in the ten years of the Great Depression, and that the cycle of boom and bust is not mainly due to outside shocks to the economy.

Keynes presented a powerful criticism of the macroeconomics based on Say's law. According to progressives, the booms, busts, and unemployment can be explained in detail by the normal workings of a capitalist economy of the type now prevalent. Uncertainty, insecurity, and cyclical unemployment are inherent in this type of economy. That is true even though this type of economy has brought amazing economic growth compared with all precapitalist systems. These issues are all explained from the progressive viewpoint in the rest of the chapters of Part III. The conflict between these two points of view in economics continues to the present.

REVIEW QUESTIONS FOR APPENDIX 40.1

Compare and contrast the arguments of critiques of classical economics and Say's law.

1. How do Marx and Mitchell refute Say's law?
2. Compare and contrast Marx and Mitchell's arguments to that of Keynes.

PART III, SECTION 2

UNDERSTANDING INSTABILITY

CHAPTER 41

How to Measure Instability

The main tools for careful measurement of the instability caused by the business cycle were developed by the great American economist Wesley Mitchell (1874–1948). This chapter follows his approach.

LEARNING OBJECTIVES

After reading this chapter, you should be able to:

- Explain how to find the peaks and troughs of the business cycle.
- Explain how to measure the path of any economic series over the cycle.
- Describe how much an economic series rises from trough to peak and falls from peak to trough.

DATING BUSINESS CYCLE PEAKS AND TROUGHS

Mitchell studied a wide range of the available indicators of business activities, from newspapers to statistics, to find out exactly when recessions and depressions occurred. A business cycle is defined by the peaks and troughs in aggregate business activity where business activity is measured by a group of indicators. For careful understanding of business cycle turning points, years are too big and clumsy. We mainly use quarterly data, such as 1970.4, which means the fourth quarter of 1970. Measurement of business cycles by the U.S. Department of Commerce is based on quarterly data that are now published officially based on Wesley Mitchell's method. Although Mitchell calculated business cycles dates going all the way back to 1800, we use only the data since 1970 in the following chapters.

The *highest point measured by the business indicators* is called a **business cycle peak**. Each peak in American history has been followed by a recession or depression. These downturns have lasted from as short a time as three quarters to as long as ten years. The *lowest point of the cycle* is called a **business cycle trough**. After each trough in American history, there have been expansions up to a peak. A **business cycle** is *the rise of the economy from trough to peak, as well the following decline from peak to trough*. In the years from 1854 to 2007, there were thirty-two business cycles.

How long has the average cycle been? In the thirty-two cycles, the average expansion lasted 36

Table 41.1

Troughs and Peaks of the Business Cycle

Initial Trough	Peak	Final Trough
1970.4	1973.4	1975.1
1975.1	1980.1	1980.3
1980.3	1981.3	1982.4
1982.4	1990.3	1991.2
1991.2	2001.1	2001.4

Source: Bureau of Economic Analysis, U.S. Department of Commerce (www.bea.gov). All data in this chapter are from that same source.

months. The average contraction lasted 17 months. On the average, the whole business cycle lasted 55 months. But circumstances change, so a cycle may last much longer or much shorter than the average. The actual quarterly dates for the last five cycles are given in Table 41.1.

Table 41.1 shows that there have been five full cycles in the United States since 1970. These cycles ranged in length from a little over a year to ten years. Although the same pattern of events unfolds in a remarkably similar way in every cycle, the length of the cycle changes, and the amplitude changes. **Amplitude** here means *the amount of rise in the expansion and the amount of decline in the contraction.*

Nine Stages

After finding the dates of each cycle, Mitchell divided each business cycle into nine stages. Stage 1 is the initial trough or low point at the beginning of the cycle. Stage 5 is the peak of business activity. Stage 9 is the final trough or low point at the end of the cycle. By definition, stages 1, 5, and 9 are each one quarter in length.

During the expansion period, between stages 1 and 5, there are three stages of equal length. Stages 2, 3, and 4 divide all of those quarters into three equal stages. Of course, every cycle expansion has a different length, but the expansion is always divided into three parts in this method, so different expansions are easy to compare. In a similar way, in the contraction period, there are three stages between 5 and 9. These three stages, 6, 7, and 8, divide the quarters into three equal stages.

As an example, let us examine the actual data in an important economic series: aggregate investment. The Department of Commerce in the national income accounts defines aggregate investment to be "gross, domestic, private investment." This long name just means that investment as used here includes all equipment and buildings bought by individuals or businesses in the United States. The investment data in the series used here are adjusted each year for inflation. The data is also seasonally adjusted, so quarterly data are not distorted by seasonal changes that occur every year and that are not part of a business cycle.

Table 42.2 shows the expansion of investment spending from stage 1 to stage 5 of the cycle. It also shows the contraction of investment spending from stage 5 to stage 9 of the cycle.

Cycle Base

Next, we may calculate *the average of an economic series for one whole cycle.* This average is called the **cycle base**. In the 1991–2001 business cycle, the average aggregate investment or cycle base was $1,297 billion per quarter.

Table 41.2

Nine Stages of Investment at the Nine Stages of the 1991–2001 Cycle

	Expansion				
Stages	1. initial trough	2. expand	3. expand	4. expand	5. peak
Investment	$809	$960	$1,235	$1,643	$1,662

	Contraction				
Stages	5. peak	6. decline	7. decline	8. decline	9. final trough
Investment	$1,662	$1,584	$1,573	$1,563	$1,490

Investment in this table refers to gross domestic investment, in billions of dollars, seasonally adjusted and adjusted for inflation.

Source: Bureau of Economic Analysis, U.S. Department of Commerce (www.bea.gov).

Table 41.3

Investment, Shown in Cycle Relatives at Nine Stages of the 1991–2001 Cycle

	Expansion				
Stages	1. initial trough	2. expand	3. expand	4. expand	5. peak
Investment	62	74	95	127	128

	Contraction				
Stages	5. peak	6. decline	7. decline	8. decline	9. final trough
investment	128	122	121	121	115

Investment in this table refers to gross domestic investment, in billions of dollars, seasonally adjusted and adjusted for inflation divided by the cycle base.

Source: Bureau of Economic Analysis, U.S. Department of Commerce (www.bea.gov).

Cycle Relatives

Wesley Mitchell coined the concept of a cycle relative. This relative is not your aunt or uncle, but shows economic levels relative to the cycle base. The **cycle relative** is defined as *the original data in a stage divided by the cycle base*. We simply divide the amount in each stage by the average or cycle base. The result is called a cycle relative. It is always multiplied by 100 to make it a percentage of the base.

For example, the original value of aggregate investment for the quarter in Stage 1 was $809 billion. The cycle base, or average, was $1,297 billion. If we divide 809 by 1297, the result is 0.62. If we multiply by 100, the result is 62. Therefore, 62 is the cycle relative at stage 1. The number 62 means that the level of investment at stage 1 was 62 percent of the cycle average or base.

Table 41.3 presents the cycle relatives of investment at each of the nine stages for the 1991–2001 business cycle. Remember that each of these nine numbers is simply the original data in Table 41.2 divided by the cycle base.

We see that investment rises in the expansion period. We also see that investment falls in the

Figure 41.1   **Investment, in Cycle Relatives for the Cycle from 1991 to 2001**

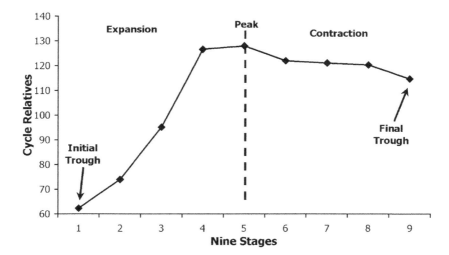

Gross domestic private investment, billions of dollars, real (inflation adjusted), seasonally adjusted is used to calculate cycle relatives. *Source:* Bureau of Economic Analysis, U.S. Department of Commerce (www.bea.gov).

contraction period. It is easy to see the percentage investment declines below the cycle average in contractions. It is also easy to see how the percentage investment rises above the average in the expansion. The cycle relatives for investment in the cycle of 1991 to 2001 (given in numbers in Table 41.2) are graphed in Figure 41.1.

Figure 41.1 shows that in the 1991–2001 cycle, investment rose during the expansion and fell during the contraction. We make use of this finding in the later chapters.

APPLICATION OF MEASUREMENT METHOD: UNEMPLOYMENT AND PRODUCTIVE CAPACITY

Two of the economic series of indicators measuring the health of the economy over the business cycle are the unemployment rate and the index of capacity utilization. The unemployment rate means the percentage of the labor force that cannot find jobs. Many economists argue that the unemployment rate tends to be understated because it does not count employees who want work but are too discouraged to look any more. It is also understated because it does not include employees who want full-time jobs but can only get part-time jobs. In fact, if you have a job for one hour a week, you are considered employed no matter how much you look for full-time work and do not find it.

The index of productive capacity of the American economy is measured by the value of all of the equipment of all the businesses in the economy. Capacity utilization measures how much of that productive capacity is actually being used. For example, an index of 90, or 90 percent of productive capacity, would mean that 90 percent of all the equipment was actually being used for production. A 100 percent use of capacity means only that all the equipment is used when the enterprise is in operation.

Figure 41.2 shows the behavior over the business cycle of the unemployment rate and of the

Figure 41.2 **Unemployment and Capacity Utilization**

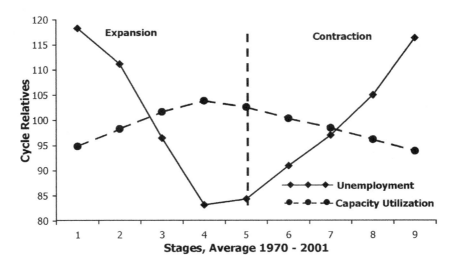

Quarterly, seasonally adjusted. Unemployment rate is the ratio of all unemployed workers to all civilian labor force, as a percentage. Capacity utilization is the index showing the ratio of equipment actually used to all equipment, as a percentage. *Source:* Bureau of Labor Statistics, U.S. Labor Department (www.bls.gov). *Note:* Average of five cycles, 1970–2001.

index of capacity utilization. It shows the average behavior of both economic series for the last five cycles, from 1970 to 2001.

The behaviors of unemployment and capacity utilization are startlingly different. The use of productive capacity rises whenever the economy expands. The reason that use of productive capacity rises in expansion is that there is more demand for the products of that capacity. The use of productive capacity declines during a recession because there is less demand for the products of that capacity. On the other hand, as more products are produced in an expansion, more employees are hired. Therefore, there are fewer unemployed people. This is why the unemployment rate falls in economic expansions. When there is a recession, the number of unemployed people rises. This is why the unemployment rate rises in recession.

SUMMARY

Business cycles are measured by indicators of aggregate business activity. There have been five whole cycles since 1970. Their peaks are where most business activity is at its highest point, and their troughs are where most business activity falls to its lowest point.

The cycle is divided into nine stages. Stage 1 is the initial trough, stage 5 is the peak, and stage 9 is the final trough. Stages 2, 3, and 4 are the expansion. Stages 6, 7, and 8 are the contraction. The cycle base is the average of an economic variable over the whole cycle. Cycle relatives are found by dividing the original nine numbers by the cycle base (and multiplying by 100 to get a percentage of the base).

KEY TERMS

amplitude
business cycle
business cycle peak

business cycle trough
cycle base
cycle relative

REVIEW QUESTIONS

Explain how to find the peaks and troughs of the business cycle.
  1. How are the peaks and troughs of the business cycle measured?
  2. What is an expansion? What is a contraction?
  3. How does unemployment behave over the business cycle?
  4. What happens to capacity utilization over the business cycle?

Explain how to measure the path of any economic series over the cycle.
  5. What is a cycle base? Explain how to find a cycle base.
  6. What is a cycle relative? Explain how to find a cycle relative.
  7. Explain how to calculate the percentage of expansion and the percentage of contraction?
  8. Name one economic series that rises in every expansion and falls in every contraction. Explain this behavior.
  9. Name one economic series that falls in expansion and rises in contraction. Explain this behavior.

Describe measuring how much an economic series rises from trough to peak and falls from peak to trough.
  10. What is a cycle relative and how is it calculated?

CHAPTER 42

═══════════════════

Consumer Spending and Labor Income

The largest single element of expenditures for the United States comes from the American consumer. This chapter looks at the long-run trends in GDP, wages and salaries, and consumption spending. Next, it explores what determines consumer demand in the aggregate for the goods and services produced. Finally, this chapter looks at how consumer demand behaves over the business cycle.

LEARNING OBJECTIVES

After reading this chapter, you should be able to:

- Explain how consumption has grown over the long run.
- Describe how consumption behaves over the business cycle.
- Compare and discuss determinants of aggregate consumption.

LONG RUN TRENDS

Part I showed that the United States economy grew rapidly in the 1950s and 1960s. In the early 1970s, many structural changes occurred as the global economy stage of capitalism became much more pronounced. One of the most spectacular changes was the change in the growth of labor income, that is, wages and salaries. Since labor income is the source of most spending on consumer goods and services, it is important to understand its trend. During the 1950s and 1960s, the United States was the undisputed economic leader of the world. American real wages and salaries rose over the period with only temporary declines. In the period of intense globalization after 1970, when the United States was challenged by other countries' rising economic strength, real wages and salaries stagnated. This trend continues all the way to the present.

We shall see in detail in Chapter 46 that stagnating real wages and salaries is very strange indeed. Real GDP rose rapidly in the 1950s and 1960s. GDP continued to rise throughout the 1970s, 1980s, and 1990s, though more slowly. While the real GDP continued to rise slowly after 1970, real wages and salaries rose little or not at all (though real labor income bounced up and down in the business cycle). Moreover, in the 1950s and 1960s, real wages and salaries rose parallel to rising labor productivity. Since 1970, productivity continued to rise, though more slowly, but real wages did not. If GDP kept rising and productivity kept rising, how come real wages and salaries for employees stagnated?

In the era of global capitalism after about 1970, corporate profits rose with increasing productivity and GDP growth. There was a slow but continuous swing of national income away from labor income and toward profit income. The share of labor income fell from the early 1970s until now, while the share of property income (profits, rent, and interest) rose. Now remember that labor income is the main source of consumer spending. Did consumer spending also stagnate? No, consumer spending did not rise as fast as GDP, but it did rise fairly consistently. How is that possible if labor income stagnated?

A small part of the answer is that wealthy owners of property increased their own consumption a great deal, but that is not enough to account for the whole rise in consumption spending. The main answer to the mystery of how real consumer spending has grown with little growth of real wages and salaries is the enormous growth of consumer debt. If your real income is stagnant, as has been true for most Americans, then you can still have rising consumption if you are willing to go ever deeper into debt.

KEYNES AND CONSUMER BEHAVIOR

What are the factors that influence consumer behavior? Part II discussed the actions of individual consumers, but now we must examine how Keynes explained consumer behavior in the aggregate, or the behavior of all consumers together. Keynes gives particular attention to understanding the basis for the decision of households to save or consume at different economic levels. For Keynes, consumer demand in the aggregate is determined primarily by the level of national income. His reasoning as to consumer behavior is based on certain broad psychological assumptions.

First, at a very low income level, the average individual still needs some minimum consumption and therefore will spend all his or her income on consumption and may even dip into savings or go into debt to spend more than his or her whole current income on consumption. Second, as the individual's income rises, a smaller percentage of it is needed to cover minimum needs. For that reason, at some break-even point, he or she reaches an equality of income received and income spent for consumption. Third, as income rises to a very high level, consumption needs and desires may be filled through the use of a smaller portion of income. An increasing percentage of income may be saved and not spent at high income levels.

This usual behavior of consumers is illustrated in Figure 42.1. The line labeled income shows the total income at each point. The income received for work is equal by definition to the income spent for consumption plus the income saved. **Savings** is defined as *the income left over after consumption*. If there were no savings so that income exactly equaled consumption at every income level, then the income line would be the same as the line for consumer spending.

In reality, consumption and income rise at different rates. The line labeled consumption shows how much consumer spending there actually is at each level of income. The space between these two lines reflects the amount by which consumption differs from income. At low levels of income, consumer spending by the poor is greater than their income, so there is **dis-saving**—*using up of reserves or going into debt*—by these consumers. At high levels of income, consumer spending by the rich is much less than their income, so there is savings by this group.

This *Keynesian schedule of aggregate consumer spending at different income levels* is called the **consumption function**. It tells us that, in the short-run, consumption is not some constant proportion of income. Rather, as income rises, consumption rises, but consumption rises more slowly than income. Therefore, as income rises, the proportion of income spent on consumption declines.

These general notions stated by Keynes have been tested in hundreds of studies, most of which bear out his statements about the usual relations of consumer spending and income at any given

Figure 42.1 **Consumption and National Income in Real Billions of Dollars, Seasonally Adjusted, Quarterly, in Annual Rate**

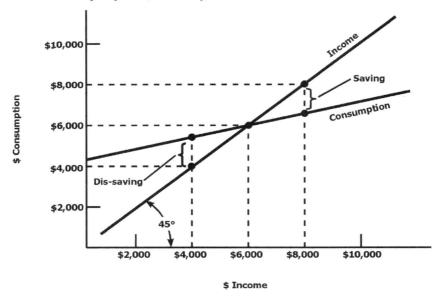

Source: Bureau of Economic Analysis, U.S. Department of Commerce (www.bea.gov).

time. The studies show somewhat different findings in different times and places, but two things are striking in all of them. The poor generally dis-save or go further into debt. The wealthy accumulate large amounts of savings each year, so their wealth rises each year. The middle class used to have some savings out of personal income. Now, however, middle class saving is about zero and some years show an aggregate increase in debt.

Let us look at aggregate personal savings in 2005. The year 2005 was the fourth year of a business expansion. We would expect the middle class to have rising savings from the earlier studies. In fact, not only were the poor slipping further into debt, but the middle class also had increasing debt. In 2005, instead of savings, in the median, American went further into debt. Even including the wealthy, aggregate personal savings was negative in some quarters and only slightly above zero for the whole year. This trend continued in 2006. This outcome is highly unusual for years 5 and 6 of an expanding economy.

Keynesian Definitions

Most economists use certain shorthand terms to describe the relationship between consumption and income. The **average propensity to consume** (APC) is *the proportion of income spent for consumption.* It is the ratio of consumption to income at any particular level of income. Let us first examine a group of high-income earners. Suppose the average income receiver among the high-income earners makes $100,000 income a year. Let us also suppose that the average high-income earner spends $80,000 a year for consumer goods. By definition, the average propensity to consume is 80/100, or 0.8. In other words, the rich, on average, spend 80 percent of their income on consumer goods.

Second, let us look at the behavior of the average income recipient of the middle-income group, which we call the middle class for short. Suppose the average income recipient of the middle class earns $40,000 income each year. Further, suppose that the average middle-class person spends $40,400 on consumer goods. In this case, the average middle-class person is spending more than his or her whole income for consumption. This assumption was true in 2007, when this chapter was being written. By definition, the APC equaled 40,400/40,000, or 1.01. In other words, under this assumption, the average middle-class person spent 101 percent of his or her income for consumer goods.

Let us look at the consumer behavior of low-income earners. Suppose the average low-income person has an income of $10,000 a year. Suppose the average poor person spends $11,000 a year on consumer goods and services. Then their average propensity to consume is 11,000/10,000, or 1.10. This means that the low-income families spend 110 percent of their income.

We have defined the relationship of consumption to income. Now what do we call the relationship of savings to income? Savings is *all income that is not spent for consumption.* The **average propensity to save** (APS) is *the proportion of savings to income.* In the previous example, on average, high-income earners saved 20 percent of their income, so their APS was 0.20.

Dis-saving means reducing your savings or borrowing. In this example, the average middle-class person dis-saved 1 percent of his or her income, so the average propensity to save was −0.01. The average low-income earner dis-saved 10 percent of his or her income, so their APS was −0.10.

There are only two more definitions to go. Economists are interested in how the economy is changing. They want to describe how your consumption changes when your income changes. Economists define the **marginal propensity to consume** (MPC), as the *increase of consumption to the increase in income.* If a person's income rises by $10,000 and she expands her consumption by $6,000 from one year to the next, then her marginal propensity to consume is 6,000/10,000, or 0.60. The **marginal propensity to save** (MPS) is *the increase in savings to an increase in income.* In this example, the woman's additional savings are $4,000 out of $10,000, so her marginal propensity to save is 0.40.

PSYCHOLOGY AND INCOME DISTRIBUTION

The use of the term *propensity* to describe consumer behavior seems to imply that consumers follow some innate psychological laws. On the contrary, consumer behavior is determined not only by natural drives but by social conditioning. We are not born with a desire for television sets, but we are conditioned to want them. Nor is there any innate compulsion to consume exactly 90 percent of our income and save 10 percent. Our desires for television sets, as well as our decisions on the ratio of consumption and savings to income, are determined by society's attitudes, ideologies, and institutions. Family background has a significant influence on consumption habits, as do secular and religious educational systems. Last but not least, the vast volume of advertising, in the United States affects the pattern of consumption.

Consumer psychology is largely socially determined. What individuals think is necessary for their existence differs greatly in every society. For example, a car isn't a necessity in the sense that one starves without a car. But try holding a job in Los Angeles without a car. It's very difficult to even search for a job without a car. The same kind idea about necessity applies in our society to a telephone and, increasingly, to the need for a computer.

Even more important than consumer psychology or desires, however, are the objective social facts of how income is distributed. Even if they have the very same psychological attitudes, an unemployed worker with a tiny income will not be able to save anything—and usually dis-saves by going into debt. On the other hand, a businessperson with a $1 million income may consume only 10 percent of his or her income. Ten percent of $1 million, however, is $100,000 a year, so he or she still has a very high consumption standard.

The data show that groups with very low incomes spend all, or more than all, of their incomes on consumption. The groups with average income now spend a little more than their total income. Groups with income much higher than average spend only a small part of it for consumption. In the terminology of Keynesian economics, low-income groups have a high propensity to consume. On the other hand, the data show that groups with very high incomes spend a smaller proportion on consumption-a low average propensity to consume. The high-income groups spend a large number of dollars on consumption, but this sometimes leaves them with a high proportion of unused income. They save this income in various forms. In the terminology of Keynesian economics, the high-income groups have a low propensity to consume and a high propensity to save.

We see, in general, that aggregate consumption is determined primarily by the desire for goods and services, but also by the amount of money in the hands of people. Remember, effective demand means not only having the desire but also having the money for goods and services. How much money is spent also depends on who gets it: one fabulously rich person or millions of middle-income people. The rich person spends a lower proportion than the average person. The average person needs to spend all of his or her income, or more, just to keep up the average standard of living.

A change in the distribution of income will affect the proportion of aggregate income spent on consumption. For example, if society taxes the rich and gives to the poor, the proportion of income spent on consumption (the APC) will usually rise. But if society taxes the poor and gives to the rich, the proportion of income spent on consumption will usually fall. The propensity to consume for the whole nation, therefore, depends mainly on two factors. First, the APC is influenced by consumer psychology. Of course, consumer psychology is influenced by all of our social experiences. Second, consumption is also influenced by how society distributes income.

CHANGE IN INCOME DISTRIBUTION

Typically, an income shift from the high income individuals to the low income individuals tends to raise the national propensity to consume. The reason is that the poor have to consume all their income, while the rich may save much of it. In the same manner, an income shift from the poor to the rich tends to lower the national propensity to consume because the rich consume a much lower proportion of their income.

Most of the income of the rich comes from ownership of property, including profits, rent, and interest. Most of the income for the middle class comes from wages and salaries. Many of the poor have either no earned income or have low-income wages. We find that most employees tend to spend all of their income for consumer goods and services (and usually more than their whole income by borrowing additional sums). On the contrary, most capitalist owners have a high income, so they are able to save a good-sized proportion of their high incomes. This theoretical expectation is confirmed by the latest data, as shown in the next section.

The effects of shifts between property income and employee income are therefore similar to those of shifts between rich and poor. If less goes to capitalist property owners and more to employees, the result is a higher propensity to consume. If less goes to employees and more to property owners, the result is a lower propensity to consume. This is because property owners consume a smaller percentage and save a considerable percentage of their income. Table 42.1 provides an example of the impact of shifting income distribution and the average propensity to consume.

Table 42.1

Consumption and Labor Share

Before income distribution shift
National income = $200 billion

Labor income = $100 billion	Property income = $100 billion
Employee APC = 100%	Capitalist APC = 15%
Employees consume = $100	Capitalists consume = $15
Total consumer demand = $115	

Therefore, national APC = 57% ($115 consumption/$200 income)

After income distribution shift
National income = $300 billion

Labor income = $100 billion	Property income = $200 billion
Employee APC = 100%	Capitalist APC = 15%
Employees consume = $100	Capitalists consume = $30
Aggregate consumer demand = $130	

Therefore, national APC = 38% ($130 consumption/$300 income).

Note: Table uses imaginary data for illustration only. Dollar amounts are in billions.

INEQUALITY AND CONSUMPTION

Consumer demand in the aggregate is affected by total income and by distribution of income. As Keynes argues, the total amount of income available is an important factor, but its distribution between people is also important. Rich, middle-income, and poor groups, as well as capitalist owners and employees, tend to have very different spending patterns. Therefore, total consumer spending is influenced by total income, but it is also influenced by the degree of inequality in the distribution of income between rich, middle-income employees, and the poor.

The latest facts of inequality in U.S. income distribution were presented in Chapter 18, so we need only summarize the data here for the present period. First, a considerable percentage of U.S. families, about 15 percent, live below the officially defined poverty level. Second, distribution of income is very unequal, with the richest 10 percent of families getting more income than the poorest 50 percent of families put together. Third, inequality has increased in the last thirty years. The gap between the top 10 percent and the bottom 90 percent keeps getting larger. Fourth, the richest one-tenth of 1 percent of families control most property, particularly corporate stock. Therefore, a very large percentage of the income of the rich is from profit, rent, or interest. Fifth, the poorest 70 percent of the population own almost no capital and obtain no interest, rent, or profit income. A very high percentage of all middle-class income is wage or salary income in return for their labor.

Consumer Behavior over the Business Cycle

The usual pattern of consumer behavior in the business cycle is illustrated in Figure 42.2, which is an average of the five cycles from 1970 to 2001. Remember, as explained in Chapter 41, that stage 1 is the low point, or trough at the beginning of the cycle, stage 5 is the cycle peak, and stage 9 is the final low point, or trough. Consumption at each of the nine stages is shown as a percentage of its average value over the cycle, called the cycle base.

Figure 42.2 **Consumption over the Business Cycle**

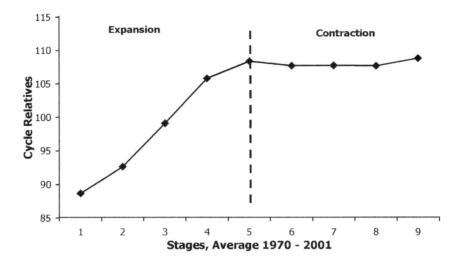

Average of five cycles, 1970–2001, in billions of real 1996 dollars, seasonally adjusted. *Source:* "Personal Consumption Expenditures," from Bureau of Economic Analysis, Department of Commerce (www.bea .gov), accessed on November 15, 2007.

Figure 42.2 reveals that on the average for these five cycles, the aggregate amount of consumption, adjusted for inflation, rose throughout the expansion. In the average recession, real consumer spending fell for a while, then rose a little. The slight rise heralded the business recovery. The typical behavior of consumer spending is to rise during the expansion of income and fall during the contraction of income.

National income rose more rapidly than consumption in expansion and fell more rapidly than consumption throughout the contraction. Remember that the average propensity to consume is the ratio of consumption to income. Since consumption expands more slowly than income, the APC falls in the expansion. Since consumption falls more slowly than income in recessions, the APC must rise in recessions. This behavior of the average propensity to consume, or consumption/income, is illustrated in Figure 42.3.

Remember the basic point that aggregate consumption rises and falls with income, just as our intuition expects. But the average ratio of consumption to income (APC) does the opposite. It is one of the few economic indicators that falls during cyclical expansions and rises during cyclical contractions. We shall find that this is an important fact for the theory of the business cycle.

Why does the average propensity to consume fall during expansions and rise during recessions? The average person's income falls in a recession and rises in an expansion. At the beginning of an expansion, the average income is relatively low, so people are forced to spend most of their money on consumer goods and series. As income rises in an expansion, people can keep the same consumer spending, but if their income increases, they can also save a little. Therefore, in an expansion, the proportion spent for consumption usually falls, while the proportion used for savings usually rises. The opposite happens in a recession, when most people have lower incomes, so they are forced to spend more on consumption and to save less.

Figure 42.3 **Ratio of Consumption to National Income**

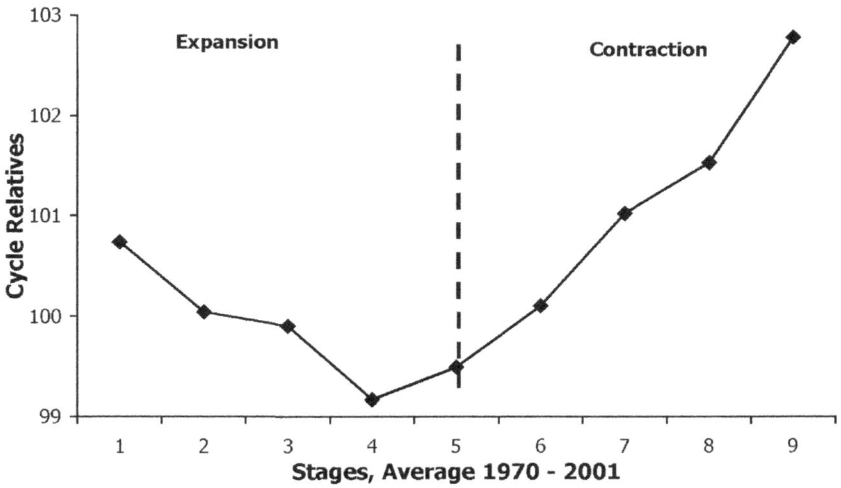

Average of five cycles, 1970–2001, in billions of real 1996 dollars, seasonally adjusted. *Source:* "Personal Consumption Expenditures," and "National Income," from Bureau of Economic Analysis, Department of Commerce (www.bea.gov).

It must be noted, however, that this fact from the average business cycle does not always happen in every year of every expansion or recession. For example, in 2005, several years into an expansion, the aggregate amount of savings was actually negative. In other words, in the strange expansion starting in 2001, instead of having more savings each year, the average American actually went more into debt each year. This new development is very important and is discussed in full when we consider consumer debt.

Consumer Behavior of Capitalist Owners and Employees

As capitalist income rises in an expansion, capitalists consume a smaller and smaller proportion of it. Partly, this is because they still consider their earlier consumption level normal and satisfactory. With a higher income, they can save more. Partly, however, it is because the profit outlook has become more optimistic, so they wish to save a larger part of their income in order to invest it in profitable enterprises. Moreover, as prosperity increases, capitalist corporations keep more profits as cash savings, ready to use when there are profitable opportunities. Interestingly, the conservative economist Milton Friedman confirmed this difference in class behavior (Friedman, pp. 69–79). Friedman found that the average business owner spent 77 percent of his or her additional income for consumption, but the average employee spent 96 percent of his or her income on consumption.

Employees, on the other hand, continue to spend in the expansion almost their whole income on consumption. Since their standard of living was below normal at the bottom of the recession, they use most of their increased income to pay off debts and buy necessities. At any rate, their propensity to consume remains very high even at the peak of the cycle. As we have seen, not only the poor but the middle class are now going further into debt, even in the present expansion. For simplicity, we can think of the usual situation as one in which many employees have little or no savings, while the property owners have rising savings out of their rising income in each expansion.

If we include not only the personal profit income of individual capitalists but also all property income from corporate profits, then the difference becomes startling. For example, in the period 1949–1982, capitalists consumed only 13 percent of all property income (including corporate profits) and saved 87 percent. Most people saved nothing and many went into debt. We shall see that this pattern continues to the present day.

Shifts in Consumption and Inequality

Why does the average propensity to consume tend to fall in each business cycle expansion and rise in each business cycle contraction? Most traditional economists simply argue in terms of psychological behavior. They claim that the average psychological propensity of consumers is fixed at the norm of their previous spending levels. It is a psychological law, they say, that consumers are slow to change their habits when their income changes. Their percentage spent on consumption falls in the upswing and rises in the downswing of the economy.

Many progressive economists, however, stress that the cause of shifts in the proportion spent in the aggregate could be shifts in income distribution between capitalist owners and employees. Since the capitalists have a much lower propensity to consume than the employees , the distribution of income between employee and capitalists is very important in determining the national average propensity to consume. Even if there were no changes in psychological propensities to consume in either class, a shift in income distribution from the middle class to the rich (or employees to capitalists) could explain a change in the average propensity to consume.

The declining average propensity to consume in an expansion may be explained by a shift of income from employees to capitalists. Employees have high propensities to consume, while capitalists have much lower propensities to consume and a high savings propensity. The declining aggregate propensity to consume in an expansion could arise from a shift of income toward the capitalist class. The rising propensity to consume in a depression could be explained by an income shift back from capitalists to employees.

What does happen to the distribution of income between capitalists and employees in expansions and in recessions? What does the data show? In every expansion, the capitalist share of income rises, while the employees' share of income falls. Income is shifting from those with low saving ratios to those with high savings ratios. Therefore, the average propensity to consume must decline, while the average propensity to save usually rises. The opposite happens in recessions. In every expansion, profits rise rapidly, while wages and salaries move up more slowly. The share of labor in the national income declines. That decline in the labor share of national income has been dramatic in the current expansion. The labor share means the proportion of all income that goes to employees for their labor, including low-paid waiter's labor and high-paid engineer's labor. The *labor share* is the aggregate employee compensation divided by national income. The declining labor share in the average expansion is shown clearly in Figure 42.4.

Figure 42.4 shows that in the average business cycle, the labor share declines for most of the business expansion but rises for most of the business recession. What does this tell us about the causes of fluctuations in aggregate consumption? Wage and salary income is the biggest part of consumption, so we would expect a close relationship.

Figure 42.4   **Labor Share Over the Business Cycle**

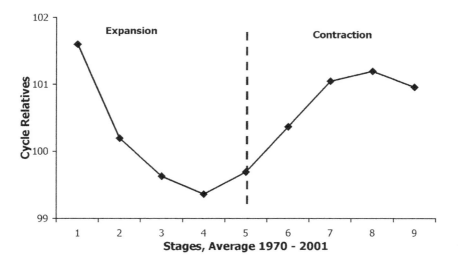

Labor share is the ratio of labor income to national income. Average of five cycles, 1970–2001, in billions of real 1996 dollars, seasonally adjusted. *Source:* Bureau of Economic Analysis, Department of Commerce (www.bea.gov).

In fact, if we compare the average propensity to consume in Figure 42.3 and the labor share in Figure 42.4, there is a very similar pattern. In the business expansion, the labor share declines (for reasons discussed later). When the labor share declines, so does the average propensity to consume. In fact, the two figures show that both ratios decline in the first four stages of expansion, then both rise a little before the peak of expansion. In the recession period, both ratios rise for four stages. Then, in the last stage of recession, the propensity to consume continues to rise, but the labor share begins to fall again.

Several studies have shown a strong statistical correlation of the propensity to consume and the labor share (see Sherman, 1991). This is no surprise because aggregate consumer spending relies mainly on labor incomes; we would expect the aggregate ratio of consumption to income to be closely related to the ratio of labor income to all income. We may safely conclude that the labor share has a strong influence on how much consumer spending there is out of income.

To avoid confusion, remember the following points. First, aggregate, real consumer spending rises and falls with business expansion and contraction. Similarly, aggregate wage and salary income also rises and falls with business expansion and contraction. On the other hand, when there is a business expansion, both the average propensity to consume and the labor share decline. Similarly, in a business recession, both the average propensity to consume and the labor share rise.

EXPLAINING THE BEHAVIOR OF THE LABOR SHARE

Why does labor income rise so slowly in expansions? In the recovery phase of the cycle, there are still large numbers of unemployed workers and professionals willing to take new jobs at relatively low pay. Looking again at the average cycle, the bargaining power of employees and unions in the early phases of business expansion is relatively weak, especially at present low levels of unionization. The weakness of unions and employees in the early expansion is partly because of the existence of a reserve of unemployed workers.

The weakness of labor is partly due to the general attitudes toward income changes. The public is sympathetic to employees resisting cuts in employee compensation but less sympathetic to fights for wage and salary increases. Even employees are more easily aroused to anger and militancy to resist wage cuts than they are enthusiastic to strike for wage increases. Another factor that prevents unions and employees from raising wages or from raising them more rapidly than productivity and prices are rising is the existence of fixed-labor contracts for two or three years.

In early expansion, the big profit increases come primarily from increased productivity. The large profit increases result partly from investment in new machinery, which increases the productivity of workers and lessens the need to hire more workers. Another reason for profit increases is that factories were running at a low percentage of capacity and are now starting to increase their use of capacity. The organization and use of labor and machines become more efficient when that level of production is reached for which the factory was designed.

Most important is that at low levels of production, capitalists may fire production-line workers. They are forced, however, to keep employed large numbers of administrative workers, maintenance workers, security people, and sales and distribution workers. The need for such workers does not decline much with lower production. Neither does it rise much with higher production. For example, a bookkeeper or a security guard is needed whether production is high or low. Therefore, as production rises toward full use of capacity, there is also a decline in the number of nonproduction workers relative to the amount of production, or per unit of production. This decline in the unit cost of production means higher profits for capitalists, but these profits are not automatically passed on to workers in higher wages. Therefore, the share of production going to labor drops in every period of industrial recovery.

Why do wages and salaries usually keep rising to the peak of expansion? At the peak of expansion, there is much less unemployment. Unions and employees therefore have greater bargaining power. Worker militancy also increases as workers become fully aware that productivity increases and higher prices are raising profits. For these reasons, real wages as well as money wages usually continue to rise to the peak of expansion.

Why do real wages fall relatively slowly in contraction? During the recession, workers strongly resist wage cuts, while prices usually rise much more slowly than in expansion (because of declining demand). Fixed-labor contracts prevent wages from declining immediately. Productivity falls mainly because there is an increasingly higher proportion of nonproduction workers. The recession usually witnesses a shift to a lower ratio of profit to wages as profits fall faster than wages. In Chapter 43, we examine why profits usually rise so rapidly in early expansion, level off in late expansion, decline rapidly in early contraction, and bottom out in late contraction.

CONSUMER DEBT

What has happened with consumer debt over the whole period from 1970 to the present (2007)? Consumer debt rose enormously in that period. If we want a scary figure, then we can say that outstanding consumer debt rose from an average $168 billion in the 1970–1975 cycle to an average of $1.21 trillion in the 1991–2001 cycle (data from the Federal Reserve Board of Governors, reported at www.economagic.com.)

The really interesting question is whether the ratio of debt to income rose or fell. If debt rose by $1 trillion in some period, it might be nothing to worry about if income rose by $10 trillion. But a rise of $1 trillion would be catastrophic if income rose by only $1 billion. What actually happened in this long period? In the 1970 to 1975 cycle, the ratio of consumer debt to national income was 64 percent on the average. This means that the debt owed by the average person was almost two-thirds of their income in an average year. That is a lot of debt burden. But what is the case during the latest cycle? In the cycle of 1991 to 2001, the total debt owed was 92 percent of national income. Average debt was getting close to average income. The debt burden on the average person rose very considerably from the beginning to the end of the period.

The ratio of debt to income is rising still further in the present expansion (see Bivens and Weller, 2006, p. 607). The immediate danger to the economy is not the total debt. The danger lies in how much interest must be paid each year to service the debt. The burden of interest is about 13 percent of the average income at this time. Before buying anything new, people must pay 13 cents out of every dollar to financial agencies on their debts. It is worth emphasizing that there is no magic ratio of debt to income after which the economy suddenly crashes. However, the greater the burden of interest payments, the worse the impact of a recession because people cannot meet their debts.

The next question is, What happens to consumer debt in a cyclical expansion and contraction? In the average cycle of the period from 1970 to 2001, the ratio of consumer debt to national income rose in the expansion by 4 percent. People owed more of their income for payments on debt at the peak of the cycle than at the beginning of the cycle.

What happened in the average recession? Real consumer debt fell by 2 percent in the average recession from 1970 to 2001. Real national income also fell 2 percent in the average recession. Therefore, the ratio of consumer debt to national income had zero movement in the average recession. In other words, in this period, people lowered their debt a little in each recession, but only as much as the decline in their income. The debt burden per dollar of income remained the same during the recession. Since the debt burden rose in every expansion, the burden has been rising over this whole period.

Why does debt rise and fall in the business cycle? As an economic expansion continues, people become more optimistic about the future. They also feel more pressure to keep up with the spending patterns of their neighbors. Therefore, the amount of credit climbs rapidly. Consumers borrow larger amounts as a proportion of their income in order to keep up in the consumption race. As long as consumers get more credit and spend it for consumption, consumer demand is improved. Therefore, the flood of consumer credit helps to postpone the recession.

Once a collapse occurs, however, this increase in credit tends to intensify the recession in several ways. Consumers who have been deeply in debt may now lose their jobs or be afraid of losing their jobs. Therefore, consumers suddenly restrict their buying, so sales may fluctuate rapidly downward. Moreover, consumers with existing debt cannot pay those debts if they lose their jobs. Businesses face both declining sales and declining revenues from consumer payments on previous debts. Eventually, if other factors continue the recession, the failure of consumers to pay back their debts is an important factor in deepening the recession.

The poor state of the consumers who borrowed money not only is painful to the consumer but often is disastrous to the lending agencies, whether a bank or other finance company. The flow of principal and interest to the bank has stopped. They own some secondhand goods, but in a recession, these are very hard to resell for anything like the original price. As a result, many lending companies and banks may go bankrupt. This hurts their depositors and stockholders and sends negative reverberations throughout the economy.

THE WEALTH EFFECT

In addition to income and credit, consumer behavior is influenced by the amount of wealth they hold. Remember that income is the amount of money a person earns in a year. Wealth is the amount that an individual has managed to save over his or her life. Wealth may be held in the form of cash or bank deposits or home ownership or corporate stock or anything else convertible to money.

For most people, the wealth effect has little importance. Many people have little or no net wealth after debts are subtracted. Only among the richest citizens of America is there enough wealth to make its rise or decline important. In recent years, more people did acquire some usable cash by borrowing on the amount of equity they own in their homes. Borrowing from home equity does increase consumption, but only temporarily. After they spend their new cash, these homeowners have nothing more to sell for ready cash. Borrowing against their home equity is a one-time thing and leaves them more vulnerable to recession. A job loss will now result in much less consumption.

The expansion of the 1990s was a long one, and many people believed that it would go on forever. They also expected the rising stock market to go on forever. Many people with relatively small savings invested in the stock market at the end of the 1990s. But then the bubble burst. Millions of small investors lost all of their savings in the stock market in the early 2000s. Their consumption declined precipitously as they realized that they had no spare assets. Even large investors lost part of their wealth in the stock market decline, so they felt poorer and lowered their propensity to consume. This is the wealth effect.

SUMMARY

This chapter looked at the long-run trends in consumption, determinants of consumer demand in the aggregate for the goods and services produced, and how consumer demand behaves over the business cycle. In order to make comparisons, some measures are introduced. The average propensity to consume (APC) means the ratio of consumption to income. The average propensity to save (APS) means the ratio of savings to income.

The marginal propensity to consume (MPC) is the change in consumption to the change in income. The marginal propensity to save (MPS) is the change in savings to the change in income.

Aggregate income, the distribution of income between labor and capital, and wealth are the primary determinants of consumption spending. Since about 1970, wages and salaries have grown far more slowly than national income. Aggregate consumption grows mostly according to the growth of wages and salaries. Aggregate consumption is also affected by the amount that consumers borrow. Most people have no savings and growing debt. The burden of interest payments on the debts owed by consumers is growing rapidly.

Income is distributed very unequally, with a few rich families having very high incomes but a large number of employee families having low incomes. The capitalist owners consume a smaller percentage of their large income than does the average employee. Therefore, they usually save a significant percentage of their income and can invest it. But since there are few capitalists and many employees, on the average, very little is saved. Aggregate consumption is also affected by wealth, but only a small percentage of consumers have significant savings and wealth.

In most business cycle expansions, consumption rises, but more slowly than income. That consumer spending rises more slowly than production means it has a limiting effect on demand for consumer goods and services. The present business expansion has been unusual in that the saved proportion of national income has not increased with rising incomes. Rather, the saved proportion has fallen. In fact, in 2005, 2006, and 2007, there has been aggregate dis-saving and growing aggregate debt. One reason for the increase in debt is that wages and salaries have grown very little, while the prices that people pay have continued to rise.

SUGGESTED READING

The usual pattern of consumer spending in the business cycle is detailed in *The Business Cycle: Growth and Crisis in Capitalism* (1991) by Howard Sherman, and the patterns of recent years are discussed in *Contours of Descent: U.S. Economic Fractures and the Landscape of Global Austerity*. (2004), by Robert Pollin.

KEY TERMS

average propensity to consume
average propensity to save
consumption function
dis-saving

marginal propensity to consume
marginal propensity to save
savings

REVIEW QUESTIONS

Explain how consumption has grown over the long run.
1. Even though labor income stagnated after 1970, consumer spending rose. Explain.
2. How does wealth and debt affect spending?

Describe how consumption behaves over the business cycle.
3. Define average propensity to consume, average propensity to save, marginal propensity to consume, marginal propensity to save.
4. Why does a decline in the labor share cause a decline in the propensity to consume for the average of all consumers?
5. Why does the labor share decline as economic expansion continues?
6. Why does the ratio of consumer debt to income rise during the average expansion?

Compare and discuss determinants of aggregate consumption.
7. Why do people purchase less if they have less wealth, even if their income remains constant?
8. How does aggregate consumption behave over the business cycle?

CHAPTER 43

Investment Spending and Profit

Economists have long realized that from the standpoint of understanding cyclical unemployment, understanding investment spending is crucial. Investment spending is one of the components of aggregate expenditures along with consumption and government and exports. Chapter 42 discussed consumption spending at length and showed that consumption fluctuates much less than national income. In Chapter 43, we shall find that investment fluctuates much more than national income. This chapter explains why investment fluctuates so strongly.

LEARNING OBJECTIVES

After reading this chapter, you should be able to:

- Compare and contrast investment and consumption spending.
- Explain why businesses invest and why investment spending fluctuates with profits.
- Discuss how investment fluctuations are a direct cause of business cycles.

GROSS AND NET INVESTMENT

Gross investment is the *total value of all capital goods produced in a year*. Gross investment has two parts. **Replacement investment** is *investment in capital goods (buildings and equipment) that have depreciated or become obsolescent*. **New investment** is *investment in additional buildings and equipment to expand the capital beyond the present level*. While the distinction between new investment and replacement investment is very useful for analysis, we must remember that it is not so clear in reality which is which. For example, do you really just "replace" a worn-out computer with the exact same vintage? Of course not. You upgrade considerably each time you get a new computer. It often becomes difficult to distinguish new and replacement investment, so the figures are always a little ambiguous.

What the Department of Commerce actually calculates is the gross investment and **depreciation**, or *the dollar value of worn-out plants and equipment*. Economists just assume that all money for depreciation of capital is spent on replacing it at the same level, unlike your upgraded computer. **Net investment** simply *equals gross investment minus depreciation*. Net investment represents the addition to the nation's productive capital.

As an example of what the data look like, in 2005, the gross domestic product (GDP) was

Figure 43.1 **Investment and Consumption**

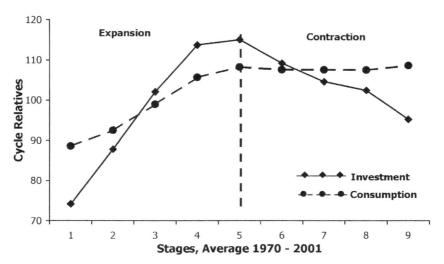

Consumption is real personal consumption spending. Investment is real gross domestic private investment. Both series are in billions of real, inflation adjusted, dollars, seasonally adjusted, quarterly data at annual rates. Average of five cycles, 1970–2001. *Source:* Bureau of Economic Analysis, Department of Commerce (www.bea.gov).

$12.5 trillion. Part of that was gross investment, which was $2.1 trillion. Depreciation was $1.6 trillion. If we subtract $1.6 trillion depreciation from $2.1 trillion gross investment, the result is a net investment of $0.5 trillion. Half a trillion of new net investment is a lot of money but pretty small compared with GDP. (Data is from the U.S. Department of Commerce, March 30, 2006, at www.bea.gov.) During the Great Depression, however, there was so little gross investment, it was less than depreciation. Therefore, net investment fell below zero for a number of years. In other words, some depreciated capital was not replaced.

INVESTMENT FLUCTUATES VIOLENTLY

In Chapter 42, it was shown that consumption fluctuates much less than national income. Here we shall find that investment fluctuates much more than national income. Businesses increase investment rapidly in expansions and decrease investment rapidly in contractions, as shown in Figure 43.1.

Figure 43.1 shows dramatically that consumer spending rises much more slowly than investment in expansions. But consumption falls much more slowly than investment in contractions.

DECISION TO INVEST

The decision to invest requires two things. One is the funds necessary to make the investment. The other is the motivation to invest, based on expectations of profit. This section looks at the funds. The next section looks at the profit motivation.

Corporations have three sources of funds for investment in modern American capitalism. First, the corporation retains some profits. It pays some profits out to stockholders, but it keeps some

Figure 43.2 **Corporate Debt (Real)**

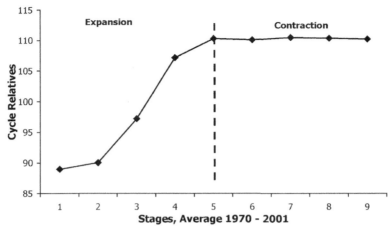

All credit market debt outstanding borrowed by nonfinancial corporate businesses real, inflation adjusted, billions of dollars, seasonally adjusted, quarterly data at annual rates, for the average of five cycles, 1970–2001. *Source:* Federal Reserve Board of Governors (www.federalreserve.gov).

for further investment. The second source of funds is borrowing from financial institutions such as banks. The third source of corporate investment is from individuals, who may invest in the stock market or bond market. Only purchase of new shares issued by the corporation, however, is a source of funds for the corporation. If one individual buys stock from another, it merely shifts the money around. It is not a source of funds for investment.

In every expansion, people and corporations become increasingly optimistic, so they borrow more. The previous chapter examined consumer borrowing. Here we look at corporate borrowing. In every expansion, corporate borrowing goes way up because of optimism about profits. In contractions, however, corporations are worried about borrowing and banks are worried about lending because some corporations will go bankrupt. In recessions, corporate borrowing stops growing and may stagnate or decline a little. This behavior is shown in Figure 43.2.

In smaller recessions, as shown in the average revealed in Figure 43.2, corporate borrowing stagnates. In large depressions, such as the Great Depression, corporate borrowing falls way down because corporations do not wish to invest anything. Moreover, banks will not support a foolish corporation that wishes to invest during the depression. During an economic expansion, corporate borrowing helps corporations expand for a longer time, so it tends to continue the expansion. But the larger corporate debt becomes, the more dangerous it becomes. If there is a huge amount of corporate debt at the end of an expansion, a small decline may cause many bankruptcies. It is possible that the greater vulnerability caused by corporate debt may turn small recessions into big depressions.

It is only when business uses funds, no matter what the source, to buy new equipment and buildings that the money becomes investment. Investment means increasing the ability to produce more goods. The corporation may also choose not to invest in productive facilities but rather to make speculative investments. A mere change in who holds an asset does not produce anything. Speculative investments include buying land to wait for it to rise in value. A corporation may also "invest" in buying back large amounts of its stock because it expects the stock to rise in value. Such purchases of assets for speculative reasons do not increase aggregate investment because they do not purchase any equipment or buildings.

In the present expansion, for example, there has been a fairly small amount of business investment to expand production to this point. Yet corporations have been rolling in cash from large profits. What have they done with the money? Mostly, they have made speculative purchases of land or stock or other assets that may rise in value. Keynes points out that such speculative spending does not help strengthen demand, nor does it help put unemployed employees back to work. Thus, even if money is not hoarded away under a bed, it may still leak out of the circulation process of production and income if it is used for speculative purposes.

Why do individuals and corporations make speculative purchases of land or stock or just hold cash rather than making productive investments? People and corporations invest to make a profit. If they see a profit down the line by installing new equipment or new buildings, then they will do that. If they do not expect to make a profit from productive investment in the economy, then they will use their funds for speculation or for hoarding in cash for safety. Both individuals and corporations like certainty when they invest. But our economy frequently generates uncertainty. When things look uncertain for the future, investors do not put money into productive investments, which may take several years to pay profits or may never turn a profit.

INVESTMENT BASED ON PROFIT MOTIVE

The businessperson who contemplates the purchase of new buildings or equipment will not decide to make the purchase unless the profit he or she expects to receive from this investment is greater than the purchase price of the buildings and equipment. Profits are exceedingly important in determining the level of investment and employment in the U.S. economy. Indeed, the prime motivation for investment in a capitalist economy is the expectation of future profit on the new investment. Yet, because future profits cannot be known with certainty, it is mainly on the basis of the present and past profits that businesspeople base their expectations. Accordingly, high or rising profits will lead to optimistic expectations and a rise in new investment.

The other reason for the importance of profits is that increased profits provide funds for increased investment. Without profits, the firm may lack funds to increase investments even if it wishes to do so. Although the investment funds can sometimes be borrowed, increased profits make it easier for the firm to obtain credit. Also, a firm with high profits in the bank looks safer, so it can borrow at lower interest rates.

There is, therefore, a close relationship between investment decisions and profits. In making a decision on whether to invest at a particular time, businesspeople seem most heavily influenced by the movements of profits in the previous few quarters and expectations of future profits. At any rate, there is no reason to doubt that investment behavior is most influenced by the recent profit performance of corporations. Statistical tests proving the close relationship of investment and profits are discussed in Sherman (1991).

PSYCHOLOGICAL ATTITUDES

Because investment decisions are based on projections of future sales, revenues, and profits, it would be easy to say that fluctuations in aggregate investment are caused by changes in investor confidence about economic conditions. Although it points to a vital aspect of economic behavior, such a formula actually explains nothing. There can be no denying the sensational effects of changes in expectations on real economic conditions in the private enterprise system. Between 1929 and 1932, children did not have enough to eat, men jumped from tall buildings, and rich women pawned their fur coats.

What caused the trouble? Pessimism? Certainly there was pessimism in the Great Depression of the 1930s. But what caused the pessimism? In 1929, most indexes of production, new investment, and profits turned down in the summer, but the stock market crash and the collapse of expectations did not occur until autumn. For example, the industrial peak was reached in June 1929, but stock prices did not peak until October 1929. In a competitive, private-enterprise economy, especially one that is increasing in complexity and interrelatedness, a single enterprise cannot accurately predict its future costs and receipts. It tends to keep an optimistic outlook until it encounters obstacles. In fact, the usual order of events in depressions appears to be that production and profit indices decline first, despite the most extreme optimism. Only then, because of the change in objective economic conditions, does the optimism change to pessimism, thus reinforcing the depression and possibly postponing the recovery. The reverse process seems to occur in economic expansions, when rises in production and profits are followed by a shift from pessimism to optimism.

Of course, after an expansion begins, it is true that the optimism of businesspeople goes beyond a rational response to profit increases, carrying the expansion far beyond the point that cold calculation would carry it. Such frenzied speculation helps make the peak conditions into a "bubble" that is easily burst. Similarly, after a depression begins, pessimistic businesspeople (usually overreacting in an irrational manner) cause a much greater decline in business activity than the objective condition warrants. But the ultimate cause of pessimism in businesspeople's attitudes is the previous recorded decline in profits or profit rates.

RELATION BETWEEN INVESTMENT AND PROFIT

In the expansion phase of the cycle, particularly in the early expansion, profits and profit rates rise rapidly. This causes a powerful spurt of investment. When the economy approaches the peak of expansion, profits and profit rates are squeezed by various forces, discussed in the next section. This profit squeeze causes pessimistic expectations of future profits. The expected decline in profits leads to a decline in investment.

The decline in investment continues throughout the contraction as profits continue to decline. Toward the end of the recession, profits bottom out and expectations become more optimistic. This ending of the profit squeeze leads to expectations of an upturn of profits. The optimistic expectations lead to the beginning of a new investment boom.

Figure 43.3 shows the behavior of investment and profits in the average of the five cycles from 1970 through 2001. Investment in this graph is defined to be gross private domestic investment, while profit is defined as profits before taxes for all corporations. Figure 43.3 reveals that in the average expansion, profits turn down first, followed by investment. In the average contraction, profits level off near the end, while investment is still declining.

Investment closely follows the movements of profits for the reasons given earlier, but investment follows with a time lag. Why is there a time lag? When conditions change and things look more profitable, there is first some time before the business knows about the improvement because it takes information a while to be recorded and read. This is true for information both about the business itself and about the whole economy. Then, if things look good enough, the business must figure out exactly what new facilities it wants to build or what equipment to buy, so there must be consultation with experts. Next, the business must usually borrow money from a financial institution. That process takes time. Any major building requires government permits, which also takes time. Finally, a building is not built in a minute, so the actual investment is paid out slowly to a contractor over time.

When there is a decline in profits, some of the same lags occur, including collection of information and waiting to see if the decline is to be deep and lengthy. Notice also that there is a floor

Figure 43.3 **Investment and Profit**

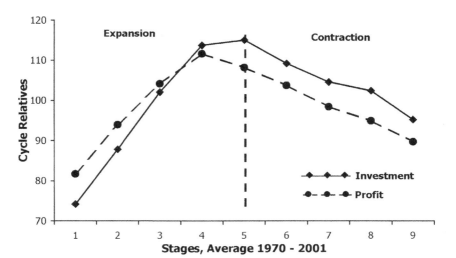

Investment is gross domestic private investment. Profit is corporate profit before taxes. Both series are seasonally adjusted, quarterly data at annual rates, billions of real, inflation adjusted dollars. Both are for the average of five cycles, 1970–2001. *Source:* Bureau of Economic Analysis, Department of Commerce (www.bea.gov).

to disinvestment because it takes time for machines to be worn out. A single firm can get rid of some of its capital investment. But in the whole economy, capital does not disappear overnight; it takes time for depreciation to occur.

WHAT DETERMINES PROFIT?

Investment is a function of profits. What, then, determines how much profit is made in the U.S. economy? In making profits, the capitalists perform three operations. First, they use their money to buy certain inputs. They buy physical capital goods, such as machinery and raw materials. They also buy labor, that is, the contractual right to use employees' power to labor for so many hours a day. Second, capitalists use the capital and labor in a production process that must produce commodities with a higher revenue than the cost of the capital and labor that went into them. Third, they sell the new commodities for money. Profit shows up here because the capitalists sell the commodities for more money than they used originally in buying the capital and labor.

Obstacles to profit can arise if (1) the cost of labor power and capital goods rises, (2) there is a decline in the productivity of the production process, or (3) there is insufficient demand for the commodities that have been produced. Some theories emphasize that profits are squeezed at the end of expansion by rising costs. Other theories emphasize that profits are squeezed at the end of expansion by inadequate demand. We shall find that profit is squeezed, like an orange in an orange squeezer, from both sides at once.

SUMMARY

Net investment spending swings rather violently up and down, fluctuating more than consumer spending. Net investment is the difference between total or gross investment and depreciation.

Investment rises because profits rise. For a number of reasons, however, the behavior of investment follows with a time lag after profits. Similarly, investment declines because profits decline, but with a time lag.

The role of the stock market is of importance and great interest in the investment process, so we discuss it in Appendix 43.1.

KEY TERMS

depreciation   new investment
gross investment   replacement investment
net investment

REVIEW QUESTIONS

Compare and contrast investment and consumption spending.
1. Define net investment, replacement investment, new investment and gross investment.
2. How do investment and consumption behave over the business cycle?

Explain why businesses invest and why investment spending fluctuates with profits.
3. Give two reasons why investment is strongly influenced by profits.
4. Where do business owners get funds to invest?

Discuss how investment fluctuations are a direct cause of business cycles.
5. Give several reasons why investment does not immediately follow profits but occurs only after a time lag.

APPENDIX 43.1
THE STOCK MARKET AND INVESTMENT

LEARNING OBJECTIVES FOR APPENDIX 43.1

After reading this appendix, you should be able to:

• Describe general movement of stock market and the business cycle.

Individual investors put money in the stock market. They do so to make a profit on it. They make profit because the corporation pays out dividends to them. But most fortunes are made in the stock market by guessing which corporations will have stock that rapidly goes up in price. The price of the stock reflects the estimates of all investors as to how much profit the corporation will make in the future. Money is made by buying a stock at a low price and selling it at a high price.

Individuals often lose money by investing in the wrong corporations. But millions also lose money just by owning stock when there is a recession. Stock prices often go way down in a recession, and small investors must sell at very low prices when they need the cash. The only advice an economist can give is that (1) all investing involves risk, and (2) if you want to invest, put the money in a fund that holds a very diverse set of stocks and is run by experts. Studies show that diversity is always the safest thing.

Figure 43.4 **Stocks**

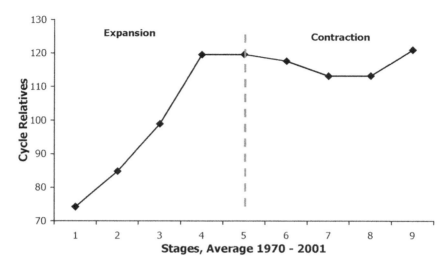

Average of five cycles, 1970–2001. Quarterly data converted from daily data. *Source:* Standard and Poor's 500 corporation stock index (www.economagic.com).

Let us now turn to the aggregate performance of the stock market, as shown in Figure 43.4. Figure 43.4 shows that the value of stocks goes up in economic expansions and down in economic contractions. Of course, this means that the investor should buy stocks at the bottom of the recession and sell all stocks at the top of the expansion. The trick is in knowing when those times have arrived. To be more precise, Figure 43.4 shows that the stock market reaches a peak one stage before the economy, and then declines. The stock market reaches its low point one stage before the bottom of the economic recession is reached, then starts to climb again. This means that investors should actually sell all of their stock about six to nine months before the cycle peak. They should buy stock a few months before the cycle trough. The problem is that every cycle is different.

REVIEW QUESTIONS FOR APPENDIX 43.1

Describe general movement of stock market and the business cycle.
1. Why do individuals invest in the stock market?
2. According to the movement of S&P 500 and the business cycle, when should investors sell? Buy? Explain.

CHAPTER 44

The Multiplier

This chapter explains how new demand for goods and services may have an effect greater than the initial spending. This is called the multiplier effect. It may come from government, investors, or foreign demand. Here we begin with government spending. The impact of government spending on the economy is a very controversial issue on which Congress spends a lot of time.

LEARNING OBJECTIVES

After reading this chapter, you should be able to:

- Explain how a given increase in spending by government, investors, or foreigners may cause a much larger (multiplied) effect on consumption and GDP.
- Discuss how the multiplied impact on the economic process may help push the economy up rapidly or help push the economy down rapidly.
- List and describe limitations of the multiplier.

THE GOVERNMENT MULTIPLIER

One objective of government policy is to increase the net flow of demand during recessions. Higher demand encourages more production and more jobs. One powerful way to increase demand is by increasing government spending. Suppose the government increases its spending for battleships and schools and roads and all sorts of other things normally purchased by government. In this case, it is obvious that aggregate demand is increased. Government may also increase private spending by lowering taxes on individuals and businesses. We shall see that this method has somewhat less impact than direct government spending.

On the other hand, government may wish to reduce demand to reduce the inflationary rise of prices. In that case a government may decide to lower its spending. Any decrease of government spending hurts someone. For example, if government lowers its spending for schools, it harms students and it harms their families. Government may also decide to reduce inflation by raising taxes. If people pay higher taxes, then they have less money to spend. This is obviously a painful way to reduce inflation.

All of these actions by government are the result of extensive discussions and debates within government and among economists, discussed in Chapter 47 on government fiscal policies. Here we ask only one question: If the government spends more money (or less money), what is the effect on consumer spending? We examine both the direct effects and the indirect effects of these government actions.

The direct effects are easy to understand. If the government spends money to hire 1,000 new teachers, then the money paid to all of them is their income. Suppose in a given length of time, the 1,000 new teachers receive an extra $1 million through government spending. If we assume the teachers spend all of it, then consumer spending goes up by $1 million.

In this case, $1 million in extra government spending leads to $1 million in extra consumer spending by the teachers. That seems obvious, so what's the fuss? By this time, you know that nothing in economics is ever as simple as it looks at first glance. In this case, we want to know not just the direct effect of the government spending on teachers but the indirect effects on the economy after the teachers spend the money.

Suppose all the teachers spend all of their income each month. Then the teachers spend $1 million each month. Somebody receives that $1 million in the form of wages, salaries, or profits. Suppose in the next month, the people who received the $1 million then spend it on other goods and services. At the end of two months, the $1 million spent by the government has been spent by the teachers and then respent by the people who sold products to the teachers. The total consumer spending at the end of two months is not $1 million but $2 million. The effect of the government spending is multiplied by respending. It may go on month after month until that $1 million has been respent many times. That is the secondary effect we wish to consider.

The multiplier is just a way of adding up how much effect a one-time government spending action will have on consumer spending, and therefore national income, over some period of time. In reality, not all people spend all of their income received within one month. Some people with a high income may save most of it for a long time. Instead of spending 100 percent on consumption, they save 75 percent of it in banks, and the banks leave it idle for some time. If all of the $1 million goes to high-income receivers, then instead of $1 million of spending, there is only 25 percent, or $250,000, of respending. Here the secondary effect is much less than if all of the $1 million were respent. The total effect of government spending is reduced whenever people save some of the money rather than spending it.

On the other hand, suppose the $1 million goes to middle-class employees who have been barely getting enough money to meet their most basic needs. As a group, they will spend most of their extra $1 million immediately. If they spend 95 percent, then $950,000 of the $1 million is immediately respent. If the people who receive this money are of the same income class, then they will again respend 95 percent of $950,000, and so forth. Clearly, when people spend most of the $1 million, the total effect of the original government spending is very great.

Calculating the Multiplier

Economists, of course, would like to say exactly what the effect is of government spending taking into account how much respending there is. That is the job of the multiplier. The secondary effects of government expenditure may be quantified in terms of the **government multiplier**. The government multiplier is a very simple idea. The government multiplier is *how much total national income is increased by an increase in government spending*. It includes the immediate effect on consumer spending and all the secondary effects.

How is the multiplier calculated? The government multiplier equals the ratio of increased national income to increased government spending. As an example, we may ask how much total increase in national income will there be from an extra $1,000 given to a teacher. How much is respent? What is the end of the process? This process is illustrated in Table 44.1.

Table 44.1

How the Government Multiplier Works

Period	Increase in Government Spending	Increase in Consumption	Increase in National Income	Increase in Savings
First	$1,000		$1,000	
Second	0	$800	800	200
Third	0	640	640	160
Fourth	0	512	512	128
Fifth	0	410	410	102
Sixth	0	328	328	82
Seventh	—	—	—	—
Eighth	—	—	—	—
Final	$1,000	$4,000	$5,000	$1,000

Government spending increases by $1,000 but then is constant. The marginal propensity to consume (MPC) is determined as MPC = 80%. We assume that investment and foreign spending are not involved, so they are set at zero.

The table makes the very simple assumption that consumer spending always reacts to an increase in the income of any individual or group. In the language of economics, their marginal propensity to consume is constant. Here it is assumed that whenever anyone gets a dollar of income, they spend 80 percent, or 4/5, on consumption. So when a teacher gets $1,000, he or she spends $800 within the first month.

The government gives the teacher $1,000. The teacher spends $800, paid to Ms. Smith for rent. How much does Ms. Smith spend? She spends 80 percent of $800, or $640. The person to whom Ms. Smith pays $640 spends 80 percent of that on consumption, and so on, until the last dollar is spent by the last person. Every increase in income automatically leads to a certain increase in consumption spending. This spending means a further increase in income, some of which will be spent for a second round of consumption. The additional spending gets smaller in each round until it reaches zero.

The key point in the table is that all consumers, such as the teachers who receive the initial income, spend 80 percent of any increase in income. Remember that the marginal propensity to consume (MPC) is simply the ratio of the additional spending on consumption to the additional income. If the marginal propensity to consume out of additional income is 80 percent, then 20 percent is saved out of each increase in income. The marginal propensity to save (MPS), or increased savings to increased income, is 20 percent.

For example, we see in Table 44.1 that government spends $1,000 in new teachers' salaries in the first period. Since it is income to teachers, it is also an increase in the national income of $1,000. We then see that in the second period, the teacher spends $800, or 80 percent, for consumer goods. Since $200 is left unspent, that is savings in the second period. The total national income is $1,000, but only $800 is spent, while $200 is saved. Similarly, in the next period, those who receive the money spent by the teacher respend 80 percent, or $640. That leaves savings of $160. The process continues the same way. In each period, consumers spend 80 percent of 80 percent of 80 percent, and so forth. At the same time, people save 20 percent of 20 percent of 20 percent, and so forth. Both consumption and savings get smaller in each round. Eventually, they reach zero in some future period and the process is ended.

The table shows only the first six rounds of spending. Imagine that the process goes on and on the same way until it reaches zero. Since the process is absolutely predictable based on our assumptions, we would like to know how will things look when the process is at an end. To calculate the end result, we may use the MPC, or 80 percent in this case. Since the savings is all that is left from income after spending, the MPS equals exactly 1 − MPC, or 20 percent in this case.

The easiest formula for the government multiplier is 1/MPS. This means that if you multiply the initial government spending by 1/MPS, you get the total spending at the end of the process. In Table 44.1, where MPS is assumed to be 20 percent, the government multiplier is 1/0.2 = 5. The multiplier is 5. Now we may simply multiply initial government spending by 5 to find out the total increase in national. In this case, the initial government spending is $1,000. Then $1,000 times 5, the multiplier, equals $5,000.

Behold the magic. By this shortcut, we have the answer. The national income will increase by $5,000 if government spends $1,000 and the MPC is 80 percent (so that the MPS is 20 percent). If you don't believe this shortcut formula, you can go ahead and repeat the calculation round by round, but $5,000 will be the end result.

Another way to state the result is that consumption rose $4,000 by the end of the process, while savings rose $1,000. Together, of course, they equal the increase in national income.

You may find it easier to think of consumption rather than savings. Remember that the marginal propensity to consume equals one minus the marginal propensity ton save. In symbols, MPC equals 1 − MPS. So if the multiplier is equal to 1/MPS, the multiplier is also 1/(1 − MPC). Notice that a lower marginal propensity to consume results in a lower multiplier. A lower multiplier means a lesser rise of national income. If the MPC is only 50 percent, the multiplier will drop to 2. A higher MPC results in a higher multiplier and a larger increase of national income. An MPC of 90 percent would mean a multiplier of 10.

Limitations of the Multiplier

Of course, the government multiplier is an artificial concept because it does not take into account all the possible complications involved. That is, the multiplier does not work so simply, and it has several limitations.

The first limitation or qualification is that the second, third, fourth, and further rounds of spending do not occur instantaneously. It takes time before income is respent for consumption. Long or varying lags make it much more difficult to speak of an exact multiplier.

Second, the multiplier explained here assumes that investment is a given and is not affected by changes in income. As was seen in earlier chapters, however, there is probably a close connection between investment and the previous change in national income. How exactly investment is affected by changes in income and in government spending is discussed in detail later in this and subsequent chapters.

The third major set of qualifications to the government multiplier arises from the fact that MPC does not remain constant, yet it is the very rock on which the multiplier theory is founded. It does not remain constant because, for one thing, consumption is actually influenced by many factors other than aggregate income. Chapter 42 went into detail about the impact on consumption of changes in the distribution of income and changes in consumer debt.

The marginal propensity to consume also varies because there are different leakages from the process at different times. For example, the effect of an increase in government spending on national income may be partly siphoned off by higher taxes or merely by automatic movements into higher tax brackets. Furthermore, it may happen that increased spending for foreign imports removes some portion of income from the domestic multiplier process. We repeat that the important effects of trade in the global economy are discussed later in this and subsequent chapters. The rising or falling national income also has important effects on international trade. These issues are so complex and important that they are treated briefly in this chapter and then later in two entire chapters on trade. For all of these reasons, MPC may change too often for any accurate prediction of the multiplier beyond a short period of only one or two rounds of the process.

The fourth and last qualification has to do with how the government spending is financed. If the government takes back through taxation the same amount that it spends, then there is no net addition to consumer spending. In that case, only the initial government spending is added to the economy, and the multiplier will be only 1. The national income will increase by the amount of the increase in government spending, but no more.

If increased government spending is financed through borrowing by sale of government bonds, the effect on the private economy depends on how the bondholders would have used the money had they not lent it to the government. If they had spent it all for consumption or investment anyway, then there would have been no net stimulation to the private economy. If they would have spent only a small percentage of it (which is often the case), then the government spending would have a very powerful net effect on the private economy.

Finally, government spending may be financed by printing money. This action is inflationary. It is disastrous if there is already some inflation.

THE INVESTMENT MULTIPLIER

The **investment multiplier** *measures the total effect on national income of an initial increase in investment.* If there is $1 billion of new investment in buildings and equipment, there will be thousands of new jobs. The new employees will use most of their new wages and salaries to buy consumer goods. Those from whom they buy will use some of the profits and wages to buy still more consumer goods. The effect on consumption is greater than the initial investment spending. The details and arithmetic are the same as for new government spending, discussed earlier.

THE EXPORT MULTIPLIER

To understand the **export multiplier**, suppose there are new exports because of increased foreign demand. Assume a demand for $1 billion of U.S. goods and services. The increased demand for American exports will result in a large amount of profits and employee compensation. Much of the profits and compensation are respent for more goods and services. Again, there is a multiplier affect, similar to that for government spending, *for it measures the total effect on national income as a result of a change in exports.*

SUMMARY

Government spending has both direct and indirect effects on national income. The direct effect is the amount of government spending, which counts as income to some people. The indirect effects occur through the additional consumer spending (and respending) the government stimulates. The indirect effects are called *multiplier effects.* The **government multiplier** *measures the total change in all spending resulting from a change in direct government spending.* Economists estimate it with the formula *multiplier = 1/MPS.* You can also calculate the multiplier with $1/(1 - MPC)$. This formula expresses a useful concept, but it is a very rough estimate because it leaves out many factors and limitations, discussed in the text.

The chapter also explained briefly that there is an investment multiplier. The investment multiplier is calculated the same way as the government multiplier. It measures the total effect on national income of an initial increase in investment.

There is also an export multiplier, resulting from an initial increase of purchases of U.S. exports by foreigners. The export multiplier is also calculated the same way. The export multiplier measures the total effect on national income of an increase in exports.

The government multiplier, investment multiplier, and export multiplier are all calculated with the same formula, so economists just call this concept *the multiplier*.

Appendix 44.1 discusses a related concept called the *accelerator*.

KEY TERMS

export multiplier   investment multiplier
government multiplier

REVIEW QUESTIONS

Explain how a given increase in spending by government, investors, or foreigners may cause a much larger (multiplied) effect on consumption and GDP.
1. Define the government multiplier. Explain how it calculates the total growth of national income that results.
2. Define the investment multiplier. Explain how it calculates the total growth of national income that results.
3. Define the import multiplier. Explain how it calculates the total growth of national income that results.

Discuss how the multiplied impact on the economic process may help push the economy up rapidly or help push the economy down rapidly.
4. Describe the process of how the multiplier impacts the economy. Explain each step of the process.
5. Explain how government would use knowledge of multiplier effect to stimulate the economy. Slow down the economy.

List and describe limitations of the multiplier.
6. What happens to the multiplier if people do not spend much (or any) of their additions to income? Explain.
7. What is the impact on the economy if the government has to borrow money to spend?

APPENDIX 44.1
THE ACCELERATOR

We saw in Chapter 43 that the basis for investment decision making is the expected profit from the investment. Yet it is difficult to estimate expected profits, so economists and businesspeople use crude substitutes to make rough guesses. A widely used index on which to base guesses of the profitability of an investment are changes in demand for output. The effect of changes in national output or income on investment is measured by the accelerator, discussed in this appendix.

LEARNING OBJECTIVES APPENDIX 44.1

After reading this appendix, you should be able to:

- Explain how a given increase in aggregate demand or national income may cause a much larger (multiplied) effect on investment.
- Discuss the impact of the accelerator model and how it may push the economy up rapidly or help push the economy down rapidly.
- List and describe limitations of the accelerator

THE ACCELERATOR MODEL

Notice that the multiplier process in the private economy moves from increased spending, in this case investment spending, to increased income. The accelerator process asks just the opposite question: Suppose consumer demand or national income increases.—What will be the effect on investment?

The **accelerator** is *the effect on investment of an increase in national income.* If national income rises slowly, investment is likely to rise slowly. If national income rises rapidly, investment will also rise rapidly. If national income stops rising and is constant, then new investment will be zero. The reason is that there is already enough capacity to produce for the present level of consumer demand. Finally, if national income declines rapidly, investment may even become negative. Capitalists will all try to get rid of their existing buildings and equipment. We learned in Chapter 43 that investment is a key variable in the economy, so the accelerator is used as one way to calculate future investment.

CALCULATION OF THE ACCELERATOR

Suppose that a machine worth $30,000 is needed in the production process to produce hats worth $10,000 in a year. A $3 investment in hat machines produces $1 of hats every year. Notice that the same machine can be used to produce hats for many, many years, so it is a very good investment in the long run. As long as the business wants to produce only $10,000 worth of hats, then only one machine is needed. Eventually, wear and tear will prevent the machine from producing more, but that takes many years, so it will be ignored here.

Now suppose the business believes that there will be a demand for another $20,000 of hats next year. How much investment will be needed in hat machines? Since each hat machine produces $1 of hats for every $3 of hat machines, it will take new machines worth $60,000 to produce hats worth an additional $20,000. In other words, the ratio of money spent on more machinery (hat machines) to more value of output (hats) is 3 to 1. This ratio of new investment to increased output is called the accelerator. In this case, the accelerator is 3.

Over many decades in the United States, the accelerator ratio for all industries has averaged about 3. If a business asks you how much to invest in new machinery (and buildings if necessary), then you ask how much increased demand the company expects in the future. You multiply the expected increase in demand by 3. Then tell the company to invest that amount in new machinery and buildings for its business.

LIMITATIONS OF THE ACCELERATOR

Of course, it is not that simple. It works only because we have made a whole bushel full of simplifying assumptions. First, your guess of $3 of machinery to $1 of new demand assumes that this particular firm has the same technology as the average for the whole economy. Second, it assumes that the same technological ratio will continue to hold in the future. An enormous amount of study would be required to tell you what to guess about these technological assumptions. You could then guess the future value of the accelerator. Moreover, to predict how much will be invested for every new dollar of demand, then the answer depends on a large number of nontechnological assumptions as well as the technological assumptions. We mention the most important ones here.

The issue for macroeconomics is not what one firm will invest but what the whole economy will invest. In the United States, the yearly output, at the moment, runs at about one-third of the value of all capital. It may therefore be assumed that roughly $3 worth of new capital is required to add $1 to national product.

The accelerator is not just a long-run technological relationship. It depends on many short-run factors and guesses by the business. First, even if the accelerator holds true for a ten-year period, does investment react exactly in that ratio to a change in demand over a two-month period or even over a whole year? In reality, there is a time lag between a change in demand and the making of new investment. The time lag between changed demand and new net investment varies among industries and even across phases of the business cycle.

A long and complicated process takes place before investment spending actually results from changes in demand. If demand improves, the corporate directors must come to expect increased future demand. But entrepreneurial expectations may also be affected by noneconomic psychological or political factors.

In the next step in the process, the directors must appropriate funds for investment purposes and perhaps arrange outside financing. After funding has been assured, engineers must design new factories or new machines. Even after the construction actually begins, it is some time before all the investment funds are fully spent. All of these time lags must be considered in trying to estimate the affect of new demand for goods and services.

Second, the accelerator theory assumes that each industry faced with higher demand is already running at full capacity. That is not true, however, in a depression or in the early stages of recovery from a recession. During a recession, there is much idle machinery and many empty, unused factories, allowing any new demand to be met easily without net investment. Thus, the accelerator is notably weaker whenever there is much unused capacity.

Third, the accelerator ignores the physical limitations on the amount of investment or disinvestments in any given period. No matter how much the demand increases at the peak of prosperity, the industries producing equipment must have enough excess capacity to produce the new equipment that is demanded.

Similarly, falling demand in a recession may indicate disinvestment. But the whole economy can disinvest (or reduce its capital stock) in one year only to the extent of the depreciation of capital in that year. In other words, capital can be reduced in the economy as a whole only as fast as it wears out or becomes obsolete.

Fourth, the simple accelerator ignores the effects of changes in the relative levels of prices and costs. At the peak of prosperity, the great demand on the capacity of the capital goods industries may raise the cost of capital goods and thus weaken investment incentives. The level of wage and salary costs also changes systematically over the cycle.

Moreover, a firm needs large amounts of financing for investment. The corporation will first try to depend on reinvestment of its own profits. If there is not enough profit, then the firm must borrow in the capital market and must face higher interest costs. On the other side, prices show long-run as well as cyclical fluctuations, which affect expected revenues. These costs and price changes, which are summarized by profit changes, affect investment as much as or more than the simple technological relation between new investment and the amount of output demanded. Therefore, the profits are a better predictor of new investment than amount demanded.

Finally, the accelerator only tries to explain net investment. Since replacement is not automatic, it is gross investment that must be explained. Replacement investment, in addition to net investment, is sometimes speeded up and sometimes postponed.

IMPORTANCE OF THE ACCELERATOR

Even after considering all of its limitations, the accelerator still has an important grain of truth. As long as demand is only as high as a firm's productive capacity, the firm can continue at that level without any new investment. When demand increases beyond its capacity, a firm can expand only by more investment in equipment and buildings. Similarly, in the aggregate economy, if demand remains unchanged for a long time, then there is no need for investing in more equipment and buildings. Net investment in the whole economy happens only when an increase in demand is expected.

To the extent that the accelerator does state a correct relationship between increased demand and investment, it helps solve some mysteries. For one thing, why does investment fluctuate up and down more than consumption? Shouldn't investment move in lock step with consumer demand? The accelerator says No! The accelerator says that no matter how high consumer spending is, if it does not change and expand further, there will be no new investment.

Thus, investment rises and falls not with the level of demand but with the *change* in demand. Changes in demand must always rise and fall by a greater percentage than demand itself. Therefore, to the extent that the accelerator is correct, it explains why investment fluctuates more than consumer demand.

CONCLUSIONS ON ACCELERATOR

The accelerator principle says net investment is related to the change in output demanded during the business cycle. Although this is roughly true, several factors indicate that there is no single, reliable, fixed figure for the accelerator ratio. First, there is a long and varying time lag from the first indication of increased demand for output to the actual investment expenditure. Second, in a recession, the accelerator is greatly weakened. Third, changes in investment cannot be as extreme as predicted because there is an upper limit given by the capacity of the capital goods industries. Fourth, the simple accelerator is modified by changes in the relationship of prices and costs because these changes affect profits and, consequently, investments. Nevertheless, the accelerator does contain a large grain of truth and emphasizes the basic fact that new capital goods are built to meet new demand. It also explains, in part, why investment fluctuates so much more violently than consumer demand. It is related not to the level of demand, but to the change in demand.

KEY TERM FOR APPENDIX 44.1

accelerator

REVIEW QUESTIONS FOR APPENDIX 44.1

Explain how a given increase in aggregate demand or national income may cause a much larger (multiplied) effect on investment.

1. Describe what effect changing national income has on investment. Why is the impact on investment larger than the change in income?
2. How does a firm decide how much money to invest in future production?

Discuss the impact of the accelerator and how it may push the economy up rapidly or help push the economy down rapidly.

3. If businesses are optimistic, how will that affect investment decisions? How will investment decisions impact output?
4. If there is a sudden drop in investment, what will happen to other macroeconomic measures of the economy?

List and describe limitations of the accelerator.

5. State some of the simplifying assumptions used to develop the multiplier. Explain what happens if the assumptions do not hold?
6. Explain how access to financing might impact investment and the accelerator.

CHAPTER 45

$$\overline{}$$

Business Cycles and Unemployment

This chapter briefly compares and contrasts the different views of conservative and progressive economists on the business cycle.

LEARNING OBJECTIVES

After reading this chapter, you should be able to:

- Compare and contrast the conservative and progressive views of the business cycle, particularly the nature and costs of unemployment.
- Explain why conservative economists argue that, left alone, the economy will adjust back to full-employment equilibrium.
- Explain why progressive economists argue that business cycles are driven by the internal workings of capitalism.

CONSERVATIVE BUSINESS CYCLE THEORIES

Until the 1930s, the main body of economic theory did not try to explain, but rather tried to explain away, the business cycle. It was argued that there was little or no general unemployment that would not be fixed by wages adjusting so that the quantity supplied and quantity demanded of labor were in equilibrium. In the 1920s, many economists claimed that recessions were gone forever. Then came the Great Depression, and it lasted ten years. In the 1960s, many conservative economists repeated that "the business cycle has disappeared." Again, in the 1980s, many conservative economists argued that at the equilibrium wage, everyone who wanted a job would be hired. Notice also that in the 1990s, some economists talked of a "new economy" such that business cycles and recessions had disappeared forever, and along came the recession of 2001 and the stock market crash. There was no more talk of the end of business cycles, and the real business cycle theory gained ground among conservative economists.

Conservative economists argued that the Great Depression, like all recessions and depressions, was caused by outside shocks to the system, including government mistakes. If the government does not interfere, the economy soon restores itself to equilibrium after a shock. Economists stressed the role of people's expectations of profits and employment. **Expectations**, or *what*

532

people think will happen, affect how markets behave. In the strongest form of this theory, all the relevant information known to buyers and sellers is reflected in the prices in the labor, product, and financial markets. This price then clears each market efficiently, so there are no shortages or excesses of quantity demanded or quantity supplied in the market for any length of time. Markets are highly competitive, and all prices are flexible. It follows that "the economy is self-regulating, that full employment is the norm, and that any government intervention into the economy will be counterproductive" (Peterson, 1987, p. 71).

Some neoclassical economists incorporated Say's law and dismissed all unemployment as voluntary. A leading economist of this school, Lucas, writes that "to explain why people allocate time to . . . unemployment, we need to know why they prefer it to all other activities" (1986, p. 38). All unemployment is by preference, and some people prefer to work and eat well, while others prefer to be idle and eat less.

These neoclassical theorists are often called equilibrium theorists because their whole approach is based on the notion that all prices are flexible. If there are any changes in conditions or external shocks to the economy, markets will rapidly adjust to a new equilibrium. In this theory, only the tools of equilibrium analysis (described in Chapter 39) are needed to understand business cycles. Lucas develops a theory of the business cycle only in the sense that it generates movements in aggregate output. These movements in aggregate output, however, are created by outside shocks, not by internal features of capitalism. "The mechanism generating these movements involves unsystematic monetary-fiscal shocks . . ." (Lucas, 1975, p. 1140). According to Lucas, the initiating cause of cycles is not the capitalist system but government mistakes. Government apparently does not have rational thought or expectations. Government does not learn from its mistakes but repeats its mistakes time after time.

Since Lucas, conservative economists argued mainly over what kind of outside shocks most commonly affect the economy. Some of them see these shocks as mainly monetary and fiscal mistakes by government. Others argue that war, bad harvests, unanticipated changes in tastes, or unanticipated changes in technology may disrupt supplies or disrupt demand. Many economists mean by an external shock such things as the large increases in oil prices in the 1970s and in 2006, which adversely affect the whole economy.

The **real business cycle theory** *argues that shocks such as new technology or higher foreign oil prices are based on real events that impact production of goods and services.* Production of goods and services affects the number of people employed by businesses. The real business cycle theory has a different view of outside shocks from most previous business cycle theories. The real business cycle theory claims that the most important shocks are not from government policy mistakes. Rather, the most important outside shocks to the economy come from technological change. Certainly such shocks as wars and bad weather do affect the economy. Such shocks, however, do not always coincide with the major swings in the economy. When there is an outside shock to the economy, it has only a minor effect when it goes contrary to a healthy expansion.

Many real business cycle theorists argue that "business cycle phenomena . . . are perfectly consistent with ideal economic efficiency" (Long and Plosser, 1983, p. 43). According to critics, it is a strange definition of efficiency that would allow us to call an economy in the midst of a recession or depression while prices adjust the economy back to full-employment equilibrium an efficient economy. In fact, some recessions occur in the absence of any apparent outside shock. Therefore, we examine the progressive theory that shows how the internal operation of the capitalist economy might produce a business cycle even in the absence of external shocks.

PROGRESSIVE CYCLE THEORIES

Progressive economists believe that outside shocks to the economy, except for major wars, play a relatively small role. The performance of the American capitalist economy is determined mainly by the internal dynamics of American and global capitalism. In fact, when we remember that the economic system is now global in nature to a very large degree, there are really very few events that are truly "outside" the global economic system.

The start of the progressive story describing how the economic system of capitalism generates business cycles is the rate of profit for businesses. The accomplishments and tensions in the economy are summed up in the rate of profit. Rising profits make business owners optimistic and create a positive outlook or expectation for the future. When profits begin to rise and expectations for the future are positive, investment follows along like a faithful puppy. After all, investment that leads to expanding production should lead to higher profits!

Profits provide funds for new investment. High profits provide a strong basis for borrowing from banks for investment purposes. Therefore, investment spending usually follows profits upward. About six to nine months after profit moves upward, investment also moves upward. When profits decline, investment also declines. Investment follows profits downward about six to nine months after profit starts declining.

While investment faithfully follows profits, investment itself plays the lead dog in a dog sled team that pulls the economy across a rough and icy surface. When business investment goes up or down, the economy slides up or down with it. While investment determines economic growth or decline, profits determine investment. When business sees a profitable opportunity, it expands its equipment, buildings, and labor force. When the outlook for profits is bad, business drastically lowers its investment in new buildings and equipment and reduces its labor force. When we understand the ups and downs of profits, we understand the ups and downs of investment and the whole economy. Recall the definition of profits:

$$\text{Profits} = \text{Revenue} - \text{Costs}$$

For an individual business, revenue minus costs tells the whole story. For the whole economy, however, how exactly do we define the strange animals called aggregate revenue and aggregate costs? As we saw in Chapter 37, in the aggregate, the revenues of business are the expenditures of:

$$\text{Revenue} = \text{Spending by consumers} + \text{Investors} + \text{Government} + \text{Foreigners}$$

Those four sources of revenue were clearly defined in previous chapters. Now what about the cost side? The costs of production generate income for the providers of input into production. For the aggregate economy, the costs of all business are:

$$\text{Costs} = \text{Payments to employees} + \text{To foreigners} +$$
$$\text{Government taxes} + \text{Interest to lenders} + \text{Miscellaneous}$$

The mysterious term *miscellaneous* covers many smaller costs and a few larger costs that have little cyclical movement.

Among the elements of aggregate revenue and aggregate costs, progressive economists differ among themselves over how important each element is in telling the story of cyclical recessions. One earlier group of economists focused exclusively on the lack of consumer demand in causing declines. Their theory, called the underconsumption theory, is detailed in Appendix 45.1. Another group of progressive economists concentrated solely on how too much investment may cause high costs and cause prices to rise. They examined the costs of employee compensation, high interest costs, and high costs of imported raw materials. Their theory, called the overinvestment theory, is detailed in Appendix 45.2. Most progressive economists today include both revenue (demand) elements as well as cost (supply) elements in their stories. They continue to differ on the importance of each element.

Here we examine aggregate revenue and cost behavior in several stages. We begin with the first stage of expansion, when all is going well. Then we look at the problems that emerge in the later stages of expansion up to the peak of profit. We consider why aggregate profit begins its initial decline. We trace how the decline in profits leads to recession. Finally, we look at the recession and how profits may eventually recover, leading to a new expansion.

FACTS ABOUT THE KEY VARIABLES

Chapters 42 and 43 looked at how consumer spending, investment spending, wages and salaries, consumer and investor credit, and profits move over the cycle. All of these variables were found to be pro-cyclical; that is, they move up with expansion and down with depression. However, they do not stay in the same ratio or proportion to each other. Consumption, as well as wages and salaries, move up and down more slowly than national income. Investment and profits move up and down faster than national income. The ratio of consumption to income (the propensity to consume) and the ratio of wages and salaries to income (the labor share) move down in business expansions and up in contractions (all data for average of last five cycles). We also saw that the ratio of consumer debt to consumer income rises in expansions and falls in contractions. Moreover, the ratio of corporate debt to corporate revenue rises in expansions and falls in contractions.

We shall see in Chapter 52 that both consumer prices and raw material prices rise in expansions and fall in contractions, but consumer prices rise and fall slowly, while raw material prices rise and fall rapidly. Thus, the ratio of raw material prices to consumer prices is pro-cyclical.

We now use these pieces of fact like a jigsaw puzzle to explain the four phases of the business cycle: recovery, prosperity, crisis, and recession.

Recovery

The first period of expansion from a recession is called **recovery**. What is happening to profits in the recovery? Revenue is rising rapidly from consumer spending and more investment spending. At the same time, costs remain low. Wages and salaries rise very, very slowly at first because of continued unemployment. Interest rates remain low as people and businesses are cautious about taking on more debt. There are still stacks of unused raw materials, so their price remains low. Since revenue is rising rapidly while costs are still low, business profit rises.

The recovery begins with income and profits expanding. The increasing employee incomes lead to more consumer spending. The increasing profits lead to business expansion of production in existing facilities and investment in new facilities.

PROSPERITY

The last half of the expansion is commonly called **prosperity** because *business is prosperous and employees' income is rising*. Once the process of recovery begins, it tends to continue. Why? It continues because every increase in consumer demand causes business to do more investment in buildings and equipment. The investment in buildings and equipment means that more employees are hired to produce the buildings and equipment. The new employees mean an increase in wages and salaries. The increased wages and salaries are used to buy more consumer goods and services. Thus, there is a tendency toward an ever-expanding production because consumption leads to investment and investment leads to still more consumption. This upward process of expansion due to the interaction between consumer spending and investor spending has sometimes been called a virtuous circle. It is discussed more fully in the language of the multiplier and accelerator in Appendix 45.3.

Crisis

Why should this happy state of affairs—high profits leading to high investment and more jobs leading to more consumption and more income—ever end? To make the problem more mysterious, a casual glance at what happens in an economic expansion makes it look like all goes smoothly until the peak is reached and a decline begins. *The decline of profits*, or **crisis**, seems to come out of nowhere. For the entire expansion, employee compensation rises, so consumption rises. For the entire expansion, profit expectations are good enough that investment in equipment and buildings continues right to the cycle peak. What is the problem? A closer examination reveals that tensions and imbalances grow in the economy throughout the whole last half of the expansion.

Problems of Spending Leading to the Crisis

The first problem is that employees' compensation remains relatively low. While profits soar, employee compensation tends to stagnate. For example, during the present expansion in 2004, the income (mostly based on profits) of the top 1 percent of Americans rose by 12.5 percent. The income of the bottom 99 percent of Americans, however, mostly based on wages and salaries, rose by only 1.5 percent (see Paul Krugman, 2006). That imbalance is a big problem because employee compensation in the form of wages and salaries is the largest source of buying power for consumer spending. As employees' wages and salaries rise far more slowly than growth of output, the portion of output that can easily be sold declines. Unsold inventories of goods held by business get much larger.

Wages and salaries are not the only source of consumer spending. Consumers also borrow and go into debt to buy more goods and services. We saw in Chapter 42 that consumer debt rose throughout the average expansion. In fact, consumer debt rose faster than consumer income. This expanding share of debt is an ever-greater burden. Moreover, consumer interest rates also rise during the expansion, so the burden is made still greater. As long as consumers are confident about their jobs and expect higher wages and salaries, they are willing to risk the burden of higher debt.

The increasing credit actually helps the expansion continue. Therefore, this rising cost to consumers is no problem for business long as consumers are willing to spend more and more. We shall see that in the current expansion, wages and salaries have been largely stagnant, but employees have been able to spend more and more on consumption by going deeper into debt. The rise of consumer debt helps business as long as consumers keep borrowing and spending more.

In addition to consumer and corporate debt, spending is also affected by financial markets. In the late 1990s, the stock market rose spectacularly, so people thought it was a road to riches that would last year after year. The stock market rise made many consumers very optimistic about their chance for riches. Therefore, they invested all of their savings in the stock market, spent more than their incomes on consumer goods, and went deeply in debt. Corporations were also very optimistic, spent a lot on investment, and went deeply into debt. However, the stock market crashed from 2001 to 2003, so many people and businesses found themselves to be much poorer. Some small investors lost all of their savings. The existence of the stock market tends to exaggerate the boom but also exaggerates the bust.

As a result of all of these tendencies—a lower share of employee compensation in the national income and the rise of consumer debt—consumer spending rises slower and slower in the expansion. This decreased spending limits demand for goods and services. Therefore, it limits profits. Historical experience shows that there is no magic number at which debt is so high as to stop consumption. In the present expansion, consumer debt is higher than their income, but consumption goes on growing somewhat. The problem for business is that when a recession starts, people suddenly quit increasing their consumption. Many consumers may not be able to pay back loans. Because loans fail to be paid back, many corporations and financial institutions are in trouble.

Yet profits depend not only on consumer spending but also on the cost per unit in production. What happens with costs in the expansion?

The Role of Costs Leading up to the Crisis

The data show that at the same time that consumer spending is rising more slowly, some types of costs are rising faster than business output. What are these costs? The largest single cost of production is employee compensation. Although employee compensation rises in every expansion, it rises more slowly than production until the peak of profits is reached. Therefore, the slow rise in employee compensation is not a cost that usually harms profits in the expansion. Let's examine some other costs.

American firms buy most of their raw materials from abroad. As America and other countries produce more, the demand for raw materials rises rapidly. It often takes a great deal of time to increase production of raw materials. As demand increases rapidly and production of raw resources increases slowly, the prices of raw materials must rise. In fact, prices of imported raw materials rise on the average far more than consumer good prices.

In the expansion in 2006, there was an enormous rise in the cost of oil. When the cost of oil and gas rises, it increases business costs in many areas. For example, higher prices of fuel means it costs a great deal more per passenger to move an airplane across the country. The higher fuel cost has pushed several airlines close to bankruptcy or into bankruptcy. Rising raw material prices across the economy mean lower rates of profit, even with the same consumer demand. When consumer demand is limited and costs are rising, profit is squeezed.

Another cost problem for business is the rise of business debt. At the beginning of an expansion, profits are rising, so businesses are optimistic about the future. They borrow large amounts of money to make new investments. Over the course of the expansion, we see that the percentage of business debt to business income keeps rising. Therefore, paying the interest on their debt becomes an increasingly higher cost. Finally, interest rates usually rise a little faster than production. Higher interest rates mean that it costs increasingly more in interest payments on borrowed money. It costs business more to pay the interest on new business debts used to expand production.

When we add together the problems of limited demand and rising costs, it is clear why profit eventually declines and brings the expansion to an end. It was shown earlier that there is slower growth of consumer demand, even with rising consumer credit.

At the same time, the prices of raw materials and the interest cost of borrowing capital are rising faster than production. The result is a **profit squeeze** toward the end of expansion. This

Figure 45.1   **Profit Squeeze at Cycle Peak**

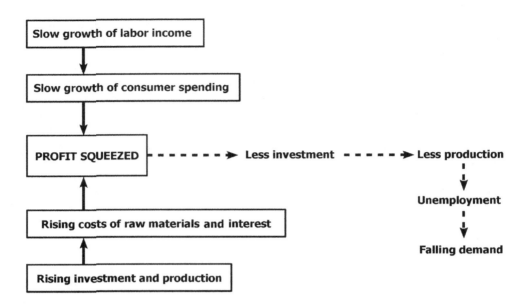

profit squeeze resembles a nut caught in a nutcracker. *The declining growth of demand and the rising growth of costs create the nutcracker effect that lowers profits. The lower profits lead to less investment.* This nutcracker effect is illustrated in Figure 45.1.

Figure 45.1 highlights the slower growth of labor income leads to slower growth of consumer spending. The reduced growth limits the amount of business revenue. At the same time in the late expansion, the figure shows rising investment and rising production lead to greater demand for raw materials and greater demand for borrowed capital. It follows that the costs of interest and raw material costs per unit rise.

The result of the profit squeeze or nutcracker effect is that aggregate business profits fall. When business profits begin to fall, businesses start to plan for less investment in equipment and buildings. Therefore, usually about six to nine months after profits begin to fall, business investment falls. Falling investment means fewer new jobs and more unemployment, less new equipment, and fewer new buildings. Lower demand for labor means lower wages and salaries as well as fewer jobs. Less labor income means less consumer spending. A recession is underway.

RECESSION

We have described the first part of the business contraction, which is called a crisis. The *crisis results in a vicious circle downward* during the **recession**. Falling consumer demand causes less investment. Falling investment causes less employment and less income. The lower income means less consumption, which causes a further decline in investment. This vicious downward circle is described in more detail in Appendix 45.3. The crisis turns into a broad recession. How far the decline will go depends not only on the business factors stated so far but also on the financial situation. How much debt do consumers have? If consumers have little debt, they can easily borrow more and continue to spend near their old levels. However, if most consumers have large debts, it is much more difficult to borrow more. In that case, consumer spending falls more rapidly.

How much debt do corporations have? Many corporations are very optimistic in the expansion, so they take on a heavy debt in order to expand. But corporations, like individuals, must eventually pay back their debts. In the recession, corporations try to reduce their debt. Rather than expanding, they wish to retrench and have a lower investment. But there is no one to take on corporate debt in a recession, so eventually some of them find that they cannot pay back their debt to the banks on time. Then these corporations go bankrupt. The same process happens with millions of individuals. They cannot pay their debts, so they go bankrupt.

Suppose a bank has many business customers and thousands of individual customers. If the businesses and individuals cannot pay back their debts and must go bankrupt, the bank is in trouble. The bank may take over from the bankrupt borrowers their factories or homes or automobiles or refrigerators. In a recession, all of this property is useless junk that cannot be sold anywhere near the prices at which it was bought. Since the bank has worthless assets, it has no stream of revenue. Then the bank cannot pay its own debts, and it too will go bankrupt. Widespread failure and bankruptcy makes the recession much deeper than it otherwise would have been.

BEGINNINGS OF RECOVERY

Even though the situation at the bottom of a recession looks terrible, profit prospects for the future may begin to improve. Wages and salaries decline, but they do not fall as fast as production. Therefore, consumers eventually are able to buy a larger percentage of the declining product. In addition, some costs fall rapidly. Interest rates remain high for a little while in the immediate crisis, but eventually they fall swiftly. Raw material prices stay up for a little while, then they fall drastically.

Eventually, most recessions tend to end as many trends reverse themselves. It is worth remembering that the Great Depression in the United States took ten years to reverse itself. The Japanese economy did not fully recover from the recession of 1991 for at least ten years. Usually, however, by the end of the recession, demand from consumers is falling very slowly. At the same time, costs are falling much faster. Finally, as costs fall faster than revenue, profits stop falling. Profits become less negative and may even be a little positive. The better outlook for profits stimulates investment and production, so a new **recovery** begins.

HUMAN IMPACT OF THE BUSINESS CYCLE

If you read most studies of the business cycle, they are abstract discussions of neat curves showing production and investment. The most important human fact of the business cycle is that there are often times of large-scale unemployment. Often, unemployed people feel useless in our present society. They do not realize that unemployment is created by the economic system. They think wrongly that their being fired is their own fault. In fact, the data on the unemployed (mentioned in Chapter 36) show that unemployment is one cause of divorce, mental health problems, feelings of helplessness, crime, and suicide. Therefore, the human impact of the business cycle is large and causes much suffering.

Chapters 52 to 56 show how international trade, international investment, and international finance shape the behavior of the business cycle in the global economy, generally making it worse than it would be if countries were isolated and their economies independent.

A STRANGE RECOVERY

The present recovery (2001–2007) has developed strangely in some ways compared with previous expansions. It turns out that these are just extremes of trends that have been going on for some time. (Data and an explanation are in Bivens and Weller, 2006.)

First, there has been very slow growth of employment. For the first four years, employment fell and never returned to its previous peak until 2004. This trend is contrary to the usual behavior of employment, which generally rises rapidly in early expansion. This behavior continues a long-run trend toward slower employment growth. This trend has included a decades-long decline in employment in manufacturing.

Second, real wages and salaries stagnated in the first four years of this expansion (2001–2005). Slow growth of real wages and salaries in the first half of expansion is usual, but lack of growth above the previous peak is *not* usual. In fact, real wages and salaries have been remarkably stagnant in the last three decades. In spite of slow growth of employment, production has risen at a rate that is average or higher than average for expansions. Productivity of labor has also grown. Since wages and salaries have been stagnant while production and productivity have grown, profits have soared at a high rate of growth.

Profits grew faster than wages and salaries not only because of the high productivity and the slow growth of employee compensation but also because much productive activity has been sent overseas (outsourced). In spite of the very slow growth of wages and salaries, consumer spending has grown enough to buy the aggregate amount supplied in the last five years. How could consumer spending grow much faster than wages and salaries, since these are the main source of consumer demand?

The answer is that middle-class employees, as well as lower paid employees and the poor, have gone more deeply into debt. This trend is very different from the average American expansion. In the usual expansion, the growth of their income has allowed most people to consume more and also to save more. In this case, the stagnant wages and salaries forced people into greater debt.

Some rising debt is usual in expansions for people with lower income. In this case, however, wages and salaries had such tiny growth that savings per year did not grow even for the middle-income group. Instead, there has been such a large increase in debt that all persons combined had an actual decrease in personal saving or increase in debt during one whole quarter of 2005 and one whole quarter of 2006. Negative savings had never happened in an expansion since our records existed. There was, of course, negative personal savings at the bottom of the Great Depression in the 1930s, but debt in the Great Depression is far from the same as negative aggregate savings in an expansion in the twenty-first century.

Although corporate profits have reached record highs, there has been relatively little new investment in equipment and buildings by historical standards for the first five years of an expansion. Rather, much of corporate profits has gone into speculation, such as purchase of real estate or buying back their own stock. The trends that have led to this new situation are documented and explained in Chapter 46.

AN OVERSIMPLIFIED STORY

The business cycle involves all aspects of the global economy, so it is complex. This chapter tells a fairly simple story about the private sector of the American economy. But that story is over-simplified, so we need to supplement it. Chapter 46 shows how the American economy grows through a series of business cycle ups and downs, but it does grow. Chapter 47 shows that ours is an economy based on vast use of credit, which exaggerates the business cycle. Chapters 48 to 51 show how government spending, taxation, and monetary policy have a very strong effect on the business cycle, modifying it in both positive and negative ways at various times.

SUMMARY

Business cycles occur in all countries with capitalist institutions. The cycle goes through phases of expansion, including recovery and prosperity, followed by phases of contraction, including crisis and recession. In the conservative view, the cause of crises and contractions is outside shocks. Without these outside shocks, the system would always expand smoothly.

Progressive economists claim business cycles are the result of the internal workings of capitalism. In the prosperity period of every business expansion, all appears well with rising profits, rising wages and salaries, and rising consumption and investment. But problems develop below the smooth surface. Employee compensation rises more slowly than production, which causes consumption to rise more slowly than the commodities for sale. At the same time that demand is slowing, costs of interest and of raw materials from abroad are rising. Thus profit is squeezed from both sides, like a nut in nutcracker. The decline in profits leads to a decline in investment, setting off a business contraction. In the recession, eventually the trends reverse themselves. Profits bottom out, with an expectation that profits will rise. This sets off a recovery. During the recession, millions of people are unemployed and miserable. Even by the end of expansion, there is still some unemployment.

SUGGESTED READINGS

For a thorough explanation of the progressive view, look at Howard Sherman, *The Business Cycle: Growth and Crisis in Capitalism*. A more recent statement of the progressive view is Howard Sherman, "Institutions and the Business Cycle" (2003).

KEY TERMS

crisis
expectations
profit squeeze
prosperity

real business cycle theory
recession
recovery

REVIEW QUESTIONS

Compare and contrast the conservative and progressive views of the business cycle, particularly the nature and costs of unemployment.

1. What are sources of disturbances to the economy according to conservative economists? Why is there unemployment?
2. What are sources of disturbances to the economy according to progressive economists?
3. What are the differences in the explanations by conservative and progressive economists?

Explain why conservative economists argue that, left alone, the economy will adjust back to full-employment equilibrium.

    4. According to conservative economists, how will the economy recover from a shock?

    5. Describe the process of recovery used by progressive economists.

Explain why progressive economists argue that business cycles are driven by the internal workings of capitalism.

    6. Identify the "internal process" that drives the economy from boom to bust and back again.

    7. Describe in detail each step of the process in #6.

    8. What are the two sides that squeeze profits near the end of expansion? Explain how the "squeeze" on profits happens.

    9. List the components of revenue and explain how revenue behaves over the business cycle. What leads to crisis? What leads to recovery?

  10. List the components of costs and explain how costs behave over the business cycle. What leads to crisis? What leads to recovery?

APPENDIX 45.1
UNDERCONSUMPTIONISM:
A DEMAND-SIDE VIEW

One group of economists used to argue that lack of effective demand for consumer goods is the most important problem or even the sole problem causing business downturns. They are called underconsumptionists. This appendix presents a brief overview of the underconsumption theory.

LEARNING OBJECTIVE FOR APPENDIX 45.1

After reading this appendix, you should be able to:

- Describe the underconsumptionist explanation of recessions and some critiques of the theory.

UNDERCONSUMPTIONISM

In addition to blaming lack of effective demand for consumer goods, underconsumptionist theorists emphasize that the problem begins in the capitalist production process (e.g., Paul Sweezy, [1942/1970]). In the production process, employees are exploited; that is, their wages and salaries are less than the product they produce. Therefore, employees cannot buy all that is produced. In addition, during an expansion, the share of labor always declines. As a result, the gap between employee income and the value of consumer goods widens. That gap leads to a cyclical downturn and unemployment.

    Figure 45.2 explains the recession step by step from the underconsumptionist view. In every expansion, employee compensation grows very slowly compared with output. Therefore, the growth

Figure 45.2 **Underconsumption at Cycle Peak**

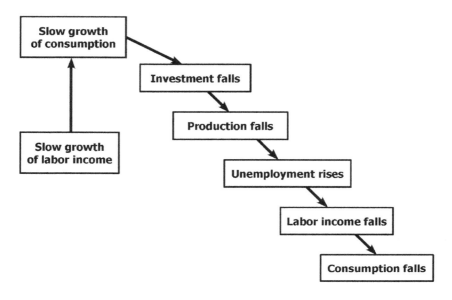

of consumption slows down. Slower growth of consumption leads to a decline in investment. If investors see slowing consumer demand, they see no reason to increase production facilities. The lower investment means less labor spent constructing new equipment and buildings. Less work means less production and less employment. With fewer people employed, there is naturally less income paid out. Finally, less income means less consumer spending. Unchecked, the process continues in a vicious circle.

The most important criticism of the underconsumptionists is that they pay no attention to costs. For example, employee compensation is an important source of consumer demand, but it is also an important cost. Every capitalist firm wants to hold its wages and salaries as low as possible. However, every capitalist firm also wants people to get high wages and salaries from other firms so consumers will have buying power. Profits may be hurt by low employee compensation in terms of consumer buying power. Low compensation, however, also means low costs of production, which helps profits. This makes the problem more complex than underconsumptionists make it sound.

REVIEW QUESTIONS FOR APPENDIX 45.1

Describe the underconsumptionist explanation of recessions and some critiques of the theory.

1. What is "underconsumption"? What causes it? How does it impact the macroeconomy?
2. What is the main criticism of underconsumption?

APPENDIX 45.2
SUPPLY-SIDE PROBLEMS:
HIGH WAGES, INTEREST, AND RAW MATERIAL

Another group of progressive economists have a version of the overinvestment theory (e.g., Boddy and Crotty, 1975). This appendix provides a brief explanation of the overinvestment theory.

LEARNING OBJECTIVE FOR APPENDIX 45.2

After reading this appendix, you should be able to:

* Describe the overinvestment theory of recessions and some critiques of the theory.

OVERINVESTMENT AND HIGH COSTS

The overinvestment theory argues that rapidly rising investment leads to a greater demand for many supplies. Those concerned with high wages costs contend that the most important cost is the cost of labor. During expansion, rising employment gives workers more bargaining power. They use their bargaining power to get higher wages and a slower pace of work. "Knowledgeable observers of the labor scene have pointed directly to an increasingly obstreperous labor force as an influence on the decline in productivity during expansion" (Boddy and Crotty, 1975, p. 8). Again, the analysis begins with workers being exploited, but now the problem is seen as a rising wage share (or falling exploitation).The higher costs and falling productivity due to the slower pace of work must lead to lower profits and a recession. Other economists with an overinvestment outlook claim that recessions are caused in part by rising interest rates and rising costs of other raw materials.

The view that recession is caused by too much investment is depicted in Figure 45.3.

According to Figure 45.3, rising aggregate demand leads to rapidly rising investment. The rapid investment in new equipment and buildings leads to hiring more employees, borrowing more money for expansion, and buying more raw materials at higher prices. The rising cost of production leads to low profit margins. Finally, a decline in investment occurs, with less production and less employment. The recession has begun.

The notion that high wages and salaries cause low profits is just as simplistic and one-sided as the underconsumption theory. A theory of lack of consumer demand ignores the fact very low costs of production might lead to more expectation of profits. A theory of rising wage and salary costs ignores the fact that more wages and salaries mean more demand. Greater consumer demand produces higher profits, though higher wages and salaries do mean high cost. Both sides of the problem are important in understanding profits.

DEBATE BETWEEN UNDERCONSUMPTION AND WAGE COST

Most modern progressive economists include both aspects of profit determination. On the one hand, limited consumption, because of limited wages and salaries, is a negative factor on profits at the peak of profits near the end of expansion. On the other hand, costs from rising wages and salaries, rising raw materials, and rising interest on consumer and business debt also are factors affecting business profits. The debate over the importance of different factors in squeezing profits has become very complex and cannot be detailed here.

Figure 45.3   **Overinvestment at Cycle Peak**

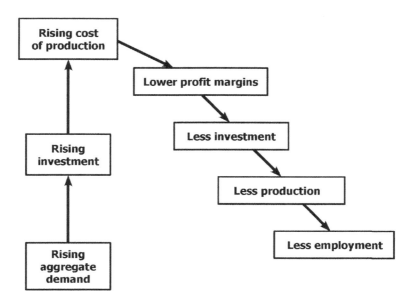

REVIEW QUESTIONS FOR APPENDIX 45.2

Describe the overinvestment theory of recessions and some critiques of the theory.
1.   What is "overinvestment"? What causes it? How does it impact the macroeconomy?
2.   What are the main criticisms of overinvestment?

APPENDIX 45.3
VIRTUOUS CIRCLES AND VICIOUS CIRCLES

This appendix discusses the virtuous circle of the prosperity period and the vicious circle of the recession period.

LEARNING OBJECTIVE FOR APPENDIX 45.3

After reading this appendix, you should be able to:

• Describe the notion of virtuous and vicious circles in the economy and why they happen.

RECOVERY AND THE VIRTUOUS CIRCLE

As shown in Chapter 44, the multiplier process acting on increased income causes a big increase in consumer spending. Once there is more consumer spending, the accelerator process causes a lot more investment. If you have forgotten the terms multiplier and accelerator, just remember two main points. According to the multiplier, investment leads to even more consumer spending than the initial investment. According to the accelerator model, increased consumer spending leads to still more investment.

In each business expansion, there is considerable momentum to continue upward after it begins. Why is that? One way to look at it is through the multiplier process and the accelerator process studied in the previous chapter. The investment multiplier measures how much is the total effect of new investment on consumer demand. New investment in buildings and equipment means more money paid out to employees in building construction and manufacturing of new equipment. That money is spent mainly for consumption. Those who receive it as profits or employee compensation then respend it for more consumer goods. Individuals consume some of their income and save some. That ratio between consumption and savings determines whether there is a high multiplier effect or a low multiplier effect. When we take into consideration all of the respending of the initial income from the investment spending, it is possible to calculate the total effect on consumption.

The process goes like this:

New investment → Multiplied respending→ More consumer demand

Remember that the accelerator asks the opposite question: How much new investment will result from an increase in consumer demand? The process goes like this:

Change in consumer demand → Accelerator process→ New investment

Thus, the investment multiplier tells us what effect investment has on consumption, while the accelerator tells us what affect a change in consumption has on investment.

In ordinary English, there is a virtuous circle in which one increase leads to another to keep the expansion going. People buy more television sets. There is then more investment to build more factories to make television sets. The investment in factories and equipment and eventually the new production of more television sets leads to more employment. The new employees are paid wages and salaries. They buy more goods and services. The virtuous circle continues.

RECESSION AND THE VICIOUS CIRCLE

The economic crisis, which ends the virtuous circle of expansion, results in a vicious circle downward during the recession. According to the accelerator, falling consumer demand leads to falling investment. According to the multiplier, falling investment leads to an even larger decline in consumer spending. Wages and salaries are falling, so downward pressure is placed on consumer demand. Costs also fall, but at first the costs do not fall as fast as demand falls. The result is a continuing decline in profits and further downward pressure on investment. This vicious circle continues downward until other tendencies stop it and a recovery begins.

REVIEW QUESTIONS FOR APPENDIX 45.3

Describe the notion of virtuous and vicious circles in the economy and why they happen.

1. What is a "virtuous circle"? What is the process that creates a virtuous circle?
2. What is a "vicious circle"? What is the process that creates a vicious circle?

CHAPTER 46

Growth and Waste

This chapter examines growth in the industrialized capitalist countries, leaving growth in less developed countries to Chapter 56 and global growth to Chapter 54. Growth in the economy is usually measured by changes in real gross domestic product (GDP). An economy is growing if real GDP is increasing from one time period to the next. What causes real GDP to increase? What enables the production of more and more goods and services? This chapter first discusses the economic growth that has resulted from capitalist economic institutions. We begin with the basics of growth that are least controversial. Next, we turn to the actual history of U.S. growth in recent decades, as well as present controversial issues surrounding growth. When the discussion of growth is completed, the chapter turns to the debate on pollution and waste.

LEARNING OBJECTIVES

After reading this chapter, you should be able to:

- Explain the role of savings and investment on growth in capitalist economies.
- Explain the role of technology and productivity on growth in capitalist economies.
- Discuss conservative policies for growth derived from the two key sources of growth.
- Describe the progressive critique of conservative policies for growth.
- Summarize patterns of growth and the explanations for the patterns of growth in recent U.S. history.
- Explain problems associated with growth in the United States.

HOW THE AMERICAN ECONOMY GROWS

The growth process in economies with capitalist economic institutions has some basic things in common. Suppose there is an entrepreneur named Betty who is in the business of producing steel. In order to produce steel, she needs machinery and buildings. In order to buy machinery and buildings for steel production, she needs a lot of money. Some money may come from her pocket. Some will come from loans from banks. Some money may come from thousands of investors through the stock market. Finally, when the steel company is working, some percentage of profits will be reinvested to expand the facilities. In short, money is raised from the savings of individuals, banks, and corporations. The money (sometimes called financial capital) is used to buy equipment and buildings (sometimes called physical capital).

Now what does the process of growth, an increase in the output of goods and services, look like when it is extended to the whole capitalist economy? The first step is to gather savings from all sources. The total savings in any one year will depend on the decisions made by all individuals and businesses. This means that some percentage of the national income is not consumed but flows into savings. *The percentage of national income that flows into savings is the average ratio of savings to income*, or the **average propensity to save** (APS). So we may say:

Average propensity to save = Savings/National income

The second step in the growth process in a capitalist type economy is that the savings must be used for investment. Classical and neoclassical economists follow Say's law and assume that all savings becomes investment. If you believe Say's Law, then the average propensity to save equals the average propensity to invest. The ratio of savings to income equals the ratio of investment to income. Keynes challenged the assumption that all savings goes into investment, but in order to see what might happen in a perfect economy, we shall also assume that all money saved gets invested for now.

Suppose that the American economy in some past year produced exactly $100 billion of goods and services. Suppose that 90 percent was consumed and 10 percent was saved. Suppose further that all savings went into investment to buy new equipment and buildings. How much new product would be produced? How much would be the rate of growth?

To answer this question, we need to know how much $100 of buildings and equipment will produce. The amount produced has changed with time and technological changes. In general, however, economists have discovered that something like $30 of goods and services a year is produced by every $100 of buildings and equipment. In other words, if Betty the capitalist bought a billion dollars worth of new buildings and equipment, we might expect her company to produce another $300 million of steel every year. Clearly, such averages are very vague and undependable because they change every year in every industry. If you go to check a particular industry, do not expect the ratio of output to capital to look anything like this. We only claim that it is a reasonable example, being in the range used by most economists for the whole U.S. economy.

At any rate, suppose the ratio of output to capital for the whole economy this year is $30 output to $100 capital. What is the rate of growth for the whole economy? We assumed that the savings ratio, the average propensity to save, is 10 percent. We assumed that the economy produces $100 billion this year. If America produces $100 billion, then the savings was $10 billion, all of which was invested in equipment and buildings.

How much will these new buildings and equipment produce? If output to capital is $3 to $10, and if America saves and invests $10 billion, then it will produce a new output of $3 billion. The result is that we will go from $100 billion output this year to $103 billion output next year. The new $10 billion capital (buildings and equipment) produces an extra $3 billion. That translates to a 3 percent increase in GDP, or a growth rate of 3 percent. That is the simplest way to look at growth.

In terms of arithmetic, we are saying that the **rate of growth** equals *the ratio of savings to output times the ratio of output to capital.* To be more concrete, let's call aggregate output GDP. Then,

Growth rate of GDP = (Savings/GDP) × (GDP/capital)

How rapidly our economy grows depends on two things. First, how much is saved out of GDP. Second, assuming that all that savings is invested in productive capital, how much GDP will be produced per dollar of investment? If all savings is invested, savings equals investment. Therefore, all investment in equipment and buildings constitutes the addition to capital. For those students who do not like equations, just remember that a certain amount of output is saved and becomes buildings and equipment. The new buildings and equipment produce a certain new amount of output, depending on our technology.

Conservative View of Growth

Conservatives interpret this model to find two important points. In their view, there are two key ways to increase our rate of growth. One is to increase our average propensity to save. The other is to increase the productivity of our capital, the ratio of output to capital. Very simply stated, these two points constitute the main classical and neoclassical views of growth, though there are many complex additions to them.

What are the policy implications? First, one way to increase growth is to increase the flow of savings. Middle-class individuals, however, have very little savings, so giving money to the middle class means that all of it goes into consumer spending and none is left for investment. Conservative economists point out that rich individuals and corporations do save. From the conservative view, it follows that giving tax breaks to the rich and to corporations will help economic growth. This is an important strategy to improve growth.

Second, conservatives emphasize that better technology will increase the product per unit of capital and therefore increase economic growth. How can we get better technology? Most technology is created by business, though some research is borrowed by business from government sources that provide it freely. How can the government encourage business to invest in new research and to invest in new equipment embodying that research? Again, the conservative answer is tax breaks for business. Those tax breaks are given at the present time specifically for corporations investing money in research or research equipment. It turns out that both avenues to faster growth can be encouraged by tax breaks for the rich or for business, especially for the large corporations that do most of the private research.

Progressive Views of Growth

The conservative conclusions seem obvious from the model of growth described previously. But that model made some controversial assumptions. In the first place, it assumed that all savings are invested. This assumption, implied by Say's law, is not accepted by most progressive economists. Let us summarize the debate on Say's law, which was presented in full in chapters 37, 38, and 39.

Say's law assumes that there is always plenty of demand for all the commodities that fit the needs of consumers. If an external shock tosses the economy off course, it will always come back to equilibrium. Whatever is saved by an individual or corporation can always be profitably invested to produce more goods and services to keep on the road of maximum growth.

Progressive economists, however, point out that it is often the case that plenty of money is available, but there is no place to invest it that looks profitable. The problem is evident in every recession. For example, in the recession of 2001, the accumulated profits of banks, stock brokers, and corporations piled up as they urgently searched for some project that would earn a profit. In 2001 and the next couple years, however, there were no such profitable projects to be found. In fact, as we saw in Chapter 45, the reason savings piled up in the first place was that the profit rate declined to a very low level. In fact, the expected profit from the average investment declined below zero in the recession of 2001.

Under capitalist economic institutions, if there is no expected profit, there is no investment. The money piles up in accounts with financial institutions that pay very little interest in a recession. It follows that, although it sounds strange, the existence of so much savings activity is a problem. These savings will not be invested unless there is a market for the goods and services they could produce. Yet there is no such market because people are not spending enough on consumption, usually because the average person does not have enough money. Increased savings by the wealthy only lowers consumption further.

Corporations invest in new technology only if they believe that it can be put to use in a profitable manner. If they see no market for the existing goods, they are very hesitant to spend a lot of money to produce even more of the goods. In a recession, they are willing to spend money on research only if they think the product of the research might be not just a little better but wildly attractive to consumers so they can get a bigger share of a limited market existing in the recession.

Even if a new invention is created, corporations are unwilling to put billions of dollars into producing it because the market is so limited. Thus, even having plenty of savings and even if new technology is created, there is no guarantee that it will be used to expand investment and increased production. Production is not held back by the lack of technological inventions but because there are not enough consumers willing or able to pay a price that would include a profit.

Some progressive reformers argue for more government money to expand research, such as stem-cell research. Other progressives call for major changes in the economic system to obtain a more democratically controlled system. If there is democratic control of the economy, then the public can decide through democratic means that they wish to devote more saving to create a more rapid growth.

Debate on Saving and Spending

Is more saving good or bad for the economy? It depends. In a long expansion at full employment, more saving allows more investment, which leads to economic growth. In a recession, however, more saving only takes money away from demand for goods and services, so it prevents recovery and leads to a deeper recession.

Is more consumer spending good or bad for the economy? It depends. If the economy is mired in recession, more consumer spending encourages more investment and leads toward an economic recovery and more growth. If the economy is at full employment for a long time, then more consumer spending can only take money away from investment and growth.

Is military spending good for the economy? It depends. In a deep recession, military spending provides employees with more money for consumer spending. That money tends to cause more investment, which means more growth. In a long period of full employment, however, any shift to more military spending means fewer dollars available for consumer goods and for investment goods. Any shift of resources from investment in equipment and building to the production of military products lowers growth. Therefore, if America has a high level of military spending over a long period of time, it will tend to help prevent deep recessions, but it will also lower the rate of growth over the course of a number of cycles.

FACTS OF THE U.S. GROWTH RATE

This section looks at what has actually happened to the rate of growth of real gross domestic product, GDP, in the last half century from 1950 to 1999 by decade. There has not yet been a full decade in the twenty-first century, so it is not included here.

Figure 46.1   **Annual Growth Rate of Real Gross Domestic Product Per Decade, 1950–1999, in Percentages**

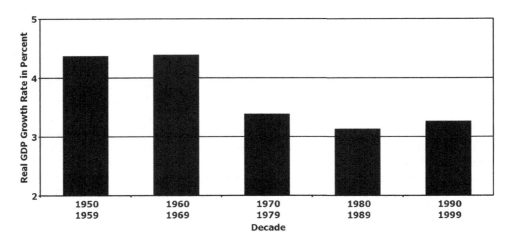

Source: Calculated from the Bureau of Economic Analysis, Department of Commerce, Table 1.2.1 at www.bea.gov: Percentage Change from Preceding Period in Real Gross Domestic Product by Major Type of Product. Seasonally adjusted at annual rates.

Table 46.1

Annual Rate of Growth Per Decade, Gross Domestic Product, Real U.S. Dollars, in Percentages

Decade	Average GDP Growth Rate
1950–1959	4.38
1960–1969	4.40
1970–1979	3.39
1980–1989	3.13
1990–1999	3.27

Calculated from the Bureau of Economic Analysis data files. Table 1.2.1: Percentage Change From Preceding Period in Real Gross Domestic Product by Major Type of Product. Seasonally adjusted at annual rates (see http://www.bea.gov).

Figure 46.1 and Table 46.1 show the experience of growth in the United States in the last half century. They show that the decades of the 1950s and 1960s had much higher growth rates than the 1970s, 1980s, and 1990s.

The figure and the table show clearly that the two decades of the 1950s and 1960s, measured from 1950 through 1969, had average growth rates of real GDP of 4.4 percent a year. The three full decades since then, measured from 1970 through 1999, had average growth rates of real GDP of just 3.3 percent a year. U.S. economic growth in the 1950s and 1960s was much higher than the average growth in the 1970s, 1980s, and 1990s. The question is, why?

The Golden Age of American Capitalism, 1950–1970

The 1950s and 1960s were a golden age of economic growth in the United States. The real GDP grew an average 4.4 percent a year from 1950 through 1969. That is very good by average historical standards. Real wages, family income, and labor productivity all grew every year. There was increasing income equality. There was declining poverty.

The main reason for this golden age was the dominant American position after World War II. Most industrial countries had a large part of their industrial base destroyed during the war. On the contrary, American industry grew very fast during the war. As a result, in the period immediately following the war, most countries produced very little and had little to trade. America produced a huge amount of all goods after converting back to peacetime production. American production of goods and services at first was greater than the production of all other countries combined.

American international trade was also greater than that of all other countries combined. If one wanted to buy a luxury automobile anywhere in the world, then one had to import an American car. This condition changed only slowly as other countries began to recover from war devastation and produce a little more.

In addition to foreign trade, there was a great deal of demand within the United States. People had accumulated savings during the war when there was full employment, but there were few civilian goods and services to buy with your income. There had also been forced savings in the form of war bonds. Money was taken from employees' paychecks for war bonds whether they liked it or not, and there was pressure on people to buy more war bonds. After the war, people could and did spend all of their money. Because of the high production, full employment, and high savings during the war, there was a relatively low amount of debt for both consumers and businesses. The low levels of debt meant that consumers and businesses felt free to borrow more and spend freely.

After a few years of disarmament, the U.S. government also began to spend more on military products than before the war. With the Korean War in 1950, military production started to rise rapidly and has never stopped since. Increased military spending added to the demand for imports from foreign countries' raw materials to be used in military production. Military production also meant more wages and salaries, so it increased the demand for consumer goods at home. Investment spending also increased greatly in this period. There were recessions in the 1950s and 1960s, but they were relatively mild. They did not stop economic growth from recovering rapidly.

Strong unions existed during this period. The strong unions, combined with rising productivity, helped to raise real wages every year. The higher wages and salaries meant a rising demand for consumer goods and services. Small business was alive and well, and competition kept prices fairly low and encouraged innovation.

Finally, since America looked so much more attractive than other countries in terms of wages and salaries, there was a brain drain of technicians and professionals from all over the world to the United Sates. This was a big help to the flood of innovations in the economy.

Slow Growth of the U.S. Economy, 1970–2001

We saw earlier that from 1970 to 1999, the annual rate of growth of U.S. real GDP dropped to 3.3 percent. This was a decline of 1.1 percent in the average growth compared to the 1950 to 1969 period. That is a major decline in annual growth when we are discussing so many years. In the years from 1970 to the present, the American economy has had years of rapid growth and years of slow growth, but there have been many more years of slow growth than in the previous period. We shall see that this slower growth was followed by the recession of 2001.

In this period, other countries surpassed the U.S. growth rate. The American economy suffered relative stagnation compared with the global economy. In other words, the American economy has been growing, but its share of the world economy has steadily declined. Within the United States, there has also been increasingly unequal distribution of income. The income of the middle class has risen much less than the whole economy. It is worth noting that America has retained its military supremacy. However, it appears that military supremacy without strong economic supremacy is not enough to preserve the old situation of U.S. dominance of the world scene.

The long period of slow growth began with a bang. The U.S. economic growth rate declined drastically in the 1970s and early 1980s. The American gross national product grew only 2.3 percent per year from 1970 to 1983. Although the rich got richer, average family income stagnated. Astonishingly, real family income was the same in 1987 as in 1973. This was a very unpleasant shock, since Americans had been used to a rising family income every year during the period from 1950 to 1970. Many middle-class families maintained the same income level only by having the wife go to work for pay. This was a new phenomenon for many in the middle class. Those families with no increase in the number of people at work had reduced income.

From 1979 to 1987, mostly years of presidents Reagan and the first George Bush, real hourly wages dropped by 7 percent. Productivity growth declined from 2.9 percent a year from 1950 to 1969 to only 0.8 percent in 1970 to 1983. Inequality increased under Reagan and Bush. Income from property ownership, including profits, rent, and interest, rose three times faster than income from labor in the 1979 to 1983 period. The percentage of people living in poverty increased.

What caused these trends? Why were there declines in growth of national product, family income, and productivity? Why was there an absolute decline in real wages? These declines in the growth rate as well as real wages resulted partly from the policies of the Reagan–Bush administration (examined later in this chapter). The decline also resulted from a number of structural changes. First, the 1950s and 1960s were influenced by major wars, including the aftermath of the Second World War, the Korean War, and the Vietnam War, as well as a continuing Cold War against the Soviet Union. As a result of these wars and anticommunist hysteria, the United States had a very high level of military spending in those years. The high military spending stimulated the economy through the flow of government money for military goods and services. The government spending made it possible to have mild recessions and quick recoveries.

This stimulus was reduced after the very high levels of the 1950s and 1960s. Because there were no significant wars, military spending declined in the 1970s and early 1980s as a percentage of GDP. Stimulation to the economy from this source declined. Of course, it meant more resources were available for investment, which could have helped growth, but we shall see that relatively little investment occurred.

A second structural change has been in the international role of the United States. In 1950, the United States was totally dominant in production and trade. There was high demand for U.S. products from the war-devastated countries of Europe and Asia and almost no competition in most industries. By the early 1970s, however, the U.S. economy faced very serious competition from Japan and Western Europe. This competition has increased ever since.

After a hundred years of trade surpluses, America suddenly faced a trade deficit. Because of competition, America sold fewer goods abroad than it bought from foreigners. To cover the trade deficit, money began to flow out of the United States. That money flow meant less demand in the United States and more demand abroad. The outflow of money rose from zero in the 1960s to more and more every year beginning in the early 1970s. The outflow of money from the United States to cover the trade deficit was over $850 billion a year by 2007.

Third, there has been a vast increase in consumer debt and business debt continuing to this day. This increase in debt made the economy of the 1970 to 2007 period much more fragile and vulnerable to economic crisis than it was in the 1950s and 1960s. When America enters a recession with large consumer debt and large business debt, people and firms cannot pay back their debts. Then financial institutions get very shaky and some banks fail.

Fourth, there has been an increase in monopoly power, continuing to this day. The increase in monopoly power has resulted in price increases, even in the midst of recession. These high prices have made recoveries more difficult.

Fifth, there has been a continuous decline in the percentage of workers in unions since 1955. This decline has lowered employees' bargaining power, resulting in lowered wages and salaries for all employees. Lower wages and salaries mean less consumer demand.

These structural changes resulted in longer and more intensive recessions in the 1970s and early 1980s than in the preceding two decades. The same structural changes have continued to cause mostly low growth ever since, though there was one short period of higher growth rates, as we shall see.

The increase in recessions also meant an increase in unemployment. From 1970 to 1982, the average unemployment rate rose to 6.8 percent. Similarly, the average use of productive capacity fell from 84 percent in the earlier period to 74 percent. The most important problem was lack of effective demand, due in part to limited wages and salaries.

Growth with Increasing Inequality, 1982–2001

Economic growth was a little better in the period from 1982 to 2001. Unemployment levels dropped. There was, however, increasing inequality between the small class of capitalist owners of business and the rest of the population, including middle-class and other employees. Let us examine a few details.

President Reagan won election on the basis that he would reduce the government deficit. In reality, in the 1980s, he tripled the deficit by spending far beyond government revenues. Most of that spending went to a huge increase in military production. The increased military spending and larger government deficits meant more profit to military producers. It also meant more interest payment to those who held government bonds.

Nevertheless, the vast increase in government spending on the military did increase demand and take the economy out of its doldrums. Economic growth led to less unemployment, so many more people had the benefit of jobs.

One of the problems of the administrations of Reagan and the first Bush was increasing inequality between classes of Americans. For example, in the business cycle of 1982 to 1991, the ratio of wages and salaries to national income fell 2.4 percent. This percentage of national income represents a lot of money that shifted from employees to property owners.

The Clinton Years

In the Clinton administration of the 1990s, the same trends continued. America took a leap forward in technology with the information revolution. The information revolution meant instant communication of words and instant computation of data available all over the world. As a result of the technological revolution, production, employment, and productivity rose. Although growth was sluggish in 1991 to 1994, it took off to a high growth rate in 1995 to 2000. For example, in the entire 1991 to 2001 business cycle, the unemployment rate fell to 5.4 percent.

But the same problems also continued. For example, the ratio of wages and salaries to national income fell another 1.4 percent in the 1991 to 2001 business cycle as income continued to shift from employees to business owners. One problem that ran through the Reagan, Bush, and Clinton years was increasing debt. As wages and salaries were held down, people paid for consumer goods and services by going into debt. In the business cycle of 1980 to 1982, consumer debt was already 144 percent of national income. In the 1982 to 1991 cycle, under Reagan and the first Bush, consumer debt rose to 173 percent of national income. Finally, at the peak of the 1991 to 2001 cycle under Clinton, the ratio of consumer debt to national income rose to 214 percent of national income. These figures mean that the average person was living with a lot of debt and paying a lot in interest payments. This trend has continued and increased under the second Bush.

Expansion of 2001–2006 Under the Second Bush

At this time (2007), the expansion under President Bush is still continuing, but it has not been a wonderful expansion for the average person. Growth has done pretty well, though is down from the previous expansion. Real corporate profits have done very well, but real wages and salaries have been mostly stagnant. The main reason is that employees lack the bargaining power to improve their wages and salaries as fast as productivity has risen. From 1950 to the early 1970s, wages and salaries rose just as rapidly as productivity. From the early 1970s until now, there has been an increasingly wide gap between rapidly rising productivity and much slower rising wages and salaries. (This gap is shown in a dramatic graph in Bivens and Weller, 2006, p. 606.) Real wages per worker rose every decade from 1930 to 1970. Since then, however, this very basic trend of American capitalism has reversed itself. Weekly wages per worker, after inflation adjustment, fell in every decade from 1974 to 2004, according to the U.S. Department of Labor (see Rick Wolff, 2006, p. 1).

It is not just wage workers, but all employees, including technicians and professionals, who have suffered from the pattern of growth in output and profits but stagnation of wages. This point has been made systematically by the president of the U.S. Federal Reserve Bank of San Francisco, Janet Yellen, who stated that growth and productivity have been very satisfactory in the last decade, but incomes of most people have done poorly. She says that "over the past three decades, much of the gain from excellent macroeconomic performance has gone to just a small segment of the population, those already in the upper part of the distribution. As a result, inequality has grown" (Yellen, 2006). Yellen adds that this inequality of income was "coupled with increased turbulence in family incomes associated with job displacement" (p. 1). She supports her view with a large amount of detailed data from the Federal Reserve.

One major cause of the lack of increases in wages and salaries to keep up with rising productivity has been the declining strength of employees versus the giant corporations. This is best seen in the decline of unionization as a percentage of the whole labor force (illustrated in a graph in Bivens and Weller, 2006, p. 611). The decline has been very considerable, so unions represent less than 20 percent of the U.S. labor force and a declining percentage each decade. At the same time as unions lost power, corporations gained power, not only in an economic sense but in power over the media and power over politics. The balance of power has shifted from labor to capital and it shows in wages and salaries.

One result of stagnant real wages and salaries has been a further large increase in the ratio of consumer debt to aggregate income. Thus, all consumer debt, including homes, was 19 percent of U.S. disposable income in the 1949 to 1953 business cycle. By the 1970 to 1973 business cycle, consumer debt had risen to 64 percent of disposable income. In the last full cycle of 1991 to 2001, all consumer debt rose to 92 percent of U.S. disposable income. Finally, in the first three years of the present expansion, all consumer debt rose to 109 percent of disposable income (see Bivens and Weller, 2006, p. 607).

What has held down jobs and employee income in the United States under the second Bush administration? We have seen that one reason is the declining strength of labor unions. Another important cause is the increased outsourcing of jobs to other countries. The term **outsourcing** means that *corporations find ways to shift jobs from high-wage workers in the United States to low-wage workers in less developed countries*. This can be done by using the worldwide computer network to let someone do calculating in India rather than in the United States. It also means moving whole factories abroad. For example, in 2006 General Motors announced that it would fire 50,000 automobile workers with high salaries. It also announced it was building large new factories in China that might employ as many as 50,000 workers.

The average Chinese wage is only about 25 cents an hour, and employers often forget to pay anything. Wal-Mart has some enterprises in China, where it was paying about 17 cents an hour. When the Chinese government announced that it was allowing unions to operate and even strike in its factories in order to raise wages, Wal-Mart was the first to object, but so did other firms.

Growth in the United States is held down by lack of demand due to slow growth of wages and salaries. The stagnant wages and salaries are partly due to the successful attempt of corporations to hold down U.S. wages and salaries, but it is also due to the corporate move to more profitable locations in the world. The most profitable countries are those that hold down wages and salaries and smash labor unions. These countries have very high rates of exploitation (see Chapter 19). This means fewer jobs and lower wages and salaries for American employees.

GROWTH AND WASTE UNDER CAPITALISM

The GDP includes much wasteful production. As was shown in Appendix 37.3, to get an estimate of how much GDP helps human happiness, we must reduce the apparent rate of profit of GDP by the amount of these wasteful products. Wasteful production should not be included in a calculation of the national product available for social welfare because no social benefit is derived.

This section examines more fully the various categories of economic waste that reduce the growth rate of useful commodities. The following types of waste should be examined in terms of their beneficial or harmful effect on human beings and on the GDP.

Military Production and Waste

Military "goods and services" are sometimes called military "evils and disservices." Military spending provides high profits for the giant corporations that produce for the military. Military spending may also increase the profits of those corporations that have investments abroad that the armed forces protect from foreign revolutions.

A dollar of military expenditure not only generates demand to that amount but also generates further spending by the employees and profit makers who receive the military spending. If the system cannot reach full employment any other way, then military spending can produce full employment. The argument of the critics is that it is a sick economic system that can only achieve full employment by military production and war. Moreover, if military spending does lead to full employment, then continued war spending will not increase employment any more. The attempt to produce more at full employment leads to inflation unless peacetime production is reduced.

If peacetime production is reduced in order to do more military production, then the result is a lower rate of economic growth.

It is a fact, however, that the U.S. capitalist system normally operates far below full employment. It is also a political fact of life that without military spending, no other kind of government spending can possibly be done on the scale needed to produce full employment. Therefore, within the present system's political and economic constraints, it is true that vast military spending is "necessary" to maintain full employment. But it is a peculiar and unwanted economic political and economic system when only the military production can actually lead to full employment. The war economy has a lower rate of economic growth than a peaceful economy in which the money is used for higher investment in expansion.

Obviously, military spending and wars also result in more taxes, inflation, wounds, deaths, and alienation and deterioration of life for millions. Conservatives believe present military spending is necessary for defense. Most progressives believe that there is more military spending than is necessary for defense and that the spending could be used better for constructive projects. Most progressives believe most military spending is unnecessary for defense and is wasteful. As we pointed out earlier, there are obstacles in the capitalist system to more peaceful, constructive projects. These obstacles include the opposition of most corporations to anything that may offer competition to them or reduce their profits, such as universal free health care. Political control by the large corporations may make peaceful, constructive government spending very limited. For this reason, many progressives believe that peaceful full employment spending could be achieved only in a system of economic democracy, discussed in Chapter 25.

Wasteful Advertising Expenses

In the United States, a very large amount of human effort is put into the peculiar occupation of convincing people to buy products they may not want or need. Obviously, every society needs to distribute its goods from the producers to the consumers, but the U.S. economy goes far beyond that. It spends billions of dollars and millions of hours of labor time for salespeople to go around from door to door or to stand in a store to persuade other people to buy things. A huge percentage of this effort is not useful, but wasteful.

A second aspect of selling is advertising. Again, some small amount of advertising is needed in any society to supply useful information to customers. More than 90 percent of all advertising in the United States and other capitalist countries, however, is not information but an attempt to persuade consumers that each of several identical products is better than the others. Therefore, hundreds of billions a year is spent on advertising that can be described as wasteful. For example, there is the advertising for smoking cigarettes, cigars, and other forms of tobacco despite the U.S. government's well-documented evidence that smoking causes cancer, heart disease, and other illness. Yet the tobacco companies continue to devote huge amounts of money to induce people to continue or begin smoking. In fact, the U.S. government still subsidizes tobacco production because of the political pressure of the tobacco farmers!

A third aspect of selling is cost estimation. In many industries, such as construction, a tremendous amount of highly skilled effort by highly paid engineers consists in providing estimates their company may use to bid for a new job, such as a public school or road or military facility. In each case, the buyer of the construction has already had its own engineers furnish an estimate. In addition to the buyer who wishes to obtain the building, there may be ten or twelve corporations who want to build it, so there will be ten or twelve sets of engineers who do this difficult work of cost estimation all over again.

A fourth aspect of selling reaches back into production. It is the designing of new products or changes in existing products, but sometimes not to make them better. The products are sometimes even made worse. The object of the changes is to make them in such a way that they will be more attractive to consumers, regardless of whether they are improved. One example is women's skirts, in which the hemline is regularly raised or lowered so that women wishing to keep in style will have to buy new skirts or dresses. Another example is the yearly change of automobile models. One year tails were put on cars, another year the tails were taken off. In some years, these automobile model changes took 1 to 3 percent of the entire GDP in totally wasted effort.

Last but not least, sales efforts take the even more despicable form of *planned obsolescence*: When firms plan obsolescance, engineers are put to work designing a product that will fall apart quicker than previous one so that the consumer will have to buy a new one.

Nuclear Waste

Atomic bombs were first exploded in 1945. The government researched, designed, and built the first nuclear energy plants. Then the government started the private nuclear industry by giving it all of the government-owned plants for a few pennies on every dollar spent by the government out of taxes. Government then subsidized the private nuclear industry by giving it huge subsidies in the form of research and development money. Finally, the government passed laws to protect the private nuclear power industry from having to pay for accidents.

In 1957, Congress passed the Price-Anderson Act, which provided federal insurance for nuclear accidents up to at least $500 million. It limited the liability of a company for a nuclear accident to $560 million. Yet a single nuclear accident could cost many billions. The government gave the nuclear industry this support because of its military uses and its promise of self-sufficiency.

In 1963, the first nonsubsidized nuclear reactor was sold. With government encouragement, the nuclear industry launched into an enormous new building program. The reactor manufacturers underestimated costs, so they charged low prices and either renegotiated contracts or incurred big losses. By 1967, seventy-five reactors had been ordered by U.S. utilities, an amazing investment in an untested product. Some orders were for nuclear reactors five times the size of any existing one.

The nuclear industry ran into three kinds of problems. First, in spite of studies proving it "impossible," there have been a large number of accidents and some very near disasters. Second, there is a limited amount of uranium, which will be used up in a few decades under present technology. The "breeder" technology would extend the use of uranium by fifty or sixty times, but would also create large amounts of plutonium wastes, which are very toxic and can be used to make atomic bombs.

Third, how do we get rid of the waste? Nuclear waste reached over 18 million cubic feet, by 1999. This waste remains toxic for a quarter of a million years (estimated costs of "safe" disposal are enormous and no clearly safe method has been discovered). These three problems mean not only dangers for all of us but much higher costs. The nuclear construction industry has fizzled, with many cancellations by the utilities. There have been no new contracts for many years now.

Conclusion on Waste

There are various kinds of economic waste: military production, monopoly misallocation, most advertising and sales expenses, planned obsolescence, and lack of conservation. Environmental destruction and pollution may be regarded as a kind of waste of resources. There is pollution of land, air, and water. Some conservatives argue that nonpollution, such as clean air, could be given a price and bought and sold in the market, thus automatically solving the problem. Progressives believe that solution is insufficient because markets are not designed to fight such a pervasive evil. In fact, pollution is caused by corporations seeking profit. Legal controls are needed to prevent pollution by private enterprise. Some progressives do not believe controls will work under capitalism, because controls go opposite to the profit motive, while those who make the profit often control government policies. For example, the Bush administration put some people into high offices in the Environmental Protection Agency who have spent their lives attacking any controls on pollution. Therefore, some progressives argue that a different type of economy is a necessary condition for an end to waste and pollution. To stop waste and pollution, they argue for democratic control of most enterprises through consumer cooperatives, employee cooperatives, and democratic public ownership.

SUMMARY

The most important points in the chapter are these: First, the classical formula said that the rate of growth depends on (1) the amount of money put by individuals into savings, and (2) assuming that all savings are invested, how the new investments in buildings and equipment affect national production. Keynes agreed with these two factors but showed that not all savings flowed into investment. In addition to low productivity or low savings, a lack of effective demand for GDP may slow growth.

Second, the rate of growth of American GDP was highest when it was most dominant in world production, particularly the post–World War II period from 1950 to 1970. When the U.S. economy began to lose dominance after 1970, the rate of growth of GDP declined significantly all the way to the present.

Third, although growth remains very significant by historical standards, the distribution of income has become more unequal. Corporate profits have risen rapidly, while employee compensation has risen far less.

Fourth, the ominous rise of consumer debt as a percentage of income has continued.

Fifth, economic growth is reduced by various kinds of waste, ranging from military waste to advertising waste to pollution.

Finally, one other variable whose importance to growth is quite controversial is the population growth, which is discussed in Appendix 46.1.

SUGGESTED READINGS

The best and most interesting text on recent achievements and problems in U.S. growth is Robert Pollin's *Contours of Descent*, 2004. An excellent but more demanding article with extensive data is Bivens and Weller, "The Job-less Economy: Not New, Just Worse" (2006). An easy to read article with plenty of data on the trend of debt accompanying U.S. growth is by Fred Magdoff, "Debt and Speculation Explode," 2006. A good book on recent growth is by Samuel Rosenberg, *American Economic Growth Since 1945* (2003).

On waste, it is still worth reading the pioneering analysis, which is both powerful and moving, by Baran and Sweezy, *Monopoly Capital* (1968). More recently, a wonderfully written book by Jared Diamond, *Collapse* (2005) tells an amazing story of lethal cases of waste and pollution in many times and places.

KEY TERMS

average propensity to save
outsourcing
rate of growth

REVIEW QUESTIONS

Explain the role of savings and investment on growth in capitalist economies.
1. What are sources of savings? What does Say's law say will happen with savings?
2. Why is investment important to economic growth? Can there be growth without investment? Explain.

Explain the role of technology and productivity on growth in capitalist economies.
3. Why is productivity important for growth? What happens if productivity falls?
4. How are technology and productivity related?

Discuss conservative policies for growth derived from the two key sources of growth.
5. What policies would conservatives argue help increase savings? Investment?
6. What would conservatives recommend to encourage technological breakthroughs?

Describe the progressive critique of conservative policies for growth.
7. How would progressive economists view conservative policies on savings and investment? Explain.

Summarize patterns of growth and the explanations for the patterns of growth in recent U.S. history.
8. Since World War II, what two decades had the highest growth rates? What three decades had lower growth rates? What were some of the factors leading to lower growth rates?

Explain problems associated with growth in the United States.
9. List the types of waste in the economy described in this chapter. Which ones do you disagree with (if any) , and why?
10. Describe one type of waste in detail and explain why it occurs.
11. Does high growth of GDP always lead to high growth of employee compensative, middle-class income, and income of the poor?

APPENDIX 46.1
POPULATION AND GROWTH

Thomas Malthus compared the need for food caused by an increase in population with the increased output from that same increased population. Malthus argued that the future growth of population would rapidly outstrip the growth of output. Therefore, starvation is a real possibility for the future. This appendix looks at the arguments of the economist responsible for giving economics the reputation of being a "dismal science."

LEARNING OBJECTIVES FOR APPENDIX 46.1

After reading this appendix, you should be able to:

- Explain why Malthus made predictions of mass starvation and why it has not always happened in developed economies.

ECONOMICS: THE DISMAL SCIENCE

Why did Malthus argue that food grows slowly while population grows rapidly? He argued that, historically, humans multiply rapidly in good times. However, he claims that food is limited by the law of diminishing returns. As the population grows faster than the supply of food, there is trouble. Let us examine the details.

The law of diminishing returns states that each additional worker adds less output than the previously hired worker. It holds true only if capital, natural resources, and technology remain unchanged and after some minimum scale of employment has been reached. Given these assumptions, the law of diminishing returns is a truism; it cannot be other than true. All other things remaining the same, it is obvious that if enough workers are crowded onto a single plot of land or even into the entire world, the crowding alone will eventually cause the product of an additional worker to decline. However, many of the classical economists, like Malthus, went much further with the truism. He predicted that diminishing returns per worker in the economy as a whole would come about in actual fact. Malthus reached this dismal conclusion on the grounds that population increase would be very rapid and would far outweigh the slow increase of capital, technology, and natural resources.

The gloomy long-run prediction based on this interpretation of the law of diminishing returns has not been borne out by the facts of historical progress. First, it is not even clear that the world population is at the minimum level at which further additions to the working force would bring diminishing returns, even if natural resources, capital, and technology were to remain constant. Second, labor itself improves in quality with advances in scientific and technical education. Third, while it was usual to argue that the earth is only so large and that its natural resources are slowly being depleted, the supply of known natural resources is steadily expanding as a result of continual discoveries of new reserves. Furthermore, there have been important discoveries of new uses for previously neglected materials. For example, coal was once merely a hard black stone of no use for fuel or heating purposes. Moreover, better ways have been found to use available resources. For example, there is power production by atomic fusion and food production by hydroponics farming. Of course, the last two means of resource expansion are also aspects of technological improvement.

Another reason there have not been diminishing returns per worker in the economy as a whole is the increasing use of capital per worker. This allows a single worker to produce far more than previously.

The final and most important reason for the defeat of diminishing returns is that development of technology in the past century meant a much more efficient use of the available capital, natural resources, and labor. At the early date Malthus wrote, it was still possible largely to ignore technological progress. Today, even the blindest economist is forced to take into account the startling advances continually being made in production techniques.

Empirically, the evidence shows that population in the developed countries has not outraced technology, natural resources, and capital but that, on the contrary, product per person has grown enormously. In the United States, the increase of agricultural output has far outrun increase of employment. In fact, between 1870 and 1940, employment in agriculture rose by only 34 percent while output rose by 279 percent. The United States thus has no lack of food but rather a surplus relative to effective cash demand. The problem of food is not the physical lack of food but that some Americans do not have enough money for a healthy diet.

It may be concluded that in the industrialized private enterprise economies, slower progress or recessions are not caused by natural and technical problems. Slow growth and recessions are caused by economic institutions that give rise to recurrent economic recessions and depressions. The natural sciences have given us ample power to obtain in the future fantastic levels of abundance or to blow to pieces the entire world.

How fast is population likely to grow? Many Malthusian theorists mechanically project the present world rate of population growth into the near future and easily arrive at quite astronomical figures for total population. It was demonstrated earlier, though, that to date, capital and technology have had no trouble keeping ahead of population growth. They probably could even keep pace with massive population growth in the coming years.

The mechanical prognostications of vast population growth, however, do not seem to have taken into account the best present knowledge of population growth patterns. Malthus described people breeding like animals and population exploding with only a few kinds of checks to its expansion. He spoke of "preventive checks" as those that cause lower birth rates. He recognized only abstention from sex or "vice and sexual deviation" and did not consider voluntary birth control through family planning and contraceptive methods. When preventive checks fail, according to Malthus, the result will be "positive checks" to population, where positive means a higher death rate. These positive checks include wars, famine, and disease.

It is true that in many less developed economies with low levels of productivity, we often find very high birthrates. At this stage, however, population may be constant for centuries because it is held in check by equally high death rates caused by wars, disease, and starvation. A second stage of rapid population growth usually follows the beginnings of industrialization and the introduction of modern methods of public health sanitation. With better control of disease and enough food production, death rates decline. As long as birth rates remain high, the population soars.

At the third stage, however, as the economy matures, we find culture and education spreading to all the population. Knowledge of contraception also spreads, as does the desire to use these means in order to keep families to a manageable size. All of the more industrialized countries have shown some tendency toward lower birth rates during the past 100 years, although there have been some upward spurts in the rate for short periods.

REVIEW QUESTIONS FOR APPENDIX 46.1

Explain why Malthus made predictions of mass starvation and why it has not always happened in developed economies.
1. What did Malthus assume about increasing production? Why?
2. What is the relationship of increasing production and population growth? Why would this be a problem?
3. Why have developed countries not experienced mass starvation as their populations grew? Explain.

PART III, SECTION 3

GOVERNMENT FISCAL POLICY

CHAPTER 47

Fiscal Policy

Fiscal policy is defined to mean all government policy dealing with government spending and government collection of revenue, mostly taxation. The first part of this chapter briefly explains the tools of fiscal policy and gives a brief history of how fiscal policy has been used in the United States. The second part describes the furious debate over fiscal policy between conservative and progressive economists. The third part stresses the immense role of military spending in the budget and takes up the "guns versus butter" debate.

LEARNING OBJECTIVES

After reading this chapter, you should be able to:

- Define and describe fiscal policy tools, and give historical examples of how they have been used.
- Compare and contrast conservative and progressive views on fiscal policy.
- Discuss how budget deficits, budget surpluses, and debt enter into the debate on fiscal policy.
- Explain how fiscal policy should be used in a recession or if there is inflation, and describe how the appropriate fiscal policy affects recession and inflation.
- List and describe the problems of using fiscal policy.
- Explain how military spending affects the economy.

MODERN FISCAL POLICY

The economic role of government that most directly influences the level of output, income, and employment is its taxing and spending of money. **Fiscal policy** *consists of decisions to spend and to tax.* The effects of fiscal policy on output, income, and employment were ignored by most economists until the depression of the 1930s. The prevailing economic philosophy was that taxes should be used only to finance necessary government expenditures. It was thought to be an unsound financial practice for governments to run a **deficit** in which *expenditures were greater than the tax revenue in a given year.* Economists preferred a **balanced budget** in which *expenditures equaled taxes under all circumstances.* They thought, however, that it was not very bad to have *taxes exceed expenditures* so that government had a **surplus**. **Debt** is when *the accumulated yearly deficits are greater than the surpluses.* By having a surplus of taxes over spending, any debts incurred in the past could be paid down or retired. In fact, in the early nineteenth century under President Andrew Jackson, there were considerable surpluses. The whole national debt was paid off for the only time in our history, while the remaining surplus was given away to the states.

The Great Depression and World War II forced a change in this viewpoint among economists. Since that time, the view has spread that government spending and taxation should help stabilize the economy. Federal government spending in the United States in 1929 was only 1 percent of gross domestic product (GDP). In the period 1930 to 1940, as the New Deal responded to the Depression, federal government spending increased to 4 percent of GDP. It included some spending to put the unemployed, who were 25 percent of the labor force, to work on government projects, such as road building.

With World War II, government spending rose to the incredible height of 42 percent of GDP in 1944, almost all for military products. After the war, it fell somewhat, but it bounced up again to 18 percent of GDP during the Korean War, went up to 20 percent during the Vietnam War, and averaged 24 percent in the 1980s. In addition to this federal spending, the amount spent by the states has also skyrocketed.

In addition to federal spending for goods and services, the federal government makes transfer payments. **Transfer payments** are *payments by the government to some group of people without any service in return.* An example is subsidies to farmers whenever prices decline. Transfer payments amount to a large percentage of the budget because they include interest on the national debt, which is now very high. They are called transfer payments because they transfer money from taxpayers to those who receive subsidies or interest on the government debt.

Transfer payments among citizens include huge subsidies to big business and large farms, small amounts of funding for welfare payments and for unemployment compensation to individuals, interest payments on government bonds to bondholders, and pension payments to people who paid Social Security taxes before retirement.

Discretionary fiscal policies are *policies adopted by Congress and the president to meet particular situations.* For example, government spending decisions were made to help rescue victims of Hurricane Katrina and to fund rebuilding efforts. As another example, Congress might decide to meet a recession by paying contractors and workers to build more roads.

There are also nondiscretionary or **automatic fiscal policies**. Automatic fiscal policies are *policies that are fixed in place by law for the indefinite future.* For example, Social Security payments are automatic because they are fixed by law for the long term, though they could be changed by a new law. These and other payments, such as unemployment compensation, do not need to be voted on when the economy changes; they are already in place.

GOVERNMENT AND AGGREGATE DEMAND

Money flows to and from government to households and businesses. The personal income tax takes money away from households, reducing demand. The corporate profit tax takes money away from business, reducing demand. Contributions to Social Security are taken from employee households, reducing demand. The sales tax also reduces the flow of money and demand going to business. On the other hand, there is an enormous flow of demand from government to business for the purchase of goods and services. Finally, there is a large flow of transfer payments both to households and businesses.

We know that when spending is greater than taxes, there is a government deficit. A deficit for government means a net flow from government to households and business, thus increasing demand. On the other hand, we know that when taxes are greater than spending, there is a government surplus. A surplus by government means a net flow from households and from business to government. Since a surplus reduces the money held by consumers and businesses, it reduces demand.

CONSERVATIVE VIEWS OF FISCAL POLICY

Views of fiscal policy go back as far as Adam Smith, whose most famous book, *The Wealth of Nations*, was written in 1776. Although Smith is conservative by present standards, he was comparatively forward looking for his time. The most famous conservative fiscal economist of the late twentieth century was Milton Friedman, whose views are the basis of some conservative thought to this day. While all conservatives agree on their basic outlook, they disagree on many details, so we largely follow the views of Friedman in presenting the conservative position.

Friedman argues that no discretionary fiscal measures are needed to fight inflation or depression. The private enterprise capitalist economy will always automatically adjust back to equilibrium at full employment after any shock if it is left alone. Therefore, the government should stay out of the economy. Friedman argues that the less government the better. He attributes many of our economic problems to too much interference with private enterprise by government. If it were not for government interference, the private economy would otherwise automatically adjust to all situations. This topic was discussed Chapter 45.

Although Friedman contends that government should have no economic role, he does allow for certain types of taxes and spending. Although he blasts government interference in the economy, he does believe that government must provide the necessary framework or foundation for a private enterprise capitalist economy. In the fiscal area, he believes, as do most conservatives, that the government must take all measures to protect private property. Protection of private property includes spending on lawmaking, judges, police, prisons, army, navy, and air force. These expenditures amount to hundreds of billions of dollars. Nevertheless, conservatives like Friedman believe they are necessary and do not violate the ban on interference with the economy.

Contrary to the liberal Keynesian view that government spending can employ workers and increase demand, Milton Friedman contends:

> Government spending does not increase employment. First, government spending has increased for the last 25 years, but so has unemployment. Two, government spending just takes money from private people who would have spent it, so there is no net increase in demand for labor. (Friedman, 1968)

Friedman contends that government spending has zero net impact on demand because it lowers private spending by the same amount.

PROGRESSIVE FISCAL POLICIES

There are a wide range of different progressive views of fiscal policy, but all of them agree that it is the duty of society and government to make sure that all employees have decent jobs to provide the necessities of living. We begin with the views of the most famous economist of the twentieth century, progressive John Maynard Keynes.

Keynes created modern macroeconomics. He focused on aggregate demand, which classical economists had ignored. Aggregate demand is composed of four flows of expenditures from consumers, business investment, net foreign demand, and government. He addressed the two problems of inflation and unemployment. In this framework, a simplified Keynesian view of fiscal policy dominated economics in the 1940s and 1950s. Basically the policy said that in a recession, it was necessary to combat unemployment by two means. First, government spending should be increased. Keynes stressed that all government spending generates demand for goods and services. It does not matter if the spending is for constructive projects, such as hospitals, or for useless projects, such as pyramids or nuclear bombs. Any government spending will increase demand and reduce unemployment. Of course, peaceful, constructive government spending may have very different effects on long-run economic growth from military spending (discussed in Chapter 46).

The simplest Keynesian view also argued that government must combat inflation by fiscal measures, contrary to the basic conservative view that fiscal measures do no good. First, inflation, which means rising prices, can be combated by reducing all government spending, both useless and constructive. Second, to fight inflation, taxes should be increased.

Suppose that business cycle recessions cause unemployment (while prices fall). The proper prescription is for government to increase spending and to lower taxes. That means there will be deficits in recessions. But that deficit spending, meaning spending greater than taxes, will help reduce unemployment and prepare the way for an economic recovery.

On the contrary, in the expansion, there are rising prices due to greater demand, but falling unemployment. The proper prescription in an expansion is to lower government spending and raise taxes. This will cause surpluses, meaning taxes greater than spending. Such government surpluses will help absorb excess demand. The lower demand will reduce prices.

Progressives in the 1950s maintained that spending and taxation measures can successfully bring about full employment with stable prices. Other progressives admitted that economists have not developed a method for ending inflation and maintaining full employment at the same time: "Experts do not yet know . . . an incomes policy that will permit us to have simultaneously . . . full employment and price stability" (Samuelson, 1973, p. 823). These worries about the relation of unemployment and inflation are one aspect of the many problems that have been raised by economists about the simplest Keynesian policy prescriptions.

PROBLEMS WITH KEYNESIAN FISCAL POLICY

Let us consider the Keynesian argument that government intervention can prevent large-scale unemployment or runaway inflation. The basic fiscal formula is to raise taxes and lower spending to fight inflations during expansions, while lowering taxes and raising spending to fight unemployment during depressions. There are, however, administrative, political, and economic problems with this formula.

Administrative Problems of Fiscal Policies

Before an intelligent fiscal policy can be carried out, one must know the economic situation, decide what to do, and get it done, but all that takes time. First, information must be gathered, and someone, usually economists, must decide if a change in the economy is temporary or permanent. Second, before spending, such as for a new bridge, engineers must design the bridge. Third, Congress must decide exactly what spending will be done or what taxes cut. Fourth, the president must agree. Fifth, the actual spending must be done. If, however, the government builds a dam, it may take five years for all the construction to be complete and for the spending to occur.

The point is that there are many time lags between an economic change and the implementation of a new fiscal policy. Often, by the time the new policy takes effect, the economic situation is totally different. In that case, the policy has an opposite effect to what was planned and throws the economy off track.

Political Problems for Fiscal Policy

The problems remain: Which spending? Whose taxes? Suppose we agree to spend the large amounts of money necessary to maintain full employment. Many outlets that would be socially beneficial conflict with the interests of large corporations or wealthy individuals. For example, higher spending for education tends to raise taxes, and many people do not want to pay these taxes. Government investment in electrical power facilities to provide cheap power to the population reduce the monopolistic power of private electric companies. The result is political constraints to government economic policies, pitting the vested interests of big corporations against the interests of all the population.

In Chapter 24, we discovered that the government is greatly influenced by the money used by large corporations to buy lobbyists or directly by money paid to members of Congress. There are great conflicts between groups, but more often than not, the winners are the owners of large corporations who can pour massive amounts of money into the political process. Therefore, most fiscal policies reflect the interests of the large corporations and are often contrary to the interests of the rest of the population.

Political Problems with Tax Cuts

In addition to government spending, another popular cure for recession is reduction of taxes to allow more money to flow into private spending. Given the interests dominating the U.S. government, however, tax cuts always end up benefiting mainly the rich and the corporations. The redistribution of income from the poor and middle class to the rich, however, especially during a recession, causes a major problem, not just for those who get little out of the tax cut but for the whole country. The consumption of the wealthy remains at adequate levels even by their standards during a recession, so lower taxes does not necessarily increase their consumption any more than before the tax cut. Moreover, the wealthy have no desire to invest during a recession in the face of probable losses.

Similarly, many economists, and even many businesspeople, may see a need for increasingly vast government spending under capitalism. There has been a continuous fight in the discussion of federal spending over "guns versus butter." Should money be spent for military purposes or for peaceful, constructive services to Americans, such as health and education? It is here that vested interests come into play.

Even small expenditures on medical care have sometimes been defeated by the money and lobbying of the insurance companies. When President Clinton proposed a very mild public health care program, the insurance companies paid for a television ad that was seen many times by everybody in the nation at the cost of billions of dollars, which told the big lie that the average person would lose the right to choose their own doctor. Clinton's plan allowed people to choose any doctor in any HBO. Instead, after its defeat, millions of people remained without health care.

Powerful interests oppose almost every item in the civilian budget as soon as recovery begins. What interests must be defeated to have the necessary spending to fill a deficiency in demand of many hundreds of billions of dollars? Constructive projects, such as a Missouri Valley Authority's efforts to develop dams, irrigation, and cheap power, were fought by the power companies tooth and nail. It is clear that in California near the end of the twentieth century, the power companies deliberately caused a severe shortage of power and made enormous profits from selling power under those conditions. Thus, government provision of water and power were opposed by the private power interests.

In 2007, President Bush asked for $481 billion in "total" military spending, almost a half trillion dollars for one year. But this total did not include other military requests, including some for the Iraq and Afghanistan wars, military projects for space, and other military-related items in the budget. This very complex subject is partly stated in a popular newspaper article, "Tank-size defense request: Bush is expected to ask for $481 billion. But the military seeks more" (Spiegel, 2007, p. 1).

Economic Constraints on Fiscal Policy

Both conservative and liberal presidents end up with remarkably similar fiscal performances in most peacetime periods (shown in great detail in the next chapter). Why does this happen? Not only are there administrative and political constraints on fiscal policy but there are also objective economic constraints, given our capitalist economic institutions. These economic constraints are given by the structure of capitalism. The three major constraints are limits on the redistribution of income, competition with private enterprise, and the incompatibility of policies to combat unemployment and policies to combat inflation at the same time.

First, if drastic redistribution of income toward equality were to be seriously legislated by a strongly progressive government, then capitalists might refuse to invest. A really drastic redistribution policy might "lower business confidence" and make capitalists hoard or flee the country with their capital. This did happen, for example, under the democratic socialist government of President Allende in Chile. Of course, capital wants places to go that are safer or that give higher returns. Such places might be difficult to find for very large amounts of capital fleeing redistribution policies in the United States. Usually, capital fleeing progressive governments has come to the United States because it has been viewed as a safe haven for profits.

Second, the U.S. government tries to avoid competition with private enterprise. If the government sponsored a successful public energy corporation, the lower prices would compete with present private energy corporations. These private energy corporations might then go on strike by not investing or by fleeing overseas. As conservatives frequently and correctly point out, any peaceful, constructive, direct investment by government does compete with private capital. Therefore, enough government investment might cause an investment strike or capital flight.

The same constraint may apply to regulations on elite professionals or government competition with elite professionals. For example, if free national health care were instituted, doctors might get reasonable payments instead of outrageous monopoly revenues. Doctors might also flee, but where would they go? Almost every other industrialized country already has free national health care.

Finally, fiscal policies for higher employment may conflict with anti-inflation policies. Policies to end unemployment require higher demand, but policies to end inflation require lower demand. A drastic enough rise in demand to cause full employment would also probably lead to much greater inflation. A drastic enough decrease in demand to cause stable prices (zero inflation) would also probably cause much more unemployment. There is simply no simple fiscal cure within capitalism to a situation of simultaneous unemployment and inflation.

THE MILITARY SOLUTION

To find some peaceful, civilian item worth hundreds of billions on which there is general agreement but no opposition from the big corporations is very difficult or impossible. There are also economic constraints facing many peaceful, constructive forms of government spending. As mentioned earlier, progressive economists from Marx to Keynes believed that it is possible to have an economy in which there is sufficient demand without war and military spending. Progressives argue that an economy based on a huge amount of military spending may prevent large recessions, but it will also reduce the rate of growth of the economy in the long run because it takes money away from consumption and investment. First, however, let us follow out the implications the of spending for war.

Dollars for military supplies do not violate any vested interests. Military spending is considered an ideal antirecession policy by big business for three reasons. First, such expenditures have the same effect in raising employment and profits as would expenditures on more socially useful projects. Yet the profits are very high because there is little competition for many kinds of military contracts. Second, military spending means big and stable profits. Civilian peacetime spending may shift up or down very easily, so it is not as reliable a source of demand as military spending. Third, the effect of expansion of military production is even more favorable in a capitalist economy because the expanded industry does not compete with peacetime industries for the consumer market. The reason is that military spending creates no new production that would compete with existing output. For example, nuclear bombs do not compete in the market with eggs or butter or any goods and services produced for private demand.

These favorable effects of military spending for business profits say nothing about the long-run unfavorable effects of military production on the growth of the goods and services used by all civilians. A dramatic example of military effects came in World War II and its aftermath. Before the war, in 1938 during the Great Depression, 18 percent of all workers were still unemployed by official statistics. During the war, the amount of government spending rose to an astonishing 40 percent of GDP. As a result of that vast increase in demand, the rate of unemployment fell to 1 percent, and that was just brief movement of people from one job to another.

But this scenario does not mean a wise citizen should pray for military spending! On the contrary, consider what would have happened if the United States continued to spend 40 percent of GDP on military production. Forty percent of GDP would have been lost for the purpose of constructive economic growth in the last sixty years. We would all be enormously poorer than we are.

One way of clarifying these two opposite effects is to see what actually happened in World War II. The war did create full employment. Full employment is very good. But the employment was all in the production of guns and tanks and bombs. The amount of civilian goods was very limited. It was so limited that physical rationing had to be initiated. No matter how much money you earned at a job, you could only buy a certain amount of eggs or milk or meat or any other food. The government issued ration stamps each month, and it was illegal to buy more than the allotted amount of food. Military spending means more production and employment, but it is all military, reducing the percentage of GDP for consumption.

Suppose there is a recession and unemployment. If it were politically possible, the whole amount of government expenditure could be spent on useful public commodities, such as housing or health or education, rather than on military. These useful types of public spending are not politically feasible in such large amounts, however, as long as the U.S. government is dominated by big business.

Military Spending versus Peaceful Spending

From all of the facts just given, we conclude that peaceful, constructive spending on a large scale is opposed by too many special interests to be politically feasible. Our hypothesis is that only large-scale military spending brought the United States out of the Great Depression of the 1930s, and only large-scale military spending has kept the United States out of another major depression.

This view is contrary to those writers who believe it would be easy to change production from guns to plows. Certainly, it is technically possible to divert money from bombs to cleaning up rivers, from tanks to education, or from military to civilian aircraft.

The problem is only political. Do those few wealthy people and corporations who benefit from military spending have more political power than those millions of people who would benefit from spending on health and education and other peaceful government spending? This is not an academic question but one at the heart of contemporary political struggle.

As this book is being written, the Iraq war is eating up $100 to $150 billion a year. Suppose the United States withdrew from Iraq all troops and all private contractors (who cost the taxpayer more in various ways). Suppose it did so in one month. This action would mean a sudden decline in military demand. The decline in demand could lead to a recession. In fact, there were economic expansions during World War II, the Korean War, and the Vietnam War. In each case, military spending was reduced after the war. In each case, there was a recession after the war.

If the Iraq war ends, then there will be a recession unless there is an equal amount of peaceful government spending. The answer to how can we pay for comprehensive health care and education for everyone is that the money saved by reduction of military spending could be spent for health and education. The problem is that vested interests will exert political power to attempt to prevent that change.

POLITICS OF FISCAL POLICY

The political reality is that vested interests oppose social programs with violent rhetoric. One example was the successful, multimillion-dollar advertising campaign against Clinton's mild health care program. Because of corporate opposition, Congress seldom talks about using the unemployed in major government building projects for peaceful use. In fact, the Eisenhower administration sold profitable nuclear energy plants to private capitalists for tiny sums of money. Presidents Nixon and Ford, both of whom were supported primarily by big business, vetoed a large number of liberal Keynesian bills to stimulate employment by more public jobs or by more spending for health, education, or welfare.

President Carter promised in his 1976 campaign some Keynesian-type spending to bring the economy to full employment. Yet he also had many ties to business and had many conservative economic advisors. Therefore, Carter did not launch constructive projects of the magnitude needed to approach full employment but continued to allow a relatively high level of unemployment. Carter kept nonmilitary spending to a constant or declining amount in terms of purchasing power. This freeze on constructive spending restricted some existing programs and prohibited new programs in national health care, public housing, or public energy production. Instead of public programs, he used subsidies to business to promote energy production. On the other hand, Carter, in spite of his explicit promise to cut military spending, increased military spending.

We have seen that political constraints make military spending the only allowable solution to unemployment. The political nature of the problem became even more apparent in the inflationary situation of the 1970s and 1980s. The Korean and Vietnam wars caused so much government demand for military supplies that inflation resulted, with prices rising especially in 1950 to 1953 and in 1967 to 1981.

To cure inflation, the simple Keynesian prescription is to increase taxes and reduce spending. But whose taxes are to be raised? Which spending is to be cut: spending for objectives of the rich or spending for middle-class needs? Major increases in taxes on the wealthy are not easily passed by our government. And there is not that much room for further taxes on the poor and the middle class without provoking rising discontent.

Therefore, it is politically easier to reduce government spending than to increase taxes. But military spending is different. Politicians and spokespersons for industry and the military continue to convince the nation that these expenditures are absolutely necessary. Thus, peaceful, constructive spending is cut time after time. Already a tiny percentage of the American government budget, it has nevertheless been cut even further every time there is a need to fight inflation through spending cuts. Hence, the burden of inflation has fallen on the common person in the form of rising prices, rising taxes, and falling constructive spending.

The question of social and political priorities often boils down to a conflict between the genuine needs of the majority versus the desires of the tiny minority that possesses immense economic and political power. The majority of Americans need more education, health, and social security, but a powerful minority favors military spending.

THE MILITARY ECONOMY

Fiscal policy is strongly influenced by the present high degree of militarization of our economy. The U.S. Department of Defense runs the largest planned economy in the world. It spends more than the net income of all U.S. corporations. It has over 8,000 major and minor installations, owns 39 million acres of land, spends over half a trillion dollars a year, uses 22,000 primary contractors and 100,000 subcontractors, and employs about 10 percent of the American labor force in the armed forces and military production.

How big is U.S. military spending in relation to all public spending? It certainly includes all Department of Defense spending, but it goes considerably beyond that. How far it goes is controversial, but the most careful study to date (see Cypher, 1974) includes half of all "international affairs" spending, veterans benefits, nuclear energy spending, and space appropriations. All of this spending is closely related to American military goals.

In addition, military spending includes about 75 percent of the interest on the public debt, since that percentage of the debt was used to pay for wars. Other military activities, on which it is too difficult to obtain exact expense data, are major parts of the research and development budget, the CIA, and other intelligence agencies. Another part of military costs are the deaths, wounds, and alienation of young Americans who fight the wars. Leaving aside the deaths, physical wounds, and mental wounds, the quantifiable items go far beyond the usual military budget.

Yet this amount of direct military spending (even if it included the things that cannot be quantified) still underestimates the impact of military spending on the U.S. economy. There is a very large indirect or secondary effect. First, the spending of those who receive dollars from military spending adds to consumer spending. Second, there is additional investment in plant, equipment, and business inventories by military industries. Economists measure the secondary effects of military spending by the government multiplier (discussed in Chapter 44). Remember that the government multiplier measures the ratio of the total increase in all spending to every dollar of increase in government spending. Estimates of the multiplier from military spending range from about $1.85 to $3.50 of total spending for every dollar of military spending.

The effect of additional military spending or reductions in military spending is greatly magnified by the secondary effects, measured by the multiplier. Therefore, if we ended all military spending, there would be a great decrease in demand. On the other hand, when military spending is increased (as in the Vietnam and Iraq wars), there is a large decrease in demand. Remember, however, that increases in military spending also mean increased deficits, increased inflation, and greater taxes and interest payments by the public. Also note that in the long run, military spending reduces our growth rate.

HOW MUCH PROFIT IN MILITARY CONTRACTS?

Why is big business normally happy with such a high level of military spending? On the aggregate level, we saw that it is used to protect U.S. investments abroad, to pull the economy out of recessions, and to prevent a major depression. There is yet an additional incentive for the individual defense contractor: the rate of profit is very high in military production, and most of these profits go to a few very large firms. Almost all military contracts go to some 205 of the top 500 corporations, and just 100 of them get 85 percent of all military contracts.

There are some studies of military profits, but all of them understate the profit rates. In reporting to the government, the military firms often overstate their costs. Since they operate in a relationship with the Pentagon, not under competition, they probably overstate costs more than most firms. Thus, they allocate costs from other parts of their business to military contracts and add in all sorts of other unrelated costs. In addition, much of the profits can be hidden. The profits can be hidden through the use of complex subcontracting procedures to subsidiaries, unauthorized use of government-owned property, and obtaining patents on research done for the government.

The profits of military contractors have been studied many times by the General Accounting Office of the U.S. government. The studies generally found that the military contractors admit to a much higher than average profit in their industry. It was also found, however, that even these admissions of high profits were sometimes only half of the actual profits made.

ALTERNATIVES TO THE MILITARY SOLUTION

In light of the well-known problems of fiscal policies, economists have had several reactions. Some conservatives see all military spending as fully justified, so they see no problem with the military solution to the lack of demand. Other conservatives do not like any fiscal policy because it interferes in the private economy, where they believe it usually does more harm than good. While they oppose all fiscal policy, they do argue for certain types of monetary policy, as we shall see in Chapter 51.

Some progressives have argued for the need to combine fiscal policy with monetary and price and wage policy. They argue, for example, that peaceful government spending can replace any amount of military spending, provided the government spending is coordinated with monetary policy and price controls.

Finally, some progressives believe that a deficiency of demand, along with rising costs, is so pervasive in capitalist expansions that no fiscal, monetary, or price measures can ever stop its main rhythm of cyclical booms and busts. Therefore, fundamental change is needed. A regime of economic democracy could directly raise demand through investment in enterprises under its control. (The democratic economy is discussed in Chapter 25.) These progressives argue that democratic planning in the economy could provide the stability and balance now lacking.

SUMMARY

This chapter discussed fiscal policy in detail. The tools of fiscal policy, government spending and taxes, were discussed. There are discretionary and autonomous fiscal policies. Depending on the value of tax revenue and how much the government spends in a year, there may be a budget surplus or deficit. Economists are divided on the importance and value of a balanced budget, especially if there is inflation or a recession.

Remember that conservative economists believe that the economy is always at full employment equilibrium unless there is an external shock. After a shock, the economy adjusts back to full-employment equilibrium. Any government interference with the economy will tend to hurt the economy; for example, government spending reduces private investment. Therefore, there should be no discretionary fiscal policy, only a balanced budget in which spending equals revenue.

Progressive Keynesians believe that the economy itself sometimes produces recessions or inflation. Increased government spending and lower taxes add to aggregate demand. Reduced government spending and higher taxes lower aggregate demand. Therefore, to fight recession and unemployment, increase demand by more government spending and lower taxes. To fight inflation and an overheated economy, raise taxes and lower government spending.

This basic and simple Keynesian view meets several problems: administrative problems, such as getting the correct timing on fiscal policy; political problems, such as resistance to constructive government spending by most of the wealthy and corporations because they pay taxes and because it might compete with them; economic problems, such as what do you do if there is both unemployment and inflation, a common occurrence in recent decades.

How can these problems be resolved? Conservatives say that the problems cannot be resolved, so Keynesian fiscal policy should never be used (though most conservatives are in favor of military spending as a special case). Progressive economists reply that fiscal policy can be effective provided it is combined with the correct monetary policy (discussed in the next few chapters). Some progressives go beyond liberal Keynesians to urge that recessions and inflation should be controlled by a democratically run economy.

Military spending is the largest single component of the U.S. federal budget. It has two main effects: if there is unemployment, it puts people to work, but these billions of dollars are paying for weapons and soldiers to kill people. Therefore, at full employment for the whole economy, the military sector is taking money away from investment in equipment and buildings, so it lowers the rate of economic growth.

SUGGESTED READINGS

The influence of interest groups on policy in congress is described in clear and readable detail in Barbara Sinclair's *Party Wars* (2006). The history of U.S. military spending, with emphasis on the Reagan, Bush, and Clinton years, is revealed in powerful prose in an article by Ronald V. Dellums, "Stealth Bombing America's Future: Beyond the B-2 Thunderdome" (1995). Dellums was a very progressive African American who chaired the Armed Services Committee of the U.S. House of Representatives. Instructors may find useful an excellent discussion of the fiscal policy of Clinton and Bush in Robert Pollin's *Contours of Descent: U.S. Economic Fractures and the Landscape of Global Austerity* (2004).

KEY TERMS

automatic fiscal policy
balanced budget
debt
deficit

discretionary fiscal policy
fiscal policy
surplus
transfer payments

REVIEW QUESTIONS

Define and describe fiscal policy tools, and give historical examples of how they have been used.

1. What is the difference between automatic and discretionary fiscal policy?
2. What fiscal policy finally brought the U.S. out of the Great Depression of the 1930's? Explain.

Compare and contrast conservative and progressive views on fiscal policy.

3. What problems are created by active fiscal policies according to conservative economists?
4. Give some examples of fiscal policy that progressive economists would use to help the economy. How would progressive economists counter conservative criticisms of fiscal policy?

Discuss how budget deficits, budget surpluses, and debt enter into the debate on fiscal policy.

5. Describe how fiscal policy decisions can be constrained by high debt.
6. How would budget deficits be erased through the use of fiscal policy, according to progressive economists?

Explain how fiscal policy should be used in a recession or if there is inflation, and describe how the appropriate fiscal policy affects recession and inflation.

7. What fiscal policies should be used if there is a recession? Explain how they would work.
8. What fiscal policies should be used if there is inflation? Explain how they would work.

List and describe the problems of using fiscal policy.

9. State some of the political issues/problems with fiscal policy. Give an historical example.
10. How might the use of fiscal policy have a negative impact on some private businesses? Explain.

Explain how military spending affects the economy.

11. Why is military spending usually politically popular? Who benefits? Who does not benefit?
12. What are some opportunity costs to military spending?
13. Explain the "guns versus butter" debate. Where would you stand on this debate? Why?

APPENDIX 47.1
FISCAL POLICIES OF PRESIDENTS CLINTON AND BUSH

We now turn to the actual fiscal policies of the Clinton and second Bush administrations to see what light they may cast on the problems raised about fiscal policies.

LEARNING OBJECTIVES FOR APPENDIX 47.1

After reading this appendix, you should be able to:

- Compare and contrast the fiscal policies of the Clinton and Bush administrations.
- Explain why there was a budget surplus in the later Clinton years.
- Explain why there is a budget deficit in the Bush years.

THE CLINTON YEARS, 1993–2001

The first part of the 1990s, partly under the first Bush presidency and partly under Clinton, was a period of slow growth of GDP, stagnant wages and salaries, and a generally weak recovery from recession. The last half of the 1990s, however, witnessed fairly rapid economic growth. There was a rapid rise in corporate profits and the stock market, with a slower rise in real wages. This accomplishment seemed so important that some economists declared that America had a new economy, not subject to recessions. A recession occurred in 2001.

Although wages and salaries were stagnant in the early 1990s, they did rise significantly in the late 1990s. The rise of corporate profits, however, was much faster than all employee compensation. Therefore, the labor share of all national income continued to fall in this period. There was thus in the late 1990s good growth, but only limited benefit for most employees, including low-paid workers, the middle class, and even high-paid technicians and professionals. Why did the labor share decline in the late 1990s? One obvious problem was that productivity of labor continued to rise much faster than the compensation of labor. But that only restates the problem. Why did real wages and salaries rise less than productivity and national product?

The national product rose in the expansion of the late 1990s because of considerable investment. The GDP was helped to rise faster than it had for many years by the information revolution. This revolution consisted of the extraordinary rise of computers and the ability to instantaneously send information around the world. The rapid rise in technology and communications was a large leap forward that allowed American firms to produce and sell a great deal more than they could have without it.

Since technology and productivity were rising very rapidly, increases could be given in wages and salaries, while profit rose much faster. However, wages and salaries were held down to a lower growth than the national product or income for several reasons. As usual in any expansion, unemployment was slow to go down. Public opinion did not support strikes because employees did make some gains, so further gains seemed less important. Even employees did not want strikes when their wages and salaries were already rising, even though they rose more slowly than soaring profits.

In addition, the share of labor depends not only on wages and salaries but also on other benefits and welfare going to all employees. In the late 1990s, it was also true that the number of people without medical insurance declined a little. The number of unemployed declined. The number of people living in poverty declined. These were significant gains, but they were nowhere near as fast as the rise of corporate profits and the rise of the stock market. Therefore, income of the propertied class, including corporate owners and stock holders, rose far faster than wages, salaries, and benefits.

Besides the information revolution and its help to corporate profits, there was another somewhat new factor in the economy. Firms made more and more investment overseas rather than in the United States. Firms also hired workers to sit at computers in faraway countries to do work previously done by American employees. The foreign employees receive very low wages, while American employees receive much higher wages and salaries because of the long U.S. history of rising productivity. Also, some American employees have unions. Unions were weak or nonexistent in some of the countries to which job were moved.

As employees perceived rising competition from abroad with the use of cheap labor there, they feared for their jobs. Since firms were moving some portion of their jobs overseas, their threats to fire American employees and move even more overseas were taken very seriously by employees. Therefore, in spite of the higher growth rate of GDP and profits, employees were very hesitant about going on strike. Taken together, this period of high growth also witnessed an ever-smaller share of national income going to American employees.

In addition to the higher growth of GDP and profits in the last half of the 1990s, there was another dramatic change relating to fiscal performance. The first Bush presidency saw a large rise in the deficit of the United States. In other words, under the first Bush, far more money was being paid out than the government was taking in.

This situation changed dramatically in the last half of the 1990s under Clinton. The deficit became smaller and smaller until finally there was a government surplus for three years, a rare occurrence in recent history. Why did the surplus grow for such a period under Clinton?

Some reasons relate to the usual way the government and the economy perform in most expansions, but the Clinton fiscal policies also contributed to the surplus. In the next chapter, we see that it is usual for deficits to decline in almost all business expansions. For a long period of history, it was also common to see surpluses toward the end of expansion. In brief, in the average expansion, regardless of which president is in power, government spending tends to rise, but at a slower rate. At the same time in the expansion, tax revenues rise very rapidly. Therefore, the revenue of government is rising much faster than its expenditures. This means lower deficits or even eventually a surplus. The reasons government spending and taxes act this way are given in the next chapter.

In the strong expansion of the late 1990s, these tendencies were encouraged by the Clinton administration's policies. The end of the Cold War against the Soviet Union allowed military spending to be reduced. After the Republicans took power in Congress in 1994, they made a deal with Clinton that froze most constructive, but not military, programs for several years. There were thus large declines of spending relative to GDP in the fields of education, health care, scientific research, and many others (including school lunches for children). Welfare spending to those in need was drastically reduced by another deal between Clinton and the Republicans over the objections of most Democrats. Clinton ensured that government discretionary spending was almost frozen, while government taxes were rising rapidly. As a result, the deficit was quickly reduced and there were yearly surpluses in the last three years of the Clinton administration.

FISCAL POLICIES OF THE SECOND BUSH, 2001–2006

The economy went into recession at the same time that the second President Bush took power in 2001. The GDP declined, unemployment rose, real wages and salaries declined, and the number of bankrupt firms rose. The stock market declined rapidly for several years. What did President Bush and the Republican congress do about the recession? They followed conservative economic views, so they did very little. There was one tax rebate for everyone, but it was very small, so it caused only a brief upswing in the economy.

Bush made a number of tax cuts. Most of Bush's tax cuts went to the richest 5 percent of the population. The other 95 percent of the population received very little. The wealthy spend a much lower percentage of their income on consumption than the middle class because the wealthy are able to save more out of a much higher income. Therefore, tax cuts that are mainly for the wealthy have very little affect on aggregate consumer spending. The argument for Bush's tax cuts for the wealthy and for corporations was that these are the ones who invest in the economy. According to conservative economists, if the wealthy have higher incomes after taxes, they will invest more in the economy, thus causing a strong recovery.

In fact, in the early years of the present recovery, the wealthy and the corporations did not invest much more in new capital goods, equipment, and buildings. Why should a corporation want to expand its productive facilities if it already cannot sell all that it produces? In a recession, there appear to be few profitable opportunities to invest. New investment would likely produce losses. Therefore, in spite of the tax breaks to the wealthy and tax breaks to the corporations, very little investment in new productive facilities occurred for several years.

On the spending side of government, the Bush administration did its best to reduce all discretionary, nonmilitary, spending. The Republicans left untouched only those programs that were embedded in the law as permanent entitlements. Even entitlement programs were attacked. Social Security payments were assailed in conservative rhetoric. President Bush said he wanted to save the Social Security system by cutting benefits and by privatizing the program. Privatizing meant that much of Social Security would be changed from secure government payments to investments in the unpredictable stock market. Since the stock market had just declined rapidly for three years, Bush's proposal horrified most voters. Millions of people had lost their savings in the stock market decline. Why would they entrust the stock market with their Social Security payments? This proposal was dropped.

President Bush and the Republicans did succeed in cutting the percentage of GDP going to health care, education, scientific research, and welfare. These peacetime programs were then replaced by an enormous expansion of military spending. The military spending rose so fast that the federal budget changed from surpluses to huge deficits. We shall see in Chapter 48 that deficits usually increase in recessions, but Bush's policy of increasingly large military spending greatly increased the deficits. Thus, while all kinds of peaceful services were drastically reduced, the budget went from surpluses to unprecedented deficits because of the military spending and the decline in taxes.

To give life to the generalities, an example may help. In 2006, President Bush proposed a budget with $2.7 trillion spending. It included a 5 percent increase in military spending. The annual request for military spending, however, did not include Iraq. The Republicans passed so-called "emergency requests" for at least $100 billion more for the Iraq war.

At the same time, almost every domestic program for the middle class was cut to some extent, with no increases for inflation or for larger numbers of people in the country. Altogether, the cuts in domestic programs amounted to $14.5 billion before worrying about inflation. The cuts included everything from A to Z, agricultural aid to veteran's benefits, with cuts in education, health care, and children's programs among others. There were cuts in Medicare, child support, and student loans, and a small program that distributed food to the elderly was cut entirely. In fact, aid to the elderly and the poor would be cut by $65 billion over the next five years (see Havemann, 2006, p. 1).

REVIEW QUESTIONS FOR APPENDIX 47.1

Compare and contrast the fiscal policies of the Clinton and Bush administrations.
1. Name some key fiscal policies used by the Bush administration (2001–2006). What was their impact?
2. Name some key fiscal policies used by the Clinton administration (1993–2001). What was their impact?
3. Explain why wages grew more slowly than productivity and GDP during the 1990s.

Explain why there was a budget surplus in the later Clinton years.
4. Other than expansion, what contributed to a budget surplus? What spending was cut and why?
5. What role did investment play in the expansion of the 1990s?

Explain why there is a budget deficit in the Bush years.
6. How and why has the amount of military spending differed from the Clinton administration of the 1990s to the Bush administration of 2001–2006?
7. What spending has been cut during the Bush administration? Increased? What has happened to taxes?

APPENDIX 47.2
FISCAL POLICY IN WARS

The largest discretionary fiscal changes take place during wars. This appendix briefly explores spending and taxes during periods of war.

LEARNING OBJECTIVES FOR APPENDIX 47.2

After reading this appendix, you should be able to:

• Describe and explain patterns of spending and taxes during recent U.S. wars.

WAR!

In World War II, the American government under Franklin Roosevelt spent 40 percent of the GDP to support the war. It would have been very unpopular and harmful to the war effort to raise taxes by that much. Therefore, there was an enormous amount of borrowing. The government borrows money by selling government bonds. The large borrowing by the government led to high deficit spending. Since there was a large deficit every year, this meant a rapidly growing national debt. Naturally, there was full employment so long as the government spent so much money. There was a recession when the war ended.

In the Korean War business cycle (1949–1954) military spending again was the dominant economic factor. In the expansion of 1949 to 1953 under Truman during the war, total federal spending grew at 4 percent per quarter. Taxes (or total receipts) grew by only 0.6 percent per quarter. Taxes grew very slowly because Truman did not want to be made unpopular by large increases in taxes. Therefore, in the wartime expansion, the deficit grew by over 3 percent per quarter and the national debt rose. Production and employment continued to rise as long as the war continued. When the war ended, there was a recession.

Similarly, under President Johnson, spending on the Vietnam War rose rapidly from about 1965 to 1968. There are no precise dates for the Vietnam War, and it did not take up the entire 1961 to 1969 expansion, but it certainly prolonged that expansion. In the actual war years, total government spending rose very rapidly. To remain popular, however, Johnson did not raise taxes. Therefore, there was more borrowing, the deficit rose, and the national debt increased rapidly. When the war ended, there was a recession.

The fiscal policy of the present Iraq war follows the same pattern. President Bush increased the military spending at a very rapid pace, spending hundreds of billions in Iraq and Afghanistan, while continuing to expand non-Iraq military spending. At the same time, he holds firmly to the principle of no more taxes (because his rich financial backers expect him to hold down their taxes). Since tax rates are not increasing (and have even declined), while government spending has leaped forward, the government is naturally going further into debt. The yearly deficit in government finances is added each year to the total government debt. Of course, so much military spending has helped production and employment in an otherwise weak recovery.

When the Iraq war ends and military spending declines, there will be a recession if there is no substitute for military production. It is perfectly possible in technical terms to switch to more constructive spending, such as health and education. If the government substitutes the same amount of spending for civilian goods and services at the time it reduces war spending, a recession could be avoided. We saw earlier that there is always much resistance to peaceful government spending from the large corporations.

To sum up, in wartime, military spending rises enormously. The large government demand ensures that production and employment continue to rise until the war ends. Taxes go up much less rapidly. Deficit spending balloons, and the national debt increases rapidly. Increase of the national debt means that the government must pay more interest to the people who hold the government bonds. When a war ends, there is always a recession unless there is some constructive substitute for the military spending.

REVIEW QUESTIONS FOR APPENDIX 47.2

Describe and explain patterns of spending and taxes during recent U.S. wars.
1. Use historical examples to demonstrate what happens to government spending during periods of war.
2. What happens to taxes during periods of war? Why?

Explain why there is an expansion during periods of war and recessions after the war.
3. Explain why there is an expansion during periods of war and recessions after the war.

CHAPTER 48

Government Spending and Taxes

In American society, the government exerts an enormous influence on the economy, although the government is itself dominated to a large extent by powerful corporations. While the U.S. government has always affected the economy in many ways, an essentially new relationship has emerged since the beginning of World War II in 1941. The government has become, by far, the largest single source of demand.

LEARNING OBJECTIVES

After reading this chapter, you should be able to:

- Explain how the amount of government spending and government spending as a proportion of GDP behave over the business cycle.
- Explain how government deficit behaves over the business cycle.
- Explain how taxes behave over the business cycle.
- Compare and contrast how spending and deficit spending differ in times of war and of peace.

THE TREND OF GOVERNMENT SPENDING, 1970–2001

What was the trend in government spending in the period from 1970 to 2001? In the cycle of 1970 to 1975, total local, state, and federal spending amounted to an average $918 billion per year. In the cycle of 1990 to 2001, in real terms after adjustment for inflation, total government spending at all levels was $1,469 billion per year, a very large increase. After the Cold War was over in the early 1990s, the share of military spending declined. In a change of direction, the military share of GDP started rising again after the U.S. occupation of Iraq.

Government and Aggregate Demand

Figure 48.1 depicts the flows of money to and from government to households and businesses.

As the figure shows, and as discussed in Chapter 47, the personal income tax takes money away from households, reducing demand. The corporate profit tax takes money away from business,

Figure 48.1   **Circular Flow of Money in Public and Private Sectors**

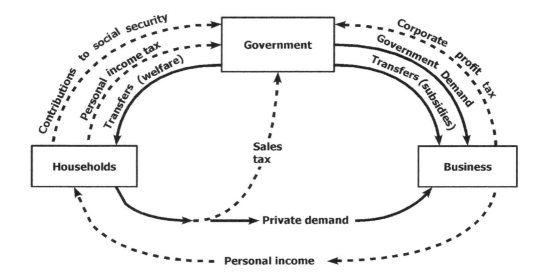

Exports and imports do not appear here and will be analyzed later.

reducing demand. Contributions to Social Security are taken from employees, before any income goes to households, reducing demand. The sales tax also reduces the flow of money and demand going to business. On the other hand, there is an enormous flow of demand from government to business for the purchase of goods and services. There is also a large flow from government to individuals and businesses in the form of transfer payments. Remember that a transfer payment is any money that flows from government to a person or business that is not in payment for goods and services.

What are some examples of transfer payments? Unemployment compensation is paid to unemployed workers because they are unemployed through no fault of their own, but obviously they are not producing goods and services for the department. A subsidy to a tobacco farmer is paid because Congress decided it is in the national interest to do so if the price of tobacco drops, but government does not buy tobacco. Interest is paid to people who buy government bonds, but no goods and services are produced by them to give to the government. Social Security payments are also transfer payments, but they are viewed as transfers from those who pay Social Security taxes to those who once paid the tax but are now retired.

Discretionary and Automatic Government Spending

Chapter 47 defined fiscal policy to mean decisions on government spending and taxing. Those types of spending that are deeply imbedded in our present political fundamentals and legal structure, such as Social Security, are called automatic fiscal policy. Congress does not need to vote on Social Security every year. The payments are made every year unless Congress changes it. Many things

Figure 48.2   **Federal Spending**

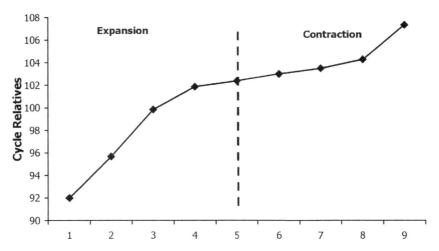

Federal spending is all U.S. government expenditures on goods and services. Average of five cycles, 1970–2001, billions of real, inflation adjusted dollars, quarterly, seasonally adjusted, annual rates.
Source: Bureau of Economic Analysis, Department of Commerce (www.bea.gov).

are fixed in concrete in the budget because they are inherited from prior commitments made in the laws. For example, in the 1930s, Congress decided to have unemployment compensation for those who are unemployed. There would be a firestorm if Congress tried to eliminate unemployment compensation altogether after all of these years, though Congress can change the amount of compensation.

As another example, Social Security payments were also pledged in the 1930s. Congress can change the amount to a small degree, but if it tried to eliminate Social Security altogether, there would be a political earthquake and Congress members who voted for it would disappear. In fact, the second President Bush tried for some years to push a campaign with all the power of the president to change Social Security from fixed payments to recipients to a new program of private investments in the stock market. He called this a reform to "save" Social Security, but most people felt that it destroyed Social Security as a secure retirement fund.

Congress has discretion to spend what is left after automatic spending. Since the automatic spending is much larger than discretionary spending, the course of government spending has the same pattern in every peacetime cycle. The pattern of spending and taxing over the business cycle, which is largely automatic spending, changes only when there is a large war. The previous chapter discussed policy views on government spending. Now let us see what government has actually done in spending in the average of the last five cycles. A distinction must be made between the amount of government spending and government spending as a share of GDP. In the usual expansion, the amount of government spending rises, but it rises more slowly than GDP. Therefore, we first consider how government spending rises in expansions, then why it rises slower than GDP.

What does Figure 48.2 tell us about federal spending? During each expansion, federal spending rises slowly over the whole expansion. The continuous but slow rise of government spending in expansions is not mysterious because there are always needs for expanding or improving infrastructure, such as roads and bridges. We shall see shortly that government revenue rises in expansions, so it is easy to spend some proportion on important projects. The expansion of government continues regardless of which party is in power and regardless of what is promised by candidates.

Figure 48.2 also shows that government spending continues to climb in economic contractions. In contractions, governments have less money and strong pressure to cut back their spending. Why does it rise? The answer is automatic spending that has been built in by laws over many decades. For example, unemployment compensation automatically increases because unemployment increases. Welfare automatically increases because the number of poor increases in contractions. Farm subsidies automatically increase because farm prices fall. Many other subsidies to business also automatically increase because they are often in trouble during recessions.

What is even more remarkable is that because of the automatic increases in government spending, not only the amount of spending but also the growth rate of spending increases in recessions. In the five cycles from 1970 to 2001, during the average economic expansion, federal government spending rose rather slowly at 1.8 percent per year. This rate of growth was far slower than the rise of GDP in those expansions. During the same period, in the average contraction, however, government spending rose much faster at 6 percent a year. Thus, we see that federal government spending rises only slowly in expansions but rapidly in contractions.

One conclusion is that the business cycle automatically changes the pattern of government spending from relatively slow in expansions to relatively fast in contractions. This is so in every cycle except when there are enormous changes in discretionary spending, such as during wars. The second conclusion is that government spending will have a different effect on aggregate demand in expansions and contractions. Remember, from the analysis of aggregate demand, that government spending is part of total demand. When government spending rises more slowly than GDP in expansions, it contributes only a little to the growth of aggregate demand.

In fact, since government spending falls further as a percentage of GDP, it has less effect on holding demand up to the level of the total GDP supplied to the market. As private spending weakens and rises more slowly near the peak of the cycle, the slowness of government spending growth also helps weaken the growth of demand.

In contractions, however, when government spending rises rapidly, it is one of the things that helps stimulate the economy and start a new recovery. There were many economic recoveries in American history before government played a significant role, so government spending is not the sole cause of recovery. However, the increased government spending does help the private sector to recover a little faster than it might otherwise have done. It must also be noted, however, that in arguments over policy, many negative effects of government spending are always asserted. Spending might have some long-run importance especially if the government debt keeps rising.

GOVERNMENT TAXATION

Government spending is only half the picture. We must also examine taxes. Taxation behaves quite differently from government spending and is much easier to understand. Federal taxes rise when people have more income. Federal income taxes are some fixed percentage at every level of income. They are called "progressive" because the percentage of taxation increases as the income bracket increases. Under President Roosevelt's Democratic administration in World War II, the tax percentage rose very steeply as income rose from bracket to bracket. The tax was then very progressive! Under several conservative Republican presidents, including the present President

Figure 48.3 **Federal Tax**

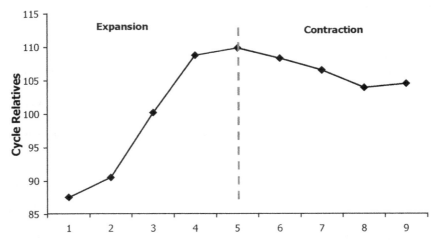

Federal revenue consists of all payments to the government from taxes and fees. Average of five cycles, 1970–2001. Billions of real, inflation adjusted dollars. Seasonally adjusted, quarterly data, at annual rates. *Source:* Bureau of Economic Analysis, Department of Commerce (www.bea.gov).

Bush, the tax rates on the rich were sharply reduced. Therefore, the federal income tax has become much less progressive.

It should also be noted that the federal income tax is a great deal less progressive in reality than it looks on paper. The problem is that there are major loopholes for high-income earners. For example, if a rich person owns stock in a corporation, then sells it after a few years at a big profit, it is called a capital gain. Capital gains from stocks are charged a much lower tax than the ordinary income of employees. For some years under President Clinton, the lower taxes for capital gains were abolished, but they were reestablished under President Bush and the Republican congress. The new tax cut for capital gains of rich stock owners made income distribution more unequal than it had been. This regressive feature of taxation means that the rich are taxed less than the poor.

Nevertheless, the federal tax is still progressive enough that when national income rises and people go into higher tax brackets, the government not only collects higher taxes but actually collects a higher percentage. On the other hand, when there is a recession, tax payers have lower income and pay a lower percentage of their income in taxes.

Because it is progressive, the federal income tax tends to rise rapidly in expansions and to fall rapidly in contractions, as shown in Figure 48.3.

Figure 48.3 shows that taxes rise when income expands and fall when income contracts. In fact, income taxes rise somewhat faster than national income, but they also fall somewhat faster than national income.

Remember that higher taxes mean less demand for goods and services. Lower taxes mean more demand for goods and services. When we discussed government policy in the previous chapter, we saw that many problems may arise when Congress tries to lower taxes. The most obvious problem is that lower taxes mean fewer government services, such as less education for children and teenagers as well as less medical care for the elderly. Another problem is that lower taxes may mean more deficits. Finally, there may be a vehement fight over whose taxes are to be lowered, those of the rich or those of the middle class.

GOVERNMENT DEFICITS AND SURPLUSES

Remember the definition of a government deficit? By definition, the federal government deficit means that federal revenues (mainly taxes) are less than government spending. A government surplus in the budget means that government revenue (mostly taxes) is greater than government spending. Some politicians talk as if a government deficit has the same effect as the deficit of an individual citizen. Both are similar in some ways. There may be a good reason for debt, such as an individual buying a house or a government building a hospital.

One difference is that an individual may judge the effect of borrowing as a good or bad thing merely in terms of its effect on himself or herself. Government deficits have major effects on the whole economy. Sometimes a government deficit hurts the economy, but sometimes it helps the economy. It depends on the economic situation. Government spending that results in a deficit (usually called deficit spending) means a flood of money into the economy. This large increase in demand means that many more people are employed. Government deficit spending, in a moderate amount, stimulates the economy. In a recession, it may help restore employment. That does not mean it is a perfect policy. Of course, if the economy is already at full employment, as during a war, the deficit spending will mean that demand far exceeds the possible supply. Therefore, under full employment, deficit spending cannot increase output any further, but it may cause inflation and many other problems.

Another difference is that an individual with too much debt may go bankrupt because he or she is unable to pay back the debt. The federal government cannot go bankrupt because it can usually manage to borrow money or it can even print money. Of course, government borrowing or printing money may cause other problems, as we shall see.

There is also a very different result depending on whether the government goes into debt to its own citizens or to foreigners. When the government sells bonds to raise money when tax revenues do not cover all of its spending (a deficit), it has to pay back the money. A government can always pay its own citizens in paper money that is worth less and less. Doing so may have catastrophic political and economic effects if it is a very large amount, but a government can certainly do it to some limited extent. If a government defaults on its debts to foreigners, they may react by ending all trade and making no future loans. In come cases, powerful countries have even invaded or otherwise taken over weak countries to recover debts.

What actually happens to the government deficit in the average peacetime business cycle? The deficit is shown in Figure 48.4.

The figure shows that in the typical economic expansion, the deficit declines. It declines because government spending rises only slowly, while taxes automatically rise rapidly. Figure 48.4 also reveals that the deficit rises in the typical recession. It rises because government spending automatically balloons in a recession. One reason is that there are increases in transfer payments such as unemployment compensation. On the other hand, as income falls, so does the federal income tax. Since spending is rising while tax receipts are falling, the deficit must rise.

What are the implications of this alternating decline and rise of the deficit? This issue was discussed in Chapter 47. As a recap of the main points, remember that in the expansion, deficit spending falls because taxes rise faster than spending. As government deficit spending falls, it becomes an element of aggregate demand that is falling in the expansion rather than rising. Therefore, the decline of government deficit spending means that the government contributes less to aggregate demand. Demand is weakened enough that other factors may then cause a recession (as explained in Chapter 45). Therefore, the declining government deficit is one of the reasons for limited demand that may lead to recession.

Figure 48.4 **Federal Deficit**

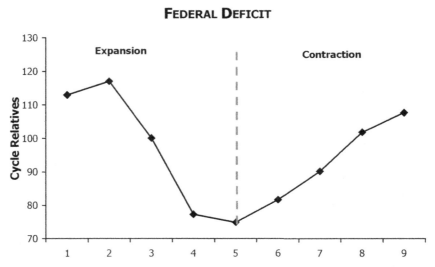

The deficit is the amount by which spending is greater than revenue. Average of five cycles, 1970–2001. *Source:* Bureau of Economic analysis, Department of Commerce (www.bea.gov).

One point needs clarifying. Why does it matter whether the decline is in all government spending or just deficit spending? All government spending keeps rising throughout the business cycle. In the expansion, while all government demand keeps rising, deficit spending falls. The point is that deficit spending does not mean the total amount of government spending, only the net flow of government spending after we subtract tax revenues. The yearly deficit measures the net flow of spending flowing from the government to individuals. It measures the net flow of demand from government. Thus, it is the deficit spending only that stimulated demand. If all government spending is offset by taxes, then there is no net flow.

In a recession, on the contrary, the government deficit automatically rises under existing laws about government spending and taxes. The rising deficit means a flood of government demand into the economy. In a recession, this may help stimulate production and employment. Although it has other effects, The rising government deficit may be one reason for economic recovery. Its possible adverse effects are fully discussed in Chapter 47.

THE GOVERNMENT DEFICIT IN WAR AND PEACE

In peacetime, the deficit tends to fall in expansions and rise in contractions, as we just described. However, the deficit tends to do the exact opposite in wartime cycles. Why is that?

In wartime, government spending rises rapidly. Government demand for military goods and services is virtually unlimited during a war. For example, in 1938 at the end of the Great Depression, 18 percent of the workforce still lived in miserable unemployment. Yet by 1943 in World War II, there was zero unemployment, except for people moving from one job to another. Frictional unemployment, movement from one job to another in 1943, was only about 1 percent of the labor force.

Why was there full employment? It was because the U.S. government spent 40 percent of the GDP on military production and soldiers. That flood of spending used up all of the millions of unemployed people and then hunted for more. Indeed, a great many women went into economic production for the first time.

The government in World War II, as in all wars, found that it could not raise taxes enough to pay for the war. That always happens because governments do not want to be unpopular in a war, so they are afraid to raise the necessary taxes. In this case, taxes would have had to have risen from 1 or 2 percent of the GDP to 40 percent of GDP.

Since government spending zoomed upward, while taxes rose very slowly, there was a huge deficit in World War II. This also happens in every war. At present, the Iraq war has driven military spending to around a half a trillion dollars a year. For political reasons, taxes have risen very little. Therefore, the war has also produced a record deficit.

Moreover, the operations of the economy pay no attention to the ideology and promises of presidents and political parties. In the expansion of World War II under Roosevelt, a Democratic president, the deficit rose dramatically. In the Korean War, under the Democratic President Truman and the Republican President Eisenhower, the deficit rose. In the Vietnam War, under the Democratic President Johnson, the deficit rose. In the two Iraq wars, the first under the Republican President George Bush and the second under his son, George W. Bush, also a Republican president, the deficit rose.

Yet in all of the time since World War II, the deficit has fallen in every peacetime expansion under every president, whether Democrat or Republican. The reason is, as shown earlier, that most government spending is automatic under existing laws and rises only very slowly in expansions. However, taxes rise rapidly in every expansion under existing laws. Therefore, in peacetime expansions, the deficit must fall. Only extreme changes in the laws would change this cause and effect. Only in a war does the discretionary spending rocket upward, producing a deficit in an expansion.

SUMMARY

The chapter showed how money flows from government to households and businesses. At the same time, money flows from households and businesses to government. Government spending puts money into the economy, but government taxes take money out of the economy. Usually, in a recession, the U.S. government runs a deficit. The reason is that automatic expenditures of government, such as unemployment compensation, must increase. Yet the falling income means that tax collections decrease. Since taxes are falling while spending is increasing, a deficit results. In a recession, deficit spending by government increases demand and helps cause a recovery.

In peacetime expansions, the deficit declines and there may be a surplus. The deficit declines in peacetime expansions because spending rises very slowly, while taxes automatically increase rapidly. If there is a surplus near the peak of the cycle, then the fact that money is flowing out of the economy to government will reduce demand. The reduced demand may help cause a recession if the private economy is moving in that direction.

We conclude that if automatic policies prevail as usual in a peacetime recession, the government deficit tends to help the private economy rise and recover at the end of the recession. On the other hand, if the automatic policies prevail as usual in an expansion, the U.S. government automatically tends to weaken demand, so it does less and less to prevent a recession at just the time when trends in the private economy are producing a recession.

REVIEW QUESTIONS

Explain how the amount of government spending and government spending as a proportion of GDP behave over the business cycle.

1. What are some automatic types of government spending? Does automatic government spending tend to go up or down in a recession?
2. What are some discretionary types of government spending?

Explain how government deficit behaves over the business cycle.

3. Does deficit spending help or hurt aggregate demand? Explain.
4. Does the deficit usually go up or down in an expansion? Explain.
5. Does the deficit usually go up or down in a recession? Explain.

Explain how taxes behave over the business cycle.

6. Does automatic taxation tend to go up or down in a recession?
7. Explain why tax rates and tax revenues often decrease in recessions and increase in expansions.

Compare and contrast how spending and deficit spending differ in times of war and peace.

8. How is government spending for war financed? What does this mean for the deficit if taxes are not raised? If taxes are raised?
9. Does military spending always decrease during peacetime? What are other programs that may receive extra funds during times of peace? What does this mean for the deficit if taxes are not raised? If taxes are raised?

PART III, SECTION 4

MONEY AND MONETARY POLICY

CHAPTER 49

Money, Banking, and Credit

Before we can fully understand government policy, we must consider the financial system on which our economy is based. This chapter begins by describing our monetary and credit system as well as the evolution of money from early times to the present. The banking system is extremely important not only to the individual depositors but also to the macroeconomy. Why? Because banks create money. This chapter examines the money creation process, and finally, it discusses the problems caused by money and credit.

LEARNING OBJECTIVES

After reading this chapter, you should be able to:

- List and explain the three functions of money.
- Describe the evolution of money and banking.
- Discuss how credit and interest rates are related to business cycles.

MONEY AND THE FUNCTIONS OF MONEY

Why is a dollar bill different from an index card? They are both pieces of paper. Why can't I take an index card into the store and leave with a bag of cookies? To understand what money is, you have to understand what money does. Money fulfills three functions: it serves as a **medium of exchange**, it serves as **a unit of account** for transactions and debts, and it is a **store of value**. A dollar bill serves as a medium of exchange. *I can go into the store with a dollar bill and the clerk will accept it in exchange for the bag of cookies.* In fact, the dollar also serves as a unit of account. *The value of the bag of cookies is measured in dollars.* If I sign an IOU (a debt) for the cookies, the terms of payment will be in dollars. A dollar is also a store of value because I can put it away and still use it in five or ten years to purchase goods and services. *It is still a dollar and can be used for payments in the future.*

Many things can store value or purchasing power into the future, but I cannot take my jewelry or art work or an index card into the store to buy cookies. Cookies will also not be valued in terms of jewelry. What makes money unique is that it fulfills all three of the functions listed. In the United States, the dollar is the medium of exchange, a unit of account, and a store of value.

To understand money more clearly, we examine a brief history of the evolution of money and credit, what money is, and what money does. This history discusses the general stages in West European financial history but does not examine the particular details of money in every country.

A HISTORY OF MONEY

Among the earliest tribes, exchange was conducted by the barter system. Barter means that one commodity is directly traded for another in the market without the use of money. For example, we may find trade in this form: 1 coat = 2 hats. If this exchange ratio persists for some time, people may come to think of one coat as worth two hats, or they may think of one hat as worth half a coat. Barter means that if you have some hats and you want a coat, you must find someone with some coats who wants to trade with you. As populations grew, trading increased, and as economies became more complex, simple barter became very difficult.

The second evolutionary step was to the crudest kind of money, a stage in which some particular commodity was used as money. Goods and services were given a value in terms of a commodity such as corn, cows, or rocks. For example, in a community in which cows are scarce and desirable, the number of cows owned would be a status symbol. Suppose cows played the role of money. A man might pay a certain number of cows for a bride. In the market, we might find that 2 coats = 1 cow = 4 hats. People in this society would calculate all their production and wealth in terms of cows. They might actually sell or trade coats for cows and then use the "cow money" to buy hats, or vice versa. This was a tremendous innovation and greatly enhanced the ability to make complex transactions.

Cows, however, are not a very convenient money commodity. They are perishable and not easily divisible, problems that could be solved by using precious metals. Imagine trying to make change with a cow! Large numbers of pieces of money that are of equal value led to the third step of the evolution: the development of metallic money. Precious metals have several virtues as a medium of exchange: (1) one need carry only a small amount to buy other commodities; (2) they are easily divisible—uniform coins of various values can be made by melting, and thus the exact amount necessary for any purchase can be used; (3) they are nonperishable and hence can be stored indefinitely.

The durability and portability of metallic money means that it may be used not only for calculating values of different goods but also in every type of exchange. Thus, trade takes this form: 1 coat = 1 oz. gold = 2 hats. Any commodity (such as a coat) may be sold for metallic money. Then the metallic money is put away until its holder wishes to buy another commodity (such as a hat).

The fourth step in the evolution came when paper claims were substituted for metallic money. Ultimately, the paper claims were still payable in metallic money, such as gold. The paper claims were originally issued by goldsmiths, private bankers, and merchants. Governments soon followed suit by issuing their own paper money. The paper money issued by government essentially represented IOUs—that is, promises by the government to pay in gold on demand. Of course, it was possible to issue more paper money than the gold held by government because not everyone demanded gold at the same time. We shall see later how banks create money in this way.

In the fifth step in the evolution of money, governments issued paper money but ruled that it could not be exchanged for gold. Paper money looked the same as before, but the government would no longer convert or pay its paper IOUs in gold on demand. In other words, the government was creating money by running the printing press. This method of money creation financed the American and French revolutions and the U.S. Civil War. Almost all governments at one time or another have printed money to pay expenses, especially in the monetary chaos following World War I.

The value of paper money today has no direct connection with gold reserves because no one is allowed to demand that the government convert it to gold. At the same time, governments usually prohibited private individuals or institutions from issuing paper money. One way governments made their paper money more acceptable to the populace was to accept it for tax payments. Governments also passed laws to declare that paper money is legal tender. The term **legal tender** means that *the paper must be accepted as payment for all debts.*

A further evolution of money is the checking account with a bank or other financial institution. Sums of money in checking accounts are bookkeeping entries called deposits. They do not exist in the form of metallic or paper money. They are actually promises to pay; that is, they are debts of the bank. Checks written against these accounts are orders to transfer deposit funds to other accounts or to convert some of the deposit account into paper currency. The owner of such an account may have brought currency to the bank or may have deposited checks from other parties.

The depositor may also have signed a note to the bank and borrowed the money from the bank. In such a case, the bank and the individual merely exchange IOUs. The bank's IOU, the deposit, serves all the functions of legal tender. Checks drawn against the balance make payment without the use of currency or coin. Although a check is not legal tender, the deposit is convertible into legal tender. Therefore, the deposit account is money.

THE EVOLUTION OF MODERN BANKING

Centuries ago, when the market system was evolving, goldsmiths had large quantities of precious metals. To protect them, secure storage facilities had to be constructed. Other individuals sought the same security for their money but did not have enough money to justify the expense of constructing such facilities. The local goldsmith began to accept the deposit of their coin (coins were the sole form of money at the time) and precious metals. As evidence of these deposits, the depositor was provided with a receipt. The goldsmith earned income by demanding payment from the individual depositor for the safekeeping of the coins and metal.

In time, goldsmiths who had developed reputations for honesty found that these deposit receipts could be used by the individuals holding them in payment of debt. These receipts began to circulate among buyers and sellers as a medium of exchange. For example, merchants, instead of carrying coin on business trips, would deposit it with a reputable and renowned goldsmith. The receipt could then be used to settle accounts in distant lands. As long as the goldsmith was willing and able to redeem these deposit receipts, or paper claims, on demand for coin, they performed the function of money. Here we see the initial stages in the development of both the banking system and paper claims as money. The validity of the paper claims as money was a function of their general acceptability as money. Their acceptance as money depended on the confidence that the public had in the goldsmith's ability to convert the paper claims into coin on demand.

Thus far, however, goldsmiths had not performed the primary distinguishing function of bankers, the creation of money. All they had done was match their metallic assets with paper claims. Their balance sheets probably would have resembled this:

Assets	Liabilities
Coin in vault $1,000	Deposits $1,000

The deposits were a liability for the goldsmith because he "owed" that money to the depositor.

Goldsmiths eventually realized they could issue loans based on the coin they were holding.

They issued loans by giving out paper (demand deposits and notes payable on demand) in excess of the coin they held in their vaults. How were they able to do this? First, people had confidence in their ability to redeem the depositors' paper claims in coin on demand. Second, this confidence led other people to accept the paper claims in settlement of their debts. Therefore, at any given time, only a small portion of the paper claims needed to be converted into coin.

As long as goldsmith-bankers could readily meet this small portion of claims for coin, they were in a position to increase their total loans beyond the actual amount of coin they had in their vaults. In other words, they were able to create money.

The total of coin, bank notes, and deposit receipts now in circulation exceeds the amount of coin that has been minted by government authority. The bank notes (issued by the goldsmith-bankers to those who borrow from them) and the deposit receipts are money. They are money in the same way coin is money, because people are willing to accept them in payment for any debt. It makes no difference to an individual whether payment is made in the form of coin, bank note, or deposit receipt, as long as the person can use them interchangeably for making their own payments.

Goldsmiths became bankers because they created money. These bankers kept in their vaults an amount of coin large enough to meet the demands for coin they expected to be made on them. In fact, they could roughly estimate these demands from their experience. A banker-goldsmith might have deposits of coin of $800 but make loans of $1,000. The banker knows that everyone will not come at the same time to get their coins.

The banker's liabilities in this example clearly exceeded the coin in his or her vault (we assume this banker was a man, though there are now many women bankers). What he had done was lend money to individuals. He paid out $200 in coins. However, people were willing to hold the other $800 of loans in the form of bank deposits with receipts. Thus, the banker created total liabilities of $1,000 in IOUs while holding only part of his total liabilities ($800) in the form of coin. He now had an additional form of income: the interest earned from the loans he made. The banker had created money in excess of the coin in his vault in the amount of $200.

The bankers' ability to create money was limited by the portion of notes and deposits they were forced to maintain in the form of coin because of depositors' habits or other considerations. In our example, because the banker had to hold 80 percent of deposits and note liabilities in the form of coin, he could expand the money supply by only 20 percent of the amount of coin in his vault.

Here we see the development, in its initial stages, of the modern banking system. The bankers created debts that circulated freely as money and slowly came to form an increasing part of the total money supply. They successfully converted their idle coins, which earned no money, into loans for which they charged a rate of interest. The lending function, formerly performed by moneylenders, became the function of bankers. The uniqueness of bankers, however, was that, unlike moneylenders, they could make loans in excess of the actual coin in their vaults.

OPERATION OF MODERN COMMERCIAL BANKS

The bankers' business consists of taking the money deposited with them, on some of which they pay interest, and lending it out at higher rates of interest. Bankers are torn between two objectives. On the one hand, they want to make as much profit as possible by lending out as much as they can. Moreover, the riskiest loans pay the highest interest rates, so risky loans may make more profit for banks if they are paid back. On the other hand, bankers want safety. Bankers want to be able to pay off easily any depositor who demands his or her money.

Technically, the banker is said to seek liquidity. **Liquid assets** are *those easily converted into money to pay off depositors.* The most liquid asset is money in paper currency and coin (or even gold). These assets are safe and liquid, but they pay no interest to the banker. The next most liquid assets are government notes and bonds. Because they are so liquid, they are sometimes called *near money*. Government bonds pay low interest because they are very safe. Government bonds can be cashed immediately, although at variable prices determined by the market if cashed before the final date payable. Least liquid are risky private loans, which may pay high interest but cannot be cashed until the payable date and may never be paid back to the bank if the individual goes bankrupt.

Banks have both assets and liabilities. **Liabilities** are *what the banks owe to someone else.* Bank liabilities consist mainly of the amount that is owed to depositors. Every depositor has the right to ask for payment. Some have the right to ask for payment at any time. So these are called demand deposits. Others have the right to be paid only after some certain time. For example, I may buy a one-year certificate of deposit from a bank for $1,000. If the interest rate is 3 percent, then after one year, the bank must pay me $1,030.

Assets are *those things owned by the bank or owed to the bank.* The assets of the banking system include gold, but gold can be held only by the government's Federal Reserve System (which is discussed in Chapter 51 on monetary policy). Another asset is currency in coins and paper, but currency is a very small part of the banks assets. A large part of bank assets consists of U.S. government bonds, certificates that say the government owes the owner interest plus repayment of the original amount. By far the banks' largest assets, however, are the loans that banks will someday collect from individuals and businesses.

Let's update the balance sheet of the goldsmith to look more like the balance sheet of a modern bank. For purposes of analysis, we often classify assets as *reserves*, or cash in the vault or on deposit with the Federal Reserve, or as loans to businesses, individuals, and governments. We shall soon discover that modern banks are required by the government to keep a certain percentage of their deposits in the form of reserves. These reserve requirements, policed by the Federal Reserve System, limit a bank's ability to make loans.

Assets	Liabilities
Coin or cash in vault (reserves)	Deposits
Government bonds	Borrowed funds
Loans to households and businesses	Capital

To recap, a bank's assets are its cash, loans to businesses and individuals, and government bonds. Its liabilities are its deposits, which represent money owed to depositors, plus shares of stock in the bank owned by stockholders, plus amounts the bank has borrowed from other sources.

CREDIT AND INSTABILITY

Throughout the nineteenth century, there were a number of monetary and banking panics, sometimes leading to recession. What is a *panic*? Remember that the banks of the nineteenth century were unregulated. If a bank wished to do so, it could loan out 100 percent of its deposits. Often, that would cause no problem because if some people take their deposits out of the bank, others put in new deposits. But suppose that there was a rumor that a bank was losing money on loans and could not pay back its depositors. What would you do if you thought that your bank might not be able to repay your deposit to you? You would rush to the bank and try to get your deposit out in cash.

When everyone rushes to the bank at the same time to get their money out, it is the beginning of a monetary panic. Since the bank cannot repay all of its depositors at one time, it must refuse to pay some depositors. Soon the panic spreads to all depositors. Soon the bank closes its doors, and all of its depositors are left without any money in their accounts. Then people are without any money to pay bills. This situation causes the panic to spread to businesses to which people owe money.

In this situation, some banks of the nineteenth century went bankrupt and no one was paid. The monetary panic then spread to other banks. In some cases, people just became generally afraid, so they wanted their money from all banks. Then there was a general money panic, with many banks going bankrupt and many people losing all of their money. Since many people could not pay back businesses for things they had bought on credit, and since banks could offer no credit, many businesses also went bankrupt. A monetary panic often led to a recession or depression.

The terrible consequences of a panic led to attempts to regulate the banking system. There was increasing regulation in the first half of the twentieth century. However, as the economic climate changed and bankers gained more political power, there has been less regulation in the last half of the twentieth century and beginning of the twenty-first century. This evolution of regulation and deregulation is described in Chapter 51 on monetary policy. Here we discuss the present role of credit with few regulations in the modern American economy from 1970 to the present.

Credit affects the economy both through the total amount of credit available and through the interest rate or price of borrowing. In Chapter 42, we discussed the amount of consumer credit. It was shown that consumer credit rises during the economic expansion because consumers are confident that they will have jobs, so they will have the income to repay their loans. The increase of consumer credit was shown to support and lengthen the expansion by increasing consumer spending.

The problem is that there is an increasingly higher ratio of consumer credit to their incomes. The situation becomes more fragile and dangerous. If there is a small decline in production and employment, many consumers cannot pay their loans or the interest on them. Consumers then may lose their homes and cars and other things they have bought on credit. This means that the corporations and banks they owe money to are weakened and may go bankrupt. The existence of credit makes a recession much worse, greatly exaggerating the downswing.

Too much credit is a problem not just of consumer debt but also of corporate debt. In every expansion, corporations and other businesses become highly optimistic, so they expand their equipment and buildings through large investments. But few corporations have the money for such large investments. They borrow money from financial institutions. Their increasing credit allows them to invest and expand the economy. The problem, however, is that the ratio of corporate debt to corporate profits keeps rising during the expansion. The data were presented in Chapter 43.

As the ratio of debt to profit becomes larger, corporations face greater danger of bankruptcy and the economy becomes more fragile. Eventually, when the profit perspective dims for any reason and a recession begins, many corporations are in great trouble. A decline in their revenue not only means lack of money to pay employees, it also means that they cannot repay their debts to financial corporations. Many corporations may go bankrupt. For this reason, a small decline in production in the whole economy has the potential to lead to a recession. Weakness and fragility of the financial system has been a major reason that recessions have turned into depressions.

Besides the desires of consumers and businesses to borrow or not to borrow, a closely related factor is the credit policy of financial institutions. During the middle of expansion, they are free and easy with credit at relatively low interest rates. This may encourage unrealistic speculative purchases by both consumers and businesses. Then, as the speculative frenzy increases, banks begin to worry about repayment. At that point, the higher demand allows them to raise interest rates. The higher interest rate makes it more difficult for individuals and businesses to borrow more money.

In recessions, banks become very pessimistic about the ability of individuals and businesses to repay loans, so they become very tight-fisted about doing any loans. Even loans that would be easily funded in expansion are refused in recessions, thus worsening the recession.

We may conclude that in addition to the rise and fall of the amount of credit outstanding, the rise and fall of interest rates also greatly influences the economic system and exaggerates instability. We next turn to interest rates.

INTEREST RATES

Interest is the amount paid to borrow money. Interest is paid on loans to businesses as well as loans to individuals. We discussed consumer credit in relation to consumer spending in Chapter 42. Here we focus on business borrowing.

The cost of borrowing money rises and falls with the business cycle, though with a time lag. Availability and cheapness of credit affect profits and investment. There are many types of interest rates reflecting the many kinds of borrowing in our society. One of the most frequently cited is the prime rate, which is the interest rate paid by a bank's best customers. It is usually lower than rates paid by other customers.

The pattern of movement of the prime rate over the business cycle is shown in Figure 49.1.

Figure 49.1 reveals two important points. First, the prime rate (and most other interest rates) rises in economic expansions and declines in recessions. Second, the prime rate (and most other interest rates) lags behind the overall business peak and trough. At the beginning of expansion, when most other economic series are rising, the interest rate still falls in the first stage of expansion.

Why does the interest rate rise and fall with the cycle, and why does it lag at the turning points? During the expansion, businesses become increasingly confident that the economy will continue to grow. Therefore, corporations want to increase their investment in equipment and buildings, but they need to borrow money to do it. As a result of the demand for bigger and bigger loans, the interest rate for corporate loans must rise.

Households also increase the amount of consumer loans borrowed in the expansion. We saw in Chapter 46 that growth in the economy does not necessarily mean increases of wages and salaries for most people. In the expansion, as the economy seems to be doing so well, many employees find that their own incomes are barely keeping up with necessary spending because of inflation. In a time of expansion, employees' hopes for the future may rise, and they feel confident about going into more debt to keep up with their standard of living as prices continue to rise.

Wealthy households usually save more as the economy and their incomes expand. But in recent expansions, the wealthy have greatly increased their consumer spending. They also used more of their income to invest. As the expansion proceeds and profit expectations rise, many investors actually borrow money to make speculative investments in land or stocks.

Why does the interest rate fall during economic contractions? During economic contractions, the process reverses itself. Declining demand means that corporations are scared to make new investments. The demand for corporate loans declines, thereby reducing business interest rates. At the same time, the falling demand means a rise in unemployment. Consumers become very pessimistic about the outlook for their jobs and salaries. As a result, consumers cut back their loans. The lower demand for loans means that the interest rate is forced down.

Why does the interest rate lag behind the economy and continue to drop when expansion begins? Even though expansion has begun, many people and many corporations still owe a lot of money, still have low incomes, and still are pessimistic for some time. Therefore, there is no big

Figure 49.1 **Interest Rate (Prime Rate)**

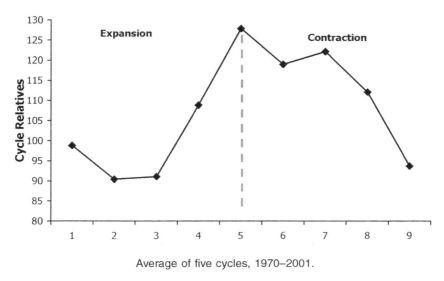

Average of five cycles, 1970–2001.

Source: Federal Reserve Board of Governors (federalreserve.gov).

demand for loans at the beginning of an expansion. Interest rates continue to drop for a while in spite of the improving economy.

Similarly, after the business peak, the interest rate remains high or falls only a little. It is not until well into the recession that interest rates begin to decline rapidly. Why do interest rates lag behind the economy on the way down into a recession? At the beginning of a recession, many people are forced into new loans. They may have been spending beyond their income and suddenly find that they have no job or they have lower pay. In order to buy necessities and to pay current debts, they are forced to go further into debt. This need for emergency loans is also true for some businesses. They may have made big investments in the expansion, but now these investments suddenly produce very little income. In order to pay current expenses, some businesses are forced to take out more loans at the beginning of the recession. As the recession deepens, neither people nor corporations want new loans. Eventually, as is the usual case in recessions, interest rates must drop.

What is the impact of interest rates and credit on the business cycle? We saw earlier that more credit in expansions helps the expansion continue. As interest rates rise, they tend to limit the amount of credit. Both consumers and businesses are more reluctant to borrow money as interest rates rise. Higher interest rates tend to limit expansion because it costs more and more to borrow. For those corporations that do continue to borrow and invest, the rate of profit is lowered somewhat by higher interest rates. Combined with other causes, this may lead to lower profit rates, causing less investment and a recession. The other causes for declining profits are almost always more important than the rising interest rates, but rising interest rates do play a negative role near the cycle peak.

In recessions, credit usually declines or at least grows very slowly (after an initial period of emergency loans). The reduction of credit means that consumers and businesses can spend less. Eventually, however, in the recession, interest rates fall. Falling interest rates is one factor helping to cause recovery.

In addition to borrowing from banks, one other way of raising money for corporations is the stock market. As we saw in Chapter 43, the stock market also rises in expansion and falls in contractions. It actually turns down before the peak of expansion. Money flowing from the stock market to corporations is reduced even before the peak. After the peak, the stock market falls considerably in every recession.

In the Great Depression, the stock market crashed and fell very drastically. This was another factor limiting money available to corporations. In 2001 to 2003, the stock market also went down very drastically, bursting an optimistic bubble of high stock prices. This reduced money flowing into corporations. It also left millions of small investors with greatly reduced savings, so they were forced to lower their consumption.

SUMMARY

Money went through a long evolution from barter in the medieval period to credit money to the present use of purely electronic entries. Both business and consumer credit rise during expansions and fall during recessions. The expansion and decline of credit tends to exaggerate the business cycle.

Interest rates for both consumers and business tend to rise in expansion and fall in recession, though they rise after business activity reaches a peak. Higher interest rates reduce profit rates toward the end of expansion, helping to bring on a recession. Lower interest rates at the end of recession are one factor helping to cause a recovery.

SUGGESTED READINGS FOR CHAPTER 49

An exciting book on why the economy has had panics in the financial sector many times in history is told by Martin Wolfson in *Financial Crises* (1994). An outstanding scholarly book on consumer debt is Robert Pollin's *Deeper in Debt: The Changing Financial Conditions of U.S. Households* (1990).

KEY TERMS

assets	medium of exchange
legal tender	store of value
liabilities	unit of account
liquid assets	

REVIEW QUESTIONS

List and explain the three functions of money.
1. State each function of money. Which function is money's most exclusive function? Why? Which function is money's least exclusive function? Why?
2. Explain why an index card or a cow does not fulfill all three functions of money.
3. What are the four "stages" of money? What drove the changes from one stage to the next? Explain.
4. What was the role of the earliest bankers? Why? How did bankers eventually begin to "create" money.

Discuss how credit and interest rates are related to business cycles.

7. Why do interest rates rise in expansions and fall in contractions?
8. Why do interest rates lag at the peak, still rising for a little while (or at least holding steady), while a recession has already started?
9. Why have many households fallen deeper into debt over the last thirty years?

APPENDIX 49.1
HOW BANKS CREATE MONEY

Exactly how much new money can banks create with a given amount of new deposits? That is the question taken up in this appendix. The appendix explains the deposit multiplier and how an initial deposit in the banking system may lead to more money in the economy.

LEARNING OBJECTIVES FOR APPENDIX 49.1

After reading this appendix, you should be able to:

*   Explain why there are reserve requirements on deposits.
*   Explain why an initial deposit in the banking system leads to the creation of new deposits.
*   Calculate the change in deposits or money supply from an initial deposit.
*   State and explain the meaning of the assumptions made when using the money multiplier and what happens when the assumptions don't hold.

MAKING MONEY

How do banks create money? To begin the story, we must revisit a bit of history. Remember that banks take in deposits and then loan money based on those deposits. Over time, there have been occasions when banks lent out all their depositors' money or lost their depositors' money on bad loans and risky investment. As word leaked out that the bank had no money, there would be a panic and loss of faith in the banking system. After the panic in the banking system at the start of the Great Depression of the 1930s, several reforms were put into place. One of those reforms was the *legal restriction that banks lend out only a certain proportion of their deposits.* This proportion, known as **required reserves**, is set by the Federal Reserve. Banking reforms, including required reserves, are discussed in detail in Chapter 51.

How the expansion of deposits and therefore the money supply works can be seen in Figure 49.2 and in Table 49.1.

Part of each new deposit must be held in reserve, and part may be lent out. For convenience assume that the Federal Reserve ratio is set at 20 percent for all kinds of deposits in all kinds of banks. If a bank receives a $1,000 deposit, it deposits the $1,000 at the bank, increasing the bank's reserves by $1,000. The bank may then lend out $800.

According to Figure 49.2 and Table 49.1, when the $800 in new loans from Bank A (Figure 49.2) is spent, it becomes new deposits in Bank B, which are the basis for new reserves of $800 for Bank B. With required reserves of 20 percent, the bank must keep $160 and may lend out $640. The process continues until all of the original new deposit ($1,000) become required reserves in various banks. The total in reserves held in all banks is $1,000, but there were $4,000 in new

Figure 49.2 **How the Money Multiplier Works (Imaginary Data)**

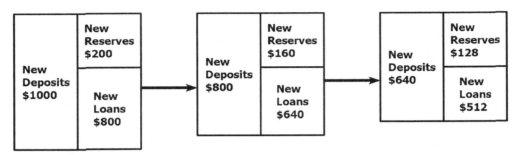

deposits from loans. Based on an initial new deposit of $1,000 in money, the banking system now has deposits of $5,000 (assumed to be demand deposits and therefore counted as money)!

For our analysis we use the concept of the **money multiplier**, which is analogous to, but not to be confused with, other multipliers we looked at in earlier chapters on investment and government spending. This multiplier *measures the effect of bank deposits on the expansion of the money supply.* A simple formula for deriving the money multiplier is

Multiplier = 1/Required Federal Reserve ratio

Assuming that each banker has to keep 20 percent of his or her deposit liabilities in the form of cash, the money supply can be expanded to five times the amount of cash that the banking system holds:

Multiplier = 1/0.20 = 5

To calculate the total amount of deposits generated, the formula is

Multiplier × Deposit = Total deposits created

Using our example, the initial new deposit of $1,000 is multiplied by 5 to get a $5,000 total increase in deposits (or in the money supply). The total deposits consist of the initial deposit of $1,000 and the $4,000 of loans and deposits generated, for a grand total of $5,000.

The analysis does not yet take into account several kinds of leakages that may occur. For

Table 49.1

Example of How Banks Multiply Money

Bank Name	Increase in Loans	Increase in Deposits	Increase in Reserves
Bank A	$800	$1,000	$200
Bank B	$640	$800	$160
Bank C	$512	$640	$128
Bank D	$410	$512	$102
Bank E	$328	$410	$82
Bank F	$262	$328	$66
All Banks	$4,000	$5,000	$1,000

Notes:
1. Assume an initial increase in deposits of $1,000.
2. Assume a required Federal Reserve ratio of 20 percent.
3. Assume that banks are always fully loaned out.

one thing, we assumed that banks lent out all they are allowed to lend by law. The assumption that banks are always fully loaned up is not consistent with the facts. There are often some **excess reserves**, or *reserves above the legal requirement*. The volume of expansion of deposits therefore depends on the degree to which bankers decide to make the maximum loans on their reserves. It also depends on the degree to which businesspeople wish to accept these loans. We also assumed in our example that people redeposit all loans back into the bank as deposits. Someone may cash the loan check and spend it, putting a stop to the multiplier process. Finally, the whole process takes time, and only a certain amount of the predicted expansion will occur in any given period. It is nevertheless generally true that banks lend in some multiple of their reserves and that total expansion of the money supply will be greater, the smaller the required Federal Reserve ratio.

SUMMARY OF APPENDIX 49.1

Banks do not have to keep 100 percent of their money in reserve to pay depositors. Banks can create new money through the credit system, arriving at some multiple of the money with which they start. This is what is meant when an economist says that banks have power to "create" money.

KEY WORDS IN APPENDIX 49.1

excess reserves   required reserves
money multiplier

REVIEW QUESTIONS FOR APPENDIX 49.1

Explain why there are reserve requirements on deposits.
  1. U.S. banks operate on a "fractional reserve system." What does this mean? How can this cause problems for the banking system and the economy?

2. Why are bank panics so destructive? What was the response of government after the Great Depression to try and stop panics?

Explain why an initial deposit in the banking system leads to the creation of new deposits.

3. Why does a bank make loans?

4. How does the bank manage the asset side of its "T" account in order to make money?

Calculate the change in deposits or money supply from an initial deposit.

5. How do changes in the reserve requirement affect the deposit multiplier?

6. Given an initial deposit of $100, how much money is created if the reserve requirement is 5%, 10%, 15%?

State and explain the meaning of the assumptions made when using the money multiplier and what happens when the assumptions don't hold.

7. What happens to the money creation process if banks do not lend out all their excess reserves?

8. What happens to the money creation process if people do not redeposit all money into the bank?

CHAPTER 50

Inflation

Inflation is an increase in the overall price level. This chapter discusses several types of inflation. First, there is inflation during every ordinary business cycle expansion. Second there is inflation during every war. Third, during the last half century, there has also been inflation in the midst of recession.

LEARNING OBJECTIVES

After reading this chapter, you should be able to:

- Describe how inflation is measured and, given appropriate data, calculate inflation.
- Compare and contrast the different causes of inflation.
- Explain why there has been inflation in every recession of the last fifty years.

HOW IS INFLATION MEASURED?

Inflation is *a rise in the overall price level*. It is not just the price of one or two goods and services increasing, it is the prices of many goods and services throughout the economy rising. The overall price level in the macroeconomy is captured by several measures. One measure is the consumer price index (CPI). The CPI measures the changes in prices of a fixed basket of goods and services. The contents of the "basket" don't change from year to year, just the prices of the goods. Designating a year as base year prices, the index is calculated by taking the price index in the current year and dividing it by base year prices, then multiplying by 100. The gross domestic product (GDP) deflator is another measure of the change of prices in the overall economy. It measures the change in prices of all goods and services in the economy, not just a few. While it is certainly a more time-consuming and expensive measure, the GDP deflator is more accurate than the CPI.

Inflation is measured by the percentage change in a price index. For example, if the CPI rises from 107 to 111 from one year to the next, the inflation would be calculated as the percentage change: $(111 - 107)/107 \times 100$. Two examples are given in Table 50.1.

WHY DOES INFLATION MATTER?

In a period of inflation when prices are rising rapidly, there tends to be a shift in income distribution. Anyone with a relatively fixed income, such as retirees on pensions, and any employee on a

Table 50.1

Mythical Example of Calculation for Inflation

Year	CPI	Second Year– First Year =	Divide by Previous Year =	Multiply by 100 =
2012	107			
		4	0.0374	3.74%
2013	111			
		2	0.0180	1.80%
2014	113			

fixed wage or salary will be hurt more by rising prices than will those whose income may go up with prices. One reason that real wages and salaries often fall behind during periods of inflation is the increased difficulty of getting higher real wages and salaries. With constant prices, a rise of 1 percent in money wages and salaries means a rise of 1 percent in real wages and salaries. It may be possible in a labor struggle to win that 1 percent. If, however, there is an inflation rate of 13 percent, then it requires a money wage increase of 14 percent to get a real wage increase of 1 percent. This may be much more difficult for employees to obtain. It is even harder to convince a state legislature to give such an increase to employees in the public sector.

People may turn more and more to the use of credit to keep up the same level of consumption as prices rise. If a recession hits, it will be much harder on households that are deep in debt, and it may lead to the bankruptcy of the banks and finance agencies who have lent them money.

While some businesses producing goods and services may be able to raise their prices to keep up with the overall inflation, capitalists who earn interest from lending money generally lose from inflation. Lenders lose because the purchasing power of the money that is repaid has declined. Financial markets therefore are very concerned about periods of inflation.

Rapid inflation, especially if it is unexpected, hurts everyone. It hurts capitalists by weakening the economic system and making it unmanageable. Businesses are unable to make plans for the future because they do not know what is happening to future prices. Households cannot plan for the future because they do not know what will be happening to their future purchasing power. Therefore, the U.S. government—and all governments in which capitalists have great influence—worries far more about inflation than about unemployment.

THE KEYNESIAN EXPLANATION OF INFLATION: DEMAND PULL

The Keynesian explanation of inflation boils down to the idea that inflation results when aggregate demand is greater than aggregate supply. It assumes that there is no way for supply to rise as fast as demand in some circumstances. For example, at the beginning of an expansion when the economy is just emerging from a recession, there are plenty of underemployed workers, and as demand increases, there are plenty of workers available for hire, so supply can rapidly increase. As the expansion approaches its peak, almost everyone is employed. In the last half of expansion, supply cannot be increased much, if at all. Therefore, aggregate demand rises faster than aggregate supply, and there is price inflation.

The aggregate demand in money terms, including both desire for products and the money for products, is called **effective demand**. This demand in money terms, or effective demand, includes not just coins and paper money and bank deposits but all the forms of credit in the economy. Effective demand includes anything that allows an individual or business or government to purchase goods and services now, whether they pay now or later. Effective demand may be expanded to some extent by banks and financial institutions or by government manipulation of the financial system and the availability of credit.

This Keynesian explanation of inflation by excess aggregate demand, including credit, is adequate to explain most of the inflation of past U.S. capitalist history through the 1940s. In the 1950s and 1960s, however, a new kind of inflation emerged that was confusing for Keynesians. The inflation of the 1970s was definitely a new variety that the usual Keynesian model cannot explain. It is *inflation at a time of deficient aggregate demand and rising costs of production* rather than excess demand. This type of inflation is called **stagflation**.

Let us take a detailed look at those types of inflation that a simple Keynesian model can explain. Then we turn to stagflation, which it cannot explain.

NORMAL INFLATION IN EXPANSIONS

In most expansions in the United States, prices rise. In most U.S. contractions, prices fall. For example, in the Great Depression of the 1930s, prices fell about 50 percent. In fact, in twenty-three of the twenty-six cyclical expansions and contractions between 1890 and 1938, prices moved in the same direction as business activity and production.

As Keynes argued, prices usually moved up in expansions because effective demand for all products was moving upward faster than the physical supply of products. On the other hand, in recessions, prices usually moved down because effective demand for all products was moving downward faster than the physical supply of products was decreasing. Lower prices were part of the reaction to decreased demand in contraction.

Why does the flow of aggregate demand in money terms rise so rapidly during a period of expansion? One factor is that the financial institutions are willing to give more credit. At the same time, businesses want to borrow in order to take advantage of profitable opportunities. Banks and other financial institutions want to lend because it appears that businesses can easily repay the loans with interest. Therefore, aggregate demand (in money terms) increases rapidly during expansions.

Not only is there more money in circulation because of lending, but it turns over faster because consumers and businesses both spend more rapidly. In Keynesian terms, the level of consumer spending and investment spending both rise. Consumers wish to get bargains before prices rise further and also because they feel assured of future income. Businesses likewise dig into their savings, borrow more on credit, and make new investments. Business invests because the future looks profitable. In times of expansion, the trend is for businesses and households to spend in order to buy goods rather than to keep idle money.

In a recession, on the other hand, the flow of money demand usually decreases even faster than production of goods and services. Banks call in their loans, while businesses do not want to borrow more. In most recessions, consumers have cut their borrowing and reduced their outstanding debts. Therefore, in most U.S. recessions, the money supply rapidly declines. Furthermore, individuals and businesses keep idle savings for the rainy days ahead, especially because there are no attractive opportunities for investment. As a result, money circulates more slowly and idle money increases considerably in a recession. For these reasons, during most of U.S. history until the 1950s, recession was normally a time of price deflation.

INFLATION IN WARTIME

The usual inflation experienced during peacetime prosperity has been moderate compared with the rapid and spectacular inflation stimulated by wartime spending. Rapid price inflation accompanied the Revolutionary War, the War of 1812, the Civil War, World War I, World War II, the Korean War, and the Vietnam War. The large amount of spending on the two Iraq wars was too small, compared with the whole U.S. economy, to cause a major inflation. The war spending contributed to inflation, but only a small amount. During wartime, there is less production of consumer goods or private producer goods. At the same time, there is full employment with high wages and salaries and profits. Most of the increased goods and services are in the military sphere, and all are bought by the government. When the federal government controls prices by legal controls, as it did during World War II, inflation was repressed. **Repressed inflation** means that *there were few price rises during the war, but strong price rises as soon as the controls were ended.*

The government finances most of its wartime purchases by borrowing, with only limited tax increases. If government then spends this money, it is deficit depending, which produces inflation if there is full employment. With little increase in taxes, civilians still have the same amount of disposable income, but the amount of available civilian goods and services is limited, since most production goes to the government. As prices begin to rise rapidly, people rush to buy goods before prices rise further. This more rapid spending and borrowing means that total spending flow can rise even faster than income rises. In the language of economics, one additional cause of rising prices is that propensities to consume and invest are rising. As the government borrows money for military spending, the deficits and debt tend to increase. When government goes into debt, the country faces all the problems that come with government debt, including higher interest payments (government debt is discussed in Chapter 49).

It is worth emphasizing that when government spends by printing money, it directly contributes to inflation. The government usually prints money to cover spending only in the most extreme conditions.

STAGFLATION: INFLATION IN THE MIDST OF STAGNATION

When there is high unemployment and production is falling, as in a recession, but there is still price inflation, some economists call this situation *stagflation*. Stagflation is the combination of a stagnant economy with inflation, a very unpleasant situation. Stagflation is a relatively new phenomenon, seen only in the last five decades of U.S. history. In the Great Depression of the 1930s, there was vast unemployment, and prices declined rapidly between 1929 and 1933. Prices recovered a little until a new recession in 1938 caused another sharp decline in prices. During World War II, large military demand created intense inflationary pressure. Prices were held down by direct price controls, so there was repressed inflation. Following World War II, price controls were ended, so prices rose rapidly in 1946 to 1950. Then, in 1949, a recession caused prices to fall. The Korean War in 1950 caused more inflation.

Stagflation in Modern Recessions, 1953–2001

Until the end of World War II and the recovery of the peacetime economy that followed, prices behaved as Keynesian theory predicts, rising in expansions and declining in recessions. In the 1950s, however, a new phenomenon became evident. In the recession of 1954, overall prices remained constant. In the recession of 1958, prices actually rose. This was the first time in U.S. history that rising prices accompanied a period of rising unemployment. In the 1961 recession, prices were again steady.

Since then, in the recessions of 1970, 1974, 1980, 1981, 1991, and 2001, price inflation continued throughout the contraction period! In these recessions, although prices continued to rise, they usually rose more slowly than prices had risen in the previous expansion. This phenomenon

Figure 50.1 **Inflation and Unemployment**

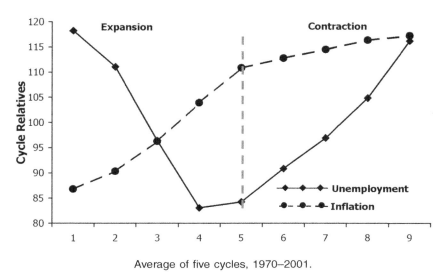

Average of five cycles, 1970–2001.

Inflation from Federal Reserve Board of Governors. Unemployment is a percentage rate comparing the number of unemployed with the total civilian labor force. *Source:* Bureau of Labor Statistics, Department of Labor (www.bls.gov).

of rising prices in expansions, but also slower price rises in recessions (called stagflation), is illustrated in Figure 50.1.

Figure 50.1 shows that in the average of the five cycles from 1970 to 2001, the phenomena of stagflation were present. Prices rose throughout the business expansion. Prices continued to rise during the average recession of this period. The rate of growth of prices is much lower in recessions than in expansions. The slower growth rate of prices in recessions is caused by the decline of aggregate demand. The fact that prices rise at all in recessions, however, shows the existence of a new situation in these recessions.

Ordinary inflation in expansions is caused by the upward pull of aggregate demand. Here, instead, prices apparently are pushed upward above their costs by individual firms to improve their profits. The *traditional inflation is caused by the upward pull of aggregate demand*, so it is called **demand-pull inflation**. The *new inflation, which occurs in both expansions and recessions, is due to firms pushing up prices to get maximum profits*, so it is called **profit-push inflation**.

How do firms push prices up? Remember that in a purely competitive market, there are thousands of small firms. Each small firm has no power to affect the market by itself, so it must accept whatever price is set by competition in the market. It would seem that a firm cannot set a market price, but only accept what is. How can we say that firms push prices up for profits?

The answer to this apparent contradiction is that a firm with monopoly or oligopoly power can decide to set the price higher or lower depending on what price will make the most profit. A competitive firm has no power to change prices at will. If the firm sets a price that is just a little higher (say 50 cents) than the market price (say 40 cents), then every consumer goes next door to another store and buys the object at the lower price.

But monopoly power means the ability to affect the market. Suppose a firm is one of only two firms that make a product. Suppose that the firm uses advertising to convince many people that it makes a better product than the other firm. If it raises the price a little, the firm may lose a few customers, but not all of its customers. If Honda raises its price by $50, it may lose a few customers to Toyota, but it will still keep many who think Honda makes a better car. In other words, demand is relatively inelastic or unresponsive to a change in price. Thus, firms with some monopoly power can set their prices as they wish. They may lose some customers if they set a higher price, or they may gain some customers if they set a lower price, but they can choose what price to set.

In the present day in America, even in a peacetime expansion, there will be some inflation for the traditional reason that aggregate demand is rising a little faster than supply. For small, competitive firms, that is the end of the story. Firms with monopoly power must decide whether to raise their prices at all or how high to raise them. Many giant firms with monopoly power choose to keep their prices slightly below the market in an expansion in order to increase their share of the market. This strategy eventually makes them even more profit. In a business expansion, all firms increase prices, but some firms with monopoly power can choose to increase them more or less than the average.

In a recession, aggregate demand falls faster than supply for some time, so competitive prices are forced down. But in sectors with a high degree of monopoly power, most of the giant firms resist any reduction of prices. Some even raise their prices in order to make more profit, even though the higher price may lose them a few customers. In a modern recession (stagflation), the average price level tends to remain constant or even rise a little.

COST-PUSH INFLATION

Most inflation in recessions, according to the previous section, is caused by profit maximization by corporations with monopoly power. This is the view of most progressive economists. Some conservative economists reject this view, saying that monopoly power has little effect on prices. Rather, they argue that *input costs, including high wages and salaries, cause inflation.* They call this type of inflation **cost-push inflation**.

Other explanations for rising prices during recessions include pressures from the production side. The rising costs of production due to rising input prices forces businesses to try to pass those increased costs on to consumers. Businesses thereby cause cost-push inflation. Interestingly, the ability of firms to pass on their increased costs to consumers may be dependent on whether or not they are in a highly competitive market, so the inflation caused by their increased prices may resemble profit-push inflation.

Rising input prices may come from many sources. In the 1970s, stagflation was generally blamed on the spike of petroleum prices during the rise of OPEC. Since the U.S. economy was still strongly based on manufacturing, and plants relied heavily on petroleum products for energy and as inputs into many products, the increased input prices affected almost every sector of the U.S. economy. There was an acute shortage of gasoline for transportation during the period as well, which also lead to increased costs.

Another source of cost-push inflation is wages and salaries. If wages and salaries increase, then business again try to pass on their increased costs of production to consumers. The labor costs to businesses would indeed increase if those costs were increasing faster than productivity or labor output.

This conservative view has been criticized on several grounds. There is no evidence that labor unions obtain such high wages and salaries as to cause inflation. The most important fact is that real wages and salaries decline in each recession. In other words, although money wages and salaries have risen somewhat in recent recessions, they have risen much less than prices. This means that inflation during the recession periods cannot be blamed on wages and salaries because they lag behind prices. In human terms, the employee's standard of living declines in each recession-plus-inflation period.

Nor can price inflation in expansions be blamed on high wages and salaries. If productivity is rising, real labor cost per unit declines in most of the expansion. Therefore, the cost of paying wages and salaries cannot possibly be the cause for higher prices in most of the expansion period. The slight rise in labor costs in the later expansion period is not enough for wages and salaries to catch up with the earlier productivity rises.

SUMMARY

In all American business cycles up until World War II, prices rose in expansions and fell in recessions. These rises and falls may be called the pattern of ordinary cyclical inflation and deflation. In every U.S. war, government demand rose very rapidly, so prices rose very rapidly. If there were price controls, the inflation was repressed during the war but took place after the controls were lifted. Later, when the war boom had ended, there was a recession with falling prices. This is the pattern of wartime inflation.

The wartime inflation as well as the old pattern of rising inflation in expansions, with deflation in contractions, was easily explained by the Keynesian notion of aggregate supply and demand. If demand rises faster than supply of products, there is inflation. If demand falls faster than the supply of products, there is deflation. Since the 1950s, recessions have witnessed a new phenomenon, not seen before that time. Prices rose not only during business expansions but also, though more slowly, during recessions. This pattern of inflation in the midst of stagnation or recession is called stagflation.

Many progressive economists explain the stagflation process as the result of monopoly power. Monopoly power has grown increasingly greater throughout both the American economy and the global economy. Since there are *only a few large corporations in each market*, each of them is called an **oligopoly** firm. As a result of their power, most giant corporations have been able to raise prices even in recessions if they found it in their interest.

Other issues related to inflation are discussed in detail in the following appendices. Appendix 50.1 discusses the price effect of market power exercised by monopolies and oligopolies. Appendix 50.2 describes the most dramatic episodes of government control of wages and prices in certain periods of American history.

KEY TERMS

cost-push inflation   oligopoly
demand-pull inflation   profit-push inflation
effective demand   repressed inflation
inflation   stagflation

REVIEW QUESTIONS

Describe how inflation is measured and, given appropriate data, calculate inflation.

1. What are two measures of price levels introduced in this chapter? How are they similar; how are they different?
2. Assume the CPI rose from 117 to 123 between 2005–2006. What was the inflation rate?

Compare and contrast the different causes of inflation.

    3.   In most cyclical expansions, do prices go up or down? Why?

    4.   What happens to prices in a major war situation? Why

Explain why there has been inflation in every recession of the last fifty years.

    5.   What has happened to prices in recessions since the 1950s? Why?

    6.   In most cyclical recessions up until the 1950s, did prices go up or down? Why?

APPENDIX 50.1

MARKET POWER AND ADMINISTERED PRICES

The debate over profit-push inflation by corporations has gone on for a long time. This appendix explores this topic in more detail.

LEARNING OBJECTIVES

After reading this appendix, you should be able to:

- Compare and contrast price movements in competitive markets and monopoly/oligopoly markets.
- Explain the relationship of oligopolies and profit-push inflation.

MONOPOLIES AND OLIGOPOLIES

In the Great Depression of the 1930s, Gardiner Means (1975) found what he called "administered prices" in the monopoly sector. What Means called the monopoly sector would now be called the oligopoly sector, meaning those industries dominated by a few corporations with a high degree of market power.

Since oligopoly means that market power is concentrated in a few corporations in the industry, economists measure the degree of concentration, meaning the percentage of sales or assets controlled by just a small number of corporations. Means found that prices were not set in a competitive market but were carefully administered or set in noncompetitive markets in the best interests of the oligopolies. He found that the competitive prices changed frequently, but the administered or monopoly prices changed very seldom.

More specifically, Means found that the prices in the competitive sector registered large declines in the depression, whereas the administered prices in the oligopoly sector declined very little. Means defines the competitive sector as the 20 percent least concentrated industries. The oligopoly sector is defined as the 20 percent most concentrated industries. From 1929 to 1932, prices in the more competitive sector fell 60 percent. Prices in the monopoly sector fell only 10 percent. A few prices in the monopoly sector even rose a little in the face of the Great Depression.

As shown in Table 50.2, in the Great Depression, the industries with large oligopoly power lowered their prices very little. They kept prices from going down only by reducing their production by very large percentages. The more competitive sectors had no choice but to let their prices be forced down by lack of demand. Production in the competitive sector declined less because of greater demand at the lower prices. The oligopoly sector thus held up its prices and profit per unit

Table 50.2

Price and Production Behavior in Depression, 1929–1932

Industry	Price Decline as Percentage of 1929 Price	Production Decline as Percentage of 1929 Production
High Level of Oligopoly Power		
Motor vehicles	12	74
Agricultural implements	14	84
Iron and steel	16	76
Cement	16	55
Automobile tires	25	42
Intermediate Levels of Monopoly Power		
Leather and leather products	33	18
Petroleum products	36	17
Textile products	39	28
More competitive Industries		
Food products	39	10
Agricultural commodities	54	1

Source: Howard Sherman, *The Business Cycle: Growth and Crisis under Capitalism.* Princeton, NJ: Princeton University Press, 1991, p. 302.

at the expense of great decreases in production and large-scale unemployment. The competitive sector lowered production less, fired fewer employees, but suffered much greater declines in prices and profits per unit. A highly concentrated economy, with most industries dominated by a few oligopoly firms, is thus more apt to produce high rates of unemployment in every decline.

Since the 1930s, monopoly power has increased dramatically. In most industries, only four or five firms sell most of the product. Most of these top four or five firms are now owned by conglomerates with power in a number of industries in many different countries of the global economy.

Data for contractions of the 1950s, 1960s, and 1970s also show the dramatic differences between price behavior by small competitive firms versus large, oligopoly firms in recessions. The competitive sector is defined in Table 50.3 as all those industries in which concentration of sales by eight firms is under 50 percent. The oligopoly sector is defined as all those industries in which concentration of sales by eight firms is over 50 percent.

Table 50.3, on the behavior of prices in the oligopoly sector and of prices in the competitive sector, is very revealing. It reveals that the pattern for the 1950 recession was the same as in the 1929 depression. In all three cycles, oligopoly prices declined a little, whereas competitive prices declined by an enormous amount. In the 1954 and 1958 recessions, we see the first indications of the new stagflation behavior. Competitive prices declined as usual, though by a small amount, but oligopoly prices actually rose in the recessions, though again by a small amount. The new situation is very clear in the 1970 recession in which competitive prices declined by a significant amount, but monopoly prices rose considerably.

Price data on the 1973 to 1975 recession indicate that monopoly prices rose in the recession by an astounding percentage. This very large price increase throughout the now-dominant oligopoly sector caused even competitive prices to show a considerable rise in the depression for the first

Table 50.3

Competitive and Oligopoly Prices

Dates of Cycle Peaks and Troughs	Changes in Competitive Prices	Changes in Oligopoly Prices
Nov. 1948–Oct. 1949	–7.8%	–1.9%
July 1953–Aug. 1954	–1.5	+1.9
July 1957–Apr. 1958	–0.3	+0.5
May 1960–Feb. 1961	–1.2	+0.9
Nov. 1969–Nov. 1970	–3.0	+5.9
Nov. 1973–Mar. 1975	+11.7	+32.8

Source: Howard Sherman, *The Business Cycle: Growth and Crisis Under Capitalism.* Princeton, NJ: Princeton University Press, 1991, p. 304.

Note: Changes in price indexes from cyclical peak to trough.

time on record. This unexpected situation undoubtedly caused great disruption in the competitive sector, decreased production, increased bankruptcies, and increased unemployment.

It was shown in this chapter that in the 1980s, 1990s, and early 2000s, prices continued to rise in each recession. It was also shown in Chapter 21 that the market power of the oligopoly corporations has continued to rise in this period.

OLIGOPOLY AND CYCLICAL STABILITY OF PROFIT RATES

Many studies have found that large, oligopoly corporations have the market power to pursue a price-setting tactic over the whole business cycle to maximize their profits. Thus, they do not try to set prices as high as possible in an expansion but rather set them just low enough to increase their share of the market. In recessions, they are not forced to set their prices so low as to make losses. Rather, they attempt to keep their prices high enough (or even raise them) to make a significant profit per unit, though they must lower the amount of production to maintain the higher prices. (For a more detailed explanation of the price behavior of oligopolies and a discussion of the literature, see Sherman, 1991.) The bottom line is that many of the large oligopoly corporations do not suffer as great a profit loss in recessions as do the smaller, more competitive corporations (see Sherman, 1991, Chapter 15).

REVIEW QUESTIONS FOR APPENDIX 50.1

Compare and contrast price movements in competitive markets and monopoly/oligopoly markets.
1. What are the differences between a competitive market and monopoly/oligopoly markets? How does that impact prices and price formation?
2. Describe differences in historical price movements between competitive and monopoly/oligopoly markets?

Explain the relationship of oligopolies and profit-push inflation.
3. Describe how monopoly/oligopoly firms protect their profits. Can a firm owner in a competitive market do this? Explain.
4. What is profit-push inflation?

APPENDIX 50.2
WAGE AND PRICE CONTROLS

In addition to fiscal policy, there have also been attempts at direct control of wages and prices. This appendix explores historical examples of price controls. In this appendix, the word *wages* means wages and salaries, since the term *wages* is used that way in this area.

LEARNING OBJECTIVES FOR APPENDIX 50.2

After reading this appendix, you should be able to:

- Explain the goal of wage and price controls.
- Compare and contrast the criticisms of price controls by conservative and progressive economists.

WAGE-PRICE CONTROLS

The most dramatic example of wage-price controls occurred during World War II. War production and related government activities absorbed 40 percent of all American output. The huge governmental expenditures raised demand so much that the Great Depression was left behind. There was full employment. Workers earned good wages, and capitalists made extremely high profits from war production.

However, consumer goods production was greatly reduced by wartime planning through government orders to the whole economy. Physical rationing of all producer goods assured that firms doing the most for the war would get the scarce machines and raw materials. Physical rationing of scarce consumer goods rigorously limited the production of consumer goods, but each person got an equal amount of goods through the rationing system.

Since there was a very large, unsatisfied demand for all goods and services, but no way to increase civilian production, there was a high agree of inflationary pressure. Therefore, the system of physical rationing was supplemented by controls on all wages and prices. Paying anyone higher prices in order to get scarce goods on the black market was a crime. This system kept legal prices low throughout the war, but prices exploded when controls were removed after the war. People used their accumulated savings, which were forced savings during the war, and went on a buying spree, leading to more inflation.

Price controls were not used again until the early 1970s. The early 1970s witnessed both stagnant economic growth and inflation, a combination that has often been called stagflation. Since neither the usual monetary nor fiscal policy does much good against stagflation, in the early 1970s, some liberal economists, especially John Kenneth Galbraith, began to call for direct wage-price controls over the economy. Knowing that the conservative President Nixon would never use such controls, the liberal Democrats in Congress gave the president power to use controls just to embarrass him politically before the 1972 election. Nixon, however, wanted to win the election and knew that he might lose it if he did nothing to end unemployment and inflation. Therefore, despite the conservative ideology against controlling the economy, on August 15, 1971, Nixon imposed wage and price controls to reduce inflation. He also increased military spending to reduce unemployment. He won the election. The military spending increased employment, while the controls held down inflation.

Why should this ancient history concern us? Because this is the only case of wage and price controls in America during peacetime. The Vietnam War was just ending. We can learn much from studying it. Nixon's price controls lasted from August 1971 to April 1974. In some phases of the policy, the controls were voluntary. It was clear, however, that voluntary controls did no good at all. For most of the period, the controls were mandated by law and regulation. In all of the periods of mandatory controls, there were controls on wages and salaries, rents, and prices. There were never any controls on profits. It was said that controls on profits would not allow the economic system to operate.

A board appointed by Nixon ran the controls and could decide to raise or lower any price. Because of the board decisions, wages and salaries were led down to very small increases. Prices were allowed to rise higher. As a result, in these years, the data show that real wages actually declined. Real wages are money wages adjusted for inflation. Since prices rose faster than money wages, the real wage had to decline. Since prices were allowed to rise faster than costs, corporate profits rose.

CRITICISMS OF PRICE CONTROLS

Economists of both right and left political views criticized the controls of 1971 to 1974, but for different reasons. Conservatives, such as Milton Friedman, were horrified at the violation of the First Commandment of laissez-faire economics: Thou shalt not interfere with the market process of setting wages and prices (see Friedman, 1982, p. 45).

Conservative economists have always argued that resources, including capital and labor, cannot be efficiently allocated if prices are not set by competition in the market. If the government arbitrarily sets prices, how can a businessperson calculate most efficiently what to produce or what technology to use? If a business calculates rationally on the basis of the arbitrary prices set by the government, then it will not choose the inputs that would be cheapest in a purely competitive market, so it will not produce in the cheapest possible way in the light of available resources. Thus, wage-price controls doom a capitalist economy to inefficiency.

Conservatives also argued that a huge, inefficient bureaucracy would be needed to administer the program. It was argued by some economists that comprehensive wage-price controls in a capitalist system combine the worst aspects of capitalism and dictatorship: a huge, inefficient, and corrupt bureaucracy plus private greed for profits.

Progressive economists agreed that the controls led to inefficiency and corruption. They also argued, however, that controls under a government dominated by big business automatically led to income shifts always from wages and salaries to corporate profits.

They were right to worry and wrong to applaud at all. Nixon actually (1) held down wages, (2) allowed prices and corporate profits to continue to rise, and (3) did nothing other than some military spending to cure unemployment.

President Nixon was much more blunt about his biases than most presidents. A theme in many of his speeches was that all Americans benefit from high corporate profits because this is the only way to ensure investment in an expanding economy. Vice-President Agnew gave many speeches repeating the theory. His speeches argued that the plan would result in corporate profits and that corporate profits would trickle down to the middle class and the poor.

One way Nixon achieved the shift of income from workers and professionals to corporations was by appointing a probusiness Pay Board to make wage decisions. The appointed union representatives first joined it, hoping to salvage some crumbs, then withdrew when they found they were to be allowed nothing. The AFL-CIO said:

We joined the Pay Board in good faith, desiring—despite our misgivings—to give it a fair chance. . . . The so-called public members are neither neutral nor independent. They are tools of the Administration, and imbued with its viewpoint that all of the nation's economic ills are caused by high wages. As a result, the Pay Board has been completely dominated and run, from the very start, by a coalition of the business and so-called public members. . . . The trade union movement's representatives on the board have been treated as outsiders—merely as a facade to maintain the pretense of a tripartite body (AFL-CIO Executive Committee, 1970, p. 7).

Most progressive economists conclude that the inevitable results of wage-price controls under a capitalist government are (1) additional corruption and inefficiency and (2) a shift in income distribution away from wages and toward profits.

REVIEW QUESTIONS FOR APPENDIX 50.2

Explain the goal of wage and price controls.
1. Why would wage and price controls be used? What are the "controls" attempting to control?
2. Describe historical examples of wage and price controls. Were they effective?

Compare and contrast the criticisms of price controls by conservative and progressive economists.
3. What are conservative criticisms of price and wage controls? Progressive criticisms? How are they similar? Different?

CHAPTER 51

Monetary Policy

This chapter explores the American government's attempts to use monetary policy to help control the swings of the business cycle, inflationary trends, and monetary panics. After a brief examination of the early evolution of monetary policy, this chapter looks at the Federal Reserve system and the tools it uses to carry out monetary policy.

LEARNING OBJECTIVES

After reading this chapter, you should be able to:

- Describe a brief history of the evolution of the Central Bank and the Federal Reserve.
- Discuss the evolution and impact of regulation and deregulation of the financial system.
- Describe the structure the Federal Reserve.
- List the tools used by the Federal Reserve, and discuss how and why they are used in periods of recession and inflation.
- Compare and contrast the main views of monetary policy.
- Discuss the actual history of recent monetary policy under President George W. Bush.

EVOLUTION OF BANKS AND REGULATIONS

Early in U.S. history, attempts were made to set up a central bank that would oversee the banking system, but they met with great resistance from many populist politicians who believed that a central bank would solidify the control of the bankers and big business over the economy. Alexander Hamilton was able to create a Bank of the United States, but it was ended after a struggle. Another Bank of the United States was set up, but it was also ended by President Andrew Jackson in 1837. After 1837, the policy of the United States was to let the banks do as they please. Banks were private business that should not be regulated.

As a result of the policy of unregulated banking, the banks often lent so much money that they ran out of money when many depositors wanted to withdraw their money at the same time. When a bank could not pay out money to depositors, the depositors were terrified of losing their money. Therefore, all depositors tried to withdraw all of their money. The bank soon went bankrupt. Usually, the spectacle of one bank going bankrupt inspired depositors at all other banks to begin withdrawing their money. Soon *many banks went bankrupt and millions of people lost all of their savings*. This is called a **panic**.

Monetary panics were seen a number of times in the nineteenth century, often setting off a recession or making an existing recession much worse. The only **monetary policy**, *policy designed to increase or decrease the flow of money and credit*, was the issuance of gold or silver for use as money. There were continuous fights over whether to use paper money (called greenbacks) or gold or silver. It was felt that only the wealthy had gold and that its use benefited only them, so many people fought to expand the system to silver money and, even further, to paper money. The money of the Untied States was mostly built on holding gold until the gold standard was ended in the Great Depression of the 1930s.

As long as the monetary system was based on gold, it prevented banks from issuing just any old paper money. But the use of gold also impeded economic progress. If the amount of goods and services expanded more quickly than there was money available to purchase those goods and services, the economy would stagnate. The result was that the late nineteenth century witnessed a twenty-four-year period of **deflation**. Deflation means *overall falling prices*. Falling prices hurt business and tend to cause lengthier periods of high unemployment. Lower prices especially hurt farmers. In the nineteenth century a protest movement was organized by farmers through the Populist Party, built around opposition to the use of the gold standard. The farmers wanted mild **inflation**, or *an increase in prices*, but bankers hate inflation because it lowers the value of the money they get in later years as loans are repaid.

There was an especially bad panic in 1907. The 1907 panic inspired the movement to form the Federal Reserve System, which was supposed to control the banking system. On December 23, 1913, President Woodrow Wilson signed the Federal Reserve Act establishing the Federal Reserve System (called the Fed for short). It was the government's answer to the banking failures and monetary panics of the nineteenth century and early 1900s. It was also supposed to be a "lender of last resort." As the **lender of last resort**, *the Federal Reserve, in times of financial panic, could lend money to banks if necessary.* These loans would also counteract the decline of credit going on in the private sector among households and businesses by shoring up the banks.

Even after the Federal Reserve System was formed, however, the forces unleashed in the Great Depression of the 1930s were so strong that a monetary panic resulted. The monetary panic was a major factor in turning a recession into a deep depression. Once the depression began, many other factors prevented a recovery for ten whole years after 1929 (the nonmonetary, structural factors causing recessions and depressions are discussed in Chapter 45). When Franklin Roosevelt assumed the presidency in 1933, the banking system was in a state of collapse with many states declaring "bank holidays," that is, closing the banks to all transactions. One of his first acts was to close all the banks. Congress then gave him emergency powers to determine which banks were sound and could reopen.

These short-term emergency actions ended the banking panic, but they were followed by more significant reforms to restore the banks and the economy. Roosevelt's reforms and regulations, called the New Deal, attempted to reduce economic instability and end the Great Depression. Among the New Deal policies were many that changed the rules of the game by regulating the banking system. For example, the power of the Federal Reserve was centralized in Washington and expanded. Banks were not allowed to operate in more than one state. Banks were prohibited from operating as stock brokers. Stock brokers were prohibited from acting as banks. The percentage of a stock purchase that one could buy on credit—called buying on margin—was subject to strict controls by the Federal Reserve.

The most important innovation occurred with the creation of the **Federal Deposit Insurance Corporation (FDIC)**. The FDIC *insured bank accounts up to a certain amount of money.* Depositors with accounts in FDIC-insured banks would know that they would always get their money from the bank (up to the insured amount) even if the bank failed. Since the bank accounts of most people were fully insured, they no longer had any reason to make a run on the bank or to take their money out of the banking system. This measure has tended to prevent monetary panics.

As the memory of the Great Depression grew dim, many conservative presidents and congresses did their best to remove the regulations and controls established by the New Deal. Confident in their view that modern monetary and fiscal policy has made the economy "depression proof," policymakers have been confident as they remove one regulation after another. Now banks can operate in all states at once. Banks can act as stock brokers, and stock brokers can operate as bankers.

As a result, financial corporations are now among the world's largest businesses, controlling previously unimaginable amounts of money. Many banks have made too many dangerous loans and are financially fragile. Because of the size of some of these financial institutions, they are often willing to take extraordinary risks, since they know the policymakers will rescue them because they are "too big to fail."

The conservative argument for deregulation is that bank regulations prevented banks from operating efficiently in the global market. On the basis of that free-market criticism of monetary regulations, various conservative administrations in Washington have slowly eroded away most of the bank regulations put in during the Great Depression. The progressive critics argue that the result of deregulation has been increased monetary instability in the economy. For example, the stock market expanded to a tremendous bubble up through June of 2000, when the bubble burst. The stock market crash continued to a low point in 2003. Many businesses and some banks went bankrupt.

Conservatives believe that if there are no regulations, the economy will automatically recover rapidly from any recession. But real economic recovery from the 2001 recession was very slow. The expansion from the recession was fueled by a bubble in the real estate market, which in 2006 began to decline and was still declining as this book went to press. The expansion has also been fueled by a dramatic rise in credit, leaving the economy vulnerable to a credit collapse.

THE STRUCTURE OF FEDERAL RESERVE SYSTEM

The Federal Reserve is the central bank of the United States, corresponding to the Bank of England or the Bank of France. Its original purposes were to give the country a currency flexible enough to meet its needs and to improve the supervision of banking. Today, however, these are only a part of broader and more important objectives, which include maintaining price stability, fostering a high rate of economic growth, and promoting a high level of employment. By law, the Federal Reserve is required to attempt to reach goals of no more than 4 percent unemployment and no more than 3 percent inflation. In practice, its main focus has been to restrain inflation at all costs, with a goal of zero inflation, regardless of other official objectives.

When the Federal Reserve has to deal with both inflation and unemployment at the same time, it usually concentrates on inflation. For example, in 1981, when inflation was very high, the Federal Reserve maintained a very tight monetary policy, squeezing inflation out of the economy even though the result was the highest level of unemployment and the worst cyclical downturn since the Great Depression. Only after extremely loud complaints from Congress and the general public did the Federal Reserve relent and adopt a more expansive policy.

The Federal Reserve functions are carried out through twelve Federal Reserve banks and their twenty-four branches. There is also central coordination by the Board of Governors in Washington. The Board of Governors consists of seven members appointed by the president and confirmed by the Senate. One of the Board's duties is to supervise all Federal Reserve operations. The Board participates in all of the principal monetary actions of the Federal Reserve.

It has full authority over changes in the legal reserve requirements of banks (within limits prescribed by Congress). The Board "reviews and determines" the interest rates of the individual Federal Reserve banks. The Board also has the authority to establish the maximum rates of interest member banks may pay on various kinds of deposits. In addition, the Federal Reserve's Board of Govenors is responsible for the regulation of how much stock an investor can buy in the stock market on credit. Going into debt to buy stock, called buying on margin, is not only dangerous for an individual but also adds to the instability for the stock market.

The presidents of the twelve regional Federal Reserve banks are not publicly elected nor are they appointed by any elected official. Rather, the president of each Federal Reserve Bank is appointed by the board of directors of that bank. Each board of directors has nine members. Six of the nine are elected by the member commercial banks of the region. Usually, these six are elected on the advice of the state bankers' association, which is the bankers' lobbying group. Not surprisingly, these six members of the regional Federal Reserve Bank board are usually conservative bankers.

The other three directors (called Class C directors) are supposed to be representative of a broader public. In fact, they often represent the same narrow interests as the bankers' representatives. Many of these so-called public directors are executives or directors of large corporations. Thus, all nine members of the boards of each of the Federal Reserve banks are usually bankers or corporate executives closely tied to banks.

As a result, they are alert to the interests of banks and large corporations. They are supposed to represent the public interest, but most of the time they sincerely believe that the public interest would be best served by policies that are also in the interest of banks and large corporations.

Perhaps the most important institution of the Federal Reserve is the **Federal Open Market Committee (FOMC)**. The FMOC has the important function *of buying and selling government bonds on the open market.* The FOMC is composed of the seven members of the Board of Governors of the Federal Reserve. The other economists on the board are often academic economists, but they are chosen by a political process so that most of them have been mainly concerned with the interests of bankers and big business.

Finally, the FMOC includes five presidents of the regional Federal Reserve banks. The twelve presidents take turns on the FOMC, but they are all bankers or represent the interests of bankers. These are the people who determine the major part of U.S. monetary policy.

The Federal Reserve System controls the money supply in order to achieve its purposes. The real basis of the value of the nation's money supply are the goods and services produced as well as confidence in the government. Until 1934, however, the money supply of the United States had as its legal base the country's gold stock. Although the Federal Reserve banks still hold gold certificates, this is merely one of several types of assets. Gold certificates need bear no necessary relationship to Federal Reserve liabilities. This means that the gold certificates bear no necessary connection to the U.S. money supply. The other principal types of assets of the Federal Reserve are government securities and loans to the member banks. The liabilities of the Federal Reserve include the paper currency held by the public and member bank reserves.

The Federal Reserve specifies exactly how much **reserves**, *a percentage of the bank's deposits*, each member bank must hold. Congress sets the minimum and maximum limits on reserve ratios that the Federal Reserve may require. Different types of banks, such as big city or rural banks, have different requirements as to what their reserves must be. Banks in the rural areas are given a lower required reserve ratio, apparently on the theory that they may also use loans from the larger city banks as part of their emergency reserves. Banking reserves may be kept either in the bank vault or in the nearest Federal Reserve bank. If it is kept as a deposit in a Federal Reserve bank, the member bank may even earn a small interest on its money reserves.

One might think the purpose of the reserve system is to ensure that each bank has sufficient funds to meet its depositors' withdrawals. However, in the Great Depression, thousands of banks failed because runs on the banks by depositors exhausted their reserves. The prevention of such panics is now met by the Federal Deposit Insurance Corporation (FDIC). The FDIC guarantees all deposits up to some level specified by Congress, such as $100,000, but the number keeps increasing with inflation. The reserves held by the Federal Reserve are not usually used to bail out banks. Rather, the reserves serve to give the Federal Reserve added control over bank behavior, increasing its ability to control the money supply so as to influence the economy.

THREE TOOLS OF MONETARY POLICY

Monetary policy is government policy, operated through the semi-independent Federal Reserve, designed to increase or decrease the flow of money and credit. It is hoped that such increases or decreases in the flow will stimulate or depress demand. What are the tools with which the Federal Reserve influences money and credit? In an inflationary situation, exactly how should monetary policy be applied, and how effective is it?

The supply of money and credit may be restricted by monetary policy through three major controls: (1) raising the bank reserve ratio required by Federal Reserve, (2) raising the interest rate the Federal Reserve charges banks, called the discount rate, and (3) selling government bonds by the Federal Reserve. Let us see how each of these controls is supposed to work.

First, in order to restrict credit, the Federal Reserve may raise the ratio of reserves banks are required to hold against their deposits. Furthermore, as soon as one bank decreases its loans, the effect on all banks may be several times as great by virtue of the money multiplier (see Appendix 49.1). In theory, raising the required reserve ratio from 10 to 20 percent would lower the potential multiplication of money by banks from tenfold to only fivefold. If all banks were fully loaned out, this would cause a great decrease of loans. A reduction in the volume of loans usually causes a decline in consumer and investment spending.

Second, the Federal Reserve may also raise the interest rate that banks must pay if they wish to borrow from the Federal Reserve banks. Changes in the discount rate have relatively small effects. If the Federal Reserve raises the rate it charges banks, this should lower the amount that banks will be able to loan, but the effect is miniscule compared with other policy tools. Their main importance is that they are assumed to signal the general direction of all of the Federal Reserve's policies. Therefore, discount rate changes can have a major effect on speculative areas, such as the stock market.

Third, the Federal Reserve may sell more government bonds to banks or individuals. The money to pay for the bonds must come from bank reserves or from individual bank deposits. In either case, the ability of banks to make loans is reduced many fold, according to the money multiplier described in Appendix 49.1. This is the primary tool of monetary policy.

During an inflationary period, in attempting to reduce the money supply, the Federal Reserve runs into obstacles that were assumed away in the discussion so far. First, the ability to limit the money supply assumes that banks have already made loans up to the maximum ratio of deposits to reserves. But banks often keep extra reserves above even the highest possible required reserve ratio and can keep lending until these reserves are exhausted.

Second, the monetary controls assume that corporations must borrow from banks all the money they need for new investments. Corporations often keep their own internal savings, which they may decide to use regardless of government policies.

Third, in cases in which the government succeeds only in getting banks to raise their interest rates by lowering the growth of the money supply, there may be little effect on investment. If expected profit rates are rising even faster than interest rates, corporations may still be willing to borrow and invest more rapidly. In all of these cases, the government may be able to restrict the growth of the money supply, but the speed of spending the present money supply may increase even more rapidly.

Despite these weaknesses, monetary policy, if applied strongly enough, can choke off a general inflation. The policies must also be applied rapidly enough, because time is required for it to take effect. Of course, too severe a remedy may cause instability in the bond and stock markets, loss of confidence by domestic and foreign investors, and eventually a business downturn.

There is, indeed, considerable evidence that Federal Reserve's attempts to reduce inflation were one part of the causes of the downturns of 1969 to 1970, 1973 to 1975, 1980, 1981 to 1982, and 2001. The clearest case was in 1981 to 1982 under President Carter. His advisors told him that the very high rate of inflation in 1980 must be stopped immediately or else he would lose the election of 1980. Therefore, he requested very strong measures by the Federal Reserve acting in coordination with the president. The controls were very drastic, strong, and restrictive on credit. As a result, the high inflation of 1980 was greatly reduced, but the rapid credit reduction triggered a recession. Carter lost the election.

In a recession, the Federal Reserve may apply exactly the opposite monetary policy that it uses in fighting inflation. The supply of money and credit may be expanded by (1) lowering the required Federal Reserve ratio, (2) lowering the discount rate, or (3) having the Federal Reserve purchase government bonds in the open market to put more cash into the hands of individuals and banks. These measures are designed to increase the volume of borrowing and thus the volume of spending by increasing the supply of money for loans and lowering interest rates.

Obstacles to monetary policies intended to combat recession include most of those obstacles met by counterinflationary policies. There are a few additional obstacles more difficult to surmount. First, the interest rate cannot go below zero, and in actual practice, lenders will not go below a floor that is somewhat above a zero rate. Yet during a depression, it may require a zero or even negative interest rate to stimulate borrowing.

Second, during periods of recession, neither consumers nor most investors seem much stimulated by slightly lower interest rates to borrow. Businesspeople apparently consider their pessimistic expectations of smaller profits or even losses to be quantitatively much more important than low interest rates in investment decisions. Moreover, if possible, many large businesses prefer to invest from internal funds. When profits fall drastically in a depression, businesses are not much attracted by any kind of loan.

The government may increase the banks' supply of money in order to combat a depression, but consumers and businesses may reduce the amount of borrowing and spending even more rapidly. In short, monetary policies may have some effect in minor recessions, but in a major depression, monetary policy may be able to do little or nothing to expand the volume of spending. The most dramatic example was the decade-long stagnation of the Japanese economy in the 1990s. The Japanese government used every expansionary monetary policy ever suggested, but nothing worked. Finally, a fiscal policy of large government spending helped start a recovery.

PRESIDENT BUSH'S MONETARY POLICY

In 2001, when President George W. Bush entered office, a recession began a few months later. We saw in Chapter 47 that his fiscal policy answer to recession was tax cuts, mainly for the rich. These tax cuts were supposed to stimulate investment. There was one small tax rebate for everyone besides the rich. This small rebate pushed up the growth rate of GDP very quickly for a short period.

The other response by the administration to the recession of 2001 was monetary policy as determined by the Federal Reserve. The main technique used by the Federal Reserve in the Bush era has been expansionary open market purchases of federal bonds. When engaging in these purchases, the Federal Reserve attempted to influence the Federal Funds interest rate. Remember that the **federal funds rate (FFR)** is *the interest rate that bankers charge each other for overnight loans.* The Federal Funds rate strongly influences all short-run interest rates. Whether it affects the interest rates for consumers and corporations, and whether interest rates affect the economy, are the questions that must be answered in assessing its usefulness.

In response to the 2001 recession and its aftereffects, the Federal Reserve pushed the Federal Funds rate down eleven times between 2001 and 2003. By the end of those cuts, the Federal Funds rate was down to 1.25 percent. This was a very low rate in U.S. monetary history. What effect did it have?

The object of pushing down this rate is to influence all other interest rates so that they will also fall. If all interest rates fall, the theory of the Federal Reserve is that lower interest rates will get consumers and corporations to borrow more. Consumers will then spend more money on consumption, and investors will spend more money on investment. The result will be an expanding economy. Unfortunately, in this case, cutting the FFR did not have as much impact on other interest rates as hoped, especially the interest rates that stimulate investment. Because the decline of interest rates did not have as large an effect as expected on corporate investment, it had little effect on jobs. This should not be surprising. There have been many studies of the effect of interest rates on investment, but few have shown any clearly significant effect (see Sherman, 1991, chapter 14).

From 2004 through 2006, the Federal Reserve decided that the economy was advancing fast enough, so it worried instead about preventing inflation. For this reason, the Federal Reserve repeatedly, month after month, raised the Federal Funds rate. What was the effect on other interest rates? Not as much as was hoped. There was a considerable effect on many short-run interest rates, but not much on long-term rates. It is long-term interest rates that affect investment. Short-term rates just represent temporary borrowing.

The higher short-run rates encouraged much speculation on land, stocks, and short-run bonds, but it had little effect, if any, on business investment. Low interest rates did lead to a big speculative bubble in real estate. The high real estate prices allowed people to get money through mortgaging their homes. They used the money to finance a giant consumption mania. Consumption based on credit kept the economy growing even as job creation and investment were sluggish.

The Federal Reserve attempted to dampen consumer spending in order to reduce inflation. This attempt did not succeed. Why did consumers continue to borrow even in the face of higher interest rates? Consumers continued to borrow and spend in order to keep up a reasonable standard of living in the face of stagnant wages. They considered their spending absolutely necessary, so they continued to borrow and spend. The bubble in housing prices helped make this credit possible.

SUMMARY

In this chapter, we examined the money supply and its evolution from barter to paper money to credit. Today, one important component of the money supply is the checking deposits owed to customers by the banks. The other big component of the money supply is credit money from lenders. The Federal Reserve System (Fed) was established to regulate banks and stabilize the money supply. It is controlled by the banks, with representatives on every regional Federal Reserve bank's board. As a result, it acts to control inflation, because inflation worries bankers. But tight controls on credit often reduce consumer and investor spending, so they increase unemployment.

Credit supports each business expansion, often beyond reasonable expectations of real economic growth. This favorable effect, however, lasts only until a recession begins. In a recession, the existence of huge debts has a massive negative effect, causing mild recessions to become deep declines in output and employment.

The Federal Reserve uses three tools to try to control the money supply in order to control inflation. They are (1) changes in reserve requirements; (2) buying or selling treasury bonds, which changes the federal funds rate; and (3) changing the discount rate (which has little direct effect but influences investors as a signal of Federal Reserve policy. All three tools are designed to alter the rate of credit creation by the banking system, which indirectly changes the interest rates faced by consumers and businesses.

The problem seen by critics is that the reasonable use of monetary policy has very limited effects. Small changes in the use of the three tools have little effect on inflation in an expansion, but they also have little effect on unemployment in a recession. If the tools are used to an extreme, then an inflation will be defeated, but at the cost of creating a recession. There have been many vehement debates on monetary policy, and some of the highlights of these debates are presented in Appendix 51.1.

SUGGESTED READINGS

An excellent discussion of the monetary policies of Clinton and Bush is in the readable but advanced *Contours of Descent: U.S. Economic Fractures and the Landscape of Global Austerity* by Robert Pollin (2005). Another excellent book is Michael Allen Meeropol's *Surrender: How the Clinton Administration Completed the Reagan Revolution* (2000).

KEY TERMS

deflation
Federal Deposit Insurance Corporation
federal funds rate (FFR)
Federal Open Market Committee
Inflation

lender of last resort
monetary policy
panic
reserves

REVIEW QUESTIONS

Describe a brief history of the evolution of the Central Bank and the Federal Reserve.
1. How has the role of the Central Bank and the Federal Reserve changed over time?
2. List and describe key policies implemented to increase stability in the banking sector.

Discuss the evolution and impact of regulation and deregulation of the financial system.
3. What are the conservative arguments for deregulating the banks?
4. What are the progressive arguments for not deregulating the banks?

Describe the structure of the Federal Reserve.
    5. Draw a "map" of the basic structure of the Federal Reserve system.
    6. What is the role of the Federal Open Market Committee and why is it so important?

List the tools used by the Federal Reserve, and discuss how and why they are used in periods of recession and inflation.
    7. What are the three main tools used by the Federal Reserve to affect inflation or unemployment?
    8. Discuss the effectiveness of each tool.

Compare and contrast the main views of monetary policy.
    9. What should the Federal Reserve do according to conservatives economists?
   10. What should the Federal Reserve do according to progressive economists?

Discuss the actual history of recent monetary policy under President George W. Bush.
   11. Describe some monetary policy decisions under the Bush administration.
   12. What are the conservative arguments supporting Bush's monetary policies? Progressive criticisms?

APPENDIX 51.1
FURIOUS DEBATES ON MONETARY POLICY

There have been many lively debates on monetary policy. What exactly were the debates that caused so much verbal vehemence and even physical attack?

LEARNING OBJECTIVES FOR APPENDIX 51.1

After reading this appendix, you should be able to:

- Compare and contrast the debates about money and monetary policy in the U.S. economy.

CLASSICAL AND PROGRESSIVE ECONOMISTS ON MONEY

The chapter discussed the Federal Reserve System and the mechanisms by which it tries to influence the monetary system. Let us now examine some of the main points of the blistering controversies that have rocked economics over what should be the tactics of monetary policy. Even very old controversies can provide some clarification of these issues.

The classical economists and early progressives argued over the importance of money. Is money just a useful thing that helps the operation of the system in a passive sort of way, or is money a very active part of the process leading to great instability? In the period of feudalism in Western Europe, barter was used in many transactions. When money (such as silver coins) was used, it was simply an intermediary between two commodities. A person might bring a pig to market and sell it for so many coins. Then the person used the coins to buy a coat or some other commodity. Money played no active role, just made the exchange of commodities more convenient.

In the early days of capitalism, some of the classical economists (discussed in Part I) thought of money in the same terms as in the feudal period. Although the classical economists had complex theories in many areas, they often simplified the analysis of money to make their basic policy point. They argued that money was only a medium of exchange, meaning that money only entered the picture as follows:

$$\text{Commodity} \rightarrow \text{Money} \rightarrow \text{Commodity}$$

For example, a pig is exchanged for coins, then the coins are exchanged for a coat. This was not a bad description of the medieval situation in which there were only occasional markets, but it is very misleading for capitalism, with its markets that work all the time and include very complex financial transactions. The point of the classical economists was that the important thing was the growth of the physical economy, not the accumulation of gold and silver.

Some earlier economists urged the accumulation of gold and silver as the basis of a country's wealth but said nothing about physical production of goods. On the contrary, according to most of the classical economists, money's role was passive. They urged the government not to use any monetary controls on trade. Rather, they urged the government to allow free trade in foreign commerce. They said there should be freedom from monetary controls both in domestic commerce and foreign commerce.

The classical economists holding such theories have been criticized by many progressive economists. Progressives agree that money played a purely passive role in the occasional markets of the feudal period. The money and credit system, however, plays a major role in the capitalist economy. Money and credit lead to the possibility of the instability that characterizes capitalism. As discussed in Chapters 38 and 45, use of money is not without problems, and the existence of money and credit tend to intensify the instability of capitalism.

The simplest progressive argument was this: in earlier, precapitalist economies, commodities are exchanged with other commodities, with money merely acting as an intermediary. In such economies and in the classical model of economics, the process is from commodity to money to commodity. But this is no longer the dominant process under capitalism. In capitalism, the main preoccupation of capitalists is to turn money into more money. The most important form of exchange for business people is:

$$\text{Money} \rightarrow \text{Commodities} \rightarrow \text{More money}$$

In the economic process of capitalism, money is used to buy commodities, including capital and labor. Then capital and labor are used to produce more commodities. The finished commodities are sold for more money. The progressive's point was that capitalism is a process for making profit, and profit is calculated in money.

When there is insufficient money to satisfy all the credit needs of businesses, an interruption in production could occur, which could spell trouble for the entire economy. Monetary policy may attempt to solve that trouble. Cyclical instability, however, is inherent in capitalism, as we saw in Chapter 45. Therefore, some progressive economists argue that monetary policy can only reduce, not end, the effects of instability. Other progressive economists argue that as long as the capitalist economic system lasts, monetary policy can be an important tool against instability.

In addition to its use as a medium of exchange, money is also borrowed and must be paid back. The existence of credit, however, means that what is borrowed may be paid back, but it is also possible that it will not be paid back. This is another path to trouble. If banks and other suppliers of credit cannot collect on mounting debt, they may also go bankrupt.

It is worth emphasizing that the nineteenth-century debates over monetary policy did not remain among peaceful academics but spread in the United States into the center of politics. One important debate, as noted in this chapter, was over the currency system. Bankers wanted a system based on gold to make sure their loans were paid back at full value. Farmers wanted paper money so as to allow a little inflation, which would make it easier to pay back the oppressive mortgages owed to the banks. Indignant farmers first organized mass protests and then formed the Populist Party. Reform of the monetary system was a major battle cry of the Populist Party and was central to many political struggles.

DEBATES ON MONETARY POLICY IN THE MID-TWENTIETH CENTURY

Let us jump from the debates of progressives versus classical economists in the mid-nineteenth century to the mid-twentieth century. In the mid-twentieth century, neoclassical economists still took the view that money is just a medium of exchange between two commodities. Thus, money can cause no problem as long as government does not interfere with money in some improper way. Even during the Great Depression, they said that government should leave money alone. Many neoclassical claimed that interference in the monetary system by the Federal Reserve caused the Depression or made it last longer.

Progressives such as John M. Keynes argued during the Great Depression in the 1920s and 1930s that money is not just an intermediary between two commodities that could do no harm. Rather, if money is used to buy commodities in order to produce more commodities for sale and profit, then it is possible that there will be insufficient money to demand all the commodities at a high enough price to make profit. The system of private profit means that the capitalist must end up with more money at the end of the process than at the beginning. If capitalists expect no profit, they cut back on production, and unemployment ensues.

Contrary to the neoclassical economists, progressive economists argued that the circulation of money may not always be smooth. Money circulation may slow up if there is no expectation of profit. The money sits idle for some time because capitalists do not see a profitable opportunity in which to invest. Money still exists, but the neoclassical assumption that money will always be used to buy more commodities is wrong. Keynes argued that demand is not effective under capitalist institutions unless it combines both desire and money income. Those who want to buy may have no money, while those who have money may not wish to spend it. The lack of effective demand, that is, demand backed by money income, leads to recession.

Unlike the neoclassical economists, progressives saw money as more than just a medium of exchange. It could be used to store value in a bank or other financial institution, so it might be idle. While it sits in a bank, it is a form of wealth, and in that form, it is a source of power to command resources under capitalism. But it may or may not be spent and become effective demand. Some progressives argued that sometimes the government must step in and take monetary action. When capitalists are unwilling to utilize their wealth to produce goods and create jobs, the government can override their objections by inducing them to circulate that wealth and create more demand.

Progressives went further to note the vital importance of credit in the modern economy. Credit allows consumers to buy beyond their income. Credit allows businesses to buy capital goods beyond their income. Money in the form of credit can be used not just as a medium of exchange but as a promise for future payment. Thus, credit is the usual source for an exaggerated boom. Excessive credit leads to a bubble in which expectations of investors go far beyond the reality of actual production.

But what happens when the bubble bursts? In a depression or recession, consumers cannot pay their debts, businesses cannot pay their debts, and creditors (such as banks) go bankrupt along with those who owe them money. Obviously, progressives argued that money and credit were very important in changing small recessions into deep recessions.

Unfortunately, there are definite limits to the effectiveness of monetary policy in ending unemployment. These limits were discussed earlier in relation to the obstacles to the use of the three policy instruments of the Federal Reserve. We explained the limitations of the manipulation of interest rates. We explained the limitations of the Federal Reserve's setting the maximum amounts of loans that banks can make. We explained the limitations of the Federal Reserve's buying and selling government bonds.

The basic problem of monetary policy in a recession may be stated this way. Monetary policy can drive down interest rates and make it much easier to get a loan, but corporations do not want loans unless they see investment opportunities. An investment opportunity means that the corporation expects to make profit by expanding. In a recession, there seems to be too much of everything for the effective demand to purchase. Therefore, there is no profit on the horizon. If there is no profit to be made, then loans are not taken on any interest rate. The Federal Reserve can lead the capitalist corporations to water, but it cannot make them drink unless the water looks clear and appealing.

As a result of these limitations on monetary policy, Keynesians in the 1950s and 1960s downplayed the importance of monetary theory and monetary policy. When Keynesians were in power in the United States government during this period, they used some monetary policy, but only in coordination with strong fiscal policy. Thus, the Federal Reserve reduced the Federal Funds rate significantly in response to the 1958 and 1961 recessions, but the government also used strong fiscal measures.

Keynesian economists remained skeptical that monetary policy could alone respond to the ups and downs of the economy. When Keynesian economists were in control of economic policy, they routinely used monetary policy to attempt to supplement government fiscal policy when seeking either to combat recessions or to restrain inflation. Fiscal policy consists of government spending and tax cuts and was discussed in Chapters 47 and 48.

MONETARISM

At the University of Chicago in the 1950s, economist Milton Friedman was publishing a series of articles in an effort to revitalize the more traditional monetary theories. From this effort, an entire school of thought called monetarism eventually emerged. **Monetarism** holds that *the economic system works very well except when government messes it up through mistakes in monetary policy*. Therefore, government should follow some minimum rules to provide the economy with an adequate amount of money but should otherwise never interfere with the monetary system or the economy.

Generally, a strict monetarist would agree with the following propositions:

1. Unfettered free markets are efficient and will promote growth. Free markets will generally solve their own problems without government assistance. Serious economic disturbances are the consequence of random shocks, such as a bad harvest or the formation of a foreign oil cartel. No one can control these shocks. Other shocks are due to misguided economic policy from a government that should not be interfering.

2. The expansion and contraction of the money stock will directly and unambiguously affect

the level of nominal spending in the economy. **Nominal spending** means *spending that is not corrected for inflation.* Real spending is the amount of spending after correction for inflation. The amount or supply of money in use in society directly affects consumer and investor spending. More money in circulation means more spending, while less money in circulation means less spending. More spending means higher prices. Less spending means lower prices.

According to monetarism, an increase in the money supply will raise prices but will have no lasting effect on output. Therefore, an excessive monetary expansion through government spending will generate inflation, and larger government spending will not much improve output and employment. In the long run, expanding the money supply does not fight unemployment.

In the short run, monetarists believe that it is impossible to get the correct timing for discretionary monetary policy. Even a correct-looking policy on the money supply may cause the wrong effects on the real output of the country for a while. It is better to abstain from short-run discretionary monetary policy and just rely on strict long-run monetary rules.

Why do monetarists believe that higher government spending has no effect on the amount of output? According to monetarists, the economy has a self-correcting mechanism whereby over time, in effect, demand always rises to meet supply. Therefore, there can be no addition to employment, only a rise in prices. Mistaken discretionary monetary measures can lead to monetary contractions, which can lead to recessions. Such mistaken monetary policy set off the Great Depression. Most monetarists would also agree that inflations usually have excessive monetary expansions as their ultimate cause.

3. There is a lag between changes in the money stock and their impact on spending. That lag is variable and unknown. Discretionary monetary policy means using monetary policy to attempt to correct problems, such as unemployment. Because of the time lag, however, discretionary changes in the money supply can only make problems worse. Any attempt to use discretionary monetary policy will tend to either overreact or underreact to economic problems because of the uncertainty of when the impact will happen.

The problem, according to Friedman, is that the change in policy first impacts the real economy for a short period. Then, however, the real economy goes back to where it was. In other words, there is higher inflation but no more output. If, on the other hand, the government leaves well enough alone, there may be a short recession, but then the economy will snap back to long-run growth. On the contrary, as seen earlier, the Keynesians believe that the correct policy of spending and taxation can prevent a recession and cause real economic growth.

The monetarists conclude that policymakers will ultimately end up trying to chase down and stamp out the results of their own misguided policy. Discretionary monetary and fiscal policy is very dangerous and often harmful. It is better to merely follow a strict rule that the monetary supply should rise at the same rate as long-run economic growth. In this way, in the opinion of Milton Friedman, the money supply will not be the source of instability.

4. When government fiscal actions try to raise demand, the actions usually favor the government at the expense of the private sector. For example, if the government borrows more money to spend, interest rates rise because of the new demand for borrowed money. Private investors are forced to pay higher interest rates. The increase of government spending at the expense of private spending is called "crowding out." Since government spending causes higher interest rates, it crowds private investment out of the money market.

Milton Friedman has gone even further, arguing that to the extent that government spending produces some useful product, such spending will preempt private investment opportunities. For example, if there were no public Tennessee Valley Authority (TVA) supplying electricity to parts of eleven states in the Southeast United States, there would be private utilities doing it. Dollars spent on facilities for the TVA are dollars not spent by private utilities to do the same thing.

CRITICISMS OF MONETARISM

Critics have attacked each of the main propositions of monetarism.

1. The monetarist assertion that the economy automatically corrects recessions and returns rapidly to growth is wrong. As shown in Chapter 45, the capitalist market system results in periodic recessions and depressions. Growth is uneven and much slower than it need be. Some critics, such as liberal Keynesians, argue that fiscal and monetary policy can reduce or end recessions. Other critics, such as Marxists, argue that no policy of reforms can get rid of the system of booms and busts, which is an integral part of the way that the capitalist system grows. Only a change in the basic institutions of the economic system itself can eliminate the cycle of booms and busts.

Contrary to the monetarist view that the only problem is outside shocks or government mistakes, the business cycle of boom and bust is internal to the system. This is shown by the fact that recessions keep recurring in the same patterns time and again.

2. Contrary to the monetarists, the critics point out that the money supply does not have any clear effect on spending in the short run for two reasons. First, the monetarists use a very narrow definition of money, such as cash and some bank deposits. Critics note that the economy today really operates mainly on credit. Therefore, it is not the money supply but the expansion and contraction of the broader credit aggregates that is really important.

Furthermore, whether one speaks of money narrowly defined or of credit, why do money and credit expand? They expand when economic activity expands. It is more accurate to say that economic expansion causes money and credit to expand than vice versa. When the economy is expanding rapidly, the corporations and the consumers wish to borrow, the banks are happy to comply, and the Federal Reserve System is under pressure to allow it. In the contraction, everyone is afraid to borrow or to lend; this causes the supply and speed of circulation of money and credit to decline.

3. Monetarists claim that no discretionary money policy is any good. Some progressive critics argue that enough is known so that discretionary monetary policy, combined with fiscal policy, can achieve some short-run success. Other progressives might agree that it is difficult to know what time lags will affect the money supply with a given policy, but they argue that this also undermines the monetarist idea that the money stock directly and unambiguously affects spending. How can it be unambiguous when the time lag is variable and unpredictable?

4. The monetarist argument says that fiscal expansionary policies lead to deficits, but these deficits must crowd out private investment. This argument has been vigorously challenged. It is argued that public spending, through the multiplier mechanism, has a very strong positive effect on the economy. This positive effect of deficit spending is much stronger than any negative effect on borrowing for private investment. The evidence on this point has been strongly disputed ever since Keynes wrote about it in the 1930s.

KEY TERMS IN APPENDIX 51.1

monetarism
nominal spending

REVIEW QUESTIONS FOR APPENDIX 51.1

Compare and contrast the debates about money and monetary policy in the U.S. economy.
1. How does the focus on production for money profits introduce instability into the economy? Explain.
2. What are problems using monetary policy to lower unemployment?
3. What are the major propositions of monetarists? How do these related to the conclusion of how monetary policy should be conducted?
4. What are the criticisms of monetarism? How do these impact conclusions about the conduct of monetary policy?

PART IV

INTERNATIONAL AND GLOBAL POLICY

CHAPTER 52

Exports and Imports

This chapter explains the relationship of U.S. exports and imports, trade deficits and trade surpluses, and how they affect the U.S. economy. It also explains how the price of imported raw materials may cause problems for the U.S. economy.

LEARNING OBJECTIVES

After reading this chapter, you should be able to:

- Explain the relationship of positive or negative net exports and aggregate demand.
- Explain why prices of imported raw materials, such as oil, cause problems in the U.S. economy.

INTERNATIONAL TRADE: EXPORTS AND IMPORTS

Exports are *those goods that Americans sell abroad.* If someone in Germany wants a Dell computer, he or she can buy it at a local store. But how did the computer get to the store? When the supply of Dell computers in Germany gets too low, the storekeeper asks Dell to send more computers. Dell then exports computers to Germany.

In exchange for the computers, the German store sends money to Dell. The German store has imported computers. **Imports** are *goods and services purchased from abroad.* In order to import, it is necessary to send money abroad.

When an American corporation receives money from abroad, it uses the money to pay employees, give dividends to stockholders, and buy investment goods to expand its business. Exports lead to a flow of money into America and an increase in demand for American goods. The demand goes both for the goods and services that are exported and for the additional demand by the corporation when it receives the money from abroad.

Similarly, when an American company imports goods and services from abroad, it pays out money to foreign businesses. Therefore, imports diminish the demand in America. If an American buys a Volkswagen car from Germany, the car comes to the United States. The money flows to Germany as demand for goods.

Net exports describes the relationship between imports and exports. **Net exports** is *the dollar value of exports minus the dollar value of imports. When exports are larger than imports, net exports is positive* and there is a **trade surplus**. If the net exports is positive, then it means that goods are flowing out of the country and money is flowing into the country. Of course, it is also possible that *imports are greater than exports. In this case, net exports is negative* and there is a **trade deficit**. The trade deficit means that more goods and services are flowing into America than are flowing out. The trade deficit also means that money and demand are flowing out of America to pay for the net inflow of goods and services. The money and demand go to some other country, such as Germany.

ACTUAL TRENDS IN EXPORTS AND IMPORTS

For about a hundred years, from roughly 1870 to 1970, the United States exported more than it imported so that net exports were positive. This was a trade surplus. Every year, the net difference between exports and imports meant that goods and services flowed out of foreign countries, while money flowed into America. In other words, the trade surplus (or positive net exports) increased demand in America by that net inflow of money.

Since about 1970, however, imports have been greater than exports. There is a trade deficit pulling money out of America every year. Moreover, the trade deficit has grown larger over time. On the average, for every year from 1970 to 1975 (the first cycle examined here), exports were $195 billion but imports were $256 billion. Therefore, net exports were negative $61 billion. (All statistics here are in real 1996 dollars, quarterly data from trough to trough of the cycle, seasonally adjusted at annual rates, from the Bureau of Economic Analysis, Department of Commerce.)

In the average of all quarters in the most recent cycle from 1991 to 2001, exports were $878 billion, but imports had risen to $1,047 billion (over a trillion dollars). Net exports went down to negative $169 billion average for the cycle. This trade deficit meant a net of $169 billion of money flowing out each year to become demand in other countries.

Since 2001, the negative net exports, or trade deficit, has risen rapidly. In the fourth quarter of 2005, the trade deficit (or negative net exports) was minus $655 billion at an annual rate, seasonally adjusted. Over $650 billion a year was the net outflow of money from America, an enormous reduction of demand for domestic American goods and services. To put it in perspective, this means that the trade deficit had risen to five percent of all gross domestic product, so it was very significant.

CYCLICAL BEHAVIOR OF EXPORTS AND IMPORTS

How do exports and imports behave over the business cycle? Imports are easy to understand and very predictable. Whenever the national income of the United States rises, Americans spend more money on imports. When there is a recession, Americans have less money and they spend less on imports. This behavior of import spending is shown in Figure 52.1.

Figure 52.1 reveals that imports rise quickly throughout the average U.S. expansion as a result of rising buying power of Americans. Every increase in American imports means that more dollars flow out of the United States to foreign countries. The increase in dollars flowing out of America means less money available for domestic demand. In the average contraction, on the other hand, American imports fall because Americans have less money to spend. Every decrease in American imports means that fewer dollars flow out of the United States to foreign countries, thus leaving more dollars for domestic demand.

Figure 52.1 **Imports**

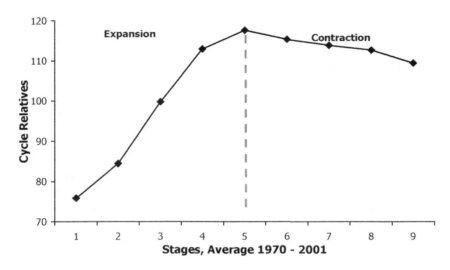

Source: U.S. Department of Commerce, www.bea.gov.

American exports to the rest of the world do not depend on U.S. demand but on world demand for U.S. goods and services. When a company in Singapore buys an American computer, this means that U.S. exports rise. Export demand cannot be easily predicted. Usually, American cycles coincide with those of the rest of the world for reasons discussed shortly. Therefore, exports usually rise somewhat during American expansions and fall somewhat during American expansions. But the movements are sluggish because many other things are happening in the rest of the world, so the correlation with American cycles is far from perfect.

The actual movement of exports in the average cycle from 1970 to the present is shown in Figure 52.2.

Figure 52.2 shows that in the average business cycle expansion, the value of exports rose steadily. This meant a growing demand for American products in every expansion. This usual rise of American exports in the expansion is a help to American business. Rising exports, however, is not the only thing happening.

The behavior of imports may contradict this trend, as shown in the next section. Figure 52.2 also shows that in the average contraction, American exports decline a little. This means less money coming into American firms, so American wages, salaries, and profits are hurt. This decline in income is harmful to domestic demand for American goods and services.

TRADE SURPLUS OR TRADE DEFICIT?

As shown earlier, net exports have been negative since 1970. America has a growing trade deficit, with the amounts shown previously. Increasingly larger amounts of money have flowed out of the American economy each year to pay for imports. The behavior of net exports over the business cycle is shown in Figure 52.3.

The path of net exports is highly significant and clearly marked in Figure 52.3. During the expan-

Figure 52.2 **Exports**

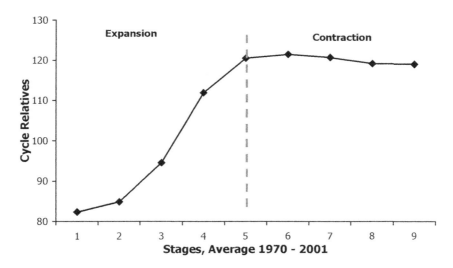

Source: U.S. Department of Commerce, www.bea.gov.

Figure 52.3 **Net Exports**

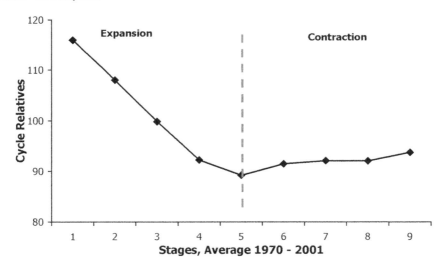

Source: U.S. Department of Commerce, www.bea.gov.

sion, net exports decreases constantly from the beginning to the end of expansion. Remember that positive net exports is the same thing as a trade surplus, but since 1970, the United States has had negative net exports, which means that we have a trade deficit. In the business cycle expansion, when the American net exports declines, the U.S. trade deficit increases. When the trade deficit increases, more and more money is flowing out of the United States to foreign countries every year.

Why has the American trade deficit risen in every business cycle expansion since the 1970s? The U.S. trade deficit rises because imports from foreign countries are greater than exports to foreign countries. In a business cycle expansion, imports rise rapidly because Americans have more money to spend. With more money, we buy more Hondas and Toyotas and all other foreign goods. For this reason, in every expansion on record, more and more money has flowed out to pay for more and more imports.

What about exports? Exports are always bringing a flow of money into the United States. Why don't exports rise in an expansion? In fact, exports do rise in expansions, but usually not as much as imports. The key fact is that U.S. exports depend on the demand of the rest of the world. If the rest of the world goes into a deep depression, they will buy much less from the United States. It is usual that most of the economies of the world expand together with the United States, but not at exactly the same pace and not at exactly the same time. Therefore, the demand for American goods during an American business cycle expansion does not rise as fast as does the American demand for imports.

The bottom line is that the American trade deficit usually rises in a U.S. expansion. In most expansions, the rising trade deficit siphons off more and more money to foreign countries. This loss of money abroad means a reduction of demand for American goods in the domestic markets.

In the average business cycle recession, as we see in Figure 52.3, net exports rises again, though at a slow pace. This rise helps support the demand for American goods in total. More precisely, it means we have less drain of demand abroad. Again, the cycles of various countries are somewhat synchronized (like some ragged synchronized swimming in the Olympics). Therefore, in the U.S. cyclical contraction, American demand for foreign imports declines quickly, but foreign demand for American exports declines more slowly. Since there is less trade deficit, there is less of a negative effect on profits.

COST OF IMPORTS, ESPECIALLY RAW MATERIALS

All imports into the United States cause money to flow out to other countries. If television sets are imported from Japan, then money must flow from America to Japan. Therefore, all imports by Americans lead to less demand in the United States for goods and services produced here.

Imports of raw materials pose special problems for American business. A very large portion of all raw materials used in America is produced abroad and imported by the United States. Suppose the price of raw materials from abroad, such as the price of oil from Venezuela or tin from Bolivia, rises in an expansion more rapidly than the price of consumer goods in the United States. If an American company produces tin cans and the price of tin cans remains constant while the price of tin in the world market goes up, the U.S. company will have lower profits per can. Figure 52.4 shows what actually happens to the price of raw materials in relation to the price of consumer goods over the average business cycle.

Figure 52.4 shows that the ratio of raw material prices to consumer goods prices declines a little at the beginning of an expansion but then rises rapidly to the cycle peak. This means that American producers of consumer goods are helped by the low price of raw materials (mostly imported) in the early expansion, so their profits are higher. Raw material prices rise more rapidly than consumer prices in the last half of expansion. American profits are hurt more and more by this increase. On the other hand, in each recession, raw material prices fall much faster than consumer prices, which helps American companies in consumer goods. It means that profits of American business do not decline as fast in a recession as they otherwise would.

To understand all of these movements, remember that it is harder to change the output of raw materials than to change the production of finished goods. For example, to increase tin or oil

Figure 52.4   **Ratio of Crude Materials Prices to Consumer Prices**

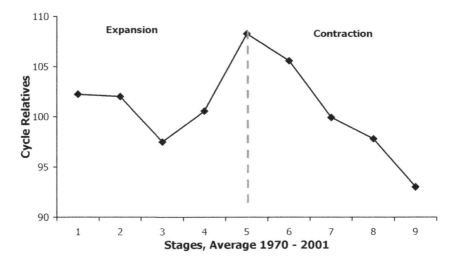

Source: U.S. Department of Commerce, www.bea.gov.

production requires new mines or new oil wells. Changing tin can production is much easier: the manufacturer simply buys more supplies. On the other hand, it is difficult to reduce production of some raw materials. For example, cotton is a raw material used by American industry. After cotton has been planted, the cotton farmer is committed to that crop and cannot, for example, decide midseason that the demand for cotton is too low and therefore replace the cotton with soybeans. The farmer must accept lower prices if the demand for cotton is lower than anticipated. Only in the following year can the crop be reduced.

One very important raw material is oil. The limited amount of oil in the world and the fact that it takes millions of years to create more has caused sharp competition for supplies and vast disruption worldwide when the supply is reduced for any reason. Sometimes, the biggest oil producers cut back the supply in a coordinated effort to force the price higher.

At the beginning of an expansion, there are large amounts of raw materials in storage, which tends to keep the price low for some time. This helps the recovery of U.S. profits. Eventually, the existing supplies are exhausted. If demand for raw materials rises still further, then there is a long time lag until more cotton can be planted and harvested, more oil wells dug, or more tin mines opened. Therefore, the price of raw materials rises rapidly in the last half of expansion. American manufacturers can simply hire more workers and use more machines, so their output rises faster while their prices rise much less. This is why high raw material prices hurt American profits in the last half of expansion. In a recession, the more rapid fall of raw material prices actually helps keep American profits from falling faster. Therefore, in a recession, the rapid decline of raw material prices is one factor that helps the recovery of American business.

SUMMARY

U.S. imports of foreign goods rise in an expansion as our income rises. U.S. imports of foreign goods fall in a contraction as our income falls. The rest of the world's economies tend to rise and fall with the American economy, but not at exactly the same time or rate of change. Therefore, the demand of the rest of the world for American goods rises more slowly than American imports in an expansion. World demand for American exports also falls more slowly than American imports in a recession.

Since our imports rise and fall faster than our exports, the net exports actually falls in an expansion and rises in a recession. Consequently, the trade deficit rises in American expansions but falls in American recessions. Therefore, the rising trade deficit is increasingly harmful in American expansions but less harmful in American recessions. For example, in 2006, the trade deficit rose to over three-quarters of a trillion dollars. That is a lot of money flowing out of the country, lowering U.S. domestic demand.

Finally, the price of raw materials rises rapidly in expansions and falls rapidly in recessions. Since the price of imported raw materials, such as oil, rises much faster than prices at which business can sell consumer goods as well as equipment, the profit margin of most American producers of consumer goods or equipment and factories is lowered. In a recession, on the other hand, the rapid decline in raw material prices helps the recovery of American profit rates.

SUGGESTED READINGS

Instructors will find the discussion of the effect of trade on the business cycle in Howard Sherman, *The Business Cycle: Growth and Crisis in Capitalism* (1991). On U.S. international dominance in finance after World War II, see the excellent study by Harry Magdoff, *Imperialism Without Colonies* (2003).

KEY TERMS

exports   trade surplus
imports   trade deficit
net exports

REVIEW QUESTIONS

Explain the relationship of positive or negative net exports and aggregate demand.
1. How does the usual pattern of American trade over the cycle tend to reduce demand for American products?
2. How does a trade surplus affect aggregate expenditures? Explain. How does a trade deficit affect aggregate expenditures? Explain.

Describe why the trade deficit rises further in economic expansions but declines in contractions.
3. Describe why the trade deficit rises further in economic expansions but declines in contractions.
4. How does the high price of raw materials in an expansion hurt the American economy?

CHAPTER 53

International Trade, Investment, and Finance
How Instability Spreads Around the World

Generally, in the modern world, most capitalist countries have recessions around the same time. Why? There are three ways expansions and recessions are transmitted from one country to another: through international trade, international investment, and international finance. This chapter explains how business cycles may be spread through these three international mechanisms in today's global economy.

LEARNING OBJECTIVES

After reading this chapter, you should be able to:

- Explain the mechanisms of global trade, investment, and finance by which instability in one country spreads to other countries.
- Compare and contrast the impact of global trade, investment, and finance on small and large economies.
- Discuss why capitalist economies in the global economy rise and fall roughly at the same time.

HOW TRADE SPREADS INSTABILITY

International trade affects all countries. In the last chapter, we saw how the rest of the world affects the U.S. economy through trade. Now let us examine how every country of the world is affected by the other economies through trade.

Slow economic growth in any country leads to less growth of its imports from the rest of the world. The slower growth of imports in some countries means less demand for goods and services from other countries. That lowered demand may help set off a recession in those countries. As an example of the effect of trade, suppose Americans usually buy hundreds of thousands of German automobiles. If there is a recession in America, Americans will have less money, so they will spend less on imported German automobiles. This decrease in demand will tend to lower German production, employment, and profits. However, Germany has a very large economy, so the loss of some American demand for automobiles will have a very small effect on the whole German economy. A recession will occur only if many other factors are turning down.

On the other hand, the American economy is very large relative to many other countries: when American demand for the goods of a small country declines, it is often devastating to smaller countries. Although the removal of U.S. trade can cause a recession in some small countries, the flow of U.S. money for imports from those countries can also cause a large expansion. For example, suppose that the small, underdeveloped country of Honduras produces nothing but bananas. Suppose that most of these bananas are exported to the United States. If America suffers a recession, Americans will have less money to buy bananas imported from Honduras. This lowered demand will be a deadly blow to the Honduran economy, since America is its largest buyer and all of its gross domestic product (GDP) comes from bananas. Finally, if America and Honduras are both suffering in a recession, a recovery in the United States is very good news for Honduras. With more money, Americans will buy more bananas. This will be a big boost for the Honduran economy.

In addition, in every global recession, a country like Bolivia that relies on exports of tin will lose a large amount of sales because manufacturing declines in the rest of the world. Moreover, the price of tin will drop in the world market as a result of a lack of demand. Therefore, profits from tin will drop dramatically not only because the volume of tin sold declines but also because the price of tin declines drastically. Thus, when the United States and other advanced capitalist countries go into recession, the less developed countries, like Honduras or Bolivia, will suffer very much from the decline in trade and from the decline in the prices of their leading exports.

We saw that the American economy affects most countries through its trade. America has an especially large effect on the smallest countries if they rely on just one product to sell to the United States. But what is the effect of the trade of other countries on the U.S. economy? Suppose Germans buy computers from U.S. computer corporations. If Germany goes into recession, then Germans will have less money to spend on imports of American computers. Therefore, exports of U.S. computers will drop. This lowered demand will hurt U.S. computer production and will help send America into recession. Computer production is only one factor, however, in the American economy, so this will be only one of a great many factors affecting the U.S. economy.

If the German economy recovers, Germans will spend more for American computers. This increase in demand will have a positive effect on the American economy, helping it recover from its own recession.

Notice that there is a feedback from one economy to another. If Germans buy more French goods, the French will have more money to buy German goods. But not all money that comes to the French for sale of additional goods and services goes back abroad. Some may be saved in France. How much the effect of increased trade reverberates back and forth, with higher and higher trade, depends on how much leaks out of the process into saving in each country.

There is a similar process of reverberation back and forth if demand declines from one country. If German demand for French goods declines, then the French get less income. In that case, they spend less on German imports to France, so there may be a vicious circle downward of trade between countries.

HOW INVESTMENT SPREADS BUSINESS CYCLES

We saw that international trade is one transmitter of booms and busts around the world. A second transmitter of instability is through **foreign investment**, which is *spending by foreign citizens on plants and equipment in a country.* If profit conditions look uncertain in other countries for economic or for political reasons, then American investors are afraid to invest in those countries. American corporations will also invest less in those countries. In countries where American investment is very important, a large decline of American investment may leave a high percentage of people unemployed in that country. If that country then goes into recession, it will have less income to spend on American imports and less money to invest in America. Thus, there is sometimes a vicious circle downward in investment as well as trade in the world economy.

As an example, if the Japanese firm Toyota invests in new automobile plants in the United States, then usually part of the money is spent in Japan on equipment. Then part of the money is spent in the United States on equipment, buildings, and construction labor. Once the buildings and equipment are ready, Toyota hires thousands of American employees. The Japanese employ a broad array of skilled American employees. These American employees include production workers, engineers, secretaries, and bookkeepers. Thus, foreign investment results in an injection of effective demand into the receiving economy. On the other hand, suppose Toyota closes a facility in the United States and withdraws as much as possible of its investment. This closing of the Toyota factory means that employees are fired and American national income loses the amount of their income.

It appears that the immediate effect of foreign investment is an increase of investment spending and consequent consumer spending. An end to an investment means an end to that source of employment and consumer demand. In the long run, however, looking at economic growth and development of an economy, the results of foreign investment are far more controversial. Are the profits reinvested in the country where the investment is located, or do they flow back to the investor country? Does this enterprise compete with native enterprises? These issues are discussed in the chapter on development (Chapter 56).

Suppose the United States enters a recession. How does that affect its foreign investment? First, business has less money during a recession, so it has fewer funds available for foreign investment. Second, business will be happy to invest the rest of its funds in foreign countries, but it must be convinced that those countries are safe for investment. Safety may refer to rebellions, wars, and political security. Usually, however, the biggest issue is simply the profit outlook in the foreign country.

Because they are interconnected by trade and in other ways, all countries with capitalist institutions usually rise and fall together in their economic movements. They often look like synchronized swimmers. If they move together, then corporations that see little opportunity for profit in the United States in a recession will also find few profitable opportunities in foreign countries because they are also in recession. Worried U.S. investors and corporations tend to cut back their investments abroad during every U.S. recession. If American corporations cut back their investment spending abroad, then their demand in those countries for equipment, buildings, and labor is reduced.

In expansions, American corporations invest abroad to buy equipment and buildings. When a country goes into a recession, it usually reduces its flow of investment to other countries. During an expansion, a country's investors have more optimism and more funds, so they increase the flow of investment to other countries. Investment problems and worries in one country are transmitted around the world in seconds in the modern global economy to cause another vicious circle downward. Investment is thus another path by which one country's booms and busts are transmitted to another.

It is also worth noting that foreign investment is subject to greater swings up and down than domestic investment. The main reason is that investing corporations are far more cautious about making investments abroad than domestically. They are cautious because they understand foreign economies less than their own. They also worry that there may be political upheaval or even military actions in foreign countries. They worry that their investments may be subject to various restrictions, including restrictions on the amount of profit that may be sent back to the investing country. Finally, they worry about partial or total confiscation of their investments. These uncertainties lead to greater fluctuations.

After the American recession of 1991, foreign investors reduced their total new investment in the United States to about $15 billion a year. As the American expansion continued, but remained weak, foreign investment increased slowly until 1997. When foreign investors saw a strong expansion of the American economy at the end of the 1990s, foreign investment jumped to $215 billion in 1998, $275 billion in 1999, and finally $335 billion in 2000. After the American recession of 2001, foreign investment in America declined precipitously to $54 billion in 2002. In the present expansion, foreign investment has slowly increased again.

The conclusion is that foreign investment in the United States follows the American business cycle, but with a short time lag because foreign investors hesitate until they are sure of the direction of the U.S. economy. Thus, the U.S. business cycle causes foreign investment in America to follow its ups and downs. Foreign investment then reinforces the expansion or reinforces the recession. (All data on foreign investment from a June 1, 2007, news release of the U.S. Department of Commerce, Bureau of Economic Analysis.)

Similarly, in the expansion that began in 2002, American investors have slowly increased their investment in Europe. U.S. investment in Europe follows the European business cycle but reinforces it. This reinforcing effect between investors of different countries is seen worldwide.

HOW INTERNATIONAL FINANCE SPREADS BUSINESS CYCLES

The third mechanism for spreading instability is **international finance**, which is *buying and selling of financial instruments (such as stocks, bonds, and government securities) of a country by citizens of another country.* Financial institutions send trillions of dollars across borders every day. Business decline in one country may lead to less money available to lend to businesses in other countries. The increase or decrease of ability or willingness to make international loans has a major affect on many countries that want loans for industrial development.

The direct financial effect of one country on another may also be seen in the stock market. For example, on February 27, 2007, the Chinese stock market fell a precipitous 8 percent in one day. Since China is now a major industrial producer and its economy is closely watched, the U.S. stock market declined 4 percent on the same day, being triggered by the Chinese collapse. All other major stock markets around the world also declined.

After World War II, the U.S. dominance in production and trade carried over into financial dominance. One reflection of this dominance was the negotiation of the Bretton Woods agreement soon after the war. It was designed in the way desired by the United States, making the U.S. dollar the international currency. Having the U.S. dollar as the accepted international currency was very important because it meant that other countries had to keep quantities of American dollars as a reserve. Thus, even if the United States lost some money abroad in its trade, the position of the dollar would still be strong because others wanted to acquire it.

American banks also spread their branches and influence around the world. By the 1970s, however, things changed. There was a decline of U.S. production and trade relative to other countries. America slowly began to lose some of its financial dominance. This loss of dominance was reflected in many ways. One way that American financial dominance was challenged was through stiff competition in finance from banks of other countries. There is now extreme competition among the leading financial powers.

Yet that competition takes place within an increasingly close set of ties of international money flows. The evidence on the present high degree of international integration of financial markets is clear. For example, one major characteristic of global financial integration is that financial capital is mobile across international frontiers. Because of the international integration of financial markets, trillions of dollars of capital flow in a short time from one country to another. When funds leave an economy, that economy is weakened. When funds flow into another economy, that economy is strengthened.

There is, however, considerable controversy over the effects of this integrated global financial market. International integration of financial transactions does not mean eternal peace and quiet and smooth economic growth. On the contrary, it often means sudden financial shifts from one country to another, following the path of profits. Such shifts are a major cause of instability around the world. For example, the countries of Southeast Asia, such as Thailand and Singapore, had very good growth for many years. Then, in the late 1990s, their financial framework deteriorated badly. One reason was that the International Monetary Fund, dominated by the United States, forced these countries to repay loans to banks and other financial institutions in the United States and other advanced capitalist countries. They were unable to pay on time, so banks refused further credit.

The financial crashes were followed by economic declines in all of the Southeast Asian countries. The economies of all of these countries are closely tied together by trade and finance, so it was not surprising that one crash immediately followed another. But the ripple effect of this Southeast Asian crisis spread further. It disrupted their trade with other countries around the world. It meant immediate lowering of profits flowing to other countries from the ruined investments made in Southeast Asia. It meant that bankers around the world suddenly were getting less interest and less repayment of loans from Southeast Asia.

Many other countries felt the effects of the Asian crisis, but some did not. The United States, for example, was not drastically affected by the Asian crisis, so the U.S. economy continued to expand until 2001. Why did the American economy escape a recession following the Asian collapse? One reason was that international organizations forced Asian countries to continue payments to banks as a price of aid. More important was the fact that the American economy was in the middle of a strong expansion. Since the American economy is very large relative to these countries, it was able to shrug off the damage because of its internal strength. If the Asian crash had come during the American recession and financial decline of 2001 to 2003, it probably would have had a major negative effect on the American economy.

The United States is such a big elephant in the global economy that it affects all of the smaller countries more than it is affected by them. When the American elephant sneezes, others get a cold. But when other countries get a cold, the American elephant is less likely to suffer. Thus, if the American economy declined, many countries that produce only one main export and that export mainly to the United States would be very badly hurt.

This description of the overwhelmingly powerful role of the American economy in the world was perfectly true right after World War II. From 1945 through the 1950s, most other countries' economies were devastated, while the American economy was stronger than ever. Immediately after that war, America produced 80 percent of all manufactured goods in the world. American exports and imports were each only about 5 percent of American GDP. The size of the American economy meant that it had an extremely large role in the economy of most countries.

In the period of globalization, however, from the early 1970s to the present, all this changed. The U.S. economy is still the largest, but others are catching up every year. Since the early 1970s, Europe and Japan have been big competitors. If a small country cannot sell to the United States, it can often sell elsewhere. Thus, the effect of American trade, investment, and finance is no longer as overwhelming a factor as it once was. This shift has allowed many other countries to be much more independent of the United States, both economically and politically.

At the same time, imports and exports have each risen from about 5 percent of GDP as late as 1950 to over 15 percent in the twenty-first century. The United States is therefore far more vulnerable to the economic ups and downs of other countries. Moreover, many giant firms based in the United States make more of their profits from abroad than in the domestic market. Conditions in other countries thus have a very strong effect on total American profits. Even the American national debt is now owned in large part by foreigners, making the United States more dependent on their continued good opinion of the U.S. economic future.

GLOBAL INTEGRATION

The global integration of trade, investment, and finance are now a dominant fact of life in the world. Any attempt to understand an economy must see the whole global picture as a starting point. Of course, such notions of global markets can be carried too far by claiming that individual nations no longer matter in the global economy. It is true that the powers of individual nations have declined. This means that all government policies must consider the rest of the world. However, individual governments can affect the global economy by very intelligent policies or by very stupid policies, as we shall see.

One example of the need to consider the global economy when a government makes decisions is the case of France under the socialist government of President Mitterrand. The Mitterrand government did much public spending designed to increase the incomes of millions of employees. The idea was that their incomes would be used to buy French goods, which would give a much-needed boost to the French economy. Unfortunately, much of the increase in French income went to buy foreign goods. This left France in an economic slowdown. Investment also went to other countries. Financial institutions moved their assets to foreign countries. Thus, domestic policies must be framed with one eye on the global economy.

The situation in France was even more difficult than for most countries. France tried counter-cyclical expansionary policies, but France was out of synch with the rest of the capitalist world. When France was trying hard to expand, other economies were still declining and governments retrenching. Since French income rose, the French demand for imports rose. But since other economies were stagnating, there was no increase in the demand for French exports. There was a rapidly increasing gap between the amount of money that France received for its exports and the amount that foreigners spent to buy French goods.

There has also been greater use of computer-facilitated information flow in the global financial market, so all developments around the world are known in seconds. National stock markets have opened up to foreign nationals. The major stock markets are now, in 2007, discussing a global integration of their markets. The increase in international banking has made it very easy to move funds. Government controls on international capital flows have been greatly reduced. Increases in European financial integration are also reflected in the growth of the market by the Euro. The Euro is a common currency among most European countries. Currently, the Euro is stronger than the dollar.

As we have seen, however, the instantaneous information flow has not resulted in a perfect international equilibrium. It has made it easier for global corporations to spread into other countries because they can make use of the integrated financial market for funds anywhere. On the other hand, it also means that a financial disaster in one country causes ripples all over the world in minutes. The area of disaster may spread much quicker than in the old days of slower communication. Since the communication is instantaneous, the problems spread instantaneously. For example, in the steep decline of the American stock markets in October 1987, the news traveled immediately. Therefore, the American, Japanese, and European stock markets all fell in unison. They fell at very different rates, but they all fell. In this example, close financial integration did not result in smooth global operations but in the spread of instability.

As another example, many countries deregulated the flow of money capital in and out of their countries. Their notion was that a freely operating market in money capital would be most efficient and would help their economies. Instead, money capital flows moved rapidly from one country to another. Whenever the grass looks greener in another country, money flows rapidly to that country. Such fickleness can cause massive disruption of the economy in the country that suddenly has much less investment.

It is true that the global financial system is highly integrated, but integration exacerbates economic problems because, as we have seen, the instability of one country is rapidly transmitted to all other countries. The tendency toward spreading instability from one country to another has been very clear since the old financial order, dominated by the United States, disappeared in the mid- to late 1960s. The old order of U.S. domination has slowly been replaced by fierce competition and considerable chaos in international financial dealings. Trillions of dollars flow from various countries to others, sometimes in one day. The rate at which one currency can be converted into another may change very quickly. Global corporations move money around very rapidly in order to maximize their profits. While their profits are maximized, it may cause great misery to millions of people.

Another financial mechanism for spread of business cycle instability is through the banking system. From financial panics of the nineteenth century to the Great Depression of the 1930s to the recession of 2001, it is clear that even a small decrease in physical output can cause tremendous damage. This damage happens if the financial system is weak and vulnerable enough to cause a major financial decline. In 2001, for example, there was a small recession in real output of goods and services in the United States, lasting less than a year. On the other hand, the financial decline in the United States and Europe lasted three years. The decline in the stock market was about 50 percent. This financial decline prevented any strong rise in investment for a long time.

If there is no financial problem, then a recession is usually short and mild by historical standards. If banks go bankrupt, then credit dries up, the stock market crashes, and the recession becomes long and deep. The phenomenon of bank failures leading to other bank failures is not new. What is new in the global economy of the twenty-first century is the instantaneous flow of information and the consequent spread of bank failures all over the world. Another new development is the spread of bank branches to many other countries. This integration and speed of news may make the international repercussions of a bank failure even greater today than previously.

In today's world, a fairly small decline in the real, physical economy of one country may be turned into a worldwide crisis by the global financial system. In 2001, a small decline in American GDP was followed by a very large decline of the American stock market, which immediately affected the financial system of many countries. The big bubble in U.S. stock prices burst, the U.S. stock market dived, and the impact spread around the world. The result was a stagnant global economy with tens of millions of unemployed workers.

One other mechanism of transmission of instability is especially important at the present time. There is an enormous amount of debt in the less-developed, poor countries. The debt is owned by American, Japanese, and European banks. Repayment of these debts is improbable because the debts are so large relative to export earnings of these countries. The inability to pay their debts resulted in crisis conditions for a long time in Latin America, Asia, and Africa. If these debts are not repaid, they must be written off as bad debts by the banks. The bank's own position then becomes visibly weaker. In each past crisis, billions of debts ended this way.

COMBINED EFFECTS OF TRADE, INVESTMENT, AND FINANCE

International trade, international investment, and international finance all tend to push every economy with capitalist economic institutions up or down in the same direction at any given time. Almost all countries now have capitalist economic institutions, so all tend to move in the same direction. As a result, almost all of the global economy tends to move up and down together.

In the global economy of today, major dealings between countries often involve a combination of trade, investment, and finance that must be understood as a single process. For example, China has agreed to buy hundreds of billions of dollars of oil from Iran. However, more than trade is involved. In a complex deal, China also agreed to invest in many immense projects in Iran, involving Chinese workers, as well as construction of equipment and buildings. The very large flows of money in the China–Iran deal present many problems of finance. One problem is how to move such tremendous sums of money from China to Iran without disturbing their banking systems. Thus, this single complex deal involved trade, investment, and finance all together.

SUMMARY

Instability is spread by three mechanisms: international trade, investment, and finance. First, international trade makes growth more rapid, but also makes declines more rapid. During an expansion, American imports rise when American incomes expand. This increases demand in other countries. With their increased income, they may then demand more from America and other countries. Expanding imports in one country may reverberate around the world in a virtuous circle upward.

Similarly, American imports decline when the American economy declines. This means fewer exports for other countries. Their lower exports mean that they have lower income. With less money to spend, they buy less from America and from all other countries. Thus, recession in one country spreads to other countries. When a country's income from exports rises less than spending for imports, it develops a trade deficit. The trade deficit means a net flow of money out of the country. Therefore, a trade deficit lowers demand for domestic products. At the present time, the American economic expansion is hurting from just such a trade deficit. As more and more money flows out each year, it hurts domestic demand for goods and services. If the U.S. economy contracts, it causes a decline in U.S. imports from other countries. This causes declines in some of those countries. Their decline leads to declines in still other countries, so there is a vicious circle downward.

Second, international investment spreads instability. Large corporations invest in many other countries. If, for some reason, these corporations become more pessimistic about future profits in some country, they reduce their flow of investment to that country. Widespread foreign investments in the world may increase instability, causing greater booms or greater declines.

Finally, integration of global finance may increase instability. Loans from one country to another must be repaid. The original loan may mean more expansion, but the repayment may constitute an enormous burden on a country and cause a financial crisis there. Stock market expansion and stock market decline spread instantaneously from one country to another.

We conclude that international trade, investment, and finance may all spread recession and unemployment around the world. The issues of global integration are further discussed and controversial points debated in the next chapter.

SUGGESTED READINGS

The literature on the international spread of business cycles is discussed in Howard Sherman's *The Business Cycle: Growth and Crisis in Capitalism* (1991). The international relations of countries in the present global economy, as well as the actions of international organizations such as the World Bank and the International Monetary Fund, are discussed in detail in the excellent study by Robert Pollin, *Contours of Descent: U.S. Economic Fractures and the Landscape of Global Austerity* (2004). A clear introduction to these issues is in Robin Hahnel's *Panic Rules! Everything You Need to Know About the Global Economy* (1999).

KEY TERMS

foreign investment
international finance

REVIEW QUESTIONS

Explain the mechanisms of global trade, investment, and finance by which instability in one country spreads to other countries.

1. How does international trade transmit expansions and recessions from one country to another?
2. How does international investment transmit expansions and recessions from one country to another?
3. How does international finance transmit expansions and recessions from one country to another?
4. Explain why foreign investment is subject to wider fluctuations than domestic investment.

Compare and contrast the impact of global trade, investment, and finance on small and large economies.

5. What is the impact of changes in patterns of trade, investment and finance on smaller countries? Larger countries?
6. What explains the differences in the impact on large and small economies?

Discuss why capitalist economies in the global economy rise and fall roughly at the same time.

7. How are business cycles transmitted from one country to another? Explain.

CHAPTER 54

Debate on Globalization

Globalization is *the process by which the world is moving toward increasing economic unification and integration.* Recent decades saw a greater globalization of economic affairs throughout most of the world. One aspect of globalization is instant communication and rapid transportation around the world. No one objects to quicker communication, quicker transportation, and closer economic ties around the world. But who controls the process of globalization, who benefits from it, and who loses from it are controversial issues.

One key issue in the debate is that the present process of globalization has been dominated by the giant corporations. The debate is between the conservative view that corporate-led globalization is a good thing and the progressive view that corporate-led globalization is a bad thing and should be changed to a more democratic process.

LEARNING OBJECTIVES

After reading this chapter, you should be able to:

- Compare and contrast the conservative and progressive views of corporate-led globalization.
- Discuss the positive aspects of globalization.
- Discuss the negative aspects of globalization.

THE PROCESS OF GLOBALIZATION

Because of better transportation and communications systems, more and more people are going overseas for vacations or work commitments. Businesses can more easily trade goods internationally. Services such as education are increasingly bought and sold internationally. The flows of goods and services are being integrated through international commodity chains and production networks. We can buy products from all over the world, from stores anywhere in the world, often finding the same selection and quality available in all countries. The Internet has made these global activities easier through cheap and easy communication and information. This kind of globalization cannot be stopped, and few would want to stop it.

The basic issue under debate is exactly what kind of globalization is to occur and who is to control it. The academic debate on this vital issue has sometimes been reflected in massive protests met with police violence. As you read this chapter, keep in mind the vital questions: Who is to control the global economy? Who is to benefit from it?

THE CONSERVATIVE VIEW

The conservative view is based on the neoclassical economics discussed systematically in Chapters 26 to 35 of this book. Conservative economists emphasize the positive aspects of globalization and claim that everyone will benefit from (1) free movement of money across borders; (2) free trade in goods and services; (3) freedom from government controls and government economic intervention; and (4) freedom from environmental regulations.

The first point is that money used for capital investment must be free to move across borders with no hindrance. Conservative economists argue that any national restriction on the movement of money capital will prevent it going to the place where it can operate most efficiently. If capital is free to flow where it can do the best job, it will be most productive. This free flow of capital benefits all nations in the world economy because production will be as cheap as possible and will produce whatever the world is demanding.

Whenever a country does not allow the free entry of any money that a corporation wishes to invest in that country, it harms itself and the whole globe. Whenever a country does not allow profits and interest to flow out of it to other places where it will be most efficiently used, it harms itself and the whole globe. Therefore, the welfare of all people on the globe will be increased the most if all money capital is allowed to flow freely in and out of every country.

This argument is not a purely academic one among friends but is rather a policy enforced by economic coercion and military might if necessary. For example, South Korea in 1998 wanted a loan from the International Monetary Fund (IMF), which is controlled by the advanced capitalist countries. In order to get that loan, it had to agree to a large number of conditions, stated in a letter of intent signed by the South Korean government on May 2, 1998 (see Hahnel, 2005). South Korea agreed to shift many publicly owned firms to private hands. Thus, the IMF coerced South Korea into *giving away public property to private individuals*, a process known as **privatization**.

South Korea agreed to the following:

to allow foreigners to be bank managers;
to let Korean firms borrow without any limits from foreign banks;
to let foreigners buy any amount of South Korean land and real estate;
to allow foreigners to increase ownership of the national telephone company from 33 percent to 49 percent;
to allow foreigners to invest without restriction in any South Korean company;
that foreigners may take over any South Korean firm without government approval;
that foreigners may participate without limit in any stock deals, insurance transactions, and land leases.

This lengthy list of concessions reveals the concrete meaning of the free flow of money and capital.

Second, free trade helps the global corporations. **Free trade** is used here to mean that *all goods and services must be allowed to travel freely in global trade without any barriers such as taxes on goods (tariffs) or caps on some goods (quotas)*. Conservative economists argue that when two countries, such as the United States and Mexico, trade freely with each other, the result will be the most efficient production in both countries. Thus, free trade always benefits both of them. Each country will produce those goods and services that it can produce most efficiently and cheaply. When they each exchange their efficiently produced goods, the result is that both sides get the goods as cheaply as possible. In general, if every country in the world produces what it is best suited to produce, then the free exchange of all goods without any barriers will result in the most efficient production all over the world. Thus, free trade helps everyone.

Why do the giant corporations favor this policy of free trade? Suppose a corporation has the technology to produce shoes more cheaply than any enterprise in a less developed country. If the shoe corporation is allowed to compete freely in the less developed country, then all of the shoemakers of that country that use the older technology of making shoes by hand will be driven out of business. The corporation expands into that country and sells millions more shoes for a profit.

Corporations of the advanced capitalist countries and their governments have used every means available to open weaker countries to "free trade." For example, in the nineteenth century, England was able to get cheap opium from other colonies, so English merchants wanted to sell the opium in China. China had a potential market of hundreds of millions of people. The result was the Opium War fought to ensure free trade in opium in China. When England won the war, opium was made legal in China so that English merchants could freely sell it to Chinese consumers.

Third, it is a strongly held view of conservative economists that all government regulations restricting corporations causes economic inefficiency. For example, for several decades in the early twentieth century, there was a movement in the United States to have laws preventing the use of children below a certain age in production. Procorporate economists and lawyers fought against child labor prohibitions on the basis that the free market alone should decide who works. Any prohibition of a group from working at all, or from working in some dangerous way, would create inefficiency. They also argued that the free market allowed poor families to survive by putting their children to work in sweatshops at an early age. In the 1920s, a constitutional amendment to prohibit child labor was passed by the U.S. congress. Ratification by the states, however, was defeated by opponents using the free-market argument that it would lower economic efficiency. Of course, corporations paid children very low wages, so high rates of profit were derived from child labor. This argument has been transferred to the international scene where it is used to prevent all rules for protection and safety of labor. In China and other countries today, there are few rules protecting workers. The U.S. corporations investing in China are among those trying to keep it that way.

Similarly, conservatives argue that government expenditure to help people, such as health care and education, is harmful. Such government expenditures prevent the free-market competition from handling health care and education in the most efficient way. On the international scene, strong pressure is put on governments to reduce their spending in such constructive areas. The argument is that these reductions in social spending would reduce deficits and allow poor governments to pay back loans from international banks. In many Latin American countries, international agencies have long put on such pressure to restrict all constructive government spending, but the same pressures are now exerted all over the world.

The fourth pillar of the globalization process is freedom from environmental regulations. Conservative economists argue that any such regulations are harmful. For example, prohibition of a certain level of smoke from factories or automobiles prevents free-market competition from determining what kind of factories or automobiles should be produced. Therefore, all such regulations hurt global economic efficiency. In Los Angeles, where automobiles create terrible smog on warm days, the automobile corporations argue that if the emission standard is set too low, it will prevent them from making enough profit to continue in the world market. This same argument is used worldwide by the global corporations to attempt to prevent all environmental regulations, such as those against global warming. President Bush, on behalf of the giant corporations, denied that there is any such thing as global warming.

Table 54.1

Positive Performance Indicators, Global Economy, 1970–2005

	1970–1979	1980–1989	1990–1999	2000–2005
GDP growth, annual rate	3.3	3.43	3.72	4.18
Internet users (millions)	0.00 (1970)	0.00	0.07 (1990)	501 (2001)
Cell phone users (per 1,000 population)	0.00	0.00 (1980)	6.00 (1992)	157 (2001)
Global inflation (Consumer Price Index; annual average; weighted)	10.4 (1975)	5.21 (1985)	2.51 (1995)	2.32 (2004)
World real interest rate	−1.3 (1975)	5.72 (1985)	4.32 (1995)	2.70 (2004)
World trade volume growth (average annual)	6.0	6.32	6.81	7.42 (2000–03)

Source: Adapted from World Bank, World Development Index Database, Washington, D.C., 2005. Access limited by subscription. Also from International Monetary Fund, "World Economic Outlook: The Global Demographic Transition," Washington, D.C., 2004.

POSITIVE ASPECTS OF GLOBALIZATION

Global corporations dominate the present process of globalization and benefit greatly from it. Conservative economists emphasize the positive aspects of present procorporate globalization. In their view, there is a potential for everyone to benefit from the new means of spreading information, such as the Internet, mobile phones, more complex computers, and complex accounting systems. These innovations make life easier and more pleasurable for hundreds of millions of people. More innovation may also enable prices to decline, inflation to moderate, interest rates to fall, and world trade to grow. Indeed, those who praise procorporate globalization show evidence for a pattern of growth and development in the world economy resulting from these positive features.

Conservatives have pointed out six positive features of the last 35 years during the process of procorporate globalization, detailed in Table 54.1. The table shows six distinct indices reflecting economic growth.

1. The growth rate of the gross product of the global economy has increased in each decade.
2. The number of Internet users has grown from zero to half a billion.
3. The number of cell phone users has increased from zero to 16 per 100 people in the world.
4. Global inflation has decreased every decade.
5. The interest rate (adjusted for inflation) has decreased from the 1960s to the present.
6. The volume of global trade has increased every decade.

Adherents of procorporate globalization believe that progress was enhanced by enabling the process of competition to work unhindered. They believe that declining tariffs and subsidies enabled world GDP growth and encouraged trade to expand. Keeping government activities very limited, with a small money supply, supposedly lowered inflation. Declining inflation enabled interest rates to fall from the highs of the 1980s to very low rates in the 2000s. More favorable trade, less inflation, lower interest rates, and more innovation are thus natural results of procorporate globalization, according to most free-market adherents.

According to conservative economists, individual freedom exists in the choice of products, employment, and business and technology. These types of freedom, it is argued, will optimize social welfare. For conservative economists, competition provides free markets with both opportunities and risks. Some businesses are bound to go into obsolescence and bankruptcy because of the dynamic process of discovery and creation. At the same time, the innovative, productive, or lucky firms survive and even expand. While industries are forever being created, others are continuously being destroyed. Skills need to be continuously updated, so workers should be prepared to endure the pain of changing jobs and industries according to market conditions. The important thing is to ensure that the process of change and improvement not be impeded.

Therefore, in the conservative view, government regulations should be kept to a minimum. Pollution controls, union power over wages, subsidies to inefficient businesses, and welfare benefits are likely to slow down the process of adjustment. The crucial thing is that economic growth will be strong and sustainable because it is devoid of government controls. Governments should not upset the dynamics of markets through sudden changes in monetary policy, which tend to distort production dynamics. They should also not undertake active fiscal policy designed to reduce unemployment or inflation, because such policies interfere with market efficiency and may make matters worse. Conservatives argue that high levels of unemployment benefits reduce the effective supply of labor. Lazy workers know that they will get their benefits with little work. All major social welfare benefits, such as health care and Social Security, reduce the productive potential of the economy.

The process of destruction and creation of new enterprises is argued to be a global process. Therefore, there should be no obstruction to this process from tariffs, export quotas, strong unions in shipping or railroads, or other limitations on the flow of money and capital. Public activities, such as postal services, schools, and hospitals, can all be taken over by private corporations and run for private profit.

The only role for government, in the conservative view, is in providing a suitable legal structure and security. A suitable structure includes business law, contract and property law, judges, police, and prisons. An army, navy, and air force will protect the private property of the country. This will be a constitutional and security apparatus that enables innovation, competition, and trade to be propelled without public intervention.

THE PROGRESSIVE VIEW

In the presentation of the conservative view, four arguments were given for a procorporate path of globalization. Progressive economists have disputed each of these four arguments.

First, conservatives argue that all controls on the movement of money around the world are bad. However, allowing billions of dollars to leave a country in one day, especially if it is a small economy, is not good for stable economic growth. Therefore, restrictions on the flow of money capital into and out of a country may allow a much more stable economic development.

The power of the global corporations has been used to get rid of democratic controls on capital and allow it to move exactly as it wishes. To accomplish this goal, controls by nations on the international movement of money have been mostly demolished. For example, some underdeveloped countries used to have controls to prevent all profit being shipped back to the advanced capitalist countries. Now, profit on investments can be taken out of an underdeveloped county and moved back to an advanced country. This movement of profit out of the underdeveloped countries has held back economic growth in the underdeveloped country.

Some underdeveloped countries have large sectors of publicly owned firms protected by controls against investment by global corporations to take over these industries. Some publicly owned firms may be more efficient than the average private firm. By allowing private foreign investors to take over and make private profit from what had been a publicly owned industry of a developing country may severely hurt the citizens of that country. For example, every time the International Monetary Fund (IMF) gives a loan to a developing country, it requires that the country change all, or at least many, of its public firms into private ones. An early controversy, in the 1950s and 1960s, was the demand that India should privatize its steel mills. A recent controversy in the late 1990s was the demand that South Korea allow foreigners to buy more than half of the ownership in all of its public firms. At the time of this writing, the United States government is exerting pressure on the Iraqi government, which owns all the oil in Iraq, to allow foreign oil companies to own 85 percent of Iraqi oil. The Iraqi parliament has resisted this demand for several years.

Second, conservatives argue that all trade should be free of controls. Progressives point out that free trade, as defined by global corporations, may severely hurt the development of a less developed country. The fierce debate on free trade versus protection of a less developed country's industry is discussed in Chapter 55.

Third, conservatives argue that corporations should not be regulated in any way. Progressive economist argue that many regulations on corporations are necessary and vital to the welfare of most citizens. For example, regulations to prevent disease in food are necessary because experience shows that corporations do not pay enough attention to food safety unless they are forced to do so. However, inspecting food costs money, so it is contrary to the profit motive.

Progressives argue that certain government regulations and spending, such as for health and education, may be very helpful to economic development. If people are starving, then it is not harmful to pay money to those who need it to stay alive. Life is more important than some measure of efficiency. It has been said that those who starve in the short run are not comforted by more industrial efficiency in the long run. Furthermore, healthy people are more productive, so giving people enough to eat helps economic development.

Some underdeveloped countries have imposed high tax rates on corporations. Conservatives attacked those high tax rates on behalf of procorporate globalization. National tax rates are being forced into line with the global average as governments must encourage firms to move into local areas. Governments are frequently forced to compete by imposing very low taxes, or even no taxes, on global firms for a given number of years. Some governments have competed by passing pro-business labor laws, reducing protection to employees of the global firms and even prohibiting unions in these firms.

Fourth, the conservative view states that the free market should not be hampered by any environmental regulations. Progressive economists argue that environmental regulations may be necessary to accomplish goals that are for the good of everyone, but are contrary to the profit motive of particular companies at a particular time.

NEGATIVE ASPECTS OF GLOBALIZATION

According to progressive economists, global data show that globalization from 1970 to the present failed to achieve anything like the performance record of the 1950s and 1960s, when globaliza-

Table 54.2

Global Investment, Profit, and GDP, 1960–2002 (Decade Annual Averages)

	1960–1969	1970–1979	1980–1989	1990–1999	2000–2002
Real global investment growth rate	7.78	3.97	3.24	2.24	2.1
U.S. largest 500 TNCs profit rate	7.15	6.30	5.30	4.02	3.30
Real per capita global GDP growth	3.19	2.11	1.27	1.05	1.00

TNC = transnational corporations (global corporations).

Source: Real global investment growth and real per capita global GDP growth calculated from raw data from World Bank, World Development Index Database, Washington D.C., 2005; TNC profit rates calculated from assets and profits data taken from various issues of *Fortune Magazine*, 1955–2005.

tion was much weaker. First, progressive economists find falling growth rates of production. We saw earlier that conservative advocates of procorporate globalization showed (as in Table 54.1) that growth rates of production have risen. So who is correct? As usual in economics, it depends on your definition. Conservatives measure the rate of growth of the total product. However, total production does not tell you much about what ordinary people get. The issue is not the total product, but how much is available for each human being. The problem is that world population has grown more than the global product in the period of corporate globalization.

When we want to know about people rather than the total product, economists look at the growth per person. The growth rate per person is shown in Table 54.2. This table adjusts the growth rate of global product (gross domestic product for all countries added together) by the number of people and the amount of inflation.

The global product growth rate per person, adjusted for inflation, was a hefty 3 percent a year in the 1950s and 1960s, but it has declined steadily since then. In the latest cycle, from 1990 through 2001, the growth rate of output per person, adjusted for inflation, dropped to 1 percent a year. Critics argue that the 1970–2001 trend of declining growth has to be seen as a failure of the policy of procorporate globalization.

Before looking at the reasons for the decline, we must note two other facts that also point to a failure of growth, or even a decline, for billions of people. For one thing, the product in a country is not evenly distributed between the rich and everyone else. Rather, distribution is unequal and getting worse, as we saw in Chapter 18. For another thing, there is not equal distribution between rich and poor countries, and the distribution has been worsening, as we shall show in Chapter 56.

Why, according to the critics, has the procorporate growth policy failed as measured by output per person? The reason is simply that there have been deteriorating levels of profit and investment. Growth rates are determined by investment in equipment and buildings. The data in the table also reveal that global business investment growth has deteriorated over successive decades from a high of 8 percent during the 1960s to 2 percent in the 1990s and early 2000s. This is a very major decline.

Investment in turn depends on the profit outlook. The decline in profit is what caused the decline in investment growth. Business does not invest if there is a poor prospect for future profit. Not surprisingly, therefore, the table shows that the profits of the largest 500 U.S. corporations have been growing at a slower and slower rate, similar to investment and productivity. Global GDP growth has thus deteriorated as a result of the inability to propel sufficient investment because of low profit in most regions and continents.

On the demand side, the problem is that there has not been enough demand for goods and ser-vices in many global markets. Why is there a lack of demand? The fact is that capitalist owners of the giant corporations have been receiving more and more profits, but their demand is only a very small part of the total. The billions of employees around the world have had relatively stagnant income. Since these billions of employees are the mass market for most goods and services, that market has fallen short. In other words, increasing inequality in the global economy has limited the demand in most regions.

The growth of demand and production is actually very uneven in different areas of the world. Currently, one major new area of high growth is East Asia, especially China. Another emerging high-growth area is Eastern Europe, especially Poland, Hungary, and the Czech Republic. On the other hand, as we shall see in detail in Chapter 56, much of the world is making little progress. Latin America, sub-Saharan Africa, the Middle East, Russia, the Ukraine, Western Europe, and North America are not growing fast enough to sustain the system.

Globally there are insufficient new markets for a long upswing. Rather, it is a time when periods of average growth end in recessions, resulting in low growth over several decades. In other words, there has been considerable growth in the advanced capitalist countries and in China. That growth has gone mainly to wealthy owners of corporations. Very few of the benefits of growth have gone to most employees in the advanced countries.

According to critics, the conservative policies of globalization made the problem worse. On the supply side, the corporations and governments under their control worked very hard to keep wages and salaries low, to keep raw material costs low, and to have as many innovations and increases of output at costs as low as possible. These policies mean low wages and salaries for billions of employees. Low rates of employee compensation mean low incomes and a low standard of living. The result is a low demand for goods and services, which discourages investment.

These policies have been applied for a long time to the less developed economies, as we shall see in Chapter 56. In the period of globalization, the policy of low compensation for employees and stagnant real wages has been applied more strongly to the advanced countries such as Japan, the United States, and Europe. The close-knit global economy has allowed the corporations to reduce high wages at home in the advanced countries, while they move many economic activities to low-wage areas in the less developed world.

CONFLICT BETWEEN LABOR AND CAPITAL IN THE GLOBAL ECONOMY

According to progressive economists, the conflict between the owners of capital and the employees who provide labor is relevant here because changes in the relative power of these two groups or classes impact economic performance. There have historically been varying degrees of conflict between these two classes, as explained in Part I. Capitalist owners worry about the interests of business, while labor unions represent the interests of employees.

There are periods when both parties agree to a truce. But there are other periods when the parties are in considerable conflict. During the 1950s and 1960s, for instance, throughout most of the advanced capitalist countries, there was an unwritten accord between the two parties. This agreement was aided by a healthy economy, so both employees and capitalist owners could ad-vance to higher income levels. Productivity gains were distributed between profit and employee compensation. In one of the best economic periods ever in the advanced nations, the domestic consumption and production were undergoing sustained growth with only brief recessions. As productivity began to fall in the 1970s, corporations felt that labor had become too strong. When the profit rate and economic growth declined in the 1970s and 1980s, corporations took measures to reverse this perceived power imbalance. Thus, procorporate globalization was in part a strategy to reverse the power of labor and enhance business interests so as to restore profit.

This policy was attempted through deregulating the safety and hour regulations of the labor market, reducing the power of the government to recognize and protect unions from illegal attacks, enhancing foreign worker competition by letting some activities go abroad, and promoting the global power of corporations. Such a conservative response can only work if global markets are rapidly expanding through time, which is not happening according to the data presented earlier.

Linked to this process of weakening employee power was the ongoing attempt of corporations to control the governments of all countries. In virtually all nations, governments began to take steps to turn public enterprises into private enterprises.

There was also a trend to reduce government activities aiding the population. Among other things, governments reduced welfare payments, lessened environmental regulation, and reduced regulation of unsafe labor practices. Also, most controls of international flows of money were dismantled. In brief, in many areas, capitalism was given a free rein almost devoid of hindrance.

This has had a major impact on international performance. Globally, the procorporate policy has seen an expansion of unproductive government spending on military industries plus subsidies to various businesses. Government spending on productive areas of education, health, infrastructure, and communications has declined relative to GDP. According to critics of procorporate globalization, this change in the composition of government spending from health, education, and infrastructure to military spending fully explains the low growth experience of the United States and most other countries since the 1970s.

According to an extensive report measuring the wealth of individuals in all countries (see Henderson, 2006), global wealth is $125 trillion in U.S. dollars. The report finds that the richest 1 percent of households possess 40 percent of all the world's wealth. The bottom 50 percent of the world's households own just 1 percent of the world's wealth.

This extreme inequality of wealth in the world is the result of the control of the giant corporations and the actions of the governments that they largely control. Most of the wealthiest 1 percent reside in just a few countries. Of these wealthy people, 34 percent live in the United States; 27 percent live in Japan; 6 percent live in England; and 5 percent live in France. The report also found immense inequality among countries between the advanced capitalist countries and the least developed countries, a subject discussed further in Chapter 56.

Another important aspect of the attempt of global corporations to lower wages and salaries in the advanced capitalist world has been the transfer of their economic activity to low-wage areas of the developing countries. There are two ways to do this. One way is to close factories in high-wage locations such as Europe and the United States and open similar plants in low-wage areas such as Asia. American automobile companies, for example, are terminating whole factories in the United States, eliminating thousands of U.S. jobs, and opening factories in China, where they pay workers substantially less money.

The second way of moving jobs to low-wage areas is called outsourcing. *Outsourcing* means domestic work taking some jobs from American and European workers and giving the jobs to workers in foreign countries. Today's communications systems and information technology enable businesses to outsource hundreds of jobs: call-center support, telemarketing, medical transcription services, order processing, publishing services, even digital-imaging (MRI and x-ray) analysis, to name just a few.

Much outsourced work is done in India, where millions of skilled and educated people are available to work at wages far below U.S. wages. One indicator of the increasing number of jobs going to Indian workers from U.S. firms is the number of tax returns filed with the U.S. Internal Revenue Service from India. In 2003, there were 25,000 U.S. tax returns from India. In 2004, there were 100,000. In 2005, the number rose again to 400,000. The skilled Indian workers earn much more than, for instance, Indian agricultural workers but as much as ten times less than similar American workers.

In this way, global corporations are reaching their goal of a global labor market in which a corporation can choose the lowest paid but well-qualified workers anywhere in the world. They are attempting to create one global market in which all wage or salary rates for the same job are equal. There is nothing wrong with a global labor market, provided there is full employment, strong protections for all employees in terms of safety and other rights, and equally strong unions in all areas.

In fact, global corporations have moved—and continue to move—jobs from areas of high employment, strong workers' rights, and strong unions to countries with high unemployment, few workers' rights, few safety laws, no minimum wage, and weak or prohibited unions. The result is some equalizing of wages and salaries around the world. This equalization is occurring not by raising the wages and salaries of the lowest paying countries to match those of the highest paying countries. Rather, global corporations are doing everything in their power to lower the wages and salaries of employees in the highest paying countries while maintaining incredibly low wages in the less developed countries. They do so by moving jobs to countries where there are millions of hungry, unemployed workers, no laws to protect workers, and few or no strong unions.

PROFIT VERSUS ENVIRONMENT IN THE GLOBAL ECONOMY

According to progressive economists and other critics, a prime conflict that has been worsened by procorporate globalization is that between profit and the environment. Conservative, procorporate globalization has led to fewer controls on corporations, including fewer safeguards against pollution. The conservative fight against pollution controls has been especially strong in the major polluting nations such as the United States, Russia, and China.

Procorporate globalization has seen an expansion of global corporations and their polluting industries and polluting products. The industries with polluting practices and products spread into new regions such as China and Russia. Air pollution is worsened in these regions by increased motor vehicle pollution as well as pollution from the new factories. Without environmental protection laws, vast forests are destroyed, wetlands are devastated, water is contaminated, and quality of life is further reduced.

The largest polluting country, the United States, refuses to sign the Kyoto Protocol, which sets limits on global warming. Instead, U.S. corporations seek to expand oil, gas, and mineral production in formerly protected areas. For example, the Republican party attempted to open up wildlife refuges in Alaska to oil drilling. The process of creating new products and innovations along established lines of energy, which use vast nonrenewable sources, create the potential for greater profit at the expense of environmental protection. The objection by conservatives is that environmental protection costs additional money.

Under procorporate rule, environmental protection is minimal. There is thus a trade-off between profit and the environment—profit wins out. The trend in environmental degradation can be seen clearly in Table 54.3.

This table shows that global atmospheric concentrations of carbon dioxide have expanded progressively, especially through the 1980s, 1990s, and 2000s. Thus, global warming has become an increasingly serious concern. The conflict between environmental protection and business profit is a crucial problem. The public interests of a clean climate, species survival, and relative climate

Table 54.3

Global Environmental Decline: Carbon Dioxide Concentration, Temperature, and Ozone Concentration, 1960–2000

	1960	1970	1980	1990	2000
Atmospheric concentration of carbon dioxide (ppm; Mauna Loa Observatory Data)	317	326	339	354	369
Global temperature change (compared with 1961–1990 average)	0 (1960)	–0.05 (1970)	+0.12 (1980)	+0.26 (1990)	+0.38 (2000)

ppm = parts per million.

Source: Adapted from EarthTrends: Concentrations of Greenhouse and Ozone-Depleting Gases in the Atmosphere, 1744–2001. World Resources Institute, 2002; and Donella H. Meadows, Jorgen Randers, and Dennis L. Meadows, *Limits to Growth: The 30-Year Update*. London: Earthscan, 2005.

stability have deteriorated in the procorporate global economy. If procorporate globalization continues, greenhouse gasses will get worse, global warming will expand, species habitats will be destroyed, and biodiversity will decline even further. As a result of increasing carbon dioxide levels, there is a slow increase in global warming, as shown in Table 54.3. Critics lay the blame for this deadly trend on the nature of procorporate globalization.

Another major problem is the theory called weak sustainability. *Weak sustainability* means that it is acceptable to trade off lower levels of ecological sustainability and livability (called ecological capital) for higher levels of physical and human capital. Such a trade-off leads, in the long run, to lower levels of well-being as the declining stock of ecological capital leads to fewer species, more overcrowding, greater stress levels , and inferior quality of life. The long-term viability of ecological capital thus requires that we end deregulated markets and restore pollution controls.

PSYCHOLOGICAL EFFECTS OF CORPORATE GLOBALIZATION

Conservative economists often talk as if all corporate growth and innovation is positive and helps everyone. In addition to the falling growth rate of GDP per person, we have discussed the increasing inequality between employees and corporate owners, the increasing inequality between rich and poor countries, and environmental destruction. This rapidly changing world also means that industries relocate, so people are tossed from one job to another and are often unemployed between jobs for varying lengths of time.

A central aspect of the procorporate global economy is the conflict between individuals and corporate-dominated society. When individual greed becomes dominant, the critics allege that society is adversely affected. Procorporate globalization praises individual self-interest and greed. Conservative economists argue that each of us should look only at the material and economic benefits for ourselves in each project. Conservatives argue that self-interest will promote economic performance through competition. This process of social benefits through individual self-interest is called the invisible hand.

Completely ignored in this conservative viewpoint are the adverse effects of strong individual greed. These adverse effects include a breakdown in the ability of people to trust one another, as well as a decline in nurturance and love. In a society built on capitalist foundations and the desire to make as much money as possible, old community bonds among people break down. Each

Table 54.4

Levels of Trust: The World and Various Nations, Percentage Who Think "People Can Be Trusted," 1981–1982, 1990–1991, 1995–1996, 1999–2001

	World	U.K.	U.S.	Argentina	Brazil	South Africa	Russia	Poland
1981–82	38.4	43.3	40.5	26.1	n.a.	29.0	n.a.	n.a.
1990–91	34.6	43.7	51.1	23.3	6.5	29.1	37.5	34.5
1995–96	24.3	29.1	35.9	17.6	2.8	15.4	23.2	16.9
1999–2001	27.5	28.9	36.3	15.9	n.a.	13.2	24.0	18.4

Source: Adapted from Institute for Social Research, World Value Surveys, 1981, 1990, 1995–1997. Ann Arbor: University of Michigan, 2000; and Institute for Social Research, World Value Surveys, 1999–2001. Ann Arbor: University of Michigan, 2004.

person feels like a tiny boat on a great ocean. Many people feel that their survival depends on a cold, competitive drive without attention to the needs of others.

There is a conflict between individual self-interest and concern for others. The result is that people have a low level of trust in their society's dominant institutions and practices. For example, according to every poll, a large majority of Americans distrust the U.S. Congress. In addition, people are coming to distrust every other individual. Global society has been slowly entering greater disarray through low and declining levels of trust of all other people over the past several decades. This trend is clearly visible in Table 54.4.

The data in Table 54.4 show the results of the World Values Survey for the four years of interviews in 1982, 1991, 1996, and 2001. People from approximately 60 nations were asked to respond whether "most people can be trusted" or "you need to be very careful" with other people. The international results for the four periods show the percentage who replied that "people can be trusted" declined from 38 percent in 1981 to 28 percent in 2001. In the United States, trust in others declined from 41 percent to 36 percent. The table shows similar declines in trust in England, Russia, Poland, Argentina, Brazil, and South Africa.

People tend not to trust others, in general terms, since there are fewer linkages between people locally. Specifically, individual self-interest has strengthened. Markets and work have replaced social solidarity and family ties. More and more people are not marrying and prefer to live alone. More detailed results show that levels of trust have declined more in conservative, procorporate nations that have reduced the role of government and sociality than in other nations. Trust is the critical social cement that binds people together and without which various disorders arise. These disorders include lack of information, inadequate interpersonal communication, and weak networks and relationships. The result of these disorders is individual feelings of aloneness and mental problems as well as higher divorce rates. They also result in lack of trust and participation in social institutions, such as the election system. For example, only half of Americans vote in presidential elections and even fewer vote in state and local elections. Finally, distrust of people and institutions results in uncertainty and unwillingness to invest in the economy.

SUMMARY

This chapter discussed some of the issues surrounding procorporate globalization. Some of the positive tendencies of the system are said to be better communication, better transportation, and greater innovation, all of which lead to higher growth rates of total GDP. Critics allege that the positive fact of innovation is connected not only to positive aspects of growth but also to the negative aspects, such as obsolete skills, business bankruptcy, environmental degradation, employer–employee conflict, more unequal distribution of income, and the destruction of non-market, human relationships.

We then examined performance indicators and specific data for some of the crucial conflicts. We considered the problems of inadequate demand creating low investment, profit, and growth of real product per person. The low growth rates of product per person have been seen in almost all regions, one exception being rapid growth in China.

We also looked at the conflict between employees and owners of corporations. We found that in the period of rapid growth in the 1950s and 1960s, some growth went to rising employee incomes for the middle class. In the period of slower growth per person since 1970, corporations have fiercely resisted any increases in wages and salaries. This anti-employee position has been supported by changes in labor regulations by most governments. As a result, wages and salaries have fallen far below the growth of productivity. Employees' share in national income has fallen, and the share of profits has risen.

The procorporate form of globalization has worsened the conflict between corporate profit and a livable environment. For capitalists, profits take precedence over clean air, safe drinking water, and the health and well-being of Earth's inhabitants.

Another problem we examined is that the procorporate globalization process has generated low and declining trust among people and in governments and social institutions.

Progressive critics allege that conservative, procorporate globalization has led to the problems we discussed in this chapter. Because of these problems, various countries have begun movements for a more democratic global economic system.

SUGGESTED READINGS

The historical background of globalization, including the important role of international organizations, was discussed extensively in Chapter 16, and useful readings were listed there. The most readable and interesting article on globalization is Robin Hahnel's "What Mainstream Economists Won't Tell You About Neoliberal Globalization" (2005).

A very readable article on the affects of globalization on the incomes of the wealthy and of ordinary people is Michael Yates's "Poverty and Inequality in the Global Economy" (2004). A brief newspaper article gives more recent United Nations data in James Henderson's "World's Richest 1% Own 40% of All Wealth, U.N. Report Discovers" (2006).

Two excellent academic studies provide a good starting place for a deeper understanding of globalization. One is Dean Baker, Gerald Epstein, and Robert Pollin's *Globalization and Progressive Economic Policy* (1998). The other is Phillip O'Hara's *Global Political Economy and the Wealth of Nations* (2004).

KEY TERMS

free trade   privatization
globalization

REVIEW QUESTIONS

Compare and contrast the conservative and progressive views of corporate-led globalization.
1. What is the "process of globalization"? What distinguishes the corporate-led globalization process?
2. Explain the arguments of free-market economists that procorporate globalization is a predominantly positive trend in the world economy.

Discuss the positive aspects of globalization.
3. How do progressive economists view corporate-led globalization?
4. What are indicators used to measure the positive aspects of globalization?
5. What enabled growth in countries due to the process of globalization?

Discuss the negative aspects of globalization.
6. Examine the major conflicts emerging from globalization, such as those associated with employee–employer interests, insufficient trust, and environmental destruction.

CHAPTER 55

Debate on Free Trade

This chapter looks at some of the history and arguments in the vehement and sometimes violent debate over free trade.

LEARNING OBJECTIVES

After reading this chapter, you should be able to:

- Compare and contrast the arguments for and against free trade between countries.
- Explain the comparative advantage model of trade (including the assumptions for the model) and how it is used to argue for free trade.
- Cite historical and current examples of protectionism and the free trade debate.

THE DEBATE ON THE EVE OF THE CIVIL WAR

As the United States approached the bloodiest war of the nineteenth century, the American Civil War, the most important disagreement, outside of slavery, was the issue of tariffs. A **tariff** is a *tax on imported goods*, whereas a **quota** is a *quantity restriction on imported goods*. The North had a rapidly growing amount of industry. Therefore, the North wanted tariffs on imported industrial goods to protect the relatively new and weak American industry from the competition of more mature foreign competitors, especially England. The South, on the contrary, had little industry. It relied heavily on the export of its cotton to England. England had extensive textile mills, which used the cotton from the South. In return, England exported to the South a great many industrial goods. The South wanted those industrial goods as cheaply as possible, so it did not want any tariffs on them.

England was the world's economic superpower with the most modern and efficient industry in the world. In any open and free competition with foreigners in a trade war, England would win. Therefore, England strongly advocated free trade. The doctrine of **free trade** simply means that governments should impose no obstacles, such as tariffs, on trading between countries. Southern politicians made use of the arguments coming from England to argue against tariffs and for free trade.

Until the early nineteenth century, many economists believed that international trade was a zero sum game and that the exporter's gains exactly offset the importer's losses. This reasoning was the prime motivation behind the early mercantilist doctrine that trade policies should be designed to encourage exports and discourage imports. That all changed with economist David Ricardo (1772–1823). Ricardo showed that both parties gained from free trade, even if one was a "technological giant" and the other a less developed nation. Here is a classic story that economics professors have used for years to explain the law of comparative advantage.

COMPARATIVE ADVANTAGE

In support of free trade, the classical English economists developed the concept known as the principle of comparative advantage. **Comparative advantage** as *a measure of efficiency means producing a good or service at the lowest opportunity cost.* It starts from the idea that every country produces some products more efficiently than other products. The argument concludes that each country should produce those goods and services that it can produce most efficiently. Each country should then export the products it produces. At the same time, each country should import from others those commodities that it produces inefficiently. This way, each country would do what it can do best.

Through free and open trade, competition among firms from every country would create the most efficient production for the whole world. All countries would benefit by concentrating on those goods and services in which each had its comparative advantage. This is not an obvious result. At first glance, one would think it would be most advantageous for a country with an **absolute advantage**, *producing goods and services with the fewest inputs or at the lowest cost*, in everything to produce all that it needs. Instead, the classical economists argued that if different countries are at different levels of development and productivity in different industries, it will pay to have each specialize and trade its products. Both countries will benefit if they specialize. In fact, this specialization will benefit the whole world if every country specializes in what it can do best.

It seems counterintuitive to think that specialization is better for all even if one country has an absolute advantage in all goods. This counterintuitive notion of relative or comparative advantage, rather than absolute advantage, is the key to the usual free trade argument. Therefore, this idea is explained in full. The view of progressive economists, who attack the theories of free trade and comparative advantage, is explained in full in Appendix 55.2.

ABSOLUTE AND COMPARATIVE ADVANTAGE

One of the most important applications of conservative analysis is the idea of comparative advantage based on the production possibilities curve model presented in Chapter 26. Put forward by David Ricardo, this idea serves as the basic principle underlying the doctrine of free trade. The doctrine of comparative advantage says that nations should produce and export those goods that can be produced at the lowest relative opportunity cost. Given the assumptions of the model, all nations benefit from this arrangement, and world output will increase when nations specialize and trade.

Suppose that you are a most highly paid lawyer and charge a fee of $2,000 per hour. Suppose further that you are also the world's best typist and are able to type 400 words per minute. Should you do your own typing? Certainly not, if you have enough legal work to keep you busy full time. Every hour you spend typing incurs an opportunity cost of $2,000 in foregone legal fees. That makes typing pretty expensive. What you might do is hire eight 50-words-per-minute typists, pay them each $10 per hour, and thus pay only $80 per hour to type 400 words per minute. The opportunity cost of practicing law (and earning $2,000 per hour) is only $80 per hour. The best way for you to spend your time is to do what you do at the lowest opportunity cost.

How does this example relate to trade between nations? The lawyer is the technological giant able to produce everything more efficiently than any other country in the world. However, resources are scarce even for technological giants, so resources should be used to produce goods that can be produced at the lowest opportunity cost. Goods that incur high opportunity costs of production (typing) should be imported.

As with all models, there are simplifying assumptions behind the Ricardian theory of comparative advantage:

1. Nations are operating on their production possibility curves, and there is no unemployment of resources.
2. There are no direct impediments to trade, such as tariffs, subsides, transport costs, and tax concessions to help producers.
3. There are constant costs, since as production increases the unit costs do not change.
4. There is perfect competition among producers, both for capitalists and workers.
5. Labor is the dominant factor of production, as capital goods, knowledge, technology, and so on are relatively invariant.

THE LAW OF COMPARATIVE ADVANTAGE

Like Adam Smith and Karl Marx, Ricardo believed in the labor theory of value. According to this theory, value depends on the amount of labor embodied in the production process, and goods exchange on the market based on the amount of labor. For example, if a textile worker could make two shirts or one coat per day, the price of a coat would be twice as high as the price of a shirt. Many contemporary economists have dismissed the labor theory of value, in part, because it says nothing about the demand side of the market. However, it is useful for illustrating the basic concepts of comparative advantage.

Table 55.1 shows the amount of wine (W) and cheese (C) that can be produced with one hour of labor in both the United States and the United Kingdom. Notice that more wine and cheese can be produced per hour in the United States than in the United Kingdom. An hour of labor produces 3 units of wine or 4 units of cheese in the United States versus only 1 unit of wine or 2 units of cheese in the United Kingdom. Therefore, the United States has an absolute advantage in the production of both goods. (In this case, the United States would be classified as the "technological giant" compared to the United Kingdom.) It might seem that the United States, given the absolute advantage, stands to gain nothing from trade with the United Kingdom. Why import goods if you can produce everything with more absolute efficiency than the other nation? Remember our lawyer-typist example.

It is comparative advantage, not absolute advantage, that forms the basis for trade. Countries should produce and export those goods in which they have a comparative advantage, and they should import those goods for which they have a comparative disadvantage. To find out which goods will be imported and exported, we must first determine comparative advantage.

The entries in the table represent the output from one hour of labor input. In the United States, one unit of labor can produce either 3 units of wine or 4 units of cheese. Thus, the opportunity cost of a unit of wine is 1.33 units of cheese ($3W = 4C$ or $1W = 1.33C$). In the United Kingdom, one unit of labor can produce either 1 unit of wine or 2 units of cheese, so the opportunity cost of a unit of wine is 2 units of cheese ($1W = 2C$). The opportunity cost of wine is lower in the United

Table 55.1

Comparative Advantage Matrix

Commodity	United Kingdom	United States
Wine (W)	1	3
Cheese (C)	2	4

States than in the United Kingdom, so the United States has a comparative advantage in wine production. The United Kingdom has a comparative advantage in cheese production: $1C = 0.5W$ versus $1C = 0.75W$. The United States has an absolute advantage in both products.

Comparative advantage is found by calculating the relative opportunity costs of production. In the United States, each hour of labor can produce 3 units of wine or 4 units of cheese. This can be written as

$$US: 3W = 4C$$

But if we solve for 1W (divide both sides by 3) or 1C (divide both sides by 4), we can better see the opportunity costs of wine or cheese:

$$US: 1W = 1.33C \text{ or } 1C = 0.75W$$

In other words, each unit of wine that is produced in the United States means giving up 1.33 units of cheese, and each unit of cheese represents the lost production of 0.75 units of wine.

The opportunity costs of production differ in the United Kingdom. Using data from the first column in Table 55.1, it is apparent that each unit of wine produced in the United Kingdom involves giving up 2 units of cheese, while each unit of cheese incurs an opportunity cost of 0.5 units of wine:

$$UK: 1W = 2C \text{ or } 1C = 0.5W$$

Now we have enough information to determine comparative advantage. Notice that each unit of wine costs 2 units of cheese in the United Kingdom but only 1.33 units of cheese in the United States. This means that the relative opportunity costs of wine is lower in the United States, so the United States has a comparative advantage in wine production. In short, wine production is cheaper in the United States in terms of relative opportunity costs. In contrast, the United Kingdom has a comparative advantage in cheese production. Each unit of cheese costs only 0.5 units of wine in the United Kingdom but 0.75 units of wine in the United States. Cheese production is cheaper in the United Kingdom in terms of relative opportunity cost. The United States should produce and export wine in exchange for cheese; the United Kingdom should produce and export cheese in exchange for wine.

The remarkable implication of the law of comparative advantage is that world output will rise without additional factor inputs when countries specialize in the production of the goods in which they have a comparative advantage and then engage in trade. Suppose that the United Kingdom and the United States are the only countries in the world and that they each have 100 workers. Suppose further that survival mandates that each worker have one unit of cheese. This means that the United Kingdom must devote at least 50 workers to cheese production ($50 \times 2 = 100$) and the

Table 55.2

Production Possibilities

	Cheese	Wine
U.K.: 50(2) =	100	50(1) = 50
U.S.: 25(4) =	100	75(3) = 225
World:	200	275

Table 55.3

Both Nations Benefit

	Cheese	Wine
U.K.: 100(2) =	200	0
U.S.:	0	100(3) = 300
World:	200	300

United States must employ at least 25 workers in the cheese industry (25 × 4 = 100). This leaves 50 workers for the wine industry in the United Kingdom and 75 workers for the wine industry in the United States. Pretrade production is shown in Table 55.2.

Now, suppose that once trade commences, there is complete specialization; that is, the United States produces only wine and the United Kingdom produces only cheese. World output would be as shown in Table 55.3.

This is a remarkable result! World output has increased! There is the same amount of cheese but more wine, so the consumers of the world are better off. Further, because wages are related to productivity, wages are likely to have risen in both countries. All that is necessary to realize these gains is for the United States to trade some of its wine for cheese.

The result we have just demonstrated holds even if we relax the seemingly restrictive assumptions of two countries, such as looking at two goods or zero transportation costs. The only qualification of note is that in the real world, complete specialization does not take place. It did in this example only because we assumed that there were constant costs no matter how much wine was produced in the United States.

In most situations, costs begin to rise before complete specialization occurs, but the general (and important!) result holds. If countries produce goods with low opportunity costs and import goods with high opportunity costs, world output increases and every nation gains from free trade. However, it must be stressed that while the nation as a whole clearly gains from free trade, some individuals within the nation may not gain. For example, free trade will mean that the dairy farmers in the United States will find that their dairy farms have suddenly fallen in value. Dairy farmers may also find it difficult to acquire the skills necessary to enter the wine industry. This is one reason there are always groups opposed to free trade.

HISTORICAL CONTINUATION OF THE FREE TRADE DEBATE

In the argument for free trade, since following their comparative advantage is to the benefit of all countries, free trade with no obstacles will lead to the best result for all. If there were no trade, the principle of comparative advantage said that everyone would be worse off. These were the classical British arguments used by Southern politicians before the Civil War.

In the mid-nineteenth century, many countries, including the northern United States and Germany, had just started industrial development. They were called **infant industries** because *their development was so new*. They were still too weak to compete with English firms, so the economists of Germany and the northern United States usually argued that their infant industries *had to be protected from the competition of more advanced economies*. If the infant American industries were protected for a few years, they would have the opportunity to develop and become strong enough for full competition. If the young American industries were not protected, little or no industry would ever develop in the United States.

Economists and politicians from the South used the free trade argument to oppose tariffs for industrial goods. But the Northern economists and politicians said that if the new Northern industries were not protected by tariffs, then the industry would be stopped and the United States would remain an underdeveloped, purely agricultural country forever. From the Civil War to the present, similar arguments have continued in various forms between the more agricultural nations and the more industrialized nations. This argument for protection from the industry of the advanced countries has remained the main argument of the underdeveloped countries ever since.

DEBATE ON TRADE IN THE TWENTY-FIRST CENTURY

There is controversy over trade between the more developed and the less developed nations. In the early twenty-first century, there are a considerable number of well-developed countries, especially Western Europe, the United States, and Japan. But there are also a very large number of less developed countries in Asia, Latin America, and Africa. There are millions of people in the less developed countries, and many of them starve to death every year. For them, industry and trade are literally matters of life and death.

The World Trade Organization (WTO) was organized under U.S. leadership to persuade countries to get rid of all barriers to trade. The advanced capitalist countries argued that the principle of comparative advantage should be followed. There should be universal free trade with no obstacles such as tariffs or quotas. The less developed capitalist countries argued that their infant industries needed protection, just as the United States had protected its infant industries. If they were not allowed to protect their industries from the devastating competition of more advanced industry, then the division of the world between affluent, advanced countries and the poor, less developed countries would last forever.

In addition, Europe and the United States want to maintain subsidies for their own agriculture. A **subsidy** is a *payment from the government to support production of a good or service*. However, a subsidy protects that product against competition, so a subsidy for agricultural products acts just like a tariff on agricultural goods. Either way, a subsidy prevents the free and fair competition of agricultural goods from other countries. Therefore, the agricultural countries of the less developed areas complained that the advanced countries, led by the United States, were being completely hypocritical. The U.S. policy meant that the advanced capitalist countries would have free trade in industry, useful for them because they had strong industries, so they could easily outcompete the less developed countries. On the other hand, the U.S. policy meant that the advanced countries could use subsidies in weak areas that required protection.

The less developed countries were outraged and said that the principle of free trade turned out to be just another argument for unequal policies that would profit the advanced countries but hurt the less developed countries. For a long time, the less developed countries were too weak to offer much protest. By the beginning of the twenty-first century, however, the less developed countries would no longer accept such blatantly unfair policies.

This argument has never been resolved. It was impossible to agree on anything, and the battle lines hardened. Therefore, the WTO was often unable to even meet in the last few years. When it did meet in the first few years of the twenty-first century, there were usually riots outside the meeting place. The riots were caused by the fact that people in the poor countries perceived the WTO as a major obstacle to their economic progress. They saw the policies of the WTO condemning millions of people to poverty and death.

At one WTO meeting in the United States, there was a large riot by Americans. If free trade benefits Americans, then why did so many vehemently protest against the WTO? The answer is that in the view of most of the American labor movement, free trade benefits global corporations controlled from the United States but harms most American employees. American corporations have been moving away from the United States to lower wage areas. For example, in 2006 Wal-Mart corporation expanded large enterprises in China. It paid the Chinese workers 17 cents an hour and required workers, if they wished to keep their jobs, to work six days a week rather than five. This practice was against Chinese law, but the workers were afraid they would lose their jobs if they spoke to inspectors. The Chinese government then discussed changing the law so that workers could form independent unions that could protest and even strike over the poor pay and conditions. Wal-Mart was the first American corporation to protest the proposed law, saying that the law violated free competition and free trade.

The goods produced in China at very low wages compete against goods made in America at much higher wages. This competition tends to drive down American wages. Furthermore, it gives the corporations an excuse for cutting American wages and salaries. Therefore, the free trade pacts are opposed by a considerable number of U.S. Congress members unless there are clear provisions to protect labor around the world and to protect the environment around the world. They argue that only with provisions for labor standards and environmental standards would free trade become fair trade.

SUMMARY

Free trade means that all obstacles to trade are ended. Comparative advantage argues that each country should produce only those goods it produces at the lowest opportunity cost at the present time and import other goods from foreign countries. It contends that this arrangement will benefit all countries. The most obvious problem with the theory of comparative advantage is that it makes static assumptions that every economic advantage will remain the same, but we live in a dynamic, changing world. If the theory is followed, then all less developed nations will be frozen in their poor status relative to the rich nations forever.

Protectionism is the view that infant industries in countries just beginning to industrialize should be protected against foreign competitors by tariffs, quotas, and other import/export costs. Protectionists argue that if each country produces only what it does best at the present time, the present situation will be frozen. Some countries will remain rich and industrial while others remain poor and agricultural for all eternity. Therefore, infant industries should be protected until they are strong enough to compete.

There are additional arguments about fairness. First, the less developed countries argue that the advanced countries cannot demand free trade in industry yet use subsidies in agriculture to keep out agricultural goods. Second, labor unions in America and Europe argue that it is unfair to have so-called free trade when trade is based on terrible labor conditions in many countries. Third, many members of the U.S. Congress argue that it is unfair to have so-called free trade when it is based on complete lack of environmental protection in many countries.

Since the debate rests to some degree on the different views of the theory of comparative advantage, we discuss this theory in a more detailed debate in two appendices. In Appendix 55.1, we examine the detailed arguments in favor of free trade and comparative advantage. Appendix 55.2 presents the detailed arguments critical of the free trade and comparative advantage theories.

KEY TERMS

absolute advantage	quota
comparative advantage	subsidy
free trade	tariff
infant industry	

REVIEW QUESTIONS

Compare and contrast the arguments for and against free trade between countries.
1. What is the difference between a tariff and a quota? Why would advocates of free trade see these policy tools as reducing consumer welfare?
2. What would be arguments used to justify barriers to free trade, such as tariffs and quotas?

Explain the comparative advantage model of trade (including the assumptions for the model) and how it is used to argue for free trade.
3. Explain how comparative advantage differs from absolute advantage.
4. What are the assumptions behind the simple static theory of comparative advantage?
5. Following are the production possibilities curves for the fictional nations of Bergsakeria and Solbergia showing their respective capacities for producing gizmos (G) and widgets (W). Use this information to answer the questions that follow.

Bergsakeria's PPC		Solbergia's PPC	
G	W	G	W
50	0	40	0
45	1	30	1
40	2	20	2
35	3	10	3
30	4	0	4
25	5		
20	6		
15	7		
10	8		
5	9		
0	10		

a. Which nation has an absolute advantage in producing gizmos (and widgets for that matter)? Explain.
b. Which nation has a comparative advantage in producing gizmos? How do you know? Which nation has a comparative advantage in producing widgets? Explain.

Cite historical and current examples of protectionism and the free trade debate.

6.   Why do Europe and the U.S. both want to maintain agricultural subsidies? Why do developing countries argue the U.S. and Europe should drop the subsidies?
7.   What is the WTO? Is it effective in enforcing trade policies? Why or why not?

APPENDIX 55.1
CONSERVATIVE DEFENSE OF COMPARATIVE ADVANTAGE

The technical argument over comparative advantage underpins the highly explosive and exciting debate over free trade. This appendix continues the exploration of the comparative advantage model by asking how the terms of trade are determined. Finally, there is a discussion of what the model suggests should be the outcome of free trade.

LEARNING OBJECTIVES FOR APPENDIX 55.1

After reading this appendix, you should be able to:

- Use the comparative advantage model to explain the terms of trade.
- Explain the predicted and actual outcomes of free trade based on the comparative advantage model.

THE CONSERVATIVE SIDE OF THE DEBATE

According to the neoclassical view, if there is free trade of all products between countries, then each country will be able to concentrate on producing those items in which it is comparatively strong. The neoclassical view provides students with a scarcity-based framework for thinking about the trade-offs inherent in production. If a country decides to spend more on war products, then fewer resources will be available for the production of civilian goods, such as automobiles, movies, health care, and college courses. At the individual level, if a student chooses to spend more time studying economics, she or he has less time available to read literature or study chemistry. There are only 24 hours in a day, after all. Time spent doing one thing means you can't do something else at the same time.

The neoclassical perspective is to include the notion of comparative advantage introduced earlier in this chapter. This notion serves as an important argument for free trade. At a minimum, free trade advocates seek the elimination of tariffs and quotas.

Most of the shortcomings of comparative advantage concern its restrictive assumptions. For example, it assumes perfect competition, which is an unrealistic assumption. Before further discussing the shortcomings of the model, we extend the technical analysis of comparative advantage to explore not just the decision about what to produce but the terms of trade as well.

THE TERMS OF TRADE

In an earlier example, we looked at the production of wine and cheese. In the example, the United States has a comparative advantage in wine and the British have a comparative advantage in the production of wine. Unless the United States is able to trade some wine for cheese, the U.S. workers will not get much work done. Likewise, the British certainly do not need the cholesterol of all that cheese and might wish to imbibe on occasion. Therefore, trade takes place. The question we need to answer now is, What are the terms of trade? **Terms of trade** are *how much of one good a country must give up to get a given quantity of another foreign-produced good.* That is, how much wine must the United States give in exchange for each unit of cheese?

In our example, before trade takes place, each unit of cheese costs 0.75 units of foregone wine in the United States. There would be no incentive to trade unless the United States could get cheese for less than 0.75 units of wine. Likewise, before trade takes place, each unit of cheese trades for 0.50 units of wine in the United Kingdom. The British will not be willing to trade cheese for wine unless they can get more than 0.50 units of wine in exchange for a unit of cheese. Putting these facts together, we get a terms of trade inequality:

$$\text{Terms of trade inequality: } 0.50W < 1C < 0.75W$$

The United Kingdom benefits if it gets more than 0.50 units of wine per 1 unit of cheese. The United States benefits if it gives less than 0.75 units of wine per 1 unit of cheese.

Let's look at the terms of trade from another perspective. Before trade, each unit of wine carries an opportunity cost of 1.33 units of cheese in the United States and 2.00 units of cheese in the United Kingdom. The United States is going to import cheese, so it wants more than 1.33 units of cheese per unit of wine. The United Kingdom is going to export cheese, so it wants to give less than 2.00 units of cheese per unit of wine. The corresponding terms of trade inequality is

$$\text{Terms of trade inequality: } 1.33C < 1W < 2.00C$$

This equation is mathematically identical to the previous inequality of $0.50W < 1C < 0.75W$. To see relationship, take the reciprocal of either inequality to get the other. Remember to reverse the inequality signs when you take the reciprocal.

Without more information, we cannot determine precisely where within the inequality the terms of trade will rest. It will depend, in part, on the relative negotiating strength of each country. The United States is clearly better off getting more cheese per unit of wine, and the United Kingdom would prefer to give as little cheese as possible per unit of wine. In the example that follows, we assume some specific terms of trade to keep things simple.

TRADE AND THE PRODUCTION POSSIBILITIES CURVE

Everything we have just discussed can be illustrated graphically with the production possibilities curve we introduced earlier in the chapter. To make the example simple, we continue to assume that production exhibits the constant costs shown in Table 55.1 and that each country has 100 units of labor. This information is enough to derive the production possibilities curves for the two countries.

Table 55.4 shows the wine/cheese production possibilities for the United States and the United Kingdom.

Point a shows how much cheese is produced if all workers are assigned to the wine industry; points b through f are found by successive movements of 20 workers from the wine production into cheese production in the United States. Points g through l give the wine and cheese production as workers are moved out of the wine industry in the United Kingdom.

Table 55.4

Wine and Cheese Production Possibilities for the United States and the United Kingdom

U.S. Production	a	b	c	d	e	f
U.S. wine	300	240	180	120	80	0
U.S. cheese	0	80	160	240	320	400

U.K. Production	g	h	i	j	k	l
U.K. wine	100	80	60	40	20	0
U.K. cheese	0	40	80	120	160	200

The data from Table 55.4 are plotted on Figure 55.1. The top panel gives the production and consumption possibilities for the United States and the bottom panel gives the same information for the United Kingdom The solid lines are the production possibilities curves (PPC) for each country. Notice that the production possibilities curves are linear, an indication of the constant opportunity costs assumption. The slope of the production possibilities curve is the opportunity cost of wine production.

Panel (a) presents the production and consumption possibilities for the United States. The opportunity cost of wine in the United States is 1.33 units of cheese, so the slope of the production possibilities curve is −1.33. The bottom panel gives the production and consumption possibilities for the United Kingdom. The opportunity cost of wine in the United Kingdom is 2 units of cheese, so the slope of its production possibilities curve is −2.0. Therefore, the United States has a comparative advantage in wine production and will export wine because the opportunity cost of wine is lower in the United States than in the United Kingdom.

If the terms of trade are $1W = 1.6C$ or $1C = 0.625W$, the consumption possibilities curve (CPC) will intersect at 480C for the United States and 125W for the United Kingdom. The consumption possibilities curves for the two countries are parallel and represent the terms of trade. The area between the consumption possibilities curves and the production possibilities curves represents the potential gains from trade. If the United Kingdom exports 100C to the United States, it will earn 62.5W. Posttrade consumption in the United Kingdom will be 100C + 62.5W. Posttrade consumption in the United States will be 100C + 237.5W.

In the *absence of trade*, a situation denoted as **autarky** in economic terminology, consumption is constrained by domestic production, so the production possibilities curve is also the consumption possibilities curve. However, once trade commences and specialization takes place, consumption possibilities expand beyond the production possibilities. How much consumption possibilities exceed production possibilities depends on the terms of trade. To illustrate, let's assume that the terms of trade are

$$1W = 1.6C \text{ or } 1C = 0.625W$$

This means that the United States can earn 1.6 units of cheese from each unit of wine that is exported. This represents a gain because each unit of wine foregone generated only 1.33 units of cheese before trade. The United Kingdom gets 0.625 units of wine for each unit of cheese it exports. This too is a gain over the pretrade value of 0.5 units of wine per unit of cheese.

Finding the slope of the consumption possibilities curve is simple. The United States will

Figure 55.1   **Comparative Advantage: The Gains from Free Trade**

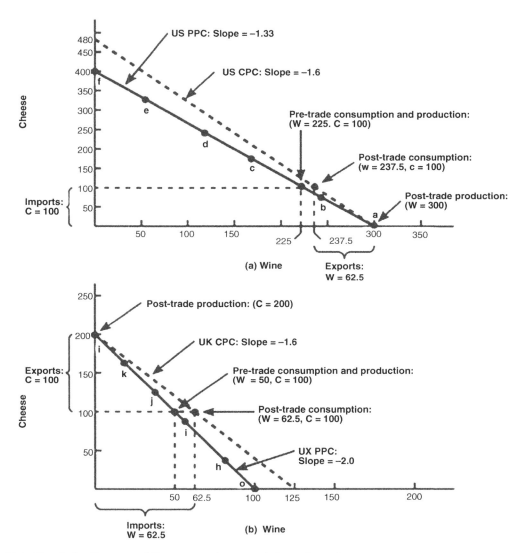

Note: For clarity, the axes of the two graphs are not drawn to scale.

continue to produce wine, so the horizontal intercept remains at 300. Now if all wine were traded for cheese at the rate of 1W = 1.6C, then the 300 units of wine could earn 300(1.6) = 480 units of cheese. This is the vertical intercept of the consumption possibilities curve for the United States. For the United Kingdom, the cheese (vertical axis) intercept is 200. If 200 units of cheese were traded for wine at a rate of 1C = 0.625W, the United Kingdom could import 200(0.625) = 125W. This is the horizontal intercept of the U.K. consumption possibilities curve. The area between the consumption possibilities curve and the production possibilities curve represents the potential gains from trade.

Without knowing the specific preferences of the two countries, we cannot determine exactly how much trade will take place, but let's suppose that each country decides that it requires 100 units of cheese. If there were no trade, this requirement would mean that the United States produced 100 units of cheese and 225 units of wine, while the United Kingdom produced 100 units of cheese and 50 units of wine. However, if we allow for specialization and free trade, each will be better off because they can consume the same amount of cheese but more wine. With complete specialization, the United Kingdom can produce 200 units of cheese. If it exports 100 units, it will be able to consume 100 units of domestic cheese and 62.5 units of imported wine—a gain of 12.5 units of wine. If the United States specializes and produces 300 units of wine and exports 62.5 units for 100 units of cheese, it will be able to consume 100 units of imported cheese and 237.5 units of domestic wine—also a gain of 12.5 units of wine. Both points are on the countries' respective consumption possibilities curves—and beyond their initial production possibilities curves. Free trade has increased world output and consumption, so both countries are better off.

Before going on, we should note that the gains from trade depend on the terms of trade. For example, if the terms of trade were 1C = 0.56W (instead of the assumed 1C = 0.625W), the United States would be even better off and the United Kingdom would be worse off. The United States would have to trade only 56 units of wine to get 100 units of cheese; U.S. consumption would be 244W plus 100C. U.K. consumption would be 100C plus 56W. Note that this arrangement is still better than what the countries were doing without international trade.

THE PREDICTIVE POWER OF COMPARATIVE ADVANTAGE

According to neoclassical economists, the theory of comparative advantage can predict several things (though the critics say it can predict nothing). It predicts, first, that if nations specialize, then they are all able to gain from trade, even if some nations have an absolute advantage in the production of most goods. It is not, therefore, absolute advantage that matters, but comparative advantage. It is certainly true that most highly developed nations have benefited from trade and that it is a major reason for their high standard of living.

Second, it predicts that nations will export goods for which they have a comparatively high level of labor productivity. Empirical evidence tends to support this proposition. Historically, nations have found it very difficult to trade in commodities for which they have a low level of productivity. It is usually the productivity that enables such nations to export these goods in return for others for which they have a comparatively lower level of productivity.

Third, it predicts that higher productivity will lead to higher wages. It is certainly true that nations that have increased their level of labor productivity have been able to give workers higher real wages and better conditions. In general, being able to benefit from trade has enabled nations to specialize and to enhance the living conditions of their population.

SUMMARY OF APPENDIX 55.1

This chapter introduced students to comparative advantage, the most important and useful application of the production possibilities curve. This appendix continued the analysis by using the comparative advantage model to find the terms of trade. By engaging in specialization and trade, comparative advantage shows that two nations can increase their production possibilities. Some predictions of comparative advantage have some validity, such as successful trading nations having relatively high productivity in the export industries and that this higher productivity will likely lead to higher wages in the long term.

KEY TERMS IN APPENDIX 55.1

autarky
terms of trade

REVIEW QUESTIONS FOR APPENDIX 55.1

Use the comparative advantage model to explain the terms of trade.

1. Demonstrate using a PPF graph why both countries can be made better off by specialization and trade.
2. Describe how two countries might arrive at mutually agreeable terms of trade.

Explain the predicted and actual outcomes of free trade based on the comparative advantage model.

3. Explain why would both countries be better off specializing and trading even if one country produces more of all goods.
4. In the real world, what might interfere with the results predicted by the model?

APPENDIX 55.2
CRITICISMS OF COMPARATIVE ADVANTAGE

Being a relatively abstract theory with many simplifying assumptions, the comparative advantage model was likely to encounter problems when it came to the complexities of the real world. We discuss the major problems in this appendix. We also introduce and discuss some other models of trade.

LEARNING OBJECTIVES FOR APPENDIX 55.2

After reading this appendix, you should be able to:

- Compare and contrast alternative models of trade.
- Discuss how alternative models seek to address weaknesses in the comparative advantage model.

DISTRIBUTIONAL PROBLEMS WITHIN A NATION

A major shortcoming of comparative advantage is that it ignores distributional problems within a nation. It might be true (assuming full employment) on average that both countries benefit. However, it seems likely that results within each country might differ significantly. We might presume that the owners of firms who are now enabled to import lower-cost foreign goods will benefit far more than the workers who lose their jobs or who face greater international competition. International trade creates winners and losers within countries. Free trade advocates often overlook this fact. The production possibilities curve analysis done here examines only the country as a whole and ignores the winning and losing groups within those countries.

HECKSCHER-OHLIN MODEL AND CAPITAL INTENSITY

The distributional problems ignored by comparative advantage led to the emergence of the **Heckscher-Ohlin model (HOM)**. *This model can be seen as a critique of the simple Ricardian comparative advantage theory. Rather than labor being the only factor of production, this model includes labor, capital, and resource inputs. It predicts that scarce factors will lose from trade, while abundant factors will benefit.* For instance, if a nation has an abundant supply of raw materials, it will likely gain a factor proportions comparative advantage for intensively extracting such resources. A nation that has a factor proportions relative advantage in capital goods, such as machinery and equipment, will likely come to specialize in these goods. Nations moving from one factor to another to take advantage of such specialization will find the old factors and those dependent upon them losing income.

This more sophisticated theory of comparative advantage seems logical enough, since nations are able to take advantage of the cost benefits of factor abundance by importing goods that use factors for which they have a relative lack of. However, when efforts were made to empirically test this HOM theory, it failed to live up to expectations. Wassily Leontief (1953), in fact, came to conclusions opposite of what was expected when he found that United States exports were less capital intensive than imports. Other studies have supported these findings for other nations. How could this be? It has been suggested the main problem with the HOM theory is its inability to satisfactorily deal with complexities associated with the dynamics of technology and knowledge. The United States may not have so much an abundance of capital, such as machinery and equipment, but rather an abundance of knowledge and technology, which is changeable through time. Like its Ricardian predecessor, the HOM is too static and inadequately incorporates complexities.

INTRA-INDUSTRY TRADE, ECONOMIES OF SCALE, AND THE PRODUCT CYCLE

Given the empirical problems with the simple Ricardian and even slightly more complex HOM versions of comparative advantage, other theories and empirical directions in international trade have emerged. Some of the predictions of comparative advantage were not so forthcoming, such as the idea that nations would specialize intensely, that supply conditions mostly determine trade patterns, and that competitive firms and free trade would reign supreme in the world. Comparative advantage ignores the fact that economies of scale are common, that companies internalize trade within their own organizations and networks, that nations and firms export and import within the same general product category, and that the product cycle may determine trade of nations.

First, both exports and imports of a specific nation are often in the same general product category (intra-industry trade) and also for the same product. This is especially the case for manufactured goods among highly developed capitalist economies. The most developed nations of the world tend to trade among themselves, leaving the much less developed in large measure out of the trade patterns. Hence, most trade occurs among nations with similar factor endowments, human capital levels, and stages of advancement.

One of the main reasons for this near-exclusive trade is cultural. The world of business involves several dominant production chains and commodity networks. They are linked together by relationships of class, cultural background, family ties, and trust and organizational arrangements. Joining the network involves becoming part of the cultural and organizational dynamics of global competition. Parts of Asia have joined this web of relationships by enhancing their business acumen. For instance, the computer technology production network increasingly involves the export

Figure 55.2 **Phases in the Product Cycle: Innovator and Imitator**

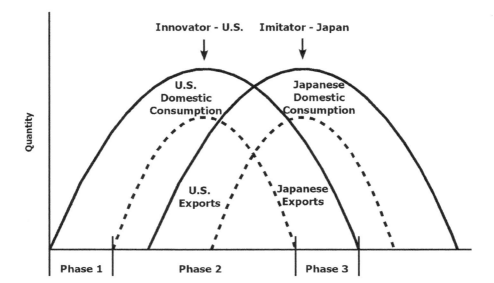

of knowledge and specialist from Silicon Valley and Europe to China, where the basic computer parts are assembled and then sold globally. Highly sophisticated knowledge capital from the core capitalist nations is linked to the hard-working laboring power of the Chinese to produce information technology that is exported and imported around the world. Various components are supplied from different nations and areas, even within the same production chain, with usually a production backup being available in cases of supply bottlenecks. East Asia is playing a leading role in these networks, along with the United States and Europe, while Africa and South America are mostly left out of these arrangements.

The **product cycle** is another *factor to consider in global trading patterns. Products tend to undergo a cycle of different phases, such as development, expansion, peak, maturity, and demise* (Vernon, 1966). Consider, for instance, the automobile industry. When a nation is going through the first phase, development of the automobile industry in this case, it tends to sell the goods only domestically, as did the United States in the 1910s and 1920s. But as it becomes successful, developing more knowledge, human capital, and expertise, economies of scale pick up and costs decline—hence, the expansion of U.S. exports of the Ford motor vehicle, along with many others, in the 1930s and 1940s. Exports grow, along with the domestic market, through the peak phase of development—for the U.S. automobile industry, the 1960s. Over time, though, the United States moved relatively to other sectors, leading other nations, such as Japan, to take over larger shares of the export market, especially into the 1970s and through the 2000s. Shifts in the export market lead to changes in cities and urban areas where working-class people are affected by industrial metamorphosis and evolution. The product cycle has an impact on trade, as shown in Figure 55.2.

There are three major phases in the development of the product cycle: (1) the initial development of the industry for home consumption following the successful innovation; (2) success of the export market as economies of scale, learning by doing, and marketing achieve some success; and (3) maturation and demise as imitators take over and succeed in gaining domestic and overseas markets. Comparative advantage fails to take into account the evolutionary process by which industries and markets change and adjust through historical time. The product cycle is an excellent example of changes in trade due to industrial metamorphosis.

TERMS OF TRADE AND THE PREBISCH-SINGER HYPOTHESIS

Another problem with the static comparative advantage theory of trade is that it assumes that free trade and concentrating on existing comparative cost structures will necessarily lead to growth and development. Scholars in Africa and Latin America, for instance, have long considered the comparative advantage theory to be a tool of imperial hegemony: a theory designed by economists in the advanced nations to reinforce the inferior position of the underdeveloped areas. Nations such as the United States and the United Kingdom tend to keep underdeveloped countries at a disadvantage by making policy recommendations for these countries to behave in ways that are quite different than the sucessful behavior of the United States and United Kingdom when they were developing. When the United States and the United Kingdom were developing, they each protected their industries and molded them into a powerful force before relaxing barriers somewhat.

Nations of sub-Saharan Africa, Latin America, and Southeast Asia have found that using the simple or even slightly more complex theory of comparative advantage for policy purposes can be disastrous. The reason is that they have been concentrating on agricultural and mining goods, which have been, more often than not, experiencing declining terms of trade compared with manufacturing, high-technology, and knowledge-based goods and services. Primary goods industries tend to suffer from oversupply, lack of value added, excess competition, constant or declining returns, and lack of effective production networks. Manufacturing and high-technology goods and services, on the other hand, tend to benefit from high-value-added innovations, barriers to entry, economies of scale, government support, and major links to successful production networks.

This *theory of the declining tendency for the terms of trade in primary products*, called the **Prebisch-Singer hypothesis (PSH)**, was developed by Raul Prebisch (1950) and Hans Singer (1950). Empirical evidence for declining terms of trade is supported for both the net barter terms of trade (NBTOT) and commodity terms of trade (CTOT); the NBTOT is an index of the price of an underdeveloped nation's export prices divided by import prices, and CTOT is an index of primary product prices divided by manufacturing prices. The major periods of decline have been in the 1920s and 1970s through 1980s.

Figure 55.3 illustrates the trend to declining CTOT over time.

Declining relative primary product terms of trade have been due to the relatively low income elasticity of demand for primary products relative to manufactured products. For instance, prices of rice, rubber, sugar, wheat, corn, and wool have declined very considerably over the period 1900 to 2000, while prices of laser censor technology, robotic equipment, and leading-edge medical pharmaceuticals have increased markedly over recent decades.

The problem is not just declining relative primary terms of trade but also the relative price volatility of primary products. Primary products tend to be produced in more competitive markets than are manufactured and high-technology goods and services, resulting in more price volatility and hence greater uncertainty. Post-Keynesian economists have shown empirically that there is a positive relationship between uncertainty and lower levels of investment, productivity, and growth. The declining primary terms of trade also leads to lower real-wage increases for nations specializing in primary products compared with those specializing in manufactured and high-technology goods.

The PSH has critical implications for economic and social policy, best seen through the lens of the experience of developing nations that have succeeded versus those that have not. The ex-

Figure 55.3 **Global Primary Product Commodity Price Index, 1900–1998**

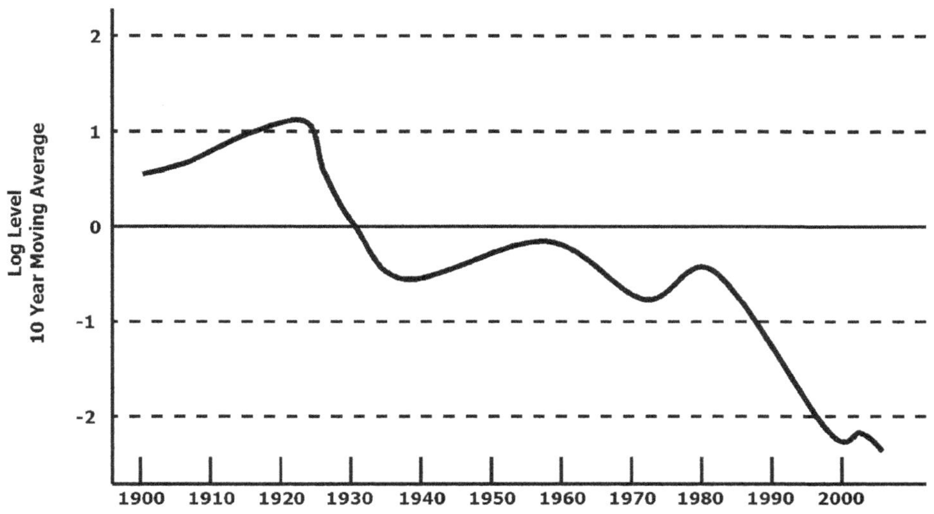

This figure is a Grilli-Yang Primary Commodity Price Index, deflated by the MUV. *Source:* Adapted from Cuddington, Ludema, and Jayasuriya (2002: 18).

perience of South Korea and Chile illustrates the potential and the problems very well. Over the past thirty years, the terms of trade of South Korea have been very positive, while that of Chile has been very negative. Why? In South Korea's case, against World Bank recommendations, in the 1940s and 1950s, the government selected various industries for assistance and development through industry policy; as a result, South Korea was able to make a successful transformation from a primary product–producing nation to a high-technology one. Government assistance included subsidies, tax advantages, and tariffs as well as infrastructure and education and health development. The government sought a partnership with businesses to guide them to success in the competitive world of business and trade. They were able to concentrate on sectors with rising prices for their goods.

Chile, on the other hand, was the Latin American nation with the greatest potential, having had a history of parliamentary democracy and a good system of education and health. In the 1970s, the government sought advice from Chicago economists and then undertook a series of radical free-market reforms directed by dictatorial government. These free-market reforms were continued after free elections were instituted into the 1980s and early 2000s. Foreign investment was encouraged, free trade advanced, and business interests were fostered. Chile continued to develop along lines of static comparative advantage, especially in copper and other primary products. As a result, Chile has failed to develop a viable manufacturing and high-technology base comparable with that of South Korea.

The key fact is that underdeveloped nations have three main options: first, to concentrate on products that have a potential for having a cartel status, such as OPEC nations attempted in the 1960s and 1970s; second, to follow the pattern of some primary products that do have a rising relative price; and third, more generally, to industrialize and/or concentrate on niche markets. The industrialization alternative has been the most successful for East Asian nations such as Taiwan, South Korea, and China. Taking that road requires state support of selected industries through industry policy, having a balance of state and market, and encouraging productive spending that stimulates long-term development and growth.

SUMMARY OF APPENDIX 55.2

Comparative advantage has many weaknesses. Assumptions of full employment and a failure to consider distribution problems within a country leave the theory incomplete. Further, predictions of specialization have not been borne out in international trade. Since the theory assumes capital to be fixed, it is ironic and logically flawed for free-trade advocates to use comparative advantage to argue in favor of international capital mobility. Static comparative advantage is problematic when it comes to the need to examine the role of factor proportions, leading to the contribution of the Heckscher-Ohlin Model (HOM), which added to labor the role of durable fixed capital such as machinery and equipment. Evidence initially obtained by Leontief found that advanced nations such as the United States, however, were not capital intensive. This anomaly was resolved by the recognition of the role of knowledge and human capital in trade, which the static theories ignored.

Other nations therefore examined the role of economies of scale and monopolistic competition in the trade process, further removing the analysis from static comparative advantage theory. Counter to static comparative advantage, highly developed nations tend to trade among themselves rather than including the underdeveloped areas in trade. This exclusive trade is due to intra-industry relationships, production networks, strategic alliances, and other complementary processes involved in trade. Cultural relations, class, and family background all play a role in trade.

Static comparative advantage theory is also problematic when it comes to comparing the terms of trade between primary and manufacturing products on a global scale. Undeveloped nations tend to export primary products that have low prices, little value added, competitive markets, little embedded knowledge and human capital, and a low-income elasticity of demand. Many East Asian nations engaged in industry policy through protection, building long-term capabilities in knowledge, innovation and skills, and promoting public infrastructure and research and development–enhancement policies. Other nations, such as those in OPEC, started a cartel and took advantage of their relative monopoly position in petroleum.

KEY TERMS IN APPENDIX 55.2

Heckscher-Ohlin model   product cycle
Prebisch-Singer hypothesis

REVIEW QUESTIONS FOR APPENDIX 55.2

Compare and contrast alternative models of trade.
1. How does the Heckscher-Ohlin model challenge the traditional model of comparative advantage? What are problems with both models?
2. How does the Prebisch-Singer hypothesis challenge the comparative advantage model of trade?

Discuss how alternative models seek to address weaknesses in the comparative advantage model.

3. Explain the need to go beyond the analysis of static comparative advantage according to modifications of the assumptions, paying particular attention to
   a. Transportation costs
   b. Factor proportions
   c. Human capital and knowledge
   d. Distribution of benefits and costs of trade
   e. Economies of scale and monopolistic competition
   f. The product cycle and industrial metamorphoses
   g. Anomalous terms of trade between primary and manufactured goods
4. Explain the possible policy implications for the need to develop along the lines of South Korea rather than Chile. Pay particular attention to (a) free trade versus protection, (b) industry, and (c) education and infrastructure spending.
5. Counter to the predictions of static comparative advantage, explain why advanced nations trade mostly among themselves (along with the select new areas that become part of their strategic alliances and partnerships).
6. Why might the product cycle provide an explanation for export success and then failure, while static comparative advantage fails to comprehend the evolutionary aspects of trade?
7. Why may developing nations find it advantageous to protect their new technology industries and provide infrastructure such as roads, education, and health services to stimulate human capital when they currently do not have a static comparative advantage in new technology products?
8. Why have South Korea, Taiwan, and Singapore been so successful at technologically advanced processes and products when static comparative advantage indicated that they should have concentrated on low-value-added goods forty years ago? Why, on the other hand, have such apparently promising nations such as Chile and Brazil not advanced that much in development compared with these previously low-development East Asian nations?

CHAPTER 56

Development

The problems of economic growth in developed industrial economies, using the United States as an example, were considered in Chapter 46. In Chapter 54, we considered the problem of growth in the global economy. Here we examine *economies that have not industrialized*, called the **less developed**, or underdeveloped, **economies**. The problems of economic growth in the less developed world are substantially different, with different relations and institutions, from those already examined in this book. We examine how underdeveloped countries have transformed their institutions in the past to lead to development as well as the prospects for other countries to transform themselves in the future.

LEARNING OBJECTIVES

After reading this chapter, you should be able to:

- Compare and contrast characteristics of developed and less developed countries.
- Discuss the impacts of colonialism and neocolonialism on less developed countries and developed countries.
- Describe and discuss the various obstacles to development.

ECONOMIC GROWTH

The economic, social, and political obstacles to industrialization in less developed countries are enormous. Before meaningful growth in output and income per person can take place in these economies, they must undertake a complete change to the institutions leading to industrialization. The economic, social, and political obstacles to industrialization in such countries are enormous. In contrast, economic growth in the developed countries merely means incremental additions to output within an established structure. Development of the less developed countries means basic social, political, and structural economic changes to lay the foundations for growth.

The countries of the world used to be divided into three groups: (1) industrially developed capitalist countries, (2) noncapitalist countries, and (3) less developed or underdeveloped capitalist countries, often called the Third World. Since the end of the Soviet Union and the transition of China toward capitalism, there are almost no noncapitalist countries still in existence. It is with this third group that we are concerned in this chapter. The terms *underdeveloped* and *less developed*

Table 56.1

Gross National Income Per Capita, U.S. Dollars, 2005

Area	Income
United States	43,740
Japan	38,980
European Monetary Union	31,914
World	6,987
Russian Federation	4,460
Latin America and Caribbean	4,008
Middle East and North Africa	2,241
China	1,740
East Asia and Pacific	1,627
Sub-Saharan Africa	745
South Asia	684
Least developed countries (U.N. classification)	378

Source: Adapted from the World Bank national accounts data and OECD National Accounts data files. GNI per capita, Atlas method (current U.S. dollars). (2006). See http://devdata.worldbank.org/data-query.

are used interchangeably in the literature, and neither term is perfectly accurate. We use *less developed* to emphasize that development is relative, not absolute. A country may be less developed than others or less developed than it could be if certain obstacles had not existed.

FACTS OF ECONOMIC UNDERDEVELOPMENT

There are at least two generally accepted definitions of a less developed country, one based on an economic index and the other based on a number of distinguishing characteristics. The economic index generally used is average income per person or per capita. The income per person is calculated by dividing gross domestic product (GDP) by the number of people in the country. According to this criterion, a country with an average income per person of less than some amount per year is classified as less developed. Of course, what is "less developed" is purely relative to the income of the more developed countries. Therefore, this figure changes over time.

If the term *underdeveloped* is based on just one index, however, it can be misleading. For example, there is no correlation between level of income and level of cultural or social development. A country might have a highly developed culture and very low average income levels. Further, an average may hide wide disparities in individual incomes. A small country sitting on an oil well may have a very high average income. Suppose, however, that the average includes a ruler who has all of the income and lives in luxury. The average also includes the rest of the people who have next to nothing.

As another example of a misleading average, we may use data on average income. The average income for everyone in the world in 2005 in U.S. dollars was almost $7,000. That would be considered a poverty level in the United States, but it is far above starvation level in the least developed countries. Data on average incomes is shown in detail in Table 56.1 and Figure 56.1.

The American average income is misleading. In 2005, the average American income was almost $44,000. This average includes the incredibly rich and incredibly poor. In contrast to the average

Figure 56.1 **Gross National Income Per Capita, U.S. Dollars, 2005**

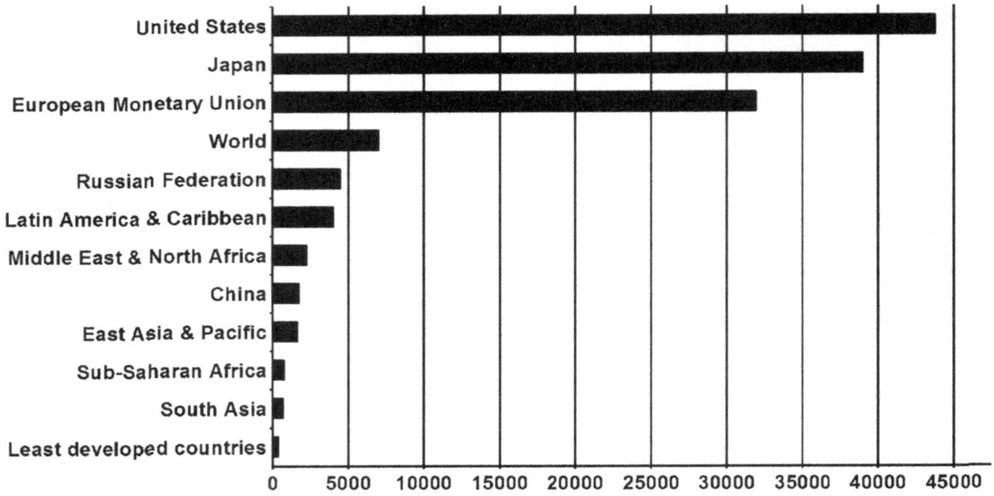

Source: Adapted from the World Bank national accounts data and OECD National Accounts data files. GNI per capita, Atlas method (current U.S. dollars). (2006). See http://devdata.worldbank.org/data-query.

American income, the average income per person for a whole year in the least developed countries (as defined by the World Bank) was only $378. We can certainly call $378 a starvation wage. But these are data for whole countries, so that average also includes extremely rich people as well as millions who toil for a year for much less than $378. Those people well below $378 a year are among the thousands in almost every less developed country who starve to death every year.

There are also many countries between the American average and the average of the least developed countries. Japan is just below the United States in Figure 56.1. The European Union is also near the United States with an average of about $32,000 per citizen. Again, Europe includes very rich countries and quite poor countries, extraordinarily rich people who raise the average and very poor people who lower the average. The United States, Japan, and the rich countries of Western Europe are the advanced capitalist countries, and their income is far above the others.

In the middle, according to the figure, is Latin America, where the income per person in the year is about $4,000. The average Latin American was ten times richer than the average person in the least developed countries but ten times poorer than the average American. Was the average Latin American rich or poor?

IS THE GAP INCREASING OR DECREASING?

In the 1950s and 1960s, the advanced capitalist countries (mainly the United States, Western Europe, and Japan) had rapid growth of GDP per person. In fact, the real GDP growth per person in the advanced capitalist countries was 3.7 percent a year. This growth was well above the global average and far above that for many less developed regions. All data in this section are from Table 56.2.

The less developed countries had fairly good rates of growth compared to their historical performance, but not as good rates as those of the advanced countries. The different regions perform

Table 56.2

Growth of Real GDP per capita in the Global Economy

	World	Advanced Capitalist Nations	Latin America	Africa	Eastern Europe	Asia (Excluding Japan)
1950–1973	2.93	3.72	2.52	2.07	3.49	2.92
1973–2001	1.43	1.98	1.08	−0.38	−1.10	3.54
1980–1990	1.43	2.67	−0.77	−1.09	1.60	6.8*
1990–2001	1.13	1.77	1.64	−0.24	−2.26	4.2

* Newly industrialized Asian nations only.

Source: Adapted from *Angus Maddison, The World Economy: A Millennial Perspective* (Paris: OECD, 2000, pp. 126, 129); and World Bank, World Development Index Database. Washington, DC, 2005.

differently, so it is interesting to look at some of the main regions of less developed countries. From 1950 to 1973, Latin America grew at 2.5 percent a year, which is good but less than the advanced capitalist countries. Africa grew at 2.1 percent, still less than the advanced capitalist countries. Asia (outside of Japan) grew at 2.9, a respectable pace, though less than the advanced capitalist countries. The only exception among the less developed countries was Eastern Europe, which was still under the Soviet economic system, which grew at 3.5 percent or just below the advanced capitalist countries.

All of these comparatively pleasant results changed downward in the period from 1973 to the present. In the latest business cycle, from 1990 to 2001, the advanced capitalist countries did less well than in the earlier period. In fact, the advanced capitalist countries had a real growth rate per person of only 1.8 percent a year. Among the less developed countries, the growth rate of Latin America fell to 1.6, close to, but still less than, the advanced countries. The two worst cases were Africa at −0.2 percent growth and Eastern Europe at −2.3 percent growth rates. Eastern Europe had moved from the Soviet system to capitalism but never fully adjusted and had not attracted enough investment.

We need not remember all of this data. It is worth knowing, however, that the advanced capitalist countries did very well in the 1950s and 1960s but have experienced declining real growth rates of GDP per person since then. The reasons for this decline in growth rates were discussed in Chapter 46 on American growth and Chapter 54 on global growth.

In the earlier period, the 1950s and 1960s, the less developed capitalist countries had considerable growth. Yet they fell further behind the advanced capitalist countries. Since 1973, the less developed capitalist countries have mostly had very strong declines in their growth rates. Many had negative growth rates in the 1990s, while advanced capitalist countries continued to grow. This widening gap in production per person accounts for much of the anger in these countries toward the United States and other advanced capitalist countries.

A BROADER DEFINITION OF DEVELOPMENT

Dissatisfaction with the use of a single, purely economic measure of development has led to a definition based on several distinguishing characteristics of less developed countries. First, they have a relatively low income per person. Second, they have a relatively high portion, often 60 percent or more, of their population engaged in agriculture. Third, they have a relatively low level of the technology used in production. Fourth, they have a relatively low level of education. Fifth, they have a relatively low level of investment in equipment and industrial buildings. According to any definition of developed and less developed, more than 50 percent of the world's population live in countries that can be classified as less developed. Moreover, the gap continues to widen as shown previously. We can better understand the current economic, social, and political conditions of less developed countries if we briefly examine some aspects of their history. In particular, we are interested in their relationships with the economically more advanced countries over the last several centuries.

COLONIALISM AND NEOCOLONIALISM

Imperialism has been around ever since the ancient empires conquered other countries for land and for slaves. Its dominant modern form was colonialism in the nineteenth and early twentieth centuries. Colonialism is the system in which the advanced countries held colonies. To be a colony meant that a country suffered military occupation by a foreign country, was dominated politically, and was exploited economically. Since the global economy became very strong in the 1970s, there has mostly been neocolonialism. **Neocolonialism** means that *there is no military occupation, but the government is dominated by a foreign power and the economy is exploited by foreign powers.*

From the fifteenth century onward, the developing capitalist economies of Europe grew economically and militarily at a rate then unparalleled in human history. From the fifteenth to the nineteenth centuries, they slowly came to dominate much of the rest of the world. They plundered, enslaved, and ruled so as to extract the maximum from their subjects. Such havoc was created that ancient and culturally advanced civilizations disappeared, as in Peru and West Africa. Progress was set back hundreds of years by the destruction of native industries, as in India. For the Europeans, the plunder was so great that it constituted the main element in the formation of European capital and eventual industrialization.

By the end of the nineteenth century, almost all of the present less developed countries were under the colonial rule of the more advanced countries. The advanced countries with colonies reaped astoundingly high profit rates from investments in the colonial countries. The profits were primarily because of a cheap labor supply and enforced lack of competition from native industry. European capital was invested mainly in extractive industries that exported raw materials to the country owning the colonies. There, the cheap raw materials were profitably turned into manufactured goods. Part of those manufactured goods was exported back, tariff-free, to the colonial country. The country owning the colony, for all practical purposes, monopolized the colonial market.

The tariff-free importation of manufactured goods completed the destruction, of the colonial country's manufacturing industries. An example of this may be seen in colonial India, especially in its textile industry:

> India, still an exporter of manufactured products at the end of the eighteenth century, becomes an importer. From 1815 to 1832, India's cotton exports dropped by 92 percent. In 1850, India was buying one quarter of Britain's cotton exports. All industrial products shared this fate. The ruin of the traditional trades and crafts was the result of British commercial policy. (Bettleheim, 1968, p. 47).

The development of the colonial areas was thus held back by the countries owning the colony. At the same time, development of the colony-owning countries was greatly speeded by the flow of plunder and profits from the colonies. The exception that proves the rule is Japan. Japan escaped colonialism as a result of several more or less accidental factors. Among the countries of Asia, Africa, and Latin America, Japan alone was able to industrialize independently and develop its own advanced capitalist economy. Japan achieved this because the others had all been reduced to colonies or to semi-colonial status, preventing their further development.

Similarly, American evolution in trade and industry was held back until it became independent of England. It is worth emphasizing that America did not become independent easily. During the Revolutionary War, the British referred to the American rebels specifically as "terrorists" and killed 25,000 American terrorists from a small population on the East coast.

The half-century from 1890 to World War II was the peak period of colonialism. At that time, Western European colonial powers ruled most the world, except for Japan, the United States, and some of Latin America (though Latin America remained heavily influenced by the West European powers). In the late 1940s and 1950s, a new era began with formal independence achieved by hundreds of millions of people throughout Asia and Africa as a result of bloody anticolonial struggles. These struggles were caused by the impact of two world wars, the Russian and Chinese revolutions, and long-pent-up pressures for liberation.

The day of open colonialism is over. The economic pattern of many ex-colonial countries, however, remains the same as under colonialism. *A country that has formal independence but retains the colonial economic pattern* is called **neocolonial**.

What do we mean by the colonial economic pattern? First, cheap raw materials and food crops are the main export. Second, the country has little or no manufacturing but relies on the importation of manufactured goods. Profit and interest continue to flow out of the neocolony. In fact, profits and interest flow out of the neocolonial country in much larger amounts than the investment that flows into it.

The problems of the underdeveloped, neocolonial countries under the regime of procorporate globalization have been summed up by Joseph Stiglitz (2006), former chief Economic Advisor to President Clinton and former head of the World Bank. He describes how the global corporations control trade and are supported by several international organizations, such as the International Monetary Organization. "We see an unfair global trade regime that hampers development." He says that the procorporate globalization process has caused "an unstable global financial system in which poor countries repeatedly find themselves with unmanageable debt burdens." Finally, he makes the key point that the international flow of money is in the wrong direction. "Money should flow from the rich to the poor countries, but increasingly, it goes in the opposite direction" (all quotes in this paragraph from Stiglitz, 2006).

Another point made by Stiglitz in the same article is that global corporations and their owners based in the United States have benefited from the profits that procorporate globalization has brought to the United States. He stresses, however, that little or none of those profits have trickled down to most Americans. America has many riches from the underdeveloped countries, but also has a relatively poor middle class slipping further and further behind the rich, who get much wealth from the underdeveloped countries. He writes: "In the U.S., tax policies have become less progressive; the bulk of recent tax cuts went to the winners, those who had already benefited both from globalization and changes in technology. Increasingly, we are becoming rich countries with poor people" (Stiglitz, 2006).

In addition, many of the neocolonies remain under the political influence of the former occupying power, even though the foreign troops have left. Many of the underdeveloped countries continue to be ruled by the same old landed elite as well as some new industrial elites. While most of the elite are now natives of the country, most of the profits still flow to foreign corporations. Although the old colonial power no longer has troops in the neocolony, it continues to exert its strong political influence through the native elite, who receive a small share of the corporate profits. For the poorest of the underdeveloped countries, especially in Africa, formal independence has changed the essential economic relationships very little.

On the one side are almost all the underdeveloped, newly independent countries, still under foreign economic domination, still poor and agricultural, and still facing all the old obstacles to development. On the other side are the advanced capitalist countries, still extracting large profits from the dependent countries. The group who benefits from neocolonialism includes all the countries that extract profits by trade and investment from the former colonies. The countries extracting profit from the neocolonies include most of Western Europe, Japan, and the United States. Neocolonial profits, meaning those profits extracted from the poor, less developed, former colonial countries in the same old ways, flow to the whole area of the advanced capitalist countries. In the age of global capitalism, the profits from the neocolonial countries flow through the global corporations even to countries like Switzerland that never held colonial power over any less developed country.

Since the 1970s, however, some of the neocolonial countries have shown a new economic pattern. These countries now are producing and exporting light manufactured goods. This step toward full industrialization is very important. The neocolonial countries that now have very considerable manufacturing include some in Asia, such as Thailand, South Korea, and India, and some in South America, such as Chile and Argentina. Yet these countries still have to import most of their capital equipment and technology. Foreign investment often dominates their industries. Foreign profits flowing back to the advanced capitalist countries are enormous. Because of the continuance of the underlying colonial economic pattern, we are justified in describing this situation as neocolonialism in spite of formal political independence and the growth of manufacturing.

Neocolonial control in the world today comes through economic and monetary penetration together with political alliances between the advanced capitalist powers and the ruling elites in the neocolonial countries. This influence is exercised partly in blatant forms, such as subsidies to the ruling groups and large amounts of free military supplies. But influence is also exercised through highly sophisticated and complex monetary agreements. The influence of the strong capitalist powers has also been maintained by granting independence to small territories, tiny divisions of former colonial domains. These tiny ex-colonies have no political or economic power with which to resist continued domination.

It should also be noted that the economic control is often not direct from one country to another but is built up in a complex pyramid in the age of global corporations. For example, some American companies directly invest in northeast Brazil. More control of that area, however, is achieved through American domination of major southern Brazilian companies, which, in turn, buy controlling interests in companies in the Brazilian northeast. Still more control is achieved through American domination of some Western European companies, which, in turn, own some major Brazilian firms or directly own some of the local firms in the Brazilian northeast. Finally, control is achieved by U.S. and West European control of international organizations, such as the World Trade Organization, the International Monetary Fund, and the World Bank. On the military level, it is worth emphasizing the existence of American military bases in many countries around the world.

Finally, since the end of communism in 1990, the old communist areas of Russia, China, and Eastern Europe have moved strongly toward capitalism. During the communist period, they developed much heavy industry. Now they are using their industry to produce goods for the world market. Much of their industry is now controlled by global corporations, so the degree of their independence is a question. Russia and Eastern Europe have had a poor economic record on the road to capitalism, so they are still at only medium levels of income and development. China has been a success story, with rapid and seemingly uninterrupted economic development.

CONSERVATIVE EXPLANATIONS OF UNDERDEVELOPMENT

In the nineteenth century, conservatives explained the poverty of the colonies mainly by noting that most colonial countries were inhabited by brown, black, yellow, or red people. Many claimed "everyone knew" that these people were "inferior." Because they were inferior, the people of the colonies must be lazy and inefficient, which accounts for underdevelopment. It is impossible to overstate the racism of nineteenth century Europeans and white Americans. All such theories have been completely exploded by biological science. Such theories are no longer discussed in any respectable social science journal, so they are not discussed here.

In both the nineteenth and the twentieth centuries, many conservative economists argued that the cause of underdevelopment in the colonies and neocolonies is overpopulation. In Chapter 46 on growth in the advanced capitalist countries, we discussed in detail the population theory of Thomas Malthus, so it need not be repeated here. In brief, Malthus said that the human population grows like rabbits because of our sexual behavior, but production grows very slowly because there are diminishing returns to inputs of labor.

We showed in detail in Chapter 46 that Malthus's theory is incorrect, so the argument against it need not be repeated here. Remember, though, that some underdeveloped countries have few people per square mile of land and few people relative to their abundant resources, yet they have poverty. Some advanced countries, such as Belgium and Japan, have relatively many people with little land and not many resources, yet they have high-level incomes.

It is also worth remembering that the United States had one of the highest rates of population growth in history in the late nineteenth century because of both big families and immigration, yet U.S. output rose rapidly and it changed from an underdeveloped agricultural country to an advanced industrialized country at the end of the period. Development does not depend on low population growth. In fact, highly developed countries have lower and lower population growth, so development tends to make the problem of population disappear.

Finally, in the late twentieth century and the early twenty-first century, conservative economists focused on the theme that underdevelopment is caused by the faulty policies of the governments of underdeveloped counties. According to conservatives, the neocolonial economies are held back by a high percentage of government-controlled industry, by high government expenditures for social improvements, and by a great deal of government regulations. We saw in discussing globalization (Chapters 16 and 54) that the international organizations, controlled by the advanced capitalist powers, have argued strongly that some features of governments in the underdeveloped countries have been obstacles to growth. The International Monetary Fund, the World Bank, and the World Trade Organization have imposed conditions against continuing these policies as requirements for loans or for membership. Let us examine these policies.

Many less developed countries do have publicly owned enterprises in some economic areas. For example, education is publicly owned and controlled in many underdeveloped countries. Many utilities, such as water and power, are public. The international organizations assumed that publicly owned enterprises are less productive than privately owned enterprises. This is clearly untrue. For example, in the United States, the Los Angeles Department of Water and Power (LADWP) has been very successful. When the private energy firms in California had shortages of power that created blackouts, the LADWP had no problems and loaned power to the private firms. In the educational area, the state-owned University of California is one of the great universities of the world and competes very well against most private universities. (Publicly owned firms are discussed in Chapter 25.)

These international organizations, WTO, IMF, and World Bank, have also described the governments of the undeveloped countries as big spenders. These conservative international organizations have attacked governments for spending money on health care, education, and free lunches for hungry children. They claim that these expenditures undermine the free market by competing with private enterprise. They argue that the money should be paid back to banks of the capitalist countries for loans. Since they assume that all government expenditure is less productive than private expenditure, they consider that they are doing the country a favor by stopping these expenditures, which hold back development.

It may be pointed out, however, that the Asian countries with a high degree of government ownership and expenditure, such as China, have very rapid rates of economic growth compared with most underdeveloped countries. Many studies have shown that government investment in education has very high rates of return in terms of economic growth. We certainly cannot generalize that high levels of government expenditure on peaceful, nonmilitary goods and services are all less productive than private ones.

Another good example from the United States is the health care system. Our health system is mostly privately owned and controlled by the insurance companies. Health care systems in all other industrialized countries (except South Africa) are mostly publicly run. The American health care system spends more than twice as much as the publicly owned systems as a percentage of GDP but provides less care, according to most indices (see sources and details in Chapter 24).

The third and last part of the conservative argument as to the policy "mistakes" of the governments of the underdeveloped countries is that they have too many government regulations. All government regulations are bad because they interfere with the free market, so they cause inefficiency. But is this always true? Suppose there are strict government regulations to attempt to prevent the terrible disasters in mines that cause the deaths of so many miners. Is this inefficient? These regulations help preserve the lives of the miners, but they lower the profits of the mine owners. Is that inefficient? There is nothing in the private competition in the mining industry that would cause firms to add more safety protection for miners. On the contrary, the dictates of competitive profit making are against expenditure of money on anything that does not produce profit. Safety measures have been enforced only by the power of the mine workers' unions or the government.

Another government regulation to which the conservative economists object is the restrictions on the flow of capital and profits into and out of countries. Some countries have been forced to end these restrictions. The result in some cases has been catastrophic. If billions of dollars can suddenly leave a small, poor country to go elsewhere for more profit, it can create monetary chaos and shortages of goods and services in that country.

THE PROGRESSIVE CONCEPT OF THE SURPLUS: A TOOL FOR UNDERSTANDING UNDERDEVELOPMENT

Chapters 19 and 20 discussed the individual surplus created by every employee that flows into corporate profits. Here we look at the **national surplus**, which is *produced by underdeveloped, neocolonial countries and flows into the profits of the global corporations as well as into the wealth of the local ruling class.*

What defines a national surplus? People must eat, wear clothes, and have some kind of shelter.

Some of the national product of each underdeveloped country is distributed to the people for basic needs. If they do not receive their basic needs from the products of their labor, then they will die of starvation or they will revolt. The native rulers and the global corporations need employees who are alive and who do not revolt. Therefore, they usually pay enough for minimum food, clothing, and shelter. Let us assume that employees and independent farmers in the underdeveloped countries do earn some minimum amount from their hard work.

Beyond this minimum going to the population of employees and farmers, there is usually a large surplus. The surplus is just the difference between the national product and the minimum kept to themselves by the struggles of the employees and farmers. The question is, What happens to that surplus? If all of the surplus is invested in new equipment and building used for production in the underdeveloped country, then there will be rapid growth. In fact, that happy situation does not exist in the underdeveloped countries, almost all of which are neocolonies.

Most of the surplus is used in one of two ways. First, the native ruling classes use their high incomes for luxury consumption and speculation. Second, most of the foreign corporations' enormous profits are removed from the poor country to the advanced capitalist countries. As a result, there is a lack of capital for investment in development. Lack of investment means not only little construction but also little new equipment and little technological improvement. It also means that few funds are available for education and training, let alone research. Lack of investment also means that millions of workers cannot be employed at a sufficient rate of profit, so they are left unemployed or underemployed. It is not the laziness or sexual activity of the people that are the cause of underdevelopment. It is the economic institutions that extract the surplus and send it to other countries that are the real obstacles to development.

INTERNAL OBSTACLES TO DEVELOPMENT: HOW PART OF THE SURPLUS IS USED BY THE NATIVE ELITE

Let us begin with the internal obstacles to development created by the political-economic systems of the underdeveloped countries. We shall find that the ruling group in most of the underdeveloped countries uses some of the surplus for investment but wastes the rest in several ways.

The typical situation in most of the underdeveloped countries finds millions of peasants with tiny farms engaged in subsistence farming. Some peasants own their little farms, but many pay rent or pay a share of their product to a landlord. These peasants are often obligated to pay high rents or high product shares to landlords. They also pay high interest rates to money-lenders for money to buy supplies until the crop is harvested. Finally, they pay high taxes to local and national governments. From their original small net product, the peasants usually pay more than half to meet these obligations. Thus they retain hardly enough for their bare subsistence and none for major improvement or investment.

What other domestic groups can make new investments in these countries? The landlords and money-lenders take much of the surplus from the peasant, so they have a surplus in the form of money. But they spend most of it on conspicuous luxury consumer goods and services. If they reinvest at all, they make extremely conservative investments. They tend to make speculative investments in more land, since land is considered the safest investment. Of course, this does not produce any further growth. Otherwise, they send the money to some safe foreign country, such as the United States. Little, if any, is invested in the industry of their own country.

Furthermore, the governments of the poorest countries are mostly dominated by a small elite of wealthy landlords and merchants, plus foreign corporations. Such governments may invest little government funds in constructive projects. Government revenue is often spent on military goods for the purpose of internal repression. Governments spend some on showcase projects, such as sports arenas or beautification of the capital city.

In the cities, there are many owners or renters of tiny stores, but they have no surplus for major investments. The prosperous merchants usually spend their money on luxury consumption, land speculation, or send it abroad for safety. The few owners of larger businesses may do some investment but often rely on foreign corporations for the largest part of new investments.

We have said that the elite take the benefits of growth and keep them from most people. This abstract concept needs a concrete example to make it clear. As an example of the relation of the elite with new technology, consider the "revolution" in agriculture experienced by several underdeveloped countries. In this green revolution, new types of grains were introduced in countries like India and Pakistan. They brought much higher yields than the original crops, and so it would seem that one of the technical barriers to feeding the population was lowered.

However, making efficient use of the processes for growing the new grain requires considerable investment in irrigation, fertilizers, and insecticides. The large landowners, who can afford this investment, enhanced their profits by evicting tenants and mechanizing the grain-production process. Indeed, this has been taking place on a growing scale, helping to explain the persisting and often worsening poverty, even where growth is taking place. The dispossessed peasants swell the ranks of the unemployed in the cities. Thus, the present economic relationships between the poor farmers and the elite form a barrier that is aggravating the very problems that development is expected to cure.

FOREIGN OBSTACLES TO PROGRESS: HOW GLOBAL CORPORATIONS TAKE PART OF THE SURPLUS

Conservative governments in many underdeveloped countries are useless in building the economy, but they are sometimes supported by the United States or some other advanced capitalist country. They receive subsidies from the United States government if they support the U.S. foreign policy and fight against internal left-wing movements. For example, the United States supported military coups by conservative groups in the past in Greece, Iran, Brazil, Nicaragua, and Chile. Such governments may get some economic growth by opening their country to foreign investors on any terms that are required. The terms of investment have often included getting rid of unions or reducing social services. All of the benefits of the growth tend to go to a very small elite as well as to the global corporations. The conditions of most of the peasant farms and city employees are not improved.

The lack of buying power by most people means that when any industry is developed by the foreign investors, it is concentrated mostly in just a few cities. Moreover, most of the new products are sold for exports. Within the country, there is no process of economic growth that is independent of foreign investors and the export market.

Because the surplus is taken by the local elite for unproductive purposes or is sent as profit or interest to foreign countries, even poor countries that are supposed to be politically independent often have low rates of economic growth. Their economic pattern remains the same as during the colonial pattern, so they are called neocolonial.

The problem is made clearer if we summarize the mechanisms that cause the low growth. First, in the colonial period, many underdeveloped countries were forced by the colonial occupiers to remain in low-productivity agriculture. The exception was a small amount of industry controlled mainly by foreigners in the coastal cities.

Second, in recent decades, many of the underdeveloped countries have developed industry.

Much of the industry is owned by global corporations. Therefore, most of the industrial profit is taken overseas, so it is not available for development of the underdeveloped country.

Third, most of their exports remain agricultural products or raw materials such as tin or oil. Since the mining companies and oil companies usually remain under foreign control, their profit is sent abroad. We have seen that much of new manufacturing is also controlled by the global corporations, so a lot of their profit is sent out of the country.

Fourth, there is little domestic production of goods and services for the population because most people have so little money that they have little effective demand. Therefore, most of the finished goods for the needs of the population have to be imported from abroad. Again, the profits on these imports flow abroad.

Because of this structure, based on the unchanged conditions of dependency and loss of their surplus, there is limited flow of money from the international market into these countries. Instead of aid flowing into these underdeveloped countries, the net flow of money is out of these countries.

Specifically, there are three roads by which the net flow of the money is out of the underdeveloped countries into the advanced capitalist countries: trade, investment, and finance. In the trade area, the countries export oil, metals, and various raw agricultural materials, such as lumber. These exports bring fairly low prices because all of these goods are relatively cheap in the international market compared with finished goods. If large amounts of money can be made by such exports, then control and profits usually are in the hands of the giant corporations of the advanced capitalist countries.

The raw materials are then used by the advanced countries to make finished goods. For example, most of the raw materials used in the United States come from the underdeveloped, neocolonial countries. After the raw materials are made into finished goods, such as lamps or cars, some of these products are then exported back to the underdeveloped neocolonial countries.

The finished goods sell on the international market at far higher prices than the raw materials that went into them. Therefore, in the trade between the neocolonial countries and the advanced capitalist countries, a river of profits flows from the less developed, neocolonial countries to the advanced capitalist countries. Often, the trade of a small country is almost all with just one advanced country on whom they are dependent economically and politically.

The second flow of profit comes from foreign investment. Many of the advanced countries have had investments in the underdeveloped countries for many years. Most such investment is in valuable raw materials such as oil. Over time, the investments become very large. The large investments return large amounts of profit to the advanced country.

For example, for a long time, in the 1960s and 1970s, there was a flow of about $1 billion a year from the United States to Latin America. The same pattern, a net flow of money from Latin America to the United States, has continued till today, at higher and higher levels. That investment built up for many years, and the flow of profits on a total investment of, say, $10 billion was about $2 billion a year from Latin America to the United States. In fact, for many decades, the flow of U.S. corporate investment into Latin America has been about half of the flow of profits back to U.S. corporations from Latin America.

Financial Crises

The third net flow of money from the underdeveloped, neocolonial countries to the advanced capitalist countries is through financial transactions. Let us examine the main type of financial transaction with regard to development.

The banks of the more advanced countries have loaned the governments of the less developed

Table 56.3

Domestic Banking Crises in the World: 1970s, 1980s, 1990s: Percentage of All Crises During 1970–1999

	1970s–1990s	1970s	1980s	1990s
Industrial nations	26	4	11	11
Less developed nations	55	2	25	28
Transitional nations	20	0	0	20
Percentage	100	6	35	59

Source: Adapted from Phillip O'Hara, "A Global Neoliberal State Social Structure of Accumulation for Sustainable Global Growth and Development?" In Steve Pressman (Ed.), *Alternative Theories of the State* (London: Palgrave, 2006, p. 75).

countries much money since their independence. That money is often loaned at fairly high interest rates. The interest on the loans has now reached a level at which it takes away a high proportion of the national income of many of the less developed countries. They borrowed the money out of necessity as the only way to survive, but then found their hopes for progress with new investments from this money were not fulfilled. With very poor economies at low rates of growth, but high proportions of debt, they are mostly unable to pay the interest on the loans. They certainly could not pay back the whole loan.

This has become a very crucial issue for many countries. A large number of international conferences have been held on the issue. One proposal was to put heavy pressure on these debtor countries to cut back on social services so that they could pay back the loans. This approach was tried in many places but did not succeed. The problem is that social services are a small amount compared with the debt. Cutting social services harms millions of people, causing vehement protest demonstrations. Some protests became full-scale revolutions, leading to changes of governments.

The other suggested solution to the unpaid loans was to cancel payments by the poor countries on loans then outstanding to underdeveloped countries. This proposal was debated with great vehemence on both sides. It was tried to some limited extent. However, the problems of the underdeveloped countries could not be solved merely by debt reduction. More drastic measures affecting the underdeveloped countries, and the foreign firms located within them, are still necessary.

One aspect of the financial crises that resulted in the underdeveloped countries was the rising number of financial panics. A financial panic results when an institution begins to run out of money to pay its depositors or investors. Frightened depositors or investors rush to pull their money out of the institution, making the situation much worse. These panics are shown in Table 56.3.

According to the table, all the underdeveloped countries together had only two financial crises in the 1970s but 25 in the 1980s and 28 in the 1990s. There has thus been a dramatic rise in the financial problems of the underdeveloped countries. This rise has followed their integration into the world financial system.

In addition to the problems of trade, investment, and finance, the underdeveloped countries were also affected by two other problems, which affected all of global capitalism. As shown in Chapter 54, these problems were environmental devastation and decline in trust for economic institutions, governments, and other human beings.

HAS GLOBALIZATION AFFECTED DEVELOPMENT?

In the colonial stage, colonies were looted of all their treasures, then they were reduced to agriculture and raw material production. They exported those commodities, and they imported their finished goods at high prices. The colonies had little industry. After the World War II, the colonies became free. But most became neocolonies. The neocolonies still kept most workers in agriculture and raw material production at very low wages. The raw materials were mostly owned by foreign corporations. Most exports were agricultural goods and raw materials, and most imports were finished goods at relatively high prices. The economic pattern of the neocolonial countries up until the 1970s resembled the pattern of colonial countries.

The very strong globalization process beginning in the 1970s produced drastic changes in the economies of the neocolonial, poor countries. Of course, globalization has been going on for hundreds of years, so there had been smaller effects for a long time. There were some exceptions to the neocolonial pattern in some countries from the 1960s to the 1970s. Yet a comparison from 1970 to 2000 shows startling changes.

Unfortunately, little change came to most of Africa, so the pattern for most of its countries remains. Most of the people are in low-productivity agriculture. Some get low wages working for foreign corporations in raw material extraction. Only a small number in the coastal cities work in industry, also mostly owned by foreign corporations with some kind of relation usually to a small number of domestic capitalists.

Much of Asia and Latin America has changed. In these countries, the new situation is marked by large-scale foreign investment in manufacturing and some service industries. There are still a large number of very poor farmers, indebted to money-lenders or landlords, but there are also a large percentage of workers and professionals in the cities, who run the industrial enterprises. There are also many more domestic capitalists. Thus, these countries have moved up to a middle level of income. As we saw, where global income per person is $7,000, these countries have moved up to the $4,000 range. The peasant farmers are still very poor, but the professionals are very well off, and the domestic capitalists are rich.

Does this mean that neocolonialism has ended in these countries? The old pattern has ended, but the new industrial pattern still allows for foreign domination and exploitation that may still be called neocolonial in most of these countries. In other words, much of the manufacturing and mining and some services are still mainly foreign owned. The foreign ownership means that a great deal of profit and interest goes abroad. The river of money still flows from the less developed world, even in the middle-income countries, to the advanced capitalist countries such as the United States.

China is one of the most dynamic of the neocolonial countries, but it has a unique background and it is moving toward a new status. China had a Communist revolution in 1948 that ended all foreign ownership of any significance. It then tried to grow without world trade except for help from the Soviet Union. It grew pretty well for a while, and then ran into troubles when it tried to speed up. A series of crises drove it to try a new system. It now has a political dictatorship, a declining area of government ownership, and a rapidly rising area of private capitalist ownership.

In the cities of China, there are rich capitalists, affluent professionals, and poorly paid workers, but even the workers have a much higher income than the peasants of rural China. The average income in the cities has been rising rapidly for the last two or three decades. In the countryside, however, the vast majority of Chinese still live by agriculture at very low income levels. The national average income per person of close to $2,000 a year represents an amazing achievement, but it mostly represents the affluent classes in the cities, with no participation from hundreds of millions of people in the countryside.

China's rapid growth represents partly the dynamic of a newly emerging capitalist power. Partly, however, the growth comes from large-scale investment by global corporations. The Chinese invested heavily in infrastructure such as roads and railroads and airports. This made possible the wave of foreign investment.

An important part of China's most rapidly growing economic sectors are in foreign hands. For example, American corporations are very obvious in China. Two American fast-food chains compete in opening store after store in China to sell fried chicken. Wal-Mart has many stores in China, where it pays employees about $0.17 per hour and sometimes forces them to work six days a week. Wal-Mart also protested to the Chinese government that it does not want any unions in their stores. General Motors and Ford have been firing workers in the United States, while building new plants in China.

China is growing rapidly, but large profits are flowing out to foreign countries. Many enterprises are jointly owned by Chinese and foreigners, but the Chinese claim that they are rapidly learning new technology and will soon not need foreigners. Such an economy is not the old neocolonial country that produced only agriculture and raw materials. Rather, its growth is based on a vast amount of new industry. Chinese industrial goods are sold all over the world, and China has a trade surplus, not a deficit. Instead of borrowing and going far into debt, China is mainly loaning money to other developing nations. There is growth and a new industrial pattern, but still an exploitation of Chinese workers by global corporations that send huge profits abroad.

Sticking to the facts rather than the optimistic predictions of some economists, we can say two things. First, in the sixty years since World War II, the gap between average incomes in the less developed countries and average income in the advanced capitalist countries has actually become wider. There are exceptions, such as in China in recent decades, but the gap on the average has increased. Second, within each country, the gap between the average income of the rich and the poor has widened. That is not true in all countries, but it is true on the average and in the world as a whole.

The process of globalization has led toward a unified global economy. A unified global economy may help all nations, including the underdeveloped nations. Moreover, within the underdeveloped, neocolonial countries, there has been a startling change. Most of the African countries are still poor and agricultural, but large parts of Asia and Latin America have developed some industry. Industrialization has long been considered a first step toward a fully developed, independent, and affluent economy.

There is evidence that the procorporate form of globalization has led, as shown in Chapter 54, to a low rate of global growth per person. In fact, the growth per person has slowed in the advanced capitalist countries but has slowed even more in the underdeveloped countries on average. As a result, the gap between rich and poor countries has grown during the process of globalization.

Finally, since the process of procorporate globalization has increased the net flow of money to the advanced capitalist countries, it has increased the anger of the people of the underdeveloped countries against those who extract profit and interest from them. The result has been conflict between those who would loosen the control exercised by the global corporations and those who would strengthen that control. Most of the conflicts have been fought by peaceful economic means. Some, such as the war in Iraq, have been fought by military force. The military solution of conflicts between the United States and underdeveloped countries has had an affect on U.S. economic growth and other areas of U.S. development. As this chapter is solely concerned with the development of the underdeveloped countries, the effects of war and militarism on the United States are discussed in Appendix 56.1.

SUMMARY

The underdeveloped capitalist countries are not only poor but are growing more slowly than the advanced capitalist countries. Why? Some nineteenth-century conservatives argued that the people of the poor countries are inferior, but that myth has been thoroughly destroyed. Some modern conservatives argue that there is too much population in the underdeveloped countries, but that myth has also been destroyed. Other modern conservatives argue that the governments of these underdeveloped countries are corrupt and have many inefficient government-owned enterprises. This view has also been severely criticized by progressives.

The main progressive view begins with the effect of colonialism on the underdeveloped countries. A colony is a country that has been conquered and occupied by another country. Many conquerors take all of the movable treasure from the occupied country. After that, the conqueror uses economic means to extract more profit every year. For example, when England owned the United States before 1776, it extracted profit by buying cheap lumber and other agricultural goods. English manufacturers then manufactured goods from the raw materials. Finally, English merchants transported some of these goods back to America and sold them at high prices to the colonists. England tried hard to stop Americans from getting any new technology and doing any manufacturing. Such has been the pattern of colonialism every since.

Colonies and colonial wars, however, are not common these days. In the era of global capitalism since about 1970, almost all colonies have become independent. Global corporations extract very high profits from these former colonies, but they do it mainly by peaceful means. Rather than colonies, most of the newly independent countries have become neocolonies. The surplus of the neocolonial underdeveloped countries is the amount that each country produces above the bare minimum of consumption of food, clothing, and shelter for the survival of its people. Most of the people of the neocolonies are very poor, some starving, but a small elite is very rich.

The elite group in most underdeveloped countries is composed of landlords, merchants, and bankers, and some capitalist manufacturers. There are now a growing number of native capitalist manufacturers and exporters, but they mostly work with, and are dependent on, global corporations. As long as they obey these corporations, they have a chance at getting rich.

The internal elite take part of the neocolony's surplus but do very little productive investment with it. They spend some of it for luxury consumer goods and services. They spend some for speculative investments in land, which do not produce any additional goods. They send a large part of it to relatively safe investments in the advanced capitalist countries. The rest of the surplus goes to the global corporations. In the form of profit and interest, it flows to the advanced capitalist countries. Since most of its surplus is used unproductively by the elite or goes to foreign countries, the rate of growth of such neocolonial underdeveloped countries is drastically slowed compared with the fully developed capitalist countries.

SUGGESTED READINGS

A well-written, progressive book on neocolonialism, especially in Iraq, is John B. Foster's *Naked Imperialism* (2006). An article stating and attacking the neoclassical view of development is Remy Herrera, "The New Development Economics: A Neoliberal Con?" (2006).

KEY TERMS

less developed economies	neocolonial
national surplus	neocolonialism

REVIEW QUESTIONS

Compare and contrast characteristics of developed and less developed countries.
1. What are measures used to compare economic outcomes of developed and less developed countries?
2. Why is underdevelopment based on several measures instead of just one?

Discuss the impacts of colonialism and neocolonialism on less developed countries and developed countries.
3. Define underdeveloped country, colony, neocolony, and surplus of a country.
4. How do the native elite of underdeveloped countries use the surplus?

Describe and discuss the various obstacles to development.
5. What are the roles played by trade, investment, and finance in extracting the surplus from an underdeveloped country and sending it abroad?
6. What are some obstacles to development? Describe how the obstacles impact some of the specific measures discussed in questions 1 and 2.

APPENDIX 56.1
EFFECTS OF MILITARISM ON U.S. DEVELOPMENT

We have discussed the effects of neocolonialism and military force on the underdeveloped world. How do the wars and military spending affect the United States? That is the question explored in this appendix.

LEARNING OBJECTIVES FOR APPENDIX 56.1

After reading this appendix, you should be able to:

- Compare and contrast the benefits and costs of militarism.

THE IMPACT OF MILITARISM

Neocolonial wars and **militarism** have both benefits and costs for the United States; militarism in this context means *support of a strong military along with the idea that war can be beneficial to a country.* Wars to hold neocolonies, such as Vietnam and Iraq, as well as military spending for these wars, do create some jobs in the short run. They also create inflation, high taxation, reduction in welfare services, and thousands of dead and wounded Americans. In the long run, high military production must reduce the amount of national income flowing into the production of consumer goods and investment, so it lowers the growth rate of GDP.

The benefits and costs of colonial wars and militarism are not spread equally among all Americans. Wars and military spending provide vast benefits for a small number of giant corporations that make very high profit rates on foreign investment and on military production. Most people lose from colonial wars through higher taxes, higher prices, and dead or wounded loved ones. Progressive economists believe that wars and military spending are not necessary to create jobs.

There are more rational and constructive ways of creating employment, such as health care and education. In the long run, war spending hurts growth, whereas better health and education help growth.

Most wars now are fought by guerrilla rather then conventional warfare. On the whole, however, global capitalism has shown some preference for peace. The military industry does make extremely high rates of profit from war production, but most economic sectors and most global corporations make more profits in peace, particularly because they pay less in taxes in peacetime. The rational path for a global corporation and those governments that it strongly influences is peace. Under President Clinton, for example, American corporations made giant steps toward conquering the whole world through peaceful, economic penetration. The Clinton administration continued to build the world's largest military power, but it mostly used it to threaten, making only very small military adventures.

KEY TERMS IN APPENDIX 56.1

militarism

REVIEW QUESTIONS FOR APPENDIX 56.1

Compare and contrast the benefits and costs of militarism.
1. Does the average American have a net benefit or a net loss from wars conducted to hold neocolonies?
2. Do any corporations benefit directly or indirectly from such wars?

GLOSSARY

Note: The parenthetical numbers following the definition indicate the chapter in which the definition can be found.

Ability-to-Pay Principle: the idea that people with higher income should pay proportionately more taxes than poor people because they can afford to (35)

Absolute Advantage: producing goods and services with the fewest inputs or at the lowest cost (55)

Accelerator: the effect on investment of an increase in national income (44.1)

Accounting Profit: the total revenue received from production and sales ($p * q$) minus direct or explicit costs like labor, rent, and payments for machinery (30)

Accumulated Net Marginal Revenue Product: the area under the marginal revenue product curve above the wage line (31.1)

Aggregate: the entire economy comprised of all the buyers and all the sellers (10)

Aggregate Demand: the total dollar amount of goods that consumers, investors, foreigners, and governments plan to buy at a given price level (38, 46)

Aggregate Supply: the total output that business produces and plans to sell at a given price level (10, 38)

Allocative Efficiency: market condition in which the marginal benefit of the last unit consumed is equal to the marginal cost of production (35.1)

Amplitude: the amount of rise in the expansion and the amount of decline in the contraction (41)

Assets: things of value that can be owned (7); those things owned by the bank or owed to the bank (49)

Autarky: the absence of trade (55.1)

Automatic Fiscal Policies: policies that are fixed in place by law for the indefinite future (47)

Average Fixed Cost: found by dividing fixed costs by total product (30)

Average Product of Labor: a measure calculated by dividing total output by the number of variable inputs (29.1)

Average Propensity to Consume: the proportion of income spent for consumption (42)

Average Propensity to Save: the proportion of savings to income (42, 46)

Average Total Cost: found by dividing total costs by total product (30)

Average Variable Cost: found by dividing variable costs by total product (30)

B.C.E.: before the Common Era (2)

Balance of Trade: the relationship between a country's exports and imports (6)

Balanced Budget: condition under which government expenditures equal taxes (47)

Benefits-Received Principle: people should pay higher taxes if they receive higher benefits from government programs (35)

Budget Surplus: occurs when the government takes in more money than it spent in a year; government revenues are greater than government expenditures (16)

Bullionism: the earliest phase of mercantilism (6)

Business: entity that produces profits for wealthy absentee owners and often sabotages industry (13)

Business Cycle Peak: highest point in the business cycle as measured by business indicators (41)

Business Cycle Trough: lowest point of the business cycle as measured by business indicators (41)

Business Cycles: upward or downward trends of output that deviate from the overall trend in output over time (6); an expansion in economic activity (measured by indicators such as output, employment, and profits) followed by a contraction in economic activity (including declining production, unemployment, business losses, and bankruptcies) (36); the rise of the economy from trough to peak, as well as the following decline from peak to trough (41)

Business Losses: condition occurring when businesses cannot sell their goods at a profit (36)

C.E.: Common Era; since year 1 of our calendar (3)

Cap-and-Trade or Emissions Trading System: an administrative process by which emissions are limited, but polluters are required to buy and sell pollution permits

Capital: materials, buildings, and equipment used in the production of goods and services (5)

Carbon Tax: a type of pollution tax on energy sources, such as coal or gasoline, that varies in proportion to the amount of carbon dioxide their use emits into the atmosphere

Cardinal Utility: the idea that the consumer satisfaction (utility or joy) received from a particular good can be numerically measured in countable units (28)

Cartel: a group of firms that acts as a monopoly (34)

Celler-Kefauver Act of 1950: forbade the purchase of either the stock of a competing corporation (which had already been illegal) or the assets of competing corporations (21)

Change in Demand: a situation in which the entire demand schedule or line shifts either out (to the right) or in (to the left) (27.1)

Change in Supply: a situation in which the entire supply schedule or line shifts either out (to the right) or in (to the left) (27.1)

Changes in Quantity Demanded: when a change in price causes the quantity demanded for a good to change (27.1)

Changes in Quantity Supplied: when a change in price causes the quantity supplied for a good to change (27.1)

Choice: the producer's decision of what raw materials and technology to use; the consumer's decision of which goods he or she wants to consume (26)

Christian Paternalist Ethic: Judeo-Christian moral code as interpreted in the medieval period (4)

Circular Flow: the supply of goods and services moves in one direction, while demand in the form of money moves in the other direction (37)

Class: a group of people who obtain their income in a way that distinguishes them from other groups and shows their relationship to other groups in the economic process (18)

Classical Liberalism: new individualistic philosophy that arose in the eighteenth century advocating less government intervention in the management of the economy (6)

Clayton Act of 1914: forbade corporations to engage in price discrimination and prohibited interlocking directorates where this would lead to a substantial reduction of competition (21)

Climate Change: refers to variations in the earth's prevailing weather conditions over time

Coase Theorem: states that externalities do not lead to resource misallocation as long as there is a system of well-defined property rights (35.1)

Collusion: a secret agreement between two or more parties, usually for fraudulent, deceitful, or illegal purposes (11)

Commercial Farming: production of food for the market (5)

Commons: land where peasants could collect wood, graze animals, and receive other benefits (5)

Communal Societies: family-based collectives (1)

Comparative Advantage: producing a good or service at the lowest opportunity cost (55)

Compensating Differentials: higher wages offered in jobs that involve danger, tedium, or significant physical labor (31)

Complementary Goods: goods that are typically consumed together and characterized by a positive cross-price elasticity of demand (27.2)

Conglomerate Merger: situation in which a giant corporation absorbs other corporations that have no relation to its primary product line (21)

Conservative: characterizing aversion to rapid change and bound to tradition (4)

Conspicuous Consumption: buying things to show off or to enhance one's social status (13, 28)

Constant Returns to Scale: occurs if output increases by the same proportion as all inputs, e.g., a tripling of inputs leads to a tripling of output (29)

Consumption: the money that individuals spend for food, clothing, shelter,and everything else they buy (37)

Consumption Function: Keynesian schedule of aggregate consumer spending at different income levels; as income increases consumption increases by some fraction (42)

Contraction: downward turn in the business cycle (36)

Cooperative Enterprise: concern in which each employee/owner has one vote on how to run the enterprise (25)

Cooperative Socialism: a system that asserts that capitalism exploits workers, and that all production decisions in a socialist society must be made by democratic votes of all the employees in an enterprise or by a plan democratically voted on by everyone in a local, state, national, or global society (9)

Corporation: a business in which all of the assets are owned by people who buy shares of stock, or shares of ownership, in the business (7)

Cost-Push Inflation: inflation caused by input costs, including high wages and salaries (50)

Creditor Nation: a country that is owed more by other countries than it owes to other countries; a country that lends more than it borrows from others on an ongoing basis (16)

Crisis: the decline of profits in a capitalist system (45)

Cross-Price Elasticity: a measure of the relative responsiveness of the demand for one good to the relative price change of another good (27.2)

Cycle Base: the average of an economic series for one whole cycle (41)

Cycle Relative: the original data in a stage divided by the cycle base (41)

Debt: occurs when the accumulated yearly budget deficits of government are greater than the budget surpluses (47)

Debtor Nation: a country that owes more money to foreign countries than foreign countries owe to it—the United States is an example; a country that borrows more than it lends from others on an ongoing basis (16)

Decreasing Returns to Scale: occurs when output increases by less than inputs; for example if inputs triple but output only doubles (29)

Deficit: occurs when government spends more than it earns in taxes and fees in a year (16); or when expenditures were greater than the tax revenue in a given year (47)

Deflation: overall falling prices (51)

Demand: the quantity of the good buyers would be willing and able to purchase during a given period, at various price levels, holding all other things constant (27)

Demand Curve: illustrates graphically the relationship between prices and the quantity demanded (27)

Demand Schedule: relates various prices of a good with the amounts of that good people would like to buy at various prices (27)

Demand-Pull Inflation: traditional inflation caused by the upward pull of aggregate demand (50)

Democracy: rule by the people (24)

Depreciation: decrease in the value of plants and equipment over time (14); the funds set aside to replace the machinery and factory buildings that are used up or eventually worn out in the process of production (37); the dollar value of worn-out plants and equipment (43)

Depression: severe downturn in production and output (6, 36)

Derived Demand: the demand for the factors of production are derived, or arise from, the output or production of goods and services that use the various factors of production (31)

Diffusion: the spread of knowledge by the movement of ideas from one village to another, as in the spread of early farming (2)

Diminishing Marginal Productivity: stage in which additional inputs cause output to increase, but at a diminishing rate (29.1)

Diminishing Marginal Utility: decline in the incremental increase in utility that takes place after a certain point as more units of an item are consumed (28)

Direct Democracy: government by the entire population, usually through elected representatives (1)

Discretionary Fiscal Policies: policies adopted by Congress and the president to address particular situations (47)

Discrimination: the adverse treatment of an individual based on group membership instead of individual productivity (22)

Diseconomies of Scale: situation in which average costs will rise if the scale of operation is expanded (30.1)

Disposable Personal Income: the amount of money at the disposal of individuals and households for spending after taxes are paid (37)

Dis-savings: using up of reserves or going into debt (42)

Division of Labor: subdivided tasks, each worker producing only the commodity for which his or her abilities are best suited (8)

Economic Democracy: the people rule the economy, not just politics (25)

Economic Institutions: sets of relations between people doing economic activities and the ways that people interact in the economy (1)

Economic Profit: starts with the accounting profit and subtracts the indirect or opportunity costs of the owner (30)

Economic Rent: a factor payment over and above the payment necessary to bring that factor into production (31.1)

Economies of Scale: condition in which average total costs (or per unit costs) fall as output increases (21); average costs fall as plant size increases (30.1)

Economy: the process through which a society provisions itself with the goods and services that it needs to survive and grow (1)

Effective Demand: demand based on spending of money by consumers and investors (37); when someone has both desire and money (40); the aggregate demand in money terms, including both desire for products and the money for products (50)

Effective Political Democracy: system existing when a country not only has all of the mechanisms and forms of democracy, but is also characterized by a situation in which all citizens have a significant amount of power and no minority with wealth or military control has disproportionate power (25)

Egalitarian: belief in equal social, political, and economic rights for all people (9)

Elastic: characterizes price elasticity of demand that is greater than one, or a percentage change in quantity demanded that is much larger than the percentage change in the price (27.2)

Empire: an extensive area of land or countries under a single authority, with no democracy (3)

Employee Compensation: wages, salaries, bonuses, commissions, and fringe benefits (37)

Emulative Consumption: trying to equal or surpass the consumption of someone else (13)

Encyclicals: letters from the pope intended for wide circulation (12)

Equilibrium: when the quantity supplied and the quantity demanded for a particular good are equal at a particular price (27.1); the point at which supply and demand come to be equal (38)

Equilibrium Wage Rate: the wage rate that clears the labor market (31)

Euler's Theorem: factor payments must "add up" to exhaust the value of output (31.1)

Excess Demand: the quantity demanded exceeds the quantity supplied (27.1)

Excess Reserves: reserves above the legal requirement (49.1)

Excess Supply: the quantity supplied will exceed the quantity demanded (27.1)

Exclusion Principle: a person using a private good can exclude others from using it (35)

Expansion: upward turn in the business cycle (36)

Expectations: what people think will happen (45)

Expenditures: the flow of money for spending (37)

Exploitation: an economic relation that occurs when the average length of the working day exceeds the time necessary for a laborer to produce the value equivalent of his subsistence wage, enabling the capitalist to appropriate the surplus produced over and above this subsistence (10); a situation in which one group or class appropriates the labor of another group or class without paying the market price for all the commodities produced by that labor (19)

Export Multiplier: measures the total effect on national income as a result of a change in exports (44)

Exports: what a country sells to foreigners (6, 52)

External Debt: the portion of the funds a government borrows by selling government-issued bonds to investors in foreign countries (16)

Externality: exists whenever the market does not recognize all of the costs or benefits of production or consumption (35)

Fascism: a system of government led by a dictator having complete power and forcibly suppressing opposition and criticism and emphasizing an aggressive nationalism and racism (14)

Federal Deposit Insurance Corporation (FDIC): institution that insures bank accounts up to a certain amount of money (51)

Federal Funds Rate (FFR): the interest rate that bankers charge each other for overnight loans (51)

Federal Open Market Committee (FOMC): has the function of buying and selling government bonds on the open market (51)

Federal Trade Commission (FTC) Act of 1914: outlawed unfair methods of competition and established the FTC to investigate the methods of competition used by business firms (21)

Feudalism: a system based on serfdom, where political power was mainly decentralized from kings to lords of estates known as feudal manors (3)

Financial Capital: money (31.1)

Fiscal Policy: consists of decisions to spend and to tax (47)

Fixed Costs: costs that do not vary with output (30)

Forces of Production: tools, factories, and equipment; the labor force and its level of knowledge; natural resources; and the general level of technology (10)

Foreign Direct Investment: an investment that gives the investor a controlling interest in a foreign company (16)

Foreign Investment: spending by foreign citizens on plant and equipment in a country (53)

Formal Political Democracy: in practice this has meant an ongoing struggle among groups in which the corporate elite, who control the economy, often win the important battles due to their economic power (25)

Free Rider: a person who receives benefits from public goods without paying for them (35.1)

Free Trade: condition under which all goods and services must be allowed to travel freely in global trade without any barriers (54)

Free Trade Zones: geographical locations within which countries agree to lower barriers to trade such as tariffs and quotas (16)

Gini Coefficient: a calculation of income inequality that falls between zero and one (18)

Global Capitalism: latest stage of capitalism in which capitalist institutions dominate most of the world and global corporations are found in every country (16)

Global Mergers: international mergers between corporations in different countries (21)

Globalization: the process of growing interdependence among countries (16, 54)

Government: institutions that regulate and implement policies on behalf of the state in domestic and global settings (24)

Government Debt: the sum of accumulated surpluses and deficits over time when the accumulated deficits are greater than accumulated surpluses (16)

Government Multiplier: expresses the amount by which total national income is increased by a one-time increase in government spending (44)

Government Spending: spending by the government on consumption and investment (37)

Grassroots: groups of people organized at the local level rather than organized by traditional or existing power structures (11)

Great Depression: a worldwide economic downturn that started in 1929 (14)

Greenhouse Effect: just as a florist's greenhouse uses glass panels to let in light and keep in heat, greenhouse gases, such as carbon dioxide, allow in light and trap heat in the earth's atmosphere

Gross Domestic Product (GDP): the current dollar value of all final goods and services produced within the country in one year (7); the total value of all the finished goods and services produced and sold by a nation during some period of time (37)

Gross Investment: the total value of all capital goods produced in a year (43)

Gross Investment Spending: spending on all capital equipment including capital that replaces worn-out machinery and plants (37)

Gross Private Investment: the total dollar amount of spending for plants, equipment, and other items in one year (11)

Growth: percentage change in real output in a country over a specific time period (5)

Heckscher-Ohlin Model (HOM): a mathematical comparative advantage model that assumes similar technology across countries and where countries differ primarily by relative differences in capital and labor (55.2)

Historical Materialism: an analytical approach that saw each social, political, and economic institution and each intellectual tradition or ideology as related in a complex web of cause and effect to all the others in that particular social-economic system (10)

Horizontal Mergers: mergers with competitors on the same level of production (21, 14); a big corporation absorbs other corporations that are direct competitors

Human Capital: the education, training, and experience that increase worker productivity and therefore income (31, 55.2)

Identification Problem: the data available cannot be identified as being on either a single demand or supply curve (27.2)

Ideological Superstructure: includes all of our ideas, ideologies, and traditions, plus all of the institutions that spread those ideas, such as churches, schools, and the media of communication (10)

Ideology: a more or less coherent system of ideas about how society works and how we should behave within a given society (1)

Imperialism: a policy of acquiring dependent territories or extending a country's influence through foreign trade (13)

Imports: what a country buys from foreigners (6, 51)

Income: the stream of receipts from work or property generated by an individual or household over a specific time period (18)

Income Elasticity: a measure of the relative responsiveness of a change in quantity demanded to a change in income; defined as the percentage change in quantity demanded divided by the percentage change in income (27.2)

Increasing Marginal Productivity: condition in which, if the capital stock is fixed, adding additional workers will result in more output per worker because of specialization (29.1)

Increasing Returns to Scale: increase in output such that output increases proportionally more than inputs; doubling of inputs causes output to triple (29)

Individualistic Socialism: philosophy asserting that capitalism exploits workers, but that an effective socialist economy must retain individual decision making through the market mechanism (9)

Industry: a grouping of companies in a similar type of production; produces needed articles for human well-being (13)

Inelastic: the price elasticity of demand is less than one; the percentage change in demand is less than the percentage change in price (27.2)

Inert: unable to move or act, sluggish, lethargic (8)

Infant Industries: characterizes many industries in the mid-nineteenth century, when many countries had just started industrial development (55)

Inferior Goods: goods that people would prefer not to consume and do so only because of their low income; as income rises, the demand for inferior goods falls (27.2)

Inflation: a general increase in prices (6); the rate at which the overall price level increases (50); Keynesian view of inflation arises whenever aggregate spending is higher than aggregate production (40, 51)

Inputs: land, labor, and time

Instinct of Workmanship: an idea of Veblen's that stressed cooperation rather than competition, individual equality and independence rather than pervasive relations of subordination, logical social interrelationships rather than ceremonial role playing, and peaceable rather than predatory dispositions generally (13)

Institutions: sets of customs, laws, and norms that influence, enable, or constrain human behavior (1, 26, 26.1)

Intensity of Labor: the effort an employee exerts each hour (19)

Internal Debt: borrowing of money by the government through the sale of government-issued bonds. (16)

International Finance: buying and selling of financial instruments (such as stocks, bonds, and government securities) of a country by citizens of another country (53)

Investment: all private investment in the United States for fixed capital, which includes buildings and equipment (37); the acquisition of plants and machinery that can be undertaken only by firms (31.1)

Investment Multiplier: measures the total effect on national income of an initial increase in investment (44)

Invidious Distinctions: differences that give rise to envy (13)

"-isms": subordination of members of targeted groups by members of dominant groups with relatively more economic and social power (22)

Just Price: a price that would compensate the seller for his efforts in transporting the good and in finding the buyer at a rate that was just sufficient to maintain the seller at his customary or traditional station in life (4)

Keynesian Cross: a model that illustrates the relationship between aggregate production and aggregate expenditures; it can be used to explain why unemployment can be a persistent condition (40)

Labor Power: one's capacity to work for a definite period of time, say in a typical working day (10, 20)

Labor Theory of Value: the exchange value of a commodity, determined by the amount of labor time necessary for its production (10)

Laissez-faire: a policy of leaving the coordination of individuals pursuing their own self-interest to the market—that the government should not be involved (8)

Law of Demand: says there is an inverse relationship between price and quantity demanded (27)

Law of Diminishing Returns: if at least one input is fixed, output will eventually increase at a diminishing rate as additional units of inputs are added (29)

Law of Supply: declares that a positive relationship exists between price and the quantity supplied of any good (27)

Leakage: money income that is not spent on consumption or investment; caused by funds used for savings, imports, and taxes (40)

Legal Tender: the paper that must be accepted as payment for all debts (49)

Lender of Last Resort: the Federal Reserve, in times of financial panic, can lend money to banks if necessary (51)

Less Developed Economies: economies that have not industrialized (56)

Liabilities: what the banks owe to someone else (49)

Liberal: someone who favors political and social reform or change (6)

Limited Liability: the corporate form that allows a large group of investors to work together with liability limited to their investments (7)

Liquid Assets: those assets easily converted into money to pay off depositors (49)

Long Run: the period of time during which a firm can change any or all of it inputs (29)

Long-Run Average Cost Curve: an "envelope" that contains all of the short-run cost curves representing different plant sizes (30.1)

Luxury Good: a good with an income elasticity greater than one (27.2)

Macroeconomics: the study of the economy as a whole with primary interest in growth, unemployment, inflation, and business cycles (15); the part of economics that deals with the behavior of the economy as a whole (36)

Malthusian Argument: based on the philosophy of Thomas Robert Malthus that rising population and rising production together doom us to ecological catastrophe and to eventual poverty as our resources are depleted (23)

Marginal Cost: the incremental cost of producing the next unit of output (26.1, 30)

Marginal Physical Product: a measure of the output of labor in terms of goods and services (31)

Marginal Product of Labor: the extra output associated with adding one additional unit of the variable input (29.1)

Marginal Productivity Rent: the rent on improved land (31.1)

Marginal Propensity to Consume: increase of consumption to the increase in income (42)

Marginal Propensity to Save: the increase in savings to an increase in income (42)

Marginal Revenue: the change in the total revenue a firm will receive as a result of the sale of one additional unit. (33)

Marginal Revenue Product: the additional revenue earned from hiring one more worker (31)

Marginal Utility: the change in satisfaction caused by consuming one more unit of a good (28)

Market Capitalism: an economic system based on production for markets in which the ownership of the means of production—land, buildings, and equipment—is in the hands of a small group of individuals called capitalists (5)

Market Failure: a situation in which market outcomes are not socially optimal or desirable; caused by externalities, public goods, and the existence of market power (35)

Market Power: the ability of an individual firm to influence or manipulate prices or output in the market (21)

Mass Production: a system of production in quantity using standardized parts, task-specific capital, and unskilled labor (29)

Mercantilism: an important school of economic thought from 1500 to 1800 in Europe, serving as a transition between feudalism and capitalism, that provided morally justified individualization, greed, and profit seeking (6)

Medium of Exchange: payment for goods and services (15, 49)

Microeconomics: the study of individual firms, individual employees, and individual consumers (15); investigates the behavior of individual consumers, individual business owners, and individual employees (36)

Militarism: support of a strong military along with the idea that war can be beneficial to a country but there are costs (56.1)

Mode of Production: consists of two elements: (1) the forces of production, and (2) the relations of production (10)

Monetarism: a school of economic thought that believes the economic system works very well except when government messes it up through mistakes in monetary policy (51.1)

Monetary Policy: policy designed to increase or decrease the flow of money and credit with the aim of managing the rates of growth, unemployment, and/or inflation (51)

Money Multiplier: multiplier = 1/required Federal Reserve ratio (49.1); measures the effect of bank deposits on the expansion of the money supply

Monopolistic Competition: a market structure with elements of perfect competition and monopoly (32); exists in an industry composed of many small firms, each producing a slightly differentiated product (34)

Monopoly: a market characterized by a single seller (5. 19)

Monopsony: a market characterized by a single buyer (19); situation in which a firm is the only buyer of a particular resource or intermediate product (33.1)

National Income: the revenues received by all businesses and households (37)

National Surplus: the flows of profit produced by underdeveloped, neocolonial countries for the benefit of global corporations as well as members of the local ruling class (56)

Natural Monopolies: firms in which the technology used creates an average total cost curve on which the minimum is not reached until the firm is producing a very large quantity (33.1)

Natural Selection: process whereby nature selects from the existing individuals the ones best suited for survival under particular conditions; eventually this type of individual has the highest reproduction rate, and over a long period of time that fact leads to changes in the species (1)

Necessary Labor: hours worked to produce an amount of output equal to the value of one's wages (19)

Necessity Good: a normal good with an income elasticity of demand of less than one (27.2)

Negative Economic Profit: condition in which the owner is not doing as well as the next best alternative (30)

Negative Externalities: social costs of production that are not reflected in price (35)

Negative Marginal Productivity: additional inputs cause output to decline (29.1)

Negative Marginal Utility: the decline in marginal utility to the point of its becoming negative, which results as additional units of a good are consumed; if marginal utility becomes negative, total utility also declines (28)

Neoclassical Economics: asserts a basic policy conclusion that free-market capitalism works well as long as government does not intervene in the economy (17)

Neocolonial or Neocolonialism: characterizes a country where there is no military occupation, but the government is dominated by a foreign power and the economy is exploited by foreign powers; for example, even after the United States had formal independence and no occupying troops, its economic relationship to England remained similar to a colonial one (7, 56)

Neolithic Revolution: period that saw the better tools, the invention of agriculture (farming and herding), and the invention of effective pottery (2)

Net Exports: the difference between what is sold to other countries and what is purchased from other countries (37, 52)

Net Investment: gross investment minus depreciation (43)

New Deal: a series of progressive programs and reforms initiated during the period 1933–1937 under President Franklin D. Roosevelt designed to take the United States out of the Depression (14)

New Investment: firm's investment in additional buildings and equipment to expand capital beyond the present level (43)

Nominal Spending: spending that is not corrected for inflation (51.1)

Normal Goods: goods whose consumption increases when income increases (27.2)

Oligopoly: a market characterized by very few firms and strategic interaction (10); industry has a few giant sellers, each of which controls a significant share of the market (32); exists when a few business firms dominate an industry (34); only a few large corporations in each market (50)

Opportunity Cost: the value of what is given up when a choice is made to do something else (26.1)

Optimal Plant Size: attained by the plant that minimizes average total costs in the long run (30.1)

Ordinal Utility: the idea that consumers can rank consumption bundles but cannot precisely measure the quantity of utility with cardinal numbers generated by those bundles (28)

Out Sourcing: process whereby corporations shift jobs from high-wage workers in the United States to low-wage workers in less developed countries (46)

Outside Shocks: disturbances from outside the system that affect the economy (39)

Panic: widespread apprehension about the financial system leading to impulsive reactions; during the 1930s banking panics where sparked by bank failures and millions of people lost their savings (51)

Pecuniary: concerning money (13)

Perfect Monopoly: situation in which only one firm in the market or industry (21), there is only one seller of a product that has no close substitutes (32), or a single firm constitutes the entire industry (33)

Perfectly Competitive Market: each buyer demands so small a percentage of output that the buyer's purchases alone also have virtually no effect on the price at which the industry sells the product; similarly, sellers have no market power (32)

Perfectly Elastic: situation in which the demand curve is perfectly horizontal and elasticity approaches infinity (27.2)

Perfectly Inelastic: situation in which there is no change in the quantity demanded regardless of the change in price; the demand curve is perfectly vertical (27.2)

Personal Savings: consumption expenditures subtracted from personal disposable income (37)

Positive Economic Profit: situation in which the owner is not only earning an accounting profit but is also doing better than his or her next best alternative (30)

Positive Externalities: benefits that are not reflected in price (35)

Prebisch-Singer Hypothesis (PSH): theory of the declining tendency for the terms of trade in primary products (55.2)

Predatory Instinct: the admiration of predatory skills, acceptance of the hierarchy of subordination, and the widespread substitution of myth and ceremony for knowledge (13)

Prehistoric: before written history (1)

Prejudice: subjective dislike of a person or a group (usually based on stereotypes) (22)

Price Controls: administrative limits placed on the price of goods by government (16)

Price Elasticity of Demand: the percentage change in quantity demanded divided by the percentage change in its own price (27.2)

Price Elasticity of Supply: measures the relative responsiveness of the quantity supplied to the change in price (27.2)

Price-Maker: an economic agent whose actions can influence the market price; a monopolist or monopsonist are examples (32)

Price-Taker: an economic agent that must accept the price as determined in the market; both buyers and sellers in perfect competition are price-takers (32)

Private Debt: the amount that business and households owe (16)

Private Property Rights: control over an asset and the right to exclude anyone else from using it (2)

Privatization: giving away or selling public property to private individuals (54)

Process Technology: the application of knowledge for producing products as efficiently as possible (29)

Product Cycle: process in which products tend to undergo different phases, such as development, expansion, peak, maturity, and demise (55.2)

Product Technology: the application of knowledge to create new goods and/or services (29)

Production Function: the mathematical relationship between output and the factors of production (typically labor) (29)

Production in the Long Run: a logical period in which the factors of production are variable and the law of diminishing returns is not applicable (29)

Production in the Short Run: conditions in which at least one factor of production is fixed, as additional units of variable factors are added (29)

Production Possibilities Curve (PPC): a curve showing the production combinations available to an economy given finite inputs and technology (26.1)

Productivity: the amount of output produced by each input (1)

Profit: total revenue less total costs (5); *see Accounting Profit and Economic Profit*

Profit Squeeze: the declining growth of demand and the rising growth of costs, which create the nutcracker effect that lowers profits; the lower profits lead to less investment (45)

Profit-Push Inflation: new inflation, which occurs in both expansions and recessions, due to firms pushing up prices to achieve maximum profits (50)

Progressive Tax: a tax whose percentage rate, or proportion of income, increases as income increases (24)

Progressive Political Economist: a scholar who does not believe that the existing market system is perfect; one who analyzes the economic system in order to see how to change it so as to improve it in the interest of better social outcomes (17)

Propaganda: selected information and publicity used to support and spread certain ideas (2)

Property Income: all the income that derives from ownership of various types of property, for example, rent and interest (37)

Proportional Tax: a tax whose percentage rate, or proportion to income, stays the same as income increases (24)

Prosperity: the last half of an expansion, when business is lucrative and employees' incomes are rising (45)

Psychological Hedonism: the concept that all actions are motivated by the desire to achieve pleasure and avoid pain (8)

Public Enterprises: enterprises under government ownership (25)

Public Good: a good that is not subject to the exclusion principle or rival consumption (35)

Quota: a quantity restriction on imported goods (55)

Racist Discrimination: differential treatment of people based on prejudices or myths about differences in physical characteristics or ethnicity (1)

Rate of Exploitation: the ratio of surplus hours to necessary hours (19)

Rate of Growth: the ratio of savings to output times the ratio of output to capital (46)

Rate of Profit per Worker: equals the profit divided by the costs to the corporation for a worker and his or her used-up material goods (20)

Rationality: the tendency of consumers to make purposeful choices based on their own self-interest (28)

Real Business Cycle Theory: the belief that shocks are based on real events that impact production of goods and services (45)

Real Wages: the actual purchasing power of the money made from employment, or the value of the dollars earned after adjusting for inflation (16)

Recession: an economic crisis that results in a vicious downward cycle (36, 45)

Recovery: the first period of expansion following a recession (45)

Regressive Tax: a tax whose percentage rate, or proportion of income, decreases as income increases (24)

Regulatory Capture: a situation that occurs when a government regulatory agency, which is supposed to act in the public interest, becomes dominated by the industry it is assigned to regulate and acts in its interest instead (21)

Relations of Production: the social relationships among people, particularly the relationship of people to the means of production (10)

Replacement Investment: investment in capital goods (buildings and equipment) that have depreciated or become obsolescent (43)

Repressed Inflation: there were few price rises during Second World War, but strong price rises as soon as the controls were ended (50)

Republic: a nation in which power is held by the people or their elected representatives (3)

Required Reserves: the legal restriction that banks lend out only a certain proportion of their deposits (49.1)

Reserves: a percentage of the bank's deposits held as vault cash or on deposit at the Fed (51)

Resources Inputs: the assets needed in production and development of an economy, including land, labor, capital, and time (21, 21.1)

Retained Earnings: profits not distributed to shareholders (14)

Returns to Scale: long-run changes in output that occur when the firm proportionally increases all factors of production (29)

Revised Sequence: the idea that production is driven not by sovereign consumers pursuing their own satisfaction, but that instead businesses use advertising and salesmanship to create consumer demand for their products (28)

Risk: an action whose outcome is unknown (31.1)

Rival Consumption: the concept that my consumption of a good makes it impossible for you to consume the good as well (35)

Rule for Maximizing Profit Under Competition: produce at the quantity that equates marginal cost and price (32)

Runs on the Bank: a situation in which many of a banks' depositors, on hearing a rumor or report that the bank was in trouble, would withdraw all their deposits (14)

Sabotage: a conscious withdrawal of efficiency (13)

Savings: all income that is not spent for consumption (42)

Say's Law: any amount of output supplied to the market will always generate an equal amount of demand (15); the supply of goods and services calls forth its own demand (38, 40, 40.1)

Scabs: nonunion workers who replace striking union workers or work for below union wages on nonunion terms (14)

Scarcity: the concept that there is never enough production to satisfy the wants and desires of all individuals (26)

Secular: not related to religion or religious beliefs (4)

Serf: someone who owes service to a landowner or lord for a certain number of days a year, but is given his or her own small amount of land for subsistence farming (3)

Sexist Discrimination: differential treatment of people based on prejudices or myths about their gender (1)

Sharecropper: tenant farmer who pays a share of his crop as rent, had to share half of his or her crop with the landlord

Sherman Anti-Trust Act of 1890: forbade any contract, combination, or conspiracy to restrain trade (21)

Short Run: the period of time when at least one of a firm's inputs is fixed (29)

Social Institutions: all the noneconomic settings in which people interact, such as the political process, the family, or religious organizations (1)

Social Losses: losses to society from the contractions that occur during business cycles (36)

Socialism: a theory of social organization that advocates ownership and control of production by the community as a whole (9)

Stagflation: inflation at a time of deficient aggregate demand and high unemployment (50)

Stereotype: standardized, oversimplified image of a particular group (22)

Stock Market Bubble: situation in which the price of a share of stock is not supported by economic fundamentals (16)

Store of Value: something that maintains its worth and can be used for payments in the future (49)

Subsidies: grants of money from the government (6, 55)

Subsistence: the minimal level of goods and services needed to support life (2)

Substitute Goods: goods that can be used interchangeably and are characterized by a negative cross-price elasticity of demand (27.2)

Supply: the quantity of a good sellers would like to sell during a given period, at various prices, holding all other things constant (27)

Supply Curve: illustrates graphically the quantities the seller would like to sell at various prices (27)

Supply Schedule: expresses the amount of a good the seller would desire to sell at various prices (27)

Surplus: food above the level needed for survival (2); the amount above costs that goes as profit to the owners of industry (20); occurs government tax revenues exceed expenditures (47)

Surplus Labor: the amount of labor that produces a company's profits (19)

Taft-Harley Act: a U.S. federal legislative action passed in 1947 that greatly restricted the activities and power of unions (19)

Tariff: a tax on imported goods (55)

Tax Loophole: a way that the tax law allows an individual or firm to pay less than the rate for the group to which the individual or firm belongs (37)

Technology: the way in which human beings produce goods and services (1); the existing level of knowledge, techniques, and types of tools available for the production of goods and services (26.1)

Teleological: characterizes events that are guided by natural and mechanical forces toward a final outcome in which each succeeding generation is superior to the preceding one (12)

Terms of Trade: how much of one good a country must give up to get a given quantity of another foreign-produced good (55.1)

Time Preference: how people rank current versus future consumption (31.1)

Total Costs: found by adding together fixed and variable costs; also average total cost times quantity (30)

Total Product: quantity that is produced (29.1)

Total Revenue: the entire amount of money that a firm receives from selling a product (27.2)

Total Utility: the amount of satisfaction one gets from consuming a good (28)

Trade Deficit: when imports exceed exports (16, 52); exports are less than imports (37)

Trade Surplus: when exports exceed imports (16); exports are greater than imports (37, 52)

Transaction Costs: the costs involved in conducting a transaction (35.1)

Transfer Payments: payments by the government to people for reasons other than current services to government (37); payments by the government to some group of people without any service in return (47)

Transformation Problem: question of how values given in labor hours can be transformed into prices in money terms under capitalism (20.1)

Trust: a combination of firms or corporations with the goal of reducing competition and controlling prices (11)

Unit Elastic or Unitary Elastic: price elasticity of demand equals one, or the percentage change in price is the same as the percentage change in quantity demanded; an elasticity coefficient equal to one (27.2)

Unit of Account: measures the value of goods and services (49)

Usury: the lending of money at interest, or lending money at exorbitant or illegal rates of interest (4)

Utility: a measure of pleasure or satisfaction (12); the satisfaction derived from consuming a good or service (28)

Utopians: impractical social reformers with a vision of social and political perfection (10)

Variable Costs: costs that change with the level of output (30)

Vertical Mergers: mergers of firms along production path from the raw materials to the factory to the wholesale and retail sales places (14); occurring between firms producing goods in sequence (21)

Wage Ceiling: the limit above which an employee's compensation may not rise (19)

Wage Floor: that compensation level below which an employee knows that she cannot provide necessary food, clothing, and shelter for her family (19)

Wartime Inflation: the increase in government demand during a war that leads to a rapid increase in prices, which ends after the boom of the war is over (50)

Wealth: the accumulated assets minus liabilities held by a particular household or individual (18)

Zero Economic Profit: situation in which the owner is doing at least as well as her or his next best alternative (30)

REFERENCES

Ackerman, F., et al. 1971. "Income Distribution in the United States." *Review of Radical Political Economy* (Summer).

AFL-CIO Executive Committee. 1970. *The National Economy.* Washington, D.C.: American Federation of Labor-Congress of Industrial Organizations.

Alexander, S. S. 1967. "Human Values and Economists' Values." In *Human Values and Economic Policy*, ed. S. Hook. New York: New York University Press.

Alvarez, Walter. 1998. *T Rex and the Crater of Doom.* New York: Vintage Books.

Ambrose, Stephen. 2001. *Nothin Like It in the World.* New York: Simon and Schuster.

Amundsen, Kirsten. 1971. *The Silenced Majority.* Englewood Cliffs, NJ: Prentice-Hall.

Anderson, Perry. 1974. *Passages from Antiquity to Feudalism.* London: New Left Books.

Andrews, Edward L. 2004. "How Tax Bill Gave Business More and More." *The New York Times*, October 13, pp. 1, 14.

Arnold, Thurman. 1969. "Economic Reform and the Sherman Anti-Trust Act." In *Historical Viewpoints Since 1865*, volume 2 (of 2 volume series), ed. J. A. Garraty. New York: Harper & Row.

Aston, T. H., and C. H. E. Philpin. 1985. *The Brenner Debate.* Cambridge: Cambridge University Press.

Bain, J. S. 1948. "Price and Production Policies." In *A Survey of Contemporary Economics*, ed. Howard S. Ellis. New York: McGraw-Hill.

Baker, Dean, Gerald Epstein, and Robert Pollin. 1998. *Globalization and Progressive Economic Policy.* Cambridge, England: Cambridge University Press.

Baran, Paul A. 1962. *The Political Economy of Growth.* New York: Monthly Review Press.

Baran, Paul, and Paul Sweezy. 1968. *Monopoly Capital.* New York: Monthly Review Press.

Barber, Richard. 1970. *The American Corporation.* New York: Dutton.

Barera, Mario. 1980. *Race and Class in the Southwest.* Notre Dame, Indiana: Notre Dame University Press.

Beer, M., ed. 1920. *Life of Robert Owen.* New York: Alfred Knopf.

Bell, Garret, ed. 1970. *The Environmental Handbook.* New York: Ballantine.

Bendix, Reinhard. 1963. *Work and Authority in Industry.* New York: Harper & Row, Torchbooks.

Bentham, Jeremy. 1955. "An Introduction to the Principles of Morals and Legislation." In *Ethical Theories*, ed. A. I. Meiden. Englewood Cliffs, NJ: Prentice-Hall.

Bergmann, Barbara. 1973. "Economics of Women's Liberation." *Challenge* 16 (May–June): 11–17.

Bernstein, Eduard. [1899] 1961. *Evolutionary Socialism.* New York: Schocken Books.

Bettleheim, Charles. 1968. *India Independent.* New York: Monthly Review Press.

Bird, Carolyn. 1971. *Born Female.* New York: Pocket Books.

Birnie, Arthur. 1936. *An Economic History of the British Isles.* London: Methuen.

Bivens, L. Josh, and Christian Weller. 2006. "The Job-Less Recovery: Not New, Just Worse." *Journal of Economic Issues* 40 (September): 603–628.

Blair, John. 1972. *Economic Concentration.* New York: Harcourt Brace Jovanovich.

Bolles, Edmund Blair. 1999. *The Ice Finders: How a Poet, A Professor, and a Politician Discovered the Ice Age.* Washington, DC: Counterpoint Press.

Bonnen, James. 1972. "The Effect of Taxes and Government Spending on Inequality." In *The Capitalist System*, ed. Richard Edwards, Michael Reich, and Thomas Weisskopf. Englewood Cliffs, NJ: Prentice-Hall.

Bowles, Samuel, and Herbert Gintis. 1986. *Democracy and Capitalism*. New York: Basic Books.

Boyer, Richard O., and Herbert Morais. 1970. *Labor's Untold Story*. New York: United Electrical Workers.

Brenner, Harvey. 1976. "Estimating the Social Costs of National Economic Policy: Implications for Mental Health and Criminal Aggression." In *Proceedings*, The Joint Economic Committee, U.S. Congress. Washington, DC: United States Government Printing Office.

Brenner, Johanna. 2000. *Women and the Politics of Class*. New York: Monthly Review Press.

Burton, Maureen, and Reynold Nesiba. 2004. "Transnational Financial Institutions, Global Financial Flows, and the International Monetary Fund." In *Global Political Economy and the Wealth of Nations: Performance, Institutions, Problems, and Policies*, ed. Philip O'Hara, pp. 147–69. New York and London: Routledge.

Cantor, Arnold. 1974. "State Local Taxes: A Study of Inequity." *AFL-CIO American Federationist*. (February).

Carnegie, Andrew. 1949. "Wealth." In *Democracy and the Gospel of Wealth*, ed. Gail Kennedy. Lexington, MA: Raytheon, Heath.

Ceram, C. W. 1986. *Gods, Graves and Scholars*, 2nd ed. New York: Vintage Books.

Chandler, Lester V. 1970. *America's Greatest Depression, 1929–1941*. New York: Harper & Row.

Chang, Ha-Joon, and Ilene Grabel. 2004. *Reclaiming Development: An Alternative Economic Policy Model*. New York: Palgrave Macmillan.

Chase, Anthony. 1997. *The American Legal System: The Evolution of the American Legal System*. New York: The New Press.

Chernow, Ron. 1998. *House of Morgan: An American Banking Dynasty and the Rise of Modern Finance*. New York: Grove Press.

Chernow, Ron. 1999. *Titan: Biography of John D. Rockefeller*. New York: Vintage Books.

Childe, V. Gordon. 1957 *What Happens in History*. New York: Penguin Press.

Clapham, J. H., and Eileen E. Powers, eds. 1966. *The Agrarian Life of the Middle Ages*, 2nd ed. London: Cambridge University Press.

Claudin, Fernando. 1975. *The Communist Movement*. New York: Monthly Review Press.

Cole, G. D. H. 1953. *A History of Socialist Thought*. 5 vols. New York: St. Martin's Press.

Collins, Chuck, and Felice Yeskel. 2000. *Economic Apartheid in America*. Boston: New Press.

Collins, Chuck, Betsy Leondar-Wright, and Holly Sklar. 1999. *Shifting Fortunes: The Perils of the Growing American Wealth Gap*. Boston: United for a Fair Economy.

Commoner, Barry. 1970. *The Poverty of Power: Environment and Economic Crisis*. New York: Alfred Knopf.

Congressional Quarterly. 1978. "Financial Disclosure." Vol. 36, September 2.

Coontz, Sydney H. 1966. *Productive Labor and Effective Demand*. New York: Augustus M. Kelley.

Cranford, John. 2007. "Political Economy: In a Pigovian's Eye." *CQWeekly* (Nov. 10), online at http://www.cqpolitics.com/wmspage.cfm?docid=weeklyreport-000002625588, accessed on November 15, 2007.

Cuddington, John T., Rodney Ludema, and Shamila A. Jayasuriya. 2002. *Prebisch-Singer Redux*. Working Paper no. 40, Reserve Bank of Chile. Santiago, Chile.

Cummings, Milton, and F. Wise. 1971. *Democracy Under Pressure*. New York: Harcourt Brace Jovanovich.

Cypher, James. 1974. "Capitalist Planning and Military Expenditures." *Review of Radical Political Economics* 6 (Fall): 1–19.

Dahl, Robert, and Charles Lindblom. 1953. *Politics, Economics and Welfare*. New York: Harper & Row.

Dahlberg, Frances, ed. 1981. *Woman the Gatherer*. New Haven, CT: Yale University Press.

Deckard, Barbara Sinclair. 1983. *The Women's Movement*. New York: Harper & Row.

Dellums, Ronald. 1995. "Stealth Bombing America's Future: Beyond the B-2 Thunderdome." *The Nation*, October 2: 350–352.

Diamond, Jared. 1997. *Guns, Germs, and Steel*. New York: W. W. Norton.

Diamond, Jared. 2004. *Collapse*. New York: Viking.

Dicey, Albert V. 1926. *Law and Public Opinion in England*, 2nd ed. London: Macmillan.

Dickens, Peter. 2003. *Global Shift: Reshaping the Global Economic Map in the 21st Century*, 4th ed. London: Sage Publications.

Dillard, Dudley. 1967. *Economic Development of the North Atlantic Community*. Englewood Cliffs, NJ: Prentice-Hall.

Dobb, Maurice H. 1946. *Studies in the Development of Capitalism*. London: Routledge & Kegan Paul.

Dobb, Maurice. 1973. *Theories of Value and Distribution Since Adam Smith*. Cambridge: Cambridge University Press.

Dowd, Douglas F. 1965. *Modem Economic Problems in Historical Perspective*. Lexington, MA: Raytheon/Heath.

DuBoff, Richard. 1989. *Accumulation and Power: An Economic History of the United States*. Armonk, NY: M.E. Sharpe.

Dugger, William M., and Howard J. Sherman, eds. 2003. *Evolutionary Theory and the Social Sciences*. 4 vols. New York and London: Routledge.

Dugger, William M., and Howard J. Sherman. 2000. *Reclaiming Evolution*. New York: Routledge.

Dymski, Gary, Gerald Epstein, and Robert Pollin, eds. 1992. *Transforming the U.S. Financial System: Equity and Efficiency for the 21st Century*. Armonk, NY: M.E. Sharpe.

Edel, Mathew. 1973. *Economics of the Environment*. Engelwood Cliffs, New Jersey: Prentice-Hall.

Edwards, Richard. 1972. "Who Fares Well in the Welfare State." In *The Capitalist System,* ed. Richard Edwards, Michael Reich, and Thomas Weisskopf. Englewood Cliffs, NJ: Prentice-Hall.

Engels, Friedrich. 1935. "Anti-Duhring." In *Handbook of Marxism*. New York: Random House.

Engels, Friedrich. 1958. *The Condition of the Working Class in England in 1844*. New York: Macmillan.

Federal Reserve Bank of New York. 1992. "Build-Down." *Quarterly Review* 17, no. 3 (Autumn).

Feiner, Susan, ed. 2002. *Race and Gender in the U.S. Economy: Views from Across the Spectrum*. Englewood Cliffs, NJ: Prentice-Hall.

Feinman, Jay M. 2004. *Unmaking Law: The Conservative Campaign to Roll Back the Common Law*. Boston: Beacon Press.

Fine, Sidney. 1964. *Laissez Faire and the General Welfare State*. Ann Arbor: University of Michigan Press.

Flexner, Eleanor. 1975. *Century of Struggle: The Women's Rights Movement in the United States*. Cambridge, MA: Beklnap Press of Harvard University Press.

Foner, Eric. 1988. *Reconstruction*. New York: Harper & Row.

Foner, Philip. 1947–1980. *History of the Labor Movement in the United States*. 5 vols. New York: International Publishers.

Foster, John Bellamy. 1984. *The Vulnerable Planet: A Short Economic History of the Environment*. New York: Monthly Review Press.

Foster, John Bellamy. 2006. *Naked Imperialism*. New York: Monthly Review Press.

Frank, Thomas. 2004. *What's the Matter With Kansas: How Conservatives Won the Heart of America*. New York: Henry Holt and Co., Metropolitan Books.

Franklin, Ray, and Solomon Resnick. 1973. *The Political Economy of Racism*. New York: Holt, Rinehart and Winston.

Freeman, A., B. Haveman, and A. Kneese. 1973. *The Economics of Environmental Policy*. New York: Wiley.

Friedan, Betty. 1963. *The Feminine Mystique*. New York: Dell.

Friedman, Milton. 1982. *Capitalism and Freedom*, 2nd ed. Chicago, IL: University of Chicago Press.

Friedman, Milton. 1968. "The Role of Monetary Policy." *American Economic Review* 72 (January): 1–24.

Fullerton, Kemper. 1959. "Calvinism and Capitalism: an Explanation of the Weber Thesis." In *Protestantism and Capitalism: The Weber Thesis and Its Critics*, ed. Robert W. Green. Lexington, MA: Heath.

Fusfeld, Daniel R. 1966. *The Age of the Economist*. Glenview, IL: Scott, Foresman.

Galbraith, John Kenneth. 1956. *America Capitalism, the Concept of Countervailing Power*. Boston: Houghton Mifflin.

Galbraith, John Kenneth. 2004. "The Iraq War." *Guardian*, Thursday, July 15.

Genovese, Eugene. 1976. *Roll, Jordan, Roll: The World the Slaves Made*. New York: Vintage Books.

Genovese, Eugene. 1989. *The Political Economy of Slavery: Studies in the Economy and Society of the Slave South*. Middletown, CT: Wesleyan University Press.

Gintis, Herbert, and Samuel Bowles. 1981. "Structure and Practice in the Labour Theory of Value." *Review of Radical Political Economics* 12, no. 4: 1–26.

Girvetz, Harry K. 1963. *The Evolution of Liberalism*. New York: Colliers.

Goldberg, Marilyn. 1970. "The Economic Exploitation of Women." *Review of Radical Political Economics* 2 (Spring): 35–47.

Gosselin, Peter. 2004. "Poor and Uninsured Americans Increase for Third Straight Year." *Los Angeles Times*, August 27, pp. 1, 7.

Gould, Stephen Jay. 1977. *Ever Since Darwin*. New York: W. W. Norton.

Grampp, William D. 1965. *Economic Liberalism*. Vol. 1. New York: Random House.

Gray, Alexander. 1963. *The Socialist Tradition*. London: Longmans.

Green, Mark, James Fallows, and David Zwick. 1972. *Who Runs Congress?* New York: Bantam.

Gruchy, Allan G. 1967. *Modern Economic Thought: The American Contribution*. New York: Augustus M. Kelley.

Guerin, Daniel. 1970. *Anarchism*. New York: Monthly Review Press.

Gunn, Christopher. 1984. *Workers' Self-Management in the United States*. Ithaca, NY: Cornell University Press.

Gunn, Christopher. 2004. *Third Sector Development: Making Up for the Market*. Ithaca, NY: Cornell University Press.

Gurley, John. 1967. "Federal Tax Policy." *National Tax Journal* (September).

Hacker, Louis M. 1970. *The Course of American Economic Growth and Development*. New York: Wiley.

Hahnel, Robin. 1999. *Panic Rules! Everything You Need to Know About the Global Economy*. Boston: South End Press.

Hahnel, Robin. 2002. *The ABCs of Political Economy: A Modern Approach*. London: Pluto.

Hahnel, Robin. 2005. *Economic Justice and Democracy: From Competition to Cooperation*. New York and London: Routledge.

Hahnel, Robin. 2005. "What Mainstream Economists Won't Tell You About Neoliberal Globalization." *Socialist Studies: The Journal of the Society for Socialist Studies* 1, no. 1 (Spring): 5–29.

Hammond, J. L., and Barbara Hammond. 1969. *The Rise of Modern Industry*. New York: Harper & Row, Torchbooks.

Hansen, Alvin. 1951. *A Guide to Keynes*. New York: McGraw-Hill.

Havemann, Joel. 2006. "Bush Budget Plan Strikes Home, Not Deficit." *Los Angeles Times*, February 6, p. A1.

Havemann, Joel. 2006. "Taxes Flatten Out, Deep Pockets Still Bulge." *Los Angeles Times*, April 17, pp. A1, A6.

Heilbroner, Robert L. 1962. *The Making of Economic Society*. Englewood Cliffs, NJ: Prentice-Hall.

Henederson, James. 2006. "World's Richest 1% Own 40% Of All Wealth, United Nations Report Discovers." *The Guardian*, December 10 (http://www.guardian.co.uk).

Henry, John. 1990. *The Making of Neoclassical Economics*. Winchester, MA: Unwin Hyman.

Herrera, Remy. 2006. "The New Development Economics: A Neoliberal Con?" *Monthly Review* 58, no. 1 (May): 38–50.

Hill, Christopher. 1966. "Protestantism and the Rise of Capitalism." In *The Rise of Capitalism*, ed. D. S. Landes. New York: Macmillan.

Hilton, Rodney. H., ed. 1976. *The Transition From Feudalism to Capitalism*. London: Verso.

Hobbes, Thomas. 1955. *Leviathan*. Reprinted in *Ethical Theories*, series ed. A. I. Meiden. Englewood Cliffs, NJ: Prentice-Hall.

Hobsbawm, Eric J. 1968. *Industry and Empire: An Economic History of Britain Since 1750*. London: Weidenfeld & Nicolson.

Hodgskin, Thomas. 1922. *Labour Defended Against the Claims of Capital*. London: Labour Publishing.

Holy Bible. n.d. "Deuteronomy," "Ecclesiastes," "Luke," "Mark," "Matthew." Cleveland, OH: World Publishing Company.

Hook, Sidney. 1933. *Towards the Understanding of Karl Marx*. New York: Day.

Howe, Florence, and Paul Pautner. 1972. "How the School System Is Rigged." In *The Capitalist System*, ed. Richard Edwards, Michael Reich, and Thomas Weisskopf. Englewood Cliffs, NJ: Prentice-Hall.

Huberman, Leo. 1961. *Man's Worldly Goods*. New York: Monthly Review Press.

Huberman, Leo, and Paul A. Sweezy. 1965. "The Road to Ruin." *Monthly Review* (April).

Hunt, E. K. 1970. "Simon N. Patten's Contribution to Economics." *Journal of Economic Issues* (December).

Hunt, E. K. 1971. "Religious Parable Versus Economic Logic: An Analysis of the Recent Controversy in Value, Capital and Distribution Theory." *Inter-Mountain Economic Review* (Fall).

Hunt, E. K. 1971. "A Neglected Aspect of the Economic Ideology of the Early New Deal." *Review of Social Economy* (September).

Hunt, E. K. 2002. *History of Economic Thought: A Critical Perspective.* Armonk, NY: M.E. Sharpe.

Hunt, E. K., and Jesse Schwartz. 1972. *Critique of the Economic Theory.* London: Penguin.

Irish, Marian, and James Protho. 1965. *The Politics of American Democracy.* Englewood Cliffs, NJ: Prentice-Hall.

Iritani, Evelyn. 2004. "New Trade Pact Could Cut Clout of U.S. in Asia." *Los Angeles Times,* November 30, pp. C1, C6.

Ivins, Molly. 2006. "I Will Not Support Hillary Clinton for President." January 20. http://www.freepress.org/columns/display/1/2006/1304.

Jevons, William Stanley. 1871. *The Theory of Political Economy,* 1st ed. London: Macmillan.

Johnston, David C. 2006. "Corporate Wealth Share Rises for Top-Income Americans." *New York Times,* January 29, p. A1.

Josephson, Matthew. 1962. *The Robber Barons.* New York: Harcourt-Brace Jovanovich, Harvest Books.

Kennedy, Robert. 1960. *The Enemy Within,* New York: Harper & Row.

Keynes, John Maynard. 1936. *The General Theory of Employment, Interest and Money.* New York: Harcourt Brace Jovanovich.

Kipnis, Ira. 1952. *The American Socialist Movement, 1897–1912.* New York: Columbia University Press.

Kolko, Gabriel. 1962. *Wealth and Power in America.* New York: Praeger.

Kolko, Gabriel. 1963. *The Triumph of Conservatism.* New York: Free Press.

Krugman, Paul. 2006. "Left Behind Economics." *Los Angeles Times,* 14 July: A19.

Lachmann, Conway. 1979. "Value Added Tax vs. the Property Tax." *Real Estate Law Journal* 8 (Summer): 34–46.

Lampman, Robert J. 1962. *Tile Share of Top Wealth-holders in National Wealth 1922–1956.* Princeton, NJ: Princeton University Press.

Lechman, J., and B. Okner. 1972. "Individual Income Tax Erosion by Income Classes." In *Economics of Federal Subsidy Programs,* ed. Joint Economic Committee, U.S. Congress, Washington, D.C.: Government Printing Office.

Lekachman, Robert, ed. 1962. *The Varieties of Economics.* 2 vols. New York: Meridian.

Lenin, V. I. 1939. *Imperialism: The Highest Stage of Capitalism.* London: Lawrence & Wishart.

Leontief, Wassily. 1956. "Factor Proportions and the Structure of American Trade: Further Theoretical and Empirical Analysis." *Economia Internazionale* (February): 3–32.

Lomborg, Bjorn. 2006. "Climate Change Can Wait. World Health Can't." *The Observer Comment,* London. July 6. Available at http://observer.guardian.co.uk/comment/story/0,,1810738,00.htm. Accessed November 15, 2007.

Los Angeles Times. 1985. "The Poor Get Poorer; the Rich Get Richer." February 3.

Luxemburg, Rosa. 1964. *The Accumulation of Capital.* New York: Monthly Review Press.

Magdoff, Fred. 2006. "Debt and Speculation Explode." *Monthly Review* 58 (6): 1–15.

Magdoff, Harry. 2003. *Imperialism Without Colonies.* New York: Monthly Review Press.

Malthus, Thomas Robert. 1961. *Essay on the Principle of Population.* Vol. 2. New York: Dutton.

Mandeville, Bernard. 1714. *The Fable of the Bees: or Private Vices, Publick Benefits.*

Mantoux, Paul. 1927. *Industrial Revolution in the Eighteenth-Century.* New York: Harcourt Brace.

Marable, Manning. 1997. *Black Liberation in Conservative America.* Boston: South End Press.

Markham, F. M. H., ed. 1952. *Henri Comte de Saint-Simon, Selected Writings.* Oxford: Blackwell.

Marshall, Alfred. [1890] 1961. *Principles of Economics.* London: Macmillan.

Marx, Karl, and Friedrich Engels. [1848] 1965. "The Communist Manifesto." In *Essential Works of Marxism,* ed. Arthur P. Mendel. New York: Bantam.

Marx, Karl. 1959. *Economic and Philosophic Manuscripts of 1844.* Moscow: Progress Publishers.

Marx, Karl. 1961. *Capital.* 3 vols. Moscow: Foreign Languages Publishing House.

Marx, Karl. 1970. *Critique of Political Economy.* New York: New World Paperbacks.

McAfee, Kathy, and Myrna Wood. 1972. "Bread and Roses." In *Female Liberation,* ed. Roberta Salper. New York: Alfred Knopf.

McChesney, Robert. 1999. *Rich Media, Poor Democracy: Communication Politics in Dubious Times.* Urbana, IL: University of Illinois Press.

McConnell, Grant. 1970. "Self-Regulation, the Politics of Business." In *Economics: Mainstream Readings and Radical Critiques,* ed. D. Mermelstein. New York: Random House.

McDonald, Lee Cameron. 1962. *Western Political Theory: The Modem Age.* New York: Harcourt Brace Jovanovich.

McNamara, Robert. 1970. "Introduction." In *Economic Development and Population Growth: A Conflict?* eds. H. Gray and S. Tangri. Lexington, MA: Heath.

Meeropol, Michael. 2000. *Surrender: How the Clinton Administration Completed the Reagan Revolution.* Ann Arbor, MI: University of Michigan Press.

Means, Gardiner. 1975. "Inflation and Unemployment." In *The Roots of Inflation,* ed. John Blair. New York: Burt Franklin.

Mintz, Sidney. 1986. *Sweetness and Power: The Place of Sugar in Modern History.* New York: Penguin Books.

Mitchell, Wesley C., and W. L. Thorp. 1926. *Business Annals.* New York: National Bureau of Economic Research.

Monthly Review. 2001. "Prisons and Executions: The U.S. Model." Vol. 53, no. 3 (July–August): entire issue.

Monthly Review. 2006. "Aspects of Class in the U.S." Vol. 58, no. 3 (July–August): entire issue.

Morgan, Robin, ed. 1970. *Sisterhood Is Powerful.* New York: Vintage.

National Academy of Sciences of the United States of America. 1971. *Proceedings* 68, no. 7 (July): 1385–1388, 1389A-1392A. Available online at http://links.jstor.org/sici?sici=0027-8424%28197107%2968%3A7%3C1385%3ANAOSAM%3E2.0.CO%3B2-N.

National Bureau of Economic Research. 2004. "Foreign Investment." News release, June 30.

Navarro, Vincente. 1993. *Dangerous to Your Health.* New York: Monthly Review Press.

Nelson, Jack. 1980. "Pollution Curbed, Reagan Says: Attacks Air Cleanup." *Los Angeles Times,* December 20, p. 1.

Nevins, Allan. 1940. *John D. Rockefeller: The Heroic Age of American Enterprise.* Vol. 1. New York: Scribner's.

O'Hara, Phillip. 2004. *Global Political Economy and the Wealth of Nations.* London: Routledge.

Owen, Robert. 1962. "The Book of the New Moral World." Reprinted in part in *Communism, Fascism, and Democracy,* ed. Carl Cohen. New York: Random House.

Patel, Kant, and Mark Rushefsky. 2006. *Health Care Politics and Policy in America.* Armonk, NY: M.E. Sharpe.

Patten, Simon. 1902. *The Theory of Prosperity.* New York: Macmillan.

Patten, Simon. 1907. *The New Basis of Civilization.* New York: Macmillan.

Patten, Simon. 1922. *Mud Hollow.* Philadelphia: Dorrance.

Patten, Simon. 1924. "The Reconstruction of Economic Theory." Reprinted in Simon Nelson Patten, *Essays in Economic Theory.* Edited by Rexford Guy Tugwell. New York: Alfred Knopf.

Pechman, Joseph. 1969. "The Rich, the Poor, and the Taxes They Pay." *The Public Interest* (Fall).

Perry, Rebecca. 2004. "Late Exit Poll Data." *Los Angeles Times,* November 4, pp. 1, 23.

Pershing, Ben, and Erin P. Billings. 2005. "GOP Pulls Reconciliation Bill From Floor." *Roll Call,* November 10.

Plummer, Anne. 2005. "GOP tells Bush NO on Defense Appropriations Torture Provision." *Congressional Quarterly* 10 (October): 2725.

Pollin, Robert. 1990. *Deeper in Debt: The Changing Financial Conditions of U.S. Households.* Washington, DC: Economic Policy Institute.

Pollin, Robert. 2004. *Contours of Descent: U.S. Economic Fractures and the Landscape of Global Austerity.* New York: Verso.

Powers, Eileen. [1924] 2000. *Medieval People.* New York: Barnes & Noble.

Prebisch, Raul. 1950. *The Economic Development of Latin America and its Principal Problems.* New York: United Nations Department of Economic Affairs.

Pryor, Frederick. 2001. "Dimensions of the World-Wide Merger Boom." *Journal of Economic Issues* 35, no. 4: 825–840.

Ramparts, editors of. 1970. "Eco-Catastrophe." San Francisco: Canfield Press.

Ransom, Roger. 1999. *Conflict and Compromise: The Political Economy of Slavery, Emancipation, and the Civil War.* Cambridge, England: Cambridge University Press.

Ransom, Roger, and Richard Sutch. 1977. *One Kind of Freedom: The Economic Consequences of Emancipation.* New York: Cambridge University Press.

Reich, Michael. 1971. "The Economics of Racism." In *Problems in Political Economy: An Urban Perspective,* ed. D. Gordon. Lexington, MA: Raytheon/Heath.

Reich, Michael. 1980. *Racial Inequality, Economic Theory, and Class Conflict.* Princeton: Princeton University Press.

Reiman, Jeffrey. 2006. *The Rich Get Richer and the Poor Get Prison*, 8th ed. Boston: Allyn & Bacon.

Ricardo, David. [1817] 1962. *Principles of Political Economy and Taxation*. London: Dent.

Riverside Press-Enterprise. 1976. "Vote Would Close Loopholes for Rich." May 13.

Riverside Press-Enterprise. 1982. "Business Outspends Labor 7 to 1 in State Elections." October 7.

Roemer, John. 1982. *A General Theory of Exploitation and Class*. Cambridge: Harvard University Press.

Rogin, Leo. 1935. "The New Deal: A Survey of Literature." *Quarterly Journal of Economics*, (May).

Rosenberg, Samuel. 2003. *American Economic Growth Since 1945*. New York: Palgrave-Macmillian.

Samuels, Warren J. 1966. *The Classical Theory of Economic Policy*. New York: World Publishing.

Samuelson, Paul. 1973. *Economics*. 9th ed. New York: McGraw-Hill.

Sapsford, D. and V.N. Balasubramanyam. 1999. "Trend and Volatility in the Net Barter Terms of Trade, 1900–92: New Results from the Application of a (Not So) New Method." *Journal of International Development* 11, no. 6: 851–857.

Schlesinger, Arthur M., Jr. 1959. "The Broad Accomplishments of the New Deal." In *The New Deal: Revolution,* ed. Edwin C. Rozwenc. Lexington, MA: Raytheon/Heath.

Schlesinger, Arthur M., Jr. 1965. *The Coming of the New Deal*. Boston: Houghton Mifflin.

Schweickart, David. 2002. *After Capitalism*. London: Rowman & Littlefield.

Sherman, Howard. 1991. *The Business Cycle: Growth and Crisis in Capitalism*. Princeton, NJ: Princeton University Press.

Sherman, Howard. 1995. *Reinventing Marxism*. Baltimore, MD: Johns Hopkins University Press.

Sherman, Howard. 1997. "Theories of Cyclical Profit Squeeze." *Review of Radical Political Economics*, 29, no. 1 (Winter): 9–17.

Sherman, Howard. 2003. "Institutions and the Business Cycle." *Journal of Economic Issues* 37, no. 3 (September): 621–642.

Sherman, Howard. 2006. *How Society Makes Itself: Evolution of Political and Economic Institutions*. Armonk, NY: M.E. Sharpe.

Sinclair, Barbara. 2006. *Party Wars*. Norman, OK: University of Oklahoma Press.

Singer, Hans. 1950. "The Distribution of Gains Between Investing and Borrowing Countries." *American Economic Review: Papers and Proceedings* (May).

Smith, Adam. [1776] 1937. *An Inquiry Into the Nature and Causes of the Wealth of Nations*. New York: Modern Library.

Stampp, Kenneth M. 1967. *The Era of Reconstruction, 1865–1877*. New York: Random House, Vintage Books.

Stiglitz, Joseph. 2002. *Globalization and Its Discontents*. New York: W. W. Norton.

Tawney, Richard H. 1954. *Religion and the Rise of Capitalism*. New York: Mentor Books.

The Nation. 1976. "Editorial Column." November 6.

Thompson, William. [1824] 1850. *An Inquiry into the Principles of the Distribution of Wealth Most Conducive to Human Happiness*. London: Wm. S. Orr & Co.

Tigar, Michael, and Madeline Levy, 1977. *Law and the Rise of Capitalism*. New York: Monthly Review Press.

U.S. Congress. 1964. *Senate Report Number 970*. Washington, D.C.: Government Printing Office.

U.S. Department of Commerce. 1961. *Historical Statistics of the United States*. Washington, D.C.: Government Printing Office.

United Nations Economic Commission of Europe. 1957. *Incomes in Postwar Europe: A Survey of Policies, Growth, and Distribution*. Geneva: United Nations.

Veblen, Thorstein. 1964a. *Absentee Ownership and Business Enterprise in Recent Times*. New York: Augustus M. Kelley.

Veblen, Thorstein. 1964b. "The Beginnings of Ownership." *Essays in Our Changing Order*. New York: Augustus M. Kelley.

Veblen, Thorstein. 1964c. "The Instinct of Workmanship and the Irksomeness of Labor." *Essays in Our Changing Order*. New York: Augustus M. Kelley.

Veblen, Thorstein. 1965a. *The Engineers and the Price System*. New York: Augustus M. Kelley.

Veblen, Thorstein. 1965b. *The Theory of Business Enterprise*. New York: Augustus M. Kelley.

Veblen, Thorstein. 1965c. *The Theory of the Leisure Class*. New York: Augustus M. Kelley.

Vernon, Raymond. 1979. "The Product Cycle Hypothesis in a New International Environment." *Oxford Bulletin of Economics and Statistics* 41 (November): 255–267.

Wachtel, Howard. 1971. "Looking at Poverty from a Radical Perspective." *Review of Radical Political Economics* (Summer).

Walras, Leon. 1957. *Elements d'economie politique pure* [Elements of Pure Economics]. Homewood, IL: Irwin.

Weber, Max. 1958. *The Protestant Ethic and the Spirit of Capitalism*. New York: Scribner's.

White, Lynn, Jr. 1962. *Medieval Technology and Social Change*. Oxford: Clarendon.

Wilson, Woodrow. 1914. *The New Freedom*. Garden City, NY: Doubleday.

Williams, William Appleman. 1966. *The Contours of American History*. New York: Quadrangle.

Wirzbicki, Alan. 2004. "Divide Seen in Voter Knowledge." *Boston Globe*, October 22, pp. 1, 13.

Wise, David, and Thomas B. Ross. 1964. *The Invisible Government*. New York: Random House.

Wolff, Rick. 2006. "The Fallout from Falling US Wages." *Monthly Review* 12 (June): 1–10.

Wolfson, Martin. (1994). *Financial Crises: Understanding the Postwar U.S. Experience*. Armonk, NY: M.E. Sharpe.

Wood, Ellen Meiksins. 2002. *The Origins of Capitalism*. London: Verso.

Woodward, C. Vann. 1974. *The Strange Career of Jim Crow*, 3rd ed. New York: Oxford University Press.

Wright, Eric Olin. 1985. *Classes*. New York: Verso.

Yates, Michael. 2004. "Poverty and Inequality in the Global Economy." *Monthly Review*, 55, no. 9 (February): 37–48.

Yellen, Janet L. 2006. President and CEO, Federal Reserve Bank of San Francisco, speech at the Center for the Study of Democracy, 2006–2007 Economics of Governance Lecture, University of California, Irvine, November 6, 2006.

Zarembo, Alan. 2007. "Global Warming: What Can't Be Stopped Can Be Slowed." *Los Angeles Times*, February 5, p. 1.

Zimbalist, Andrew, Howard Sherman, and Stuart Brown. 1988. *Comparing Economic Systems: A Political-Economic Approach*, 2nd ed. San Diego: Harcourt Brace Jovanovich.

Zinn, Howard. 1999. *A People's History of the United States*. New York: Harper Collins.

INDEX

Made in United States
North Haven, CT
05 February 2023

32065902R00415